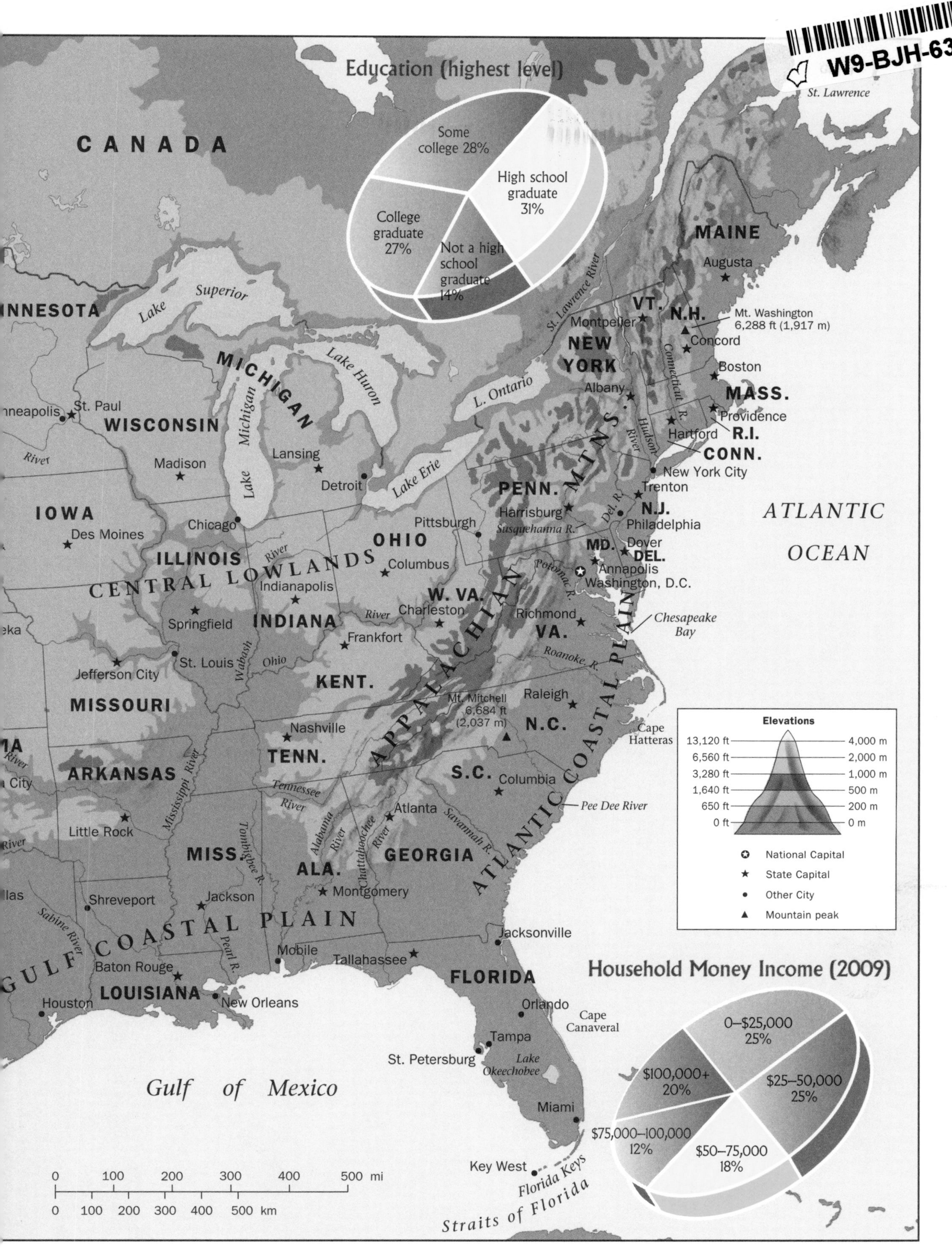

Education (highest level)
Some college 28%
High school graduate 31%
College graduate 27%
Not a high school graduate 14%
CANADA
St. Lawrence
MAINE
Augusta
VT.
N.H.
Mt. Washington 6,288 ft (1,917 m)
Montpelier
Concord
NEW YORK
Boston
MASS.
Albany
Providence
R.I.
Hartford
CONN.
New York City
Trenton
N.J.
Philadelphia
PENN.
Harrisburg
Susquehanna R.
Del. R.
Pittsburgh
MD.
Dover
DEL.
Annapolis
Washington, D.C.
Potomac R.
Chesapeake Bay
Richmond
VA.
W. VA.
Charleston
Roanoke R.
Raleigh
N.C.
Cape Hatteras
Mt. Mitchell 6,684 ft (2,037 m)
S.C.
Columbia
Pee Dee River
ATLANTIC OCEAN
St. Lawrence River
Connecticut R.
Hudson River
APPALACHIAN MTNS.
ATLANTIC COASTAL PLAIN
Lake Superior
Lake Michigan
Lake Huron
L. Ontario
Lake Erie
MINNESOTA
Minneapolis
St. Paul
WISCONSIN
MICHIGAN
Madison
Lansing
Detroit
River
IOWA
Des Moines
Chicago
ILLINOIS
OHIO
Columbus
CENTRAL LOWLANDS
Indianapolis
INDIANA
Springfield
Frankfort
Ohio River
Wabash
St. Louis
Jefferson City
MISSOURI
KENT.
Nashville
TENN.
Tennessee River
ARKANSAS
Mississippi River
Little Rock
MISS.
Tombigbee R.
Alabama River
Chattahoochee River
Atlanta
Savannah R.
GEORGIA
ALA.
Montgomery
Shreveport
Jackson
Sabine River
GULF COASTAL PLAIN
Pearl R.
Mobile
Tallahassee
Jacksonville
Baton Rouge
LOUISIANA
New Orleans
Houston
FLORIDA
Orlando
Cape Canaveral
Tampa
St. Petersburg
Lake Okeechobee
Miami
Key West
Florida Keys
Straits of Florida
Gulf of Mexico
Elevations
13,120 ft — 4,000 m
6,560 ft — 2,000 m
3,280 ft — 1,000 m
1,640 ft — 500 m
650 ft — 200 m
0 ft — 0 m
National Capital
State Capital
Other City
Mountain peak
Household Money Income (2009)
0–$25,000 25%
$25–50,000 25%
$50–75,000 18%
$75,000–100,000 12%
$100,000+ 20%
0 100 200 300 400 500 mi
0 100 200 300 400 500 km

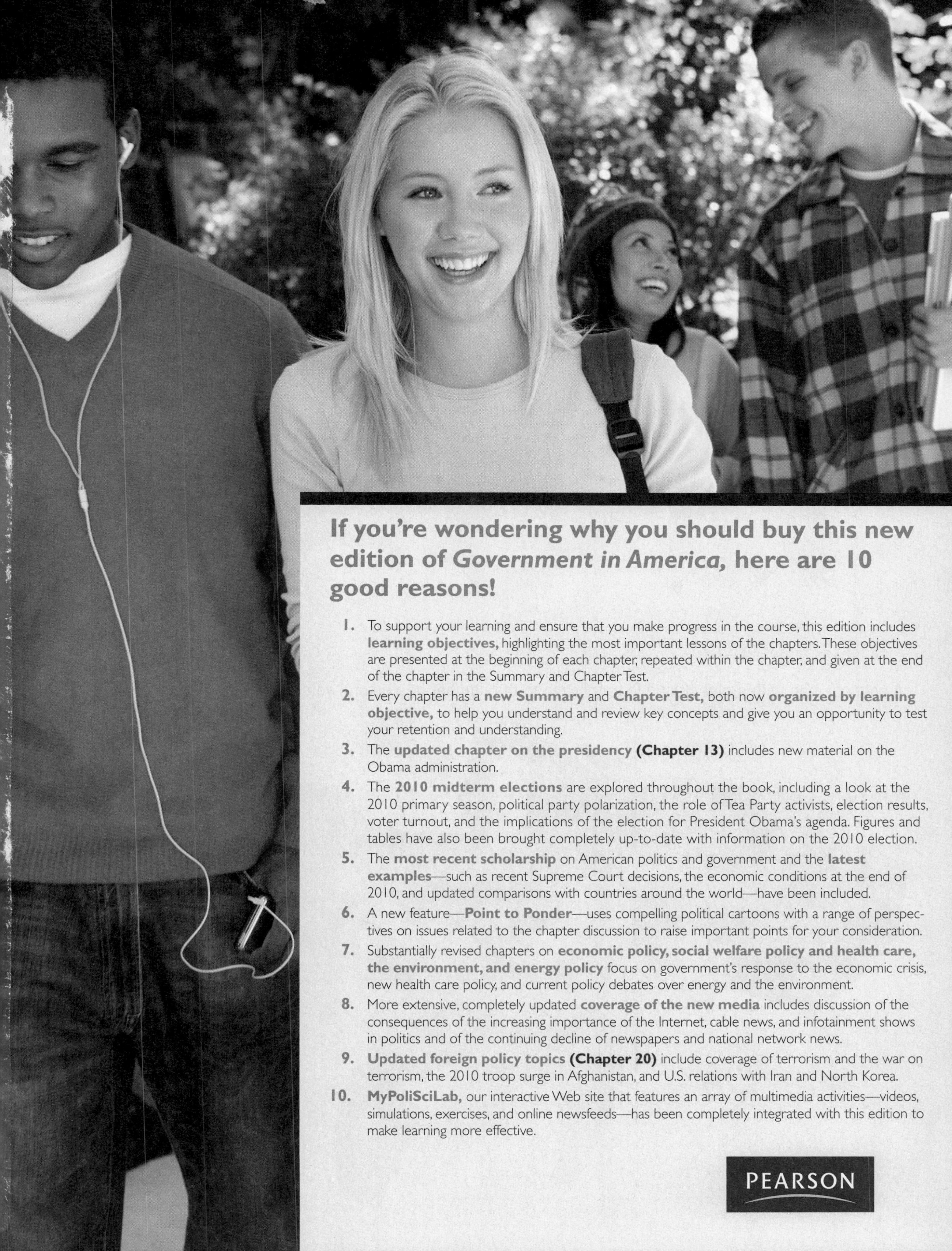
If you're wondering why you should buy this new edition of Government in America, here are 10 good reasons!
1. To support your learning and ensure that you make progress in the course, this edition includes learning objectives, highlighting the most important lessons of the chapters. These objectives are presented at the beginning of each chapter, repeated within the chapter, and given at the end of the chapter in the Summary and Chapter Test.
2. Every chapter has a new Summary and Chapter Test, both now organized by learning objective, to help you understand and review key concepts and give you an opportunity to test your retention and understanding.
3. The updated chapter on the presidency (Chapter 13) includes new material on the Obama administration.
4. The 2010 midterm elections are explored throughout the book, including a look at the 2010 primary season, political party polarization, the role of Tea Party activists, election results, voter turnout, and the implications of the election for President Obama's agenda. Figures and tables have also been brought completely up-to-date with information on the 2010 election.
5. The most recent scholarship on American politics and government and the latest examples—such as recent Supreme Court decisions, the economic conditions at the end of 2010, and updated comparisons with countries around the world—have been included.
6. A new feature—Point to Ponder—uses compelling political cartoons with a range of perspectives on issues related to the chapter discussion to raise important points for your consideration.
7. Substantially revised chapters on economic policy, social welfare policy and health care, the environment, and energy policy focus on government's response to the economic crisis, new health care policy, and current policy debates over energy and the environment.
8. More extensive, completely updated coverage of the new media includes discussion of the consequences of the increasing importance of the Internet, cable news, and infotainment shows in politics and of the continuing decline of newspapers and national network news.
9. Updated foreign policy topics (Chapter 20) include coverage of terrorism and the war on terrorism, the 2010 troop surge in Afghanistan, and U.S. relations with Iran and North Korea.
10. MyPoliSciLab, our interactive Web site that features an array of multimedia activities—videos, simulations, exercises, and online newsfeeds—has been completely integrated with this edition to make learning more effective.
PEARSON

ELECTORAL COLLEGE VOTES IN THE 2008 ELECTION

THE UNITED STATES
A political map showing the number of electoral votes per state

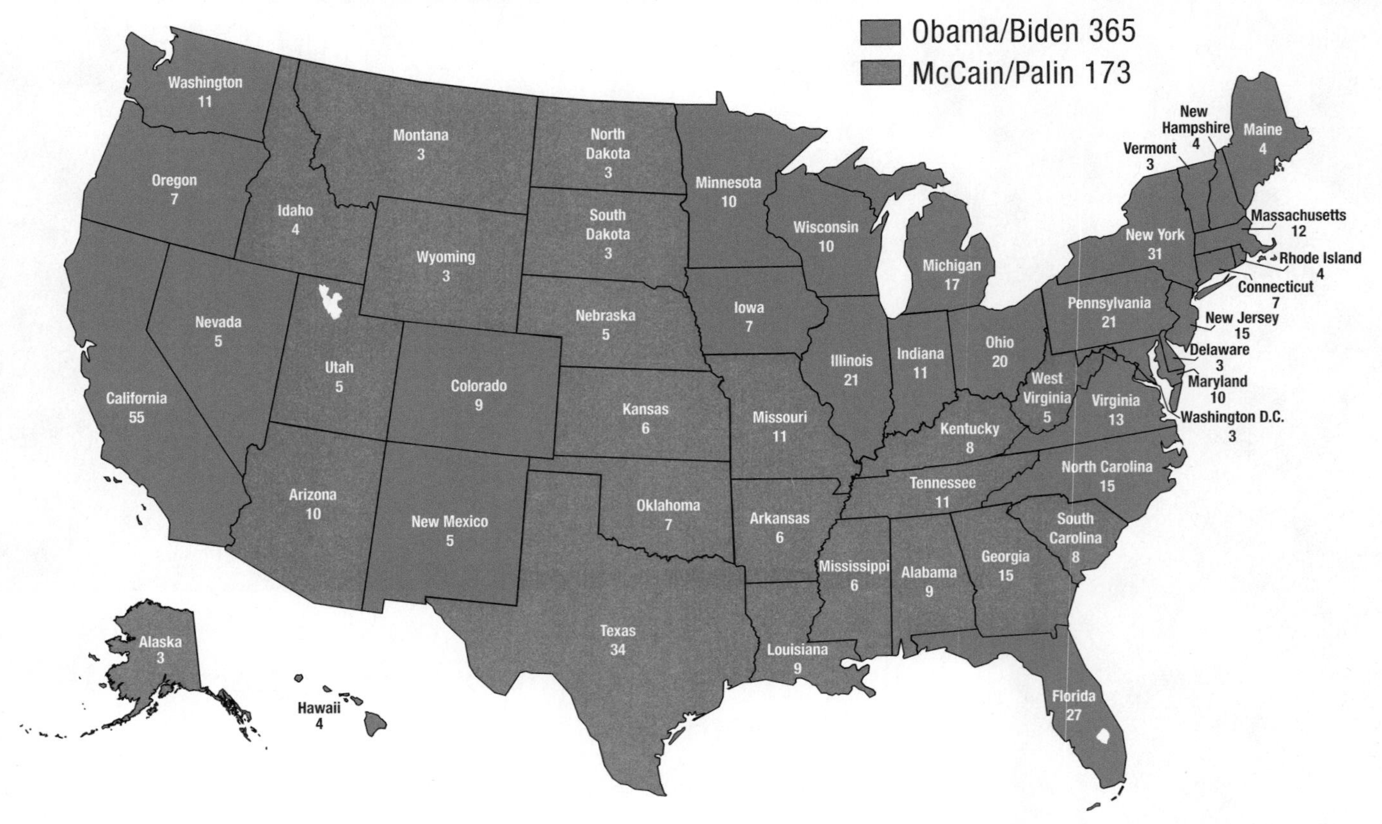

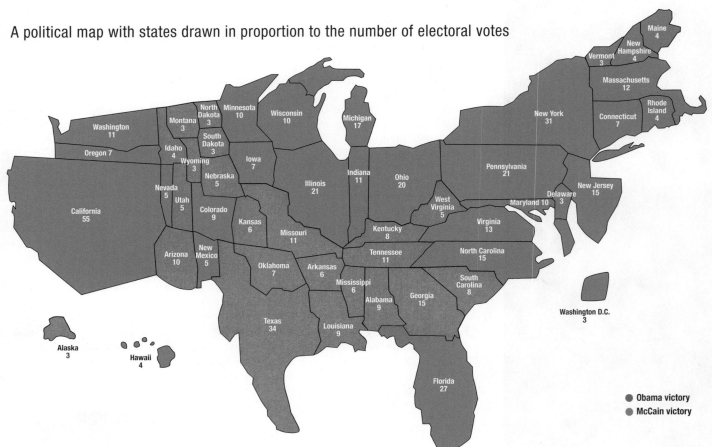

A political map with states drawn in proportion to the number of electoral votes

GOVERNMENT IN AMERICA

Fifteenth Edition

GOVERNMENT IN AMERICA

People, Politics, and Policy

GEORGE C. EDWARDS III

Texas A & M University

MARTIN P. WATTENBERG

University of California, Irvine

ROBERT L. LINEBERRY

University of Houston

Longman

Boston Columbus Indianapolis New York San Francisco Upper Saddle River
Amsterdam Cape Town Dubai London Madrid Milan Munich Paris Montreal Toronto
Delhi Mexico City São Paulo Sydney Hong Kong Seoul Singapore Taipei Tokyo

Executive Editor: Reid Hester
Editorial Assistant: Elizabeth Alimena
Director of Development: Meg Botteon
Development Editor: Randee Falk
Senior Marketing Manager: Lindsey Prudhomme
Associate Development Editor: Donna Garnier
Media Supplements Editor: Regina Vertiz
Production Manager: Denise Phillip
Project Coordination, Text Design, and Electronic Page Makeup: PreMediaGlobal
Cover Design Manager: John Callahan
Cover Designer: Base Art
Cover Images: (c) Jeff Vanuga/Corbis and (c) David Dea/Stockphoto
Photo Researcher: Connie Gardner
Senior Manufacturing Buyer: Roy Pickering
Printer and Binder: Quad/Graphics/Dubuque
Cover Printer: The Lehigh Press/Phoenix Color Corporation

For permission to use copyrighted material, grateful acknowledgment is made to the copyright holders on pp. 695–696 which are hereby made part of this copyright page.

Library of Congress Cataloging-in-Publication Data

Government in America: people, politics, and policy / George C. Edwards III, Martin P. Wattenberg, Robert L. Lineberry.—Fifteenth ed.
p. cm.
Includes bibliographical references and index.
ISBN 978-0-205-80637-9 (alk. paper)
1. United States—Politics and government. I. Edwards, George C. II. Wattenberg, Martin P., 1956 III. Lineberry, Robert L.
JK276.E39 2010b
320.473--dc22

2010044177

Longman
is an imprint of

www.pearsonhighered.com

2 3 4 5 6 7 8 9 10—QDB—13 12 11

ISBN-13: 978-0-205-80637-9
ISBN-10: 0-205-80637-6

Brief Contents

Detailed Contents

Preface

Politics matters. The national government provides important services, ranging from retirement security and health care to recreation facilities and weather forecasts. The national government may also send us to war or negotiate peace with our adversaries, expand or restrict our freedom, raise or lower our taxes, and increase or decrease aid to education. In the twenty-first century, decision makers of both political parties are facing difficult questions regarding American democracy and the scope of our government. Students need a framework for understanding these questions.

We write *Government in America* to provide our readers with a better understanding of our fascinating political system. This fifteenth edition of *Government in America* continues to frame its content with a public policy approach to government in the United States. We continually ask—and answer—the question, "What difference does politics make to the policies that governments produce?" It is one thing to describe the Madisonian system of checks and balances and separation of powers or the elaborate and unusual federal system of government in the United States; it is something else to ask how these features of our constitutional structure affect the policies governments generate.

We do not discuss policy at the expense of politics, however. We provide extensive coverage of five core subject areas: constitutional foundations, patterns of political behavior, political institutions, public policy outputs, and state and local government, but we try to do so in a more analytically significant—and interesting—manner. We take special pride in introducing students to relevant work from current political scientists, such as the role of political action committees (PACs) or the impact of divided government—something we have found instructors appreciate.

New to This Edition

Government in America, Fifteenth Edition has been substantially revised and updated to reflect recent, and often historic, changes in politics, policy, and participation. All figures and tables include the most recent data available. A large percentage of the photos and their captions are new to this edition. We have also added new features to help students understand and master the material in this book.

The Fifteenth Edition includes:

- learning objectives, presented at the beginning of each chapter and repeated within and at the end of the chapter to highlight for students the most important lessons of the chapter
- new chapter summaries, organized by learning objective
- improved chapter tests at the end of each chapter—including multiple choice, true/false, and short answer—also organized by learning objective and giving students an opportunity to test their retention and understanding of key chapter concepts
- questions to encourage critical thinking in boxed features, as well as in some photo and figure captions
- a new feature—**Point to Ponder**—in which a political cartoon is used to make a point about some aspect of American government or politics and raise a question for students to consider

- expanded and updated coverage of immigration to reflect the policy's prominence in American politics
- the latest Supreme Court decisions on civil liberties and civil rights
- improved coverage of Hispanic civil rights issues
- coverage of the 2010 midterm congressional elections
- material on the Obama presidency, including its challenges and presidential power
- data on the increases in political interest and voting participation among young Americans during the 2008 presidential election
- new material on how public opinion polling is beginning to be conducted via the Internet and how telephone polls are adapting to the replacement of landline phones with cell phones
- more extensive, completely updated coverage of the new media; the increasing importance of the Internet, cable news, and infotainment shows in politics; and the continuing decline of newspapers and national network news
- new material on Blue Dog Democrats
- a substantially revised and updated review of the presidential nomination process and campaign finance laws
- additional material on lobbying and policy change
- expanded coverage of the impact of globalization on economic policymaking
- the latest budgetary data
- coverage of the most recent appointees to the Supreme Court
- material examining the state of the economy and the government's intervention in it
- a substantially improved chapter on social welfare policy
- a substantially improved chapter on health care, the environment, and energy to reflect their increased importance in the national agenda
- new material on the war in Afghanistan and the war on terrorism in the chapter on national security
- a substantial number of new figures to increase the visual appeal of the book and to make data more accessible and understandable to students

Two Themes

To render the policy focus in concrete terms, two important themes appear throughout the book: the nature of democracy and the scope of government. Each chapter begins with a preview of the relevancy of these themes to the chapter's subject, refers to the themes at points within the chapter, and ends with specific sections on the two themes under the heading "Understanding . . ." that show how the themes illuminate the chapter's subject matter.

The first great question central to governing, a question every nation must answer, is, *How should we govern?* In the United States, our answer is by "democracy." Yet democracy is an evolving and somewhat ambiguous concept. In Chapter 1, we define democracy as a means of selecting policymakers and of organizing government so that policy represents and responds to citizens' preferences. As with previous editions, we continue to incorporate theoretical issues in our discussions of different models of American democracy. We try to encourage students to think analytically about the theories and to develop independent assessments of how well the American system lives up to citizens' expectations of democratic government. To help them do this, in every chapter we raise questions about democracy. For example, does Congress give the American people the policies they want? Is a strong presidency good for democracy? Does our mass media make us more democratic? Are powerful courts that make policy decisions compatible with democracy?

The second theme, the scope of government, focuses on another great question of governing: *What should government do?* Here we discuss alternative views concerning the proper role and size for American government and how the workings of institutions and politics influence this scope. The government's scope is the core question around which politics revolves in contemporary America, pervading many crucial issues: To what degree should Washington impose national standards for health care or speed limits on state policies? How high should taxes be? Do elections encourage politicians to promise more governmental services? Questions about the scope of government are policy questions and thus obviously directly related to our policy approach. Since the scope of government is *the* pervasive question in American politics today, students will have little problem finding it relevant to their lives and interests.

We hope that students—long after reading *Government in America*—will employ these perennial questions about the nature of our democracy and the scope of our government when they examine political events. The specifics of policy issues will change, but questions about whether the government is responsive to the people or whether it should expand or contract its scope will always be with us.

Politics Matters

In its relevant, balanced treatment of politics and policymaking, *Government in America* refers to two key themes: *the nature of democracy* and *the scope of government*. Each chapter begins with a preview of these two themes, establishing them as a context for the discussion to follow.

Chapter 6

Public Opinion and Political Action

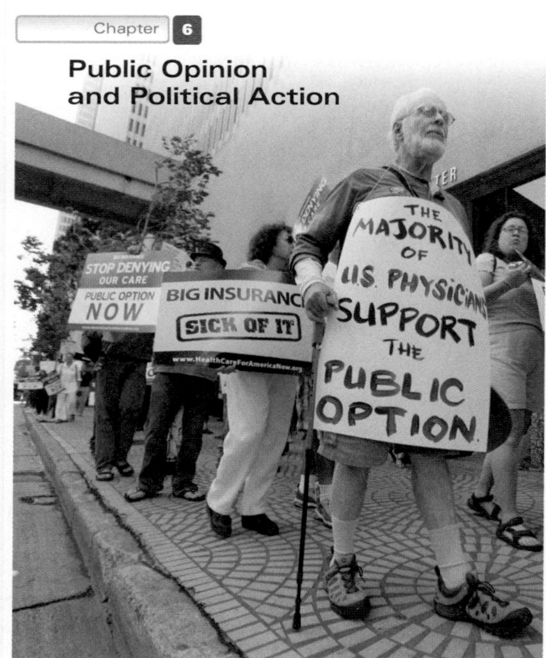

Learning Objectives

- 6.1 Identify demographic trends and their likely impact on American politics.
- 6.2 Outline how various forms of socialization shape political opinions.
- 6.3 Explain how polls are conducted and what can be learned from them about American public opinion.
- 6.4 Assess the influence of political ideology on Americans' political thinking and behavior.
- 6.5 Classify forms of political participation into two broad types.
- 6.6 Analyze how public opinion about the scope of government guides political behavior.

POLITICS IN ACTION: THE LIMITS OF PUBLIC UNDERSTANDING OF HEALTH CARE REFORM

One of the biggest issues early in the Obama administration was health care reform. President Obama made his proposal to guarantee health insurance coverage for almost all Americans a centerpiece of his plan for economic recovery. One of the most discussed elements of the original proposal supported by most Democrats was "the public option," a shorthand term for the creation of a government-administered health insurance program that would be available to individuals and small companies at competitive market rates. This proposal tapped straight into the fundamental issue of the proper scope of government, and sparked public demonstrations both for and against it.

One problem that Democrats faced was getting the public to understand the essence of their proposal. In August 2009, with the debate over the public option drawing much media attention, just 37 percent of respondents in a nationwide poll commissioned by AARP correctly identified the public option from a list of three choices provided to them. Commenting on these disappointing results on his popular political blog, Nate Silver wrote, "This is *mostly* a debate being had among policy elites and the relatively small fraction of the public that is highly knowledgeable and engaged about health care reform; for most others, the details are lost on them."[1]

Public opinion polling has become a major growth industry in recent years. The media seem to love to report on the latest polls. If there is nothing new in their findings, journalists can always fall back on one sure pattern: the lack of public attention to matters of public policy. Whether it's health care reform, cap-and-trade policy, or the question of immigration reform, the safest prediction that a public opinion analyst can make is that many people will be unaware of the major elements of the legislative debate going on in Washington.

In a democracy, the people are expected to guide public policy. But do people pay enough attention to public affairs to fulfill their duty as citizens? As we shall see in this chapter, there is much reason to be concerned about the level of public information about the American public; yet, a case can also be made that most people know enough for democracy to work reasonably well. Like public opinion itself, evaluating the state of public knowledge of public policy is complex.

Politicians and columnists commonly intone the words the American people " and then claim their view as that of the citizenry. Yet it would be hard to find a statement about the American people—who they are and what they believe—that is either entirely right or entirely wrong. The American people are wondrously diverse. There are over 300 million Americans, forming a mosaic of racial, ethnic, and cultural groups. America was founded on the principle of tolerating diversity and individualism, and it remains one of the most diverse countries in the world. Most Americans view this diversity as among the most appealing aspects of their society.

The study of American **public opinion** aims to understand the distribution of the population's beliefs about politics and policy issues. Because there are many groups and a

Chapter OUTLINE
page 168
The American People
page 173
How Americans Learn About Politics: Political Socialization
page 176
Measuring Public Opinion and Political Information
page 183
What Americans Value: Political Ideologies
page 186
How Americans Participate in Politics
page 190
Understanding Public Opinion and Political Action
page 191
Summary

Each chapter concludes with a section titled "Understanding . . . ," which reviews the chapter's content in light of the two themes.

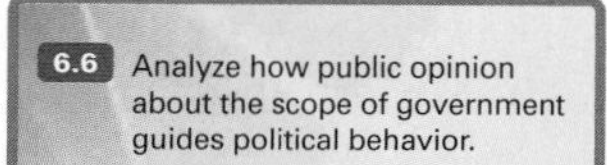

Understanding Public Opinion and Political Action

In many third world countries, there have been calls for more democracy in recent years. One often hears that citizens of developing nations want their political system to be like America's in the sense that ordinary people's opinions determine how the government is run. However, as this chapter has shown, there are many limits on the role public opinion plays in the American political system. The average person is not very well informed about political issues, including the crucial issue of the scope of government.

Public Attitudes Toward the Scope of Government

Central to the ideology of the Republican Party is the belief that the scope of American government has become too wide. According to Ronald Reagan, probably the most admired Republican in recent history, government was not the solution to society's problems—it was the problem. He called for the government to "get off the backs of the American people."

Reagan's rhetoric about an overly intrusive government was reminiscent of the 1964 presidential campaign rhetoric of Barry Goldwater, who lost to Lyndon Johnson in a landslide. Indeed, Reagan first made his mark in politics by giving a televised speech on behalf of the embattled Goldwater campaign. Although the rhetoric was much the same when Ronald Reagan was first elected president in 1980, public opinion about the scope of

Illuminating Themes

Several times in each chapter's margin, Why It Matters insets encourage students to think critically about an aspect of government, politics, or policy and to consider the repercussions—including for themselves—if things worked differently. Each Why It Matters feature extends the book's policy emphasis to situate it directly within the context of students' daily lives.

Youth Turnout

Young people typically have very low turnout rates in the United States. Who votes matters not only because these individuals decide who wins elections but also because politicians pay attention primarily to voters. The fact that so few young people vote means that politicians are not likely to pay too much attention to their opinions or to promote policies that will particularly help them.

YOU ARE THE POLICYMAKER

Balancing the Budget

You have seen that the national government is running large budget deficits and that the national debt continues to grow. Here is the situation you would face as a budget decision maker: According to the OMB, in fiscal year 2011 the national government will have revenues (including Social Security taxes) of about $2.567 trillion. Mandatory expenditures for domestic policy (entitlements such as Social Security and other prior obligations) total about $2.165 trillion. Nondiscretionary payments on the national debt cost another $251 billion. National defense will c an additional $750 billion. That leaves you with a deficit of $599 billion. Moreover, you have yet to spend on discretionary domestic policy program: The president's proposals for these discretionary programs will take $671 billion. If you spend this amount, you will run a deficit of $1.267 trillion—a you will not even have had a chance to fund any significant new programs. Moreover, you may have to ask Congress for additional funds to pay for the wars in Iraq and Afghanistan.

What do you think? Would you drastically reduce defense expenditures? Or would you leave them alone and close down substantial portions of the rest of the

YOU ARE THE JUDGE

The Case of the New Haven Firefighters

New Haven, Connecticut, used objective examinations to identify those firefighters best qualified for promotion. When the results of such an exam to fill vacant lieutenant and captain positions showed that white candidates had outperformed minority candidates, the city threw out the results based on the statistical racial disparity. White and Hispanic firefighters who passed the exams but were denied a chance at promotions by the city's refusal to certify the test results sued the city alleging that discarding the test results discriminated against them based on their race in violation of Title VII of the Civil Rights Act of 1964. The city responded that if they had certified the test results, they could have faced Title VII liability for adopting a practice having a disparate impact on minority firefighters.

You be the judge: Did New Haven discriminate against white and Hispanic firefighters?

Decision: In *Ricci v. DeStefano* (2009), the Court held that if an employer uses a hiring or promotion test, it generally has to accept the test results unless the employer has strong evidence that the test was flawed and improperly favored a particular group. New Haven could not reject the test results simply because the higher scoring candidates were white.

You Are the Policymaker asks students to read arguments on both sides of a specific current issue—such as whether we should prohibit PACs—and then to make a policy decision. In Chapters 4 and 5 (Civil Liberties and Civil Rights), this feature is titled You Are the Judge and presents the student with an actual court case.

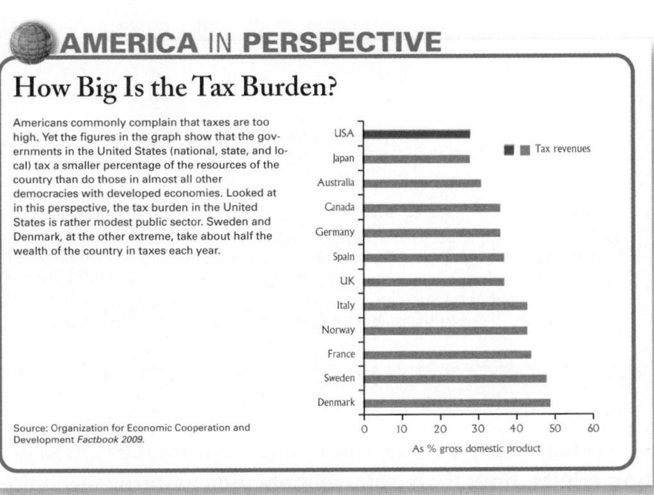
AMERICA IN PERSPECTIVE

How Big Is the Tax Burden?

Americans commonly complain that taxes are too high. Yet the figures in the graph show that the governments in the United States (national, state, and local) tax a smaller percentage of the resources of the country than do those in almost all other democracies with developed economies. Looked at in this perspective, the tax burden in the United States is rather modest public sector. Sweden and Denmark, at the other extreme, take about half the wealth of the country in taxes each year.

Source: Organization for Economic Cooperation and Development *Factbook 2009*.

The America in Perspective feature examines how the United States compares to other countries on topics such as tax rates, voter turnout, and the delivery of public services. By reading these boxes and comparing the United States to other nations, students can obtain a better perspective on the size of our government and the nature of democracy.

Politics Matters

MyState

State and Local Spending on Public Education

The downside of the public policy diversity fostered by federalism is that states are largely dependent on their own resources for providing public services; these resources vary widely from state to state. This map shows the great variation among the states in the money spent on children in the public schools.

QUESTIONS FOR DISCUSSION

- How does your state rank in terms of education spending?
- Would you have been better off if there had been a national standard for spending?

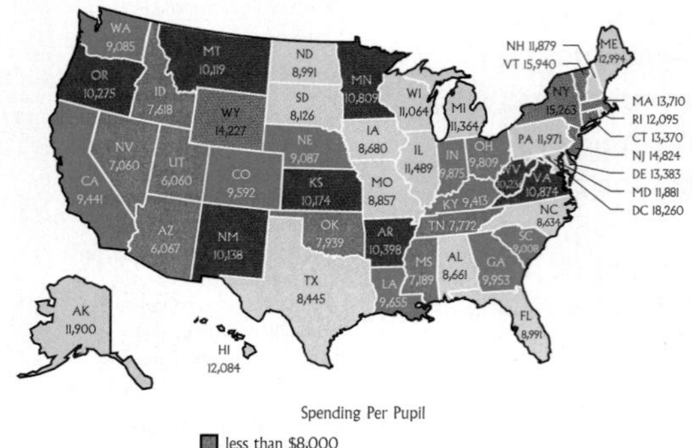

Spending Per Pupil

- less than $8,000
- $8,000–8,999
- $9,000–9,999
- $10,000–10,999
- $11,000–12,999
- $13,000+

Source: U.S. Department of Commerce, Statistical Abstract of the United States, 2010 (Washington, DC: U.S. Government Printing Office, 2010), Table 253. The data are for 2007.

The My State feature brings the lessons of national politics home to the state level, putting important political issues in the students' own backyards. Figures on issues—ranging from the percentage of minorities in a state's population to spending on public education—both inform readers about political circumstances in their own states and illustrate their state's position on the topic in relation to the rest of the country.

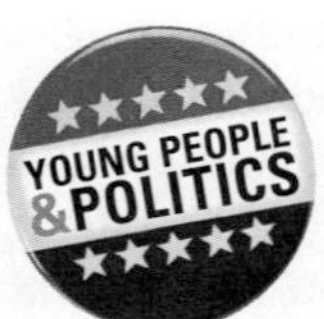

The Parties Face an Independent Youth

Younger people have always had a tendency to be more independent of the major political parties than older people. But this has rarely been as evident in survey data as it is now. As you can see from the 2008 national survey data displayed here, 54 percent of people between the ages of 18 and 24 said they were political independents. In contrast, only 31 percent of people over 65 called themselves independents. Data over time indicate that as people get older, they become more likely to identify with one of the major parties. But whether this will be true for the current generation of youth remains to be seen.

AGE	DEMOCRAT	INDEPENDENT	REPUBLICAN
18–24	29	54	17
25–34	30	49	21
35–44	32	40	28
45–54	35	33	33
55–64	37	38	25
65+	36	31	33

QUESTIONS FOR DISCUSSION

- Do you think that as the current generation of young people ages they will become more likely to identify with the major political parties?
- Because younger people are so likely to be independent, does this mean that many young voters are particularly open to persuasion during campaigns? If so, why don't the Democrats and Republicans pay special attention to getting them on their side?

Source: Authors' analysis of the 2008 American National Election Study.

The popular Young People and Politics feature illustrates how policies specifically impact young adults, how their political behavior patterns are unique and important, and how their particular policy desires are being met or ignored by public officials.

Making Politics Matter to Students

The Decline of Executions

Supreme Court decisions, new DNA technology, and perhaps a growing public concern about the fairness of the death penalty have resulted in a dramatic drop in the number of death sentences—from 98 in 1998 to 42 in 2009. Although the number of executions in Texas been relatively constant, the state's share of total executions nationwide has increased: from 32 percent in 2005 to 57 percent in 2009. Texas prosecutors and juries are no more apt to seek and impose death sentences than those in the rest of the country. However, once a death sentence is imposed there, prosecutors, the courts, the pardon board, and the governor are united in moving the process along.

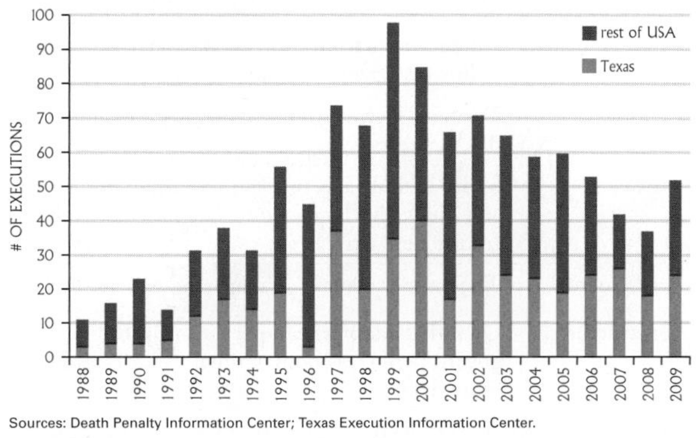

Sources: Death Penalty Information Center; Texas Execution Information Center.

Because students often have little idea of just how much things have changed in their lifetimes (a student who is 18 in 2011 was born in 1993, when President Bill Clinton took office), A Generation of Change provides students some historical perspective—based on their very own life spans. Topics include changes in network news broadcasts, partisan realignment in the South, and the increase in polarization of Democratic and Republican voters.

Learning Objectives

7.1 Describe how American politicians choreograph their messages through the mass media.

7.2 Outline the key developments in the history of mass media and American politics.

7.3 List the major criteria that determine which news stories receive the most media attention.

7.4 Analyze the impact the media has on what policy issues Americans think about.

7.5 Explain how policy entrepreneurs employ media strategies to influence the public agenda.

7.6 Assess the impact of the mass media on the scope of government and democracy in America.

Learning objectives listed at the beginning of and within chapters, and chapter summaries organized by learning objectives, highlight the most important lessons of the chapter.

A POINT TO PONDER

During the nomination process, candidates and the media pay far more attention to Iowa and New Hampshire than to most other states.

What do you think—is this a serious problem? Why or why not?

The new Point to Ponder feature uses political cartoons to raise questions for students to consider.

Chapter Test

7.1 Describe how American politicians choreograph their messages through the mass media.

1. The emergence of media events has contributed to each of the following trends EXCEPT
   a. Increasing news coverage of candidates as individuals
   b. Increasing politicians' control over the political agenda
   c. Increasing the importance of image for presidents
   d. Increasing negativity in American political campaigns
   e. All of the above are true
2. In recent years, most presidential election campaign television advertisements have been negative.

   True_____ False_____
3. How important are the news media
4. The trend toward more negative and cynical news coverage began during
   a. The Great Depression
   b. World War II
   c. The Korean War
   d. The Vietnam War
   e. The Persian Gulf War
5. Those who watch the news on television tend to be more engaged in politics than those who read the news.

   True_____ False_____
6. The Internet appears to be in creasing public interest in political news.

   True_____ False_____
7. Evaluate the shift from broadcasting toward narrowcasting. What impact has this shift had on the quality of political journalism? What impact do you think the

provide a better model? Why or why not?

7.3 List the major criteria that determine which news stories receive the most media attention.

9. Which of the following factors best account(s) for what is considered newsworthy?
   a. A story's high entertainment value
   b. A story's high informational value
   c. A story's high sophistication value
   d. A story's high political value
   e. All of the above
10. News coverage of political campaigns pays relatively little attention to policy issues.

    True_____ False_____

End-of-chapter Chapter Tests, also organized by learning objectives, enable students to assess their understanding of key points before they move on to the next topic.

Resources in Print and Online

NAME OF SUPPLEMENT	PRINT	ONLINE	ONLINE	AVAILABLE TO DESCRIPTION
MyClassPrep		✓	Instructor	This new resource provides a rich database of figures, photos, videos, simulations, activities, and much more that instructors can use to create their own lecture presentation. For more information visit www.mypoliscilab.com
Instructor's Manual 0205059538		✓	Instructor	Offers chapter overviews, lecture outlines, teaching ideas, discussion topics, and research activities. All resources hyperlinked for ease of navigation.
Test Bank 0205043321		✓	Instructor	Contains over 100 questions per chapter in multiple-choice, true-false, short answer, and essay format. Questions are tied to text Learning Objectives and have been reviewed for accuracy and effectiveness.
MyTest 020505952X		✓	Instructor	All questions from the Test Bank can be accessed in this flexible, online test generating software.
Study Guide 0205056938	✓		Student	Contains learning objectives, chapter summaries, key terms, and practice tests.
PowerPoint Presentation 0205059511		✓	Instructor	Slides include a lecture outline of the text, graphics from the book, and quick check questions for immediate feedback on student comprehension.
Transparencies 0205075665		✓	Instructor	These slides contain all maps, figures, and tables found in the text.
Pearson Political Science Video Program	✓		Instructor	Qualified adopters can peruse our list of videos for the American government classroom. Contact your local Pearson representative for more details.
Classroom Response System (CRS) 0205082289		✓	Instructor	A set of lecture questions, organized by topic, for use with "clickers" to garner student opinion and assess comprehension.
American Government Study Site		✓	Instructor/ Student	Online package of practice tests, flashcards and more organized by major course topics. Visit *www.pearsonamericangovernment.com*
You Decide! Current Debates in American Politics, 2011 Edition 020511489X	✓		Student	This debate-style reader by John Rourke of the University of Connecticut examines provocative issues in American politics today by presenting contrasting views of key political topics.
Voices of Dissent: Critical Readings in American Politics, Eighth Edition 0205697976	✓		Student	This collection of critical essays assembled by William Grover of St. Michael's College and Joseph Peschek of Hamline University goes beyond the debate between mainstream liberalism and conservatism to fundamentally challenge the status quo.
Diversity in Contemporary American Politics and Government 0205550363	✓		Student	Edited by David Dulio of Oakland University, Erin E. O'Brien of Kent State University, and John Klemanski of Oakland University, this reader examines the significant role that demographic diversity plays in our political outcomes and policy processes, using both academic and popular sources.
Writing in Political Science, Fourth Edition 0205617360	✓		Student	This guide, written by Diane Schmidt of California State University—Chico, takes students through all aspects of writing in political science step-by-step.
Choices: An American Government Database Reader		✓	Student	This customizable reader allows instructors to choose from a database of over 300 readings to create a reader that exactly matches their course needs. For more information go to *www.pearsoncustom.com/database/choices.html.*
Ten Things That Every American Government Student Should Read 020528969X	✓		Student	Edited by Karen O'Connor of American University. We asked American government instructors across the country to vote for the ten things beyond the text that they believe every student should read and put them in this brief and useful reader. Available at no additional charge when packaged with the text.
American Government: Readings and Cases, Eighteenth Edition 0205697984	✓		Student	Edited by Peter Woll of Brandeis University, this longtime best-selling reader provides a strong, balanced blend of classic readings and cases that illustrate and amplify important concepts in American government, alongside extremely current selections drawn from today's issues and literature. Available at a discount when ordered packaged with this text.
Penguin-Longman Value Bundles	✓		Student	Longman offers 25 Penguin Putnam titles at more than a 60 percent discount when packaged with any Longman text. Go to *www.pearsonhighered.com/penguin* for more information.
Longman State Politics Series	✓		Student	These primers on state and local government and political issues are available at no extra cost when shrink-wrapped with the text. Available for Texas, California, and Georgia.

*Visit the Instructor Resource Center to download supplements at www.pearsonhighered.com/educator

Acknowledgments

Many colleagues have kindly given us comments on the drafts of the fifteenth edition of *Government in America* and eleventh edition of *Government in America, Brief:* Malcolm Cross, Tarleton State University; Gregory Culver, University of Southern Indiana; Yolanda Hake, South Texas College; Thomas Marshall, University of Texas at Arlington; Darrial Reynolds, South Texas College; John Roche, Palomar College; Barbara Trish, Grinnell College; Ruth Ann Alsobrook, Paris Junior College; Michael Cobb, North Carolina State University ; Scott Comparato, Southern Illinois University–Carbondale; Matthew Eshbaugh-Soha, University of North Texas; Philip Habel, Southern Illinois University–Carbondale; Ronald Rubin, Borough of Manhattan Community College–CUNY; Carmine Scavo, East Carolina University; Justin Vaughn, Cleveland State University; and David Weiden, Indiana University-Purdue University Indianapolis.

There are also many reviewers of previous editions to whom we owe our continued gratitude:

Donald Aiesi, Furman University
David Gray Alder, Idaho State University
Phillip J. Ardoin, Appalachian State University
Shari Garber Bax, Central Missouri State University
Craig Bauer, Our Lady of Holy Cross College
Valentine J. Beliglio,Texas Woman's University
Nancy L. Bednar, Del Mar College
Jeffrey C. Berry, South Texas Community College
William Biano, Pennsylvania State University
Richard Bilsker, College of Southern Maryland
Allison Calhoun-Brown, Georgia State University
Karen Callaghan, Texas Southern University
Myles L. Clowers, San Diego City College
Sara Trowbridge Combs, Virginia Highlands Community College
Don Cothran, Northern Arizona State University
Jim Cox, Georgia Perimeter College
Malcolm L. Cross, Tarleton State University
Robert De Luna, St. Philip's College
Donald Kent Douglas, Long Beach City College
Andrew Dowdle, University of Arkansas
Gialisa Gaffaney, Cerritos College
Herbert Gooch, California Lutheran University
Forest Grieves, University of Montana
Martin Gruberg, University of Wisconsin
Dick Hernandez, Orange Coast College
Martin James, Henderson State University
E. Terrence Jones, University of Missouri, St. Louis
Haroon A. Khan, Henderson State University
Manoucher Khosrowshahi, Tyler Junior College
Richard Kiefer,Waubonsee Community College
Ashlyn Kuersten, Western Michigan University
Lisa Langenbach, Middle Tennessee State University
Michael Leuy, Southeast Missouri State University
Cecilia G. Manrique, University of Wisconsin–La Crosse
Nancy Marion, University of Akron
Thomas R. Marshall, University of Texas, Arlington
Craig Matthews, Fullerton College
Derrick Moffitt, Georgia Military College
Michael K. Moore, University of Texas at Arlington
Amy S. Patterson, Elmhurst College
Geoff Peterson, James Rhodes, Luther College; University of Wisconsin–Eau Claire
John Roche, Palomar College

Joseph Romance, Drew University
Gregory Schaller, Villanova University
Robert Speel, Pennsylvania State University, Erie
Bruce Stinebrickner, DePauw University
Glen Sussman, Old Dominion University
William R. Thomas, Georgia State University
R. Mark Tiller, Houston Community College, Northwest
Reed Welch, West Texas A & M University
Harry L. Wilson, Roanoke College
John Wood, Oklahoma State University
Heather Wyatt-Nichol, Stephen F. Austin State University
Kathryn Yates, Richland College

A number of editors have provided valuable assistance in the production of this edition of *Government in America*. Editor-in-Chief Eric Stano provided valuable guidance. Randee Falk was a superb developmental editor, coordinating every aspect of the book. We are grateful to both of them. Finally, we owe a special debt of gratitude to Professor Donald Haider-Markel of the University of Kansas, who did an outstanding job drafting Chapter 21.

George C. Edwards III
Martin P. Wattenberg
Robert L. Lineberry

About the Authors

George C. Edwards III is Distinguished Professor of Political Science at Texas A&M University. He also holds the George and Julia Blucher Jordan Chair in Presidential Studies, has served as the Olin Professor of American Government at Oxford and the John Adams Fellow at the University of London, and held senior visiting appointments at Sciences Po-Paris, Peking University, Hebrew University of Jerusalem, and the U.S. Military Academy at West Point. He is an associate member of Nuffield College at the University of Oxford and was the founder and from 1991–2001 the director of The Center for Presidential Studies.

When he determined that he was unlikely to become shortstop for the New York Yankees, he turned to political science. Today, he is one of the country's leading scholars of the presidency and has authored dozens of articles and written or edited 24 books on American politics and public policy making. He is also editor of *Presidential Studies Quarterly* and general editor of the *Oxford Handbook of American Politics* series. Among his latest books, *On Deaf Ears: The Limits of the Bully Pulpit* examines the effectiveness of presidential leadership on public opinion; *Why the Electoral College Is Bad for America* evaluates the consequences of the method of electing the president; *Governing by Campaigning* analyzes the politics of the Bush presidency; and *The Strategic President* offers a new formulation for understanding presidential leadership.

Professor Edwards has served as president of the Presidency Research Section of the American Political Science Association, which has named its annual dissertation prize in his honor and awarded him its Career Service Award. A member of Phi Beta Kappa and a Woodrow Wilson Fellow, he has received the Decoration for Distinguished Civilian Service from the U.S. Army and the Pi Sigma Alpha Prize from the Southern Political Science Association. He is also a member of the Council on Foreign Relations. He has spoken to more than 200 universities and other groups in the U.S. and abroad, keynoted numerous national and international conferences, done hundreds of interviews with the national and international press, and can be heard on National Public Radio. Grants from the National Science Foundation, the Smith-Richardson Foundation, and the Ford Foundation have funded his work. He has served on the Board of Directors of the Roper Center, the Board of Trustees of the Center for the Study of the Presidency, and on many editorial boards.

Dr. Edwards also applies his scholarship to practical issues of governing, including advising Brazil on its constitution and the operation of its presidency, Russia on building a democratic national party system, Mexico on elections, and Chinese scholars on democracy. He also authored studies for the 1988 and 2000 U.S. presidential transitions.

When not writing, speaking, or advising, he prefers to spend his time with his wife Carmella, sailing, skiing, scuba diving, traveling, or attending art auctions.

Martin P. Wattenberg is a professor of political science at the University of California, Irvine. His first regular paying job was with the Washington Redskins, from which he moved on to receive a Ph.D. at the University of Michigan. He is the author of *Is Voting for Young People?,* part of Longman's Great Questions in Politics series. In addition, he is the author of several books published by Harvard University Press: *Where Have All the Voters Gone?* (2002), *The Decline of American Political Parties* (1998), and *The Rise of Candidate-Centered Politics* (1991).

Professor Wattenberg has lectured about American politics on all of the inhabited continents. His travels have led him to become interested in electoral politics around the world. He has coedited two books published by Oxford University Press—one on party systems in the advanced industrialized world and the other on the recent trend toward mixed-member electoral systems.

Robert L. Lineberry is a professor of political science at the University of Houston and has been its senior vice president. He served from 1981 to 1988 as dean of the College of Liberal Arts and Sciences at the University of Kansas in Lawrence.

A native of Oklahoma City, he received a B.A. degree from the University of Oklahoma in 1964 and a Ph.D. in political science from the University of North Carolina in 1968. He taught for seven years at Northwestern University.

Dr. Lineberry has been president of the Policy Studies Section of the American Political Science Association and has been editor of *Social Science Quarterly.* He is the author or coauthor of numerous books and articles on political science. In addition, for the past 37 years he has regularly taught the introductory course in American government.

He has been married to Nita Lineberry for 45 years. They have two children, Nikki, who works in Denver, and Keith, who works in Houston. They have six grandchildren—Lee, Hunter, Callie, Arwen, Elijah, and Eleanor.

Chapter 1

Introducing Government in America

Learning Objectives

1.1 Identify the key functions of government and explain why they matter.

1.2 Define politics in the context of democratic government.

1.3 Assess how citizens can have an impact on public policy and how policies can impact people.

1.4 Identify the key principles of democracy and outline theories regarding how it works in practice and the challenges democracy faces today.

1.5 Outline the central arguments of the debate in America over the proper scope of government.

POLITICS AND GOVERNMENT MATTER—that is the single most important message of this book. Consider, for example, the following list of ways that government and politics may have already impacted your life:

- Any public schools you attended were prohibited by the federal government from discriminating against females and minorities and from holding prayer sessions led by school officials. Municipal school boards regulated your education, and the state certified and paid your teachers.
- The ages at which you could get your driver's license, drink alcohol, and vote were all determined by state and federal governments.
- Before you could get a job, the federal government had to issue you a Social Security number, and you have been paying Social Security taxes every month that you have been employed. If you worked at a low-paying job, your starting wages were likely determined by state and federal minimum-wage laws.
- As a college student, you may be drawing student loans financed by the government. The government even dictates certain school holidays.
- Even though gasoline prices have risen substantially in recent years, federal policy continues to make it possible for you to drive long distances relatively cheaply compared to citizens in most other countries. In many other advanced industrialized nations, such as England and Japan, gasoline is twice as expensive as in the United States because of the high taxes their governments impose on fuel.
- If you apply to rent an apartment, by federal law landlords cannot discriminate against you because of your race or religion.

This list could, of course, be greatly extended. And it helps explain the importance of politics and government. As Barack Obama said when he first ran for public office in 1993, "Politics does matter. It can make the difference in terms of a benefits check. It can make the difference in terms of school funding. Citizens can't just remove themselves from that process. They actually have to engage themselves and not just leave it to the professionals."[1]

More than any other recent presidential campaign, Obama's 2008 run for the White House was widely viewed as having turned many young Americans on to politics. *Time* magazine even labeled 2008 as the "Year of the Youth Vote," noting that Obama was "tapping into a broad audience of energized young voters hungry for change."[2] And young people did more than display enthusiasm at massive rallies for Obama. By supporting Obama by a two-to-one margin, they provided him with a key edge in the election. Many observers proclaimed that the stereotype of politically apathetic American youth should finally be put to rest.

Stereotypes can be outdated or even off the mark; unfortunately, the perception that young Americans are less engaged in politics than older people has been and continues to be supported by solid evidence. In past editions of this book we wrote:

> *Whether because they think they can't make a difference, the political system is corrupt, or they just don't care, many young Americans are clearly apathetic about public affairs. And while political apathy isn't restricted to young people, a tremendous gap has opened up between young adults and the elderly on measures of political interest, knowledge, and participation.*

Chapter OUTLINE

Although there were some positive developments for young people's political involvement in 2008, it would be premature to declare an end to the era of youth political apathy—the gap between young and older Americans remains. Consider some data from the National Election Study, a nationally representative survey conducted each presidential election year.

In 2008, when the National Election Study asked a nationwide sample about their general level of interest in politics, over half of Americans under the age of 30 said they rarely followed politics, compared to less than a quarter of those over the age of 65. Notice, in Figure 1.1, that although this gap is less than that which was found at the time of the 2000 election, in the early 1970s, when 18- to 20-year-olds became eligible to vote, there was no generation gap in political interest. Back then, young people actually reported following politics a bit more regularly than did senior citizens.

Lack of interest leads to lack of information. The National Election Study always asks a substantial battery of political knowledge questions. As you can see in Figure 1.2, which shows the average percentage of correct answers for various age groups in 1972 and 2008, in 2008 young people were correct only 20 percent of the time whereas people over 65 were correct more than twice as often.[3] Whether the question concerned identifying partisan control of the House and Senate, or accurately estimating the unemployment rate, the result was the same: young people were clearly less knowledgeable than the elderly. This pattern between age and political knowledge has been found time and time again in surveys in recent years.[4] By contrast, in 1972 there was virtually no pattern by age, with those under 30 actually scoring 4 percent higher than those over 65.

Thomas Jefferson once said that there has never been, nor ever will be, a people who are politically ignorant and free. If this is indeed the case, write Stephen Bennett and Eric Rademacher, then "we can legitimately wonder what the future holds" if young people "remain as uninformed as they are about government

FIGURE 1.1 Political Apathy Among Young and Old Americans, 1972–2008

In every presidential election from 1972 to 2008, the American National Election Studies has asked a cross-section of the public the following question: "Some people seem to follow what's going on in government and public affairs most of the time, whether there's an election going on or not. Others aren't that interested. Would you say you follow what's going on in government and public affairs most of the time, some of the time, only now and then, or hardly at all?" Below we have graphed the percentage who said they only followed politics "only now and then" or "hardly at all." Lack of political interest among young people hit a record high during the 2000 campaign between Bush and Gore, when over two-thirds said they rarely followed public affairs. Since then, political interest among young people has recovered somewhat; however, compared to senior citizens, they are still twice as likely to report low political interest.

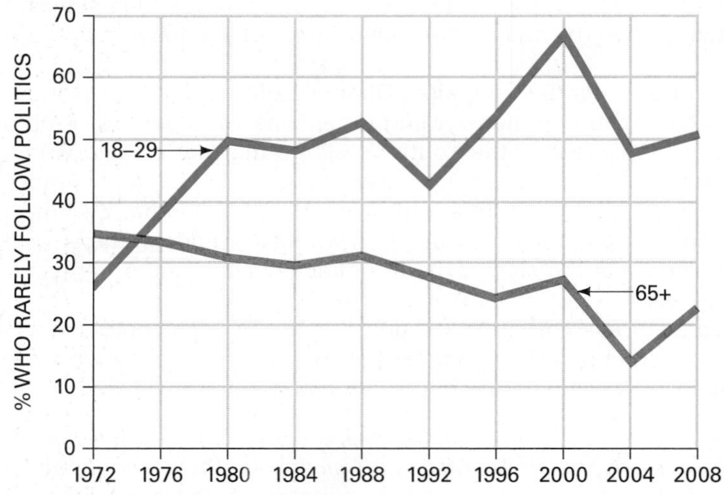

Source: Authors' analysis of 1972–2008 American National Election Studies data.

FIGURE 1.2 Age and Political Knowledge, 1972 and 2008

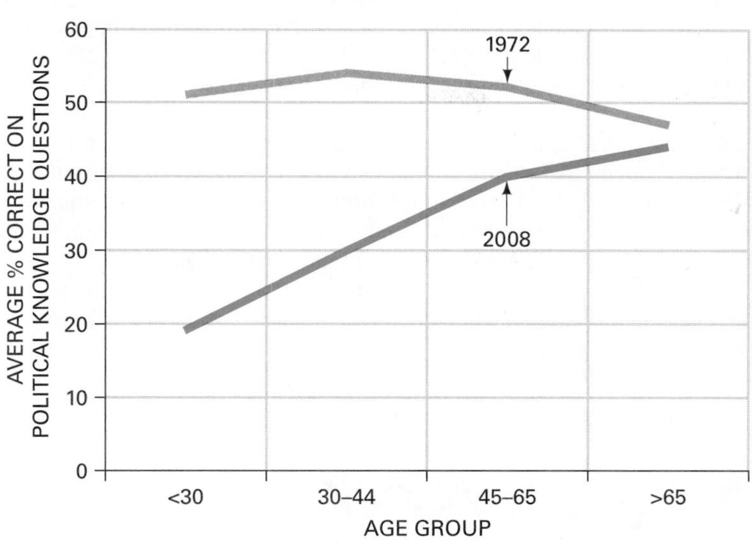

This figure shows the percentage of correct answers to five questions in 1972 and three questions in 2008 by age group. In 1972, the relationship between age and political knowledge was basically flat: Each age group displayed roughly the same level of information about basic political facts, such as which party currently had more seats in the House of Representatives. By 2008, the picture had changed quite dramatically, with young people being substantially less likely to know the answer to such questions than were older people.

Source: Authors' analysis of 1972 and 2008 National Election Studies data.

and public affairs."[5] While this may well be an overreaction, there definitely are important consequences when citizens lack political information. In *What Americans Know About Politics and Why It Matters*, Michael Delli Carpini and Scott Keeter make a strong case for the importance of staying informed about public affairs. Political knowledge, they argue, (1) fosters civic virtues, such as political tolerance; (2) helps citizens to identify what policies would truly benefit them and then incorporate this information in their voting behavior; and (3) promotes active participation in politics.[6] If you've been reading about the debate on immigration reform, for example, you'll be able to understand the proposed legislation, and that knowledge will then help you identify and vote for candidates whose views agree with yours.

As you will see throughout this book, those who participate in the political process are more likely to benefit from government programs and policies. Young people often complain that the elderly have far more political clout than they do—turnout statistics make it clear why this is the case. As shown in Figure 1.3, in recent decades the voter turnout rate for people under 25 has consistently been much lower than that for senior citizens, particularly for midterm elections. Whereas turnout rates for the young have generally been going down, turnout among people over 65 years of age has actually gone up slightly since 1972. Political scientists used to write that the frailties of old age led to a decline in turnout after age 60; now such a decline occurs only after 80 years of age. Greater

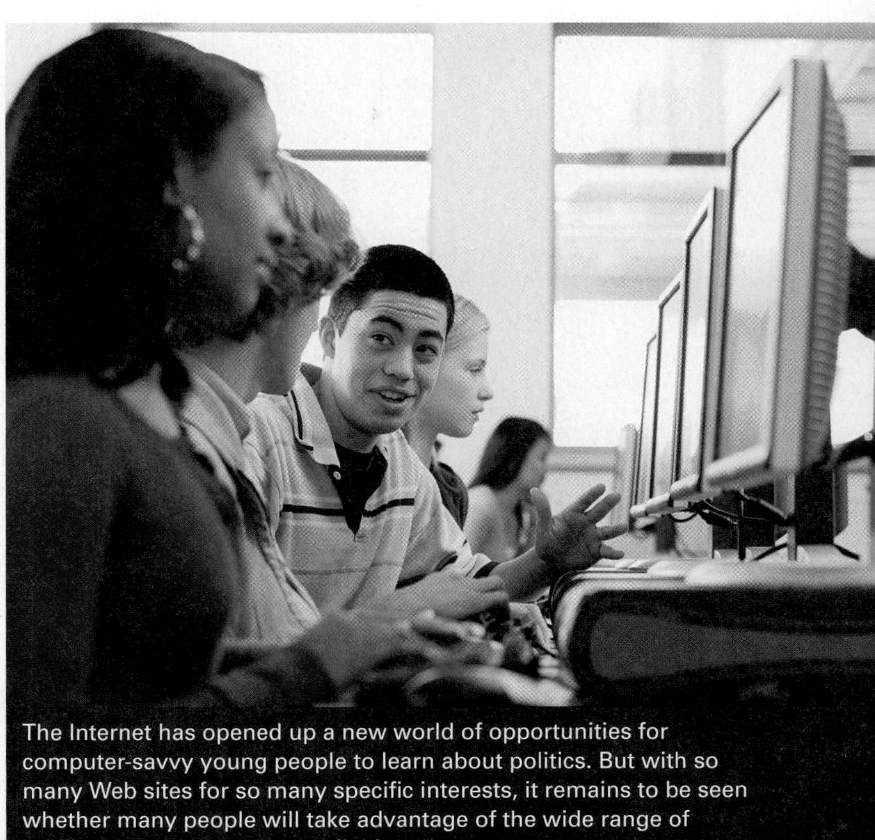

The Internet has opened up a new world of opportunities for computer-savvy young people to learn about politics. But with so many Web sites for so many specific interests, it remains to be seen whether many people will take advantage of the wide range of political information now available.

FIGURE 1.3 Presidential Election Turnout Rates of Young and Old Americans, 1972–2008

This graph shows the turnout gap between young and old Americans in all presidential and midterm elections from 1972 through 2008. The sawtooth pattern of both lines illustrates how turnout always drops off between a presidential election and a midterm election (e.g., from 2004 to 2006). The ups and downs in the graph are much more evident among young people because they are less interested in politics and hence less likely to be regular voters.

In 2008, turnout among young people rose to the highest level that has been measured by the Census Bureau since 1972. A close examination of the Census results reveals that this surge of youth participation can be traced to minorities. For the first time ever, young African-Americans had a higher turnout rate than young whites. Furthermore, record rates of turnout were set by young Hispanics and Asian-Americans. It will be interesting to see if these record turnout rates can be maintained after the enthusiasm over Barack Obama's historic 2008 candidacy subsides. A generation ago, the surge of youth participation that accompanied Bill Clinton's election in 1992 was followed by a sharp drop-off in participation in 1994. If you are reading this in the spring of 2011 or later, then you can go to the Census Web page on voting and registration (http://www.census.gov/hhes/www/socdemo/voting/index.html) to see what percentage of young Americans voted in 2010.

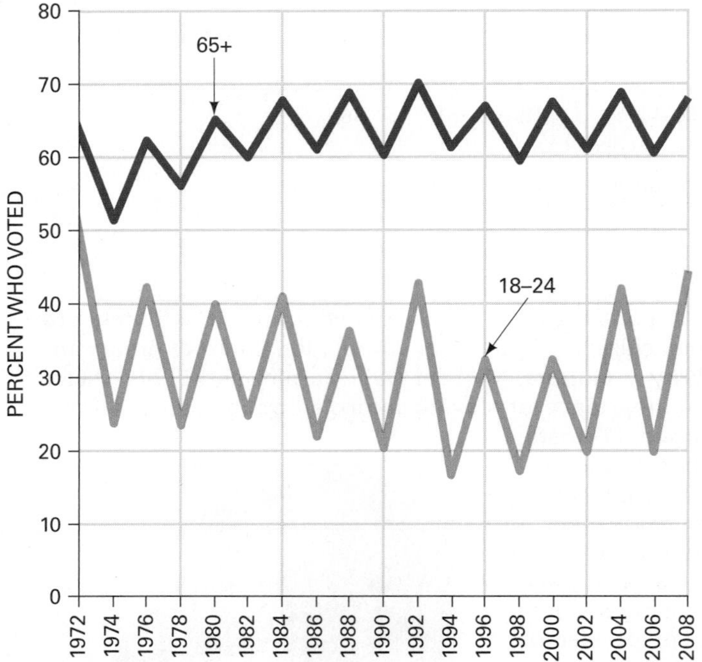

Source: U.S. Census Bureau Current Population Surveys. Data can be found at http://www.census.gov/hhes/www/socdemo/voting/publications/historical/index.html.

access to medical care because of the passage of Medicare in 1965 must surely be given some of the credit for this change. Who says politics doesn't make a difference?

Of course, today's youth have not had any policy impact them in the way that, say, the introduction of Medicare or the draft and the Vietnam War affected previous generations. However, the cause of young people's political apathy probably runs deeper. A broader reason is that today's young adults have grown up in an environment in which news about political events has been increasingly more avoidable and less shared than in the past. When CBS, NBC, and ABC dominated the airwaves, in the 1960s and 1970s, their extensive coverage of presidential speeches, political conventions, and presidential debates frequently left little else to watch on TV. As channels proliferated over subsequent decades, it became much easier to avoid exposure to politics by switching the channel—and of course the Internet has exponentially broadened the choices. Major political events were once shared national experiences. But for many young people today, September 11, 2001, represents the only time that they closely followed a major national event along with everyone else.

Consider some contrasting statistics. Whereas President Nixon got an average Nielsen rating of 50 for his televised addresses and press conferences (meaning that half the population was watching), President Obama averaged only about 24 for his seven major nationally televised appearances in 2009, despite the public's anxiety about the economy.[7] Political conventions, which once received more TV coverage than the Summer Olympics, have been relegated to an hour per night and draw abysmal ratings. The 2008 presidential debates averaged a respectable Nielsen rating of 35, but this was only about three-fifths of the size of the typical debate audience from 1960 to 1980.

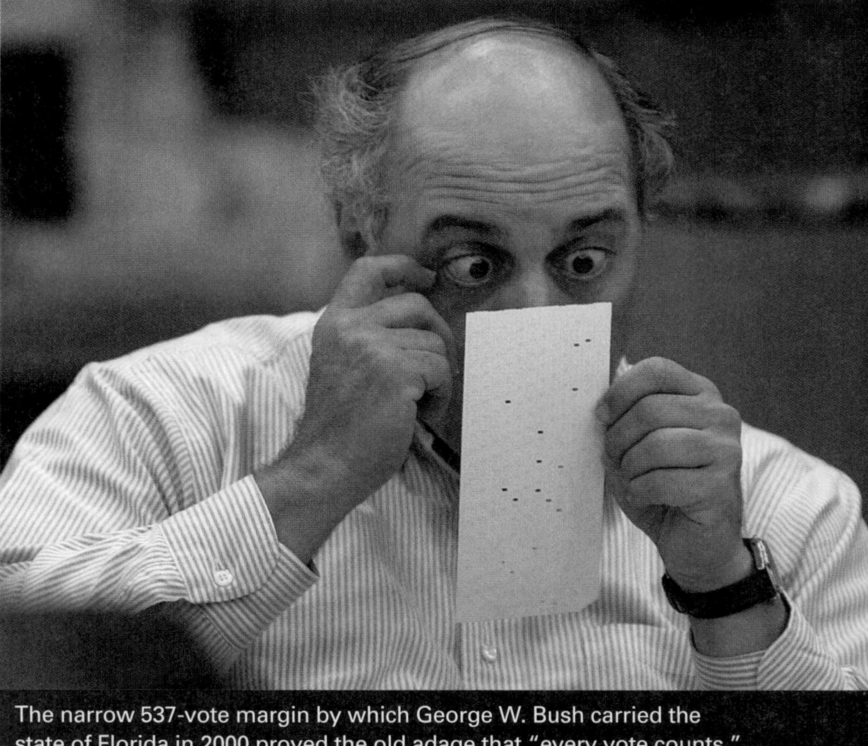

The narrow 537-vote margin by which George W. Bush carried the state of Florida in 2000 proved the old adage that "every vote counts." Here, an election official strains to figure out how to interpret a voter's punch in the tedious process of recounting ballots by hand.

In sum, young people today have never known a time when most citizens paid attention to major political events. As a result, most of them have yet to get into the habit of following and participating in politics. In a 2009 Pew Research Center survey, 38 percent of young adults said they enjoyed keeping up with the news, compared to 68 percent of senior citizens. And young people have grown up in a fragmented media environment, in which hundreds of TV channels and millions of Internet sites have provided them with a rich and varied socialization experience but have also enabled them to easily avoid political events. It has become particularly difficult to convince a generation that has channel and Internet surfed all their lives that politics really does matter.

How will further expansion of channels and, especially, blogs and other Web sites, affect youth interest in and knowledge of politics? Political scientists see both opportunities and challenges. Some optimistic observers see these developments as offering "the prospect of a revitalized democracy characterized by a more active and informed citizenry."[8] Political junkies will certainly find more political information available than ever before, and electronic communications will make it easier for people to express their political views in various forums and directly to public officials. However, with so many media choices for so many specific interests, it will also be easy to avoid the subject of public affairs. It may also be easier to avoid a range of opinion. Political scientist Jeremy Mayer argues that "if we all get to select exactly how much campaign news we will receive, and the depth of that coverage, it may be that too many Americans will choose shallow, biased sources of news on the Internet."[9]

Groups that are concerned about low youth turnout are focusing on innovative ways of reaching out to young people via new technologies, such as social networking sites like Facebook, to make them more aware of politics. In doing so, they are encouraged and spurred by the fact that young people are far from inactive in American society and in recent years have been doing volunteer community service at record rates. As Harvard students Ganesh Sitaraman and Previn Warren write in *Invisible Citizens: Youth Politics After September 11*, "Young people are some of the most active members of their communities and are devoting increasing amounts of their time to direct service work and volunteerism."[10] It is only when it comes to politics that young people seem to express indifference about getting involved.

It is our hope that after reading this book, you will be persuaded that paying attention to politics and government is important. Government has a substantial impact on all our lives. But it is also true that we have the opportunity to have a substantial impact on government. Involvement in public affairs can take many forms, ranging from simply becoming better informed by browsing through political Web sites to running for elected office. In between are countless opportunities for everyone to make a difference.

1.1 Identify the key functions of government and explain why they matter.

Government

government
The institutions and processes through which **public policies** are made for a society.

The institutions that make decisions for a society are collectively known as **government**. In the case of our own national government, these institutions are Congress, the president, the courts, and federal administrative agencies ("the bureaucracy"). Thousands of state and local governments also decide on policies that influence our lives. There are about 500,000 elected officials in the United States. Thus, policies that affect you are being made almost constantly.

Because government shapes how we live, it is important to understand the process by which decisions are made as well as what is actually decided. Two fundamental questions about governing will serve as themes throughout this book:

- ***How should we govern?*** Americans take great pride in calling their government democratic. This chapter examines the workings of democratic government; the chapters that follow will evaluate the way American government actually works compared to the standards of an "ideal" democracy. We will continually ask, Who holds power and who influences the policies adopted by government?
- ***What should government do?*** This text explores the relationship between *how* American government works and *what* it does. In other words, it addresses the question, Does our government do what we want it to do? Debates over this question concerning the scope of government are among the most important in American political life today. Some people would like to see the government take on more responsibilities; others believe it already takes on too much.

public goods
Goods, such as clean air and clean water, that everyone must share.

While citizens often disagree about what their government should do for them, all governments have certain functions in common. National governments throughout the world perform the following functions:

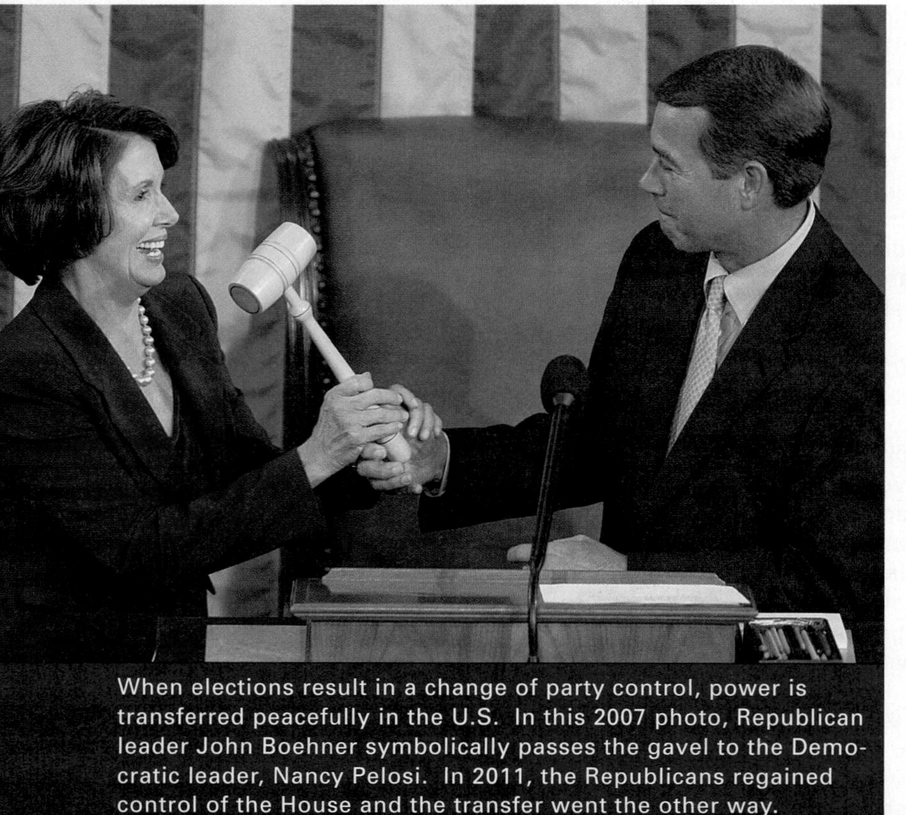
When elections result in a change of party control, power is transferred peacefully in the U.S. In this 2007 photo, Republican leader John Boehner symbolically passes the gavel to the Democratic leader, Nancy Pelosi. In 2011, the Republicans regained control of the House and the transfer went the other way.

- ***Maintain a national defense.*** A government protects its national sovereignty, usually by maintaining armed forces. In the nuclear age, some governments possess awesome power to make war through highly sophisticated weapons. The United States currently spends over $650 billion a year on national defense. Since September 11, 2001, the defense budget has been substantially increased in order to cope with the threat of terrorism on U.S. soil.
- ***Provide public services.*** Governments in this country spend billions of dollars on schools, libraries, hospitals, and dozens of other public institutions. Some of these services, called **public goods**, are such that, if they exist, by their very nature they cannot be denied to anyone and therefore must be shared by everyone; access to highways, for example, cannot be denied. National defense is in effect a public good. Such services can only be provided by government, as the private sector would have no incentive to provide them. Other services, such as a college education or medical care, can be provided to some individuals

without being provided to all; these services are also widely provided by the private sector.

- ***Preserve order.*** Every government has some means of maintaining order. When people protest in large numbers, governments may resort to extreme measures to restore order. For example, the National Guard was called in to stop the looting and arson after rioting broke out in Los Angeles following the 1992 Rodney King verdict.
- ***Socialize the young.*** Governments politically socialize the young—that is, instill in children knowledge of and pride in the nation and its political system and values. Most modern governments pay for education, and school curricula typically include a course on the theory and practice of the country's government. Rituals like the daily Pledge of Allegiance seek to foster patriotism and love of country.
- ***Collect taxes.*** Approximately one out of every three dollars earned by American citizens goes to national, state, and local taxes—money that pays for the public goods and services the government provides.

Governments provide a wide range of public services, including providing a national defense. Because of the threat from Al Qaeda, U.S. troops have been in Afghanistan since 2001. In late 2009, President Obama ordered that an additional 30,000 troops be sent there. Here, a U.S. Marine Sgt. and translator can be seen talking to a local elder in southern Afghanistan.

All these governmental tasks add up to weighty decisions that our political leaders must make. For example, how much should we spend on national defense as opposed to education? How high should taxes for Medicare and Social Security be? We answer such questions through politics.

Politics

1.2 Define politics in the context of democratic government.

Politics determines whom we select as our governmental leaders and what policies these leaders pursue. Political scientists often cite Harold D. Lasswell's famous definition of politics: "Who gets what, when, and how."[11] It is one of the briefest and most useful definitions of politics ever penned. Admittedly, this broad definition covers a lot of ground (office politics, sorority politics, and so on) in which political scientists are generally not interested. They are interested primarily in politics related to governmental decision making.

The media usually focus on the *who* of politics. At a minimum, this includes voters, candidates, groups, and parties. *What* refers to the substance of politics and government—benefits, such as medical care for the elderly, and burdens, such as new taxes. *How* refers to the ways in which people participate in politics. People get what they want through voting, supporting, compromising, lobbying, and so forth. In this sense, government and politics involve winners and losers. Behind every arcane tax provision or item in an appropriations bill, there are real people getting something, or getting something taken away.

The ways in which people get involved in politics make up their **political participation**. Many people judge the health of a government by how widespread political participation is. America does quite poorly when judged by its voter turnout, which is one of the lowest in the world. Low voter turnout has an effect

politics
The process by which we select our governmental leaders and what policies these leaders pursue. Politics produces authoritative decisions about public issues.

political participation
All the activities by which citizens attempt to influence the selection of political leaders and the policies they pursue. Voting is the most common means of political participation in a **democracy**. Other means include protest and civil disobedience.

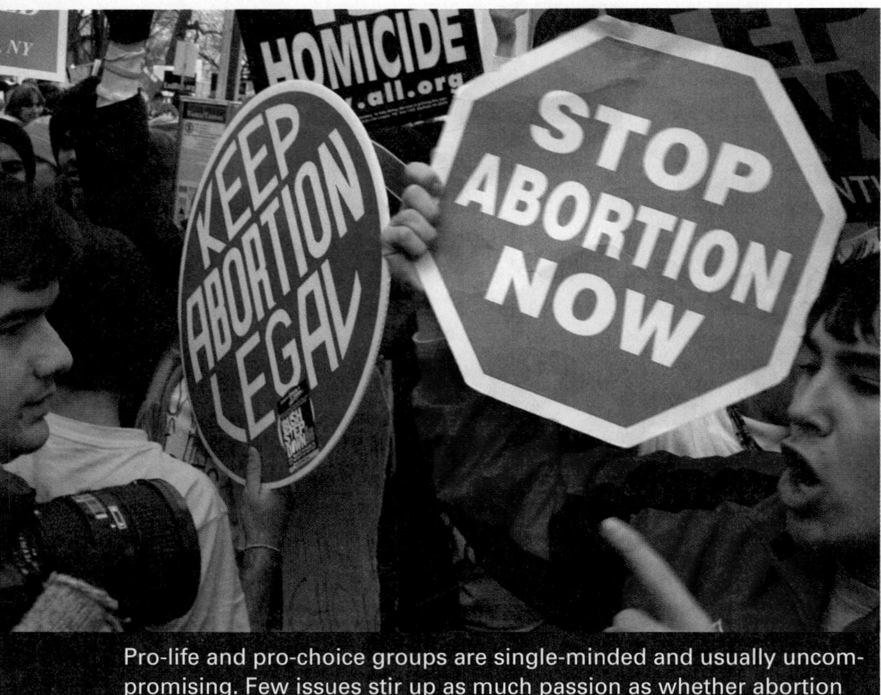

Pro-life and pro-choice groups are single-minded and usually uncompromising. Few issues stir up as much passion as whether abortion should be permitted and, if so, under what conditions.

on who holds political power. Because so many people do not show up at the polls, voters are a distorted sample of the public as a whole. Groups with a high turnout rate, such as the elderly, benefit, whereas those with a low turnout rate, such as young people, lack political clout.

Voting is only one form of political participation. (See Chapter 6 for a discussion of other forms of participation.) For a few Americans, politics is a vocation: They run for office, and some even earn their livelihood from holding political office. In addition, there are many Americans who treat politics as critical to their interests. Many of these people are members of **single-issue groups**—groups so concerned with one issue that members often cast their votes on the basis of that issue only, ignoring a politician's stand on everything else. Groups of activists dedicated either to outlawing abortion or to preserving abortion rights are good examples of single-issue groups.

Individual citizens and organized groups get involved in politics because they understand that public policy choices made by governments affect them in significant ways. Will all those who need student loans receive them? Will everyone have access to medical care? Will people be taken care of in their old age? Is the water safe to drink? These and other questions tie politics to policymaking.

single-issue groups
Groups that have a narrow interest, on which their members tend to take an uncompromising stance.

The Policymaking System

1.3 Assess how citizens can have an impact on public policy and how policies can impact people.

Americans frequently expect government to do something about their problems. For example, the president and members of Congress are expected to keep the economy humming along; voters will penalize them at the polls if they do not. The **policymaking system** reveals the way our government responds to the priorities of its people. Figure 1.4 shows a skeletal model of this system. The rest of this book will flesh out this model, but for now it will help you understand how government policy comes into being and evolves over time.

policymaking system
The process by which policy comes into being and evolves. People's interests, problems, and concerns create political issues for government policymakers. These issues shape policy, which in turn impacts people, generating more interests, problems, and concerns.

People Shape Policy

The policymaking system begins with people. All Americans have interests, problems, and concerns that are touched on by public policy. Some people may think the government should help train people for jobs in today's increasingly technology-oriented economy; others may think that their taxes are too high and that the country would be best served by a large tax cut. Some people may expect government to do something to curb domestic violence; others may be concerned about prospects that the government may make it much harder to buy a handgun.

What do people do to express their opinions in a democracy? As mentioned, people have numerous avenues for participation, such as voting for candidates who represent their opinions, joining political parties, posting messages to Internet chat groups, and forming *interest groups*—organized groups of people with a common interest. In this way, people's concerns enter the linkage institutions of the policymaking system. **Linkage institutions**—parties, elections, interest groups, and the

linkage institutions
The political channels through which people's concerns become political issues on the policy agenda. In the United States, linkage institutions include elections, political parties, interest groups, and the media.

FIGURE 1.4 The Policymaking System

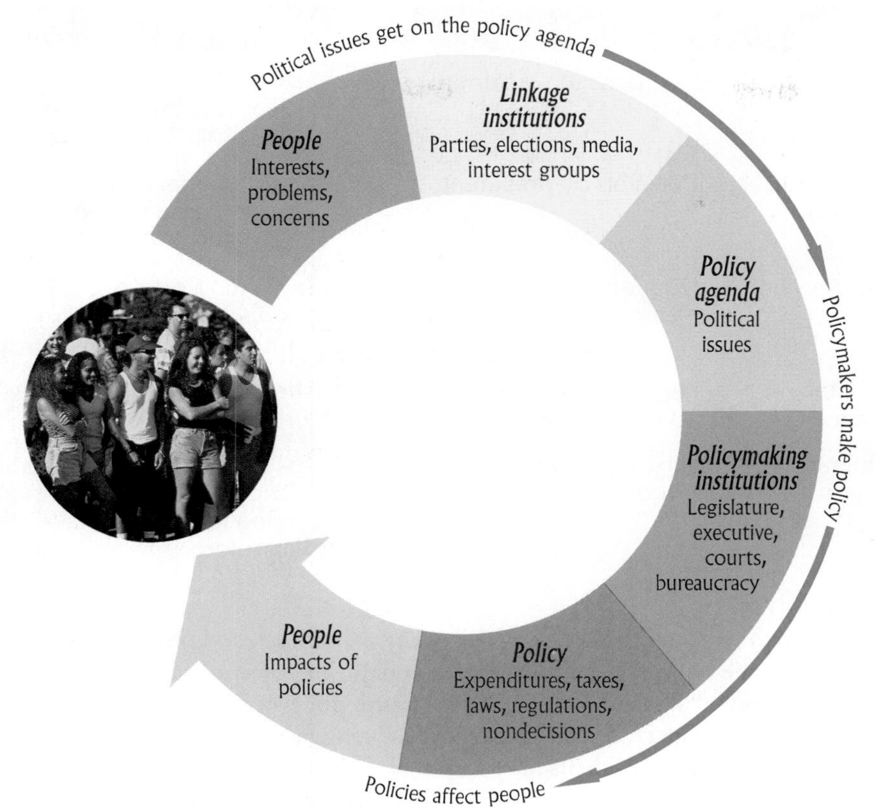

media—transmit Americans' preferences to the policymakers in government. Parties and interest groups strive to ensure that their members' concerns receive appropriate political attention. The media investigate social problems and inform people about them. Elections provide citizens with the chance to make their opinions heard by choosing their public officials.

All these institutions help to shape the government's **policy agenda**, the issues that attract the serious attention of public officials and other people actively involved in politics at a given time. Some issues will be considered, and others will not. If politicians want to get elected, they must pay attention to the problems that concern voters. When you vote, you are partly looking at whether a candidate shares your agenda. If you are worried about rising health care costs and a certain candidate talks only about America's moral decay and ending legalized abortions, you will probably support another candidate.

policy agenda
The issues that attract the serious attention of public officials and other people involved in politics at a point in time.

A government's policy agenda changes regularly. When jobs are scarce and business productivity is falling, economic problems occupy a high position on the government's agenda. If the economy is doing well and trouble spots around the world occupy the headlines, foreign policy questions are bound to dominate the agenda. In general, bad news—particularly about a crisis situation—is more likely than good news to draw sufficient media attention to put a subject on the policy agenda. As the old saying goes, "Good news is no news." When unemployment rises sharply, it leads the news; when jobs are plentiful, the latest unemployment report is much less of a news story. Thus, the policy agenda responds more to societal failures than successes. The question politicians constantly ask is, How can we as a people do better?

political issue
An issue that arises when people disagree about a problem and how to fix it.

policymaking institutions
The branches of government charged with taking action on political issues. The U.S. Constitution established three policymaking institutions—Congress, the presidency, and the courts. Today, the power of the bureaucracy is so great that most political scientists consider it a fourth policymaking institution.

People, of course, do not always agree on what government should do. Indeed, one group's positions and interests are often at odds with those of another group. A **political issue** is the result of people disagreeing about a problem or about the public policy needed to fix it. There is never a shortage of political issues; government, however, will not act on any issue until it is high on the policy agenda.

Policymakers stand at the core of the system, working within the three **policymaking institutions** established by the U.S. Constitution: Congress, the presidency, and the

TABLE 1.1 Types of Public Policies

TYPE	DEFINITION	EXAMPLE
Congressional statute	Law passed by Congress	The $787 billion American Recovery and Reinvestment Act of 2009 is enacted.
Presidential action	Decision by president	An additional 30,000 troops are ordered to deploy to Afghanistan.
Court decision	Opinion by Supreme Court or other court	Supreme Court rules that individuals have a constitutional right to own a gun.
Budgetary choices	Legislative enactment of taxes and expenditures	The federal budget resolution is enacted.
Regulation	Agency adoption of regulation	The Department of Education issues guidelines for qualifying for the federal student loan forgiveness program.

public policy
A choice that government makes in response to a political issue. A policy is a course of action taken with regard to some problem.

policy impacts
The effects a policy has on people and problems. Impacts are analyzed to see how well a policy has met its goal and at what cost.

courts. Policymakers scan the issues on the policy agenda, select those they consider important, and make policies to address them. Today, the power of the bureaucracy is so great that most political scientists consider it a fourth policymaking institution.

Very few policies are made by a single policymaking institution. Environmental policy is a good example. Some presidents have used their influence with Congress to urge clean-air and clean-water policies. When Congress responds by passing legislation to clean up the environment, bureaucracies have to implement the new policies. The bureaucracies, in turn, create extensive volumes of rules and regulations that define how policies are to be implemented. In addition, every law passed and every rule made can be challenged in the courts. Courts make decisions about what policies mean and whether they conflict with the Constitution.

AIDS was relatively low on the political agenda until well-known celebrities contracted the disease. AIDS activists have found, however, that getting the problem on the agenda is only half the political battle. Getting the government to take aggressive action to find and approve new treatments has proved to be at least as difficult.

Policies Impact People

Every decision that government makes—every law it passes, budget it establishes, and ruling it hands down—is **public policy**. Public policies are of various types, depending in part on which policymaking institution they originated with. Some of the most important types—statute, presidential action, court decision, budgetary choice, regulation—are defined and exemplified in Table 1.1.

Policies can be established through inaction as well as through action. Doing nothing—or nothing different—can prove to be a very consequential governmental decision. Reporter Randy Shilts's book traces the dramatic increase in the number of people with AIDS and reveals how governments in Washington and elsewhere did little or debated quietly about what to do.[12] Shilts claims that because politicians initially viewed AIDS as a gay person's disease, they were reluctant to support measures to deal with it, fearful of losing the votes of antigay constituents. The issue thus remained a low priority on the government's policy agenda until HIV and AIDS spread to the general population—and to celebrities like basketball star Earvin "Magic" Johnson.

Once policies are made and implemented, they affect people. **Policy impacts** are the effects that a policy has on people and on society's problems. People want policy that effectively addresses their interests, problems, and concerns; clearly, a new law, executive order, bureaucratic regulation, or court judgment doesn't mean much if it doesn't work. Environmentalists want an industrial emissions policy that not only claims to prevent air pollution but also does so. Minority groups want a civil rights policy that not only promises them equal treatment but also ensures it.

Having a policy implies having a goal. Whether we want to reduce poverty, cut crime, clean the water, or hold down inflation, we have a goal in mind. Policy impact analysts ask how well a policy achieves its goal—and at what cost. The analysis of policy impacts carries the policymaking system back to its point of origin: the interests, problems, and concerns of the people. Translating people's desires into effective public policy is crucial to the workings of democracy.

Democracy

1.4 Identify the key principles of democracy and outline theories regarding how it works in practice and the challenges democracy faces today.

Democracy is a system of selecting policymakers and of organizing government so that policy reflects citizens' preferences. Today, the term *democracy* takes its place among terms like *freedom, justice,* and *peace* as a word that seemingly has only positive connotations. As you can see in Figure 1.5, currently most people in most democracies around the world believe that, although democracy may have its faults, it is the best form of government. Yet the writers of the U.S. Constitution had no fondness for democracy, as many of them doubted the ability of ordinary Americans to make informed judgments about what government should do. Roger Sherman, a delegate to the Constitutional Convention, said the people "should have as little to do as may be with the government." Only much later did Americans come to cherish democracy and believe that all citizens should actively participate in choosing their leaders.

democracy
A system of selecting policymakers and of organizing government so that policy represents and responds to the public's preferences.

Most Americans would probably say that democracy is "government by the people." These words are, of course, part of the famous phrase by which Abraham Lincoln defined democracy in his Gettysburg Address: "government of the people, by the people, and for the people." The extent to which each of these three aspects of democracy holds true is a matter crucial to evaluating how well our government is working. Certainly, government has always been "of the people" in the United States, for the Constitution

FIGURE 1.5 Assessment of Democracy by Citizens in Various Countries

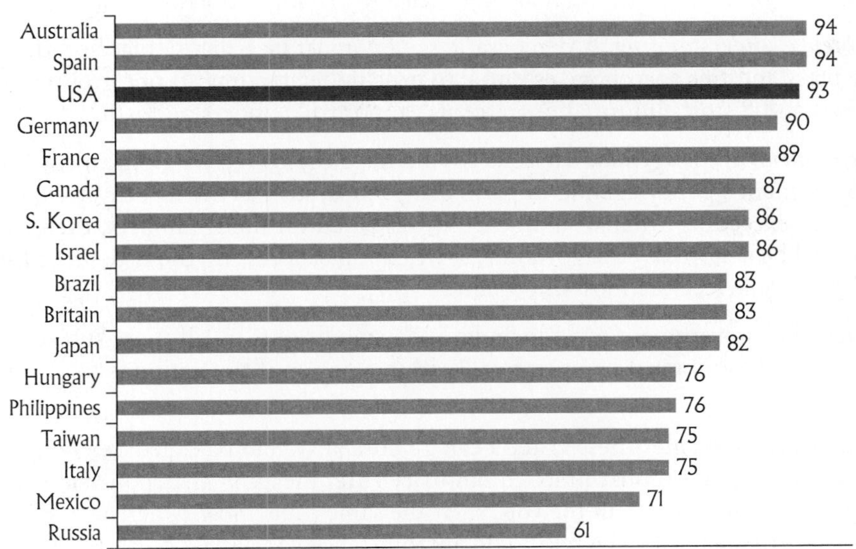

Most citizens in most democracies believe that democracy is the best form of government. This figure shows the percentages in various democracies who said "strongly agree" or "agree" in response to the following: "Please tell me how strongly you agree or disagree with the following statement: 'Democracy may have problems but it's better than any other form of government.' Do you agree strongly, agree, disagree, or disagree strongly with this statement?"

Source: Authors' analysis of the Comparative Study of Electoral Systems, module 2 (2001–2006).

"Isn't that the real genius of democracy? The voters are ultimately to blame."

forbids the granting of titles of nobility—a status of privilege within the government, usually passed down from generation to generation. On the other hand, it is a physical impossibility for government to be "by the people" in a nation of over 300 million people. Therefore, our democracy involves choosing people from among our midst to govern. Where the serious debate begins is whether political leaders govern "for the people," as there always are significant biases in how the system works. Democratic theorists have elaborated a set of goals to use in evaluating this crucial question.

Traditional Democratic Theory

Traditional democratic theory rests on a number of key principles that specify how governmental decisions are made in a democracy. Robert Dahl, one of America's leading theorists, suggests that an ideal democratic process should satisfy the following five criteria:

- ***Equality in voting.*** The principle of "one person, one vote" is basic to democracy. Voting need not be universal, but it must be representative.
- ***Effective participation.*** Citizens must have adequate and equal opportunities to express their preferences throughout the decision-making process.
- ***Enlightened understanding.*** A democratic society must be a marketplace of ideas. A free press and free speech are essential to civic understanding. If one group monopolizes and distorts information, citizens cannot truly understand issues.
- ***Citizen control of the agenda.*** Citizens should have the collective right to control the government's policy agenda. If particular groups, such as the wealthy, have influence far exceeding what would be expected based on their numbers, then the agenda will be distorted—the government will not be addressing the issues that the public as a whole feels are most important.
- ***Inclusion.*** The government must include, and extend rights to, all those subject to its laws. Citizenship must be open to all within a nation if the nation is to call itself democratic.[13]

majority rule
A fundamental principle of traditional democratic theory. In a democracy, choosing among alternatives requires that the majority's desire be respected. See also **minority rights**.

minority rights
A principle of traditional democratic theory that guarantees rights to those who do not belong to majorities. See also **majority rule**.

Ideally, only if it satisfies these criteria can a political system be called democratic. Furthermore, democracies must practice **majority rule**, meaning that policies made should reflect the will of over half the voters. At the same time, most Americans would not want to give the majority free rein to do anything they can agree on. Restraints on the majority are built into the American system of government in order to protect the minority. Thus, the majority cannot infringe on **minority rights**; freedom of assembly, freedom of speech, and so on are freedoms for those in a minority as well as the majority.

In a society too large to make its decisions in open meetings, a few must look after the concerns of the many. The relationship between the few leaders and the many citizens is one of **representation**. The literal meaning of representation is to "make present once again." In politics, this means that the desires of the people should be replicated in government through the choices of elected officials. The closer the correspondence between representatives and their constituents, the closer the approximation to an ideal democracy. As might be expected for such a crucial question, theorists disagree widely about the extent to which this actually occurs in America.

representation
A basic principle of traditional democratic theory that describes the relationship between the few leaders and the many followers.

Three Contemporary Theories of American Democracy

Theories of American democracy are essentially theories about who has power and influence. All, in one way or another, ask the question, Who really governs in our nation? Each focuses on a key aspect of politics and government, and each reaches a somewhat different conclusion.

Pluralism One important theory of American democracy, **pluralism**, states that groups with shared interests influence public policy by pressing their concerns through organized efforts. The National Rifle Association (NRA), the National Organization for Women (NOW), and the United Auto Workers (UAW) are contemporary examples of such interest groups.

Pluralism
A theory of American democracy emphasizing that the policymaking process is very open to the participation of all groups with shared interests, with no single group usually dominating. Pluralists tend to believe that as a result, public interest generally prevails.

According to pluralist theory, because of open access to various institutions of government and public officials, organized groups can compete with one another for control over policy and no one group or set of groups dominates. Given that power is dispersed in the American form of government, groups that lose in one arena can take their case to another. For example, civil rights groups faced congressional roadblocks in the 1950s but were able to win the action they were seeking from the courts.

Pluralists are generally optimistic that the public interest will eventually prevail in the making of public policy through a complex process of bargaining and compromise. They believe that, rather than speaking of majority rule, we should speak of groups of minorities working together. Robert Dahl expresses this view well when he writes that in America "all active and legitimate groups in the population can make themselves heard at some crucial stage in the process."[14]

Group politics is certainly as American as apple pie. Writing in the 1830s, Alexis de Tocqueville called us a "nation of joiners" and pointed to the high level of associational activities as one of the crucial reasons for the success of American democracy. The recent explosion of interest group activity can therefore be seen as a very positive development from the perspective of pluralist theory. Interest groups and their lobbyists—the groups' representatives in Washington—have become masters of the technology of politics. Computers, mass mailing lists, sophisticated media advertising, and hard-sell techniques are their stock in trade. As a result, some observers believe that Dahl's pluralist vision of all groups as being heard through the American political process is more true now than ever before.

On the other hand, Robert Putnam argues that many of the problems of American democracy today stem from a decline in group-based participation.[15] Putnam theorizes that advanced technology, particularly television, has served to increasingly isolate Americans from one another. He shows that membership in a variety of civic associations, such as parent–teacher associations, the League of Women Voters, and the Elks, Shriners, and Jaycees, has been declining for decades. Interestingly, Putnam does not interpret the decline of participation in civic groups as meaning that people have become "couch potatoes." Rather, he argues that Americans' activities are becoming less tied to institutions and more self-defined. The most famous example he gives to illustrate this trend is the fact that membership in bowling leagues has dropped sharply at the same time that more people are bowling—indicating that more and more people must be bowling alone. Putnam believes that participation in interest groups today is often like bowling alone. Groups that have mushroomed lately, such as the AARP, typically just ask their members to participate by writing a check from the comfort of their own home. If people are indeed participating

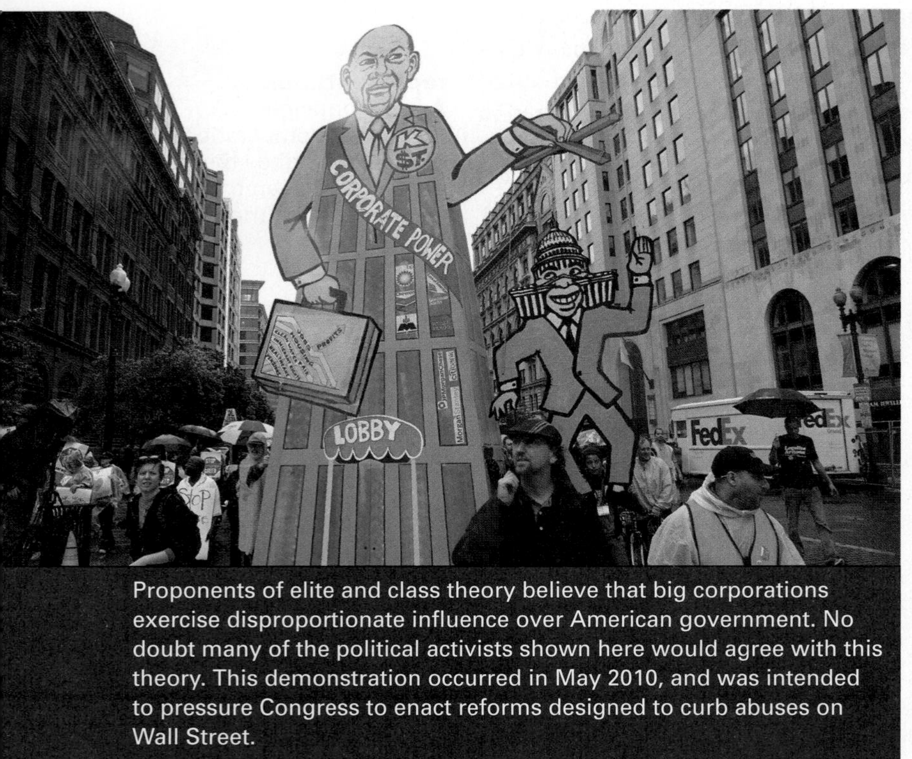

Proponents of elite and class theory believe that big corporations exercise disproportionate influence over American government. No doubt many of the political activists shown here would agree with this theory. This demonstration occurred in May 2010, and was intended to pressure Congress to enact reforms designed to curb abuses on Wall Street.

in politics alone rather than in groups, then pluralist theory is becoming less descriptive of American politics today.

Elitism Critics of pluralism believe that it paints too rosy a picture of American political life. By arguing that almost every group can get a piece of the pie, they say, pluralists miss the larger question of how the pie is distributed. The poor may get their food stamps, but businesses get massive tax deductions worth far more. Some governmental programs may help minorities, but the income gap between whites and blacks remains wide.

Elitism
A theory of American democracy contending that an upper-class elite holds the power and makes policy, regardless of the formal governmental organization.

Elitism contends that our society, like all societies, is divided along class lines and that an upper-class elite pulls the strings of government. Wealth—the holding of assets such as property, stocks, and bonds—is the basis of this power. Over a third of the nation's wealth is currently held by just 1 percent of the population. Elite and class theorists believe that this 1 percent of Americans controls most policy decisions because they can afford to finance election campaigns and control key institutions, such as large corporations. According to elite and class theory, a few powerful Americans do not merely influence policymakers—they are the actual policymakers.

At the center of all theories of elite dominance is big business. Few American presidents tried harder to help big business than did George W. Bush, and many commentators believe that he succeeded beyond all expectations. For example, political scientists Jacob Hacker and Paul Pierson wrote in 2005 that "America's political market no longer looks like the effectively functioning market that economics textbooks laud. Rather, it increasingly resembles the sort of market that gave us the Enron scandal, in which corporate bigwigs with privileged information got rich at the expense of ordinary shareholders, workers, and consumers."[16] A 2004 report on rising inequality issued by the American Political Science Association concluded, "Citizens with lower or moderate incomes speak with a whisper that is lost on the ears of inattentive government officials, while the advantaged roar with a clarity and consistency that policymakers readily hear and routinely follow."[17]

The most extreme proponents of elite theory maintain that who holds office in Washington is of marginal consequence; the corporate giants always have the power. Clearly, most people in politics would disagree with this view, noting that it did make a difference that Bush was elected in 2000 rather than Gore. According to Gore's promises in 2000, for example, the wealthiest Americans would have received no tax cuts had he become president, whereas under President Bush the wealthy and the middle class alike were granted tax cuts.

hyperpluralism
A theory of American democracy contending that groups are so strong that government, which gives in to the many different groups, is thereby weakened.

Hyperpluralism A third theory, **hyperpluralism**, offers a different critique of pluralism. Hyperpluralism is pluralism gone sour. In this view, the many competing groups are so strong that government is weakened, as the influence of so many groups cripples government's ability to make policy. The problem is not that a few groups excessively influence government action but that many groups together render government unable to act.

Whereas pluralism maintains that input from groups is a good thing for the political decision-making process, hyperpluralism asserts that there are *too* many ways for groups to control policy. Our fragmented political system made up of governments with overlapping jurisdictions is one major factor that contributes to hyperpluralism. Too many governments can make it hard to coordinate policy implementation. Any policy requiring the cooperation of the national, state, and local levels of government can be hampered by the reluctance of any one of them. Furthermore, groups use the fragmented system to their advantage, As groups that lose policymaking battles in Congress increasingly carry the battle to the courts; the number of cases brought to state and federal courts has soared. Ecologists use legal procedures to delay construction projects they feel will damage the environment, businesses take federal agencies to court to fight the implementation of regulations that will cost them money, labor unions go to court to secure injunctions against policies they fear will cost them jobs, and civil liberties groups go to court to defend the rights of people who are under investigation for possible terrorist activities. The courts have become one more battleground in which policies can be effectively opposed as each group tries to bend policy to suit its own purposes.

Hyperpluralist theory holds that government gives in to every conceivable interest and single-issue group. Groups have become sovereign, and government is merely their servant. When politicians try to placate every group, the result is confusing, contradictory, and muddled policy—if the politicians manage to make policy at all. Like elite and class theorists, hyperpluralist theorists suggest that the public interest is rarely translated into public policy.

Challenges to Democracy

Regardless of which theory is most convincing, there are a number of continuing challenges to democracy. Many of these challenges apply to American democracy as well as to other democracies around the world.

Increased Complexity of Issues Traditional democratic theory holds that ordinary citizens have the good sense to reach political judgments and that government has the capacity to act on those judgments. Today, however, we live in a society with complex issues and experts whose technical knowledge of those issues vastly exceeds the knowledge of the general population. What, after all, does the average citizen—however conscientious—know about eligibility criteria for welfare, agricultural price supports, foreign competition, and the hundreds of other issues that confront government each year? Years ago, the power of the few—the elite—might have been based on property holdings. Today, the elite are likely to be those who command knowledge, the experts. Even the most rigorous democratic theory does not demand that citizens be experts on everything; but as human knowledge has expanded, it has become increasingly difficult for individual citizens to make well-informed decisions.

Limited Participation in Government When citizens do not seem to take their citizenship seriously, democracy's defenders worry. There is plenty of evidence that Americans know little about who their leaders are, much less about their policy decisions, as we will discuss at length in Chapter 6. Furthermore, Americans do not take full advantage of their opportunities to shape government or select its leaders. Limited participation in government challenges the foundation of democracy. In particular, because young people represent the country's future, their low voting turnout rates point to an even more serious challenge to democracy on the horizon.

Escalating Campaign Costs Many political observers worry about the close connection between money and politics, especially in congressional elections. Winning a House seat these days usually requires a campaign war chest of *at least* a million dollars, and Senate races are even more costly. Candidates have become increasingly dependent on political action committees (PACs) to fund their campaigns because of the escalation of campaign costs. These PACs often represent specific economic interests, and they care little about how members of Congress vote on most issues—just the issues that particularly affect them. Critics charge that when it comes to the issues PACs care about, the members of Congress listen, lest they be denied the money they need for their reelection. When democracy confronts the might of money, the gap between democratic theory and reality widens further.

Diverse Political Interests The diversity of the American people is reflected in the diversity of interests represented in the political system. As will be shown in this book, this system is so open that interests find it easy to gain access to policymakers. When interests conflict, which they often do, no coalition may be strong enough to form a majority and establish policy. But each interest may use its influence to thwart those whose policy proposals they oppose. In effect, they have a veto over policy, creating what is often referred to as **policy gridlock**. In a big city, gridlock occurs when there are so many cars on the road that no one can move; in politics, it occurs when each policy coalition finds its way blocked by others.

policy gridlock
A condition that occurs when interests conflict and no coalition is strong enough to form a majority and establish policy, so nothing gets done.

Democracy is not necessarily an end in itself. For many, evaluations of democracy depend on what democratic government produces. Thus, a major challenge to democracy in America is to overcome the diversity of interests and fragmentation of power in order to deliver policies that are responsive to citizens' needs.

American Political Culture and Democracy

The key factor that holds American democracy together in the view of many scholars is its **political culture**—the overall set of values widely shared within American society. As Ronald Inglehart and Christian Welzel argue in their book on cultural change and democracy, "Democracy is not simply the result of clever elite bargaining and constitutional engineering. It depends on deep-rooted orientations among the people themselves. These orientations motivate them to demand freedom and responsive government. . . . Genuine democracy is not simply a machine that, once set up, functions by itself. It depends on the people."[18]

political culture
An overall set of values widely shared within a society.

Far more than most countries, the political culture of the United States is crucial to understanding its government, as Americans are so diverse in terms of ancestries, religions, and heritages. What unites Americans more than anything else is a set of shared beliefs and values. As G. K. Chesterton, the noted British observer of American politics, wrote in 1922, "America is the only nation in the world that is founded on a creed. That creed is set forth with dogmatic and even theological lucidity in the Declaration of Independence."[19] Arguing along the same lines, Seymour Martin Lipset writes that "the United States is a country organized around an ideology which includes a set of dogmas about the nature of good society."[20] Lipset argues that the American creed can be summarized by five elements: liberty, egalitarianism, individualism, laissez-faire, and populism.[21]

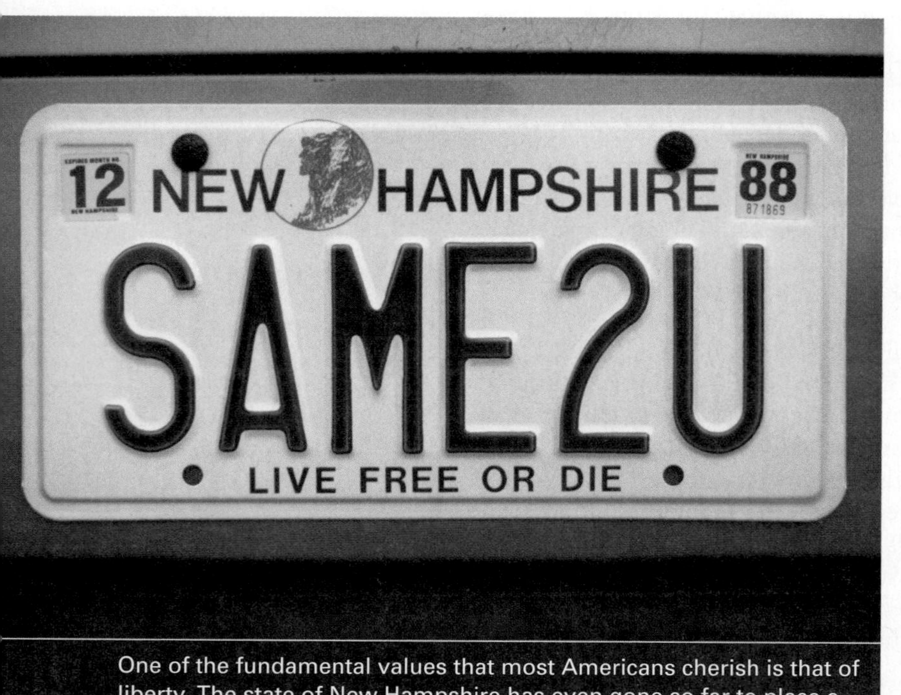

One of the fundamental values that most Americans cherish is that of liberty. The state of New Hampshire has even gone so far to place a slogan to this effect on all the automobile license plates in the state.

Liberty One of the most famous statements of the American Revolution was Patrick Henry's "Give me liberty or give me death." During the Cold War, a common bumper sticker was "Better Dead Than Red," reflecting many Americans' view that they would prefer to fight to the bitter end than submit to the oppression of communist rule. To this day, New Hampshire's official state motto is "Live Free or Die." When immigrants are asked why they came to America, by far the most common response is to live in freedom.

Freedom of speech and religion are fundamental to the American way of life. In the Declaration of Independence, Thomas Jefferson placed liberty right along with life and the pursuit of happiness as an "unalienable right" (that is, a right not awarded by human power, not transferable to another power, and not revocable).

Egalitarianism The most famous phrase in the history of democracy is the Declaration of Independence's statement "We hold these truths to be self-evident, that all men are created equal. . . ." As the French observer Alexis de Tocqueville noted long ago, egalitarianism in the United States involves equality of opportunity and respect in the absence of a monarchy and aristocracy. Americans have never been equal in terms of condition. What is most critical to this part of the American creed is that everyone has a chance to succeed in life.

Tocqueville accurately foresaw that the social equality he observed in American life in the 1830s would eventually lead to political equality. Although relatively few Americans then had the right to vote, he predicted that all Americans would be given this right because, in order to guarantee equality of opportunity, everyone must have an equal chance to participate in democratic governance. Thus, another key aspect of egalitarianism is equal voting rights for all adult American citizens.

Today, about three out of four Americans say they are proud of the fair and equal treatment of all groups in the United States. As you can see in Figure 1.6, this level of pride in the country's egalitarianism is extremely high compared to that in other democracies.

Individualism One of the aspects of American political culture that has shaped the development of American democracy has been individualism—the belief that people can and should get ahead on their own. The immigrants who founded American society may have been diverse, but many shared a common dream of America as a place where one could make it on one's own without interference from government. Louis Hartz's *The Liberal Tradition in America* is a classic analysis of the dominant political beliefs during America's formative years. Hartz argues that the major force behind limited government in America is that it was settled by people who fled from the feudal and clerical oppressions of the Old World. Once in the New World, they wanted little from government other than for it to leave them alone.[22]

Another explanation for American individualism is the existence of a bountiful frontier, at least up until the start of the twentieth century. Not only did many people come to America to escape from governmental interference, but the frontier allowed them to get away from government almost entirely once they arrived. Frederick Jackson Turner's famous work on the significance of the frontier in American history argues that "the frontier is productive of individualism."[23] According to Turner, being in the wilderness and having to survive on one's own left settlers with an aversion to any control from the outside world—particularly from the government.

FIGURE 1.6 Pride in Various Countries Regarding Equal Treatment of Groups

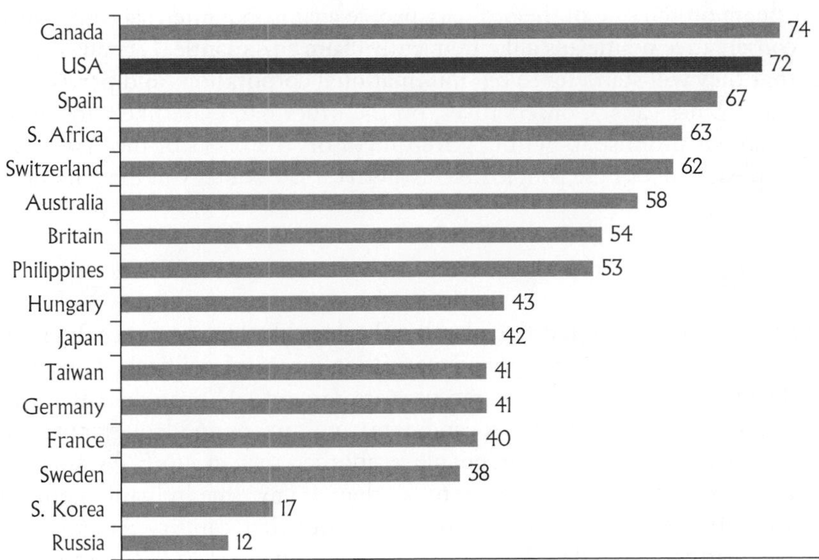

Americans rank very high in terms of being proud of their country's fair and equal treatment of all groups. This figure shows the percentages who said "very proud" or "somewhat proud" in response to the question, "How proud are you of [country] in . . . its fair and equal treatment of all groups—very proud, somewhat proud, not very proud, not proud at all?"

Source: Authors' analysis of 2003 International Social Survey Program surveys.

Former Prime Minister Tony Blair of Great Britain and President George W. Bush worked closely together as allies during the 2003 Iraqi war and formed a close friendship. But the two leaders had extremely different views regarding the proper scope of government in domestic policy. Blair was first elected to the British Parliament as a self-declared socialist, and in his position as prime minister he strived to strengthen Britain's national health care system. In contrast, President Bush favored free-market policies and opposed the idea of establishing a national health care system in the United States.

Laissez-faire An important result of American individualism has been a clear tendency to prefer laissez-faire economic policies, which promote free markets and limited government. As John Kingdon writes in his book *America the Unusual*, "Government in the United States is much more limited and much smaller than government in virtually every other advanced industrialized country on earth."[24] Compared to most other economically developed nations, the United States devotes a smaller percentage of its resources to government. As we will see in Chapter 14, Americans have a lighter tax burden than citizens of other democratic nations.

Further, all of the other advanced industrial democracies have long had a system of national health insurance that guarantees care to all their citizens; it wasn't until 2010 that the United States established a system to guarantee most Americans health insurance with the passage of the Patient Protection and Affordable Care Act. In other countries, national governments have taken it on themselves to start up airline, telephone, and communications companies. Governments have built much of the housing in most Western nations, compared to only a small fraction of the housing in America. Thus, in terms of its impact on citizens' everyday lives, government in the United States actually does less than the governments of these other democracies.

Populism Abraham Lincoln summarized American democracy as "government of the people, for the people, and by the people." Such an emphasis on *the people* is at the heart of populism, which can best be defined as a political philosophy supporting the rights of average citizens in their struggle against privileged elites. As Lipset writes, American populist thought holds that the people at large "are possessed of some kind of sacred mystique, and proximity to them endows the politician with esteem—and with legitimacy."[25]

In America, being on the side of the ordinary people against big interests is so valued that liberal and conservative politicians alike frequently claim this mantle. Liberals are inclined to argue that they will stand up to big multinational corporations and protect the interests of ordinary Americans. Conservatives, on the other hand, are likely to repeat Ronald Reagan's famous promise to get big government off the backs of the American people. A populist pledge to "put the people first" is always a safe strategy in the American political culture.

A Culture War?

Although Americans are widely supportive of cultural values like liberty and egalitarianism, some scholars are concerned that a sharp polarization into rival political camps with different political cultures has taken place in recent years. James Q. Wilson defines such a polarization as "an intense commitment to a candidate, a culture, or an ideology that sets people in one group definitively apart from people in another, rival group."[26] Wilson believes that America is a more polarized nation today than at any time in living memory. He argues that the intensity of political divisions in twenty-first-century America is a major problem, writing that "a divided America encourages our enemies, disheartens our allies, and saps our resolve—potentially to fatal effect."[27]

A POINT TO PONDER

In his first major political speech, Barack Obama proclaimed that there was no such thing as red or blue states—only the United States. For Obama, the social and political stereotypes portrayed in this Pulitzer Prize–winning cartoon are exaggerations.

What do you think—is there a cultural war going on in America?

Source: David Horsey, Seattle-Post Intelligencer, 2002

Other scholars, however, believe that there is relatively little evidence of a so-called culture war going on among ordinary American citizens. Morris Fiorina concludes, "There is little indication that voters are polarized now or that they are becoming more polarized—even when we look specifically at issues such as abortion that supposedly are touchstone issues in the culture war. If anything, public opinion has grown more centrist on such issues and more tolerant of the divergent views, values, and behavior of other Americans."[28] Wayne Baker outlines three ways in which America might be experiencing a crisis of cultural values: (1) a loss over time of traditional values, such as the importance of religion and family life; (2) an unfavorable comparison with the citizens of other countries in terms of key values such as patriotism; and (3) the division of society into opposed groups with irreconcilable moral differences. Baker tests each of these three possibilities thoroughly with recent survey data from the United States and other countries and finds little evidence of cultural division or an ongoing crisis of values in America.[29]

Preview Questions About Democracy

Throughout *Government in America* you will be asked to evaluate the state of American democracy today. The chapters that follow will acquaint you with the development of democracy in the United States. You will see that the U.S. Constitution was not originally designed to promote democracy but has slowly evolved to its current form, largely through the extension of civil liberties and civil rights.

Probably the most important civil right is the right to vote. When you look at voting behavior and elections, ask the following questions about how people form their opinions and to what extent they express these opinions via elections:

- Are people knowledgeable about matters of public policy?
- Do they apply what knowledge they have to their voting choices?
- Are American elections designed to facilitate public participation?

Linkage institutions, such as interest groups, political parties, and the media, help translate input from the public into output from the policymakers. When you explore these institutions, consider the extent to which they either help or hinder democracy:

- Does the interest group system allow for all points of view to be heard, or do significant biases give advantages to particular groups?
- Do political parties provide voters with clear choices, or do they and their candidates intentionally obscure their stands on issues in order to get as many votes as possible?
- If there are choices, do the media help citizens understand them?

It is up to public officials to actually make policy choices because American government is a representative democracy. For democracy to work well, elected officials must be responsive to public opinion. When you read about our elected officials, ask questions like the following:

- Is Congress representative of American society, and is it capable of reacting to changing times?
- Does the president look after the general welfare of the public, or has the office become too focused on the interests of the elite?

In addition to the performance of elected officials, the way our nonelected institutions—the bureaucracy and the courts—function is crucial to evaluating how well American democracy works. These institutions are designed to implement and interpret the law, but bureaucrats and judges often cannot avoid making public policy as well. A question to consider for these institutions is, When they make public policy, are they violating democratic principles for policy decisions, given that neither institution can be held accountable at the ballot box?

All these questions concerning democracy in America have more than one answer. A goal of *Government in America* is to offer different ways to evaluate and answer these questions. Moreover, closely linked to questions about democracy are questions about one of the most important issues facing modern American democracy: Is the scope of government responsibilities too vast, just about right, or not comprehensive enough?

The Scope of Government in America

1.5 Outline the central arguments of the debate in America over the proper scope of government.

In proposing a massive $787 billion economic stimulus package to deal with the nation's economic woes in January of 2009, President Obama stated, "It is true that we cannot depend on government alone to create jobs or long-term growth, but at this particular moment, only government can provide the short-term boost necessary to lift us from a recession this deep and severe." In response, Republican House Leader John Boehner countered, "This bill makes clear that the era of Big Government is back, and the Democrats expect you to pay for it." He and other conservatives opposed the stimulus bill, arguing that such increases in the scope of the federal government would result in less freedom and prosperity. Had they been in the majority in 2009, they would have pushed through tax cuts to reduce the scope of government rather than a set of spending initiatives which increased it.

Those who are inclined to support an active role for government argue that its intervention is sometimes the only means of achieving important goals in American society. How else, they ask, can we ensure that people have enough to eat, clean air and water, and affordable health care? How else can we ensure that the disadvantaged are given opportunities for education and jobs and are not discriminated against? Opponents of widening the scope of government agree that these are worthwhile goals but challenge whether involving the federal government is an effective way to pursue them. Dick Armey, who served as the Republicans' majority leader in the House from 1995 to 2002, expressed this view well when he wrote, "There is more wisdom in millions of individuals making decisions in their own self-interest than there is in even the most enlightened bureaucrat (or congressman) making decisions on their behalf."[30] Or, as Ronald Reagan argued in his farewell presidential address, "As government expands, liberty contracts."

gross domestic product The sum total of the value of all the goods and services produced in a year in a nation.

To understand the dimensions of this debate, it is important first to get some sense of the current scope of the federal government's activities.

How Active Is American Government?

In terms of dollars spent, government in America is vast. Altogether, our governments—national, state, and local—spend about a third of our **gross domestic product (GDP)**, the total value of all goods and services produced annually by the United States. Government not only spends large sums of money but also employs large numbers of people. About 24 million Americans work for our government, mostly at the state and local level as teachers, police officers, university professors, and so on. Consider some facts about the size of our national government:

- It spends about $3.8 trillion annually (printed as a number, that's $3,800,000,000,000 a year).
- It employs about 2.8 million civilians, as well as 1.4 million in the military.
- It owns one-third of the land in the United States.
- It occupies 2.6 billion square feet of office space, more than four times the office space located in the nation's 10 largest cities.

How does the American national government spend $3.8 trillion a year? National defense takes about one-sixth of

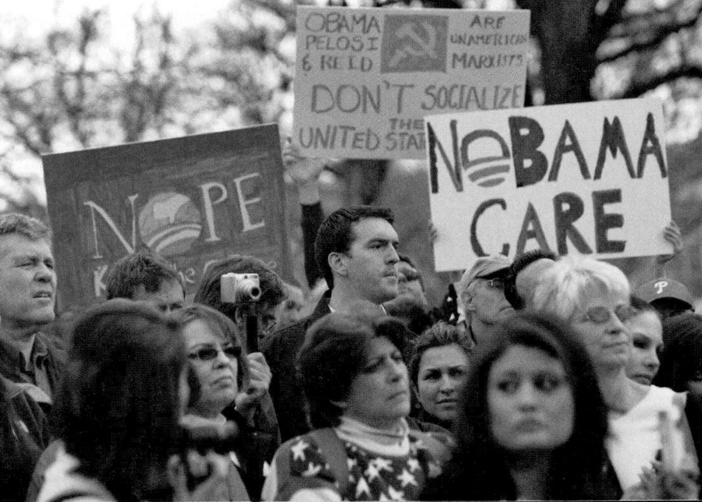

The political debate over the historic health care reform bill signed into law by President Obama in March 2010 often involved the crucial question of the proper scope of government. Opponents of the bill often denounced it as an unwarranted government takeover of health care. For example, Representative Paul Ryan said it constituted "a paternalistic ideology at odds with our historic commitment to individual liberty, limited government and entrepreneurial dynamism." In contrast, proponents argued that this is exactly the sort of role that government should be taking on. For example, Speaker of the House Nancy Pelosi said that it "would lead to healthier lives, and more liberty to pursue hopes, dreams, and happiness."

the federal budget, a much smaller percentage than it did three decades ago—even with the recent increase after September 11. Social Security consumes more than one-fifth of the budget. Medicare is another big-ticket item, requiring a little over one-tenth of the budget. State and local governments also get important parts of the federal government's budget. The federal government helps fund highway and airport construction, police departments, school districts, and other state and local functions.

When expenditures grow, tax revenues must grow to pay the additional costs. When taxes do not grow as fast as spending, a budget deficit results. The federal government ran a budget deficit every year from 1969 through 1997. The last few Clinton budgets showed surpluses, but soon after George W. Bush took over, the government was running a deficit once again due to the combination of reduced taxes and increased expenditures on national security following the events of September 11. The severe economic recession that took hold at the end of Bush's presidency led to his running up further red ink in 2008 to bail out the financial system and to Obama's doing the same in 2009 with an economic stimulus package to combat unemployment. The net result was that in fiscal year 2010 the annual deficit was a staggering $1.3 trillion. All told, the many years of deficit spending have left the country with a national debt of over $13 trillion, which will continue to pose a problem for policymakers for decades to come.

Whatever the national problem—unemployment, terrorism, AIDS, illegal immigration, energy, education—many people expect Congress and the president to solve it with legislation. Thus, American government certainly matters tremendously in terms of dollars spent, persons employed, and laws passed. Our concern, however, is less about the absolute size of government and more about whether government activity is what we want it to be.

Preview Questions about the Scope of Government

Debate over the scope of government is central to contemporary American politics, and it is a theme this text will examine in each chapter. You will explore the implications of the way politics, institutions, and policy in America affect the scope of government. By considering questions such as those listed below, you may arrive at your own conclusions about the appropriate role of government in America.

Part 1 of *Government in America* examines the constitutional foundations of American government. A concern with the proper scope of government leads to a series of questions regarding the constitutional structure of American politics, including the following:

- What role did the Constitution's authors foresee for the federal government?
- Does the Constitution favor a government with a broad scope, or is it neutral on this issue?
- Why did the functions of government increase, and why did they increase most at the national rather than the state level?
- Has bigger, more active government constrained freedom, or does the increased scope of government serve to protect civil liberties and civil rights?

Part 2 focuses on those who make demands on government, including the public, political parties, interest groups, and the media. Here you will seek answers to questions such as the following:

- Does the public favor a large, active government?
- Do competing political parties predispose the government to provide more public services?
- Do elections help control the scope of government, or do they legitimize an increasing role for the public sector?
- Are pressures from interest groups necessarily translated into more governmental regulations, bigger budgets, and the like?
- Has media coverage of government enhanced government's responsibilities and scope, or have the media been an instrument for controlling government?

Governmental institutions themselves obviously deserve close examination. Part 3 discusses these institutions and asks the following:

- Has the presidency been a driving force behind increasing the scope and power of government?
- Can the president control a government with so many programs and responsibilities?
- Is Congress, because it is subject to constant elections, predisposed toward big government?
- Is Congress too responsive to the demands of the public and organized interests?

Governmental institutions include the nonelected branches of government—the courts and bureaucracy—and these institutions are especially interesting when we consider the issue of the scope of government. For instance:

- Are the federal courts too active in policymaking, intruding on the authority and responsibility of other branches and levels of government?
- Is the bureaucracy too acquisitive, constantly seeking to expand its budgets and authority, or does it simply reflect the desires of elected officials?
- Is the bureaucracy too large and thus a wasteful menace to efficient and fair implementation of public policies?

The next 20 chapters will search for answers to these and many other questions regarding the scope of government and why it matters. You will undoubtedly add a few questions of your own as you seek to resolve the issue of the proper scope of government involvement.

Summary

1.1 Identify the key functions of government and explain why they matter.

The functions that all governments perform include maintaining a national defense, providing public services, preserving order, socializing the young, and collecting taxes. By performing these functions, governments regularly shape the way in which we live.

1.2 Define politics in the context of democratic government.

Politics determines what leaders we select and what policies they pursue. The *who* of politics is the voters, candidates, parties, and groups; the *what* is the benefits and burdens of government; the *how* is the various ways in which people participate in politics.

1.3 Assess how citizens can have an impact on public policy and how policies can impact people.

The policymaking system is in effect a cycle. Citizens' interests and concerns are transmitted through linkage institutions (parties and elections, interest groups, the media). These concerns shape the government's policy agenda, from which those in policymaking institutions (Congress, the presidency, the courts) choose issues to address. The policies that are made (laws, executive orders, regulations, and court judgments) then influence people's lives.

1.4 Identify the key principles of democracy and outline theories regarding how it works in practice and the challenges democracy faces today.

According to traditional democratic theory, the ideal democracy is characterized by "one person, one vote," equal opportunities to participate, freedom of speech and the press, citizen control of the policy agenda, and inclusion. Pluralist theory holds that American democracy works well, as competition among many organized groups means that the public interest becomes public policy. This view is disputed by elitist theory, which claims that the powerful few dominate, and by hyperpluralist theory, which sees the excessive influence of many competing groups as leading to muddled policy or inaction. Contemporary challenges to American and other democracies include the complexity of issues today, citizens' limited participation, escalating campaign costs, and the policy gridlock resulting from diverse political interests.

1.5 Outline the central arguments of the debate in America over the proper scope of government.

One of the most important issues facing modern American democracy is the proper scope of government. Politicians constantly debate whether the scope of government responsibilities is too vast, just about right, or not comprehensive enough. This debate concerns whether the goals that are agreed to be important are best achieved through government action or rather through means other than government.

Chapter Test

1.1 Identify the key functions of government and explain why they matter.

1. Which of the following is an example of a public good?
   a. Medical care
   b. College education
   c. Automobile insurance
   d. Home ownership
   e. National defense
2. Government is typically made up of the institutions that make decisions for a society.

   True______ False______
3. List and explain at least three of the functions that national governments perform, according to this textbook. To what extent do you think each of these are important functions? Explain your answer.

1.2 Define politics in the context of democratic government.

4. Politics determines who we select as our governmental leaders and what policies these leaders pursue.

   True______ False______
5. Harold Laswell defined politics as "who gets what, when, and how." Explain what he meant by this definition as you apply it to an issue area of your choice.

1.3 Assess how citizens can have an impact on public policy and how policies can impact people.

6. All of the following are considered linkage institutions EXCEPT __________
   a. the media
   b. interest groups
   c. political parties
   d. courts
   e. elections
7. How do people affect public policy within the policymaking system? Why is the policy agenda so important to the policymaking system, and how might it help or hinder public influence over policy-making institutions?

1.4 Identify the key principles of democracy and outline theories regarding how it works in practice and the challenges democracy faces today.

8. According to Robert Dahl's traditional democratic theory, an ideal democratic process should satisfy all of the following criteria EXCEPT __________
   a. Equality in voting
   b. Effective participation
   c. Enlightened understanding
   d. Citizen control of the agenda
   e. Majority rule
9. The theory of hyperpluralism is based on the assumption that input from interest groups is good for the political decision-making process.

   True______ False______
10. What are the four continuing challenges to democracy mentioned in this textbook? Of those, which do you think poses the most significant challenge to American democracy, and why? How would you attempt to meet this particular challenge?
11. What are the five central features of American political culture, or the "American creed," according to Seymour Martin Lipset? Why is political culture a key factor in holding American democracy together? Do you think there is a culture war going in the United States that may serve to polarize Americans? What is the evidence in favor of and against the existence of a culture war today?

1.5 Outline the central arguments of the debate in America over the proper scope of government.

12. How does the federal government spend its nearly $4 trillion annual budget? Based on these expenditures, do you think that the government does too much? If you think so, explain and indicate where the government should cut services.
13. What are the primary arguments in favor of and against an active role for government in today's society? Use a current policy example to support your answer.

PEARSON mypoliscilab™ Exercises

Apply what you learned in this chapter on MyPoliSciLab.

Read on mypoliscilab.com

eText: Chapter 1

Study and Review on mypoliscilab.com

Pre-Test
Post-Test

Watch on mypoliscilab.com

Video: Mexico Border Security
Video: The Bailout Hearings
Video: Vaccines: Mandatory Protection
Video: Chicago Gun Laws
Video: Facebook Privacy Concerns
Video: The President Addresses School Children

Chapter Exam
Flashcards

Explore on mypoliscilab.com

Simulation: What Are American Civic Values?

Key Terms

government (8)
public goods (8)
politics (9)
political participation (9)
single-issue groups (10)
policymaking system (10)
linkage institutions (10)
policy agenda (11)
political issue (11)
policymaking institutions (11)
public policy (12)
policy impacts (12)
democracy (13)
majority rule (14)
minority rights (14)
representation (15)
pluralism (15)
elitism (16)
hyperpluralism (16)
policy gridlock (18)
political culture (18)
gross domestic product (23)

Internet Resources

www.policyalmanac.org
Contains a discussion of major policy issues of the day and links to resources about them.

http://thomas.loc.gov/home/histdox/fedpapers.html
The complete collection of the *Federalist Papers*.

www.tocqueville.org
Information and discussion about Tocqueville's classic work *Democracy in America*.

www.bowlingalone.com
A site designed to accompany Robert Putnam's work, which contains information concerning the data he used and projects he is working on to reinvigorate American communities.

www.politicalwire.com
A good daily guide to some of the most interesting political stories of the day, as seen from a liberal's perspective.

www.realclearpolitics.com
A good daily guide to some of the most interesting political stories of the day, as seen from a conservative's perspective.

For Further Reading

Alesina, Alberto and Edward L. Glaeser. ***Fighting Poverty in the US and Europe: A World of Difference.*** New York: Oxford, 2004. A comprehensive analysis of how and why the scope of government is smaller in the United States than in Europe.

Bok, Derek. ***The State of the Nation: Government and the Quest for a Better Society.*** Cambridge, MA: Harvard University Press, 1996. An excellent analysis of how America is doing, compared to other major democracies, on a wide variety of policy aspects.

Dahl, Robert A. ***Democracy and Its Critics.*** New Haven, CT: Yale University Press, 1982. A very thoughtful work by one of the world's most articulate advocates of pluralist theory.

de Tocqueville, Alexis. ***Democracy in America.*** New York: Mentor Books, 1956. This classic by a nineteenth-century French aristocrat remains one of the most insightful works on the nature of American society and government.

Hartz, Louis. ***The Liberal Tradition in America.*** New York: Harcourt, Brace, 1955. A classic analysis of why the scope of American government has been more limited than in other democracies.

Kingdon, John W. ***Agendas, Alternatives, and Public Policies.*** 2nd ed. New York: HarperCollins, 1995. One of the best efforts by a political scientist to examine the political agenda.

Macedo, Stephen, et al. ***Democracy at Risk: How Political Choices Undermine Citizen Participation, and What We Can Do About It.*** Washington, DC: Brookings, 2005. An insightful review of many aspects of political participation in America.

Putnam, Robert. ***Bowling Alone: The Collapse and Revival of American Community.*** New York: Simon & Schuster, 2000. Putnam's highly influential work shows how Americans have become increasingly disconnected from one another since the early 1960s.

Schuck, Peter H. and James Q. Wilson, eds. ***Understanding America: The Anatomy of an Exceptional Nation.*** New York: Public Affairs, 2008. An excellent set of readings about various policy topics, with an emphasis on how American policy differs from that of other established democracies.

Sitaraman, Ganesh and Previn Warren. ***Invisible Citizens: Youth Politics After September 11.*** New York: iUniverse, Inc., 2003. Two Harvard students examine why today's youth demonstrate a commitment to community service while at the same time largely neglect involvement in politics.

Stanley, Harold W., and Richard G. Niemi. ***Vital Statistics on American Politics, 2009-2010.*** Washington, DC: CQ Press, 2010. Useful data on government, politics, and policy in the United States.

Wolfe, Alan. ***Does American Democracy Still Work?*** New Haven: Yale University Press, 2006. An influential critique of the problems of democracy in America today.

Chapter 2

The Constitution

Learning Objectives

2.1 Describe the ideas behind the American Revolution and their role in shaping the Constitution.

2.2 Analyze how the weaknesses of the Articles of Confederation led to its failure.

2.3 Describe the delegates to the Constitutional Convention and the core ideas they shared.

2.4 Categorize the issues at the Constitutional Convention and outline the resolutions reached on each type of issue.

2.5 Analyze how the components of the Madisonian system addressed the dilemma of reconciling majority rule with the protection of minority interests.

2.6 Compare and contrast the Federalists and Anti-Federalists in terms of their background and their positions regarding government.

2.7 Explain how the Constitution can be formally amended and how it changes informally.

2.8 Assess whether the Constitution establishes a majoritarian democracy and how it limits the scope of government.

POLITICS IN ACTION: AMENDING THE CONSTITUTION

Gregory Lee Johnson knew little about the Constitution, but he knew that he was upset. He felt that the buildup of nuclear weapons in the world threatened the planet's survival, and he wanted to protest presidential and corporate policies concerning nuclear weapons. Yet he had no money to hire a lobbyist or to purchase an ad in a newspaper. So he and some other demonstrators marched through the streets of Dallas, chanting political slogans and stopping at several corporate locations to stage "die-ins" intended to dramatize the consequences of nuclear war. The demonstration ended in front of Dallas City Hall, where Gregory doused an American flag with kerosene and set it on fire.

Burning the flag violated the law, and Gregory was convicted of "desecration of a venerated object," sentenced to one year in prison, and fined $2,000. He appealed his conviction, claiming that the law that prohibited burning the flag violated his freedom of speech. The U.S. Supreme Court agreed in the case of *Texas v. Gregory Lee Johnson*.

Gregory was pleased with the Court's decision, but he was nearly alone. The public howled its opposition to the decision, and President George H. W. Bush called for a constitutional amendment authorizing punishment of flag desecraters. Many public officials vowed to support the amendment, and organized opposition to it was scarce. However, an amendment to prohibit burning the American flag did not obtain the two-thirds vote in each house of Congress necessary to send it to the states for ratification.

Instead, Congress passed a law—the Flag Protection Act—that outlawed the desecration of the American flag. The next year, however, in *United States v. Eichman*, the Supreme Court found the act an impermissible infringement on free speech.

After years of political posturing, legislation, and litigation, little has changed. Burning the flag remains a legally protected form of political expression despite the objections of the overwhelming majority of the American public. Gregory Johnson did not prevail because he was especially articulate, nor did he win because he had access to political resources, such as money or powerful supporters. He won because of the nature of the Constitution.

Understanding how an unpopular protestor like Gregory Lee Johnson could triumph over the combined forces of the public and its elected officials is central to understanding the American system of government. The Constitution supersedes ordinary law, even when the law represents the wishes of a majority of citizens. The Constitution not only guarantees individual rights but also decentralizes power. Even the president could not force Congress to start the process of amending the Constitution. Power is not concentrated efficiently in the hands of one person, such as the president. Instead, there are

Chapter OUTLINE

numerous checks on the exercise of power and many obstacles to change. Some complain that this system produces stalemate, while others praise the way in which it protects minority views. Both positions are correct.

Gregory Johnson's case raises some important questions about government in America. What does democracy mean if the majority does not always get its way? Is this how we should be governed? And is it appropriate that the many limits on the scope of government action, both direct and indirect, sometimes prevent action desired by most people?

constitution
A nation's basic law. It creates political institutions, assigns or divides powers in government, and often provides certain guarantees to citizens. Constitutions can be either written or unwritten. See also **U.S. Constitution**.

A **constitution** is a nation's basic law. It creates political institutions, allocates power within government, and often provides guarantees to citizens. A constitution is also an unwritten accumulation of traditions and precedents that have established acceptable means of governing. As the body of rules that govern our nation, the U.S. Constitution has an impact on our everyday lives. Our theme of the scope of government runs throughout this chapter, which focuses on what the national government can and cannot do. A nation that prides itself on being "democratic" must evaluate the Constitution according to democratic standards, the core of our other theme. To understand government and to answer questions about how we are governed and what government does, we must first understand the Constitution.

2.1 Describe the ideas behind the American Revolution and their role in shaping the Constitution.

The Origins of the Constitution

In the summer of 1776, a small group of men met in Philadelphia and passed a resolution that began an armed rebellion against the government of what was then the most powerful nation on Earth. The resolution was, of course, the Declaration of Independence; the armed rebellion was the American Revolution.

The attempt to overthrow a government forcibly is a serious and unusual act. All countries, including the United States, consider it treasonous and levy serious punishments for it. A set of compelling ideas drove our forefathers to take such drastic and risky action. Understanding the Constitution requires an understanding of these ideas.

The Road to Revolution

By eighteenth-century standards, life was not bad for most people in America at the time of the Revolution (slaves and indentured servants being major exceptions). In fact, white colonists "were freer, more equal, more prosperous, and less burdened with cumbersome feudal and monarchical restraints than any other part of mankind."[1] Although the colonies were part of the British Empire, the king and Parliament generally confined themselves to governing America's foreign policy and trade. Almost everything else was left to the discretion of individual colonial governments. Although commercial regulations irritated colonial shippers, planters, land speculators, and merchants, these rules had little influence on the vast bulk of the population, who were self-employed farmers or artisans.

As you can see in Figure 2.1, Britain obtained an enormous new territory in North America after the French and Indian War (also known as the Seven Years' War) ended in 1763. The cost of defending this territory against foreign adversaries was large, and Parliament reasoned that it was only fair that those who were the primary beneficiaries—the colonists—should contribute to their own defense. Thus, in order to raise revenue for colonial administration and defense, the British Parliament passed a series of taxes on newspapers, official documents, paper, glass, paint, and tea. Britain also began tightening enforcement of its trade regulations, which were designed to benefit the mother country, not the colonists.

FIGURE 2.1 European Claims in North America

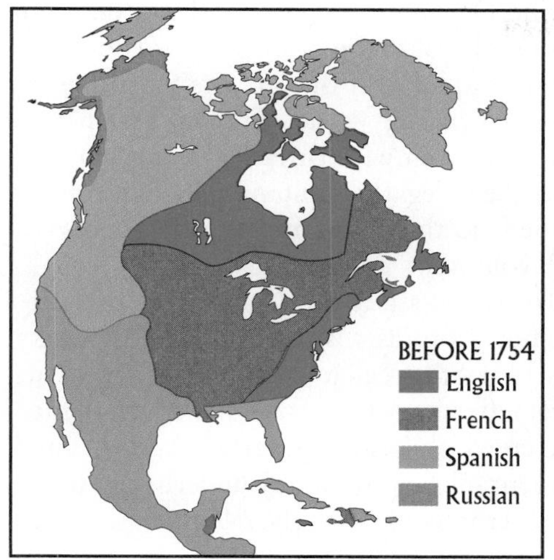

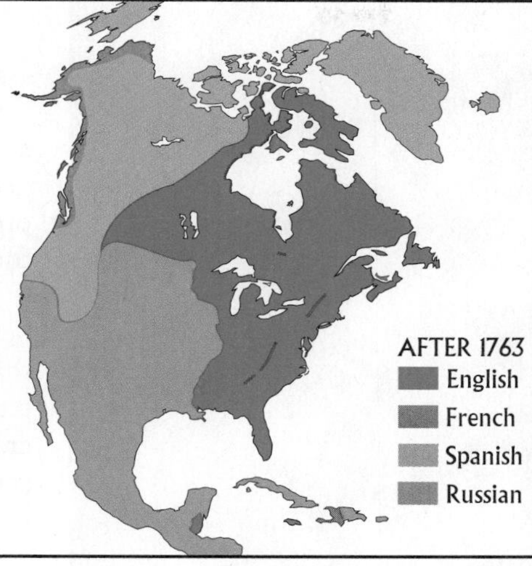

Following its victory in the French and Indian War in 1763, Britain obtained an enormous new territory to govern. To raise revenues to defend and administer the territory, it raised taxes on the colonists and tightened enforcement of trade regulations. (Britain also gained Florida from Spain as a result of the war.)

The colonists lacked direct representation in Parliament and resented the legislature imposing taxes without their consent. They protested, boycotted the taxed goods, and, as a symbolic act of disobedience, even threw 342 chests of tea into Boston Harbor. Britain reacted by applying economic pressure through a naval blockade of the harbor, further fueling the colonists' anger. The colonists responded by forming the First Continental Congress in September 1774, sending delegates from each colony to Philadelphia to discuss the future of relations with Britain.

Declaration of Independence
The document approved by representatives of the American colonies in 1776 that stated their grievances against the British monarch and declared their independence.

Declaring Independence

Talk of independence was common among the delegates. Thomas Paine's fiery tract *Common Sense* appeared in January 1776 and fanned the already hot flames of revolution. In May and June 1776, the Continental Congress began debating resolutions about independence. On June 7, Richard Henry Lee of Virginia moved "that these United States are and of right ought to be free and independent states." A committee composed of Thomas Jefferson of Virginia, John Adams of Massachusetts, Benjamin Franklin of Pennsylvania, Roger Sherman of Connecticut, and Robert Livingston of New York was formed to draft a document to justify the inevitable declaration. On July 2, Congress formally approved Lee's motion to declare independence from England. Congress adopted the **Declaration of Independence**, two days later, on July 4 (You can read it in the appendix).

The primary author of the Declaration of Independence was Thomas Jefferson, a 33-year-old, well-educated Virginia lawmaker who was a talented author steeped in the philosophical writings of European moral philosophers.[2] The Declaration quickly became one of the most widely quoted and revered documents in America. Filled with fine principles and bold language, it can be read as both a political tract and a philosophical treatise.

Politically, the Declaration was a polemic, a political argument, announcing and justifying a revolution. Most of the document—27 of its 32 paragraphs—listed the ways in which the king had abused the colonies. The delegates accused George III of all sorts of evil deeds, including inciting the "merciless Indian savages" to make war on the colonists. The delegates focused blame on the king because

COMMON SENSE;

ADDRESSED TO THE

INHABITANTS

OF

A M E R I C A,

On the following interesting

S U B J E C T S.

I. Of the Origin and Design of Government in general, with concise Remarks on the English Constitution.

II. Of Monarchy and Hereditary Succession.

III. Thoughts on the present State of American Affairs.

IV. Of the present Ability of America, with some miscellaneous Reflections.

Man knows no Master save creating HEAVEN,
Or those whom choice and common good ordain.
THOMSON.

PHILADELPHIA;
Printed, and Sold, by R. BELL, in Third-Street,
MDCCLXXVI.

Thomas Paine's *Common Sense* encouraged the colonists to declare independence from Britain.

John Adams (from right), Roger Sherman, Robert R. Livingston, Thomas Jefferson, and Benjamin Franklin submit the Declaration of Independence to Continental Congress President John Hancock. Legend has it that Hancock remarked, "We must be unanimous; there must be no pulling different ways; we must hang together," to which Franklin replied, "We must indeed all hang together, or, most assuredly, we shall hang separately."

they held that only he, not Parliament, had authority over the colonies.

The Declaration's polemical aspects were important because the colonists needed foreign assistance to take on Britain, the most powerful nation in the world. France, which was engaged in a war with Britain, was a prime target for the delegates' diplomacy and eventually provided aid that was critical to the success of the Revolution.

Today, we study the Declaration of Independence more as a statement of philosophy than as a political call to arms. In just a few sentences, Jefferson set forth the American democratic creed, the most important and succinct statement of the philosophy underlying American government—as applicable today as it was in 1776.

The English Heritage: The Power of Ideas

The Declaration articulates ideas that were by then common knowledge on both sides of the Atlantic, especially among those people who wished to challenge the power of kings. Franklin, Jefferson, James Madison of Virginia, Robert Morris of Pennsylvania, Alexander Hamilton of New York, and other intellectual leaders in the colonies were learned and widely read men, familiar with the works of English, French, and Scottish political philosophers. These leaders corresponded about the ideas they were reading, quoted philosophers in their debates over the Revolution, and applied those ideas to the new government they formed through the framework of the Constitution.

John Locke was one of the most influential philosophers read by the colonists. His writings, especially *The Second Treatise of Civil Government* (1689), profoundly influenced American political leaders. His work was "the dominant political faith of the American colonies in the second quarter of the eighteenth century."[3]

natural rights
Rights inherent in human beings, not dependent on governments, which include life, liberty, and property. The concept of natural rights was central to English philosopher John Locke's theories about government and was widely accepted among America's Founders.

consent of the governed
The idea that government derives its authority by sanction of the people.

limited government
The idea that certain restrictions should be placed on government to protect the **natural rights** of citizens.

The foundation on which Locke built his powerful philosophy was a belief in **natural rights**—rights inherent in human beings, not dependent on governments. Before governments arise, Locke held, people exist in a state of nature in which there are no formal laws or governments. Instead, the laws of nature govern people, laws determined by people's innate moral sense. This natural law brings natural rights, including life, liberty, and property. Natural law can even justify a challenge to the rule of a tyrannical king because it is superior to man-made law. Government, Locke argued, must be built on the **consent of the governed**; in other words, the people must agree on who their rulers will be. It should also be a **limited government**; that is, there must be clear restrictions on what rulers can do. Indeed, the sole purpose of government, according to Locke, was to protect natural rights. The idea that certain things were beyond the realm of government contrasted sharply with the traditional notion that kings had been divinely granted absolute rights over their subjects.

Two limits on government were particularly important to Locke. First, governments must provide standing laws so that people know in advance whether their acts will be acceptable. Second, and Locke was very forceful on this point, "the supreme power cannot take from any man any part of his property without his consent." To Locke, "the preservation of property was the end of government." The sanctity of property was one of the few ideas absent in Jefferson's draft of the Declaration of Independence, which altered Locke's phrase "life, liberty, and property" to "life, liberty, and the pursuit of happiness." We shall soon see, however, how the Lockean idea of the sanctity of property figured prominently at the Constitutional Convention. James Madison, the most influential member of that body, directly echoed Locke's view that the preservation of property is the purpose of government.

Locke argued that in an extreme case, people have a right to revolt against a government that no longer has their consent. Locke anticipated critics' charges that this right would lead to constant civil disturbances. He emphasized that people should not revolt until injustices become deeply felt. The Declaration of Independence accented the same point, declaring that "governments long established should not be changed for light and transient causes." But when matters went beyond "patient sufferance," severing these ties was not only inevitable but also necessary.

Locke represented only one element of revolutionary thought from which Jefferson and his colleagues borrowed. In the English countryside, there was also a well-established tradition of opposition to the executive power of the Crown and an emphasis on the rights of the people. Moreover, an indigenous American set of ideas—stressing moral virtue, patriotism, relations based on merit, and the equality of independent citizens—intensified the radicalism of the British "country" ideology and linked it with older currents of European thought, stretching back to antiquity, regarding the rights of citizens and the role of government.

The American Creed

There are some remarkable parallels between Locke's thought and Jefferson's language in the Declaration of Independence (see Table 2.1). Jefferson, like Locke, finessed his way past the issue of how the rebels knew that men had rights. Jefferson simply declared that it was "self-evident" that men were equally "endowed by their Creator with certain unalienable rights," including "life, liberty, and the pursuit of happiness." Because it was the purpose of government to "secure" these rights, the people could form a new government if it failed to do so.[4]

It was in the American colonies that the powerful ideas of European political thinkers took root and grew into what Seymour Martin Lipset termed the "first new nation."[5] With these revolutionary ideas in mind, Jefferson claimed in the Declaration of Independence that people should have primacy over governments, that they should rule instead of be ruled. Moreover, each person was important as an individual, "created equal," and endowed with "unalienable rights." Consent of the governed, not divine rights or tradition, made the exercise of political power legitimate.

No government had ever been based on these principles. Ever since 1776, Americans have been concerned about fulfilling the high aspirations of the Declaration of Independence.

Winning Independence

The pen may be mightier than the sword, but declaring independence did not win the Revolution—it merely announced its beginning. John Adams wrote to his wife Abigail, "You will think me transported with enthusiasm, but I am not. I am well aware of the toil, blood, and treasure that it will cost us to maintain this Declaration, and support and defend these states." Adams was right. The colonists seemed little match for the finest army in the world, whose size was nearly quadrupled by hired guns from the German state of Hesse and elsewhere. In 1775, the British had 8,500 men stationed in the colonies and had hired nearly 30,000 mercenaries. Initially, the colonists had only 5,000 men in uniform, and their number waxed and waned as the war progressed. Nevertheless, in 1783, the American colonies won their war of independence. How they eventually won is a story best left to history books. However, in the following sections we will explore how they formed a new government.

TABLE 2.1 Locke and the Declaration of Independence: Some Parallels

LOCKE	DECLARATION OF INDEPENDENCE
Natural Rights "The state of nature has a law to govern it" "life, liberty, and property"	"Laws of Nature and Nature's God" "life, liberty, and the pursuit of happiness."
Purpose of Government "to preserve himself, his liberty, and property"	"to secure these rights"
Equality "men being by nature all free, equal and independent"	"all men are created equal"
Consent of the Governed "for when any number of men have, by the consent of every individual, made a community, with a power to act as one body, which is only by the will and determination of the majority"	"Governments are instituted among men, deriving their just powers from the consent of the governed."
Limited Government "Absolute arbitrary power, or governing without settled laws, can neither of them consist with the ends of society and government." "As usurpation is the exercise of power which another has a right to, so tyranny is the exercise of power beyond right, which nobody can have a right to."	"The history of the present King of Great Britain is a history of repeated injuries and usurpations."
Right to Revolt "The people shall be the judge.... Oppression raises ferments and makes men struggle to cast off an uneasy and tyrannical yoke."	"Prudence, indeed, will dictate that Governments long established should not be changed for light and transient causes.... But when a long train of abuses and usurpations, pursuing invariably the same Object evinces a design to reduce them under absolute Despotism, it is their right, it is their duty, to throw off such Government."

The "Conservative" Revolution

Revolutions such as the 1789 French Revolution, the 1917 Russian Revolution, and the 1978–1979 Iranian Revolution produced great societal change—as well as plenty of bloodshed. The American Revolution was different. Although many people lost their lives during the Revolutionary War, the Revolution itself was essentially a conservative movement that did not drastically alter the colonists' way of life. Its primary goal was to restore rights that the colonists felt were already theirs as British subjects and to live as they had before Britain tightened its regulations after the Seven Years' War.

American colonists did not feel the need for great social, economic, or political upheavals. Despite their opposition to British rule, they "were not oppressed people; they had no crushing imperial shackles to throw off."[6] As a result, the Revolution did not create class conflicts that would split society for generations to come. The colonial leaders' belief that they needed the consent of the governed blessed the new nation with a crucial element of stability—a stability the nation would need.

The Government That Failed: 1776–1787

2.2 Analyze how the weaknesses of the Articles of Confederation led to its failure.

The Continental Congress that adopted the Declaration of Independence was only a voluntary association of the states. In 1776, Congress appointed a committee to draw up a plan for a permanent union of the states. That plan, our first constitution, was the **Articles of Confederation**.[7]

Articles of Confederation
The first constitution of the United States, adopted by Congress in 1777 and enacted in 1781. The Articles established a national legislature, the Continental Congress, but most authority rested with the state legislatures.

The Articles of Confederation

The Articles established a government dominated by the states. The United States, according to the Articles, was a confederation, a "league of friendship and perpetual union" among 13 states. The Articles established a national legislature with one house; states could send as many as seven delegates or as few as two, but each state had only one vote. There was no president and no national court, and the powers of the national legislature were strictly limited. Most authority rested with the state legislatures because the new nation's leaders feared that a strong central government would become as tyrannical as British rule.

Because unanimous consent of the states was needed to put the Articles into operation, the Articles adopted by the Continental Congress in 1777 did not go into effect until 1781, when laggard Maryland finally ratified them. In the meantime, the Continental Congress barely survived, lurching from crisis to crisis. At one point during the war, some of Washington's troops threatened to create a monarchy with him as king unless Congress paid their overdue wages.

Even after the states ratified the Articles of Confederation, many logistical and political problems plagued Congress. State delegations attended haphazardly. Congress had few powers outside maintaining an army and navy—and little money to do even that. It had to request money from the states because it had no power to tax. If states refused to send money (which they often did), Congress did without. In desperation, Congress sold off western lands (land east of the Mississippi and west of the states) to speculators, issued securities that sold for less than their face value, or used its own presses to print money that was virtually worthless. Congress also voted to disband the army despite continued threats from Britain and Spain.

Congress lacked the power to regulate commerce, which inhibited foreign trade and the development of a strong national economy. It did, however, manage to develop sound policies for the management of the western frontiers, passing the Northwest Ordinance of 1787 that encouraged the development of the Great Lakes region.

In general, the weak and ineffective national government could take little independent action. All government power rested in the states. The national government could not compel the states to do anything, and it had no power to deal directly with individual citizens. The weakness of the national government prevented it from dealing with the hard times that faced the new nation. There was one benefit of the Articles, however: When the nation's leaders began to write a new Constitution, they could look at the provisions of the Articles of Confederation and know some of the things they should avoid.

A Strong National Government

One of the most important features of the Constitution is the creation of a strong national government. If the Framers had retained a weak national government, as under the Articles of Confederation, Congress could not create a great national economic market through regulating interstate commerce, the president could not conduct a vigorous foreign policy, federal courts could not issue orders to protect civil rights, and the federal government could not raise the funds to pay for Social Security benefits or grants and loans for college students.

Changes in the States

What was happening in the states was as important as what was happening in Congress. The most significant change was a dramatic increase in democracy and liberty, at least for white males. Many states adopted bills of rights to protect freedoms, abolished religious qualifications for holding office, and liberalized requirements for voting. Expanded political participation brought a new middle class to power.

This middle class included farmers who owned small homesteads rather than manorial landholders and artisans instead of lawyers. Before the Revolution, almost all members of New York's assembly were either urban merchants or wealthy landowners. In the 1769 assembly, for example, 25 percent of the legislators were farmers, even though nearly 95 percent of New Yorkers were farmers. But after the Revolution, a major power shift occurred. With expanded voting privileges, farmers and craftworkers became a decisive majority, and the old elite of professionals, wealthy merchants, and large landholders saw its power shrink. The same change occurred in other states as power shifted from a handful of wealthy individuals to a more broad-based group (see Figure 2.2). Democracy was taking hold everywhere.

The structure of government in the states also became more responsive to the people. State constitutions concentrated power in the legislatures because most people considered legislators to be closer to the voters than governors or judges. Legislatures often selected the governors and kept them on a short leash, with brief tenures and limited veto and appointment powers. Legislatures also overruled court decisions and criticized judges for unpopular decisions.

The idea of equality, at least among white males, was driving change throughout the nation. Although the Revolutionary War itself did not transform American society, it unleashed the republican tendencies in American life. Americans were in the process of becoming "the most liberal, the most democratic, the most commercially minded, and the most modern people in the world."[8] Members of the old colonial elite found this turn of affairs quite troublesome because it challenged their hold on power.

FIGURE 2.2 Power Shift: Economic Status of State Legislators Before and After the Revolutionary War

After the Revolution, power in the state legislatures shifted from the hands of the wealthy to those with more moderate incomes and from merchants and lawyers to farmers. This trend was especially evident in the northern states.

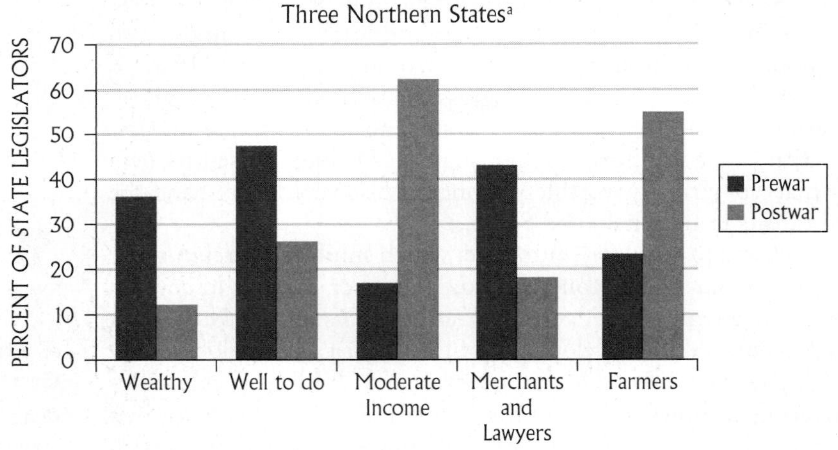

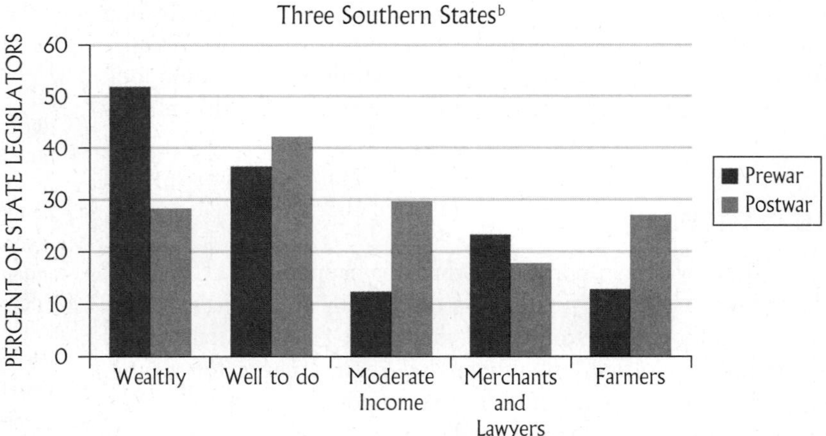

[a]New York, New Jersey, New Hampshire

[b]Maryland, South Carolina, Virginia

Economic Turmoil

Economic issues were at the top of the political agenda. A postwar depression had left many small farmers unable to pay their debts and threatened them with mortgage foreclosures. Now under control of people more sympathetic to debtors, the state legislatures listened to the demands of small farmers. A few states, notably Rhode Island, demonstrated their support of debtors, passing policies favoring them over creditors. Some printed tons of paper money and passed "force acts" requiring reluctant creditors to accept the almost worthless money. Debtors could thus pay big debts with cheap currency.

Policies favoring debtors over creditors did not please the economic elite, who had once controlled nearly all the state legislatures. They were further shaken when, in 1786, a small band of farmers in western Massachusetts rebelled at losing their land to creditors. Led by Revolutionary War Captain Daniel Shays, this rebellion, called **Shays' Rebellion**, was a series of armed attacks on courthouses to prevent judges from foreclosing on farms. Farmers in other states—although never in large numbers—were also unruly. The economic elite were scared at the thought that people had taken the law into their own hands and violated the property rights of others. Neither Congress nor the state was able to raise a militia to stop Shays and his followers, so elites assembled a privately paid force to do the job. This necessity further fueled dissatisfaction with the weakness of the Articles of Confederation system.

Shays' Rebellion, in which farmers physically prevented judges from foreclosing on farms, helped spur the birth of the Constitution. News of the small rebellion spread quickly around the country, and some of the Philadelphia delegates thought a full-fledged revolution would result. The event reaffirmed the Framers' belief that the new federal government needed to be a strong one.

The Aborted Annapolis Meeting

In September 1786, a handful of leaders assembled in Annapolis, Maryland, to discuss problems with the Articles of Confederation and suggest solutions. The assembly was an abortive attempt at reform. Only five states—New York, New Jersey, Delaware, Pennsylvania, and Virginia—were represented at the meeting; the 12 delegates were few enough in number to meet around a dinner table. Called to consider commercial conflicts that had arisen among the states under the Articles of Confederation, the Annapolis delegates decided that a larger meeting and a broader proposal were needed to organize the states. Holding most of their meetings at a local tavern, this small and unofficial band of reformers issued a call for a full-scale meeting of the states in Philadelphia the following May—in retrospect, a rather bold move by so small a group. The Continental Congress granted their request, however, and called for a meeting of all the states. In May 1787, what we now call the Constitutional Convention got down to business in Philadelphia.

Shays' Rebellion
A series of attacks on courthouses by a small band of farmers led by Revolutionary War Captain Daniel Shays to block foreclosure proceedings.

Making a Constitution: The Philadelphia Convention

2.3 Describe the delegates to the Constitutional Convention and the core ideas they shared.

Representatives from 12 states came to Philadelphia to heed the Continental Congress's call to "take into consideration the situation in the United States." Only Rhode Island, a stronghold of paper-money interests and thus skeptical of reforms favoring creditors, refused to send delegates. Virginia's Patrick Henry (the colonial firebrand who had declared, "Give me liberty or give me death!") feared a centralization of power and also did not attend.

The delegates were ordered to meet "for the sole and express purpose of revising the Articles of Confederation." The Philadelphia delegates did not pay much attention to this order, however, because amending the Articles required the unanimous consent of the states, which they knew would be impossible. Thus, the 55 delegates ignored their instructions and began writing what was to become the **U.S. Constitution**. (You will find the entire text of the Constitution in the Appendix.)

U.S. Constitution
The document written in 1787 and ratified in 1788 that sets forth the institutional structure of U.S. government and the tasks these institutions perform. It replaced the Articles of Confederation.

Gentlemen in Philadelphia

Who were these 55 men? They may not have been "demigods," as Jefferson, perhaps sarcastically, called them, but they were certainly an elite group of economic and political notables. They were mostly wealthy planters, successful (or once-successful) lawyers and merchants, and men of independent wealth. Many were college graduates, and most had practical political experience. Most were coastal residents rather than residents of the expanding western frontiers, and a significant number were urbanites rather than part of the primarily rural American population.

Philosophy into Action

The delegates in Philadelphia were an uncommon combination of philosophers and shrewd political architects. The debates moved from high principles on the big issues to self-interest on the small ones.[9] The delegates devoted the first two weeks mainly to general debates about the nature of republican government (government in which ultimate power rests with the voters). After that, practical and divisive issues sometimes threatened to dissolve the meeting.

Obviously, these 55 men did not share the same political philosophy. Democratic Benjamin Franklin held very different views from a number of delegates who were wary of democracy. Yet at the core of their ideas existed a common center. The group agreed on questions of (1) human nature, (2) the causes of political conflict, (3) the objects of government, and (4) the nature of a republican government.

Human Nature In his famous work titled *Leviathan,* written in 1651, Thomas Hobbes argued that man's natural state was war and that a strong absolute ruler was necessary to restrain man's bestial tendencies. Without a strong government, Hobbes wrote, life would be "solitary, poor, nasty, brutish, and short." The delegates opposed Hobbes' powerful monarch, however, siding with Locke's argument that government should be limited.

Nevertheless, the delegates held a cynical view of human nature. People, they thought, were self-interested. Franklin and Hamilton, poles apart philosophically, both voiced this sentiment. Said Franklin, "There are two passions which have a powerful influence on the affairs of men: the love of power and the love of money." Hamilton agreed in his characteristically straightforward manner: "Men love power." The men at Philadelphia believed that government should play a key role in containing the natural self-interest of people.[10]

Alexander Hamilton, a New York delegate to the Convention, favored a strong central government. Hamilton was less influential at the Convention than he would be later as an architect of the nation's economic policy.

Political Conflict Of all the words written by and about the delegates, none have been more widely quoted than these by James Madison from *Federalist 10* (reprinted in the Appendix): "The most common and durable source of factions has been the various and unequal distribution of property." In other words, *the distribution of wealth* (land was the main form of wealth in those days) *is the source of political conflict.* "Those who hold and those who are without property," Madison went on, "have ever formed distinct interests in society." Other sources of conflict included religion, views of governing, and attachment to various leaders.[11]

Arising from these sources of conflict are **factions**, which we might call parties or interest groups. A majority faction might well be composed of the many who have little or no property; the minority faction, of those with property. If unchecked, the delegates thought, one of these factions would eventually tyrannize the other. The majority would try to seize the government to reduce the wealth of the minority; the minority would try to seize the government to secure its own gains. Governments run by factions, the Founders believed, are prone to instability, tyranny, and even violence. The Founders intended to check the effects of factions.

factions
Parties or interest groups that James Madison saw as arising from the unequal distribution of property or wealth and attacked as having the potential to cause instability in government.

Objects of Government To Gouverneur Morris of Pennsylvania, the preservation of property was the "principal object of government." Morris was outspoken and plainly overlooked some other objects of government, including security from invasion, domestic tranquility, and promotion of the general welfare. However, Morris's remark typifies the philosophy of many of the delegates. As property holders themselves, these delegates could not imagine a government that did not make its principal objective an economic one: the preservation of individual rights to acquire and hold wealth. A few (like Morris) were intent on shutting out the propertyless altogether. "Give the votes to people who have no property," Morris claimed, "and they will sell them to the rich who will be able to buy them."

Pennsylvania delegate Gouverneur Morris was a man of considerable means and was concerned primarily with protecting property holders. He was responsible for the style and wording of the Constitution.

Nature of Government Given their beliefs about human nature, the causes of political conflict, the need to protect property, and the threat of tyranny by a faction, what sort of government did the delegates believe would work? They answered in different ways, but the message was always the same. Power should be set against power so that no one faction would overwhelm the others. The secret of good government is "balanced" government. They were influenced in their thinking by the writings of a French aristocrat, Baron Montesquieu, who advocated separate branches of government with distinct powers and the ability to check the other branches. The Founders agreed, concluding that a limited government would have to contain checks on its own power. So long as no faction could seize the whole of government at once, tyranny could be avoided. A balanced government required a complex network of checks, balances, and separation of powers.

Critical Issues at the Convention

2.4 Categorize the issues at the Constitutional Convention and outline the resolutions reached on each type of issue.

The delegates in Philadelphia could not merely construct a government from ideas. They wanted to design a government that was consistent with their political philosophy, but they also had to confront some of the thorniest issues facing the fledgling nation at the time—issues of equality, the economy, and individual rights.

The Equality Issues

The Declaration of Independence states that all men are created equal; the Constitution, however, is silent on equality. Nevertheless, some of the most important issues on the policy agenda in Philadelphia concerned equality. Three issues occupied more attention than almost any others: whether the states were to be equally represented, what to do about slavery, and whether to ensure equality in voting.

New Jersey Plan
The proposal at the Constitutional Convention that called for equal **representation** of each state in Congress regardless of the state's population.

Virginia Plan
The proposal at the Constitutional Convention that called for **representation** of each state in Congress in proportion to that state's share of the U.S. population.

Connecticut Compromise
The compromise reached at the Constitutional Convention that established two houses of Congress: the House of Representatives, in which **representation** is based on a state's share of the U.S. population; and the Senate, in which each state has two representatives.

Equality and Representation of the States

One crucial policy issue was how to constitute the new Congress. The **New Jersey Plan**, proposed by William Paterson of New Jersey, called for each state to be equally represented in the new Congress. The opposing strategy, suggested by Edmund Randolph of Virginia, is usually called the **Virginia Plan**. It called for giving each state representation in Congress based on the state's share of the American population.

The delegates resolved this conflict with a compromise devised by Roger Sherman and William Johnson of Connecticut. The solution proposed by this **Connecticut Compromise** was to create two houses in Congress. One body, the Senate, would have two members from each state (the New Jersey Plan), and the second body, the House of Representatives, would have representation based on population (the Virginia Plan). The U.S. Congress is still organized in exactly the same way. Each state has two senators, and the state's population determines its representation in the House.

Although the Connecticut Compromise was intended to maximize equality among the states, it actually gives more power to people who live in states with small populations than to those who live in more heavily populated states. Every state has two senators and at least one member of the House, no matter how small its population. To take the most extreme case, Wyoming and California have the same number of votes in the Senate (two), although Wyoming has less than 2 percent of California's population. Thus, a citizen of Wyoming has about *70 times* the representation in the Senate as does a citizen of California.[12]

Because it is the Senate, not the House, that ratifies treaties, confirms presidential nominations, and hears trials of impeachment, citizens in less populated states have a greater say in these key tasks. In addition, the electoral college (the body that actually elects the president and is discussed in Chapter 10) gives small states greater weight. If no presidential candidate receives a majority in the electoral college, the House of Representatives makes the final decision—with each state having one vote. In such a case (which has not occurred since 1824), the votes of citizens of Wyoming would again carry about 70 times as much weight as those of Californians.

Whether representation in the Senate is "fair" is a matter of debate. What is not open to question is that the delegates to the 1787 convention had to accommodate various interests and viewpoints in order to convince all the states to join an untested union.

Representation in the Senate

The Senate both creates a check on the House and overrepresents states with small populations. If there were only one house of Congress, governance would be more efficient. If representation were based solely on population, interests centered in states with small populations would lose an advantage and there might be a closer correspondence between public opinion and public policy. At the same time, there would be one less important check on government action. Which do you prefer?

Slavery

The second equality issue was slavery. The contradictions between slavery and the sentiments of the Declaration of Independence are obvious, but in 1787 slavery was legal in every state except Massachusetts. It was concentrated in the South, however, where slave labor was commonplace in agriculture. Some delegates, like Gouverneur Morris, denounced slavery in no uncertain terms. But the Convention could not accept Morris's position in the face of powerful Southern opposition led by Charles C. Pinckney of South Carolina. The delegates did agree that Congress could limit *future importing* of slaves (they allowed it to be outlawed after 1808), but they did not forbid slavery itself. The Constitution, in fact, inclines toward recognizing slavery; it states that persons legally "held to service or labour" (referring to slaves) who escaped to free states had to be returned to their owners.

Another difficult question about slavery arose at the Convention. How should slaves be counted in determining representation in Congress (and thus also electoral votes)? Southerners were happy to see slaves counted toward determining their representation in the House of Representatives (though reluctant to count them for apportionment of taxation). Here the result was the famous *three-fifths compromise*. Representation and taxation were to be based on the "number of free persons," plus three-fifths of the number of "all other persons." Everyone, of course, knew who those other persons were.

Equality in Voting

The delegates dodged one other issue on equality. A handful of delegates, led by Franklin, suggested that national elections should require universal manhood suffrage (that is, a vote for all free adult males). This still would have left a majority of the population disenfranchised, but for those still smarting from Shays' Rebellion and the fear of mob rule, the suggestion was too democratic. Many delegates

A POINT TO PONDER

The Framers could not reach agreement regarding slavery. As a result, it persisted for several generations until the Civil War resolved the issue. Yet one could argue that leaving difficult decisions to future generations is a primary reason for the survival of the nation.

What do you think—were the Framers copping out, or smartly trying not to take on too much conflict at once and leaving flexibility for future generations?

DOONESBURY Garry Trudeau

wanted to include property ownership as a qualification for voting. Ultimately, as the debate wound down, they decided to leave the issue to the states. People qualified to vote in state elections could also vote in national elections. Table 2.2 summarizes how the Founders dealt with the three issues of equality.

The Economic Issues

The Philadelphia delegates were deeply concerned about the state of the American economy. Economic issues were high on the Constitution writers' policy agenda. People disagreed (in fact, historians still disagree) as to whether the postcolonial economy was in a shambles.[13] The writers of the Constitution, already committed to a strong national government, charged that the economy was indeed in disarray and that they needed to address the following problems:

- The states had erected tariffs against products from other states.
- Paper money was virtually worthless in some states; however, many state governments, which were controlled by debtor classes, forced it on creditors anyway.
- Congress was having trouble raising money because the economy was in a recession.

Understanding something about the delegates and their economic interests gives us insight into their views on the role of government in the economy. They were, by all accounts, the nation's postcolonial economic elite. Some were budding capitalists. Others were creditors whose loans were being wiped out by cheap paper money. Many were merchants who could not even carry

When the Constitution was written, many Northern and Southern delegates assumed that slavery, being relatively unprofitable, would soon die out. A single invention—Eli Whitney's cotton gin—made it profitable again. Although Congress did act to control the growth of slavery, the slave economy became entrenched in the South. • ***Could the Founders have prohibited slavery in the new nation?***

TABLE 2.2 How the Constitution Resolved Three Issues of Equality

PROBLEM	SOLUTION
Equality of the States	
Should states be represented equally (the New Jersey Plan) or in proportion to their population (the Virginia Plan)?	Both, according to the Connecticut Compromise. States have equal representation in the Senate, but representation in the House is proportionate to population.
Slavery	
What should be done about slavery?	Although Congress was permitted to stop the importing of slaves after 1808 and states were required to return runaway slaves from other states, the Constitution is mostly silent on the issue of slavery.
How should slaves be counted for representation in the House of Representatives?	Give states credit for three-fifths of slaves in determining population for representation.
Equality in Voting	
Should the right to vote be based on universal manhood suffrage, or should it be very restricted?	Finesse the issue. Let the states decide qualifications for voting.

on trade with a neighboring state. Virtually all of them thought a strong national government was needed to bring economic stability to the chaotic union of states that existed under the Articles of Confederation.[14]

It is not surprising, then, that the Framers of the Constitution would seek to strengthen the economic powers (and thus the scope) of the new national government. One famous historian, Charles A. Beard, claimed that their principal motivation for doing so was to increase their personal wealth. The Framers, he said, not only were propertied, upper-class men protecting their interests, but also held bonds and investments whose value would increase if the Constitution were adopted. The best evidence, however, indicates that although they were concerned about protecting property rights, the Founders' motivations were in the broad sense of building a strong economy rather than in the narrow sense of increasing their personal wealth.[15]

The delegates made sure that the Constitution clearly spelled out the economic powers of Congress (see Table 2.3). Consistent with the general allocation of power in the

TABLE 2.3 Economics in the Constitution

Powers of Congress

1. Levy taxes.
2. Pay debts.
3. Borrow money.
4. Coin money and regulate its value.
5. Regulate interstate and foreign commerce.
6. Establish uniform laws of bankruptcy.
7. Punish piracy.
8. Punish counterfeiting.
9. Create standard weights and measures.
10. Establish post offices and post roads.
11. Protect copyrights and patents.

Prohibitions on the States

1. States cannot pass laws impairing the obligations of contract.
2. States cannot coin money or issue paper money.
3. States cannot require payment of debts in paper money.
4. States cannot tax imports or exports from abroad or from other states.
5. States cannot free runaway slaves from other states.

Other Key Provisions

1. The new government assumes the national debt contracted under the Articles of Confederation.
2. The Constitution guarantees a republican form of government.
3. The states must respect civil court judgments and contracts made in other states.

Constitution, Congress was to be the chief economic policymaker. It could obtain revenues through taxing and borrowing. These tools, along with the power to appropriate funds, became crucial instruments for influencing the economy (as we will see in Chapter 17). By maintaining sound money and guaranteeing payment for the national debt, Congress was to encourage economic enterprise and investment in the United States. The Constitution also allocates to Congress power to build the nation's infrastructure by constructing post offices and roads and to establish standard weights and measures. To protect property rights, Congress was charged with punishing counterfeiters and pirates, ensuring patents and copyrights, and legislating rules for bankruptcy. Equally important (and now a key congressional power, with a wide range of implications for the economy) was Congress's new ability to regulate interstate and foreign commerce. In sum, the Constitution granted Congress the power to create the conditions within which markets could flourish.

In addition, the Framers prohibited practices in the states that they viewed as inhibiting economic development, such as maintaining individual state monetary systems, placing duties on imports from other states, and interfering with lawfully contracted debts. Moreover, the states were to respect civil judgments and contracts made in other states, and they were to return runaway slaves to their owners. To help the states, the national government guaranteed them "a republican form of government" to prevent a recurrence of Shays' Rebellion, in which some people used violence, instead of legislation and the courts, to resolve commercial disputes.

The Constitution also obligated the new government to repay all the public debts incurred under the Continental Congress and the Articles of Confederation—debts that totaled $54 million. Paying off the debts would ensure from the outset that money would flow into the American economy and would also restore the confidence of investors in the young nation.

The Individual Rights Issues

Another major item on the Constitutional Convention agenda for the delegates was designing a system that would preserve individual rights. There was no dispute about the importance of safeguarding individualism, and the Founders believed that this would be relatively easy. After all, they were constructing a limited government that, by design, could not threaten personal freedoms. In addition, they dispersed power among the branches of the national government and between the national and state governments so that each branch or level could restrain the other. Also, most of the delegates believed that the various states were already doing a sufficient job of protecting individual rights.

As a result, the Constitution says little about personal freedoms. The protections it does offer are the following:

- It prohibits suspension of the **writ of habeas corpus** (except during invasion or rebellion). Such a court order enables persons detained by authorities to secure an immediate inquiry into the causes of their detention. If no proper explanation is offered, a judge may order their release. (Article I, Section 9)
- It prohibits Congress or the states from passing bills of attainder (which punish people without a judicial trial). (Article I, Section 9)
- It prohibits Congress or the states from passing *ex post facto* laws (which punish people or increase the penalties for acts that were not illegal or not as punishable when the act was committed). (Article I, Section 9)
- It prohibits the imposition of religious qualifications for holding office in the national government. (Article VI)
- It narrowly defines and outlines strict rules of evidence for conviction of treason. To be convicted, a person must levy war against the United States or adhere to and aid its enemies during war. Conviction requires confession in open court or the testimony of *two* witnesses to the *same* overt act. The Framers of the Constitution would have been executed as traitors if the Revolution had failed, and they were therefore sensitive to treason laws. (Article III, Section 3)
- It upholds the right to trial by jury in criminal cases. (Article III, Section 2)

writ of habeas corpus
A court order requiring jailers to explain to a judge why they are holding a prisoner in custody.

The delegates were content with their document. When it came time to ratify the Constitution, however, there was widespread criticism of the absence of specific protections of individual rights, such as free expression and the rights of the accused.

2.5 Analyze how the components of the Madisonian system addressed the dilemma of reconciling majority rule with the protection of minority interests.

The Madisonian System

The Framers believed that human nature was self-interested and that inequalities of wealth were the principal source of political conflict. Regardless, they had no desire to remove the divisions in society by converting private property to common ownership; they also believed that protecting private property was a key purpose of government. Their experience with state governments under the Articles of Confederation reinforced their view that democracy was a threat to property. Many of them felt that the nonwealthy majority—an unruly mob—would tyrannize the wealthy minority if given political power. Thus, the delegates to the Constitutional Convention faced the dilemma of reconciling economic inequality with political freedom. How could they devise a government that was responsive to the majority while protecting private property?

Thwarting Tyranny of the Majority

James Madison was neither wealthy nor a great orator. He was, however, a careful student of politics and government and became the principal architect of the government's final structure, which we sometimes refer to as the Madisonian system.[16] He and his colleagues feared both majority and minority factions. Either could take control of the government and use it to their own advantage. Factions of the minority, however, were easy to handle; the majority could simply outvote them. Factions of the majority were harder to handle. If the majority united around some policy issue, such as the redistribution of wealth, they could oppress the minority, violating the latter's basic rights.[17]

As Madison would later explain in *Federalist 51* (reprinted in the Appendix):

> Ambition must be made to counteract ambition. . . . If men were angels, no government would be necessary. If angels were to govern men, neither external nor internal controls would be necessary. In framing a government which is to be administered by men over men, the great difficulty lies in this: you must first enable the government to control the governed; and then in the next place oblige it to control itself.[18]

To prevent the possibility of a tyranny of the majority, Madison proposed the following:

1. Place as much of the government as possible beyond the direct control of the majority.
2. Separate the powers of different institutions.
3. Construct a system of checks and balances.

Limiting Majority Control Madison believed that to thwart tyranny by the majority, it was essential to keep most of the government beyond their power. His plan placed only one element of government, the House of Representatives, within direct control of the votes of the majority. In contrast, state legislatures were to elect senators, and special electors were to select the president; in other words, government officials would be elected by a small minority, not by the people themselves. The president was to nominate judges (see Figure 2.3). Even if the majority seized control of the House of Representatives, they still could not enact policies without the agreement of the Senate and the president. To further insulate governmental officials from public opinion, the Constitution gave judges lifetime tenure and senators terms of six years, with only one-third elected every two years, compared with the two-year election intervals of all members of the House of Representatives.

separation of powers A feature of the Constitution that requires each of the three branches of government—executive, legislative, and judicial—to be relatively independent of the others so that one cannot control the others. Power is shared among these three institutions.

Separating Powers The Madisonian scheme also provided for a **separation of powers**. Each of the three branches of government—executive (the president),

FIGURE 2.3 The Constitution and the Electoral Process: The Original Plan

Under Madison's plan, which was incorporated in the Constitution, voters' electoral influence was limited. Voters directly elected only the House of Representatives. Senators and presidents were indirectly elected—senators by state legislatures, and presidents by the electoral college, whose members, depending on the state, were chosen by state legislatures or by voters; the president nominated judges. Over the years, Madison's original model has been substantially democratized. The Seventeenth Amendment (1913) established direct election of senators by popular majorities. Today, the electoral college has become largely a rubber stamp, voting the way the popular majority in each state votes.

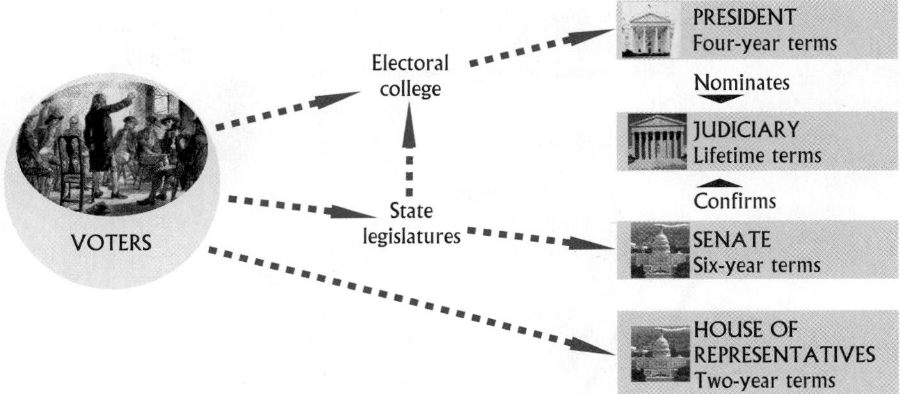

legislative (Congress), and judicial (the courts)—would be relatively independent of one another so that no single branch could control the others. The Founders gave the president, Congress, and the courts independent elements of power. The Constitution does not divide power absolutely, however; rather, it *shares* it among the three institutions.

Creating Checks and Balances Because powers were not completely separate, each branch required the consent of the others for many of its actions. This created a system of **checks and balances** that reflected Madison's goal of setting power against power to constrain government actions. He reasoned that if a faction seized one institution, it still could not damage the whole system. The system of checks and balances was an elaborate and delicate creation. The president checks Congress by holding veto power; Congress holds the purse strings of government and must approve presidential nominations.

checks and balances Features of the Constitution that limit government's power by requiring that power be balanced among the different governmental institutions. These institutions continually constrain one another's activities.

The courts also figured into the system of checks and balances. Presidents could nominate judges, but their confirmation by the Senate was required. The Supreme Court itself, in *Marbury v. Madison* (1803), asserted its power to check the other branches through judicial review: the right to hold actions of the other two branches unconstitutional. This right, which is not specifically outlined in the Constitution, considerably strengthened the Court's ability to restrain the other branches of government. For a summary of separation of powers and the checks and balances system, see Figure 2.4.

Checks and Balances

People often complain about gridlock in government, but that is a product of checks and balances. Making it difficult for either a minority or a majority to dominate easily also makes it difficult to pass legislation over which there is disagreement.

Establishing a Federal System As we will discuss in detail in Chapter 3, the Founders also established a federal system of government that divided the power of government between a national government and the individual states. Most government activity at the time occurred in the states. The Framers of the Constitution anticipated that this would be an additional check on the national government.

The Constitutional Republic

When asked what kind of government the delegates had produced, Benjamin Franklin is said to have replied, "A republic . . . if you can keep it." Because the Founders did not wish to have the people directly make all decisions (as in a town meeting where everyone has

FIGURE 2.4 Separation of Powers and Checks and Balances in the Constitution

The doctrine of separation of powers allows the three institutions of government to check and balance one another. Judicial review—the power of courts to hold executive and congressional policies unconstitutional—was not explicit in the Constitution but was asserted by the Supreme Court in *Marbury v. Madison.*

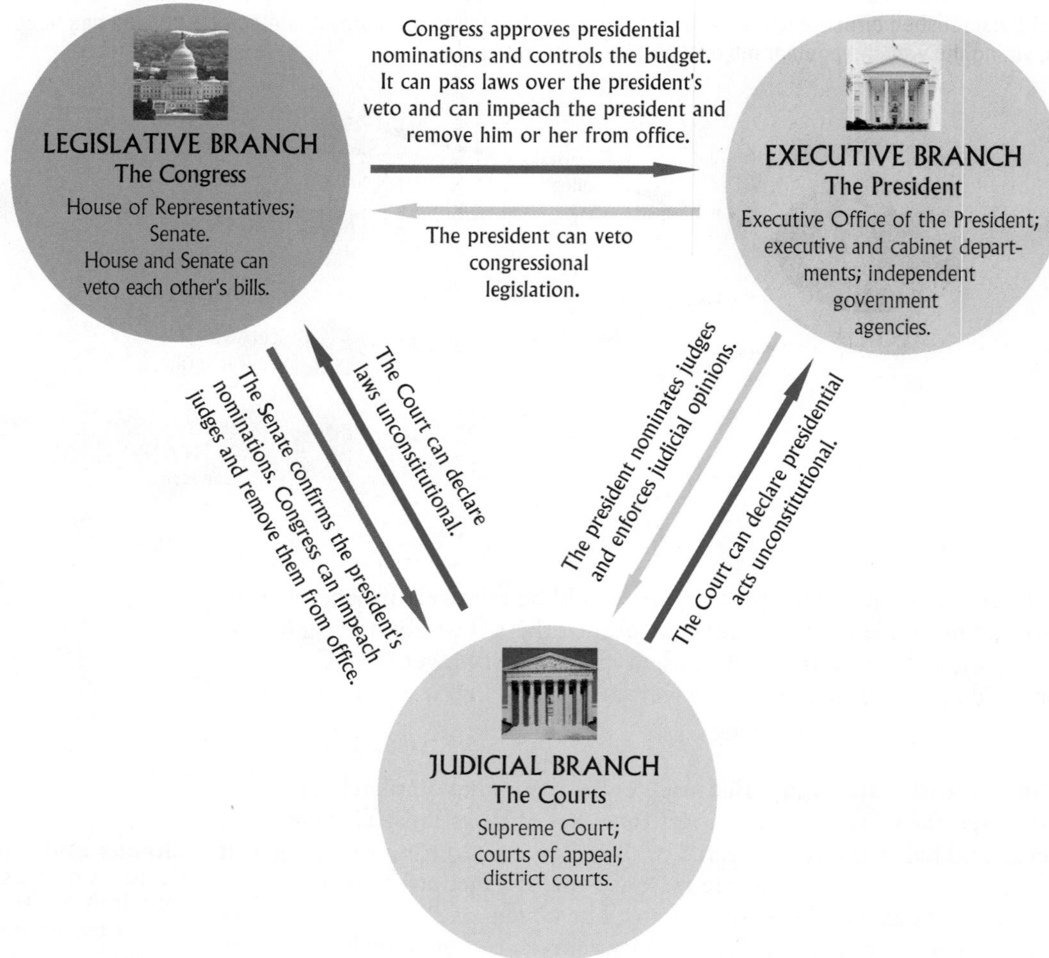
LEGISLATIVE BRANCH
The Congress
House of Representatives; Senate.
House and Senate can veto each other's bills.
Congress approves presidential nominations and controls the budget. It can pass laws over the president's veto and can impeach the president and remove him or her from office.
The president can veto congressional legislation.
EXECUTIVE BRANCH
The President
Executive Office of the President; executive and cabinet departments; independent government agencies.
The Senate confirms the president's nominations. Congress can impeach judges and remove them from office.
The Court can declare laws unconstitutional.
The president nominates judges and enforces judicial opinions.
The Court can declare presidential acts unconstitutional.
JUDICIAL BRANCH
The Courts
Supreme Court; courts of appeal; district courts.

republic
A form of government in which the people select representatives to govern them and make laws.

one vote), and because even then the country was far too large for such a proposal to be feasible, they did not choose to create a direct democracy. Their solution was to establish a **republic**: a system based on the consent of the governed in which representatives of the public exercise power. This deliberative democracy required and encouraged reflection and refinement of the public's views through an elaborate decision-making process.

The system of checks and balances and separation of powers favors the status quo. People who desire change must usually have a sizable majority, not just a simple majority of 51 percent. Those opposed to change need only win at one point in the policymaking process—say in obtaining a presidential veto—whereas those who favor change must win *every* battle along the way. Change usually comes slowly, if at all. As a result, the Madisonian system encourages moderation and compromise and slows change. It is difficult for either a minority or a majority to tyrannize, and both property rights and personal freedoms (with only occasional lapses) have survived.

Franklin was correct that such a system is not easy to maintain. It requires careful nurturing and balancing of diverse interests. Some critics argue that the policymaking process lacks efficiency, preventing effective responses to pressing matters. We will examine this issue closely throughout *Government in America.*

The End of the Beginning

On the 109th day of the meetings, in stifling heat made worse because the windows of the Pennsylvania statehouse were closed to ensure secrecy, the final version of the Constitution was read aloud. Then Dr. Franklin rose with a speech he had written; however, he was so enfeebled that he had to ask James Wilson to deliver it. Franklin noted, "There are several parts of this Constitution of which I do not at present approve, but I am not sure that I shall never approve them," and then asked for a vote. Ten states voted yes, and none voted no, but South Carolina's delegates were divided. After signing the document (Edmund Randolph, Elbridge Gerry, and George Mason of Virginia refused to sign), the members adjourned to a tavern. The experience of the last few hours, when conflict intermingled with consensus, reminded them that implementing this new document would be no small feat.

George Washington presides over the signing of the Constitution. "The business being closed," he wrote, "the members adjourned to the City Tavern, dined together and took cordial leave of each other."

Ratifying the Constitution

2.6 Compare and contrast the Federalists and Anti-Federalists in terms of their background and their positions regarding government.

The Constitution did not go into effect once the Constitutional Convention in Philadelphia was over. It had to be ratified by the states. Our awe of the Founders sometimes blinds us to the bitter politics of the day. There is no way of determining the public's feelings about the new document, but as John Marshall (who later became chief justice) suggested, "It is scarcely to be doubted that *in some of the adopting states, a majority of the people were in opposition*" (emphasis added).[19] The Constitution itself required that only 9 of the 13 states approve the document before it could be implemented, ignoring the requirement that the Articles of Confederation be amended only by unanimous consent.

Federalists and Anti-Federalists

Throughout the states, a fierce battle erupted between the **Federalists**, who supported the Constitution, and the **Anti-Federalists**, who opposed it. Newspapers were filled with letters and articles, many written under pseudonyms, praising or condemning the document. In praise of the Constitution, three men—James Madison, Alexander Hamilton, and John Jay—wrote a series of articles under the name Publius. These articles, known as the **Federalist Papers**, are second only to the Constitution itself in reflecting the thinking of the Framers. (You will find two of the most famous of these articles, *Federalist 10* and *51*, in the Appendix.)

Federalists
Supporters of the U.S. Constitution at the time the states were contemplating its adoption.

Anti-Federalists
Opponents of the American Constitution at the time when the states were contemplating its adoption.

Federalist Papers
A collection of 85 articles written by Alexander Hamilton, John Jay, and James Madison under the name "Publius" to defend the Constitution in detail.

Beginning on October 27, 1787, barely a month after the Convention ended, the *Federalist Papers* began to appear in New York newspapers as part of the ratification debate in New York. Eighty-five were eventually published. They not only defended the Constitution detail by detail but also represented an important statement of political philosophy. (The essays influenced few of the New York delegates, however, who voted to ratify the Constitution only after New York City threatened to secede from the state if they did not.)

Far from being unpatriotic or un-American, the Anti-Federalists sincerely believed that the new government was an enemy of freedom, the very freedom they had just fought a war to ensure. They launched bitter, biting, even brilliant attacks on the work

52 THE FEDERALIST.

long as it exiſts by a conſtitutional neceſſity for local purpoſes, though it ſhould be in perfect ſubordination to the general authority of the union, it would ſtill be, in fact and in theory, an aſſociation of ſtates, or a confederacy. The propoſed conſtitution, ſo far from implying an abolition of the ſtate governments, makes them conſtituent parts of the national ſovereignty by allowing them a direct repreſentation in the ſenate, and leaves in their poſſeſſion certain excluſive and very important portions of ſovereign power.—This fully correſponds, in every rational import of the terms, with the idea of a federal government.

In the Lycian confederacy, which conſiſted of twenty-three CITIES, or republics, the largeſt were intitled to *three* votes in the COMMON COUNCIL, thoſe of the middle claſs to *two*, and the ſmalleſt to *one*. The COMMON COUNCIL had the appointment of all the judges and magiſtrates of the reſpective CITIES. This was certainly the moſt delicate ſpecies of interference in their internal adminiſtration; for if there be any thing that ſeems excluſively appropriated to the local juriſdictions, it is the appointment of their own officers. Yet Monteſquieu, ſpeaking of this aſſociation, ſays, "Were I to give a model of an excellent "confederate republic, it would be that of Lycia." Thus we perceive that the diſtinctions inſiſted upon were not within the contemplation of this enlightened civilian, and we ſhall be led to conclude, that they are the novel refinements of an erroneous theory.

PUBLIUS.

NUMBER X.

The ſame Subject continued.

AMONG the numerous advantages promiſed by a well conſtructed union, none deſerves to be more accurately developed than its tendency to break and control the violence of faction. The friend of popular governments,

THE FEDERALIST. 53

governments, never finds himſelf ſo much alarmed for their character and fate, as when he contemplates their propenſity to this dangerous vice. He will not fail therefore to ſet a due value on any plan which, without violating the principles to which he is attached, provides a proper cure for it. The inſtability, injuſtice and confuſion introduced into the public councils, have in truth been the mortal diſeaſes under which popular governments have every where periſhed; as they continue to be the favorite and fruitful topics from which the adverſaries to liberty derive their moſt ſpecious declamations. The valuable improvements made by the American conſtitutions on the popular models, both ancient and modern, cannot certainly be too much admired; but it would be an unwarrantable partiality, to contend that they have as effectually obviated the danger on this ſide as was wiſhed and expected. Complaints are every where heard from our moſt conſiderate and virtuous citizens, equally the friends of public and private faith, and of public and perſonal liberty; that our governments are too unſtable; that the public good is diſregarded in the conflicts of rival parties; and that meaſures are too often decided, not according to the rules of juſtice, and the rights of the minor party; but by the ſuperior force of an intereſted and overbearing majority. However anxiouſly we may wiſh that theſe complaints had no foundation, the evidence of known facts will not permit us to deny that they are in ſome degree true. It will be found indeed, on a candid review of our ſituation, that ſome of the diſtreſſes under which we labor, have been erroneouſly charged on the operation of our governments; but it will be found at the ſame time, that other cauſes will not alone account for many of our heavieſt misfortunes; and particularly, for that prevailing and increaſing diſtruſt of public engagements, and alarm for private rights, which are echoed from one end of the continent to the other. Theſe muſt be chiefly, if not

E 3 wholly,

As an explanation and defense of the Constitution, the *Federalist Papers* were often discussed at dinner parties and debated in public places. Today, the U.S. has higher literacy rates than in the 1780s. • ***Do you think that a similar set of documents, so rich in political philosophy, would be so widely read in modern America?***

of delegates such as Washington, Madison, Franklin, and Hamilton, and frankly questioned the motives of the Constitution's authors.

One objection was that the new Constitution was a class-based document, intended to ensure that a particular economic elite controlled the public policies of the national government.[20] Another fear of the Anti-Federalists was that the new government would erode fundamental liberties. Why, they asked, was there no list of rights in the Constitution? You can compare the views of the Federalists and Anti-Federalists in Table 2.4.

To allay fears that the Constitution would restrict personal freedoms, the Federalists promised to add amendments to the document specifically protecting individual liberties. They kept their word; James Madison introduced 12 constitutional amendments during the First Congress in 1789. Ten were ratified by the states and took effect in 1791. These first 10 amendments to the Constitution, which restrain the national government from limiting personal freedoms, have come to be known as the **Bill of Rights** (see Table 2.5). Another of Madison's original 12 amendments, one dealing with congressional salaries, was ratified 201 years later as the Twenty-seventh Amendment.

Bill of Rights
The first 10 amendments to the **U.S. Constitution**, drafted in response to some of the **Anti-Federalist** concerns. These amendments define such basic liberties as freedom of religion, speech, and press and guarantee defendants' rights.

Opponents also feared that the Constitution would weaken the power of the states (which it did). Patrick Henry railed against strengthening the federal government at the expense of the states. "We are come hither," he told his fellow delegates to the Virginia ratifying convention, "to preserve the poor commonwealth of Virginia."[21] Many state political leaders feared that the Constitution would diminish their own power as well.

Finally, not everyone wanted the economy placed on a more sound foundation. Creditors opposed the issuance of paper money because it would produce inflation and make the money they received as payment on their loans decline in value. Debtors favored paper money, however. Their debts (such as the mortgages on their farms)

TABLE 2.4 Federalists and Anti-Federalists Compared

ANTI-FEDERALISTS	FEDERALISTS
Backgrounds	
Small farmers, shopkeepers, laborers	Large landowners, wealthy merchants, professionals
Government Preferred	
Strong state government	Weaker state governments
Weak national government	Strong national government
Direct election of officials	Indirect election of officials
Shorter terms	Longer terms
Rule by the common man	Government by the elite
Strengthened protections for individual liberties	Expected few violations of individual liberties

TABLE 2.5 The Bill of Rights (Arranged by Function)

Protection of Free Expression	
Amendment 1:	Freedom of speech, press, and assembly Freedom to petition government
Protection of Personal Beliefs	
Amendment 1:	No government establishment of religion Freedom to exercise religion
Protection of Privacy	
Amendment 3:	No forced quartering of troops in homes during peacetime
Amendment 4:	No unreasonable searches and seizures
Protection of Defendants' Rights	
Amendment 5:	Grand jury indictment required for prosecution of serious crime No second prosecution for the same offense No compulsion to testify against oneself No loss of life, liberty, or property without due process of law
Amendment 6:	Right to a speedy and public trial by a local, impartial jury Right to be informed of charges against oneself Right to legal counsel Right to compel the attendance of favorable witnesses Right to cross-examine witnesses
Amendment 7:	Right to jury trial in civil suit where the value of controversy exceeds $20
Amendment 8:	No excessive bail or fines No cruel and unusual punishments
Protection of Other Rights	
Amendment 2:	Right to bear arms
Amendment 5:	No taking of private property for public use without just compensation
Amendment 9:	Unlisted rights are not necessarily denied
Amendment 10:	Powers not delegated to the national government or denied to the states are reserved for the states or the people

would remain constant, but if money became more plentiful, it would be easier for them to pay off their debts.

Ratification

Federalists may not have had the support of the majority, but they made up for it in shrewd politicking. They knew that many members of the legislatures of some states were skeptical of the Constitution and that state legislatures were populated with political leaders who would lose power under the Constitution. Thus, the Federalists specified that the Constitution be ratified by special conventions in each of the states—not by state legislatures.

Delaware was the first to approve, on December 7, 1787. Only six months passed before New Hampshire's approval (the ninth) made the Constitution official. Virginia and New York then voted to join the new union. Two states were holdouts: North Carolina and Rhode Island made the promise of the Bill of Rights their price for joining the other states.

With the Constitution ratified, it was time to select officeholders. The Framers of the Constitution assumed that George Washington would be elected the first president of the new government—even giving him the Convention's papers for safekeeping—and they were right. The general was the unanimous choice of the electoral college for president. He took office on April 30, 1789, in New York City, the first national capital. New Englander John Adams became the vice president—or, as Franklin called him, "His Superfluous Excellence."

2.7 Explain how the Constitution can be formally amended and how it changes informally.

Changing the Constitution

"The Constitution," said Jefferson, "belongs to the living and not to the dead." The U.S. Constitution is frequently—and rightly—referred to as a living document. It is constantly being tested and altered.

Constitutional changes are made either by formal amendments or by a number of informal processes. Formal amendments change the letter of the Constitution. There is also an unwritten body of tradition, practice, and procedure that, when altered, may change the spirit of the Constitution.

The Formal Amending Process

The most explicit means of changing the Constitution is through the formal process of amendment. Article V of the Constitution outlines procedures for formal amendment. There are two stages to the amendment process—proposal and ratification—and each stage has two possible avenues (see Figure 2.5). An amendment may be proposed either by a two-thirds vote in each house of Congress or by a national convention called by Congress at the request of two-thirds of the state legislatures. An amendment may be ratified either by the legislatures of three-fourths of the states or by special state conventions called in three-fourths of the states. The president has no formal role in amending the Constitution, although the chief executive may influence the success of proposed amendments. In general, it is difficult to formally amend the Constitution (see "America in Perspective: The Unusual Rigidity of the U.S. Constitution").

All but one of the successful amendments to the Constitution have been proposed by Congress and ratified by the state legislatures. The exception was the Twenty-first Amendment, which repealed the short-lived Eighteenth Amendment—the prohibition amendment that outlawed the sale and consumption of alcohol. The amendment was ratified by special state conventions rather than by state legislatures. Because

FIGURE 2.5 How the Constitution Can Be Amended

The Constitution sets up two alternative routes for proposing amendments and two for ratifying them. One of the four combinations has been used in every case but one.

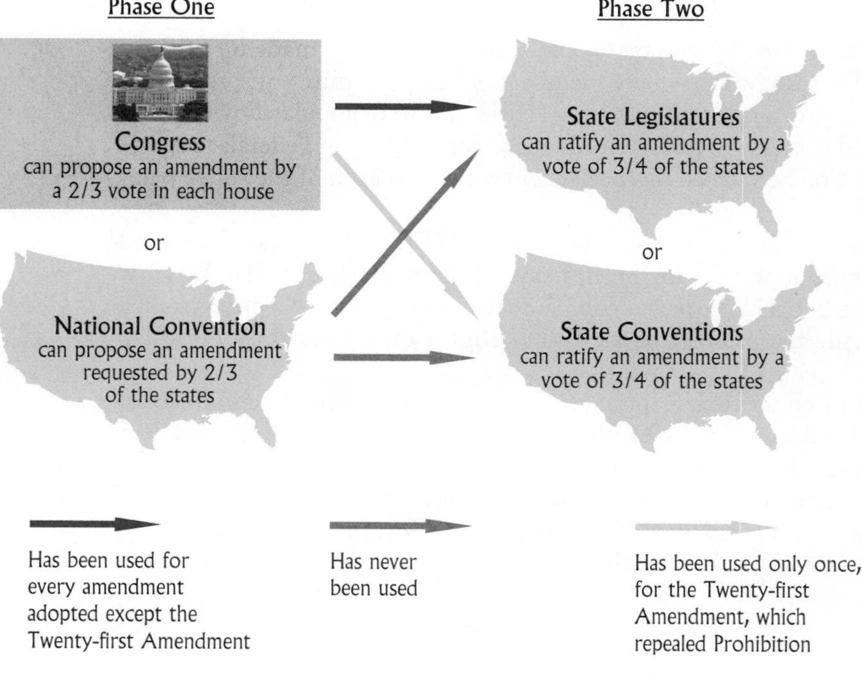
Phase One
Phase Two
Congress
can propose an amendment by a 2/3 vote in each house
or
National Convention
can propose an amendment requested by 2/3 of the states
State Legislatures
can ratify an amendment by a vote of 3/4 of the states
or
State Conventions
can ratify an amendment by a vote of 3/4 of the states
Has been used for every amendment adopted except the Twenty-first Amendment
Has never been used
Has been used only once, for the Twenty-first Amendment, which repealed Prohibition

AMERICA IN PERSPECTIVE

The Unusual Rigidity of the U.S. Constitution

In the *Federalist* 43, James Madison wrote that the Founders designed a process for adopting amendments to the U.S. Constitution that "guards equally against that extreme facility, which would render the Constitution too mutable; and that extreme difficulty, which might perpetuate its discovered faults." In other words, Madison felt that the American Constitution was rigid enough to provide stability in government, yet also flexible enough to allow adaptation over time.

Most other democracies have a procedure for adopting constitutional amendments, but few of the world's established democracies have made it as difficult as it is in the United States. Arend Lijphart developed a measure of constitutional rigidity based on the percentage vote required at the most demanding stage of the amending process. In the U.S., this would be 75 percent because at least three-quarters of the state legislatures or of conventions in three-quarters of the states must approve constitutional amendments. As you can see in the table below, only 4 of the other 22 established democracies require a majority of greater than two-thirds to amend their national constitution. In this regard, then, the U.S. Constitution is unusually rigid.

Requirements for Constitutional Amendments in Developed Democracies

SIMPLE MAJORITY (50% PLUS 1)	BETWEEN A SIMPLE MAJORITY AND TWO-THIRDS	TWO-THIRDS MAJORITY	SUPERMAJORITY (GREATER THAN TWO-THIRDS)
Great Britain	Denmark	Austria	Australia
Iceland	France	Belgium	Canada
Israel	Greece	Finland	Japan
New Zealand	Ireland	Germany	Switzerland
	Italy	Netherlands	U.S.
	Sweden	Norway	
		Portugal	
		Spain	

Source: Arend Lijphart, *Patterns of Democracy* (New Haven, CT: Yale University Press, 1999), p. 220.

proponents of repeal doubted that they could win in conservative legislatures, they persuaded Congress to require that state conventions be called.

Unquestionably, formal amendments have made the Constitution more egalitarian and democratic. Amendments that emphasize equality and increase the ability of a popular majority to affect government now provide a balance to the emphasis on economic issues in the original document. The Bill of Rights, which Chapter 4 will discuss in detail, heads the amendments (see Table 2.5). Later amendments, including the Thirteenth Amendment abolishing slavery, forbid various political and social inequalities based on race, gender, and age (Chapter 5 discusses these amendments). Other amendments, discussed later in this chapter, have democratized the political system, making it easier for voters to influence the government. Only one existing amendment specifically addresses the economy—the Sixteenth, or "income tax," Amendment. Overall, it is clear that the most important effect of these constitutional amendments has been to expand liberty and equality in the United States.

Some amendments have been proposed but not ratified. The best known of these in recent years is the **Equal Rights Amendment (ERA)**. First introduced in Congress in 1923 by the nephew of suffragist Susan B. Anthony, the ERA had to wait 49 years—until 1972—before Congress passed it and sent it to the states for ratification. The ERA stated simply, "Equality of rights under the law shall not be denied or abridged by the United States or by any State on account of sex." This seemingly benign amendment sailed through Congress and the first few state legislatures.[22] Public opinion polls showed substantial support for the ERA. Surveys revealed that even people who held traditional views of women's roles still supported it. Nevertheless, the ERA was not ratified.[23] It failed, in part, because of the system of checks and balances. Three-fourths of

Equal Rights Amendment
A constitutional amendment passed by Congress in 1972 stating that "equality of rights under the law shall not be denied or abridged by the United States or by any state on account of sex." The amendment failed to acquire the necessary support from three-fourths of the state legislatures.

Amending the Constitution to give women the right to vote was an important step in the women's rights movement.

the states, not simply a national majority, had to approve the ERA for it to become part of the Constitution. Many conservative Southern states opposed it, thus exercising their veto power despite approval by a majority of Americans.

Of course, supporters of the ERA can propose it again, and proponents of other constitutional amendments have been active in recent years. You can consider the issue of frequently amending the Constitution in "You Are the Policymaker: How Frequently Should We Amend the Constitution?"

The Informal Process of Constitutional Change

Think for a moment about all the changes in American government that have taken place without altering a word or a letter of the written document. In fact, there is not a word in the Constitution that would lead us to suspect any of the following developments:

- The United States has the world's oldest two-party system.
- Abortions through the second trimester of pregnancy (when the fetus cannot live outside the mother's womb) are legal in the United States.
- Members of the electoral college almost always follow the preference of their state's electorate.
- Television influences our political agenda and guides our assessments of candidates and issues.

None of these things is "unconstitutional." The parties emerged, first technology and then the law permitted abortions, television came to prominence in American life—all without having to tinker with the Founders' handiwork. These developments could occur because the Constitution changes *informally* as well as formally. There are several ways in which the Constitution changes informally: through judicial interpretation, through political practice, and as a result of changes in technology and changes in the demands on policymakers.

Judicial Interpretation Disputes often arise about the meaning of the Constitution. If it is the "supreme law of the land," then someone has to decide how to interpret the Constitution when disputes arise. In 1803, in the famous case of ***Marbury v. Madison***, the Supreme Court decided it would be the one to resolve differences of opinion (Chapter 16 discusses this case in detail). It claimed for itself the power of **judicial review**. Implied but never explicitly stated in the Constitution,[24] this power gives courts the right to decide whether the actions of the legislative and executive branches of state and national governments are in accord with the Constitution.

Marbury v. Madison
The 1803 case in which the **Supreme Court** asserted its right to determine the meaning of the **U.S. Constitution**. The decision established the Court's power of judicial review over acts of Congress.

judicial review
The power of the courts to determine whether acts of Congress and, by implication, the executive are in accord with the **U.S. Constitution**. Judicial review was established by ***Marbury v. Madison***.

Judicial interpretation can profoundly affect how the Constitution is understood because the Constitution usually means what the Supreme Court says it means. For example, in 1896, the Supreme Court decided that the Constitution allowed racial discrimination despite the presence of the Fourteenth Amendment. Fifty-eight years later, it overruled itself and concluded that segregation by law violated the Constitution. In 1973, the Supreme Court decided that the Constitution protected a woman's right to an abortion during the first two trimesters of pregnancy when the fetus is not viable outside the womb—an issue the Founders never imagined. (We discuss these cases in Chapters 4 and 5.)

Changing Political Practice Current political practices also change the Constitution—stretching it, shaping it, and giving it new meaning. Probably no changes are more important to American politics than those related to parties and presidential elections.

YOU ARE THE POLICYMAKER

How Frequently Should We Amend the Constitution?

Since the ratification of the Bill of Rights in 1791, there have been only 17 amendments to the Constitution—an average of one amendment every 13 years. It is now common, however, for political activists—and even political party platforms—to call for amendments. Some recent examples include prohibiting gay marriage, the burning of the American flag, and abortion; permitting prayer in public schools; requiring a balanced national budget; limiting the length of congressional terms; guaranteeing women's rights (the ERA); and protecting victims' rights.

Conservatives have been in the forefront of most recent calls for amendments (the ERA being an exception); many of the proposals for constitutional change are designed to overcome liberal Supreme Court decisions. Liberals, quite naturally, have opposed these amendments. There is a larger question here than just the particular changes that advocates of amending the Constitution support, however. The big question is, how frequently should we change the fundamental law of the land?

Those who support amending the Constitution argue that it should reflect the will of the people. If the overwhelming majority of the public wants to prohibit burning the American flag, for example, why shouldn't the Constitution reflect its preference? There is little possibility that a minority or even a narrow majority will be able to impose its will on the people, they argue, because the Constitution requires an extraordinary majority to ratify an amendment. So why should we be reluctant to test the waters of change?

Opponents of changing the Constitution frequently have their own arguments. It is ironic, they say, that conservatives, who typically wish to preserve the status quo, should be in the forefront of fundamental change. They argue that the Constitution has served the United States very well for more than two centuries with few changes. Why should we risk altering the fundamentals of the political system? And if we do, will we be setting a dangerous precedent that will encourage yet more change in the future? Will such changes undermine the very nature of a constitution that is designed to set the basic rules of the game and be above the political fray?

What do you think? Are the arguments simply a reflection of ideologies? Should the Constitution reflect the current sentiment of the public and be changed whenever that opinion changes? Or should we show more caution in amending the Constitution no matter how we feel about a specific amendment?

Political parties as we know them did not exist when the Constitution was written. In fact, its authors would have disliked the idea of parties, which encourage factions. Regardless, by 1800 a party system had developed, and it plays a key role in making policy today. American government would be radically different if there were no political parties, even though the Constitution is silent about them.

Changing political practice has also reduced the electoral college to a clerical role in selecting the president. The writers of the Constitution intended that there be no popular vote for the president; instead, state legislatures or the voters (depending on the state) would select wise electors who would then choose a "distinguished character of continental reputation" (as the *Federalist Papers* put it) to be president. These electors formed the electoral college.

In 1796, the first election in which George Washington was not a candidate, electors scattered their votes among 13 candidates. By the election of 1800, domestic and foreign policy issues had divided the country into two political parties. To avoid dissipating their support, the parties required electors to pledge in advance to vote for the candidate who won their state's popular vote, leaving electors with a largely clerical function. Nothing in the Constitution prohibits an elector from voting for any candidate (which occasionally happens). Nevertheless, the idea of electors exercising independent judgments is a constitutional anachronism, changed not by formal amendment but by political practice.

Technology Technology has also greatly changed the Constitution. The media have always played an important role in politics—questioning governmental policies, supporting candidates, and helping shape citizens' opinions. Modern technology, however, has spurred the development of a *mass* media that can rapidly reach huge audiences, something unimaginable in the eighteenth century. The bureaucracy has grown in importance with the development of computers, which create new potential for bureaucrats to serve the public (such as writing over 40 million Social Security checks each month)—and, at times, create mischief. Electronic communications and the development of atomic weapons have given the president's role as commander in chief added significance, increasing the power of the president in the constitutional system. More recently, the Internet has fundamentally changed the way in which we select elected officials.

Increasing Demands on Policymakers The significance of the presidency has also grown as a result of increased demands for new policies. The evolution of the United States in the realm of international affairs—from an insignificant country that kept to itself to a superpower with an extraordinary range of international obligations—has concentrated additional power in the hands of the chief executive, whom the Constitution designates to take the lead in foreign affairs. Similarly, the increased demands of domestic policy have positioned the president in a more prominent role in preparing the federal budget and a legislative program.

All wars increase presidential power because they place additional demands on the commander in chief. Congress of necessity delegates to the president the authority to prosecute a war, which involves a multitude of decisions, ranging from military strategy to logistics. The war on terrorism has taken delegation of authority one step further, however. Because the enemy may be not a country but rather an amorphous group of people who employ the weapons of terrorism as political instruments, it is more difficult for Congress to specify the president's authority. Thus, a few days following the terrorist attacks of September 11, 2001, Congress passed a broad resolution authorizing the president to use force against those nations, organizations, or persons that he alone determined were involved in the attacks. In other words, Congress asked the president to determine the identity of the enemy. This resolution served as the legal basis for the war in Afghanistan that began in 2001.

In October 2002, Congress passed another resolution authorizing the president to use "all means necessary and appropriate," which included the use of military force, to defend the United States against Iraq and enforce UN resolutions regarding Iraq. Congress delegated to the president the right to determine if and when the United States would go to war. This broad grant of power provided the authority to invade Iraq in March 2003. The president also interpreted this resolution as authorizing him to order the National Security Agency to secretly monitor the international telephone calls and e-mail messages of people inside the United States who might be communicating with terrorists abroad.

In addition to fighting terrorists abroad, securing the homeland also became a highly salient issue. Only six weeks after the terrorist attacks, Congress passed the USA Patriot Act. This law gave the executive branch broad new powers for the wiretapping, surveillance, and investigation of terrorism suspects. The act gave the federal government the power to examine a suspect's records held by third parties, such as doctors, libraries, bookstores, universities, and Internet service providers. It also allowed searches of private property without probable cause and without prior notice to the owner, limiting a person's opportunities to challenge a search.

Thus, the war on terrorism has altered the balance of power in our constitutional system. It has substantially increased demands on the president and accorded the president a notable increase in authority to meet those demands. Some also see it as resulting in the loosening of protections of personal privacy.

The Importance of Flexibility

The Constitution, even with all 27 amendments, is a short document containing fewer than 8,000 words. It does not prescribe in detail the structure and functioning of the national government. Regarding the judiciary, the Constitution simply tells Congress to create a court system as it sees fit. The Supreme Court is the only court required by the Constitution, and even here the Constitution leaves the number of justices and their qualifications up to Congress. Similarly, many of the governing units we have today—such as the executive departments, the various offices in the White House, the independent regulatory commissions, and the committees of Congress, to name only a few examples—are not mentioned at all in the Constitution.

It is easy to see that the document the Framers produced over 200 years ago was not meant to be static, written in stone. Instead, the Constitution's authors created a flexible system of government, one that could adapt to the needs of the times without sacrificing personal freedom. The Framers allowed future generations to determine their own needs. (The constitutions of the various states tend to be much longer and much more detailed, as you can see in "My State: The Length of State Constitutions.") As muscle grows on the constitutional skeleton, it inevitably gives new shape and purpose to the government. This flexibility has helped ensure the Constitution's—and the nation's—survival. Although the United States is young compared to other Western nations, it has the oldest functioning Constitution. France, which experienced a revolution in 1789, the same year the Constitution took effect, has had 12 constitutions over the past two centuries. Despite the great diversity of the American population, the enormous size of the country, and the extraordinary changes that have taken place over the nation's history, the U.S. Constitution is still going strong.

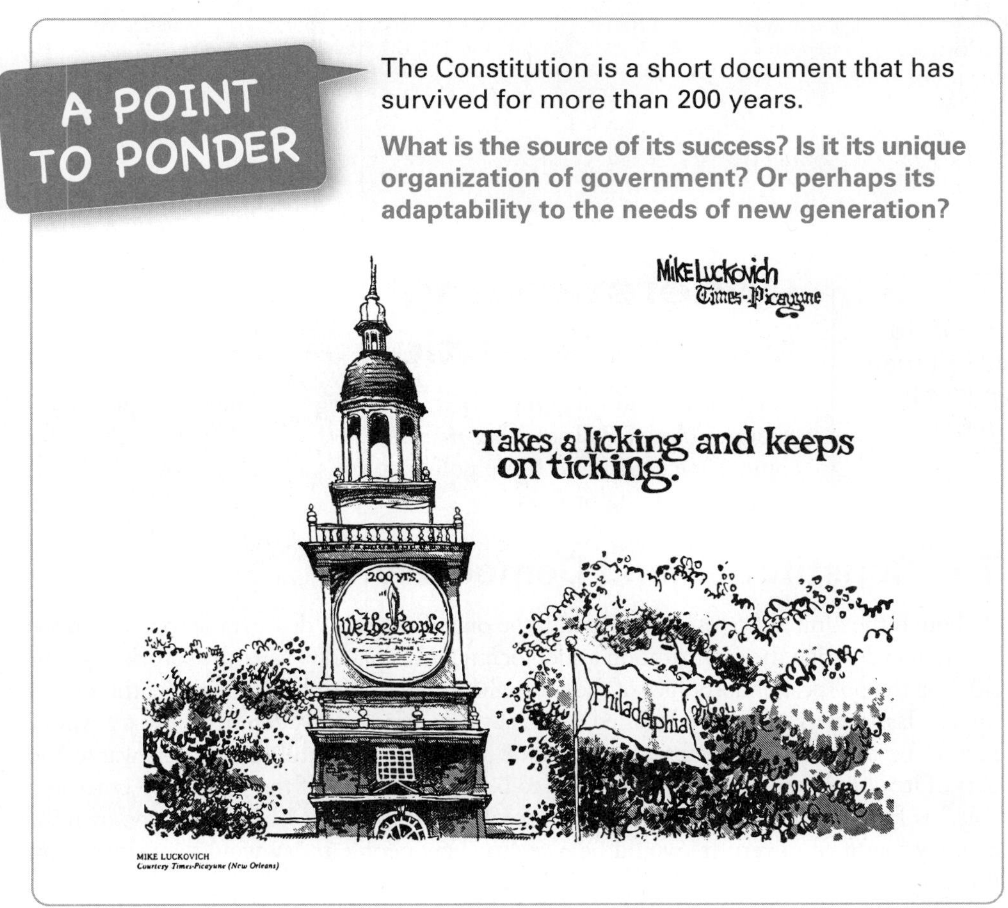

A POINT TO PONDER

The Constitution is a short document that has survived for more than 200 years.

What is the source of its success? Is it its unique organization of government? Or perhaps its adaptability to the needs of new generation?

MIKE LUCKOVICH
Courtesy Times-Picayune (New Orleans)

The Length of State Constitutions

In contrast to the U.S. Constitution, state constitutions tend to be long and very detailed, with numerous amendments. They average about four times the length of the U.S. Constitution. In addition, the average state constitution has been amended approximately 100 times. Only 6 of the 50 state constitutions have fewer than the 27 amendments to the U.S. Constitution. Greater length usually means greater specificity of detail about how a government must work and what it can do, which in turn reduces its flexibility.

The adjacent map classifies the constitutions of the 50 states according to their length in terms of number of words. The word count includes amendments to each constitution.

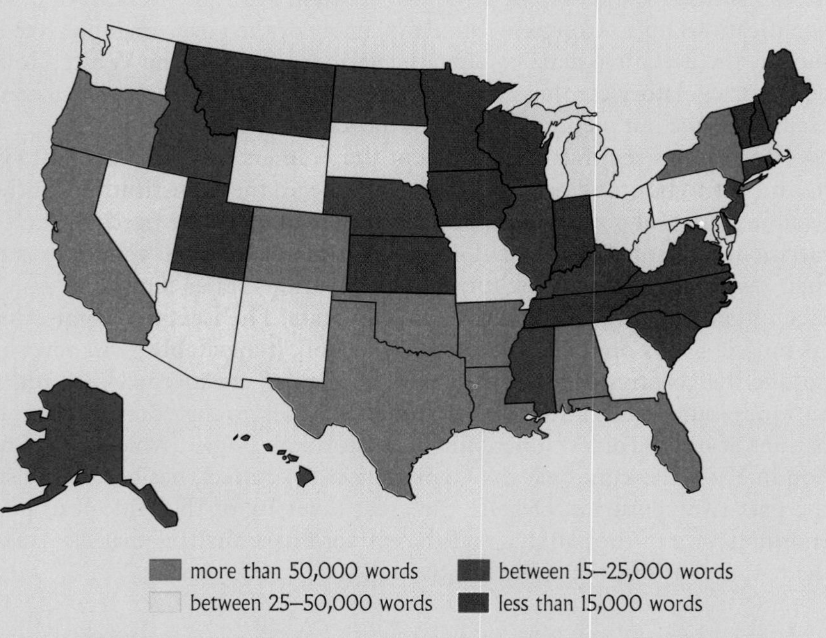

more than 50,000 words
between 25–50,000 words
between 15–25,000 words
less than 15,000 words

Source: Adapted from Harold W. Stanley and Richard G. Niami, *Vital Statistics on American Politics, 2007–2008* (Washington, DC: CQ Press, 2008), pp. 308–310.

QUESTIONS FOR DISCUSSION

- How does your state rank in terms of the length of its constitution?
- Do you think it would better if your state's constitution were as flexible as the U.S. Constitution?

2.8 Assess whether the Constitution establishes a majoritarian democracy and how it limits the scope of government.

Understanding the Constitution

The Constitution sets the broad rules for government and politics in America. As we will see, *these rules are never neutral*. Instead, they give some participants and some policy options advantages over others in the policymaking process.

The Constitution and Democracy

Although the United States is often said to be one of the most democratic societies in the world, few describe the Constitution as democratic. This paradox is hardly surprising, considering the political philosophies of the men who wrote it. Members of eighteenth-century upper-class society generally despised democratic government. If democracy was a way of permitting the majority's preference to become policy, the Constitution's authors wanted no part of it. The American government was to be a government of the "rich, well-born, and able," as Hamilton said, a government where John Jay's wish that "the people who own the country ought to govern it" would be a reality. Few people today would consider these thoughts democratic.

The Constitution did not, however, create a monarchy or a feudal aristocracy. It created a republic, a representative form of democracy modeled after the Lockean tradition of limited government. Thus, the undemocratic—even antidemocratic—Constitution established a government that permitted substantial movement toward democracy.

One of the central themes of American history is the gradual democratization of the Constitution. What began as a document characterized by numerous restrictions on direct voter participation has slowly become much more democratic. Today, few people share the Founders' fear of democracy. The expansion of voting rights has moved the American political system away from the elitist model of democracy and toward the pluralist model.

The Constitution itself offered no guidelines on voter eligibility, leaving it to each state to decide. As a result, only a small percentage of adults could vote; states excluded women and slaves entirely. Of the 17 constitutional amendments passed since the Bill of Rights, five focused on the expansion of the electorate. The Fifteenth Amendment (1870) prohibited discrimination on the basis of race in determining voter eligibility (although it took the Voting Rights Act of 1965, discussed in Chapter 5, to make the amendment effective). The Nineteenth Amendment (1920) gave women the right to vote (although some states had already done so). The Twenty-third Amendment (1961) accorded the residents of Washington, DC, the right to vote in presidential elections. Three years later, the Twenty-fourth Amendment prohibited poll taxes (which discriminated against the poor). Finally, the Twenty-sixth Amendment (1971) lowered the voter eligibility age to 18 (see "Young People and Politics: Lowering the Voting Age").

Not only are more people eligible to vote, but voters now have more officials to elect. The Seventeenth Amendment (1913) provided for direct election of senators. The development of political parties has fundamentally altered presidential elections.

Lowering the Voting Age

The 1960s was a tumultuous era, and massive protests by students and other young people regarding the war in Vietnam were common in the last half of the decade. Many young people felt that protesting was the best they could do because the voting age was 21 in most states—even though 18-year-olds were old enough to marry, work, and pay taxes as others adults did. In the Vietnam War, the average age of U.S. soldiers was 19, and young citizens often asserted, "If we're old enough to fight, we're old enough to vote." (Imagine the response today if soldiers fighting in Afghanistan and Iraq could not vote.)

Majorities in both houses of Congress agreed that the voting age was unfair and passed the Voting Rights Act of 1970, lowering the voting age to 18 in both federal and state elections. The Supreme Court, however, held that Congress had exceeded its authority and only could set voting ages in national elections.

In 1971, Senator Jennings Randolph, a Democrat from West Virginia, proposed a constitutional amendment to lower the voting age to 18 years: "The right of citizens of the United States, who are eighteen years of age or older, to vote shall not be denied or abridged by the United States or by any State on account of age." Randolph was a warrior for peace and had great faith in young people, arguing, "They possess a great social conscience, are perplexed by the injustices in the world, and are anxious to rectify those ills."

Randolph had introduced legislation lowering the voting age 11 times, beginning in 1942. This time, aided by appreciation of the sacrifices of young soldiers in Vietnam, he was successful. The amendment passed the Senate unanimously, and it passed the House of Representatives by a vote of 400 to 19. It was then sent to the states to be ratified. No state wanted to maintain two sets of voter registration books and go to the expense of running separate election systems for federal elections and for all other elections. Thus, the states were receptive to the proposed amendment, and in just 100 days three-fourths of the states ratified it.

On July 5, the Twenty-sixth Amendment was formally adopted into the Constitution, adding 11 million potential voters to the electorate. Half of these young voters cast their ballots in the 1972 presidential election.

QUESTIONS FOR DISCUSSION

- There are proposals in some states to lower the voting age below 18. What is the appropriate age for voting?
- Would it be appropriate for different states to have different ages for voting?

By placing the same candidate on the ballot in all the states and requiring members of the electoral college to support the candidate who receives the most votes, parties have increased the probability that the candidate for whom most Americans vote will also receive a majority of the electoral college vote. (For more on the electoral college, see Chapter 10.) Nevertheless, it is possible for the candidate who receives the most popular votes to lose the election, as occurred in 1824, 1876, 1888, and 2000.

Technology has also diminished the separation of the people from those who exercise power. Officeholders communicate directly with the public through television, radio, and targeted mailings. Air travel makes it easy for members of Congress to commute regularly between Washington and their districts. Similarly, public opinion polls, the telephone, e-mail, and the Internet enable officials to stay apprised of citizens' opinions on important issues. Even though the American population has grown from fewer than 4 million to more than 300 million people since the first census was taken in 1790, the national government has never been closer to those it serves.

The Constitution and the Scope of Government

The Constitution created political institutions and the rules for politics and policymaking. Many of these rules limit government action. This limiting function is what the Bill of Rights and related provisions in the Constitution are all about. No matter how large the majority, for example, it is unconstitutional to establish a state-supported church.

The goal of most of these limitations is primarily to protect liberty and to open the system to a broad range of participants. The potential range of action for the government is actually quite wide. Thus, it is constitutionally permissible, although highly unlikely, for the national government either to abolish Social Security payments to the elderly or to take over ownership of the oil industry or the nation's airlines.

The appropriate scope of government, such as government support for the social welfare efforts of religious organizations, is one of the most important–and most difficult–constitutional issues. Here President George W. Bush visits a Washington, DC charity, SOME, that feeds the needy and the homeless.

Yet the system of government created by the Constitution has profound implications for what the government does. On one hand, the system reinforces individualism at every turn. The separation of powers and the checks and balances established by the Constitution allow almost all groups some place in the political system where their demands for public policy can be heard. Because many institutions share power, groups can usually find at least one sympathetic ear in government. Even if the president opposes the policies a particular group favors, Congress, the courts, or some other institution can help the group achieve its policy goals. In the early days of the civil rights movement, for example, African Americans found Congress and the president unsympathetic, so they turned to the Supreme Court. Getting their interests on the political agenda would have been much more difficult if the Court had not had important constitutional power.

On the other hand, the Constitution encourages stalemate. By providing effective access for so many interests, the Founders created a system of policymaking in which it is difficult for the government to act. The separation of powers and the system of checks and balances promote the politics of bargaining, compromise, and playing one institution against another. The system of checks and balances implies that one institution is checking another.

Some scholars suggest that so much checking was built into the American political system that effective government is almost impossible.[25] If the president, Congress, and the courts all pull in different directions on policy, the result may be either no policy at all (gridlock) or an inadequate, makeshift policy. The outcome may be nondecisions when the country requires that difficult decisions be made. If government cannot respond effectively because its policymaking processes are too fragmented, then its performance will be inadequate. Perhaps the Constitution limits the ability of government to reach effective policy decisions. Certainly, radical departures from the status quo are atypical in American politics.

Summary

2.1 Describe the ideas behind the American Revolution and their role in shaping the Constitution.

The American Revolution was built on the foundation of belief in natural rights, consent of the governed, limited government, the responsibility of government to protect private property, and the equality of citizens. The Constitution would reflect all these ideas.

2.2 Analyze how the weaknesses of the Articles of Confederation led to its failure.

The Articles of Confederation established a government dominated by the states, without a permanent executive or national judiciary. A weak central government could not raise sufficient funds to support a national defense, regulate commerce to encourage trade, protect property rights, or take action without the unanimous consent of the states.

2.3 Describe the delegates to the Constitutional Convention and the core ideas they shared.

The Framers of the Constitution were more educated, wealthy, and urban than most Americans. They shared some core ideas, including that people were self-interested, that the distribution of wealth was the principal source of political conflict, that the main object of government was protecting private property, and that power should be set against power to balance government.

2.4 Categorize the issues at the Constitutional Convention and outline the resolutions reached on each type of issue.

Conflicts over equality led to the Connecticut Compromise, the three-fifths compromise on slavery, and the decision to leave the issue of voting rights to the states. The greatest inequality of all, that of slavery, was so contentious an issue that the Framers simply avoided addressing it.

The Framers, many of whom belonged to the economic elite, believed that the American economy was in a shambles and intended to make the national government an economic stabilizer. They also knew that a strong national government would be better able to ensure the nation's security. The specificity of the powers assigned to Congress left no doubt that Congress was to forge national economic policy.

Because they believed that the limited government they had constructed would protect freedom, the Framers said little about individual rights in the Constitution. They did, however, take a number of specific steps, including substantially limiting the suspension of the writ of habeas corpus.

2.5 Analyze how the components of the Madisonian system addressed the dilemma of reconciling majority rule with the protection of minority interests.

The Founders reconciled majority rule with minority interests by constraining both the majority and the minority. The Madisonian system did this primarily by dispersing power among separate branches of government, each with a somewhat different constituency, and giving them shared powers so that each branch had a check on the others.

2.6 Compare and contrast the Federalists and Anti-Federalists in terms of their background and their positions regarding government.

Ratification of the Constitution was not a foregone conclusion. The Federalists, who were largely from the economic elite, supported a strong national government, and preferred to insulate public officials from public opinion. Anti-Federalists, largely from the middle class, supported a weaker national government and direct forms of democracy, and wanted stronger protection of individual liberties than the original Constitution offered. As a result, the Federalists promised to propose what became the Bill of Rights.

2.7 Explain how the Constitution can be formally amended and how it changes informally.

Constitutional change—both formal and informal—continues to shape and alter the letter and the spirit of the Madisonian system. The formal amendment process, requiring supermajorities in both houses of Congress and among the states, poses difficult hurdles to overcome. However, judicial interpretation, changing political practices, technology, and the increasing demands on policymakers have also changed the constitutional system in fundamental ways, providing a valuable flexibility.

2.8 Assess whether the Constitution establishes a majoritarian democracy and how it limits the scope of government.

The Constitution did not create a majoritarian democracy. Majorities do not always rule in America. Nevertheless, there has been a gradual democratization of the Constitution as the right to vote has expanded, senators have become elected, electors have become agents of political parties, and technology has facilitated direct, two-way communication between office holders and the public.

By protecting individual rights, and thus limiting the ability of officials to restrict them, the Constitution limits the scope of government. By dispersing power among institutions, it increases the access of interests to government but also allows these interests to check each other and produce a stalemate.

Chapter Test

2.1 Describe the ideas behind the American Revolution and their role in shaping the Constitution.

1. The notion that the people must agree on who their rulers will be is referred to as
   a. Sanctity of property rights
   b. Natural rights
   c. Consent of the governed
   d. Limited government
   e. Direct democracy

2. What were John Locke's views of the purpose of and limits on government?

3. Why is the American Revolution called a "conservative" revolution? Do you agree with this interpretation? Why or why not?

2.2 Analyze how the weaknesses of the Articles of Confederation led to its failure.

4. The primary result of Shays' Rebellion was
   a. To spread similar, unruly behavior to ever larger and more effective groups
   b. To force states to pass "force acts" and print money
   c. To calm the elite's fears about the economic climate
   d. To serve as a factor motivating the American Revolution
   e. To precipitate a review of the Articles of Confederation in Annapolis

5. The Articles of Confederation established a strong central government to respond to issues of economic and national crisis.

   True______ False______

6. Although it was ultimately a failure, the Articles of Confederation positively influenced the subsequent Constitution. How was it a failure and yet a positive influence?

2.3 Describe the delegates to the Constitutional Convention and the core ideas they shared.

7. According to James Madison, which of the following is the primary source of political conflict?
   a. Differing political ideologies
   b. Different religious views
   c. The distribution of wealth
   d. Self-interested human nature
   e. The lack of education

8. The delegates at the Philadelphia Convention believed that humans were primarily self-interested.

   True______ False______

9. What were the four core ideas on which the delegates at the Philadelphia Convention agreed? Briefly explain each.

2.4 Categorize the issues at the Constitutional Convention and outline the resolutions reached on each type of issue.

10. The Connecticut Compromise did which of the following?
    a. It guaranteed that slaves would count as three-fifths of a person in calculating a state's representation in Congress.
    b. It ensured that states would continue to influence the national government through a federalist system.
    c. It created two houses of Congress with different bases for determining congressional representation.
    d. It established that a state's representation in Congress would be based solely on the state's population of free citizens.
    e. It ensured that citizens of larger states would have more power than citizens of smaller states.

11. Which of the following economic powers are given to Congress in the U.S. Constitution?
    a. The power to tax and borrow money

b. The power to regulate interstate and foreign commerce
c. The power to broadly protect property rights
d. The power to print and coin money
e. All of the above

12. The U.S. Constitution in its original form, prior to amendment
a. Dealt more thoroughly with economic issues than with issues of equality
b. Dealt more thoroughly with issues of equality than with economic issues
c. Emphasized both economic and equality issues to a large degree
d. Mentioned both economic and equality issues only in passing
e. Dealt with neither economic nor equality issues

13. The Virginia Plan called for each state to be equally represented in the new Congress.

True______ False______

2.5 Analyze how the components of the Madisonian system addressed the dilemma of reconciling majority rule with the protection of minority interests.

14. The system of governance set up in the U.S. constitutional republic tends to
a. Favor the status quo and limit political change
b. Be relatively efficient in producing political results
c. Encourage direct democracy
d. Centralize power
e. All of the above

15. The Framers believed that, like the separation of powers and checks and balances, federalism would act as a check on the national government.

True______ False______

16. What provisions did Madison write into the Constitution in his attempt to limit the possibility of a "tyranny of the majority"?

17. Historian and political scientists James McGregor Burns has argued that the extensive system of checks and balances in the Constitution has made effective government almost impossible. Do you agree or disagree with him, and why? Explain, using concrete examples.

2.6 Compare and contrast the Federalists and Anti-Federalists in terms of their background and their positions regarding government.

18. The Bill of Rights was adopted primarily to
a. Allay fears that the Constitution would restrict freedom
b. Ensure that the Constitution had the support of the Federalists
c. Protect the states against the potential for abuses by the national government
d. Guarantee that Congress had sufficient authority to address national economic crises
e. Satisfy Madison's concerns about factions and to check their effects

19. The Constitution went into effect once the delegates in Philadelphia had voted to approve the document.

True______ False______

20. What were three issues the Federalists and Anti-Federalists disagreed on, and what positions did they take on these issues?

21. Why did the Federalists support amending the Constitution with a Bill or Rights even though the original (unamended) Constitution contained several protections for individuals?

2.7 Explain how the Constitution can be formally amended and how it changes informally.

22. Which of the following means of amending the Constitution has never been used to date?
a. Proposal by two-thirds support in both houses of Congress
b. Ratification by three-fourths of state legislatures
c. Ratification by three-fourths of state conventions
d. Proposal through a national convention called by Congress
e. Each of the above has been used at least once

23. The Equal Rights Amendment is an example of a constitutional amendment that failed to be ratified.

True______ False______

24. How is the formal amendment process consistent with our Madisonian system of government, designed to thwart tyranny of the majority?

25. Although the Constitution is difficult to change through the formal amendment process, the Framers created a "living" document, one that is broad, interpretable, and changing. Using examples of how the Constitution has changed over time, what is your assessment of how well this original intention of the Framers been met?

2.8 Assess whether the Constitution establishes a majoritarian democracy and how it limits the scope of government.

26. That the Constitution has been amended five times to expand the electorate illustrates how it has become more democratic over time.

True______ False______

27. How has the expansion of voting rights moved the American political system away from the elitist model of democracy and toward more of a pluralist model?

28. If democracy is defined as a way for the majority's preferences to become law, then the Framers would not be considered to be in favor of democracy. However, the Constitution also has clear provisions for formal and informal change that permitted movement toward greater democracy. Based on what you have learned about the Constitution and democracy, do you think that the Framers would approve or disapprove of American democracy today?

PEARSON mypoliscilab Exercises

Apply what you learned in this chapter on MyPoliSciLab.

Read on **mypoliscilab.com**

eText: Chapter 2

Study and **Review** on **mypoliscilab.com**

Pre-Test
Post-Test
Chapter Exam
Flashcards

Watch on **mypoliscilab.com**

Video: Animal Sacrifice and Free Exercise
Video: Polygamy and the U.S. Constitution

Explore on **mypoliscilab.com**

Simulation: You Are James Madison
Simulation: You Are Proposing a Constitutional Amendment
Comparative: Comparing Constitutions
Timeline: The History of Constitutional Amendments
Visual Literacy: The American System of Checks and Balances

Key Terms

constitution (30)
Declaration of Independence (31)
natural rights (32)
consent of the governed (32)
limited government (32)
Articles of Confederation (35)
Shays' Rebellion (37)
U.S. Constitution (38)
factions (39)
New Jersey Plan (40)
Virginia Plan (40)
Connecticut Compromise (40)
writ of habeas corpus (43)
separation of powers (44)
checks and balances (45)
republic (46)
Federalists (47)
Anti-Federalists (47)
Federalist Papers (47)
Bill of Rights (48)
Equal Rights Amendment (51)
Marbury v. Madison (52)
judicial review (52)

Internet Resources

http://www.colonialhall.com/biography.php
Biographies of the Founders.

http://www.earlyamerica.com/earlyamerica/milestones/commonsense/
Thomas Paine's *Common Sense.*

http://www.usconstitution.net/articles.html
The Articles of Confederation.

http://thomas.loc.gov/home/histdox/fedpapers.html
Federalist Papers in support of the ratification of the Constitution.

http://www.wepin.com/articles/afp/index.htm
Anti-Federalist writings opposing the ratification of the Constitution.

http://www.usconstitution.net/constframedata.html
Background of the Framers.

http://www.archives.gov/exhibits/charters/constitution.html
The Constitution.

http://www.usconstitution.net/constamfail.html
Important failed constitutional amendments.

http://www.usconstitution.net/constamprop.html
Recently proposed constitutional amendments.

For Further Reading

Bailyn, Bernard. ***The Ideological Origins of the American Revolution.*** Cambridge, MA: Harvard University Press, 1967. A leading work on the ideas that spawned the American Revolution.

Becker, Carl L. ***The Declaration of Independence:*** *A Study in the History of Political Ideas.* New York: Random House, 1942. Classic work on the meaning of the Declaration.

Dahl, Robert A. ***How Democratic Is the American Constitution?*** 2nd ed. New Haven, CT: Yale University Press, 2003. Questions the extent to which the Constitution furthers democratic goals.

Hamilton, Alexander, James Madison, and John Jay. ***The Federalist Papers.*** 2nd ed. Edited by Roy P. Fairfield. Baltimore: Johns Hopkins University Press, 1981. Key tracts in the campaign for the Constitution and cornerstones of American political thought.

Higginbotham, A. Leon, Jr. ***In the Matter of Color: Race and the American Legal Process, the Colonial Period.*** New York: Oxford University Press, 1978. Chronicles how colonial governments established the legal foundations for the enslavement of African Americans.

Jensen, Merrill. ***The Articles of Confederation.*** Madison: University of Wisconsin Press, 1940. Definitive and balanced treatment of the Articles.

Jillson, Calvin C. ***Constitution Making: Conflict and Consensus in the Federal Convention of 1787.*** New York: Agathon, 1988. Sophisticated analysis of the drafting of the Constitution.

Lipset, Seymour Martin. ***The First New Nation.*** New York: Basic Books, 1963. Political sociologist Lipset sees the early American experience as one of nation building.

Maier, Pauline. *American Scripture.* New York: Knopf, 1997. Argues that the Declaration was the embodiment of the American mind and historical experience.

McDonald, Forrest B. ***Novus Ordo Seclorum: The Intellectual Origins of the Constitution.*** Lawrence: University Press of Kansas, 1986. Discusses the ideas behind the Constitution.

Morris, Richard B. ***The Forging of the Union, 1781–1789.*** New York: Harper & Row, 1987. Written to coincide with the bicentennial of the Constitution, this is an excellent history of the document's making.

Norton, Mary Beth. ***Liberty's Daughters.*** Boston: Little, Brown, 1980. Examines the role of women during the era of the Revolution and concludes that the Revolution transformed gender roles, setting women on the course to equality.

Rakove, Jack N. ***Original Meanings: Politics and Ideas in the Making of the Constitution.*** New York: Alfred A. Knopf, 1996. Shows the difficulty of divining the original intentions of the Framers.

Rossiter, Clinton. ***1787: The Grand Convention.*** New York: Macmillan, 1966. A well-written study of the making of the Constitution.

Storing, Herbert J. ***What the Anti-Federalists Were For.*** Chicago: University of Chicago Press, 1981. Analysis of the political views of those opposed to ratification of the Constitution.

Wood, Gordon S. ***The Creation of the American Republic.*** Chapel Hill: University of North Carolina Press, 1969. In-depth study of American political thought prior to the Constitutional Convention.

Wood, Gordon S. ***Empire of Liberty: A History of the Early Republic, 1789-1815.*** New York: Oxford University Press, 2009. Excellent account of America's pivotal first quarter-century.

Wood, Gordon S. ***The Radicalism of the American Revolution.*** New York: Vintage, 1993. Shows how American society and politics were thoroughly transformed in the decades following the Revolution.

Chapter 3

Federalism

Learning Objectives

3.1 Define federalism and explain its consequences for American politics and policy.

3.2 Outline what the Constitution says about division of power between national and state governments and states' obligations to each other, and trace the increasing importance of the national government.

3.3 Characterize the shift from dual to cooperative federalism and the role of fiscal federalism in intergovernmental relations today.

3.4 Assess the impact of federalism on democratic government and the scope of government.

POLITICS IN ACTION: AIDING DISASTER VICTIMS

On August 29, 2005, Hurricane Katrina, a Category 5 storm, swept across the Mississippi Gulf Coast, devastating New Orleans and parts of Mississippi and Alabama. Levees that had protected New Orleans for generations gave way to the force of the storm, stranding thousands of citizens without electricity, food, water, health care, communications, or police protection.

State and local governments are the first responders to natural disasters, but the breadth of the disaster quickly overwhelmed most of the local infrastructure. The national government is supposed to supplement state and local efforts; instead, a virtual standoff between hesitant federal officials and besieged authorities in Louisiana deepened the crisis in New Orleans.

Chaos reigned as the fractured division of responsibility meant no one person or agency was in charge. Federal and state officials clashed over the issue of "federalizing" the Louisiana National Guard, which the governor was reluctant to do because she feared losing authority over it and lacked confidence in the national government.

State and local officials assumed that Washington would provide rapid and substantial aid, but leaders in Louisiana and New Orleans were not always sure what they needed. Thus, desperate state and local officials made open-ended pleas for help, which federal officials found difficult to interpret. Rather than initiate relief efforts—such as providing buses, food and water, troops, diesel fuel, and rescue boats—federal officials waited for specific requests and, weighing legalities and logistics, proceeded at a deliberate pace.

As a result, Americans watched in horror as their favorite news anchors reported from New Orleans standing beside suffering victims while federal officials were still unable to move the necessary personnel (including members of the world's mightiest military force) and supplies to aid those stricken by the storm.

Aid did arrive eventually, but it was followed very closely by a public relations battle to assign blame for what everyone agreed was a wholly inadequate response at all levels.

The issue was not whether to aid disaster victims. Everyone agreed with that. Instead, the issue was determining the appropriate federal and state powers and responsibilities. The complications surrounding the government response to Hurricane Katrina illustrate the importance of understanding American federalism, the complex relationships between different levels of government in the United States.

In exploring American federalism, we will be especially attentive to our themes of democracy and the scope of government. Does federalism, the vertical division of power, enhance democracy in the United States? Does the additional layer of policymakers at the state level make government more responsive to public opinion or merely more complicated? Does it enhance the prospects that a national majority of Americans will have their way in public policy? And what are the implications of federalism for the scope of the national government's activities? Why has the national government grown so much relative to state governments, and has this growth been at the expense of the states?

Chapter OUTLINE

The relationships between governments at the local, state, and national levels often confuse Americans. These confusions stem from the complexities of the relationships. Locally elected school boards run neighborhood schools, but the schools also receive state and national funds, and with those funds come state and national rules and regulations. Local airports, sewage systems, pollution control systems, and police departments also receive a mix of local, state, and national funds, so they operate under a complex web of rules and regulations imposed by each level of government.

3.1 Define federalism and explain its consequences for American politics and policy.

Defining Federalism

Federalism is a rather unusual system for governing, with particular consequences for those who live within it. This section explains the federal system and how it affects Americans living in such a system.

What Is Federalism?

federalism
A way of organizing a nation so that two or more levels of government have formal authority over the same land and people. It is a system of shared power between units of government.

Federalism is a way of organizing a nation so that two or more levels of government have formal authority over the same area and people. It is a system of shared power between units of government. For example, the state of California has formal authority over its inhabitants, but the national government can also pass laws and establish policies that affect Californians. We are subject to the formal authority of both state and national governments.

Although federalism is not unique to the United States, it is not a common method of governing. Only 11 of the 190 or so nations of the world have federal systems, and these countries, which include Germany, Mexico, Argentina, Canada, Australia, India, and the United States, share little else as a group (see "America in Perspective: Why Federalism?").

unitary governments
A way of organizing a nation so that all power resides in the central government. Most national governments today are unitary governments.

Most nations instead have **unitary governments**, in which all power resides in the central government. If the French Assembly, for instance, wants to redraw the boundaries of local governments or change their forms of government, it can (and has). In contrast, if the U.S. Congress wants to, say, abolish Alabama or redraw its boundary with Georgia, it cannot.

American states are unitary governments with respect to their local governments. That is, local governments receive their authority from the states, which can create or abolish local governments and can make rules for them, telling them what their speed limits will be, how they will be organized, how they can tax people, on what they can spend money, and so forth. States, in contrast, receive their authority not from the national government but *directly* from the Constitution.

There is a third form of governmental structure, a *confederation*. The United States began as a confederation under the Articles of Confederation. In a confederation, the national government is weak, and most or all power is in the hands of the country's components—for example, the individual states. Today, confederations are rare and mainly take the form of international organizations such as the United Nations (see Chapter 20). Table 3.1 provides a summary of the authority relations in the three systems of government.

intergovernmental relations
The workings of the federal system—the entire set of interactions among national, state, and local governments, including regulations, transfers of funds, and the sharing of information.

The workings of the federal system are sometimes called **intergovernmental relations**. This term refers to the entire set of interactions among national, state, and local governments, including regulations, the transfers of funds, and the sharing of information.

Why Is Federalism So Important?

One consequence of the federal system in America is that it *decentralizes our politics*. Voters elect senators as representatives of individual states, not of the entire nation. Even the presidential election, choosing a leader for the national government, is actually

TABLE 3.1 Authority Relations in Three Systems of Government

	UNITARY	CONFEDERATE	FEDERAL
Central government	Holds primary authority Regulates activities of states	Limited powers to coordinate state activities	Shares power with states
State government	Few or no powers Duties regulated by central government	Sovereign Allocates some duties to central government	Shares power with central government
Citizens	Vote for central government officials	Vote for state government officials	Vote for both state and central government officials

51 presidential elections, one in each state and one in Washington, D.C. (see Chapter 10). It is even possible—as happened in 2000—for a candidate who receives the most popular votes in the country to lose the election because of the way in which the Constitution distributes electoral votes by state.

The federal system decentralizes our politics in more fundamental ways than does our electoral system. With more layers of government, more opportunities exist for

AMERICA IN PERSPECTIVE

Why Federalism?

Only 11 countries have federal systems. Trying to determine why these particular nations chose a federal system is an interesting but difficult task. All three North American nations have federal systems, but the trend does not continue in South America, where only two nations have federal systems. Countries large in size—such as Canada and Australia—or large in both size and population—such as India, the United States, Brazil, and Mexico—tend to have federal systems, which decentralize the administration of governmental services. Nevertheless, China and Indonesia—two large and heavily populated countries—have unitary governments, and tiny Malaysia and Switzerland have federal systems.

A nation's diversity may also play a role in the development of a federal system. Brazil, Canada, India, Malaysia, Switzerland, and the United States have large minority ethnic groups, often distinct in language and religion. Many nations with unitary systems, however, ranging from Belgium to most African countries, are also replete with ethnic diversity.

Most federal systems are democracies, although most democracies are not federal systems. Authoritarian regimes generally do not wish to disperse power away from the central government. However, both the former Soviet Union and the former Yugoslavia, perhaps reflecting the extraordinary diversity of their populations, had federal systems—of a sort: In both countries, the central government retained ultimate power. As democracy swept through these countries, their national governments dissolved, and several smaller nations were formed.

NATION	POPULATION	AREA (THOUSANDS SQUARE MILES)	DIVERSITY (ETHNIC, LINGUISTIC, AND RELIGIOUS)
Argentina	40,913,584	1,068	Low
Australia	21,262,641	2,968	Low
Austria	8,210,281	32	Low
Brazil	198,739,269	3,286	Medium
Canada	33,487,208	3,852	High
Germany	82,329,758	138	Low
India	1,166,079,217	1,269	High
Malaysia	25,715,819	127	High
Mexico	111,211,789	762	Low
Switzerland	7,604,467	16	Medium
United States	307,212,123	3,718	Medium

Source: Central Intelligence Agency, *The World Factbook, 2010*

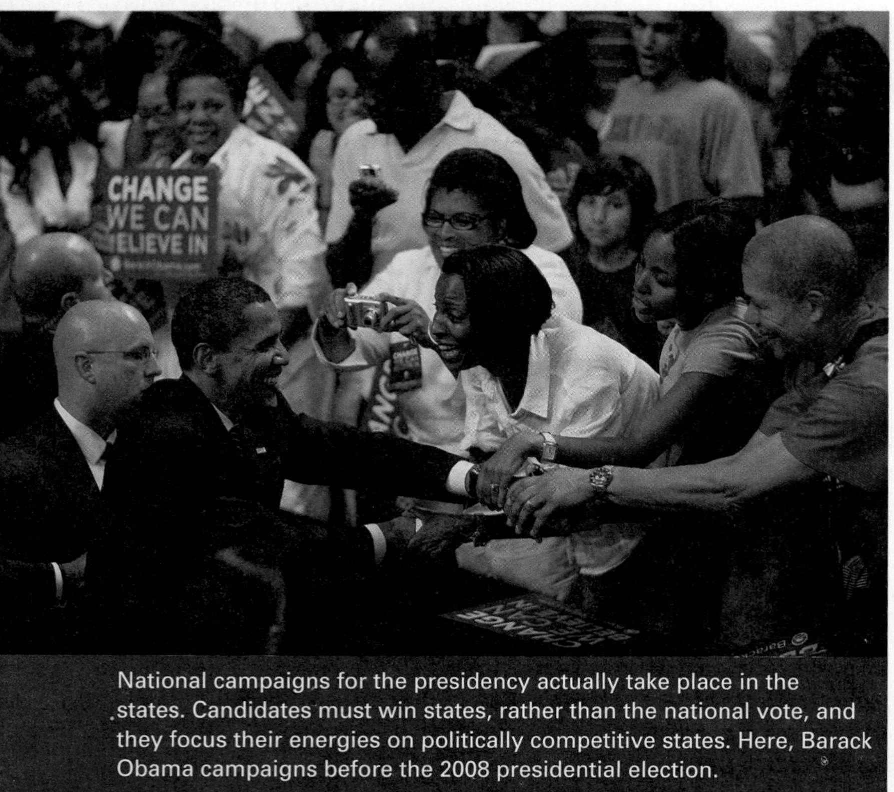

National campaigns for the presidency actually take place in the states. Candidates must win states, rather than the national vote, and they focus their energies on politically competitive states. Here, Barack Obama campaigns before the 2008 presidential election.

political participation. With more people wielding power, there are more points of access in government and more opportunities for government to satisfy the demands of interests for public policies. With states making more decisions, fewer issues need to be decided at the national level, lessening conflict there.

As we will see, federalism also enhances judicial power. Dividing government power and responsibilities necessitates umpires to resolve disputes between the two levels of government. In the American system, judges serve as the umpires. Thus, when the national government places prohibitions or requirements on the states, inevitably issues arise for the courts to decide.

The federal system not only decentralizes our politics but also *decentralizes our policies*. The history of the federal system demonstrates the tension between the states and the national government about policy—about who controls it and what it should be. In the past, people debated whether the states or the national government should regulate the railroads, pass child labor laws, or adopt minimum-wage legislation. Today, people debate whether the states or the national government should regulate abortions, set standards for public schools, determine speed limits on highways, protect the environment, provide health care for the poor, or tell 18-year-olds they cannot drink alcohol.[1]

Policies about health care, the economy, the environment, and other matters are subject to both the centralizing force of the national government and the dispersing force of the states. The overlapping powers of the two levels of government mean that most of our public policy debates are also debates about federalism.

States are responsible for most public policies dealing with social, family, and moral issues. The Constitution does not give the national government the power to pass laws that *directly* regulate drinking ages, marriage and divorce, or speed limits. These policy prerogatives belong to the states. They become national issues, however, when aggrieved or angry groups take their cases to Congress or the federal courts in an attempt to use the power of the national government to *influence* states or to convince federal courts to find a state's policy unconstitutional.

A good example of this process is the federal requirement that states raise their drinking age to 21 in order to receive highway funds. Candy Lightner, a Californian whose 13-year-old daughter had been killed by a drunk driver, formed Mothers Against Drunk Driving (MADD) in 1980. MADD lobbied Congress to pass a law withholding federal highway funds from any state that did not raise its drinking age. Today, every state has a legal drinking age of 21.

The American states have always been policy innovators.[2] The states overflow with reforms, new ideas, and new policies. From clean-air legislation to welfare reform, the states constitute a national laboratory to develop and test public policies and share the results with other states and the national government. Almost every policy that the national government has adopted had its beginnings in the states. One or more states pioneered child labor laws, minimum-wage legislation, unemployment compensation, antipollution legislation, civil rights protections, and the income tax. More recently, states have been active in reforming health care, education, and welfare—and the national government is paying close attention to their efforts.

The Constitutional Basis of Federalism

> **3.2** Outline what the Constitution says about division of power between national and state governments and states' obligations to each other, and trace the increasing importance of the national government.

The word *federalism* is absent from the Constitution, and not much was said about it at the Constitutional Convention. Eighteenth-century Americans had little experience in thinking of themselves as Americans first and state citizens second. In fact, loyalty to state governments was so strong that the Constitution would have been resoundingly defeated had it tried to abolish them. In addition, a central government, working alone, would have had difficulty trying to govern eighteenth-century Americans. The people were too widely dispersed and the country's transportation and communication systems too primitive to allow governing from a central location. There was no other practical choice in 1787 but to create a federal system of government.

The Division of Power

The Constitution's writers carefully defined the powers of state and national governments (see Table 3.2). Although they favored a stronger national government, the Framers still made states vital components in the machinery of government. The Constitution guaranteed states equal representation in the Senate (and even made this provision unamendable, in Article V). It also made states responsible for both state and national elections—an important power. Further, the Constitution virtually guaranteed the continuation of each state; Congress is forbidden to create new states by chopping up old ones, unless a state's legislature approves (an unlikely event).

The Constitution also created obligations of the national government toward the states; it is to protect states against violence and invasion, for example. At times,

TABLE 3.2 The Constitution's Distribution of Powers

TO THE NATIONAL GOVERNMENT	TO BOTH THE NATIONAL AND STATE GOVERNMENT	TO THE STATE GOVERNMENTS
	SOME POWERS GRANTED BY THE CONSTITUTION	
Coin money Conduct foreign relations Regulate commerce with foreign nations and among states Provide an army and a navy Declare war Establish courts inferior to the Supreme Court Establish post offices Make laws necessary and proper to carry out the foregoing powers	Tax Borrow money Establish courts Make and enforce laws Charter banks and corporations Spend money for the general welfare Take private property for public purposes, with just compensation	Establish local governments Regulate commerce within a state Conduct elections Ratify amendments to the federal Constitution Take measures for public health, safety, and morals Exert powers the Constitution does not delegate to the national government or prohibit the states from using
	SOME POWERS DENIED BY THE CONSTITUTION	
Tax articles exported from one state to another Violate the Bill of Rights Change state boundaries	Grant titles of nobility Permit slavery (Thirteenth Amendment) Deny citizens the right to vote because of race, color, or previous servitude (Fifteenth Amendment) Deny citizens the right to vote because of gender (Nineteenth Amendment)	Tax imports or exports Coin money Enter into treaties Impair obligations of contracts Abridge the privileges or immunities of citizens or deny due process and equal protection of the law (Fourteenth Amendment)

however, the states find the national government deficient in meeting its obligations, as we will discuss later in this chapter.

As Table 3.2 shows, the states and the national government have overlapping responsibilities for important matters, such as maintaining law and order, protecting citizens' health and safety, and regulating financial institutions. In Article VI of the Constitution, the Framers dealt with what remains a touchy question: In a dispute between the states and the national government, which prevails? The answer that the delegates provided, often referred to as the **supremacy clause**, is reasonably clear. They stated that the following three items were the supreme law of the land:

supremacy clause
The clause in Article VI of the Constitution that makes the Constitution, national laws, and treaties supreme over state laws as long as the national government is acting within its constitutional limits.

1. The Constitution
2. Laws of the national government (when consistent with the Constitution)
3. Treaties (which can be made only by the national government)

Judges in every state were specifically directed to obey the Constitution, even if their state constitutions or state laws directly contradicted it. Today, all state executives, legislators, and judges are bound by oath to support the Constitution.

The national government, however, can operate only within its appropriate sphere. It cannot usurp the states' powers. But what are the boundaries of the national government's powers? According to some commentators, the **Tenth Amendment** provides part of the answer. It states that the "powers not delegated to the United States by the Constitution, nor prohibited by it to the states, are reserved to the states respectively, or to the people." To those advocating states' rights, the amendment clearly means that the national government has only those powers that the Constitution specifically assigned to it. The states or people have supreme power over any activity not mentioned there. Despite this interpretation, in 1941, the Supreme Court (in *United States v. Darby*) called the Tenth Amendment a constitutional truism, a mere assertion that the states have independent powers of their own—not a declaration that state powers are superior to those of the national government.

Tenth Amendment
The constitutional amendment stating, "The powers not delegated to the United States by the Constitution, nor prohibited by it to the states, are reserved to the states respectively, or to the people."

The Court seemed to backtrack on this ruling in favor of national government supremacy in a 1976 case, *National League of Cities v. Usery,* in which it held that extending national minimum-wage and maximum-hours standards to employees of state and local governments was an unconstitutional intrusion of the national government into the domain of the states. In 1985, however, in *Garcia v. San Antonio Metro*, the Court overturned the *National League of Cities* decision. The Court held, in essence, that it was up to Congress, not the courts, to decide which actions of the states should be regulated by the national government. Once again, the Court ruled that the Tenth Amendment did not give states power superior to that of the national government for activities not mentioned in the Constitution.

Protecting Rights

State constitutions guarantee many basic rights. However, few Americans would feel comfortable with only state protections for their liberties. The Bill of Rights in the U.S. Constitution is the ultimate legal defense of freedom.

Occasionally, issues arise in which states challenge the authority of the national government. Several states have challenged federal education regulations resulting from the 2002 No Child Left Behind Act. Some states began a challenge of the requirement that every American purchase health insurance even before the 2010 health care reform bill passed Congress. In such cases, the federal government usually wins.

Federal courts can order states to obey the Constitution or federal laws and treaties. However, in deference to the states, the *Eleventh Amendment* prohibits individual damage suits against state officials (such as a suit against a police officer for violating one's rights) and protects state governments from being sued against their consent by private parties in federal or state[3] courts or before federal administrative agencies.[4] In 2001, the Court voided the application of the Americans with Disabilities Act to the states, finding it a violation of the Eleventh Amendment (*Board of Trustees of University of Alabama, et al. v. Garrett, et al.*). Cases arising under the Fourteenth Amendment (usually cases regarding racial discrimination) are an exception.[5] The federal government may also bring suits against states in federal courts, as may individuals seeking to prohibit future illegal actions of state officials.

The Supreme Court has also made it easier for citizens to control the behavior of local officials. The Court ruled that a federal law passed in 1871 to protect newly freed slaves permits individuals to sue local governments for damages or seek injunctions against any local official acting in an official capacity who they believe has deprived them of any right secured by the Constitution or by federal law.[6] Such suits are now common in the federal courts.

Establishing National Supremacy

Over the years, the federal government has gained power relative to the states. Four key events have largely settled the issue of how national and state powers are related: (1) the elaboration of the doctrine of implied powers, (2) the definition of the commerce clause, (3) the Civil War, and (4) the long struggle for racial equality.

Implied Powers As early as 1819, the issue of state versus national power came before the Supreme Court in the case of ***McCulloch v. Maryland***. The new American government had moved quickly on many economic policies. In 1791, it created a national bank, a government agency empowered to print money, make loans, and engage in many other banking tasks. A darling of Alexander Hamilton and his allies, the bank had numerous opponents—including Thomas Jefferson, farmers, and state legislatures—who were against strengthening the national government's control of the economy and who saw the bank as an instrument of the elite. Congress allowed the First Bank of the United States to expire; however, during James Madison's presidency it created the Second Bank, fueling a great national debate.

McCulloch v. Maryland
An 1819 Supreme Court decision that established the supremacy of the national government over state governments. The Court, led by Chief Justice John Marshall, held that Congress had certain implied powers in addition to the powers enumerated in the Constitution.

Railing against the "Monster Bank," the state of Maryland passed a law in 1818 taxing the national bank's Baltimore branch $15,000 a year. The Baltimore branch refused to pay, whereupon the state of Maryland sued the cashier, James McCulloch, for payment. When the state courts upheld Maryland's law and its tax, the bank appealed to the U.S. Supreme Court. John Marshall was chief justice, and two of the country's most capable lawyers argued the case before the Court. Daniel Webster, widely regarded as one of the greatest senators in U.S. history, argued for the national bank, and Luther Martin, a delegate to the Constitutional Convention, argued for Maryland.

Martin maintained that the Constitution was very clear about the powers of Congress (outlined in its Article I). The power to create a national bank was not among them. Thus, Martin concluded, Congress had exceeded its powers, and Maryland had a right to tax the bank. On behalf of the bank, Webster argued for a broader interpretation of the powers of the national government. The Constitution was not meant to stifle congressional powers, he said, but rather to permit Congress to use all means "necessary and proper" to fulfill its responsibilities.

enumerated powers
Powers of the federal government that are specifically addressed in the Constitution; for Congress, including the powers listed in Article I, Section 8, for example, to coin money and regulate its value and impose taxes.

In their decision, Marshall and his colleagues set forth two great constitutional principles. The first was the *supremacy of the national government over the states*. Marshall wrote, "the government of the United States, though limited in its power, is supreme within its sphere of action." As long as the national government behaved in accordance with the Constitution, its policies took precedence over state policies, as the supremacy clause said. Because of this principle, federal laws or regulations, such as many civil rights acts and rules regulating hazardous substances, water quality, and clean-air standards, *preempt* state or local laws or regulations and thus preclude their enforcement.

implied powers
Powers of the federal government that go beyond those enumerated in the Constitution, in accordance with the statement in the Constitution that Congress has the power to "make all laws necessary and proper for carrying into execution" the powers enumerated in Article I.

The other key principle of *McCulloch* was that *the national government has certain implied powers that go beyond its enumerated powers*. The Court held that Congress was behaving consistently with the Constitution when it created the national bank. Congress had certain **enumerated powers**, powers *specifically* listed in Article I, Section 8, of the Constitution. These included coining money and regulating its value, imposing taxes, and so forth. The Constitution did not enumerate creating a bank, but Article I, Section 8, concluded by stating that Congress has the power to "make all laws necessary and proper for carrying into execution the foregoing powers." That, said Marshall, gave Congress certain **implied powers**. It could make economic policy consistent with the Constitution, including by establishing a national bank.

elastic clause
The final paragraph of Article I, Section 8, of the Constitution, which authorizes Congress to pass all laws "necessary and proper" to carry out the enumerated powers.

Commentators often refer to the "necessary and proper" clause of the Constitution as the **elastic clause**. Hundreds of congressional policies, especially in the economic domain, involve powers not specifically mentioned in the Constitution. Federal policies to regulate food and drugs, build interstate highways, protect consumers, clean up dirty air and water, and do many other things are all justified as implied powers of Congress.

Commerce Power The Constitution gives Congress the power to regulate interstate and international commerce. American courts have spent many years trying to define commerce. In 1824, the Supreme Court, in deciding the case of ***Gibbons v. Ogden***, defined commerce very broadly to encompass virtually every form of commercial activity. Today, commerce covers not only the movement of goods, but also radio signals, electricity, telephone messages, the Internet, insurance transactions, and much more.

Gibbons v. Ogden
A landmark case decided in 1824 in which the Supreme Court interpreted very broadly the clause in Article I, Section 8, of the Constitution giving Congress the power to regulate interstate commerce, as encompassing virtually every form of commercial activity.

The Supreme Court's decisions establishing the national government's implied powers (*McCulloch v. Maryland*) and a broad definition of interstate commerce (*Gibbons v. Ogden*) established the power of Congress to promote economic development through subsidies and services for business interests. In the latter part of the nineteenth century, however, Congress sought to use its interstate commerce power to *regulate* the economy, for example, by requiring safer working conditions for laborers or protecting children from working long hours. The Court then ruled that the interstate commerce power did not give Congress the right to regulate local commercial activities.

The Great Depression placed new demands on the national government, and beginning in 1933, the New Deal of President Franklin D. Roosevelt produced an avalanche of regulatory and social welfare legislation. Although initially the Supreme Court voided much of this legislation, after 1937 the Court began to loosen restrictions on the national government's regulation of commerce. In 1964, when Congress prohibited racial discrimination in places of public accommodation such as restaurants, hotels, and movie theaters, it did so on the basis of its power to regulate interstate commerce. Thus, regulating commerce is one of the national government's most important sources of power.

In recent years, the Supreme Court has scrutinized the use of the commerce power with a skeptical eye, however. In 1995, the Court held in *United States v. Lopez* that the federal Gun-Free School Zones Act of 1990, which forbade the possession of firearms in public schools, exceeded Congress's constitutional authority to regulate commerce. Guns in a school zone, the majority said, have nothing to do with commerce. Similarly, in 2000, the Court ruled in *United States v. Morrison* that the power to regulate interstate commerce did not provide Congress with the authority to enact the 1994 Violence Against Women Act, which provided a federal civil remedy for the victims of gender-motivated violence. Gender-motivated crimes of violence are not, the Court said, in any sense economic activity.

Several other recent cases have had important implications for federalism. In *Printz v. United States* (1997) and *Mack v. United States* (1997), the Supreme Court voided the congressional mandate in the Brady Handgun Violence Prevention Act that the chief law enforcement officer in each local community conduct background checks on prospective gun purchasers. According to the Court, "The federal government may neither issue directives requiring the states to address particular problems, nor commend the states' officers, or those of their political subdivision, to administer or enforce a federal regulatory program."

The Civil War What *McCulloch* pronounced constitutionally, the Civil War (1861–1865) settled militarily. We typically think of the Civil War as mainly a struggle over slavery, but it was also a struggle between states and the national government. In fact, Abraham Lincoln announced in his 1861 inaugural address that he would support a constitutional amendment guaranteeing slavery if it would save the Union. Instead, it took a bloody civil war for the national government to assert its power over the Southern states' claim of sovereignty.

The Struggle for Racial Equality A century later, conflict between the states and the national government again erupted over states' rights and national power. In 1954, in *Brown v. Board of Education,* the Supreme Court held that school segregation was unconstitutional. Southern politicians responded with what they called "massive resistance" to the decision. When a federal judge ordered the admission of two African-American students to the University of Alabama in 1963, Governor George Wallace literally blocked the school entrance to prevent federal marshals and the students from entering the admissions office. Despite Wallace's efforts, the students were admitted, and throughout the 1960s the federal government enacted laws and policies to end segregation in schools, housing, public accommodations, voting, and jobs. The conflict between states and the national government over equality issues was decided in favor of the national government. National standards of racial equality prevailed.

The establishment of the doctrine of the federal government's implied powers, the evolution of the commerce power, the Civil War, and the struggle for racial equality have made the national government supreme within its sphere. Nevertheless, the sphere for the states remains a large and important one.

In 1963, Alabama Governor George Wallace made a dramatic stand at the University of Alabama to resist integration of the all-white school. Federal marshals won this confrontation, and since then the federal government in general has been able to impose national standards of equal opportunity on the states.

States' Obligations to Each Other

Federalism involves more than relationships between the national government and state and local governments. The states must deal with each other as well, and the Constitution outlines certain obligations that each state has to every other state.

Full Faith and Credit Suppose that, like millions of other Americans, a person divorces and then remarries. This person purchases a marriage license, which registers the marriage with a state. On the honeymoon, the person travels across the country. Is this person married in each state he or she passes through, even though the marriage license is with only one state? Can the person be arrested for bigamy because the divorce occurred in only one state?

The answer, of course, is that a marriage license and a divorce, like a driver's license and a birth certificate, are valid in all states. Article IV of the Constitution requires that states give **full faith and credit** to the public acts, records, and civil judicial proceedings of every other state. This reciprocity is essential to the functioning of society and the economy. Without the full faith and credit clause, people could avoid their obligations, say, to make payments on automobile loans simply by crossing a state boundary. In addition, because courts can enforce contracts between business firms across state boundaries, firms incorporated in one state can do business in another.

full faith and credit
A clause in Article IV of the Constitution requiring each state to recognize the public acts, records, and judicial proceedings of all other states.

Usually, the full faith and credit provision in the Constitution poses little controversy. An exception occurred in 1996, when courts in Hawaii recognized same-sex marriages. What would happen in other states that did not recognize Hawaiian marriages between same-sex partners? Congress answered with the Defense of Marriage Act, which permits states to disregard gay marriages, even if they are legal elsewhere in the United States. Hawaii has since overturned recognition of gay marriage. However, as we discuss in Chapter 5, several states have legalized same-sex marriages, while others recognize same-sex "civil unions" or provide domestic partnership benefits to same-sex couples. It remains to be seen whether courts will uphold Congress's power to make exceptions to the full faith and credit clause, but opponents of gay marriage, concerned they might not, have focused on amending the Constitution to allow states not to recognize same-sex marriages.

Extradition What about criminal penalties? Almost all criminal law is state law. If someone robs a store, steals a car, or commits a murder, the chances are that this person is breaking a state, not a federal, law. The Constitution says that states are

Because of the full faith and credit clause of the Constitution, marriage certificates issued by one state are valid in every state. People are also entitled to most of the benefits—and subject to most of the obligations—of citizenship in any state they visit, thanks to the privileges and immunities clause. Gay marriage is straining these principles, however, as most states refuse to recognize marriages between same-sex partners.

required to return a person charged with a crime in another state to that state for trial or imprisonment, a practice called **extradition**. Although there is no way to force states to comply, they usually are happy to do so, not wishing to harbor criminals and hoping that other states will reciprocate. Thus, a lawbreaker cannot avoid punishment by simply escaping to another state.

Privileges and Immunities The most complicated obligation among the states is the requirement that citizens of each state receive all the **privileges and immunities** of any other state in which they happen to be. The goal of this constitutional provision is to prohibit states from discriminating against citizens of other states. If, for example, a Texan visits California, the Texan will pay the same sales tax and receive the same police protection as residents of California.

There are many exceptions to the privileges and immunities clause, however. Many of you attend public universities. If you reside in the state that your university is located in, you generally pay a tuition substantially lower than that paid by your fellow students from out of state. Similarly, only residents of a state can vote in state elections. States often attempt to pass some of the burdens of financing the state government to those outside the state, for example, through taxes on minerals mined in the state but consumed elsewhere or special taxes on hotel rooms rented by tourists.

The Supreme Court has never clarified just which privileges a state must make available to all Americans and which privileges can be limited to its own citizens. In general, the more fundamental the right—such as owning property or receiving police protection—the less likely it is that a state can discriminate against citizens of another state. In 1999, the Supreme Court held in *Saenz v. Roe* that California could not require a new resident to wait a year before becoming eligible for welfare benefits that exceeded those available in the state from which the new resident came.

extradition
A legal process whereby a state surrenders a person charged with a crime to the state in which the crime is alleged to have been committed.

privileges and immunities
The provision of the Constitution according citizens of each state the privileges of citizens of other states.

3.3 Characterize the shift from dual to cooperative federalism and the role of fiscal federalism in intergovernmental relations today.

Intergovernmental Relations Today

The past two centuries have seen dramatic changes in American federalism. These changes are most apparent in two areas. First, there has been a gradual shift in the nature of power sharing between two levels of government.[7] The second major change has been the rise of fiscal federalism, the elaborate assortment of federal grants-in-aid to the states and localities.

From Dual to Cooperative Federalism

dual federalism
A system of government in which both the states and the national government remain supreme within their own spheres, each responsible for some policies.

One way to understand the changes in American federalism over the past 200 years is to contrast two types of federalism. The first type is **dual federalism**, in which both the national government and the states remain supreme within their own spheres. The states are responsible for some policies, the national government for others. For example, the national government has exclusive control over foreign and military policy, the postal system, and monetary policy. States are exclusively responsible for schools, law enforcement, and road building. In dual federalism, the powers and policy assignments of the two layers of government are distinct, as in a layer cake, and proponents of dual federalism believe that the powers of the national government should be interpreted narrowly.

Most politicians and political scientists today argue that dual federalism is outdated. They are more likely to describe the current American federal system as one of **cooperative federalism**, where states and the national government share powers and policy assignments.[8] Instead of a layer cake, they see American federalism as more like a marble cake, with mingled responsibilities and blurred distinctions between the levels of government. After the terrorist attacks on September 11, 2001, the national government asked state and local governments to investigate suspected terrorists, and both national and state public health officials dealt with the threat caused by anthrax in the mail in Florida, New York, and Washington, D.C.

cooperative federalism
A system of government in which powers and policy assignments are shared between states and the national government.

Initially, before the national government began to assert its dominance, the American federal system leaned toward dual federalism. However, it was never characterized by a neat separation into purely state and purely national responsibilities. A look at the area of education, which is usually thought of as being mainly a state and local responsibility, illustrates this point and also shows the movement toward cooperative federalism.

Even under the Articles of Confederation, Congress set aside land in the Northwest Territory to be used for schools. During the Civil War, the national government adopted a policy to create land grant colleges. Important American universities such as Wisconsin, Texas A&M, Illinois, Ohio State, North Carolina State, and Iowa State owe their origins to this national policy. (To learn more about how federalism affects college education, see "Young People and Politics: Federal Support for Colleges and Universities.")

In the 1950s and 1960s, the national government began supporting public elementary and secondary education. In 1958, Congress passed the National Defense Education Act, largely in response to Soviet success in the space race. The act provided federal grants and loans for college students and financial support for elementary and secondary education in science and foreign languages. In 1965, Congress passed the Elementary and Secondary Education Act, which provided federal aid to numerous schools. Although these policies expanded the national government's role in education, they were not a sharp break with the past.

Cooperative federalism began during the Great Depression of the 1930s and continues into the twenty-first century. This photo shows the Big Dig in Boston, the largest and most complex highway and tunnel project in the nation's history. The federal government provided about half of the funds for this extraordinarily expensive public work.

Today, the federal government's presence is felt in every schoolhouse. Almost all school districts receive some federal assistance. To do so, they must comply with federal rules and regulations; for example, they must maintain desegregated and nondiscriminatory programs. The No Child Left Behind Act established standards of performance along with sanctions, including loss of federal aid, for failing to meet the standards. In addition, as we will see in Chapters 4 and 5, federal courts have ordered local schools to implement elaborate desegregation plans and have placed constraints on school prayers.

Highways are another example of the movement toward cooperative federalism. In an earlier era, states and cities were largely responsible for building roads, although the

Constitution does authorize Congress to construct "post roads." In 1956, Congress passed an act creating an interstate highway system. Hundreds of red, white, and blue signs were planted at the beginnings of interstate construction projects. The signs announced that the interstate highway program was a joint federal–state project and specified the cost and sharing of funds. In this and many other areas, the federal system has promoted a partnership between the national and state governments.

Cooperative federalism today rests on several standard operating procedures in programs and their administration. For hundreds of programs, cooperative federalism involves the following:

- *Shared costs.* Cities and states can receive federal money for airport construction, sewage treatment plants, youth programs, and many other programs, but only if they pay part of the bill.
- *Federal guidelines.* Most federal grants to states and cities come with strings attached. Congress spends billions of dollars to support state highway construction, for example; however, as we have seen, to get their share, states must adopt and enforce limits on the legal drinking age.
- *Shared administration.* State and local officials implement federal policies, but they have administrative powers of their own. The U.S. Department of Labor, for example, gives billions of dollars to states for job training, but states have considerable latitude in spending the money.

The cooperation between the national government and state governments is such an established feature of American federalism that it persists even when the two levels of government are in conflict on certain matters. For example, in the 1950s and 1960s, Southern states cooperated well with Washington in building the interstate highway system while they clashed with the national government over racial integration.

Federal Support for Colleges and Universities

Because most colleges and universities are public institutions created by state and local governments, federalism has direct consequences for the students who attend them. State and local governments provide most of the funding for public colleges and universities, but almost everyone agrees that this funding is inadequate. In response to this problem, the national government has stepped in to support postsecondary education programs.

One could argue that the federal government makes it possible for many students to attend college at all because it is the primary source of financial aid. The federal government provides nearly $100 billion in financial assistance (including grants, loans, and work-study assistance) to about 23 million postsecondary students each year. Nearly two-thirds of all full-time undergraduates receive some form of financial aid from the federal government.

The federal government also provides several billion dollars of direct grants to colleges and universities across the nation. Billions more in federal funds support research and training in certain areas, especially science and engineering—which receive about $30 billion a year. The library, laboratories, and the buildings in most colleges and universities have received funds from the federal government.

Each year the federal government provides about 13 percent of the revenue for both public and private, not-for-profit colleges and universities. Few colleges and universities could withstand a 13 or 14 percent budget cut and the loss of most of the financial assistance for its students. Federalism, then, matters quite a lot to college students.

QUESTIONS FOR DISCUSSION

- Why do state institutions of higher education require aid from the federal government? Why don't the states provide adequate funds to run their own colleges and universities?
- Federal aid comes with strings attached. Would it be better to rely completely on state support?

Source: U.S. Department of Education, National Center for Education Statistics, *Digest of Education Statistics*, 2010, Tables 350, 351, 353, 380; U.S. Department of Commerce, *Statistical Abstract of the United States, 2010* (Washington, DC: U.S. Government Printing Office, 2010), Table 280.

Devolution?

For most of the twentieth century, Democrats supported increasing the power of the federal government in order to advance national policies ranging from child labor laws and education to Social Security and health care. Republicans, on the other hand, generally opposed these policies and favored states taking responsibility for these issues. They often articulated their opposition to increased federal power in terms of a defense of state authority in a federal system.

In his first inaugural address, Ronald Reagan articulated a traditional conservative view when he argued that the states had primary responsibility for governing in most policy areas, and he promised to "restore the balance between levels of government." Few officials at either the state or the national level agreed with Reagan about reducing the national government's role in domestic programs. Nevertheless, Reagan's opposition to the national government's spending on domestic policies and the huge federal deficits of the 1980s forced a reduction in federal funds for state and local governments and shifted some responsibility for policy back to the states.

When the Republicans captured Congress in the 1994 elections, the first time they had majorities in both houses in 40 years, they spoke of a "revolution" in public policy, one aimed primarily at restricting the scope of the national government and returning responsibility for policies to the states. **Devolution**, transferring responsibility for policies from the federal government to state and local governments, was at the center of their rhetoric. They followed this rhetoric with action as they repealed federal speed limits, allowed states more latitude in dealing with welfare policy, and made it more difficult for state prisoners to seek relief in federal courts.

devolution
Transferring responsibility for policies from the federal government to state and local governments.

Since the mid-1990s, however, Republicans have been less concerned with abstract principles and more with adopting a pragmatic approach to federalism to accomplish their goals. They found turning to the federal government—and *restricting* state power—the most effective way to achieve a wide range of policy objectives, including loosening economic and environmental regulations, controlling immigration, setting health insurance standards, restricting the expansion of government health care coverage, stiffening penalties for criminals, extending federal criminal penalties, and tracking child-support violators. During the presidency of George W. Bush, Republicans passed a law removing most class-action lawsuits from state courts. Most significantly, they passed the No Child Left Behind Act, the largest expansion of the federal role in education since Lyndon Johnson's Great Society and a policy that has allowed more federal intrusion into a state domain than almost any other in U.S. history. Many states have complained loudly about the problems and the cost of implementing the legislation.

Today, most Americans embrace a pragmatic view of governmental responsibilities, seeing the national government as more capable of—and thus responsible for—handling some issues (such as managing the economy, ensuring access to health care and the safety of food and drugs, preserving the environment, and providing income security for the elderly), and state and local governments as better at handling others (such as crime, welfare, and education).[9] Nevertheless, both levels of government are, of necessity, involved in most policy areas.

Fiscal Federalism

The cornerstone of the national government's relations with state and local governments is **fiscal federalism**—the pattern of spending, taxing, and providing grants in the federal system. States can influence the national government through local elections for national officials, but the national government has a powerful source of influence over the states—money. *Grants-in-aid*, federal funds appropriated by Congress for distribution to state and local governments, are the main instrument that the national government uses for both aiding and influencing states and localities.

fiscal federalism
The pattern of spending, taxing, and providing grants in the federal system; it is the cornerstone of the national government's relations with state and local governments.

Federal aid (including loan subsidies) amounted to about $646 billion in 2011. Figure 3.1 illustrates the growth in the amount of money spent on federal grants. Federal aid, covering a wide range of policy areas (see "A Generation of

FIGURE 3.1 Fiscal Federalism: Federal Grants to State and Local Governments

Federal grants to state and local governments have grown rapidly in recent decades and now amount to more than $600 billion per year. The sharp increase in grants for 2010 and 2011 was the result of the stimulus package designed to counter the country's financial crisis.

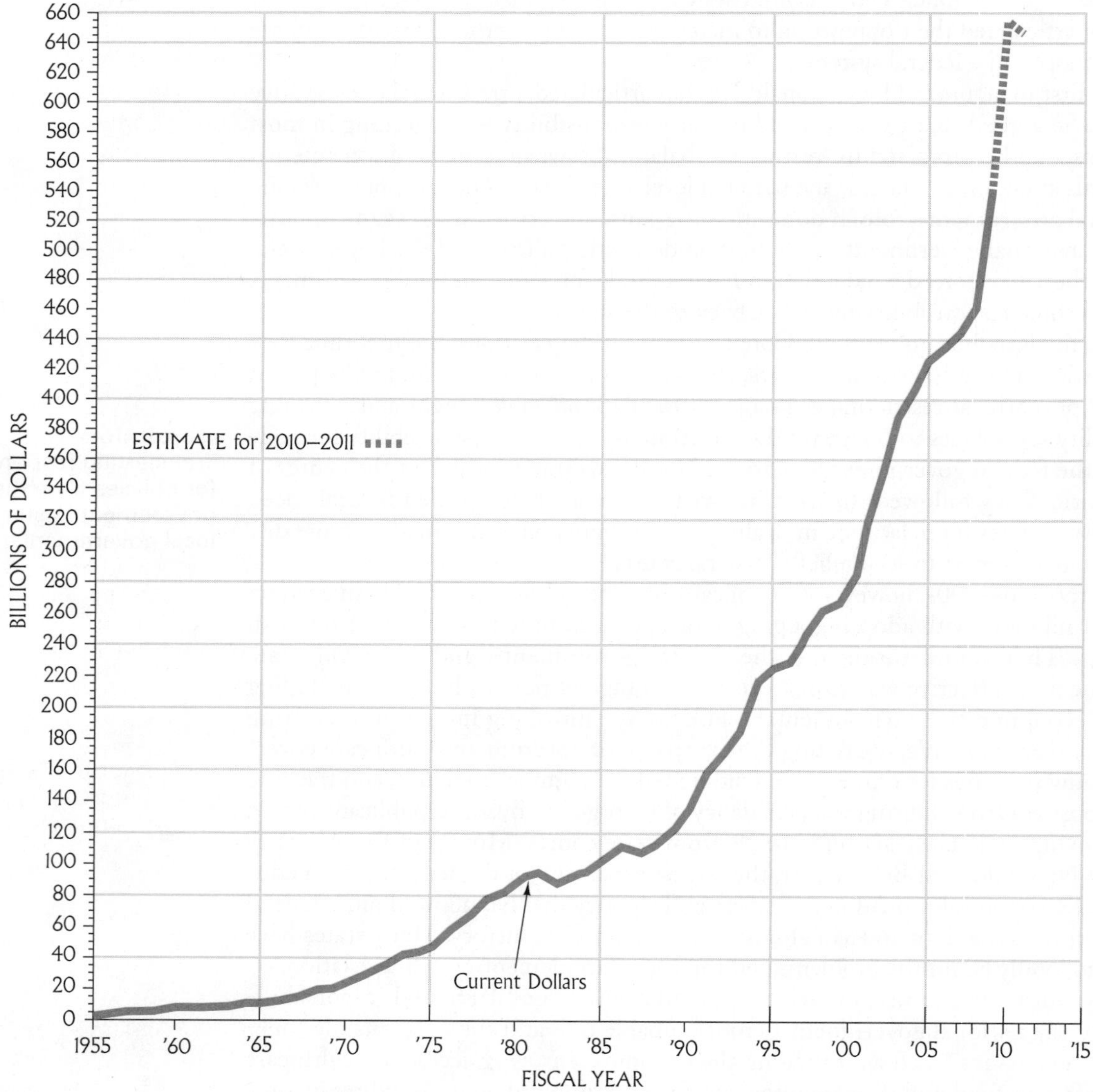

Source: Office of Management and Budget, *Budget of the United States Government, Fiscal Year 2011: Historical Tables* (Washington, DC: U.S. Government Printing Office, 2010), Table 12.1.

Change: Functions of Federal Grants"), accounts for about 22 percent of all the funds spent by state and local governments and for about 18 percent of all federal government expenditures.[10]

categorical grants
Federal grants that can be used only for specific purposes, or "categories," of state and local spending. They come with strings attached, such as nondiscrimination provisions. Compare **block grants**.

The Grant System: Distributing the Federal Pie The national government regularly publishes the *Catalogue of Federal Domestic Assistance,* a massive volume listing the federal aid programs available to states, cities, and other local governments. The book lists federal programs that support energy assistance for the elderly poor, housing allowances for the poor, drug abuse services, urban rat control efforts, community arts programs, state disaster preparedness programs, and many more.

There are two major types of federal aid for states and localities: *categorical grants* and *block grants*. **Categorical grants** are the main source of federal aid to state and local governments. These grants can be used only for specific purposes, or categories, of state and local spending.

Because direct orders from the federal government to the states are rare (an exception is the Equal Opportunity Act of 1982, which bars job discrimination by state and local governments), most federal regulation is accomplished in a more indirect manner: Congress attaches conditions to the grants that states receive. Such restrictions on grants have become especially common since the 1970s.

One string commonly attached to categorical and other federal grants is a nondiscrimination provision, stating that aid may not be used for purposes that discriminate against minorities, women, or other groups. Another string, a favorite of labor unions, is that federal funds may not support construction projects that pay below the local union wage. Other restrictions may require an environmental impact statement for a federally supported construction project or provisions for community involvement in the planning of the project.

The federal government may also employ *crossover sanctions*—using federal dollars in one program to influence state and local policy in another, such as when funds are withheld for highway construction unless states raise the drinking age to 21 or establish highway beautification programs.

Crosscutting requirements occur when a condition on one federal grant is extended to all activities supported by federal funds, regardless of their source. The grandfather of these requirements is Title VI of the 1964 Civil Rights Act (see Chapter 5), which bars discrimination in the use of federal funds because of race, color, national origin, gender, or physical disability. For example, if a university discriminates illegally in one program—such as athletics—it may lose the federal aid it receives for all its programs. There are also crosscutting requirements dealing with environmental protection, historic preservation, contract wage rates, access to government information, the care of experimental animals, the treatment of human subjects in research projects, and a host of other policies.

There are two types of categorical grants. **Project grants**, the more common type, are awarded on the basis of competitive applications. National Science Foundation grants obtained by university professors are an example of project grants. In contrast, **formula grants**, as their name implies, are distributed according to a formula. These formulas vary from grant to grant and may be computed on the basis of population, per capita income, percentage of rural population, or some other factor. A state or local government does not apply for a formula grant; a grant's formula determines how much money the particular government will receive. As a result, Congress is the site of vigorous political battles over the formulas themselves. The most common formula grants are those for Medicaid, child nutrition programs, sewage treatment plant construction, public housing, community development programs, and training and employment programs.

Complaints about the cumbersome paperwork and the many strings attached to categorical grants led to the adoption of the second major type of federal aid, **block grants**. These grants are given more or less automatically to states or communities, which then have discretion within broad areas in deciding how to spend the money. First adopted in 1966, block grants support programs in areas like community development and social services.

The Scramble for Federal Dollars With more than $600 billion in federal grants at stake, most states and many cities have

WHY IT MATTERS

Grants-in-Aid

The federal system of grants-in-aid sends revenues from federal taxes to state and local governments. This transfers the burden of paying for services from those who pay state and local taxes, such as taxes on sales and property, to those who pay national taxes, especially the federal income tax.

project grants
Federal **categorical grant** given for specific purposes and awarded on the basis of the merits of applications.

formula grants
Federal **categorical grants** distributed according to a formula specified in legislation or in administrative regulations.

block grants
Federal grants given more or less automatically to states or communities to support broad programs in areas such as community development and social services.

The federal government often uses grants-in-aid as a carrot and stick for the states. For example, aid has been withheld from some cities until police departments have been racially and sexually integrated.

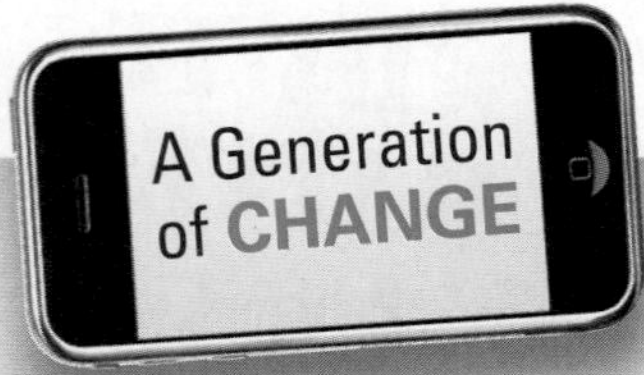

Functions of Federal Grants

Federal grants support many policies, and the distribution of grants is not static. The priorities of federal grants have changed over the past generation. The percentage of grants devoted to health care, especially Medicaid, has increased substantially, mostly at the expense of income security and education and training programs.

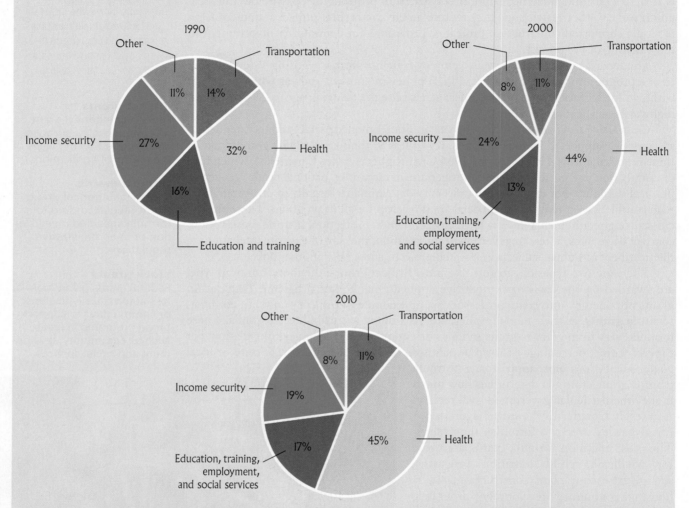

Source: Office of Management and Budget, Budget of the United States Government, *Fiscal Year 2011: Historical Tables* (Washington, DC: U.S. Government Printing Office, 2010), Table 12.2.

established full-time staffs in Washington.[11] Their task is to keep track of what money is available and to help their state or city get some of it. There are many Washington organizations of governments—the U.S. Conference of Mayors and the National League of Cities, for example—that act like other interest groups in lobbying Congress. Senators and representatives regularly go to the voters with stories of their influence in securing federal funds for their constituencies. They need continued support at the polls, they say, so that they will rise in seniority and get key posts to help "bring home the bacon."

Despite some variations, on the whole federal grant distribution follows the principle of *universalism*: something for everybody. The vigilance of senators and representatives keeps federal aid reasonably well spread among the states. This equality makes good politics, but it also may undermine public policy. Chapter I of the 1965 Elementary and Secondary Education Act is the federal government's principal endeavor to assist public schools. The primary intent of Chapter I was to give extra help to poor children. Yet the funds are allocated to 95 percent of all the school districts in the country. President Clinton's proposal to concentrate Chapter I funds on the poorest students failed when it ran into predictable opposition in Congress.

The Mandate Blues States and localities are usually pleased to receive aid from the national government, but there are times when they would just as soon not have it. For example, say Congress decides to expand a program administered by the states and funded, in part, by the national government. It passes a law requiring the states to expand the program if they want to keep receiving aid, which most states do. Requirements that direct states or local governments to provide additional services under threat of penalties or as a condition of receipt of a federal grant are a type of *mandate*.

States usually are pleased to accept federal funds, revenue they do not have to raise themselves. The states are not always happy with the strings that come attached with federal funds, however.

Would it be better if states raised their own funds rather than depending on federal aid? Are there obstacles to states raising their own revenues?

Congress usually appropriates some funds to help pay for the new policy, but whether it does or does not, the states suddenly have to budget more funds for the program just to receive federal grant money.

Medicaid, which provides health care for poor people, is a prime example of a federal grant program that puts states in a difficult situation. Administered by the states, Medicaid receives wide support from both political parties. The national government pays the majority of the bill, and the states pick up the rest. In the past two decades, Congress has moved aggressively to expand Medicaid to specific populations, requiring the states to extend coverage to certain children, pregnant women, and elderly poor. Congress has also increased its funding for the program, but new requirements have meant huge new demands on state budgets as well. In effect, Congress has set priorities for the states.

A related problem arises when Congress passes a law creating financial obligations for the states but provides no funds to meet these obligations. For example, in 1990 Congress passed the Americans with Disabilities Act, requiring states to make facilities, such as state colleges and universities, accessible to individuals with disabilities, but did not allocate funds to implement this policy. Similarly, the Clean Air Act of 1970 established national air quality standards but requires states to implement them and to appropriate funds for that purpose.

In 1995, Congress passed and President Clinton signed a law that requires the Congressional Budget Office to estimate the costs of all bills that impose such mandates. All antidiscrimination legislation and most legislation requiring state and local governments to take various actions in exchange for continued federal funding (such as grants for transportation) are exempt from this requirement. The bill also ordered federal agencies to design new processes to allow greater input by state and local officials into the development of regulations imposing mandates.

Mandates coupled with insufficient funds continue to pose problems for state and local governments. As we saw in the discussion of the Hurricane Katrina aftermath, such governments are the first responders in most emergencies: Their police forces provide most of the nation's internal security, they maintain most of the country's transportation infrastructure, and they are responsible for protecting the public's health and providing emergency health care. The heightened concern for homeland security since September 11, 2001, led Congress to impose sizable new mandates on the states to increase their ability to deal with acts of terrorism, but Congress has not provided all the resources necessary to increase state and local capabilities. Similarly, as we saw, the No Child Left Behind Act, passed in 2002, threatens school systems with the loss of federal funds if their schools do not improve student performance, but the federal government has provided only a modest increase in funding to help the school systems bring about those improvements.

Policies of the federal government may have major impacts on core policies of state and local governments, like elementary and secondary education, and determine how much is spent on these policies. Here, President George W. Bush speaks about his No Child Left Behind education policy, in Nashville, Tennessee.

Federal courts, too, create unfunded mandates for the states. In recent years, federal judges have issued states orders in areas such as prison construction and management, school desegregation, and facilities in mental health hospitals. These court orders often require states to spend funds to meet standards imposed by the judge.

A combination of federal regulations and inadequate resources may also put the states in a bind. The national government requires that a local housing authority build or acquire a new low-income housing facility for each one it demolishes. But for years Congress has provided little money for the construction of public housing. As a result, a provision intended to help the poor by ensuring a stable supply of housing actually hurts them because it discourages local governments from demolishing unsafe and inadequate housing.

The federal government may also unintentionally create financial obligations for the states. In 1994, California, New York, Texas, Florida, and other states sued the federal government for reimbursement for the cost of health care, education, prisons, and other public services that the states provide to illegal residents. The states charged that the federal government's failure to control its borders was the source of huge new demands on their treasuries and that Washington, not the states, should pay for the problem. Although the states did not win their cases, their point is a valid one.

Understanding Federalism

3.4 Assess the impact of federalism on democratic government and the scope of government.

The federal system is central to politics, government, and policy in America. The division of powers and responsibilities among different levels of government has implications for both the themes of democracy and the scope of government.

Federalism and Democracy

One of the reasons that the Founders established a federal system was to allay the fears of those who believed that a powerful and distant central government would tyrannize the states and limit their voice in government. By decentralizing the political system, federalism was designed to contribute to democracy—or at least to the limited form of democracy supported by the Founders. Has it done so?

The more levels of government, the more opportunities there are for participation in politics. State governments provide thousands of elected offices for which citizens may vote and/or run.

Additional levels of government also contribute to democracy by increasing access to government. Some citizens and interest groups are likely to have better access to state-level governments and others to the national government, so the two levels increase the opportunities for government to be responsive to demands for policies.[12] For example, in the 1950s and 1960s, when advocates of civil rights found themselves stymied in Southern states, they turned to the national level for help in achieving racial equality. Business interests, on the other hand, have traditionally found state governments to be more responsive than the national government to their demands. Organized labor is not well established in some states, but it can usually depend on some sympathetic officials at the national level who will champion its proposals.

Different economic interests are concentrated in different states: energy in Texas, citrus growing in Florida and California, and copper mining in Montana, for example. The federal system allows an interest concentrated in a state to exercise substantial influence in the election of that state's officials, both local and national. In turn, these officials promote policies advantageous to the interest in both the state capital and Washington. This is a pluralism of interests that James Madison, among others, valued within a large republic.

State and local bases have another advantage. Even if a party loses at the national level, it can rebuild in its areas of strength and develop leaders under its banner at the state and local levels. As a result, losing an election becomes more acceptable, and the peaceful transfer of power is more probable. This was especially important in the early years of the nation before our political norms had become firmly established.

Because the federal system assigns states important responsibilities for public policies, it is possible for the diversity of opinion within the country to be reflected in different public policies among the states. If the citizens of Texas wish to have a death penalty, for example, they can vote for politicians who support it, even if other states move to abolish the death penalty (see "You Are the Policymaker: Should *Whether* You Live Depend on *Where* You Live?").

States may also take initiatives on what most people view as national policies when the federal government acts contrary to the views of people within those states. Many states raised the minimum wage when Congress did not. Some states funded stem cell research after George W. Bush severely restricted it on the federal level. Similarly, many states have taken the lead in raising the standards for environmental protection after they concluded the national government was too lenient.

By handling most disputes over policy at the state and local levels, federalism also reduces decision making and conflict at the national level. If every issue had to be resolved in Washington, the national government would be overwhelmed.

Despite its advantages for democracy, relying on states to supply public services has some drawbacks. States differ in the resources they can or will devote to services like public education. Thus, the quality of education a child receives is heavily dependent on

YOU ARE THE POLICYMAKER

Should *Whether* You Live Depend on *Where* You Live?

Because the federal system allocates major responsibilities for public policy to the states, policies often vary with the views of the population in different locations. The differences among public policies are especially dramatic in the criminal justice system.

A conviction for first-degree murder in 35 states may well mean the death penalty for the convicted murderer. In 15 other states and the District of Columbia, first-degree murderers are subject to a maximum penalty of life behind bars.

What do you think? Some people see diversity in public policy as one of the advantages of federalism. Others may argue that citizens of the same country ought to be subject to uniform penalties. Should *whether* you live depend on *where* you live?

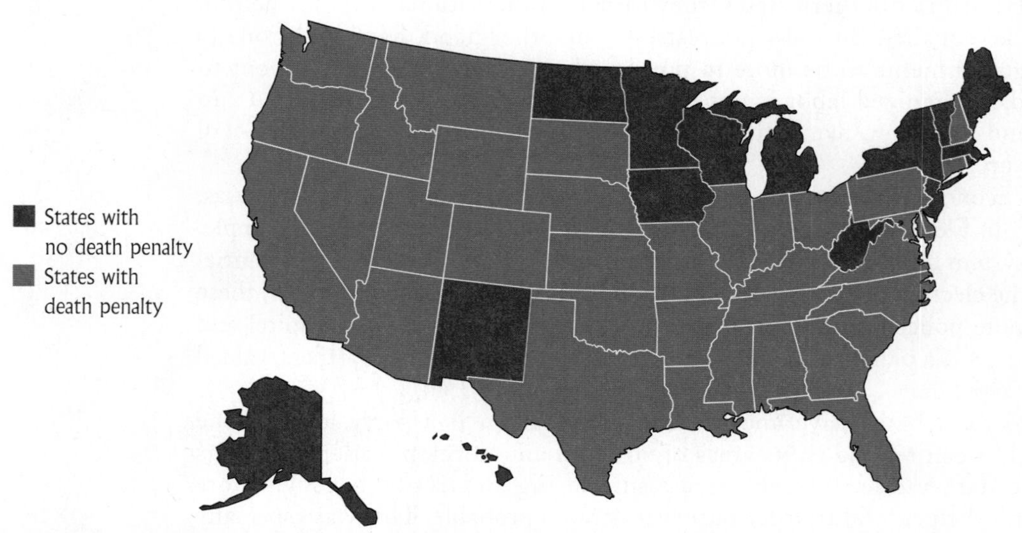

the state in which the child's parents happen to reside. In 2007, the District of Columbia and Vermont spent $18,260 and $15,940 per student, respectively, while Utah spent only $6,060 (see "My State: State and Local Spending on Public Education).

Diversity in policy can also discourage states from providing services that they might otherwise provide. Political scientists have found that generous welfare benefits can strain a state's treasury by attracting poor people from states with lower benefits. As a result, states may be deterred from providing generous benefits to those in need. A national program with uniform welfare benefits would provide no incentive for welfare recipients to move to another state in search of higher benefits.[13]

Federalism may also have a negative effect on democracy insofar as local interests are able to thwart national majority support of certain policies. As we discussed earlier in this chapter, in the 1960s, the states—especially those in the South—became battlegrounds when the national government tried to enforce national civil rights laws and court decisions. Federalism complicated and delayed efforts to end racial discrimination because state and local governments were responsible for public education and voting eligibility, for example, and because they had passed most of the laws supporting racial segregation.

Finally, the sheer number of governments in the United States is, at times, as much a burden as a boon to democracy. Program vendors at baseball games say, "You can't tell the players without a scorecard"; unfortunately, scorecards are not available for local governments, where the players are numerous and sometimes seem to be involved in different games. The U.S. Bureau of the Census counts not only people but also governments. Its latest count revealed an astonishing 89,527 American governments (see Table 3.3).

State and Local Spending on Public Education

The downside of the public policy diversity fostered by federalism is that states are largely dependent on their own resources for providing public services; these resources vary widely from state to state. This map shows the great variation among the states in the money spent on children in the public schools.

QUESTIONS FOR DISCUSSION

- How does your state rank in terms of education spending?
- Would you have been better off if there had been a national standard for spending?

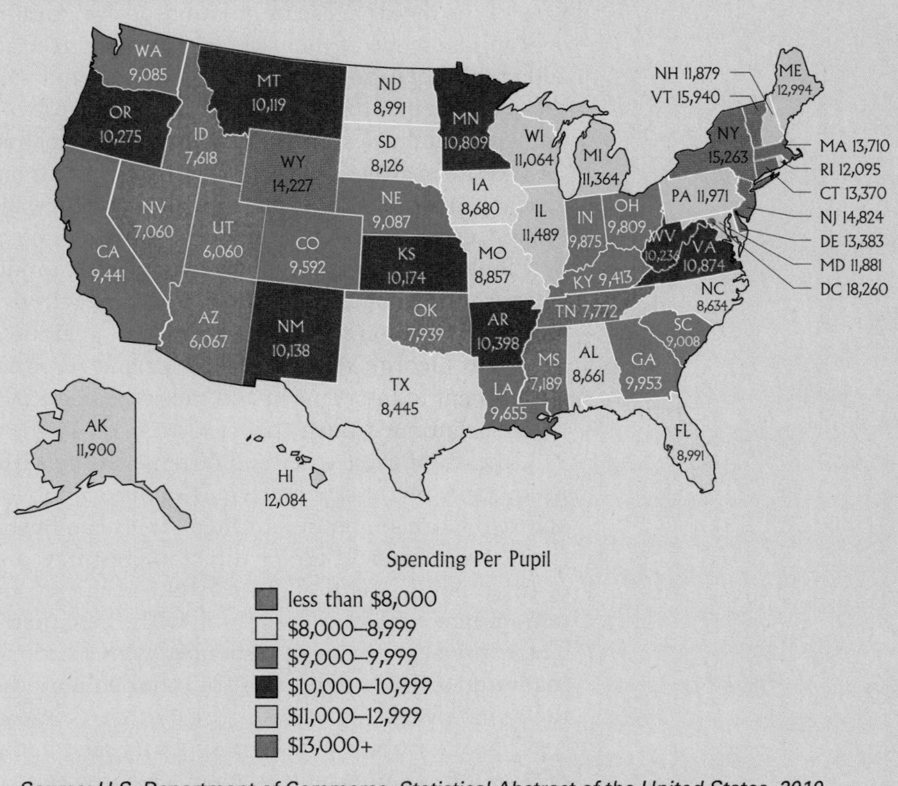

Source: U.S. Department of Commerce, Statistical Abstract of the United States, 2010 (Washington, DC: U.S. Government Printing Office, 2010), Table 253. The data are for 2007.

TABLE 3.3 The Number of Governments in America

GOVERNMENT LEVEL	NUMBER OF GOVERNMENTS
U.S. government	1
States	50
Counties	3,033
Municipalities	19,492
Townships or towns	16,519
School districts	13,051
Special districts	37,381
Total	89,527

Source: U.S. Department of Commerce, *Statistical Abstract of the United States, 2010* (Washington, DC: U.S. Government Printing Office, 2010), Table 416.

Certainly, 90,000 governments ought to be enough for any country. Are there too many? Americans speak eloquently about their state and local governments as grassroots governments, close to the people. Yet having so many governments makes it difficult to know which governments are doing what. Exercising democratic control over them is even more difficult; voter turnout in local elections is often less than 20 percent.

Federalism and the Scope of the National Government

One of the most persistent questions in American politics has been the question of the appropriate scope of the national government relative to that of state governments. To address this question, we must first understand why the national government grew and then ask whether this growth was at the expense of the states or occurred because of the unique capabilities and responsibilities of the national government.

President Ronald Reagan negotiated quotas on imports of Japanese cars in order to give advantages to the American auto industry, raising the price of all automobiles in the process. At the behest of steel companies, he placed quotas on the amount of steel that could be imported (thereby making steel products more expensive). After airplanes were grounded because of the terrorist attacks of September 11, 2001, Congress approved $15 billion in subsidies and loan guarantees to the faltering airlines. In 2008, President George W. Bush asked for and received extensive authority for the federal government to intervene in and subsidize financial institutions and automakers. Barack Obama continued Bush's policies.

In each of these cases and dozens of others, the national government has involved itself (some might say interfered) in the economic marketplace with quotas, subsidies, and regulations intended to help American businesses. As Chapter 2 explained, the national government took a direct interest in economic affairs from the very founding of the republic. As the United States changed from an agricultural to an industrial nation, new problems arose and, with them, new demands for governmental action. The national government responded with a national banking system, subsidies for railroads and airlines, and a host of other policies that dramatically increased its role in the economy.

The industrialization of the country raised other issues as well. With the formation of large corporations in the late nineteenth century—Cornelius Vanderbilt's New York Central Railroad and John D. Rockefeller's Standard Oil Company, for example—came

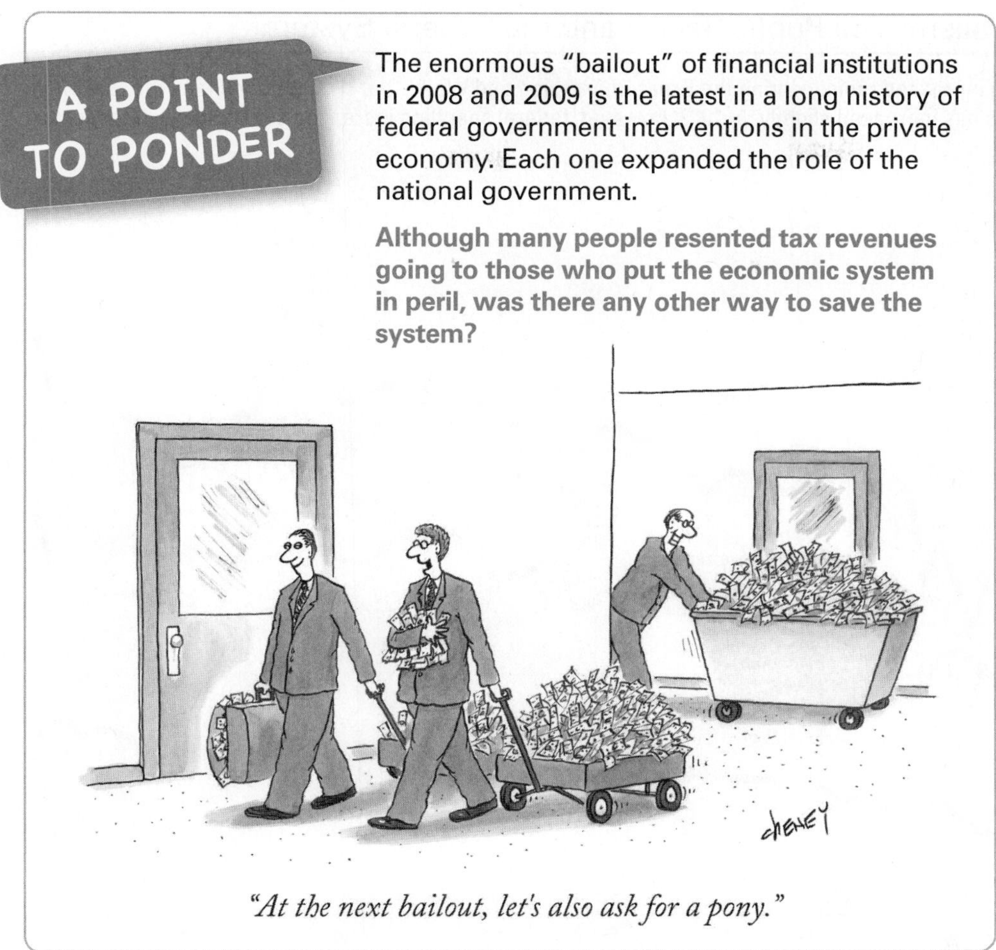
A POINT TO PONDER
The enormous "bailout" of financial institutions in 2008 and 2009 is the latest in a long history of federal government interventions in the private economy. Each one expanded the role of the national government.
Although many people resented tax revenues going to those who put the economic system in peril, was there any other way to save the system?
cheney

"At the next bailout, let's also ask for a pony."

the potential for such abuses as monopoly pricing. If there is only one railroad in town, it can charge farmers inflated prices to ship their grain to market. If a single company distributes most of the gasoline in the country, it can set the price at which gasoline sells. Thus, many interests asked the national government to restrain monopolies and to encourage open competition.

There were additional demands on the national government for new public policies. Farmers sought services such as agricultural research, rural electrification, and price supports. Unions wanted the national government to protect their rights to organize and bargain collectively and to help provide safer working conditions, a minimum wage, and pension protection. Along with other groups, labor unions supported a wide range of social welfare policies, from education to health care, that would benefit the average worker. As the country became more urbanized, new problems arose in the areas of housing, welfare, the environment, and transportation. In each case, the relevant interest turned to the national government for help.

Why not turn to the state governments instead? The answer in most cases is simple: A problem or policy requires the authority and resources of the national government; to deal with it otherwise would be at best inefficient. National defense is somewhat special, in that the Constitution forbids states from having independent defense policies. But even if it did not, how many states would want to take on a responsibility that represents more than half the federal workforce and about one-fifth of federal expenditures? A wide range of other issues would not be sensible for the states to handle. It makes little sense for Louisiana to pass strict controls on polluting the Mississippi River if most of the river's pollution occurs upstream, where Louisiana has no jurisdiction. Rhode Island has no incentive to create an energy policy because it has no natural energy reserves. Similarly, how effectively can any state

FIGURE 3.2 Fiscal Federalism: The Public Sector and the Federal System

The federal government's spending increased rapidly during the Great Depression and World War II. In recent years, the role of both federal and state governments has increased slightly. In 2009, however, federal spending increased substantially in response to the economic crisis.

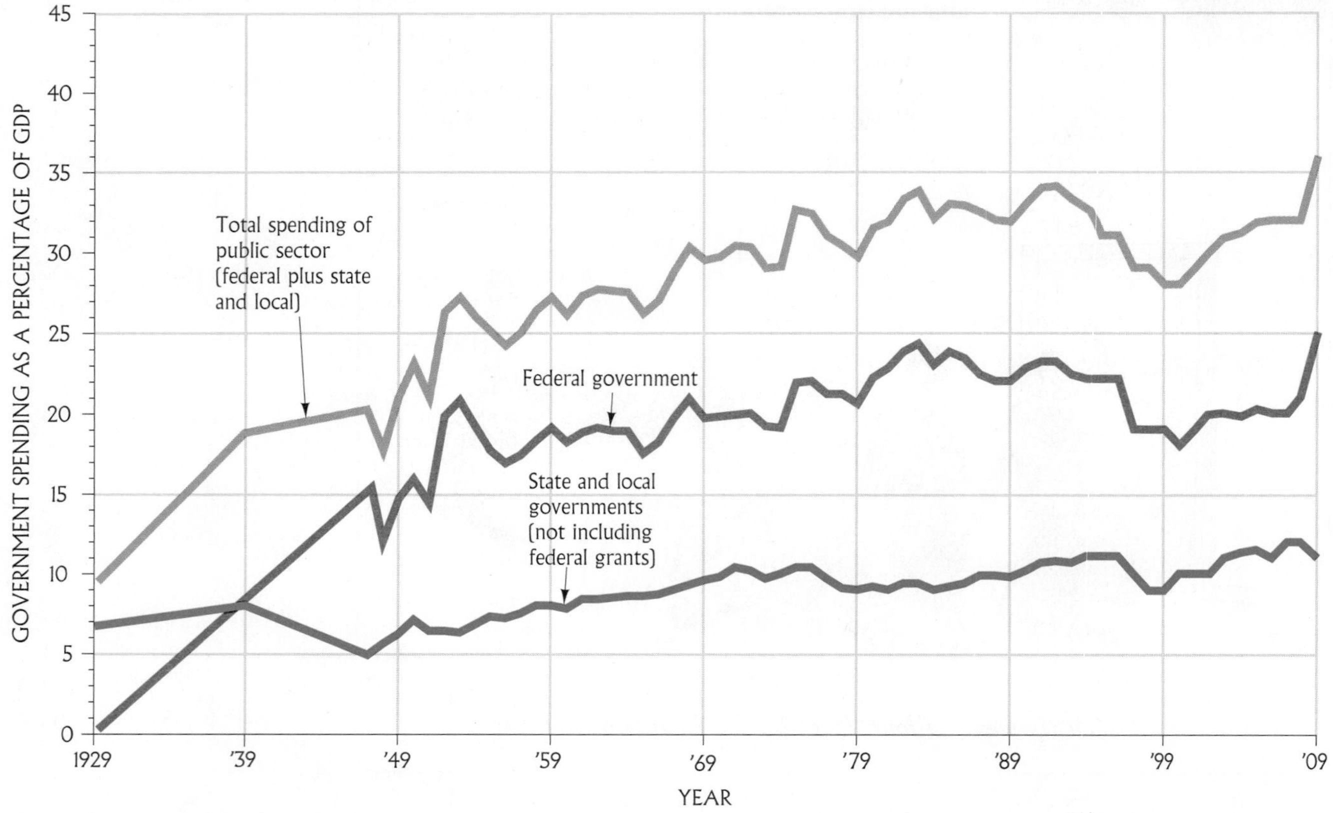

Source: Office of Management and Budget, *Budget of the United States Government, Fiscal Year 2011: Historical Tables* (Washington, DC: U.S. Government Printing Office, 2010), Table 15.3.

regulate an international conglomerate such as General Motors? How can each state, acting individually, manage the nation's money supply? Although each state could have its own space program, combining efforts in one national program is much more efficient. The largest category of federal expenditures is that for economic security, including the Social Security program. If each state had its own retirement program, would retirees who moved to Florida or Arizona be paid by their new state or the state they moved from? A national program is the only feasible method of ensuring the incomes of the mobile elderly of today's society.

Figure 3.2 shows that the national government's share of American governmental expenditures has grown rapidly since 1929. The most rapid period of growth was the 1930s and 1940s, a period that included the Great Depression and World War II. Before that time, the national government spent an amount equal to only 2.5 percent of the size of the economy, the gross domestic product (GDP); today, it spends more than a fifth of our GDP of our GDP (this includes grants to states and localities). The proportion of our GDP spent by state and local governments has grown less rapidly than the national government's share. States and localities spent 7.4 percent of our GDP in 1929; they spend about 12 percent today (not including federal grants).[14]

Figure 3.2 demonstrates that the states have not been supplanted by the national government; indeed, they carry out virtually all the functions they always have. Instead, with the support of the American people, the national government has taken on new responsibilities. In addition, the national government has added programs to help the states meet their own responsibilities.

Summary

3.1 Define federalism and explain its consequences for American politics and policy.

Federalism is a way of organizing a nation so that two or more levels of government have formal authority over the same area and people. It decentralizes both politics and policy in the United States.

3.2 Outline what the Constitution says about division of power between national and state governments and states' obligations to each other, and trace the increasing importance of the national government.

The Constitution divides power between the national (federal) government and state governments and makes the national government supreme within its sphere. The national government has implied as well as enumerated powers, as *McCulloch v. Maryland* made clear. The Civil War also helped establish the preeminence of the national government, and over the years the Supreme Court has interpreted these powers—particularly Congress's interstate commerce power—broadly, as Washington has taken on more responsibilities to deal matters such as the economy and civil rights. States have obligations to give full faith and credit to the public acts, records, and civil judicial proceedings of other states, return a person charged with a crime in another state to that state, and accord citizens of other states the privileges and immunities enjoyed by their own citizens.

3.3 Characterize the shift from dual to cooperative federalism and the role of fiscal federalism in intergovernmental relations today.

States no longer have exclusive responsibility for those government functions that are within its sphere but instead share these responsibilities with the federal government. Through categorical and block grants, the federal government provides state and local governments with substantial portions of their budgets, and it uses this leverage to influence policy by attaching conditions to receiving the grants. Sometimes the Washington mandates state policy without providing the resources to implement the policy.

3.4 Assess the impact of federalism on democratic government and the scope of government.

On the positive side, federalism reduces conflict at the national level, encourages acceptance of losing elections, and increases the opportunities for citizens to participate in government and see their policy preferences reflected in law. On the negative side, it may increase inequities between states with different levels of resources, discourage states from providing services, allow local interests to thwart national policy, and complicate efforts to make government responsive.

The national government has grown in response to the demands of Americans for public services it can best provide, but it has not in any way supplanted the states.

Chapter Test

3.1 Define federalism and explain its consequences for American politics and policy.

1. A country in which all power resides in a central government has ______
   a. A unitary government
   b. A confederacy
   c. An intergovernmental system
   d. A federal system of government
   e. An enumerated government

2. Federalism is a system of government in which three or more levels of government (local, state, and federal) have formal authority over the same area and people.

   True______ False______

3. What are two pros and two cons of the decentralized politics and policies of a federal system? Use specific policy examples to illustrate your answer.

3.2 Outline what the Constitution says about division of power between national and state governments and states' obligations to each other, and trace the increasing importance of the national government.

4. The "full faith and credit" clause in Article IV of the Constitution is primarily designed to ensure ______ between states.
   a. Communication
   b. Reciprocity
   c. Honesty
   d. Commerce
   e. Goodwill

5. According to the regulation of privileges and immunities between states, a citizen of Texas who buys a product while visiting a store in California ______
   a. Pays the Texas sales tax
   b. Pays the California sales tax
   c. Pays both the California and the Texas sales tax
   d. Can choose whether s/he wants to pay the California or Texas sales tax
   e. Pays the California sales tax, but can ask to be reimbursed when returning to Texas

6. When the Supreme Court interpreted the commerce clause broadly, it contributed to the expansion of national supremacy over the states.

   True______ False______

7. Explain how a shift in the balance of power between states and the national government has shaped the history of federalism in the United States. In your answer, explain how different interpretations of the Tenth Amendment, including in several important Supreme Court decisions, relate to the debate regarding the boundaries of state and national power.

3.3 Characterize the shift from dual to cooperative federalism and the role of fiscal federalism in intergovernmental relations today.

8. The shift from dual to cooperative federalism ______
   a. Required an initial devolution in federal influence over states
   b. Involved a clear, discrete shift, related to implementation of the New Deal
   c. Involved gradual change in many policy areas, including education
   d. Involved a shift from presidential to congressional dominance over policy
   e. Resulted primarily from largely partisan efforts by Republicans in the 1950s

9. Over the past generation, the percentage of federal grants devoted to education and training programs has decreased in favor of grants devoted to health care.

   True______ False______

10. Suppose that you are a state official in charge of creating a new program designed to reduce high school dropout rates. To finance your program, you require assistance through federal grants. Based on your knowledge of the different types of grants available from the federal government, which type would you prefer to receive for your program, and why? Which do you think would be most effective in helping you achieve your goals? Explain your answer.

11. The United States has undergone a gradual shift from dual to cooperative federalism. In your opinion, what are some of the factors that have explained this shift? What are some possible positive and negative consequences? Use specific examples to explain your answer.

3.4 Assess the impact of federalism on democratic government and the scope of government.

12. An examination of the historical growth of federal responsibilities over policy reveals that
    a. The federal government can handle many policy areas more efficiently than can the states
    b. The federal government responds to interest group demands to take a more active policy role
    c. The federal government expanded its role over policy as the nation industrialized
    d. The federal government's share of governmental expenditures has grown rapidly since the New Deal
    e. All of the above are true

13. Based on your understanding of the federalism and the framing of the Constitution, why did the Founders establish a federal system of government? In what ways does federalism contribute to and/or limit democracy? In your opinion, does federalism make government more or less democratic? Explain your answer.

14. How does federalism affect the scope of government? Did the national government grow at the expense of state power or did this growth occur because of the unique capabilities and responsibilities of the national government? What are some examples of policies that best support your answer?

PEARSON mypoliscilab Exercises

Apply what you learned in this chapter on MyPoliSciLab.

Read on **mypoliscilab.com**

eText: Chapter 3

Study and **Review** on **mypoliscilab.com**

Pre-Test
Post-Test
Chapter Exam
Flashcards

Watch on **mypoliscilab.com**

Video: Proposition 8
Video: The Real ID
Video: Water Wars

Explore on **mypoliscilab.com**

Simulation: You Are a Restaurant Owner
Simulation: You Are a Federal Judge
Comparative: Comparing Federal and Unitary Systems
Timeline: Federalism and the Supreme Court
Visual Literacy: Federalism and Regulations

Key Terms

federalism (66)
unitary governments (66)
intergovernmental relations (66)
supremacy clause (70)
Tenth Amendment (70)
McCulloch v. Maryland (71)
enumerated powers (71)
implied powers (71)
elastic clause (71)
Gibbons v. Ogden (72)
full faith and credit (73)
extradition (74)
privileges and immunities (74)
dual federalism (74)
cooperative federalism (75)
devolution (77)
fiscal federalism (77)
categorical grants (78)
project grants (79)
formula grants (79)
block grants (79)

Internet Resources

www.cfda.gov/index?cck=1&au=&ck=
The Catalog of Federal Domestic Assistance allows you to search through hundreds of federal grants.

www.ncsl.org/statefed/StateFederalCommittees/tabid/773/Default.aspx
Information and discussion of issues on federal–state relations from the National Conference of State Legislatures.

www.census.gov/compendia/statab/
The *Statistical Abstract of the United States* contains a wealth of data on state public policies.

www.csg.org
Council of State Governments Web site offers information on states and state public policies.

usgovinfo.about.com/od/rightsandfreedoms/a/federalism.htm
The powers of the national and state governments.

www.federalismproject.org
Original research on American federalism, sponsored by the American Enterprise Institute.

www.cas.sc.edu/poli/courses/scgov/History_of_Federalism.htm
The history of U.S. federalism.

For Further Reading

Beer, Samuel H. ***To Make a Nation: The Rediscovery of American Federalism***. Cambridge, MA: Harvard University Press, 1993. An excellent study of the philosophical bases of American federalism.

Conlan, Timothy J. ***From New Federalism to Devolution: Twenty-Five Years of Intergovernmental Reform.*** Washington, DC: Brookings Institution, 1998. An analysis of the efforts to restructure intergovernmental relations since the late 1960s.

Elazar, Daniel J. ***American Federalism: A View from the States***, 3rd ed. New York: Harper&Row, 1984. A well-known work surveying federalism from the standpoint of state governments.

Gerston, Larry N. ***American Federalism***. New York: M. E. Sharpe, 2007. A concise introduction to federalism.

Miller, Lisa L. ***The Perils of Federalism: Race, Poverty, and the Politics of Crime Control***. New York: Oxford University Press, 2008. How federalism affects the making and implementation of policy regarding crime.

O'Toole, Laurence. ***American Intergovernmental Relations***, 4th ed. Washington, DC: CQ Press, 2006. Essays on many aspects of federalism.

Peterson, Paul E. ***The Price of Federalism***. Washington, DC: Brookings Institution, 1995. A good assessment of the costs and benefits of federalism.

Posner, Paul L., and Timothy J. Conlan. ***Intergovernmental Management for the 21st Century***. Washington, DC: Brookings Institution, 2007. Assesses the state of intergovernmental relations in the U.S. and an agenda for improving them.

Schapiro, Robert A. ***Polyphonic Federalism: Toward the Protection of Fundamental Rights***. Chicago: University of Chicago Press, 2009. Argues that the multiple perspectives on policy provided by federalism are a great advantage for the United States.

Walker, David B. ***The Rebirth of Federalism***. 2nd ed. Chatham, NJ: Chatham House, 2000. A history of American federalism and an analysis of its current condition.

Chapter 4

Civil Liberties and Public Policy

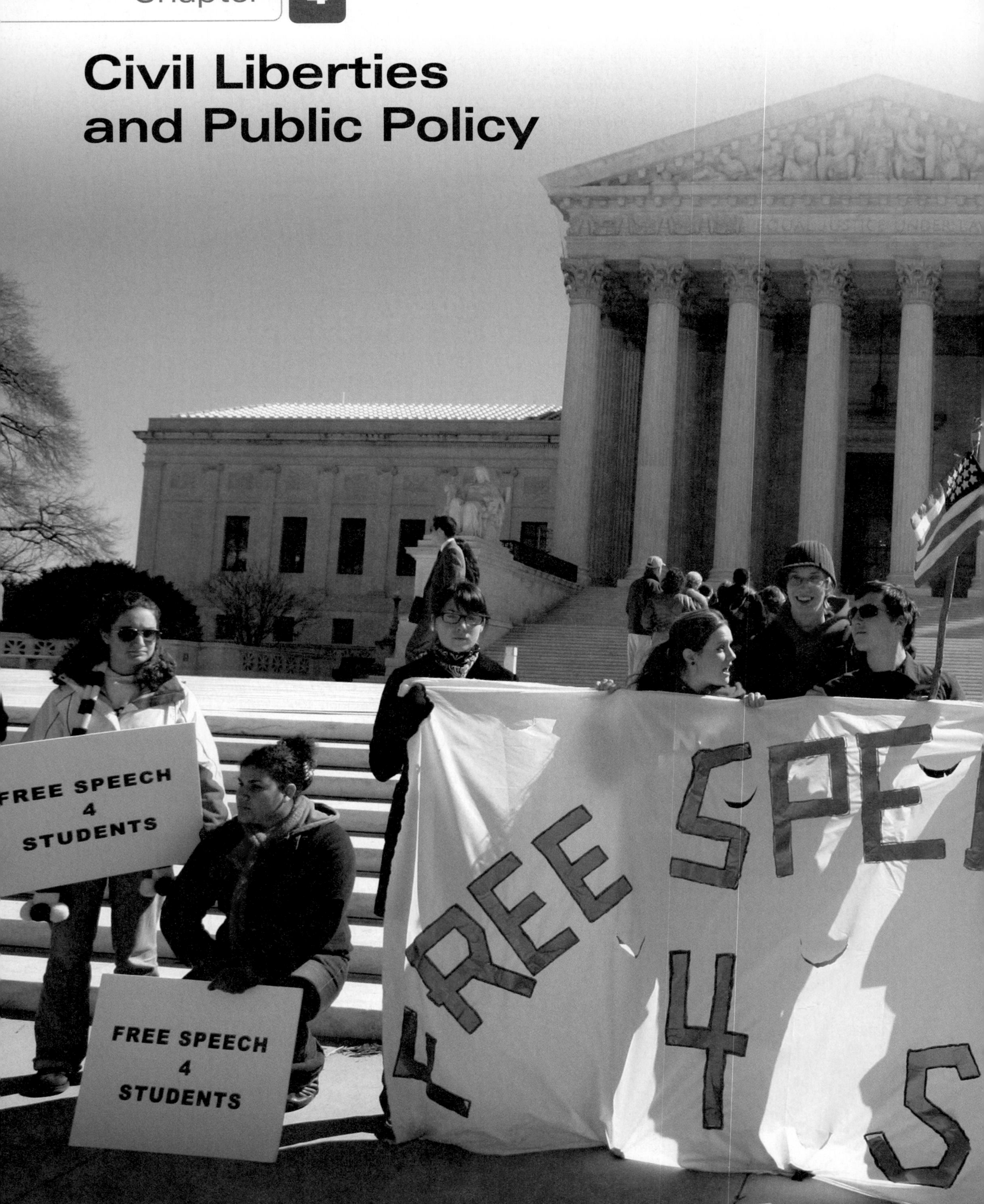

Learning Objectives

4.1 Trace the process by which the Bill of Rights has been applied to the states.

4.2 Distinguish the two types of religious rights protected by the First Amendment and determine the boundaries of those rights.

4.3 Differentiate the rights of free expression protected by the First Amendment and determine the boundaries of those rights.

4.4 Describe the rights to assemble and associate protected by the First Amendment and their limitations.

4.5 Describe the right to bear arms protected by the Second Amendment and its limitations.

4.6 Characterize defendants' rights and identify issues that arise in their implementation.

4.7 Outline the evolution of a right to privacy and its application to the issue of abortion.

4.8 Assess how civil liberties affect democratic government and how they both limit and expand the scope of government.

Chapter OUTLINE

POLITICS IN ACTION: FREE SPEECH ON CAMPUS

The Board of Regents of the University of Wisconsin System requires students at the university's Madison campus to pay an activity fee that supports various campus services and extracurricular student activities. In the university's view, such fees enhance students' educational experiences by promoting extracurricular activities, stimulating advocacy and debate on diverse points of view, enabling participation in campus administrative activity, and providing opportunities to develop social skills—all consistent with the university's broad educational mission. Registered student organizations (RSOs) engaging in a number of diverse expressive activities are eligible to receive a portion of the fees, which are administered by the student government subject to the university's approval.

There has been broad agreement that the process for reviewing and approving RSO applications for funding is administered in a viewpoint-neutral fashion. RSOs may also obtain funding through a student referendum. Some students, however, sued the university, alleging that the activity fee violated their First Amendment rights and that the university must grant them the choice not to fund RSOs that engage in political and ideological expression offensive to their personal beliefs.

In 2000, the Supreme Court held in a unanimous decision in *Board of Regents of University of Wisconsin System v. Southworth* that if a university determines that its mission is well served if students have the means to engage in dynamic discussion on a broad range of issues, it may impose a mandatory fee to sustain such dialogue. The Court recognized that it was all but inevitable that the fees will subsidize speech that some students find objectionable or offensive. Thus, the Court required that a university provide some protection to its students' First Amendment interests by requiring viewpoint neutrality in the allocation of funding support.

The University of Wisconsin case is the sort of complex controversy that shapes American civil liberties. Debates about the right to abortion, the right to bear arms, the separation of church and state, and similar issues are constantly in the news. Some of these issues arise from conflicting interests. The need to protect society against crime often conflicts with society's need to protect the rights of people accused of crime. Other conflicts derive from strong differences of opinion about what is ethical, moral, or right. To some Americans, abortion is murder, the taking of a human life. To others, a woman's choice whether to bear a child, free of governmental intrusion, is a fundamental right. Everyone, however, is affected by the extent of our civil liberties.

Deciding complex questions about civil liberties requires balancing competing values, such as maintaining an open system of expression while protecting individuals from the excesses such a system may produce. As we learned in Chapter 1, civil liberties are essential to democracy. How could we have free elections without free speech, for example? But does it follow that critics of officials should be able to say whatever they want, no matter how untrue? And who should decide the extent of our liberty? Should it be a representative institution such as Congress or a judicial elite such as the Supreme Court?

The role of the government in resolving civil liberties controversies is also the subject of much debate. Conservatives usually advocate narrowing the scope of government, yet many strongly support government-imposed limits on abortion and government-sanctioned prayers in public schools. They also want government to be less hindered by concern for defendants' rights. Liberals, who typically support a broader scope of government, usually want to limit government's role in prohibiting abortion and encouraging religious activities and to place greater constraints on government's freedom of action in the criminal justice system.

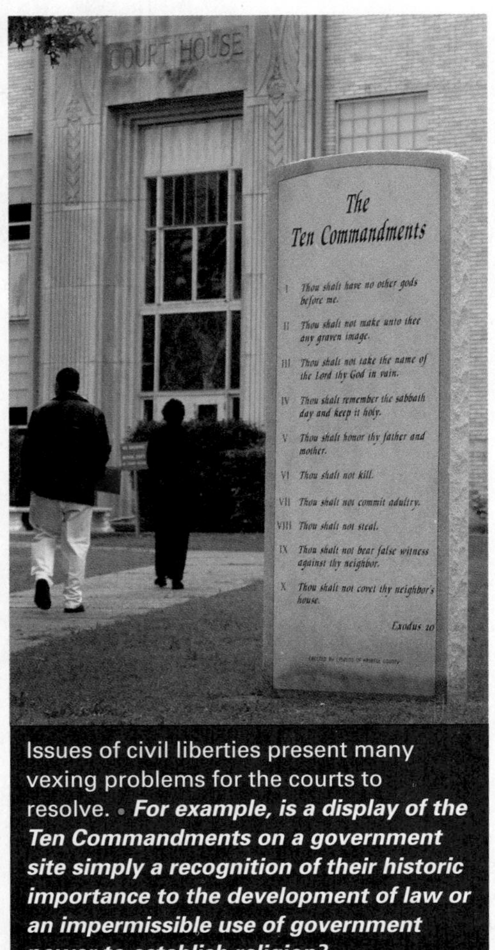

Issues of civil liberties present many vexing problems for the courts to resolve. • ***For example, is a display of the Ten Commandments on a government site simply a recognition of their historic importance to the development of law or an impermissible use of government power to establish religion?***

Civil liberties are individual legal and constitutional protections against the government. Americans' civil liberties are set down in the **Bill of Rights**, the first 10 amendments to the Constitution. At first glance, many questions about civil liberties look easy to resolve. The Bill of Rights' guarantee of a free press seems straightforward; either Americans can write what they choose or they cannot. In the real world of American law, however, these issues are subtle and complex.

Disputes about civil liberties often end up in court. The Supreme Court of the United States is the final interpreter of the content and scope of our liberties; this ultimate power to interpret the Constitution accounts for the ferocious debate over presidential appointments to the Supreme Court.

Throughout this chapter you will find special features titled "You Are the Judge." Each feature describes an actual case brought before the courts and asks you to compare the decision you would make with that of the judge who heard the case.

To understand the specifics of American civil liberties, we must first understand the Bill of Rights.

4.1 Trace the process by which the Bill of Rights has been applied to the states.

The Bill of Rights

By 1787, all state constitutions had bills of rights, some of which survive, intact, to this day. Although the new U.S. Constitution had no bill of rights, the state ratifying conventions made its inclusion a condition of ratification. The First Congress passed the Bill of Rights in 1789 and sent it to the states for ratification. In 1791, these amendments became part of the Constitution.

civil liberties
The legal constitutional protections against government. Although our civil liberties are formally set down in the **Bill of Rights**, the courts, police, and legislatures define their meaning.

Bill of Rights
The first 10 amendments to the U.S. Constitution, which define such basic liberties as freedom of religion, speech, and press and guarantee defendants' rights.

The Bill of Rights—Then and Now

The Bill of Rights ensures Americans' basic liberties, such as freedom of speech and religion, and protection against arbitrary searches and being held for long periods without trial (see Table 4.1). The Bill of Rights was ratified when British abuses of the colonists' civil liberties were still a fresh and bitter memory. Colonial officials had jailed newspaper editors, arrested citizens without cause, and detained people and forced them to confess at gunpoint or worse. Thus, the first 10 amendments enjoyed great popular support.

Political scientists have discovered that people are devotees of rights in theory but that their support wavers when it comes time to put those rights into practice.[1] For example, Americans in general believe in freedom of speech, but many citizens would not let the Ku Klux Klan speak in their neighborhood or allow their public schools to teach about atheism or homosexuality. In addition, Americans seem willing to trade civil liberties for security when they feel that the nation is threatened, as in the case of terrorism.[2] Few rights are absolute; we cannot avoid the difficult questions of balancing civil liberties and other individual and societal values.

TABLE 4.1 The Bill of Rights

These amendments were passed by Congress on September 25, 1789, and ratified by the states on December 15, 1791.

Amendment I—Religion, Speech, Assembly, Petition
Congress shall make no law respecting an establishment of religion, or prohibiting the free exercise thereof; or abridging the freedom of speech, or of the press; or the right of the people peaceably to assemble, and to petition the Government for a redress of grievances.

Amendment II—Right to Bear Arms
A well-regulated militia, being necessary to the security of a free State, the right of the people to keep and bear arms, shall not be infringed.

Amendment III—Quartering of Soldiers
No Soldier shall, in time of peace be quartered in any house, without the consent of the owner, nor in time of war, but in a manner to be prescribed by law.

Amendment IV—Searches and Seizures
The right of the people to be secure in their persons, houses, papers, and effects, against unreasonable searches and seizures, shall not be violated, and no warrants shall issue, but upon probable cause, supported by oath or affirmation, and particularly describing the place to be searched, and persons or things to be seized.

Amendment V—Grand Juries, Double Jeopardy, Self-Incrimination, Due Process, Eminent Domain
No person shall be held to answer to a capital, or otherwise infamous crime, unless on a presentment or indictment of a Grand Jury, except in cases arising in the land or naval forces, or in the militia, when in actual service in time of war or public danger: nor shall any person be subject for the same offense to be twice put in jeopardy of life or limb; nor shall be compelled in any criminal case to be a witness against himself, nor be deprived of life, liberty, or property, without due process of law; nor shall private property be taken for public use, without just compensation.

Amendment VI—Criminal Court Procedures
In all criminal prosecutions, the accused shall enjoy the right to a speedy and public trial, by an impartial jury of the State and district wherein the crime shall have been committed, which district shall have been previously ascertained by law, and to be informed of the nature and cause of the accusation; to be confronted with the witnesses against him; to have compulsory process for obtaining witnesses in his favor, and to have the assistance of counsel for his defense.

Amendment VII—Trial by Jury in Common-Law Cases
In Suits at common law, where the value in controversy shall exceed twenty dollars, the right of trial by jury shall be preserved, and no fact tried by a jury, shall be otherwise re-examined in any Court of the United States.

Amendment VIII—Bails, Fines, and Punishment
Excessive bail shall not be required, nor excessive fines imposed, nor cruel and unusual punishments inflicted.

Amendment IX—Rights Retained by the People
The enumeration in the Constitution, of certain rights, shall not be construed to deny or disparage others retained by the people.

Amendment X—Rights Reserved to the States
The powers not delegated to the United States by the Constitution, nor prohibited by it to the States, are reserved to the States respectively, or to the people.

The Bill of Rights and the States

Take another look at the **First Amendment**. Note the first words: "Congress shall make no law. . . ." The Founders wrote the Bill of Rights to restrict the powers of the new national government. In 1791, Americans were comfortable with their state governments; after all, every state constitution had its own bill of rights. Thus, a literal reading of the First Amendment suggests that it does not prohibit a state government from passing a law prohibiting the free exercise of religion, free speech, or freedom of the press.

First Amendment
The constitutional amendment that establishes the four great liberties: freedom of the press, of speech, of religion, and of assembly.

What happens, however, if a state passes a law violating one of the rights protected by the federal Bill of Rights and the state's constitution does not prohibit this abridgment of freedom? In 1833, the answer to that question was "nothing." The Bill of Rights, said the Court in ***Barron v. Baltimore***, restrained only the national government, not states and cities.

Almost a century later, however, the Court ruled that a state government must respect some First Amendment rights. The 1925 ruling in ***Gitlow v. New York*** relied not on the First Amendment but on the Fourteenth—the second of three "Civil War Amendments" that ended slavery, gave former slaves legal protection, and ensured their voting rights. Ratified in 1868, the **Fourteenth Amendment** declared,

> No state shall make or enforce any law which shall abridge the privileges or immunities of citizens of the United States nor shall any state deprive any person of life, liberty, or property, without due process of law; nor deny to any person within its jurisdiction the equal protection of the laws.

In *Gitlow*, the Court announced that freedoms of speech and press "were fundamental personal rights and liberties protected by the **due process clause** of the Fourteenth Amendment from impairment by the states." In effect, the Court interpreted the Fourteenth Amendment to say that states could not abridge the freedoms of expression protected by the First Amendment. This decision began the development of the **incorporation doctrine**, the legal concept under which the Supreme Court has nationalized the Bill of Rights by making most of its provisions applicable to the states through the Fourteenth Amendment.

Initially, the Supreme Court held only parts of the First Amendment to be binding on the states as a result of *Gitlow*. Gradually, especially during the 1960s, the Court applied most of the Bill of Rights to the states (see Table 4.2). Many of the judicial decisions that empowered the Bill of Rights were controversial, but today, the Bill of Rights guarantees individual freedoms against infringement by state and local governments as well as by the national government. Only the Third and Seventh Amendments, the grand jury requirement of the Fifth Amendment, and the prohibition against excessive fines and bail in the Eighth Amendment have not been applied specifically to the states.

Barron v. Baltimore
The 1833 Supreme Court decision holding that the **Bill of Rights** restrained only the national government, not the states and cities.

Gitlow v. New York
The 1925 Supreme Court decision holding that freedoms of press and speech are "fundamental personal rights and liberties protected by the due process clause of the **Fourteenth Amendment** from impairment by the states" as well as by the federal government. Compare ***Barron v. Baltimore***.

Fourteenth Amendment
The constitutional amendment adopted after the Civil War that declares "No State shall make or enforce any law which shall abridge the privileges or immunities of citizens of the United States; nor shall any state deprive any person of life, liberty, or property, without due process of law; nor deny to any person within its jurisdiction the equal protection of the laws." See also **due process clause**.

4.2 Distinguish the two types of religious rights protected by the First Amendment and determine the boundaries of those rights.

Freedom of Religion

The First Amendment contains two elements regarding religion and government. These elements are commonly referred to as the establishment clause and the free exercise clause. The **establishment clause** states that "Congress shall make no law respecting an establishment of religion." The **free exercise clause** prohibits the abridgment of citizens' freedom to worship or not to worship as they please. Sometimes these freedoms conflict. The government's practice of providing chaplains on military bases is one example of this conflict; some accuse the government of establishing religion in order to ensure that members of the armed forces can freely practice their religion. Usually, however, establishment clause and free exercise clause cases raise different kinds of conflicts.

The Establishment Clause

Some nations, such as Great Britain, have an established church that is officially supported by the government and recognized as a national institution. A few American colonies had official churches, but the religious persecutions that incited many colonists to move to America discouraged any desire that the First Congress might have had to establish a national church in the United States. Thus, the First Amendment prohibits an established national religion.

It is much less clear, however, what else the First Congress intended to include in the establishment clause. Some people argued that it meant only that the government

due process clause
Part of the **Fourteenth Amendment** guaranteeing that persons cannot be deprived of life, liberty, or property by the United States or state governments without due process of law. See also ***Gitlow v. New York***.

incorporation doctrine
The legal concept under which the Supreme Court has nationalized the **Bill of Rights** by making most of its provisions applicable to the states through the **Fourteenth Amendment**.

establishment clause
Part of the **First Amendment** stating that "Congress shall make no law respecting an establishment of religion."

TABLE 4.2 The Nationalization of the Bill of Rights

DATE	AMENDMENT	RIGHT	CASE
1925	First	Freedom of speech	*Gitlow v. New York*
1931	First	Freedom of the press	*Near v. Minnesota*
1937	First	Freedom of assembly	*De Jonge v. Oregon*
1940	First	Free exercise of religion	*Cantwell v. Connecticut*
1947	First	Establishment of religion	*Everson v. Board of Education*
1958	First	Freedom of association	*NAACP v. Alabama*
1963	First	Right to petition government	*NAACP v. Button*
2010	Second	Right to bear arms	*McDonald v. Chicago*
	Third	No quartering of soldiers	Not incorporated[a]
1949	Fourth	No unreasonable searches and seizures	*Wolf v. Colorado*
1961	Fourth	Exclusionary rule	*Mapp v. Ohio*
1897	Fifth	Guarantee of just compensation	*Chicago, Burlington, and Quincy RR v. Chicago*
1964	Fifth	Immunity from self-incrimination	*Mallory v. Hogan*
1969	Fifth	Immunity from double jeopardy	*Benton v. Maryland*
	Fifth	Right to grand jury indictment	Not incorporated
1932	Sixth	Right to counsel in capital cases	*Powell v. Alabama*
1948	Sixth	Right to public trial	*In re Oliver*
1963	Sixth	Right to counsel in felony cases	*Gideon v. Wainwright*
1965	Sixth	Right to confrontation of witnesses	*Pointer v. Texas*
1966	Sixth	Right to impartial jury	*Parker v. Gladden*
1967	Sixth	Right to speedy trial	*Klopfer v. North Carolina*
1967	Sixth	Right to compulsory process for obtaining witnesses	*Washington v. Texas*
1968	Sixth	Right to jury trial for serious crimes	*Duncan v. Louisiana*
1972	Sixth	Right to counsel for all crimes involving jail terms	*Argersinger v. Hamlin*
	Seventh	Right to jury trial in civil cases	Not incorporated
1962	Eighth	Freedom from cruel and unusual punishment	*Robinson v. California*
	Eighth	Freedom from excessive fines or bail	Not incorporated
1965	Ninth	Right of privacy	*Griswold v. Connecticut*

[a]The quartering of soldiers has not occurred under the Constitution.

could not favor one religion over another. In contrast, Thomas Jefferson argued that the First Amendment created a "wall of separation" between church and state, forbidding not just favoritism but also any support for religion at all. These interpretations continue to provoke argument, especially when religion is mixed with education, as occurs with the issues of government aid to church-related schools and prayer in public schools.

free exercise clause
A **First Amendment** provision that prohibits government from interfering with the practice of religion.

Proponents of aid to church-related schools argue that it does not favor any specific religion. Some opponents reply that the Roman Catholic Church has by far the largest religious school system in the country and gets most of the aid. It was Protestant Lyndon Baines Johnson who obtained the passage of the first substantial aid to parochial elementary and secondary schools in 1965. He argued that the aid went to students, not schools, and thus should go wherever the students were, including church-related schools.

Lemon v. Kurtzman
The 1971 Supreme Court decision that established that aid to church-related schools must (1) have a secular legislative purpose; (2) have a primary effect that neither advances nor inhibits religion; and (3) not foster excessive government entanglement with religion.

In ***Lemon v. Kurtzman*** (1971), the Supreme Court declared that aid to church-related schools must do the following:

1. Have a secular legislative purpose
2. Have a primary effect that neither advances nor inhibits religion
3. Not foster an excessive government "entanglement" with religion

Since that time, the Court has had to draw a fine line between aid that is permissible and aid that is not. For instance, the Court has allowed religiously affiliated colleges and universities to use public funds to construct buildings. Public funds may also be used to provide students in parochial schools with textbooks, computers and other instructional equipment, lunches, and transportation to and from school and to administer standardized testing services. However, schools may not use public funds to pay teacher salaries or to provide transportation for students on field trips. The theory underlying these decisions is that it is possible to determine that buildings, textbooks, lunches, school buses, and national tests are not used to support sectarian education. However, determining how teachers handle a subject in class or focus a field trip may require complex and constitutionally impermissible regulation of religion.

In an important loosening of its constraints on aid to parochial schools, the Supreme Court decided in 1997 in *Agostini v. Felton* that public school systems could send teachers into parochial schools to teach remedial and supplemental classes to needy children. In a landmark decision in 2002, the Court in ***Zelman v. Simmons-Harris*** upheld a program that provided some families in Cleveland, Ohio, with vouchers they could use to pay tuition at religious schools.

Zelman v. Simmons-Harris
The 2002 Supreme Court decision that upheld a state program providing families with vouchers that could be used to pay for tuition at religious schools.

Controversy over aid to schools is not limited to Roman Catholic schools. In 1994, the Supreme Court ruled in *Kiryas Joel v. Grumet* that New York state had gone too far in favoring religion when it created a public school district for the benefit of a village of Hasidic Jews.

At the same time, the Supreme Court has been opening public schools to religious activities. The Court decided that public universities that permit student groups to use their facilities must allow student religious groups on campus to use the facilities for religious worship.[3] In the 1984 Equal Access Act, Congress made it unlawful for any public high school receiving federal funds (almost all of them do) to keep student groups from using school facilities for religious worship if the school opens its facilities for other student meetings.[4] In 2001, the Supreme Court extended this principle to public elementary schools.[5] Similarly, in 1993, the Court required public schools that rent facilities to organizations to do the same for religious groups.[6]

In 1995, the Court held that the University of Virginia was constitutionally required to subsidize a student religious magazine on the same basis as other student publications.[7] However, in 2004, the Court held that the state of Washington was within its rights when it excluded students pursuing a devotional theology degree from its general scholarship program.[8]

Engel v. Vitale
The 1962 Supreme Court decision holding that state officials violated the **First Amendment** when they wrote a prayer to be recited by New York's schoolchildren.

School District of Abington Township, Pennsylvania v. Schempp
A 1963 Supreme Court decision holding that a Pennsylvania law requiring Bible reading in schools violated the establishment clause of the ***First Amendment***.

The threshold of constitutional acceptability becomes higher when public funds are used in a more direct way to support education. Thus, school authorities may not permit religious instructors to come into public school buildings during the school day to provide religious education,[9] although they may release students from part of the compulsory school day to receive religious instruction elsewhere.[10] In 1980, the Court also prohibited the posting of the Ten Commandments on the walls of public classrooms.[11]

School prayer is perhaps the most controversial religious issue. In 1962 and 1963, the Court aroused the wrath of many Americans by ruling that voluntary recitations of prayers or Bible passages, when done as part of classroom exercises in public schools, violated the establishment clause. In ***Engel v. Vitale*** and ***School District of Abington Township, Pennsylvania v. Schempp***, the justices observed that "the place of religion in our society is an exalted one . . . [but] in the relationship between man and religion, the State is firmly committed to a position of neutrality."

It is *not* unconstitutional, of course, to pray in public schools. Students may pray silently as much as they wish. What the Constitution forbids is the sponsorship or encouragement of prayer, directly or indirectly, by public school authorities. Thus, in 1992, the Court ruled that a school-sponsored prayer at a public school graduation violated the constitutional separation of church and state.[12] In 2000, the Court held that student-led prayer at football games was also unconstitutional.[13] Three Alabama laws authorized schools to hold one-minute periods of silence for "meditation or voluntary prayer," but the Court rejected this approach because the state made it clear that the purpose of the statute was to return prayer to the schools. The Court did indicate, however, that a less clumsy approach would pass its scrutiny.[14]

A great ferment in the relationship between religion and American political life has marked recent years. Religious issues and controversies have assumed much greater importance in political debate than they commanded before.[15] Much of this new importance is due to fundamentalist religious groups that have spurred their members to political action. Many school districts have simply ignored the Supreme Court's ban on school prayer and continue to allow prayers in their classrooms. Some religious groups and many members of Congress, especially conservative Republicans, have pushed for a constitutional amendment permitting prayer in school. A majority of the public consistently supports school prayer.[16]

Fundamentalist Christian groups have pressed some state legislatures to mandate the teaching of "creation science"—their alternative to Darwinian theories of evolution—in public schools. Louisiana, for example, passed a law requiring schools that taught Darwinian theory to teach creation science, too. Regardless, the Supreme Court ruled in 1987 that this law violated the establishment clause.[17] The Court had already held in a 1968 case that states cannot prohibit Darwin's theory of evolution from being taught in the public schools.[18] More recently, some groups have advocated "intelligent design," the view that living things are too complicated to have resulted from natural selection and thus must be the result of an intelligent cause, as an alternative to evolution. Although they claim that their belief has no religious implications, lower courts have begun to rule that requiring teachers to present intelligent design as an alternative to evolution is a constitutionally unacceptable promotion of religion in the classroom.

The Supreme Court's struggle to interpret the establishment clause is also evident in areas other than education. In 2005, the Supreme Court found that two Kentucky counties violated the establishment clause value of official religious neutrality when they posted large, readily visible copies of the Ten Commandments in their courthouses. The Court concluded that the counties' ostensible and predominant purpose was to advance religion.[19] However, the Court did not hold that a governmental body can never integrate a sacred text constitutionally into a governmental display on law or history. Thus, in 2005, the Court also upheld the inclusion of a monolith inscribed with the Ten Commandments among the 21 historical markers and 17 monuments surrounding the Texas State Capitol. The Court argued that simply having religious content or promoting a message consistent with a religious doctrine does not run afoul of the establishment clause. Texas's placement of the Commandments monument on its capitol grounds was a far more passive use of those texts than their posting in elementary school classrooms and also served a legitimate historical purpose.[20]

WHY IT MATTERS

The Establishment Clause

What if the Constitution did not prohibit the establishment of religion? If a dominant religion received public funds and were in a position to control health care, public education, and other important aspects of public policy, these policies might be quite different from what they are today. In addition, the potential for conflict between followers of the established religion and adherents of other religions would be substantial.

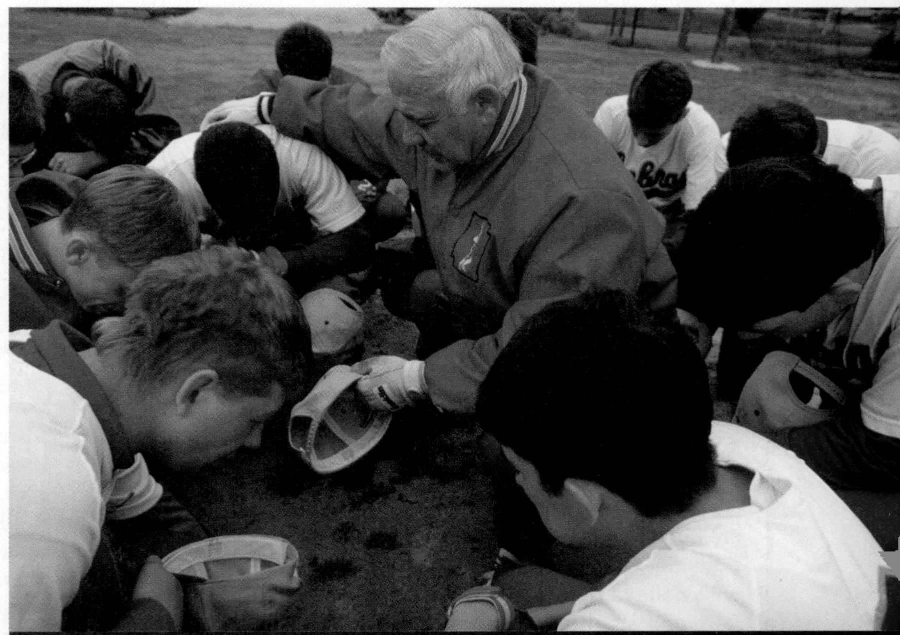

One of the most controversial issues regarding the First Amendment's prohibition of the establishment of religion is prayer in public schools. Although students may pray on their own, school authorities may not sponsor or encourage prayer. Some schools violate the law, however. • ***What was your experience with prayer in school?***

Displays of religious symbols during the holidays have prompted considerable controversy. In 1984, the Court found that Pawtucket, Rhode Island, could set up a Christmas nativity scene on public property—along with Santa's house and sleigh, Christmas trees, and other symbols of the Christmas season.[21] Five years later, the Court extended the principle to a Hanukkah menorah placed next to a Christmas tree. The Court concluded that these displays had a secular purpose and provided little or no benefit to religion. At the same time, the Court invalidated the display of the nativity scene without secular symbols in a courthouse because, in this context, the county gave the impression of endorsing the display's religious message.[22]

The Court's basic position is that the Constitution does not require complete separation of church and state; it mandates accommodation of all religions and forbids hostility toward any. At the same time, the Constitution forbids government endorsement of religious beliefs. Drawing the line between neutrality toward religion and promotion of it is not easy; this dilemma ensures that cases involving the establishment of religion will continue to come before the Court.

The Free Exercise Clause

The First Amendment also guarantees the free exercise of religion. This guarantee seems simple enough. Whether people hold no religious beliefs, practice voodoo, or go to church, temple, or mosque, they should have the right to practice religion as they choose. In general, Americans are tolerant of those with religious views outside the mainstream, as you can see in "America in Perspective: Tolerance for the Free Speech Rights of Religious Extremists."

The matter is, of course, more complicated. Religions sometimes forbid actions that society thinks are necessary; or, conversely, religions may require actions that society finds unacceptable. For example, what if a religion justifies multiple marriages or the use of illegal drugs? Muhammad Ali, the boxing champion, refused induction into

AMERICA IN PERSPECTIVE

Tolerance for the Free Speech Rights of Religious Extremists

Despite 9/11, Americans are more tolerant of the free speech rights of religious extremists than are people in other democracies with developed economies. Why do you think Americans are so tolerant?

Question: There are some people whose views are considered extreme by the majority. Consider religious extremists, that is people who believe that their religion is the only true faith and all other religions should be considered as enemies. Do you think such people should be allowed to hold public meetings to express their views?

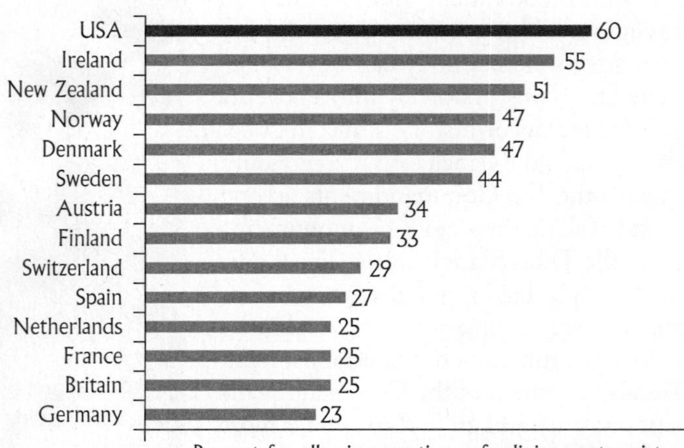

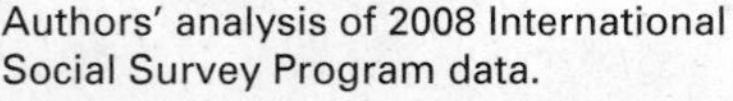
Authors' analysis of 2008 International Social Survey Program data.

the armed services during the Vietnam War because, he said, military service would violate his Muslim faith. Amish parents often refuse to send their children to public schools. Jehovah's Witnesses and Christian Scientists may refuse to accept blood transfusions and certain other kinds of medical treatment for themselves or their children.

Cassius Clay was the world heavyweight boxing champion before he converted to Islam, changed his name to Muhammad Ali, and was drafted during the war in Vietnam. Arguing that he opposed war on religious grounds, he refused to join the army. The federal government prosecuted him for draft dodging, and he was stripped of his title. In 1971, the Supreme Court overturned his conviction for draft evasion. He is pictured here at the Houston induction center in 1967.

Consistently maintaining that people have an inviolable right to *believe* what they want, the courts have been more cautious about the right to *practice* a belief. What if, the Supreme Court once asked, a person "believed that human sacrifices were a necessary part of religious worship?" Over the years, the Court has upheld laws and regulations forbidding polygamy, prohibiting business activities on Sunday (restricting the commerce of Orthodox Jews, for whom Sunday is a workday), denying tax exemptions to religious schools that discriminate on the basis of race,[23] allowing the building of a road through ground sacred to some Native Americans, and even prohibiting a Jewish air force captain from wearing his yarmulke while on duty (Congress later intervened to permit military personnel to wear yarmulkes).

At the same time, Congress and the Supreme Court have granted protection to a range of religiously motivated practices. The Court allowed Amish parents to take their children out of school after the eighth grade. Reasoning that the Amish community was well established and that its children would not burden the state, the Court held that religious freedom took precedence over compulsory education laws.[24] More broadly, although a state can compel parents to send their children to an accredited school, parents have a right to choose religious schools rather than public schools for their children's education. A state may not require Jehovah's Witnesses or members of other religions to participate in public school flag-saluting ceremonies. Congress has also decided—and the courts have upheld—that people can become conscientious objectors to war on religious grounds. You can examine another free exercise case in "You Are the Judge: The Case of Animal Sacrifices."

In 1988, the Court upheld the state of Oregon's prosecution of persons using the drug peyote as part of their religious rituals (*Employment Division v. Smith)*. The Court discarded its previous requirement for a *compelling interest* before a government could even indirectly limit or prohibit religious practices and decided that state laws interfering with religious practices but not specifically aimed at religion were constitutional. As long as a law does not single out and ban religious practices because they are engaged in for religious reasons or only because of the religious belief they display, a general law may be applied to conduct even if the conduct is religiously inspired.[25]

In the Religious Freedom Restoration Act of 1993, Congress attempted to overturn the principle that the Court had articulated in *Smith*. This act conferred on all persons the right to perform their religious rituals unless the government could show that the law or regulation in question was narrowly tailored and in pursuit of a "compelling interest." In 1997, however, the Supreme Court declared this act, as applied to the states, was an unconstitutional intrusion by Congress into the states' prerogatives for regulating the health and welfare of citizens.[26] The Religious Freedom Restoration Act does apply to the national government, however, and in 2006, the Court allowed a small religious sect to use a hallucinogenic tea in its rituals despite the federal government's attempts to bar its use.[27]

In 2000, Congress passed narrower legislation that, in accordance with the "compelling interest" standard, made it more difficult for local governments to enforce zoning or other regulations against religious groups and required governments to allow those institutionalized in state facilities (such as prisons) to practice their faith. The Supreme Court upheld this law in 2005.[28]

YOU ARE THE JUDGE

The Case of Animal Sacrifices

The church of Lukumi Babalu Aye, in Hialeah, Florida, practiced Santeria, a Caribbean-based mix of African ritual, voodoo, and Catholicism. Central to Santeria is the ritual sacrifice of animals—at birth, marriage, and death rites as well as at ceremonies to cure the sick and initiate new members.

Offended by these rituals, the city of Hialeah passed ordinances prohibiting animal sacrifices in religious ceremonies. The church challenged the constitutionality of these laws, claiming they violated the free exercise clause of the First Amendment because the ordinances essentially barred the practice of Santeria. The city, the Santerians claimed, was discriminating against a religious minority. Besides, many other forms of killing animals were legal, including fishing, using animals in medical research, selling lobsters to be boiled alive, and feeding live rats to snakes.

You be the judge: Do the Santerians have a constitutional right to sacrifice animals in their religious rituals? Does the city's interest in protecting animals outweigh the Santerians' requirement for animal sacrifice?

Decision: In 1993, the Court overturned the Hialeah ordinances that prohibited the use of animal sacrifice in religious ritual. In *Church of the Lukumi Babalu Aye, Inc. v. City of Hialeah*, the justices concluded that governments that permit other forms of killing animals may not then ban sacrifices or ritual killings. In this instance, the Court found no compelling state interest that justified the abridgment of the freedom of religion.

4.3 Differentiate the rights of free expression protected by the First Amendment and determine the boundaries of those rights.

Freedom of Expression

A democracy depends on the free expression of ideas. Thoughts that are muffled, speech that is forbidden, and meetings that cannot be held are the enemies of the democratic process. Totalitarian governments know this, which is why they go to enormous trouble to limit expression.

Americans pride themselves on their free and open society. Freedom of conscience is absolute; Americans can *believe* whatever they want. The First Amendment plainly forbids the national government from limiting freedom of *expression*—that is, the right to say or publish what one believes. Is freedom of expression, then, like freedom of conscience, also *absolute*? Supreme Court Justice Hugo Black thought so; he was fond of pointing out that the First Amendment said that Congress shall make *no* law. "I read no law abridging to mean no law abridging." In contrast, Justice Oliver Wendell Holmes offered a classic example of impermissible speech in 1919: "The most stringent protection of free speech would not protect a man in falsely shouting 'fire' in a theater and causing a panic."

The courts have been called on to decide where to draw the line separating permissible from impermissible speech. First, can the government censor speech that it thinks will violate the law? Second, what constitutes *speech* (or press) within the meaning of the First Amendment and thus deserves constitutional protection, and what does not? Holding a political rally to attack an opposing candidate's stand on important issues receives First Amendment protection. Obscenity and libel and incitements to violence and overthrow of the government do not. But just how do we know, for example, what is obscene? To make things more complicated, certain forms of nonverbal speech, such as picketing, are considered symbolic speech and receive First Amendment protection. Judges also have had to balance freedom of expression against competing values, such as public order, national security, and the right to a fair trial. Then there are questions regarding commercial speech. Does it receive the same protection as religious and political speech? Regulating the publicly owned airwaves raises yet another set of difficult questions.

One controversial freedom of expression issue involves so-called hate speech. Advocates of regulating hate speech forcefully argue that, for example, racial insults, like fighting words, are "undeserving of First Amendment protection because the perpetrator's intent is not to discover the truth or invite dialogue, but to injure the victim."[29] In contrast, critics of hate speech policy argue that "sacrificing free speech rights is too high a price to pay to advance the cause of equality."[30] In 1992, the Supreme Court ruled that legislatures and universities may not single out racial, religious, or sexual insults or threats for prosecution as "hate speech" or "bias crimes."[31]

Prior Restraint

In the United States, the First Amendment ensures that even if the government frowns on some material, a person's right to publish it is all but inviolable. That is, it ensures there will not be **prior restraint,** government actions that prevent material from being published—or, in a word, censorship. A landmark case involving prior restraint is ***Near v. Minnesota*** (1931). A blunt newspaper editor called local officials a string of names including "grafters" and "Jewish gangsters." The state closed down his business, but the Supreme Court ordered the paper reopened.[32] Of course, the newspaper editor—or anyone else—could later be punished for violating a law or someone's rights *after* publication.

prior restraint
A government preventing material from being published. This is a common method of limiting the press in some nations, but it is usually unconstitutional in the United States, according to the **First Amendment** and as confirmed in the 1931 Supreme Court case of ***Near v. Minnesota***.

Near v. Minnesota
The 1931 Supreme Court decision holding that the protects newspapers from **prior restraint.**

The extent of an individual's or group's freedom from prior restraint does depend in part, however, on who that individual or group is. Expressions of students in public school may be limited more than those of adults in other settings. In 1988, the Supreme Court ruled that a high school newspaper was not a public forum and could be regulated in "any reasonable manner" by school officials.[33] In 2007, the Court held that the special characteristics of the school environment and the governmental interest in stopping student drug abuse allow schools to restrict student expressions that they reasonably regard as promoting such abuse.[34]

The Supreme Court has also upheld restrictions on the right to publish in the name of national security. Wartime often brings censorship to protect classified information. These restrictions often have public support; few would find it unconstitutional if a newspaper, for example, were hauled into court for publishing troop movement plans during a war. During the Persian Gulf War, reporters could get to the field only in the company of official Pentagon press representatives. Nor have the restrictions upheld been limited to wartime censorship. The national government has successfully sued former CIA agents for failing to meet their contractual obligations to submit books about their work to the agency for censorship, even though the books revealed no classified information.[35]

Nevertheless, the courts are reluctant to issue injunctions prohibiting the publication of material even in the area of national security. The most famous case regarding prior restraint and national security involved the publication of stolen Pentagon papers. You can examine this case in "You Are the Judge: The Case of the Purloined Pentagon Papers."

Free Speech and Public Order

In wartime and peacetime, considerable conflict has arisen over the trade-off between free speech and the need for public order. During World War I, Charles T. Schenck, the secretary of the American Socialist Party, distributed thousands of leaflets urging young men to resist the draft. Schenck was charged with impeding the war effort. The Supreme Court upheld his conviction in 1919 (***Schenck v. United States***). Justice Holmes declared that government could limit speech if it provokes a clear and present danger of substantive evils. Only when such danger exists can government restrain speech. It is difficult to say, of course, when speech becomes dangerous rather than simply inconvenient for the government.

Schenck v. United States
A 1919 decision upholding the conviction of a socialist who had urged young men to resist the draft during World War I. Justice Holmes declared that government can limit speech if the speech provokes a "clear and present danger" of substantive evils.

The courts confronted the issue of free speech and public order during the 1950s. In the late 1940s and early 1950s, there was widespread fear that communists had infiltrated the government. American anticommunism was a powerful force, and the national government was determined to jail the leaders of the Communist Party. Senator Joseph McCarthy and others in Congress persecuted people whom they thought were subversive, based on the Smith Act of 1940, which forbade advocating the violent overthrow of the American government. In *Dennis v. United States* (1951), the Supreme Court upheld prison sentences for several Communist Party leaders for conspiring to advocate the violent overthrow of the government—even in the absence of evidence that they actually urged people to commit specific acts of violence. Although the activities of this tiny, unpopular group resembled

YOU ARE THE JUDGE

The Case of the Purloined Pentagon Papers

During the Johnson administration, the Department of Defense amassed an elaborate secret history of American involvement in the Vietnam War that included hundreds of documents, many of them secret cables, memos, and war plans. Many documented American ineptitude and South Vietnamese duplicity. One former Pentagon official, Daniel Ellsberg, who had become disillusioned with the Vietnam War, managed to retain access to a copy of these Pentagon papers. Hoping that revelations of the Vietnam quagmire would help end American involvement, he decided to leak the Pentagon papers to the *New York Times*.

The Nixon administration pulled out all the stops in its effort to embarrass Ellsberg and prevent publication of the Pentagon papers. Nixon's chief domestic affairs adviser, John Ehrlichman, approved a burglary of Ellsberg's psychiatrist's office, hoping to find damaging information on Ellsberg. (The burglary was bungled, and it eventually led to Ehrlichman's conviction and imprisonment.) In the courts, Nixon administration lawyers sought an injunction against the *Times* that would have ordered it to cease publication of the secret documents. Government lawyers argued that national security was being breached and that Ellsberg had stolen the documents from the government. The *Times* argued that its freedom to publish would be violated if an injunction were granted. In 1971, the case of *New York Times v. United States* was decided by the Supreme Court.

You be the judge: Did the *Times* have a right to publish secret, stolen Department of Defense documents?

Decision: In a 6-to-3 decision, a majority of the justices agreed that the "no prior restraint" rule prohibited prosecution before the papers were published. The justices also made it clear that if the government brought prosecution for theft, the Court might be sympathetic. No such charges were filed.

yelling "Fire!" in an empty theater rather than a crowded one, the Court ruled that a communist takeover was so grave a danger that government could squelch their threat. Thus, it concluded that protecting national security outweighed First Amendment rights.

The prevailing political climate often determines what limits the government will place on free speech. During the early 1950s, Senator Joseph McCarthy's persuasive—if unproven—accusations that many public officials were communists created an atmosphere in which the courts placed restrictions on freedom of expression—restrictions that would be unacceptable today.

Soon the political climate changed, however, and the Court narrowed the interpretation of the Smith Act, making it more difficult to prosecute dissenters. In later years, the Court has found that it is permissible to advocate the violent overthrow of the government in the abstract but not actually to incite anyone to imminent lawless action (*Yates v. United States* [1957]; *Brandenburg v. Ohio* [1969]).

The 1960s brought waves of protest over political, economic, racial, and social issues and, especially, the Vietnam War. Many people in more recent times have engaged in public demonstrations, such as those opposing the war in Iraq. Courts have been quite supportive of the right to protest, pass out leaflets, or gather signatures on petitions—as long as it is done in public places. People may even distribute campaign literature anonymously.[36] Constitutional protections diminish once a person steps on private property, such as most shopping centers. The Supreme Court has held that federal free speech guarantees did not apply when a person was on private property.[37] However, it upheld a state's power to include politicking in shopping centers within its own free speech guarantee,[38] and in 1994, the Supreme Court ruled that cities cannot bar residents from posting signs on their own property.[39]

Obscenity

Obscenity is one of the more perplexing of free speech issues. In 1957, The Supreme Court held that "obscenity is not within the area of constitutionally protected speech or press"

(***Roth v. United States***). Deciding what is obscene, however, has never been an easy matter. Obviously, public standards vary from time to time, place to place, and person to person. Much of today's MTV would have been banned only a few decades ago. What might be acceptable in Manhattan's Greenwich Village would shock residents of some other areas of the country. Works that some people call obscene might be good entertainment or even great art to others. At one time or another, the works of Aristophanes, Mark Twain, and even the "Tarzan" stories by Edgar Rice Burroughs were banned. The state of Georgia banned the acclaimed film *Carnal Knowledge (*a ban the Supreme Court struck down in 1974).[40]

The Court tried to clarify its doctrine by spelling out what could be classified as obscene and thus outside First Amendment protection in the 1973 case of ***Miller v. California***. Warren Burger, chief justice at the time, wrote that materials were obscene under the following circumstances:

1. The work, taken as a whole, appealed "to a prurient interest in sex."
2. The work showed "patently offensive" sexual conduct that was specifically defined by an obscenity law.
3. The work, taken as a whole, lacked "serious literary, artistic, political, or scientific value."

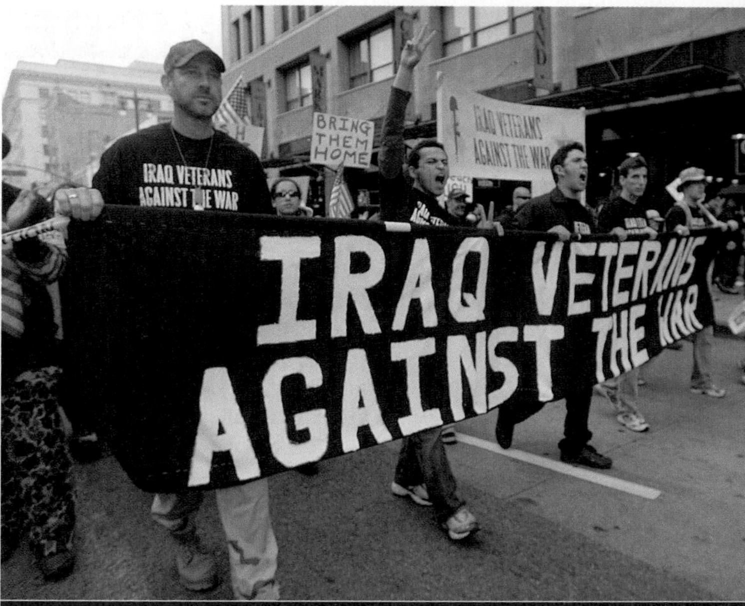

Free speech sometimes conflicts with public order. The Constitution protects the rights of protestors, such as those pictured here opposing the war with Iraq, to have their say.

Roth v. United States
A 1957 Supreme Court decision ruling that "obscenity is not within the area of constitutionally protected speech or press."

Miller v. California
A 1973 Supreme Court decision that avoided defining obscenity by holding that community standards be used to determine whether material is obscene in terms of appealing to a "prurient interest" and being "patently offensive" and lacking in value.

Decisions regarding whether material was obscene, said the Court, should be based on average people (in other words, juries) applying the contemporary standards of local—not national—communities.

The Court did provide "a few plain examples" of what sort of material might fall within this definition of obscenity. Among these examples were "patently offensive representations of ultimate sexual acts . . . actual or simulated," "patently offensive representations of masturbation or excretory functions," or "lewd exhibition of the genitals." Cities throughout the country duplicated the language of *Miller* in their obscenity ordinances. The qualifying adjectives *lewd* and *offensive* prevent communities from banning anatomy texts, for example, as obscene. The difficulty remains in determining what is *lewd* or *offensive*.

In addition to the difficulty in defining obscenity, another reason why obscenity convictions can be difficult to obtain is that no nationwide consensus exists that offensive material should be banned—at least not when it is restricted to adults. In many communities the laws are lenient regarding pornography, and prosecutors know that they may not get a jury to convict, even when the disputed material is obscene as defined by *Miller*. Thus, obscene material is widely available in adult bookstores, video stores, and movie theaters.

Despite the Court's best efforts to define obscenity and determine when it can be banned, state and local governments continue to struggle with the application of these rulings. In one famous case, a small New Jersey town tried to get rid of a nude dancing parlor by using its zoning power to ban all live entertainment. The Court held that the measure was too broad, restricting too much expression, and thus unlawful.[41] However, the Court has upheld laws specifically banning nude dancing when their effect on overall expression was minimal.[42] Jacksonville, Florida, tried to ban drive-in movies containing nudity. You can examine the Court's reaction in "You Are the Judge: The Case of the Drive-in Theater."

Regulations aimed at keeping obscene material away from the young, who are considered more vulnerable to its harmful influences, have wide support, and courts have consistently ruled that states may protect children from obscenity. The rating

YOU ARE THE JUDGE

The Case of the Drive-in Theater

Almost everyone concedes that *sometimes* obscenity should be banned by public authorities. One instance might be when a person's right to show pornographic movies clashes with another's right to privacy. Presumably, no one wants hard-core pornography shown in public places where schoolchildren might see it. Showing dirty movies in an enclosed theater or in the privacy of your own living room is one thing. Showing them in public is something else. Or is it?

The city of Jacksonville, Florida, wanted to limit the showing of certain kinds of movies at drive-in theaters. Its city council reasoned that drive-ins were public places and that drivers passing by would be involuntarily exposed to movies they might prefer not to see. Some members of the council argued that drivers distracted by steamy scenes might even cause accidents. So the council passed a local ordinance forbidding movies showing nudity (defined in the ordinance as "bare buttocks . . . female bare breasts, or human bare pubic areas") at drive-in theaters.

Arrested for violating the ordinance, a Mr. Erznoznik challenged the constitutionality of the ordinance. He claimed that the law was overly broad and banned nudity, not obscenity. The lawyers for the city insisted that the law was acceptable under the First Amendment. The government, they claimed, had a responsibility to forbid a "public nuisance," especially one that might cause a traffic hazard.

You be the judge: Did Jacksonville's ban on nudity in movies at drive-ins go too far, or was it a constitutional limit on free speech?

Decision: In *Erznoznik v. Jacksonville* (1975), the Supreme Court held that Jacksonville's ordinance was unconstitutionally broad. The city council had gone too far; it could end up banning movies that might not be obscene. The ordinance would, said the Court, ban a film "containing a picture of a baby's buttocks, the nude body of a war victim or scenes from a culture where nudity is indigenous." Said Justice Powell for the Court, "Clearly, all nudity cannot be deemed obscene."

scheme of the Motion Picture Association of America is one example, as is the more recent TV ratings system. Also strongly supported are laws designed to protect the young against pornographic exploitation. It is a violation of federal law to receive sexually explicit photographs of children through the mail or over the Internet, and in 1990 the Supreme Court upheld Ohio's law forbidding the possession of child pornography.[43]

Advances in technology have created a new wrinkle in the obscenity issue. The Internet and the World Wide Web make it easier to distribute obscene material rapidly, and a number of online information services have taken advantage of this opportunity. In 1996, Congress passed the Communications Decency Act, banning obscene material and criminalizing the transmission of indecent speech or images to anyone under 18 years of age. This law made no exception for material that has serious literary, artistic, political, or scientific merit as outlined in *Miller v. California*, and in 1997, the Supreme Court overturned it as being overly broad and vague and a violation of free speech.[44] In 2002, the Court overturned a law banning virtual child pornography on similar grounds.[45] (Apparently the Supreme Court views the Internet similarly to print media, with similar protections against government regulation.) In 1999, however, the Court upheld prohibitions on obscene e-mail and faxes.

libel
The publication of false or malicious statements that damage someone's reputation.

New York Times v. Sullivan
Decided in 1964, this case established the guidelines for determining whether public officials and other public figures could win damage suits for **libel**. To do so, individuals must prove that the defamatory statements were made with "actual malice" and reckless disregard for the truth.

Libel and Slander

Another type of expression not protected by the First Amendment is **libel**, the publication of false statements that are malicious and damage a person's reputation. *Slander* refers to spoken defamation, whereas libel refers to written defamation.

Of course, if politicians could collect damages for every untrue thing said about them, the right to criticize the government—which the Supreme Court termed "the central meaning of the First Amendment"—would be stifled. No one would dare be critical for fear of making a factual error. To encourage public debate, the Supreme Court has held in cases such as ***New York Times v. Sullivan*** (1964) that statements about public figures are libelous only if made with malice and reckless disregard for the truth. Public figures have to prove to a jury, in effect, that whoever wrote or said untrue statements about them knew that the statements were untrue and intended to harm them. This standard makes libel cases difficult for public figures to win because it is difficult to prove that a publication was intentionally malicious.[46]

Private individuals have a lower standard to meet for winning libel lawsuits. They need show only that statements made about them were defamatory falsehoods and that the author was negligent. Nevertheless, it is unusual for someone to win a libel case, and most people do not wish to draw attention to critical statements about themselves.

If public debate is not free, there can be no democracy, yet in the process of free debate some reputations will be damaged (or at least bruised), sometimes unfairly. Libel cases must thus balance freedom of expression with respect for individual reputations. In one widely publicized case, General William Westmoreland, once the commander of American troops in South Vietnam, sued CBS over a documentary it broadcast called *The Uncounted Enemy*. It claimed that American military leaders in Vietnam, including Westmoreland, systematically lied to Washington about their success there to make it appear that the United States was winning the war. The evidence, including CBS's own internal memoranda, showed that the documentary made errors of fact. Westmoreland sued CBS for libel. Ultimately, the power of the press—in this case, a sloppy, arrogant press—prevailed. Fearing defeat at the trial, Westmoreland settled for a mild apology.[47]

An unusual case that explored the line between parody and libel came before the Supreme Court in 1988, when Reverend Jerry Falwell sued *Hustler* magazine. *Hustler* editor Larry Flynt had printed a parody of a Campari Liquor ad about various celebrities called "First Time" (in which celebrities related the first time they drank Campari, but with an intentional double meaning). When *Hustler* depicted the Reverend Jerry Falwell having had his "first time" in an outhouse with his mother, Falwell sued. He alleged that the ad subjected him to great emotional distress and mental anguish. The case tested the limits to which a publication could go to parody or lampoon a public figure. The Supreme Court ruled that they can go pretty far—all nine justices ruled in favor of the magazine.

Libel Law

It is difficult for public figures to win libel cases. Public figures will likely lose even if they can show that the defendant made defamatory falsehoods about them. This may not be fair, but it is essential for people to feel free to criticize public officials. Fear of losing a lawsuit would have a chilling effect on democratic dialogue.

A POINT TO PONDER

It is easy to take rights for granted and to focus on interests of more immediate concern. Determining the boundaries of freedom has been an ongoing process.

Do you think we will ever have a final statement regarding the protections in the Bill of Rights?

Symbolic Speech

Freedom of speech, more broadly interpreted, is a guarantee of freedom of expression. In 1965, school authorities in Des Moines, Iowa, suspended Mary Beth Tinker and her brother John when they wore black armbands to protest the Vietnam War. The Supreme Court held that the suspension violated the Tinkers' First Amendment rights. The right to freedom of speech, said the Court, went beyond the spoken word.[48]

Texas v. Johnson
A 1989 case in which the Supreme Court struck down a law banning the burning of the American flag on the grounds that such action was symbolic speech protected by the **First Amendment**.

symbolic speech
Nonverbal communication, such as burning a flag or wearing an armband. The Supreme Court has accorded some symbolic speech protection under the **First Amendment**.

When Gregory Johnson set a flag on fire at the 1984 Republican National Convention in Dallas to protest nuclear weapons, the Supreme Court decided that the state law prohibiting flag desecration violated the First Amendment (***Texas v. Johnson*** [1989]). Burning the flag, the Court said, constituted speech and not just dramatic action.[49] When Massachusetts courts ordered the organizers of the annual St. Patrick's Day parade to include the Irish-American Gay, Lesbian, and Bisexual Group of Boston, the Supreme Court declared that a parade is a form of protected speech, and thus that the organizers are free to include or exclude whomever they want.

Wearing an armband, burning a flag, and marching in a parade are examples of **symbolic speech**: actions that do not consist of speaking or writing but that express an opinion. Court decisions have classified these activities somewhere between pure speech and pure action. The doctrine of symbolic speech is not precise; for example, although burning a flag is protected speech, burning a draft card is not.[50] In 2003, the Court held that states may make it a crime to burn a cross with a purpose to intimidate, as long as the law clearly gives prosecutors the burden of proving that the act was intended as a threat and not as a form of symbolic expression.[51] The relevant cases make it clear, however, that First Amendment rights are not limited by a rigid definition of what constitutes speech.

Free Press and Fair Trials

The Bill of Rights is an inexhaustible source of potential conflicts among different types of freedoms. One is the conflict between the right of the press to print what it wants and the right to a fair trial. The quantity of press coverage given to the trial of Michael Jackson on charges of child sexual abuse was extraordinary, and little of it was sympathetic to Jackson. Defense attorneys argue that such publicity can inflame the community—and potential jurors—against defendants and compromise the fairness of a trial. It may very well.

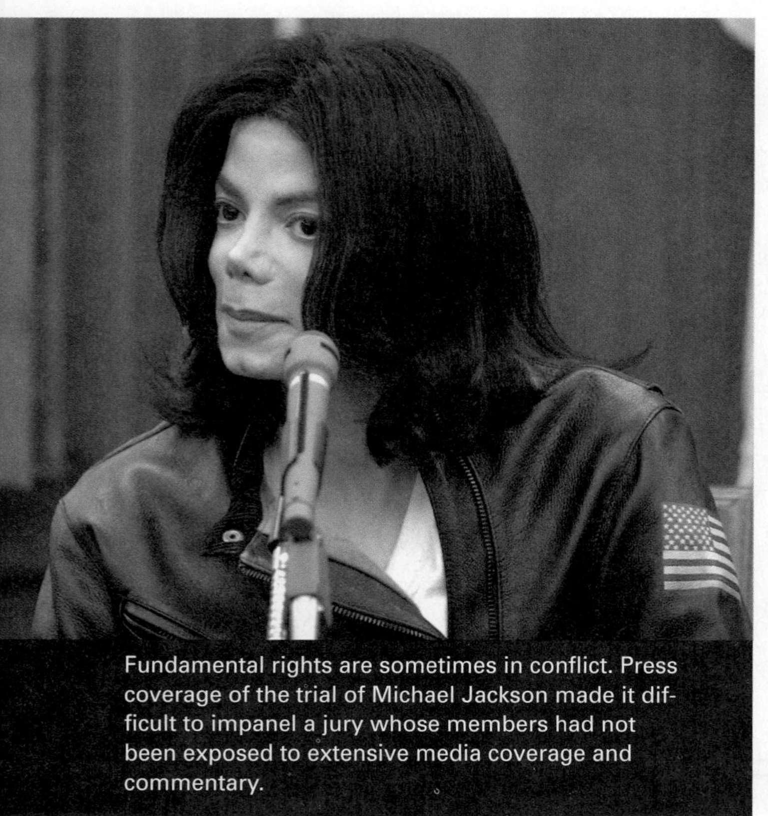
Fundamental rights are sometimes in conflict. Press coverage of the trial of Michael Jackson made it difficult to impanel a jury whose members had not been exposed to extensive media coverage and commentary.

Nevertheless, the Court has *never* upheld a restriction on the press in the interest of a fair trial. The Constitution's guarantee of freedom of the press entitles journalists to cover every trial. When a Nebraska judge issued a gag order forbidding the press to report any details of a particularly gory murder (or even to report the gag order itself), the outraged Nebraska Press Association took the case to the Supreme Court. The Court sided with the editors and revoked the gag order.[52] In 1980, the Court reversed a Virginia judge's order to close a murder trial to the public and the press. "The trial of a criminal case," said the Court, "must be open to the public."[53] A pretrial hearing, though, is a different matter. In a 1979 case, the Supreme Court permitted a closed hearing on the grounds that pretrial publicity might compromise the defendant's right to fairness. Ultimately, the only feasible measure that the judicial system can take against the influence of publicity in high-profile cases is to sequester the jury, thereby isolating it from the media and public opinion.

Occasionally a reporter withholds some critical evidence that either the prosecution or the defense wants in a criminal case, information that may be essential for a fair trial. Reporters argue that "protecting their sources" should exempt them from revealing notes from confidential informants. Some states have passed *shield laws* to protect reporters in these situations. In most states, however, reporters have no more rights than other citizens once a case has come to trial. The Supreme Court ruled in *Branzburg v. Hayes* (1972) that in the absence of shield laws, the right of a fair trial preempts the reporter's right to protect sources. After a violent confrontation with student protestors at Stanford University, the police got a search warrant and marched off to the *Stanford Daily*, which they believed to have pictures of the scene—from which they could make arrests. The paper argued that its files were protected by the First Amendment, but the decision in ***Zurcher v. Stanford Daily*** (1978) sided with the police, not the paper.

Zurcher v. Stanford Daily
A 1978 Supreme Court decision holding that a proper search warrant could be applied to a newspaper as well as to anyone else without necessarily violating the **First Amendment** rights to freedom of the press.

Commercial Speech

Not all forms of communication receive the full protection of the First Amendment. Laws restrict **commercial speech**, such as advertising, far more extensively than expressions of opinion on religious, political, or other matters. The Federal Trade Commission (FTC) decides what kinds of goods may be advertised on radio and television and regulates the content of such advertising. These regulations have responded to changes in social mores and priorities. Thirty years ago, for example, tampons could not be advertised on TV, whereas cigarette commercials were everywhere. Today, the situation is just the reverse.

commercial speech
Communication in the form of advertising. It can be restricted more than many other types of speech but has been receiving increased protection from the Supreme Court.

The FTC attempts to ensure that advertisers do not make false claims for their products, but "truth" in advertising does not prevent misleading promises. For example, when ads imply that the right mouthwash or deodorant will improve one's love life, that dubious message is perfectly legal.

Nevertheless, laws may regulate commercial speech on the airwaves in ways that would clearly be impossible in the political or religious realm—even to the point of forcing a manufacturer to say certain words. For example, the makers of Excedrin pain reliever were forced to add the words "on pain other than headache" in their commercials describing tests that supposedly supported the product's claims of superior effectiveness. (The test results were based on the pain that women experienced after giving birth.)

Although commercial speech is regulated more rigidly than other types of speech, the courts have been broadening its protection under the Constitution. For years, many states had laws that prohibited advertising for professional services—such as legal and engineering services—and for certain products ranging from eyeglasses and prescription drugs to condoms and abortions. Advocates of these laws claimed that they were designed to protect consumers against misleading claims, while critics charged that the laws prevented price competition. In recent years, the courts have struck down many such restrictions as violations of freedom of speech. In 1999, the Supreme Court overturned restrictions on advertising casino gambling in states where such gambling is legal.[54] In general, the Supreme Court has allowed the regulation of commercial speech when the speech concerns unlawful activity or is misleading, but otherwise regulations must advance a substantial government interest and be no more extensive than necessary to serve that interest.[55]

Regulation of the Public Airwaves

The Federal Communications Commission (FCC) regulates the content, nature, and very existence of radio and television broadcasting. Although newspapers do not need licenses, radio and television stations do. A licensed station must comply with regulations, including the requirement that it devote a certain percentage of broadcast time to public service, news, children's programming, political candidates, or views other than those its owners support. The rules are more relaxed for cable channels, which can specialize in a particular type of broadcasting because consumers pay for, and thus have more choice about, the service.

This sort of governmental interference would clearly violate the First Amendment if it were imposed on the print media. For example, the state of Florida passed

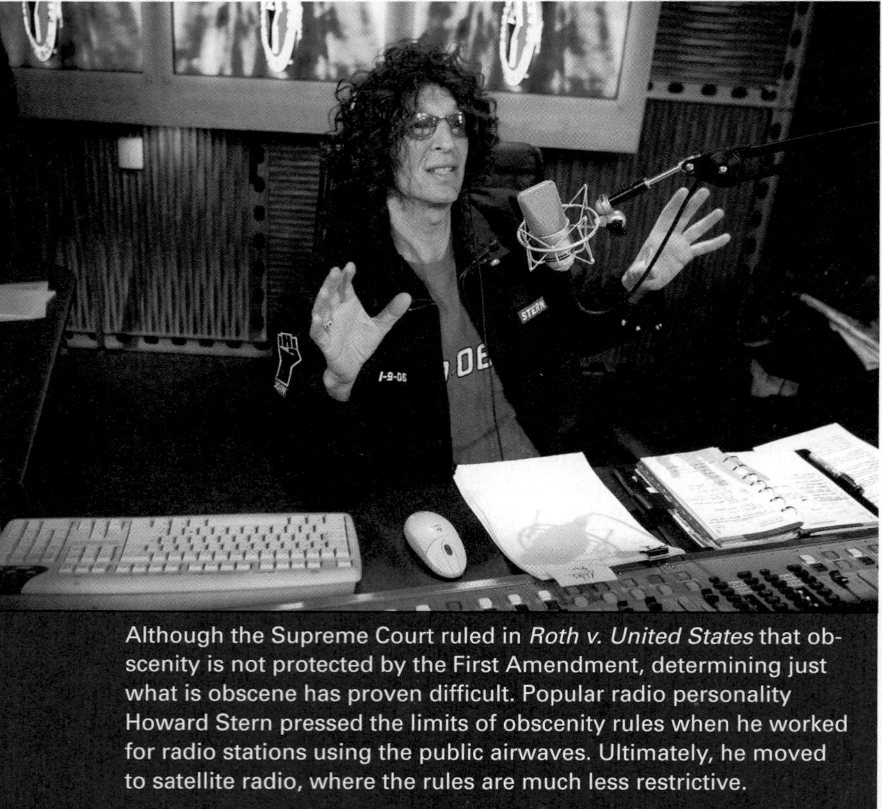

Although the Supreme Court ruled in *Roth v. United States* that obscenity is not protected by the First Amendment, determining just what is obscene has proven difficult. Popular radio personality Howard Stern pressed the limits of obscenity rules when he worked for radio stations using the public airwaves. Ultimately, he moved to satellite radio, where the rules are much less restrictive.

a law requiring newspapers in the state to provide space for political candidates to reply to newspaper criticisms. The Supreme Court, without hesitation, voided this law (***Miami Herald Publishing Company v. Tornillo*** [1974]). Earlier, in ***Red Lion Broadcasting Company v. Federal Communications Commission*** (1969), the Court upheld similar restrictions on radio and television stations, reasoning that such laws were justified because only a limited number of broadcast frequencies were available.

One FCC rule regulating the content of programs restricts the use of obscene words. Comedian George Carlin had a famous routine called "Filthy Words" that could never be said over the airwaves. A New York City radio station tested Carlin's assertion by airing his routine. The ensuing events proved Carlin right. In 1978, the Supreme Court upheld the commission's policy of barring these words from radio or television when children might hear them.[56] Similarly, the FCC twice fined New York radio personality Howard Stern $600,000 for indecency. It is especially interesting to note that if Stern's commentaries had been carried by cable or satellite instead of the airwaves, he could have expressed himself with impunity. (In 2006, he made the move to satellite transmission.)

Miami Herald Publishing Company v. Tornillo
A 1974 case in which the Supreme Court held that a state could not force a newspaper to print replies from candidates it had criticized, illustrating the limited power of government to restrict the print media.

Red Lion Broadcasting Company v. Federal Communications Commission
A 1969 case in which the Supreme Court upheld restrictions on radio and television broadcasting. These restrictions on the broadcast media are much tighter than those on the print media because there are only a limited number of broadcasting frequencies available.

Technological change has blurred the line between broadcasting and private communications between individuals. With cable television now in most American homes, the Supreme Court is faced with ruling on the application of free speech guidelines to cable broadcasting.

Federal law requires cable television operators providing channels "primarily dedicated to sexually oriented programming" either to "fully scramble or otherwise fully block" those channels or to limit their transmission to hours when children are unlikely to be viewing, set by administrative regulation as between 10:00 P.M. and 6:00 A.M. The Playboy Entertainment Group pointed out that banning transmission restricts sexually oriented programming even to households without children. It challenged the law as an unconstitutional violation of the First Amendment free speech guarantee, arguing that Congress had less restrictive ways to accomplish its goals. In *United States v. Playboy Entertainment Group* (2000), the Supreme Court agreed. It held that although government had a legitimate right to regulate sexually oriented programming, any such regulation must be narrowly tailored to promote a compelling government interest. If a less restrictive alternative would serve the government's purpose, Congress must use that alternative. The Court concluded that targeted blocking, in which subscribers can ask their cable companies to block a signal to their homes, is less restrictive than banning and is a feasible and effective means of furthering its compelling interests. Thus, the more restrictive option of banning a signal for most of the day cannot be justified.

4.4 Describe the rights to assemble and associate protected by the First Amendment and their limitations.

Freedom of Assembly

The last of the great rights guaranteed by the First Amendment is the freedom to "peaceably assemble." Commentators often neglect this freedom in favor of the more trumpeted freedoms of speech, press, and religion, yet it is the basis for forming interest groups, political parties, and professional associations as well as for picketing and protesting.

Right to Assemble

There are two facets of the freedom of assembly. First is the literal right to assemble—that is, to gather together in order to make a statement. This freedom can conflict with other societal values when it disrupts public order, traffic flow, peace and quiet, or bystanders' freedom to go about their business without interference. Within reasonable limits, called *time, place,* and *manner restrictions*, freedom of assembly includes the rights to parade, picket, and protest. Whatever a group's cause, it has the right to demonstrate, but no group can simply hold a spontaneous demonstration anytime, anywhere, and anyway it chooses. Usually, a group must apply to the local city government for a permit and post a bond of a few hundred dollars—a little like making a security deposit on an apartment. The governing body must grant a permit as long as the group pledges to hold its demonstration at a time and place that allows the police to prevent major disruptions. There are virtually no limitations on the content of a group's message. One important case arose when the American Nazi Party applied to march in the streets of Skokie, Illinois, a Chicago suburb with a sizable Jewish population, including many survivors of Hitler's death camps. You can examine the Court's decision in "You Are the Judge: The Case of the Nazis' March in Skokie."

Protest that verges on harassment tests the balance between freedom and order. Protestors lined up outside abortion clinics have been a common sight. Members of groups such as "Operation Rescue" try to shame clients into staying away and may harass them if they do visit a clinic. Rights are in conflict in such cases: A woman seeking to terminate her pregnancy has the right to obtain an abortion; the demonstrators have the right to protest the very existence of the clinic. The courts have acted to restrain these protestors, setting limits on how close they may come to the clinics and upholding damage claims of clients against the protestors. In one case, pro-life demonstrators in a Milwaukee, Wisconsin, suburb paraded outside the home of a physician who was reported to perform abortions. The town board forbade future picketing in residential neighborhoods. In 1988, the Supreme Court agreed that the right of residential privacy was a legitimate local concern and upheld the ordinance.[57] In 1994, Congress passed a law enacting broad new penalties against abortion protestors.

NAACP v. Alabama
The Supreme Court protected the right to assemble peaceably in this 1958 case when it decided the NAACP did not have to reveal its membership list and thus subject its members to harassment.

Right to Associate

The second facet of freedom of assembly is the right to associate with people who share a common interest, including an interest in political change. In a famous case at the height of the civil rights movement, Alabama tried to harass the state chapter of the National Association for the Advancement of Colored People (NAACP) by requiring it to turn over its membership list. The Court found this demand an unconstitutional restriction on freedom of association (***NAACP v. Alabama*** [1958]).

In 2006, some law schools argued that congressional legislation that in effect required them to grant military recruiters access to their students violated the schools' freedoms of speech and association. The Supreme Court concluded that the law regulates conduct, not speech. In addition, nothing about recruiting suggests that law schools agree with any speech by recruiters, and nothing in the law restricts what they may say about the military's policies. Nor does the law force a law school to accept members it does not desire, and students and faculty are free to voice their disapproval of the military's message.[58]

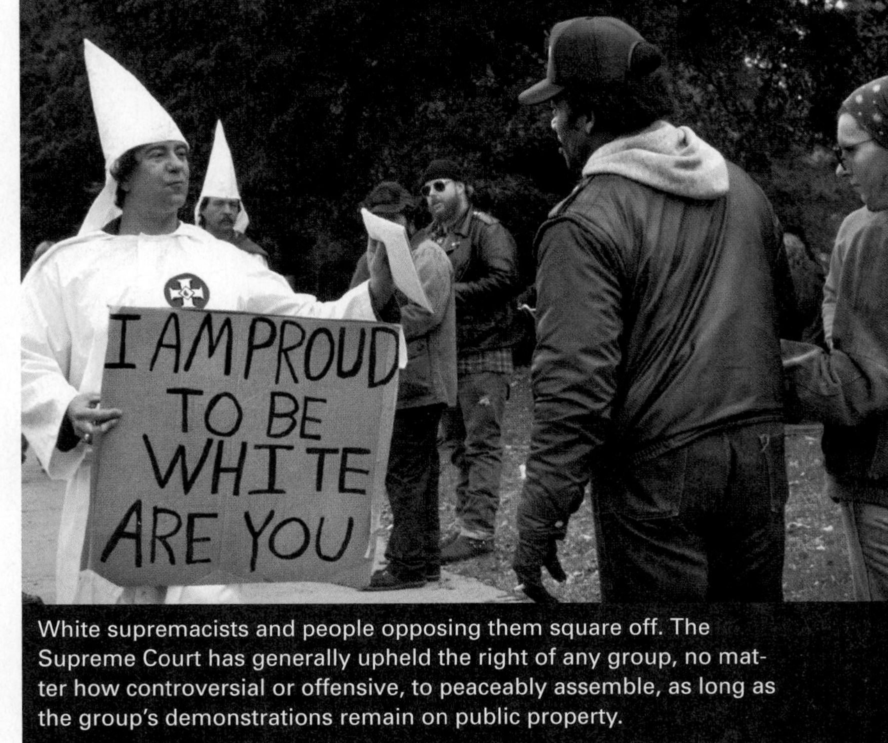

White supremacists and people opposing them square off. The Supreme Court has generally upheld the right of any group, no matter how controversial or offensive, to peaceably assemble, as long as the group's demonstrations remain on public property.

YOU ARE THE JUDGE

The Case of the Nazis' March in Skokie

Hitler's Nazis slaughtered 6 million Jews in death camps like Bergen-Belsen, Auschwitz, and Dachau. Many of the survivors migrated to the United States, and thousands settled in Skokie, Illinois, a suburb just north of Chicago with a heavily Jewish population.

The American Nazi Party in the Skokie area was a ragtag group of perhaps 25 to 30 members. Its headquarters was a storefront building on the West Side of Chicago, near an area with an expanding African American population. After Chicago denied them a permit to march in an African American neighborhood, the American Nazis announced their intention to march in Skokie. Skokie's city government required that they post a $300,000 bond to obtain a parade permit. The Nazis claimed that the high bond was set in order to prevent their march and that it infringed on their freedoms of speech and assembly. The American Civil Liberties Union (ACLU), despite its loathing of the Nazis, defended the Nazis' claim and their right to march. The ACLU lost half its Illinois membership because it took this position.

You be the judge: Do Nazis have the right to parade, preach anti-Jewish propaganda, and perhaps provoke violence in a community peopled with survivors of the Holocaust? What rights or obligations does a community have to maintain order?

Decision: A federal district court ruled that Skokie's ordinance did restrict freedom of assembly and association. No community could use its power to grant parade permits to stifle free expression. In *Collins v. Smith* (Collins was the Nazi leader, and Smith was the mayor of Skokie), the Supreme Court let this lower-court decision stand. In fact, the Nazis did not march in Skokie, settling instead for some poorly attended demonstrations in Chicago.

A POINT TO PONDER

In its humorous way, this cartoon shows that constitutional rights are sometimes in conflict.

Is there any way to prioritize our basic rights?

"The way I see it, the Constitution cuts both ways. The First Amendment gives you the right to say what you want, but the Second Amendment gives me the right to shoot you for it."

Right to Bear Arms

4.5 Describe the right to bear arms protected by the Second Amendment and its limitations.

Few issues generate as much controversy as gun control. In an attempt to control gun violence, many communities have passed restrictions on owning and carrying handguns. National and state and local laws have also mandated background checks for gun buyers and limited the sale of certain types of weapons altogether. Yet other laws have required that guns be stored in a fashion to prevent their theft or children from accessing and firing them. Some groups, most notably the National Rifle Association, have invested millions of dollars to fight almost all gun control efforts, arguing that they violate the Second Amendment's guarantee of a right to bear arms. Many advocates of gun control argue that the Second Amendment apply only to the right of states to create militias. Surprisingly, the Supreme Court has rarely dealt with gun control.

In 2008, however, the Court directly faced the issue. A law in the District of Columbia restricted residents from owning handguns, excluding those registered prior to 1975 and those possessed by active and retired law enforcement officers. The law also required that all lawfully owned firearms, including rifles and shotguns, be unloaded and disassembled or bound by a trigger lock or similar device. The Supreme Court in *District of Columbia v. Heller* (2008) held that the Second Amendment protects an individual right to possess a firearm unconnected with service in a militia, and to use that arm for traditionally lawful purposes, such as self-defense within the home. Similarly, the requirement that any lawful firearm in the home be disassembled or bound by a trigger lock is unconstitutional because it makes it impossible for citizens to use arms for the core lawful purpose of self-defense. In 2010 in *McDonald v. Chicago*, the Court extended the Second Amendment's limits on restricting an individual's right to bear arms to state and local gun control laws.

Nevertheless, like most rights, the Second Amendment right is not unlimited. It is not a right to keep and carry any weapon whatsoever in any manner whatsoever and for whatever purpose. For example, prohibitions on concealed weapons are permissible, as are limits on the possession of firearms by felons and the mentally ill, laws forbidding the carrying of firearms in sensitive places such as schools and government buildings, laws imposing conditions and qualifications on the commercial sale of arms, and laws restricting "dangerous and unusual weapons" that are not typically used for self-defense or recreation.

Defendants' Rights

4.6 Characterize defendants' rights and identify issues that arise in their implementation.

The Bill of Rights contains only 45 words that guarantee the freedoms of religion, speech, press, and assembly. Most of the remaining words concern the rights of people accused of crimes. The Founders intended these rights to protect the accused in *political* arrests and trials; British abuse of colonial political leaders was still fresh in the memory of American citizens. Today the courts apply the protections in the Fourth, Fifth, Sixth, Seventh, and Eighth Amendments mostly in criminal justice cases.

It is useful to think of the stages of the criminal justice system as a series of funnels decreasing in size. Generally speaking, a *crime* is (sometimes) followed by an *arrest*, which is (sometimes) followed by a *prosecution*, which is (sometimes) followed by a *trial*, which (usually) results in a *verdict* of innocence or guilt. The funnels get smaller and smaller, each dripping into the next. Many more crimes occur than are reported, many more crimes are reported than arrests are made (the ratio is about five to one), many more arrests are made than prosecutors prosecute, and many more prosecutions occur than jury trials. At each stage of the criminal justice system, the Constitution protects the rights of the accused (see Table 4.3).

Interpreting Defendants' Rights

The language of the Bill of Rights comes from the late 1700s and is often vague. For example, just how speedy is a "speedy trial"? How "cruel and unusual" does a punishment have to be in order to violate the Eighth Amendment? The courts continually must rule

TABLE 4.3 The Constitution and the Stages of the Criminal Justice System

Although our criminal justice system is complex, it can be broken down into stages. The Constitution protects the rights of the accused at every stage.

STAGE	PROTECTIONS
1. Evidence gathered	"Unreasonable search and seizure" forbidden (Fourth Amendment)
2. Suspicion cast	Guarantee that "writ of habeas corpus" will not be suspended, forbidding imprisonment without evidence (Article I, Section 9)
3. Arrest made	Right to have the "assistance of counsel" (Sixth Amendment)
4. Interrogation held	Forced self-incrimination forbidden (Fifth Amendment); "Excessive bail" forbidden (Eighth Amendment)
5. Trial held	"Speedy and public trial" by an impartial jury required (Sixth Amendment); "Double jeopardy" (being tried twice for the same crime) forbidden (Fifth Amendment); Trial by jury required (Article III, Section 2) Right to confront witnesses (Sixth Amendment)
6. Punishment imposed	"Cruel and unusual punishment" forbidden (Eighth Amendment)

on the constitutionality of actions by police, prosecutors, judges, and legislatures—actions that a citizen or group could claim violate certain rights. Defendants' rights, just like those rights protected by the First Amendment, are not clearly defined in the Bill of Rights.

One thing is clear, however. The Supreme Court's decisions have extended specific provisions of the Bill of Rights—one by one—to the states as part of the general process of incorporation we discussed earlier. Virtually all the rights we discuss in the following sections affect the actions of both national and state authorities.

Searches and Seizures

Police cannot arrest a citizen without reason. They need evidence to arrest, and courts need evidence to convict. Before making an arrest, police need what the courts call **probable cause**, reasonable grounds to believe that someone is guilty of a crime. Often police need to get physical evidence—a car thief's fingerprints, a snatched purse—to use in court. The Fourth Amendment forbids **unreasonable searches and seizures**. To prevent abuse of police power, the Constitution requires that no court issue a **search warrant** unless probable cause exists to believe that a crime has occurred or is about to occur. These written warrants must specify the area to be searched and the material sought in the police search.

probable cause
The situation occurring when the police have reason to believe that a person should be arrested. In making the arrest, police are allowed legally to search for and seize incriminating evidence.

unreasonable searches and seizures
Obtaining evidence in a haphazard or random manner, a practice prohibited by the Fourth Amendment. Probable cause and/or a search warrant are required for a legal and proper search for and seizure of incriminating evidence.

search warrant
A written authorization from a court specifying the area to be searched and what the police are searching for.

A warrant is not a constitutional requirement for a reasonable police search, however. Most searches in this country take place without warrants. Such searches are valid if probable cause of a crime exists, if the search is necessary to protect an officer's safety, or if the search is limited to material relevant to the suspected crime or within the suspect's immediate control. The Supreme Court has also held that police may enter a home without a warrant when they have an objectively reasonable basis for believing that an occupant is seriously injured or imminently threatened with such injury.[59]

The Supreme Court has upheld aerial searches to secure key evidence in cases involving marijuana growing and environmental violations, roadside checkpoints in which police randomly examine drivers for signs of intoxication,[60] the use of narcotics-detecting dogs at a routine stop for speeding,[61] and the search of a passenger and car following a routine check of the car's registration.[62] The Court also has approved warrantless "hot pursuit" of criminal suspects; warrantless car stops and "stop-and-frisk" encounters with passengers and pedestrians based on reasonable suspicion (not probable cause) of criminal activity; and mandatory drug testing of transportation workers and high school athletes with no individualized suspicion at all. Searches of K–12 students require only that there be a reasonable chance of finding evidence of wrongdoing, rather than the higher standard of probable cause.[63]

However, some decisions offer more protection against searches. The Court has held that although officers may order a driver and passengers out of a car while issuing a traffic citation and may search for weapons to protect themselves from danger, they cannot search a car if there is no threat to the officer's safety.[64] In 2009, the Court decided that the police may search a vehicle incident to an arrest only if it is reasonable to believe the arrestee might access the vehicle at the time of the search (to obtain a weapon or destroy evidence, for example) or that the vehicle contains evidence of the offense of arrest. They cannot search vehicles for evidence of other crimes.[65] Similarly, the Supreme Court prohibited highway checkpoints designed to detect ordinary criminal wrongdoing, such as possessing illegal drugs,[66] and it ruled that an anonymous tip that a person is carrying a gun is not sufficient justification for a police officer to stop and frisk that person.[67] In addition, the Court found that police use of a thermal imaging device to detect abnormal heat (needed for growing marijuana) in a home violated the Fourth Amendment.[68]

Since 1914, the Supreme Court has used an **exclusionary rule** to weigh evidence in criminal cases. This rule prevents prosecutors from introducing illegally seized evidence in court, but until 1961 it applied only to the federal government. The Supreme Court broadened the application in the case of a Cleveland woman named Dollree Mapp, who was under suspicion for illegal gambling activities. The police broke into her home looking for a fugitive, and while there, they searched the house and found a cache of obscene materials. Mapp was convicted of possessing them. She appealed her case to the federal courts, claiming that the exclusionary rule should be made a part of the Fourth Amendment. Since the local police had no probable cause to search for obscene materials—only for materials related to gambling—she argued, the evidence should not be used against her. In an important decision (***Mapp v. Ohio*** [1961]), the Supreme Court ruled that the evidence had been seized illegally, and the Court reversed Mapp's conviction. Since then, the exclusionary rule has been part of the Fourth Amendment and has been incorporated within the rights that restrict the states, as well as the federal government.

exclusionary rule
The rule that evidence cannot be introduced into a trial if it was not constitutionally obtained. The rule prohibits use of evidence obtained through **unreasonable search and seizure.**

Mapp v. Ohio
The 1961 Supreme Court decision ruling that the **Fourth Amendment's** protection against **unreasonable searches and seizures** must be extended to the states.

Critics of the exclusionary rule, including some Supreme Court justices, argue that its strict application may permit guilty persons to go free because of police carelessness or innocent errors. The guilty, they say, should not go free because of a "technicality." Supporters of the exclusionary rule respond that the Constitution is not a technicality and that—because everyone is presumed innocent until proven guilty—defendants' rights protect the *accused*, not the guilty. You can examine one contemporary search-and-seizure case in "You Are the Judge: The Case of Ms. Montoya."

The Exclusionary Rule

The exclusionary rule, in which courts disregard evidence obtained illegally, has been controversial. Although critics view the rule as a technicality that helps criminals to avoid justice, this rule protects defendants (who have not been proven guilty) from abuses of police power.

Beginning in the 1980s, the Court has made some exceptions to the exclusionary rule, including allowing the use of illegally obtained evidence when this evidence led police to a discovery that they eventually would have made without it.[69] The justices also decided to establish the good-faith exception to the rule; evidence can be used if the police who seized it mistakenly thought they were operating under a constitutionally valid warrant.[70] In 1995, the Court held that the exclusionary rule does not bar evidence obtained illegally as the result of clerical errors.[71] In 2006, it held that a police violation of the knock-and-announce rule was not a justification for suppressing the evidence they found upon entry with a warrant.[72] The Court even allowed evidence illegally obtained from a banker to be used to convict one of his customers.[73] In a 2009 decision, *Herring v. United States*, the Court made it clear that to trigger the exclusionary rule, police conduct must be sufficiently deliberate that the exclusion of evidence can meaningfully deter it. The rule does not apply when there is isolated negligence rather than systemic error or reckless disregard of constitutional requirements.

The War on Terrorism. The *USA Patriot Act*, passed just six weeks after the September 11, 2001, terrorist attacks, gave the government broad new powers for the wiretapping, surveillance, and investigation of terrorism suspects. Attorney General John Ashcroft also eased restrictions on domestic spying in counterterrorism operations,

YOU ARE THE JUDGE

The Case of Ms. Montoya

Rosa Elvira Montoya de Hernandez arrived at the Los Angeles International Airport on Avianca Flight 080 from Bogotá, Colombia. Her first official encounter was with U.S. Customs inspector Talamantes, who noticed that she spoke no English. Interestingly, Montoya's passport indicated eight recent quick trips from Bogotá to Los Angeles. She had $5,000 in cash but no pocketbook or credit cards.

Talamantes and his fellow customs officers were suspicious. Stationed in Los Angeles, they were hardly unaware of the fact that Colombia was a major drug supplier. They questioned Montoya, who explained that her husband had a store in Bogotá and that she planned to spend the $5,000 at Kmart and JC Penney, stocking up on items for the store.

The inspector, somewhat wary, handed Montoya over to female customs inspectors for a search. These agents noticed what the Supreme Court later referred to delicately as a "firm fullness" in Montoya's abdomen. Suspicions, already high, increased. The agents applied for a court order to conduct pregnancy tests, X-rays, and other examinations, and eventually they found 88 balloons containing 80 percent pure cocaine in Montoya's alimentary canal.

Montoya's lawyer argued that this constituted unreasonable search and seizure and that her arrest and conviction should be set aside. There was, he said, no direct evidence that would have led the officials to suspect cocaine smuggling. The government argued that the arrest had followed from a set of odd facts leading to reasonable suspicion that something was amiss.

You be the judge: Was Montoya's arrest based on a search-and-seizure incident that violated the Fourth Amendment?

Decision: The Supreme Court held that U.S. Customs agents were well within their constitutional authority to search Montoya. Even though collection of evidence took the better part of two days, Justice Rehnquist, the opinion's author, remarked wryly that "the rudimentary knowledge of the human body which judges possess in common with the rest of mankind tells us that alimentary canal smuggling cannot be detected in the amount of time in which other illegal activities may be investigated through brief . . . stops."

allowing agents to monitor political or religious groups without any connection to a criminal investigation. The Patriot Act gave the federal government the power to examine a terrorist suspect's records held by third parties, such as doctors, libraries, bookstores, universities, and Internet service providers. It also allowed searches of private property without probable cause and without notice to the owner until after the search has been executed, limiting a person's opportunities to challenge a search. Congress reauthorized the law in 2006 with few changes.

In December 2005, reports revealed that President George W. Bush had ordered the National Security Agency, without the court-approved warrants ordinarily required for domestic spying, to monitor the international telephone calls and e-mail messages of people inside the United States. In 2008, Congress overhauled the nation's surveillance law, the Foreign Intelligence Surveillance Act, allowing officials to use broad warrants to eavesdrop on large groups of foreign targets at once rather than requiring individual warrants for wiretapping purely foreign communications, like phone calls and e-mail messages that pass through American telecommunications switches. In targeting and wiretapping Americans, however, officials must obtain individual court orders from the special intelligence court, although in "exigent" or emergency circumstances, they can wiretap for at least seven days without a court order if it they assert that "intelligence important to the national security of the United States may be lost."

Fifth Amendment
A constitutional amendment designed to protect the rights of persons accused of crimes, including protection against double jeopardy, **self-incrimination**, and punishment without due process of law.

self-incrimination
The situation occurring when an individual accused of a crime is compelled to be a witness against himself or herself in court. The **Fifth Amendment** forbids involuntary self-incrimination.

Self-Incrimination

Suppose that evidence has been gathered and suspicion directed toward a particular person, and the police are ready to make an arrest. In the American system, the burden of proof rests on the police and the prosecutors. The **Fifth Amendment** forbids forced **self-incrimination**, stating that no person "shall be compelled to be a witness against himself." Whether in a congressional hearing, a courtroom, or a police station, suspects need not provide evidence that can later be used against them. However, the government may guarantee suspects *immunity*—exemption from prosecution in exchange for suspects' testimony regarding their own and others' misdeeds.

You have probably seen television shows in which an arrest is made and the arresting officers recite, often from memory, a set of rights to the arrestee. These rights are authentic and originated from a famous court decision—perhaps the most important modern decision in criminal law—involving an Arizona man named Ernesto Miranda.[74]

One of the most important principles of constitutional law is that defendants in criminal cases have rights. Probable cause and/or a search warrant are required for a legal search for and seizure of incriminating evidence. Here police officers read the suspect his rights based on the Supreme Court's decision in *Miranda v. Arizona.*

Miranda was picked up as a prime suspect in the rape and kidnapping of an 18-year-old girl. Identified by the girl from a police lineup, he was questioned by police for two hours. During this time, they did not tell him of either his constitutional right against self-incrimination or his right to counsel. In fact, it is unlikely that Miranda had even heard of the Fifth Amendment. He said enough to lead eventually to a conviction. The Supreme Court reversed his conviction on appeal, however. In ***Miranda v. Arizona*** (1966), the Court established guidelines for police questioning. Suspects must be told that:

- They have a constitutional right to remain silent and may stop answering questions at any time
- What they say can be used against them in a court of law
- They have a right to have a lawyer present during questioning and that the court will provide an attorney if they cannot afford their own lawyer

Miranda v. Arizona
The 1966 Supreme Court decision that sets guidelines for police questioning of accused persons to protect them against **self-incrimination** and to protect their right to counsel.

Police departments throughout the country were originally disgruntled by *Miranda.* Most departments today, however, seem to take *Miranda* seriously and usually read a *Miranda* card advising suspects of their rights. Ironically, when Ernesto Miranda himself was murdered, police read the suspect his rights from a *Miranda* card.

A POINT TO PONDER

Rights are only as meaningful as the officials who implement them. U.S. courts attempt to protect defendants' rights by denying prosecutors improperly obtained evidence.

Is there a better way to ensure these rights?

THE WIZARD OF ID

In the decades since the *Miranda* decision, the Supreme Court has made a number of exceptions to its requirements. In 1991, for example, the Court held that a coerced confession introduced in a trial does not automatically taint a conviction. If other evidence is enough for a conviction, then the coerced confession is a "harmless error" that does not necessitate a new trial.[75] Nevertheless, in 2000 in *Dickerson v. U.S.*, the Court made it clear that it supported the *Miranda* decision and that Congress was not empowered to change it. In 2010, the Court held that police may take a second run at questioning a suspect who has invoked his Miranda rights, but they must wait until 14 days after the suspect has been released from custody.[76] The Court also declared that criminal suspects seeking to protect their right to remain silent must speak up to invoke it.[77]

The Fifth Amendment prohibits not only coerced confessions but also coerced crimes. The courts have overturned convictions based on *entrapment*—when law enforcement officials encourage persons to commit crimes (such as accepting bribes or purchasing illicit drugs) that they otherwise would not commit. "You Are the Judge: The Case of the Enticed Farmer" addresses this issue.

The Right to Counsel

Sixth Amendment
A constitutional amendment designed to protect individuals accused of crimes. It includes the right to counsel, the right to confront witnesses, and the right to a speedy and public trial.

Gideon v. Wainwright
The 1963 Supreme Court decision holding that anyone accused of a felony where imprisonment may be imposed, however poor he or she might be, has a right to a lawyer. See also **Sixth Amendment**.

One of the most important of the *Miranda* rights is the right to counsel. Even lawyers who are taken to court hire another lawyer to represent them. (There is an old saying in the legal profession that a lawyer who defends himself has a fool for a client.) The **Sixth Amendment** has always ensured the right to counsel in federal courts, but until 1932, individuals were frequently tried, and sometimes convicted, for capital offenses (those in which the death penalty could be imposed) in state courts without a lawyer. In that year, the Supreme Court ordered the states to provide an attorney for indigent (poor) defendants accused of a capital crime (*Powell v. Alabama*).

Most crimes are not capital crimes, however, and most crimes are tried in state courts. It was not until 1963, in ***Gideon v. Wainwright***,[78] that the Supreme Court extended the right to an attorney for everyone accused of a felony in a state court. Subsequently, the Court went a step further than *Gideon* and held that whenever imprisonment could be imposed, a lawyer must be provided for the accused (*Argersinger v. Hamlin* [1972]). In addition, the Supreme Court found that a trial court's erroneous deprivation of a criminal defendant's *choice* of counsel entitles him to reversal of his conviction.[79]

YOU ARE THE JUDGE

The Case of the Enticed Farmer

In 1984, Keith Jacobson, a 56-year-old farmer who supported his elderly father in Nebraska, ordered two magazines and a brochure from a California adult bookstore. He expected nude photographs of adult males but instead found photographs of nude boys. He ordered no other magazines.

Three months later, Congress changed federal law to make the receipt of such materials illegal. Finding his name on the mailing list of the California bookstore, two government agencies repeatedly enticed Jacobson through five fictitious organizations and a bogus pen pal with solicitations for sexually explicit photographs of children. After 26 months of enticement, Jacobson finally ordered a magazine and was arrested for violating the Child Protection Act.

He was convicted of receiving child pornography through the mail, which he undoubtedly did. Jacobson claimed, however, that he had been entrapped into committing the crime.

You be the judge: Was Jacobson an innocent victim of police entrapment, or was he truly seeking child pornography?

Decision: The Court agreed with Jacobson. In *Jacobson v. United States* (1992), it ruled that the government had overstepped the line between setting a trap for the "unwary innocent" and the "unwary criminal" and failed to establish that Jacobson was independently predisposed to commit the crime for which he was arrested. Jacobson's conviction was overturned.

Trials

Television's portrayal of courts and trials is almost as dramatic as its portrayal of detectives and police officers—and both often vary from reality. Highly publicized trials are dramatic but rare. The murder trial of O. J. Simpson made headlines for months. CNN even carried much of the pretrial and trial live. But in reality, most cases, even ones in which the evidence is solid, do not go to trial.

If you visit a typical American criminal courtroom, you will rarely see a trial complete with judge and jury. In American courts, 90 percent of all cases begin and end with a guilty plea. Most cases are settled through a process called **plea bargaining**. A plea bargain results from a bargain struck between a defendant's lawyer and a prosecutor to the effect that a defendant will plead guilty to a lesser crime (or fewer crimes) in exchange for a state not prosecuting that defendant for a more serious (or additional) crime.

plea bargaining
A bargain struck between the defendant's lawyer and the prosecutor to the effect that the defendant will plead guilty to a lesser crime (or fewer crimes) in exchange for the state's promise not to prosecute the defendant for a more serious (or additional) crime.

Critics of the plea-bargaining system believe that it permits many criminals to avoid the full punishment they deserve. The process, however, works to the advantage of both sides; it saves the state the time and money that would otherwise be spent on a trial, and it permits defendants who think they might be convicted of a serious charge to plead guilty to a lesser one.

Whether plea bargaining serves the ends of justice is much debated. Its critics are concerned that plea bargaining unduly benefits defendants. A study of sentencing patterns in three California counties discovered that a larger proportion of defendants who went to trial (rather than plea bargained) ended up going to prison compared with those who pleaded guilty and had no trial. In answer to their question "Does it pay to plead guilty?" the researchers gave a qualified yes.[80] Good or bad, plea bargaining is a practical necessity. Only a vast increase in resources would allow the court system cope with a trial for every defendant.

The defendants in the 300,000 cases per year that actually go to trial are entitled to many rights, including the Sixth Amendment's provision for a speedy trial by an impartial jury. An impartial jury includes one that is not racially biased.[81] These days, defendants (those who can afford it, at least) do not leave jury selection to chance. A sophisticated technology of jury selection has developed. Jury consultants—often psychologists or other social scientists—develop profiles of jurors likely to be sympathetic or hostile to a defendant. Lawyers for both sides spend hours questioning prospective jurors in a major case.

The Constitution does not specify the size of a jury; in principle, it could be anywhere from 1 to 100 people. Tradition in England and America has set jury size at 12, although in petty cases six jurors are sometimes used, and traditionally a jury had to be unanimous in order to convict. The Supreme Court has eroded those traditions, permitting states to use fewer than 12 jurors and to convict with a less-than-unanimous vote. Federal courts still employ juries of 12 persons and require unanimous votes for a criminal conviction.

In recent years, the Supreme Court has aggressively defended the jury's role in the criminal justice process—and limited the discretion of judges in sentencing. In several cases, the Court has held that other than a previous conviction, any fact that increases the penalty for a crime beyond the prescribed statutory maximum or even the ordinary range must be submitted to a jury and proved beyond a reasonable doubt.[82] These decisions ensure that the judge's authority to sentence derives wholly from the jury's verdict.

There are yet additional rights related to trials. Defendants have the right to confront the witnesses against them. The Supreme Court has held that prosecutors cannot introduce testimony into a trial unless the accused can cross-examine the witness,[83] even if the witness is providing facts such as lab reports.[84]

The Sixth Amendment (and the protection against the suspension of the writ of *habeas corpus*) also guarantees that persons who are arrested have a right to be brought before a judge. This occurs at two stages of the judicial process. First, those detained have a right to be informed of the accusations against them. Second, they have a right to a *speedy and public trial*.

Prisoners held at the U.S. naval base at Guantánamo Bay, Cuba, present difficult issues of prisoners' rights.

The War on Terrorism. Normally, these guarantees present few issues. However, in the aftermath of the September 11, 2001, terrorist attacks, the FBI detained more than 1,200 persons as possible dangers to national security. Of these persons, 762 were illegal aliens (mostly Arabs and Muslims), and many of them languished in jail for months until cleared by the FBI. For the first time in U.S. history, the federal government withheld the names of detainees, reducing their opportunities to exercise their rights for access to the courts and to counsel. The government argued that releasing the names and details of those arrested would give terrorists a window on the terror investigation. In 2004, the Supreme Court refused to consider whether the government properly withheld names and other details about these prisoners. However, in other cases, the Court found that detainees held both in the United States and at the naval base at Guantánamo Bay, Cuba, had the right to challenge their detention before a judge or other neutral decision maker (*Hamdi v. Rumsfeld* and *Rasul v. Bush* [2004]).

In an historic decision in 2006 (*Hamdan v. Rumsfeld*), the Supreme Court held that the procedures President Bush had approved for trying prisoners at Guantánamo Bay lacked congressional authorization and violated both the Uniform Code of Military Justice and the Geneva Conventions. The flaws the Court cited were the failure to guarantee defendants the right to attend their trial and the prosecution's ability under the rules to introduce hearsay evidence, unsworn testimony, and evidence obtained through coercion. Equally important, the Constitution did not empower the president to establish judicial procedures on his own.

Later that year, Congress passed the Military Commissions Act (MCA), which specifically authorized military commissions to try alien unlawful enemy combatants and denied access to the courts for any alien detained by the United States government who was determined to be an enemy combatant or who was awaiting determination regarding enemy combatant status. This allowed the United States government to detain such aliens indefinitely without prosecuting them in any manner. However, in June 2008, the Supreme Court held in *Boumediene v. Bush* that foreign terrorism suspects held at Guantánamo Bay have constitutional rights to challenge their detention in U.S. courts. "The laws and Constitution are designed to survive, and remain in force, in extraordinary times," the Court proclaimed as it declared unconstitutional the provision of the MCA that stripped the federal courts of jurisdiction to hear habeas corpus petitions from detainees seeking to challenge their designation as enemy combatants. The Court also found that the truncated review procedure provided by the Detainee Treatment Act of 2005 fell short of being a constitutionally adequate substitute because it failed to offer the fundamental procedural protections of habeas corpus.

Eighth Amendment
The constitutional amendment that forbids cruel and unusual punishment, although it does not define this phrase. Through the **Fourteenth Amendment**, this provision applies to the states.

cruel and unusual punishment
Court sentences prohibited by the **Eighth Amendment**. Although the Supreme Court has ruled that mandatory death sentences for certain offenses are unconstitutional, it has not held that the death penalty itself constitutes cruel and unusual punishment.

Cruel and Unusual Punishment

Citizens convicted of a crime can expect punishment ranging from mild to severe, the mildest being some form of probation and the most severe, of course, being the death penalty. The **Eighth Amendment** forbids **cruel and unusual punishment**, although it does not define the phrase. Through the Fourteenth Amendment, this provision of the Bill of Rights applies to the states.

Although the Court held in 2010 that it is a violation of the cruel and unusual punishment clause to sentence a juvenile offender to life in prison without parole for a nonhomicide crime,[85] almost the entire constitutional debate over cruel and unusual punishment has centered on the death penalty (an exception can be found in "You Are the Judge: The Case of the First Offender"). More than 3,300 people are currently on death row, nearly half of them in California, Texas, and Florida.

The Court first confronted the question of whether the death penalty is inherently cruel and unusual punishment in *Furman v. Georgia* (1972), when it overturned Georgia's death penalty law because the state imposed the penalty in a "freakish" and "random" manner. In response to this decision, 35 states passed new laws permitting the death penalty. Some states, to prevent arbitrariness in punishment, mandated death penalties for some crimes. In *Woodson v. North Carolina* (1976), the Supreme Court ruled against mandatory death penalties. Since then the Court has come down more clearly on the side of the death penalty. In ***Gregg v. Georgia*** (1976), the Court upheld capital punishment, concluding that it was "an expression of society's outrage at particularly offensive conduct. . . . It is an extreme sanction, suitable to the most extreme of crimes."

Shortly before retiring from the bench in 1994, Supreme Court Justice Harry Blackmun declared that the administration of the death penalty "fails to deliver the fair, consistent and reliable sentences of death required by the Constitution" (*Callins v. Callins* [1994]). Social scientists have shown that minority defendants and murderers whose victims were white are more likely to receive death sentences than are white murderers or those whose victims were not white. For example, about 80 percent of the murder victims in cases resulting in an execution were white, even though only 50 percent of murder victims generally are white. Nevertheless, in ***McCleskey v. Kemp*** (1987), the Supreme Court concluded that the death penalty did not violate the equal protection of the law guaranteed by the Fourteenth Amendment. The Court insisted that the unequal distribution of death penalty sentences was constitutionally acceptable because there was no evidence that juries intended to discriminate on the basis of race.

Today, the death penalty is a part of the American criminal justice system, and about 1,100 persons have been executed since the Court's decision in *Gregg*. The Court has also made it more difficult for death row prisoners to file petitions that would force legal delays and appeals to stave off their appointed executions; it has made it easier for prosecutors to exclude jurors opposed to the death penalty (*Wainwright v. Witt*, 1985); and it has allowed "victim impact" statements detailing the character of murder victims and their families' suffering to be used against a defendant. Most Americans support the death penalty, although there is evidence that racism plays a role in the support of whites.[86] It is interesting to note that the European Union prohibits the death penalty in member countries.

In recent years, however, evidence that courts have sentenced innocent people to be executed has reinvigorated the debate over the death penalty. Attorneys have employed

Gregg v. Georgia
The 1976 Supreme Court decision that upheld the constitutionality of the death penalty, stating, "It is an extreme sanction, suitable to the most extreme of crimes." The Court did not, therefore, believe that the death sentence constitutes **cruel and unusual punishment**.

McCleskey v. Kemp
The 1987 Supreme Court decision that upheld the constitutionality of the death penalty against charges that it violated the **Fourteenth Amendment** because minority defendants were more likely to receive the death penalty than were white defendants.

YOU ARE THE JUDGE

The Case of the First Offender

Ronald Harmelin of Detroit was convicted of possessing 672 grams of cocaine (a gram is about one-thirtieth of an ounce). Michigan's mandatory sentencing law required the trial judge to sentence Harmelin, a first-time offender, to life imprisonment without possibility of parole. Harmelin argued that this was cruel and unusual punishment because it was "significantly disproportionate," meaning that, as we might say, the punishment did not fit the crime. Harmelin's lawyers argued that many other crimes more serious than cocaine possession would net similar sentences.

You be the judge: Was Harmelin's sentence cruel and unusual punishment?

Decision: The Court upheld Harmelin's conviction in *Harmelin v. Michigan* (1991), spending many pages to explain that severe punishments were quite commonplace, especially when the Bill of Rights was written. Severity alone does not qualify a punishment as "cruel and unusual." The severity of punishment was up to the legislature of Michigan, which, the justices observed, knew better than they the conditions on the streets of Detroit. Later, Michigan reduced the penalty for possession of small amounts of cocaine and released Harmelin from jail.

the new technology of DNA evidence in a number of states to obtain the release of dozens of death row prisoners. Governor George Ryan of Illinois declared a moratorium on executions in his state after researchers proved that 13 people on death row were innocent. Later, he commuted the death sentences of all prisoners in the state. In general, there has been a decline in executions, as you can see in "A Generation of Change: The Decline in Executions."

In addition, the Supreme Court has placed constraints on the application of the death penalty, holding that the Constitution barred the execution of the mentally ill (*Ford v. Wainwright*, 1986); mentally retarded persons (*Atkins v. Virginia*, 2002); those under the age of 18 when they committed their crimes (*Roper v. Simmons*, 2005); and those convicted of raping adult women (*Coker v. Georgia*, 1977) and children (*Kennedy v. Louisiana*, 2008) where the crime did not result, and was not intended to result, in the victim's death. In *Kennedy*, the Court went beyond the question in the case to rule out the death penalty for any individual crime—as opposed to offenses against the state, like treason or espionage—where the victim's life was not taken. In addition, the Court has required that a jury, not just a judge, find an aggravating circumstance necessary for imposition of the death penalty (*Ring v. Arizona*). The Court also required lawyers for defendants in death penalty cases to make reasonable efforts to fight for their clients at a trial's sentencing phase (*Rompilla v. Beard* [2005]).

Debate over the death penalty continues. In 2008, the Supreme Court upheld the use of lethal injection, concluding that challengers to this method of execution must

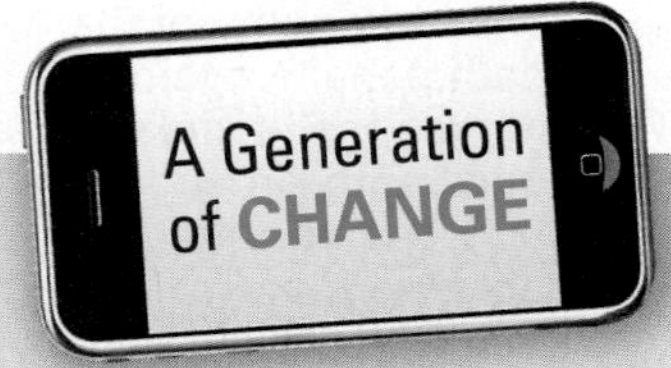

The Decline of Executions

Supreme Court decisions, new DNA technology, and perhaps a growing public concern about the fairness of the death penalty have resulted in a dramatic drop in the number of death sentences—from 98 in 1999 to 42 in 2009. Although the number of executions in Texas been relatively constant, the state's share of total executions nationwide has increased: from 32 percent in 2005 to 57 percent in 2009. Texas prosecutors and juries are no more apt to seek and impose death sentences than those in the rest of the country. However, once a death sentence is imposed there, prosecutors, the courts, the pardon board, and the governor are united in moving the process along.

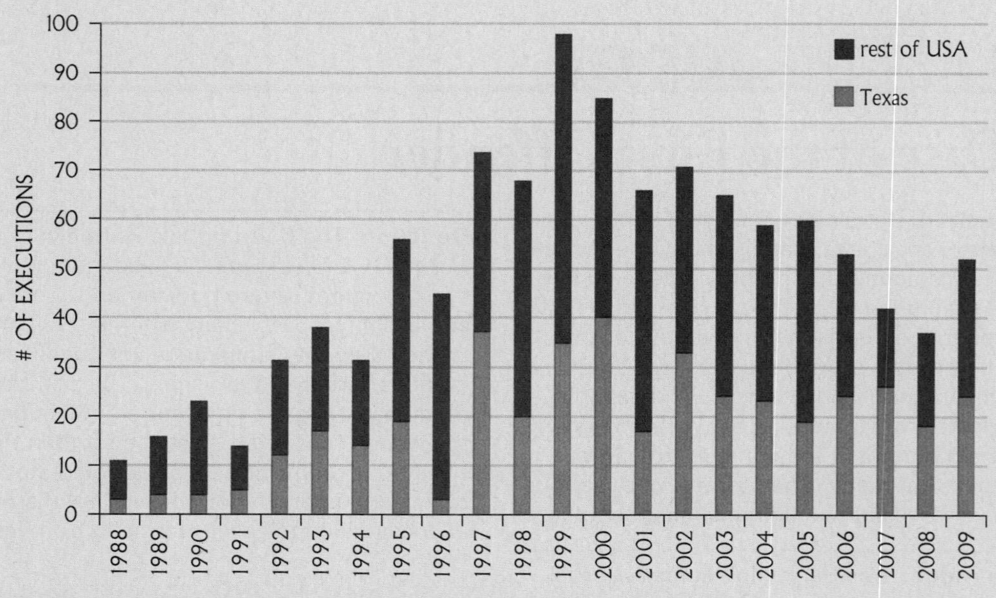

Sources: Death Penalty Information Center; Texas Execution Information Center.

College Students Help Prevent Wrongful Deaths

The Center on Wrongful Convictions at Northwestern University investigates possible wrongful convictions and represents imprisoned clients with claims of actual innocence. The young staff, including faculty, cooperating outside attorneys, and Northwestern University law students, pioneered the investigation and litigation of wrongful convictions—including the cases of nine innocent men sentenced to death in Illinois.

Undergraduates as well as law students have been involved in establishing the innocence of men who had been condemned to die. One instance involved the case of a man with an IQ of 51. The Illinois Supreme Court stayed his execution, just 48 hours before it was due to be carried out, because of questions about his mental fitness. This stay provided a professor and students from a Northwestern University investigative journalism class with an opportunity to investigate the man's guilt.

They tracked down and reinterviewed witnesses. One eyewitness recanted his testimony, saying that investigators had pressured him into implicating the man. The students found a woman who pointed to her ex-husband as the killer. Then a private investigator interviewed the ex-husband, who made a videotaped statement claiming he killed in self-defense. The students literally helped to save the life of an innocent man.

On January 11, 2003, Governor George H. Ryan of Illinois chose Lincoln Hall at Northwestern University's School of Law to make an historic announcement. He commuted the death sentences of all 167 death row prisoners in Illinois (he also pardoned 4 others based on innocence the previous day). The governor felt it was fitting to make the announcement there, before "the students, teachers, lawyers, and investigators who first shed light on the sorrowful conditions of Illinois' death penalty system."

In addition to saving the lives of wrongfully convicted individuals in Illinois, the Northwestern investigations have also helped trigger a nationwide reexamination of the capital punishment system. To learn more about the Center on Wrongful Convictions, visit its Web site at http://www.law.northwestern.edu/wrongfulconvictions/.

QUESTIONS FOR DISCUSSION

- Why do you think college students and others were better able to determine the truth about the innocence of condemned men than were the police and prosecutors at the original trials?
- Are there other areas of public life in which students can make important contributions through their investigations?

show not only that a state's method "creates a demonstrated risk of severe pain," but also that there were alternatives that were "feasible" and "readily implemented" that would "significantly" reduce that risk.[87] You can see what some students are doing about the injustices they perceive in the death penalty system in "Young People and Politics: College Students Help Prevent Wrongful Deaths."

The Right to Privacy

4.7 Outline the evolution of a right to privacy and its application to the issue of abortion.

The members of the First Congress who drafted the Bill of Rights and enshrined American civil liberties would never have imagined that Americans would go to court to argue about wiretapping, surrogate motherhood, abortion, or pornography. New technologies have raised ethical issues unimaginable in the eighteenth century. Today, one of the greatest debates concerning Americans' civil liberties lies in the emerging area of privacy rights.

Is There a Right to Privacy?

right to privacy
The right to a private personal life free from the intrusion of government.

Nowhere does the Bill of Rights say that Americans have a **right to privacy**. Clearly, however, the First Congress had the concept of privacy in mind when it crafted the first 10 amendments. Freedom of religion implies the right to exercise private beliefs; the

Third Amendment prohibited the government from forcing citizens to quarter soldiers in their homes during times of peace; protections against "unreasonable searches and seizures" make persons secure in their homes; and private property cannot be seized without "due process of law." In 1928, Justice Brandeis hailed privacy as "the right to be left alone—the most comprehensive of the rights and the most valued by civilized men."

The idea that the Constitution guarantees a right to privacy was first enunciated in a 1965 case involving a Connecticut law forbidding the use of contraceptives. It was a little-used law, but a doctor and a family planning specialist were arrested for disseminating birth control devices. The state reluctantly brought them to court, and they were convicted. The Supreme Court, in the case of *Griswold v. Connecticut*, wrestled with the privacy issue. Seven justices finally decided that various portions of the Bill of Rights cast "penumbras" (or shadows)—unstated liberties implied by the explicitly stated rights—protecting a right to privacy, including a right to family planning between husband and wife. Supporters of privacy rights argued that this ruling was reasonable enough, for what could be the purpose of the Fourth Amendment, for example, if not to protect privacy? Critics of the ruling—and there were many of them—claimed that the Supreme Court was inventing protections not specified by the Constitution.

There are other areas of privacy rights, including the sexual behavior of gays and lesbians, which we discuss in the next chapter. The most important application of privacy rights, however, came in the area of abortion. The Supreme Court unleashed a constitutional firestorm in 1973 that has not yet abated.

Roe v. Wade
The 1973 Supreme Court decision holding that a state ban on all abortions was unconstitutional. The decision forbade state control over abortions during the first trimester of pregnancy, permitted states to limit abortions to protect the mother's health in the second trimester, and permitted states to ban abortion during the third trimester.

Controversy over Abortion

In 1972, the Supreme Court heard one of the most controversial cases ever to come before the Court. Under the pseudonym of "Jane Roe," a Texas woman named Norma McCorvey sought an abortion. She argued that the state law allowing the procedure only to save the life of a mother was unconstitutional. Texas argued that states had the power to regulate moral behavior, including abortions. The Court's opinion in ***Roe v. Wade*** (1973) followed medical authorities in dividing pregnancy into three equal trimesters. *Roe* forbade any state control of abortions during the first trimester; it permitted states to regulate abortion procedures, but only in a way that protected the mother's health, in the second trimester; and it allowed the states to ban abortion during the third trimester, except when the mother's life or health was in danger. This decision unleashed a storm of protest.

Passions sometimes rule in the debate over abortion. Paul Hill went so far as to murder a physician who performed abortions, arguing that he had the right to do so to save the lives of the unborn. The jury did not agree, and Hill was sentenced to death.

Since *Roe v. Wade*, women have received more than 50 million legal abortions in the United States, more than a million in 2009. Abortion is a common experience: at current rates, about one in three American women will have had an abortion by the time she reaches age 45. Moreover, a broad cross section of U.S. women has abortions. Fifty-six percent of women having abortions are in their twenties; 61 percent have one or more children; 67 percent have never married; 57 percent are economically disadvantaged; and 78 percent report a religious affiliation. No racial or ethnic group makes up a majority: 41 percent of women obtaining abortions are white non-Hispanic, 32 percent are black non-Hispanic, 20 percent are Hispanic, and 7 percent are of other racial backgrounds.[88]

Yet the furor has never subsided. Congress has passed numerous statutes forbidding the use of federal funds for abortions. Many states have passed similar restrictions. For example, Missouri forbade the use of state funds or state employees to perform abortions. The Court upheld this law in *Webster v. Reproductive Health Services* (1989).

In 1991, the Court went even further in upholding restrictions on abortions. In *Rust v. Sullivan*, it found to be constitutional a Department of Health and Human Services ruling specifying that family planning services receiving federal funds could not provide women any counseling regarding abortion. This decision was greeted by a public outcry that the rule would deny many poor women abortion counseling and limit the First Amendment right of a medical practitioner to counsel a client. On his third day in office, President Clinton lifted the ban on abortion counseling.

In 1992, in ***Planned Parenthood v. Casey***, the Court changed its standard for evaluating restrictions on abortion from one of "strict scrutiny" of any restraints on a "fundamental right" to one of "undue burden" that permits considerably more regulation. The Court upheld a 24-hour waiting period, a parental or judicial consent requirement for minors (you can see variations among the states on this restriction in "My State: Laws on Abortions for Minors"), and a requirement that doctors present women with information on the risks of the operation. The Court struck down a provision requiring a married woman to tell her husband of her intent to have an abortion, however, and the majority also affirmed their commitment to the basic right of a woman to obtain an abortion.

Planned Parenthood v. Casey
A 1992 case in which the Supreme Court loosened its standard for evaluating restrictions on abortion from one of "strict scrutiny" of any restraints on a "fundamental right" to one of "undue burden" that permits considerably more regulation.

In 2000, the Court held in *Sternberg v. Carhart* that Nebraska's prohibition of "partial birth" abortions was unconstitutional because the law placed an undue burden on women seeking an abortion by limiting their options to less safe procedures, provided no exception for cases where the health of the mother was at risk, and did not clearly specify prohibited procedures. In 2003, Congress passed a law banning partial birth abortions, providing an exception to the ban in order to save the life of a mother but no exception to preserve a mother's health, as it found that the procedure was never necessary for a woman's health. In *Gonzales v. Carhart* (2007), the Supreme Court upheld

Laws on Abortions for Minors

Abortions are legal in the United States. However, for teenagers under the age of 18, the laws on abortions differ from state to state. In some states, parental permission is required before a girl under age 18 can have an abortion. Some states allow a judge to bypass this rule, enabling a minor to obtain permission from a court instead.

This map shows which states require parental consent before a minor can obtain an abortion.

QUESTIONS FOR DISCUSSION

- What are the restrictions in your state on abortions for minors?
- Do you favor parental consent for abortions for minors?

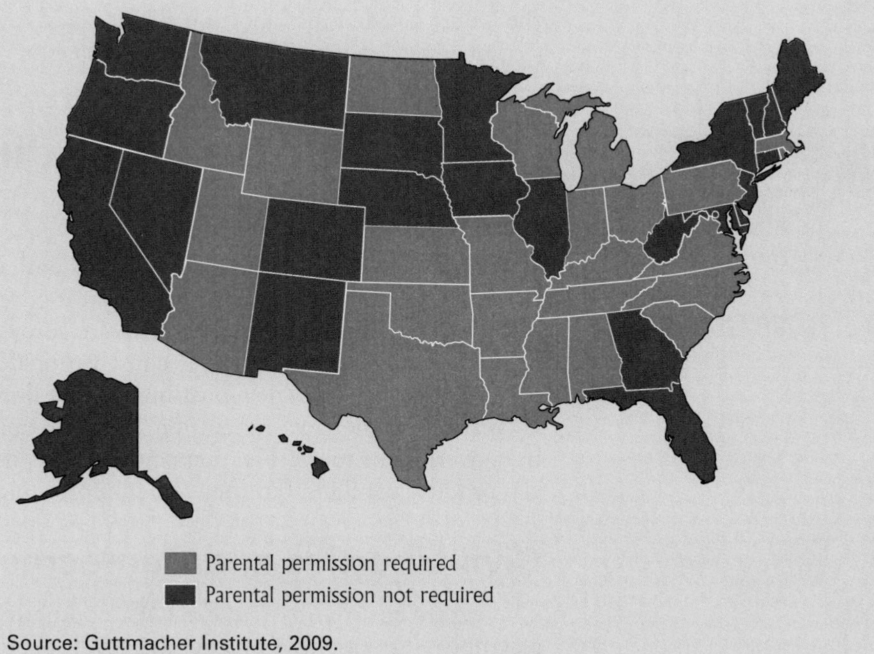

Source: Guttmacher Institute, 2009.

FIGURE 4.1 The Abortion Debate

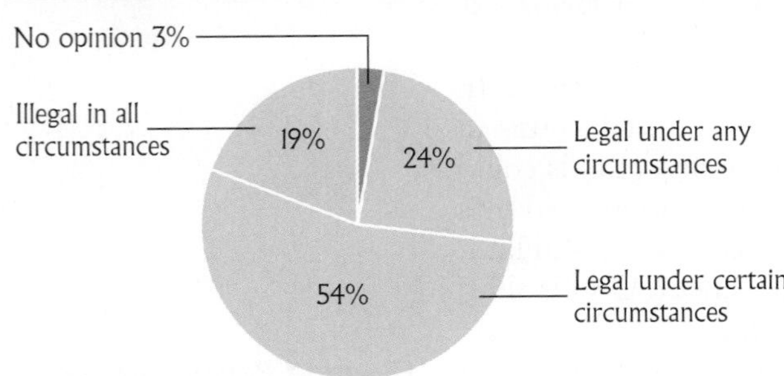

In few areas of public opinion research do scholars find more divided opinion than abortion. Some people feel very strongly about the matter, enough so that they are "single-issue voters" unwilling to support any candidate who disagrees with them. Most take a middle position, one that supports the principle of abortion but that also accepts restrictions on access to abortions.

Question: Do you think abortions should be legal under any circumstances, legal only under certain circumstances, or illegal in all circumstances?

Source: Gallup Poll, May 3–6, 2010.

that law, finding it was specific and did not subject women to significant health risks or impose an undue burden on a woman's right to an abortion. The Court also took pains to point out that the law would not affect most abortions, which are performed early in a pregnancy, and that safe alternatives to the prohibited procedure are available.

Americans are deeply divided on the issue of abortion (see Figure 4.1). Proponents of choice believe that access to abortion is essential if women are to be fully autonomous human beings. Opponents call themselves pro-life because they believe that the fetus is fully human and that an abortion therefore deprives a human of the right to life. These positions are irreconcilable, making abortion a politician's nightmare. Wherever a politician stands on this divisive issue, a large number of voters will be enraged.

Because passions run so strongly on the issue, advocates may take extreme action. In the last two decades, abortion opponents have bombed a number of abortion clinics and murdered several physicians who performed abortions.

Efforts to protect women's access to clinics sometimes clash with protesters' rights to free speech and assembly. In 1994, the Court consolidated the right to abortion established in *Roe* with the protection of a woman's right to enter an abortion clinic to exercise that right. Citing the government's interest in preserving order and maintaining women's access to pregnancy services, the Court upheld a state court's order of a 36-foot buffer zone around a clinic in Melbourne, Florida.[89] That same year, Congress passed the Freedom of Access to Clinic Entrances Act, which makes it a federal crime to intimidate abortion providers or women seeking abortions. In 2000, it upheld a 100-foot restriction on approaching someone at a health care facility to discourage abortions.[90] In another case, the Court decided that abortion clinics could invoke the federal racketeering law to sue violent antiabortion protest groups for damages.[91]

4.8 Assess how civil liberties affect democratic government and how they both limit and expand the scope of government.

Understanding Civil Liberties

American government is both democratic and constitutional. America is democratic because it is governed by officials who are elected by the people and, as such, are accountable for their actions. The American government is constitutional because it has a fundamental organic law, the Constitution, that limits the things that government may do. By restricting the government, the Constitution limits what the people can empower the government to do. The democratic and constitutional components of government can produce conflicts, but they also reinforce one another.

Civil Liberties and Democracy

The rights ensured by the First Amendment—the freedoms of speech, press, and assembly—are essential to a democracy. If people are to govern themselves, they need access to all available information and opinions in order to make intelligent, responsible, and accountable decisions. If the right to participate in public life is to be open to all, then Americans—in all their diversity—must have the right to express their opinions.

Individual participation and the expression of ideas are crucial components of democracy, but so is majority rule, which can conflict with individual rights. The majority does not have the freedom to decide that there are some ideas it would rather not hear, although at times the majority tries to enforce its will on the minority. The conflict is even sharper in relation to the rights guaranteed by the Fourth, Fifth, Sixth, Seventh, and Eighth Amendments. These rights protect all Americans, but they also make it more difficult to punish criminals. It is easy—although misleading—for the majority to view these guarantees as benefits for criminals at the expense of society.

With some notable exceptions, the United States has done a good job in protecting the rights of diverse interests to express themselves. There is little danger that a political or economic elite will muffle dissent. Similarly, the history of the past five decades is one of increased protections for defendants' rights, and defendants are typically not among the elite. Ultimately, the courts have decided what constitutional guarantees mean in practice. Although federal judges, appointed for life, are not directly accountable to popular will,[92] "elitist" courts have often protected civil liberties from the excesses of majority rule.

Civil Liberties and the Scope of Government

Civil liberties in America are both the foundation for and a reflection of our emphasis on individualism. When there is a conflict between an individual or a group attempting to express themselves or worship as they please and an effort by a government to constrain them in some fashion, the individual or group usually wins. If protecting the freedom of an individual or group to express themselves results in inconvenience or even injustice for the public officials they criticize or the populace they wish to reach, so be it. Every nation must choose where to draw the line between freedom and order. In the United States, we generally choose liberty.

Today's government is huge and commands vast, powerful technologies. Americans' Social Security numbers, credit cards, driver's licenses, and school records are all on giant computers to which the government has immediate access. It is virtually impossible to hide from the police, the FBI, the Internal Revenue Service, or any governmental agency. Because Americans can no longer avoid the attention of government, strict limitations on governmental power are essential. The Bill of Rights provides these vital limitations.

Thus, in general, civil liberties limit the scope of government. Yet substantial government efforts are often required to protect the expansion of rights that we have witnessed thus far. Those seeking abortions may need help reaching a clinic, defendants may demand that lawyers be provided them at public expense, advocates of unpopular causes may require police protection, and litigants in complex lawsuits over matters of birth or death may rely on judges to resolve their conflicts. It is ironic—but true—that an expansion of freedom may require a simultaneous expansion of government.

Summary

4.1 Trace the process by which the Bill of Rights has been applied to the states.

Under the incorporation doctrine, most of the freedoms outlined in the Bill of Rights limit the states as well as the national government. The due process clause of the Fourteenth Amendment provides the basis for this protection of rights.

4.2 Distinguish the two types of religious rights protected by the First Amendment and determine the boundaries of those rights.

The establishment clause of the First Amendment prohibits government sponsorship of religion, religious exercises, or religious doctrine, but government may support religious-related activities that have a secular purpose if this does not foster excessive entanglement with religion. The free exercise clause guarantees that people may hold any religious views they like, but government may at times limit practices related to those views.

4.3 Differentiate the rights of free expression protected by the First Amendment and determine the boundaries of those rights.

Americans enjoy wide protections for expression, both spoken and written (as in the press), including symbolic and commercial speech. Free expression is protected even when it conflicts with other rights, such as the right to a fair trial. However, the First Amendment does not protect some expression, such as libel, fraud, obscenity, and incitement to violence, and government has more leeway to regulate expression on the public airwaves.

4.4 Describe the rights to assemble and associate protected by the First Amendment and their limitations.

The First Amendment protects the right of Americans to assemble to make a statement, although time, place, and manner restrictions on parades, picketing and protests are permissible. Citizens also have the right to associate with others who share a common interest.

4.5 Describe the right to bear arms protected by the Second Amendment and its limitations.

Most people have a right to possess firearms and use them for traditionally lawful purposes. However, government may limit this right to certain classes of people, certain areas, and certain weapons, and may require qualifications for purchasing firearms.

4.6 Characterize defendants' rights and identify issues that arise in their implementation.

The Bill of Rights provides defendants with many rights, including protections against unreasonable searches and seizures, self-incrimination, entrapment, and cruel and unusual punishment (although the death penalty is not inherently constitutionally unacceptable). Defendants also have a right to be brought before a judicial officer when arrested, to have the services of counsel, to receive a speedy and fair trial (including by an impartial jury), and to confront witnesses who testify against them. They also must be told of their rights. Nevertheless, the implementation of each of these rights requires judges to make nuanced decisions about the meaning of relevant provisions of the Constitution.

4.7 Outline the evolution of a right to privacy and its application to the issue of abortion.

Beginning in the 1960s, the Supreme Court articulated a right to privacy, as implied by the Bill of Rights. This right has been applied in various domains and is the basis for a woman's right to an abortion under most, but not all, circumstances.

4.8 Assess how civil liberties affect democratic government and how they both limit and expand the scope of government.

The rights of speech, press, and assembly are essential to democracy. So is majority rule. When any of the Bill of Rights, including defendants' rights, conflict with majority rule, rights prevail.

There is a paradox about civil liberties and the scope of government. Civil liberties, by definition, limit the scope of government action, yet substantial government efforts may be necessary to protect the exercise of rights.

Chapter Test

4.1 Trace the process by which the Bill of Rights has been applied to the states.

1. Prior to the Supreme Court ruling in *Gitlow v. New York*, how were state governments restricted by the Bill of Rights?
   a. Only the First Amendment restricted state governments, with the Bill of Rights in its entirety applying just to the national government
   b. The Bill of Rights restricted state governments just as it did the national government
   c. The Bill of Rights did not restrict state governments but only the national government
   d. The Bill of Rights restricted state governments on a case-by-case basis as it did the national government
   e. The Bill of Rights restricted state action only on a case-by-case basis while restricting the national government generally

2. The legal concept under which the Supreme Court has nationalized the Bill of Rights is the
   a. Incorporation doctrine
   b. Establishment doctrine
   c. Inclusion doctrine
   d. Privileges and immunities clause
   e. Due process clause

3. What was the Supreme Court's decision in the case of *Gitlow v. New York,* and what was its reasoning? Why was this decision significant?

4.2 Distinguish the two types of religious rights protected by the First Amendment and determine the boundaries of those rights.

4. Which of the following statements best explains the Supreme Court's interpretation of what the government may do to regulate religion?
   a. It can prohibit religious beliefs and practices it considers inappropriate

b. It can prohibit religious beliefs and practices so long as it does not specifically target a religion
c. It can prohibit religious practices but not religious beliefs
d. It can prohibit neither religious beliefs nor religious practices
e. It can prohibit religious practices and beliefs for only certain religions

5. Imagine that you are an administrator at a public university and the Christian Fellowship has petitioned to use university facilities. According to Supreme Court decisions on the matter of religion and public schools, you
   a. Can deny the Christian Fellowship the use of the university facilities
   b. Must allow the Christian Fellowship to use the facilities, just like the Political Science Club and other student organizations
   c. Must allow the Christian Fellowship to use the facilities as long as its activities there do not include worship
   d. Must put the question to a vote of your student body
   e. Must require the Christian Fellowship group to file a religious exemption before you grant its request

6. Concerning the establishment clause of the First Amendment, the Supreme Court has found that drawing the line between neutrality toward religion and promotion of it is difficult. Identify and discuss three Supreme Court cases that illustrate this. Why do you think drawing this line is so difficult?

4.3 Differentiate the rights of free expression protected by the First Amendment and determine the boundaries of those rights.

7. Court decisions concerning symbolic speech
   a. Have clearly defined symbolic speech and what type of symbolic speech is protected
   b. Have clearly defined symbolic speech but have ruled that it is never protected
   c. Have extended protections to only some forms of symbolic speech
   d. Have ruled that symbolic speech is always protected
   e. Have not directly addressed the matter of symbolic speech

8. What measures can a court take in order to guarantee the right to a fair trial in the face of media scrutiny?
   a. The court can limit journalists' access to particularly sensitive trials
   b. The court can exercise prior restraint against the publication of information that might influence the jury
   c. The court can force journalists to hold back sensitive information until after the trial has ended
   d. The court can threaten journalists with fines and imprisonment for revealing sensitive information
   e. The Supreme Court has never upheld a restriction on the press in the interest of a fair trial

9. The right to freedom of speech applies differently on public and private property.

   True______ False______

10. Why does the Supreme Court allow more rigid regulation of commercial than other forms of speech?

11. The First Amendment to the U.S. Constitution reads, "Congress shall make no law . . . restricting the freedom of speech." Based on your understanding of the Constitution and numerous Supreme Court cases, how well do you think the Supreme Court has protected the First Amendment protections of freedom of speech? Explain your answer.

4.4 Describe the rights to assemble and associate protected by the First Amendment and their limitations.

12. Because the First Amendment mentions only assembly, there is no constitutional freedom of association.

    True______ False______

13. Suppose that you are in charge of deciding whether to provide permits to pro-choice and pro-life supporters who wish to assemble in your community and advocate their political positions. How might you balance this right to assemble with the government's necessity to ensure order, consistent with your understanding of this constitutional protection and Supreme Court decisions?

4.5 Describe the right to bear arms protected by the Second Amendment and its limitations.

14. Which of the following are constitutional limits to the right to keep and bear arms?
    a. Limits on concealed weapons
    b. Limits on firearms possession by the mentally ill
    c. Limits on carrying firearms in schools
    d. Limits on the commercial sales of firearms
    e. All of the above restrictions on the right to keep and bear arms are permissible

15. In the case of *District of Columbia v. Heller* (2008), the Supreme Court struck down a law that outlawed the possession of handguns in our nation's capital. What was the Court's primary reasoning? Do you agree or disagree with the decision? In your opinion, how did the Court balance the right to bear arms with the need of the government to provide order in society? Explain your answer.

4.6 Characterize defendants' rights and identify issues that arise in their implementation.

16. Each of the following protections is found in the Fifth and Sixth Amendments, except
    a. The right to a speedy trial by an impartial jury
    b. The right to counsel
    c. The right to plea bargain
    d. The right to remain silent
    e. All of the above are rights protected in the Fifth and Sixth Amendments

17. The Fourth Amendment to the Constitution requires police officers to have a warrant to search or arrest a criminal suspect.

    True______ False______

18. What is the exclusionary rule and what are some exceptions to it, as identified by the U.S. Supreme Court?

19. What are the main arguments advanced by advocates and critics of the death penalty? Which set of arguments do you agree with more, and why? Has the Supreme Court ruled that the death penalty is "cruel and unusual punishment"? Why or why not?

4.7 Outline the evolution of a right to privacy and its application to the issue of abortion.

20. Which of the following is NOT a constitutional restriction on abortion?
    a. States may forbid the use of state funds for abortions
    b. States may require parental consent for a minor seeking an abortion
    c. States may require married women to tell their husbands of their intent to have an abortion
    d. States may ban "partial birth" abortions
    e. States may require doctors to present women with the risks of having an abortion

21. Is there a right to privacy in the Bill of Rights and, if so, how has it evolved over time? Defend your answer, referring to Supreme Court cases.

4.8 Assess how civil liberties affect democratic government and how they both limit and expand the scope of government.

22. When thinking about citizens' rights, one can distinguish between the rights of an individual citizen and the rights of society as a whole. Based on what you have learned in this chapter, under what circumstances are the courts and the government more likely to give preference to individual rights over the rights of society? By the same token, under what circumstances are concerns for society as a whole likely to override individual rights?

23. The Bill of Rights was designed to protect individuals from the tyranny of government. But as civil liberties have expanded, promoting democracy, they have also expanded the scope of government. How might you resolve the apparent contradiction between the expansion of democracy and scope of government? How well do you think the Bill of Rights balances these two considerations?

PEARSON mypoliscilab™ Exercises

Apply what you learned in this chapter on MyPoliSciLab.

Read on **mypoliscilab.com**

eText: Chapter 4

Study and **Review** on **mypoliscilab.com**

Pre-Test
Post-Test
Chapter Exam
Flashcards

Watch on **mypoliscilab.com**

Video: Funeral Protestors Push the Limits of Free Speech
Video: D.C.'s Right to Bear Arms
Video: Water Wars

Explore on **mypoliscilab.com**

Simulation: You Are a Police Officer
Simulation: You Are a Supreme Court Justice Deciding a Free Speech Case
Simulation: Balancing Liberty and Security in a Time of War
Comparative: Comparing Civil Liberties
Timeline: Civil Liberties and National Security

Key Terms

civil liberties (94)
Bill of Rights (94)
First Amendment (95)
Fourteenth Amendment (96)
due process clause (96)
incorporation doctrine (96)
establishment clause (96)
free exercise clause (97)
prior restraint (103)
libel (106)
symbolic speech (108)
commercial speech (109)
probable cause (114)
unreasonable searches and seizures (114)
search warrant (114)
exclusionary rule (115)
Fifth Amendment (116)
self-incrimination (116)
Sixth Amendment (118)
plea bargaining (119)
Eighth Amendment (120)
cruel and unusual punishment (120)
right to privacy (123)

Key Cases

Barron v. Baltimore (1833)
Gitlow v. New York (1925)
Lemon v. Kurtzman (1971)
Zelman v. Simmons-Harris (2002)
Engel v. Vitale (1962)
School District of Abington Township, Pennsylvania v. Schempp (1963)
Near v. Minnesota (1931)
Schenck v. United States (1919)
Roth v. United States (1957)
Miller v. California (1973)
New York Times v. Sullivan (1964)
Texas v. Johnson (1989)
Zurcher v. Stanford Daily (1978)
Miami Herald Publishing Company v. Tornillo (1974)
Red Lion Broadcasting Company v. Federal Communications Commission (1969)
NAACP v. Alabama (1958)
Mapp v. Ohio (1961)
Miranda v. Arizona (1966)
Gideon v. Wainwright (1963)
Gregg v. Georgia (1976)
McCleskey v. Kemp (1987)
Roe v. Wade (1973)
Planned Parenthood v. Casey (1992)

Internet Resources

www.freedomforum.org
Background information and recent news on First Amendment issues.

www.eff.org
Web site concerned with protecting online civil liberties.

www.aclu.org
Home page of the American Civil Liberties Union, offering information and commentary on a wide range of civil liberties issues.

www.firstamendmentcenter.org/rel_liberty/overview.aspx
Background on freedom of religion in the United States and discussion of major church–state cases.

www.firstamendmentcenter.org/Speech/index.aspx
Background on freedom of speech in the United States and discussion of major free speech issues.

www.firstamendmentcenter.org/faclibrary/index.aspx
Cases on freedom of religion, speech, press, and assembly and background material.

www.cc.org
Christian Coalition home page, containing background information and discussion of current events.

www.deathpenaltyinfo.org
The Death Penalty Information Center, providing data on all aspects of the death penalty.

www.guttmacher.org
The Guttmacher Institute, a nonpartisan source of information on all aspects of abortion.

http://reproductiverights.org/en
Center for Reproductive Rights Web site.

www.nrlc.org
National Right to Life Web site.

For Further Reading

Adler, Renata. ***Reckless Disregard.*** New York: Knopf, 1986. The story of two monumental conflicts between free press and individual reputations.

Baker, Liva. ***Miranda: The Crime, the Law, the Politics.*** New York: Atheneum, 1983. An excellent book-length treatment of one of the major criminal cases of our time.

Baumgartner, Frank R., Suzanne L. De Boef, and Amber E. Boydstun. ***The Decline of the Death Penalty and the Discovery of Innocence.*** New York: Cambridge University Press, 2008. Explains changes in public support for the death penalty and the number of executions.

Garrow, David J. ***Liberty and Sexuality.*** New York: Macmillan, 1994. The most thorough treatment of the development of the law on the right to privacy and abortion.

Heymann, Philip B. ***Terrorism, Freedom, and Security.*** Cambridge, MA: MIT Press, 2004. Thoughtfully balances concerns for freedom with those of safety from terrorism.

Irons, Peter. ***The Courage of Their Convictions: Sixteen Americans Who Fought Their Way to the Supreme Court.*** New York: Penguin Books, 1990. Accounts of 16 Americans over a period of 50 years who took their cases to the Supreme Court in defense of civil liberties.

Levy, Leonard W. ***The Emergence of a Free Press.*** New York: Oxford University Press, 1985. A major work on the Framers' intentions regarding freedom of expression.

Levy, Leonard W. ***The Establishment Clause: Religion and the First Amendment.*** New York: Macmillan, 1986. The author argues that it is unconstitutional for government to provide aid to any religion.

Lewis, Anthony. ***Make No Law: The Sullivan Case and the First Amendment.*** New York: Random House, 1991. A well-written story of the key case regarding American libel law and an excellent case study of a Supreme Court case.

Rose, Melody. ***Safe, Legal, and Unavailable: Abortion Politics in the United States.*** Washington, DC: CQ Press, 2007. Explores how many women do not have the ability to exercise their constitutional right to an abortion.

Rosenblatt, Roger. *Life Itself: Abortion in the American Mind.* New York: Random House, 1992. The author seeks to reconcile the clash of absolutes in the abortion controversy with scholarly analysis and interview data.

Chapter 5

Civil Rights and Public Policy

Learning Objectives

5.1 Differentiate the Supreme Court's three standards of review for classifying people under the equal protection clause.

5.2 Trace the evolution of protections of the rights of African Americans and explain the application of nondiscrimination principles to issues of race.

5.3 Relate civil rights principles to progress made by other ethnic groups in the United States.

5.4 Trace the evolution of women's rights and explain how civil rights principles apply to gender issues.

5.5 Show how civil rights principles have been applied to seniors, people with disabilities, and gays and lesbians.

5.6 Trace the evolution of affirmative action policy and assess the arguments for and against it.

5.7 Establish how civil rights policy advances democracy and increases the scope of government.

POLITICS IN ACTION: LAUNCHING THE CIVIL RIGHTS MOVEMENT

A 42-year-old seamstress named Rosa Parks was riding in the "colored" section of a Montgomery, Alabama, city bus on December 1, 1955. A white man got on the bus and found that all the seats in the front, which were reserved for whites, were taken. He moved on to the equally crowded colored section. J. F. Blake, the bus driver, then ordered all four passengers in the first row of the colored section to surrender their seats because the law prohibited whites and blacks from sitting next to or even across from one another.

Three of the African Americans hesitated and then complied with the driver's order. But Rosa Parks, a politically active member of the National Association for the Advancement of Colored People, said no. The driver threatened to have her arrested, but she refused to move. He then called the police, and a few minutes later two officers boarded the bus and arrested her.

At that moment the civil rights movement was born. There had been substantial efforts—and some important successes—to use the courts to end racial segregation, but Rosa Parks's refusal to give up her seat led to extensive mobilization of African Americans. Protestors employed a wide range of methods, including nonviolent resistance. A new preacher in town, Martin Luther King, Jr., organized a boycott of the city buses. He was jailed, his house was bombed, and his wife and infant daughter were almost killed, but neither he nor the African American community wavered. Although they were harassed by the police and went without motor transportation by walking or even riding mules, they persisted in boycotting the buses.

It eventually took the U. S. Supreme Court to end the boycott. On November 13, 1956, the Court declared that Alabama's state and local laws requiring segregation on buses were illegal. On December 20, federal injunctions were served on the city and bus company officials, forcing them to follow the Supreme Court's ruling.

On December 21, 1956, Rosa Parks boarded a Montgomery city bus for the first time in over a year. She could sit wherever she liked and chose a seat near the front.

Americans have never fully come to terms with equality. Most Americans favor equality in the abstract—a politician who advocated inequality would not attract many votes—yet the concrete struggle for equal rights under the Constitution has been our nation's most bitter battle. It pits person against person, as in the case of Rosa Parks and the nameless white passenger, and group against group. Those people who enjoy privileged positions in American society have been reluctant to give them up.

Individual liberty is central to democracy. So is a broad notion of equality, such as that implied by the concept of "one person, one vote." Sometimes these values conflict, as when individuals or a majority of the people want to act in a discriminatory fashion.

Chapter **OUTLINE**

How should we resolve such conflicts between liberty and equality? Can we have a democracy if some citizens do not enjoy basic rights to political participation or suffer discrimination in employment? Can we or should we try to remedy past discrimination against minorities and women?

In addition, many people have called on government to protect the rights of minorities and women, increasing the scope and power of government in the process. Ironically, this increase in government power is often used to *check* government, as when the federal courts restrict the actions of state legislatures. It is equally ironic that society's collective efforts to use government to protect civil rights are designed not to limit individualism but to enhance it, freeing people from suffering and from prejudice. But how far should government go in these efforts? Is an increase in the scope of government to protect some people's rights an unacceptable threat to the rights of other citizens?

The phrase "all men are created equal" is at the heart of American political culture; yet implementing this principle has proved to be one of our nation's most enduring struggles. Throughout our history, a host of constitutional questions have been raised by issues involving African Americans and other minorities and women, ranging from slavery and segregation to equal pay. The rallying cry of minorities and women has been **civil rights**, which are policies designed to protect people against arbitrary or discriminatory treatment by government officials or individuals.

civil rights
Policies designed to protect people against arbitrary or discriminatory treatment by government officials or individuals.

The resulting controversies have been fought in the courts, Congress, and the bureaucracy, but the meaning of *equality* remains as elusive as it is divisive. Today's equality debates center on these key types of inequality in America:

- ***Racial and ethnic discrimination.*** Two centuries of discrimination against racial and ethnic minorities have produced historic Supreme Court and congressional policies that seek to eliminate such discrimination from the constitutional fabric. Americans have yet to resolve issues such as the appropriate role of affirmative action programs, however.
- ***Gender discrimination.*** The role of women in American society has changed substantially since the 1700s. However, equal rights for women have yet to be constitutionally guaranteed. The Equal Rights Amendment was not ratified, and women continue to press for equality and to seek protection from sexual harassment.
- ***Discrimination based on factors including age, disability, and sexual orientation.*** As America is "graying," older Americans are demanding a place under the civil rights umbrella. Also seeking constitutional protections against discrimination are people with disabilities and gays and lesbians.

5.1 Differentiate the Supreme Court's three standards of review for classifying people under the equal protection clause.

The Struggle for Equality

The struggle for equality has been a persistent theme in our nation's history. Slaves sought freedom, free African Americans fought for the right to vote and to be treated as equals, women pursued equal participation in society, and the economically disadvantaged called for better treatment and economic opportunities. This fight for equality affects all Americans. Philosophically, the struggle involves defining the term *equality*. Constitutionally, it involves interpreting laws. Politically, it often involves power.

Conceptions of Equality

What does *equality* mean? Jefferson's statement in the Declaration of Independence that "all men are created equal" did not mean that he believed everybody was exactly alike or that there were no differences among human beings. The Declaration went on to speak, however, of "inalienable rights" to which all are equally entitled. American society does not emphasize *equal results* or *equal rewards*; few Americans argue that everyone should earn the same salary or have the same amount of property. Instead, a belief in *equal rights* has led to a belief in *equality of opportunity*; in other words, everyone should have the same chance to succeed. What individuals make of that equal chance depends on their abilities and efforts.

The Constitution and Inequality

The delegates to the Constitutional Convention created a plan for government, not guarantees of individual rights. Not even the Bill of Rights mentions equality. It does, however, have implications for equality in that it does not limit the scope of its guarantees to specified groups within society. It does not say, for example, that only whites have freedom from compulsory self-incrimination or that only men are entitled to freedom of speech. The First Amendment guarantees of freedom of expression, in particular, are important because they allow those who are discriminated against to work toward achieving equality. As we will see, this kind of political activism has proven important for groups fighting for civil rights.

The first and only place in which the idea of equality appears in the Constitution is in the **Fourteenth Amendment**, one of the three amendments passed after the Civil War. (The Thirteenth abolishes slavery, and the Fifteenth extends the right to vote to African Americans.) Ratified in 1868, the Fourteenth Amendment forbids the states from denying to anyone "**equal protection of the laws**." This equal protection clause became the principal tool for waging struggles for equality. Laws, rules, and regulations inevitably classify people. For example, some people are eligible to vote while others are not; some people are eligible to attend a state university while others are denied admission. Such classifications cannot violate the equal protection of the law.

Fourteenth Amendment
The constitutional amendment adopted after the Civil War that states "No State shall make or enforce any law which shall abridge the privileges or immunities of citizens of the United States; nor shall any state deprive any person of life, liberty, or property, without due process of law; nor deny to any person within its jurisdiction the **equal protection of the laws.**"

equal protection of the laws
Part of the **Fourteenth Amendment** emphasizing that the laws must provide equivalent "protection" to all people.

How do the courts determine whether a classification in a law or regulation is permissible or violates the equal protection of the law? For this purpose, the Supreme Court developed three levels of scrutiny, or analysis, called *standards of review* (see Table 5.1). The Court has ruled that to pass constitutional muster, most classifications must only be *reasonable*. In practice, this means that a classification must bear a rational relationship to some legitimate governmental purpose, for example, to educating students in colleges. The courts defer to rule makers, typically legislatures, and anyone who challenges these classifications has the burden of proving that they are not reasonable, but arbitrary. (A classification that is arbitrary—a law singling out, say, people with red hair or blue eyes for inferior treatment—would be invalid.) Thus, for example, the states can restrict the right to vote to people over the age of 18; age is a reasonable classification and hence a permissible basis for determining who may vote.

The African American struggle for equality paved the way for civil rights movements by women and other minorities. Here, civil rights leaders Roy Wilkins, James Farmer, Martin Luther King Jr., and Whitney Young meet with President Lyndon B. Johnson.

With some classifications, however, the burden of proof is with the rule maker. The Court has ruled that racial and ethnic classifications, such as those that would prohibit African Americans from attending school with whites or that would deny a racial or ethnic group access to public services such as a park or swimming pool, are *inherently suspect*. Courts presume that these classifications are invalid and uphold them only if they serve a "compelling public interest" and there is no other way to accomplish the

TABLE 5.1 Supreme Court's Standards for Classifications Under the Equal Protection Clause of the Fourteenth Amendment

BASIS OF CLASSIFICATION	STANDARD OF REVIEW	APPLYING THE TEST
Race and ethnicity	Inherently suspect (difficult to meet)	Is the classification necessary to accomplish a compelling governmental purpose and the least restrictive way to reach the goal?
Gender	Intermediate scrutiny (moderately difficult to meet)	Does the classification bear a substantial relationship to an important governmental goal?
Other (age, wealth, etc.)	Reasonableness (easy to meet)	Does the classification have a rational relationship to a legitimate governmental goal?

purpose of the law. In the case of a racial or ethnic classification, the burden of proof is on the government that created it to prove that the classification meets these criteria. It is virtually impossible to show that a classification by race or ethnicity that serves to disadvantage a minority group serves a compelling public interest. What about classifications by race and ethnicity, such as for college admissions, that are designed to *remedy* previous discrimination? As we will see in our discussion of affirmative action, the Court is reluctant to approve even these laws.

Classifications based on gender receive *intermediate scrutiny*; the courts presume them to be neither constitutional nor unconstitutional. A law that classifies by gender, such as one that makes men but not women eligible for a military draft, must bear a substantial relationship to an important governmental purpose, a lower threshold than serving a "compelling public interest."

Conditions for women and minorities would be radically different if it were not for the "equal protection" clause.[1] The following sections show how equal protection litigation has worked to the advantage of minorities, women, and other groups seeking protection under the civil rights umbrella.

5.2 Trace the evolution of protections of the rights of African Americans and explain the application of nondiscrimination principles to issues of race.

African Americans' Civil Rights

Throughout American history, African Americans have been the most visible minority group in the United States. Thus, African Americans have blazed the constitutional trail for securing equal rights for all Americans. They made very little progress, however, until well into the twentieth century.

The Era of Slavery

For the first 250 years of American settlement, most African Americans lived in slavery. Slaves were the property of their masters. They could be bought and sold, and they could neither vote nor own property. The Southern states, whose plantations required large numbers of unpaid workers, were the primary market for slave labor. Policies of the slave states and the federal government accommodated the property interests of slave owners, who were often wealthy and enjoyed substantial political influence.

Scott v. Sandford
The 1857 Supreme Court decision ruling that a slave who had escaped to a free state enjoyed no rights as a citizen and that Congress had no authority to ban slavery in the territories.

In 1857, the Supreme Court bluntly announced in ***Scott v. Sandford*** that a black man, slave or free, was "chattel" and had no rights under a white man's government and that Congress had no power to ban slavery in the western territories. This decision invalidated the hard-won Missouri Compromise, which had allowed Missouri to become a slave state on the condition that northern territories would remain free of slavery. As a result, the *Scott* decision was an important milestone on the road to the Civil War.

The Union victory in the Civil War and the ratification of the **Thirteenth Amendment** ended slavery. The promises implicit in this amendment and the other two Civil War amendments introduced the era of reconstruction and segregation, in which these promises were first honored and then broken.

Thirteenth Amendment
The constitutional amendment ratified after the Civil War that forbade slavery and involuntary servitude.

The Era of Reconstruction and Segregation

After the Civil War ended, Congress imposed strict conditions on the former Confederate states before it would seat their representatives and senators. No one who had served in secessionist state governments or in the Confederate army could hold state office, the legislatures had to ratify the new amendments, and the military would govern the states like "conquered provinces" until they complied with the tough federal plans for reconstruction. Many African American men held state and federal offices during the 10 years following the war. Some government agencies, such as the Freedmen's Bureau, provided assistance to former slaves who were making the difficult transition to independence.

To ensure his election in 1876, Rutherford Hayes promised to pull the troops out of the South and let the Southern states do as they pleased. Southerners lost little time reclaiming power and imposing a code of *Jim Crow laws*, or segregationist laws, on African Americans. ("Jim Crow" was the name of a stereotypical African American in a nineteenth-century minstrel song.) These laws relegated African Americans to separate public facilities, separate school systems, and even separate restrooms. Not only had most whites lost interest in helping former slaves, but much of what the Jim Crow laws mandated in the South was also common practice in the North. Indeed, the national government practiced segregation in the armed forces, employment, housing programs, and prisons.[2] In this era, racial segregation affected every part of life, from the cradle to the grave. African Americans were delivered by African American physicians or midwives and buried in African American cemeteries. Groups such as the Ku Klux Klan terrorized African Americans who violated the norms of segregation, lynching hundreds of people.

Plessy v. Ferguson
An 1896 Supreme Court decision that provided a constitutional justification for segregation by ruling that a Louisiana law requiring "equal but separate accommodations for the white and colored races" was constitutional.

The Supreme Court was of little help. Although it voided a law barring African Americans from serving on juries (*Strauder v. West Virginia* [1880]), in the *Civil Rights Cases* (1883), it held that the Fourteenth Amendment did not prohibit racial discrimination by private businesses and individuals.

The Court then provided a constitutional justification for segregation, in the 1896 case of ***Plessy v. Ferguson***. The Louisiana legislature had required "equal but separate accommodations for the white and colored races" in railroad transportation. Although Homer Plessy was seven-eighths white, he had been arrested for refusing to leave a railway car reserved for whites. The Court upheld the law, saying that segregation in public facilities was not unconstitutional as long as the separate facilities were substantially equal. Moreover, the Court subsequently paid more attention to the "separate" than to the "equal" part of this ruling, allowing Southern states to maintain high schools and professional schools for whites even where there were no such schools for blacks. Significantly, until the 1960s, nearly all the African American physicians in the United States were graduates of two medical schools, Howard University in Washington, D.C., and Meharry Medical College in Tennessee.

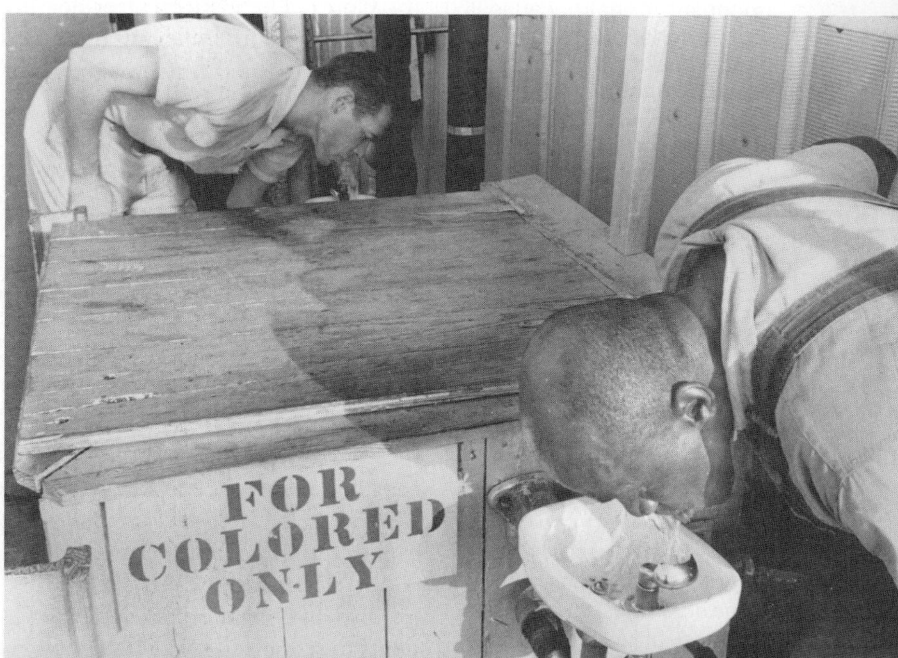

In the era of reconstruction and segregation, Jim Crow laws, such as those requiring separate drinking fountains for African Americans and whites, governed much of life in the South.

Nevertheless, some progress on the long road to racial equality was made in the first half of the twentieth century. The Supreme Court voided some of the most egregious practices limiting the right to vote (discussed later in this chapter). In 1941, President Franklin D. Roosevelt issued an executive order forbidding racial discrimination in defense industries, and in 1948, President Harry S. Truman ordered the desegregation of the armed services. The leading edge of change, however, was in education.

Equal Education

Education is at the core of Americans' beliefs in equal opportunity. It is not surprising, then, that civil rights advocates focused many of their early efforts on desegregating schools. To avoid the worst of backlashes, they started with higher education. The University of Oklahoma admitted George McLaurin, an African American, as a graduate student but forced him to use separate facilities, including a special table in the cafeteria, a designated desk in the library, and a desk just outside the classroom doorway. In *McLaurin v. Oklahoma State Regents* (1950), the Court ruled that a public institution of higher learning could not provide different treatment to a student solely because of his or her race. In the same year, the Court found the "separate but equal" formula generally unacceptable for professional schools in *Sweatt v. Painter*.

At this point, civil rights leaders turned to elementary and secondary education. After searching carefully for the perfect case to challenge legal public school segregation, the Legal Defense Fund of the National Association for the Advancement of Colored People (NAACP) selected the case of Linda Brown. Brown was an African American student in Topeka, Kansas, required by Kansas law to attend a segregated school. In Topeka, African American schools were fairly equivalent to white schools with regard to the visible signs of educational quality—teacher quality, facilities, and so on. Thus, the NAACP chose the case in order to test the *Plessy v. Ferguson* doctrine of "separate but equal." It wanted to force the Court to rule directly on whether school segregation was inherently unequal and thereby violated the Fourteenth Amendment's requirement that states guarantee "equal protection of the laws."

Brown v. Board of Education
The 1954 Supreme Court decision holding that school segregation was inherently unconstitutional because it violated the **Fourteenth Amendment**'s guarantee of **equal protection**. This case marked the end of legal segregation in the United States.

President Eisenhower had just appointed Chief Justice Earl Warren. So important was the case that the Court heard two rounds of arguments, one before Warren joined the Court. The justices, after hearing the oral arguments, met in the Supreme Court's conference room. Believing that a unanimous decision would have the most impact, the justices negotiated a broad agreement and then determined that Warren himself should write the opinion.

In ***Brown v. Board of Education*** (1954), the Supreme Court set aside its precedent in *Plessy* and held that school segregation was inherently unconstitutional because it violated the Fourteenth Amendment's guarantee of equal protection. Legal segregation had come to an end.

Brown v. Board of Education

In *Brown v. Board of Education,* the Supreme Court overturned its decision in *Plessy v. Ferguson.* This decision was a major step in changing the face of America. Just imagine what the United States would be like today if we still had segregated public facilities and services like universities and restaurants.

A year after its decision in *Brown*, the Court ordered lower courts to proceed with "all deliberate speed" to desegregate public schools. Desegregation proceeded slowly in the South, however. A few counties threatened to close their public schools; white enrollment in private schools soared. In 1957, President Eisenhower had to send troops to desegregate Central High School in Little Rock, Arkansas. In 1969, 15 years after its first ruling that school segregation was unconstitutional and in the face of continued massive resistance, the Supreme Court withdrew its earlier grant of time to school authorities and declared, "Delays in desegregating school systems are no longer tolerable" (*Alexander v. Holmes County Board of Education*). Thus, after nearly a generation of modest progress, Southern schools were suddenly integrated (see Figure 5.1).

In general, the Court found that if schools were legally segregated before, authorities had an obligation to overcome past discrimination. This could include assigning students to schools in a way that would promote racial balance. Some federal judges ordered the busing of students to achieve racially balanced schools, a practice upheld (but not required) by the Supreme Court in *Swann v. Charlotte-Mecklenberg County Schools* (1971).

Not all racial segregation is what is called *de jure* ("by law") segregation. *De facto* ("in reality") segregation results, for example, when children are assigned to schools

FIGURE 5.1 Percentage of Black Students Attending School with Any Whites in Southern States

Despite the Supreme Court's decision in *Brown v. Board of Education* in 1954, school integration proceeded at a snail's pace in the South for a decade. Most Southern African American children entering the first grade in 1955 never attended school with white children. Things picked up considerably in the late 1960s, however, when the Supreme Court insisted that obstruction of implementation of its decision in *Brown* must come to an end.

These table entries are based on elementary and secondary students in 11 Southern states—Virginia, North Carolina, South Carolina, Georgia, Alabama, Mississippi, Louisiana, Texas, Arkansas, Tennessee, and Florida.

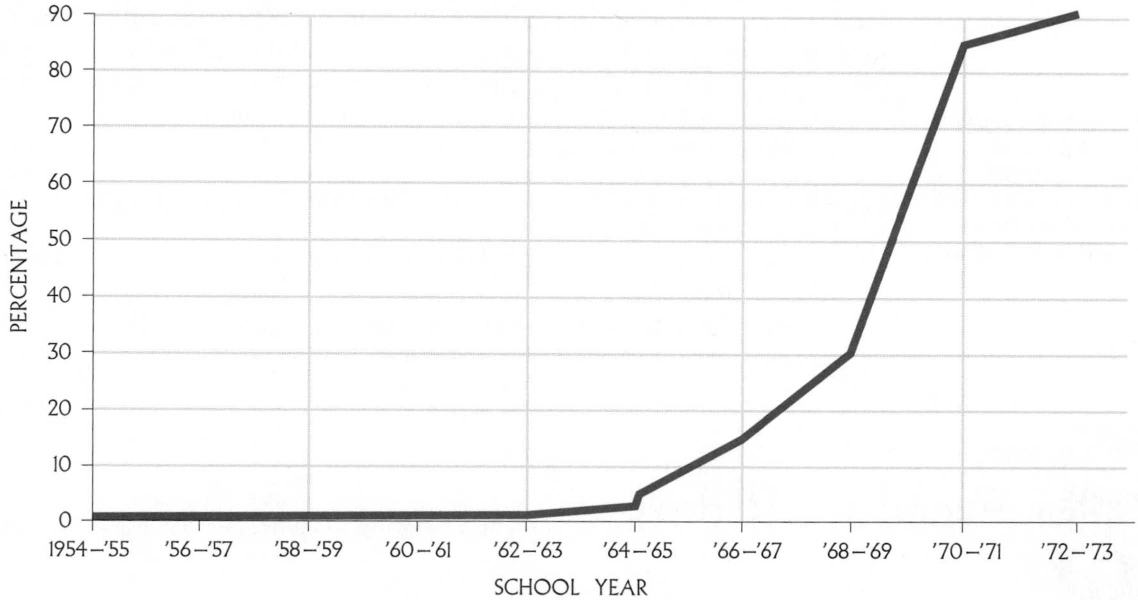

Source: Lawrence Baum, *The Supreme Court*, 10th ed. (Washington, DC: CQ Press, 2010), 192.

near their homes and those homes are in neighborhoods that are racially segregated for social and economic reasons. Sometimes the distinction between *de jure* and *de facto* segregation has been blurred by past official practices. Because minority groups and federal lawyers demonstrated that Northern schools, too, had purposely drawn district lines to promote segregation, school busing came to the North as well. Denver, Boston, and other cities instituted busing for racial balance, just as Southern cities did.

Majorities of both whites and blacks have opposed busing, which is one of the least popular remedies for discrimination. In recent years, it has become less prominent as a judicial instrument.

Courts do not have the power to order busing between school districts; thus, school districts that are composed largely of minorities must rely on other means to integrate. Kansas City, Missouri, spent years and $1.5 billion under federal court orders to attract white students from the city's suburbs, but with limited success. In 1995, in *Missouri v. Jenkins*, the Supreme Court indicated that it would not look favorably on continued federal court control of the district.

The Civil Rights Movement and Public Policy

The civil rights movement organized both African Americans and whites, and using tactics such as sit-ins, marches, and civil disobedience, sought to establish equal opportunities in the political and economic sectors and to end the policies and practices of segregation (see "Young People and Politics: Freedom Riders"). The movement's trail was long and sometimes bloody. Police turned their dogs on nonviolent marchers in Birmingham, Alabama. Racists murdered other activists in Meridian, Mississippi, and Selma, Alabama. Fortunately, the goals of the civil rights movement appealed to the national conscience. By the 1970s, overwhelming majorities of white Americans supported racial integration.[3] Today, the principles established in *Brown* have near-universal support.

It was the courts as much as the national conscience that put civil rights goals on the nation's policy agenda. In other areas as well as in education, *Brown v. Board of Education* was the beginning of a string of Supreme Court decisions holding various forms of discrimination unconstitutional. *Brown* and these other cases gave the civil rights movement momentum that would grow in the years that followed.

As a result of national conscience, the courts, the civil rights movement, and the increased importance of African American voters, the 1950s and 1960s saw a marked increase in public policies seeking to foster racial equality. These innovations included policies to promote voting rights, access to public accommodations, open housing, and nondiscrimination in many other areas of social and economic life. The **Civil Rights Act of 1964** did the following:

Civil Rights Act of 1964
The law making racial discrimination in hotels, motels, and restaurants illegal and forbidding many forms of job discrimination.

- Made racial discrimination illegal in hotels, motels, restaurants, and other places of public accommodation
- Forbade discrimination in employment on the basis of race, color, national origin, religion, or gender[4]
- Created the Equal Employment Opportunity Commission (EEOC) to monitor and enforce protections against job discrimination

Freedom Riders

Most political activity is quite safe. There have been occasions, however, when young adults have risked bodily harm and even death to fight for their beliefs. Years after *Brown v. Board of Education* (1954), segregated transportation was still the law in some parts of the Deep South. To change this system, the Congress of Racial Equality (CORE) organized freedom rides in 1961. Young black and white volunteers in their teens and early twenties traveled on buses through the Deep South. In Anniston, Alabama, segregationists destroyed one bus, and men armed with clubs, bricks, iron pipes, and knives attacked riders on another. In Birmingham, the passengers were greeted by members of the Ku Klux Klan with further acts of violence. At Montgomery, the state capital, a white mob beat the riders with chains and ax handles.

The Ku Klux Klan hoped that this violent treatment would stop other young people from taking part in freedom rides. It did not. Over the next six months, more than a thousand people took part in freedom rides. A young white man from Madison, Wisconsin, James Zwerg, was badly injured by a mob and left in the road for over an hour. White-run ambulances refused to take him to the hospital. In an interview afterward, he reflected the grim determination of the freedom riders: "Segregation must be stopped. It must be broken down. Those of us on the Freedom Ride will continue. No matter what happens we are dedicated to this. We will take the beatings. We are willing to accept death."

As with the Montgomery bus boycott and the conflict at Little Rock, the freedom riders gave worldwide publicity to the racial discrimination suffered by African Americans, and in doing so they helped to bring about change. Attorney General Robert Kennedy petitioned the Interstate Commerce Commission (ICC) to draft regulations to end racial segregation in bus terminals. The ICC was reluctant, but in September 1961 it issued the necessary orders.

The freedom riders did not limit themselves to desegregating buses. During the summer of 1961, they also sat together in segregated restaurants, lunch counters, and hotels. Typically they were refused service, and they were often threatened and sometimes attacked. The sit-in tactic was especially effective when it focused on large companies that feared boycotts in the North and that began to desegregate their businesses.

In the end, the courage of young people committed to racial equality prevailed. They helped to change the face of America.

QUESTIONS FOR DISCUSSION

- What are young adults doing to fight racism today?
- Does civil disobedience have a role in contemporary America?

- Provided for withholding federal grants from state and local governments and other institutions that practiced racial discrimination
- Strengthened voting rights legislation
- Authorized the U.S. Justice Department to initiate lawsuits to desegregate public schools and facilities

The Voting Rights Act of 1965 (discussed next) was the most extensive federal effort to crack century-old barriers to African American voting in the South. The Court decided in *Jones v. Mayer* (1968) that Congress could regulate the sale of private property to prevent racial discrimination and Congress passed the *Open Housing Act of 1968* to forbid discrimination in the sale or rental of housing.

In short, in the years following *Brown,* congressional and judicial policies attacked virtually every type of segregation. By the 1980s, there were few, if any, forms of racial discrimination left to legislate against. Efforts for legislation were successful, in part, because by the mid-1960s federal laws effectively protected the right to vote, in fact as well as on paper. Members of minority groups thus had some power to hold their legislators accountable.

Voting Rights

The early Republic limited **suffrage**, the legal right to vote, to a handful of the population—mostly property-holding white males. The **Fifteenth Amendment**, adopted in 1870, guaranteed African Americans the right to vote—at least in principle. It said, "The right of citizens to vote shall not be abridged by the United States or by any state on account of race, color, or previous condition of servitude." The gap between these words and their implementation, however, remained wide for a full century. States seemed to outdo one another in developing ingenious methods of circumventing the Fifteenth Amendment.

Many states required potential voters to complete literacy tests before registering to vote. Typically the requirement was that they read, write, and understand the state constitution or the U.S. Constitution. In practice, however, registrars rarely administered the literacy tests to whites, while the standard of literacy they required of blacks was so high that few were ever able to pass the test. In addition, Oklahoma and other Southern states used a *grandfather clause* that exempted persons whose grandfathers were eligible to vote in 1860 from taking these tests. This exemption did not apply, of course, to the grandchildren of slaves but did allow illiterate whites to vote. The law was blatantly unfair; it was also unconstitutional, said the Supreme Court in the 1915 decision *Guinn v. United States.*

To exclude African Americans from registering to vote, most Southern states also relied on **poll taxes**, which were small taxes levied on the right to vote that often fell due at a time of year when poor sharecroppers had the least cash on hand. To render African American votes ineffective, most Southern states also used the **white primary**, a device that permitted political parties to exclude African Americans from voting in primary elections. Because the South was so heavily Democratic, white primaries had the effect of depriving African Americans of a voice in the most important contests and letting them vote only when it mattered least, in the general election. The Supreme Court declared white primaries unconstitutional in 1944 in *Smith v. Allwright.*

The civil rights movement put suffrage high on its political agenda; one by one, the barriers to African American voting fell during the 1960s. The **Twenty-fourth Amendment**, which was ratified in 1964, prohibited poll taxes in federal elections. Two years later, the Supreme Court voided poll taxes in state elections in *Harper v. Virginia State Board of Elections.*

To combat the use of discriminatory voter registration tests—requiring literacy or an understanding of the Constitution, for example—the **Voting Rights Act of 1965** prohibited any government from using voting procedures that denied a person the vote on the basis of race or color and abolished the use of literacy requirements for anyone who had completed the sixth grade. The federal government sent election registrars to

suffrage
The legal right to vote, extended to African Americans by the **Fifteenth Amendment**, to women by the **Nineteenth Amendment**, and to people over the age of 18 by the **Twenty-sixth Amendment.**

Fifteenth Amendment
The constitutional amendment adopted in 1870 to extend suffrage to African Americans.

poll taxes
Small taxes levied on the right to vote. This method was used by most Southern states to exclude African Americans from voting. Poll taxes were declared void by the **Twenty-fourth Amendment** in 1964.

white primary
Primary elections from which African Americans were excluded, an exclusion that, in the heavily Democratic South, deprived African Americans of a voice in the real contests. The Supreme Court declared white primaries unconstitutional in 1944.

Twenty-fourth Amendment
The constitutional amendment passed in 1964 that declared **poll taxes** void in federal elections.

Voting Rights Act of 1965
A law designed to help end formal and informal barriers to African American suffrage. Under the law, hundreds of thousands of African Americans were registered, and the number of African American elected officials increased dramatically.

The Voting Rights Act of 1965 produced a major increase in the number of African Americans registered to vote in Southern states. Voting also translated into increased political clout for African Americans. President Lyndon Johnson is shown here signing the bill.

areas with long histories of discrimination, and these same areas had to submit all proposed changes in their voting laws or practices to a federal official for approval. As a result of these provisions, hundreds of thousands of African Americans registered to vote in Southern states.

The effects of these efforts were swift and certain, as the civil rights movement turned from protest to politics.[5] When the Voting Rights Act passed in 1965, only 70 African Americans held public office in the 11 Southern states. By the early 1980s, more than 2,500 African Americans held elected offices in those states, and the number has continued to grow. There are currently more than 9,400 African American elected officials in the United States.[6]

The Voting Rights Act of 1965 not only secured the right to vote for African Americans but also attempted to ensure that their votes would not be diluted through racial gerrymandering (drawing district boundaries to advantage a specific group). For example, in many cities, the residences of minorities were clustered in one part of the community. If members of the city council were elected from districts within the city, minority candidates would have a better chance to win some seats. In response, some cities chose to elect all council members in at-large seats (in which council members were elected from the entire city), thereby reducing the chances of a geographically concentrated minority from electing a minority council member. When Congress amended the Voting Rights Act in 1982, it further insisted that minorities be able to "elect representatives of their choice" when their numbers and configuration permitted. Thus, redrawing district boundaries was to avoid discriminatory *results* and not just discriminatory *intent*. In 1986, the Supreme Court upheld this principle in *Thornburg v. Gingles*.

> **WHY IT MATTERS**
>
> **The Voting Rights Act**
>
> In passing the Voting Rights Act of 1965, Congress enacted an extraordinarily strong law to protect the rights of minorities to vote. There is little question that officials pay more attention to minorities when they can vote. And many more members of minority groups are now elected to high public office.

Officials in the Justice Department, which was responsible for enforcing the Voting Rights Act, and state legislatures that drew new district lines interpreted the amendment of the Voting Rights Act and the *Thornburg* decision as a mandate to create minority-majority districts, districts in which a minority group accounted for a majority of the voters. Consequently, when congressional district boundaries were redrawn following the 1990 census, several states, including Florida, North Carolina, Texas, Illinois, New York, and Louisiana, created odd-shaped districts designed to give minority-group voters a numerical majority. Fourteen new U.S. House districts were drawn specifically to help elect African Americans to Congress, and six districts were drawn to elect new Hispanic members (these efforts worked, as we will see in Chapter 12).

However, in 1993, the Supreme Court heard a challenge to a North Carolina congressional district that in some places was cut no wider than a superhighway to create an African American majority winding snakelike for 160 miles. In its decision in *Shaw v. Reno*, the Court decried the creation of districts based solely on racial composition, as well as the district drawers' abandonment of traditional redistricting standards such as compactness and contiguity. Thus, the Court gave legal standing to challenges to any congressional map with an oddly shaped minority-majority district that may not be defensible on grounds other than race (such as shared community interest or geographical compactness).

In 1994, in *Johnson v. DeGrandy*, the Court ruled that a state legislative redistricting plan that does not create the greatest possible number of minority-majority districts is not in violation of the Voting Rights Act. In 1995, in *Miller v. Johnson*, the Court rejected the efforts of the Justice Department to achieve the maximum possible number of minority districts. It held that the use of race as a "predominant factor" in drawing district lines should be presumed to be unconstitutional. The next year, in *Bush v. Vera* and *Shaw v. Hunt*, the Supreme Court voided three convoluted districts in Texas and one in North Carolina on the grounds that race had been the primary reason for abandoning compact district lines and that the state legislatures had crossed the line into unconstitutional racial gerrymandering.

In yet another turn, in 1999, the Court declared in *Hunt v. Cromartie* that conscious consideration of race is not automatically unconstitutional if the state's primary motivation was potentially political (African Americans tend to be Democrats, for example) rather than racial. We can expect continued litigation concerning this question, especially since the Court has decided that state legislatures may redraw district boundaries at any time and not only after a census.[7]

The Rights of Other Minority Groups

5.3 Relate civil rights principles to progress made by other ethnic groups in the United States.

As we discuss in Chapter 6, America is heading toward a *minority majority*: a situation in which Americans who are members of minority groups will outnumber Americans of European descent (see "My State: A Nation of Minorities"). African Americans are not the only minority group that has suffered legally imposed discrimination. Even before the civil rights struggle, Native Americans, Hispanics, and Asians learned how powerless they could become in a society dominated by whites. The civil rights laws for which African Americans fought have benefited members of these groups as well. In addition, social movements tend to beget new social movements; thus, the African American civil rights movement of the 1960s spurred other minorities to mobilize to protect their rights.

Native Americans

The earliest inhabitants of the continent, the American Indians, are, of course, the oldest minority group. About 4.5 million people identify themselves as at least part Native American or Native Alaskan, including 11 percent of Oklahomans and New Mexicans and 18 percent of Alaskans. The history of poverty, discrimination, and exploitation experienced by American Indians is a long one. For generations, U.S. policy promoted westward expansion at the expense of Native Americans' lands. The government isolated Native Americans on reservations, depriving them of their lands and their rights. Then, with the Dawes Act of 1887, the federal government turned to a strategy of forced assimilation, sending children to boarding schools off the reservations, often against the will of their families, and banning tribal rituals and languages.

Finally, in 1924, Congress made American Indians citizens of the United States and gave them the right to vote, a status that African Americans had achieved a half century before. Not until 1946 did Congress establish the Indian Claims Act to settle Indians' claims against the government related to land that had been taken from them.[8] Today, most Native Americans still live in poverty and ill health, almost half on or near a reservation. American Indians know, perhaps better than any other group, the significance of the gap between public policy regarding discrimination and the realization of that policy.

But progress is being made. The civil rights movement of the 1960s created a more favorable climate for Native Americans to secure guaranteed access to the polls, to housing, and to jobs and to reassert their treaty rights. The Indian Bill of Rights was adopted as Title II of the Civil Rights Act of 1968, applying most of the provisions of the Constitution's Bill of Rights to tribal governments. In *Santa Clara Pueblo v. Martinez* (1978), the Supreme Court strengthened the tribal power of individual tribe members and furthered self-government by Indian tribes.

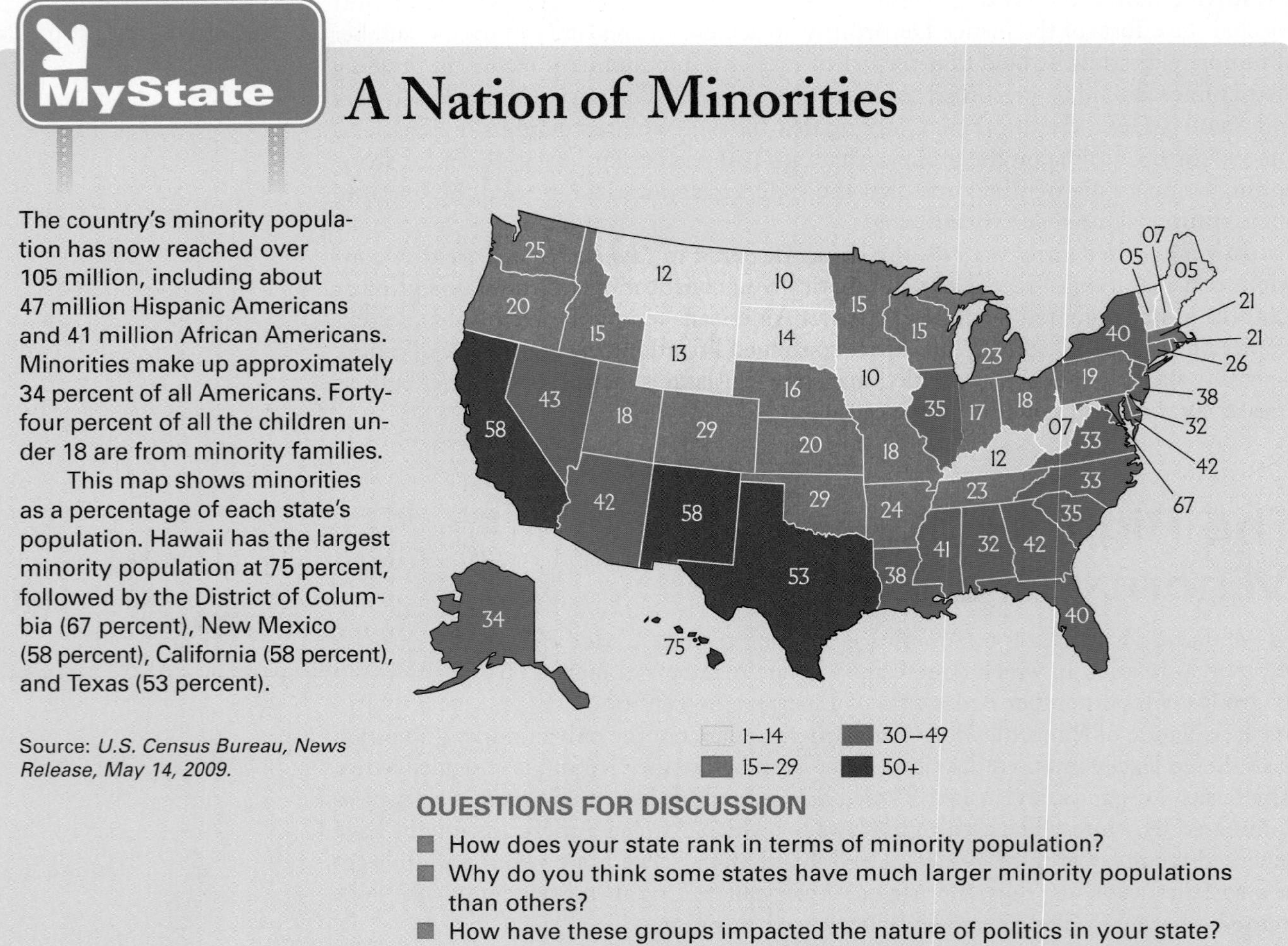

MyState

A Nation of Minorities

The country's minority population has now reached over 105 million, including about 47 million Hispanic Americans and 41 million African Americans. Minorities make up approximately 34 percent of all Americans. Forty-four percent of all the children under 18 are from minority families.

This map shows minorities as a percentage of each state's population. Hawaii has the largest minority population at 75 percent, followed by the District of Columbia (67 percent), New Mexico (58 percent), California (58 percent), and Texas (53 percent).

Source: *U.S. Census Bureau, News Release, May 14, 2009.*

QUESTIONS FOR DISCUSSION

- How does your state rank in terms of minority population?
- Why do you think some states have much larger minority populations than others?
- How have these groups impacted the nature of politics in your state?

Progress came in part through the activism of Indians such as Dennis Means of the American Indian Movement (AIM), Vine Deloria, and Dee Brown, who drew attention to the plight of American Indian tribes. In 1969, for example, some Native Americans seized Alcatraz Island in San Francisco Bay to protest the loss of Indian lands. In 1973, armed members of AIM seized 11 hostages at Wounded Knee, South Dakota—the site of an 1890 massacre of 200 Sioux (Lakota) by U.S. cavalry—and remained there for 71 days until the federal government agreed to examine Indian treaty rights.

Equally important, Indians began to use the courts to protect their rights. The Native American Rights Fund (NARF), founded in 1970, has won important victories concerning hunting, fishing, and land rights. Native Americans are also retaining access to their sacred places and have had some success in stopping the building of roads and buildings on ancient burial grounds or other sacred spots. Several tribes have won court cases protecting them from taxation of tribal profits.

As in other areas of civil rights, the preservation of Native American culture and the exercise of Native American rights sometimes conflict with the interests of the majority. For example, some tribes have gained special rights to fish and even to hunt whales. Anglers concerned with the depletion of fishing stock and environmentalists worried about loss of the whale population have voiced protests. Similarly, Native American rights to run businesses denied to others by state law and to avoid taxation on tribal lands have made running gambling casinos a lucrative option for Indians. This has irritated both those who oppose gambling and those who are offended by the tax-free competition.

Hispanic Americans

Hispanic Americans (or Latinos, as some prefer to be called)—chiefly from Mexico, Puerto Rico, and Cuba but also from El Salvador, Honduras, and other countries in Central and South America—have displaced African Americans as the largest minority group. Today they number more than 47 million and account for about 15 percent of the U.S. population. Hispanics make up 45 percent of the population of New Mexico and more than a third of the population of both California and Texas.

In Texas and throughout much of the Southwestern United States in the first half of the twentieth century, people of Mexican origin were subjected to discrimination, and worse. They were forced to use segregated public restrooms and attend segregated schools. Hundreds of them were killed in lynchings. Approximately 500,000 Latinos served in the U.S. armed forces in World War II, but many of these veterans faced discrimination upon their return. Dr. Hector P. Garcia founded the American GI Forum, the country's first Latino veterans' advocacy group, in 1948 after he saw the Naval Station at Corpus Christi refusing to treat sick Latino veterans. Garcia's organization received national attention when the remains of Felix Longoria, a Mexican American soldier killed while on a mission in the Pacific, were returned to his relatives in Three Rivers, Texas, for final burial. The only funeral parlor in his hometown would not allow Longoria's family to hold services for Longoria because of his Mexican heritage. Soon the incident became the subject of outrage across the country. With the help of the Forum and the sponsorship of then Senator Lyndon B. Johnson, Longoria was buried in Arlington National Cemetery.

In Jackson County, Texas, where Mexican Americans made up 14 percent of the population by the early 1950s, not a single person with a Spanish surname had been allowed to serve on a jury in 25 years. Some 70 Texas counties had similar records of exclusion. When an all-Anglo jury convicted Pete Hernandez, a migrant cotton picker, of murder in Jackson County, a team of Hispanic civil rights lawyers from the American GI Forum and the League of United Latin American Citizens (LULAC) filed suit, arguing that the jury that convicted him of murder could not be impartial because of the exclusion of Hispanics from the jury. This case eventually reached the Supreme Court, the first time that Hispanic lawyers had argued before the Court. The Supreme Court unanimously ruled in Hernandez's favor in ***Hernandez v. Texas* (1954)**, holding that in excluding Hispanics from jury duty, Texas had unreasonably singled out a class of people for different treatment. The defendant had been deprived of the equal protection guaranteed by the Fourteenth Amendment, a guarantee "not directed solely against discrimination between whites and Negroes." This landmark decision, which protected Hispanics and the right to fair trials, helped widen the definition of discrimination beyond race.

Hernandez v. Texas
A 1954 Supreme Court decision that extended protection against discrimination to Hispanics.

Hispanic leaders drew from the tactics of the African American civil rights movement, using sit-ins, boycotts, marches, and related activities to draw attention to their cause. Inspired by the NAACP's Legal Defense Fund, they also created the Mexican American Legal Defense and Education Fund (MALDEF), in 1968, to help argue their cause in court. In the 1970s, MALDEF established the Chicana Rights Project to challenge sex-discrimination against Mexican American women. In addition, Hispanic groups began mobilizing in other ways to protect their interests. An early prominent example was the United Farm Workers, led by César Chávez, who in the 1960s publicized the plight of migrant workers, a large proportion of whom are Hispanic.

Their growing numbers have made Hispanic Americans the largest minority group in the United States. Their political power is reflected in the two dozen members of the U.S. House of Representatives, such as Loretta and Linda Sanchez of California, the first set of sisters to serve simultaneously in Congress.

The rights of illegal immigrants have been a matter of controversy for decades. In 1975, Texas revised its education laws to withhold state funds for educating children who had not been legally admitted to the United States and authorized local school districts to deny enrollment to such students. In *Plyler v. Doe* (1982), the Supreme Court struck down the law as a violation of the Fourteenth Amendment because illegal immigrant children are people and therefore had protection from discrimination unless a substantial state interest could be shown to justify it. The Court found no substantial state interest that would be served by denying an education to students, who had no control over being brought to the United States, and observed that denying them an education would likely contribute to "the creation and perpetuation of a subclass of illiterates within our boundaries, surely adding to the problems and costs of unemployment, welfare, and crime."

A major concern of Latinos has been discrimination in employment hiring and promotion. Using the leverage of discrimination suits, MALDEF has won a number of consent decrees with employers to increase the opportunities for employment for Latinos.

Like Native Americans, Hispanic Americans benefit from the nondiscrimination policies originally passed to protect African Americans. Provisions of the Voting Rights Act of 1965 covered San Antonio, Texas, and thereby helped Hispanic voters to elect Henry Cisneros as mayor of San Antonio in 1981. There are now more than 5,200 elected Hispanic officials in the United States,[9] and Hispanic Americans play a prominent role in the politics of such major cities as Houston, Miami, Los Angeles, and San Diego. In 1973, Hispanics won a victory when the Supreme Court found that multimember electoral districts (in which more than one person represents a single district) in Texas discriminated against minority groups because they decreased the probability of a minority being elected.[10] Nevertheless, poverty, discrimination, and language barriers continue to depress Hispanic voter registration and turnout.

Korematsu v. United States
A 1944 Supreme Court decision that upheld as constitutional the internment of more than 100,000 Americans of Japanese descent in encampments during World War II.

Asian Americans

Asian Americans are the fastest-growing minority group: the 16 million persons who are at least part Asian make up about 5 percent of the U.S. population. For more than a hundred years prior to the civil rights acts of the 1960s, Asian Americans suffered discrimination in education, jobs, and housing as well as restrictions on immigration and naturalization. Discrimination was especially egregious during World War II when the U.S. government, beset by fears of a Japanese invasion of the Pacific Coast, rounded up more than 100,000 Americans of Japanese descent and herded them into encampments. These internment camps were, critics claimed, America's concentration camps. The Supreme Court, however, in ***Korematsu v. United States*** (1944), upheld the internment as constitutional. Congress has since authorized benefits for the former internees. As with other groups, policy changes have led to changes in status and in political strength for Asian Americans. Today, Americans of Chinese, Japanese, Korean, Vietnamese, and other Asian ethnicities have assumed prominent positions in U.S. society.

One of the low points in the protection of civil rights in the United States occurred during World War II when more than 100,000 Americans of Japanese descent were moved to internment camps.

Arab Americans and Muslims

There are about 3.5 million persons of Arab ancestry in the United States, and about 6 million Muslims. Since the terrorist attacks of September 11, 2001, Arab, Muslim, Sikh, and South Asian Americans and those perceived to be members of these groups have been the victims of increased numbers of bias-related assaults, threats, vandalism, and arson. The incidents have consisted of telephone, Internet, mail, and face-to-face threats; minor assaults as well as assaults with dangerous weapons and assaults resulting in serious injury and death; and vandalism, shootings, arson, and bombings directed at homes, businesses, and places of worship. Members of these groups have also experienced discrimination in employment, housing, education, and access to public accommodations and facilities.

As we saw in Chapter 4, in the wake of the September 11, 2001, terrorist attacks, the FBI detained more than 1,200 persons as possible threats to national security. About two-thirds of these persons were illegal aliens—mostly Arabs and Muslims—and many of them languished in jail for months until cleared by the FBI. This process seemed to violate the Sixth Amendment right of detainees to be informed of accusations against them, as well as the constitutional protection against the suspension of the writ of habeas corpus. As we have seen, in 2004 the Supreme Court declared that detainees had the right to challenge their detention before a judge or other neutral decision maker.

The struggle for equal rights has not been limited to minority groups, however. Political activity on behalf of women has been so energetic and so far-reaching that a separate section is needed to examine this struggle for equality.

Women and Public Policy

5.4 Trace the evolution of women's rights, and explain how civil rights principles apply to gender issues.

The first women's rights activists were products of the abolitionist movement, where they often encountered sexist opposition. Noting that the status of women shared much in common with that of slaves, some leaders resolved to fight for women's rights. Two of these women, Lucretia Mott and Elizabeth Cady Stanton, organized a meeting at Seneca Falls in upstate New York. They had much to discuss. Not only were women denied the vote, but they were also subjected to patriarchal (male-dominated) family law and denied educational and career opportunities. The legal doctrine known as *coverture* deprived married women of any identity separate from that of their husbands; wives could not sign contracts or dispose of property. Divorce law was heavily biased in favor of husbands. Even abused women found it almost impossible to end their marriages, and men had the legal advantage in securing custody of the children.

The Battle for the Vote

On July 19, 1848, 100 men and women signed the Seneca Falls Declaration of Sentiments and Resolutions. Patterned after the Declaration of Independence, it proclaimed, "The history of mankind is a history of repeated injuries and usurpations on the part of man toward woman, having in direct object the establishment of an absolute tyranny over her." Thus began the movement that would culminate, 72 years later, in the ratification of the **Nineteenth Amendment**, giving women the vote. Charlotte Woodward, 19 years old in 1848, was the only signer of the Seneca Falls Declaration who lived to vote for the president in 1920.

Nineteenth Amendment The constitutional amendment adopted in 1920 that guarantees women the right to vote. See also **suffrage**.

Although advocates of women's suffrage had hoped that the Fifteenth Amendment would extend the vote to women as well as to the newly freed slaves, this hope was disappointed, and as it turned out, the battle for women's suffrage was fought mostly in the late nineteenth and early twentieth centuries. Leaders like Stanton and Susan B. Anthony were prominent in the cause, which emphasized the vote but also addressed women's other grievances. The suffragists had considerable success in the states, especially in the West. Several states allowed women to vote before the constitutional amendment passed. The feminists lobbied, marched, protested, and even engaged in civil disobedience.[11]

The "Doldrums": 1920–1960

Winning the right to vote did not automatically win equal status for women. In fact, the feminist movement seemed to lose rather than gain momentum after winning the vote, perhaps because the vote was about the only goal on which all feminists agreed. There was considerable division within the movement on other priorities.

Many suffragists accepted the traditional model of the family. Fathers were breadwinners, mothers bread bakers. Although most suffragists thought that women should have the opportunity to pursue any occupation they chose, many also believed that women's primary obligations revolved around the roles of wife and mother. Many suffragists had defended the vote as basically an extension of the maternal role into public life, arguing that a new era of public morality would emerge when women could vote. These *social feminists* were in tune with prevailing attitudes.

Public policy toward women continued to be dominated by protectionism rather than by the principle of equality. Laws protected working women from the burdens of overtime work, long hours on the job, and heavy lifting. The fact that these laws also protected male workers from female competition received little attention. State laws tended to reflect—and reinforce—traditional family roles. These laws concentrated on limiting women's work opportunities outside the home so they could concentrate on their duties within it. The laws in most states required husbands to support their families (even after a divorce) and to pay child support, though divorced fathers did not always pay. When a marriage ended, mothers almost always got custody of the children, although husbands had the legal advantage in custody battles. Public policy was designed to preserve traditional motherhood and hence, supporters claimed, to protect the family and the country's moral fabric.[12]

Equal Rights Amendment
A constitutional amendment originally introduced in Congress in 1923 and passed by Congress in 1972, stating that "equality of rights under the law shall not be denied or abridged by the United States or by any state on account of sex." Despite public support, the amendment fell short of the three-fourths of state legislatures required for passage.

Only a minority of feminists challenged these assumptions. Alice Paul, the author of the original **Equal Rights Amendment** (ERA), was one activist who claimed that the real result of protectionist law was to perpetuate gender inequality. Simply worded, the ERA reads, "Equality of rights under the law shall not be denied or abridged by the United States or by any state on account of sex." Most people saw the ERA as a threat to the family when it was introduced in Congress in 1923. It gained little support. In fact, women were less likely to support the amendment than men were.

The Second Feminist Wave

The civil rights movement of the 1950s and 1960s attracted many female activists, some of whom also joined student and antiwar movements. These women often met with the same prejudices as had women abolitionists. Betty Friedan's book *The Feminine Mystique*, published in 1963, encouraged women to question traditional assumptions and to assert their own rights. Groups such as the National Organization for Women (NOW) and the National Women's Political Caucus were organized in the 1960s and 1970s.

Reed v. Reed
The landmark case in 1971 in which the Supreme Court for the first time upheld a claim of gender discrimination.

Before the advent of the contemporary feminist movement, the Supreme Court upheld virtually every instance of gender-based discrimination. The state and federal governments could discriminate against women—and, indeed, men—as they chose. In the 1970s, the Court began to take a closer look at gender discrimination. In ***Reed v. Reed*** (1971), the Court ruled that any "arbitrary" gender-based classification violated the equal protection clause of the Fourteenth Amendment. This was the first time the Court declared any law unconstitutional on the basis of gender discrimination.

Craig v. Boren
In this 1976 ruling, the Supreme Court established the "intermediate scrutiny" standard for determining gender discrimination.

Five years later, the Court heard a case regarding an Oklahoma law that prohibited the sale of 3.2 percent beer to males under the age of 21 but allowed females over the age of 18 to purchase it. In ***Craig v. Boren*** (1976), the Court voided the statute and established an "intermediate scrutiny" standard: The Court would not presume gender discrimination to be either valid or invalid. The courts were to show less deference to gender classifications than to more routine classifications but more deference than to racial classifications. Nevertheless, the Court has repeatedly said that there must be an "exceedingly persuasive justification" for any government to classify people by gender.

The Supreme Court has struck down many laws and rules for discriminating on the basis of gender. For example, the Court voided laws giving husbands exclusive control over family property.[13] The Court also voided employers' rules that denied women equal monthly retirement benefits because they live longer than men.[14]

Despite *Craig v. Boren*, men have been less successful than women in challenging gender classifications. The Court upheld a statutory rape law applying only to men[15] and the male-only draft, which we will discuss shortly. The Court also allowed a Florida law giving property tax exemptions only to widows, not to widowers.[16]

Contemporary feminists have suffered defeats as well as victories. The ERA was revived when Congress passed it in 1972 and extended the deadline for ratification until 1982. Nevertheless, the ERA was three states short of ratification when time ran out. Paradoxically, whereas the 1920 suffrage victory had weakened feminism, losing the ERA battle stimulated the movement. Proponents have vowed to keep reintroducing the amendment in Congress and continue to press hard for state and federal action on women's rights.

Women in the Workplace

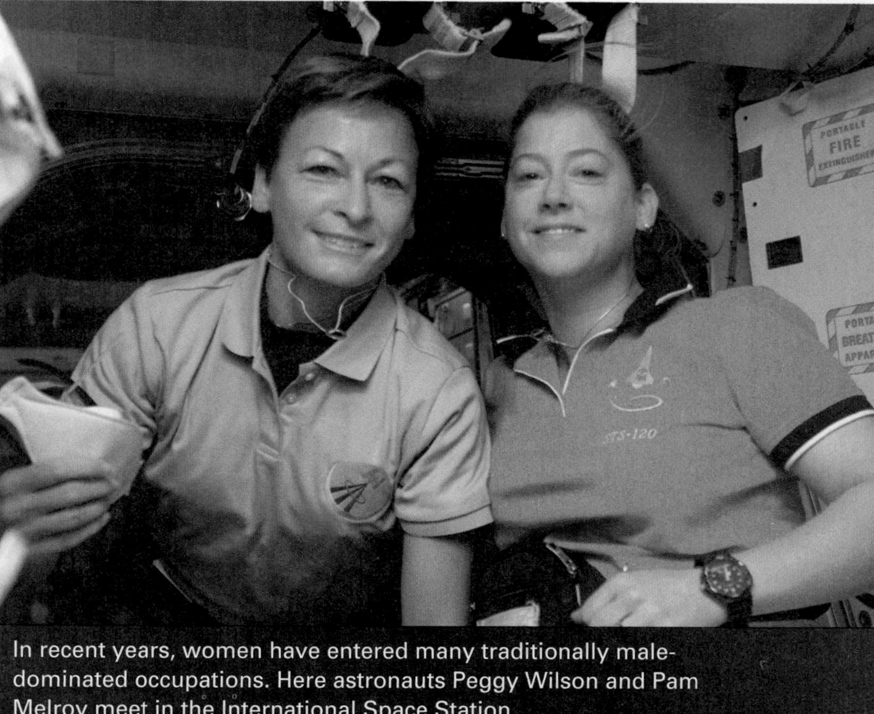

In recent years, women have entered many traditionally male-dominated occupations. Here astronauts Peggy Wilson and Pam Melroy meet in the International Space Station.

One reason why feminist activism persists has nothing to do with ideology or other social movements. The family pattern that traditionalists sought to preserve—father at work, mother at home—is becoming a thing of the past. There are 72 million women in the civilian labor force (compared to 83 million males), representing 60 percent of adult women. Sixty-two percent of these women are married and living with their spouse. There are also 34 million female-headed households (8 million of which include children), and about 70 percent of American mothers who have children below school age are in the labor force.[17] As conditions have changed, public opinion and public policy demands have changed, too.

Congress has made some important progress, especially in the area of employment. The Civil Rights Act of 1964 banned gender discrimination in employment. The protection of this law has been expanded several times. For example, in 1972, Congress gave the EEOC the power to sue employers suspected of illegal discrimination. The Pregnancy Discrimination Act of 1978 made it illegal for employers to exclude pregnancy and childbirth from their sick leave and health benefits plans. The Civil Rights and Women's Equity in Employment Act of 1991 shifted the burden of proof in justifying hiring and promotion practices to employers, who must show that a gender requirement is necessary for the particular job.

The Supreme Court also weighed in against gender discrimination in employment and business activity. In 1977, it voided laws and rules barring women from jobs through arbitrary height and weight requirements (*Dothard v. Rawlinson*). Any such prerequisites must be directly related to the duties required in a particular position. Women have also been protected from being required to take mandatory pregnancy leaves from their jobs[18] and from being denied a job because of an employer's concern for harming a developing fetus.[19] Many commercial contacts are made in private business and service clubs, which often have excluded women from membership. The Court has upheld state and city laws that prohibit such discrimination.[20]

Education is closely related to employment. Title IX of the Education Act of 1972 forbids gender discrimination in federally subsidized education programs (which include almost all colleges and universities), including athletics. But what about single-gender schooling? In 1996, the Supreme Court declared that Virginia's categorical exclusion of women from education opportunities at the state-funded Virginia Military Institute (VMI) violated women's rights to equal protection of the law.[21] A few days later, The Citadel, the nation's only other state-supported all-male college, announced that it would also admit women.

Women have made substantial progress in their quest for equality, but debate continues as Congress considers new laws. Three of the most controversial issues that legislators will continue to face are wage discrimination, sexual harassment, and the role of women in the military.

WHY IT MATTERS

Changes in the Workplace

Laws and Supreme Court decisions striking down barriers to employment for women are not just words. They have had important consequences for employment opportunities for many millions of women and have helped women make substantial gains in entering careers formerly occupied almost entirely by men.

Wage Discrimination and Comparable Worth

Traditional women's jobs often pay much less than men's jobs that demand comparable skill; for example, a female secretary often earns far less than a male accounts clerk with the same qualifications. Median weekly earnings for women working full time are only

Hillary Clinton, shown here speaking to supporters during her 2008 run for the Democratic presidential nomination, is symbolic of the increasing prominence of women in American society.

80 percent those for men working full time.[22] In other words, although the wage gap has narrowed, women still earn only $0.80 for every $1.00 men make. You can see the trend in wage ratios in "A Generation of Change: The Shrinking Gap Between Men's and Women's Wages."

The first significant legislation that Barack Obama signed as president was a 2009 bill outlawing "discrimination in compensation," which is broadly defined to include wages and employee benefits. The law also makes it easier for workers to win lawsuits claiming pay discrimination based on gender, race, religion, national origin, age, or disability.

Sexual Harassment

Whether in the military, on the assembly line, or in the office, women for years have voiced concern about sexual harassment, which, of course, does not affect only women. The U.S. Equal Employment Opportunity Commission defines sexual harassment as "unwelcome sexual advances, requests for sexual favors, and other verbal or physical conduct of a sexual nature . . . when this conduct explicitly or implicitly affects an individual's employment, unreasonably interferes with an individual's work performance, or creates an intimidating, hostile, or offensive work environment."[24]

In 1986, the Supreme Court articulated this broad principle: Sexual harassment that is so pervasive as to create a hostile or abusive work environment is a form of gender discrimination, which is forbidden by the 1964 Civil Rights Act.[25] In 1993, in *Harris v. Forklift Systems*, the Court reinforced its decision. No single factor, the Court said, is required to win a sexual harassment case under Title VII of the 1964 Civil Rights Act. The law is violated when the workplace environment "would reasonably be perceived, and is perceived, as hostile or abusive." Thus, workers are not required to prove that the workplace environment is so hostile as to cause them "severe psychological injury" or that they are unable to perform their jobs. The protection of federal law comes into play before the harassing conduct leads to psychological difficulty.[26] The Court has also made it clear that employers are responsible for preventing and eliminating harassment at work,[27] and they cannot retaliate against someone filing a complaint about sexual harassment.[28] Addressing harassment in public schools, the Court ruled that school districts can be held liable for sexual harassment in cases of student-on-student harassment.[29]

Sexual harassment may be especially prevalent in male-dominated occupations such as the military. A 1991 convention of the Tailhook Association, an organization of naval aviators, made the news after reports surfaced of drunken sailors jamming a hotel hallway and sexually assaulting female guests, including naval officers, as they stepped off the elevator. After the much-criticized initial failure of the navy to identify the officers responsible for the assault, heads rolled, including those of several admirals and the secretary of the navy. In 1996 and 1997, a number of army officers and noncommissioned officers were discharged—and some went to prison—for sexual harassment of female soldiers in training situations. Behavior that was once viewed as simply male high jinks is now recognized as intolerable. The Pentagon removed top officials at the Air Force Academy in 2003 following charges that female cadets were frequently raped by male cadets. With more women serving in

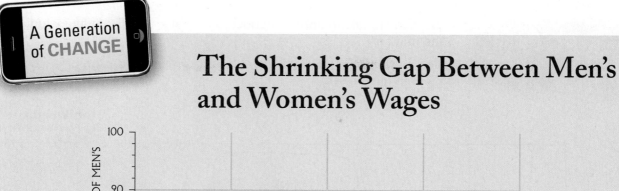

The Shrinking Gap Between Men's and Women's Wages

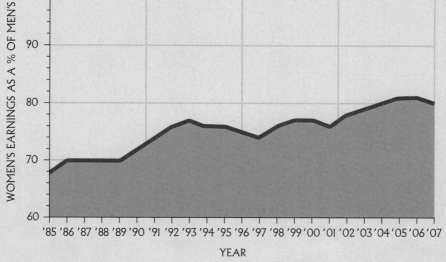

WOMEN'S EARNINGS AS A % OF MEN'S

100
90
80
70
60

'85 '86 '87 '88 '89 '90 '91 '92 '93 '94 '95 '96 '97 '98 '99 '00 '01 '02 '03 '04 '05 '06 '07

YEAR

Source: U.S. Department of Labor, Bureau of Labor Statistics, *Women in the Labor Force: A Databook* (2009 edition), Table 16.

Over the past generation, the gap between the earnings of a typical American woman and that of a typical American man has narrowed. In 1985, women's median weekly earnings were 68 percent of that of men, in contrast to about 80 percent today.

QUESTIONS FOR DISCUSSION

- Do you think the gender gap in earnings will continue to shrink as your generation moves into the work force? Why or why not?
- Some people think that the government should take steps to promote pay equity between men and women. For some proposals along these lines, see *http://www.pay-equity.org/cando.html.* What do you think? Is this the sort of area where the government should take action, or is this a matter best left to private enterprise?

the military, the issue of protecting female military personnel from sexual harassment becomes ever more pressing.

Women in the Military

Military service is another controversial aspect of gender equality. Women have served in every branch of the armed services since World War II. Originally, they served in separate units such as the WACS (Women's Army Corps), the WAVES (Women Accepted for Volunteer Emergency Service in the navy), and the Nurse Corps. Until the 1970s, the military had a 2 percent quota for women (which was never filled). Now women are part of the regular service. They make up about 14 percent of the active duty armed forces,[23] and compete directly with men for promotions. Congress opened all the service academies to women in 1975. Women have done well, sometimes graduating at the top of their class.

A POINT TO PONDER

Women are taking important positions in every walk of life, including the military.

Do you think the United States should continue the prohibition against women in combat?

Don Wright
The Palm Beach Post
Tribune Media Services

Two important differences between the treatment of men and that of women persist in military service. First, only men must register for the draft when they turn 18 (see "You Are the Judge: Is Male-Only Draft Registration Gender Discrimination?"). Second, statutes and regulations also prohibit women from serving in combat. A breach exists between policy and practice, however, as the Persian Gulf War and the wars in Iraq and Afghanistan have demonstrated. Women fly jets, pilot helicopters at the front, operate antimissile systems, patrol streets with machine guns, dispose of explosives, and provide unit and convoy security; some have been taken as prisoners of war. Women are now permitted to serve as combat pilots in the navy and air force and to serve on navy warships, including submarines. However, they are still not permitted to serve in ground combat units in the army or marines.

Women's participation in recent conflicts has reopened the debate over whether women should serve in combat. Some experts insist that because women, on average, have less upper-body strength than men, they are less suited to combat. Others argue that men will not be able to fight effectively beside wounded or dying women. Critics of these views point out that some women surpass some men in upper-body strength and that we do not know how well men and women will fight together. This debate is not only a controversy about ability; it also touches on the question of whether engaging in combat is a burden or a privilege. Clearly some women—and some who would deny them combat duty—take the latter view.

YOU ARE THE **JUDGE**

Is Male-Only Draft Registration Gender Discrimination?

Since 1973 the United States has had a volunteer force, and in 1975, registration for the draft was suspended. However, in 1979, after the Soviet Union invaded Afghanistan, President Jimmy Carter asked Congress to require both men and women to register for the draft. Registration was designed to facilitate any eventual conscription. Congress reinstated registration in 1980, but, as before, for men only. In response, several young men filed a suit. They contended that the registration requirement was gender-based discrimination that violated the due process clause of the Fifth Amendment.

You be the judge: Does requiring only males to register for the draft unconstitutionally discriminate against them?

Decision: The Supreme Court displayed its typical deference to the elected branches in the area of national security when it ruled in 1981 in *Rostker v. Goldberg* that male-only registration did not violate the Fifth Amendment. The Court found that male-only registration bore a substantial relationship to Congress's goal of ensuring combat readiness and that Congress acted well within its constitutional authority to raise and regulate armies and navies when it authorized the registration of men and not women. Congress, the Court said, was allowed to focus on the question of military need rather than "equity."

Other Groups Active Under the Civil Rights Umbrella

5.5 Show how civil rights principles have been applied to seniors, people with disabilities, and gays and lesbians.

Policies enacted to protect one or two groups can be applied to other groups as well. Three recent entrants into the civil rights arena are aging Americans, people with disabilities, and gays and lesbians. All these groups claim equal rights, as racial and ethnic minorities and women do, but they each face and pose different challenges.

Civil Rights and the Graying of America

America is aging rapidly. About 37 million people are 65 or older, accounting for 12 percent of the total population. Nearly 4.5 million people are 85 or older.[30] People in their eighties are the fastest-growing age group in the country.

When the Social Security program began in the 1930s, 65 was chosen as the retirement age for the purpose of benefits. The choice was apparently arbitrary, but 65 soon became the usual age for mandatory retirement. Although many workers might prefer to retire while they are still healthy and active enough to enjoy leisure, not everyone wants or can afford to do so. Social Security is not—and was never meant to be—an adequate income, and not all workers have good pension plans or retirement savings plans. Nevertheless, employers routinely refused to hire people over a certain age. Nor was age discrimination limited to older workers. Graduate and professional schools often rejected applicants in their thirties on the grounds that their professions would get fewer years—and thus less return—out of them. This policy had a severe impact on housewives and veterans who wanted to return to school.

As early as 1967, in the Age Discrimination in Employment Act, Congress banned some kinds of age discrimination. In 1975, a civil rights law was passed denying federal funds to any institution that discriminated against people over the age of 40 because of their age. Today, for most workers there can be no compulsory retirement. In 1976, the Supreme Court, however, declared that it would not place age in the suspect classification category, when it upheld a state law requiring police officers to retire at the age of 50. Thus, age classifications still fall under the reasonableness standard of review,[31] and employers need only show that age is related to the ability to do a job to require workers to retire.

Job bias is often hidden, and proving it depends on inference and circumstantial evidence. The Supreme Court made it easier to win cases of job bias in 2000 when it held in *Reeves v. Sanderson* that a plaintiff's evidence of an employer's bias, combined with sufficient evidence to find that the employer's asserted justification is false, may permit juries and judges to conclude that an employer unlawfully discriminated. Five years later, the Court found that employers can be held liable for discrimination even if they never intended any harm. Older employees need only show an employer's policies disproportionately harmed them—and that there was no reasonable basis for the employer's policy.[32] Thus, employees can win lawsuits without direct evidence of an employer's illegal intent. In 2008, the Supreme Court ruled that it is up to the employer to show that action against a worker stems form reasonable factors other than age (*Meacham v. Knolls Atomic Power Laboratory*). The impact of these decisions is likely to extend beyond questions of age discrimination to the litigation of race and gender discrimination cases brought under Title VII of the Civil Rights Act of 1964 as well as cases brought under the Americans with Disabilities Act.

Civil Rights and People with Disabilities

Americans with disabilities have suffered from both direct and indirect discrimination. Governments and employers have often denied them rehabilitation services, education, and jobs. And even when there has been no overt discrimination, many people with disabilities have been excluded from the workforce and isolated. Throughout most of American history, public and private buildings have been hostile to the blind, deaf, and mobility impaired. Stairs, buses, telephones, and other necessities of modern life have been designed in ways that keep the disabled out of offices, stores, and restaurants. As one slogan said, "Once, blacks had to ride at the back of the bus. We can't even get on the bus."

Americans with Disabilities Act of 1990
A law passed in 1990 that requires employers and public facilities to make "reasonable accommodations" for people with disabilities and prohibits discrimination against these individuals in employment.

The first rehabilitation laws were passed in the late 1920s, mostly to help veterans of World War I. Accessibility laws had to wait another 50 years. The Rehabilitation Act of 1973 added people with disabilities to the list of Americans protected from discrimination. Because the law defines an inaccessible environment as a form of discrimination, wheelchair ramps, grab bars on toilets, and Braille signs have become common features of American life. The Education of All Handicapped Children Act of 1975 entitled all children to a free public education appropriate to their needs. The **Americans with Disabilities Act of 1990** (ADA) strengthened these protections, requiring employers and administrators of public facilities to make "reasonable accommodations" and prohibiting employment discrimination against people with disabilities.

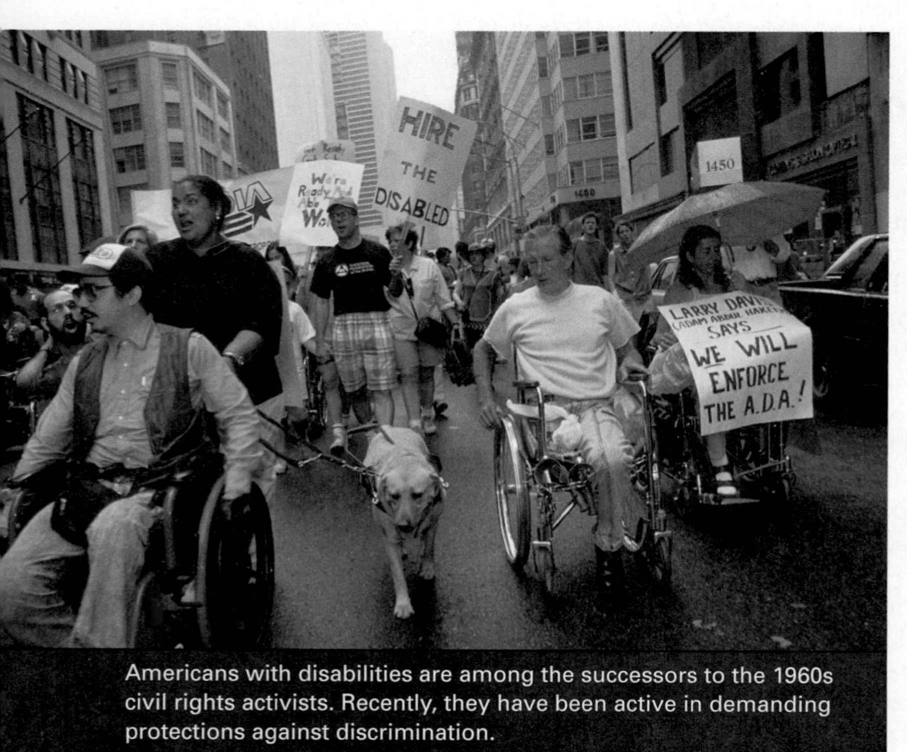

Americans with disabilities are among the successors to the 1960s civil rights activists. Recently, they have been active in demanding protections against discrimination.

Determining who is "disabled" has generated some controversy. Are people with AIDS entitled to protections? In 1998, the Supreme Court answered yes. It ruled that the ADA offered protection against discrimination to people with AIDS.[33] In 2008, Congress expanded the definition of disability, making it easier for workers to prove discrimination. Accordingly, in deciding whether a person is disabled, courts are not to consider the effects of "mitigating measures" like prescription drugs, hearing aids and artificial limbs. Moreover, "an impairment that is episodic or in remission is a disability if it would substantially limit a major life activity

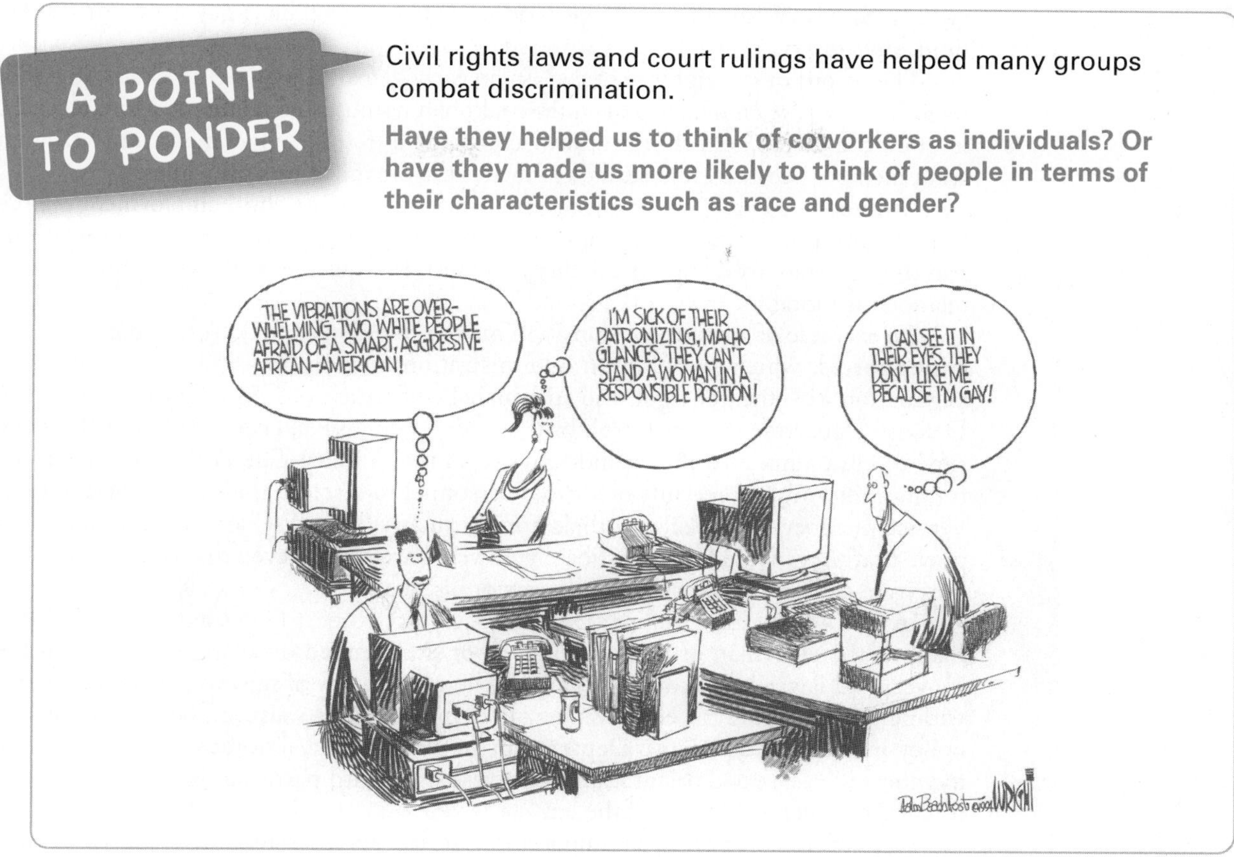

Civil rights laws and court rulings have helped many groups combat discrimination.

Have they helped us to think of coworkers as individuals? Or have they made us more likely to think of people in terms of their characteristics such as race and gender?

when active." Otherwise, the more successful a person is at coping with a disability, the more likely it is that a court would find that they are no longer disabled and therefore no longer covered under the ADA.

Nobody wants to oppose policies beneficial to people with disabilities. Nevertheless, civil rights laws designed to protect the rights of these individuals have met with opposition and, once passed, with sluggish enforcement. The source of this resistance is concern about the cost of programs. Such concern is often shortsighted, however. People forget that changes allowing people with disabilities to become wage earners, spenders, and taxpayers are a gain rather than drain on the economy.

Gay and Lesbian Rights

Even by conservative estimates, several million Americans are homosexual, representing every social stratum and ethnic group. Yet gays and lesbians have often faced discrimination in hiring, education, access to public accommodations, and housing, and they may face the toughest battle for equality.

Homophobia—fear and hatred of homosexuals—has many causes. Some of these causes are very deep-rooted, relating, for example, to the fact that certain religious groups condemn homosexuality. Homophobia has even led to killings, including the brutal 1998 killing of Matthew Shepard, a 21-year-old political science freshman at the University of Wyoming. Shepard was found tied to a fence, having been hit in the head with a pistol 18 times and repeatedly kicked in the groin.

The growth of the gay rights movement was stimulated by a notorious incident in a New York City bar in 1969. Police raided the Stonewall bar, frequented by gay men. Such raids were then common. This time, customers at the bar resisted the police. Unwarranted violence, arrests, and injury to persons and property resulted. In the aftermath of Stonewall, gays and lesbians organized in an effort to protect their civil rights, in the process developing political skills and forming effective interest groups. Significantly, most colleges and universities now have gay rights organizations on campus.

The record of gay rights is mixed. In an early defeat, the Supreme Court, in 1986, ruled in *Bowers v. Hardwick* that states could ban homosexual relations. More recently, in 2000 the Court held that the Boy Scouts could exclude a gay man from being an adult member because homosexuality violates the organization's principles.[34]

Attitudes are changing, however. Few Americans oppose equal employment opportunities for homosexuals, and majorities support the legality of homosexual relations and the acceptability of homosexuality as a lifestyle. Half the public views homosexual relations as moral.[35]

An example of attitudes in transition may be the "don't ask, don't tell" policy for the armed forces, which the Clinton administration adopted in 1993, after months of negotiation with the Pentagon and an avalanche of criticism. This policy reaffirmed the Defense Department's strict prohibition against homosexual conduct but at the same time did not automatically exclude gays from the military. The Pentagon was barred from asking military recruits or service personnel to disclose their sexual orientation. Service members who declared their homosexuality faced discharge unless they could prove that they would remain celibate and were barred from even disclosing to a friend in private conversation that they were gay or bisexual.

In 2010, President Obama, Defense Secretary Robert Gates and Admiral Mike Mullen, the chairman of the Joint Chiefs of Staff, called on Congress to repeal the 17-year-old law. The Pentagon began an extensive review of how to change the policy without undermining the effectiveness of the military. Gates also announced an interim policy in which the Defense Department would not take action to discharge service members whose sexual orientation was revealed by third parties or jilted partners, one of the most onerous aspects of the law.

Gay activists have also won important victories. Several states, including California, and more than 100 communities have passed laws protecting homosexuals against some forms of discrimination.[36] In 1996, in *Romer v. Evans*, the Supreme Court voided a state constitutional amendment approved by the voters of Colorado that denied homosexuals protection against discrimination. The Court found that the Colorado amendment violated the U.S. Constitution's guarantee of equal protection of the law. In 2003, in *Lawrence v. Texas*, the Supreme Court overturned *Bowers v. Hardwick* when it voided a Texas antisodomy law on the grounds that such laws were unconstitutional intrusions of the right to privacy.

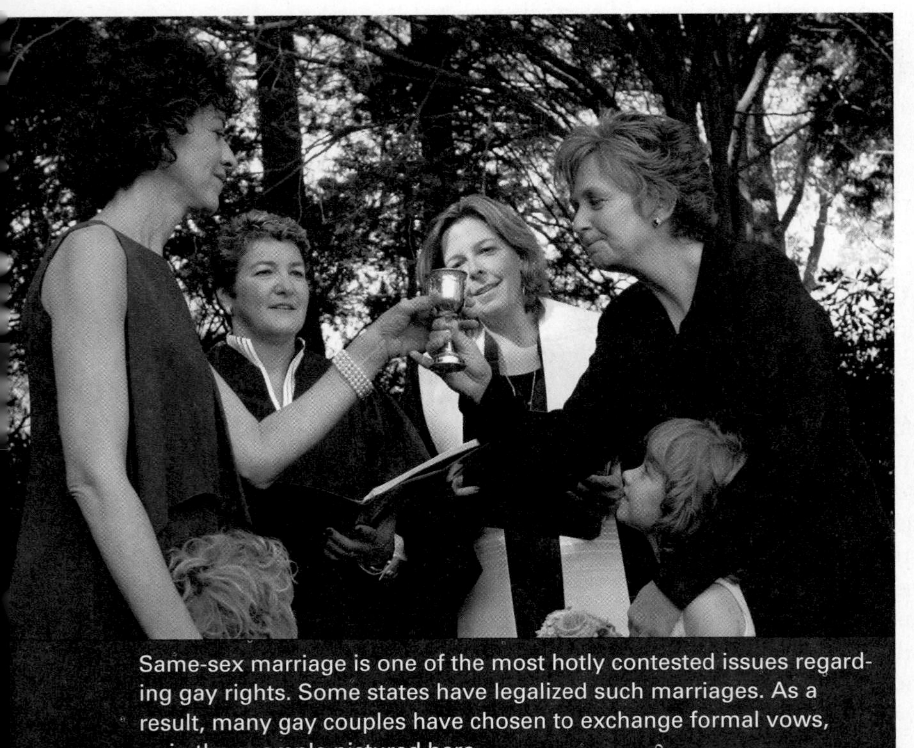
Same-sex marriage is one of the most hotly contested issues regarding gay rights. Some states have legalized such marriages. As a result, many gay couples have chosen to exchange formal vows, as in the example pictured here.

Today the most prominent issue concerning gay rights may be same-sex marriage. Most states have laws banning such marriages and the recognition of same-sex marriages that occur in other states. In 1996, Congress passed the Defense of Marriage Act, which permits states to disregard same-sex marriages even if they are legal elsewhere in the United States. However, Vermont, Massachusetts, Connecticut, New Hampshire, Iowa, and Washington, DC have legalized same-sex marriages. New York recognizes such marriages performed elsewhere. Several other states, including California, New Jersey, Hawaii, Maine, Washington, and Oregon, recognize same-sex "civil unions" or provide domestic partnership benefits to same-sex couples. When given the opportunity, gay and lesbian couples have rushed to the altar, provoking a strong backlash from social conservatives. President George W. Bush called for a constitutional amendment to ban same-sex marriage, but Congress has yet to pass such an amendment. With the prospects for gay marriage remaining uncertain, gays also continue to push for benefits associated with marriage, including health insurance, taxes, Social Security payments, hospital visitation rights, and much else that most people take for granted.

Affirmative Action

5.6 Trace the evolution of affirmative action policy and assess the arguments for and against it.

Some people argue that groups that have suffered invidious discrimination require special efforts to provide them with access to education and jobs. In 1965, President Lyndon Johnson signed Executive Order 11246, prohibiting federal contractors and federally assisted construction contractors and subcontractors from discriminating in employment decisions on the basis of race, color, religion, sex, or national origin. The order also required contractors to take "affirmative action" to ensure against employment discrimination, including the implementation of plans to increase the participation of minorities and women in the workplace.

Affirmative action involves efforts to bring about increased employment, promotion, or admission for members of groups who have suffered from discrimination. The goal is to move beyond *equal opportunity* (in which everyone has the same chance of obtaining good jobs, for example) toward *equal results* (in which different groups have the same percentage of success in obtaining those jobs). This goal might be accomplished through special rules in the public and private sectors that recruit or otherwise give preferential treatment to previously disadvantaged groups. Numerical quotas that ensure that a certain portion of government contracts, law school admissions, or police department promotions go to minorities and women are the strongest and most controversial form of affirmative action. The constitutional status of affirmative action is not clear.

affirmative action
A policy designed to give special attention to or compensatory treatment for members of some previously disadvantaged group.

At one point, the federal government mandated that all state and local governments, as well as each institution receiving aid from or contracting with the federal government, adopt an affirmative action program. The University of California at Davis (UC–Davis) introduced one such program. Eager to produce more minority physicians in California, the medical school set aside 16 of 100 places in the entering class for "disadvantaged groups." One white applicant who did not make the freshman class was Allan Bakke. After receiving his rejection letter from Davis for two straight years, Bakke learned that the mean scores on the Medical College Admissions Test of students admitted under the university's program were the 46th percentile on verbal tests and the 35th on science tests. Bakke's scores on the same tests were at the 96th and 97th percentiles, respectively. He sued UC–Davis, claiming that it had denied him equal protection of the laws by discriminating against him because of his race.

The result was an important Supreme Court decision in Bakke's favor, ***Regents of the University of California v. Bakke*** (1978).[37] The Court ordered Bakke admitted, holding that the UC–Davis Special Admissions Program did discriminate against him because of his race. Yet the Court refused to order UC–Davis never to use race as a criterion for admission. A university could, said the Court, adopt an "admissions program where race or ethnic background is simply one element—to be weighed fairly against other elements—in the selection process." It could *not*, as the UC–Davis Special Admissions Program did, set aside a quota of spots for particular groups.

Regents of the University of California v. Bakke
A 1978 Supreme Court decision holding that a state university could weigh race or ethnic background as one element in admissions but could not set aside places for members of particular racial groups.

Although Bakke ended up in medical school, Brian Weber did not get into the company apprenticeship program he wanted to enter. In *United Steelworkers of America, AFL-CIO v. Weber* (1979), the Court found that the Kaiser Aluminum Company, Weber's employer, intended its special training program, which had a quota for minorities, to rectify years of past employment discrimination at Kaiser. Thus, said the Court, a voluntary union- and management-sponsored program to take more African Americans than whites did *not* discriminate against Weber.

Until 1995, the Court was more deferential to Congress than to local government in upholding affirmative action programs. In 1989, the Court found a Richmond, Virginia, plan that reserved 30 percent of city subcontracts for minority firms to be unconstitutional.[38] In 1980, on the other hand, the Court upheld a federal rule setting aside 10 percent of all federal construction contracts for minority-owned firms.[39] In 1990, the Court agreed that Congress may require preferential treatment for minorities to increase their ownership of broadcast licenses.[40] This event marked the first time that the Supreme Court upheld a specific affirmative action program that was not devised to remedy past discrimination. On other matters, the Court approved preferential treatment of minorities in promotions,[41] and it ordered quotas for minority union memberships.[42]

Adarand Constructors v. Pena
A 1995 Supreme Court decision holding that federal programs that classify people by race, even for an ostensibly benign purpose such as expanding opportunities for minorities, should be presumed to be unconstitutional.

Things changed in 1995, however. In ***Adarand Constructors v. Pena***, the Court overturned the decision regarding broadcast licenses and cast grave doubt on its holding regarding contracts set aside for minority-owned firms. It held that federal programs that classify people by race, even for an ostensibly benign purpose such as expanding opportunities for members of minorities, should be presumed to be unconstitutional. Such programs must be subject to the most searching judicial inquiry and can survive only if they are "narrowly tailored" to accomplish a "compelling governmental interest." In other words, the Court applied criteria for evaluating affirmative action programs similar to those it applies to other racial classifications, the less-benign suspect standard we discussed earlier in the chapter. These are the same criteria the Court has applied to state affirmative action programs since 1989. Although *Adarand Constructors v. Pena* did not void federal affirmative action programs in general, it certainly limited their potential impact.

In addition, in 1984, the Court ruled that affirmative action does not exempt recently hired minorities from traditional work rules specifying the "last hired, first fired" order of layoffs.[43] And in 1986, it found unconstitutional an effort to give preference to African American public school teachers in layoffs because this policy punished innocent white teachers and the African American teachers had not been the actual victims of past discrimination.[44] We examine a more recent case of a public employer using affirmative action promotions to counter underrepresentation of minorities in the workplace in "You Are the Judge: The Case of the New Haven Firefighters."

A POINT TO PONDER
While supporters see affirmative action as a policy designed to provide greater opportunities for minorities to excel, opponents see it as a violation of the merit principle.
Is it possible to design a policy that meets both our concern for equality and the principle of merit as the basis of advancement?
I WONDER HOW HE FEELS ABOUT O.J.?
I WONDER HOW HE FEELS ABOUT FARRAKHAN?
I WONDER HOW HE FEELS ABOUT AFFIRMATIVE ACTION?
CHENEY

Opposition to affirmative action comes also from the general public. Such opposition is especially strong when affirmative action is seen as *reverse discrimination*—in which, as in the case of Allan Bakke, individuals are discriminated against when people who are less qualified are hired or admitted to programs because of their minority status. In 1996, California voters passed Proposition 209, which banned state affirmative action programs based on race, ethnicity, or gender in public hiring, contracting, and educational admissions (Washington State passed a similar ban in 1998). There is little question that support for Proposition 209 represented a widespread skepticism about affirmative action programs.

In 2003, the Supreme Court made two important decisions on affirmative action in college admissions. First, the Court agreed that there was a compelling interest in promoting racial diversity on campus. The Court upheld the University of Michigan law school's use of race as one of many factors in admission in *Grutter v. Bollinger* (2003). The Court found that the law school's use of race as a plus in the admissions process was narrowly tailored and that it made individualistic, holistic reviews of applicants in a nonmechanical fashion. In response, in 2006, Michigan voters passed a ballot initiative banning affirmative action in college admissions and government hiring.

In *Gratz v. Bollinger* (2003), however, the Court struck down the University of Michigan's system of undergraduate admissions in which every applicant from an underrepresented racial or ethnic minority group was automatically awarded 20 points of the 100 needed to guarantee admission. The Court said that the system was tantamount to using a quota, which it outlawed in *Bakke*, because it made the factor of race decisive for virtually every minimally qualified underrepresented minority applicant. The 20 points awarded to minorities were more than the school awarded for some measures of academic excellence, writing ability, or leadership skills.

In 2007, the Supreme Court addressed the use of racial classification to promote racial balance in public schools in Seattle, Washington, and Jefferson County, Kentucky. Some parents filed lawsuits contending that assigning children to different public schools based solely on their race violated the Fourteenth Amendment's equal protection guarantee. In *Parents Involved in Community Schools v. Seattle School District No. 1* (2007), the Court agreed that the school districts' use of race in their voluntary integration plans, even for the purpose of preventing resegregation, violated the equal protection guarantee and therefore was unconstitutional. Using the inherently suspect standard related to racial classifications, the Court found that the school districts lacked the compelling interest of remedying the effects of past intentional discrimination and concluded that racial balancing by itself was not a compelling state interest. The Court

YOU ARE THE JUDGE

The Case of the New Haven Firefighters

New Haven, Connecticut, used objective examinations to identify those firefighters best qualified for promotion. When the results of such an exam to fill vacant lieutenant and captain positions showed that white candidates had outperformed minority candidates, the city threw out the results based on the statistical racial disparity. White and Hispanic firefighters who passed the exams but were denied a chance at promotions by the city's refusal to certify the test results sued the city alleging that discarding the test results discriminated against them based on their race in violation of Title VII of the Civil Rights Act of 1964. The city responded that if they had certified the test results, they could have faced Title VII liability for adopting a practice having a disparate impact on minority firefighters.

You be the judge: Did New Haven discriminate against white and Hispanic firefighters?

Decision: In *Ricci v. DeStefano* (2009), the Court held that if an employer uses a hiring or promotion test, it generally has to accept the test results unless the employer has strong evidence that the test was flawed and improperly favored a particular group. New Haven could not reject the test results simply because the higher scoring candidates were white.

did indicate that school authorities might use a "race conscious" means to achieve diversity but that the school districts must be sensitive to other aspects of diversity besides race and narrowly tailor their programs to achieve diversity.

Whatever the Court may rule in the future with regard to affirmative action, the issue is clearly a complex and difficult one. Opponents of affirmative action argue that merit is the only fair basis for distributing benefits and that any race or gender discrimination is wrong, even when its purpose is to rectify past injustices rather than to reinforce them. Proponents of affirmative action argue in response that what constitutes merit is highly subjective and can embody prejudices of which the decision maker may be quite unaware. For example, experts suggest, a man might "look more like" a road dispatcher than a woman and thus get a higher rating from interviewers. Many affirmative action advocates also believe that increasing the number of women and minorities in desirable jobs is such an important social goal that it should be considered when looking at individuals' qualifications. They claim that what white males lose from affirmative action programs are privileges to which they were never entitled in the first place; after all, nobody has the right to be a doctor or a road dispatcher. Moreover, research suggests that affirmative action offers significant benefits for women and minorities with relatively small costs for white males.[45]

5.7 Establish how civil rights policy advances democracy and increases the scope of government.

Understanding Civil Rights and Public Policy

The original Constitution is silent on the issue of equality. The only direct reference in the Constitution to equality is in the Fourteenth Amendment, which forbids the states to deny "equal protection of the laws." Those five words have been the basis for major civil rights statutes and scores of judicial rulings protecting the rights of minorities and women. These laws and decisions, granting people new rights, have empowered groups to seek and gain still more victories. The implications of their success for democracy and the scope of government are substantial.

Civil Rights and Democracy

Equality is a basic principle of democracy. Every citizen has one vote because democratic government presumes that each person's needs, interests, and preferences are neither any more nor any less important than the needs, interests, and preferences of every other person. Individual liberty is an equally important democratic principle, one that can conflict with equality.

Equality tends to favor majority rule. Because under simple majority rule everyone's wishes rank equally, the policy outcome that most people prefer seems to be the fairest choice in cases of conflict. What happens, however, if the majority wants to deprive the minority of certain rights? In situations like these, equality threatens individual liberty. Thus, the principle of equality can invite the denial of minority rights, whereas the principle of liberty condemns such action.[46] In general, Americans today strongly believe in protecting minority rights against majority restrictions, as you can see in "America in Perspective: Respect for Minority Rights."

Majority rule is not the only threat to liberty. Politically and socially powerful minorities have suppressed majorities as well as other minorities. Women have long outnumbered men in America, about 53 percent to 47 percent. In the era of segregation, African Americans outnumbered whites in many Southern states. Inequality persisted, however, because customs that reinforced it were entrenched within the society and because inequality often served the interests of the dominant groups. When slavery and segregation existed in an agrarian economy, whites could get cheap agricultural labor. When men were breadwinners and women were homemakers, married men had a source of cheap domestic labor.

Both African Americans and women made many gains even when they lacked one essential component of democratic power: the vote. They used other rights—such as

Respect for Minority Rights

Americans rate the importance of protection of minority rights relatively highly compared to other democracies. Why do you think that is?

Question: There are different opinions about people's rights in a democracy. On a scale of 1 to 10, where 1 is not at all important and 7 is very important, how important is it that government authorities respect and protect rights of minorities?

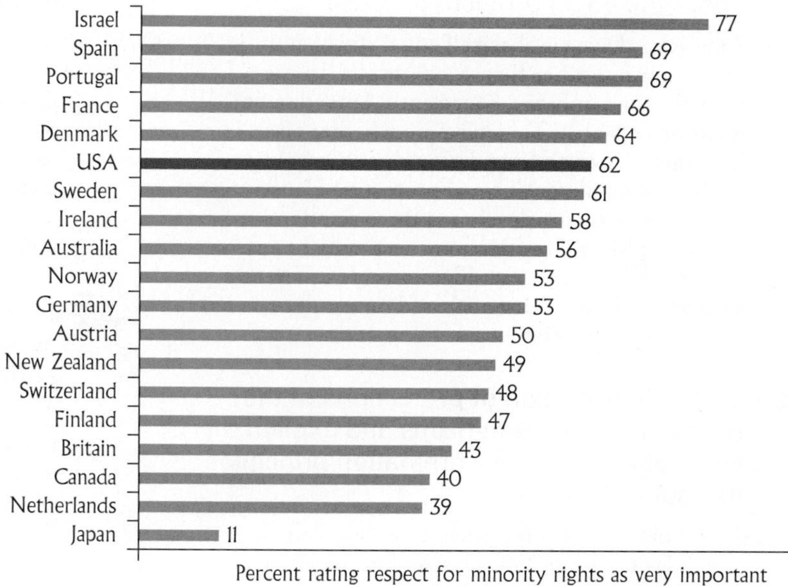

Source: Authors' analysis of 2004 International Society Survey Program data.

their First Amendment freedoms—to fight for equality. When Congress protected the right of African Americans to vote in the 1960s, the nature of Southern politics changed dramatically. The democratic process is a powerful vehicle for disadvantaged groups to press their claims.

Civil Rights and the Scope of Government

The Founders might be greatly perturbed if they knew about all the civil rights laws the government has enacted; these policies do not conform to the eighteenth-century idea of limited government. But the Founders would expect the national government to do whatever is necessary to hold the nation together. The Civil War showed that the original Constitution did not adequately deal with issues like slavery that could destroy the society the Constitution's writers had struggled to secure.

Civil rights laws increase the scope and power of government. These laws regulate the behavior of individuals and institutions. Restaurant owners must serve all patrons, regardless of race. Professional schools must admit women. Employers must accommodate people with disabilities and make an effort to find minority workers, whether they want to or not.

However, civil rights, like civil liberties, is an area in which increased government activity in protecting basic rights also represents limits on government and protection of individualism. Remember that much of segregation was *de jure*, established by governments. Moreover, basic to the notion of civil rights is that individuals are not to be judged according to characteristics they share with a group. Thus, civil rights protect the individual against collective discrimination.

The question of where to draw the line in the government's efforts to protect civil rights has received different answers at different points in American history, but few Americans want to turn back the clock to the days of *Plessy v. Ferguson* and Jim Crow laws or to the exclusion of women from the workplace.

Summary

5.1 Differentiate the Supreme Court's three standards of review for classifying people under the equal protection clause.

Americans have emphasized equal rights and opportunities rather than equal results. In the Constitution, only the Fourteenth Amendment mentions equality. To determine whether classifications in laws and regulations are in keeping with the amendment's equal protection clause, the Supreme Court developed three standards of review: Most classifications need only be reasonable, racial or ethnic classifications are inherently suspect, and classifications based on gender receive intermediate scrutiny.

5.2 Trace the evolution of protections of the rights of African Americans and explain the application of nondiscrimination principles to issues of race.

Racial discrimination is rooted in the era of slavery, which lasted about 250 years, and persisted in an era of segregation, especially in the South, into the 1950s. The civil rights movement achieved victories through civil disobedience and through the Court rulings, beginning with *Brown v. the Board of Education,* voiding discrimination in education, transportation, and other areas of life. In the 1960s, Congress prohibited discrimination in public accommodations, employment, housing, and voting through legislation such as the 1964 Civil Rights Act and the 1965 Voting Rights Act. Through their struggle for civil rights, African Americans blazed the constitutional trail for securing equal rights for all Americans.

5.3 Relate civil rights principles to progress made by other ethnic groups in the United States.

Native Americans, Hispanic Americans, Asian Americans, and Arab Americans and Muslims have suffered discriminatory treatment. Yet each group has benefitted from the application of Court decisions and legislation of the civil rights era. These groups have also engaged in political action to defend their rights.

5.4 Trace the evolution of women's rights, and explain how civil rights principles apply to gender issues.

After a long battle, women won the vote, with the passage of the Nineteenth Amendment, in 1920. Beginning in the 1960s, a second feminist wave successfully challenged gender-based classifications regarding employment, property, and other economic issues. Despite increased equality, issues remain, including lack of parity in wages, participation in the military, and combating sexual harassment.

5.5 Show how civil rights principles have been applied to seniors, people with disabilities, and gays and lesbians.

Seniors and people with disabilities have successfully fought bias in employment, and the latter have gained greater access to education and public facilities. Gays and lesbians have faced more obstacles to overcoming discrimination and have been more successful in areas such as employment and privacy than in obtaining the right to marry.

5.6 Trace the evolution of affirmative action policy and assess the arguments for and against it.

Affirmative action policies, which began in the 1960s, are designed to bring about increased employment, promotion, or admission for members of groups that have suffered from discrimination. In recent years, the Supreme Court has applied the inherently suspect standard to affirmative action policies and prohibited quotas and other means of achieving more equal results.

5.7 Establish how civil rights policy advances democracy and increases the scope of government.

Civil rights policies advance democracy because equality is a basic principle of democratic government. When majority rule threatens civil rights, the latter must prevail. Civil rights policies limit government discrimination but also require an active government effort to protect the rights of minorities.

Chapter Test

5.1 Differentiate the Supreme Court's three standards of review for classifying people under the equal protection clause.

1. Which of the following best characterizes the original Constitution's treatment of equality?
   a. The Constitution treats equality as corresponding with the phrase "all men are created equal"
   b. The Constitution treats equality as corresponding with equal results and equal rewards
   c. The Constitution treats equality as corresponding with the equal protection of the laws

d. The Constitution treats equality as corresponding with equal representation in Congress
e. The Constitution does not address equality

2. Courts presume classifications based on race to be
a. Constitutional
b. Remedial
c. Offensive
d. Reasonable
e. Inherently suspect

3. Based on your understanding of the U.S. Constitution, what do you think are the primary reasons why the Framers did not prioritize equality? Be specific and support your answer with examples.

5.2 Trace the evolution of protections of the rights of African Americans and explain the application of nondiscrimination principles to issues of race.

4. Which of the following statements best characterizes post-Reconstruction developments for African Americans?
a. The Supreme Court continued to strike down antidiscriminatory laws
b. The departure of federal troops from Southern states led to a surge of segregationist laws
c. African Americans increasingly sought employment in the federal government, which did not segregate by race
d. African Americans held seats in Congress and in state legislatures
e. All of the above are accurate characterizations

5. Which of the following did the Civil Rights Act of 1964 NOT accomplish?
a. It strengthened voting rights legislation
b. It forbade discrimination in the sale or rental of housing
c. It created the Equal Employment Opportunity Commission (EEOC)
d. It forbade discrimination in employment on the basis of race, color, national origin, religion, or gender
e. It authorized the U.S. Justice Department to initiate lawsuits to desegregate public schools

6. Civil rights laws only restrict *de jure* segregation.

True______ False______

7. Discuss the several court cases that built up to the landmark decision in *Brown v. Board of Education*. Why do you think segregation was addressed first in education and not in other areas, such as employment or housing?

8. Although the Fifteenth Amendment appeared to grant African Americans the right to vote, the gap in time between this amendment and its implementation was large. What were some of the primary means used by states to limit voting by African Americans? How were they able to do so in light of the specific wording of the Fifteenth Amendment?

5.3 Relate civil rights principles to progress made by other ethnic groups in the United States.

9. The Supreme Court has held that children not legally admitted to the United States are not protected by the Fourteenth Amendment.

True______ False______

10. The history of discrimination in the United States often focuses on the discrimination faced by African Americans, but other minority groups have also struggled for civil rights. In what ways were these struggles similar to the struggle of African Americans? In what ways were they different?

5.4 Trace the evolution of women's rights, and explain how civil rights principles apply to gender issues.

11. Which of the following statements best characterizes what occurred after ratification of the Nineteenth Amendment gave women the right to vote?
a. The movement for women's rights turned to promoting equality through public policy
b. The feminist movement continued to gain strength as women were able to vote for officials who supported their goals
c. New state laws began to expand opportunities for women in the workplace
d. The feminist movement lost momentum as it lacked unified support for its goals
e. A backlash led to more restricted social conditions for women

12. In *Craig v. Boren*, the Supreme Court held gender discrimination, like racial discrimination, to a strict scrutiny standard.

True______ False______

13. What are arguments (social, political, practical, and other) for and against opening up combat branches of the military to women? In what ways, if any, do you believe advances in technology have affected this issue?

5.5 Show how civil rights principles have been applied to seniors, people with disabilities, and gays and lesbians.

14. Which of the following is the standard for evaluating age discrimination claims?
a. The reasonableness standard
b. The medium scrutiny standard
c. The strict scrutiny standard
d. The employer's bias standard
e. The Supreme Court has yet to rule on a proper classification for age discrimination

15. The Americans with Disabilities Act prohibits employment discrimination against people with disabilities.

True______ False______

16. Imagine that you are a justice on the Supreme Court and, not having ruled on this issue before, the Court has an opportunity to set clear precedent on same-sex marriage. Based on your understanding of the Constitution, equality, and previous Court decisions concerning gays and lesbians, would you rule to support or oppose same-sex marriage? Justify your answer.

5.6 Trace the evolution of affirmative action policy and assess the arguments for and against it.

17. Which statement about affirmative action best reflects current Supreme Court precedent?
    a. Quotas or set-asides may be used in both employment and education to redress past discrimination
    b. Quotas or set-asides may be used in employment to redress past discrimination
    c. Racial set-asides can be used by universities and colleges in order to promote diversity
    d. Although racial set-asides are unconstitutional, race may be considered as one among many factors in determining college admissions
    e. Affirmative action in any form is reverse discrimination and is therefore unconstitutional under the Civil Rights Act of 1964

18. What are some of the arguments for and against affirmative action? In your answer, consider both the historical and the current context of affirmative action. Do you think affirmative action is constitutional? Explain your answer.

5.7 Establish how civil rights policy advances democracy and increases the scope of government.

19. How might civil rights laws, despite their intent to promote democratic values, actually work to threaten the liberties of individuals?

20. Based on what you know about the Framers' conception of equality, how do you think they would view the historical development of civil rights laws?

PEARSON mypoliscilab Exercises

Apply what you learned in this chapter on MyPoliSciLab.

Read on **mypoliscilab.com**

eText: Chapter 5

Study and **Review** on **mypoliscilab.com**

Pre-Test
Post-Test
Chapter Exam
Flashcards

Watch on **mypoliscilab.com**

Video: Should Don't Ask Don't Tell Go Away?
Video: Supreme Court: No Race-Based Admissions

Explore on **mypoliscilab.com**

Simulation: You Are the Mayor and Need to Make Civil Rights Decisions
Comparative: Comparing Civil Rights
Timeline: The Civil Rights Movement
Timeline: The Mexican-American Civil Rights Movement
Timeline: The Struggle for Equal Protection
Timeline: Women's Struggle for Equality
Visual Literacy: Race and the Death Penalty

Key Terms

civil rights (134)
Fourteenth Amendment (135)
equal protection of the laws (135)
Thirteenth Amendment (137)
Civil Rights Act of 1964 (140)
suffrage (141)
Fifteenth Amendment (141)
poll taxes (141)
white primary (141)
Twenty-fourth Amendment (141)
Voting Rights Act of 1965 (141)
Nineteenth Amendment (147)
Equal Rights Amendment (148)
Americans with Disabilities Act of 1990 (154)
affirmative action (157)

Key Cases

Scott v. Sandford (1857)
Plessy v. Ferguson (1896)
Brown v. Board of Education (1954)
Hernandez v. Texas (1954)
Korematsu v. United States (1944)
Reed v. Reed (1971)
Craig v. Boren (1976)
Regents of the University of California v. Bakke (1978)
Adarand Constructors v. Pena (1995)

Internet Resources

www.usdoj.gov/crt/
Home page of the Civil Rights Division of the U.S. Department of Justice, containing background information and discussion of current events.

www.usdoj.gov/crt/ada/adahom1.htm
Home page of the Americans with Disabilities Act of the U.S. Department of Justice, containing background information and discussion of current events.

www.naacp.org
Home page of the NAACP, containing background information and discussion of current events.

www.lulac.org
League of United Latin American Citizens home page, with information on Latino rights and policy goals.

www.civilrightsproject.ucla.edu/aboutus.php
Home page of the Civil Rights Project at UCLA, with background information and other resources on civil rights.

www.now.org
Home page of the National Organization of Women, containing material on issues dealing with women's rights.

www.hrc.org
Human Rights Campaign home page, with information on lesbian, gay, bisexual, and transgender rights.

www.usccr.gov
U.S. Commission on Civil Rights home page, with news of civil rights issues around the country.

For Further Reading

Anderson, Terry H. ***The Pursuit of Fairness.*** New York: Oxford University Press, 2005. A history of affirmative action.

Arsenault, Raymond. ***Freedom Riders: 1961 and the Struggle for Racial Justice.*** New York: Oxford University Press, 2006. The story of the freedom riders' efforts to desegregate the South.

Baer, Judith A. ***Women in American Law: The Struggle Toward Equality from the New Deal to the Present,*** 3rd rev. ed. New York: Holmes and Meier, 2003. An excellent analysis of women's changing legal status.

Berger, Raoul. ***Government by Judiciary: The Transformation of the Fourteenth Amendment.*** Cambridge, MA: Harvard University Press, 1977. Berger is not one who favors use of the Fourteenth Amendment to expand equality.

Bergman, Barbara R. ***In Defense of Affirmative Action.*** New York: Basic Books, 1996. An argument on behalf of affirmative action policies.

Bowen, William G., and Derek Bok. ***The Shape of the River: The Long-Term Consequences of Considering Race in College and University Admissions.*** Princeton, NJ: Princeton University Press, 1998. Former presidents of Harvard and Princeton discuss affirmative action in higher education.

García, John A. ***Latino Politics in America: Community, Culture, and Interests.*** Lanham, MD: Rowman & Littlefield, 2003. An insightful view of Latino politics.

Mansbridge, Jane. ***Why We Lost the ERA.*** Chicago: University of Chicago Press, 1986. The politics of women's rights.

McClain, Paula D., and Joseph Stewart. ***Can't We All Get Along?,*** 5th ed. Boulder, CO: Westview, 2009. Racial and ethnic minorities in American politics.

McGlen, Nancy, Karen O'Connor, Laura Van Assendelft, and Wendy Gunther. ***Women, Politics, and American Society,*** 4th ed. New York: Longman, 2004. Explores the efforts, achievements, and setbacks in the movement toward equality for women.

Nakanishi, Don T., and James S. Lai, eds. ***Asian American Politics: Law, Participation, and Policy.*** Lanham, MD: Rowman & Littlefield, 2003. Essays focusing on Asian American politics.

Perry, Barbara A. ***The Michigan Affirmative Action Cases.*** Lawrence, KS: University Press of Kansas, 2007. Behind-the-scenes story of the politics and law of attempting to overturn affirmative action programs in higher education.

Pinello, Daniel R. ***America's Struggle for Same-Sex Marriage.*** New York: Cambridge University Press, 2006. The social movement for same-sex marriage and the political controversies surrounding it.

Rimmerman, Craig A. ***The Lesbian and Gay Movements.*** Boulder, CO: Westview, 2008. Examines the strategies and issues of gay and lesbian politics.

Urofsky, Melvin I. ***A Conflict of Rights: The Supreme Court and Affirmative Action.*** New York: Scribner's, 1991. A case study of the issues, people, and events surrounding the case of *Joyce v. Johnson.*

Wilkins, David E. ***American Indian Politics and the American Political System,*** rev. ed. Lanham, MD: Rowman & Littlefield, 2003. Excellent treatment of Native American issues and politics.

Woodward, C. Vann. ***The Strange Career of Jim Crow,*** 2nd ed. New York: Oxford University Press, 1966. Examines the evolution of Jim Crow laws in the South.

Chapter 6

Public Opinion and Political Action

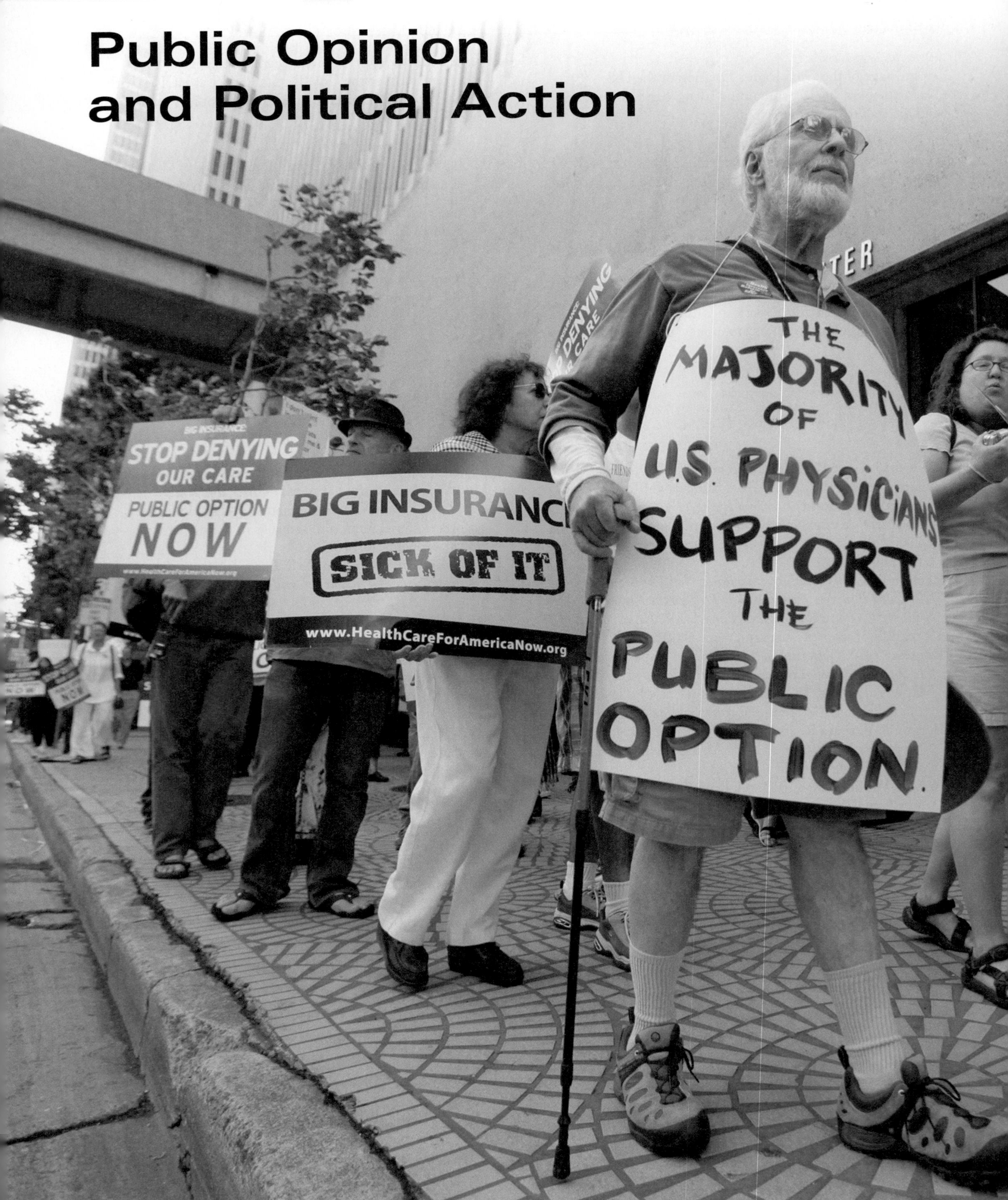

Learning Objectives

6.1 Identify demographic trends and their likely impact on American politics.

6.2 Outline how various forms of socialization shape political opinions.

6.3 Explain how polls are conducted and what can be learned from them about American public opinion.

6.4 Assess the influence of political ideology on Americans' political thinking and behavior.

6.5 Classify forms of political participation into two broad types.

6.6 Analyze how public opinion about the scope of government guides political behavior.

POLITICS IN ACTION: THE LIMITS OF PUBLIC UNDERSTANDING OF HEALTH CARE REFORM

One of the biggest issues early in the Obama administration was health care reform. President Obama made his proposal to guarantee health insurance coverage for almost all Americans a centerpiece of his plan for economic recovery. One of the most discussed elements of the original proposal supported by most Democrats was "the public option," a shorthand term for the creation of a government-administered health insurance program that would be available to individuals and small companies at competitive market rates. This proposal tapped straight into the fundamental issue of the proper scope of government, and sparked public demonstrations both for and against it.

One problem that Democrats faced was getting the public to understand the essence of their proposal. In August 2009, with the debate over the public option drawing much media attention, just 37 percent of respondents in a nationwide poll commissioned by AARP correctly identified the public option from a list of three choices provided to them. Commenting on these disappointing results on his popular political blog, Nate Silver wrote, "This is *mostly* a debate being had among policy elites and the relatively small fraction of the public that is highly knowledgeable and engaged about health care reform; for most others, the details are lost on them."[1]

Public opinion polling has become a major growth industry in recent years. The media seem to love to report on the latest polls. If there is nothing new in their findings, journalists can always fall back on one sure pattern: the lack of public attention to matters of public policy. Whether it's health care reform, cap-and-trade policy, or the question of immigration reform, the safest prediction that a public opinion analyst can make is that many people will be unaware of the major elements of the legislative debate going on in Washington.

In a democracy, the people are expected to guide public policy. But do people pay enough attention to public affairs to fulfill their duty as citizens? As we shall see in this chapter, there is much reason to be concerned about the level of public information about the American public; yet, a case can also be made that most people know enough for democracy to work reasonably well. Like public opinion itself, evaluating the state of public knowledge of public policy is complex.

Politicians and columnists commonly intone the words "the American people" and then claim their view as that of the citizenry. Yet it would be hard to find a statement about the American people—who they are and what they believe—that is either entirely right or entirely wrong. The American people are wondrously diverse. There are over 300 million Americans, forming a mosaic of racial, ethnic, and cultural groups. America was founded on the principle of tolerating diversity and individualism, and it remains one of the most diverse countries in the world. Most Americans view this diversity as among the most appealing aspects of their society.

The study of American **public opinion** aims to understand the distribution of the population's beliefs about politics and policy issues. Because there are many groups and a

Chapter
OUTLINE

public opinion
The distribution of the population's beliefs about politics and policy issues.

great variety of opinions in the United States, this is an especially complex task. This is not to say that public opinion would be easy to study even if America were a more homogeneous society; as you will see, measuring public opinion involves painstaking interviewing procedures and careful wording of questions.

For American government to work efficiently and effectively, the diversity of the American public and its opinions must be faithfully channeled through the political process. This chapter reveals just how difficult this task is.

6.1 Identify demographic trends and their likely impact on American politics.

The American People

demography
The science of population changes.

census
An "actual enumeration" of the population, which the Constitution requires that the government conduct every 10 years. The census is a valuable tool for understanding demographic changes.

One way of looking at the American public is through **demography**—the science of human populations. The most valuable tool for understanding demographic changes in America is the **census**. The U.S. Constitution requires that the government conduct an "actual enumeration" of the population every 10 years. The first census was conducted in 1790; the most recent census was done in 2010.

The Census Bureau tries to conduct the most accurate count of the population possible. It isn't an easy job, even with the allocation of billions of federal dollars to the task. In 2010, a census form was mailed out to all 134 million residential addresses in the United States. Despite the fact that federal law requires a response from every household—a fact that is noted on the mailing envelope—only 72 percent of households responded, ranging from a high of 81 percent in Wisconsin to a low of 62 percent in Alaska. Thus, 800,000 people were hired to follow up with the remaining 28 percent through door-to-door canvassing. In explaining on its Web site why participation was so important, the Census Bureau noted that "the information the census collects helps to determine how more than $400 billion dollars of federal funding each year is spent on infrastructure and services like: 1) hospitals; 2) job training centers; 3) schools; 4) senior centers; 5) bridges, tunnels and other public works projects; and 6) emergency services."[2] Communities that are usually undercounted in the census—primarily those with high concentrations of minorities, people with low incomes, and children—end up getting less from the federal government than they should.

Changes in the U.S. population, which census figures reflect, also impact our culture and political system in numerous ways, as will be examined in the next few sections.

In an attempt to get more people to fill out their Census form, the Census Bureau advertised heavily in 2010 to try to increase public awareness of the Census and its importance. One controversial allocation of money was $1.2 million to sponsor NASCAR driver Greg Biffle during three auto races in March. Critics derided this is as an absurd use of taxpayer money. In response, Census Director Robert Groves argued that millions of Americans followed NASCAR races, and that an increase in the initial response to the Census of just 0.1 percent could cut the cost of conducting the Census by $8.5 million.

The Immigrant Society

The United States has always been a nation of immigrants. As John F. Kennedy said, America is "not merely a nation but a nation of nations."[3] All Americans except Native Americans are either descended from immigrants or are immigrants themselves. Today, federal law allows for about 1 million new immigrants a year, and in recent years about 500,000 illegal immigrants a year have also entered the United States. Combined, this is equivalent to adding roughly the population of Phoenix every year. The Census Bureau estimates that currently 12 percent of the nation's population are immigrants and that 41 percent of this group have already become U.S. citizens. States vary substantially in the percentage of their residents who are foreign born—from a high of 27 percent in California to a low of 1 percent in West Virginia.

There have been three great waves of immigration to the United States:

- In the first wave, in the early and mid-nineteenth century, immigrants were mainly northwestern Europeans (English, Irish, Germans, and Scandinavians).
- In the second wave, in the late nineteenth and early twentieth centuries, many immigrants were southern and eastern Europeans (Italians, Jews, Poles, Russians, and others). Most came through Ellis Island in New York (now a popular museum).
- In the most recent wave, since the 1960s, immigrants have been especially Hispanics (particularly from Cuba, Central America, and Mexico) and Asians (from Vietnam, Korea, the Philippines, and elsewhere).

Immigrants bring with them their aspirations and their political beliefs. For example, Cubans in Miami, who constitute nearly half of the city's population, came to America to escape Fidel Castro's Marxist regime and brought their anticommunist sentiments with them. The Vietnamese, too, came after communists took power in their homeland. As with past waves of immigration, many immigrants today come, not to flee an oppressive government, but to escape poverty, and immigrants' aspirations as well as their political beliefs can influence the policy agenda. For example, to meet the needs of immigrant children who are poor and speak little English, many Hispanic leaders have advocated that bilingual education be offered in American public schools (see "You are the Policymaker: Should Some Schools Offer Bilingual Education?").

melting pot
A term often used to characterize the United States, with its history of immigration and mixing of cultures, ideas, and peoples.

The American Melting Pot

With its long history of immigration, the United States has often been called a **melting pot**, in which cultures, ideas, and peoples blend into one. As the third wave of immigration continues, policymakers have begun to speak of a new **minority majority**, meaning that America will eventually cease to have a non-Hispanic white majority. As of 2008, the Census Bureau reported an all-time low in the percentage of non-Hispanic white Americans—just 66 percent of the population. Hispanics made up the largest minority

minority majority
The situation, likely beginning in the mid-twenty-first century, in which the non-Hispanic whites will represent a minority of the U.S. population and minority groups together will represent a majority.

YOU ARE THE POLICYMAKER

Should Some Schools Offer Bilingual Education?

Bilingual education is the attempt to teach students in two languages. In 1968, Congress first mandated bilingual education for school districts with substantial non-English-speaking populations. A policy of bilingual education can be implemented in different ways. In a *maintenance* approach, students are taught in both English and their native language. In a *transitional* approach, students are at first taught in both languages but gradually, as their English skills improve, the other language is phased out. A slightly different approach from bilingual education is *English as a second language*, in which instruction is primarily in English but with concentrated instruction given to non-English speakers.

Each of these three approaches makes significant assumptions, which have larger policy implications. The first assumes that the United States can be a multilingual country and that it is good to preserve a multicultural heritage. The second and third assume (as some state laws have tried to proclaim) that America is a society in which everyone's primary language should be English.

The issue of bilingual education provokes strong public disagreements. Proponents of bilingual education contend that being placed into English-only classes guarantees poor learning by the children of many immigrants. Opponents argue that time spent educating students bilingually is time taken away from working on subjects like mathematics and science, and that these children will only become further disadvantaged. Both sides think they know what's best for these children, thereby leaving policymakers with a difficult choice.

What do you think? Would you encourage your local or state government to support special educational programs for non-English-speakers? If you support such programs, do you favor the *maintenance* version of *bilingual education*, the *transition* version, or *English as a second language*?

FIGURE 6.1 The Coming Minority Majority

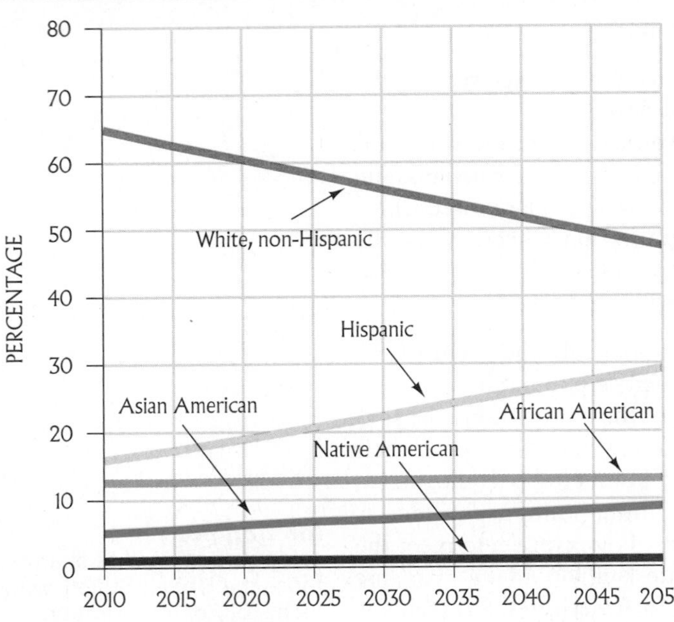

Based on current birthrates and immigration rates, the Census Bureau estimates that the demographics of the United States should change as shown in the accompanying graph. As of 2008, the Census estimated that minority groups should be in the majority nationwide by the year 2045. Of course, should rates of birth and immigration change, so would these estimates. Hawaii, New Mexico, California, and Texas already have minority majorities. Five other states—Maryland, Mississippi, Georgia, New York, and Arizona—have minority populations of about 40 percent.

Source: U.S. Census Bureau, http://www.census.gov/population/www/projections/summarytables.html.

group, accounting for 15 percent of the U.S. population, with African Americans making up 13 percent, Asian Americans 5 percent, and Native Americans 1 percent. In recent years, minority populations have been growing at a much faster rate than the white non-Hispanic population. As you can see in Figure 6.1, the Census Bureau estimates that by the middle of the twenty-first century, non-Hispanic whites will represent only 48 percent of the population.

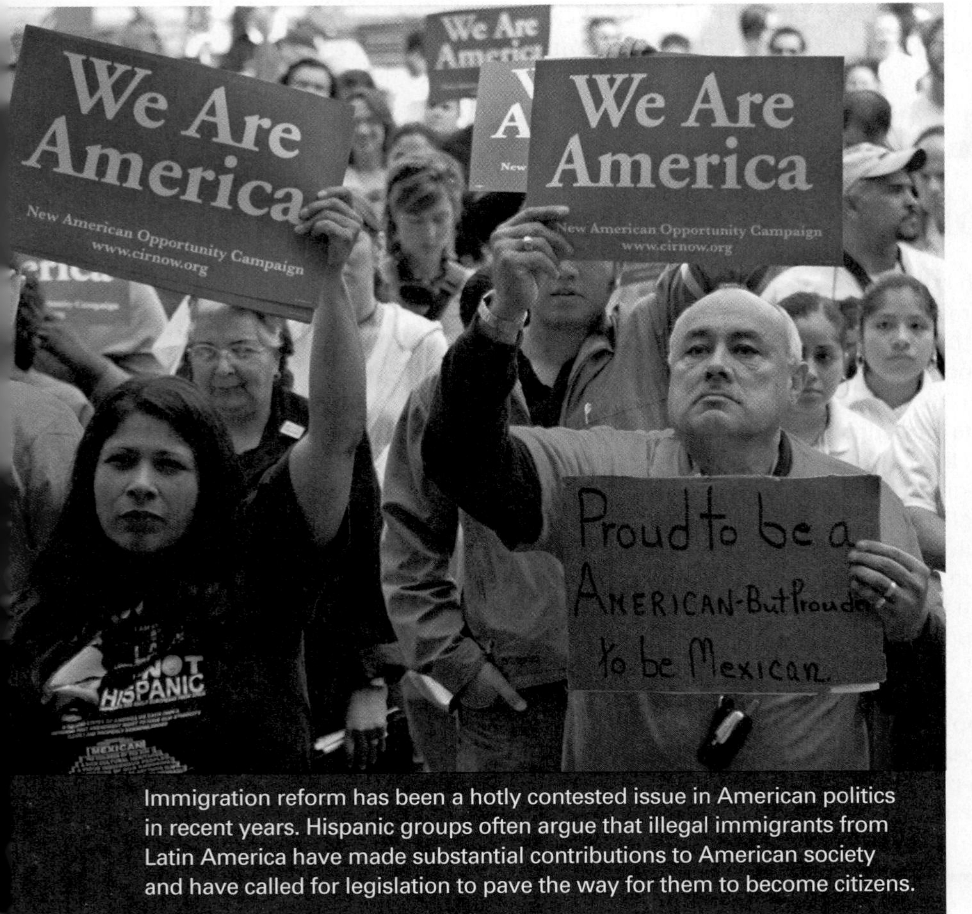

Immigration reform has been a hotly contested issue in American politics in recent years. Hispanic groups often argue that illegal immigrants from Latin America have made substantial contributions to American society and have called for legislation to pave the way for them to become citizens.

Until recently, African Americans were the largest minority group in the country. One in eight Americans is a descendant of these reluctant immigrants—Africans brought to America by force as slaves. A legacy of centuries of racism and discrimination (discussed in Chapter 5) is that a relatively high proportion of African Americans are economically disadvantaged—in 2008, according to Census Bureau data, 24 percent of African Americans lived below the poverty line compared to 9 percent of non-Hispanic whites.

Although this economic disadvantage persists, African Americans have been exercising more political power, and the number of African Americans serving in an elected office has increased by over 600 percent since 1970.[4] African Americans have been elected as mayors of many of the country's biggest cities, including Los Angeles, New York, and Chicago. Under George W. Bush, two African Americans, Colin Powell and Condoleezza Rice, served as secretary of state. And the biggest African American political breakthrough of all occurred when Barack Obama was elected president in 2008.

In the 2000 census, the Hispanic population outnumbered the African American population for the first time. Like African

Americans, Hispanics are concentrated in cities. Hispanics are rapidly gaining political power in the Southwest, and cities such as San Antonio and Los Angeles have elected mayors of Hispanic heritage. As of 2010, the state legislatures of New Mexico, Texas, Arizona, and California had at least 10 percent Hispanic representation.[5]

An issue of particular relevance to the Hispanic community is that of illegal immigration. According to the Department of Homeland Security, there were about 10.8 million unauthorized persons residing in the United States in 2009, 75 percent of whom were from Mexico and other Central American countries.[6] Although presidents Bush and Obama both pledged to address the problems of illegal immigration, no significant reform has been enacted since the 1986 Simpson-Mazzoli Act. This law requires that employers document the citizenship of their employees. Whether people are born in Canton, Ohio, or Canton, China, they must prove that they are either U.S. citizens or legal immigrants in order to work. Civil and criminal penalties can be assessed against employers who knowingly employ undocumented immigrants. However, it has proved difficult for authorities to establish that employers have knowingly accepted false social security cards and other forged identity documents, and, as a result, the Simpson-Mazzoli Act has not significantly slowed illegal immigration.

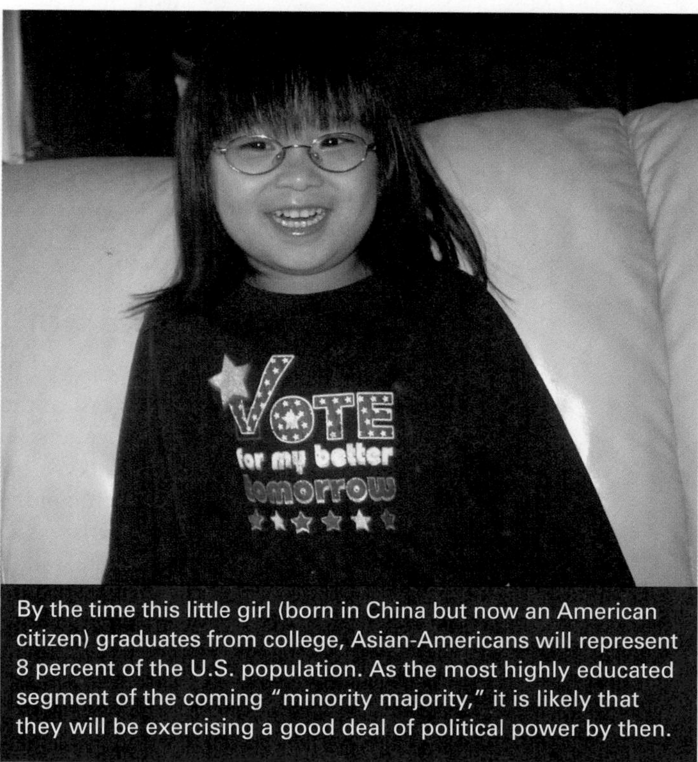

By the time this little girl (born in China but now an American citizen) graduates from college, Asian-Americans will represent 8 percent of the U.S. population. As the most highly educated segment of the coming "minority majority," it is likely that they will be exercising a good deal of political power by then.

Unlike Hispanics who have come to America to escape poverty, the recent influx of Asians, which began with the 1965 Immigration Act,[7] has been driven by a new class of professional workers looking for greater opportunity. Indeed, the new Asian immigrants are the most highly skilled immigrant group in American history,[8] and Asian Americans have often been called the superachievers of the emerging minority majority. Significantly, 53 percent of Asian Americans over the age of 25 hold a college degree, almost twice the national average.[9] As a result, their median family income has already surpassed that of non-Hispanic whites. Although still a very small minority group, Asian Americans have had some notable political successes. For example, in 1996 Gary Locke (a Chinese American) was elected governor of Washington, in 2001 Norman Mineta (a Japanese American) was appointed secretary of transportation, and in 2007 Bobby Jindal (an Indian American) was elected governor of Louisiana.

By far the worst off of America's minorities is its one indigenous minority, American Indians or Native Americans. Before the arrival of Europeans, America was home to 12 million to 15 million Native Americans. War and disease had reduced their numbers to a mere 210,000 by 1910. Currently, about 4.5 million Americans list themselves as being of Native American heritage. As a group, statistics show, they are the least healthy, the poorest, and the least educated in the American melting pot. Although some tribes have successfully exploited oil or other resources on their land and others have opened profitable casinos, many Native Americans remain economically and politically disadvantaged. In the Dakotas, site of the largest Sioux reservations, census data show that roughly half the Native Americans live below the poverty line.

Americans live in an increasingly multicultural and multilingual society. Yet, regardless of ethnic background, Americans have a common **political culture**—an overall set of values widely shared within the society. For example, there is much agreement across ethnic groups about such basic American values as the principle of treating all equally. However, not all observers view this most recent wave of immigration without concern. Ellis Cose, a prominent journalist, has written that "racial animosity has proven to be both an enduring American phenomenon and an invaluable political tool." Because America has entered a period of rapid ethnic change, Cose predicts immigration "will be a magnet for conflict and hostility."[10] For Robert Putnam, the concern takes a different form, as he finds that

political culture
An overall set of values widely shared within a society.

"diversity does *not* produce 'bad race relations' or ethnically defined group hostility" but, rather, that "inhabitants of diverse communities tend to withdraw from collective life" and to distrust their neighbors.[11] Putnam thus recommends a renewed emphasis on the motto on our one dollar bill—*e pluribus unum* (out of many, one) to deal with the challenge created by the growing diversity within American communities.

The emergence of the minority majority is just one of several major demographic changes that are altering the face of American politics. In addition, the population has been moving and aging.

The Regional Shift

For most of American history, the most populous states were concentrated north of the Mason–Dixon Line and east of the Mississippi River. However, as you can see in "My State: Shifting Population Centers," much of America's population growth since World War II has been centered in the West and South. In particular, the populations of Arizona, Texas, and Florida have grown rapidly as people moved to the Sun Belt. From 2000 to 2010, the rate of population growth was 29 percent in Arizona, 19 percent in Texas, and 16 percent in Florida. In contrast, population growth in the Northeast was a scant 3 percent.

reapportionment
The process of reallocating seats in the House of Representatives every 10 years on the basis of the results of the census.

Demographic changes are associated with political changes. States gain or lose congressional representation as their population changes, and thus power shifts as well. This **reapportionment** process occurs once a decade, after each census, when the 435 seats in the House of Representatives are reallocated to reflect population changes. Thus, as Texas grew in population, its representation in the House increased from just 21 in 1950 to 35 after the 2010 census. New York, on the other hand, lost over one-third of its delegation during the same period.

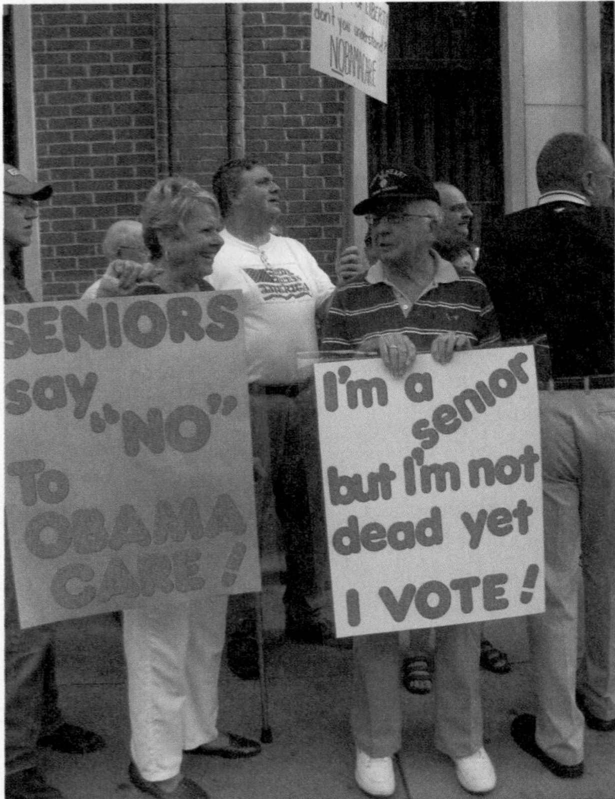

Senior citizens have been exercising more and more political power in recent decades. They not only vote in relatively high percentages, but also frequently make their political views heard through political actions, such as demonstrations. Here, some senior citizens in Lebanon, Pennsylvania are shown taking part in a protest against President Obama's health care reform bill.

The Graying of America

Florida, currently the nation's fourth most populous state, has grown in large part as a result of its attractiveness to senior citizens. Nationwide, citizens over 65 are the fastest-growing age group in America. Not only are people living longer as a result of medical advances, but in addition the fertility rate has dropped substantially—from 3.6 children per woman in 1960 to about 2.1 today.

The aging of the population has enormous implications for Social Security. Social Security is structured as a pay-as-you-go system, which means that today's workers pay the benefits for today's retirees. In 1960, there were 5.7 workers per retiree; today there are 3. By 2040, there will be only about two workers per retiree. This ratio will put tremendous pressure on the Social Security system, which, even today, is exceeded only by national defense as America's most costly public policy. The current group of older Americans and those soon to follow can lay claim to trillions of dollars guaranteed by Social Security. People who have been promised benefits naturally expect to collect them, especially benefits for which they have made monthly contributions. Thus, both political parties have long treated Social Security benefits as sacrosanct. For example, whenever President George W. Bush spoke on behalf of his proposal to allow younger workers to put part of their Social Security payroll taxes into personal retirement accounts, he carefully stated his view that Social Security should remain unchanged for anyone born before 1950. (For more on the future of Social Security, see Chapter 18.)

Shifting Population Centers

These maps paint a portrait of the regional shift in the population of the United States over the past 60 years. The states are drawn to scale on the basis of population. (Because Alaska and Hawaii were not states in 1950, they are not included in the first map.) In 1950, the most populous states were concentrated in the North and the East; New York, Pennsylvania, and Illinois stand out. By 2010 the national population picture had changed considerably. The country's population of over 300 million people is scattered more widely, and states such as California, Texas, and Florida have experienced huge increases.

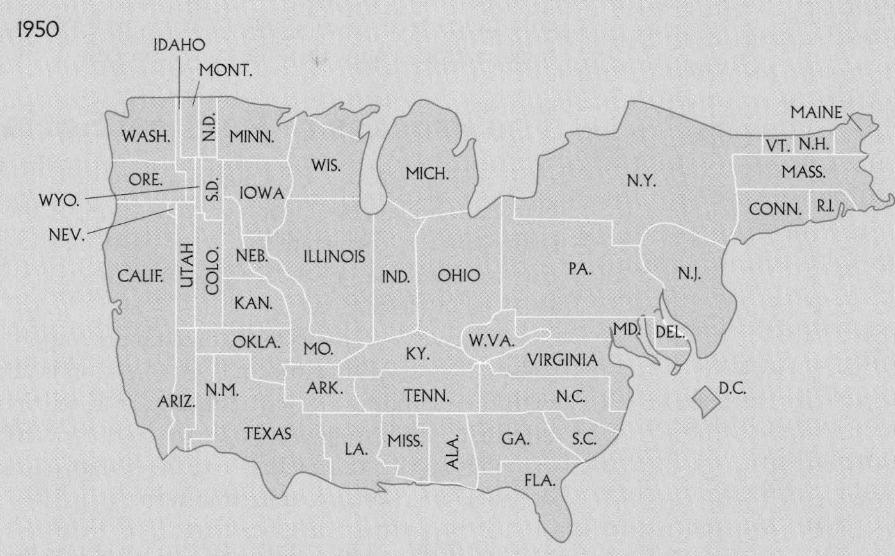

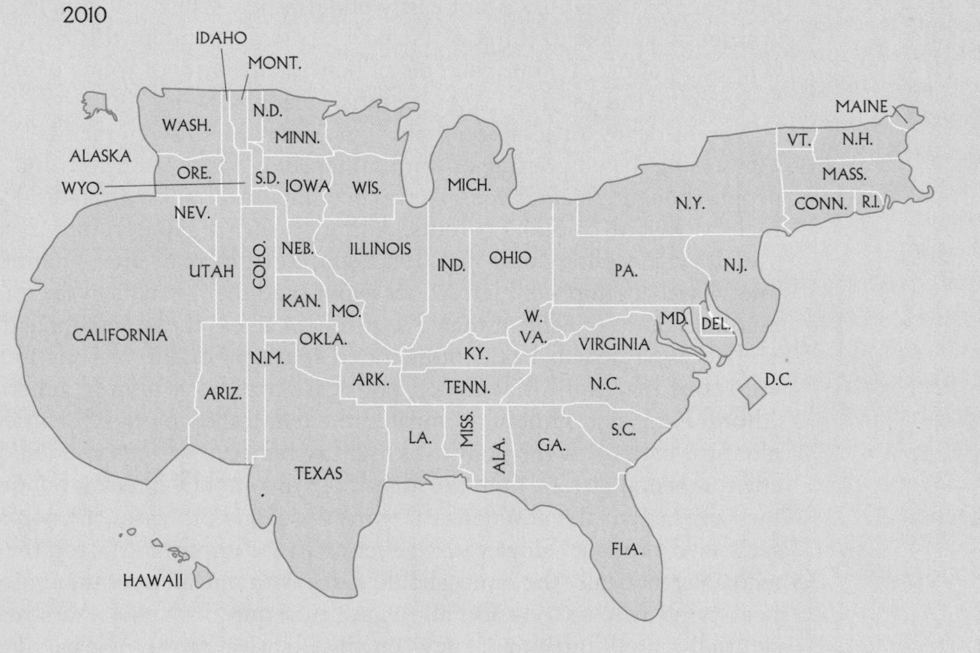

How Americans Learn About Politics: Political Socialization

6.2 Outline how various forms of socialization shape political opinions.

Central to the formation of public opinion is **political socialization**, or "the process through which an individual acquires his or her particular political orientations—his or her knowledge, feelings, and evaluations regarding his or her political world."[12] As people become more socialized with age, their political orientations

political socialization The process through which individuals in a society acquire political attitudes, views, and knowledge, based on inputs from family, schools, the media, and others.

grow firmer. Not surprisingly, governments aim their socialization efforts largely at the young. Authoritarian regimes are particularly concerned with indoctrinating their citizens at an early age. For example, youth in the former Soviet Union were organized into the Komsomol—the Young Communist League. Membership in these groups was helpful in gaining admission to college and entering certain occupations. In the Komsomol, Soviet youth were taught their government's view of the advantages of communism (though apparently not well enough to keep the system going). Political socialization is a much more subtle process in the United States.

The Process of Political Socialization

Only a small portion of Americans' political learning is formal. Civics or government classes in high school teach citizens some of the nuts and bolts of government—how many senators each state has, what presidents do, and so on. But such formal socialization is only the tip of the iceberg. Americans do most of their political learning without teachers or classes.

Informal learning is really much more important than formal, in-class learning about politics. Most of this informal socialization is almost accidental. Few parents sit down with their children and say, "Johnny, let us tell you why we're Republicans." Instead, the informal socialization process might be best described by words like *pick up* and *absorb*.

The family, the media, and the schools all serve as important agents of political socialization. We look at each in turn.

The Family The family's role in socialization is central because of its monopoly on two crucial resources in the early years: time and emotional commitment. The powerful influence of the family is not easily undermined. Most students in an American government class like to think of themselves as independent thinkers, especially when it comes to politics. Yet one can predict how the majority of young people will vote simply by knowing the political leanings of their parents.[13]

Some degree of adolescent rebellion against parents and their beliefs does take place. Witnessing the outpouring of youthful rebellion in the late 1960s and early 1970s, many people thought a generation gap was opening up. Supposedly, radical youth condemned their backward-thinking parents. Although such a gap occurred in some families, the overall evidence for it was slim. For example, eight years after Jennings and Niemi first interviewed a sample of high school seniors and their parents in the mid-1960s, they still found far more agreement than disagreement across the generational divide.[14]

Recent research has demonstrated that one of the reasons for the long-lasting impact of parental influence on political attitudes is simply genetics. In one study, Alford, Funk, and Hibbing compared the political opinions of identical twins and nonidentical twins.[15] If the political similarity between parents and children is due just to environmental factors, then the identical twins should agree on political issues to about the same extent the nonidentical twins do, as in both cases the twins are raised in the same environment. However, if genetics are an important factor, then identical twins, who are genetically the same, should agree with one another more often than nonidentical twins, who are not. On all the political questions they examined, there was substantially more agreement between the identical twins—clearly demonstrating that genetics play an important role in shaping political attitudes.

The Mass Media The mass media are the "new parent," according to many observers. Average grade-school youngsters spend more time each week watching television than they spend at school. And television displaces parents as the chief source of information as children get older.

Unfortunately, today's generation of young adults is significantly less likely to watch television news and read newspapers than their elders. Many studies have attributed the relative lack of political knowledge of today's youth to their media consumption or, more appropriately, to their lack of it.[16] In 1965, Gallup found virtually no difference between age categories in frequency of following politics through the media. In recent years, however, a considerable age gap has opened up, with older people paying the most attention to the news and young adults the least. The median age of viewers of CBS, ABC, and

NBC news programs in 2008 was 61—19 years older than the audience for a typical prime-time program.[17] If you have ever turned on the TV news and wondered why so many of the commercials seem to be for various prescription drugs, now you know why.

School Political socialization is as important to a government as it is to an individual. Governments, including our own, often use schools to promote national loyalty and support for their basic values. In most American schools, the day begins with the Pledge of Allegiance. During the 1988 presidential campaign, George H. W. Bush argued that teachers should be required to lead students in the pledge. His opponent, Michael Dukakis, had vetoed a bill to require this in Massachusetts, claiming that it was unconstitutional. Underlying Bush's argument was the assumption that proper socialization in the schools was crucial to the American political system—a position Dukakis disagreed with more with respect to means than ends.

As part of promoting support for the basic values of the system, American children have long been successfully educated about the virtues of free enterprise and democracy. In the hands of an unscrupulous government, though, educational socialization can be a dangerous tool. For example, in Nazi Germany, textbooks were used to promote acceptance of murderous policies. Consider the following example from a Nazi-era math book:

> If a mental patient costs 4 Reichsmarks a day in maintenance, a cripple 5.50, and a criminal 3.50, and about 50,000 of these people are in our institutions, how much does it cost our state at a daily rate of 4 Reichsmarks—and how many marriage loans of 1,000 Reichsmarks per couple could have been given out instead?[18]

Both authoritarian and democratic governments have an interest in students' learning the positive features of their political system because this helps ensure that youth will grow up to be supportive citizens. David Easton and Jack Dennis have argued that "those children who begin to develop positive feelings toward the political authorities will grow into adults who will be less easily disenchanted with the system than those children who early acquire negative, hostile sentiments."[19] Of course, this is not always the case. Well-socialized youths of the 1960s led the opposition to the American regime and the war in Vietnam. It could be argued, however, that even these protestors had been positively shaped by the socialization process, for the goal of most activists was to make the system more democratically responsive rather than to change American government radically.

Most American schools are public schools, financed by the government. Their textbooks are often chosen by the local and state boards, and teachers are certified by the state government. Schooling is perhaps the most obvious intrusion of the government into Americans' socialization. And education does exert a profound influence on a variety of political attitudes and behavior. Better-educated citizens are more likely to vote in elections, they exhibit more knowledge about politics and public policy, and they are more tolerant of opposing (even radical) opinions.

The payoffs of schooling thus extend beyond better jobs and better pay. Educated citizens also more closely approximate the model of a democratic citizen. A formal civics course may not make much difference, but the whole context of education does. As Albert Einstein once said, "Schools need not preach political doctrine to defend democracy. If they shape men and women capable of critical thought and trained in social attitudes, that is all that is necessary."

Political Learning over a Lifetime

Political learning does not, of course, end when one reaches 18 or even when one graduates from college. Politics is a lifelong activity. Because America is an aging society, it is important to consider the effects of growing older on political learning and behavior.

Aging increases political participation as well as strength of party attachment. Young adults lack experience with politics. Because political behavior is to some degree learned behavior, there is some learning yet to do. Political participation rises steadily with age until the infirmities of old age make it harder to participate, as can be seen in Figure 6.2. Similarly, strength of party identification increases as people often develop a pattern of usually voting for one party or the other.

FIGURE 6.2 Turnout Increases with Age

In the 2006 congressional elections, as in most midterm elections, the relationship between age and turnout was particularly pronounced. Although the data for the 2010 midterm elections were not available when this book went to press, analysts expected pretty much the same turnout pattern by age. Because today's young adults lean in the liberal direction, political analysts noted throughout the 2010 campaign that the usual low turnout rate of young people would hurt the Democrats.

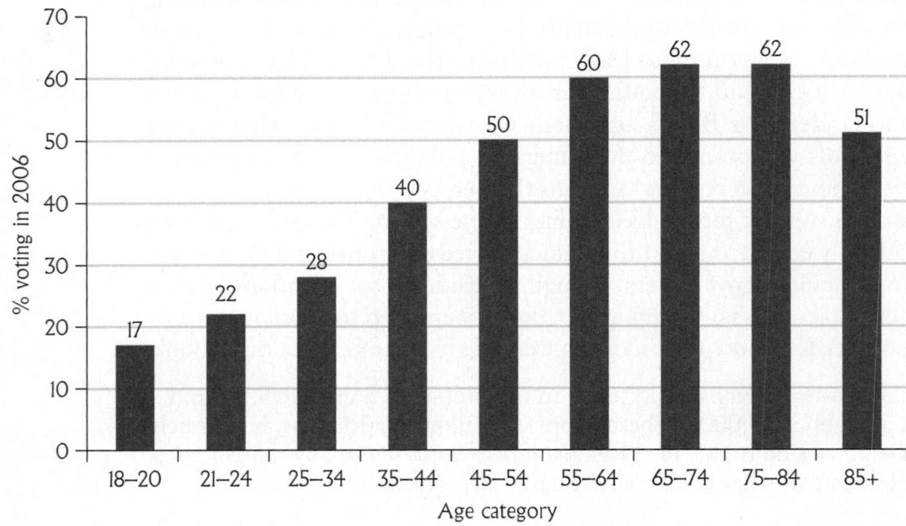

Source: Authors' analysis of 2006 Census Bureau data.

Politics, like most other things, is thus a learned behavior. Americans learn to vote, to pick a political party, and to evaluate political events in the world around them. One of the products of all this learning is what is known as public opinion.

6.3 Explain how polls are conducted and what can be learned from them about American public opinion.

Measuring Public Opinion and Political Information

Before examining the role that public opinion plays in American politics, it is essential to learn about the science of public opinion measurement. How do we really know the approximate answers to questions such as what percentage of young people favor abortion rights, how many Hispanics supported Barack Obama's 2008 campaign, or what percentage of the public is looking for a job but cannot find one? Polls provide these answers, but there is much skepticism about polls. Many people wonder how accurately public opinion can be measured by interviewing only 1,000 or 1,500 people around the country. This section provides an explanation of how polling works; it is hoped that this will enable you to become a well-informed consumer of polls.

How Polls Are Conducted

Public opinion polling is a relatively new science. It was first developed by a young man named George Gallup, who initially did some polling for his mother-in-law, a long-shot candidate for secretary of state in Iowa in 1932. With the Democratic landslide of that year, she won a stunning victory, thereby further stimulating Gallup's interest in politics. From that little acorn the mighty oak of public opinion polling has grown. The firm that Gallup founded spread throughout the democratic world, and in some languages *Gallup* is actually the word used for an opinion poll.[20]

sample
A relatively small proportion of people who are chosen in a survey so as to be representative of the whole.

It would be prohibitively expensive and time-consuming to ask every citizen his or her opinion on a whole range of issues. Instead, polls rely on a **sample** of the population—a relatively small proportion of people who are chosen to represent the whole. Herbert Asher draws an analogy to a blood test to illustrate the principle of sampling.[21] Your doctor does not need to drain a gallon of blood from you to determine whether you have mononucleosis, AIDS, or any other disease. Rather, a small sample of blood will reveal its properties.

In public opinion polling, a sample of about 1,000 to 1,500 people can accurately represent the "universe" of potential voters. The key to the accuracy of opinion polls is the technique of **random sampling**, which operates on the principle that everyone should have an equal probability of being selected as part of the sample. Your chance of being asked to be in the poll should therefore be as good as that of anyone else—rich or poor, black or white, young or old, male or female. If the sample is randomly drawn, about 13 percent of those interviewed will be African American, slightly over 50 percent female, and so forth, matching the population as a whole.

random sampling
The key technique employed by survey researchers, which operates on the principle that everyone should have an equal probability of being selected for the sample.

Remember that the science of polling involves estimation; a sample can represent the population with only a certain degree of confidence. The level of confidence is known as the **sampling error**, which depends on the size of the sample. The more people interviewed in a poll, the more confident one can be of the results. A typical poll of about 1,500 to 2,000 respondents has a sampling error of ±3 percent. What this means is that 95 percent of the time the poll results are within 3 percent of what the entire population thinks. If 60 percent of the sample say they approve of the job the president is doing, one can be pretty certain that the true figure is between 57 and 63 percent.

sampling error
The level of confidence in the findings of a public opinion poll. The more people interviewed, the more confident one can be of the results.

In order to obtain results that will usually be within sampling error, researchers must follow proper sampling techniques. In perhaps the most infamous survey ever, a 1936 *Literary Digest* poll underestimated the vote for President Franklin Roosevelt by 19 percent, erroneously predicting a big victory for Republican Alf Landon. The well-established magazine suddenly became a laughingstock and soon went out of business. Although the number of responses the magazine obtained for its poll was a staggering 2,376,000, its polling methods were badly flawed. Trying to reach as many people as possible, the magazine drew names from the biggest lists they could find: telephone books and motor vehicle records. In the midst of the Great Depression, the people on these lists were above the average income level (only 40 percent of the public had telephones then; fewer still owned cars) and were more likely to vote Republican. The moral of the story is this: Accurate representation, not the number of responses, is the most important feature of a public opinion survey. Indeed, as polling techniques have advanced over the past 70 years, typical sample sizes have been getting smaller, not larger.

random-digit dialing
A technique used by pollsters to place telephone calls randomly to both listed and unlisted numbers when conducting a survey.

Computer and telephone technology has made surveying less expensive and more commonplace. In the early days of polling, pollsters needed a national network of interviewers to traipse door-to-door in their localities with a clipboard of questions. Now most polling is done on the telephone with samples selected through **random-digit dialing**. Calls are placed to phone numbers within randomly chosen exchanges (for example, 512-471-XXXX) around the country. In this manner, both listed and unlisted numbers are reached at a cost of about one-fifth that of person-to-person interviewing. There are a couple of disadvantages, however. About 2 percent of the population does not have a phone, and people are substantially less willing to participate over the telephone than in person—it is easier to hang up than to slam the door in someone's face. These are small trade-offs for political candidates running for minor offices, for whom telephone polls are the only affordable method of gauging public opinion.

Public opinion polls these days are done mostly over the telephone. Interviewers, most of whom are young people (and frequently college students), sit in front of computer terminals and read the questions that appear on the screen to randomly chosen individuals they have reached on the phone. They then enter the appropriate coded responses directly into the computer database. Such efficient procedures make it possible for analysts to get survey results very quickly.

However, in this era of cell phones, many pollsters are starting to worry whether this methodology will continue to be affordable. As of 2010, government studies showed that about one in four households had cell phone service only. This percentage is significantly higher among young adults, minorities, and people who are transient. Because federal law prohibits use of automated dialing programs to cell phones, pollsters have to use the far more expensive procedure of dialing cell phones numbers manually. In addition, studies have shown that people are much less likely to agree to be interviewed when they are reached on a cell phone as compared to a landline. All told, Mark Mellman, one of America's top political pollsters, estimates that it is 5 to 15 times as expensive to gather interviews from the cell cell-phone-only segment of the population as from landline users.[22] Although big firms like Gallup have successfully made the adjustment so far, the costs of conducting phone polls are likely to further escalate as more people give up their landlines.

As with many other aspects of commerce in America, the future of polling may lie with the Internet. Internet pollsters, such as Knowledge Networks, assemble representative panels of the population by first contacting people on the phone and asking them whether they are willing to participate in Web-based surveys on a variety of topics. If they agree, they are paid a small sum every time they participate. And if they don't have Internet access, they are provided with it as part of their compensation. Once someone agrees to participate, they are then contacted exclusively by e-mail. As Knowledge Networks proclaims, "This permits surveys to be fielded very quickly and economically. In addition, this approach reduces the burden placed on respondents, since e-mail notification is less obtrusive than telephone calls, and most respondents find answering Web questionnaires to be more interesting and engaging than being questioned by a telephone interviewer."[23]

From its modest beginning, with George Gallup's 1932 polls for his mother-in-law in Iowa, polling has become a big business. That it has grown so much and spread throughout the world is no surprise: From Manhattan to Moscow, from Tulsa to Tokyo, people want to know what other people think.

The Role of Polls in American Democracy

Polls help political candidates detect public preferences. Supporters of polling insist that it is a tool for democracy. With it, they say, policymakers can keep in touch with changing opinions on the issues. No longer do politicians have to wait until the next election to see whether the public approves or disapproves of the government's course. If the poll results shift, then government officials can make corresponding midcourse corrections. Indeed, it was George Gallup's fondest hope that polling could contribute to the democratic process by providing a way for public desires to be heard at times other than elections.

Critics of polling, by contrast, say it makes politicians more concerned with following than leading. Polls might have told the Constitutional Convention delegates that the Constitution was unpopular or might have told President Thomas Jefferson that people did not want the Louisiana Purchase. Certainly they would have told William Seward not to buy Alaska, a transaction known widely at the time as "Seward's Folly." Polls may thus discourage bold leadership, like that of Winston Churchill, who once said,

> Nothing is more dangerous than to live in the temperamental atmosphere of a Gallup poll, always taking one's pulse and taking one's temperature.... There is only one duty, only one safe course, and that is to try to be right and not to fear to do or say what you believe.[24]

Based on their research, Jacobs and Shapiro argue that the common perception of politicians pandering to the results of public opinion polls may be mistaken. Their examination of major policy debates in the 1990s finds that political leaders "track public opinion not to make policy but rather to determine how to craft their public presentations and win public support for the policies they and their supporters favor."[25] Staff members in both the White House and Congress repeatedly remarked that their purpose in conducting polls was not to set policies but rather to find the key words and phrases with which to promote policies already in place. Thus, rather than using polls to identify centrist approaches that will have the broadest popular appeal, Jacobs and Shapiro argue that elites use them to formulate strategies that enable them to avoid compromising on what they want to do. As President Obama's chief pollster, Joel Benenson, said in 2009 about his team's work for the president: "Our job isn't to tell him what to do. Our job is to help him figure out if he can strengthen his message and persuade more people to his side. The starting point is where he is and then you try to help strengthen the message and his reasons for doing something."[26]

Yet, polls might weaken democracy in another way—they may distort the election process by creating a *bandwagon effect*. The wagon carrying the band was the centerpiece of nineteenth-century political parades, and enthusiastic supporters would literally jump on it. Today, the term refers to voters who support a candidate merely because they see that others are doing so. Although only 2 percent of people in a recent CBS/*New York Times* poll said that poll results had influenced them, 26 percent said they thought others had been influenced (showing that Americans feel that "it's the other person who's susceptible"). Beyond this, polls play to the media's interest in who's ahead in the race. The issues of recent presidential campaigns have sometimes been drowned out by a steady flood of poll results.

Probably the most widely criticized type of poll is the Election Day **exit poll.** For this type of poll, voting places are randomly selected around the country. Workers are then sent to these places and told to ask every tenth person how they voted. The results are accumulated toward the end of the day, enabling the television networks to project the outcomes of all but very close races before hardly any votes are actually counted. In some presidential elections, the networks declared a national winner while millions on the West Coast still had hours to vote. Critics have charged that this practice discourages many people from voting and thereby affects the outcome of some state and local races.

exit poll
Public opinion surveys used by major media pollsters to predict electoral winners with speed and precision.

Perhaps the most pervasive criticism of polling is that by altering the wording of a question, pollsters can manipulate the results. Small changes in question wording can sometimes produce significantly different results. For example, in February 2010, the *New York Times*/CBS News poll found that 70 percent favored permitting "gay men and lesbians" to serve in the military whereas only 44 percent favored military service by "homosexuals" who "openly announce their sexual orientation." Thus, proponents of gays and lesbians in the armed forces could rightly say that a solid public majority favored their military service while opponents could rightly counter that only a minority favored lifting the ban on open military service by homosexuals. This example illustrates why, in evaluating public opinion data, it is crucial to carefully evaluate how questions are posed. Fortunately, most major polling organizations now post their questionnaires online, thereby making it much easier than ever before for everyone to scrutinize their work.

A nuts-and-bolts knowledge of how polls are conducted will help you avoid the common mistake of taking poll results for solid fact. But being an informed consumer of polls also requires that you think about whether the questions are fair and unbiased. The good—or the harm—that polls do depends on how well the data are collected and how thoughtfully the data are interpreted.

What Polls Reveal About Americans' Political Information

Thomas Jefferson and Alexander Hamilton had very different views about the wisdom of common people. Jefferson trusted people's good sense and believed that education would enable them to take the tasks of citizenship ever more seriously. Toward that end, he founded the University of Virginia. In contrast, Hamilton lacked confidence in people's capacity for self-government. His response to Jefferson was the infamous phrase, "Your people, sir, is a great beast."

If there had been polling data in the early days of the American republic, Hamilton would probably have delighted in throwing some of the results in Jefferson's face. If public opinion analysts agree about anything, it is that the level of public knowledge about politics is dismally low. As discussed in Chapter 1, this is particularly true for young people, but the level of knowledge for the public overall is not particularly encouraging either. For example, in October 2008, the National Annenberg Election Survey asked a set of factual questions about some prominent policy stands taken by Obama and McCain during the campaign. The results were as follows:

- 63 percent knew that Obama would provide more middle-class tax cuts
- 47 percent knew McCain favored overturning *Roe v. Wade*

A POINT TO PONDER

Pollsters sometimes ask people about policy issues with which they are largely unfamiliar.

What do you think—should one take the findings from such polls with a big grain of salt?

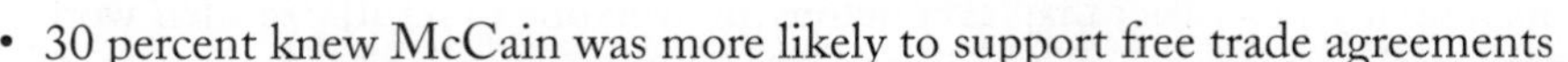

- 30 percent knew McCain was more likely to support free trade agreements
- 8 percent knew that both candidates supported stem cell research funding

If so many voters did not know these hotly debated issues, then there is little doubt that most were also unaware of the detailed policy platforms the candidates were running on.

No amount of Jeffersonian faith in the wisdom of the common people can erase the fact that Americans are not well informed about politics. Polls have regularly found that less than half the public can name their representative in the House, and much less say how he or she generally votes. Asking people to explain their opinion on whether trade policy toward China should be liberalized, or whether the proposed "Star Wars" missile defense system should be implemented, or whether the strategic oil reserve should be tapped when gasoline prices skyrocket often elicits blank looks. When trouble flares in a far-off country, polls regularly find that people have no idea where that country is. In fact, surveys show that citizens in the United States and, to different extents, around the globe lack a basic awareness of the world around them (see "America in Perspective: Citizens Show Little Knowledge of Geography").

As Lance Bennett points out, these findings provide "a source of almost bitter humor in light of what the polls tell us about public information on other subjects."[27] Slogans from TV commercials are better recognized than famous political figures. In a Zogby national poll in 2006, 74 percent of respondents were able to name each of the "Three Stooges"—Larry, Curly, and Moe—whereas just 42 percent could name each of the three branches of the U.S. government—judicial, executive, and legislative.

WHY IT MATTERS

Political Knowledge of the Electorate

The average American clearly has less political information than most analysts consider to be desirable. While this level of information is surely adequate to maintain our democracy, survey data plainly show that citizens with above-average levels of political knowledge are more likely to vote and to have stable and consistent opinions on policy issues. If political knowledge were to increase overall, it would in all likelihood be good for American democracy.

How can Americans, who live in the most information-rich society in the world, be so ill informed about politics? Some blame the schools. E. D. Hirsch, Jr., criticizes schools for a failure to teach "cultural literacy."[28] People, he says, often lack the basic contextual knowledge—for example, where Afghanistan is, or what the Vietnam War

AMERICA IN PERSPECTIVE

Citizens Show Little Knowledge of Geography

In 2002, a major cross-national study sponsored by *National Geographic* interviewed representative samples of 18- to 24-year-olds to assess their knowledge of world geography. As this test shows, the results were discouraging—particularly with regard to American youth, who came in last in placing countries accurately on the map. The average young person in the United States got less than half the questions right. Believe it or not, 11 percent of young Americans could not even find their own country on the map. Despite the American military campaign in Afghanistan after September 11, only 17 percent could correctly place that country on the map. Such lack of basic geographic knowledge is fairly common throughout the world. Here is the average score for each of the 9 countries in which the test was administered:

COUNTRY	AVERAGE % CORRECT
Sweden	79
Germany	77
Italy	75
France	71
Japan	62
Canada	56
United Kingdom	54
Mexico	49
United States	46

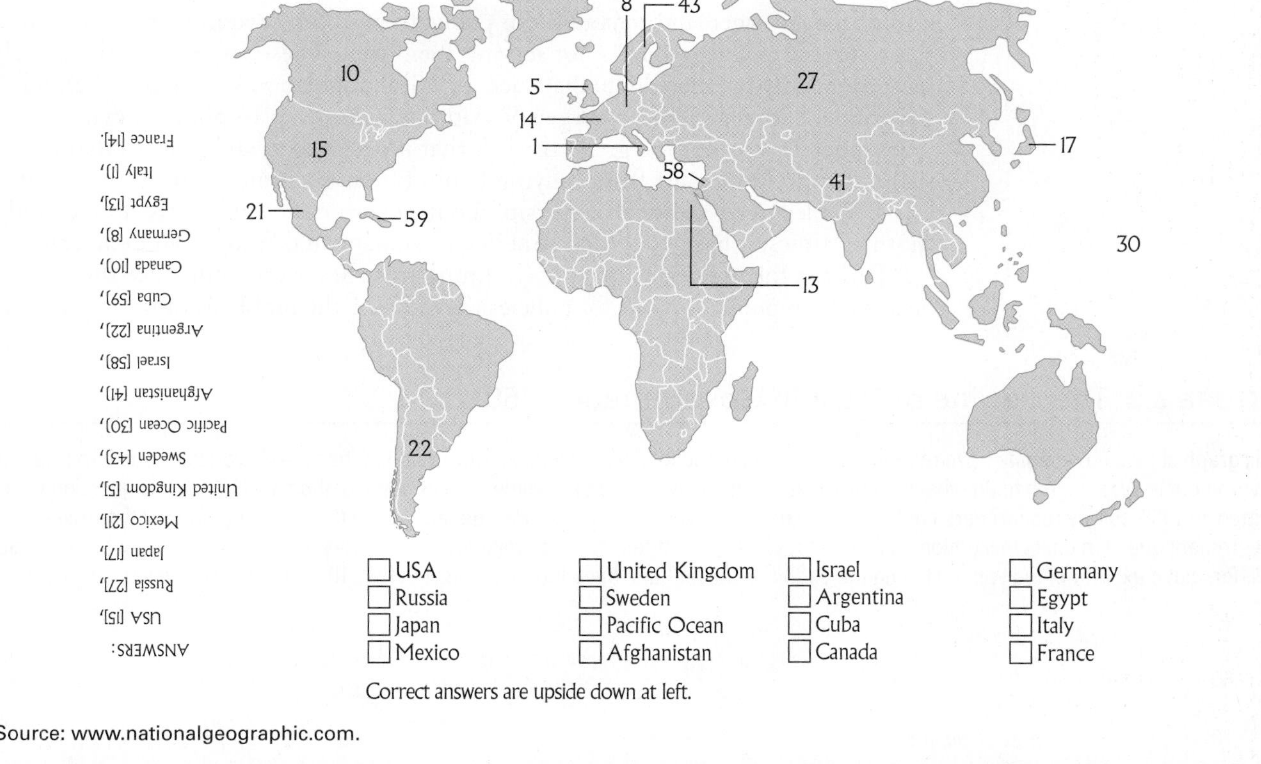

Correct answers are upside down at left.

Source: www.nationalgeographic.com.

was about—necessary to understand and use the information they receive from the news media or from listening to political candidates. Nevertheless, it has been found that increased levels of education over the past five decades have scarcely raised public knowledge about politics.[29] Despite the apparent glut of information provided by the media, Americans do not remember much about what they are exposed to through the media. (Of course, there are many critics who say that the media fail to provide much meaningful information, a topic that will be discussed in Chapter 7.)

The "paradox of mass politics," says Russell Neuman, is that the American political system works as well as it does given the discomforting lack of public knowledge about politics.[30] Scholars have suggested numerous ways that this paradox can be resolved. Although many people may not know the ins and outs of most policy questions, some will base their political behavior on knowledge of just one issue that they really care about, such as abortion or environmental protection. Others will rely on simple information regarding which groups are for and against a proposal, siding with the group or groups they trust the most.[31] And finally, some people will simply vote for or against incumbent officeholders based on how satisfied they are with the job the government is doing.

The Decline of Trust in Government

Sadly, the American public has become increasingly dissatisfied with government over the past five decades, as shown in Figure 6.3. In the late 1950s and early 1960s, nearly three-quarters of Americans said that they trusted the government in Washington to do the right thing always or mostly. By the late 1960s, however, researchers started to see a precipitous drop in public trust in government. First Vietnam and then Watergate shook the people's confidence in the federal government. The economic troubles of the Carter years and the Iran hostage crisis helped continue the slide; by 1980, only one-quarter of the public thought the government could be trusted most of the time or always. Since then, trust in government has occasionally risen for a while, but the only time a majority said they could trust the government most of the time was in 2002, after the events of September 11.

Some analysts have noted that a healthy dose of public cynicism helps to keep politicians on their toes. Others, however, note that a democracy is based on the consent of the governed and that a lack of public trust in the government is a reflection of their belief that the system is not serving them well. These more pessimistic analysts have frequently wondered whether such a cynical population would unite behind their government in a national emergency. Although the drop in political cynicism after September 11 was not too great, the fact that it occurred at all indicates that cynicism will not stop Americans from rallying behind their government in times of national crisis. Widespread political cynicism about government apparently applies only to "normal" times; it has not eroded Americans' fundamental faith in our democracy.

Perhaps the greatest impact of declining trust in government since the 1960s has been to drain public support for policies that address the problems of poverty and racial

FIGURE 6.3 The Decline of Trust in Government, 1958–2010

This graph shows how people have responded over time to the following question: How much of the time do you think you can trust the government in Washington to do what is right—just about always, most of the time, or only some of the time? When this question was written, in 1958, survey researchers could not imagine that anyone would respond "never," so the traditional wording of the trust in government question omits this option. In 2008, about 2 percent of respondents volunteered that they never trusted the government. Some pollsters have experimented with including the option of "never" and have found that as much as 10 percent of their sample will choose it.

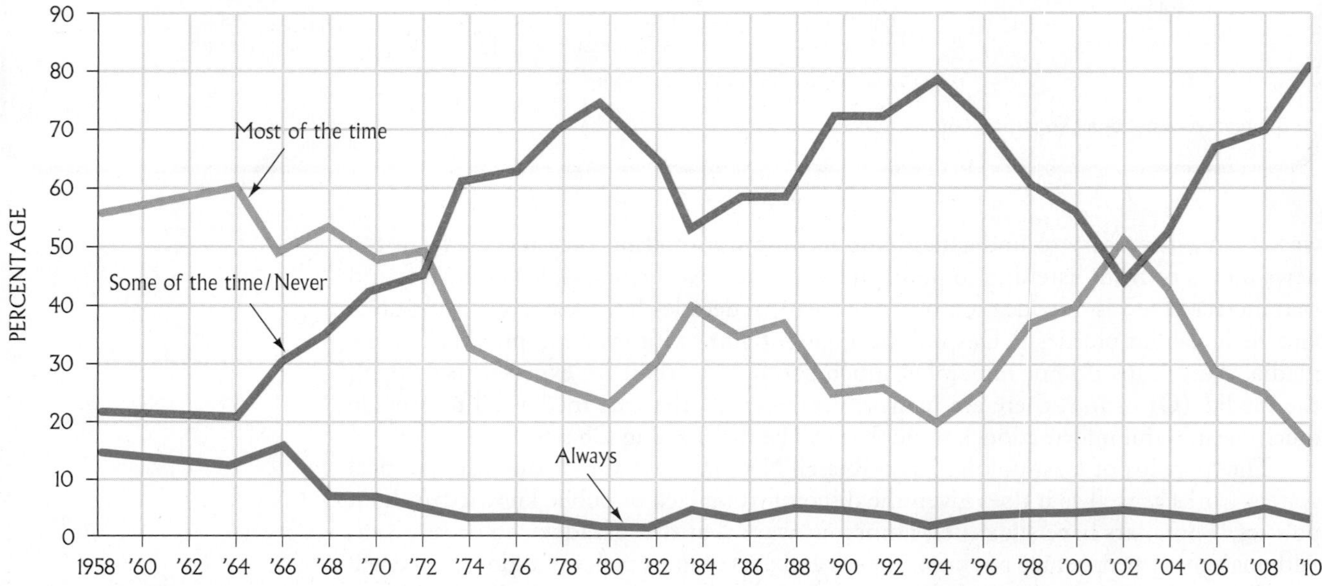

Sources: Authors' analysis of 1958–2008 American National Election Study data; December 2006 Pew Research Center poll; February 5–10, 2010 *New York Times*/CBS News Poll.

inequality. Mark Hetherington argues, "People need to trust the government when they pay the costs but do not receive the benefits, which is exactly what antipoverty and race-targeted programs require of most Americans. When government programs require people to make sacrifices, they need to trust that the result will be a better future for everyone."[32] Hetherington's careful data analysis shows that declining trust in government has caused many Americans to believe that "big government" solutions to social problems are wasteful and impractical, thereby draining public support from them. Indeed, during the debate over health care reform, President Obama's advisers argued that the primary obstacle they faced was not persuading the public of the need for health care reform but, rather, convincing them to put sufficient trust in the government's ability to carry out the reform.[33] Obama acknowledged the problem in his 2010 State of the Union Address, saying, "We have to recognize that we face more than a deficit of dollars right now. We face a deficit of trust—deep and corrosive doubts about how Washington works that have been growing for years."

political ideology
A coherent set of beliefs about politics, public policy, and public purpose, which helps give meaning to political events.

What Americans Value: Political Ideologies

6.4 Assess the influence of political ideology on Americans' political thinking and behavior.

A coherent set of values and beliefs about public policy is a **political ideology**. Liberal ideology, for example, supports a wide scope for the central government, often involving policies that aim to promote equality. Conservative ideology, in contrast, supports a less active scope of government that gives freer rein to the private sector. Table 6.1 attempts to summarize some of the key differences between liberals and conservatives.

TABLE 6.1 How to Tell a Liberal from a Conservative

Here, in attempt to clarify *liberal* and *conservative*—those labels that are so often thrown around—are some of the political views likely to be taken by liberals and conservatives. This table, to be sure, is oversimplified.

	LIBERALS	CONSERVATIVES
Foreign Policy		
Military spending	Believe we should spend less	Believe we should maintain peace through strength
Use of force	Less willing to commit troops to action, such as the war in Iraq	More likely to support military intervention around the world
Social Policy		
Abortion	Support "freedom of choice"	Support "right to life"
Prayer in schools	Are opposed	Are supportive
Affirmative action	Favor	Oppose
Economic Policy		
Scope of government	View government as a regulator in the public interest	Favor free-market solutions
Taxes	Want to tax the rich more	Want to keep taxes low
Spending	Want to spend more on the poor	Want to keep spending low
Crime		
How to cut crime	Believe we should solve the problems that cause crime	Believe we should stop "coddling criminals"
Defendants' rights	Believe we should guard them carefully	Believe we should stop letting criminals hide behind laws

Who Are the Liberals and Conservatives?

Decades of survey data have consistently shown that more Americans choose the ideological label of conservative over liberal. The 2008 General Social Survey found that of those who labeled themselves, 36 percent were conservatives, 38 percent were moderates, and just 26 percent were liberals. The predominance of conservative thinking in America is one of the most important reasons for the relatively restrained scope of government activities compared to most European nations.

Yet there are some groups that are more liberal than others and thus would generally like to see the government do more. Among people under the age of 30, there are slightly more liberals than conservatives, as shown in "Young People and Politics: How Younger and Older Americans Compare on the Issues." The younger the individual, the less likely that person is to be a conservative. The fact that younger people are also less likely to vote means that conservatives are overrepresented at the polls.

In general, groups with political clout tend to be more conservative than groups whose members have often been shut out from the halls of political power. This is in large part because excluded groups have often looked to the government to rectify the inequalities they have faced. For example, government activism in the form of the major civil rights bills of the 1960s was crucial in bringing African Americans into the mainstream of American life. Many African American leaders currently place a high priority on retaining social welfare and affirmative action programs in order to assist African Americans' progress. It should come as little surprise, then, that African Americans are more liberal than the national average. Similarly, Hispanics also are less

How Younger and Older Americans Compare on the Issues

The following table compares young adults and senior citizens on a variety of issues. Because younger citizens are much less likely to vote than older people, the differences between the two groups give us some indication of how public opinion is not accurately reflected at the polls. As you can see, younger people are substantially more likely to call themselves liberal than are senior citizens. Befitting their liberalism, they are more supportive of government spending on health care and environmental protection, and less inclined than seniors to spend more on the military. Younger voters are also more supportive of abortion rights and gay rights.

However, younger people are not always more likely to take the liberal side of an issue. Younger people are more supportive of investing Social Security funds in the stock market—a reform proposal that has been primarily championed by conservative politicians such as George W. Bush.

QUESTIONS FOR DISCUSSION

- Only a few issues could be covered in this table because of space limitations. On what other issues do you think there are likely to be differences of opinion between young and old people?
- Do you think the differences shown in the table are important? If so, what difference might it make to the American political agenda if young people were to vote at the same rate as the elderly?

	18–29	65+
Liberal	29	13
Moderate or don't know	47	43
Conservative	25	44
Believe abortion should be a matter of personal choice	48	26
Believe same sex couples should be allowed to marry	60	19
Favor government paying for all necessary medical care for all Americans	60	34
Believe the environment must be protected even if it costs some jobs	47	23
Favor the federal government making it make it more difficult to buy guns	53	43
Favor spending more spending on the military	31	59
Oppose investing Social Security funds in stocks and bonds	24	55

Source: Authors' analysis of the 2008 American National Election Study.

conservative than non-Hispanic whites, and the influx of more Hispanics into the electorate may well move the country in a slightly more liberal direction.

Women are not a minority group—making up, as they do, about 54 percent of the population—but they have been politically and economically disadvantaged. Compared to men, women are more likely to support spending on social services and to oppose the higher levels of military spending, which conservatives typically advocate. These issues concerning the priorities of government rather than the issue of abortion—on which men and women actually differ very little—lead women to be significantly less conservative than men. This ideological difference between men and women has resulted in the **gender gap**, a regular pattern in which women are more likely to support Democratic candidates. In his 1996 reelection, for example, Bill Clinton carried the women's vote whereas Bob Dole won more support from men. In 2008, surveys showed that women were about 7 percent more likely to support Barack Obama than men.

gender gap
The regular pattern in which women are more likely to support Democratic candidates, in part because they tend to be less conservative than men and more likely to support spending on social services and to oppose higher levels of military spending.

The gender gap is a relatively new predictor of ideological positions, dating back only to 1980, when Ronald Reagan was first elected. A more traditional source of division between liberals and conservatives has been financial status, or what is often known as social class. But in actuality, the relationship between family income and ideology is now relatively weak; social class has become much less predictive of political behavior than it used to be.[34]

The role of religion in influencing political ideology has also changed greatly in recent years. Catholics and Jews, as minority groups who struggled for equality, have long been more liberal than Protestants. Today, Jews remain by far the most liberal demographic group in the country.[35] However, the ideological gap between Catholics and Protestants is now smaller than the gender gap. Ideology is now determined more by religiosity—that is, the degree to which religion is important in one's life—than by religious denomination. What is known as the new Christian Right consists of Catholics and Protestants who consider themselves fundamentalists or "born again." The influx of new policy issues dealing with matters of morality and traditional family values has recently tied this aspect of religious beliefs to political ideology. Those who identify themselves as born-again Christians are currently the most conservative demographic group. On the other hand, people who say they have no religious affiliation (roughly 15 percent of the population) are more liberal than conservative.

Just as some people are very much guided by their religious beliefs whereas others are not, political ideology doesn't necessarily guide political behavior. It would probably be a mistake to assume that when conservative candidates do better than they have in the past, this necessarily means people want more conservative policies, for not everyone thinks in ideological terms.

Do People Think in Ideological Terms?

The authors of the classic study *The American Voter* first examined how much people rely on ideology to guide their political thinking.[36] They divided the public into four groups, according to ideological sophistication. Their portrait of the American electorate was not flattering. Only 12 percent of the people showed evidence of thinking in ideological terms. These people, classified as *ideologues*, could connect their opinions and beliefs with broad policy positions taken by parties or candidates. They might say, for example, that they liked the Democrats because they were more liberal or the Republicans because they favored a smaller government. Forty-two percent of Americans were classified as *group benefits* voters. These people thought of politics mainly in terms of the groups they liked or disliked; for example, "Republicans support small business owners like me" or "Democrats are the party of the working person." Twenty-four percent of the population were *nature of the times* voters. Their handle on politics was limited to whether the times seemed good or bad to them; they might vaguely link the party in power with the country's fortune or misfortune. Finally, 22 percent of the voters expressed no ideological or issue content in making their political evaluations. They were called the *no issue content* group. Most of them simply voted routinely for a party or judged the candidates solely by their personalities. Overall, at least during the 1950s, Americans seemed to care little about the differences between liberal and conservative politics.

There has been much debate about whether this portrayal has been and continues to be an accurate characterization of the public. In the 1970s, Nie, Verba, and Petrocik argued that voters were more sophisticated than they had been in the 1950s.[37] Others, though, have concluded that people have seemed more informed and ideological only because the wording of the questions changed.[38] Recently, the authors of *The American Voter Revisited* updated the analysis of *The American Voter* using survey data from the 2000 election. They found that just 20 percent of the population met the criteria for being classified as an ideologue in 2000—not that much more than the 12 percent in 1956. Echoing the analysts of the 1950s, they conclude that "it is problematic to attribute ideological meaning to aggregate voting patterns when most of the individuals making their decisions about the candidates are not motivated by ideological concepts."[39]

These findings do not mean that the vast majority of the population does not have a political ideology. Rather, for most people the terms *liberal* and *conservative* are just not as important as they are for members of the political elite, such as politicians, activists, and journalists. Relatively few people have ideologies that organize their political beliefs as clearly as in the columns of Table 6.1. Thus, the authors of *The American Voter* concluded that to speak of election results as indicating a movement of the public either left (to more liberal policies) or right (to more conservative policies) is not justified because most voters do not think in such terms. Furthermore, those who do are actually the least likely to shift from one election to the next.

Morris Fiorina makes a similar argument with regard to the question of whether America is in the midst of a political culture war. In the media these days, one frequently hears claims that Americans are deeply divided on fundamental political issues, making it seem like there are two different nations—the liberal blue states versus the conservative red states. After a thorough examination of public opinion data, Fiorina concludes that "the views of the American citizenry look moderate, centrist, nuanced, ambivalent—choose your term—rather than extreme, polarized, unconditional, dogmatic."[40] He argues that the small groups of liberal and conservative activists who act as if they are at war with one another have left most Americans in a position analogous to "unfortunate citizens of some third-world countries who try to stay out of the crossfire while Maoist guerrillas and right-wing death squads shoot at each other."[41]

One of the topics that many commentators believe have led to a political culture war is that of gay rights. However, as shown in "A Generation of Change: Attitudes Toward Gays and Lesbians," the survey data over the past two decades show a growing acceptance of homosexuals among liberals, moderates, and conservatives alike. Rather than an ideological culture war, this example shows how all ideological groups have changed with the changing social mores of the times.

6.5 Classify forms of political participation into two broad types.

How Americans Participate in Politics

In politics, as in many other aspects of life, the squeaky wheel gets the grease. The way citizens "squeak" in politics is to participate. Americans have many avenues of political participation open to them:

- Mrs. Jones of Iowa City goes to a neighbor's living room to attend her local precinct's presidential caucus.
- Demonstrators against abortion protest at the Supreme Court on the anniversary of the *Roe v. Wade* decision.
- Parents in Alabama file a lawsuit to oppose textbooks that, in their opinion, promote "secular humanism."
- Mr. Smith, a Social Security recipient, writes to his senator to express his concern about a possible cut in his cost-of-living benefits.
- Over 120 million people vote in a presidential election.

political participation
All the activities used by citizens to influence the selection of political leaders or the policies they pursue. The most common means of political participation in a democracy is voting; other means include **protest** and civil **disobedience**.

All these activities are types of **political participation**, which encompasses the many activities in which citizens engage to influence the selection of political leaders or the

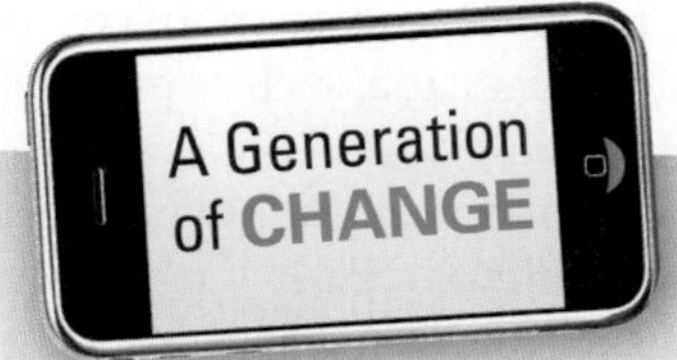

Attitudes Toward Gays and Lesbians

It is often said that public opinion surveys are merely "snapshots in time." Thus, public opinion can change from one time point to the next, as people's attitudes are subject to change. Furthermore, generational replacement can often produce substantial changes in public opinion over an extended period of time, as the attitudes of new entrants into the electorate are sometimes quite different from those of the generations that are dying out. Such is the case with attitudes toward gays and lesbians over the past six presidential elections.

The American National Election Studies have regularly asked respondents to rate gays and lesbians on a "feeling thermometer" scale ranging from 0 to 100. They are told that 0 represents very cool feelings, whereas 100 represents very warm feelings, with 50 being the neutral point. The following graph displays the average ratings that liberals, moderates, and conservatives gave gays and lesbians from 1988 to 2008. It is interesting to note that as recently as 1988, all three ideological groups expressed more negative than positive feelings toward gays and lesbians—for all groups the average rating was well below 50. If reports of a culture war were correct, then we would predict that as liberals have become more positive toward homosexuals, conservatives have become even more negative. This has certainly not been the case. By 2008, the average rating given to gays and lesbians had risen by roughly 20 points among all three ideological groups. Thus, societal attitudes have changed across the political spectrum. A key reason for this change is that young people within each ideological group have expressed more favorable ratings toward gays and lesbians. This is clearly a case of a generation of change being driven by a new generation of voters.

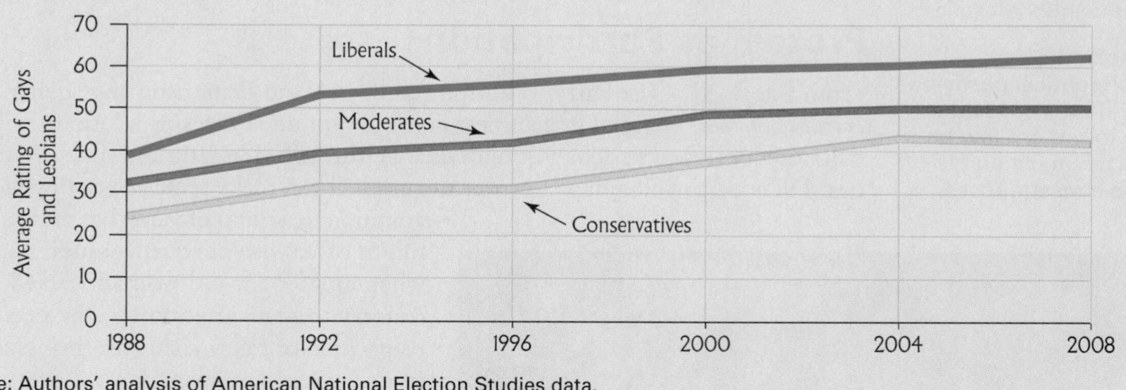

Source: Authors' analysis of American National Election Studies data.

policies they pursue.[42] Participation can be overt or subtle. The mass protests against communist rule throughout Eastern Europe in the fall of 1989 represented an avalanche of political participation, yet quietly writing a letter to your congressperson also represents political participation. Political participation can be violent or peaceful, organized or individual, casual or consuming.

Generally, the United States has a culture that values political participation. Americans express very high levels of pride in their democracy: the General Social Survey has consistently found that over 80 percent of Americans say they are proud of how democracy works in the United States. Nevertheless, just 62 percent of adult American citizens voted in the presidential election of 2008, and only about 40 percent turned out for the 2010 midterm elections. At the local level, the situation is even worse, with elections for city council and school board often drawing less than 10 percent of the eligible voters. (For more on voter turnout and why it is so low, see Chapter 10.)

Conventional Participation

Although the line is hard to draw, political scientists generally distinguish between two broad types of participation: conventional and unconventional. Conventional participation includes many widely accepted modes of influencing government—voting, trying to persuade others, ringing doorbells for a petition, running for office, and so on. In contrast, unconventional participation includes activities that are often dramatic, such as protesting, civil disobedience, and even violence.

For a few, politics is their lifeblood; they run for office, work regularly in politics, and live for the next election. These Americans, who number at most in the tens of thousands, are as familiar with policy questions as the average citizen is with slogans on TV commercials. They are the political elites—activists, party leaders, interest group leaders, judges, members of Congress, and other public officials. (Part 3 of this book will discuss the political elite in detail.)

Millions take part in political activities beyond simply voting. In two comprehensive studies of American political participation conducted by Sidney Verba and his colleagues, in 1967 and 1987 samples of Americans were asked about their role in various kinds of political activities, such as voting, working in campaigns, contacting government officials, signing petitions, working on local community issues, and participating in political protests.[43] Recently, Russell Dalton has extended the time series for some of these dimensions of political participation into the twenty-first century.[44] All told, voting is the only aspect of political participation that a majority of the population reported engaging in but also the only political activity for which there is evidence of a decline in participation in recent years. Substantial increases in participation have been found on the dimensions of giving money to candidates and contacting public officials, and small increases are evident for all the other activities. Thus, although the decline of voter turnout is a development Americans should rightly be concerned about (see Chapter 10), a broader look at political participation reveals some positive developments for participatory democracy.

protest
A form of **political participation** designed to achieve policy change through dramatic and unconventional tactics.

civil disobedience
A form of **political participation** based on a conscious decision to break a law believed to be unjust and to suffer the consequences.

Protest as Participation

From the Boston Tea Party to burning draft cards to demonstrating against abortion, Americans have engaged in countless political protests. **Protest** is a form of political participation designed to achieve policy change through dramatic and unconventional tactics. The media's willingness to cover the unusual can make protests worthwhile, drawing attention to a point of view that many Americans might otherwise never encounter. For example, when an 89-year-old woman walked across the country to draw attention to the need for campaign finance reform, she put this issue onto the front page of newspapers most everywhere she traveled. Using much more flamboyant means, the AIDS activist group appropriately called "ACT-UP" interrupts political gatherings to draw attention to the need for AIDS research. In fact, protests today are often orchestrated to provide television cameras with vivid images. Demonstration coordinators steer participants to prearranged staging areas and provide facilities for press coverage.

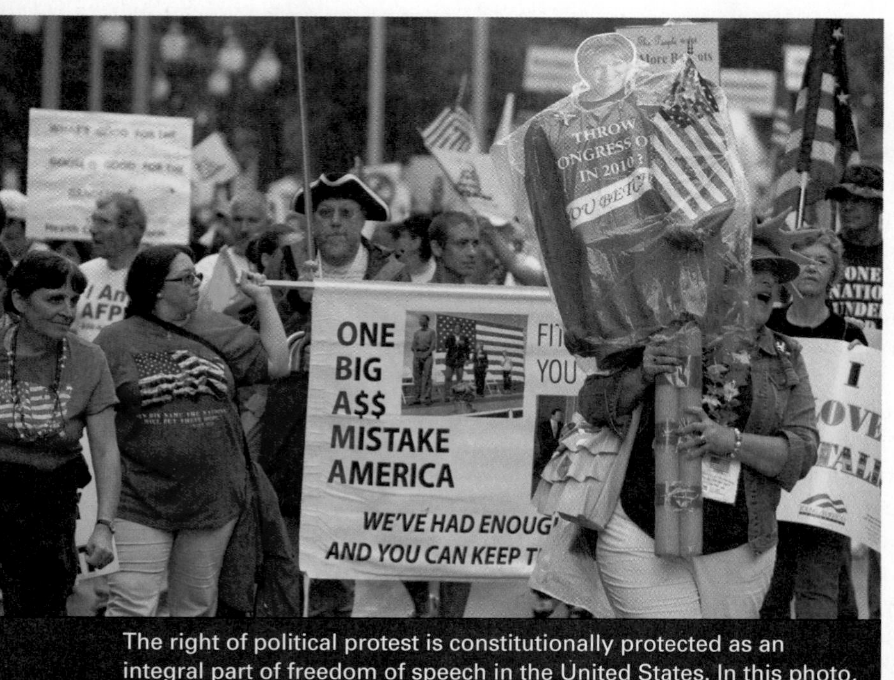

The right of political protest is constitutionally protected as an integral part of freedom of speech in the United States. In this photo, some Tea Party activists are shown taking part in the Taxpayer March on Washington as they walk down Pennsylvania Avenue toward the U.S. Capitol on September 12, 2010.

Throughout American history, individuals and groups have sometimes used **civil disobedience** as a form of protest; that is, they have consciously broken a law that they thought was unjust. In the 1840s, Henry David Thoreau refused to pay his taxes as a protest against the Mexican War and went to jail; he stayed only overnight because his friend Ralph Waldo Emerson paid the taxes. Influenced by India's Mahatma Gandhi, the Reverend Martin Luther King, Jr., and others in the civil rights movement engaged in civil disobedience in the 1950s and 1960s to bring an end to segregationist laws. His "Letter from a Birmingham Jail" is a classic defense of civil disobedience.[45] In 1964, King was awarded a Nobel Peace Prize at the age of 35—the youngest person ever to receive this honor.

Sometimes political participation can be violent. The history of violence in American politics is a long one—not surprising, perhaps, for a nation born in rebellion. The turbulent 1960s included many outbreaks of violence. African American neighborhoods in American cities were torn by riots. College campuses sometimes turned into battle zones as protestors against the Vietnam War fought police and National Guard units; students were killed at Kent State and Jackson State in 1970. Although supported by few people, throughout American history violence has been a means of pressuring the government to change its policies.

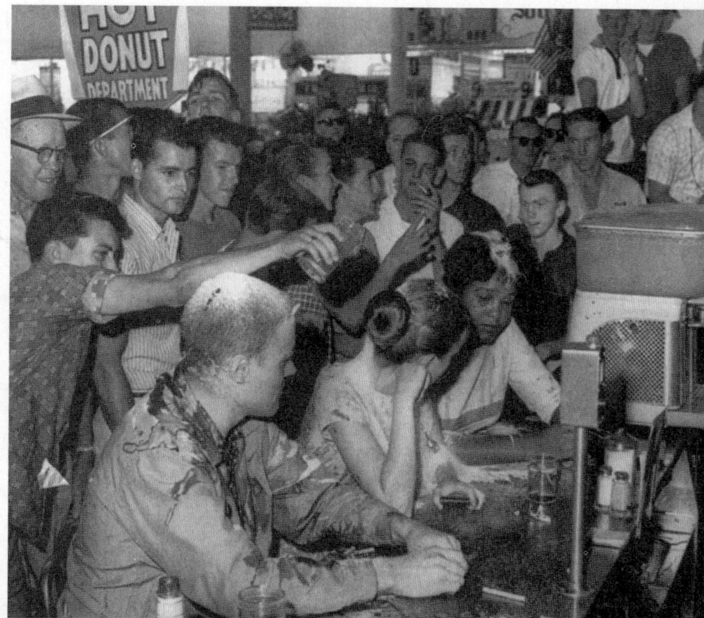

Nonviolent civil disobedience was one of the most effective techniques of the civil rights movement in the American South. Young African Americans sat at "whites only" lunch counters to protest segregation. Photos such as this drew national attention to the injustice of racial discrimination.

Class, Inequality, and Participation

Rates of political participation are unequal among Americans. Virtually every study of political participation has come to the conclusion that "citizens of higher social economic status participate more in politics. This generalization . . . holds true whether one uses level of education, income, or occupation as the measure of social status."[46] Figure 6.4 presents recent evidence on this score. Note that people with higher incomes are more likely not only to donate money to campaigns but also to participate in other ways that do not require financial resources, such as attending meetings. Theorists who believe that America is ruled by a small, wealthy elite make much of this fact to support their view.

To what extent does race affect participation? When the scenes of despair among poor African Americans in New Orleans during the aftermath of Hurricane Katrina refocused attention on racial inequalities, some commentators speculated that one reason that the federal government was so slow in coming to the aid of African Americans is that they are less likely to vote. But in actuality, the difference in turnout rates between whites and blacks in Louisiana has been relatively small in recent years; in 2004, for example, 60 percent of whites voted compared to 54 percent of blacks.[47] (Notably, in the area that encompasses the poverty-stricken lower Ninth Ward, the turnout rate of African Americans was exactly the same as it was statewide).

One reason for this relatively small participation gap is that minorities have a group consciousness that gives them an extra incentive to vote. Political scientists have long recognized that when blacks and whites with equal levels of education are compared, the former actually participate more in politics.[48] For example, the Census Bureau's 2008 survey on turnout found that among people without a high school diploma, blacks were 11 percent more likely to vote than were whites.

Perhaps the best-known image of American political violence from the late 1960s to early 1970s: A student lies dead on the Kent State campus, one of four killed when members of the Ohio National Guard opened fire on anti–Vietnam War demonstrators.

People who believe in the promise of democracy should definitely be concerned with the inequalities of political participation in America. Those who participate are easy to listen to; nonparticipants are easy to ignore. Just as the makers of denture cream do not worry too much about people with healthy teeth, many politicians

WHY IT MATTERS

Political Participation

Inequality in political participation is a problem in a representative democracy. Public policy debates and outcomes would probably be substantially different if people of all age groups and income groups participated equally. If young adults participated more, politicians might be more inclined to seek ways by which the government could help young people get the training necessary to obtain good jobs in a changing economy. And if the poor participated at higher levels, government programs to alleviate poverty would likely be higher on the political agenda.

FIGURE 6.4 Political Participation by Family Income

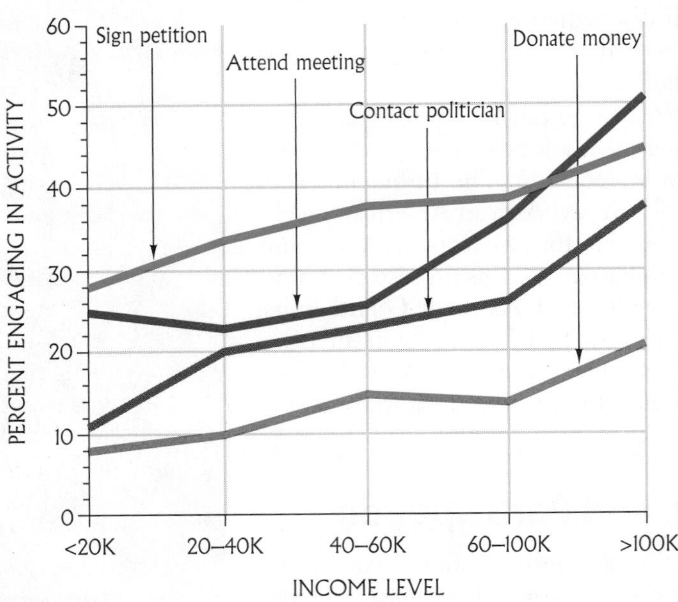

The graph shows, by income status, the percentage of the adult population who said they participated in various forms of political activity during the past year.

Source: Authors' analysis of 2004 General Social Survey data.

don't concern themselves much with the views of groups with low participation rates, such as the young and people with low incomes. Who gets what in politics therefore depends in part on who participates.

6.6 Analyze how public opinion about the scope of government guides political behavior.

Understanding Public Opinion and Political Action

In many third world countries, there have been calls for more democracy in recent years. One often hears that citizens of developing nations want their political system to be like America's in the sense that ordinary people's opinions determine how the government is run. However, as this chapter has shown, there are many limits on the role public opinion plays in the American political system. The average person is not very well informed about political issues, including the crucial issue of the scope of government.

Public Attitudes Toward the Scope of Government

Central to the ideology of the Republican Party is the belief that the scope of American government has become too wide. According to Ronald Reagan, probably the most admired Republican in recent history, government was not the solution to society's problems—it was the problem. He called for the government to "get off the backs of the American people."

Reagan's rhetoric about an overly intrusive government was reminiscent of the 1964 presidential campaign rhetoric of Barry Goldwater, who lost to Lyndon Johnson in a landslide. Indeed, Reagan first made his mark in politics by giving a televised speech on behalf of the embattled Goldwater campaign. Although the rhetoric was much the same when Ronald Reagan was first elected president in 1980, public opinion about the scope of government had changed dramatically. In 1964, only 30 percent of the population thought the government was getting too powerful; by 1980, this figure had risen to 50 percent.

For much of the population, however, questions about the scope of government have consistently elicited no opinion at all. Indeed, when this question was asked in the 2000 American National Election Study, 42 percent of those interviewed said they had not thought about the question (among those under 25 years of age, this figure was 60 percent). The question of government power is a complex one, but as we will continue to emphasize, it is one of the key controversies in American politics today. Once again, it seems that the public is not nearly as concerned with political issues as would be ideal in a democratic society.

Nor does public opinion on different aspects of the same issue exhibit much consistency. Thus, although more people today think that overall the government is too big, a plurality has consistently called for more spending on such programs as education, health care, aid to cities, protecting the environment, and fighting crime. Many political scientists have looked at these contradictory findings and concluded that Americans are ideological conservatives but operational liberals—meaning that they oppose the idea of big government in principle but favor it in practice. The fact that public opinion is often contradictory in this respect may contribute to policy gridlock because it is hard for politicians to know which aspect of the public's attitudes to respond to.

Democracy, Public Opinion, and Political Action

Remember, though, that American democracy is representative rather than direct. As *The American Voter* stated many years ago, "The public's explicit task is to decide not what government shall do but rather who shall decide what government shall do."[49] When individuals under communist rule protested for democracy, what they wanted most was the right to have a say in choosing their leaders. Americans can—and often do—take for granted the opportunity to replace their leaders at the next election. Protest is thus directed at making the government listen to specific demands, not overthrowing it. In this sense, it can be said that American citizens have become well socialized to democracy.

If the public's task in democracy is to choose who is to lead, we must still ask whether it can do so wisely. If people know little about where candidates stand on issues, how can they make rational choices? Most choose performance criteria over policy criteria. As Morris Fiorina has written, citizens typically have one hard bit of data to go on: "They know what life has been like during the incumbent's administration. They need not know the precise economic or foreign policies of the incumbent administration in order to see or feel the results of those policies."[50] Thus, even if they are voting only based on a general sense of whether the country is moving in the right or wrong direction, their voices are clearly being heard—holding public officials accountable for their actions.

Summary

6.1 Identify demographic trends and their likely impact on American politics.

Immigration—both legal and illegal—has accelerated in America in recent decades. Largely as a consequence, the size of the minority population has increased greatly. If current trends continue, by the middle of the twenty-first century non-Hispanic whites will represent less than half of the population. The American population has also been aging and moving to Sunbelt states such as California, Texas, and Florida.

6.2 Outline how various forms of socialization shape political opinions.

Much of the process of political socialization is informal. People pick up and absorb political orientations from major actors in their everyday environment. The principal actors in the socialization process are the family, the media, and schools. As people age, the firmness with which they hold political attitudes, such as party identification, tends to increase.

6.3 Explain how polls are conducted and what can be learned from them about American public opinion.

Polls are conducted through the technique of random sampling, in which every member of the population has an equal probability of being selected for an interview. A random sample of about 1,000 Americans will yield results that are normally within plus or minus three percentage points of what would be found if everyone were interviewed. The responses from such samples can be important tools for democracy, measuring what the public thinks about political matters between elections. Polls also help analysts assess the age-old question of how well informed people are about political issues.

6.4 Assess the influence of political ideology on Americans' political thinking and behavior.

A political ideology is a coherent set of values and beliefs about public policy. The two most prominent ideologies in American politics are conservatism and liberalism. These ideologies guide people's thinking on policy issues. Although roughly 60 percent of the American public call themselves either conservatives or liberals, even many of these individuals are not necessarily ideologically consistent in their political attitudes. Often they are conservative in principle but liberal in practice; that is, they are against big government but favor more spending on a wide variety of programs.

6.5 Classify forms of political participation into two broad types.

Conventional forms of political participation include voting, writing letters or e-mails to public officials, attending political meetings, signing petitions, and donating money to campaigns and political groups. Unconventional participation involves activities such as attending protest demonstrations and acts of civil disobedience. Many studies have found that citizens of higher social economic status participate more in American politics.

6.6 Analyze how public opinion about the scope of government guides political behavior.

Conservatives typically believe that the scope of American government has become too wide in recent decades. They look to Ronald Reagan's pledge to get the government "off the backs of the American people" as inspiration. In contrast, liberals believe the scope of government should be further increased, and support policies like the 2010 Health Insurance Reform Act.

Chapter Test

6.1 Identify demographic trends and their likely impact on American politics.

1. Which of the following is the fastest-growing group in the United States?
   a. African Americans
   b. Asian Americans
   c. Non-Hispanic whites
   d. Hispanics
   e. Native Americans

2. Based on the regional shift, which of these states would have been expected to gain representation following the 2010 census?
   a. Arizona
   b. Illinois
   c. Michigan
   d. New York
   e. Tennessee

3. What are some possible consequences—political, social, and economic—of each of important demographic changes that are occurring—the emergence of a minority majority, the regional shift, and the graying of America? Do you think that these changes will strengthen or weaken political culture in the United States? Explain your answer.

6.2 Outline how various forms of socialization shape political opinions.

4. The main source of political socialization WITHIN the school context is government and civics classes.

   True______ False______

5. Growing older increases political participation but not strength of party attachment.

   True______ False______

6. Discuss how family, media, and school each contribute to the political socialization process in the United States. Why is political socialization crucial to a democracy? Given that it is crucial, how might the socialization process in the United States be improved?

6.3 Explain how polls are conducted and what can be learned from them about American public opinion.

7. Which of the following ensures that the opinions of several hundred million Americans can be inferred through polling?
   a. Random sampling
   b. Sampling error
   c. Population sampling
   d. Sample size of at least 1,500 people
   e. All of the above

8. Years of polling data reveal that Americans tend to be very engaged in and well informed about politics.

   True______ False______

9. The biggest consequence of declining trust in government has been a lack of support for the government during times of international crisis.

   True______ False______

10. What are the benefits of polling in a democracy, and what are some possible problems? What are three main obstacles to conducting a reliable public opinion poll? How serious are these obstacles, and how might they be partly overcome? Explain your answer.

6.4 Assess the influence of political ideology on Americans' political thinking and behavior.

11. Americans are more likely to be conservative than liberal.

   True______ False______

12. Women tend to be more liberal and supportive of Democratic presidential candidates than men.

   True______ False______

13. What did the classic study The *American Voter* conclude about whether Americans think in ideological terms? What have more recent studies on the subject found?

14. Have differences between liberals and conservatives in American politics today contributed to a culture war? Give an opinion and support it with concrete examples.

6.5 Classify forms of political participation into two broad types.

15. Which of the following type of political participation is most common in the United States?
   a. Protesting a governmental policy
   b. Litigating through the court system
   c. Writing to a member of Congress
   d. Voting in elections
   e. Campaigning on behalf of a candidate

16. Civil disobedience is a form of conventional political participation.

   True______ False______

17. What are some of the main inequalities in American political participation? In your opinion, to what extent are these inequalities a potential problem for American democracy? Explain.

6.6 Analyze how public opinion about the scope of government guides political behavior.

18. What do public opinion polls reveal about Americans and their views concerning the size of government? How might the contradictory nature of public opinion affect political decision making?

19. What do the public opinion data that show Americans to be uninformed and uninvolved in politics say about the strength of American democracy? Are there any shortcuts that citizens may take to evaluate the government rationally but without extensive knowledge of government and policy?

PEARSON mypoliscilab™ Exercises

Apply what you learned in this chapter on MyPoliSciLab.

Read on mypoliscilab.com

eText: Chapter 6

Study and Review on mypoliscilab.com

Pre-Test
Post-Test
Chapter Exam
Flashcards

Watch on mypoliscilab.com

Video: America's Aging Population
Video: Obama Approval Rating
Video: Opinion Poll on the U.S. Economy
Video: Candidates Court College Students
Video: Chicago Worker Protest
Video: Who is in the Middle Class?
Video: L.A. Riots: 15 Years Later
Video: Teen Sues for Equal Protection

Explore on mypoliscilab.com

Simulation: You Are a Polling Consultant
Simulation: You Are the Leader of Concerned Citizens for World Justice
Comparative: Comparing Political Landscapes
Comparative: Comparing Governments and Public Opinion
Timeline: War, Peace and Public Opinion
Visual Literacy: Using the Census to Understand Who Americans Are
Visual Literacy: Who Are Liberals and Conservatives? What's the Difference?

Key Terms

public opinion (168)
demography (168)
census (168)
melting pot (169)
minority majority (169)
political culture (171)
reapportionment (172)
political socialization (174)
sample (176)
random sampling (177)
sampling error (177)
random-digit dialing (177)
exit poll (179)
political ideology (183)
gender gap (185)
political participation (186)
protest (188)
civil disobedience (188)

Internet Resources

www.census.gov
The census is the best source of information on America's demography. Go to the list of topics to find out the range of materials that are available.

www.gallup.com
The Gallup Poll regularly posts reports about its political surveys at this site.

www.census.gov/compendia/statab/
The *Statistical Abstract of the United States* contains a wealth of demographic and political information that can be downloaded in Adobe Acrobat format from this site.

www.pollster.com
A good source of information about current polls and the polling business.

For Further Reading

Asher, Herbert. *Polling and the Public: What Every Citizen Should Know,* 7th ed. Washington, DC: Congressional Quarterly Press, 2007. A highly readable introduction to the perils and possibilities of polling and surveys.

Bean, Frank D., and Gillian Stevens. *America's Newcomers and the Dynamics of Diversity.* New York: Russell Sage Foundation, 2003. A balanced examination of the positive and negative consequences of immigration to the United States.

Bryan, Frank M. *Real Democracy: The New England Town Meeting and How It Works.* Chicago: University of Chicago Press, 2004. This book reviews data collected by undergraduates at roughly 1,500 Vermont town meetings in order to test numerous theories of political participation at the local level.

Campbell, Andrea Louise. *How Policies Make Citizens: Senior Political Activism and the American Welfare State.* Princeton, NJ: Princeton University Press, 2003. Senior citizens have become more active in politics in recent years; Campbell explains why.

Campbell, Angus, et al. *The American Voter.* New York: Wiley, 1960. The classic study of the American voter, based on data from the 1950s.

Conway, M. Margaret. *Political Participation,* 3rd ed. Washington, DC: Congressional Quarterly Press, 2000. A good review of the literature on political participation.

Delli Carpini, Michael X., and Scott Keeter. *What Americans Know About Politics and Why It Matters.* New Haven, CT: Yale University Press, 1996. The best study of the state of political knowledge in the electorate.

DeSipio, Louis. *Counting on the Latino Vote: Latinos as a New Electorate.* Charlottesville: University Press of Virginia, 1998. An examination of the current state of Latino public opinion and how more Latinos could be politically mobilized in the future.

Fiorina, Morris P. *Culture War? The Myth of a Polarized America,* 3rd ed. New York: Longman, 2010. This book argues that the so-called culture war between the red and blue states is highly exaggerated, as most Americans possess relatively moderate and nuanced opinions on political issues.

Hetherington, Marc J. *Why Trust Matters.* Princeton, NJ: Princeton University Press, 2005. The author argues that the decline of trust in government in recent decades has weakened support for progressive policies to address problems of poverty and racial inequality.

Jacobs, Lawrence R., and Robert Y. Shapiro. *Politicians Don't Pander.* Chicago: University of Chicago Press, 2000. Contrary to popular notions that politicians hold their fingers to the wind and try to follow the polls, Jacobs and Shapiro argue that politicians use polls to figure out how to best persuade the public to support their preferred policies.

Jennings, M. Kent, and Richard G. Niemi. *Generations and Politics: A Panel Study of Young Adults and Their Parents.* Princeton, NJ: Princeton University Press, 1981. A highly influential study of the class of 1965, their parents, and how both generations changed over the course of eight years.

Lewis-Beck, Michael S., et al. *The American Voter Revisited.* Ann Arbor, MI: University of Michigan Press, 2008. A replication of the classic analysis in *The American Voter* employing data from the 2000 and 2004 American National Election Studies.

Nie, Norman H., Jane Junn, and Kenneth Stehlik-Barry. *Education and Democratic Citizenship in America.*

Chicago: University of Chicago Press, 1996. An in-depth investigation of the role of education in fostering political tolerance and participation.

Persily, Nathaniel, Jack Citrin, and Patrick J. Egan. ***Public Opinion and Constitutional Controversy.*** New York: Oxford University Press, 2008. A review of public opinion data on major issues that have recently come before the Supreme Court, such as abortion, the death penalty, and affirmative action.

Tate, Katherine. ***From Protest to Politics: The New Black Voters in American Elections,*** enlarged ed. Cambridge, MA: Harvard University Press, 1998. An excellent examination of public opinion and participation among the African American community.

Verba, Sidney, and Norman H. Nie. ***Participation in America.*** New York: Harper & Row, 1972. A landmark study of American political participation.

Verba, Sidney, Kay Lehman Schlozman, and Henry E. Brady. ***Voice and Equality: Civic Voluntarism in American Politics.*** Cambridge, MA: Harvard University Press, 1995. A worthy update and extension to *Participation in America.*

Chapter 7

The Mass Media and The Political Agenda

Learning Objectives

7.1 Describe how American politicians choreograph their messages through the mass media.

7.2 Outline the key developments in the history of mass media and American politics.

7.3 List the major criteria that determine which news stories receive the most media attention.

7.4 Analyze the impact the media has on what policy issues Americans think about.

7.5 Explain how policy entrepreneurs employ media strategies to influence the public agenda.

7.6 Assess the impact of the mass media on the scope of government and democracy in America.

POLITICS IN ACTION: THE INCREASING DIFFICULTY OF GETTING OUT A PRESIDENTIAL MESSAGE

Because policymaking often depends upon politicians' power to persuade, the ability to communicate with the American public is a key tool for policymakers. When presidents speak to the nation, they expect a large viewing audience and anticipate that their message will continue to reach the public through news reports for days afterwards. But a series of changes in the mass media environment has made it much less likely that these expectations will be fulfilled today compared to just several decades ago. A tale of the initial speeches given to Congress by President Reagan in 1981 and President Obama in 2009 provides a good illustration of the profound changes in the presidential media environment discussed in this chapter.

President Ronald Reagan addressed Congress during prime time on February 18, 1981, to outline his proposed policies for economic recovery. Reagan's speech was covered live on CBS, NBC, and ABC and garnered a Nielsen rating of 60, meaning that three-fifths of the American public watched it. Beyond reaching this enormous live audience, Reagan knew he could communicate his message to the many people who would soon read and view news about his remarks. The next day, at least 55 percent of the public—the percentage surveys back then found read a newspaper every day—could be expected to pick up a newspaper containing stories about the president's speech. Later that evening, roughly 38 percent could be expected to view some coverage of the president's speech on the highly rated national newscasts at dinnertime.

The situation was markedly different when President Barack Obama went to Capitol Hill on February 24, 2009, to set forth his proposals for dealing with the economic crisis. Obama's speech, too, was covered live on CBS, NBC, and ABC—and on FOX, FOX News, CNN, MSNBC, CNBC, Telemundo, and Univision. Yet, whereas Reagan received a rating of 60 on the three networks, Obama achieved a rating of just 32 on 10 channels. In this age of narrowcasting, in which a plethora of channels appeal to specialized audiences, large audiences are increasingly rare—and even presidents usually do not achieve them. Not only was the audience rating for Obama's speech about half of Reagan's, but he also could not count on a regular audience of news consumers learning about his remarks the next day. By the time Obama assumed office, the percentage of the public who read the newspaper daily had fallen from the 55 percent of the early 1980s to only about 32 percent. And the typical ratings of the nightly newscasts on the three traditional broadcast networks had plummeted from 38 to just 16. (Of course, there are now also cable news shows available to most viewers. But these shows, which typically get ratings of less than 2, scarcely make up for the lost audience of the network broadcasts.)

The diminishing audience for presidential messages, as well as for national news, means that President Obama faces a significantly more difficult task in getting messages

Chapter **OUTLINE**

through to the entire public than did his predecessors in the mass media age. For politicians other than the president, of course, this problem is even more acute. Moreover, the problem is one that may have considerable consequences. Democracy depends upon an informed citizenry, and the citizenry depends on the mass media for its information. If only a fraction of the public is paying attention to political events, then democracy may well suffer. As with many areas of American life, the future of the mass media may lie with the Internet. Yet, so far, the promise of the Internet for broadening political discourse remains unfulfilled.

high-tech politics
A politics in which the behavior of citizens and policymakers and the political agenda itself are increasingly shaped by technology.

mass media
Television, radio, newspapers, magazines, the Internet, and other means of popular communication.

media events
Events that are purposely staged for the media and that are significant just because the media are there.

Since the latter part of the twentieth century, the American political system has been in a period of **high-tech politics**—a politics in which the behavior of citizens and policymakers, as well as the political agenda itself, is increasingly shaped by technology. A key part of this evolving technology is the **mass media**, including television, radio, newspapers, magazines, and the Internet. These and other means of popular communication are called *mass media* because they reach and profoundly influence not only the elites but also the masses.

This chapter examines media politics, focusing on the rise of modern media in America's advanced technological society, the making of the news and its presentation through the media, biases in the news, and the impact of the media on policymakers and the public. It also reintroduces the concept of the policy agenda, in which the media play an important role.

7.1 Describe how American politicians choreograph their messages through the mass media.

The Mass Media Today

Whether one is promoting a candidate, drawing attention to a social issue, or proposing a government program, political success depends on effectively communicating a message. The key is gaining control over the political agenda, which today, as throughout the period of high-tech politics, involves getting one's priorities presented at the top of the daily news.

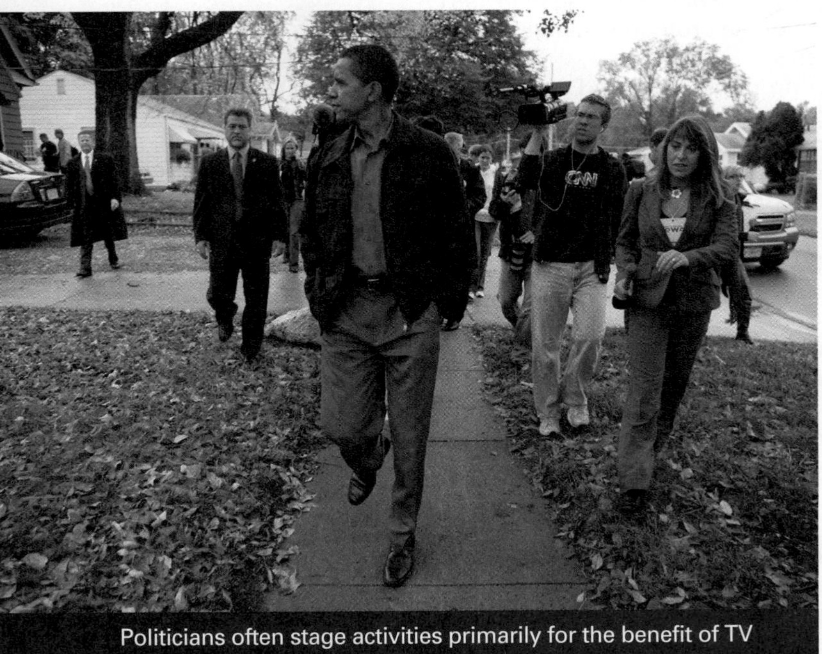

Politicians often stage activities primarily for the benefit of TV cameras. For example, the sight of a major national candidate going door-to-door asking ordinary people for their support is something that the media finds difficult to pass up. In this swing through an Iowa neighborhood, Barack Obama met perhaps 30 of the 90,000 people that voted for him in the Iowa caucuses. But the number of people who saw pictures like this in their newspaper or viewed the video footage on TV was far, far greater.

Politicians have learned that one way to guide the media's focus successfully is to give the media carefully scripted events to report on. A **media event** is staged primarily for the purpose of being covered; if the media were not there, the event would probably not happen or would have little significance. For example, while campaigning for the presidency in Iowa, Barack Obama went door-to-door one day in a middle-class neighborhood with TV crews in tow. The few dozen people he met could scarcely have made a difference, but Obama was not really there to win votes by personal contact. Rather, the point was to get television coverage of him reaching out to ordinary people. Getting the right image on the TV news for just 30 seconds can have a much greater payoff than a whole day's worth of handshaking. Whereas once a candidate's G.O.T.V. program stood for "Get Out the Vote," today it is more likely to mean "Get on TV."

Slickly produced TV commercials are another important tool in high-tech politics. For example, approximately 60 percent of presidential campaign spending is now devoted to TV ads. Moreover, in this case, the message being communicated is largely a negative one: In recent presidential elections, about two-thirds of the prominently aired ads were negative ads.[1] Some political scientists have expressed concern that the tirade of accusations, innuendoes, and countercharges in political advertising may be poisoning the American political process.[2]

Media events and TV commercials are largely about image making. Such image making does not stop with the campaign; it is also a critical element in day-to-day governing. Politicians' images in the press are seen as good indicators of their clout. Image is especially important for presidents, who in recent decades have devoted much attention to maintaining a well-honed public image, as reflected in this excerpt from an internal White House memo written by President Nixon:

> When I think of the millions of dollars that go into one lousy 30-second television spot advertising a deodorant, it seems to me unbelievable that we don't do a better job in seeing that presidential appearances always have the very best professional advice whenever they are to be covered on TV. . . . The President should never be without the very best professional advice for making a television appearance.[3]

Few, if any, administrations devoted so much effort and energy to the president's media appearance as did Ronald Reagan's. It has often been said that Reagan played to the media as he had played to the cameras in Hollywood, with his aides choreographing his public appearances. According to journalist Mark Hertsgaard, news management in the Reagan White House operated on the following seven principles: (1) plan ahead, (2) stay on the offensive, (3) control the flow of information, (4) limit reporters' access to the president, (5) talk about the issues you want to talk about, (6) speak in one voice, and (7) repeat the same message many times.[4]

If Reagan was exceptional in his ability to handle the media, he was far from alone in his realization of its importance to the presidency. In today's high-tech age, presidents can hardly lead the country if they cannot communicate effectively with it. President Clinton once reflected on *Larry King Live*: "The thing that has surprised me most is how difficult it is . . . to really keep communicating what you're about to the American people. That to me has been the most frustrating thing." According to journalist Bob Woodward, Clinton confided to a friend that "I did not realize the importance of communications and the overriding importance of what is on the evening television news. If I am not on, or there with a message, someone else is, with their message."[5]

The Development of Media Politics

7.2 Outline the key developments in the history of mass media and American politics.

There was virtually no daily press when the U.S. Constitution was written. The daily newspaper is largely a product of the mid-nineteenth century; radio and television have been around only since the first half of the twentieth century. As recently as the presidency of Herbert Hoover (1929–1933), reporters submitted their questions to the president in writing, and he responded in writing—if at all. As Hoover put it, "The President of the United States will not stand and be questioned like a chicken thief by men whose names he does not even know."[6]

Hoover's successor, Franklin D. Roosevelt (1933–1945), practically invented media politics. To Roosevelt, the media were a potential ally. Roosevelt promised reporters two presidential **press conferences**—meetings with reporters—a week, resulting in about 1,000 press conferences during his 12 years in the White House. He used presidential wrath to warn reporters off material he did not want covered, and he chastised news reports he deemed inaccurate. His wrath was rarely invoked, however, and the press revered him, never even reporting to the American public that the president was confined to a wheelchair. The idea that a political leader's health status might be public business was alien to journalists in FDR's day.

press conferences
Meetings of public officials with reporters.

This relatively cozy relationship between politicians and the press lasted through the early 1960s. ABC's Sam Donaldson said that when he first came to Washington in

1961, "many reporters saw themselves as an extension of the government, accepting, with very little skepticism, what government officials told them."[7] And coverage of a politician's personal life was generally off limits. For example, as a young reporter, R. W. Apple, Jr., of the *New York Times* once observed a beautiful woman being escorted to President Kennedy's suite. Thinking he had a major scoop, he rushed to tell his editor. But he was quickly told, "Apple, you're supposed to report on political and diplomatic policies, not girlfriends. No story."[8]

With the events of the Vietnam War and the Watergate scandal, though, unquestioning acceptance soon gave way to skepticism and even cynicism. Newspeople have come to assume that politicians rarely tell the whole story and that their own job is to ferret out the truth. As Sam Donaldson of ABC News wrote in his book, *Hold On, Mr. President!*,

> If you send me to cover a pie-baking contest on Mother's Day, I'm going to ask dear old Mom whether she used artificial sweetener in violation of the rules, and while she's at it, could I see the receipt for the apples to prove she didn't steal them. I maintain that if Mom has nothing to hide, no harm will have been done. But the questions should be asked.[9]

Thus, for example, when the Clinton–Lewinsky scandal broke, so strong was the desire to find out what the president had to hide in his personal life that 75 percent of the questions asked during the daily White House press briefings that week concerned the scandal.[10] The importance that journalists give to scrutinizing the claims of government officials can be seen in Figure 7.1. Many political scientists, however, are critical of such **investigative journalism**—the use of detective-like reporting methods to check up on the statements of governmental officials. They see the adversarial role of the media, in which reporters pit themselves against political leaders, as contributing to public cynicism and negativity about politics.[11]

investigative journalism The use of in-depth reporting to unearth scandals, scams, and schemes, at times putting reporters in adversarial relationships with political leaders.

In his analysis of media coverage of presidential campaigns since 1960, Thomas Patterson found that news coverage of presidential candidates has become increasingly less favorable. Patterson's careful analysis uncovers two major aspects of this trend toward more negative coverage: The emphasis of campaign reporting has changed dramatically from "what" to "why," and whereas the "what" was primarily candidates' policy statements, today's "why" focuses on the campaign as horse race. This emphasis on

FIGURE 7.1 The Importance Journalists Assign to Various Roles of the Mass Media

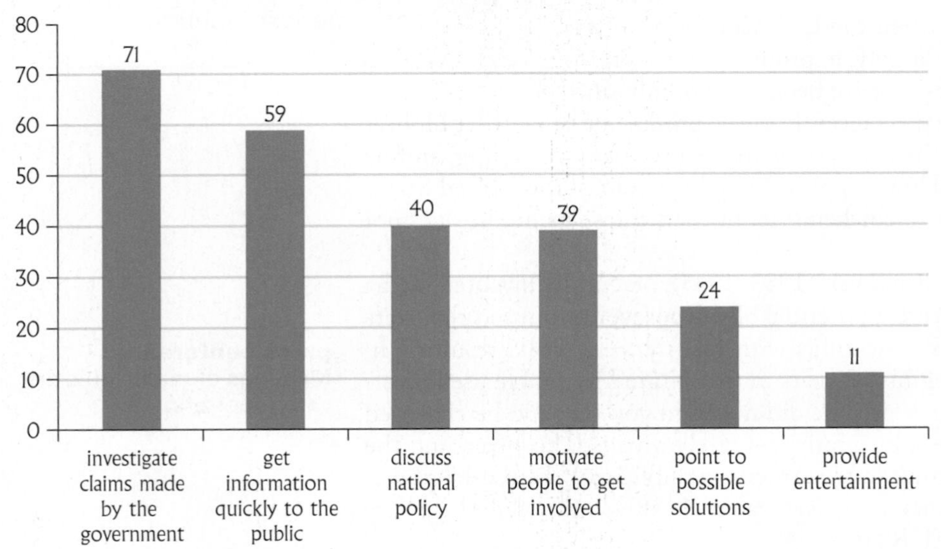

A recent national survey of journalists in America asked them to rate the importance of "a number of things that the news media do or try to do today." To the left are the percentages of journalists who ranked each of these media roles as "extremely important."

Source: Adapted from David. H. Weaver et al., *The American Journalist in the 21st Century* (Mahwah, NJ: Lawrence Erlbaum, 2007), 140.

hard-biting analysis of political maneuvering and campaign controversies naturally leads to unfavorable impressions of the candidates. Clearly, little favorable could come of coverage of such issues as how much Barack Obama knew about the incendiary comments of Reverend Wright or whether George W. Bush fulfilled his military obligations. Those who run campaigns naturally complain about such coverage. As Karl Rove, one of George W. Bush's top political advisers, said after the 2000 election,

> The general nature of the tone of the coverage was very much in keeping with what Patterson suggests, that it is process oriented, highly cynical, negative, dismissive of issue positions, focused on the internals of the campaign and not on the big messages and really serves to trivialize the whole contest.[12]

The White House press secretary battles daily with the press corps, as correspondents attempt to obtain ever more information while the president's spokesperson tries to control the news agenda and spin stories in the administration's favor. Symbolizing this conflict, Obama's press secretary Robert Gibbs offered to give members of the press a chance to dunk him in a tank at the annual White House luau one year. Four reporters stepped up to take a shot at dunking Gibbs and two succeeded in dunking him in the tank.

Whether or not such media coverage is ultimately in the public's best interest is much debated. The press maintains that the public is now able to get a complete, accurate, and unvarnished look at the candidates. Critics of the media charge the controversial aspects of the campaign are emphasized at the expense of an examination of the major issues.

To explore the development of media politics, we need to distinguish between two kinds of media: the **print media**, which include newspapers and magazines, and the **electronic media**, which include radio, television, and the Internet. Newspapers, radio, and television have each reshaped political communication at some point in American history. It is difficult to assess the likely impact of the Internet at this point, but there is at least some reason to believe that political communication is being reshaped once again.

print media
Newspapers and magazines, as compared with **electronic media.**

electronic media
Television, radio, and the Internet, as compared with **print media.**

The Print Media

The first American daily newspaper was printed in Philadelphia in 1783, but such papers did not proliferate until the technological advances of the mid-nineteenth century. The ratification of the First Amendment in 1791, guaranteeing freedom of speech, gave even the earliest American newspapers freedom to print whatever they saw fit. In so doing, it gave the media a unique ability to display the government's dirty linen, an ability that, as we've seen, the American press today makes ample use of.

Thomas Jefferson famously said, "If I had to choose between government without newspapers, and newspapers without government, I wouldn't hesitate to choose the latter." Our first mass medium, newspapers have continued to play a crucial role down through the centuries. Even in recent decades, with the emergence of other media, most political scientists who have researched media and politics agree on the value of newspapers as a source of information. Studies invariably find that regular newspaper readers are better informed and more likely to vote.[13] For example, Robert Putnam, in his highly influential book entitled *Bowling Alone,* finds that "those who *read* the news are more engaged and knowledgeable about the world than those who only *watch* the news." Putnam concludes that "newspaper reading and good citizenship go together."[14] All of this should hardly be surprising given that newspapers have so much more information than TV. A major metropolitan newspaper averages roughly 100,000 words daily, whereas a typical broadcast of the nightly news on TV amounts to only about 3,600 words.[15]

Despite the continued value of newspapers, ever since the rise of TV and TV news, American newspaper circulation rates have been declining. And with the rise of the Internet, this trend has been greatly accelerated. Whereas in 1960 one newspaper was sold for every two adults, by 2008 this ratio had plummeted to one paper for every five adults. With young adults reading newspapers at record low rates, the accelerated decline in readership is likely to continue.

Many people believe the future of the newspaper business lies with the Internet. For most major newspapers, online editions have become a source of advertising revenue. However, this advertising revenue falls far short of what newspapers need to maintain a full staff of reporters and editors; as of mid-2009, it represented only about 10 percent of newspapers' total take from advertising.[16] Some newspapers have tried charging for access to their reporting. But this strategy of selling Internet subscriptions has proved successful only for papers that focus on business news, such as the *Wall Street Journal* and the *Financial Times*. As Howard Kurtz writes, most newspapers are facing the problem that "in a world of Twitter feeds and gigabytes of gossip and a thousand other distractions, most people will see no need to pay for news. There will always be enough aggregators out there for them to cherry-pick the latest headlines, photos and video."[17] The financial situation of many major city newspapers is now so tenuous that some policymakers have proposed making it possible for newspapers to become tax-exempt nonprofit organizations, as you can read about in "You Are the Policymaker: Should Newspapers Be Allowed to Be Nonprofit Organizations?"

Magazines, the other component of the print media, are also struggling in the Internet age. For the few magazines that focus on political events, this struggle is especially dire, since their circulation levels are not among the industry's highest. The so-called newsweeklies, intended for a wide audience—*Time, Newsweek,* and *U.S.*

YOU ARE THE POLICYMAKER

Should Newspapers Be Allowed to Be Nonprofit Organizations?

The newspaper business is clearly in financial trouble. Long-established newspapers in Denver and Seattle went out of business in 2009, and papers in Philadelphia, Chicago, Los Angeles, Minneapolis, and Baltimore, among others, have recently filed for Chapter 11 bankruptcy. The red ink that the newspaper business is facing is of concern to many policymakers today. President Obama, a self-proclaimed "big newspaper junkie," has said that "it's something that I think is absolutely critical to the health of our democracy."

One plan to help out the struggling newspaper industry is a bill proposed by Senator Benjamin Cardin, called the Newspaper Revitalization Act. This bill would offer newspapers the option of operating as nonprofit organizations for educational purposes. Such a classification would give them a tax status similar to public broadcasting companies. With this tax status, newspapers would no longer have to pay taxes on any advertising or subscription revenue they generate. In addition, much like PBS radio and TV stations, they could receive tax-deductible contributions.

Although most policymakers are supportive of the goal of keeping newspapers in operation, many have raised serious questions about the wisdom of this bill. Some are concerned that, if newspapers were to receive a tax break, they would become beholden to politicians and thus less likely to pursue critical stories and investigations. Others are troubled by the fact that newspapers operating as nonprofits could no longer speak out with editorial commentaries or endorsements. Any nonprofit newspaper would also have to be wary of seeming to support a particular point of view lest it risk its tax-exempt status. Proponents of the bill acknowledge these drawbacks, but reply that any newspaper in a community is better than none at all.

What do you think? Would you favor allowing newspapers to operate as nonprofit entities?

News & World Report—rank well behind such popular favorites as *Reader's Digest, TV Guide,* and *National Geographic.* More serious magazines of political news and opinion—for example, the *New Republic, National Review,* and the *Atlantic Monthly*—tend to be read only by the educated elite, and they are outsold by other magazines meant for specific audiences, such as *Hot Rod, Weightwatchers Magazine,* and *Organic Gardening.*

The Emergence of Radio and Television

Gradually, electronic media have displaced the print media as Americans' principal source of news and information. This displacement began with radio, and then television. By the middle of the 1930s, radio ownership had become almost universal in America, and during World War II, radio went into the news business in earnest, taking the nation to the war in Europe and the Pacific. A decade later, the public was getting its news from television as well. Then, in 1960, John Kennedy faced off against Richard Nixon in the first ever televised presidential debate. Haggard from a week in the hospital, and with his five-o'clock shadow and perspiration clearly visible, Nixon looked awful compared to the crisp, clean, attractive Kennedy. The poll results from this debate illustrate the visual power of television in American politics: People listening on the radio gave the edge to Nixon, but those who saw the debate on television thought Kennedy had won. Russell Baker, who covered the event for the *New York Times,* writes in his memoirs that "television replaced newspapers as the most important communications medium in American politics" that very night.[18] Nixon blamed his poor appearance in this debate for his narrow defeat in the election.[19]

Much like radio and World War II in the 1940s, television took the nation to the war in Vietnam in the 1960s. Television exposed governmental naïveté—and sometimes outright lying—about the progress of the war. Every night, Americans watched the horrors of war in living color on television. President Johnson soon had two wars on his hands, one in faraway Vietnam and the other at home with antiwar protesters—both covered in detail by the media. In 1968, CBS anchor Walter Cronkite journeyed to Vietnam for a firsthand look at the state of the war. In an extraordinary TV special, Cronkite reported that the war was not being won nor was it likely to be. Watching from the White House, Johnson sadly remarked that if he had lost Cronkite, he had lost the support of the American people.[20]

Walter Cronkite on CBS, and his counterparts on ABC and NBC, highly trusted and influential, brought about and symbolized the golden era of network news. That era is clearly coming to an end, as cable news and the Internet have increasingly supplanted the nightly news shows. As *New York Times* media critic Frank Rich recently wrote, "The No. 1 cliché among media critics is that we're watching the 'last hurrah' of network news anchors as we have known them for nearly half a century."[21] You can see the evidence for this trend in "A Generation of Change: How Network News Broadcasts Are Going the Way of the Dinosaurs."

Government Regulation of Electronic Media

With the invention of radio, a number of problems that the government could help with—such as overlapping use of the same frequency—soon became apparent. In 1934, Congress created the Federal Communications Commission (FCC) to regulate the use of airwaves. Today, the FCC regulates communications via radio, television, telephone, cable, and satellite. The FCC is an independent regulatory body, although, like other such bodies, it is subject to political pressures, including through Congress's control over its budget and the president's appointing its members.

The FCC's regulation takes several important forms. First, to prevent near monopolies of control over a broadcast market, the FCC has instituted rules to limit

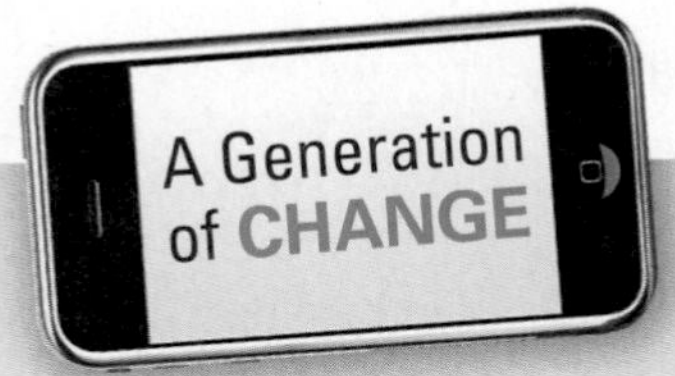

How Network News Broadcasts Are Going the Way of the Dinosaurs

Over the past quarter century, the NBC, ABC, and CBS nightly news broadcasts have gone from being instrumental in setting the nation's agenda to the TV equivalent of dinosaurs on the verge of extinction.

In 1981, one could make a legitimate argument that, in their short existence, network newscasts had played a significant role in the political downfall of three presidents—Presidents Johnson, Nixon, and Carter—because of the way they had drawn attention to their shortcomings. Writing in 1983, media historian Barbara Matusow said of the evening news anchors, "They have taken their place beside presidents, congressmen, labor leaders, industrialists, and others who shape public policy and private attitudes."*

Between 1983 and 2004, Tom Brokaw, Peter Jennings, and Dan Rather, who anchored the nightly news at NBC, ABC, and CBS, respectively, saw their Nielsen ratings slip lower and lower, as shown in this graph. When Tom Brokaw was asked near the end of his career as anchor of the *NBC Evening News* what he perceived his mission to be, he responded simply "to survive." Because of the loyal viewership they had built up, these three longtime anchors were able to keep their news shows going. Whether their successors, whose ratings continue to set new lows, can do the same for another generation remains to be seen.

In its heyday, network TV news broadcasts put afternoon newspapers out of business. Too few people felt they needed an afternoon paper once the nightly news was available on television. Today, in this era of 24-hour cable news channels and the Internet, turning on the television to get the news at a set time early in the evening itself seems like a quaint remnant of the past.

*Barbara Matusow, *The Evening Stars: The Making of the Network News Anchor* (Boston: Houghton Mifflin, 1983), 1.

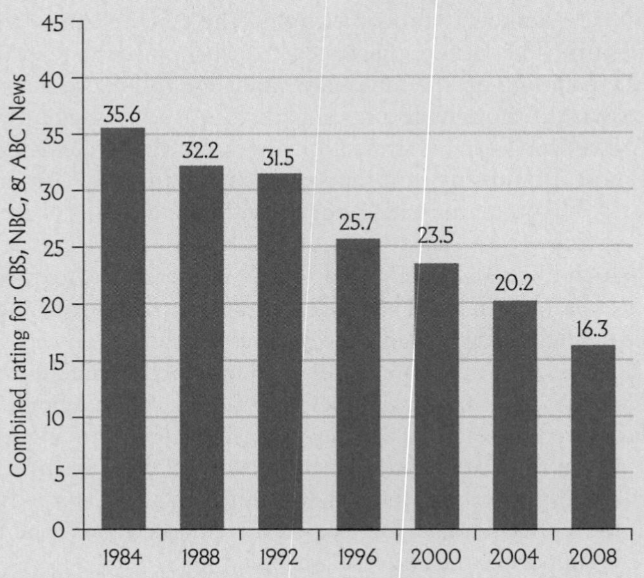

Source: *State of the News Media, 2009,* http://www.stateofthemedia.org/2009/index.htm. Ratings are for November of each year.

the number of stations owned or controlled by one company. Since a simplification in 1996, the rule has been just that no single owner can control more than 35 percent of the broadcast market. Second, the FCC conducts periodic examinations of the goals and performance of stations as part of its licensing authority. Congress long ago stipulated that in order to receive a broadcasting license, a station must serve the public interest. The FCC has on only rare occasion withdrawn licenses for failing to do so, as when a Chicago station lost its license for neglecting informational programs and for presenting obscene movies. Third, the FCC has issued a number of fair treatment rules concerning access to the airwaves for political candidates and officeholders. The equal time rule stipulates that if a station sells advertising time to one candidate, it must be willing to sell equal time to other candidates for the same office. And the right-of-reply rule states if a person is attacked on a broadcast other than the news, then that person has a right to reply via the same station. For many years, the fairness doctrine required broadcasters to give time to opposing views if they broadcast a program slanted to one side of a controversial issue. But with the development of so many TV channels via cable, by the late 1980s this rule was seen as unnecessary and was abolished.

From Broadcasting to Narrowcasting: The Rise of Cable and Cable News

The first major networks—ABC, NBC, and CBS—included the term "broadcasting" in their name because their signal was being sent out to a broad audience. Each of these networks dealt with various subjects that had widespread public appeal, including politics and government. But with the development of cable TV, market segmentation took hold. Sports buffs can watch ESPN all day, music buffs can tune in to MTV or VH1, history buffs can stay glued to the History Channel, and so forth. If you are interested in politics, you can switch between C-SPAN, C-SPAN2, CNN, MSNBC, Fox News Channel, and others. Rather than appealing to a general audience, channels such as ESPN, MTV, and C-SPAN focus on a narrow, particular interest. Hence, their mission can be termed **narrowcasting**, as opposed to the traditional broadcasting.

narrowcasting
Media programming on cable TV (e.g., on MTV, ESPN, or C-SPAN) or the Internet that is focused on a particular interest and aimed at a particular audience, in contrast to broadcasting.

Narrowcasting has significantly affected media usage patterns, especially for young adults. Having grown up with narrowcasting alternatives, young adults are less likely than other age groups to be using newspapers and broadcast media as news and information sources. Interestingly, one source of information about politics that young people are more likely than other age groups to rely on is humorous shows that cover current events, or "infotainment," as you can see in "Young People and Politics: Learning from Comedy Shows?"

Narrowcasting clearly has great potential for disseminating news to the American public. With the growth of cable TV news channels, television can be said to have entered a new era of bringing the news to people—and to political leaders, as it happens. Michael Bohn, a former high-ranking government intelligence officer, writes that during the George W. Bush administration cable news became a valuable source of breaking information in the White House Situation Room.[22] President Bush and his aides regularly turned to cable news stations when major terrorist incidents grabbed worldwide attention.

Currently, about two-thirds of the American public subscribe to cable television and thereby have access to dozens of channels. Sometime in the not-too-distant future it is expected that most cable systems will offer 500 channels. As the number of channels increases, anyone who is really interested in politics will find political information readily available.

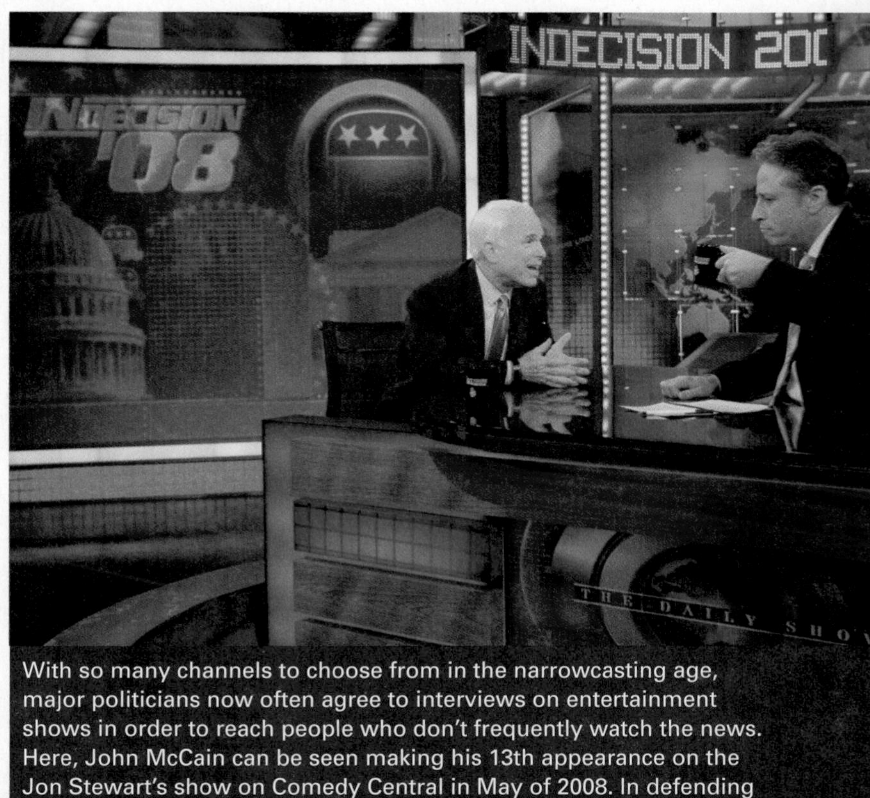

With so many channels to choose from in the narrowcasting age, major politicians now often agree to interviews on entertainment shows in order to reach people who don't frequently watch the news. Here, John McCain can be seen making his 13th appearance on the Jon Stewart's show on Comedy Central in May of 2008. In defending his decision to appear frequently on this show, McCain has called it his "avenue to young voters."

Yet, at least so far, the potential of cable news is generally not realized in practice. One common criticism is that cable news channels fail to systematically cover political events and issues, perhaps because their resources are far from up to the task. A content analysis of CNN, Fox News, and MSNBC programming confirms just how little substantive information cable news channels tend to convey. In this analysis, Columbia University's Project for Excellence in Journalism looked at 240 hours of cable news programming during 2003. Its report provides a telling indictment of the medium. Among the many findings were that (1) only 11 percent of the time was taken up with written and edited stories; (2) the role of the reporter was primarily to talk extemporaneously; (3) stories were repeated frequently, usually without any important new information; and (4) coverage of the news was spotty, ignoring many important topics. All in all, this comprehensive study paints a very unflattering portrait of what is shown on cable news networks, labeling much of it as simply "talk radio on television."[23]

Learning from Comedy Shows?

In December 2007, the Pew Research Center asked a representative sample of Americans how they learned about the presidential campaign. One of its most interesting findings was that young people were much more likely than older people to say they regularly or sometimes learned about the campaign from comedy programs like *The Daily Show* or *Saturday Night Live,* as you can see in the figure below. Commenting on this survey finding, Jon Stewart of *The Daily Show* at first dismissed out of hand any notion that young people were turning to his comedy show to learn about political events. Subsequently, his show adopted the slogan of "Keeping America Informed—Unintentionally." Is this slogan in fact accurate? How much do comedy shows contribute to their viewers' store of political information?

Scholars have found that by wrapping bits of political content into an amusing package, entertainment shows that cover current events can make politics more appealing to viewers who might otherwise ignore the subject, and thereby add to their political knowledge. Barry Hollander specifically examined what young adults take away from infotainment shows and concluded that they glean "at least modest amounts of campaign information from such content."[a] Matthew Baum found that exposure to entertainment-oriented TV talk shows among voters with lower-than-average political interest had a significant impact on how they evaluated the candidates.[b]

Although infotainment programs are clearly an element of political discourse today, some academic studies have revealed their limitations in terms of actually helping viewers understand the political world. Kim and Vishak conducted an experimental study to compare learning from traditional news and infotainment coverage of the same political events. They found that subjects who were shown Jon Stewart's coverage of the Supreme Court nomination process then in progress learned less factual information than those who were shown a similar amount of coverage of this topic culled from the nightly news. The title of their article—"Just Laugh! You Don't Need to Remember"—nicely summarizes their most important finding with regard to infotainment shows.[c] A recent study of how young adults react to *The Colbert Report* provides especially compelling evidence of how political messages can be obscured amidst laughter. Baumgartner and Morris found that young people who were shown some of Stephen Colbert's ridicule of conservative media figures like Bill O'Reilly actually became *more* supportive of conservative policies. Colbert's criticism of conservatives is indirect, performed through what knowledgeable observers would consider to be not-so-subtle mockery. However, for casual, less-informed viewers, the right-wing arguments that Colbert exaggerates apparently get through much better than his portrayal of them as absurd. As Baumgartner and Morris theorize, "the humor may block, disrupt, or distract" processing of the central political message "by increasing the likeability or trustworthiness of the source (Colbert)."[d]

Ironically, it is the fact that infotainment shows are not designed to convey political information that makes them desirable as shows for politicians to appear on in person. As the old saying goes, "If you want to go duck hunting, you need to go where the ducks are." People who are not much interested in politics can often only be reached by appearing on shows that don't normally do politics.

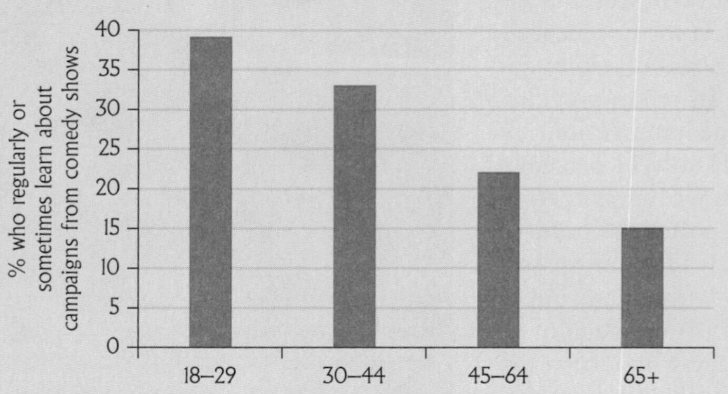

Source: Authors' analysis of a December 2007 survey by the Pew Research Center for the People & the Press.

[a]Barry A. Hollander, "Late-Night Learning: Do Entertainment Programs Increase Political Campaign Knowledge for Young Viewers?" *Journal of Broadcasting and Electronic Media* (December 2005): 412.

[b]Matthew A. Baum, "Talking the Vote: Why Presidential Candidates Hit the Talk Show Circuit," *American Journal of Political Science* (April 2005): 213–34.

[c]Young Mie Kim and John Vishak, "Just Laugh! You Don't Need to Remember: The Effects of Entertainment Media on Political Information Acquisition and Information Processing in Political Judgment," *Journal of Communication* (June 2008): 338–60.

[d]Jody C. Baumgartner and Jonathan S. Morris, "One 'Nation,' Under Stephen? The Effects of *The Colbert Report* on American Youth," *Journal of Broadcasting and Electronic Media* (December 2008): 635.

QUESTIONS FOR DISCUSSION

- How much do you think can really be learned about politics from the comedy shows that so many young people say they learn from?
- Do you think presidential candidates should go on these shows in order to reach people who do not watch traditional news shows, or do you think the nature of comedy shows demeans serious politicians who appear on them?

Two other common criticisms of cable news channels are that too much of the time they show people yelling at one another and that when a story breaks they tend to sensationalize it. President Obama recently remarked that he doesn't watch the cable news channels because "it feels like WWF wrestling." Softening this derogatory remark, the president went on to say that "it's not even necessarily that there's not good reporting on it; it's just that everyone is having to accelerate to get the next story, the new story, and if there's a story that people think is going to sell, then they overdo it."[24]

In view of these issues, it is not surprising that many scholars of the media feel that the shift from network news to cable news has reduced the overall quality of political journalism. As media critic Thomas Rosensteil writes, "Network journalism originally was designed not to make a profit but to create prestige. Cable is all about profit and keeping costs low. What is disappearing is an idealism about the potential of TV as a medium to better our politics and society."[25]

The Impact of the Internet

Some scholars have optimistically predicted that the Internet will be a boon for American democracy, by enabling citizens to become well informed about politics. Indeed, as any college student knows, the Internet is the ultimate research tool. Want to know something specific? The answer can usually be found by searching the Internet using a few key words. If you want to know how presidential candidates stand on federal support for higher education, an Internet search should quickly reveal the answers. Or if you want to know how your two U.S. senators voted on Medicaid appropriations, the records of the Senate roll calls can be found on the Internet. In short, for anyone with basic computing skills, gaining information about political issues is now easier than ever before.

Yet the fact that so much political information is at one's fingertips via the Internet doesn't necessarily mean that people will take advantage of this unprecedented opportunity to become well informed about politics. To a far greater extent than TV, the Internet is purposive—that is, what people see is the product of their own intentional choices. Politics is only one of a myriad of subjects that one can find out about on the Internet. As we saw in the previous chapter on public opinion, most Americans' interest in politics is fairly limited. Most people with limited political interest will probably not be motivated to use the Internet to look up detailed information about politics very often, let alone to follow politics on a regular basis. Indeed, the data on Lycos searches displayed in Table 7.1 indicate that even during the week of the first 2008 presidential election debate, Americans were more likely to be looking for information on pop culture than politics. In the most comprehensive study of the Internet and politics to date, Matthew Hindman finds that traffic to political sites accounts for just 0.12 percent of

TABLE 7.1 The Top 25 Lycos Searches for the Week of the First 2008 Presidential Debate

Every week, the search engine Lycos lists the search terms that its users have most frequently used to seek information on the Internet. Here you can find the top 25 searches for the week ending September 30, 2008—the week of the first Obama–McCain presidential debate. As you can see, only 2 of the top 25 search items reflect an interest in the election or news events. More people used the Internet to get information about pop culture figures such as Clay Aiken and Paris Hilton than to learn about the stunning news of Lehman Brothers' bankruptcy or about the presidential candidates.

The rankings reflect what Internet users are most interested in. Political scientists have long argued that politics are only a peripheral part of most people's lives, and these rankings clearly reflect that fact.

RANK	SEARCH TERM	RANK	SEARCH TERM
1.	Clay Aiken	14.	Naruto
2.	Paris Hilton	15.	WWE
3.	YOUTUBE	16.	Kanye West
4.	Travis Barker	17.	Lance Armstrong
5.	Pamela Anderson	18.	Biggest Loser
6.	Kim Kardashian	19.	Bristol Palin
7.	Facebook	20.	Lehman Brothers Bankruptcy
8.	DJ AM	21.	RUNESCAPE
9.	Britney Spears	22.	Kendra Wilkinson
10.	Dragonball	23.	Carmen Electra
11.	Lindsay Lohan	24.	Jennifer Hudson
12.	Sarah Palin	25.	Eva Mendes
13.	Megan Fox		

Source: http://50.lycos.com.

all Web traffic, with the most frequently visited political site—HuffingtonPost.com—ranking 796th in terms of viewing hits.[26]

So far, the Internet has had its main impact on politics largely by facilitating more communication in every conceivable direction. Through the Internet, journalists, politicians, and interest group organizers can communicate more readily with the public at large, and ordinary citizens can respond far more easily and frequently than before. As a result, there have been some important changes in the nature of campaigning as well as in political communication.

For campaigns, the ability to post information and communicate with supporters via the Internet appears to help somewhat with political mobilization. Bruce Bimber and Richard Davis's study of campaigning online found that "campaign web sites attract supporters of the candidates who display them, and the messages of these sites have a modest tendency to strengthen and reinforce voters' predispositions."[27] As these authors point out, with the decline of traditional neighborhood-based party organizations, the Internet is providing a much-needed means to bring activists together, employing such vehicles as Meetup and Facebook.

Blogs in particular have provided political activists with a means to make their concerns heard to an extent that was previously possible only for professional journalists. Indeed, Brian Williams of NBC News remarks that because of blogs, the news media now faces competition from "people who have an opinion, a modem, and a bathrobe." He further laments, "All of my life, developing credentials to cover my field of work,

A POINT TO PONDER

President Obama recently said that he was "concerned that if the direction of the news is all blogosphere, all opinions, with no serious fact-checking, no serious attempts to put stories in context, that what you will end up getting is people shouting at each other across the void but not a lot of mutual understanding."

What do you think—is this something to be concerned about? Why, or why not?

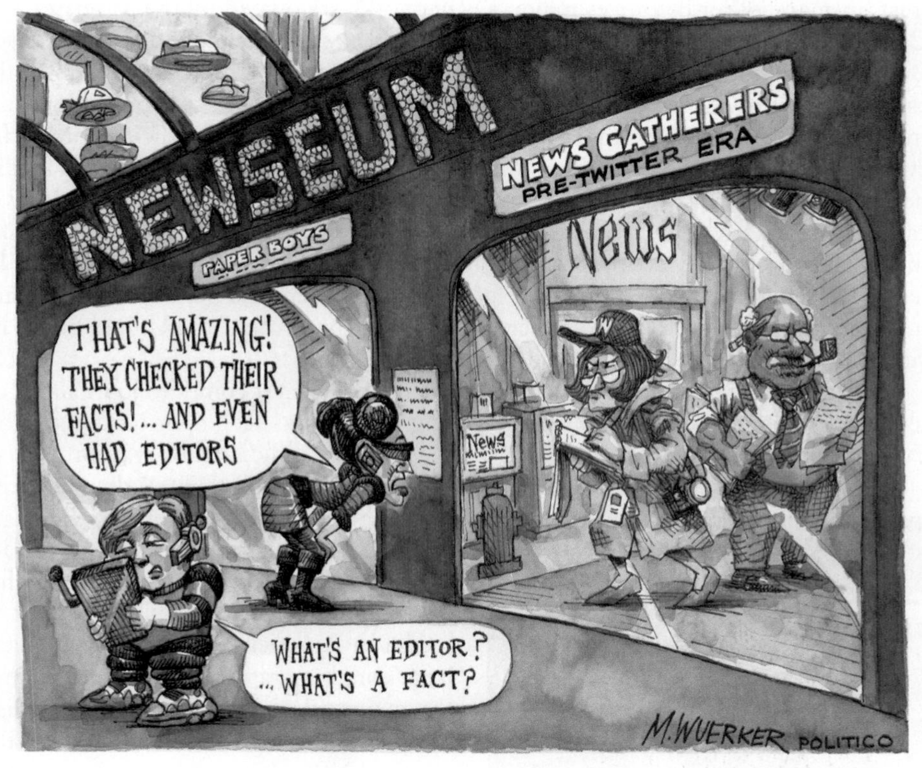

and now I'm up against a guy named Vinny in an efficiency apartment in the Bronx who hasn't left the efficiency apartment in two years."[28] His lament appears to be somewhat exaggerated, however. In theory anyone can challenge Brian Williams in the blogosphere, but in practice few bloggers are ever going to be able to reach as many people as a network anchor. Posting a blog entry is easy, but getting it national attention is difficult. Matthew Hindman analyzed the most successful political bloggers and found that in their credentials they are far more similar to the leading traditional journalists than to Brian Williams' "Vinny." In particular, the major political bloggers like Markos Moulitsas Zuniga and Hugh Hewitt all have strong analytic training, excellent writing skills, and an encyclopedic knowledge of politics. Hindman concludes that, in fact, blogs have "given a small group of educational, professional, and technical elites new influence in U.S. politics" but "have done far less to amplify the political voice of average citizens."[29]

Even if blogs remain largely a tool of elites, they have on occasion made it possible for citizens without journalistic credentials to get the media to pay attention to stories that might otherwise be ignored and to serve as watchdogs over the media. For example, when Dan Rather and CBS News ran a story in 2004 about documents that allegedly showed that George W. Bush had shirked his duties with the National Guard in the 1970s, a number of bloggers quickly raised questions concerning their authenticity. The bloggers were ultimately proven right, and CBS News apologized for running the story.

WHY IT MATTERS

Media as a Business

In his classic book *Understanding Media*, Marshall McLuhan coined the famous phrase, "The medium is the message." By this, McLuhan meant that the way we communicate information can be more influential than the information itself. In the United States, news is a commodity controlled by the media, not a public service. Therefore, the news media have far more incentive to make their reports interesting than informative about policy issues. The public would probably be exposed to more policy information were it not for this incentive system.

Private Control of the Media

As we have seen, America has a rich diversity of media sources. One of the main reasons that this has long been the case is that journalism has long been big business in the United States, with control of virtually all media outlets being in private hands. Only a relatively small number of TV stations are publicly owned in America, and these PBS stations play a minimal role in the news business, attracting very low ratings. In contrast, in many other countries major TV networks are owned by the government. In Canada, the most prominent stations are part of the state-run network (the Canadian Broadcasting Company); this is the case in most European countries, as well. In these established democracies, government ownership is not supposed to inhibit journalists from criticizing the government because the journalists are assured autonomy. However, in some countries, like China, that do not have democratic systems, the media—newspapers as well as television—are typically government enterprises and have to carefully avoid any criticism of the government. Because of private ownership of the media and the First Amendment right to free speech, American journalists have long had an unfettered capacity to criticize government leaders and policies. As you can see in "America in Perspective: Press Freedom Around the World," the United States rates very well in terms of freedom of the press.

Although the American media are independent when it comes to journalistic content, they are totally dependent on advertising revenues to keep their businesses going. Public ownership means that the media can serve the public interest without worrying about the size of their audience; private ownership means that getting the biggest possible audience is the primary—indeed, sometimes the only—objective. This focus on audience is exacerbated by the fact that media in America today tend to be part of large conglomerates. Consider, for example, the major television networks. The Disney Corporation bought ABC, General Electric acquired NBC, Viacom (a conglomerate that owns many entertainment companies, including Blockbuster, Paramount Pictures, MTV, and Simon & Schuster) took over CBS, and CNN became part of Time Warner. In the newspaper business, **chains**, such as Gannett, Knight-Ridder, and Newhouse, control newspapers that together represent over 80 percent of the nation's daily circulation.[30]

Blogs are playing an increasing important role in the reporting of political news. In 2005, 23-year old Garrett Graff, who was writing a blog about the news media in Washington became the first person to receive a White House press pass for the specific purpose of writing a blog. In 2008, as shown in this photo, the Democratic National Convention set up a lounge specifically for bloggers who were posting from the convention.

This increasing profit orientation has had repercussions for American journalism and, specifically, political reporting. For example, the major television networks once had bureaus all over the world; however, these foreign bureaus became a target for cost cutting, as they were expensive to operate and surveys showed that the public was not much interested in news from overseas. The decline in coverage was precipitous.

Press Freedom Around the World

Freedom of the press varies substantially around the world. In general, the United States and other well-established democracies value freedom of the press, allowing journalists to openly criticize their government without fear of physical threats or censorship.

Journalists in some other countries are not so fortunate. They sometimes work directly for the state and dare not contradict government policy or criticize their country's leaders. In countries where freedom of the press is restricted, journalists often work in fear of physical threats, imprisonment, and even being murdered. They find that their offices can be searched at any time or their work confiscated, and their stories must be cleared by government censors.

Based on various criteria for freedom of the press, the international organization known as Reporters Without Borders produces an annual index of press freedom. The graph below shows the 2009 scores for 20 selected countries among the approximately 170 countries surveyed. A low score indicates extensive freedom of the press, whereas a high score indicates many restrictions on journalists.

Like almost other established democracies, the United States ranked very favorably in terms of press freedom in 2009.

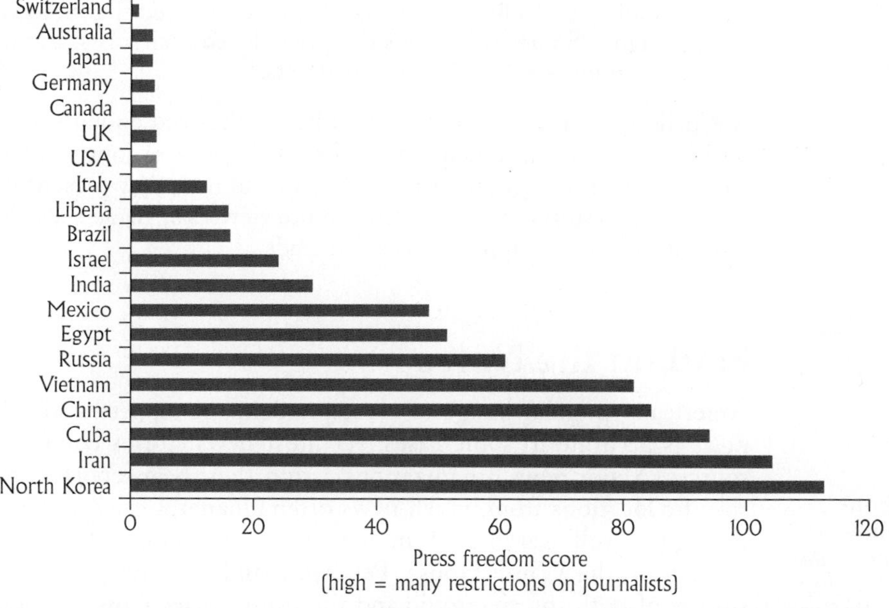

Source: Reporters Without Borders, "Worldwide Press Freedom Index," 2009, http://www.rsf.org/en-classement1003-2009.html.

A study found that ABC, NBC, and CBS broadcast just 1,382 minutes of foreign news in 2000 compared to 4,032 minutes in 1989.[31] Not surprisingly, following the terrorist attacks of September 11, 2001, the TV networks had to scramble to establish an ability to cover foreign news, for a public that had become unfamiliar with foreign news. As we shall see in the following section, striving for profits greatly shapes how the news is reported in America.

chains
Groups of newspapers published by media conglomerates and today accounting for over four-fifths of the nation's daily newspaper circulation.

Reporting the News

7.3 List the major criteria that determine which news stories receive the most media attention.

As journalism students will quickly tell you, news is what is timely and different. It is a man biting a dog, not a dog biting a man. An often-repeated speech on foreign policy or a well-worn statement on the need for immigration reform is less newsworthy than an odd episode. The public rarely hears about the routine ceremonies at state dinners, but when President George Bush threw up all over the Japanese prime minister in 1992, the world's media jumped on the story. Similarly, when Howard Dean screamed to a crowd of supporters after the 2004 Iowa caucuses, the major networks and cable news channels played the clip over 600 times in the following four days, virtually obliterating any serious discussion of the issues. In its search for the unusual, the news media can give its audience a peculiar, distorted view of events and policymakers.

Millions of new and different events happen every day; journalists must decide which of them are newsworthy. A classic look into how the news is produced can be found in Edward J. Epstein's *News from Nowhere*,[32] which summarizes his insights from a year of observing NBC's news department from inside the organization. Epstein found that in the pursuit of high ratings, news shows are tailored to a fairly low level of audience sophistication. To a large extent, TV networks define news as what is entertaining to the average viewer. A dull and complicated story would have to be of enormous importance to get on the air; in contrast, relatively trivial stories can make the cut if they are interesting enough. Leonard Downie, Jr., and Robert Kaiser of the *Washington Post* argue that entertainment has increasingly pushed out information in the TV news business. They write that the history of TV news can be summarized in a couple sentences:

> As audiences declined, network executives decreed that news had to become more profitable. So news divisions sharply reduced their costs, and tried to raise the entertainment value of their broadcasts.[33]

Regardless of the medium, it cannot be emphasized enough that news reporting is a business in America. The quest for profits shapes how journalists define what is newsworthy, where they get their information, and how they present it. And the pursuit of types of news stories that will attract more viewers or readers also leads to certain biases in what the American public sees and reads.

Finding the News

Americans' popular image of correspondents or reporters somehow uncovering the news is accurate in some cases; yet most news stories come from well-established sources. Major news organizations assign their best reporters to particular **beats**—specific locations from which news often emanates, such as Congress. For example, during the Gulf War in 1991, more than 50 percent of the lead stories on TV newscasts came from the White House, Pentagon, and State Department beats.[34] Numerous studies of both the electronic and the print media show that journalists rely almost exclusively on such established sources to get their information.[35]

beats
Specific locations from which news frequently emanates, such as Congress or the White House. Most top reporters work a particular beat, thereby becoming specialists in what goes on at that location.

trial balloons
Intentional news leaks for the purpose of assessing the political reaction.

Politicians depend on the media to spread certain information and ideas to the general public. Sometimes they feed stories to reporters in the form of **trial balloons**, information leaked to see what the political reaction will be. For example, a few days prior to President Clinton's admission that he had had an "inappropriate relationship" with Monica Lewinsky, top aides to the president leaked the story to Richard Berke of the *New York Times*. The timing of the leak was obvious; the story appeared just before Clinton had to decide how to testify before Kenneth Starr's grand jury. When the public reacted that it was about time he admitted this relationship, it was probably easier for him to do so—at least politically.

Journalists and politicians have a symbiotic relationship, with politicians relying on journalists to get their message out and journalists relying on politicians to keep them in the know. When reporters feel that their access to information is being impeded, complaints of censorship become widespread. During the Gulf War in 1991, reporters' freedom of movement and observation was severely restricted. After the fighting was over, 15 influential news organizations sent a letter to the secretary of defense complaining that the rules for reporting the war were designed more to control the news than to facilitate it.[36] Largely because of such complaints, during the 2003 military campaign to oust Saddam Hussein the Pentagon "embedded" about 500 reporters with coalition fighting forces, thus enabling them to report on combat activity as it happened. The result was an increased ability to transmit combat footage. A content analysis by Farnsworth and Lichter found that 35 percent of major TV network stories contained combat scenes compared to just 20 percent in 1991.[37] The public response to this new form of war reporting was largely positive.[38]

In 2003, during the Iraq War, a number of journalists were embedded with fighting units, meaning that they traveled along with them day after day and literally became part of the unit. Being right in with the action enabled an immediacy of reporting that was never possible before. One much-praised example of embedded reporting was that of NBC's David Bloom, who sent back stunningly clear pictures of what it was like to move through the desert with an infantry division. Sadly, Bloom was one of a number of journalists who died during the conflict with Iraq. He suffered a pulmonary embolism, a condition that may have been brought on by long hours confined to a very small space inside an armored tank.

Although journalists are typically dependent on familiar sources, an enterprising reporter occasionally has an opportunity to live up to the image of the crusading truth seeker. Local reporters Carl Bernstein and Bob Woodward of the *Washington Post* uncovered important evidence about the Watergate break-in and cover-up in the early 1970s. Ever since the Watergate scandal, news organizations have regularly sent reporters on beats to expose the uglier side of government corruption and inefficiency, and, as discussed earlier, journalists have seen such reporting as among their important roles.

There are many cases of good investigative reporting making a difference in politics and government. For example, in 1997, the *New York Times* won a Pulitzer Prize for its in-depth reports on how a proposed gold-mining operation threatened the environment of part of Yellowstone National Park. When President Clinton vacationed at nearby Jackson Hole, he decided to go up and see the mine because he had been reading about it in the *New York Times.* Soon afterward, the project was stopped, and the government gave the owners of the property a financial settlement. In 1999, the *Chicago Tribune* documented the experiences of numerous Illinois men sentenced to death who had been convicted on questionable evidence or coerced into confessing. Soon after the series was published, the governor of Illinois suspended all executions in the state. And in 2007, a reporter with the *Birmingham News* won a Pulitzer Prize for his exposure of cronyism and corruption in Alabama's two-year college system, resulting in the dismissal of the chancellor and other corrective action.

Presenting the News

Once the news has been "found," it has to be neatly compressed into a 30-second news segment or fit in among other stories and advertisements in a newspaper. If you had to pick a single word to describe news coverage by the news media, it would be *superficial.* "The name of the game," says former White House Press Secretary Jody Powell, "is skimming off the cream, seizing on the most interesting, controversial, and unusual aspects of an issue."[39] Editors do not want to bore or confuse their audience. TV news, in particular, is little more than a headline service. According to former CBS anchor Dan Rather, "You simply cannot be a well-informed citizen by just watching the news on television."[40]

Except for the little-watched but highly regarded *NewsHour* on PBS and ABC's late-night *Nightline,* analysis of news events rarely lasts more than a minute. Patterson's study of campaign coverage (see Chapter 9) found that only skimpy attention was given to the issues during a presidential campaign. Clearly, if coverage of political events during the height of an election campaign is thin, coverage of day-to-day policy questions is even thinner. Issues such as reforming the Medicare system, adjusting eligibility levels for food stamps, and regulating the financial services industry are highly complex and difficult to treat in a short news clip. A careful study of media coverage of Bill and Hillary Clinton's comprehensive health care proposal in 1993–94 found that the media focused much more on strategy and who was winning the political game than on the specific policy issues involved.[41] President Obama faced exactly the same problem in his battle to reform America's health care system in 2009–10, frequently admonishing the press, "This isn't about me. This isn't about politics."

Strangely enough, as technology has enabled the media to pass along information with greater speed, news coverage has become less thorough.[42] High-tech communication has helped reporters do their job faster but not necessarily better. Newspapers once routinely reprinted the entire text of important political speeches; now the *New York Times* is virtually the only paper that does so—and even the *Times* has cut back sharply on this practice. In place of speeches, Americans now hear **sound bites** of 10 seconds or less on TV. The average length of time that a presidential candidate was given to talk uninterrupted on the TV news declined precipitously from 43 seconds in 1968 to just 8 seconds in 2004.[43] Politicians have expressed frustration with sound-bite journalism. For example, President Jimmy Carter told a reporter that

> it's a strange thing that you can go through your campaign for president, and you have a basic theme that you express in a 15- or 20-minute standard speech . . . but the traveling press—sometimes exceeding 100 people—will never report that speech to the public. The peripheral aspects become the headlines, but the basic essence of what you stand for and what you hope to accomplish is never reported.[44]

Sound-bite journalism has meant both that politicians are unable to present the issues and that they are able to avoid the issues. Why should politicians work to build a carefully crafted case for their point of view when a catchy line will do just as well? And as Walter Cronkite wrote, "Naturally, nothing of any significance is going to be said in seven seconds, but this seems to work to the advantage of many politicians. They are not required to say anything of significance, and issues can be avoided rather than confronted."[45]

Over the past decade or so, politicians have found it increasingly difficult to get their message covered on the major networks, as ratings pressures have led to a decrease in political coverage, leaving the field to much-less-watched channels like CNN and MSNBC. The three major networks *together* devoted an average of 12.6 minutes per night to the exceedingly close 2000 presidential election campaign; just half the 24.6 minutes they devoted to the 1992 campaign.[46] Indeed, in the presidential election of 2000, voters had to bypass network television newscasts and watch TV talk shows to hear candidates deliver their messages. George W. Bush was on-screen for a total of 13 minutes during his appearance on *Late Night with David Letterman* on October 19, which exceeded his entire speaking time on all three network news shows during that month. Similarly, Al Gore received more speaking time on his September 14 *Letterman* appearance than he did during the entire month of September on the network evening newscasts.[47]

During the Cold War, presidents could routinely obtain coverage for their speeches on the three major networks anytime they requested it. Now, with the networks able to shunt the coverage to CNN and other cable news outlets, it is easy for them to say "no" to even the president. In May 2000, for example, Bill Clinton was rebuffed when he asked for time on ABC, NBC, and CBS to address U.S.–China relations. "Are you crazy? It's sweeps month!" was one of the responses.[48] In September 2009, Fox opted to show an episode of "So You Think You Can Dance" instead of Obama's address to Congress about health care.

WHY IT MATTERS

The Increasing Speed of News Dissemination

When Samuel Morse sent the first telegraph message from the U.S. Capitol building, he tapped out a question, "What hath God wrought?" The answer back was "What is the news from Washington?" Ever since, the transmission of news via electronic means has become faster and faster. As a result, over time there has been less and less time for deliberative action to deal with long-term problems, and the political agenda has come to focus more on the here and now.

sound bites
Short video clips of approximately 10 seconds. Typically, they are all that is shown from a politician's speech on the nightly television news.

Bias in the News

Some have argued that political reporting is biased in favor of one point of view—most often that the media have a liberal bias. There is limited evidence to support this charge of a liberal bias. In four comprehensive surveys of American journalists conducted between 1971 and 2002, David Weaver and his colleagues consistently found that reporters were more likely to classify themselves as liberal than the general public. For example, in 2002, 40 percent of journalists surveyed said they leaned to the left compared to only

25 percent who leaned to the right.[49] However, the vast majority of studies have found that most reporting is not systematically biased toward a particular ideology or party.

That reporting typically reflects little explicit ideological bias does not mean that it is uninfluenced by reporters' backgrounds and assumptions. Thus, former CBS News reporter Bernard Goldberg argued in his best-selling book *Bias* that "real media bias comes not so much from what party they attack. Liberal bias is the result of how they see the world."[50] According to Goldberg (who, it should be noted, is an outspoken conservative), on social issues like feminism, gay rights, and welfare the nightly news clearly leans to the left, shaped by the big-city environment in which network reporters live. He asks, "Do we really think that if the media elites worked out of Nebraska instead of New York; and if they were overwhelmingly social conservatives instead of liberals . . . do we really think that would make no difference?"[51]

Conservative Republicans often criticize the media for being biased against them. Studies have indeed shown that TV and newspaper reporters are more likely to be liberals than conservatives. However, there is little evidence that the personal views of reporters influence their coverage.

The overriding bias, however, is not an ideological bias but, rather, as we have seen, a bias toward stories that will draw the largest audience. Bernard Goldberg also writes, "In the United States of Entertainment there is no greater sin than to bore the audience. A TV reporter could get it wrong from time to time. He could be snippy and snooty. But he could not be boring."[52] Surveys show that people are most fascinated by, and most likely to follow, stories involving conflict, violence, disaster, or scandal, as is reflected in the data in Table 7.2. Such stories have the drama that brings in big audiences.

TABLE 7.2 Stories Citizens Have Tuned In and Tuned Out

Since 1986, the monthly survey of the Pew Research Center for the People & the Press has asked Americans how closely they have followed major news stories. As one would expect, stories involving disaster or human drama have drawn more attention than have complicated issues of public policy. A representative selection of their findings is presented here. The percentage in each case is the proportion who reported following the story "very closely."

The explosion of the space shuttle Challenger in 1986	80%
Terrorist attacks on the World Trade Center and Pentagon	74%
Impacts of hurricanes Katrina and Rita	73%
Los Angeles riots in 1992	70%
1987 rescue of baby Jessica McClure from a well	69%
School shootings at Columbine High School in Colorado	68%
Iraq's invasion of Kuwait in 1990	66%
2010 earthquake in Haiti	60%
Start of hostilities against Iraq in 2003	57%
Supreme Court decision on flag burning	51%
Opening of the Berlin Wall	50%
Passage of Obama's health care reform bill in 2010	49%

(*continues*)

TABLE 7.2 (Continued)

Arrest of O. J. Simpson	48%
Obama's decision to send 30,000 additional troops to Afghanistan	43%
Controversy over whether Elián González must return to Cuba	39%
2000 presidential election outcome	38%
Impeachment trial of President Clinton in the Senate	31%
Obama's speech from Egypt, addressed to the Muslim world	26%
Prescription drug benefit added to the Medicare program	25%
Confirmation of Sonia Sotomayor to the Supreme Court	22%
Congressional debate over NAFTA	21%
Jack Abramoff's admission that he bribed members of Congress	18%
2010 Supreme Court decision allowing corporations and unions to pay for ads about political candidates	18%
Ethnic violence in the Darfur region of Sudan	16%
Passage of the Communications Deregulation Bill	12%
Violent protests in Tibet against the Chinese government in 2008	12%

Source: Pew Research Center for the People & the Press.

talking head
A shot of a person's face talking directly to the camera. Because such shots are visually unstimulating, the major networks rarely show politicians talking for very long.

Television is particularly biased toward stories that generate good pictures. Seeing a **talking head** (a shot of a person's face talking directly to the camera) is boring; viewers will switch channels in search of more interesting visual stimulation. For example, during an unusually contentious and lengthy interview of George H. W. Bush by Dan Rather concerning the Iran-Contra scandal in the 1980s, CBS's ratings actually went down as people tired of watching two talking heads argue.[53] In contrast, ratings can be increased by, say, ambassadors squaring off in a fistfight at the United Nations, a scene CBS showed three times in one day—without once discussing the cause of the fight.[54] The result of this kind of bias, political scientist Lance Bennett points out, is that "the public is exposed to a world driven into chaos by seemingly arbitrary and mysterious forces."[55]

7.4 Analyze the impact the media has on what policy issues Americans think about.

The News and Public Opinion

How does the news media's depiction of a threatening, hostile, and corrupt world shape Americans' political opinions and behaviors? This question is difficult to answer, as the effects of the news media can be difficult to accurately assess. One reason is that it is hard to separate the media from other influences. When presidents, legislators, and interest groups—as well as news organizations—are all discussing an issue, it is not easy to isolate the opinion changes that come from political leadership from those that come from the news. Moreover, the effect of one news story on public opinion may be trivial but the cumulative effect of dozens of news stories may be important.

For many years, students of the subject tended to doubt that the media had more than a marginal effect on public opinion. The "minimal effects hypothesis" stemmed from the fact that early scholars were looking for direct impacts—for example, whether the media affected how people voted.[56] When the focus turned to how the media affect *what Americans think about,* the effects began to appear more significant. In a series of controlled laboratory experiments, Shanto Iyengar and Donald Kinder subtly manipulated the stories participants saw on the TV news.[57] They found that they could significantly affect the importance people attached to a given problem by splicing a few stories about it into the news over the course of a week. Iyengar and Kinder do not maintain that the networks can make something out of nothing or conceal problems that actually exist. But they do conclude that "what television news does, instead, is alter the priorities Americans attach to a circumscribed set of problems, all of which are plausible contenders for public concern."[58] Subsequent research by Miller and Krosnick has revealed that agenda-setting effects are particularly strong among politically knowledgeable citizens who trust the media. Thus, rather than the media manipulating the public, they argue that agenda setting reflects a deliberate and thoughtful process on the part of sophisticated citizens who rely on what they consider a credible institutional source of information.[59]

Nonetheless, this agenda-setting effect can have a range of far-reaching consequences. First, by increasing public attention to specific problems, the media influence the criteria by which the public evaluates political leaders. When unemployment goes up but inflation goes down, does public support for the president increase or decrease? The answer could depend in large part on which story the media emphasized. The fact that the media emphasized the country's slow economic growth in 1992 rather than the good news of low inflation and interest rates was clearly instrumental in setting the stage for Bill Clinton's ousting the incumbent president, George H. W. Bush, that year. Similarly, the emphasis on the deteriorating economic situation in 2008 rather than the good news about the success of the troop surge in Iraq was clearly an advantage for Obama and a disadvantage for McCain.

The media can even have a dramatic effect on how the public evaluates specific events by emphasizing one event over others. When, during a 1976 presidential debate, President Ford incorrectly stated that the Soviet Union did not dominate Eastern Europe, the press gave substantial coverage to Ford's misstatement, and this coverage had an impact on the public. Polls showed that most people did not realize the president had made an error until the press told them so. Afterward, the initial assessment that Ford had won the debate shifted, as voters expressed increased concern about his competence in foreign policymaking.[60] Similarly, the media's focus on misstatements by Al Gore during the first presidential debate of 2000 had an impact on public opinion. In the days immediately following this debate, the percentage who thought that Gore had beaten Bush declined markedly.[61]

Much remains unknown about the effects of the media and the news on American political opinion and behavior. Enough is known, however, to conclude that the media are a key political institution. The media control much of the technology that in turn controls much of what Americans believe about politics and government. For this reason, it is important to look at the American policy agenda and the media's role in shaping it.

Policy Entrepreneurs and Agenda Setting

7.5 Explain how policy entrepreneurs employ media strategies to influence the public agenda.

Someone who asks you "What's your agenda?" wants to know something about your priorities. As discussed in Chapter 1, governments also have agendas. John Kingdon defines **policy agenda** as "the list of subjects or problems to which government officials, and people outside of government closely associated with those officials, are paying some serious attention at any given time."[62] Interest groups, political parties, individual politicians, public relations firms, bureaucratic agencies—and, of course, the president and Congress—are all pushing for their priorities to take precedence over others. Health care, education, unemployment, and immigration reform—these and scores of other issues compete for attention from the government.

policy agenda
The issues that attract the serious attention of public officials and other people actively involved in politics at the time.

policy entrepreneurs
People who invest their political "capital" in an issue. According to John Kingdon, a policy entrepreneur "could be in or out of government, in elected or appointed positions, in interest groups or research organizations."

Political activists depend heavily on the media to get their ideas placed high on the governmental agenda. Political activists are often called **policy entrepreneurs**—people who invest their political "capital" in an issue (as an economic entrepreneur invests capital in an idea for making money). Kingdon says that policy entrepreneurs can "be in or out of government, in elected or appointed positions, in interest groups or research organizations."[63] Policy entrepreneurs' arsenal of weapons includes press releases, press conferences, and letter writing; convincing reporters and columnists to tell their side; trading on personal contacts; and, in cases of desperation, resorting to staging dramatic events.

The media are not always monopolized by political elites; the poor and downtrodden have access to them too. Civil rights groups in the 1960s relied heavily on the media to tell their stories of unjust treatment. Many believe that the introduction of television helped to accelerate the movement by showing Americans—in the North and South alike—just what the situation was.[64] Protest groups have learned that if they can stage an interesting event that attracts the media's attention, at least their point of view will be heard. Radical activist Saul Alinsky once dramatized the plight of one neighborhood by having its residents collect rats and dump them on the mayor's front lawn. The story was one that local reporters could hardly resist. In 2002, graduate students at the University of California, Irvine, camped out in tents in the campus park to protest the lack of investment in on-campus housing. The prime organizer, a teaching assistant for an introduction to American government course, issued press releases and made calls to news directors urging them to come down and take a look. Soon after several stations put the sorry scene on TV, the university administration gave in to the graduate students' demands.

Conveying a long-term, positive image through the media is more important than gaining media coverage of a few dramatic events. Policy entrepreneurs, in or out of government, depend on goodwill and good images. Thus, groups, individuals, and even countries sometimes turn to public relations firms to improve their image and their ability to peddle their issue positions.[65]

7.6 Assess the impact of the mass media on the scope of government and democracy in America.

Understanding the Mass Media

The media act as key linkage institutions between the people and the policymakers and have a profound impact on the political policy agenda. Bernard Cohen goes so far as to say, "No major act of the American Congress, no foreign adventure, no act of diplomacy, no great social reform can succeed unless the press prepares the public mind."[66] If Cohen is right, then the growth of government in America would have been impossible without the media having established the need for it.

The Media and the Scope of Government

The media's watchdog function helps to keep politicians in check. Notably, this is one aspect of the media's job performance that Americans consistently evaluate positively. For over two decades, the Pew Research Center for People & the Press has consistently found that a clear majority of the public has said that press criticism of political leaders does more good than harm. In 2009, a Pew Research Center poll found that 62 percent said that press criticism of political leaders is worth it because it keeps leaders from doing things that should not be done, while 22 percent believed criticism keeps political leaders from doing their jobs.[67] Reporters themselves consider exposing officeholders to be an essential role of the press in a free society, as we saw in Figure 7.1. They often hold disparaging views of public officials, seeing them as self-serving, hypocritical, lacking in integrity, and preoccupied with reelection. Thus, it is not surprising that journalists frequently see a need to debunk public officials and their policy proposals.

As every new policy proposal is met with media skepticism, constraints are placed on the scope of what government can do. The watchdog orientation of the press can be characterized as neither liberal nor conservative but reformist. Reporters often see their job as crusading against foul play and unfairness in government and society. This focus on injustice in society inevitably encourages enlarging the scope of government. Once the media identify a problem in society—such as poverty, inadequate medical care for the elderly, or poor education for certain children—reporters usually begin to ask what the government is doing about it. Could it be acting more effectively to solve the problem? What do people in the White House and Congress (as well as state and local government) have to say about it? In this way, the media portray government as responsible for handling almost every major problem. Although skeptical of what politicians say and do, the media report on America's social problems in a manner that often also encourages government to take on more and more tasks.

Individualism and the Media

More than any other development in the past century, the rise of television broadcasting has reinforced and furthered individualism in the American political process. Candidates are now much more capable of running for office on their own by appealing to people directly through television. Individual voters can see the candidates "up close and personal" for themselves, and they have much less need for political parties or social groups to help them make their decisions.

Television finds it easier to focus on individuals than on groups. As a result, candidate personality is more important than ever. In part because of this focus on individuals, TV has also affected the relative amount of coverage accorded to the three branches of government. Whereas there are 535 members of Congress, there is only one president. Doris Graber's study of nightly news broadcasts in 2008–09 found that 65 percent of the coverage devoted to the three branches was devoted to the president as compared to 29 percent for Congress. The Supreme Court, which does not allow TV cameras to cover its proceedings and whose members rarely give interviews, is almost invisible on TV newscasts, receiving a mere 6 percent of the coverage.[68]

Democracy and the Media

As Ronald Berkman and Laura Kitch remark, "Information is the fuel of democracy."[69] Widespread access to information could be the greatest boon to democracy since the secret ballot, yet most observers think that the great potential of today's high-tech media has yet to be realized. Noting the vast increase in information available through the news media, Berkman and Kitch state, "If the sheer quantity of news produced greater competency in the citizenry, then we would have a society of political masters. Yet, just the opposite is happening."[70] The rise of the "information society" has not brought about the rise of the "informed society."

Whenever the media are criticized for being superficial, their defense is to say that this is what people want. Network executives remark that if people suddenly started to watch in-depth shows such as PBS's *NewsHour,* then they would gladly imitate them—if people wanted serious coverage of the issues, they would be happy to provide it. They point out that they are in business to make a profit and that, to do so, they must appeal to the maximum number of people. As Matthew Kerbel observes, "The people who bring you the evening news would like it to be informative *and* entertaining, but when these two values collide, the shared orientations of the television news world push the product inexorably toward the latter."[71] It is not their fault if the resulting news coverage is superficial, network executives argue; blame capitalism or blame the people—most of whom like news to be more entertaining than educational. Thus, if people are not better informed in the high-tech age, it is largely because they do not care to hear about complicated political issues. In this sense, one can say that the people really do rule through the media.

A POINT TO PONDER

Studies have found that the focus of television news in recent years has shifted toward more human interest stories, with the result being less coverage of national and international politics.

Do you think TV news producers are just responding to what Americans want? And, if so, do you think that is what TV news *should* be doing?

"Responding to viewer sentiment, we have eliminated world news and expanded our entertainment and sports news."

Summary

7.1 Describe how American politicians choreograph their messages through the mass media.

Politicians stage media events for the primary purpose of getting attention from the media. These events are artfully stage-managed to present the intended message. Campaign commercials are also carefully crafted to convey specific images and information.

7.2 Outline the key developments in the history of mass media and American politics.

Newspapers were long the dominant media through which Americans got their news. But ever since the emergence of television they have been on the decline. The Internet has further accelerated the decline of newspaper reading; newspapers have thus far failed to establish profitability for their online editions. The nightly network news broadcasts on CBS, NBC, and ABC were the #1 means by which Americans got their news from the 1960s through the 1980s. But ever since the emergence of cable and cable news they have seen their audiences shrink, as American television has moved from the broadcasting to the narrowcasting era. The Internet provides more access to political information than ever possible before. How much typical citizens will take advantage of these opportunities remains to be seen. But certainly campaigns and political activists have been able to use the Internet to organize for political action and to get specially targeted messages out.

7.3 List the major criteria that determine which news stories receive the most media attention.

The media define "news" largely as events that are unusual and out of the ordinary. Because of economic pressures, the media are biased in favor of stories with high drama that will attract people's interest instead of extended analyses of complex issues.

7.4 Analyze the impact the media has on what policy issues Americans think about.

The media are instrumental in setting the American political agenda—that is, the issues that get seriously addressed by politicians. What issues Americans think about is much influenced by which issues the media choose to cover. It has often been said that the media are like a searchlight, bringing one episode and then another out of darkness and into the public eye.

7.5 Explain how policy entrepreneurs employ media strategies to influence the public agenda.

Policy entrepreneurs seek to influence the policy agenda by getting the media to pay attention to the issues that they are particularly concerned with. They employ a variety of strategies to obtain media coverage, including press releases, press conferences, and letter writing. Sometimes they will resort to staging dramatic events that are so interesting and unusual that reporters can hardly resist covering them.

7.6 Assess the impact of the mass media on the scope of government and democracy in America.

The media's role as a watchdog over government sometimes constrains expansions of the scope of government by fomenting skepticism about what government can accomplish. On the other hand, media crusades against injustices sometimes serve to encourage government to take on increased responsibilities. The media's superficial coverage of policy issues is criticized by many democratic theorists. Yet, members of the media argue in their own defense that they are only providing the sort of coverage of politics that draws the biggest audiences.

Chapter Test

7.1 Describe how American politicians choreograph their messages through the mass media.

1. The emergence of media events has contributed to each of the following trends EXCEPT
   a. Increasing news coverage of candidates as individuals
   b. Increasing politicians' control over the political agenda
   c. Increasing the importance of image for presidents
   d. Increasing negativity in American political campaigns
   e. All of the above are true

2. In recent years, most presidential election campaign television advertisements have been negative.

   True______ False______

3. How important are the news media today for presidents who hope to govern successfully? In answering this question, discuss efforts by recent presidents to choreograph their messages through media.

7.2 Outline the key developments in the history of mass media and American politics.

4. The trend toward more negative and cynical news coverage began during
   a. The Great Depression
   b. World War II
   c. The Korean War
   d. The Vietnam War
   e. The Persian Gulf War

5. Those who watch the news on television tend to be more engaged in politics than those who read the news.

   True______ False______

6. The Internet appears to be increasing public interest in political news.

   True______ False______

7. Evaluate the shift from broadcasting toward narrowcasting. What impact has this shift had on the quality of political journalism? What impact do you think the trend toward narrowcasting will have on political participation and awareness?

8. Compare and contrast private and public media. How might the business model of privately owned media both contribute to and detract from the free flow of information to American citizens? In your opinion, does public ownership of the media provide a better model? Why or why not?

7.3 List the major criteria that determine which news stories receive the most media attention.

9. Which of the following factors best account(s) for what is considered newsworthy?
   a. A story's high entertainment value
   b. A story's high informational value
   c. A story's high sophistication value
   d. A story's high political value
   e. All of the above

10. News coverage of political campaigns pays relatively little attention to policy issues.

    True______ False______

11. Evaluate the symbiotic relationship between the press and government. How might this relationship promote positive coverage of the government? How might it encourage critical news coverage, instead? Provide specific examples in your answer.

12. It is commonly thought that media favor one political point of view in

their coverage of politics. Does social science research support this belief? Why or why not? If bias does exist in news coverage, how does it influence news coverage?

7.4 Analyze the impact the media has on what policy issues Americans think about.

13. Each of the following characterizes how media affect public opinion EXCEPT
    a. Media affect public opinion to a marginal extent
    b. Media affect which issues the public finds to be important
    c. Media affect the public's evaluation of elected officials
    d. Media affect knowledgeable citizens' policy agendas
    e. All of the above are true

14. How do the media affect public evaluation of different political events? Provide specific examples to support your answer.

7.5 Explain how policy entrepreneurs employ media strategies to influence the public agenda.

15. Political activists use media coverage to push their ideas high onto the policy agenda.

    True______ False______

16. Who are policy entrepreneurs and how do they seek to affect the policy agenda through the media? Give some examples. What appears to most contribute to their success?

7.6 Assess the impact of the mass media on the scope of government and democracy in America.

17. Television's emphasis on the individual has the effect of encouraging
    a. Greater news coverage of the Supreme Court
    b. Greater news coverage of interest groups
    c. Greater news coverage of Congress
    d. Greater news coverage of ordinary voters
    e. Greater news coverage of the presidency

18. How does the media's role as watchdog affect the scope of government? Why do you think the public supports this role of the news media?

19. Explain the phrase "information is the fuel of democracy" and evaluate its accuracy in the context of today's high-tech media society. If the media fall short in "fueling" democracy, is this a problem and what do you think can be done? Are the media are justified in giving people what they want? Defend your answer.

PEARSON mypoliscilab™ Exercises

Apply what you learned in this chapter on MyPoliSciLab.

Read on **mypoliscilab.com**

eText: Chapter 7

Study and **Review** on **mypoliscilab.com**

Pre-Test
Post-Test
Chapter Exam
Flashcards

Watch on **mypoliscilab.com**

Video: YouTube Politics
Video: The Pentagon's Media Message

Explore on **mypoliscilab.com**

Simulation: You Are the News Editor
Comparative: Comparing News Media
Timeline: Three Hundred Years of American Mass Media
Visual Literacy: Use of the Media by the American Public

Key Terms

high-tech politics (198)
mass media (198)
media event (198)
press conferences (199)
investigative journalism (200)
print media (201)
electronic media (201)
narrowcasting (205)
chains (211)
beats (212)
trial balloons (212)
sound bites (214)
talking head (216)
policy agenda (217)
policy entrepreneurs (218)

Internet Resources

www.journalism.org
The Pew Research Center's Project for Excellence in Journalism regularly posts studies about the mass media at this site.

www.appcpenn.org
The Annenberg Public Policy Center conducts studies that analyze the content of TV coverage of politics.

www.usnpl.com
Listings for newspapers all over the country, including Web links, where available.

www.cmpa.com
The Center for Media and Public Affairs posts its studies of the content of media coverage of politics at this site.

www.livingroomcandidate.org
A great collection of classic and recent political commercials from 1952 through 2008.

For Further Reading

Baum, Matthew A. ***Soft News Goes to War: Public Opinion and American Foreign Policy in the New Media Age.*** Princeton, NJ: Princeton University Press, 2003. A path-breaking examination of how people learn about major foreign policy events from entertainment news shows like *Oprah* and *Dateline.*

Davis, Richard. ***Typing Political: The Role of Blogs in American Politics.*** New York: Oxford University Press, 2009. A comprehensive assessment of the growing role played by political blogs and their relationship with the mainstream media.

Downie, Leonard, Jr., and Robert G. Kaiser. ***The News About the News: American Journalism in Peril.*** New York: Alfred A. Knopf, 2002. A good look at how the changing economics of the news profession is altering media values and practices.

Epstein, Edward J. ***News from Nowhere: Television and the News.*** New York: Random House, 1973. A classic analysis of how financial considerations shape what is presented on TV news broadcasts.

Farnsworth, Stephen J., and S. Robert Lichter. ***The Mediated Presidency: Television News and Presidential Governance.*** Lanham, MD: Rowman & Littlefield, 2006. An in-depth content analysis of how the news media covered the administrations of Ronald Reagan, Bill Clinton, and George W. Bush.

Goldberg, Bernard. ***Bias: A CBS Insider Exposes How the Media Distort the News.*** Washington, DC: Regnery, 2002. A best-selling account of the network news that argues there is a liberal bias on many issues, especially social policies.

Hindman, Matthew. ***The Myth of Digital Democracy.*** Princeton, NJ: Princeton University Press, 2009. Hindman presents much evidence to argue that rather than broadening political discourse, the Internet has empowered a small set of elites—some new, but most familiar.

Graber, Doris A. ***Mass Media and American Politics,*** 8th ed. Washington, DC: Congressional Quarterly Press, 2010. The standard textbook on the subject.

Hamilton, James T. ***All the News That's Fit to Sell.*** Princeton, NJ: Princeton University Press, 2004. An examination of how marketing considerations shape what does and does not make the news.

Iyengar, Shanto, and Donald R. Kinder. ***News That Matters.*** Chicago: University of Chicago Press, 1987. Two political psychologists show how the media can affect the public agenda.

Kingdon, John W. ***Agendas, Alternatives, and Public Policy,*** 2nd ed. New York: HarperCollins, 1995. The best overall study of the formation of policy agendas.

Mindich, David T. Z. ***Tuned Out: Why Americans Under 40 Don't Follow the News.*** New York: Oxford University Press, 2005. An interesting examination of why today's young people are not following political news nearly as closely as older people.

Patterson, Thomas E. ***Out of Order.*** New York: Knopf, 1993. A highly critical and well-documented examination of how the media cover election campaigns.

Prior, Markus. ***Post-Broadcast Democracy: How Media Choice Increases Inequality in Political Involvement and Polarizes Elections.*** New York: Cambridge University Press, 2007. The best book so far on how the transition from broadcasting to narrowcasting has impacted American politics.

Weaver, David H. et al. ***The American Journalist in the 21st Century.*** Mahwah, NJ: Lawrence Erlbaum, 2007. A thorough examination of journalists in America—who they are, what they believe about politics, and how their professional values and practices have evolved over the past three decades.

West, Darrell M. ***Air Wars: Television Advertising in Election Campaigns, 1952–2008.*** Washington, DC: Congressional Quarterly Press, 2009. An analysis of how TV campaign ads have evolved over the past four decades and what impact they have had on elections.

Chapter 8

Political Parties

Learning Objectives

8.1 Identify the functions that political parties perform in American democracy.

8.2 Determine the significance of party identification in America today.

8.3 Describe how political parties are organized in the United States.

8.4 Evaluate how well political parties generally do in carrying out their promises.

8.5 Differentiate the various party eras in American history.

8.6 Assess both the impact of third parties on American politics and their limitations.

8.7 Evaluate the advantages and disadvantages of responsible party government.

POLITICS IN ACTION: HOW POLITICAL PARTIES CAN MAKE ELECTIONS USER FRIENDLY FOR VOTERS

In the 2010 elections, the Republicans gained control of the House of Representatives just two years after Barack Obama's historic election to the presidency. One of the strategies they pursued was to compile a list of proposals that most Republicans supported entitled "A Pledge to America." With unemployment hovering near 10 percent, the Republican proposals concentrated on specific agenda items that they argued would be better suited to revive the nation's economy than those of Obama and the Democrats. Among the items in this list were extending the tax cuts passed under President Bush, providing for new tax deductions for small businesses, and repealing newly enacted health care mandates on business.

"A Pledge to America" was sometimes referred to in the media as the "Contract with America, Part II." In 1994, the original Contract with America was credited by many with helping the Republicans gain control of the House of Representatives after 40 years of Democratic majorities. It outlined 10 bills that the Republicans promised to focus on during the first 100 days of a Republican-controlled House of Representatives. The contract was the brainchild of Newt Gingrich and Richard Armey, who were both college professors before they were elected to Congress. Gingrich and Armey thought the Republicans needed a stronger message in 1994 than simply stating their opposition to President Clinton's policies. The contract was an attempt to offer voters a positive program for reshaping American public policy and reforming how Congress works. Without actually knowing much about the individual candidates themselves, voters would know what to expect of the signers of the contract and would be able to hold them accountable for these promises in the future. In this sense, the contract endeavored to make politics user friendly for the voters.

America's Founding Fathers were more concerned with their fear that political parties could be forums for corruption and national divisiveness than they were with the role that parties could play in making politics user friendly for ordinary voters. Thomas Jefferson spoke for many when he said, "If I could not go to heaven but with a party, I would not go there at all." In his farewell address, George Washington also warned of the dangers of parties.

Today, most observers would agree that political parties have contributed greatly to American democracy. In one of the most frequently—and rightly—quoted observations about American politics, E. E. Schattschneider said that "political parties created democracy . . . and democracy is unthinkable save in terms of the parties."[1] Political scientists and politicians alike believe that a strong party system is desirable.

The strength of the parties has an impact not only on how we are governed but also on what government does. Major expansions or contractions of the scope of government have generally been accomplished through the implementation of one party's platform.

Chapter OUTLINE

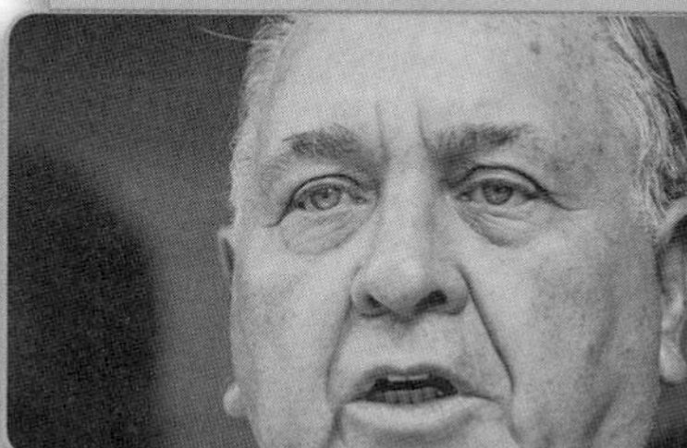

Currently, the Democrats and Republicans differ greatly on the issue of the scope of government. Which party controls the presidency and whether the same party also controls the Congress make a big difference.

party competition
The battle of the parties for control of public offices. Ups and downs of the two major parties are one of the most important elements in American politics.

The alternating of power and influence between the two major parties is one of the most important elements in American politics. **Party competition** is the battle between Democrats and Republicans for the control of public offices. Without this competition there would be no choice, and without choice there would be no democracy. Americans have had a choice between two major political parties since the early 1800s.

8.1 Identify the functions that political parties perform in American democracy.

The Meaning of Party

Almost all definitions of political parties have one thing in common: Parties try to win elections. This is their core function and the key to their definition. By contrast, interest groups do not nominate candidates for office, though they may try to influence elections. For example, no one has ever been elected to Congress as the nominee of the National Rifle Association, though many nominees have received the NRA's endorsement. Thus, Anthony Downs defined a **political party** as a "team of men [and women] seeking to control the governing apparatus by gaining office in a duly constituted election."[2]

political party
According to Anthony Downs, a "team of men [and women] seeking to control the governing apparatus by gaining office in a duly constituted election."

The word *team* is the slippery part of this definition. Party teams may not be as well disciplined and single-minded as teams fielded by top football coaches. Party teams often run every which way and are difficult to lead. Party leaders often disagree about policy, and between elections the party organizations seem to all but disappear. So who are the members of these teams? A widely adopted way of thinking about parties in political science is as "three-headed political giants." The three heads are (1) the party in the electorate, (2) the party as an organization, and (3) the party in government.[3]

The *party in the electorate* is by far the largest component of an American political party. Unlike many European political parties, American parties do not require dues or membership cards to distinguish members from nonmembers. Americans may register as Democrats, Republicans, Libertarians, or whatever, but registration is not legally binding and is easily changed. To be a member of a party, you need only claim to be a member. If you call yourself a Democrat, you are one—even if you never talk to a party official, never work in a campaign, and often vote for Republicans.

The *party as an organization* has a national office, a full-time staff, rules and bylaws, and budgets. In addition to its national office, each party maintains state and local headquarters. The party organization includes precinct leaders, county chairpersons, state chairpersons, state delegates to the national committee, and officials in the party's Washington office. These are the people who keep the party running between elections and make its rules. From the party's national chairperson to its local precinct captain, the party organization pursues electoral victory.

The *party in government* consists of elected officials who call themselves members of the party. Although presidents, members of Congress, governors, and lesser officeholders may share a common party label, they do not always agree on policy. Presidents and governors may have to wheedle and cajole their own party members into voting for their policies. In the United States, it is not uncommon to put personal principle—or ambition—above loyalty to the party's leaders. These leaders are the main spokespersons for the party, however. Their words and actions personify the party to millions of Americans. If the party is to translate its promises into policy, the job must be done by the party in government.

Political parties are everywhere in American politics—present in the electorate's mind, as an organization, and in government offices—and one of their major tasks is to link the people of the United States to their government and its policies.

Tasks of the Parties

The road from public opinion to public policy is long and winding. Millions of Americans cannot raise their voices to the government and indicate their policy preferences in unison. In a large democracy, **linkage institutions** translate inputs from the public into outputs from the policymakers. Linkage institutions sift through all the issues, identify the most pressing concerns, and put these onto the governmental agenda. In other words, linkage institutions help ensure that public preferences are heard loud and clear. In the United States, there are four main linkage institutions: parties, elections, interest groups, and the media.

linkage institutions The channels through which people's concerns become political issues on the government's policy agenda. In the United States, linkage institutions include elections, political parties, interest groups, and the media.

Kay Lawson writes that "parties are seen, both by the members and by others, as agencies for forging links between citizens and policymakers."[4] Here is a checklist of the tasks that parties perform—or should perform—if they are to serve as effective linkage institutions:

Parties Pick Candidates Almost no one above the local level gets elected to a public office without winning a party's endorsement.[5] A party's official endorsement is called a *nomination*; it entitles the nominee to be listed on the general election ballot as that party's candidate for a particular office. Up until the early twentieth century, American parties chose their candidates with little or no input from voters. Progressive reformers led the charge for primary elections, in which citizens would have the power to choose nominees for office. The innovation of primary elections spread rapidly, transferring the nominating function from the party organization to the party identifiers.

Parties Run Campaigns Through their national, state, and local organizations, parties coordinate political campaigns. However, television and the Internet have made it easier for candidates to build their own personal campaign organization, and thus take their case directly to the people without the aid of the party organization.

Parties Give Cues to Voters Just knowing whether a candidate is a Democrat or a Republican provides crucial information to many voters. Voters can reasonably assume that if a candidate is a Democrat, chances are good that he or she favors progressive principles and has tended to support President Barack Obama's policies. On the other side of the coin, it can be reasonably assumed that a Republican favors conservative principles and has opposed many of President Obama's policies. A voter therefore need not do extensive research on the individual candidates but rather can rely on the informational shortcut provided by their party affiliations.

Parties Articulate Policies Each political party advocates specific policy alternatives. For example, the Democratic Party platform has for many years advocated support for a woman's right to an abortion, whereas the Republican Party platform has repeatedly called for restrictions on abortion.

Political Parties

Parties perform many important tasks in American politics. Among the most important are generating symbols of identification and loyalty, mobilizing majorities in the electorate and in government, recruiting political leaders, implementing policies, and fostering stability in government. Hence, it has often been argued that the party system has to work well for the government to work well.

Parties Coordinate Policymaking When President Obama commits himself to a major policy goal, such as health insurance coverage for all Americans, the first place he usually looks for support is from his fellow Democrats. In America's fragmented government, parties are essential for coordinating policymaking between the executive and legislative branches of government.

The importance of these tasks makes it easy to see why most political scientists accept Schattschneider's famous assertion that modern democracy is unthinkable without competition between political parties.

Parties, Voters, and Policy: The Downs Model

The parties compete, at least in theory, as in a marketplace. A party competes for voters' support; its products are its candidates and policies. Anthony Downs has provided a working model of the relationship among citizens, parties, and policy, employing a

One's party affiliation is an important part of one's political identity. Although clubs of college Republicans and college Democrats are common on campuses around the country, roughly half of college-age Americans do not have a party affiliation, preferring to call themselves Independents.

rational-choice perspective.[6] **Rational-choice theory** "seeks to explain political processes and outcomes as consequences of purposive behavior. Political actors are assumed to have goals and to pursue those goals sensibly and efficiently."[7] Downs argues that (1) voters want to maximize the chance that policies they favor will be adopted by government and that (2) parties want to win office. Thus, in order to win office, the wise party selects policies that are widely favored. Parties and candidates may do all sorts of things to win—kiss babies, call opponents ugly names, even lie and cheat—but in a democracy they will use primarily their accomplishments and policy positions to attract votes. If Party A figures out what the voters want more accurately than does Party B, then Party A should be more successful.

The long history of the American party system has shown that successful parties rarely stray far from the midpoint of public opinion. In the American electorate, a few voters are extremely liberal and a few extremely conservative, but the majority are in the middle or lean just slightly one way or the other (see Figure 8.1). If Downs is right, then centrist parties will win, and extremist parties will be condemned to footnotes in the history books. Indeed, occasionally a party may misperceive voters' desires or take a risky stand on a principle—hoping

FIGURE 8.1 The Downs Model: How Rational Parties Position Themselves Near (but Not at) the Center of Public Opinion

In 2008, the American National Election Study asked a sample of the American population to classify themselves on a 7-point scale from extremely liberal to extremely conservative. The graph shows how respondents who reported voting for president located themselves on this scale. (Respondents who said they didn't know are included in the middle category, as the parties have to assume that these voters are up for grabs in the center.) The arrows indicate how the typical voter placed the two major parties on the same scale.

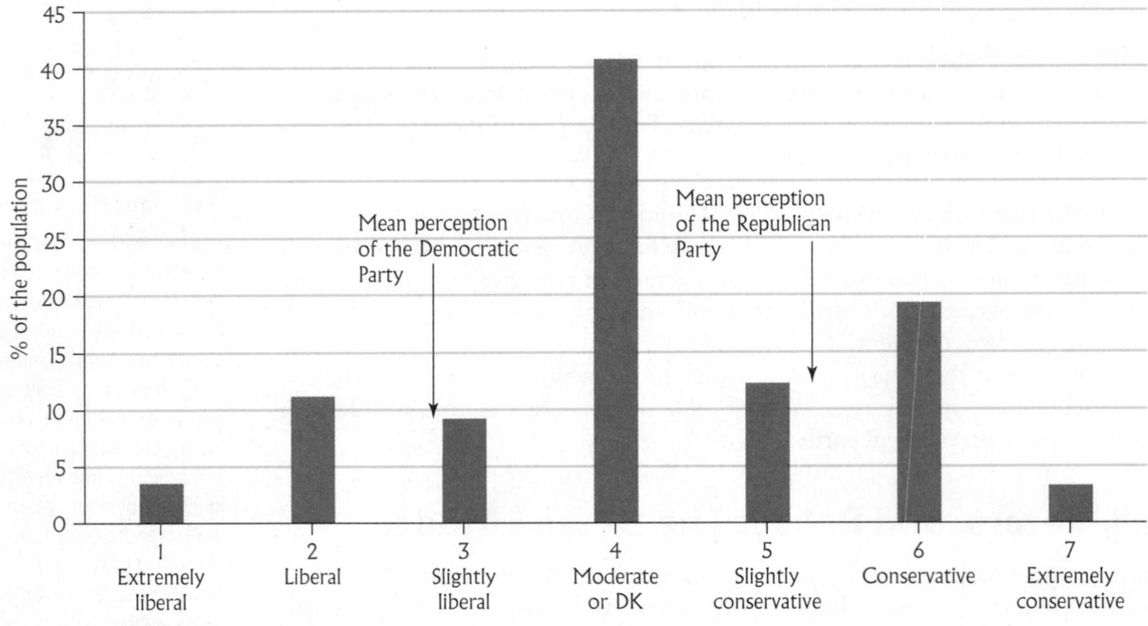

Source: Author's analysis of the 2008 American National Election Study.

to persuade voters during the campaign—but in order to survive in a system where the majority opinion is middle of the road, parties must stay fairly near the center.

We sometimes hear criticism that there is not much difference between the Democrats and the Republicans. However, given that about two-thirds of the electorate are in the middle three ideological categories of Figure 8.1, these two parties have little choice. We would not expect two competing department stores to locate at opposite ends of town when most people live on Main Street. Downs also notes, though, that from a rational-choice perspective, one should expect the parties to differentiate themselves at least somewhat. Just as Ford tries to offer something different from and better than Toyota in order to build buyer loyalty, so Democrats and Republicans have to forge substantially different identities to build voter loyalty. In 2008, the American National Election Study found that 78 percent of the population believed that important differences existed between the parties.

rational-choice theory
A popular theory in political science to explain the actions of voters as well as politicians. It assumes that individuals act in their own best interest, carefully weighing the costs and benefits of possible alternatives.

The Party in the Electorate

8.2 Determine the significance of party identification in America today.

In most European nations, being a party member means formally joining a political party. You get a membership card to carry around, you pay dues, and you vote to pick your local party leaders. In America, being a party member takes far less work. There is no formal "membership" in the parties at all. If you believe you are a Democrat or a Republican, then you are a Democrat or a Republican. Thus, the party in the electorate consists largely of symbolic images and ideas. For most people the party is a psychological label. Most voters have a **party image** of each party; that is, they know (or think they know) what the Republicans and Democrats stand for. Liberal or conservative, pro-business or pro-labor, pro-choice or pro-life—these are some of the elements of each party's images.

Party images help shape people's **party identification**, the self-proclaimed preference for one party or the other. Because many people routinely vote for the party they identify with (all else being equal), even a shift of a few percentage points in the distribution of party identification is important. Since 1952, the American National Election Study surveys have asked a sample of citizens, "Generally speaking, do you usually think of yourself as a Republican, a Democrat, or an Independent?" Repeatedly asking this question permits political scientists to trace party identification over time (see Figure 8.2). In recent presidential elections, two clear patterns have been evident. First,

party image
The voter's perception of what the Republicans or Democrats stand for, such as conservatism or liberalism.

party identification
A citizen's self-proclaimed preference for one party or the other.

FIGURE 8.2 Party Identification in the United States, 1952–2008[a]

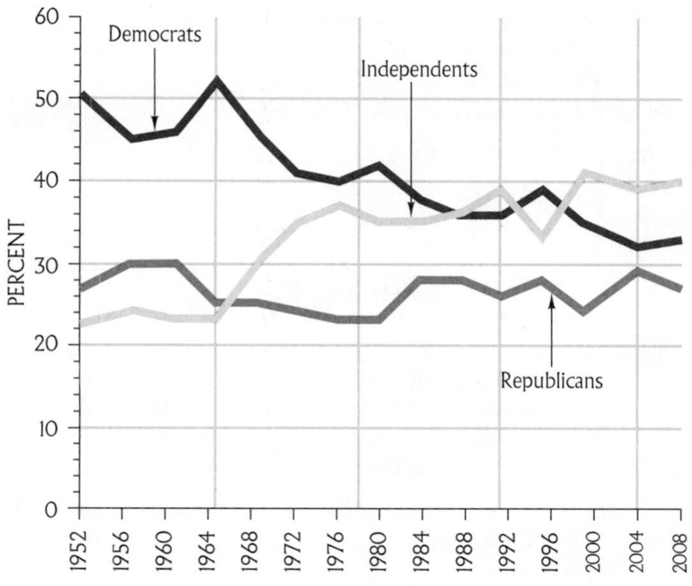

Political analysts and scholars carefully monitor changes in the distribution of party identification. Below, you can see the percentage of the population who have identified themselves as Democrats, Independents, and Republicans during each presidential election year from 1952 to 2008.

[a]In percentage of people; the small percentage who identify with a minor party or who cannot answer the question are excluded.

Source: American National Election Studies, 1952–2008.

unlike earlier periods when Democrats greatly outnumbered Republicans, the Democratic Party's edge in terms of identifiers in the electorate has lately been quite modest. In 1964, there were more than twice as many Democrats as Republicans, whereas in 2008 Republicans trailed Democrats by a mere 6 percentage points. Second, in most recent elections the most frequent response to the party identification question has been the Independent option. In 2008, 40 percent of the population called themselves independents. As you can see in "Young People and Politics: The Parties Face an Independent Youth," survey data demonstrate that the younger one is, the more likely he or she is to be a political independent.

ticket splitting
Voting with one party for one office and with another party for other offices. It has become the norm in American voting behavior.

People who call themselves Independents are the most likely voters to engage in the practice of **ticket splitting**—voting with one party for one office and the other party for another office. For example, the 2008 National Election Study found that 21 percent of Independents who voted for Obama supported a Republican for the House of Representatives, compared to just 10 percent among Democratic identifiers who voted for Obama. The result of many voters being open to splitting their tickets is that even when one party has a big edge in a state, the other party always has a decent shot at winning at least some important offices. In other words, regardless of media labels of red and blue states, the practice of ticket splitting means that no state is ever completely safe for a given party. Thus, New Jersey, Michigan, and Maine lean heavily toward the Democrats in national elections, but as of 2011 all the governors of these states were Republicans. On the other side of the coin, Democrats were serving as governors in heavily Republican states, such as West Virginia and Arkansas.

The Parties Face an Independent Youth

Younger people have always had a tendency to be more independent of the major political parties than older people. But this has rarely been as evident in survey data as it is now. As you can see from the 2008 national survey data displayed here, 54 percent of people between the ages of 18 and 24 said they were political independents. In contrast, only 31 percent of people over 65 called themselves independents. Data over time indicate that as people get older, they become more likely to identify with one of the major parties. But whether this will be true for the current generation of youth remains to be seen.

AGE	DEMOCRAT	INDEPENDENT	REPUBLICAN
18–24	29	54	17
25–34	30	49	21
35–44	32	40	28
45–54	35	33	33
55–64	37	38	25
65+	36	31	33

QUESTIONS FOR DISCUSSION

- Do you think that as the current generation of young people ages they will become more likely to identify with the major political parties?
- Because younger people are so likely to be independent, does this mean that many young voters are particularly open to persuasion during campaigns? If so, why don't the Democrats and Republicans pay special attention to getting them on their side?

Source: Authors' analysis of the 2008 American National Election Study.

The Party Organizations: From the Grass Roots to Washington

8.3 Describe how political parties are organized in the United States.

An organizational chart is usually shaped like a pyramid, with those who give orders at the top and those who carry them out at the bottom. In drawing an organizational chart of an American political party, you could put the national committee and national convention of the party at the apex of the pyramid, the state party organizations in the middle, and the thousands of local party organizations at the bottom. Such a chart, however, would provide a misleading depiction of an American political party. The president of General Motors is at the top of GM in fact as well as on paper. By contrast, the chairperson of the Democratic or Republican national committee is on top on paper but not in fact.

As organizations, American political parties are decentralized and fragmented. One can imagine a system in which the national office of a party resolves conflicts among its state and local branches, states the party's position on the issues, and then passes orders down through the hierarchy. One can even imagine a system in which the party leaders have the power to enforce their decisions by offering greater influence and resources to officeholders who follow the party line and by punishing—even expelling—those who do not. Many European parties work just that way, but in America the formal party organizations have little such power. Candidates in the United States can get elected on their own. They do not need the help of the party most of the time, and hence the party organization is relegated to a comparatively limited role.

Local Parties

The urban political party was once the main political party organization in America. From the late nineteenth century through the New Deal of the 1930s, scores of cities were dominated by **party machines**. A machine is a kind of party organization, very different from the typical fragmented and disorganized political party in America today. It can be defined as a party organization that depends on rewarding its members in some material fashion.

party machines
A type of political party organization that relies heavily on material inducements, such as patronage, to win votes and to govern.

Patronage is one of the key inducements used by party machines. A patronage job is one that is awarded for political reasons rather than for merit or competence alone. In the late nineteenth century, political parties routinely sold some patronage jobs to the highest bidder. Party leaders made no secret of their corruption, openly selling government positions to raise money for the party. Some of this money was used to buy votes, but a good deal went to line the pockets of the politicians themselves. The most notable case was that of New York City's Democratic leader William Tweed, widely known as "Boss Tweed," whose ring reportedly made between $40 million and $200 million from tax receipts, payoffs, and kickbacks.

patronage
One of the key inducements used by party machines. A patronage job, promotion, or contract is one that is given for political reasons rather than for merit or competence alone.

At one time, urban machines in Albany, Chicago, Philadelphia, Kansas City, and elsewhere depended heavily on ethnic group support. Some of the most fabled machine leaders were Irish politicians, including New York's George Washington Plunkett, Boston's James Michael Curley, and Chicago's Richard J. Daley. Daley's Chicago machine was the last survivor, steamrolling its opposition amid charges of racism and corruption. Even today there are remnants of the Chicago machine, led by Mayor Richard Michael Daley (the son of the legendary Richard J. Daley). The survival of machine politics in Chicago can be traced to its ability to limit the scope of reform legislation. A large proportion of city jobs were classified as "temporary" even though they had been held by the same person for decades, and these positions were exempted from the merit system of hiring. At its height, the Democratic political machine in Chicago dispensed 40,000 patronage jobs, the recipients of which were expected to deliver at least 10 votes

Mayor Richard J. Daley ruled the city of Chicago from 1955 until his death in 1976. His Cook County Democratic Party organization was highly organized at the precinct level. Members of the organization kept people in their neighborhoods happy by providing for their local needs, such as street maintenance, new stoplights, no-parking zones, and so on, and the people reciprocated on Election Day by supporting the organization's candidates.

each on Election Day and to kick back 5 percent of their salary in the form of a donation to the local Democratic Party.[8]

Urban party organizations are also no longer very active as a rule. Progressive reforms that placed jobs under the merit system rather than at the machine's discretion weakened the machines' power. Regulations concerning fair bidding on government contracts also took away much of their ability to reward the party faithful. As ethnic integration occurred in big cities, the group loyalties that the machines often relied on no longer seemed very relevant to many people.

Partly filling in the void created by the decline of the inner-city machines has been a revitalization of party organization at the county level—particularly in affluent suburbs. These county organizations distribute yard signs and campaign literature, get out the vote on Election Day, and help state and local candidates any way they can. Traditionally, local organizations relied on personal knowledge of individuals in the neighborhood who could be persuaded to support the party. Today, these organizations have access to computerized lists with all sorts of details about registered voters that they use to try to tailor their appeals to each individual.

The 50 State Party Systems

American national parties are a loose aggregation of state parties, which are themselves a fluid association of individuals, groups, and local organizations. There are 50 state party systems, and no two are exactly alike. In a few states, the parties are well organized, have sizable staffs, and spend a lot of money. Pennsylvania is one such state. In other states, however, parties are weak. California, says Kay Lawson, "has political parties so weak as to be almost nonexistent; it is the birthplace of campaigning by 'hired guns' and it has been run by special interests for so long that Californians have forgotten what is special about that."[9]

The states are allowed wide discretion in the regulation of party activities, and how they choose to organize elections influences the strength of the parties profoundly. In particular, the choice between holding open versus closed primaries is a crucial one, as you can read about in "You Are the Policymaker: Should Political Parties Choose Their Nominees in Open or Closed Primaries?" When it comes to the general election, some states promote voting according to party by listing the candidates of each party down a single column, whereas others place the names in random order. About a third of the states currently have a provision on their ballots that enables a voter to cast a vote for all of one party's candidates with a single act. This option clearly encourages straight-ticket voting and makes the support of the party organization more important to candidates in these states.

closed primaries
Elections to select party nominees in which only people who have registered in advance with the party can vote for that party's candidates, thus encouraging greater party loyalty.

open primaries
Elections to select party nominees in which voters can decide on Election Day whether they want to participate in the Democratic or Republican contests.

Organizationally, state parties are on the upswing throughout the country. As recently as the early 1960s, half the state party organizations did not even maintain a permanent headquarters; when the state party elected a new chairperson, the party organization simply shifted its office to his or her hometown.[10] In contrast, almost all state parties today have a permanent physical headquarters, typically in the capital city or the largest city. State party budgets have also increased greatly, as parties have acquired professional staffs and high-tech equipment. For example, as of 1999, the typical state party budget for an election year was more than eight times greater than it was 20 years earlier.[11]

In terms of headquarters and budgets, state parties are better organized than they used to be. Nevertheless, as John Bibby points out, they mostly serve to supplement the candidates' own personal campaign organizations; thus, state party organizations rarely manage campaigns. The job of the state party, writes Bibby, is merely "to provide technical services" within the context of a candidate-centered campaign.[12]

YOU ARE THE POLICYMAKER

Should Political Parties Choose Their Nominees in Open or Closed Primaries?

Some states restrict who can participate in party nomination contests far more than others. In **closed primaries** only people who have registered in advance with a party can vote in its primary. In contrast, **open primaries** allow voters to decide on Election Day whether they want to participate in the Democratic or Republican contests. Each state legislature is faced with making the choice between an open or closed primary, and the pros and cons of these two basic options are often hotly debated.

Closed primaries are generally favored by the party organizations themselves because they encourage voters to officially declare a partisan preference when they register to vote. By requiring voters to sign up in advance in order to participate in its primary, a party can be reasonably assured that most people who participate in their nomination decisions will be reasonably committed to its platform. In other words, closed primaries favor ideological purity and help to keep the policy distinctions between Democrats and Republicans clear. A further advantage for the party organizations is that a closed primary system requires the state's election authority to maintain a record of the party registration of each voter. It is, of course, a secret who you vote for, but anything you put down on your voter registration form is public information. Hence, a closed primary provides each party with invaluable information identifying voters who consider themselves to be party members. Imagine running a business and having the government collect information for you regarding who likes your product. It's no wonder that if the decision were left up to the leaders of the party organizations most would choose a closed primary.

Despite these advantages, the trend among the states in recent years has been toward more open primaries. The main advantage of open primaries is that they allow for more voters to participate in party nomination decisions. Because independents can vote in either party's primary and partisans can readily switch sides, the two major parties are faced with the task of competing for voter support in the primary round as well as the general election. In particular, young people, whose independent streak (see page 230) often leaves them on the sidelines in closed primaries, can be brought into the parties' fold in an open primary. For many policymakers, the chance to widen participation in one's own party via an open primary outweighs the advantage of limiting participation to loyal party members in a closed primary. However, even advocates of open primaries acknowledge that come with some risk for mischief. There is always a possibility that the partisans of one side will "raid" the other party's primary in order to give a boost to its least viable candidate. This would be akin to letting UCLA students participate in the choice of the quarterback for USC's football team. Though raiding is always a theoretical possibility, scholars have found that when voters cast a ballot in the other party's primary, it is usually for candidates whom they genuinely support.

What do you think? Would you choose an open or closed primary?

The National Party Organizations

The supreme power within each of the parties is its **national convention**. The convention meets every four years, and its main task is to write the party's platform and then nominate its candidates for president and vice president. (Chapter 9 will discuss conventions in detail.) Keeping the party operating between conventions is the job of the **national committee**, composed of representatives from the states and territories. Typically, each state has a national committeeman and a national committeewoman as delegates to the party's national committee. The Democratic committee also includes assorted governors, members of Congress, and other party officials.

national convention
The meeting of party delegates every four years to choose a presidential ticket and write the party's platform.

national committee
One of the institutions that keeps the party operating between conventions. The national committee is composed of representatives from the states and territories.

Day-to-day activities of the national party are the responsibility of the party's **national chairperson**. The national party chairperson hires the staff, raises the money, pays the bills, and attends to the daily duties of the party. When asked, at a joint appearance, what their biggest organizational challenge was, the chairs of the Democratic and Republican parties both promptly responded "money."[13]

The chairperson of the party that controls the White House is normally selected by the president himself (subject to routine ratification by the national committee),

national chairperson
The national chairperson is responsible for the day-to-day activities of the party and is usually handpicked by the presidential nominee.

whereas the contest for chair of the party out of power is often a hotly fought battle. In the early 1970s, two of the people who served for a while as chair of the Republican Party at the request of President Nixon were Bob Dole and George H. W. Bush, both of whom used this position as a means of political advancement. As of 2010, former governor of Virginia Tim Kaine, having been chosen by President Obama, headed the Democratic National Committee, and Michael Steele, the former lieutenant governor of Maryland, held the reins at the Republican National Committee.

8.4 Evaluate how well political parties generally do in carrying out their promises.

The Party in Government: Promises and Policy

Which party controls each of America's many elected offices matters because both parties and the elected officials who represent them usually try to turn campaign promises into action. As a result, the party that has control over the most government offices will have the most influence in determining who gets what, where, when, and how.

coalition
A group of individuals with a common interest on which every political party depends.

Voters are attracted to a party in government by its performance and policies. What a party has done in office—and what it promises to do—greatly influences who will join its **coalition**—a set of individuals and groups supporting it. Sometimes voters suspect that political promises are made to be broken. To be sure, there are notable instances in which politicians have turned—sometimes 180 degrees—from their policy promises. Lyndon Johnson repeatedly promised in the 1964 presidential campaign that he would not "send American boys to do an Asian boy's job" and involve the United States in the Vietnam War, but he did. In the 1980 campaign, Ronald Reagan asserted that he would balance the budget by 1984, yet his administration quickly ran up the largest deficit in American history. Throughout the 1988 campaign George Bush proclaimed,

It is a commonplace belief that political parties are only responsive to their big contributors.

Is this a fair assessment and, if so, what might the repercussions be?

"Read my lips—no new taxes," but he reluctantly changed course two years later when pressured on the issue by the Democratic majority in Congress. Bill Clinton promised a tax cut for the middle class during the 1992 campaign, but after he was elected, he backed off, saying that first the deficit would have to be substantially reduced.

It is all too easy to forget how often parties and presidents do exactly what they say they will do. For every broken promise, many more are kept. Ronald Reagan promised to step up defense spending and cut back on social welfare expenditures, and his administration quickly delivered on these pledges. Bill Clinton promised to support bills providing for family leave, easing voting registration procedures, and tightening gun control that had been vetoed by his predecessor. He lobbied hard to get these measures through Congress again and proudly signed them into law once they arrived on his desk. George W. Bush promised a major tax cut for every taxpayer in America, and he delivered just that in 2001. In sum, the impression that politicians and parties never produce policy out of promises is off the mark.

If parties generally do what they say they will, then the party platforms adopted at the national conventions represent blueprints, however vague, for action. Consider what the two major parties promised the voters in their 2008 platforms (see Table 8.1). There is little doubt that the choice between Democratic and Republican policies in 2008 was clear on many important issues facing the country. Furthermore, since coming to office in 2009, President Obama has clearly pursued a course of action in sync with the Democratic platform.

Indeed, two projects that are monitoring President Obama's actions on his campaign promises have found far more promises that are being followed through on than broken. As of June 2010, the *National Journal*'s "Promise Audit" (http://promises.nationaljournal.com/) had found that at least some progress had been made on keeping 84 percent of Obama's specific campaign promises. Of the remainder, another 14 percent had not been acted on and only 2 percent had been broken. Similarly, PolitiFact, a Pulitzer Prize-winning–feature of the *St. Petersburg Times* (http://www.politifact.com/truth-o-meter/promises/) reported at least some progress on 83 percent of over 500 promises, with 14 percent stalled and only 3 percent broken.

TABLE 8.1 Party Platforms, 2008

Although few people actually read party platforms, they are one of the best written sources for what the parties believe in. A brief summary of some of the contrasting positions in the Democratic and Republican platforms of 2008 illustrates major differences in beliefs between the two parties.

REPUBLICANS	DEMOCRATS
The War in Iraq To those who have sacrificed so much, we owe the commitment that American forces will leave that country in victory and with honor. That outcome is too critical to our own national security to be jeopardized by artificial or politically inspired timetables that ignore the advice of our on-the-ground commanders.	**The War in Iraq** We will give our military a new mission: ending this war and giving Iraq back to it its people. We will be as careful getting out of Iraq as we were careless getting in. We can remove our combat brigades at the pace of one to two per month and expect to complete redeployment within 16 months.
Energy Independence We simply must draw more American oil from American soil if we are to have the resources we need to achieve energy independence. We support accelerated exploration and drilling of American sources, from oilfields off the nation's coasts to proven fields. . . . Confident in the promise offered by science and technology, Republicans will pursue dramatic increases in the use of safe, affordable, reliable—and clean—nuclear power.	**Energy Independence** We know we can't drill our way to energy independence and so we must summon all of our ingenuity and legendary hard work and we must invest in research, development, and deployment of forms of new energy—solar, wind, as well as technologies to store energy through advanced batteries and clean up our coal plants. . . . We are committed to getting at least 25% of our electricity from renewable sources by 2025.

(*Continued*)

TABLE 8.1 (Continued)

REPUBLICANS	DEMOCRATS
Abortion We assert the inherent dignity and sanctity of all human life and affirm that the unborn child has a fundamental individual right to life which cannot be infringed.	**Abortion** The Democratic Party strongly and unequivocally supports *Roe v. Wade*, and a woman's right to choose a safe and legal abortion, regardless of ability to pay.
Gay Marriage A Republican Congress enacted the Defense of Marriage Act, affirming the right of states not to recognize same-sex marriages licensed in other states. . . . We urge renewed use of that Article III power to prevent activist federal judges from imposing upon the rest of the nation the judicial activism in Massachusetts and California.	**Gay Marriage** We oppose the Defense of Marriage Act and all attempts to use this issue to divide us.
Health Care The American people rejected Democrats' attempted government takeover of health care in 1993, and they remain skeptical of politicians who would send us down that road. Republicans pledge that as we reform our health care system we will not put the system on a path that empowers Washington bureaucrats at the expense of patients.	**Health Care** We believe that quality and affordable health care is a basic right. . . . Health care should be a shared responsibility between employers, workers, insurers, providers and government. All Americans should have coverage they can afford; employers should have incentives to provide coverage to their workers; insurers and providers should ensure high quality affordable care; and the government should ensure that health insurance is affordable and provides meaningful coverage.
Taxes The last thing Americans need right now is tax hikes. . . . Along with making the 2001 and 2003 tax cuts permanent so American families will not face a large tax hike, Republicans will advance tax policies to support American families, promote savings and innovation, and put us on a path to fundamental tax reform.	**Taxes** We will shut down the corporate loopholes and tax havens and use the money so that we can provide an immediate middle class tax cut that will offer relief to workers and their families. . . . For families making more than $250,000, we'll ask them to give back a portion of the Bush tax cuts to invest in health care and other key priorities.
Education To get our schools back to the basics of learning, we support initiatives to block-grant more Department of Education funding to the states, with requirements for state-level standards, assessments, and public reporting to ensure transparency. Local educators must be free to end ineffective programs and reallocate resources where they are most needed.	**Education** We will make an unprecedented national investment to provide teachers with better pay and better support to improve their skills, and their students' learning. We'll reward effective teachers who teach in underserved areas, take on added responsibilities like mentoring new teachers, or consistently excel in the classroom.

Source: Excerpts from party platforms as posted on the Web sites of each organization.

8.5 Differentiate the various party eras in American history.

Party Eras in American History

While studying political parties, remember the following: *America is a two-party system and always has been.* Of course, there are many minor parties around—Libertarians, Socialists, Reform, Greens—but they rarely have a chance of winning a major office. In contrast, most democratic nations have more than two parties represented in their national legislature. Throughout American history, one party has been the dominant majority party for long periods of time. A majority of voters identify with the party in power; thus, this party tends to win a majority of the elections. Political scientists call these periods **party eras**.

Punctuating each party era is a **critical election**.[14] A critical election is an electoral earthquake: Fissures appear in each party's coalition, which begins to fracture; new issues appear, dividing the electorate. Each party forms a new coalition—one that endures for years. A critical election period may require more than one election before change is apparent, but in the end, the party system will be transformed.

This process is called **party realignment**—a rare event in American political life that is akin to a political revolution. Realignments are typically associated with a major crisis or trauma in the nation's history. One of the major realignments, when the Republican Party emerged, was connected to the Civil War. Another was linked to the Great Depression of the 1930s, when the majority Republicans were displaced by the Democrats. The following sections look more closely at the various party eras in American history.

party eras
Historical periods in which a majority of voters cling to the party in power, which tends to win a majority of the elections.

critical election
An electoral "earthquake" where new issues emerge, new coalitions replace old ones, and the majority party is often displaced by the minority party. Critical election periods are sometimes marked by a national crisis and may require more than one election to bring about a new party era.

party realignment
The displacement of the majority party by the minority party, usually during a **critical election** period.

1796–1824: The First Party System

In the *Federalist Papers*, James Madison warned strongly against the dangers of "factions," or parties. But Alexander Hamilton, one of the coauthors of the *Federalist Papers*, did as much as anyone to inaugurate our party system.[15] Hamilton was the nation's first secretary of the treasury, for which service his picture appears on today's $10 bill. To garner congressional support for his pet policies, particularly a national bank, he needed votes. From this politicking and coalition building came the rudiments of the Federalist Party, America's first political party. The Federalists were also America's shortest-lived major party. After Federalist candidate John Adams was defeated in his reelection bid in 1800, the party quickly faded. The Federalists were poorly organized, and by 1820 they no longer bothered to offer up a candidate for president. In this early period of American history, most party leaders did not regard themselves as professional politicians. Those who lost often withdrew completely from the political arena. The ideas of a loyal opposition and rotation of power in government had not yet taken hold.[16] Each party wanted to destroy the other party, not just defeat it—and such was the fate of the Federalists.

The party that crushed the Federalists was led by Virginians Jefferson, Madison, and Monroe, each of whom was elected president for two terms in succession. They were known as the Democratic-Republicans, or sometimes as the Jeffersonians. The Democratic-Republican Party derived its coalition from agrarian interests rather than from the growing number of capitalists who supported the Federalists. This made the party particularly popular in the largely rural South. As the Federalists disappeared, however, the old Jeffersonian coalition was torn apart by factionalism as it tried to be all things to all people.

1828–1856: Jackson and the Democrats Versus the Whigs

More than anyone else, General Andrew Jackson founded the modern American political party. In the election of 1828, he forged a new coalition that included Westerners as well as Southerners, new immigrants as well as settled Americans. Like most successful politicians of his day, Jackson was initially a Democratic-Republican, but soon after his ascension to the presidency his party became known as simply the Democratic Party, which continues to this day. The "Democratic" label was particularly appropriate for Jackson's supporters because their cause was to broaden political opportunity by eliminating many vestiges of elitism and mobilizing the masses.

Whereas Jackson was the charismatic leader, the Democrats' behind-the-scenes architect was Martin Van Buren, who succeeded Jackson as president. Van Buren's one term in office was relatively undistinguished, but his view of party competition left a lasting mark. He "sought to make Democrats see that their only hope for maintaining the purity of their own principles was to admit the existence of an opposing party."[17]

A realist, Van Buren argued that a party could not aspire to pleasing all the people all the time. He argued that a governing party needed a loyal opposition to represent parts of society that it could not. This opposition was provided by the Whigs. The Whig Party included such notable statesmen as Henry Clay and Daniel Webster, but it was able to win the presidency only when it nominated military heroes such as William Henry Harrison (1840) and Zachary Taylor (1848). The Whigs had two distinct wings—Northern industrialists and Southern planters—who were brought together more by the Democratic policies they opposed than by the issues on which they agreed.

1860–1928: The Two Republican Eras

In the 1850s, the issue of slavery dominated American politics and split both the Whigs and the Democrats. Slavery, said Senator Charles Sumner, an ardent abolitionist, "is the only subject within the field of national politics which excites any real interest."[18] Congress battled over the extension of slavery to the new states and territories. In *Dred Scott v. Sandford*, the Supreme Court of 1857 held that slaves could not be citizens and that former slaves could not be protected by the Constitution. This decision further sharpened the divisions in public opinion, making civil war increasingly likely.

The Republicans rose in the late 1850s as the antislavery party. Folding in the remnants of several minor parties, in 1860 the Republicans forged a coalition strong enough to elect Abraham Lincoln president and to ignite the Civil War. The "War Between the States" was one of those political earthquakes that realigned the parties. After the war, the Republican Party thrived for more than 60 years. The Democrats controlled the South, though, and the Republican label remained a dirty word in the old Confederacy.

A second Republican era was initiated with the watershed election of 1896, perhaps the most bitter battle in American electoral history. The Democrats nominated William Jennings Bryan, populist proponent of "free silver" (linking money with silver, which was more plentiful than gold, and thus devaluing money to help debtors). The Republican Party made clear its positions in favor of the gold standard, industrialization, the banks, high tariffs, and the industrial working classes as well as its positions against the "radical" Western farmers and "silverites." "Bryan and his program were greeted by the country's conservatives with something akin to terror."[19] The *New York Tribune* howled that Bryan's Democrats were "in league with the Devil." On the other side, novelist Frank Baum lampooned the Republicans in his classic novel *The Wizard of Oz*. Dorothy follows the yellow brick road (symbolizing the gold standard) to the Emerald City (representing Washington), only to find that the Wizard (whose figure resembles McKinley) is powerless. But by clicking on her *silver* slippers (the color was changed to ruby for Technicolor effect in the movie), she finds that she can return home.

The election of 1860 proved to be a realigning election. Having only been formed six years earlier in 1854, the Republican Party suddenly became the nation's majority party with the victory of the Lincoln–Hamlin ticket.

Political scientists call the 1896 election a realigning one because it shifted the party coalitions and entrenched the Republicans for another generation. (For more on the election of 1896, see Chapter 10.) For the next three decades the Republicans continued as the nation's majority party, until the stock market crashed in 1929. The ensuing Great Depression brought about another fissure in the crust of the American party system.

1932–1964: The New Deal Coalition

President Herbert Hoover's handling of the Depression turned out to be disastrous for the Republicans. He solemnly pronounced that economic depression could not be cured by legislative action. Americans, however, obviously disagreed and voted for Franklin D. Roosevelt, who promised the country a *New Deal.* In his first 100 days as president, Roosevelt prodded Congress into passing scores of anti-Depression measures. Party realignment began in earnest after the Roosevelt administration got the country moving again. First-time voters flocked to the polls, pumping new blood into the Democratic ranks and providing much of the margin for Roosevelt's four presidential victories. Immigrant groups in Boston and other cities had been initially attracted to the Democrats by the 1928 campaign of Al Smith, the first Catholic to be nominated by a major party for the presidency.[20] Roosevelt reinforced the partisanship of these groups, and the Democrats forged the **New Deal coalition**.

Franklin Roosevelt reshaped the Democratic Party, bringing together a diverse array of groups that had long been marginalized in American political life. Many of the key features of the Democratic Party today, such as support from labor unions, can be traced to the FDR era.

The basic elements of the New Deal coalition were the following:

- *Urban dwellers.* Big cities such as Chicago and Philadelphia were staunchly Republican before the New Deal realignment; afterward, they were Democratic bastions.
- *Labor unions.* FDR became the first president to support unions enthusiastically, and they returned the favor.
- *Catholics and Jews.* During and after the Roosevelt period, Catholics and Jews were strongly Democratic.
- *The poor.* Although the poor had low turnout rates, their votes went overwhelmingly to the party of Roosevelt and his successors.
- *Southerners.* Ever since pre–Civil War days, white Southerners had been Democratic loyalists. This alignment continued unabated during the New Deal. For example, Mississippi voted over 90 percent Democratic in each of FDR's four presidential election victories.
- *African Americans.* The Republicans freed the slaves, but under FDR the Democrats attracted the majority of African Americans.

New Deal coalition
A coalition forged by the Democrats, who dominated American politics from the 1930s to the 1960s. Its basic elements were the urban working class, ethnic groups, Catholics and Jews, the poor, Southerners, African Americans, and intellectuals.

As you can see in Figure 8.3, many of the same groups that supported FDR's New Deal continue to be part of the Democratic Party's coalition today.

The New Deal coalition made the Democratic Party the clear majority party for decades. Harry S Truman, who succeeded Roosevelt in 1945, promised a Fair Deal. World War II hero and Republican Dwight D. Eisenhower broke the Democrats' grip on power by being elected president twice during the 1950s, but the Democrats regained the presidency in 1960 with the election of John F. Kennedy. His New Frontier was in the New Deal tradition, with platforms and policies designed to help labor, the working classes, and minorities. Lyndon B. Johnson became president after Kennedy's assassination and was overwhelmingly elected to a term of his own in 1964. His Great Society programs vastly increased the scope of government in America, and his War on Poverty was reminiscent of Roosevelt's activism in dealing with the Depression. Johnson's Vietnam War policies, however, tore the Democratic Party apart in 1968, leaving the door to the presidency wide open for Republican candidate Richard M. Nixon.

FIGURE 8.3 Party Coalitions Today

The two parties continue to draw support from very different social groups, many of which have existed since the New Deal era. This figure shows the percentage identifying as Democrats and Republicans for various groups in 2008.

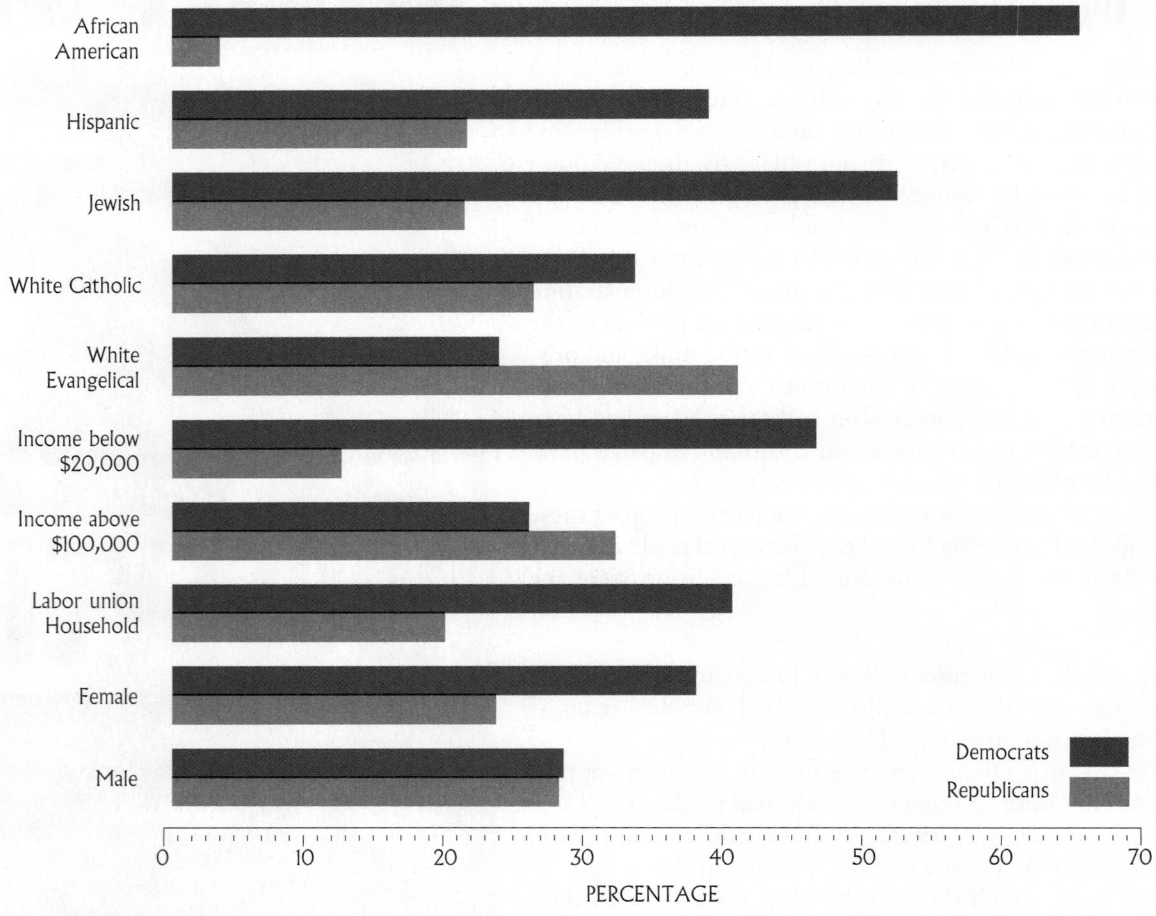

Source: Authors' analysis of Pew Research Center polls conducted in January and February 2008.

1968–Present: Southern Realignment and the Era of Divided Party Government

When Richard Nixon was first elected to the presidency in 1968, he formulated what became widely known as his "Southern strategy." Emphasizing his support for states' rights, law and order, and a strong military posture, Nixon hoped to win over Southern conservatives to the Republican Party, thereby breaking the Democratic Party's long dominance in the former confederacy. Party realignment in the South did not happen as quickly as Nixon would have liked, but it has taken place gradually over in the four decades since 1968.[21] As you can see in "A Generation of Change: Realignment in the South," the South was still a Democratic congressional stronghold as of the late-1980s, but now it clearly leans in the Republican direction.

Another noteworthy aspect of Nixon's 1968 election was that for the first time in the twentieth century, a newly elected president moved into the White House without having his party in control of both houses of Congress. Prior to 1968, most newly elected presidents had swept a wave of their fellow partisans into office with them. For example, the Democrats gained 62 seats in the House when Woodrow Wilson was elected in 1912 and 97 when FDR was elected in 1932. Nixon's inability to bring in congressional majorities with him was not to be an exception, however, but rather the beginning of a new pattern—repeated in the presidential elections won by Ronald

Reagan and George Bush. For a time, it seemed that the normal state of affairs in Washington was for American government to be divided with a Republican president and a Democratic Congress.

Bill Clinton's election in 1992 briefly restored united party government until the Republicans won both houses of Congress in the 1994 elections. After the 1994 elections, Republican leaders were optimistic that they were at last on the verge of a new Republican era in which they would control both the presidency and Congress simultaneously. On the other side, Democratic leaders were hopeful that voters would not like the actions of the new Republican Congress and would restore unified Democratic control of the government. In the end, the ambitions of both sides were frustrated as voters opted to continue divided party government, with a Republican Congress throughout Clinton's second term. During the eight years of George W. Bush's presidency, the Republicans maintained control of the Congress for just the middle four years, from 2003 through 2006. Barack Obama enjoyed Democratic majorities in Congress during his first two years as president, but divided government returned to Washington when the Republicans gained control of the House in 2010.

With only about 60 percent of the electorate currently identifying with the Democrats or Republicans, it may well be difficult for either one to gain a strong enough foothold to maintain simultaneous control of both ends of Pennsylvania

Divided Party Government

When one party controls the White House and the other party controls one or both houses of Congress, divided party government exists. Given that one party can check the other's agenda, it is virtually impossible for a party to say what it is going to do and then actually put these policies into effect. This situation is bad if you want clear lines of accountability on policy, but it is good if you prefer that the two parties be forced to work out compromises.

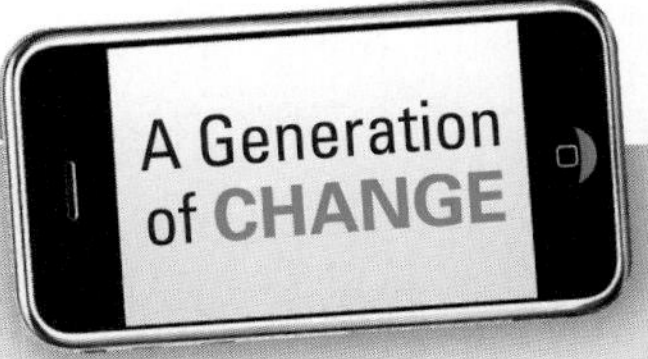

Realignment in the South

One of the most significant political changes over the past generation has been the partisan realignment in the Southern states that has transformed this region from one where Democrats occupied the majority of congressional seats to a crucial bastion of Republican support. In 1987, none of the Southern delegations to the House of Representatives had a Republican majority, and the GOP controlled only 6 of the region's 22 Senate seats. A generation later, the Republicans hold the majority of Southern House and Senate seats. Recently, the South has been the only region of the country where Republicans have consistently outnumbered Democrats in Congress.

Without strong Southern support for the Republicans in recent elections, it is doubtful that the GOP would have been able to attain majority party status in the Congress for most of the period from 1995 to 2006. The crucial role of the South in Republican politics has lately been reflected in the makeup of the GOP congressional leadership. Trent Lott of Mississippi and Bill Frist of Tennessee have served as the Republicans' majority leader in the Senate. Georgia's Newt Gingrich served as Speaker of the House for three terms, and Virginia's Eric Cantor currently holds the position of Republican House majority leader.

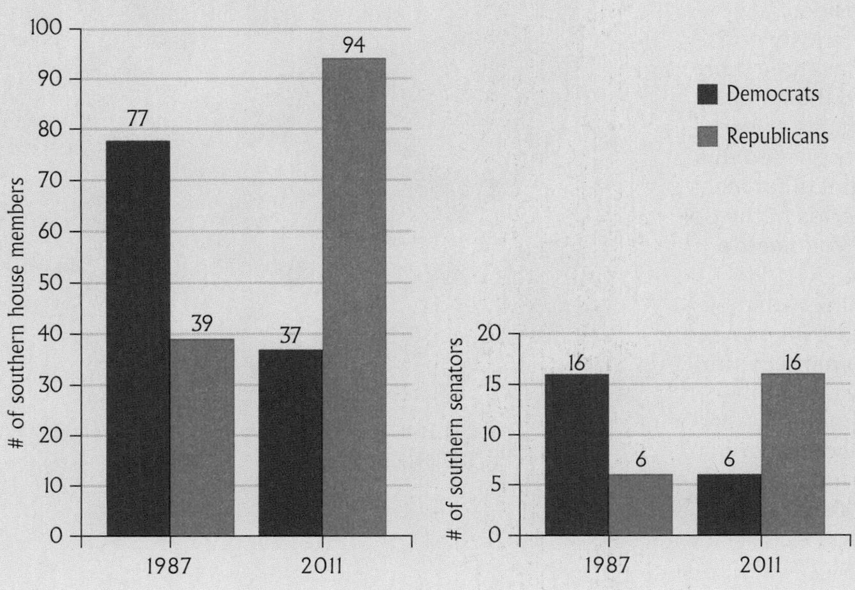

Avenue for very long. All told, both houses of Congress and the presidency have been simultaneously controlled by the same party for just 12 of the 44 years from 1969 to 2012. The regularity with which partisan control of the presidency and Congress has been divided during this period is unprecedented in American political history.

Divided party government is frequently seen not only at the federal level but at the state level as well. As Morris Fiorina shows, the percentage of states that have unified party control of the governorship and the state legislature has declined substantially over the past sixty years.[22] Whereas 85 percent of state governments had one party controlling both houses of the legislature and the governorship in 1946, by 2011 this was the case in only 60 percent of the states (see "My State: Partisan Control of State Governments, 2011"). Divided government, once an occasional oddity in state capitols, is now commonplace.

The recent pattern of divided government has caused many political scientists to believe that the party system has dealigned rather than realigned. Whereas realignment involves people changing from one party to another, **party dealignment** means that many people are gradually moving away from both parties. When your car is realigned, it is adjusted in one direction or another to improve its steering. Imagine if your mechanic were to remove the steering mechanism instead of adjusting it—your car would be useless and ineffective. This is what many scholars fear has been happening to the parties.

party dealignment
The gradual disengagement of people from the parties, as seen in part by shrinking party identification.

Partisan Control of State Governments, 2011

This map shows which states as of 2011 were totally under Democratic or Republican control—that is, had one party controlling both houses of the legislature as well as the governorship. Divided party control means that either one or both houses of the legislature are controlled by a party different than the governor. Nebraska has a nonpartisan legislature and hence cannot be classified.

QUESTIONS FOR DISCUSSION

- Why do think your state has a divided government, a Republican-controlled government, or a Democratic-controlled government? Does this reflect how your state usually votes in presidential elections? Why or why not?
- When was the last time there was a change in the partisan control of your state government? What precipitated this change, and what difference did it make in terms of the policy direction of your state's government?
- What do you think would be best for your state in the near future—divided party control of the state government, or having either the Democrats or Republicans in control of both the legislature and the governorship? Why?

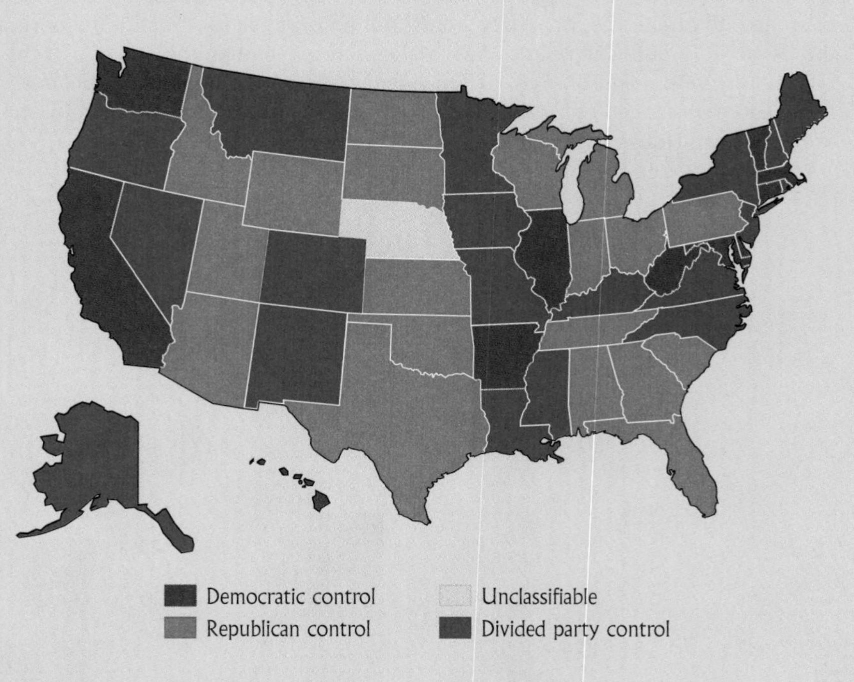

Third Parties: Their Impact on American Politics

8.6 Assess both the impact of third parties on American politics and their limitations.

The story of American party struggle is primarily the story of two major parties, but **third parties** are a regular feature of American politics and occasionally attract the public's attention. Third parties in the United States come in three basic varieties. First are parties that promote certain causes—either a controversial single issue (prohibition of alcoholic beverages, for example) or a relatively extreme ideological position such as socialism or libertarianism. Second are splinter parties, which are offshoots of a major party. Teddy Roosevelt's Progressives in 1912, Strom Thurmond's States' Righters in 1948, and George Wallace's American Independents in 1968 all claimed they did not get a fair hearing from Republicans or Democrats and thus formed their own new parties. Finally, some third parties are merely an extension of a popular individual with presidential aspirations. Both John Anderson in 1980 and Ross Perot in 1992 and 1996 offered voters who were dissatisfied with the Democratic and Republican nominees another option.

third parties
Electoral contenders other than the two major parties. American third parties are not unusual, but they rarely win elections.

Although third-party candidates almost never win office in the United States, scholars believe they are often quite important.[23] They have brought new groups into the electorate and have served as "safety valves" for popular discontent. The Free Soilers of the 1850s were the first true antislavery party; the Progressives and the Populists put many social reforms on the political agenda. George Wallace told his supporters in 1968 they had the chance to "send a message" to Washington—a message of support for tougher law and order measures, which is still being felt to this day. Ross Perot used his saturation of the TV airwaves in 1992 to ensure that the issue of the federal deficit was not ignored in the campaign. And in 2000, Green Party candidate Ralph Nader forced more attention on environmental issues and ultimately cost Gore the presidency by drawing away a small percentage of liberal votes.

Despite the regular appearance of third parties, the two-party system is firmly entrenched in American politics. Would it make a difference if America had a multiparty system, as so many European countries have? The answer is clearly yes. The most obvious consequence of two-party governance is the moderation of political conflict. If America had many parties, each would have to make a special appeal in order to stand out from the crowd. It is not hard to imagine what a multiparty system might look like in the United States. Quite possibly, African American groups would form their own party, pressing vigorously for racial equality. Environmentalists could constitute another party, vowing to clean up the rivers, oppose nuclear power, and save the wilderness. America could have religious parties, union-based parties, farmers' parties, and all sorts of others. As in some European countries, there could be half a dozen or more parties represented in Congress (see "America in Perspective: Multiparty Systems in Other Countries").

The American two-party system contributes to political ambiguity. Why should parties risk taking a strong stand on a controversial policy if doing so will only antagonize many voters? Ambiguity is a safe strategy,[24] as candidates positioned at either extreme of the

Third party candidates usually struggle to get noticed in the United States, as almost all major elected officials are affiliated with either the Democrats or Republicans. But occasionally a third party candidate will become a serious contender, as did Lincoln Chaffee when he ran successfully for governor of Rhode Island in 2010.

AMERICA IN PERSPECTIVE

Multiparty Systems in Other Countries

One of the major reasons why the United States has only two parties represented in government is structural. America has a **winner-take-all system**, in which whoever gets the most votes wins the election. There are no prizes awarded for second or third place. Suppose there are three parties; one receives 45 percent of the vote, another 40 percent, and the third 15 percent. Although it got less than a majority, the party that finished first is declared the winner. The others are left out in the cold. In this way, the American system discourages small parties. Unless a party wins, there is no reward for the votes it gets. Thus, it makes more sense for a small party to merge with one of the major parties than to struggle on its own with little hope. In this example, the second- and third-place parties might merge (if they can reach an agreement on policy) to challenge the governing party in the next election.

In a system that employs **proportional representation**, however, such a merger would not be necessary. Under this system, which is used in most European countries, legislative seats are allocated according to each party's percentage of the nationwide vote. If a party wins 15 percent of the vote, then it receives 15 percent of the seats. Even a small party can use its voice in Parliament to be a thorn in the side of the government, standing up strongly for its principles. Such has often been the role of the Greens in Germany, who are ardent environmentalists. After the 2002 German election they formed a **coalition government** along with Germany's Social Democratic Party. Together the coalition controlled over half the seats in the German parliament for three years. Coalition governments are common in Europe. Italy has regularly been ruled by coalition governments since the end of World War II, for example.

Even with proportional representation, not every party gets represented in the legislature. To be awarded seats, a party must exceed a certain minimal percentage of votes, which varies from country to country. Israel has one of the lowest thresholds at 1.5 percent. This explains why there are always so many parties represented in the Israeli Knesset—12 as of 2010. The founders of Israel's system wanted to make sure that all points of view were represented, but sometimes this has turned into a nightmare, with small extremist parties holding the balance of power.

Parties have to develop their own unique identities to appeal to voters in a multiparty system. This requires strong stands on the issues, but after the election compromises must be made to form a coalition government. If an agreement cannot be reached on the major issues, the coalition is in trouble. Sometimes a new coalition can be formed; other times the result is the calling of a new election. In either case, it is clear that proportional representation systems are more fluid than the two-party system in the United States.

QUESTIONS FOR DISCUSSION

- If the United States adopted a form of proportional representation guaranteeing that any party would get seats in the House of Representatives if it won at least 5 percent of the national vote, how many political parties do you think would obtain seats? What new parties do you think would be formed and would become important players in a proportional representation system?
- Do you think your political views would end up being better represented if we had proportional representation and there were more viable parties to choose from on Election Day? If so, how?
- Do you think the United States ought to consider using proportional representation to determine how many members of each party get elected to Congress? Why or why not?

winner-take-all system
An electoral system in which legislative seats are awarded only to the candidates who come in first in their constituencies.

spectrum, such as Barry Goldwater in 1964 and George McGovern in 1972, have found out the hard way. The two-party system thus throttles extreme or unconventional views.

8.7 Evaluate the advantages and disadvantages of responsible party government.

Understanding Political Parties

Political parties are considered essential elements of democratic government. Indeed, one of the first steps taken toward democracy in formerly communist Eastern European countries was the formation of competing political parties to contest elections. After years of one-party totalitarian rule, Eastern Europeans were ecstatic to be able to adopt a multiparty system like those that had proved successful in the West. In contrast, the founding of the world's first party system in the United States was seen as a risky adventure in the then uncharted waters of democracy. Wary of having parties at all, the Founders designed a system that has greatly restrained their political role to this day. Whether American parties should continue to be so loosely organized is at the heart of today's debate about their role in American democracy.

proportional representation
An electoral system used throughout most of Europe that awards legislative seats to political parties in proportion to the number of votes won in an election.

Democracy and Responsible Party Government: How Should We Govern?

coalition government
When two or more parties join together to form a majority in a national legislature. This form of government is quite common in the multiparty systems of Europe.

Ideally, in a democracy candidates should say what they mean to do if elected and, once they are elected, should be able to do what they promised. Critics of the American party system lament that this is all too often not the case and have called for a "more responsible two-party system."[25] Advocates of the **responsible party model** believe the parties should meet the following conditions:

responsible party model
A view about how parties should work, held by some political scientists. According to the model, parties should offer clear choices to the voters, who can then use those choices as cues to their own preferences of candidates. Once in office, parties would carry out their campaign promises.

1. Parties must present distinct, comprehensive programs for governing the nation.
2. Each party's candidates must be committed to its program and have the internal cohesion and discipline to carry out its program.
3. The majority party must implement its programs, and the minority party must state what it would do if it were in power.
4. The majority party must accept responsibility for the performance of the government.

A two-party system operating under these conditions would make it easier to convert party promises into governmental policy. A party's officeholders would have firm control of the government, so they would be collectively rather than individually responsible for their actions. Voters would therefore know whom to blame for what the government does and does not accomplish.

As this chapter has shown, American political parties fall short of these conditions. They are too decentralized to take a single national position and then enforce it. Most candidates are self-selected, gaining their nomination by their own efforts rather than the party's. Because party primaries are electoral contests for popular support, the party's organization and leaders do not have control over those who run in the general election under their labels. In America's loosely organized party system, there simply is no mechanism for a party to discipline officeholders and thereby ensure cohesion in policymaking. Party leaders can help a candidate raise money,[26] get on to the prestigious committees, and sometimes provide support in their efforts to get special benefits for their constituency. But what they cannot do is even more telling: They cannot deny them the party's nomination at the next election or take away their congressional staff support. Thus, as David Mayhew writes, "Unlike most politicians elsewhere, American ones at both legislative and executive levels have managed to navigate the last two centuries of history without becoming minions of party leaders."[27] American officeholders try to go along with their parties' platform whenever they can. But when the party line conflicts with their own personal opinion and/or the clear desires of their constituents, then they feel perfectly comfortable in voting against their party's leaders. As you can see in Table 8.2, even on the key policy votes in Congress during the presidency of George W. Bush, there were numerous disagreements among members of the same party.

Because American officeholders don't always follow the platform planks of their party, even when Democrats controlled majorities in both the House and Senate in 2009-2010, President Obama could not take for granted that his policy proposals would be enacted into law. In particular, Obama has regularly encountered resistance from members of the organized caucus known as "**Blue Dog Democrats**." Back in the days of the Solid South, Democrats would often say that they would vote for "a yellow dog" if their party wanted them to. Today's Blue Dogs say they have been squeezed so often by the liberals in the Democratic leadership that they have turned blue. Hailing mostly from Southern and/or rural areas of the country, they are more fiscally conservative than

Blue Dog Democrats
Fiscally conservative Democrats who are mostly from the South and/or rural parts of the United States.

TABLE 8.2 Partisan Divisions on Key Roll Call Votes During the Bush Presidency

During the presidency of George W. Bush, there was much discussion in the press about heightened partisan tensions between Democrats and Republicans in Congress. While it is true that congressional voting was more polarized along party lines than had usually been the case in recent times (see Chapter 12), a close look at the roll calls on nine key proposals that President Bush favored reveals a variety of patterns. On three issues, colored in orange in Table 8.2, there was bipartisan support for Bush's position. On two others, colored in blue, the majority of Democrats supported Bush's proposals whereas the majority of Republicans decided not to go along with their own party's leader. Just four of the nine key votes, colored in green, fit the very loose American criteria for a party-line vote: a majority of the president's party voting in support of his position and a majority of the opposition party voting the other way. Notably, on all these partisan votes at least some Democrats broke ranks to support President Bush, and on the Republican side there was unanimity only on the issue of cutting taxes in 2001.

	DEMS FOR	DEMS AGAINST	REPS FOR	REPS AGAINST
2008 $700 billion bailout bill	172	63	91	108
2008 $168 billion tax rebate	216	10	169	25
2007 immigration reform*	33	15	12	37
2005 USA Patriot Act reauthorization	43	156	214	14
2003 prescription drug program	16	190	204	25
2002 Iraq War	82	126	215	6
2001 USA Patriot Act	145	62	211	3
2001 No Child Left Behind	198	6	183	33
2001 tax cut	10	197	219	0

*The House of Representatives never voted on this proposal because it failed a key test in the Senate. Hence, we display the Senate vote in this case, whereas the other votes displayed are from the more numerous House.

most Democrats and are resistant to any domestic policy proposals that would enlarge the scope of government. Thus, on congressional votes like the $787 billion economic stimulus package or the even more expensive health care proposal, many Blue Dog Democrats did not support President Obama's initiatives.

Whenever a president's agenda fails to pass because of his inability to rally his own party, such as occurred with George W. Bush's plans to partially privatize Social Security and to reform our immigration policy, advocates of responsible party government bemoan the lack of centralized political parties in America. However, not everyone thinks that America's decentralized parties are a problem. Critics of the responsible party model argue that the complexity and diversity of American society are too great to be captured by such a simple model of party politics. Local differences need an outlet for expression, they say. One cannot expect Texas Democrats always to want to vote in line with New York Democrats. In the view of those opposed to the responsible party model, America's decentralized parties are appropriate for the type of limited government the Founders sought to create and most Americans wish to maintain.[28]

The Founding Fathers were very concerned that political parties would trample on the rights of individuals. They wanted to preserve individual freedom of action by various elected officials. With America's weak party system, this has certainly been the case. Individual members of Congress and other elected officials have great freedom to act as they see fit rather than toeing the party line.

American Political Parties and the Scope of Government

The lack of disciplined and cohesive European-style parties in America goes a long way to explain why the scope of governmental activity in the United States is not as broad as it is in other established democracies. The long struggle to guarantee access to health

A POINT TO PONDER

Many people believe that the gap between the two parties has become so wide that is hard to get bipartisan agreement about anything.

Based on the data shown in Table 8.2, as well as partisan behavior during the Obama presidency, how accurate is that view?

"In Washington today, the sun rose over Capitol Hill and received broad bipartisan support."

care for all Americans provides a perfect example. In Britain, the Labour Party had long proposed such a system, and after it won the 1945 election, all its members of Parliament voted to enact national health care into law. On the other side of the Atlantic, President Truman also proposed a national health care bill in the first presidential election after World War II. But even though he won the election and had majorities of his own party in both houses of Congress, his proposal never got very far. The weak party structure in the United States allowed many congressional Democrats to oppose Truman's health care proposal. Over four decades later, President Clinton again proposed a system of universal health care and had a Democratic-controlled Congress to work with. But the Clinton health care bill never even came up for a vote in Congress because of the president's inability to get enough members of his own party to go along with the plan. It wasn't until 2010 that President Truman's dream for health care for all Americans was finally realized. Notably, this historic bill only passed by a narrow margin in the Democratic-controlled House of Representatives, with 34 House Democrats opposing it despite the strong urging of President Obama. In short, substantially increasing the scope of government in America is not something that can be accomplished through the disciplined actions of one party's members, as is the case in other democracies.

On the other hand, because it is rarely the case that one single party can ever be said to have firm control over American government, the hard choices necessary to cut back on existing government spending are rarely addressed. A disciplined and cohesive governing party might have the power to say no to various demands on the government. In contrast, America's loose party structure makes it possible for many individual politicians—Democrats and Republicans alike—to focus their efforts on getting more from the government for their own constituents.

Summary

8.1 Identify the functions that political parties perform in American democracy.

Even though political parties are one of Americans' least beloved institutions, political scientists see them as a key linkage between policymakers and the people. Political parties operate at three levels: (1) in the electorate; (2) as organizations; and (3) in government. Among the functions that they perform in our democratic system are to pick candidates, run campaigns, give cues to voters, articulate policies, and coordinate policymaking between the branches of government.

8.2 Determine the significance of party identification in America today.

Party identification—one's self-proclaimed general preference for one party or the other—is the most important factor in explaining the political behavior of American voters. People who do not identify with either party are known as political independents. They are the crucial swing voters who can go either way and are also more likely to split their tickets. Young people are especially likely to be Independents.

8.3 Describe how political parties are organized in the United States.

American political party organizations are decentralized and fragmented. The national party organization can rarely tell state parties what to do. In particular, the state party organizations have a good deal of discretion as to how to choose their nominees for state and local offices. Some states opt to have closed primaries, which restrict participation to people who have registered with the party, whereas others have open primaries, which allow much broader participation. The supreme power within each of the parties is its national convention, which, every four years, nominates candidates for president and vice president and sets party policy. In between conventions, the activities of the national party are guided by each party's national chairperson.

8.4 Evaluate how well political parties generally do in carrying out their promises.

Political parties affect policy through their platforms. Despite much cynicism about party platforms, they serve as important roadmaps for elected officials once they come into office. More promises are generally kept than broken.

8.5 Differentiate the various party eras in American history.

Throughout American history, one party has generally been dominant for a substantial period of time. The first party era, from 1796 to 1824, was dominated by the Democratic-Republicans, whose agricultural base defeated the business-oriented Federalists. The newly formed Democratic Party dominated from 1828 to 1856, pushing for more power for ordinary individuals. The newly formed Republican Party came to power in 1860 and dominated American politics through 1928—first standing firm against slavery and then successfully promoting the interests of industrialization. The Great Depression led to a reversal of party fortunes, with the Democrats establishing the New Deal coalition that usually prevailed from 1932 to 1964. Since 1968, neither party has been able to hold the reins of power for long. A frequent result has been for power to be divided, with one party controlling the presidency and the other in control of the Congress.

8.6 Assess both the impact of third parties on American politics and their limitations.

Third parties in the United States have brought new groups into the electorate and have served as a vehicle for sending a protest message to the two major parties. The American winner-take-all electoral system makes it hard for third parties to win elections. In contrast, most European electoral systems use proportional representation, which guarantees that any party that has at least a certain percentage of the vote receives a proportional share of the legislative seats.

8.7 Evaluate the advantages and disadvantages of responsible party government.

Some scholars of American politics have advocated what is known as "responsible party government," in which parties offer clear policy choices which generate clearly identifiable outcomes. That is, at least in theory, parties say what they plan to do and once in office carry out these plans. The main disadvantage is that the party discipline necessary for a party to carry out its pledges requires members of the party in government to toe the line without regard to constituency preferences. Individualism in American politics would be stifled by a true responsible government.

Chapter Test

8.1 Identify the functions that political parties perform in American democracy.

1. What is a political party's core function?
   a. To field candidates for elected office
   b. To provide a voting cue to the electorate
   c. To try to win elections
   d. To organize a national office
   e. To guide policymakers' decisions

2. Successful political parties in the United States remain close to the midpoint of public opinion.

   True______ False______

3. Explain three of the five ways in which political parties act as a linkage institution. How does performing these tasks show that parties are serving as linking institutions?

4. Political parties are often called "three-headed giants." What are the three "heads" of political parties? How do they relate to each other?

8.2 Determine the significance of party identification in America today.

5. Ticket-splitting ensures that most states are safely Republican or Democrat.

   True______ False______

6. What is party identification and in the United States how does party identification affect voting?

8.3 Describe how political parties are organized in the United States.

7. The internal organization of political parties in the United States is best characterized as
   a. Hierarchical
   b. Fragmented
   c. Centralized
   d. Rigidly determined
   e. Usually marked by strong leadership

8. Party machines dominate local party organizations today.

   True______ False______

9. What role do state party organizations play in American politics today? How does the use of a closed or open primary system help or hinder state party organization influence over campaigns and elections?

10. What is the role of the national party organization between national conventions? Who runs the national organization and what is this person's primary role?

8.4 Evaluate how well political parties generally do in carrying out their promises.

11. By and large, American political parties have kept most of their platform promises and translated them into public policy.

    True______ False______

12. Based on what you know about American political parties, what are some incentives that parties have to carry out their campaign promises? Why might political parties fail to achieve their campaign promises?

8.5 Differentiate the various party eras in American history.

13. A party dealignment is considered to be
    a. The fragmentation of a political party into splinter parties
    b. The loss of party members as more people identify as Independents
    c. The loss of party members to the other party
    d. The shuffling of party coalitions
    e. The reformulation of a party's platform

14. What do the terms *party era*, *critical election*, and *party realignment* each mean? Explain how they are related to each other.

15. Trace American political parties across their several eras in American history. In what ways are these eras similar and in what ways are they different?

8.6 Assess the impact that third parties have had on American politics and why America has only two major parties.

16. Third parties in American politics typically
    a. Encourage major party candidates to take extreme positions
    b. Win elections in American politics
    c. Promote a broad range of moderate policy ideas
    d. Bring new groups into politics
    e. Replace one of the two major parties during realignments

17. The American two-party system encourages parties and candidates to offer clear choices for voters.

    True______ False______

18. Even though third parties rarely win elected office in the United States, they are still important in several respects. In what ways are third parties important to American politics? Use concrete examples to support your answer.

19. Do you think that if the United States had a multiparty system, American politics would be different? If so, in what ways would American politics be different?

8.7 Evaluate the advantages and disadvantages of responsible party government.

20. Which of the following is NOT true about the responsible party model of government?
    a. Both parties present comprehensive and distinct policy programs
    b. Both parties' candidates are committed to carrying out the party's program
    c. The majority party must accept responsibility for government's performance

d. Both parties operate much as the major parties do today
e. The minority party must state what it would do if it were in power

21. So-called Blue Dog Democrats are an example of the Democratic Party operating according to the principles of responsible party government.

True______ False______

22. How does the American two-party system limit the scope of government and yet, at the same time, prevent politicians from taking measures that would limit the scope of government? Use recent policy examples to support your answer.

PEARSON mypoliscilab™ Exercises

Apply what you learned in this chapter on MyPoliSciLab.

Read on **mypoliscilab.com**

eText: Chapter 8

Study and **Review** on **mypoliscilab.com**

Pre-Test
Post-Test
Chapter Exam
Flashcards

Watch on **mypoliscilab.com**

Video: Green Party Candidates Stay on Ballot
Video: New Ballots Bring New Complications in New York
Video: Senator Specter Switches Parties
Video: Republicans and Democrats Divide on Tax Cut
Video: Tea Party Victories Concern for GOP

Explore on **mypoliscilab.com**

Simulation: You Are a Campaign Manager: Help McCain Win Swing States and Swing Voters
Comparative: Comparing Political Parties
Timeline: The Evolution of Political Parties in the United States
Timeline: Third Parties in American History
Visual Literacy: State Control and National Platforms

Key Terms

party competition (226)
political party (226)
linkage institutions (227)
rational-choice theory (229)
party image (229)
party identification (229)
ticket splitting (230)
party machines (231)
patronage (231)
closed primaries (232)
open primaries (232)
national convention (233)
national committee (233)
national chairperson (234)
coalition (234)
party eras (237)
critical election (237)
party realignment (237)
New Deal coalition (239)
party dealignment (242)
third parties (243)
winner-take-all system (244)
proportional representation (245)
coalition government (245)
responsible party model (245)
Blue Dog Democrats (245)

Internet Resources

www.rnc.org
The official site of the Republican National Committee.

www.democrats.org
The Democratic Party online.

www.house.gov/melancon/BlueDogs/index.html
The official site of the fiscally conservative Democratic Blue Dog Coalition.

www.lp.org
Although Libertarians rarely get more than a few percent of the vote, they consistently get many of their candidates on the ballot for many offices. You can learn more about their beliefs at this official site.

www.gp.org
The official Web site for the Green Party, which emphasizes environmental protection over corporate profits.

For Further Reading

Black, Earl, and Merle Black. ***The Rise of Southern Republicanism.*** Cambridge, MA: Harvard University Press, 2002. An excellent examination of the transformation of party politics in the South.

Burden, Barry C., and David C. Kimball. ***Why Americans Split Their Tickets: Campaigns, Competition and Divided Government.*** Ann Arbor: University of Michigan Press, 2002. A good analysis of who splits their ticket and under what conditions they are most likely to do so.

Currinder, Marian. ***Money in the House: Campaign Funds and Congressional Party Politics.*** Boulder, CO: Westview Press, 2009. Examines how congressional parties define and reward loyalty through campaign contributions.

Downs, Anthony. ***An Economic Theory of Democracy.*** New York: Harper & Row, 1957. An extremely influential theoretical work that applies rational-choice theory to party politics.

Green, John C., and Daniel M. Shea. ***The State of the Parties,*** 5th ed. Lanham, MD: Rowman & Littlefield, 2007. A diverse set of articles on numerous aspects of party politics, with an emphasis on how well the party system is working.

Hershey, Marjorie Randon. ***Party Politics in America,*** 14th ed. New York: Longman, 2011. The standard textbook on political parties.

Levendusky, Matthew. ***The Partisan Sort: How Liberals Became Democrats and Conservatives Became Republicans.*** Chicago: University of Chicago Press, 2009. An insightful analysis of how the ideological gap between Democrats and Republicans has widened in recent decades.

Maisel, L. Sandy, ed. ***The Parties Respond: Changes in the American Parties and Campaigns,*** 4th ed. Boulder, CO: Westview, 2002. A good collection of readings on how parties have adapted to changes in the political system.

Mayhew, David R. ***Electoral Realignments: A Critique of an American Genre.*** New Haven, CT: Yale University Press, 2002. A critical look at the historical evidence concerning realignment theory.

Rosenstone, Steven, Roy Behr, and Edward Lazarus. ***Third Parties in America,*** 2nd ed. Princeton, NJ: Princeton University Press, 1996. An analytical study of why third parties appear, when they do, and what effect they have.

Sundquist, James L. ***Dynamics of the Party System,*** rev. ed. Washington, DC: Brookings Institution, 1983. One of the best books ever written on the major realignments in American history.

Wattenberg, Martin P. ***The Decline of American Political Parties, 1952–1996.*** Cambridge, MA: Harvard University Press, 1998. An account of the decline of parties in the electorate.

Chapter 9

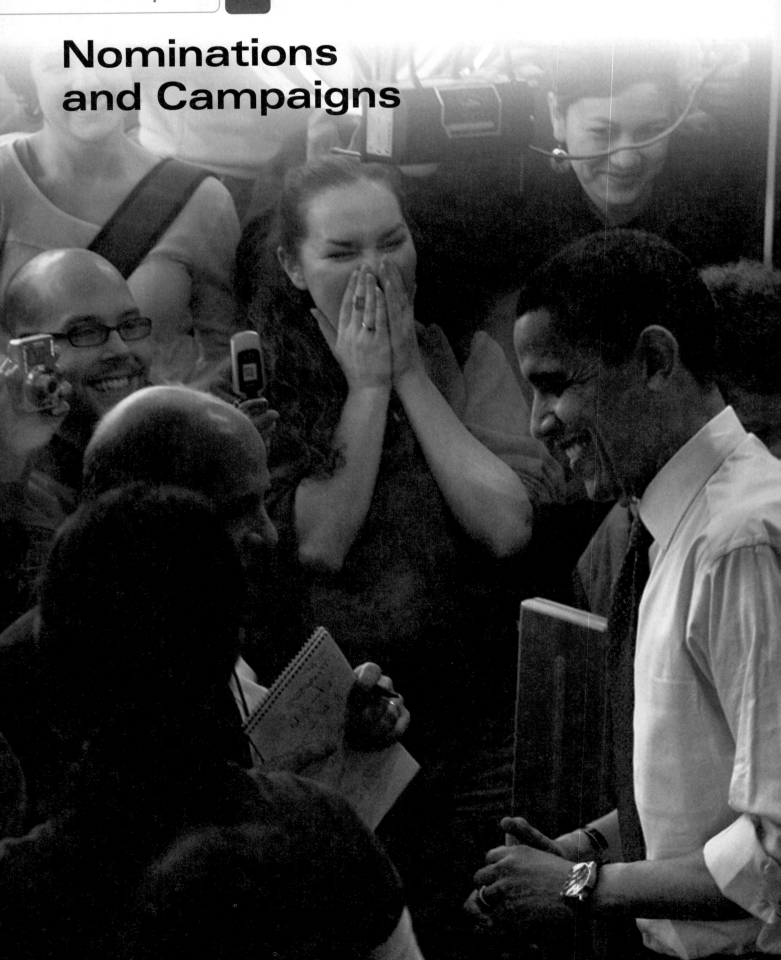

Nominations and Campaigns

Learning Objectives

9.1 Evaluate the fairness of our current system of presidential primaries and caucuses.

9.2 Explain the key objectives of any political campaign.

9.3 Outline how fund-raising for federal offices is regulated by campaign finance laws.

9.4 Determine why campaigns have an important yet limited impact on election outcomes.

9.5 Assess the advantages and disadvantages of having a long presidential campaign.

POLITICS IN ACTION: HOW RUNNING FOR OFFICE CAN BE MORE DEMANDING THAN GOVERNING

Campaigning for any major office has become a massive undertaking in today's political world. Consider Barack Obama's grueling schedule for March 21, 2008, a day in a relatively low-key period of the presidential campaign:

- The senator arrives at the Benson Hotel in Portland, Oregon, after midnight, following a 2,550-mile plane ride from Charleston, West Virginia, where he had spent the previous day campaigning.
- At 7:00 A.M., Obama leaves his hotel for a jog around downtown Portland.
- After returning to the hotel for a change of clothes, Obama meets privately with Governor Bill Richardson of New Mexico, who has just decided to endorse him. The pair then proceed to a scheduled rally at the Portland Memorial Coliseum, where the endorsement is publicly announced to an enthusiastic crowd of 12,800 people.
- Following the morning rally, Obama holds a press conference, taking questions from the corps of reporters traveling with him as well as members of the Oregon media.
- Obama then hops on his campaign bus for an hour's drive down to Oregon's capital city of Salem, where he responds to questions from ordinary Oregonians at a town-hall meeting attended by about 3,000 people.
- While in Salem, Obama manages to do six separate interviews with Oregon news organizations before getting back on the campaign bus.
- After another hour on the road, the bus pulls up in front of American Dream Pizza in Corvallis, where the candidate pops in for a slice of pizza and an impromptu chat with some pleasantly surprised fellow diners (as pictured in the photo at left).
- Obama then re-boards his bus for another hour's ride to Eugene to address a crowd of 10,000 people at the University of Oregon's basketball arena.
- Following this evening rally, the candidate goes to the Eugene airport to board his campaign plane for a 200-mile flight to Medford, Oregon. Just after 1:00 A.M., Obama walks into his hotel for the night, knowing that he has another day like this to look forward to tomorrow.

It is often said that the presidency is the most difficult job in the world, but getting elected to the position may well be tougher. It is arguable that the long campaign for the presidency puts candidates under more continuous stress than they could ever face in the White House. As Karl Rove, George W. Bush's veteran political adviser, wrote just before the first primary votes were cast in 2008, "There are few more demanding physical activities than running for president, other than military training or athletics at a very high level."[1] When asked if he was exhausted by the demands of campaigning in 2008, Barack Obama simply answered, "Sometimes, yes, of course."

The current American style of long and arduous campaigns has evolved from the belief of reformers that the cure for the problems of democracy is more democracy. Whether this approach is helpful or harmful to democracy is a question that provokes much debate with respect to American political campaigns. Some scholars believe it is

Chapter **OUTLINE**

important that presidential candidates go through a long and difficult trial by fire. Others, however, worry that the system makes it difficult for politicians with other responsibilities—such as incumbent governors and senior senators—to take a run at the White House.

The consequences for the scope of government are also debatable. Anthony King argues that American politicians do too little governing because they are always "running scared" in today's perpetual campaign.[2] From King's perspective, the campaign process does not allow politicians the luxury of trying out solutions to policy problems that might be initially unpopular but would work well in the long run. The scope of government thus stays pretty much as is, given that politicians are usually too concerned with the next election to risk fundamental change. Of course, many analysts would argue that having officeholders constantly worrying about public opinion is good for democracy and that changes in the scope of government shouldn't be undertaken without extensive public consultation.

As you read this chapter, consider whether today's nomination and campaign process provides *too much* opportunity for interaction between the public and candidates for office, and consider whether the entire process takes too much time and costs too much money. These are very important topics of debate in American politics today.

With about half a million elected officials in this country, there is always someone somewhere running for office. This chapter will focus mainly on the campaign for the world's most powerful office: the presidency of the United States. On some topics that are broadly generalizable, such as money and campaigning, we will include examples from congressional races as well. Chapter 12 will specifically discuss the congressional election process.

Campaigns in American politics can be divided into two stages: first, nominations, and, second, campaigns between the two nominees. The prize for a nomination campaign is garnering a party's nod as its candidate; the prize for an election campaign is winning an office. This chapter discusses what happens up to Election Day. Chapter 10 explores how people decide whether to vote and whom to vote for.

9.1 Evaluate the fairness of our current system of presidential primaries and caucuses.

The Nomination Game

A **nomination** is a party's official endorsement of a candidate for office. Anyone can play the nomination game, but few have any serious chance of victory. Generally, success in the nomination game requires money, media attention, and momentum. **Campaign strategy** is the way in which candidates attempt to manipulate each of these elements to achieve the nomination.

nomination
The official endorsement of a candidate for office by a **political party**. Generally, success in the nomination game requires momentum, money, and media attention.

campaign strategy
The master game plan candidates lay out to guide their electoral campaign.

Deciding to Run

Believe it or not, not every politician wants to run for president. One reason why is that campaigns have become more physically and emotionally taxing than ever. As former Speaker of the House Thomas Foley once said, "I know of any number of people who I think would make good presidents, even great presidents, who are deterred from running by the torture candidates are obliged to put themselves through."[3] Running for president is an around-the-clock endurance test for over a year: sleep deprivation and strange hotel beds, countless plane rides, junk food eaten on the run, a lack of regular exercise, and copious amounts of stress. As 1984 Democratic nominee Walter Mondale once said, "For four years, that's all I did. I mean, all I did. That's all you think about. That's all you talk about.... That's your leisure. That's your luxury... I told someone, 'The question is not whether I can get elected. The question is whether I can be elected and not be nuts when I get there.'"[4]

In most advanced industrialized countries, campaigns last no more than two months according to custom and/or law. In contrast, American campaigns seem endless; a presidential candidacy needs to be either announced or an open secret for at least a year before the election. Virtually all of the major candidates for president in 2008 had declared their candidacy and started to run at full steam ahead by the winter of 2007.

Competing for Delegates

In some ways, the nomination game is tougher than the general election game; it whittles a large number of players down to two. The goal of the nomination game is to win the support of a majority of delegates at the **national party convention**—the supreme power within each of the parties, which functions to select presidential and vice presidential candidates and to write a party platform.

national party convention
The supreme power within each of the parties. The convention meets every four years to nominate the party's presidential and vice-presidential candidates and to write the party's platform.

At each political party's convention, state delegations meet to cast their votes. Today, the choices of the delegates are well known in advance, and the real contests involve the selection of the delegates from each state in the first place. However, it was not always that way. From the invention of political party conventions in the 1830s up until the late 1960s, the vast majority of the delegates were the political elite—elected officials and heads of the local party organizations. Frequently, each state had one or two party "bosses" who ran the show, such as the state's governor or the mayor of its largest city. These "bosses" could control who went to the convention and how the state's delegates voted once they got there. They were the kingmakers of presidential politics who met in smoke-filled rooms at the convention to cut deals and form coalitions.

Early in the twentieth century, the presidential primary was promoted by reformers who wanted to take nominations out of the hands of the party bosses. The reformers wanted to let the people vote for the candidate of their choice and then bind the delegates to vote for that candidate at the national convention. Although primary elections caught on quickly as a method for nominating candidates for Congress and state government positions, the presidential primary was less quick to catch on: 35 states left the choice of convention delegates to the party elites through the 1960s.

McGovern-Fraser Commission
A commission formed at the 1968 Democratic convention in response to demands for reform by minority groups and others who sought better representation.

It wasn't until the Democratic Party's disastrous 1968 convention that pressure mounted to rethink the traditional elite-dominated closed procedures for selecting convention delegates. As the war in Southeast Asia raged, another war of sorts took place in the streets of Chicago during the Democratic convention. Demonstrators against the war battled Mayor Richard Daley's Chicago police in what an official report later called a "police riot." Beaten up in the streets and defeated in the convention hall, the antiwar faction won one concession from the party regulars: a special committee to review the party's delegate selection procedures, which they felt had discriminated against them. Minorities, women, youth, and other groups that had been poorly represented in the party leadership also demanded a more open process of convention delegate selection. The result was a committee of inquiry, which was chaired first by Senator George McGovern and later by Representative Donald Fraser.

Riots at the 1968 Democratic national convention led to the creation of the McGovern-Fraser Commission, which established open procedures and affirmative action guidelines for delegate selection. These reforms have made party conventions more representative than they once were.

After a careful review of the procedures used to select delegates to the 1968 Democratic convention, the **McGovern-Fraser Commission** famously concluded that "meaningful participation of Democratic voters in the choice of their presidential nominee was often difficult or costly, sometimes completely illusory, and, in not a few instances, impossible."[5] In order to correct this situation, they wrote new rules to make Democratic Party conventions more representative and open to input from the public. Under these new rules, party leaders could no longer handpick the convention delegates virtually in secret. All delegate selection procedures were required to be open, so that party leaders had no more clout than college students or anyone else who wanted to participate. States were told that delegates had to be selected via a method that everyone could participate in—either a state-run primary election or an open meeting at the local level. Many states decided that the easiest way to comply with these new Democratic delegate selection procedures was simply to hold a primary to select convention delegates.[6] Because state laws instituting primaries typically apply to both parties' selection of delegates, the Republican Party's nomination process was similarly transformed.

Few developments have changed American politics as much as the opening of the presidential nomination process to broad-based public participation. The elite-dominated game of bargaining for the party's nomination was transformed into a process in which candidates competed for tens of millions of votes. Delegates who were experienced politicians and knew the candidates gave way to delegates who attain their seats due to their preferred candidate's ability to pull in votes.

superdelegates
National party leaders who automatically get a delegate slot at the **national party convention**.

The only remaining vestige of the old elite-dominated system is the so-called **superdelegates**—the people who are awarded automatic slots as delegates based on the office they currently hold, such as being a member of Congress or of their party's national committee. In 2008, these members of the political elite made up 19 percent of the Democratic delegates and 6 percent of the Republican delegates.[7] Because the Democratic nomination race between Obama and Clinton was so close, a good deal of media attention focused on the possibility that the superdelegates could prove to be decisive and could even overturn the people's verdict by giving the nomination to the candidate who received fewer popular votes. However, as political scientist William Mayer notes, the principle that nominations are decided by the voters has become so ingrained in the American psyche that even when the superdelegates have "the theoretical capacity to influence the outcome of a closely contested nomination race, they are reluctant to exercise that power."[8] Thus, in 2008, as in the past nine presidential elections, the Democratic and Republican nominees were determined by the results of the primaries and caucuses in the 50 states.

The Caucuses and Primaries From January through June of the election year, the individual state parties busily choose their delegates to the national convention via either caucuses or primaries.

Since 1972, the Iowa caucuses have been the first test of candidates' vote-getting ability. Iowa is one of about a dozen mostly rural states that hold a set of meetings, known as caucuses, to select convention delegates. In a **caucus** system voters must show up at a fixed time and attend an open meeting lasting one or two hours to express their presidential preference. Because attending a caucus requires a greater time commitment than a primary election, participation in caucuses is much lower than the level of turnout for primaries. As such, caucuses represent a rather different sort of test for a presidential candidate than primaries. As Thomas Mann explains, "Caucuses test candidates' strategic acuity, organizational strength, and intensity of support, qualities not irrelevant to performance in the general election and in the White House."[9] Barack Obama's experience as a community organizer before he entered politics is widely thought to have given him special insight into how to mobilize activists to attend a caucus. David Plouffe, Obama's campaign manager, proudly proclaimed that their "organization and grassroots supporters understood how to win caucuses."[10] Indeed, starting with a victory in Iowa, the Obama campaign won the majority of delegates at stake in every caucus state in 2008—an edge that proved crucial to Obama's narrow victory over Clinton in the race for the Democratic nomination.

caucus
A system for selecting convention delegates used in about a dozen mostly rural states in which voters must show up at a set time and attend an open meeting to express their presidential preference.

Given that the Iowa caucuses are the first test of the candidates' vote-getting ability, they usually become a full-blown media extravaganza.[11] Well-known candidates like Dick Gephardt in 2004 and John Glenn in 1984 have seen their campaigns virtually fall apart as a result of poor showings in Iowa. Most important, some candidates have received tremendous boosts from unexpected strong showings in Iowa. An obscure former Georgia governor named Jimmy Carter took his first big presidential step by winning there in 1976. In 2008, Barack Obama's victory shocked the political world and landed him on the covers of the major weekly magazines, *Time* and *Newsweek*. Because of the impact that Iowa's first-in-the-nation caucus can have, candidates spend far more time during the nomination season there than they do in the big states like California, Texas, and Florida. As David Yepsen, Iowa's top political reporter, wrote in the *Des Moines Register* the day before the 2008 Iowa caucus, "For more than a year, Iowans have been carpet-bombed by record numbers of candidate visits, interest groups, commercials, mail, phone calls and people knocking on doors. Millions of dollars have been spent here and hundreds of staffers deployed, using the most advanced political tactics and technologies. Day in and day out, we have been told how important we are and how so much is at stake."[12] As in most years, the results from the 2008 Iowa caucus winnowed down the number of viable candidates for the primaries to come.

Most of the delegates to the Democratic and Republican national conventions are selected in **presidential primaries**, in which a state's voters go to the polls to express their preference for a party's nominee for president. The primary season begins during the winter in New Hampshire. As with the Iowa caucuses, the importance of the New Hampshire primary is not the number of delegates or how representative the state is but rather that it is traditionally first.[13] At this early stage, the campaign is not for delegates but for image—candidates want the rest of the country to see them as front-runners. The frenzy

presidential primaries Elections in which a state's voters go to the polls to express their preference for a party's nominee for president. Most delegates to the **national party conventions** are chosen this way.

A POINT TO PONDER

During the nomination process, candidates and the media pay far more attention to Iowa and New Hampshire than to most other states.

What do you think—is this a serious problem? Why or why not?

For a number of months, Howard Dean's formidable fund-raising and high poll standing made him the front-runner in the race for the 2004 Democratic presidential nomination. But when he repeatedly screamed during a concession speech after the first delegate contest in Iowa, his reputation took a drastic hit from which his campaign never recovered.

of political activity in this small state is given lavish attention in the national press. During the week of the primary, half the portable satellite dishes in the country can be found in Manchester, New Hampshire, and the networks move their anchors and top reporters to the scene to broadcast the nightly news. In recent years, over a fifth of TV coverage of the nomination races has been devoted to the New Hampshire primary.[14]

With so much attention paid to the early contests, more states have moved their primaries up in the calendar to capitalize on the media attention. This **frontloading** of the process resulted in about two-thirds of both Democratic and Republican delegates being chosen within six weeks of the Iowa caucus in 2008. At one time, it was considered advantageous for a state to choose its delegates late in the primary season so that it could play a decisive role. However, in recent years, states that have held late primaries have frequently proved to be irrelevant given that one candidate had already secured the nomination by the time their primaries were held. The very close race between Obama and Clinton for the Democratic nomination in 2008 is the one recent exception to this rule.

State laws determine how delegates are allocated, operating within the general guidelines set by the parties. The Democrats require all states to use some form of proportional representation in which a candidate who gets 15 percent or more of a state's vote is awarded a roughly proportional share of the delegates. Republicans believe in less regulation and consequently give states a large degree of discretion. Some states, like Florida, allocate all Republican delegates to whoever wins the most votes; others, like California, award delegates according to who wins each congressional district; and yet others employ some form of proportional representation.

WHY IT MATTERS

Early Delegate Contests

In baseball, no one would declare a team out of the pennant race after it lost the first two games of the season. But in the race for the presidential nomination, the results of the Iowa caucus and the New Hampshire primary frequently end the campaigns of many candidates after only a handful of national delegates have been selected. These contests are important not because of the number of delegates that are chosen but because they are the first indicators of public support. If a candidate does not do well in these first two contests, money and media attention dry up quickly.

Week after week, the primaries serve as elimination contests, as the media continually monitor the count of delegates won. The politicians, the press, and the public all love a winner. Candidates who fail to score early wins get labeled as losers and typically drop out of the race. Usually they have little choice since losing quickly inhibits a candidate's ability to raise the money necessary to win in other states. As one veteran fund-raiser put it, "People don't lose campaigns. They run out of money and can't get their planes in the air. That's the reality."[15]

In the 1980 delegate chase, a commonly used football term became established in the language of American politics. After George H. W. Bush scored a surprise victory over Ronald Reagan in Iowa, he proudly claimed to possess "the big mo"—momentum. Actually, Bush had only a little "mo" and quickly fell victim to a decisive Reagan victory in New Hampshire. But the term neatly describes what candidates for the nomination are after. Primaries and caucuses are more than an endurance contest, although they are certainly that; they are also proving grounds. Week after week, the challenge is to do better than expected. Learning from his father's experience, George W. Bush jokingly told the reporters on his 2000 campaign plane, "Please stow your expectations securely in your overhead bins, as they may shift during the trip and can fall and hurt someone—especially me."[16]

To get "mo" going, candidates have to beat people they were not expected to beat, collect margins above predictions, and—above all else—never lose to people they were expected to trounce. Momentum is good to have, but it is no guarantee of victory because candidates with a strong base sometimes bounce back. Political scientist Larry Bartels found that "substantive political appeal may overwhelm the impact of momentum."[17] Indeed, after being soundly trounced by John McCain in New

Hampshire in 2000, George W. Bush quickly bounced back to win the big states necessary to get the Republican nomination. Eight years later, it was John McCain who bounced back to win after Mike Huckabee scored a victory in the first 2008 Republican contest, in Iowa.

frontloading
The recent tendency of states to hold primaries early in the calendar in order to capitalize on media attention.

Evaluating the Primary and Caucus System The primaries and the caucuses are here to stay. That reality does not mean, however, that political scientists or commentators are particularly happy with the system. Criticisms of this marathon campaign are numerous; here are a few of the most important:

- ***Disproportionate attention goes to the early caucuses and primaries.*** Take a look at "My State: How Obama and Clinton Visited Some States Far More than

How Obama and Clinton Visited Some States Far More than Others During the 2008 Nomination Campaign

In 2008, for the first time in recent years, the contest for the Democratic nomination turned into a 50-state contest, with Obama and Clinton battling in a close race for every delegate. Yet, as usual, the first caucus in Iowa and the first primary in New Hampshire received far more attention from the candidates than their number of delegates would warrant. Together, these two states accounted for just 2 percent of the delegates to the 2008 Democratic National Convention but for a full 29 percent of the public events held by Obama and Clinton during the campaign. Here, you can see a map of the 50 states drawn to scale in terms of the number of events the two major Democratic candidates held in them; note how blown out of proportion Iowa and New Hampshire are on the map.

QUESTIONS FOR DISCUSSION

- Do you think your state got the attention it deserved from Obama and Clinton during the Democratic nomination campaign in 2008?
- Examine where in the calendar year your state had its Democratic primary or caucus by going to http://politics.nytimes.com/election-guide/2008/primaries/democraticprimaries/index.html. How do you think the timing of your state's delegate selection contest influenced the amount of attention it received from the major Democratic candidates?
- Do you think your state should change its position in the primary calendar for 2012 so as to attract more attention from the candidates? If so, where in the calendar do you think it should move to?

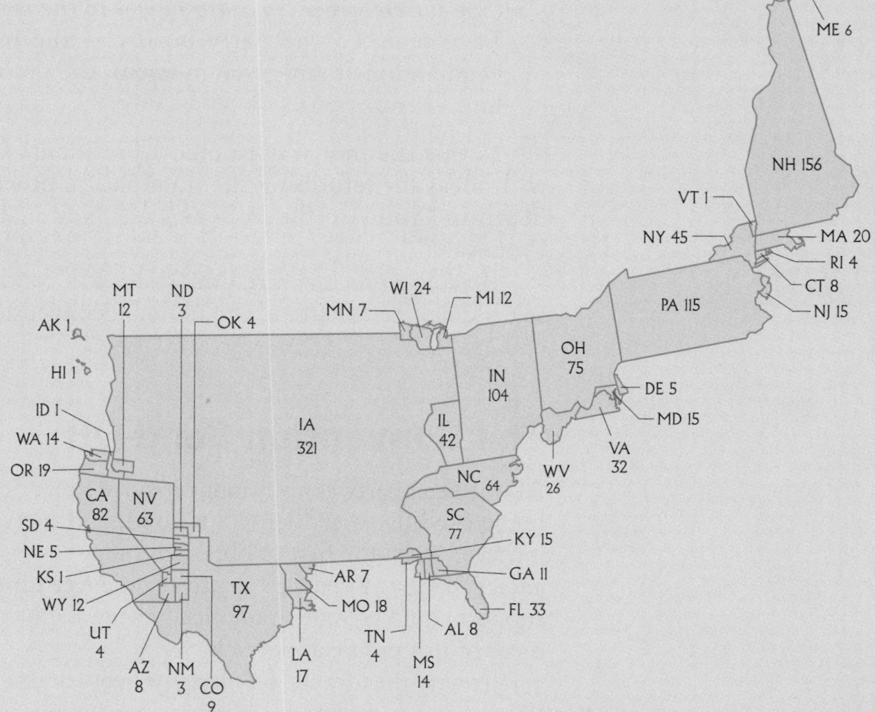

Source: *Washington Post* campaign tracker data for January 2007 through May 20, 2008, http://projects.washingtonpost.com/2008-presidential-candidates/tracker/.

Others During the 2008 Nomination Campaign," which shows that the focus of the two major Democratic candidates in 2008 was amazingly concentrated on the early contests for delegates. In particular, Iowa, with the first caucus, and New Hampshire, with the first primary, received far more attention than some of the most heavily populated states, with later contests. Although Iowa and New Hampshire are not always "make-or-break" contests, they play a key—and disproportionate—role in building momentum, by generating money and media attention.

- ***Prominent politicians find it difficult to take time out from their duties to run.*** Running for the presidency has become a full-time job. It is hard to balance the demands of serving in high public office with running a presidential campaign. Of the six U.S. senators who were candidates for the presidency in 2008, the average voting participation rate in 2007 was a mere 63 percent—far below the average senatorial attendance rate of about 95 percent.[18]
- ***Money plays too big a role in the caucuses and primaries.*** Momentum means money—getting more of it than your opponents do. Many people think that money plays too large a role in American presidential elections. (This topic will be discussed in detail shortly.) Candidates who drop out early in the process often lament that their inability to raise money left them without a chance to compete.
- ***Participation in primaries and caucuses is low and unrepresentative.*** Although about 60 percent of adult citizens vote in the November presidential election, only about 25 percent cast ballots in presidential primaries. Participation in caucuses is even lower because attending a caucus meeting takes far more time and effort than voting in a primary election. Except for Iowa, where the extraordinary media attention usually boosts the participation, only about 5 percent of registered voters typically show up for caucuses. Moreover, voters in primaries and caucuses are hardly representative of voters at large: they tend to be older and more affluent than average.
- ***The system gives too much power to the media.*** Critics contend that the media have replaced the party bosses as the new kingmakers. Deciding who has momentum at any given moment, the press readily labels candidates as winners and losers.

Is this the best way to pick a president? Critics think not, and have come up with ideas for reforming the nomination process, some of which are examined in-depth in "You Are the Policymaker: National and Regional Presidential Primary Proposals."

Barring some major reform, states will continue to hold primaries and caucuses to select delegates to attend the national conventions, where the nominees are formally chosen.

The Convention Send-Off

At one time party conventions provided great drama. Great speeches were given, dark-horse candidates suddenly appeared, and numerous ballots were held as candidates jockeyed to be the first to obtain the support of a majority of the delegates. With delegates having the chance to vote again every time there was no clear winner, candidate support could change dramatically from ballot to ballot, thereby adding to the excitement of this political spectacle.

Today, the drama has largely been drained from the conventions because the winner is a foregone conclusion. No longer can a powerful governor shift a whole block of votes at the last minute. Delegates selected in primaries and open caucuses have known preferences. The last time there was any doubt about who would win at

YOU ARE THE POLICYMAKER

National and Regional Presidential Primary Proposals

The idea of holding a **national primary** to select party nominees has been discussed virtually ever since state primaries were introduced. In 1913, President Woodrow Wilson proposed it in his first message to Congress. Since then, over 250 proposals for a national presidential primary have been introduced in Congress. These proposals do not lack public support; opinion polls have consistently shown that a substantial majority of Democrats, Republicans, and Independents alike favor such reform.

According to its proponents, a national primary would bring directness and simplicity to the process for the voters as well as the candidates. The length of the campaign would be shortened, and no longer would votes in one state have more political impact than votes in another. The concentration of media coverage on this one event, say its advocates, would increase not only political interest in the nomination decision but also public understanding of the issues involved.

A national primary would not be so simple, respond the critics. Because Americans would not want a candidate nominated with 25 percent of the vote from among a field of six candidates, in most primaries a runoff election between the top two finishers in each party would have to be held. So much for making the campaign simpler, national primary critics note. Each voter would have to vote three times for president—twice in the primaries and once in November.

Another common criticism of a national primary is that only well-established politicians would have a shot at breaking through in such a system. Big money and big attention from the national media would become more crucial than ever. Talented politicians who operate in relative national obscurity because of the small size of their state would never have a chance. Do Americans, however, really want politicians without an established reputation to become president?

Perhaps more feasible than a national primary is holding a series of **regional primaries**, in which, say, states in the Eastern time zone would vote one week, those in the Central time zone the next, and so on. This would impose a more rational structure and cut down on candidate travel. A regional primary system would also put an end to the jockeying between states for an advantageous position in the primary season. In 2005, a bipartisan commission on electoral reform led by former President Jimmy Carter and former Secretary of State James Baker endorsed a plan to establish regional primaries (see www.american.edu/ia/cfer/).

The major problem with the regional primary proposal, however, is the advantage gained by whichever region goes first. For example, if the Western states were the first to vote, any candidate from California would have a clear edge in building momentum. Although most of the proposed plans call for the order of the regions to be determined by lottery, this would not erase the fact that regional advantages would surely be created from year to year.

Another prominent proposal is to have states vote in four stages according to their population size, with the least populous states leading off and the big states like California and Texas voting last. Such a proposal received serious consideration from the Republican National Committee in 2000 and was about to be voted on at the convention until George W. Bush let it be known that he did not favor it. Bush expressed concern that the plan would be unworkable because candidates would be asked to campaign all over the country in each stage.

What do you think? Do the advantages of the reform proposals outweigh the disadvantages? Would any of them represent an improvement over the current system?

the convention was in 1976, when Gerald Ford edged out Ronald Reagan for the Republican nomination.

Without such drama, the networks have substantially scaled back the number of hours of coverage, as you can see in Figure 9.1. Even with the condensed TV coverage, the Nielsen ratings have fallen to rather low levels.[19] About 38 million people watched Barack Obama's speech to the 2008 Democratic convention, which was covered by all the major broadcast networks as well as the cable news channels. By contrast, over 97 million people tuned in to see the Giants defeat the Patriots in the 2008 Super Bowl, which was broadcast on only one network.

national primary
A proposed nationwide primary that would replace the current system of **caucuses** and **presidential primaries**.

regional primaries
A proposed series of primaries held in each geographic region that would replace the current system of **caucuses** and **presidential primaries**.

FIGURE 9.1 The Declining Coverage of Conventions on Network TV

Believe it or not, Democratic and Republican conventions once got far more coverage on the major networks (CBS, NBC, and ABC) than did the Summer Olympics. As the number of presidential primaries increased, however, and nominations came to be decided in these contests, conventions ceased to offer much political suspense. Hence, the networks drastically cut back on their coverage of these events, as you can see in the data displayed here.

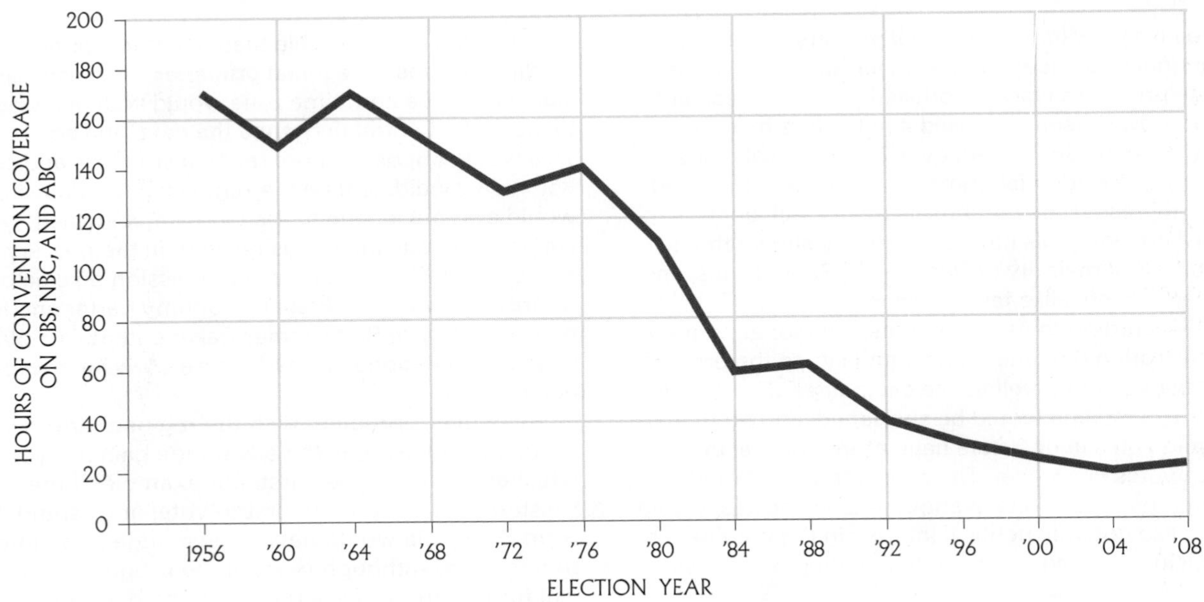

Source: For 1956–1984, calculated from data reported in Byron E. Schafer, *Bifurcated Politics: Evolution and Reform in the National Party Convention* (Cambridge, MA: Harvard University Press, 1988), 274; updated by the authors for 1988 through 2008.

Although conventions are no longer very interesting, they are a significant rallying point for the parties. As George W. Bush said prior to the Republican convention in 2000, "The convention system provides a system of rewards for hardworking, grass-roots people who end up being delegates. I view it as an opportunity for these people to go back home, energized to help me get elected."[20] Modern conventions are carefully scripted to present the party in its best light. As Barack Obama wrote in his 2006 book, *The Audacity of Hope*, the party convention "serves as a weeklong infomercial for the party and its nominee."[21] Delegates are no longer there to argue for their causes but merely to support their candidate. The parties carefully orchestrate a massive send-off for the presidential and vice-presidential candidates. The party's leaders are there in force, as are many of its most important followers—people whose input will be critical during the general election campaign. The conventions are also important in developing the party's policy positions and in promoting political representation.

In the past, conventions were essentially an assembly of party leaders, gathered together to bargain over the selection of the party's ticket. Almost all delegates were white, male, and over 40. Lately, party reformers, especially among the Democrats, have worked hard to make the conventions far more demographically representative.

Meeting in an oversized, overstuffed convention hall in a major city, a national convention is a short-lived affair. The first day usually has as its highlight the keynote speech, in which a dynamic speaker outlines the party's basic principles and touts the nominee-to-be. In 2004, John Kerry chose the little-known Barack Obama for this role at the Democratic convention, and Obama's eloquent speech instantly established him as a rising young political star.

The second day centers on the **party platform**—the party's statement of its goals and policies for the next four years. The platform is drafted prior to the convention by a committee whose members are chosen in rough proportion to each candidate's strength. Any time over 20 percent of the delegates to the platform committee disagree with the majority, they can bring an alternative minority plank to the convention floor for debate. In former times, contests over the platform were key tests of candidates' strength before the actual nomination. When a peace plank failed to be adopted by the 1968 Democratic national convention, it was clear that Vice President Hubert Humphrey would defeat antiwar candidate Eugene McCarthy. In contrast, recent contests over the platform have served mostly as a way for the minority factions in the party to make sure that their voices are heard. Since 1992, pro-choice Republicans have often tried in vain to force a vote on the solidly antiabortion plank in the GOP platform. Fearing the negative publicity the party would incur by showing open disagreement on this emotionally charged issue, pro-choice Republican leaders have dissuaded delegates from forcing such a confrontation.

The third day of the convention is devoted to formally nominating a candidate for president. One of each candidate's eminent supporters gives a speech extolling the candidate's virtues; a string of seconding speeches then follow. Toward the end of the evening, balloting begins as states announce their votes. After all the votes are counted, the long-anticipated nomination becomes official.

The vice-presidential nominee is chosen by roll-call vote on the convention's final day, though custom dictates that delegates simply vote for whomever the presidential nominee recommends. The vice-presidential candidate then comes to the podium to make a brief acceptance speech. This speech is followed by the grand finale—the presidential candidate's acceptance speech, in which the battle lines for the coming campaign are drawn. Afterward, all the party leaders come out to congratulate the party's ticket, raise their hands in unity, and bid the delegates farewell.

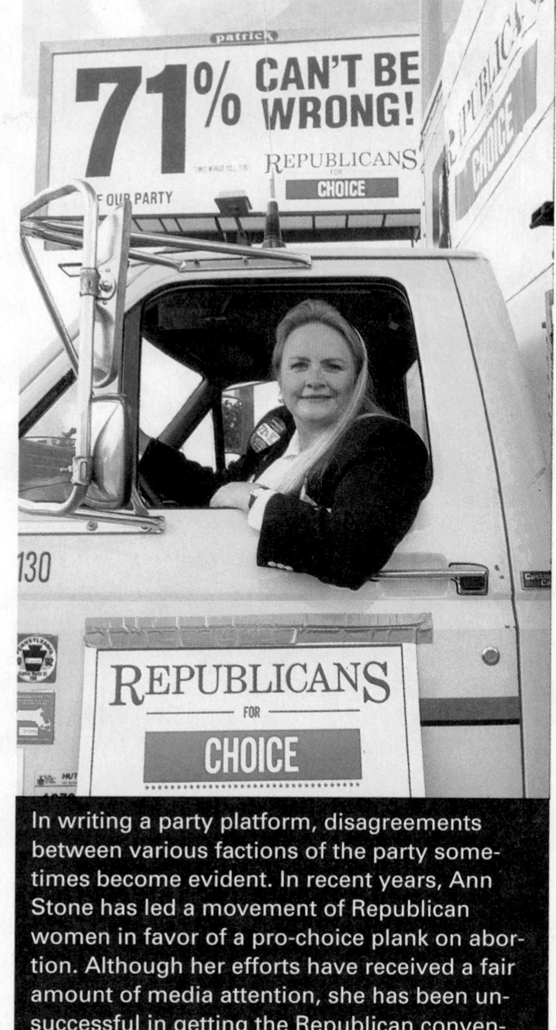

In writing a party platform, disagreements between various factions of the party sometimes become evident. In recent years, Ann Stone has led a movement of Republican women in favor of a pro-choice plank on abortion. Although her efforts have received a fair amount of media attention, she has been unsuccessful in getting the Republican convention to consider changing its pro-life platform.

The Campaign Game

9.2 Explain the key objectives of any political campaign.

Once nominated, candidates concentrate on campaigning for the general election. The word *campaign* originated as a military term: Generals mounted campaigns, using their limited resources to achieve strategic objectives. Political campaigns proceed in a similar fashion, with candidates allocating their scarce resources of time, money, and energy to achieve their political objectives.

Campaigns involve more than organization and leadership. Artistry also enters the picture, for campaigns deal in images. The campaign is the canvas on which political strategists try to paint portraits of leadership, competence, caring, and other characteristics Americans value in presidents. Campaigning today is an art and a science, heavily dependent—like much else in American politics—on technology.

party platform
A political party's statement of its goals and policies for the next four years. The platform is drafted prior to the party convention by a committee whose members are chosen in rough proportion to each candidate's strength. It is the best formal statement of a party's beliefs.

The High-Tech Media Campaign

The new machines of politics have changed the way campaigns are run. During the first half of the twentieth century, candidates and their entourage piled onto a campaign train and tried to speak to as many people as time, energy, and money would allow. Voters

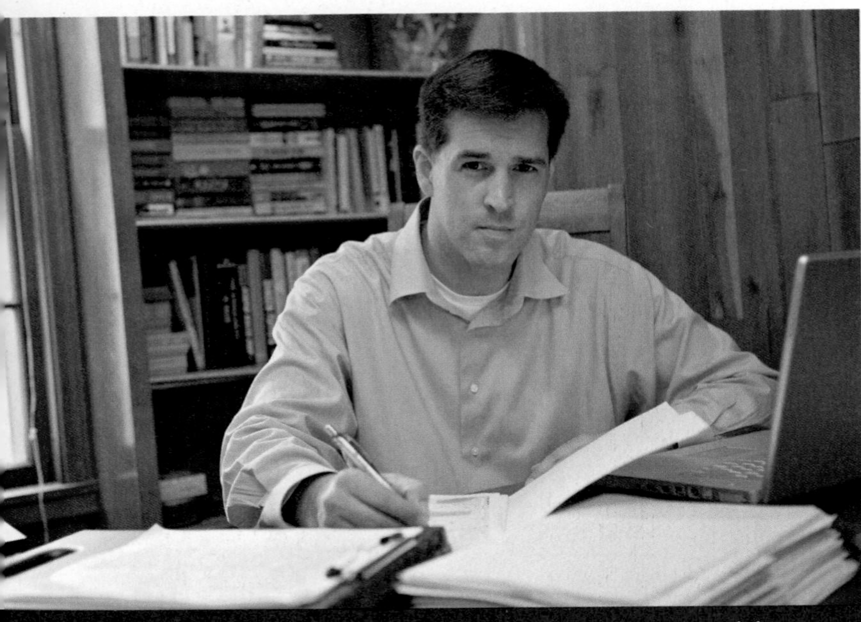

Technology has changed the way campaigns are run and the way candidates attempt to reach the people. When Sean Tevis ran for a seat in the Kansas legislature in 2008 he drew a set of clever cartoons about his campaign and posted them on his Web site. After the *Los Angeles Times* publicized his innovative Web site, small contributions came in at a rapid rate, and he ended up raising four times his goal. Nevertheless, he lost by a 52-48 margin. In 2010, he ran unsuccessfully for Congress.

journeyed from miles around to see a presidential whistle-stop tour go by and to hear a few words in person from the candidate. Today, television is the most prevalent means used by candidates to reach voters. Thomas Patterson stresses that "today's presidential campaign is essentially a mass media campaign. . . . It is no exaggeration to say that, for the majority of voters, the campaign has little reality apart from its media version."[22] Barack Obama put this into a candidate's perspective when he wrote, "I—like every politician at the federal level—am almost entirely dependent on the media to reach my constituents. It is the filter through which my votes are interpreted, my statements analyzed, my beliefs examined. For the broad public at least, I am who the media says I am."[23]

The computer revolution has also now overtaken political campaigns. At the end of the first presidential debate in 1996, Bob Dole encouraged viewers to go to his Web site for more information on his issue stands. So many people immediately tried to check it out that the server soon crashed. Today, one of the first things presidential candidates do is establish a Web site with detailed information about their issue stands and background, videos of their key speeches, a schedule of upcoming events, and a form enabling people to donate to the campaign online. A May 2008 survey by the Pew Internet & American Life Project found that 29 percent of Americans had gone online to read or watch campaign material posted on a candidate's Web site. The same study also found that 23 percent said they regularly receive e-mails with political content and that 10 percent had used sites like Facebook or MySpace for some kind of political activity.[24]

Nowhere has the impact of the Internet been greater than on political fund-raising. The Pew study found that 6 percent of American adults had donated online to a candidate in the first five months of 2008. Six percent may not sound like a big slice of the American adult population, but it amounts to about 14 million people. If the average online donor contributed just $75, that would translate into over a billion dollars in political contributions. The most prominent recipient of this flood of online donations in 2008 was the Obama campaign, which received contributions from over a million people via the Internet. The Internet is likely to increasingly impact, and may soon even revolutionize, fund-raising for political campaigns.

direct mail
A method of raising money for a political cause or candidate, in which information and requests for money are sent to people whose names appear on lists of those who have supported similar views or candidates in the past.

Computer technology has long been used by campaigns in the form of **direct mail**, a technique for locating potential supporters by sending information and a request for money to huge lists of people who have supported candidates with similar views in the past. Conservative fund-raiser Richard Viguerie pioneered the mass mailing list, including in his computerized list the names and addresses of hundreds of thousands of individuals who contributed to conservative causes. The accumulation of mailing lists enables candidates to pick an issue—be it helping the homeless, opposing abortion, aiding Israel, or anything else—and write to a list of people concerned about that issue. The ability to use e-mail has made such targeted fund-raising far easier and more cost-effective. Direct mail costs roughly 40 cents for every dollar raised through solicitations sent out via the post office. On the Internet, the main expense is just the staff time to collect addresses and write up the e-mail messages. As Robert Boatright argues, "Candidates who use the Web to raise money can raise larger sums from small donors than has traditionally been the case in campaigns; they can effectively give donors an idea of how their money will be used; and they can more easily resolicit donors throughout the campaign."[25] The e-mail list maintained by the 2008 Obama campaign reportedly exceeded 5 million addresses, whom the campaign e-mailed regularly with strategic updates and occasional requests for further contributions. The high-tech campaign is no longer a luxury. Candidates *must* use the media and computer technology just to stay competitive.

The most important goal of any media campaign is simply to get attention. Media coverage is determined by two factors: (1) how candidates use their advertising budget and (2) the "free" attention they get as news makers. The first, obviously, is relatively easy to control; the second is more difficult but not impossible. Almost every logistical decision in a campaign—where to eat breakfast, whom to include on stage, when to announce a major policy proposal—is calculated according to its intended media impact. In the first half of the twentieth century, the biggest item in a campaign budget might have been renting a railroad train. Today, the major item is unquestionably television advertising. At least half the total budget for a presidential or U.S. Senate campaign will be used for campaign commercials.

Many observers worry that we have entered a new era of politics in which the slick slogan and the image salesperson dominate—an era when Madison Avenue is more influential than Main Street. Most political scientists, however, are concluding that such fears are overblown. Research has shown that campaign advertising can be a source of information about issues as well as about images. Thomas Patterson and Robert McClure examined the information contained in TV advertising and found that viewers learned more about candidates' stands on the issues from watching their ads than from watching TV news shows. Most news coverage stresses where the candidates went, how big their crowds were, and other campaign details. The networks only occasionally delve into where the candidates stand on the issues. In contrast, political ads typically address issues; a study of 230,000 candidate ads that ran in 1998 found that spots that emphasized policy outnumbered those that stressed personal image by a 6-to-1 ratio.[26] Most candidates apparently believe that their policy positions are a crucial part of their campaign, and they are willing to pay substantial sums to communicate them to voters.

Candidates have much less control over the other aspect of the media, news coverage. To be sure, most campaigns have press aides who feed "canned" news releases to reporters. Still, the media largely determine for themselves what is happening in a campaign and what they want to cover. Campaign coverage seems to be a constant interplay between hard news about what candidates say and do and the human interest angle, which most journalists think sells newspapers or interests television viewers. Apparently, news organizations believe that policy issues are of less interest to voters than the campaign itself. The result is that news coverage is disproportionately devoted to campaign strategies, speculation about what will happen next, poll results, and other aspects of the campaign game. Once a candidate has taken a policy position and it has been reported, it becomes old news. The latest poll showing Smith ahead of Jones is thus more newsworthy. Roger Ailes, the president of Fox News, calls this his "orchestra pit" theory of American politics: "If you have two guys on stage and one guy says, 'I have a solution to the Middle East problem,' and the other guy falls in the orchestra pit, who do you think is going to be on the evening news?"[27] As you can see in Figure 9.2, a comprehensive study of 2008 campaign coverage that looked at various types of media found that far more stories dealt with the horse race and strategy than with policy and the candidates' public records.

Organizing the Campaign

In every campaign, there is too much to do and too little time to do it. Every candidate must prepare for nightly banquets and endless handshaking. More important, to organize their campaigns effectively, candidates must do the following:

- ***Get a campaign manager***. Some candidates try to run their own campaign, but they usually end up regretting it. A professional campaign manager can keep the candidate from getting bogged down in organizational details. This person also bears the day-to-day responsibility for keeping the campaign square on its message and setting its tone.

FIGURE 9.2 The Focus of Media Stories During the 2008 General Election

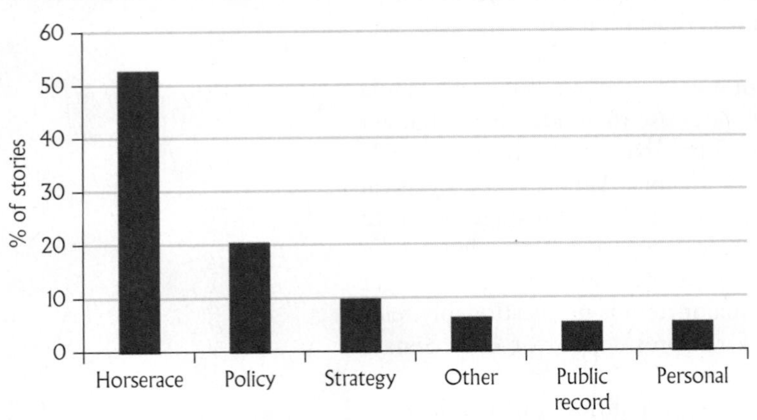

During the period from the end of the political party conventions through the final presidential debate, the Project for Excellence in Journalism coded the major focus of 2,412 stories about the campaign. These stories were randomly selected from 48 different outlets in five media sectors—newspapers, online, network TV, cable TV, and radio. The results can be seen in the figure to the left.

Source: Project for Excellence in Journalism, "Winning the Media Campaign: How the Press Reported the 2008 Presidential General Election," 33. This report can be found online at http://www.journalism.org/sites/journalism.org/files/WINNING%20THE%20 MEDIA%20CAMPAIGN%20FINAL.pdf.

- ***Get a fund-raiser.*** Money, as this chapter will soon discuss in detail, is an important key to election victory.
- ***Get a campaign counsel.*** With all the current federal regulation of campaign financing, legal assistance is essential to ensure compliance with the laws.
- ***Hire media and campaign consultants.*** Candidates have more important things to do with their time than plan ad campaigns, contract for buttons and bumper stickers, and buy TV time and newspaper space. Professionals can get them the most exposure for their money.
- ***Assemble a campaign staff.*** It is desirable to hire as many professionals as the campaign budget allows, but it is also important to get a coordinator of volunteers to ensure that envelopes are licked, doorbells rung, and other small but vital tasks addressed. Many campaign volunteers are typically young people, who are the most likely to have the energy and freedom from commitments required for this sort of intensive work. However, in recent decades high school seniors have expressed less interest in participating in campaigns (see "Young People and Politics: Declining Interest in Working in Campaigns").
- ***Plan the logistics.*** A modern presidential campaign involves jetting around the country at an incredible pace. Aides known as "advance workers" handle the complicated details of candidate scheduling and see to it that events are well publicized and well attended.
- ***Get a research staff and policy advisers.*** Candidates have little time to master the complex issues reporters will ask about. Policy advisers—often distinguished academics—feed them the information they need to keep up with events.
- ***Hire a pollster.*** Professional polling firms conduct opinion research to tell candidates how the voters view them and what is on the voters' minds.
- ***Get a good press secretary.*** Candidates running for major office have reporters dogging them every step of the way. The reporters need news, and a good press secretary can help them make their deadlines with stories that the campaign would like to see reported.
- ***Establish a Web site.*** A Web site is a relatively inexpensive way of getting a candidate's message out.

Most of these tasks cost money. Campaigns are not cheap, and the role of money in campaigns is a controversial one.

Declining Interest in Working in Campaigns

Walk into any campaign headquarters and chances are good that you'll find a lot of young people at work. Many of our nation's leaders got their political start working in a campaign when they were young. If you want to get involved in politics as a possible career, this is where you begin. The work is often tedious, the hours are long, and the financial rewards are usually minimal. Hence, full-time campaign work is not really suitable for someone with an active career or for a retired person. Campaign jobs have been and likely will continue to be filled primarily by young people.

Nevertheless, as you can see in this figure, over the past quarter-century high school seniors' interest in working on campaigns has declined. Whereas between 15 and 20 percent of those interviewed in the late 1970s and early 1980s said they planned to work on a campaign or had already done so, in recent years only about 10 percent have expressed an interest in campaign work.

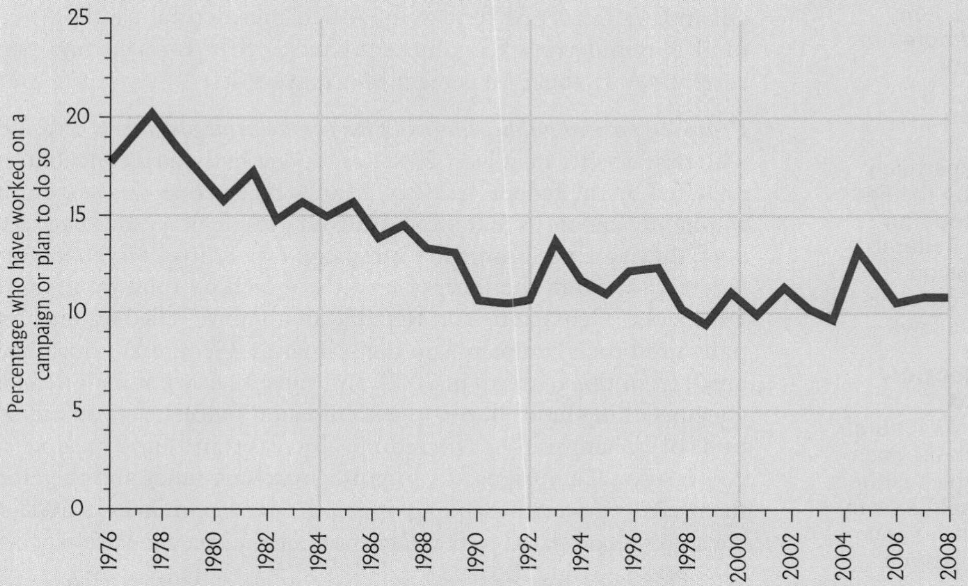

Source: Authors' analysis of the annual *Monitoring the Future* national surveys of high school seniors.

QUESTIONS FOR DISCUSSION

- At the same time that young people have been expressing less interest in working on political campaigns, they have been volunteering for community organizations at record rates. Might the decline in interest in campaign work simply be because today's young people are focusing on nonpolitical forms of community action?
- Do you think that one reason young people may not be very interested in working in campaigns may be that the issues discussed in recent campaigns, such as health care policy, aren't of much interest to them? If so, what sort of issues might stimulate more young people to sign up for campaign work?
- If more young people were to volunteer for work in campaigns, what difference might it make? How might the issue agenda of political campaigns be altered if more young people become involved?

Money and Campaigning

9.3 Outline how fund-raising for federal offices is regulated by campaign finance laws.

There is no doubt that campaigns are expensive and, in America's high-tech political arena, growing more so. Candidates need money to build a campaign organization and to get their message out. Many people and groups who want certain things from the government are all too willing to give it; thus, there is the common perception that money buys votes and influence. The following sections examine the role of money in campaigns.

The Maze of Campaign Finance Reforms

In the early 1970s, as the costs of campaigning skyrocketed with the growth of television and the Watergate scandal exposed large, illegal campaign contributions, momentum developed for campaign finance reform. Several public interest lobbies (see Chapter 11), notably Common Cause and the National Committee for an Effective Congress, led the drive. In 1974, Congress passed the **Federal Election Campaign Act**. It had two main goals: tightening reporting requirements for contributions and limiting overall expenditures. The 1974 act and its subsequent amendments did the following:

Federal Election Campaign Act
A law passed in 1974 for reforming campaign finances. The act created the **Federal Election Commission**, provided public financing for presidential primaries and general elections, limited presidential campaign spending, required disclosure, and attempted to limit contributions.

Federal Election Commission
A six-member bipartisan agency created by the **Federal Election Campaign** Act of 1974. The Federal Election Commission administers and enforces campaign finance laws.

Presidential Election Campaign Fund
Money from the $3 federal income tax check-off goes into this fund, which is then distributed to qualified candidates to subsidize their presidential campaigns.

matching funds
Contributions of up to $250 are matched from the Presidential Election Campaign Fund to candidates for the presidential nomination who qualify and agree to meet various conditions, such as limiting their overall spending.

- ***Created the Federal Election Commission.*** A bipartisan body, the six-member Federal Election Commission (FEC) administers campaign finance laws and enforces compliance with their requirements.
- ***Created the Presidential Election Campaign Fund.*** The FEC is in charge of doling out money from this fund to qualified presidential candidates. Money for this fund is raised via a $3 voluntary check-off box on income tax returns, which currently only about 10 percent of taxpayers do.
- ***Provided partial public financing for presidential primaries.*** Presidential candidates who raise $5,000 in at least 20 states can get individual contributions of up to $250 matched by the federal treasury. Money received at this stage of the campaign is commonly known as **matching funds**. If presidential candidates accept federal support, they agree to limit their campaign expenditures to an amount prescribed by federal law. From the inception of the matching fund program in 1976 through 1996, every Democratic and Republican nominee relied on matching funds to partially fund their campaigns in the primaries. George W. Bush became the first to break from this pattern, in 2000, and since then most major candidates have forgone matching funds during the nomination process. As you can see in "A Generation of Change: The Incredible Increase in Fund-raising for Presidential Nomination Campaigns," by forgoing matching funds and therefore not subjecting themselves to overall spending limits, the party nominees in 2008 spent an incredible amount compared to the party nominees just a generation ago.
- ***Provided full public financing for major party candidates in the general election.*** For the general election, each major party nominee is eligible to receive a fixed amount of money to cover his or her total campaign expenses. For 2008, this amounted to $85 million. Unlike in the primaries, federal funds come in the form of a grant, thereby making the offer much more attractive. From the inception of this system in 1976 through 2004, every Democratic and Republican nominee accepted the grant. In 2008, Barack Obama became the first major party nominee to turn it down, opting instead to raise as much money as he could in increments of up to $2,300, the limit on individual contributions. All told, Obama raised about $337 million for the general election campaign, giving him a substantial edge in campaign funds over John McCain, who opted to just take the $85 million from the Federal Election Commission.
- ***Required full disclosure.*** Regardless of whether they accept any federal funding, all candidates for federal office must file periodic reports with the FEC, listing who contributed and how the money was spent.
- ***Limited contributions.*** Scandalized to find out that some wealthy individuals had contributed $1 million to the 1972 Nixon campaign, Congress limited individual contributions to presidential and congressional candidates to $1,000. The McCain-Feingold Act increased this limit to $2,000 as of 2004 and provided for it to be indexed to rise along with inflation in the future; hence, the limit for 2008 was $2,300.

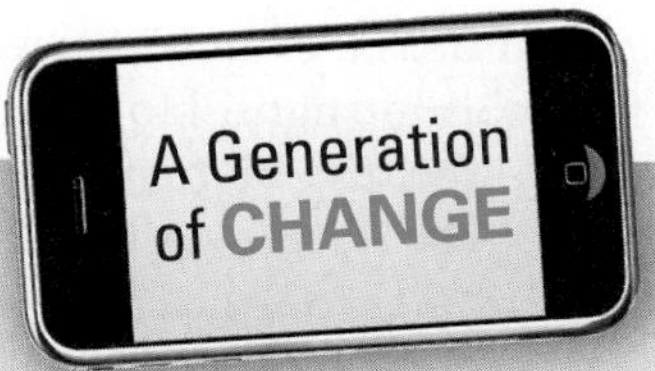

The Incredible Increase in Fund-raising for Presidential Nomination Campaigns

A generation ago, fund-raising for presidential nomination campaigns was rather limited compared to the vast sums of money that are raised by the parties' presidential nominees today. As you can see in the graph, the 1988 nomination campaigns of George Bush and Michael Dukakis cost a total of $60.3 million. About 29 percent of this amount came from federal matching funds, which were designed to supplement small contributions from individuals. Acceptance of these matching funds requires candidates to limit the total amount they raise. In 1988, both Bush and Dukakis ended up spending close to the legal limit of $32 million for that year. By 2008, the cap on nomination expenditures had risen to about $57 million as the result of inflation over the years. For both the Obama and McCain campaigns this seemed too constraining in light of what they thought they could raise on their own without matching funds. All told, the two campaigns raised a stunning $408 million just to fund their activities up to the end of the primary season in early June. Even taking inflation into account, this is about four times what the party nominees raised a generation ago.

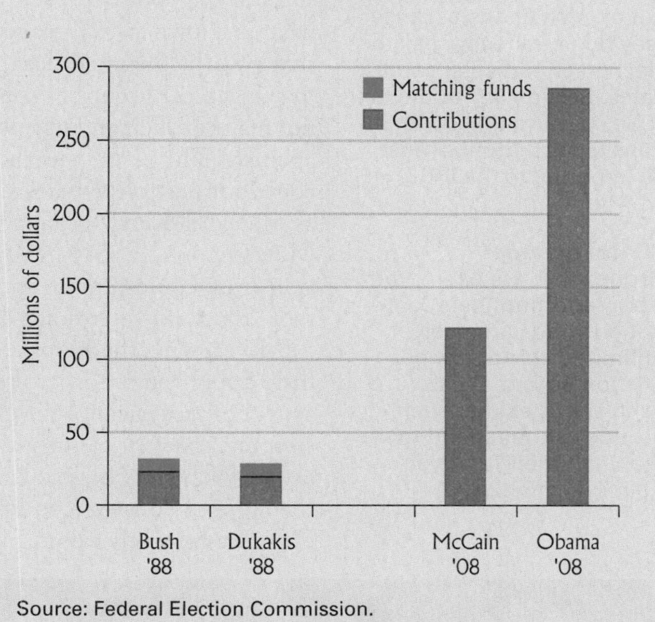

Source: Federal Election Commission.

Although the 1974 campaign reforms were generally welcomed by both parties, the constitutionality of the Federal Election Campaign Act was challenged in the 1976 case of *Buckley v. Valeo*. In this case, the Supreme Court struck down, as a violation of free speech, the portion of the act that had limited the amount that individuals could contribute to their own campaigns. This aspect of the Court ruling made it possible for Ross Perot to spend over $60 million of his own fortune on his independent presidential candidacy in 1992 and for Mitt Romney to spend $44 million out of his own pocket in pursuit of the Republican presidential nomination in 2008.

Another loophole was opened in 1979 with an amendment to the original act that made it easier for political parties to raise money for voter registration drives and the distribution of campaign material at the grass-roots level or for generic party advertising. Money raised for such purposes was known as **soft money** and for over two decades was not subject to any contribution limits. In 2000, nearly half a billion dollars was raised by the two parties via soft money contributions, with many of the contributions coming in increments of hundreds of thousands of dollars. AT&T alone gave over $3 million in soft money, as did the American Federation of State, County, and Municipal Employees.

soft money
Political contributions earmarked for party-building expenses at the grass-roots level or for generic party advertising. Unlike money that goes to the campaign of a particular candidate, such party donations are not subject to contribution limits. For a time, such contributions were unlimited, until they were banned by the McCain-Feingold Act.

Senators John McCain (R-Ariz.) and Russell Feingold (D-Wis.) crusaded for years to remove the taint of large soft money campaign contributions from the political system. Their efforts finally came to fruition in 2002 when their bill was passed by the Congress and signed into law by President George W. Bush. The major provision of the McCain-Feingold Act was to ban soft money contributions. In addition, it prohibited corporations and unions from using their general treasury funds to pay for electioneering communications in the last 60 days of federal campaigns. However, in the 2010 case of *Citizens United v. Federal Election Commission,* the Supreme Court ruled that this was an unconstitutional restriction on free speech. Both corporations and unions can now spend as much as they like to promote their political views, as long as they do so independently, that is, without coordinating their message with any candidate's campaign.

527 groups
Independent political groups that are not subject to contribution restrictions because they do not directly seek the election of particular candidates. Section 527 of the tax code specifies that contributions to such groups must be reported to the IRS.

501(c) groups
Groups that are exempted from reporting their contributions and can receive unlimited contributions. Section 501c of the tax code specifies that such groups cannot spend more than half their funds on political activities.

Although the McCain-Feingold's ban on soft money contributions remains in effect, it didn't take long for a major loophole for big contributors to be opened up. Some scholars call this the "hydraulic theory of money and politics," noting that money, like water, inevitably finds its way around any obstacle. Wealthy individuals on both sides of the political spectrum found that they could make unlimited contributions to what is known as **527 groups**, which are named after the section of the federal tax code that governs these political groups. In a controversial ruling, the FEC in 2004 declined to subject 527 groups to contribution restrictions as long as their political messages did not make explicit endorsements of candidates by using phrases like "Vote for" and "Vote against." The result was that many people who had in the past given big soft money contributions to the parties decided instead to give big donations to a 527 group, such as the anti-Kerry group Swift Boat Veterans for Truth or the anti-Bush group MoveOn.org. In 2010, **501(c) groups** emerged as vehicles for unlimited political donations that could remain anonymous. Unlike 527 groups, 501(c) groups cannot spend more than half their funds on political activities.[28]

Even with the loopholes that have developed in campaign finance law, there is little doubt that efforts to regulate campaign contributions since 1974 have made this aspect of American politics more open and honest. The Federal Election Commission makes every contribution and expenditure report publically available, and a variety of Web sites have taken on the task of making this information easy to search through. If you want to know how much money a particular candidate for federal office has recently raised for their campaign, you can easily look up their most recent quarterly statement at www.opensecrets.org. And if you want to know who among your neighbors has donated to federal campaigns, you can find this information with a simple search at www.fundrace.org. As Frank Sorauf writes, detailed reports of American campaign contributions and expenditures have "become a wonder of the democratic political world. Nowhere else do scholars and journalists find so much information about the funding of campaigns, and the openness of Americans about the flow of money stuns many other nationals accustomed to silence and secrecy about such traditionally private matters."[29]

Probably the most influential 527 group in a presidential campaign so far was the Swift Boat Veterans for Truth, who placed advertisements like this on TV in 2004. These veterans, funded in large part by multi-million-dollar donations from three Texas businessmen, alleged that John Kerry had lied about his Vietnam war record.

The Proliferation of PACs

The campaign reforms of the 1970s also encouraged the spread of **political action committees**, generally known as PACs. Before the 1974 reforms, corporations were technically forbidden to donate money to political campaigns, but many wrote big checks anyway. Unions could make indirect contributions, although limits were set on how they could aid candidates and political parties. The 1974 reforms created a new, more open way for interest groups such as business and labor to contribute to campaigns. Any interest group, large or small, can now get into the act by forming its own PAC to directly channel contributions of up to $5,000 per candidate in both the primary and the general election.

political action committees
Funding vehicles created by the 1974 campaign finance reforms. A corporation, union, or some other interest group can create a political action committee (PAC) and register it with the **Federal Election Commission**, which will meticulously monitor the PAC's expenditures.

At the end of 2008, the FEC reported that there were 4,611 PACs, which contributed $412.8 million to House and Senate candidates during the 2007–2008 election cycle. A PAC is formed when a business association or some other interest group decides to contribute to candidates whom it believes will support legislation it favors. The group registers as a PAC with the FEC and then puts money into the PAC coffers. The PAC can collect money from stockholders, members, and other interested parties. It then donates the money to candidates, often after careful research on their issue stands and past voting records. One very important ground rule prevails: All expenditures must be meticulously reported to the FEC. If PACs are corrupting democracy, as many believe, at least they are doing so openly.

Candidates need PACs because high-tech campaigning is expensive. Tightly contested races for the House of Representatives now frequently cost over $1 million; Senate races can easily cost $1 million for television alone. PACs play a major role in paying for expensive campaigns. Thus, there emerges a symbiotic relationship between the PACs and the candidates: Candidates need money, which they insist can be used without compromising their integrity; PACs want access to officeholders, which they insist can be gained without buying votes. Most any lobbyist will tell their clients that politicians will listen to any important interest group but that with a sizable PAC donation they'll listen better.

There is an abundance of PACs willing to help out candidates. There are big PACs, such as the Realtors Political Action Committee and the American Medical Association Political Action Committee. There are little ones, too, representing smaller industries or business associations: EggPAC, FishPAC, FurPAC, LardPAC, and, for the beer distributors, SixPAC.[30] Table 9.1 lists the business, labor, and

TABLE 9.1 The Big-Spending Political Action Committees (PACs) in 2008

According to an analysis of Federal Election Commission data by the Center for Responsive Politics, here are the top five business, labor, and ideological/single-issue PAC contributors to congressional candidates for the 2008 election cycle and the percentage that they gave to Democrats.

BUSINESS	AMOUNT CONTRIBUTED	PERCENTAGE GIVEN TO DEMOCRATS
National Association of Realtors	$4,020,900	58
AT&T	3,108,200	47
American Bankers Association	2,918,143	43
National Beer Wholesalers	2,869,000	53
National Auto Dealers Association	2,860,000	34
LABOR		
International Brotherhood of Electrical Workers	3,344,650	98
International Association of Fire Fighters	2,734,900	77
Operating Engineers Union	2,704,067	87
Laborers Union	2,555,350	92
Airline Pilots Association	2,422,000	85
IDEOLOGICAL/SINGLE ISSUE		
Human Rights Campaign	1,084,183	95
National Rifle Association	1,054,462	22
US–Cuba Democracy	760,500	59
National Committee to Save Social Security	458,266	95
KidsPAC	447,500	100

Source: Center for Responsive Politics.

ideological PACs that gave the most money to congressional candidates in 2008 and shows which party each favored.

Critics of the PAC system worry that all this money leads to PAC control over what the winners do once in office. Archibald Cox and Fred Wertheimer write that the role of PACs in campaign finance "is robbing our nation of its democratic ideals and giving us a government of leaders beholden to the monied interests who make their election possible."[31] On some issues, it seems clear that PAC money has made a difference. The Federal Trade Commission (FTC), for example, once passed a regulation requiring that car dealers list known mechanical defects on the window stickers of used cars. The National Association of Automobile Dealers quickly became one of the largest donors to congressional incumbents. Soon afterward, 216 representatives cosponsored a House resolution nullifying the FTC regulation. Of these House members, 186 had been aided by the auto dealers' PAC.[32]

It is questionable, however, whether such examples are the exception or the rule. Most PACs give money to candidates who agree with them in the first place. For instance, labor PACs will not waste their money trying to influence members of Congress who have consistently opposed raising the minimum wage. Frank Sorauf's careful review of the subject concludes that "there simply are no data in the systematic studies that would support the popular assertions about the 'buying' of the Congress or about any other massive influence of money on the legislative process."[33]

The impact of PAC money on presidents is even more doubtful. A small contribution from any one PAC is not likely to turn a presidential candidate's head, given the vast sums of money that are involved in running for president. Although John McCain and Hillary Clinton each accepted $1.4 million in PAC contributions for their primary campaigns in 2008, this amounted to less than one percent of their fund-raising totals. And Barack Obama declined to accept any PAC contributions to his presidential campaign.

Money matters in campaigns and sometimes also during legislative votes. Although the influence of PACs may be exaggerated, the high cost of running for office ensures their continuing major role in the campaign process.

WHY IT MATTERS

Money and Elections

As the old saying goes, "Money is the mother's milk of politics." The amount of money raised is one concrete indicator of support before the first votes are cast, and is often used by the media to judge who the leading candidates are. In addition, money provides a campaign with the ability to hire sufficient staff and advertising time to get its message out.

Party leaders often spend substantial time helping their party's candidates raise money. Here, Vice President Biden can be seen appearing at a fund-raising event for Senator Blanche Lincoln of Arkansas. Despite the help of Biden and other Democratic leaders in raising ample funds for her reelection bid, she was defeated in November 2010 by Republican John Boozman.

Are Campaigns Too Expensive?

The Center for Responsive Politics estimated in 2008 that the contests for the presidency and Congress cost over $5 billion.[34] This seems like a tremendous amount of money. Yet American elections cost, per person, about as much as a DVD movie. Bradley Smith, who served as a commissioner on the FEC, writes that the proportion of the nation's gross domestic product spent on political activity is a mere .05 percent.[35] What bothers politicians most about the rising costs of high-tech campaigning is that fund-raising takes up so much of their time. Many American officeholders feel that the need for continuous fund-raising distracts them from their jobs as legislators. They look with envy at how politicians in other countries can win major office without worrying about raising huge sums of money (see "America in Perspective: Arlene McCarthy's Election to the European Parliament").

Public financing of congressional campaigns would take care of this problem. Some

AMERICA IN PERSPECTIVE

Arlene McCarthy's Election to the European Parliament

Arlene McCarthy is one of Europe's up-and-coming young politicians. She was first elected to represent England in the European Parliament at the age of 33 in 1994, and since then she has been easily reelected three times. When asked if she could have won a similar election in the United States, she responds with a firm "No—I would never have been able to raise enough money."

A substantial bankroll, however, was not required for Ms. McCarthy to get her start in European politics. All told, she estimates that she spent about $1,600 to get the Labour Party's nomination in her district. Of this, roughly half was spent on new clothes, with the rest going for traveling costs, such as hotels, gasoline, and food. No one contributed any money to support her campaign for the nomination, and she never felt this was necessary. The party sent out information about the candidates to the voters who would decide the nomination, and the candidates were forbidden from sending out anything else. Only 4,500 dues-paying members of the party could participate in the nomination process, thus making it possible for Ms. McCarthy to speak personally with many of the activists who ultimately gave her a start in politics. Her major appeal was that she had gained much knowledge about how the European Parliament worked during her service as a staff member there and that she could effectively represent the interests of people back home in England.

About 1,800 voters returned their mail ballot, and Arlene McCarthy finished first among five candidates. The general election loomed only six weeks away when she became the Labour Party's nominee, but the party took charge of her campaign from this point on. The party provided her with about $40,000 in campaign funds, as well as staff and campaign literature. When Labour won a smashing victory across the country, Ms. McCarthy was swept into office and had suddenly gone from being a young staff member to a member of the European Parliament.

The nomination and general election campaign of Arlene McCarthy illustrates several differences between European campaigns and those of the United States. Had she run a similar campaign in the United States, she would have had to raise far more money, appeal to far more people to get her party's nomination, and run a much longer campaign.

QUESTIONS FOR DISCUSSION

- Which type of nomination campaign do you think is best—the wide-open American style or the more limited type of European campaign that Arlene McCarthy had to run?
- Do you think that with the European-style campaign it is easier than in the United States for young people and women like Arlene McCarthy to get started in politics? Why or why not?

Source: Personal interview with Arlene McCarthy, December 12, 1998.

lawmakers support some sort of public financing reform; however, it will be very difficult to get Congress to consent to equal financing for the people who will challenge them for their seats. Incumbents will not readily give up the advantage they have in raising money.

Perhaps the most basic complaint about money and politics is that there may be a direct link between dollars spent and votes received. Few have done more to dispel this charge than political scientist Gary Jacobson. His research has shown that the more congressional incumbents spend, the worse they do.[36] This fact is not as odd as it sounds. It simply means that incumbents who face a tough opponent must raise more money to meet the challenge. When a challenger is not a serious threat, as they all too often are not, incumbents can afford to campaign cheaply.

More important than having "more" money is having "enough" money. Herbert Alexander calls this "the doctrine of sufficiency." As he writes, "Enough money must be spent to get a message across to compete effectively but outspending one's opponent is not always necessary—even an incumbent with a massive ratio of higher spending."[37] One case in point is that of the late Paul Wellstone, a previously obscure political science professor who beat an incumbent senator in 1990 despite being outspent by 5 to 1.[38] In 2010, billionaire Meg Whitman spent over $140 million of her own money in her bid for Governor of California but was soundly defeated by Jerry Brown, whose campaign had about $100 million less to spend.

9.4 Determine why campaigns have an important yet limited impact on election outcomes.

The Impact of Campaigns

Almost all politicians presume that a good campaign is the key to victory. Many political scientists, however, question the importance of campaigns. Reviewing the evidence, Dan Nimmo concluded, "Political campaigns are less crucial in elections than most politicians believe."[39] For years, researchers studying campaigns have stressed that campaigns have three effects on voters: reinforcement, activation, and conversion. Campaigns can reinforce voters' preferences for candidates; they can activate voters, getting them to contribute money or ring doorbells as opposed to merely voting; and they can convert, changing voters' minds.

Over half a century of research on political campaigns leads to a single message: Campaigns mostly reinforce and activate; only rarely do they convert. The evidence on the impact of campaigns points clearly to the conclusion that the best-laid plans of campaign managers change very few votes. Given the billions of dollars spent on political campaigns, it may be surprising to find that they do not have a great effect. Several factors tend to weaken campaigns' impact on voters:

selective perception
The phenomenon that people's beliefs often guide what they pay the most attention to and how they interpret events.

- Most people pay relatively little attention to campaigns in the first place. Moreover, people have a remarkable capacity for **selective perception**—paying most attention to things they already agree with and interpreting events according to their own predispositions.
- Long-term factors, such as party identification, influence voting behavior regardless of what happens in the campaign.
- Incumbents start with a substantial advantage in terms of name recognition and a track record.

Such findings do not mean, of course, that campaigns never change voters' minds or that converting a small percentage is unimportant. Hillygus and Shields' careful analysis of survey data finds that a substantial number of voters are persuadable because they disagree with their preferred candidate on at least one issue (for example, pro-choice Republicans). They demonstrate how politicians use what are known as "wedge" issues—issues on which the other party's coalition is divided—to attempt to draw supporters from the opponent's camp into their own.[40] In tight races, a good campaign that targets specific constituencies for persuasion can make the difference between winning and losing.

9.5 Assess the advantages and disadvantages of having a long presidential campaign.

Understanding Nominations and Campaigns

Throughout the history of American politics, election campaigns have become longer and longer as the system has become increasingly open to public participation. Reformers over the decades have maintained that the solution to the problems of American democracy is yet more democracy—or as John Lennon sang, "Power to the people." In principle, more democracy always sounds better than less, but in practice it is not such a simple issue.

Are Nominations and Campaigns Too Democratic?

If American campaigns are judged solely by how open they are, then certainly the American system must be viewed favorably. In other countries, the process of leadership nomination occurs within a relatively small circle of party elites. Thus, politicians must work their way up through an apprenticeship system. In contrast, America has an entrepreneurial system in which the people play a crucial role at every stage from nomination to election. In this way, party outsiders can get elected in a way virtually unknown outside the United States. By appealing directly to the people, a candidate can emerge from obscurity to win the White House. For example, former one-term Governor Jimmy Carter was scarcely known outside of his home state a year before his election to the presidency. After serving a dozen years as governor of Arkansas, Bill Clinton was only in a slightly better position than Carter in terms of name recognition when he announced his first campaign for the presidency in 1991. In this sense, the chance to win high office is open to almost any highly skilled politician with even a small electoral base.

There is a price to be paid for all this openness, however. The process of selecting American leaders is a long and convoluted one that has little downtime before it revs up all over again. Barack Obama had scarcely been sworn into office when potential Republican candidates for 2012 started to schedule visits to Iowa and New Hampshire. Some analysts have even called the American electoral process "the permanent campaign."[41] Many wonder whether people would pay more attention to politics if it did not ask so much of them. Given so much democratic opportunity, many Americans are simply overwhelmed by the process and stay on the sidelines. Similarly, the burdens of

A POINT TO PONDER

With changes in the nominating process and with the rise of the expensive, high-tech media campaign, the road to the presidency has become ever more long and winding.

What are the pros and cons of such presidential campaigns? Do you think such long, hard-fought campaigns are really necessary to fully test presidential aspirants?

the modern campaign can discourage good candidates from throwing their hats into the ring. One of the most worrisome burdens that candidates face is amassing a sufficient campaign treasury. The system may be open, but it requires a lot of fund-raising to be able to take one's case to the people.

Today's campaigns clearly promote individualism in American politics. The current system of running for office has been labeled by Wattenberg the "candidate-centered age."[42] It allows for politicians to decide on their own to run, to raise their own campaign funds, to build their own personal organizations, and to make promises about how they specifically will act in office. The American campaign game is one of individual candidates, by individual candidates, and for individual candidates.

Do Big Campaigns Lead to an Increased Scope of Government?

Today's big campaigns involve much more communication between candidates and voters than America's Founders ever could have imagined. In their view, the presidency was to be an office responsible for seeing to the public interest as a whole. They wished to avoid "a contest in which the candidates would have to pose as 'friends' of the people or make specific policy commitments."[43] Thus, the Founders would probably be horrified by the modern practice in which candidates make numerous promises during nomination and election campaigns.

States are the key battlegrounds of presidential campaigns, and candidates must tailor their appeals to the particular interests of each major state. When in Iowa, for instance, candidates typically promise to keep agricultural subsidies high and support the ethanol program; in New York, to help big cities with federal programs; and in Texas, to help the oil and gas industry. To secure votes from each region of the country, candidates end up supporting a variety of local interests. Promises mount as the campaign goes on, and these promises usually add up to new government programs and money. The way modern campaigns are conducted is thus one of many reasons why politicians usually find it easier to promise, at least, that government will do more. Furthermore, with their finger constantly to the wind assessing all the different political crosscurrents, it is hard for politicians to promise that the scope of government will be limited through specific cuts.

Summary

9.1 Evaluate the fairness of our current system of presidential primaries and caucuses.

The current system of presidential primaries and caucuses, which leads to nomination at national party conventions, allows tens of millions of Americans to participate in the selection of the Democratic and Republican parties' nominees for president. The system gives some states much greater influence than others. In particular, Iowa, with the first caucus, and New Hampshire, with the first primary, have disproportionate power stemming from the massive media attention devoted to these early contests and the momentum generated by winning them. Some other common criticisms of the nomination process are that money plays too big a role, that turnout rates are lower than in the general election, and that the mass media exercises too much power in determining which candidates are considered to be serious contenders.

9.2 Explain the key objectives of any political campaign.

Political campaigns involve the allocation of scarce resources of time, money, and energy to achieve the goal of winning elections for political office—an allocation that requires effective organization and effective use of high-tech media. One of the most important goals of any campaign is simply to get attention. Campaigns seek to control the political agenda, getting the media and the public to focus on the issues that they wish to emphasize.

9.3 Outline how fund-raising for federal offices is regulated by campaign finance laws.

Federal election law restricts direct contributions to federal campaigns to $2,400 for individuals and $5,000 for political action committees (PACs). In the presidential nomination process, federal matching funds are available to candidates who agree to limit their overall spending. Because major candidates can now raise such large sums overall, they are now reluctant to accept matching funds. In the general election for president, a grant of approximately $85 million is available to each party nominee to finance their entire campaign; candidates who turn down the grant are free to raise an unlimited total in increments equal or less than the maximum contribution limit. The McCain-Feingold Act eliminated unlimited soft money contributions to the political parties. It also sought to restrict corporations and unions from electioneering during the last two months of a campaign, but the Supreme Court ruled that this was an unconstitutional restriction on free speech in the 2010 case of *Citizens United v. Federal Election Commission.*

9.4 Determine why campaigns have an important yet limited impact on election outcomes.

In general, politicians tend to overestimate the impact of campaigns; political scientists have found that campaigning serves primarily to reinforce citizens' views and to activate voters rather than to change views. Factors such as selective perception, party identification, and the incumbency advantage tend to weaken the ability of campaigns to influence voters' decisions.

9.5 Assess the advantages and disadvantages of having a long presidential campaign.

American election campaigns are easily the most open and democratic in the world—some say too open. They are also extraordinarily long, perhaps excessively burdening politicians and voters and leading politicians to make many promises that increase the scope of government. On the other hand, long campaigns give little-known candidates a chance to emerge and provide a strenuous test for all the candidates.

Chapter Test

9.1 Evaluate the fairness of our current system of presidential primaries and caucuses.

1. A key difference between caucuses and primaries is that
   a. Early caucuses are more important than early primaries
   b. The media cover early caucuses more than early primaries
   c. Caucuses are worth more delegates than primaries
   d. Participation in caucuses is much lower than the level of turnout for primaries
   e. Caucus participants are more representative of the national electorate than are voters in primaries

2. Superdelegates have traditionally played an important role in the presidential nomination process.

   True______ False______

3. The New Hampshire primary is especially important because it helps whittle down the number of viable candidates for the primaries that follow it.

   True______ False______

4. How has the competition for delegates changed over time? Specifically, how have the roles of party leaders and conventions changed and what impact have primaries had on the nomination of presidents? Be sure to explain the impact of the McGovern-Fraser Commission.

5. Evaluate today's primary and caucus system. What are some of the major criticisms of the current system? In your opinion, is the current system the best way to pick a president? If so, why? If not, what alternatives might be better?

9.2 Explain the key objectives of any political campaign.

6. Why is a campaign manager important to a well-organized campaign?
   a. To help ensure the candidate's compliance with campaign finance laws
   b. To assist the candidate in responding to reporters' questions
   c. To tell the candidate how he or she is viewed by voters
   d. To feed the candidate the information needed to keep up with events
   e. To keep the candidate from getting bogged down in organizational details

7. Candidates today find it relatively easy to obtain the free media attention they seek.

   True______ False______

8. Imagine that you are a campaign manager and want to create a winning image for your client. What qualities would you emphasize and how would you go about organizing your campaign to ensure that voters embrace the image you have painted of your client?

9.3 Outline how fund-raising for federal offices is regulated by campaign finance laws.

9. According to the textbook, the main benefit of campaign finance laws has been to
   a. Make American political campaigns more open and honest
   b. Limit spending by candidates
   c. Limit spending by corporations
   d. Limit unregulated money spent in campaigns
   e. Limit the proliferation of political action committees

10. So-called 527 groups spend millions of unrestricted dollars on political campaigns.

    True______ False______

11. If you had the power to change some aspect of campaign finance law and practice, which aspect of it would you change, how would you change it, and why? What would you keep the same, and why?

12. In your opinion, does money buy victory for political candidates? Why or why not?

9.4 Determine why campaigns have an important yet limited impact on election outcomes.

13. Research concerning the impact that political campaigns have on voters shows that campaigns
    a. Reinforce preferences, activate voters, and convert voters
    b. Reinforce preferences, but rarely activate or convert voters
    c. Reinforce preferences and activate voters, but rarely convert voters
    d. Convert voters, but rarely reinforce preferences or activate voters
    e. Activate voters, but rarely reinforce preferences or convert voters

14. What are the primary factors that weaken the impact of campaigns on voters? Based on your understanding of these factors, which do you think is most important and why?

9.5 Assess the advantages and disadvantages of having a long presidential campaign.

15. What are the advantages and disadvantages of having a long presidential campaign? Specifically, does a long presidential campaign ask too much of American citizens who wish to participate in the democratic process? Explain your answer.

16. According to the Founders, the presidency was to be an office responsible for seeing to the public interest as a whole. In your opinion, have the current nominating and campaign processes diminished the ability of the president to see to the public interest as a whole? Explain.

PEARSON mypoliscilab Exercises

Apply what you learned in this chapter on MyPoliSciLab.

Read on **mypoliscilab.com**

eText: Chapter 9

Study and **Review** on **mypoliscilab.com**

Pre-Test
Post-Test
Chapter Exam
Flashcards

Watch on **mypoliscilab.com**

Video: Who Are the Superdelegates?
Video: Money in the 2008 Presidential Race
Video: Oprah Fires Up Obama Campaign

Explore on **mypoliscilab.com**

Simulation: You Are a Campaign Manager: Lead Obama to Battleground State Victory
Simulation: You Are a Media Consultant to a Political Candidate
Simulation: You Are a Campaign Manager: McCain Navigates Campaign Financing
Comparative: Comparing Political Campaigns
Timeline: Television and Presidential Campaigns
Visual Literacy: Iowa Caucuses

Key Terms

nomination (254)
campaign strategy (254)
national party convention (255)
McGovern-Fraser Commission (255)
superdelegates (256)
caucus (256)
presidential primaries (257)
frontloading (259)
national primary (261)
regional primaries (261)
party platform (263)
direct mail (264)
Federal Election Campaign Act (268)
Federal Election Commission (268)
Presidential Election Campaign Fund (268)
matching funds (268)
soft money (269)
527 groups (270)
501 groups (270)
political action committees (271)
selective perception (274)

Internet Resources

www.fec.gov
The Federal Election Commission's reports on campaign spending can be found at this site.

www.fundrace.org
This site allows one to look up donations from particular individuals and to map contribution patterns for particular areas.

www.opensecrets.org
The Center for Responsive Politics posts a wealth of analysis about PAC contributions at its site.

http://politicsmagazine.com
Campaigns and Elections magazine posts some of its articles here.

For Further Reading

Bartels, Larry M. ***Presidential Primaries and the Dynamics of Public Choice.*** Princeton, NJ: Princeton University Press, 1988. An excellent analysis of voters' decision-making process in the nominating season.

Bimber, Bruce, and Richard Davis. ***Campaigning Online: The Internet in U.S. Elections.*** New York: Oxford University Press, 2003. An interesting study of how candidates use Web sites and how voters react to them.

Corrado, Anthony, and David B. Magleby, eds. ***Financing the 2008 Election: Assessing Reform.*** Washington, DC: Brookings, 2010. A comprehensive set of readings that analyze how campaign finance and spending shaped the presidential and congressional races of 2008.

Franz, Michael M., et al. ***Campaign Advertising and American Democracy.*** Philadelphia: Temple University Press, 2008. A thorough examination of the role of campaign ads in recent elections, arguing that political ads are beneficial to the working of democracy in America.

Hillygus, D. Sunshine, and Todd G. Shields. ***The Persuadable Voter: Wedge Issues in Presidential Campaigns.*** Princeton, NJ: Princeton University Press, 2008. An examination of how campaigns use issues to woo swing voters.

Hull, Christopher C. ***Grassroots Rules: How the Iowa Caucus Helps Elect American Presidents.*** Stanford, CA: Stanford University Press, 2008. A detailed study of the impact of the Iowa caucus from 1976 to 2004.

Institute of Politics, ed. ***Campaign for President: The Managers Look at 2008.*** Lanham, MD: Rowman & Littlefield, 2009. The campaign managers for all the 2008 presidential candidates gathered at Harvard to discuss their experiences in the primaries and the general election.

King, Anthony. ***Running Scared.*** New York: Free Press, 1997. King argues that American politicians campaign too much and govern too little.

Patterson, Thomas E. ***Out of Order.*** New York: Knopf, 1993. A classic review of the role of the media in elections.

Semiatin, Richard J. ***Campaigns on the Cutting Edge.*** Washington, DC: Congressional Quarterly Press, 2008. A provocative set of articles on how campaigns are taking advantage of innovative new technologies.

Smith, Bradley A. ***Unfree Speech: The Folly of Campaign Finance Reform.*** Princeton, NJ: Princeton University Press, 2001. A provocative book that argues that most regulations concerning donations to political campaigns should be eliminated.

Smith, Steven S., and Melanie J. Springer. ***Reforming the Presidential Nomination Process.*** Washington, DC: Brookings Institution Press, 2009. A good set of current readings on the presidential nomination process.

Chapter 10

Elections and Voting Behavior

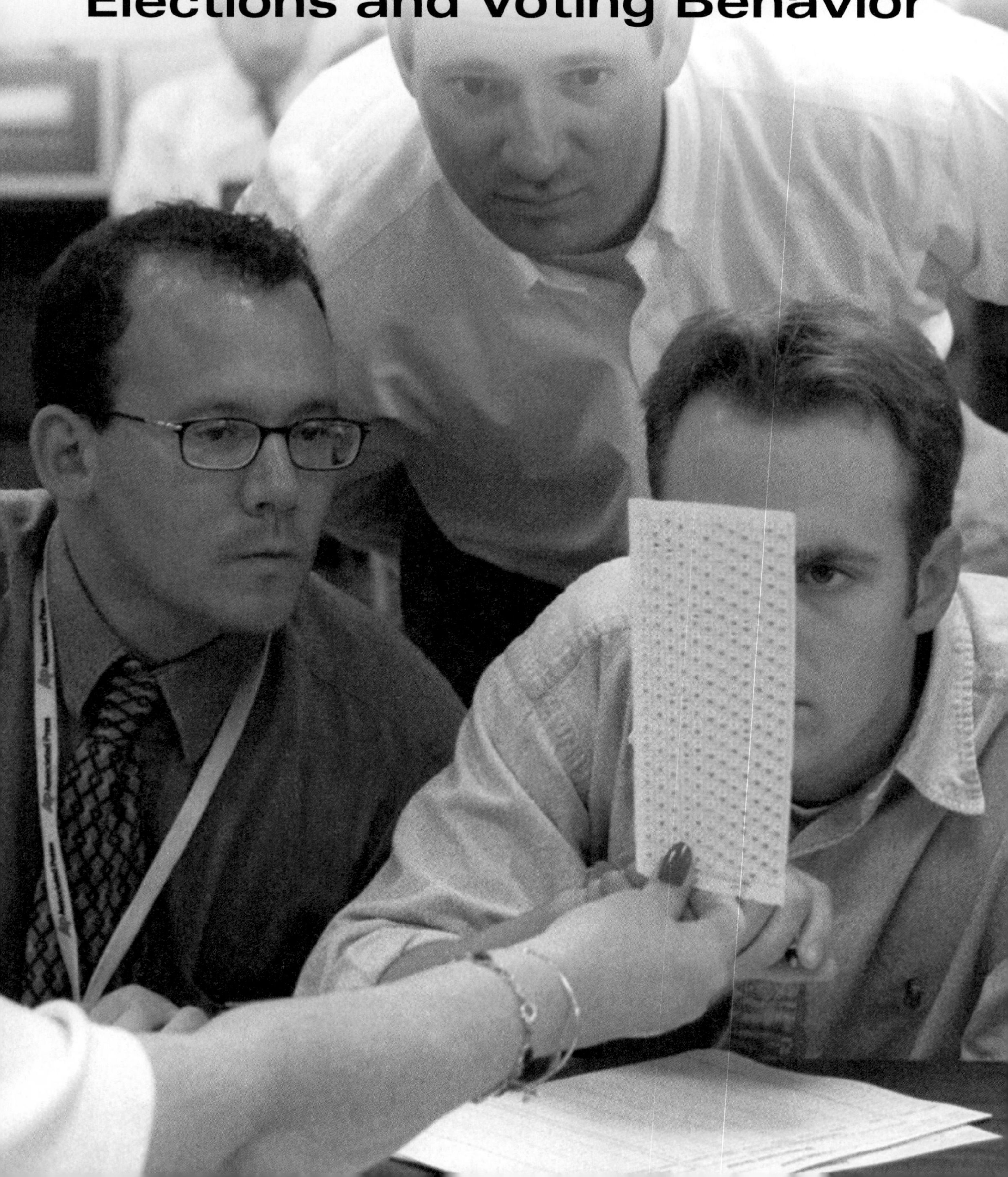

Learning Objectives

10.1 Distinguish the types of elections in the United States.

10.2 Trace the evolution of the American electoral process from 1800 to the present.

10.3 Identify the factors that influence whether people vote or not.

10.4 Assess the impact of party identification, candidate evaluations, and policy opinions on voting behavior.

10.5 Evaluate the fairness of the Electoral College system for choosing the president.

10.6 Assess the extent to which elections make government officials pay attention to what voters want.

POLITICS IN ACTION: THE CHALLENGE OF FIGURING OUT THE MEANING OF A VOTE

One of the most memorable images of the 2000 presidential election was the regularly repeated scene of Florida election officials holding up a ballot to the light to try to determine whether a punch was present. When Joseph Harris, professor of political science at the University of California at Berkeley, invented the first punch-card voting system in the early 1960s, it was hailed as a great technological innovation, enabling unprecedented speed in vote counting. But although the system was also reputed to be more accurate than previous methods of voting, by 2000 the punch cards had become antiquated technology compared to modern Scantron and touch-screen methods. Embarrassed election officials were quick to admit that they had long been aware of the problems with punch-card voting systems. Such systems theoretically worked fine as long as people followed the directions—placing the cards in the machines properly and punching the chads through the card completely. But as we saw in Florida in 2000, many people did not follow the instructions. With the election coming down to just hundreds of votes, the question became whether election officials could accurately and fairly ascertain the intent of voters whose ballots had not been properly punched. Should a vote be counted if one, two, or three of the four corners of the chad had been perforated? How about if only a dimple was visible on the chad, indicating that the voter had at least touched the stylus to the ballot at that point? Election officials struggled to do the best they could by holding them up to the light and examining them carefully. Some applauded the process as a valiant attempt to make sure every vote was counted, whereas others criticized officials for trying to "divine the intent of the voter."

Scholars who analyze elections have a seemingly easier job—figuring out the meaning of the vote totals once they have been counted. But as Walter Lippmann, one of the most astute observers of American politics, once remarked,

> *We call an election an expression of the popular will. But is it? We go into a polling booth and mark a cross on a piece of paper for one of two, or perhaps three or four names. Have we expressed our thoughts on the public policy of the United States? Presumably we have a number of thoughts on this and that with many buts and ifs and ors. Surely the cross on a piece of paper does not express them.*[1]

This chapter will discuss why it is difficult for elections to be a faithful mechanism for expressing the public's desires concerning what government should do. The fact that only about 60 percent of citizens of voting age participate is one reason. Another is that candidates sometimes obscure the issues. As you read this chapter, the crucial question to consider is: Are the people represented by elections in America?

Chapter **OUTLINE**

Elections serve a critical function in American society. They *institutionalize* political activity, making it possible for most political participation to be channeled through the electoral process rather than bubbling up through demonstrations, riots, or revolutions. Elections provide *regular access to political power*, so that leaders can be replaced without being overthrown. This is possible because elections have **legitimacy** in the eyes of the American people; that is, they are almost universally accepted as a fair and free method of selecting political leaders. Furthermore, by choosing who is to lead the country, the people—if they make their choices carefully—can also guide the policy direction of the government.

legitimacy
A characterization of elections by political scientists meaning that they are almost universally accepted as a fair and free method of selecting political leaders. When legitimacy is high, as in the United States, even the losers accept the results peacefully.

This chapter will give you a perspective on how elections function in the American system as well as on how voters generally behave—in terms of both how they decide whether to vote and how those who do vote make their choices. The focus here is primarily on presidential elections; Chapter 12 on Congress will examine congressional elections in detail.

10.1 Distinguish the types of elections in the United States.

How American Elections Work

The United States has three general kinds of elections: primary elections, in which voters select party nominees; general elections, which are contested between the nominees of the parties; and elections on specific policy questions, in which voters engage in making or ratifying legislation. Primary elections were covered in the previous chapter, and general elections will be the main topic of this chapter. But first we briefly examine elections that decide policy questions, because such contests are becoming increasingly important in many states.

referendum
A state-level method of direct legislation that gives voters a chance to approve or disapprove proposed legislation or a proposed constitutional amendment.

initiative petition
A process permitted in some states whereby voters may put proposed changes in the state law to a vote if sufficient signatures are obtained on petitions.

At present, there is no constitutional provision for specific policy questions to be decided by a nationwide vote. It is certainly conceivable that this may come to pass sometime in the twenty-first century,[2] as a number of European democracies have recently started to put questions of great importance—such as joining the European Monetary Union—to a national vote. Procedures allowing the public to pass legislation directly have been in effect for quite some time in many American states. There are two methods for getting items on a state ballot. The first is a **referendum**, whereby voters are given the chance to approve or disapprove some legislative act, bond issue, or constitutional amendment proposed by the legislature. The second method is an **initiative petition**, which typically requires citizens proposing a law to gain signatures equal to 10 percent of the number of voters in the previous election.

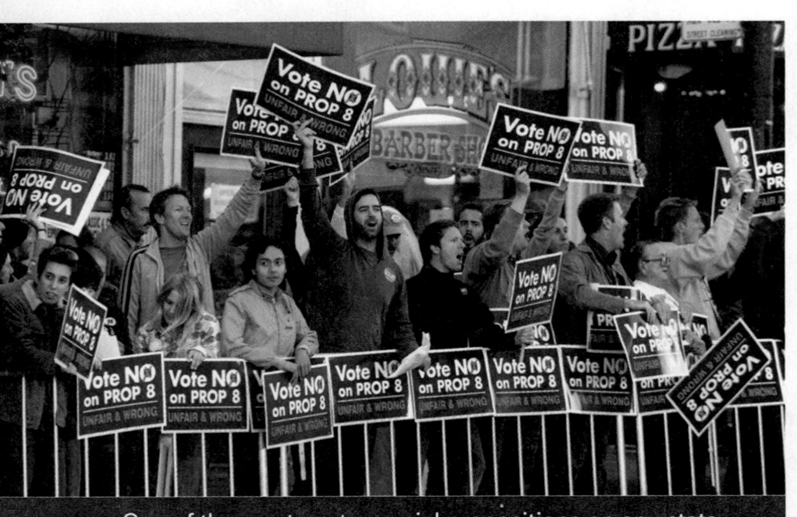

One of the most controversial propositions on any state ballot in 2008 was California's Proposition 8 regarding the state's definition of marriage. Over $75 million was spent by the two sides of the issue. In the end, the effort to outlaw gay marriage passed by a narrow margin.

Initiative petitions are often portrayed as lawmaking from the ground up, with the people taking charge of the political agenda and forcing decisions on issues on which state legislatures have failed to act. Twenty-four states, mostly in the West, currently enable voters to propose and decide legislation through an initiative petition. The most famous example is California's Proposition 13, which in 1978 put a limit on the rise in property taxes in California. Although ballot initiatives require the support of a majority of voters, Daniel Smith argues that they often stem, more than anything, from the actions of a dedicated political entrepreneur.[3] For example, he writes that Barbara Anderson—a housewife without any previous political experience—spearheaded a Massachusetts initiative that is considered one of the most significant tax-cutting measures enacted in any state. None of Smith's examples of political entrepreneurs who successfully used the initiative process were either well known or wealthy. These case studies of people who have spearheaded major initiative campaigns demonstrate how ordinary individuals can sometimes change the course of public policy.

In the November 2010 elections, many state ballot questions were voted on. By a 54-46 margin, California voters rejected a measure that would have decriminalized the possession of up to an ounce of marijuana. In Oklahoma, voters approved a measure mandating all official state actions be conducted in English. Voters in Arkansas overwhelmingly approved an amendment to the state constitution establishing the right to hunt and fish. Measures guaranteeing the right to a secret ballot in union elections were enacted into law in Arizona, South Carolina, South Dakota, and Utah. And in Washington state, voters rejected an initiative that would have created a state income tax.

A Tale of Three Elections

10.2 Trace the evolution of the American electoral process from 1800 to the present.

Times change, and so do elections. A glance at three American elections—1800, 1896, and 2008—should give you a good idea of how elections have changed over time.

1800: The First Electoral Transition of Power

By current standards, the 1800 election was not much of an election at all. There were no primaries, no nominating conventions, no candidate speeches, and no entourage of reporters. Both incumbent President John Adams and challenger Thomas Jefferson were nominated by their parties' elected representatives in Congress—Adams by Federalists and Jefferson by Democratic-Republicans. Once nominated, the candidates sat back and let their state and local organizations promote their cause. Communication and travel were too slow for candidates to get their message across themselves. Besides, campaigning was considered below the dignity of the presidential office.

At that time, however, newspapers were little concerned with dignity—or honesty for that matter. Most were rabidly partisan and did all they could to run down the opposition's candidate. Jefferson was regularly denounced as a Bible-burning atheist, the father of mulatto children (much later shown to be probably true based on DNA tests), and a mad scientist. Adams, on the other hand, was said to be a monarchist "whose grand object was to destroy every man who differed from his opinions."[4]

The focus of the campaign was not on voters but rather on the state legislatures, which had the responsibility for choosing members of the Electoral College. When the dust settled, the Jeffersonians had won a slim victory in terms of electoral votes; however, they had also committed a troubling error. In the original constitutional system, each elector cast two ballots, and the top vote getter was named president and the runner-up, vice president.[5] In 1796, Jefferson had become Adams's vice president by virtue of finishing second. Not wanting Adams to be his vice president, Jefferson made sure that all his electors also voted for his vice-presidential choice—Aaron Burr of New York. The problem was that when each and every one of them did so, Jefferson and Burr ended up tied for first. This meant that the Federalist-controlled House of Representatives would have to decide between the two Democratic-Republican candidates. Burr saw the chance to steal the presidency from Jefferson by cutting a deal with the Federalists, but his efforts failed. After 35 indecisive ballots in the House, the Federalists finally threw their support behind Jefferson. On March 4, 1801, the transition from Adams to Jefferson marked the first peaceful transfer of power between parties via the electoral process in world history.

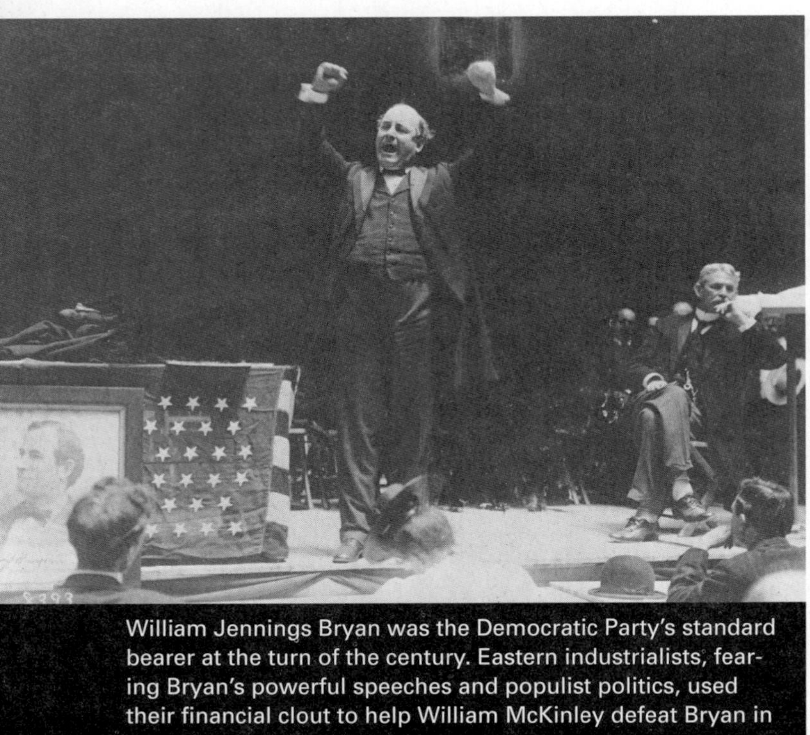

William Jennings Bryan was the Democratic Party's standard bearer at the turn of the century. Eastern industrialists, fearing Bryan's powerful speeches and populist politics, used their financial clout to help William McKinley defeat Bryan in the 1896 presidential election.

1896: A Bitter Fight Over Economic Interests

Nearly a century later the election of 1896 was largely fought over economics. By then national nominating conventions had become well established, and Republicans, meeting in St. Louis for their convention, nominated former Congressman William McKinley. The Republicans' major issues were support for the gold standard and high tariffs. The gold standard linked money to this scarce precious metal so that debtors never got a break from inflation. Tariffs protected capitalists and their workers from foreign competition. Perhaps most importantly, they were able to run against a very unpopular retiring president—Democrat Grover Cleveland—who was widely blamed for the severe economic downturn of 1893–1896 that the country was suffering through.

The Democrats met in Chicago's sticky July heat. They had an issue—unlimited coinage of silver—but no clear front-runner. The high point of the Chicago convention was a speech by 36-year-old William Jennings Bryan of Nebraska, who proclaimed the virtues of the silver rather than the gold standard. Bryan went on to win the nomination on the fifth ballot and to become the youngest nominee of a major party in American history.

The flamboyant Bryan broke with tradition and took to the stump in person. He gave 600 speeches as his campaign train traveled through 26 states, logging 18,000 miles. Debtors and silver miners were especially attracted to Bryan's pitch for cheap silver money. In contrast, the serene McKinley was advised to sit home in Ohio and run a front-porch campaign. He did, and he managed to label the Democrats as the party of economic depression ("In God We Trust, with Bryan We Bust").

Bryan won the oratory, but McKinley won the election. Eastern manufacturers contributed a small fortune to the Republicans. Only white Southerners, Westerners in the silver-producing states, and rural debtors lined up behind the Democrats. The Republicans won overwhelmingly in the industrial Northeast and Midwest and became firmly entrenched as the nation's majority party for the next several decades. McKinley triumphed by a margin of 271 to 176 in the Electoral College. Nearly 80 percent of the eligible electorate voted in one of the highest turnouts ever.

2008: An Election About Change

Late in the 2008 presidential campaign, Barack Obama told a crowd of supporters in Detroit, "You couldn't have written a novel with all the crazy stuff that has happened in this election." Indeed, Obama's rise from an obscure Illinois state senator in 2004 to the nation's first successful African American candidate for president in 2008 was truly incredible.

Like the great nineteenth-century orator William Jennings Bryan, Barack Obama was catapulted to national prominence as the result of a debut speech that electrified the Democratic Convention. In his nationally televised keynote address at the 2004 Democratic Convention, Obama told listeners:

> There is not a liberal America and a conservative America—there is the United States of America. There is not a Black America and a White America and Latino America and Asian America—there is the United States of America. The pundits like to slice-and-dice our country into Red States and Blue States; Red States for Republicans, Blue States for Democrats. But I've got news for them, too. We worship an "awesome God" in the Blue States, and we don't like federal agents poking

> around in our libraries in the Red States. We coach Little League in the Blue States and yes, we've got some gay friends in the Red States. There are patriots who opposed the war in Iraq and there are patriots who supported the war in Iraq. We are one people, all of us pledging allegiance to the stars and stripes, all of us defending the United States of America.

Newsstands from New York to Seattle quickly sold out of newspapers declaring Barack Obama the winner and the nation's first African American president. Many jubilant customers reportedly picked up multiple copies as keepsakes.

With this message of unity and multiculturalism, Obama was viewed as a rising star and potential presidential candidate from his first day as a U.S. senator in 2005. Within two years he had two books on the best-seller list—an autobiography titled *Dreams From My Father* and a collection of policy proposals titled *The Audacity of Hope*.

By the time Obama declared his presidential candidacy in February 2007, he had built a national constituency and established himself as the primary alternative to the front-runner, Senator Hillary Clinton. On a cold day in Springfield, Illinois, he proclaimed, "I recognize there is a certain presumptuousness—a certain audacity—to this announcement. I know I haven't spent a lot of time learning the ways of Washington. But I've been there long enough to know that the ways of Washington must change." Indeed, in the Democratic primaries his call for change resonated slightly more effectively than Clinton's emphasis on experience. With strong support from young people, the highly educated, and African Americans, Obama eked out one of the closest nomination victories ever, as he and Senator Clinton contested all 50 states from January to June.

In contrast, the Republican presidential nomination was wrapped up sooner and more decisively by Senator John McCain. Nevertheless, he too seemed to be an improbable nominee, having long been viewed with suspicion by the party's conservative base. But in 2008, when even many Republicans wanted change, his reputation as a maverick (someone who thinks independently and doesn't always toe the party line) had special appeal. And when he surprised everyone with his historic choice of the first Republican woman to be nominated for vice president—Alaska's little-known Governor Sarah Palin—he energized the party's base and took a short-lived lead in the polls.

As the fall campaign began, the race seemed to be shaping up as a close battle between Obama's perceived advantages on economic issues and personal intelligence versus McCain's perceived advantages on foreign policy issues and political experience. But then the nation's agenda changed dramatically as a credit crisis rocked the financial markets in late September. McCain took an aggressive approach, even suspending his campaign in order to try to stitch together a congressional coalition to address the crisis. Obama, on the other hand, approached the situation coolly, noting that the campaign should go on, as presidents have to work on multiple things all the time. When McCain's fellow Republicans in the House of Representatives voted against the financial bailout bill that both candidates had endorsed, his leadership image clearly suffered. Furthermore, the intense focus on the economy for the rest of the campaign provided Obama with opportunities to emphasize his popular plans for a middle-class tax cut, extension of health care coverage, and programs to support education.

Obama also gained ground on McCain as voters compared the choices for vice president. Although Sarah Palin proved to be an effective stump speaker, in the judgment of many observers, her one-on-one interviews with the anchors of ABC and CBS News revealed apparent gaps in her knowledge of policies. By Election Day, exit polls found that just 38 percent of voters thought that she was qualified to assume the presidency compared to 66 percent for Democratic vice presidential nominee Joe Biden.

Most importantly, Obama was able to inextricably link McCain to President George W. Bush, whose 70 percent disapproval approval rating was the worst ever recorded. In their final televised debate, McCain looked right at Obama and said, "I'm not George Bush. If you wanted to run against President Bush, you should have run four years ago." In turn, the Obama campaign responded with a powerful ad that tied the two together by showing a clip in which McCain acknowledged he had voted with President Bush 90 percent of the time.

The people's verdict in 2008, just as in 1800 and 1896, was that it was time for a change in Washington. Obama carried 53 percent of the popular vote, compared to 46 percent for McCain and 1 percent for third party candidates. As shown in Figure 10.1, this translated into a 365–173 margin in the Electoral College, with the Democrats winning nine states they had lost in 2004—Florida, Ohio, Indiana, Iowa, New Mexico, Colorado, Nevada, North Carolina, and Virginia.

In 2008, as in all election years, voters faced two key choices: whether and how to vote. The following sections will investigate how voters make these choices.

FIGURE 10.1 The Electoral College Results for 2004 and 2008

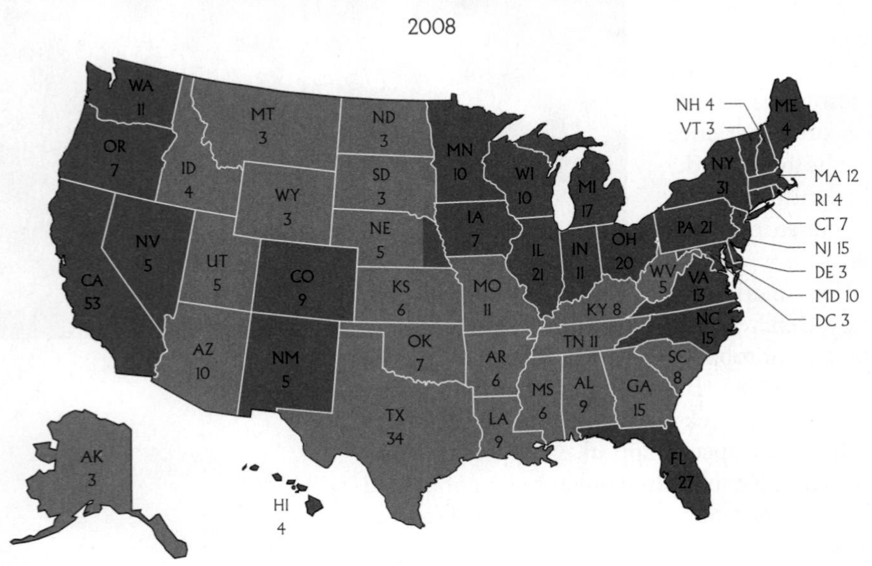

These two maps show the number of votes each state had in the Electoral College in 2004 and 2008 and which states were carried by the Democrats (BLUE) and Republicans (RED).

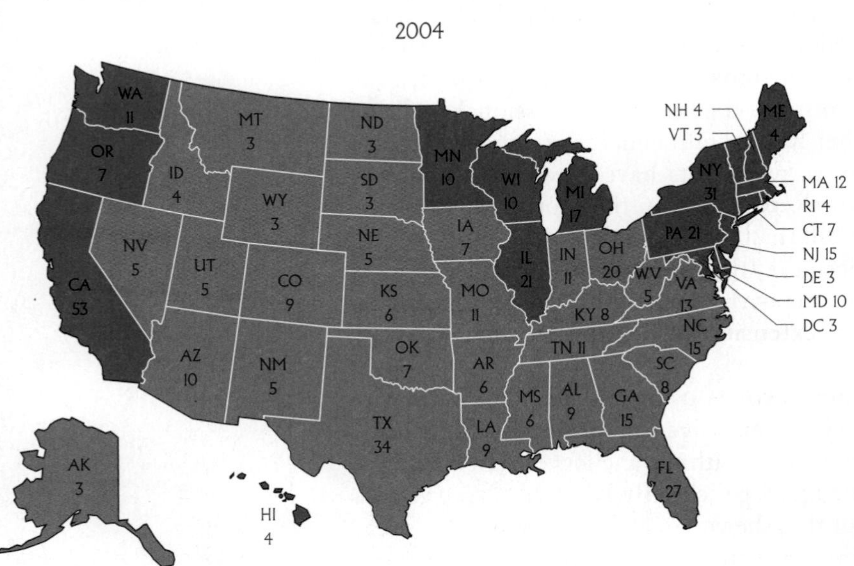

Whether to Vote: A Citizen's First Choice

10.3 Identify the factors that influence whether people vote or not.

Over two centuries of American electoral history, federal laws have greatly expanded **suffrage**—the right to vote. In the election of 1800, only property-owning white males over the age of 21 were typically allowed to vote. Now virtually everyone over the age of 18—male or female, white or nonwhite, rich or poor—has the right to vote. (For more on the expansion of suffrage, see Chapter 5.) The two major exceptions concern noncitizens and convicted criminals. No state currently permits residents who are not citizens to vote. Some immigrant groups feel that this ought to be changed at least at the local level. State law varies widely when it comes to crime and voting: Virtually all states deny prisoners the right to vote, about half extend the ban to people on parole, and 10 states impose a lifetime ban on convicted felons.

suffrage
The legal right to vote, in the United States gradually extended to virtually all citizens over the age of 18.

Interestingly, as the right to vote has been extended, proportionately fewer of those eligible have chosen to exercise that right. In the past 120 years, the 80 percent turnout in the 1896 election was the high point of electoral participation. In 2008, 61.7 percent of adult citizens voted in the presidential election.

Deciding Whether to Vote

Realistically, when over 125 million people vote in a presidential election, as they did in 2008, the chance of one vote affecting the outcome is very, very slight. Once in a while, of course, an election is decided by a small number of votes, as occurred in Florida in 2000. It is more likely, however, that you will be struck by lightning than participate in an election decided by a single vote.

political efficacy
The belief that one's **political participation** really matters—that one's vote can actually make a difference.

Not only does your vote probably not make much difference to the outcome, but voting is somewhat costly. You have to spend some of your valuable time becoming informed, making up your mind, and getting to the polls. If you carefully calculate your time and energy, you might rationally decide that the costs of voting outweigh the benefits. Indeed, the most frequent response given by nonvoters in the 2008 Census Bureau survey on turnout was that they could not take time off from work or school that day.[6] Some scholars have therefore proposed that one of the easiest ways to increase American turnout levels would be to move Election Day to Saturday or to make it a holiday, as it is in many other countries.[7]

Although civic courses routinely stress that in a democracy every vote matters, elections for public office rarely hinge on a single vote or end up in a tie. When an exception to this general rule occurs, even on the local level, it often draws national media attention. Thus, *The New York Times* and other newspapers covered the story when an election for a seat to the Cave Creek, AZ town council resulted in a 660-660 tie and the winner was decided by a card game presided over by the town judge. The candidate on the right won.

Economist Anthony Downs, in his model of democracy, tries to explain why a rational person would ever bother to vote. He argues that rational people vote if they believe that the policies of one party will bring more benefits than the policies of the other party.[8] Thus, people who see policy differences between the parties are more likely to join the ranks of voters. If you are an environmentalist and you expect the Democrats to pass more environmental legislation than the Republicans, then you have an additional incentive to go to the polls. On the other hand, if you are truly indifferent—that is, if you see no difference whatsoever between the two parties—you may rationally decide to abstain.

Another reason why many people vote is that they have a high sense of **political efficacy**—the belief that ordinary people can influence the government.

A reason often given for low turnout rates is that people do not realize the power of the ballot box.

Do you think this is a major reason why so many people don't vote?

"You mean, like, wow, we can actually get rid of, you know, incumbents with this whatchamacallit?"

Efficacy is measured by asking people to agree or disagree with statements such as, "I don't think public officials care much what people like me think." Those who lack strong feelings of efficacy are being quite rational in staying home on Election Day because they don't think they can make a difference. Yet even some of these people will vote anyway, simply to support democratic government. In this case, people are impelled to vote by a sense of **civic duty**. The benefit from doing one's civic duty is the long-term contribution made toward preserving democracy.

civic duty
The belief that in order to support democratic government, a citizen should vote.

Registering to Vote

Politicians used to say, "Vote early and often." Cases such as 159,000 votes being cast by 147,000 eligible voters in West Virginia in 1888 were not that unusual. Largely to prevent corruption associated with stuffing ballot boxes, around 1900 states adopted **voter registration** laws, which require individuals to first place their name on an electoral roll in order to be allowed to vote. Although these laws have made it more difficult to vote more than once, they have also discouraged some people from voting at all. Voter registration requirements in the United States are, in part, to blame for why Americans are significantly less likely to go to the polls than citizens of other democratic nations (see "America in Perspective: Why Turnout in the United States Is So Low Compared to Turnout in Other Countries").

voter registration
A system adopted by the states that requires voters to register prior to voting. Some states require citizens to register as much as 30 days in advance, whereas others permit Election Day registration.

Registration procedures currently differ from state to state. In sparsely populated North Dakota, there is no registration at all, and in Minnesota, Wisconsin, Iowa, Wyoming, Idaho, Montana, New Hampshire, Maine, and North Carolina, voters can

AMERICA IN PERSPECTIVE

Why Turnout in the United States Is So Low Compared to Turnout in Other Countries

Despite living in a culture that encourages participation, Americans have a woefully low turnout rate compared to citizens of other democracies. The figure below displays the most recent election turnout rates in the United States and a variety of other nations.

There are several reasons given for Americans' abysmally low turnout rate. Probably the one most often cited is the American requirement of voter registration. The governments of many (but not all) other democracies take the responsibility of seeing to it that all their eligible citizens are on the voting lists. In America, the responsibility for registration lies solely with the individual. If we were like the Scandinavian countries, where the government registers every eligible citizen, no doubt our turnout rate would be higher.

A second difference between the United States and other countries is that the American government asks citizens to vote far more often. Whereas the typical European voter may cast two or three ballots in a four-year period, many Americans are faced with a dozen or more separate elections in the space of four years. Furthermore, Americans are expected to vote for a much wider range of political offices. With one elected official for roughly every 500 citizens, and elections held somewhere virtually every week, it is no wonder that it is so difficult to get Americans to the polls. It is probably no coincidence that the one European country that has a lower turnout rate—Switzerland—has also overwhelmed its citizens with voting opportunities, typically asking people to vote three or four times every year.

Third, the stimulus to vote is low in the United States because the choices offered Americans are not as starkly different as in other countries. The United States is quite unusual in that it has always lacked a major left-wing socialist party. When European voters go to the polls, they are deciding on whether their country will be run by parties with socialist goals or by conservative (and in some cases religious) parties. The consequences of their vote for redistribution of income and the scope of government are far greater than the ordinary American voter can imagine.

Finally, the United States is one of the few democracies that still vote mid-week, when most people are working. Article I, Section III of the U.S. Constitution allows Congress to determine the timing of federal elections. Comparative research has shown that countries that hold elections on the weekend have higher turnout.

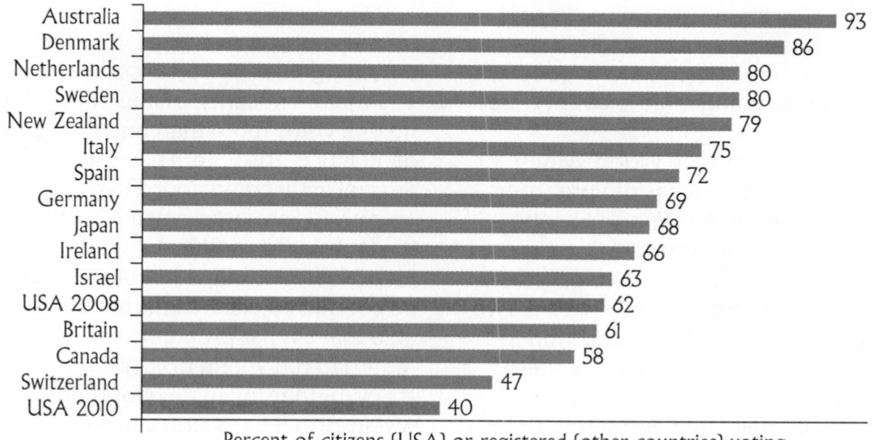

Sources: In all countries except for the United States, official reports of the percentage of registered voters casting valid votes participating. For the United States, the percentage of citizens participating was calculated based on Census Bureau reports of the number of citizens of voting age and reports from the states regarding how many people voted.

QUESTIONS FOR DISCUSSION

- Some people would like the United States to emulate other countries and have the government register everyone who is eligible to vote. Others oppose this European-style system, believing that this would lead to an intrusive big government that would require everyone to have a national identity card. What do you think?
- Do you think American turnout rates would be better if we followed the lead of most other democracies and held elections on the weekend?

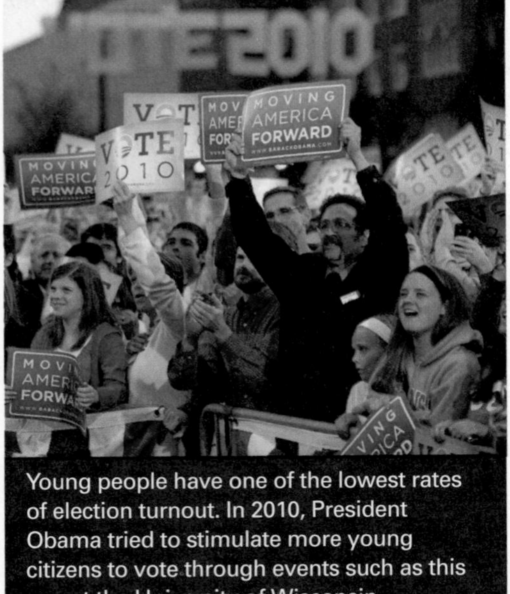

Young people have one of the lowest rates of election turnout. In 2010, President Obama tried to stimulate more young citizens to vote through events such as this one at the University of Wisconsin.

register on Election Day. Advocates of this user-friendly procedure are quick to point out that these states all ranked near the top in voter turnout in 2008. For many years, some states—particularly in the South—had burdensome registration procedures, such as requiring people to make a trip to their county courthouse during normal business hours. This situation was changed by the 1993 **Motor Voter Act**, which required states to allow eligible voters to register by simply checking a box on their driver's license application or renewal form. Nevertheless, the act's impact on turnout has thus far been largely disappointing. Turnout for the presidential election of 2008 was virtually the same as turnout for the 1992 presidential election, held before the act was passed.

Future reform designed to increase turnout may well focus on conducting elections through e-mail (see "You Are the Policymaker: Registering and Voting by E-Mail?").

Who Votes?

When just over half the population votes, the necessity of studying nonvoters takes on added importance. Table 10.1 displays data regarding the turnout rates of various groups in the 2008 presidential

YOU ARE THE POLICYMAKER

Registering and Voting by E-Mail?

Although many precincts now use computer touch screens to record votes, the high-tech age has not yet made much of an impact on the voting process. Americans have not yet harnessed much modern technology to improve democracy. There is good reason to expect that this will change in the twenty-first century.

The personal computer and the World Wide Web are likely to facilitate the process of voter registration. Already, one can go to the Web site of the Election Assistance Commission (http://www.eac.gov/files/voter/nvra_update.pdf) and download the "National Mail Voter Registration Form." Twenty-two states currently accept copies of this application printed from the computer image, signed by the applicant, and mailed in the old-fashioned way. As e-mail replaces "snail mail," the entire voter registration process may come to be mostly electronic. With the growing pervasiveness of personal computers in the home, this change would clearly make registering to vote more user-friendly.

If people can register by computer, the next step is voting by e-mail. A growing trend in the Pacific Coast states has been voting by mail. In 1998, Oregon voters approved a referendum to eliminate traditional polling places and conduct all future elections by mail. In California, approximately 40 percent of the votes cast currently come in via the post office. Again, as e-mail takes the place of regular mail, why not have people cast their votes through cyberspace?

Voting through the Internet would be less costly for the state, as well as easier for the average citizen, assuming near-universal computer literacy and access. The major concerns, of course, would be ensuring that no one votes more than once and preserving the confidentiality of the vote. These sorts of security concerns are currently being addressed by top computer programmers, as commercial enterprises increasingly use the Internet to conduct business. If the technology can be perfected to allow trillions of dollars of business to be conducted via the Internet, then it seems reasonable that similar problems can be overcome with regard to the voting process.

Whether these developments, should they occur, will improve democracy in America is debatable. Making voting more user-friendly should encourage turnout, but people will still have to be interested enough in the elections to send in their e-mail ballots. If old-style polling places are relegated to the history books and everyone votes electronically in the convenience of their own homes, the sense of community on Election Day may be lost. This loss could lead to even lower turnout.

What do you think? Do the benefits of voting by e-mail outweigh the potential costs?

TABLE 10.1 Reported Turnout Rates for Groups of U.S. Citizens in 2008

SOCIAL GROUPS	PERCENT
18–24	49
25–34	57
35–44	63
45–54	67
55–64	71
65 and over	70
No high school diploma	39
High school diploma	55
Some college	68
College degree	77
Advanced degree	83
White, non-Hispanic	66
African American	65
Hispanic	50
Asian American	48
Native Americans	53
Men	61
Women	66
Married	70
Single	56
Government workers	76
Self-employed	69
Work in private industry	62
Unemployed	55
Full-time student	56

Source: Authors' analysis of the 2008 U.S. Census Bureau survey.

Motor Voter Act
A 1993 act that requires states to permit people to register to vote when they apply for their driver's license.

election. This information reveals numerous demographic factors that are related to turnout.

- ***Education.*** People with higher-than-average educational levels have a higher rate of voting than do people with less education. Highly educated people are more capable of discerning the major differences between the candidates. In addition, their educational training comes in handy in clearing the bureaucratic hurdles imposed by registration requirements.
- ***Age.*** Older people are far more likely to vote than younger people. Younger citizens are less likely to be registered, but even just analyzing turnout patterns among registered voters yields wide differences by age. In Iowa, for example, the secretary of state reported that among those on the registration rolls, only 22 percent of those under 25 years of age voted in 2006, as compared to 72 percent among those over 65 years of age.[9]
- ***Race.*** Racial minorities are usually underrepresented among voters relative to their share of the citizenry. This was clearly evident in the 2008 turnout data for Hispanics, Asian Americans, and Native Americans. However, for the first time ever, there was no significant difference in the turnout rates between African Americans and white non-Hispanics, due to the historic nature of the 2008 Obama candidacy.
- ***Gender.*** In an earlier period many women were discouraged from voting, but today women actually participate in elections at a slightly higher rate than do men.

Youth Turnout

Young people typically have very low turnout rates in the United States. Who votes matters not only because these individuals decide who wins elections but also because politicians pay attention primarily to voters. The fact that so few young people vote means that politicians are not likely to pay too much attention to their opinions or to promote policies that will particularly help them.

- ***Marital status.*** People who are married are more likely to vote than those who are not. This pattern is true among all age categories and generally reflects the fact that married people are more tied into their community.
- ***Government employment.*** Having something at stake (their jobs and the future of the programs they work on) and being in a position to know more about government impels government workers to high levels of participation.

These differences in turnout rates are cumulative. Possessing several of these traits—say, being elderly, well educated, and married—adds significantly to one's likelihood of voting. Conversely, being, say, young, poorly educated, and single is likely to add up to a very low probability of voting. If you possess many of the demographic traits of nonvoters, then the interests of people like you are probably not drawing a great deal of attention from politicians—regardless of whether you personally vote or not. Politicians listen far more carefully to groups with high turnout rates, as they know their fate may well be in their hands. Who votes does matter.

10.4 Assess the impact of party identification, candidate evaluations, and policy opinions on voting behavior.

How Americans Vote: Explaining Citizens' Decisions

A common explanation of how Americans vote—one favored by journalists and politicians—is that they vote for the candidate whose policy views they prefer. Of course, the candidates have invested a lot of time and money to get those views implanted in the public mind. Starting from the idea that citizens vote for the candidate whose policy views they prefer, many journalists and politicians claim that the election winner has a mandate from the people to carry out the promised policies. This premise is sometimes called the **mandate theory of elections**.

mandate theory of elections
The idea that the winning candidate has a mandate from the people to carry out his or her platforms and politics. Politicians like the theory better than political scientists do.

Politicians, of course, are attracted to the mandate theory. It lets them justify what they want to do by claiming public support for their policies. As President Clinton said during the final presidential debate in 1992, "That's why I am trying to be so specific in this campaign—to have a mandate, if elected, so Congress will know what the American people have voted for." Immediately after declaring victory in the 2004 presidential election, President Bush forcefully asserted that he had a mandate to enact his proposed policies over the next four years. As Bush stated, "When you win there is a feeling that the people have spoken and embraced your point of view, and that's what I intend to tell Congress." And following his victory in 2008, President Obama said "I don't think there's any question that we have a mandate to move the country in a new direction and not continue the same old practices that have gotten us into the fix that we're in."

Political scientists, however, think little of the mandate theory of elections.[10] Whereas victorious politicians are eager to proclaim that "the people have spoken," political scientists know that voters' decisions may involve various elements. Political scientists focus on three major elements of voters' decisions: (1) voters' party identification, (2) voters' evaluation of the candidates, and (3) the match between voters' policy positions and those of the candidates and parties—a factor termed "policy voting."

Party Identification

Party identifications are crucial for many voters because they provide a regular perspective through which voters can view the political world. Once established, party identification is a label that people often adhere to for a long period of time, as they do with other elements of their social identity, such as their religious affiliation, social class, or even loyalty to a sports team. Party identification simplifies the political world for many voters and provides a reliable cue as to who is on their side. "Presumably," say Niemi and Weisberg, "people choose to identify with a party with which they generally agree. . . . As a result they need not concern themselves with every issue that comes along, but can generally rely on their party identification to guide them."[11] For example, some voters in Texas might not know anything about the issues in the race for state comptroller, but if they know which party they usually prefer, then voting based on party will probably lead to the same decision that they would reach if they were to study the issues.

In the 1950s, scholars singled out party affiliation as the best single predictor of a voter's decision. For example, it was said that many Southern Democrats would vote for a yellow dog if their party nominated one. "My party—right or wrong" was the motto of strong party identifiers. However, following the emergence of television and candidate-centered politics, the parties' hold on voters eroded substantially during the 1960s and 1970s and then stabilized at a lower level.[12] Today, many voters agree with the statement that "I choose the best person for the office, regardless of party," in part because modern technology makes it easier for them to evaluate and make their own decisions about the candidates. For these voters, the so-called floating voters, election choices have become largely a matter of individual choice; their support is up for grabs in each election (Young people are particularly likely to be floating voters and open to the possibility of voting for candidates who are neither Democrats nor Republicans, as you can read about in "Young People and Politics: How Young Voters Have Consistently Been More Supportive of Third-Party Candidates.")

Parties tend to rely on demographic groups that lean heavily in their favor to form their basic coalition. Even before an election campaign begins, Republicans usually assume they will not receive much support from African Americans or Jews. Democrats have an uphill struggle attracting groups that are staunchly Republican in their leanings, such as conservative evangelical Christians or upper-income voters. Coalitions can change over time, however; as you can see in Table 10.2, when we compare the 1960 and 2008 presidential elections, there are substantial differences in how various groups voted.

Candidate Evaluations: How Americans See the Candidates

All candidates try to present a favorable personal image. Appearance is a part of personal image, and using laboratory experiments, political psychologists Shawn Rosenberg and Patrick McCafferty showed that it is possible to manipulate a candidate's appearance in a way that affects voters' choices. Holding a candidate's policy views and party identification constant, they found that when good pictures are substituted for bad ones, a candidate's vote-getting ability is significantly increased. Although a laboratory setting may not be representative of the real world, Rosenberg and McCafferty conclude that "with appropriate pretesting and adequate control over a candidate's public appearance, a campaign consultant should be able to significantly manipulate the image projected to the voting public."[13]

To do so, a consultant would need to know what sort of candidate qualities voters are most attuned to. Research by Miller, Wattenberg, and Malanchuk shows that the three most important dimensions of candidate image are integrity, reliability, and competence.[14] In 2000, one of the key factors that helped George W. Bush was that he was rated more positively on integrity than was Al Gore. Reliability comprises such traits as being dependable and being decisive. When the Bush campaign repeatedly labeled John Kerry a "flip-flopper" during the 2004 campaign, Kerry's image of reliability clearly suffered. The personal traits most often mentioned by voters, though, involve competence. In 2008, competence ratings favored Obama

How Young Voters Have Consistently Been More Supportive of Third-Party Candidates

Over the past four decades, there have been a number of important third-party or independent candidates for the presidency. These candidates differed a great deal in political ideology. George Wallace ran in 1968 as a conservative, Ross Perot offered voters a centrist choice in the 1992 and 1996 elections, and John Anderson in 1980 and Ralph Nader in 2000 were liberals. Yet all of these candidates had one thing in common in terms of their supporters—they all drew a higher percentage of the votes of young adults than any other age group, as you can see in the national survey findings displayed here.

The reason young voters have been consistently more supportive of third-party or independent candidates is that, as we saw in Chapter 8, they are more likely to be political independents, who lack ties to Democrats or Republicans and are more open to alternatives outside the two-party system. Thus, a conservative third-party candidate is more likely to get the vote of younger conservatives than of older conservatives, and a liberal third-party candidate is more likely to get the vote of young liberals than of older liberals. Should a third-party candidate ever win nationwide, it is likely that young voters will be in forefront of his or her political supporters.

QUESTIONS FOR DISCUSSION

- Are young people sending a message to the two major parties by supporting alternative candidates?
- If America were like most European countries in using proportional representation in its elections, would young people be the supporters of new parties that might have a big impact?

PERCENT VOTING FOR:

Age Group	George Wallace 1968	John Anderson 1980	Ross Perot 1992	Ross Perot 1996	Ralph Nader 2000
18–29	15	16	28	14	5
30–44	11	11	19	11	2
45–64	12	8	17	7	2
65+	8	3	12	5	2

Sources: 1968, 1980, 1992, and 1996 American National Election Studies; 2000 National Voter Exit Poll.

over McCain, as voters rated Obama substantially higher on the specific trait of intelligence.[15]

Such evaluations of candidate personality are sometimes seen as superficial and irrational bases for judgments. Miller and his colleagues disagree with this interpretation, arguing that voters rely on their assessments of candidates' personalities to predict how they would perform in office. If a candidate is perceived as too incompetent to carry out policy promises, or as too dishonest for those promises to be trusted, it makes perfect sense for a voter to pay more attention to personality than policies. Interestingly, Miller and his colleagues find that college-educated voters are actually the most likely to view the candidates in terms of their personal attributes and to make important issue-oriented inferences from these attributes (for example, that a candidate who is unreliable may not be the right person to be the commander in chief of the armed forces). As Maureen Dowd, a Pulitzer Prize–winning columnist, has remarked, "When I first started writing about politics for the *Times*, I got criticized sometimes for focusing on the persona and not simply the policy. But as a student of Shakespeare, I always saw the person and the policy as inextricably braided. You had to know something about the person to whom you were going to entrust life and death decisions."[16]

TABLE 10.2 Changing Patterns in Voting Behavior: 1960 and 2008 Compared

The demographic correlates of presidential voting behavior have changed in a number of important ways since 1960. In 1960, Protestants and Catholics voted very differently, in part because of Kennedy's Catholicism but also because Catholics were a key element of the Roosevelt-era Democratic coalition; by 2008, Catholics were only slightly more likely to support the Democratic nominee than Protestants. Today, the major difference along religious lines involves how often one attends religious services, with those who attend regularly being substantially more likely to support Republican presidential candidates. The least likely group to support Republicans these days is African Americans. As you can see in data here, Obama clearly drew more support from African Americans than did Kennedy. Democrats also gained support from female voters, who preferred Obama by 7 percent more than men but had voted for Nixon over the handsome Kennedy. Finally, Hispanics, who tend to support Democratic candidates, accounted for only about 1 percent of voters in 1960—too small to be captured accurately in surveys—but for 9 percent in 2008.

	KENNEDY	NIXON	OBAMA	McCAIN
Protestant	36	63	45	54
Catholic	83	17	54	45
Jewish	89	11	78	21
Regularly attend religious services	49	50	43	55
Often attend religious services	36	64	53	46
Seldom attend religious services	55	44	59	39
Never attend religious services	51	49	67	30
White	48	52	43	56
African American	71	29	95	4
Hispanic	NA	NA	67	31
Male	52	48	49	48
Female	47	53	56	43
18–29	53	47	66	32
30–44	51	49	52	46
45–64	50	50	50	49
65+	39	61	45	53
No high school diploma	55	45	63	35
High school diploma	52	48	52	46
Some college	33	67	51	47
College degree	38	62	53	45

Source: 1960 American National Election Study and 2008 National Voter Exit Poll.

Policy Voting

Policy voting occurs when people base their choices in an election on their own issue preferences. True policy voting can only take place when four conditions are met. First, voters must have a clear sense of their own policy positions. Second, voters must know where the candidates stand on policy issues. Third, they must see differences between the candidates on these issues. And finally, they must actually cast a vote for the candidate whose policy positions coincide with their own.

policy voting
Electoral choices that are made on the basis of the voters' policy preferences and where the candidates stand on policy issues.

Given these conditions, policy voting is not always easy—even for the educated voter. Abramson, Aldrich, and Rohde analyzed responses to seven questions about policy issues in the 2008 American National Election Study. They found that on the average issue, 61 percent of the respondents met the first three informational criteria for policy voting. When these criteria were met—i.e., when respondents had a position, knew the candidates' stances, and saw differences between them—they voted for the candidate closest to their own position 71 percent of the time.[17] Of course, we should never expect all votes to be consistent with policy views, as many people will prefer one candidate on some policies and another candidate on other policies.

One regular obstacle to policy voting is that candidates often decide that the best way to handle a controversial issue is to cloud their positions in rhetoric. For example, in 1968 both major party candidates—Nixon and Humphrey—were deliberately ambiguous about what they would do to end the Vietnam War. This made it extremely difficult for voters to cast their ballots according to how they felt about the war. The media may not be much help, either, as they typically focus more on the "horse race" aspects of the campaign than on the policy stands of the candidates, as discussed in Chapter 9. Voters thus often have to work fairly hard just to be well informed enough to potentially engage in policy voting.

In today's political world, it is easier for voters to vote according to policies than it was in the 1960s. The key difference is that candidates are now regularly forced to take clear stands to appeal to their own party's primary voters. As late as 1968, it was still possible to win a nomination by dealing with the party bosses; today's candidates must appeal first to the issue-oriented activists in the primaries. Whatever the major issues are in the next presidential election, it is quite likely that the major contenders for the Democratic and Republican nominations will be taking stands on them in order to gain the support of these activists. Thus, what has changed is not the voters but the electoral process, which now provides much more incentive for candidates to clearly delineate their policy differences. In particular, George W. Bush took strong and clear policy stances on tax cuts, the war on terror, appointing conservative judges, and many other areas. Many scholars feel that as a result, he became a polarizing figure whom voters either loved or hated. Rather than cloud his rhetoric in ambiguity like presidents Eisenhower or Nixon, George W. Bush took pride in being straightforward and plainspoken. Part of what made Bush such a polarizing figure was stylistic, but the necessity for any modern candidate to appeal to their party's ideologically motivated activists in the primaries was also a factor. Indeed, President Obama faced these same constraints, and at the end of 2009 the Gallup Poll reported that his approval ratings were the most polarized along party lines for any first-year president in history.[19]

Mandate Theory of Elections

The mandate theory of elections asserts that voters send a policy message when they elect one candidate over another. Ideally, American democracy would work this way. The fact that it often does not means that leaders may be claiming more support from the people for their policies than is really justified.

A POINT TO PONDER

It is often claimed that candidates tend to hide their intentions with vague rhetoric whenever possible.

Do you think this is usually the case in presidential and congressional elections? If so, what are the consequences of obfuscation and how would things change if candidates were more direct?

"It's a good speech—just a couple of points that need obfuscation."

Party voting, candidate evaluation, and policy voting all play a role in elections. Their impact is not equal from one election to another, but they are the main factors affecting voter decisions. Once voters make their decisions in presidential elections, it is not just a simple matter of counting the ballots to see who has won the most support nationwide. Rather, the complicated process of determining Electoral College votes begins.

The Last Battle: The Electoral College

10.5 Evaluate the fairness of the Electoral College system for choosing the president.

It is the members of the **Electoral College**, not the people at large, who actually cast the determining votes for president and vice president of the United States. The Electoral College is a unique American institution, created by the Constitution. The American Bar Association once called it "archaic, undemocratic, complex, ambiguous, indirect, and dangerous." Many, but certainly not all, political scientists oppose its continued use, as do most voters.

Electoral College
A unique American institution, created by the Constitution, providing for the selection of the president by electors. Although the Electoral College vote usually reflects a popular majority, less populated states are overrepresented and the winner-take-all rule concentrates campaigns on close states.

The Founders wanted the president to be selected by the nation's elite, not directly by the people. They created the Electoral College for this purpose and left the decision as to how the electors are chosen to each state. Since 1828, though, political practice has been for electors to vote for the candidate who won their state's popular vote. This is how the Electoral College system works today:

- Each state, according to the Constitution, has as many electoral votes as it has U.S. senators and representatives.[21] The state parties select slates of electors, positions they use as a reward for faithful service to the party.
- Forty-eight out of the fifty states employ a winner-take-all system in which all their electors are awarded to the presidential candidate who wins the most votes statewide.
- In Maine and Nebraska, an elector is allocated for every congressional district won, and whoever wins the state as a whole wins the two electors allotted to the state for its senators. In 2008, Obama won the congressional district around Omaha, Nebraska, whereas McCain won the other two districts and the overall state vote. Therefore, Nebraska's electoral vote ended up being split with four for McCain and one for Obama.
- Electors meet in their states in December, following the November election, and then mail their votes to the vice president (who is also president of the Senate). The vote is counted when the new congressional session opens in January and is reported by the vice president. Thus, Dick Cheney had the duty of announcing the election of Barack Obama in January 2009.
- If no candidate receives an Electoral College majority, then the election is thrown into the House of Representatives, which must choose from among the top three electoral vote winners. A significant aspect of the balloting in the House is that each state delegation has one vote, thus giving the one representative from Wyoming an equal say with the 53 representatives from California. Although the Founders envisioned that the House would often have to vote to choose the president, this has not occurred since 1824.

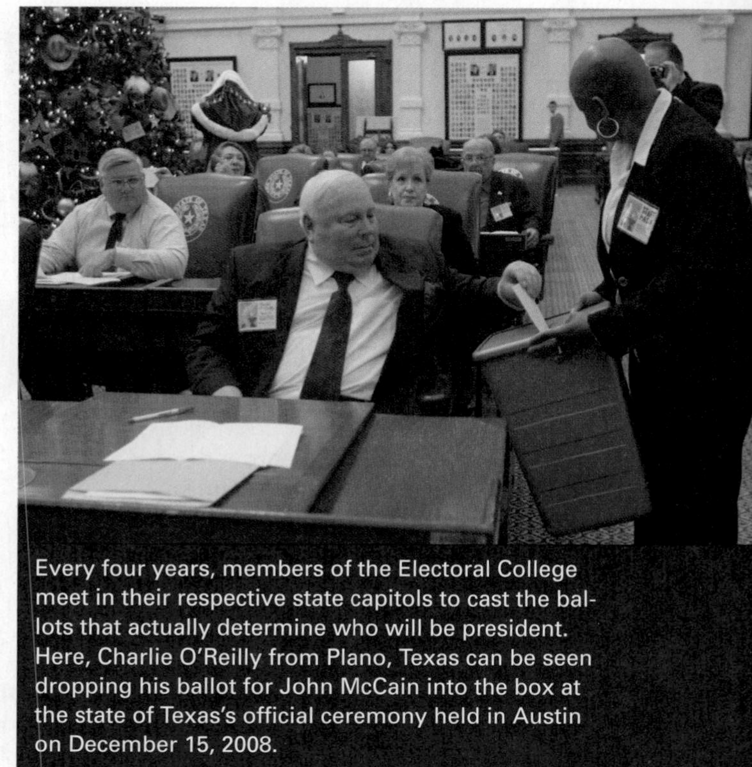

Every four years, members of the Electoral College meet in their respective state capitols to cast the ballots that actually determine who will be president. Here, Charlie O'Reilly from Plano, Texas can be seen dropping his ballot for John McCain into the box at the state of Texas's official ceremony held in Austin on December 15, 2008.

The Electoral College is important to the presidential election for two reasons. First, it introduces a bias into the campaign and electoral process. Because each state gets two electors for its senators regardless of population, the less populated states are overrepresented. One of the key reasons that

TABLE 10.3 Presidential Vote in 2000 by State Representation in the Electoral College

States with less than seven electoral votes are overrepresented in the Electoral College. Therefore, the fact that George W. Bush did especially well in these states in 2000, as shown in this table, helped him to win the presidency without winning the popular vote—the first time a candidate accomplished this feat since 1888.

	BUSH	GORE	NADER	OTHERS
Electoral votes <7	52.5%	42.3%	3.7%	1.5%
7–18	48.9%	47.6%	2.5%	1.0%
>18	45.7%	50.7%	2.7%	0.9%

Source: Calculated by the authors from official election returns.

George W. Bush won the Electoral College vote in 2000 without winning the popular vote was that he did better in the less-populated states, as shown in Table 10.3. A second reason for the importance of the Electoral College is that the winner-take-all norm means candidates will necessarily focus on winning the states where the polls show that there appears to be a close contest. As President Obama's campaign manager writes:

> Most of the country—those who lived in safely red or blue states—did not truly witness the 2008 presidential campaign. The real contest occurred in only about sixteen states, in which swing voters in particular bumped up against the campaign at every turn—at their doors; on their phones; on their local news, TV shows, and radio programs; and on the Internet. In these states, we trotted out the candidate and our surrogates, built large staffs and budgets to support our organizational work, and mounted ferocious and diversified advertising campaigns. They were the canvas on which we sketched the election.[22]

In "My State: The 2008 Battlegrounds" you can see which 16 states got the vast majority of attention from the Obama and McCain campaigns during the final phase of the 2008 presidential campaign.

The 2008 Battlegrounds

The purple states in the map below were identified by the Obama and/or the McCain campaigns in 2008 as battleground states. All the other states were regarded by both campaigns as safely in the pocket of one candidate or the other.

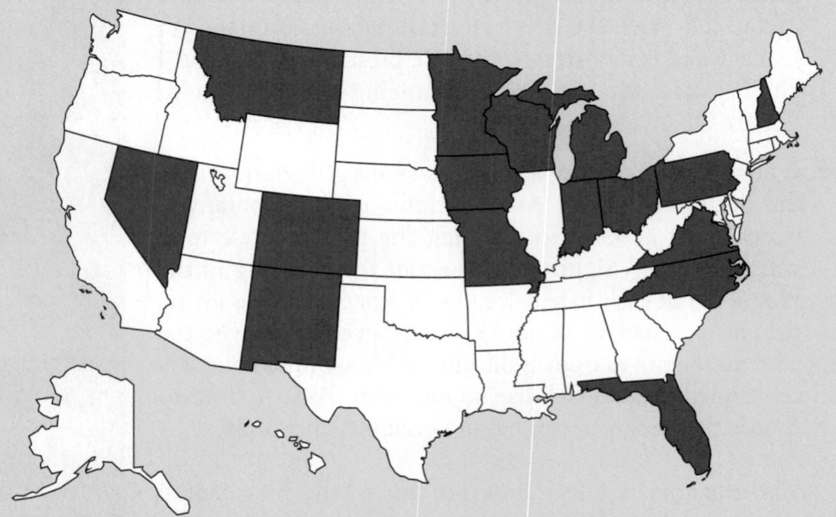

QUESTIONS FOR DISCUSSION

- If your state was a battleground state, what sorts of attention from the presidential candidates do you think it got that the nonbattleground states did not? If your state was not a battleground state, how do you think the campaign might have been different for you if the presidential election had been decided by the popular vote rather than the Electoral College?
- Do you think it makes a difference that the presidential campaigns pay so much more attention to a select set of battleground states than to the other states? Why or why not?

Understanding Elections and Voting Behavior

10.6 Assess the extent to which elections make government officials pay attention to what voters want.

Elections accomplish two tasks, according to democratic theory. First, and most obviously, they *select the policymakers*. Second, elections are supposed to help *shape public policy*. Whether elections in fact make the government pay attention to what the people think is at the center of debate concerning how well democracy works in America. In the hypothetical world of rational choice theory and the Downs model (see Chapter 8), elections do in fact guide public policy; however, over a generation of social science research on this question has produced mixed findings. It is more accurate to describe the connection between elections and public policy as a two-way street: Elections, to some degree, affect public policy, and public policy decisions partly affect electoral outcomes.

Democracy and Elections

There will probably never be a definitive answer to the question of how much elections affect public policy—for it is a somewhat subjective matter. The broad contours of the answer, however, seem reasonably clear: *The greater the policy differences between the candidates, the more likely voters will be able to steer government policies by their choices.*

Of course, the candidates do not always help to clarify the issues. One result is that the policy stands are sometimes shaped by what Benjamin Page once called "the art of ambiguity," in which "presidential candidates are skilled at appearing to say much while actually saying little."[23] Occasionally sidestepping controversial questions and hedging answers is indeed part of being a professional politician, as you can observe at almost every presidential press conference.

retrospective voting
A theory of voting according to which voters essentially make their decisions based on their answers to the question "What have you done for me lately?"

When individual candidates do offer a plain choice to the voters (what 1964 Republican nominee Barry Goldwater once called "a choice, not an echo"), voters are better able to guide the government's policy direction. Ronald Reagan followed in Goldwater's footsteps in the 1980s by making clear his intention to cut the growth of domestic spending, reduce taxes, and build up American military capability. Once elected, he proceeded to do much of what he said he would—demonstrating that elections can sometimes dramatically affect public policy.

If elections affect policies, then policies can also affect elections. Most policies have consequences for the well-being of certain groups or the society as a whole. Those who feel better off as a result of certain policies are likely to support candidates who pledge to continue those policies, whereas those who feel worse off are inclined to support opposition candidates. This is known as the theory of **retrospective voting**,[24] in which voters essentially ask the simple question, "What have you done for me lately?" Incumbents who provide desired results are rewarded; those who fail to do so are not reelected.

Nothing makes incumbent politicians more nervous than the state of the economy. When the economy takes a downturn, the call to "throw the

The final chapter of any presidential campaign is the swearing in of the winner at noon on the following January 20. Here, Chief Justice John Roberts administers the oath to Barack Obama as Michelle Obama holds the Bible. The original photograph this collage is based on was taken by a *Washington Post* photographer, and the individual "pixels" which comprise the collage were assembled from thousands of photos taken at the inauguration.

rascals out" usually sweeps the nation. In presidential elections, people unhappy with the state of the economy tend to blame the incumbent. Republican Herbert Hoover was in office when the stock market crash of 1929 sparked the Great Depression. Hoover and his fellow Republicans were crushed by Franklin Roosevelt in the 1932 elections. In 2008, Democrats were still hitting the Republicans with the memory of Hoover—calling George W. Bush a modern-day Hoover whose administration had presided over the worst annual job creation record of any president since the Great Depression.

Clearly, elections affect policy, and public policy—especially the perception of economic policy impacts—can affect elections. Once in office, politicians use fiscal policy to try to keep the American economy running on an even keel. (How they do this is considered in Chapter 17.) If economic troubles mount, voters point their fingers at incumbent policymakers, and those fingers are more likely to pull the lever for the challengers on Election Day. In recent elections people who felt the national economy had improved voted strongly for the incumbent, whereas those who thought the economy had gotten worse strongly favored the major challenger. As V. O. Key once wrote, "The only really effective weapon of popular control in a democratic regime is the capacity of the electorate to throw a party from power."[25]

Elections and the Scope of Government

While the threat of electoral punishment constrains policymakers, it also helps to increase generalized support for government and its powers. Voters know that the government can be replaced at the next election, so they are much more likely to feel that it will be responsive to their needs. Furthermore, when people have the power to dole out electoral reward and punishment, they are more likely to see government as their servant instead of their master. As Benjamin Ginsberg writes, "Democratic elections help to persuade citizens that expansion of the state's powers represents an increase in the state's capacity to serve them."[26]

Therefore, rather than wishing to be protected from the state, citizens in a democracy often seek to benefit from it. It is no coincidence that "individuals who believe they can influence the government's actions are also more likely to believe, in turn, that the government should have more power."[27] Voters like to feel that they are sending a message to the government to accomplish something. It should thus be no surprise that as democracy has spread, government has come to do more and more, and its scope has grown.

Summary

10.1 Distinguish the types of elections in the United States.

American elections can be classified into three basic types. Primary elections are held to select the political parties' nominees for elective offices. General elections are then contested between the nominees to determine who actually wins these offices. In some states, referendums are held to let the voters decide specific policy questions at the ballot box.

10.2 Trace the evolution of the American electoral process from 1800 to the present.

Elections have changed dramatically since 1800 when Adams ran against Jefferson and neither candidate participated in the campaign. By 1896, it was acceptable for candidates to campaign in person, and William Jennings Bryan did so with a vengeance. Nevertheless, at that time suffrage—the right to vote—was still limited mostly to white males. Now virtually all American citizens over the age of 18 have the right to vote. One constant throughout American electoral history is that the appeal of "it's time for a change" has been powerful when citizens are dissatisfied with the government's performance; this was the case in both 1800 and 2008.

10.3 Identify the factors that influence whether people vote or not.

In order to exercise their right to vote, citizens must go through the registration process. Although registration reform has been touted as the answer to America's low turnout problems, the Motor Voter Act of 1993 has yet to produce the benefit of greater voter participation that most people hoped for. Turnout in 2008 was virtually identical to what it was in 1992, and in 2010 only about 40 percent of the eligible electorate voted. Among the factors that make people more likely to vote are being better educated, older, and married.

10.4 Assess the impact of party identification, candidate evaluations, and policy opinions on voting behavior.

Party affiliation is the best predictor of voting behavior as it represents a standing decision to vote with one's party, all else being equal. Candidate evaluations and policy opinions are two factors that can sometimes sway people to defect from their preferred party, and play an especially important role in decision-making among Independents (voters do not identify with a party). Candidate evaluations usually involve important performance-relevant factors such as competence, integrity, and reliability. Policy voting often becomes important when voters see clear differences between the candidates and can determine whose stands on the issues best represent their own opinions.

10.5 Evaluate the fairness of the Electoral College system for choosing the president.

The Electoral College gives voters in the less-populated states somewhat greater weight in choosing the president. As a result, the winner of the national popular vote does not always prevail in the Electoral College, as was evident most recently in the 2000 contest between George W. Bush and Al Gore. Because all but two states allocate all their electors in a winner-take-all fashion and because many states lean solidly toward one party or the other, the candidates focus much of their energies on winning about fifteen so-called battleground states. These states, such as Florida and Ohio, receive a lot of attention in the general election campaign, whereas others, such as California and New York, are largely taken for granted by the candidates.

10.6 Assess the extent to which elections make government officials pay attention to what voters want.

Elections are the centerpiece of democracy. Few questions are more important in understanding American government than this: Do elections matter? Under the right conditions, elections can influence public policy, and policy outcomes can influence elections. The most important condition enabling voters to steer government policy is that the policy differences between the candidates be clear. But they can also make their voices heard by simply voting to reward or punish incumbents based on their performance in office. Elected officials who produce desired results are reelected; those fail to do are thrown out of office.

Chapter Test

10.1 Distinguish the types of elections in the United States.

1. An initiative petition can be considered what kind of lawmaking?
   a. Elitist lawmaking
   b. Top-down lawmaking
   c. Indirect lawmaking
   d. Ground-up lawmaking
   e. Lateral lawmaking

2. In many states, citizens can use referendums to approve or disapprove amendments to state constitutions.

   True______ False______

3. Based on what you have learned concerning Americans' voting behavior and participation in politics, evaluate some potential benefits and problems of direct democracy through the initiative process. How might the initiative process actually be considered undemocratic?

10.2 Trace the evolution of the American electoral process from 1800 to the present.

4. Based on the three elections described in the chapter, which of the following statements accurately characterizes the evolution of the American elections?
   a. The electoral process has become more elitist over time
   b. The same policy issues have been the focus of elections throughout the years
   c. There has been a steady increase in voter turnout over time
   d. The Electoral College has played an increasingly important role over time
   e. There has been an increase in campaigning by candidates over time

5. Presidential primaries have been a part of the presidential election process since the framing of the Constitution.

   True______ False______

6. Identify and explain three key changes in the presidential election process over time. Based on the three elections described in the chapter, how have elections become more democratic?

10.3 Identify the factors that influence whether people vote or not.

7. Which of the following is NOT true about Americans' voting behavior?
   a. A college graduate is more likely to vote than a high school graduate
   b. A single person is more likely to vote than a married person
   c. Women are more likely to vote than men
   d. A public-sector employee is more likely to vote than a private-sector employee
   e. A 50-year-old is more likely to vote than a 22-year-old

8. Citizens who have a high sense of political efficacy are more likely to actually vote than those who do not.

   True______ False______

9. The Motor Voter Act of 1993 has had a very positive impact on voter turnout.

   True______ False______

10. Imagine that you are charged with writing a brief report that outlines the possible causes of low turnout in the United States and offers some possible solutions. Specifically address possible causes and solutions for low turnout among different age groups—older, middle-aged, and, especially, younger voters.

10.4 Assess the impact of party identification, candidate evaluations, and policy opinions on voting behavior.

11. Which of the following statements best characterizes how party identification influences Americans' voting behavior?
    a. Party identification encourages voting based on cost–benefit analysis
    b. Party identification often puts voters in a tough situation of choosing between their party and their favored candidate
    c. Party identification encourages voting based on a candidate's specific policy positions and achievements
    d. Party identification simplifies the political world for many voters
    e. None of the above

12. College-educated voters are most likely to view political candidates in terms of their personal attributes.

    True______ False______

13. What is policy voting, when is it likely to occur, and who is likely to be a policy voter? Why is policy voting unlikely to occur for many voters?

10.5 Evaluate the fairness of the Electoral College system for choosing the president.

14. The Electoral College ensures that large states are overrepresented in the presidential election.

    True______ False______

15. The Electoral College encourages candidates to campaign in large, battleground states. Do you think that this aspect of the Electoral College detracts from the fairness of democratic elections? Why or why not?

10.6 Assess the extent to which elections make government officials pay attention to what voters want.

16. What is retrospective voting? How might retrospective voting encourage government officials to respond to voters' policy wishes after an election? What impact might retrospective voting have on policymaking?

17. Evaluate this statement made by Benjamin Ginsburg: "Individuals who believe they can influence the government's actions are also more likely to believe, in turn, that the government should have more power." Do agree with his assessment? Explain your answer.

PEARSON mypoliscilab™ Exercises

Apply what you learned in this chapter on MyPoliSciLab.

Read on **mypoliscilab.com**

eText: Chapter 10

Study and **Review** on **mypoliscilab.com**

Pre-Test
Post-Test
Chapter Exam
Flashcards

Watch on **mypoliscilab.com**

Video: State Primary Race

Explore on **mypoliscilab.com**

Simulation: You Are an Informed Voter Helping Your Classmates
Simulation: You Are a Campaign Manager: Countdown to 270!
Comparative: Comparing Voting and Elections
Timeline: Nominating Process
Timeline: Close Calls in Presidential Elections
Visual Literacy: Voting Turnout: Who Votes in The United States?
Visual Literacy: The Electoral College: Campaign Consequences and Mapping the Results

Key Terms

legitimacy (282)
referendum (282)
initiative petition (282)
suffrage (287)
political efficacy (287)
civic duty (288)
voter registration (288)
Motor Voter Act (291)
mandate theory of elections (292)
policy voting (295)
Electoral College (297)
retrospective voting (299)

Internet Resources

www.electionstudies.org
The American National Election Studies are a standard source of survey data about voting behavior. This site offers information about these studies, as well as some of their results.

www.annenbergpublicpolicycenter.org/ProjectDetails.aspx?myId=1
A good source of information on public views during the 2008 presidential campaign.

www.census.gov/population/www/socdemo/voting.html
The U.S. Census Bureau's studies of registration and turnout can be found at this address.

For Further Reading

Abramson, Paul R., John H. Aldrich, and David W. Rohde. ***Change and Continuity in the 2008 Elections.*** Washington, DC: Congressional Quarterly Press, 2010. A good overview of voting behavior in the 2008 elections, which also focuses on recent historical trends.

Campbell, Angus, et al. ***The American Voter.*** New York: Wiley, 1960. The classic study of the American electorate in the 1950s, which has shaped scholarly approaches to the subject ever since.

Institute of Politics, ed. ***Campaign for President: The Managers Look at 2008.*** Lanham, MD: Rowman & Littlefield, 2009. The campaign managers for all the 2008 presidential candidates gathered at Harvard to discuss their experiences in the primaries and the general election.

Kelley, Stanley G., Jr. ***Interpreting Elections.*** Princeton, NJ: Princeton University Press, 1983. Presents a theory of "the simple act of voting."

Lewis-Beck, Michael S., et al. ***The American Voter Revisited.*** Ann Arbor, MI: University of Michigan Press, 2008. A replication of the classic analysis in *The American Voter* employing data from the 2000 and 2004 American National Election Studies.

Martin, Fenton S., and Robert U. Goehlert. ***How to Research Elections.*** Washington, DC: Congressional Quarterly Press, 2001. A very useful guide to many sources of information about elections.

Nie, Norman H., Sidney Verba, and John R. Petrocik. ***The Changing American Voter.*** Cambridge, MA: Harvard University Press, 1976. Challenges some of the assumptions of Campbell et al.'s *The American Voter.*

Niemi, Richard G., and Herbert F. Weisberg, eds. ***Controversies in Voting Behavior,*** 4th ed. Washington, DC: Congressional Quarterly Press, 2001. An excellent set of readings on some of the most hotly debated facets of voting.

Smith, Daniel A. ***Tax Crusaders and the Politics of Direct Democracy.*** New York: Routledge, 1998. A collection of interesting essays about activists who have made a difference through their advocacy of tax cut initiatives.

Wattenberg, Martin P. ***Where Have All the Voters Gone?*** Cambridge, MA: Harvard University Press, 2002. A review of the reasons for declining voter turnout, both in the United States and in other advanced industrialized countries.

Wolfinger, Raymond E., and Steven J. Rosenstone. ***Who Votes?*** New Haven, CT: Yale University Press, 1980. A classic quantitative study of who turns out and why.

Chapter 11

Interest Groups

Learning Objectives

11.1 Describe the role of interest groups in American politics.

11.2 Compare and contrast the theories of pluralism, elitism, and hyperpluralism.

11.3 Analyze the factors that make some interest groups more successful than others in the political arena.

11.4 Assess the four basic strategies that interest groups use to try to shape policy.

11.5 Identify the various types of interest groups and their policy concerns.

11.6 Evaluate how well Madison's ideas for controlling the influence of interest groups have worked in practice.

POLITICS IN ACTION: HOW THE BEVERAGE INDUSTRY MOBILIZED TO STOP A SUGAR TAX

As the debate over health care reform dominated the political agenda in 2009, interest groups mobilized both for and against various policy changes that were under consideration. One of these proposals would have impacted many teenagers every day—namely, a federal tax of a penny an ounce on soft drinks and other highly sugared beverages. The consumption of sugar-sweetened beverages has been linked to risks for obesity, diabetes, and heart disease; therefore, supporters of this tax argued that it made sense to impose a levy on sugary drinks to offset health care costs and to reduce overconsumption of these beverages. They were bolstered by a report in the prestigious *New England Journal of Medicine* in April 2009, which concluded that "a penny-per-ounce excise tax could reduce consumption of sugared beverages by more than 10%." Furthermore, this report argued that such a tax "would generate considerable revenue, and as with the tax on tobacco, it could become a key tool in efforts to improve health."[1] The so-called soda tax proposal got a major boost in July 2009 when President Obama was asked about it by a reporter from *Men's Health* magazine and responded positively, saying, "I actually think it's an idea that we should be exploring. There's no doubt that our kids drink way too much soda."[2] Although Michelle Obama never spoke out about this tax, it was easy for many political observers to see how it would dovetail nicely with her initiative aimed at solving childhood obesity, called "Let's Move." With support from the White House seeming likely, some key members of the tax-writing Ways and Means Committee jumped on the bandwagon in support of this proposal.

In the world of interest groups politics, for every action there is a reaction. With the prospects for enacting a tax on sodas and other sweetened drinks looking up, the producers of such drinks soon mobilized to fight it. A reduction in the consumption of such drinks might have sounded good to public health advocates, but it would mean billions in lost revenue to the companies that make and distribute them. The American Beverage Association, which had been spending about $700,000 per year on lobbying Congress, suddenly spent $18.9 million lobbying Congress in 2009. The two biggest soda producers, Coca-Cola and PepsiCo, together spent $18.6 million on lobbying, up from about $3 million per year.[3] In addition, soft-drink producers enlisted a host of allies to work with them in trying to derail any consideration of such a tax. The milk industry quickly signed up, realizing that chocolate milk could well be taxed too. The fast-food industry also joined in, fearing that its sales of soda would suffer. But perhaps most significantly, many Latino groups joined in the alliance, arguing that this tax would disproportionately hurt low-income minority communities. In a $10 million TV and magazine campaign, the coalition known as Americans Against Food Taxes placed ads in English and Spanish that stated "They say it won't be much, but anything is too much when you're raising a family these days."

With all this lobbying against the proposed tax on sweetened drinks, members of Congress quickly dropped the idea of a federal tax. It never even came to a vote in a committee of Congress, much less the floor of either house. Depending upon one's point of

Chapter OUTLINE

Paid for by the Coalition to Scare Your Pants Off

view, the success of these groups in derailing this proposal can be interpreted as consistent with any one of the three theories of interest groups that will be reviewed in this chapter. Elitist theorists would clearly focus on the ability of big corporations like PepsiCo to suddenly devote millions of dollars to lobbying. Pluralists would point to the mobilization of potential groups and to the alliance formed between the financially powerful and ethnic minorities, which, although poor, brought crucial voting power to the table. Hyperpluralists would argue that this whole episode demonstrates how the government bends over backward to avoid alienating any organized interest group, thereby leading to policy gridlock and the inability to effect policy changes.

Our nation's capital has become a hub of interest group activity. On any given day, it is possible to observe pressure groups in action in many forums. In the morning, you could attend congressional hearings, in which you are sure to see interest groups testifying for and against proposed legislation. At the Supreme Court, you might stop in to watch a public interest lawyer arguing for strict enforcement of environmental regulations. Take a break for lunch at a nice Washington restaurant, and you may see a lobbyist entertaining a member of Congress. In the afternoon, go to any department of the executive branch (such as commerce, labor, or the interior) and you might catch bureaucrats working out rules and regulations with friendly—or sometimes unfriendly—representatives of the interests they are charged with overseeing. You could stroll past the impressive headquarters of the National Rifle Association, the AFL-CIO, or AARP to get a sense of the size of some of the major lobbying organizations. To see some lobbying done on college students' behalf, drop by One Dupont Circle, where you'll find the offices of many of the higher education groups, which lobby for student loans and scholarships, as well as for aid to educational institutions. At dinnertime, if you are able to finagle an invitation to a Georgetown cocktail party, you may see lobbyists trying to get the ear of government officials—both elected and unelected.

All this lobbying activity poses an interesting paradox: Although turnout in elections has declined since 1960, participation in interest groups has mushroomed. As Kay Schlozman and John Tierney write, "Recent decades have witnessed an expansion of astonishing proportions in the involvement of private organizations in Washington politics."[4] This chapter will explore the factors behind the interest group explosion, how these groups enter the policymaking process, and what they get out of it.

11.1 Describe the role of interest groups in American politics.

The Role of Interest Groups

All Americans have some interests they want represented. Organizing to promote these interests is an essential part of democracy. The right to organize groups is protected by the Constitution, which guarantees people the right "peaceably to assemble, and to petition the Government for a redress of grievances." This important First Amendment right has been carefully defended by the Supreme Court. The freedom to organize is as fundamental to democratic government as freedom of speech and freedom of the press.

interest group
An organization of people with shared policy goals entering the policy process at several points to try to achieve those goals. Interest groups pursue their goals in many arenas.

The term *interest group* seems simple enough to define. Interest refers to a policy goal; a group is a combination of people. An **interest group**, therefore, is an organization of people with similar policy goals who enter the political process to try to achieve those goals. Whatever their goals—outlawing abortion or ensuring the right to one or regulating tax loopholes or creating new ones—interest groups pursue them in many arenas. Every level of government, local to federal, is fair game, as is every branch of government. A policy battle lost in Congress may be turned around when it comes to bureaucratic implementation or to the judicial process.

This multiplicity of policy arenas helps distinguish interest groups from political parties. Parties fight their battles through the electoral process; they run candidates for public office. Interest groups may support candidates for office, but American interest groups do not run their own slate of candidates, as occurs in some other countries. In

other words, no serious candidate is ever listed on the ballot as a candidate of the National Rifle Association or Common Cause. It may be well known that a candidate is actively supported by a particular group, but that candidate faces the voters as a Democrat, a Republican, or a third-party candidate.

Another key difference between parties and interest groups is that interest groups are often policy specialists, whereas parties are policy generalists. Most interest groups have a handful of key policies to push: A farm group cares little about the status of urban transit; an environmental group has its hands full bringing polluters into court without worrying about the minimum wage. Unlike political parties, these groups need not limit themselves by trying to appeal to everyone.

The number of interest groups in the United States has been increasing rapidly over the past half century. In 1959, there were about 6,000 groups; by 2009, the *Encyclopedia of Associations* listed about 25,000 groups.[5] There now seems to be an organized group for just about every conceivable interest. Very few occupations or industries go without a group to represent them in Washington. Even lobbyists themselves now have groups to represent their profession, such as the American League of Lobbyists.

One of the major factors behind this explosion in the number of interest groups has been the development of sophisticated technology. A well-organized interest group can deluge members of Congress with tens of thousands of faxes and e-mail messages in a matter of hours. Technology did not create interest group politics, but it has surely made the process much easier.

Theories of Interest Group Politics

11.2 Compare and contrast the theories of pluralism, elitism, and hyperpluralism.

Understanding the debate over whether lobbying and interest groups in general create problems for government in America requires an examination of three important theories, which were introduced in Chapter 1. **Pluralism** argues that interest group activity brings representation to all. According to pluralists, groups compete and counterbalance one another in the political marketplace. In contrast, **elitism** argues that a few groups (primarily the wealthy) have most of the power. Finally, **hyperpluralism** asserts that too many groups are getting too much of what they want, resulting in government policy that is often contradictory and lacking in direction. This section looks in turn at each of these three theories' claims with respect to interest groups.

pluralism
A theory of government and politics emphasizing that many groups, each pressing for its preferred policies, compete and counterbalance one another in the political marketplace.

elitism
A theory of government and politics contending that an upper-class elite will hold most of the power and thus in effect run the government.

hyperpluralism
A theory of government and politics contending that groups are so strong that government, seeking to please them all, is thereby weakened.

Pluralism

Pluralist theory rests its case on the many centers of power in the American political system. Pluralists consider the extensive organization of competing groups as evidence that influence is widely dispersed among them. They believe that groups win some and lose some but that no group wins or loses all the time. Pluralist theorists offer a *group theory of politics*, which consists of several essential arguments.[6]

- ***Groups provide a key link between people and government.*** All legitimate interests in the political system can get a hearing from government once they are organized.
- ***Groups compete.*** Labor, business, farmers, consumers, environmentalists, and other interests constantly make competing claims on the government.
- ***No one group is likely to become too dominant.*** When one group throws its weight around too much, its opponents are likely to intensify their organization and thus restore balance to the system. For every action, there is a reaction.
- ***Groups usually play by the rules of the game.*** In the United States, group politics is a fair fight, with few groups lying, cheating, stealing, or engaging in violence to get their way.

- ***Groups weak in one resource can use another.*** Big business may have money on its side, but labor has numbers. All legitimate groups are able to affect public policy by one means or another.

Pluralists would never deny that some groups are stronger than others or that competing interests do not always get an equal hearing. Still, they can point to many cases in which a potential group organized itself and, once organized, affected policy decisions. African Americans, women, and consumers are all groups who were long ignored by government officials but who, once organized, redirected the course of public policy. In sum, pluralists argue that lobbying is open to all and is therefore not to be regarded as a problem.

Elitism

Whereas pluralists are impressed by the vast number of organized interests, elitists are impressed by how insignificant most of them are. Real power, elitists say, is held by relatively few people, key groups, and institutions. They maintain that the government is run by a few big interests looking out for themselves—a view that the majority of the public has usually agreed with in recent years, as you can see in Figure 11.1.

Elitists critique pluralist theory by pointing to the concentration of power in a few hands. Where pluralists find dispersion of power, elitists find interlocking and concentrated power centers. They note, for example, that about one-third of top institutional positions—corporate boards, foundation boards, university trusteeships, and so on—are occupied by people who hold more than one such position, resulting in so-called interlocking directorates.[7] Elitists see the rise of mighty multinational corporations as further tightening the control of corporate elites. A prime example is America's giant oil companies. Robert Engler has tried to show that government has always bent over backward to maintain high profits for the oil industry.[8] When they come up against the power of these multinational corporations, consumer interests are readily pushed aside, according to elitists.

FIGURE 11.1 Perceptions of the Dominance of Big Interests

The figure tracks responses to the question, Would you say the government is pretty much run by a few big interests looking out for themselves or that it is run for the benefit of all the people?

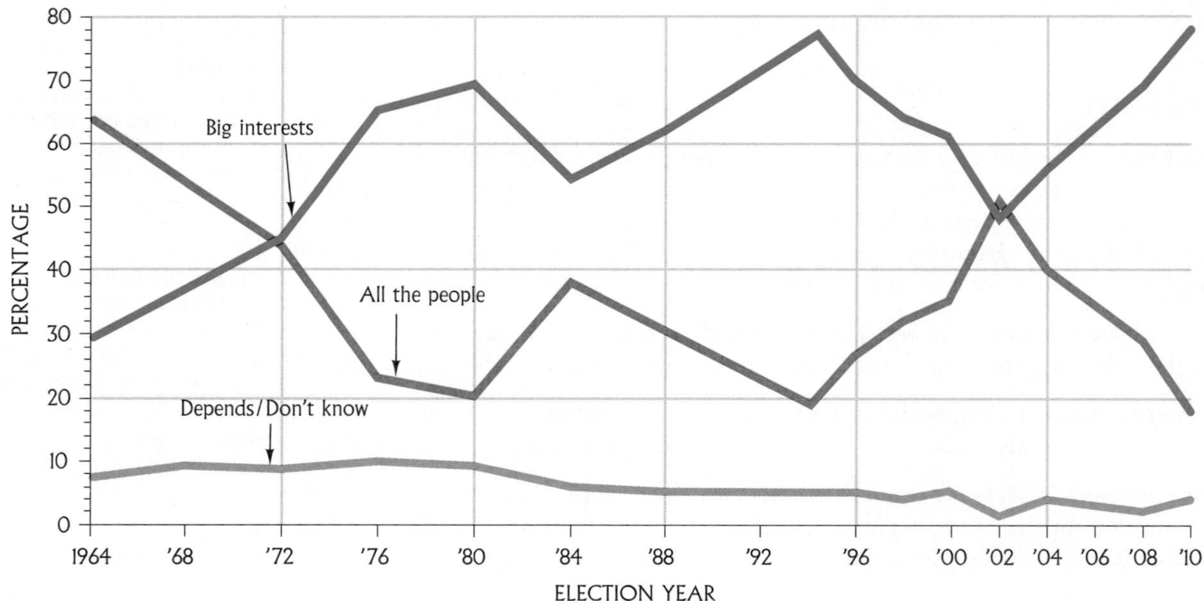

Source: Authors' analysis of 1964–2008 American National Election Study data; February 2010 *New York Times*/CBS News Poll.

In sum, the elitist view of the interest group system makes the following assertions:

- The fact that there are numerous groups proves nothing because groups are extremely unequal in power.
- Awesome power is held by the largest corporations.
- The power of a few is fortified by an extensive system of interlocking directorates.
- Other groups may win many minor policy battles, but corporate elites prevail when it comes to the big decisions.

Thus, lobbying is a problem, say elite theorists, because it benefits few at the expense of many.

Hyperpluralism

Hyperpluralists, also critical of pluralism, argue that the interest group system is out of control. For hyperpluralists, the problem is, in a phrase coined by Theodore Lowi, *interest group liberalism,* a situation in which government is excessively deferential to groups, with virtually all pressure group demands seen as legitimate and the job of government as to advance them all.[9]

As a result of this effort to please and appease every interest, agencies proliferate, conflicting regulations expand, programs multiply, and, of course, the budget skyrockets. If environmentalists want clean air, government imposes clean-air rules; if businesses complain that cleaning up pollution is expensive, government gives them a tax write-off for pollution control equipment. If the direct-mail industry wants cheap rates,

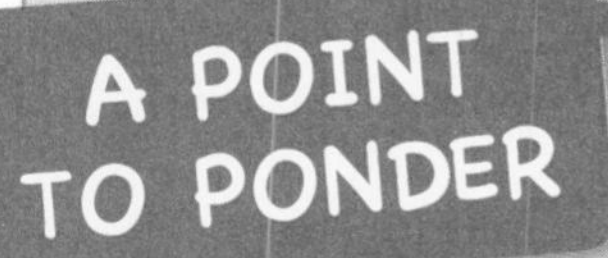

Hyperpluralists argue that there are too many special interests getting too much of what they want.

In your opinion, what is the effect of a wide range of groups pursuing their interests? Are these self-interests in reality unbridled (i.e., unrestrained)? Looking at the groups in the cartoon, what do you think pluralist and elitist theorists might say?

iron triangles
Subgovernments are composed of interest group leaders interested in a particular policy, the government agency in charge of administering that policy, and the members of congressional committees and subcommittees handling that policy; they exercise a great deal of control over specific policy areas.

government gives it to them; if people complain about junk mail, the Postal Service gives them a way to take their names off mailing lists. If cancer researchers convince the government to launch an antismoking campaign, tobacco sales may drop; if they do, government will subsidize tobacco farmers to ease their loss.[10]

According to hyperpluralists, interest group liberalism is promoted by the network of *subgovernments* in the American political system that exercise a great deal of control over specific policy areas. These subgovernments, which are generally known as **iron triangles**, are composed of key interest group leaders interested in policy X, the government agency in charge of administering policy X, and the members of congressional committees and subcommittees handling policy X.

All the elements of the iron triangle have the same goal: protecting their self-interest. The network of subgovernments in the agricultural policy area of tobacco is an excellent example. Tobacco interest groups include the Tobacco Council, the International Cigars and Pipe Retailers Association, and the tobacco growers. Various agencies in the Department of Agriculture administer tobacco programs, and they depend on the tobacco industry's clout in Congress to help keep their agency budgets safe from cuts. Finally, most of the members of the House Tobacco Subcommittee are from tobacco-growing regions. All these elements want to protect the interests of tobacco farmers. Similar iron triangles of group–agency–committee ties exist in scores of other policy areas.

Theories of Interest Group Politics

Our conclusions about how well the Madisonian system works to control the power of special interests would depend on whether we used pluralist, elitist, or hyperpluralist interpretations. A pluralist interpretation would suggest that Madison's system has worked as intended. In an elitist interpretation, however, the wealthy hold too much power, and in a hyperpluralist interpretation, too many groups have too much power.

Hyperpluralists' major criticism of the interest group system is that relations between groups and the government have become too cozy. Hard choices about national policy are rarely made. Instead of making choices between X and Y, the government pretends there is no need to choose and instead tries to favor both policies. It is a perfect script for policy gridlock. In short, the hyperpluralist position on group politics is as follows:

- Groups have become too powerful in the political process as government tries to appease every conceivable interest.
- Interest group liberalism is aggravated by numerous iron triangles—comfortable relationships among a government agency, the interest group it deals with, and congressional subcommittees.
- Trying to please every group results in contradictory and confusing policy.

Ironically, the recent interest group explosion is seen by some scholars as weakening the power of iron triangles. With so many more interest groups to satisfy, and with many of them competing against one another, a cozy relationship between groups and the government is plainly more difficult to sustain.

11.3 Analyze the factors that make some interest groups more successful than others in the political arena.

What Makes an Interest Group Successful?

In recent years, *Fortune* magazine has issued a yearly list of the 25 most powerful interest groups in politics. Table 11.1 displays one such list, and a quick look will probably reveal some surprises. Some of these powerful lobbying groups are relatively unknown.

Many factors affect the success of an interest group, as indicated by the diversity of groups in *Fortune*'s "Power 25." Among these factors are the size of the group, its intensity, and its financial resources. While greater intensity and more financial resources work to a group's advantage, surprisingly, smaller groups are more likely to achieve their goals than larger groups.

The Surprising Ineffectiveness of Large Groups

In one of the most often quoted statements concerning interest groups, E. E. Schattschneider wrote that "pressure politics is essentially the politics of small groups. . . . Pressure tactics are not remarkably successful in mobilizing general

TABLE 11.1 The Power 25

In order to rank lobbying associations according to their power, *Fortune* asked members of Congress, prominent congressional staffers, senior White House aides, and top-ranking officers of the largest lobbying groups in Washington to assess, on a scale of 0 to 100, the political clout of 87 major trade associations, labor unions, and interest groups. Here is the list of the groups that finished in the top 25 in terms of political clout back in 2001. As *Fortune* found relatively little change in this list from year to year in the past, it is likely that if it produced a more current list, most of these groups would still be on it.

1. National Rifle Association	14. National Education Association
2. American Association of Retired Persons	15. American Farm Bureau Federation
3. National Federation of Independent Business	16. Motion Picture Association of America
4. American Israel Public Affairs Committee	17. National Association of Broadcasters
5. Association of Trial Lawyers of America	18. National Right to Life Committee
6. AFL-CIO	19. Health Insurance Association of America
7. Chamber of Commerce	20. National Restaurant Association
8. National Beer Wholesalers Association	21. National Governors' Association
9. National Association of Realtors	22. Recording Industry
10. National Association of Manufacturers	23. American Bankers Association
11. National Association of Homebuilders	24. Pharmaceutical Research and Manufacturers of America
12. American Medical Association	25. International Brotherhood of Teamsters
13. American Hospital Association	

Source: *Fortune* magazine.

interests."[11] There are perfectly good reasons why consumer groups are less effective than producer groups, patients are less effective than doctors, and energy conservationists are less effective than oil companies: Smaller groups have organizational advantages over larger groups.

To shed light on this point, it is important to distinguish between a potential and an actual group. A **potential group** is composed of all people who might be group members because they share some common interest.[12] An **actual group** is composed of those in the potential group who choose to join. Groups vary enormously in the degree to which they enroll their potential membership. Consumer organizations are minuscule when compared with the total number of consumers, which includes almost every American. In contrast, organizations such as the National Beer Wholesalers Association, the American Hospital Association, and the Motion Picture Association of America include a good percentage of their potential members. These groups find it easier to get potential members to actually participate.

potential group
All the people who might be interest group members because they share some common interest.

actual group
The people in the potential group who actually join.

Economist Mancur Olson explains this phenomenon in *The Logic of Collective Action*.[13] Olson points out that all groups are in the business of providing collective goods. A **collective good** is something of value, such as clean air, that cannot be withheld from either potential or actual group members. When the AFL-CIO wins a higher minimum wage, all low-paid workers benefit, regardless of whether they are members of the union. In other words, members of the potential group share in benefits that members of the actual group work to secure. If this is the case, an obvious and difficult problem results: Why should potential members work for something if they can get it free? Why join the group, pay dues, and work hard for a goal when a person can benefit from the group's activity without doing anything at all? A perfectly rational response is thus to sit back and let other people do the work. This is commonly known as the **free-rider problem**.

collective good
Something of value that cannot be withheld from a potential group member.

free-rider problem
For a group, the problem of people not joining because they can benefit from the group's activities without joining.

The bigger the group, the more serious the free-rider problem. One reason for this is that in a small group, members' shares of the collective good are more likely to be great enough to give them an incentive to try to secure it by joining. The old saying that "everyone can make a difference" is much more credible in the case of a relatively small group. In the largest groups, in contrast, each member can expect to get only a tiny share of the policy gains. Weighing the costs of participation against the relatively small benefits, the temptation is always to "let somebody else do it." Therefore, as Olson argues, the larger the potential group, the less likely potential members are to contribute.

This distinct advantage of small groups helps explain why consumer groups have a harder time organizing for political action than do businesses. Such groups claim to seek "public interest" goals, but the gains they win are usually spread thin over millions of people. In contrast, the lobbying costs and benefits for business are concentrated. Suppose that, for example, consumer advocates take the airlines to court over charges of price fixing and force the airlines to return $10 million to consumers in the form of lower prices. This $10 million settlement, divided among tens of millions of people who use airlines, amounts to relatively small change for each consumer. Yet, for each of the 60 airline companies it amounts to a substantial sum. One can quickly see which side will be better organized in such a struggle.

In sum, the differences between large and small groups with regard to incentives to participate help explain why interest groups with relatively few members are often so effective. The power of business in the American political system is thus due to more than just money, as proponents of elite theory would have us believe. In addition to their considerable financial strength, multinational corporations have an easier time organizing themselves for political action than larger potential groups, such as consumers. Once well organized, large groups may be very effective, but it is much harder for them to get together in the first place.

selective benefits Goods that a group can restrict to those who actually join.

The primary way for large potential groups to overcome the free-rider problem is to provide attractive benefits for only those who join the organization. **Selective benefits** are goods that a group can restrict to those who pay their yearly dues, such as information publications, travel discounts, and group insurance rates. AARP, the group ranked second in Fortune's "Power 25," has built up a membership list of 35 million Americans over the age of 50 by offering a variety of selective benefits (see Figure 11.2).

FIGURE 11.2 The Benefits of AARP Membership

This chart illustrates the answers given by a sample of AARP members when they were asked why they had joined the organization.

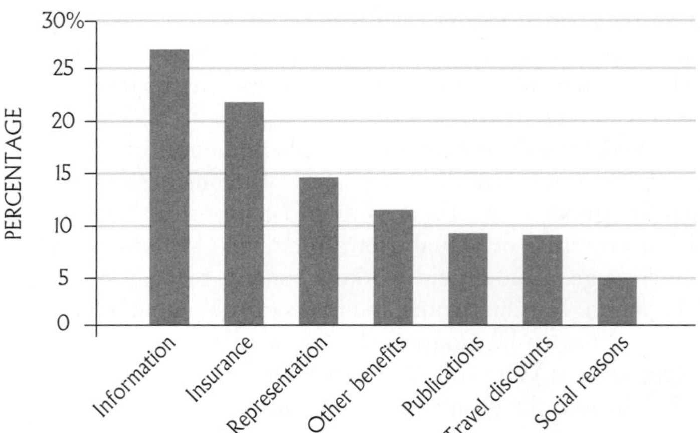

Source: AARP.

Intensity

Another way in which a large potential group may be mobilized is through an issue that people feel intensely about. Intensity is a psychological advantage that can be enjoyed by small and large groups alike. When a group shows that it cares deeply about an issue, politicians are more likely to listen; many votes may be won or lost on a single issue. The rise of single-issue groups (discussed in Chapter 1) has been one of the most dramatic political developments in recent years. Even college students have gotten into the act, forming groups to lobby against tuition increases, as you can read about in "Young People and Politics: The Virginia 21 Coalition."

A **single-issue group** can be defined as a group that has a narrow interest, dislikes compromise, and single-mindedly pursues its goal. Anti–Vietnam War activists may have formed the first modern single-issue group. Opponents of nuclear power plants, gun control (ranked number 1 in "The Power 25"), and abortion are some of the many such groups that exist today. All these groups deal with issues that evoke the strong emotions characteristic of single-interest groups.

single-issue groups
Groups that have a narrow interest, tend to dislike compromise, and often draw membership from people new to politics.

Perhaps the most emotional issue of recent times has been that of abortion. As befits the intensity of the issue, activities have not been limited to conventional means

The Virginia 21 Coalition

As budget crunches have hit most states in recent years, many state legislatures have cut back on funding for higher education and approved sharp increases in tuition at public colleges and universities. In response, college students in some states have started to form interest groups to fight for more state subsidies for higher education and for limiting tuition increases. In Virginia, a group called the "21st Century Virginia Coalition," or simply "Virginia 21" for short, has recently had some success in getting the state's politicians to listen to the opinions of college students regarding funding for higher education.

Virginia 21 first entered the political scene with a campaign to garner support for a bond referendum on the 2002 Virginia ballot to provide over $900 million to state universities for capital improvements. The group raised over $17,000 to support the campaign, made roughly 20,000 telephone calls to round up votes for it, and aired a student-written and student-produced radio commercial on behalf of the referendum, which passed with overwhelming support.

One of the organization's priorities was to push for a 1-cent increase in the state's sales tax that would be dedicated to increasing funds available for education. The organization collected over 10,000 signatures for a petition titled "Fund Virginia's Future" and presented them to the state legislature. But they grabbed more attention when they dropped off over 200,000 pennies at the office of the state treasurer in support of the proposed 1-cent increase in the sales tax. The pennies weighed approximately three-quarters of a ton, and the gesture was designed to show that college students care "a ton" about the funding of higher education. The local media could hardly ignore such a gripping visual image.

In 2006, Virginia 21 successfully lobbied the state legislature to pass a bill designed to cut the costs of textbooks for students in Virginia colleges. The measure required public universities to come up with guidelines mandating that professors acknowledge that they are aware of the exact costs of the books they assign, and to specify whether supplements sold with these books are actually required.

Virginia 21 is committed to lobbying the state legislature to substantially increase funds for higher education. It may or may not succeed in this goal, but it does seem destined to at least make sure that the views of college students are heard by policymakers. As of 2010, the Coalition had 46,000 members.

QUESTIONS FOR DISCUSSION

- Would you give money and/or volunteer for a group in your state like Virginia 21? Why or why not?
- Which of the strategies of interest group lobbying discussed later on in this chapter do you think would be most effective for a group like Virginia 21?

Source: www.virginia21.org

of political participation. Protesting—often in the form of blocking entrances to abortion clinics—has now become a common practice for antiabortion activists. Pro-choice activists have organized as well, especially in the wake of the 1989 *Webster v. Reproductive Health Services* case, which allowed states greater freedom to restrict abortions. Both groups' positions are clear, not subject to compromise, and influence their vote.

Financial Resources

One of the major indictments of the American interest group system is that it is biased toward the wealthy. When he was the majority leader in the Senate, Bob Dole once remarked that he had never been approached by a Poor People's political action committee. There is no doubt that money talks in the American political system, and those who have it get heard. All groups listed in Table 11.1 spend over a million dollars a year on lobbying and campaign contributions. A big campaign contribution may ensure a phone call, a meeting, or even a favorable vote or action on a particular policy. When Lincoln Savings and Loan Chair Charles Keating was asked in 1990 whether the $1.3 million he had funneled into the campaigns of five U.S. senators had anything to do with these senators later meeting with federal regulators on his behalf, he candidly responded, "I certainly hope so."

It is important to emphasize, however, that even on some of the most important issues, the big interests do not always win. An excellent example of this is the historic Tax Reform Act of 1986. In *Showdown at Gucci Gulch,* two reporters from the *Wall Street Journal* chronicle the improbable victory of sweeping tax reform.[14] In this case, a large group of well-organized, highly paid (and Gucci-clad) lobbyists were unable to preserve many of their most prized tax loopholes. One of the heroes of the book, former Senator Robert Packwood of Oregon, was Congress's top political action committee recipient during the tax reform struggle; he had raked in $992,000 for his reelection campaign. As chair of the Senate Finance Committee, however, Packwood ultimately turned against the hordes of lobbyists trying to get his ear on behalf of various loopholes. The only way to deal with the tax loophole problem, he concluded, was to go virtually cold turkey by eliminating all but a very few. "There is special interest after special interest that is hit in this bill," Packwood gloated, pointing out that many of them contributed to his campaign. In the end, passage of the reform bill offered "encouraging proof that moneyed interests could not always buy their way to success in Congress."[15]

A recent study of interest group activity on about 100 randomly chosen policy issues by Frank Baumgartner and his colleagues provides the most comprehensive analysis ever of who got what they lobbied for and who did not. The question of how much financial resources mattered was uppermost on the minds of these political scientists, and their results were both definitive and striking. They report, "The usual types of resources that are often assumed to 'buy' policy outcomes—PAC donations, lobbying expenditures, membership size, and organizational budgets—have no observable effect on the outcomes."[16] Based on their analysis, they offer several explanations for why the correlation between big money and lobbying success is so weak. First, they find that lobbying is a very competitive enterprise. Once one side mobilizes its resources, such as money, the other side is almost sure to mobilize whatever resources and allies it has to counter them. Second, in numerous instances one big interest faced off against another. In fact, a full 17 percent of the issues they examined involved one member of *Fortune*'s "Power 25" facing off against another. Third, their data revealed a high degree of diversity within sides active in the lobbying game, as groups with substantial financial resources often allied themselves with poor groups with whom they shared a common goal. As Baumgartner and his colleagues explain, "Where the wealthy often ally with the poor . . . it is logically impossible to observe a strong correlation between wealth and success."[17] The tale of the wealthy soda industry forming a lobbying alliance with Latino groups recounted at the beginning of this chapter is an excellent example of this phenomenon.

How Groups Try to Shape Policy

11.4 Assess the four basic strategies that interest groups use to try to shape policy.

No interest group has enough staff, money, or time to do everything possible to achieve its policy goals. Interest groups must therefore choose from a variety of tactics. The four basic strategies are lobbying, electioneering, litigation, and appealing to the public.

Lobbying

The term *lobbying* comes from the place where petitioners used to collar legislators. In the early years of politics in Washington, members of Congress had no offices and typically stayed in boardinghouses or hotels while Congress was in session. A person could not call them up on the phone or make an appointment with their secretary; the only sure way of getting in touch with a member of Congress was to wait in the lobby where he was staying to catch him either coming in or going out. These people were dubbed *lobbyists* because they spent so much of their time waiting in lobbies.

Of course, merely loitering in a lobby does not make one a lobbyist; there must be a particular reason for such action. Lester Milbrath has offered a more precise definition of the practice. He writes that **lobbying** is a "communication, by someone other than a citizen acting on his or her own behalf, directed to a governmental decision maker with the hope of influencing his or her decision."[18] Lobbyists, in other words, are political persuaders who represent organized groups. They usually work in Washington, handling groups' legislative business. They are often former legislators themselves. For example, according to a study by Public Citizen's Congress Watch, over 70 former members of Congress lobbied for the financial services sector in 2009—many of them earning sums they only could have dreamed of as lawmakers.[19]

lobbying
According to Lester Milbrath, a "communication, by someone other than a citizen acting on his or her own behalf, directed to a governmental decision maker with the hope of influencing his or her decision."

There are two basic types of lobbyists. The first type is a regular, paid employee of a corporation, union, or association. Such lobbyists may hold a title, such as vice president for government relations, but everyone knows that it is for a reason that their office is in Washington even if the company headquarters is in Houston. The second type is available for hire on a temporary basis. These lobbyists generally work for groups that are too small to afford a full-time lobbyist or that have a unique, but temporary, need for access to Congress or the executive branch.

The Lobbying Disclosure Act of 1995 established criteria for determining whether an organization or firm should register their employees as lobbyists. Those who fit the criteria must register with the Secretary of the U.S. Senate and file a report regarding each of their clients, indicating how much they were paid by them for lobbying services. This information is made public by the Senate's Office of Public Records, and combing through about 20,000 disclosure forms per year has become a substantial business in itself. The fall 2009 edition of *Washington Representatives,* a $250 reference book on participants in the federal lobbying process, advertised that it provided "in-depth profiles on 18,000 lobbyists, 12,000 clients, and 1,700 lobbying firms."[20] Since 1998, the Center for Responsive Politics has been calculating the expenditures on lobbying of each industry. In Figure 11.3, you can see the enormous amounts that the top–spending industries doled out for lobbying over the course of a decade.

Although lobbyists are primarily out to influence members of Congress, it is important to remember that they can be of help to them as well. Ornstein and Elder list four important ways in which lobbyists can help a member of Congress[21]:

- ***They are an important source of information.*** Members of Congress have to concern themselves with many policy areas; lobbyists can confine themselves to only one area and can thus provide specialized expertise. If information is power, then lobbyists can often be potent allies.
- ***They can help politicians with political strategy for getting legislation through.*** Lobbyists are politically savvy people, and they can be useful consultants. When Leon

FIGURE 11.3 The Big Spenders on Lobbying, 1998–2007

This graph presents the total amount spent on lobbying by industries that were the biggest spenders for the period 1998–2007. Keep in mind that the data are presented in terms of millions spent: $1,000 million equals $1 billion, so, for example, the pharmaceutical industry spent over $1 billion on lobbying. All told, just these 15 industries spent $9.4 billion on lobbying during these 10 years.

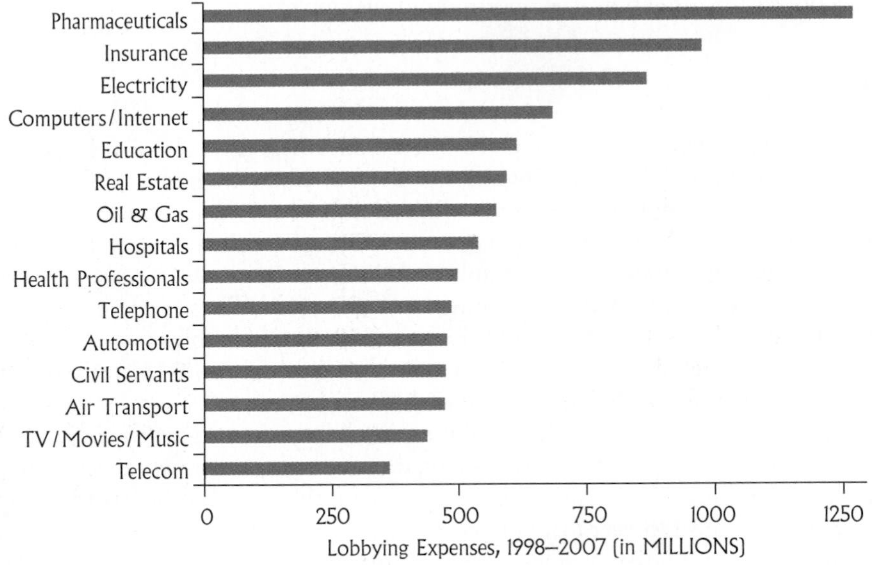

Source: Center for Responsive Politics.

Panetta served as White House chief of staff in the Clinton administration, he regularly convened a small group of Washington lobbyists to discuss how the administration should present its proposals.[22]

- ***They can help formulate campaign strategy and get the group's members behind a politician's reelection campaign.*** Labor union leaders, for example, often provide help in how to appeal to typical working people, and they often provide volunteers to help out in campaigns as well.
- ***They are a source of ideas and innovations.*** Lobbyists cannot introduce bills, but they can peddle their ideas to politicians eager to attach their name to an idea that will bring them political credit.

Like anything else, lobbying can be done crudely or gracefully. Lobbyists can sometimes be heavy-handed. They can threaten or cajole a legislator, implying that electoral defeat is a certain result of not "going along." They can even make it clear that money flows to the reelection coffers of those who cooperate. It is often difficult to tell the difference between lobbying as a shady business and lobbying as a strictly professional representation of legitimate interests.

High-priced lobbyists are often compared to the airline mechanic who is called in to fix the plane, turns just one screw and submits a bill for a thousand dollars. Asked to justify such a huge fee for such a little bit of work, the mechanic says, "Well it's $10 for turning the screw, and $990 for knowing which screw to turn." Similarly, the skilled lobbyist is paid for knowing who to contact and with what information. A recent in-depth study of lobbyists and their work by Rogan Kersh concludes that their success depends largely on their ability to deploy information strategically on behalf of their clients. As Kersh writes, "Searching for, analyzing, and presenting information compose the central activity in most lobbyists' daily work."[23] Richard Hall and Alan Deardorff have characterized lobbying as a form of "legislative subsidy," or a "matching grant of costly policy information, political intelligence, and labor to the enterprises of strategically selected legislators,"[24] and have argued that its purpose is not to change anyone's mind but rather simply to help political allies.

Other evidence, however, suggests that sometimes lobbying can persuade legislators to support a certain policy.[25] The National Rifle Association, which for years kept major gun control policies off the congressional agenda, has long been one of Washington's most effective lobbying groups.[26] In a more specific example, from the late 1980s, intensive lobbying by wealthy senior citizens, who were enraged by the tax burden the Catastrophic Health Care Act imposed on them, led Congress to repeal the act only a year after it was passed.

Nailing down the specific effects of lobbying is difficult, partly because it is difficult to isolate its effects from other influences. Lobbying clearly works best on people already committed to the lobbyist's policy position. Thus, like campaigning, lobbying is directed toward primarily activating and reinforcing supporters. For example, antiabortion lobbyists would not think of approaching California's Dianne Feinstein to attempt to convert her to their position, because Feinstein clearly supports the pro-choice position. If Senator Feinstein is lobbied by anyone on the abortion issue, it will be by the pro-choice faction, urging her not to compromise with the opposition.

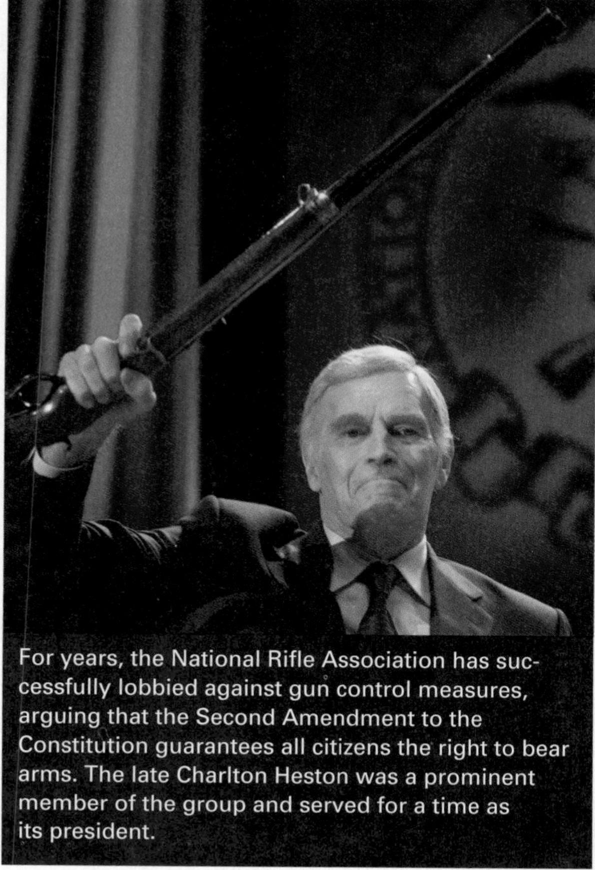

For years, the National Rifle Association has successfully lobbied against gun control measures, arguing that the Second Amendment to the Constitution guarantees all citizens the right to bear arms. The late Charlton Heston was a prominent member of the group and served for a time as its president.

Electioneering

Because lobbying works best with those already on the same side, getting the right people into office and keeping them there is also a key strategy of interest groups. Many groups therefore get involved in **electioneering**—aiding candidates financially and getting group members out to support them. Pressure group involvement in campaigns is nothing new. In the election of 1896 (see Chapter 10), silver-mining interests poured millions into the losing presidential campaign of William Jennings Bryan, who advocated unlimited coinage of silver.

electioneering
Direct group involvement in the electoral process, for example, by helping to fund campaigns, getting members to work for candidates, and forming **political action committees.**

political action committees (PACs)
Political funding vehicles created by the 1974 campaign finance reforms. An interest group can create a PAC and register it with the Federal Election Commission, which will monitor the PAC's expenditures.

A means for groups to participate in electioneering is provided by **political action committees** (PACs), discussed in Chapter 9. The number of PACs has exploded from 608 in 1974, the year they were created by campaign finance reforms, to 4,611 in 2009, according to the Federal Election Commission. No major interest group seeking to exert influence on the political process these days can pass up the opportunity to funnel money honestly and openly into the campaign coffers of its supporters. For example, Major League Baseball's PAC gave $201,500 to congressional candidates during the 2008 election cycle, mostly to members of congressional committees who were considering legislation that might impact the business of baseball.[27] As economist Roger Noll of Stanford University remarked about the activity of baseball's PAC, "Any industry that has any kind of dependence on government is pretty much forced to do what they're doing," he said. "Unfortunately, this has become the cost of doing business."[28]

As campaign costs have risen, PACs have come along to help pay the bill. In recent years, nearly half the candidates running for reelection to the House of Representatives have received the majority of their campaign funds from PACs. Furthermore, their challengers were not likely to be recipients of this PAC largesse. PACs gave a whopping $305 million to congressional incumbents during the 2008 election cycle, compared to a mere $49 million to the challengers.[29] Why does PAC money go so overwhelmingly to incumbents? The answer is that PAC contributions are basically investments for the future, and incumbents are the most likely to return the investment. When R. Kenneth Godwin and Barry J. Seldon asked a sample of PAC directors to explain why their PACs gave money to certain candidates, the top five answers were that these candidates were (1) on committees that are important to their interests, (2) very supportive of issues important to them, (3) from a district or state where they had facilities, (4) helping them with executive and regulatory agencies, and (5) in leadership positions that enabled them to influence issues that affect the PAC.[30]

A POINT TO PONDER

Some people think that lawmakers will happily take campaign contributions from any special interest that is willing to contribute.

Do you think this is actually the case for most politicians? And do you think most special interests are as indiscriminate in whom they give money to as this cartoon seems to suggest?

Only a handful of serious congressional candidates have resisted the lure of PAC money in recent years. A candidate who did resist, Democrat Steve Sovern, described his experiences trying to get on the PAC bandwagon. Running for the House from Iowa's Second District, Sovern made the now-standard pilgrimage to Washington to meet with potential contributors. "I found myself in line with candidates from all over," he reported. Each PAC had eager candidates fill out a multiple-choice questionnaire on issues important to the PAC. Candidates who shared the same concerns and views and who looked like winners got the money. Sovern later reported that "the process made me sick." After his defeat, he organized his own PAC called LASTPAC (for Let the American System Triumph), which urged candidates to shun PAC campaign contributions.[31] There have been serious calls to do away with PACs altogether, as discussed in "You Are the Policymaker: Should PACs Be Eliminated?"

WHY IT MATTERS

PACs

The great increase in the number of PACs over the past several decades has enabled far more groups to become involved in electioneering. Insofar as more participation is desirable, the increase of PACs has to be considered a positive development. But given that only groups that can successfully organize and raise substantial sums of money can take advantage of the PAC system, the increased importance of PACs has introduced some obvious biases into the electoral process.

In addition to their role in financing campaigns, interest groups participate in elections in numerous other ways. Among these are recruiting interest groups members to run as candidates for office, issuing official group endorsements, providing volunteer labor to participate in campaign work, and sending delegates to state and national party conventions to try to influence party platforms.

Litigation

If interest groups fail in Congress or get only a vague piece of legislation, the next step is to go to court in the hope of getting specific rulings. Karen Orren has linked much of the success of environmental interest groups to their use of lawsuits. "Frustrated in

YOU ARE THE POLICYMAKER

Should PACs Be Eliminated?

The effect of PAC campaign contributions on congressional votes has become a perennial issue in American politics. Critics of PACs are convinced that they distort the democratic process and corrupt our political system in favor of those who can raise the most money. Many politicians freely admit—once they are out of office—that it is a myth to think that the PACs don't want something in return. They may only want to be remembered on one or two crucial votes or with an occasional intervention with government agencies, but multiply this by the thousands of special interests that are organized today and the worst fears of the hyperpluralists could be realized—a government that constantly yields to every special interest.

Common Cause (www.commoncause.org) has made it its primary mission to expose what it sees as the evils of the PAC system. It argues that the influence of corporate PACs on Capitol Hill has led to "corporate welfare" and costs taxpayers billions of dollars. For example, Common Cause maintains that the Bush administration's decision to eliminate the roadless rule, which protected 1.9 million acres of federal forests in Oregon from logging, was a clear payback for PAC contributions by the timber industry. Along with others, Common Cause has attributed the failure of Congress to further regulate tobacco and cigarette advertising to the more than $35 million of PAC contributions from tobacco companies over the past decade. And Common Cause asserts that $3 million in PAC contributions from the biggest mortgage brokers kept Congress from scrutinizing questionable lending practices that played such a crucial role in bringing on the recession of 2008–2009.

However, others argue that connection is not causation. They believe that most members of Congress are not affected by PAC contributions, which come largely from groups they already agree with anyway. Defenders of the PAC system also point out that the PAC system further increases participation in the political process. As opposed to individual donations, PACs—which represent groups of people—allow better representation of occupational groups. The PAC system allows people with common professional interests, such as farmers, lawyers, dentists, and college professors, to express their support of candidates jointly through political contributions. Similarly, corporation PACs can represent the interests of stockholders and employees.

If James Madison's notion that the key to controlling the power of interest groups is to expand their sphere of participation, then PACs certainly do this, according to their defenders. Beyond this, the money for today's expensive media campaigns has to come from somewhere. Those who wish to maintain the PAC system typically argue that the alternative of the government providing campaign funds is impractical given that only about 1 in 10 taxpayers participates in the $3 voluntary income tax check-off system for financing federal campaigns (see Chapter 9).

What do you think? Would you consider eliminating PACs? Or, as a middle course, would you favor reducing the amount of money that they can donate directly to candidates? Or, would you prefer just to leave things as they are at present?

Congress," she wrote, "they have made an end run to the courts, where they have skillfully exploited and magnified limited legislative gains."[32] Environmental legislation, such as the Clean Air Act, typically includes provisions allowing ordinary citizens to sue for enforcement. As a result, every federal agency involved in environmental regulation now has hundreds of suits pending against it at any given time. Moreover, the constant threat of a lawsuit increases the likelihood that businesses will consider the environmental impact of what they do.

Perhaps the most famous interest group victories in court were those won by civil rights groups in the 1950s. While civil rights bills remained stalled in Congress, these groups won major victories in court cases concerning school desegregation, equal housing, and employment discrimination. More recently, consumer groups have used suits against businesses and federal agencies as a means of enforcing consumer regulations.

One tactic that lawyers employ to make the views of interest groups heard by the judiciary is the filing of *amicus curiae* briefs ("friend of the court" briefs), written arguments submitted to the courts in support of one side of a case. Through these written depositions, a group states its collective position as well as how its own welfare will be affected by the outcome of the case. Numerous groups may file *amicus* briefs in highly publicized and emotionally charged cases. For example, in the case of *Regents of the University of California v. Bakke* (see Chapter 5), which challenged affirmative action programs as reverse discrimination, over 100 different groups filed *amicus* briefs. A study of participation in *amicus* briefs by Caldeira and Wright found that the Supreme Court has been accessible to a wide array of organized interests, in terms of deciding both which cases to hear and how to rule.[33]

A more direct judicial strategy employed by interest groups is the filing of class action lawsuits, which enable a group of people in a similar situation to combine their common grievances into a single suit. For instance, in 1977 flight attendants won a class action suit against the airline industry's regulation that all stewardesses be unmarried. As one lawyer who specializes in such cases states, "The class action is the greatest, most effective legal engine to remedy mass wrongs."[34]

Going Public

Groups are also interested in the opinions of the public. Because public opinion ultimately makes its way to policymakers, interest groups carefully cultivate their public image and use public opinion to their advantage when they can. As Ken Kollman finds, even the wealthiest and most powerful groups in America appeal to public opinion to help their cause. For example, when the government instituted a requirement for tax-withholding on savings accounts, the American Bankers Association appealed to their customers to protest this to their congressional representatives. After 22 million postcards flooded into Congress, lawmakers quickly reversed the policy.[35]

Interest groups market not only their stand on issues but also their reputations. Business interests want people to see them as "what made America great," not as wealthy Americans trying to ensure large profits. The Teamsters Union likes to be known as a united organization of hardworking men and women, not as an organization that has in the past been influenced by organized crime. Farmers promote the image of a sturdy family working to put bread on the table, not the huge agribusinesses that have largely replaced family farms. In this way, many groups try to create a reservoir of goodwill with the public.

Interest groups' appeals to the public for support have a long tradition in American politics. In 1908, AT&T launched a major magazine advertising campaign to convince people of the need for a telephone monopoly. In 1948, when President Truman proposed a system of national health insurance, the American Medical Association spent millions of dollars on ads attacking "socialized medicine." In both 1994 and 2010, when Congress took up major initiatives to reform health care, many groups placed advertisements in support of and opposition to the proposals made by Presidents Clinton and Obama. In both cases, so much money was spent (over $100 million) that many observers compared this activity to a national electoral campaign.

Lately, more and more organizations have undertaken expensive public relations (PR) efforts, whether to defend their reputations or to promote their stands on issues. After *60 Minutes* ran a story in 2009 about a lawsuit against Chevron for allegedly contaminating the Ecuadorian Amazon and causing a wave of cancer in the region, Chevron hired former CNN correspondent Gene Randall to produce a video telling its side of the story and posted the video on YouTube. In other recent examples, Toyota ran ads defending itself against charges of negligence after some of its vehicles were found to have acceleration and braking problems, and Microsoft condemned its prosecution by the Justice Department for alleged monopolistic practices. Mobil Oil has long run a visible corporate PR effort to influence the public with its regular editorial-style ads in the *New York Times* and other major publications.

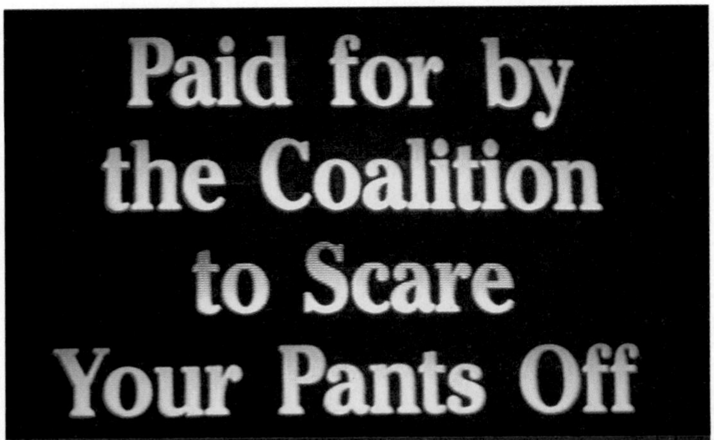

Interest groups spent over $100 million appealing to public opinion during the debate over health care in 1994. In a counter-ad produced by the Democratic National Committee, the argument was made that opponents of the Clinton health care plan were using scare tactics. You can see the tag end of the ad in this photo.

These ads typically address issues that affect the oil industry and big business in general. One was even titled "Why Do We Buy This Space?" Mobil answered its rhetorical question by saying that "business needs voices in the media, the same way labor unions, consumers, and other groups in our society do."[36] No one knows just how effective these image-molding efforts are, but many groups seem to believe firmly that advertising pays off.

Types of Interest Groups

11.5 Identify the various types of interest groups and their policy concerns.

Whether they are lobbying, electioneering, litigating, or appealing to the public, interest groups are omnipresent in the American political system. As with other aspects of American politics and policymaking, political scientists loosely categorize interest groups into clusters. Among the most important clusters are those consisting of groups that deal with either economic issues, environmental concerns, equality issues, or the interests of consumers and the public generally. An examination of these four very distinct types of interest groups will give you a good picture of much of the American interest group system.

Economic Interests

All economic interests are ultimately concerned with wages, prices, and profits. In the American economy, government does not determine these directly. Only on rare occasions has the government imposed wage and price controls. This has usually been during wartime, although the Nixon administration briefly used wage and price controls to combat inflation. More commonly, public policy in America has economic effects through regulations, tax advantages, subsidies and contracts, and international trade policy.

Business, labor, and farmers all fret over the impact of government regulations. Even a minor change in government regulatory policy can cost industries a great deal. Tax policies also affect the livelihood of individuals and firms. How the tax code is written determines whether people and producers pay a lot or a little of their incomes to the government. Government often provides subsidies to farmers, small businesses, railroads, minority businesses, and others, and every economic group wants to get its share of this direct aid and government contracts. In this era of economic global interdependence, economic interests are concerned about such matters as import quotas and tariffs (fees imposed on imports) and the soundness of the dollar. Although labor and business interests both seek to influence government because of the effect of these various aspects of economic policy, the impact on economic policy they seek is considerably different.

Labor Labor has more affiliated members than any other interest group except AARP. About 10 million workers are members of unions belonging to the AFL-CIO—itself a union of unions. And millions of other workers belong to unions not affiliated with the AFL-CIO, such as the National Education Association, the Teamsters, and the Service Employees International Union.

The major aim of American union organizations is to press for policies to ensure better working conditions and higher wages. Recognizing that many workers would like to enjoy union benefits without actually joining a union and paying dues, unions have fought hard to establish the **union shop**, which requires new employees of a business to join the union representing them within a short period of time and to remain members. In contrast, business groups have supported **right-to-work laws**, which outlaw union membership as a condition of employment. They argue that such laws deny a basic freedom—namely, the right not to belong to a group. In 1947, the biggest blow ever to the American labor movement occurred when Congress passed the Taft-Hartley Act, permitting states to adopt right-to-work laws (known within the AFL-CIO as "slave

union shop
A provision found in some collective bargaining agreements requiring all employees of a business to join the union within a short period, usually 30 days, and to remain members as a condition of employment.

right-to-work laws
A state law forbidding requirements that workers must join a union to hold their jobs. State right-to-work laws were specifically permitted by the Taft-Hartley Act of 1947.

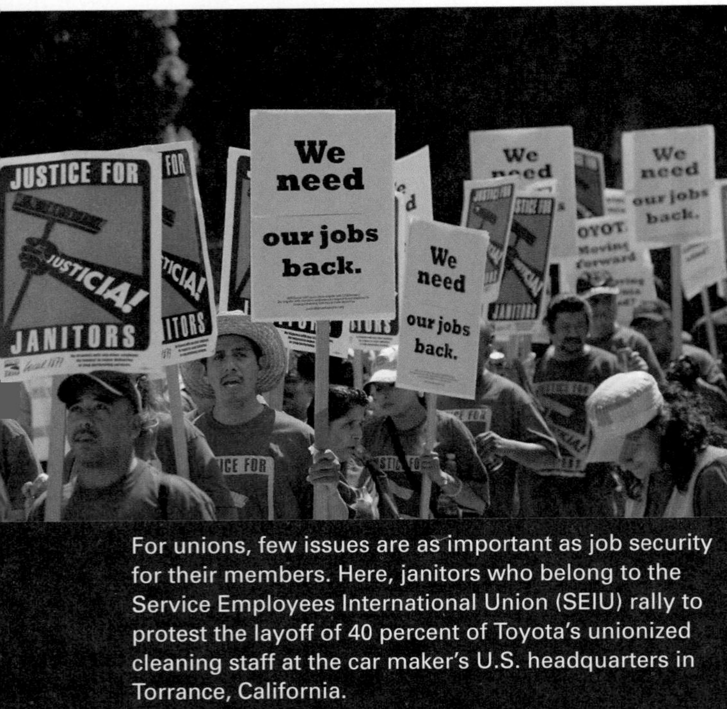

For unions, few issues are as important as job security for their members. Here, janitors who belong to the Service Employees International Union (SEIU) rally to protest the layoff of 40 percent of Toyota's unionized cleaning staff at the car maker's U.S. headquarters in Torrance, California.

labor laws"). Most of the states that have right-to-work laws are in the South, which has the lowest percentage of unionized workers, as you can see in "My State: Labor Union Membership as a Percentage of State Workforces."

The American labor movement reached its peak in 1956, when 33 percent of the nonagricultural workforce belonged to a union; since then, the percentage has declined to about 12 percent. One factor behind this decline is that low wages in other countries have adversely affected the American job market in a number of key manufacturing sectors (see Chapter 17). The U.S. steel industry, which once dominated in the domestic market, now has to compete with imports from producers based in Brazil, Korea, and other fast-developing economies. The United Auto Workers found its clout greatly reduced as Detroit faced increasingly heavy competition from Japanese automakers. Some political scientists, however, believe labor's problems result from more than the decline of blue-collar industries. Paul Johnson argues that the biggest factor causing the decline in union membership is the problems unions have in convincing today's workers that they will benefit from unionization. In particular, Johnson argues that this task has become more difficult because of employers' efforts to make nonunion jobs more satisfying.[37] Whatever the reason, it is clear that labor unions' membership and thus their potential ability to shape public policy have decreased.

Labor Union Membership as a Percentage of State Workforces

The map to the right classifies the 50 states according to the percentage of their nonagricultural workers who were members of a labor union in 2008.

QUESTIONS FOR DISCUSSION

- How does your state rank in terms of the prevalence of labor union membership in its workforce? Why do you think your state ranks as it does?
- Look up what types of labor unions, if any, are particularly prominent in your state. Have these labor unions influenced the nature of politics in your state? If so, how?
- Do you think it would best for your state if labor union membership increased or decreased over the next decade? Why?

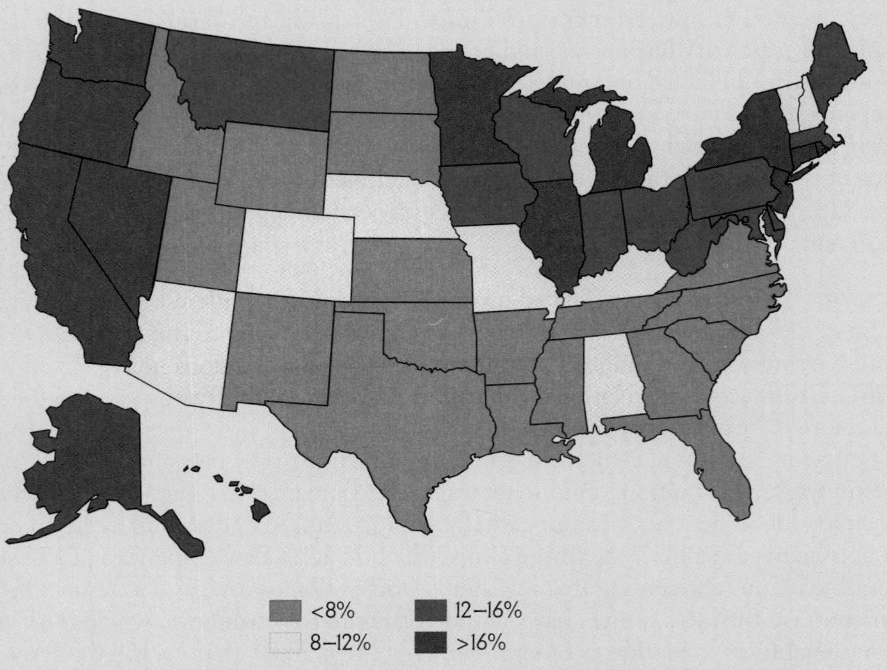

Source: *Statistical Abstract of the United States, 2010,* table 650, http://www.census.gov/compendia/statab/2010/tables/10s0650.pdf.

Business If the elite theorists are correct and there is an American power elite, it certainly must be dominated by leaders of the biggest banks, insurance companies, and multinational corporations. In any event, business is well organized for political action. Most large corporations now have offices in Washington that monitor legislative activity. So do hundreds of trade associations. And the Chamber of Commerce has become an imposing lobbying force, spending over $100 million a year lobbying on behalf of its mission to fulfill "the unified interests of American business." Business PACs have increased more dramatically than any other category of PACs over the past several decades. Many people assume that corporate and trade PAC contributions are always tilted in favor of the Republican Party and its tax-cutting and deregulatory agenda. However, as you can see in "A Generation of Change: How Non-Labor PACs Have Shifted Back and Forth," these PACs have swayed with the political winds, favoring whichever party happens to be in the majority at the time.

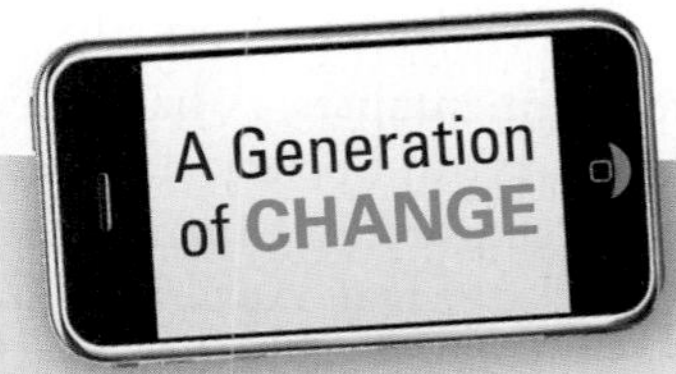

How Non-Labor PACs Have Shifted Back and Forth

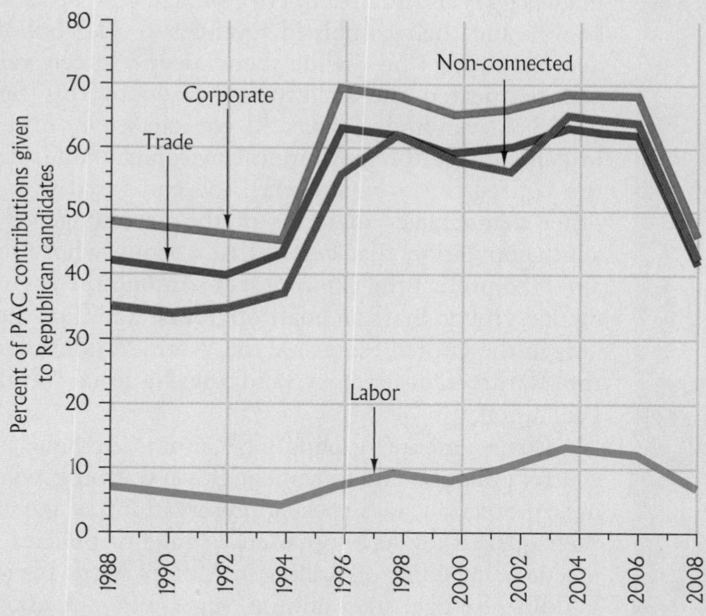

Source: Federal Election Commission.

Despite the tax-cutting and deregulatory agenda advocated by Ronald Reagan and the Republican Party in the 1980s, throughout that decade corporate and trade association PACs gave slightly more campaign contributions to Democratic candidates for the House of Representatives than they did to Republican candidates. The major reason for this pattern was that the Democrats had long held the majority in the House and therefore held the balance of power on the committees through which any legislation affecting business would have to pass. Many political analysts at the time argued that business groups gave money to the Republicans because they wanted to and the Democrats because they had to (in order to curry favor with the party in power).

As you can see in the graph, this situation changed markedly when the Republicans became the majority party in both the House and Senate, starting in 1995. Shortly afterwards, the Republican leadership in Congress started to actively encourage business interest groups and PACs to hire Republicans, as part of what has become known as the "K Street Project." The idea behind this was that if the big lobbying associations (concentrated on K Street in Washington, D.C.) were being run by Republicans, then the contributions would naturally go the GOP's way. This strategy appeared to be a successful one for the Republicans. During the 1996 through 2006 election-year cycles, when the Republicans held the majority in the House, they consistently received roughly two out of every three PAC dollars donated to House campaigns by corporate, trade, and non-connected (i.e., miscellaneous) PACs. Only labor PACs stuck with the Democrats during this period.

In the 2006 elections, despite the Republicans' advantage in PAC donations, the Democrats regained control of both houses of Congress. If the "K Street Project" has been truly successful in putting committed Republicans in charge of big lobbying associations, then PAC contributions should have continued to be tilted toward the Republicans in 2008. The results, as you can see, were disappointing to the Republicans. Once the Democrats had regained control of Congress, the PAC contributions immediately started to flow back their way.

Business interests are far from monolithic, as different business interests compete on many specific issues. Both Microsoft and Google have their lobbyists on Capitol Hill pressing their competing interests. Trucking and construction companies want more highways, but railroads do not. An increase in international trade will help some businesses expand their markets, but others may be hurt by foreign competition. In short, business interests are generally unified when it comes to promoting greater profits but are often fragmented when policy choices have to be made.

Although the trade associations are often among the least visible of Washington lobbies, they are a significant component of business interests, fighting regulations that would reduce their profits and seeking preferential tax treatment as well as subsidies and contracts. America's complex schedules of tariffs are monuments to the activities of the trade associations, whose successes are measured in amendments won, regulations rewritten, and exceptions made.

Environmental Interests

Among the newer political interest groups are the environmentalists. A handful of environmental groups, such as the Sierra Club and the Audubon Society, have been around since the nineteenth century, but many others trace their origins to the first Earth Day, April 22, 1970. On that day, ecology-minded people marched on Washington and other places to symbolize their support for environmental protection. Just two decades later, one estimate pegged the number of environmental groups at over 10,000 and their combined revenues at $2.9 billion—demonstrating "how widely and deeply green values had permeated the society."[38] No doubt this figure would be even higher today. As you can see in "America in Perspective: Membership in Environmental Groups," the United States ranks very high compared to many other democracies in terms of the percentage of the adult population that belongs to a group whose main aim is to protect the environment. Among the environmental groups that can boast of at least a million members in the United States are the World Wildlife Fund, the Nature Conservancy, and the National Wildlife Federation.

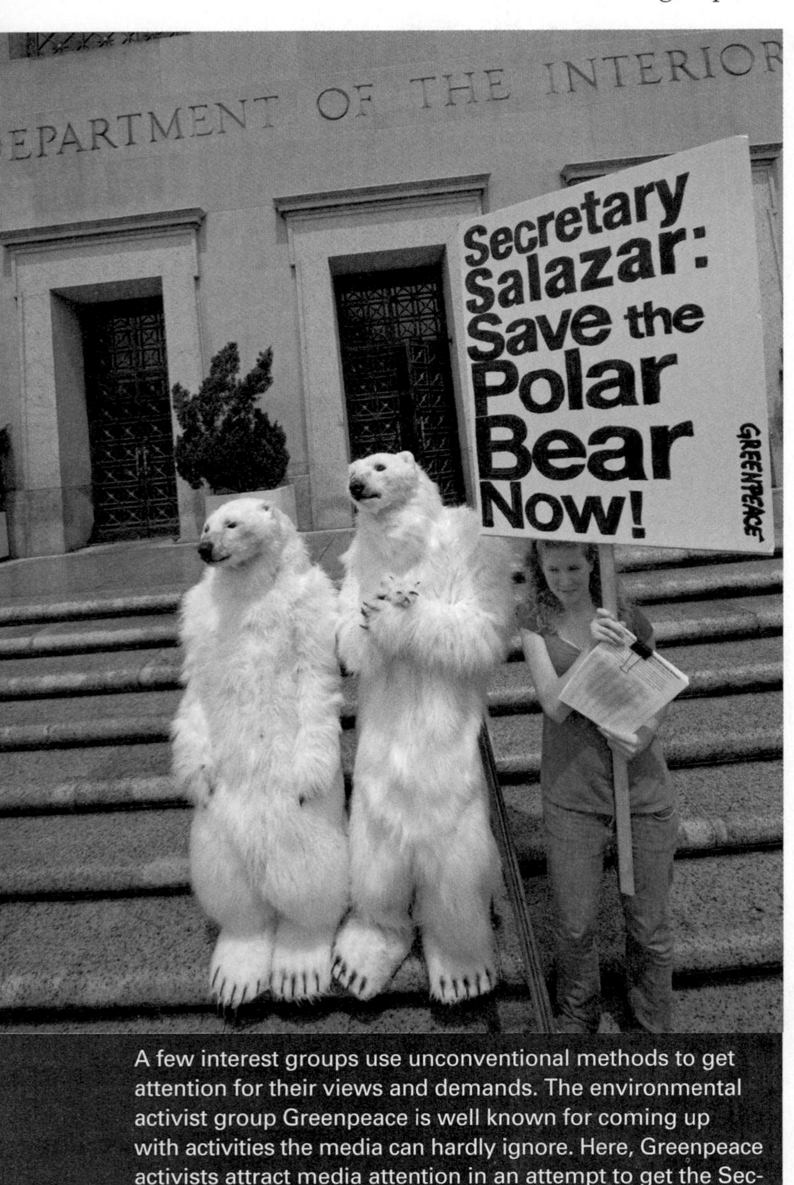

A few interest groups use unconventional methods to get attention for their views and demands. The environmental activist group Greenpeace is well known for coming up with activities the media can hardly ignore. Here, Greenpeace activists attract media attention in an attempt to get the Secretary of Interior to take regulatory action to combat global warming and help save the polar bear species.

Environmental groups have promoted policies to control pollution and to combat global warming, wilderness protection, and species preservation. In pursuing their goals, they have opposed a range of policies and practices, including oil drilling in Alaska's Arctic National Wildlife Refuge, strip mining, supersonic aircraft, and nuclear power plants. On these and other issues, environmentalists have exerted a great deal of influence on Congress and state legislatures. In particular, the arguments of environmentalists about radiation risks have had a profound impact on public policy. No new nuclear power plants have been approved since 1977, although in 2010 the Obama administration offered $8 billion in loan guarantees to two such projects that were seeking approval in the state of Georgia.[39]

Equality Interests

The Fourteenth Amendment guarantees equal protection under the law. American history, though, shows that this is easier said than done. Two sets of interest groups,

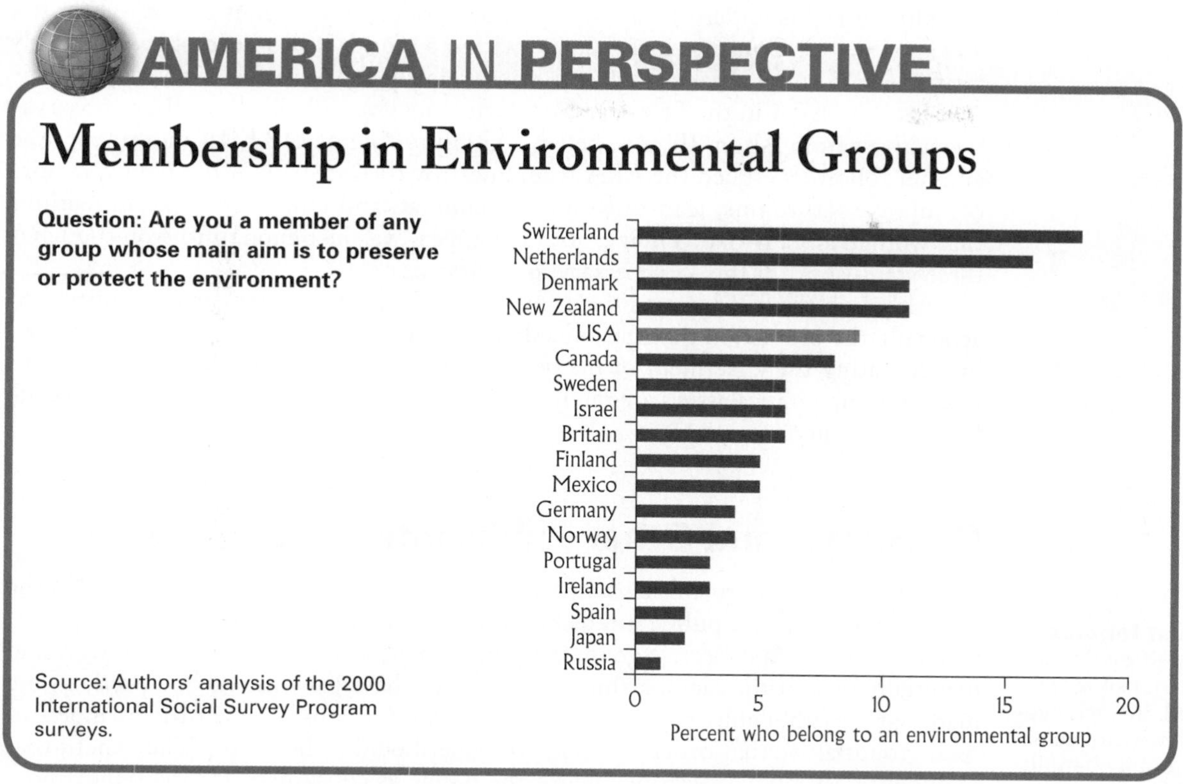

representing minorities and women, have made equal rights their main policy goal. Chapter 5 reviewed the long history of the civil rights movement; this section is concerned with its policy goals and organizational base.

Equality at the polls, in housing, on the job, in education, and in all other facets of American life has long been the dominant goal of African-American groups. The oldest and largest of these groups is the National Association for the Advancement of Colored People (NAACP). It argued and won the monumental *Brown v. Board of Education* case, in which the Supreme Court, in 1954, held that segregated schools were unconstitutional. Today, civil rights groups continue to push for equality, for example, through affirmative action programs to ensure that minority groups are given educational and employment opportunities.

Although the work of civil rights interest groups in fighting segregation and discrimination is well known, Dona and Charles Hamilton argue that "much less is known about the 'social welfare agenda'—the fight for social welfare policies to help the poor."[40] They argue that civil rights groups, since their early days, have been concerned with larger and more universal economic problems in American society.

Women gained the right to vote with the ratification of the Nineteenth Amendment in 1920, but political and economic equality for women has remained elusive. In recent decades, women's rights groups, such as the National Organization for Women (NOW), have lobbied for an end to discrimination against women. One of their top goals has

Environmental lobbies have been successful in preventing the building of any new nuclear power plants for the last 30 years. Some of the older nuclear plants are now being destroyed, as you can see in this photo.

long been the passage of the Equal Rights Amendment (ERA), which states that "equality of rights under the law shall not be abridged on account of sex." The ERA was approved by Congress in 1972, and within a month it had been overwhelmingly ratified by 15 states. Even Texas and Kansas, fairly conservative states, voted decisively for the ERA in the first year. Soon after, however, Phyllis Schlafly, a conservative activist from Alton, Illinois, began a highly visible STOP ERA movement. She and her followers argued the ERA would destroy the integrity of the family, require communal bathrooms, lead to women in combat, and eliminate legal protections that women already had. Their emotional appeal was just enough to stop the ERA three states short of the 38 necessary for ratification.

Although the ERA seems dead for the moment, NOW remains committed to achieving the protection that the amendment would have constitutionally guaranteed by advocating the enactment of many individual statutes. As is often the case with interest group politics, issues are rarely settled once and for all; rather, they shift to different policy arenas.

Consumer and Other Public Interest Lobbies

public interest lobbies According to Jeffrey Berry, organizations that seek "a collective good, the achievement of which will not selectively and materially benefit the membership or activists of the organization."

Today thousands of organized groups are championing various causes or ideas "in the public interest." These **public interest lobbies** are, in Jeffrey Berry's definition, organizations that seek "a collective good, the achievement of which will not selectively and materially benefit the membership or activists of the organization."[41] If products are made safer by the lobbying of consumer protection groups, it is not the members of such groups alone that benefit; rather, everyone should be better off. The benefit that public interest lobbies seek may be for the public as consumers, for the public more broadly defined, or for some sector of the public.

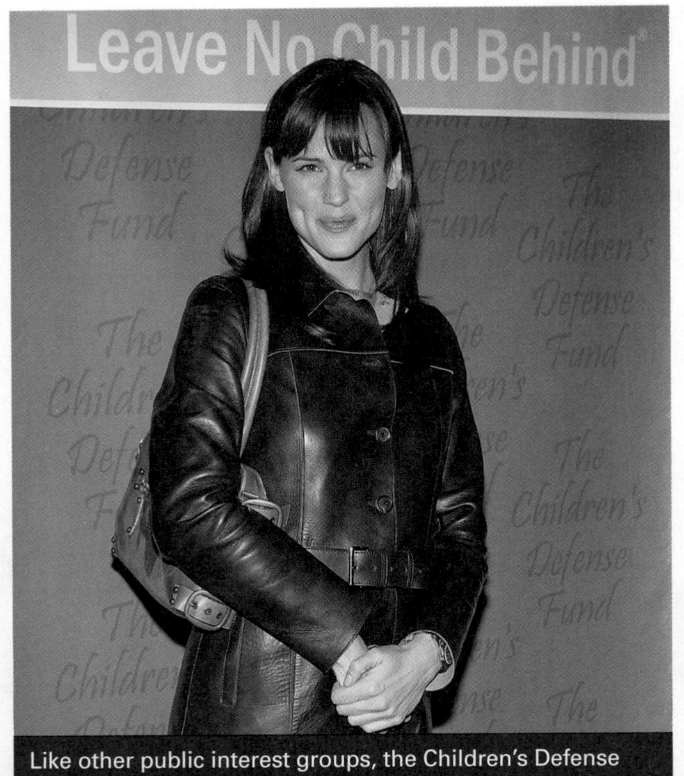

Like other public interest groups, the Children's Defense Fund faces the challenge of organizing a large potential group with broad goals. Therefore, it helps that celebrities like Jennifer Garner (shown here) are willing to publicize their support.

If ever a lobbying effort was spurred by a single person, it was the consumer movement. In the name of consumers, Ralph Nader took on American business almost single-handedly at first. He was propelled to national prominence by his 1965 book, *Unsafe at Any Speed,* which attacked General Motors' Corvair as mechanically deficient and dangerous. General Motors made the mistake of hiring a private detective to look for some dirt they could use to discredit him. Nader eventually learned about the investigation, sued General Motors for invasion of privacy, and won a hefty damage settlement. He used the proceeds to launch the first major consumer group in Washington.

Consumer groups have won many legislative victories. In 1973, for example, Congress responded to consumer advocacy by creating the Consumer Product Safety Commission, which it authorized to regulate all consumer products and to ban products that were dangerous. Products that the commission investigated included, in 2010, children's cribs reported to cause accidental strangulation and Starbucks water bottles reported to shatter in consumers' hands.

In addition to consumer groups, the wide range of public interest groups includes groups seeking to protect those who cannot speak for themselves, such as children or the mentally ill; good-government groups such as Common Cause, which push for openness and fairness in government; and religious groups like the Christian Coalition, which pursue what they consider to be moral standards for society.

Understanding Interest Groups

11.6 Evaluate how well Madison's ideas for controlling the influence of interest groups have worked in practice.

The problem of interest groups in America is much what it was over 200 years ago when James Madison defined it in speaking of his concerns about factions: A free society must allow for the representation of all groups that seek to influence political decision making, yet groups are usually more concerned with their own self-interest than with the needs of society as a whole, and for democracy to work well, it is important that they not be allowed to assume a dominant position.

Interest Groups and Democracy

Madison's solution to the problems posed by interest groups was to create a wide-open system in which many groups would be able to participate. In a wide-open system, according to Madison, groups with opposing interests would counterbalance one another. Pluralist theorists believe that a rough approximation of the public interest emerges from this competition. Indeed, with the tremendous growth of interest group politics in recent years, for every group with an interest, there now seems to be a competing group to watch over it—not to mention public interest lobbies to watch over them all. Robert Salisbury argues that "the growth in the number, variety, and sophistication of interest groups represented in Washington" has transformed policymaking such that it "is not dominated so often by a relatively small number of powerful interest groups as it may once have been."[42] He concludes that the increase in lobbying activity has actually resulted in less clout overall for interest groups—and in better democracy.

Elite theorists clearly disagree with this conclusion and point to the proliferation of business PACs as evidence of more interest group corruption in American politics than ever. A democratic process requires a free and open exchange of ideas in which candidates and voters can hear one another out, but PACs—the source of so much money in elections—distort the process. Elite theorists particularly note that wealthier interests are greatly advantaged by the PAC system. It is true that there are over four thousand PACs, but the relatively few big-spending ones dominate the fund-raising game. In 2004, a quarter of all PAC contributions came from just 48 PACs, each of which gave over a million dollars. In contrast, the 2,180 smallest PACs (in terms of donations made) accounted for just 10 percent of all PAC contributions.[43]

Hyperpluralist theorists maintain that whenever a major interest group objects strongly to proposed legislation, policymakers will bend over backward to try to accommodate it. With the formation of so many groups in recent years and with so many of them having influence in Washington, hyperpluralists argue that it has been increasingly difficult to accomplish major policy change in Washington. And this policy gridlock, so often evident in American politics today, diminishes democracy.

Interest Groups and the Scope of Government

Although individualistic, Americans are also very associational. As Alexis de Tocqueville wrote in the 1830s, "Americans of all ages, all conditions, and all dispositions constantly form associations."[44] This is not at all contradictory. By joining a number of political associations, Americans are able to politicize a variety of aspects of their own individualism. The multiplicity of the American interest group structure and the openness of American politics to inputs from interest groups allow individuals many channels for political participation and thus facilitate representation of individual interests.

Although individualism is most often treated in this book as being responsible for the relatively small scope of American government, when it works its way through interest group politics, the result is just the opposite. Individual interest groups fight to sustain government programs that are important to them, thereby making it hard for politicians ever to reduce the scope of government. Both President Carter and

President Reagan found their attempts to cut waste in federal spending frustrated by interest groups. In his farewell address, Carter "suggested that the reason he had so much difficulty in dealing with Congress was the fragmentation of power and decision making that was exploited by interest groups."[45] Similarly, a month before leaving office, Reagan remarked that "special interest groups, bolstered by campaign contributions, pressure lawmakers into creating and defending spending programs."[46] Above all, most special interest groups strive to maintain established programs that benefit them.

However, one can also argue that the growth in the scope of government in recent decades accounts for a good portion of the proliferation of interest groups. The more areas in which the federal government has become involved, the more interest groups have developed to attempt to influence policy. As William Lunch notes, "A great part of the increase was occasioned by the new government responsibility for civil rights, environmental protection, and greater public health and safety."[47] For example, once the government got actively involved in protecting the environment, many groups sprung up to lobby for strong standards and enforcement. Given the tremendous effects of environmental regulations on many industries, it should come as no surprise that these industries also organized to ensure that their interests were taken into account. As Salisbury writes, many groups have "come to Washington out of need and dependence rather than because they have influence."[48] He argues that interest groups spend much of their time merely monitoring policy developments in order to alert their membership and develop reactive strategies.

Summary

11.1 Describe the role of interest groups in American politics.

Interest groups consist of groups that participate in the political process in order to promote the policy goals which its individual members share. They usually focus their efforts on one specific issue area, unlike political parties, which have to address all issues on the public agenda.

11.2 Compare and contrast the theories of pluralism, elitism, and hyperpluralism.

The theory of pluralism asserts that the policymaking process is very open to the participation of all interest groups, with no single group usually dominating. Pluralists tend to believe that as a result the public interest generally prevails. In contrast, elitism contends that an upper-class elite holds the power and makes policy, regardless of the formal governmental organization. Hyperpluralism criticizes pluralism from a different perspective, contending that, with so many groups being so strong, government is weakened and its ability to make effective policy is crippled.

11.3 Analyze the factors that make some interest groups more successful than others in the political arena.

Groups that have large numbers of potential members are usually less effective than groups that have a smaller potential membership, because it is easier to mobilize members of a smaller group, who have more incentive to participate. Both large and small groups can benefit from the intensity of their members' beliefs. Money always helps lubricate the wheels of power, though it is hardly a surefire guarantee of success.

11.4 Assess the four basic strategies that interest groups use to try to shape policy.

Interest groups use four basic strategies to maximize their effectiveness. Lobbying is one well-known group strategy. Although the evidence on its influence is mixed, it is clear that lobbyists are most effective with those legislators already sympathetic to their side. Thus, electioneering becomes critical because it helps put supportive people in office. Often today, groups operate in the judicial as well as the legislative process, using litigation in the courts when lobbying fails or is not enough. Many also find it important to project a good image, employing public relations techniques to present themselves in the most favorable light.

11.5 Identify the various types of interest groups and their policy concerns.

Economic interest groups involve business and labor, with business focusing on governmental regulations and subsidies and labor focusing on policies to ensure good working conditions and wages. Environmental interests advocate policies to deal with problems such as global warming and pollution; they are also heavily involved in efforts to protect the wilderness and endangered species. Interest groups that are concerned with equality promote the fair treatment of groups that have been discriminated against in the past, such as African Americans and women. Public interest lobbies pursue policy objectives that they believe will benefit all citizens, such as consumer protection laws.

11.6 Evaluate how well Madison's ideas for controlling the influence of interest groups have worked in practice.

The issue of controlling interest groups remains as crucial to democracy today as it was in James Madison's time. Some scholars believe that the growth of interest groups has worked to divide political influence, just as Madison hoped it would. Critics of this point of view tend to focus on the political action committee (PAC) system as the new way in which special interests corrupt American democracy, or on the problem of too many groups having too much power to block policy change.

Chapter Test

11.1 Describe the role of interest groups in American politics.

1. Interest groups are often policy specialists, whereas political parties are policy generalists.

   True______ False______

2. What role do interest groups play in American politics? That is, what do interest groups hope to influence and why?

11.2 Compare and contrast the theories of pluralism, elitism, and hyperpluralism.

3. Which of the following is NOT an element of the pluralist group theory of politics?
   a. Groups provide a crucial link between people and government
   b. Groups usually follow the rules of the game
   c. Groups compete with each other
   d. Groups often counter-balance each other's strengths and weaknesses
   e. Groups often become too dominant

4. Elite theory relies on the notion that subgovernments exercise a great deal of control over numerous policy areas.

   True______ False______

5. What is "interest group liberalism" and how does it explain interest groups in American politics? Do you think that this theory presents an accurate depiction of interest group politics today? Explain, using a specific policy area as an example.

6. Compare and contrast pluralist, hyperpluralist, and elitist theories of interest group politics. Which paints the most favorable picture of interest groups, and how? Which do you think best depicts interest group politics today? Explain.

11.3 Analyze the factors that make some interest groups more successful than others in the political arena.

7. Which of the following is NOT true of the success of interest groups?
   a. The more intense a group, the more successful it tends to be
   b. The more financial resources a group has, the more successful it tends to be
   c. The more potential members a group has, the more successful it tends to be
   d. The smaller a group is, the more successful it tends to be
   e. All of the above are true

8. Single-issue groups often succeed by using an emotional issue to their advantage.

   True______ False______

9. Explain why large groups are often surprisingly ineffective. How might large groups improve their effectiveness? Your answer should include reference to collective goods, selective benefits, and the free-rider problem.

10. What did Frank Baumgartner and his colleagues find concerning the role that money plays in lobbying effectiveness? Do these findings change your view of interest groups and money and the role they play in American politics? Why or why not?

11.4 Assess the four basic strategies that interest groups use to try to shape policy.

11. Which of the following is NOT a tactic interest groups use?
    a. Lobbying to influence policy
    b. Forming political action committees to influence elections
    c. Fielding candidates for office in general elections
    d. Litigating to influence policy through the courts
    e. Appealing to the public to promote a positive group image

12. Political action committees contribute more or less equally to the campaigns of challengers and incumbents.

    True______ False______

13. Interest groups engage in a variety of activities to influence public policy. Discuss each of these activities and explain when each is most likely the best option for influencing public policy. Then pick a policy area that you are interested in and explain which tactic you think would be most effective and why.

14. What are the main arguments brought forth by advocates and critics of political action committees (PACs)? Which side do you agree with more, and why? Would you favor the abolition of PACs? Why, or why not?

11.5 Identify the various types of interest groups and their policy concerns.

15. Which of the following type of interest group tends to push for a collective good?
    a. Labor groups
    b. Consumer groups
    c. Environmental groups
    d. Equality groups
    e. All of the above

16. Labor groups have continued to expand their membership and influence into the twenty-first century.

    True______ False______

17. Based on the discussion in the chapter of interest group theories and of factors contributing to interest group success, which of the various types of interest groups do you think would be most successful, and why?

11.6 Evaluate how well Madison's ideas for controlling the influence of interest groups have worked in practice.

18. How have Madison's ideas for controlling interest groups fared in today's political environment? Which theory of interest groups best correlates with Madison's ideas? Based on your answer, do you think that interest groups are beneficial or harmful for democracy? Explain your answer.

19. How do interest groups affect the scope of government? Why is it difficult for politicians to reduce the scope of government when interest groups are so prevalent? Are there ways in which interest groups might tend to reduce the scope of government? Explain.

PEARSON mypoliscilab™ Exercises

Apply what you learned in this chapter on MyPoliSciLab.

Read on **mypoliscilab.com**

eText: Chapter 11

Study and **Review** on **mypoliscilab.com**

Pre-Test
Post-Test
Chapter Exam
Flashcards

Watch on **mypoliscilab.com**

Video: American Cancer Society Recommendation
Video: California Teachers Stage Sit-Ins
Video: Murtha and the PMA Lobbyists

Explore on **mypoliscilab.com**

Simulation: You Are a Lobbyist
Comparative: Comparing Interest Groups
Timeline: Interest Groups and Campaign Finance
Visual Literacy: Federal Election Rules, PACs, and the Money Trail

Key Terms

interest group (306)
pluralism (307)
elitism (307)
hyperpluralism (307)
iron triangles (310)
potential group (311)
actual group (311)
collective good (311)
free-rider problem (311)
selective benefits (312)
single-issue group (313)
lobbying (315)
electioneering (317)
political action committees (PACs) (317)
union shop (321)
right-to-work laws (321)
public interest lobbies (326)

Internet Resources

www.aarp.org
The official site of AARP.

www.aflcio.org
The nation's largest labor association, the AFL-CIO, posts material at this site.

www.nea.org
The site of the National Education Association.

www.greenpeaceusa.org
The place to go to learn more about the activities of this environmental protection group.

www.commoncause.org
The official site of Common Cause, one of the nation's oldest and largest public affairs interest groups.

www.freespeech.org
A site for an interest group that represents young people, particularly on Social Security issues.

For Further Reading

Baumgartner, Frank R. et al. ***Lobbying and Policy Change.*** Chicago: University of Chicago Press, 2008. A path-breaking study of who wins and loses in the lobbying game and why.

Berry, Jeffrey M. ***The New Liberalism: The Rising Power of Citizen Groups.*** Washington, DC: Brookings Institution, 1999. Berry argues that citizen groups have been strikingly successful in influencing the policy agenda in recent decades.

Berry, Jeffrey M., and Clyde Wilcox. ***The Interest Group Society,*** 5th ed. New York: Longman, 2008. One of the best contemporary textbooks on interest groups in American politics.

Cigler, Allan J., and Burdett A. Loomis, eds. ***Interest Group Politics,*** 7th ed. Washington, DC: Congressional Quarterly Press, 2007. An excellent collection of original articles on the modern interest group system.

CQ Press Editors. ***Public Interest Group Profiles, 2006–2007.*** Washington, DC: Congressional Quarterly Press, 2006. A comprehensive reference book about interest groups that provides information about internship and employment opportunities with many groups.

Dye, Thomas R. ***Who's Running America?*** 7th ed. Englewood Cliffs, NJ: Prentice Hall, 2002. A good summary of the elitist view of interest groups.

Herrnson, Paul S., Ronald G. Shaiko, and Clyde Wilcox, eds. ***The Interest Group Connection,*** 2nd ed. Washington, DC: Congressional Quarterly Press, 2005. A collection of essays on how interest groups attempt to influence elections and the three branches of government.

Kollman, Ken. ***Outside Lobbying: Public Opinion and Interest Group Strategies.*** Princeton, NJ: Princeton University Press, 1998. An insightful study of how many interest groups use public opinion in the lobbying process.

Lowi, Theodore J. ***The End of Liberalism,*** 2nd ed. New York: Norton, 1979. A critique of the role of subgovernments and the excessive deference to interest groups in the American political system.

Olson, Mancur. ***The Logic of Collective Action.*** Cambridge, MA: Harvard University Press, 1965. Develops an economic theory of groups, showing how the cards are stacked against larger groups.

Rauch, Jonathan. ***Demosclerosis: The Silent Killer of American Government.*** New York: Random House, 1994. A good treatment of hyperpluralism in American politics.

Rozell, Mark J., Clyde Wilcox, and David Madland. ***Interest Groups in American Campaigns,*** 2nd ed. Washington, DC: Congressional Quarterly Press, 2006. A good review of how interest groups are playing an increasingly important role in electioneering.

Chapter 12

Congress

Learning Objectives

12.1 Characterize the backgrounds of members of Congress and assess their impact on the ability of members of Congress to represent average Americans.

12.2 Identify the principal factors influencing the outcomes in congressional elections.

12.3 Compare and contrast the House and Senate, and describe the roles of congressional leaders, committees, caucuses, and staff.

12.4 Outline the path of bills to passage and explain the influences on congressional decision making.

12.5 Assess Congress's role as a representative body and the impact of representation on the scope of government.

Chapter **OUTLINE**

POLITICS IN ACTION: GOVERNING IN CONGRESS

John Boehner began serving in the House of Representatives in 1991. Twenty years later, he was elected to the chamber's highest position: Speaker of the House. As minority leader, he had often led the opposition to President Barack Obama's policies in areas ranging from economic policy to healthcare reform. He had also frequently criticized the Democratic majority, especially for, in his view, its willingness to expand government and its use of special procedures to shut Republicans out of the decision-making process.

In 2010, the Republicans won a majority of seats in the House after being in the minority for four years, and Boehner's role changed from leading the opposition to sharing responsibility for governing. The role of Speaker meant that his days would now be filled with efforts to persuade his fellow partisans to unite on supporting Republican proposals as well as on continuing to oppose the president's. However, to get proposals passed, he would need not only to unite his party but also to prevail over the objections of the Democratic Senate and the president. In short, he would need to contend with the Madisonian system of separation of powers and checks and balances—a far more difficult task. And House Democrats, feeling excluded from an effective policymaking role, would complain bitterly.

The movement of legislation through the congressional labyrinth is complicated and slow, and there are many checks on policymaking. Power is fragmented within Congress, and representatives and senators are typically fiercely independent. Former Senate Majority Leader Howard Baker declared that moving the Senate is like "trying to push a wet noodle": When Congress faces the great issues of the day, it often cannot arrive at any decision at all.

Congress is both our central policymaking branch and our principal *representative* branch. As such, it lies at the heart of American democracy. How does Congress combine its roles of representing constituents *and* making effective public policy? Some critics argue that Congress is too responsive to constituents and, especially, to organized interests and is thus unable to make difficult choices regarding public policy, such as reining in spending. Others argue that Congress is too insulated from ordinary citizens and makes policy to suit the few rather than the many. Yet other critics focus on Congress as the source of government expansion. Does Congress's responsiveness predispose the legislature to increase the size of government to please those in the public wishing more or larger government programs?

The Framers of the Constitution conceived of the legislature as the center of policymaking in America. Their plan was for the great disputes over public policy to be resolved in Congress, not in the White House or the Supreme Court. Although the prominence of Congress has ebbed and flowed over the course of American history, as often as not, Congress is the true center of power in Washington.

Congress's tasks become more difficult each year. On any given day, a representative or senator can be required to make sensible judgments about missiles, nuclear waste dumps, abortion, trade competition with China, income tax rates, the soaring costs of Social Security and Medicare, or any of countless other issues. The 2009 health care reform proposal was about 1,400 pages long and weighed six pounds. Just finding time to think about these issues—much less debate them—has become increasingly difficult. Despite the many demands of the job, there is no shortage of men and women running for congressional office. The following sections will introduce you to these people.

12.1 Characterize the backgrounds of members of Congress and assess their impact on the ability of members of Congress to represent average Americans.

The Representatives and Senators

Being a member of Congress is a difficult and unusual job. A person must be willing to spend considerable time, trouble, and money to obtain a crowded office on Capitol Hill. To nineteenth-century humorist Artemus Ward, such a quest was inexplicable: "It's easy to see why a man goes to the poorhouse or the penitentiary. It's because he can't help it. But why he should voluntarily go live in Washington is beyond my comprehension."

The Members

To many Americans, being a member of Congress may seem like a glamorous job. What citizens do not see are the 14-hour days spent dashing from one meeting to the next (members are often scheduled to be in two places at the same time),[1] the continuous travel between Washington and constituencies, the lack of time for reflection or exchange of ideas, the constant fund-raising, the partisan rancor that permeates Congress, and—perhaps most important of all—the feeling that Congress is making little headway in solving the country's problems. It is ironic that such frustrations exist in an organization whose members put so much blood, sweat, and tears into joining.

There are attractions to the job, however. First and foremost is power. Members of Congress make key decisions about important matters of public policy. In addition, members of Congress earn a salary of $174,000—about three times the income of the typical American family, although far below that of hundreds of corporate presidents—and they receive generous retirement and health benefits.

There are 535 members of Congress. An even hundred, two from each state, are members of the Senate. The other 435 are members of the House of Representatives. The Constitution specifies only that members of the House must be at least 25 years old and American citizens for seven years, that senators must be at least 30 and American citizens for nine years, and that all members of Congress must reside in the state from which they are elected.

Members of Congress are not typical or average Americans, however, as the figures in Table 12.1 reveal. Those who argue the country is run by a power elite are quick to point out that members come largely from occupations with high status and usually have substantial incomes. Although calling the Senate a "millionaire's club" is an exaggeration, the proportion of millionaires and near millionaires is much higher in Congress than in an average crowd of 535 people. Business and law are the dominant prior occupations; other elite occupations such as academia are also well represented.

The prominence of lawyers in Congress is not surprising. Law especially attracts persons interested in politics and provides the flexibility (and often the financial support of a law firm) to wage election campaigns. In addition, many government positions in which aspiring members of Congress can make their marks, such as district attorney, are reserved for lawyers.

Some prominent groups are underrepresented. African Americans make up about 10 percent of the members of the House (compared with about 13 percent of the total

TABLE 12.1 A Portrait of the 112th Congress: Some Statistics

CHARACTERISTIC	HOUSE (435 TOTAL)	SENATE (100 TOTAL)
Party**		
Democrat	191	51
Republican	244	47
Independent	–	2
Gender		
Men	363	83
Women	72	17
Race/Ethnicity		
Asian	4	2
African American	42	0
Hispanic	24	2
White and other	365	96
Religion+	Percent	Percent
Protestant	53	55
Roman Catholic	31	26
Jewish	7	12
Other and unspecified	9	7
Prior occupation*+	Percent	Percent
Public service/politics	57	48
Law	41	63
Business	52	36
Education	19	20
Other	41	29

+Data for 111th Congress.
*Some members specify more than one occupation.
**As late as mid-November 2010, votes were still being tallied.
Source: *Congressional Quarterly.*

population), but there is no African American in the Senate. There are 24 Hispanics in the House and 2 in the Senate, although Hispanics represent 16 percent of the population. Asian and Native Americans are also underrepresented. However, women may be the most underrepresented group; females account for more than half the population but for only 17 percent of members of each chamber in Congress—72 voting representatives (as well as the nonvoting representative from Washington, D.C.) and 17 senators.

Members of Congress who do not share their constituents' economic and social backgrounds can nonetheless represent their concerns. The late Senator Edward Kennedy, for example, born into one of America's wealthiest families, championed the poor and underprivileged throughout his career. Here, Kennedy spoke to workers concerned over proposed cuts in their pay and benefits.

How important are the personal characteristics of members of Congress? Can a group of predominantly white, upper-middle-class, middle-aged Protestant males adequately represent a much more diverse population? Would a group of more typical citizens be more effective in making major policy decisions? Because power in Congress is highly decentralized, the backgrounds of representatives and senators can be important if they influence how these officials prioritize issues and how they vote on issues. There is evidence that African-American members are more active than are white members in serving African-American constituents,[2] and they appear to increase African-American constituents' contact with and knowledge about Congress.[3] On the average, women legislators seem to be more active than are men in pursuing the interests of women.[4] By the same token, representatives with a business background are more pro-business than are other members.[5]

Obviously, members of Congress cannot claim *descriptive* representation—that is, representing constituents by mirroring their personal, politically relevant characteristics. They may, however, engage in *substantive* representation—representing the interests of groups.[6]

Despite their gains in recent congressional elections, women are the most underrepresented demographic group in Congress. Here women senators and representatives meet to raise awareness of domestic violence.

For example, members of Congress with a background of wealth and privilege, such as the late Senator Edward Kennedy, can be champions for the interests of the poor. Moreover, most members of Congress have lived in the constituencies they represent for many years and share the beliefs and attitudes of a large proportion of their constituents. If they do not share such perspectives, they may find it difficult to keep their seats come election time. At the same time, women and African Americans in Congress are achieving important positions on committees, increasing the chances of making descriptive representation effective.[7]

Why Aren't There More Women in Congress?

Sarah Fulton, a scholar of women in politics, found that in the 2008 elections, women won 56 percent of the House races, and 57 percent of the Senate races in which they competed.[8] Yet, despite this winning record, we have seen that women in the 111th Congress (2009–2010) occupied just 17 percent of both U.S. House and Senate seats. If women have proven themselves capable of competing with and winning against men, then why aren't there more women in Congress?

Part of the reason for women's underrepresentation is that fewer women than men become major party nominees for office. For example, a female major-party nominee contested only 31 percent of the 435 House races in 2008. In a recent article, Fulton and her coauthors report that women with children are significantly less ambitious about running for office than are their male counterparts, largely because of greater child care responsibilities; however, they find no gender disparity in ambition when looking at women without children. The authors also suggest that women's decisions to run are more sensitive than are men's to their perceptions of the odds of winning: Women are less likely than are men to run when they perceive their odds to be poor; however, they are more likely than are men to run when they detect a political opportunity.[9] If these findings are correct, remedying women's underrepresentation might require a more even distribution of childcare responsibilities between spouses as well as women's overcoming their reluctance to run when they perceive their prospects to be less than stellar.

12.2 Identify the principal factors influencing the outcomes in congressional elections.

Congressional Elections

Congressional elections are demanding, expensive,[10] and, as you will see, generally foregone conclusions—yet members of Congress are first and foremost politicians. Men and women may run for Congress to forge new policy initiatives, but they also enjoy politics and consider a position in Congress near the top of their chosen profession. Even if they dislike politics, without reelection they will not be around long enough to shape policy.

Who Wins Elections?

incumbents
Those already holding office. In congressional elections, incumbents usually win.

Incumbents are individuals who already hold office. Sometime during each term, the incumbent must decide whether to run again or to retire voluntarily. Most decide to run for reelection. They enter their party's primary, almost always emerge victorious, and typically win in the November general election, too. Indeed, the most predictable aspect of congressional elections is this: *Incumbents usually win* (see Figure 12.1).

FIGURE 12.1 The Incumbency Factor in Congressional Elections

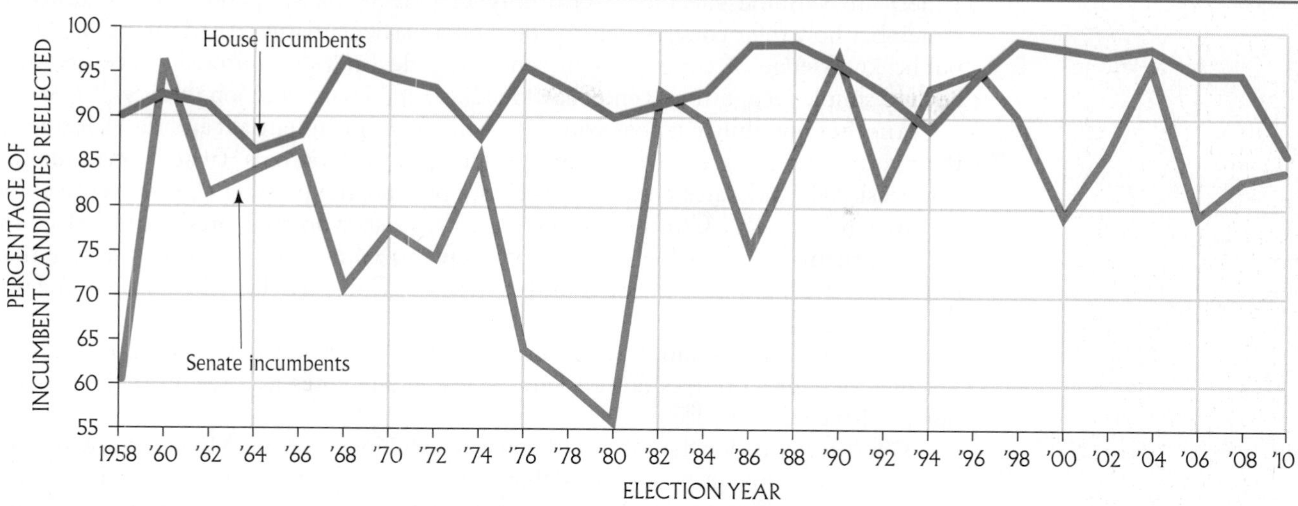

Source: Norman J. Ornstein, Thomas E. Mann, and Michael J. Malbin, *Vital Statistics on Congress, 1997–1998* (Washington, DC: Congressional Quarterly Press, 1998). Data for 1998–2010 compiled by the authors. Figures reflect incumbents running in both primary and general elections.

Even in a year of great political upheaval such as 1994, in which the Republicans gained eight seats in the Senate and 53 seats in the House, 92 percent of incumbent senators and 89 percent of incumbent representatives won their bids for reelection.

In the case of the House, not only do more than 90 percent of incumbents seeking reelection win, but most of them win with more than 60 percent of the vote. Perhaps most astonishing is the fact that even when challengers' positions on the issues are closer to the voters' positions, incumbents still tend to win.[11]

The picture for the Senate is a little different. Even though senators still have a good chance of beating back a challenge, the odds of reelection are often not as handsome as for House incumbents; senators typically win by narrower margins. One reason for the greater competition in the Senate is that an entire state is almost always more diverse than a congressional district and thus provides a larger base for opposition to an incumbent. At the same time, senators have less personal contact with their constituencies, which on average are about 10 times larger than those of members of the House of Representatives. Senators also receive more coverage in the media than representatives do and are more likely to be held accountable on controversial issues. Moreover, senators tend to draw more visible challengers, such as governors or members of the House, whom voters already know and who have substantial financial backing—a factor that lessens the advantages of incumbency.

Despite their success at reelection, incumbents often feel quite vulnerable. As Thomas Mann put it, members of Congress perceive themselves as "unsafe at any margin."[12] Thus, they have been raising and spending more campaign funds, sending more mail to their constituents, visiting their states and districts more often, and staffing more local offices than ever before.[13]

The Advantages of Incumbency

There are several possible explanations for the success of incumbents. One is that voters know how their elected representatives vote on important policy issues and agree with their stands, sending them back to Washington to keep up the good work. This, however, is usually not the case. Most citizens have trouble recalling the names of their congressional representatives (in one poll only 28 percent of the public could name their representatives in the House),[14] let alone keeping up with their representatives' voting records. One study found that only about one-fifth of Americans could make an accurate guess about how their representatives voted on any issue in Congress;[15] in an American National Election Study, only 11 percent of the people even claimed to remember how their congressperson voted on a particular issue. As Mann put it, "Mass public knowledge of congressional candidates declines precipitously once we move beyond simple recognition, generalized feelings, and incumbent job ratings."[16]

Another possibility is that voter assessments of presidential candidates influence their voting for Congress. Most stories of presidential "coattails" (when voters support congressional candidates because of their support for the president), however, seem to be just stories.[17] Bill Clinton and George W. Bush won four presidential elections between them. Yet in each election they received a *smaller* percentage of the vote than did almost every winning member of their party in Congress. They had little in the way of coattails.

Journalists often claim that voters are motivated primarily by their pocketbooks. Yet members of Congress do not gain or lose many votes as a result of the ups and downs of the economy.[18]

What accounts for the success of congressional incumbents? Members of Congress engage in three primary activities that increase the probability of their reelection: advertising, credit claiming, and position taking.[19] The lack of strong opponents and the high costs of campaigning further ensure their success.

Advertising For members of Congress, advertising means much more than placing ads in the newspapers and on television. Most congressional advertising takes place between elections in the form of contact with constituents. The goal is *visibility.*

Members of Congress work hard to get themselves known in their constituencies, and they usually succeed. Not surprisingly, members concentrate on staying visible and make frequent trips home. In a typical week, members spend some time in their home districts,[20] even though their districts may be hundreds of miles from Washington. Similarly, members use the franking privilege to mail newsletters to every household in their constituency.

More recently, members of Congress have employed technology to bring franking into the digital age. Congressional staffers track the interests of individual voters, file the information in a database, and then use e-mails or phone calls to engage directly with voters on issues they know they care about. Using taxpayers' money, legislators employ a new technology that allows them to call thousands of households simultaneously with a recorded message, inviting people in their districts to join in on a conference call. With the push of a button, the constituent is on the line with the House member—and often 1,000 or more fellow constituents. Equally important, the lawmaker knows, from the phone numbers, where the respondents live and, from what they say on the call, what issues interest them. Information gathered from these events, as well as from e-mails and phone calls from constituents, gets plugged into a database, giving the incumbent something a challenger could only dream of: a detailed list of the specific interests of thousands of would-be voters. E-mail then allows for personal interaction—and a free reminder of why the incumbent should be reelected.

Credit Claiming Congresspersons also engage in credit claiming, which involves enhancing their standing with constituents through service to individuals and the district. One member told Richard Fenno about the image he tried to cultivate in his constituency:

> [I have] a very high recognition factor. And of all the things said about me, none of them said, "He's a conservative or a liberal," or "He votes this way on such and such an issue." None of that at all. There were two things said. One, "He works hard." Two, "He works for us." Nothing more than that. So we made it our theme, "O'Connor gets things done"; and we emphasized the dams, the highways, the buildings, the casework.[21]

Morris Fiorina has emphasized this close link between service and success.[22] Members of Congress, he says, *can* go to the voters and stress their policymaking record and their stands on new policy issues on the agenda. The problem with facing the voters on one's record—past, present, and future—is that policy positions make enemies as well as friends. A member of Congress's vote for reducing government spending may win some friends, but it will make enemies of voters who link that vote with service cutbacks. Besides, a congressperson can almost never show that he or she alone was responsible for a major policy. Being only one of 435 members of the House or one of 100 senators, a person can hardly promise to end inflation, cut taxes, or achieve equal rights for women single-handedly.

One thing, however, always wins friends and almost never makes enemies: *servicing the constituency.* There are two ways in which members of Congress can do so: through casework and through the pork barrel. **Casework** is helping constituents as individuals—cutting through some bureaucratic red tape to give people what they think they have a right to get. Do you have trouble getting your check from the Social Security Administration on time? Call your congressperson; he or she can cut red tape. Does your town have trouble getting federal bureaucrats to respond to its request for federal construction money? Call your congressperson. Representatives and senators can single-handedly take credit for each of these favors.

casework
Activities of members of Congress that help constituents as individuals, particularly by cutting through bureaucratic red tape to get people what they think they have a right to get.

Another service is winning federal funds for their states and districts. The **pork barrel** is composed of federal projects, grants, and contracts available to state and local governments, businesses, colleges, and other institutions. Typically, Congress appropriates funds for grants and let institutions—such as universities—compete for funding for specific projects. In recent years, however, members of Congress have grown increasingly aggressive in "earmarking" funds that must be spent for particular projects in specific districts. The Office of Management and Budget reported that there were nearly 12,000 such earmarks in 2007, costing about $17 billion. Members of Congress love to take credit for a new highway, sewage treatment plant, or research institute. Often, they announce the awards through their offices.

pork barrel
Federal projects, grants, and contracts available to state and local governments, businesses, colleges, and other institutions in a congressional district.

As a result of the advantages of incumbency in advertising and credit claiming, incumbents, especially in the House, are usually much better known and have a more favorable public image than do their opponents.[23] Getting things done for the folks back home often wins an incumbent the chance to serve them again. Yet, for all the advantage they confer, by themselves casework and pork barrel, even shrewdly deployed, do not determine congressional elections.[24]

Position Taking Even if, in establishing their public images, members of Congress emphasize their experience, hard work, trustworthiness, and service to their constituencies—qualities unrelated to partisan or programmatic content—they must take positions on policies when they vote and when they respond to constituents' questions And the positions they take may affect the outcome of an election, particularly if the issues are on matters salient to voters and the positions are not well aligned with those of a majority of constituents. This is especially true in elections for the Senate, in which issues are likely to play a greater role than in House elections.

Weak Opponents Another advantage for incumbents, particularly in the House, is that they are likely to face weak opponents. In part because the advantages of incumbency scare off potentially effective opponents,[25] those individuals who do run are usually not well known or well qualified and lack experience and organizational and financial backing.[26] The lack of adequate campaign funds is a special burden because challengers need money to compensate for the "free" recognition incumbents receive from their advertising and credit claiming.[27]

Because credit claiming is so important to reelection, members of Congress rarely pass up the opportunity to increase federal spending in their state or district. The early 2000s witnessed a surge in earmarks of expenditures of specific projects. One of the most notorious was the down payment of $223 million for the "Bridge to Nowhere," proposed to replace the ferry connecting Ketchikan, Alaska (population of about 9,000), to the Ketchikan International Airport on Gravina Island (population of about 50). After widespread criticism, Alaska canceled the project.

Campaign Spending It costs a great deal of money to elect a Congress. In the 2007–2008 election cycle, congressional candidates and supporting party committees spent more than $2 billion to contest 435 House and 33 Senate seats. The average winner in the House spent about $1.4 million while the average Senate winner spent $8.5 million.[28]

Challengers have to raise large sums if they hope to defeat an incumbent, and the more they spend, the more votes they receive. Money buys them name recognition and a chance to be heard. Incumbents, by contrast, already have high levels of recognition among their constituents and benefit less (but still benefit) from campaign spending; what matters most is how much their opponents spend. (In contests for open seats, the candidate who spends the most usually wins.[29]) In the end, however, challengers are usually substantially outspent by incumbents. In both the Senate and House races in 2008, the typical incumbent outspent the typical challenger by a ratio of more than 3 to 1.[30]

The candidate spending the most money usually wins—but not always. In Senate races in 2006, Rick Santorum of Pennsylvania, James Talent of Missouri, and Ned Lamont of Connecticut outspent their opponents by spending $28 million, $24 million, and $21 million, respectively—and all lost. Obviously, prolific spending in a campaign is no guarantee of success.

The Role of Party Identification

At the base of every electoral coalition are the members of the candidate's party in the constituency. Most members of Congress represent constituencies in which their party is in the clear majority, giving incumbents yet another advantage. Most people identify with a party, and most party identifiers reliably vote for their party's candidates. Indeed, about 90 percent of voters who identify with a party vote for the House candidates of their party. State legislatures have eagerly employed advances in technology to draw the boundaries of House districts so that there is a safe majority for one party. In addition, it is now more common for people to live in communities where their neighbors are likely to have political and other attitudes that are similar to their own,[31] reducing the basis for party competition.

Defeating Incumbents

In light of the advantages of incumbents, it is reasonable to ask why anyone challenges them at all. One of the main reasons is simply that challengers are often naïve about their chances of winning. Because few have money for expensive polls, they rely on friends and local party leaders, who often tell them what they want to hear.

Sometimes challengers receive some unexpected help. An incumbent tarnished by scandal or corruption becomes instantly vulnerable. Clearly, voters do take out their anger at the polls. For example, representatives who bounced large numbers of checks at the House bank were much more likely to lose their seats in the 1992 elections than their more fiscally responsible colleagues.[32] In a close election, negative publicity can turn victory into defeat.[33]

Incumbents may also lose many of their supporters if the boundaries of their districts change. After each federal census, Congress reapportions its membership. States that have gained significantly in population will be given more House seats; states that have lost substantial population will lose one or more of their seats. The state legislatures must then redraw their states' district lines; one incumbent may be moved into another's district, where the two must battle for one seat.[34] A state party in the majority is more likely to move two of the opposition party's representatives into a single district than two of its own. Or it might split the district of an incumbent of the minority party to make that district more competitive. In 2004, Republicans in Texas redrew the state's congressional boundaries for the second time since 2000, removing many Democratic constituents from the districts of Democratic representatives. In the end, the Republicans gained four seats in the state's delegation in the U.S. House of Representatives.

Finally, major political tidal waves occasionally roll across the country, leaving defeated incumbents in their wake. One such wave occurred in 1994, when the public mood turned especially sour and voters took out their frustration on Democratic incumbents, defeating 34 in the House and two in the Senate. In 2006, the tide reversed as six Republican senators and 23 Republican representatives lost their seats.

Open Seats

When an incumbent is not running for reelection, and the seat is open, there is greater likelihood of competition. If the party balance in a constituency is such that either party has a chance of winning, each side may offer a strong candidate with name recognition among the voters or enough money to establish name recognition. Most of the turnover in the membership of Congress results from vacated seats.

Stability and Change

Because incumbents usually win reelection, there is some stability in the membership of Congress. This stability allows representatives and senators to gain some expertise in dealing with complex questions of public policy. At the same time, it also may insulate them from the winds of political change. Safe seats make it more difficult for citizens to "send a message to Washington" with their votes. Particularly in the House, it takes a large shift in votes to affect the outcomes of most elections. To increase turnover in the membership of Congress, some reformers have proposed *term limitations* for representatives and senators[35] (see "You Are the Policymaker: Should We Impose Term Limits on Members of Congress?").

YOU ARE THE POLICYMAKER

Should We Impose Term Limits on Members of Congress?

In the late 1980s, many reformers were concerned that the incumbency advantage enjoyed by legislators created, in effect, lifetime tenure, which served as a roadblock to change and encouraged ethics abuses. To increase turnover among legislators, these reformers proposed term limitations, generally restricting representatives to 6 or 12 consecutive years in office.

The movement to limit the terms of legislators spread rapidly across the country. Within a few years, 23 states enacted term limitations for members of their state legislatures. The House Republicans made terms limits for Congress part of their Contract with America in the 1994 election. Yet changing the terms of members of Congress requires changing the Constitution, which is difficult to do, and many members of Congress have fought term limitations fiercely.

Opponents of term limitations object to the loss of experienced legislators and of the American people's ability to vote for whomever they please. In addition, they add, there is plenty of new blood in the legislature: At the beginning of the 111th Congress (in 2009), most members of the House and Senate had served fewer than 10 years in Congress. Moreover, changes in the party make-up of the House appear to reflect changes in voter preferences for public policy.*

Proponents of term limits suffered two setbacks in 1995 when Congress failed to pass a constitutional amendment on term limitations (it also failed in 1997) and when the Supreme Court, in *U.S. Term Limits, Inc. et al. v. Thornton et al.*, decided that state-imposed term limits on members of Congress were unconstitutional. Many Americans support a constitutional amendment to impose term limitations on members of Congress. At the same time, most seem comfortable with their own representatives and senators and appear content to reelect them again and again.

What do you think? If you were a policymaker, would you favor or oppose term limits? What action, if any, would you take?

*Suzanna De Boef and James A. Stimson, "The Dynamic Structure of Congressional Elections," *Journal of Politics* 57 (August 1995): 630–48.

12.3 Compare and contrast the House and Senate, and describe the roles of congressional leaders, committees, caucuses, and staff.

How Congress Is Organized to Make Policy

Of all the senators' and representatives' roles, making policy is the toughest. Congress is a collection of generalists trying to make policy on specialized topics. Members are short on time and specific expertise. As generalists on most subjects, they are surrounded by people who know (or claim to know) more than they do—lobbyists, agency administrators, even their own staffs. Even if they had time to study all the issues thoroughly, making wise national policy would be difficult. If economists disagree about policies to fight unemployment, how are legislators to know which policies may work better than others?

When ringing bells announce a roll-call vote, representatives or senators rush into the chamber from their offices or from a hearing—often unsure of what is being voted on. Frequently, "uncertain of their position, members of Congress will seek out one or two people who serve on the committee which considered and reported the bill, in whose judgment they have confidence."[36]

The Founders gave Congress's organization just a hint of specialization when they split it into the House and the Senate.

American Bicameralism

bicameral legislature
A legislature divided into two houses. The U.S. Congress and all state legislatures except Nebraska's are bicameral.

A **bicameral legislature** is a legislature divided into two houses. The U.S. Congress is bicameral, as is every American state legislature except Nebraska's, which has one house (unicameral). As you saw in Chapter 2, the Connecticut Compromise at the Constitutional Convention created a bicameral Congress. Each state is guaranteed two senators, and the number of representatives a state has is determined by its population (California has 53 representatives; Alaska, Delaware, Montana, North Dakota, South Dakota, Vermont, and Wyoming have just 1 each). By creating a bicameral Congress, the Constitution set up yet another check and balance. No bill can be passed unless both House and Senate agree on it; each body can thus veto the policies of the other. Table 12.2 shows some of the basic differences between the two houses.

TABLE 12.2 House Versus Senate: Some Key Differences

CHARACTERISTIC	HOUSE OF REPRESENTATIVES	SENATE
Constitutional powers	Must initiate all revenue bills; Must pass all articles of impeachment	Must give "advice and consent" to many presidential nominations Must approve treaties Tries impeached officials
Membership	435 members	100 members
Term of office	Two years	Six years
Constituencies	Usually smaller	Usually larger
Centralization of power	More centralized; stronger leadership	Less centralized; weaker leadership
Political prestige	Less prestige	More prestige
Role in policymaking	More influential on budget; more specialized	More influential on foreign affairs; less specialized
Turnover	Small	Moderate
Role of seniority	More important in determining power	Less important in determining power
Procedures	Limited debate; limits on floor amendments allowed	Unlimited debate

The House More than four times as large as the Senate, the House is also more institutionalized—that is, more centralized, more hierarchical, and less anarchic.[37] Party loyalty to leadership and party-line voting are more common in the House than in the Senate. Partly because there are more members, leaders in the House do more leading than do leaders in the Senate. First-term House members have less power than senior representatives; they are more likely than first-term senators to be just seen and not heard.[38]

Both the House and the Senate set their own agendas. Both use committees, which we will examine shortly, to winnow down the thousands of bills introduced. One institution unique to the House, however, plays a key role in agenda setting: the **House Rules Committee**. This committee reviews most bills coming from a House committee before they go to the full House. Performing a traffic cop function, the Rules Committee gives each bill a "rule," which schedules the bill on the calendar, allots time for debate, and sometimes even specifies what kind of amendments may be offered. Today, the committee usually brings legislation to the floor under rules that limit or prohibit amendments and thus the opportunities for the minority to propose changes. The Rules Committee is generally responsive to the House leadership, in part because the Speaker of the House now appoints the committee's members.

House Rules Committee
The committee in the House of Representatives that reviews most **bills** coming from a House committee before they go to the full House.

The Senate The Constitution's framers thought the Senate would protect elite interests, counteracting tendencies of the House to protect the interests of the masses. They gave the House power to initiate all revenue bills and to impeach officials; they gave the Senate power to ratify all treaties, to confirm important presidential nominations (including nominations to the Supreme Court), and to try impeached officials. Despite the framers' expectations, history shows that when the same party controls both chambers, the Senate is just as liberal as—and perhaps more liberal than—the House.[39] The real differences between the bodies lie in the Senate's organization and decentralized power.

Smaller than the House, the Senate is also less disciplined and less centralized. Today's senators are more nearly equal in power than representatives are. They are also more nearly equal in power than senators have been in the past. Even incoming senators sometimes get top committee assignments; they may even become chairs of key subcommittees.

Committees and party leadership are important in determining the Senate's legislative agenda, just as they are in the House. Party leaders do for Senate scheduling what the Rules Committee does in the House.

One activity unique to the Senate is the **filibuster**. This is a tactic by which opponents of a bill use their right to unlimited debate as a way to prevent the Senate from ever voting on a bill. Unlike their fellow legislators in the House, once senators have the floor in a debate, tradition holds that they can talk as long as they wish. Strom Thurmond of South Carolina once held forth for 24 hours and 18 minutes opposing a civil rights bill in 1957. Working together, then, like-minded senators can practically debate forever, tying up the legislative agenda until the proponents of a bill finally give up their battle. In essence, they literally talk the bill to death.

filibuster
A strategy unique to the Senate whereby opponents of a piece of legislation use their right to unlimited debate to prevent the Senate from ever voting on a **bill**. Sixty members present and voting can halt a filibuster.

The power of the filibuster is not absolute, however. Sixty members present and voting can halt a filibuster by voting for *cloture* on debate. However, many senators are reluctant to vote for cloture for fear of setting a precedent to be used against them when *they* want to filibuster.

At its core, the filibuster raises profound questions about American democracy because it is used by a minority, sometimes a minority of one, to defeat a majority. Southern senators once used filibusters to prevent the passage of civil rights legislation.[40] More recently, the opponents of all types of legislation have used them. Indeed, during Bill Clinton's presidency, filibusters became the weapon of first resort for even the most trivial matters. Each senator has at least six opportunities to filibuster a single bill, and these opportunities can be used one after another. In addition, the tactical uses of a filibuster have expanded. A senator might threaten to filibuster an unrelated measure in order to gain concessions on a bill he or she opposes.

A POINT TO PONDER

Many people criticize Congress for not being able to act on policy issues. There are many ways to stop action in Congress, the Senate filibuster being the most notable. Simple majority rule would expedite decisions on controversial matters. It would also mean that minority interests would more frequently lose.

Would the United States be better off with more efficiency in Congress?

If the minority is blocking the majority, why doesn't the majority change the rules to prevent filibuster? The answer is twofold. First, changing the rules requires 67 votes. It is always difficult to obtain the agreement of two-thirds of the Senate on a controversial matter. Second, every senator knows that he or she might be in the minority on an issue at some time. A filibuster gives senators who are in the minority a powerful weapon for defending their (or their constituents') interests. Americans today commonly complain about gridlock in Congress. Nevertheless, senators have decided that they are more concerned with allowing senators to block legislation they oppose than with expediting the passage of legislation a majority favors.

Congressional Leadership

Leading 100 senators or 435 representatives in Congress—each jealous of his or her own power and responsible to no higher power than the constituency—is no easy task. "Few members of the House, fewer still in the Senate," Robert Peabody once wrote, "consider themselves followers."[41] Chapter 8 discussed the party in government. Much of the leadership in Congress is really party leadership. There are a few formal posts whose occupants are chosen by nonparty procedures, but those who have the real power in the congressional hierarchy are those whose party put them there.

Speaker of the House
An office mandated by the Constitution. The Speaker is chosen in practice by the majority party, has both formal and informal powers, and is second in line to succeed to the presidency should that office become vacant.

The House Chief among leadership positions in the House of Representatives is the **Speaker of the House**. This is the only legislative office mandated by the Constitution. In practice, the majority party selects the Speaker. Before each Congress begins, the majority party presents its candidate for Speaker, who—because this person attracts the unanimous support of the majority party—turns out to be a shoo-in. Typically, the Speaker is a senior member of the party. John Boehner of Ohio, who has served in Congress since 1991, was elected Speaker in 2011. The Speaker is also two heartbeats away from the presidency, being second in line (after the vice president) to succeed a president who resigns, dies in office, or is convicted after impeachment.

Years ago, the Speaker was king of the congressional mountain. Autocrats such as "Uncle Joe Cannon" and "Czar Reed" ran the House like a fiefdom. A great revolt in 1910 whittled down the Speaker's powers and gave some of them to committees, but six decades later, members of the House restored some of the Speaker's powers. Today, the Speaker does the following:

- Presides over the House when it is in session
- Plays a major role in making committee assignments, which are coveted by all members to ensure their electoral advantage
- Appoints or plays a key role in appointing the party's legislative leaders and the party leadership staff
- Exercises substantial control over which bills get assigned to which committees

In addition to these formal powers, the Speaker has a great deal of informal clout inside and outside Congress. When the Speaker's party differs from the president's party, as it frequently does, the Speaker is often a national spokesperson for the party. The bank of microphones in front of the Speaker of the House is a commonplace feature of the evening news. A good Speaker also knows the members well—including their past improprieties, the ambitions they harbor, and the pressures they feel.

Leadership in the House, however, is not a one-person show. The Speaker's principal partisan ally is the **majority leader**—a job that has been the main stepping-stone to the Speaker's role. The majority leader is responsible for scheduling bills in the House. More important, the majority leader is responsible for rounding up votes on behalf of the party's position on legislation. Working with the majority leader are the party's **whips**, who carry the word to party troops, counting votes before they are cast and leaning on waverers whose votes are crucial to a bill. Party whips also report the views and complaints of the party rank and file back to the leadership. The current majority leader is Republican Eric Cantor of Virginia.

The minority party is also organized, poised to take over the Speakership and other key posts if it should win a majority in the House. The Republicans had been the minority party in the House for 40 years before 1995, although they had a

majority leader
The principal partisan ally of the **Speaker of the House,** or the party's manager in the Senate. The majority leader is responsible for scheduling **bills,** influencing committee assignments, and rounding up votes in behalf of the party's legislative positions.

whips
Party leaders who work with the **majority leader** or **minority leader** to count votes beforehand and lean on waverers whose votes are crucial to a **bill** favored by the party.

John Boehner was elected Speaker of the House in 2011. Majority Leader Harry Reid of Nevada leads the Democrats in the Senate, which makes him the most powerful member of that body. Nevertheless, in the decentralized power structure in the upper chamber, even he must work for support and negotiate with Minority Leader Mitch McConnell of Kentucky.

president to look to for leadership for much of that period. After 4 years in the majority, Democrats again are experiencing minority status, led by the **minority leader**, Nancy Pelosi, of California.

minority leader
The principal leader of the minority party in the House of Representatives or in the Senate.

The Senate The Constitution makes the vice president of the United States the president of the Senate; this is the vice president's only constitutionally defined job. However, even the mighty Lyndon Johnson, who had been the Senate majority leader before becoming vice president, found himself an outsider when he returned as the Senate's president. Vice presidents usually slight their senatorial chores, except in the rare case when their vote can break a tie. Modern vice presidents are active in representing the president's views to senators, however.

It is the Senate majority leader—currently Democrat Harry Reid of Nevada—who, aided by the majority whips, serves as the workhorse of the party, corralling votes, scheduling floor action, and influencing committee assignments. The majority leader's counterpart in the opposition, the minority leader—currently Republican Mitch McConnell of Kentucky—has similar responsibilities. Power is widely dispersed in the contemporary Senate; it no longer lies in the hands of a few key members of Congress who are insulated from the public. Therefore, party leaders must appeal broadly for support, often speaking to the country directly or indirectly over television.

WHY IT MATTERS

Weak Parties

Parties organize Congress, but historically they have been relatively weak. If parties are strong, they can enforce strict party loyalty and thus are better able to keep their promises to voters. At the same time, strict party loyalty makes it more difficult for members of Congress to break from the party line to represent their constituents' special needs and interests.

Congressional Leadership in Perspective Despite their stature and power, congressional leaders cannot always move their troops. Power in both houses of Congress, but especially the Senate, is decentralized. Leaders are elected by their party members and must remain responsive to them. Except in the most egregious cases (which rarely arise), leaders cannot administer severe punishments to those who do not support the party's stand, and no one expects members to vote against their constituents' interests. Senator Robert Dole nicely summed up the leader's situation when he once dubbed himself the "Majority Pleader."

Nevertheless, party leadership, at least in the House, has been more effective in recent years. There has been more policy agreement within the parties and thus more party unity in voting on the floor. Increased agreement has made it easier for the Speaker to exercise his or her prerogatives regarding the assignment of bills and members to committees, the rules under which the House considers legislation on the floor, and the use of an expanded whip system—and thus better able to advance an agenda that reflects party preferences.[42]

The Committees and Subcommittees

Will Rogers, the famous Oklahoman humorist, once remarked that "outside of traffic, there is nothing that has held this country back as much as committees." Members of the Senate and the House would apparently disagree. Most of the real work of Congress goes on in committees, and committees dominate congressional policymaking in all its stages.

Committees regularly hold hearings to investigate problems and possible wrongdoing and to oversee the executive branch. Most of all, *they control the congressional agenda and guide legislation* from its introduction to its send-off to the president for his signature. We can group committees into four types, the first of which is by far the most important.

standing committees
Separate subject-matter committees in each house of Congress that handle **bills** in different policy areas.

joint committees
Congressional committees on a few subject-matter areas with membership drawn from both houses.

conference committees
Congressional committees formed when the Senate and the House pass a particular **bill** in different forms. Party leadership appoints members from each house to iron out the differences and bring back a single bill.

1. **Standing committees** handle bills in different policy areas (see Table 12.3). Each house of Congress has its own standing committees. In Congress today, the typical representative serves on two committees and four subcommittees (subcommittees are smaller units of a committee created out of the committee membership); senators average three committees and seven subcommittees.
2. **Joint committees** exist in a few policy areas, such as the economy and taxation, and draw their membership from both the Senate and the House.
3. **Conference committees** are formed when the Senate and the House pass different versions of the same bill (which they typically do). Appointed by the party leadership,

TABLE 12.3 Standing Committees in the Senate and in the House

SENATE COMMITTEES	HOUSE COMMITTEES
Agriculture, Nutrition, and Forestry	Agriculture
Appropriations	Appropriations
Armed Services	Armed Services
Banking, Housing, and Urban Affairs	Budget
Budget	Education and Labor
Commerce, Science, and Transportation	Energy and Commerce
Energy and Natural Resources	Financial Services
Environment and Public Works	Foreign Affairs
Finance	Homeland Security
Foreign Relations	House Administration
Health, Education, Labor, and Pensions	Judiciary
Homeland Security and Governmental Affairs	Natural Resources
Judiciary	Oversight and Government Reform
Rules and Administration	Rules
Small Business and Entrepreneurship	Science and Technology
Veterans' Affairs	Small Business
	Standards of Official Conduct
	Transportation and Infrastructure
	Veterans' Affairs
	Ways and Means

a conference committee consists of members of each house chosen to iron out Senate and House differences and to report back a compromise bill.

4. **Select committees** may be temporary or permanent and usually have a focused responsibility. The House and Senate each have a select committee on intelligence, for example.

select committees
Congressional committees appointed for a specific purpose, such as the Watergate investigation.

The Committees at Work: Legislation and Oversight With more than 9,000 bills submitted by members in the course of a two-year period, some winnowing is essential. Every bill goes to a committee, which has virtually the power of life and death over it. The whole House or Senate usually considers only bills that obtain a favorable committee report.

A new bill that the Speaker sends to a committee typically goes directly to a subcommittee, which can hold hearings on the bill. Sizable committee and subcommittee staffs conduct research, line up witnesses for hearings, and write and rewrite bills. Committees and their subcommittees produce reports on proposed legislation. A committee's most important output, however, is the "marked-up" (rewritten) bill itself, which it submits to the full House or Senate for debate and voting.

The work of committees does not stop when the bill leaves the committee room. Members of the committee usually serve as "floor managers" of the bill, helping party leaders hustle votes for it. They are also the "cue givers" to whom other members turn for advice. When the Senate and House pass different versions of the same bill, some committee members serve on the conference committee.

The committees and subcommittees do not leave the scene even after legislation passes. They stay busy in **legislative oversight**, the process of monitoring the bureaucracy and its administration of policies, most of which were established by Congress. Committees handle oversight mainly through hearings. When an agency wants a bigger budget, the relevant committee reviews its current budget. Even if no budgetary issues are involved, members of committees constantly monitor how the bureaucracy is

legislative oversight
Congress's monitoring of the bureaucracy and its administration of policy, performed mainly through hearings.

implementing a law. Agency heads and even cabinet secretaries testify, bringing graphs, charts, and data on the progress they have made and the problems they face. Committee staffs and committee members grill agency heads about particular problems. For example, a member may ask a Small Business Administration official why constituents who are applying for loans get the runaround. In short, through oversight, Congress can pressure agencies and, in extreme cases, cut their budgets in order to secure compliance with congressional wishes.[43] Oversight also provides an opportunity to refine existing policies or respond to new problems.

Occasionally, congressional oversight rivets the nation's attention. This was the case, for example, in 1987, when Congress established a special joint committee to investigate what became known as the Iran-Contra affair, involving the secret sale of arms to Iran (for which President Reagan hoped to obtain the release of American hostages held in the Middle East) and the diversion of some of the funds from these sales to the Contras fighting the Sandinista government in Nicaragua (in the face of congressional prohibition of such aid).

Congress keeps tabs on more routine activities of the executive branch through its committee staff members. These members have specialized expertise in the fields and agencies that their committees oversee and maintain an extensive network of formal and informal contacts with the bureaucracy. By reading the voluminous reports that Congress requires of the executive and by receiving information from numerous sources—agencies, complaining citizens, members of Congress and their personal staff, state and local officials, interest groups, and professional organizations—staff members can keep track of the implementation of public policy.[44]

Congressional oversight grew as the size and complexity of the national government grew in the 1960s and in response to numerous charges that the executive branch had become too powerful (and, especially, the widespread belief that Presidents Johnson and Nixon had abused their power). The tight budgets of recent years have provided additional incentives for oversight, as members of Congress have sought to protect programs they favor from budget cuts and to get more value for the tax dollars spent on them. As the publicity value of receiving credit for controlling governmental spending has increased, so has the number of representatives and senators interested in oversight.[45]

Nevertheless, members of Congress have many competing responsibilities, and there are few political payoffs for carefully watching a government agency to see whether it is implementing policy properly. It is difficult to go to voters and say, "Vote for me. I oversaw the routine handling of road building." Because of this lack of incentives, problems may be overlooked until it is too late to do much about them. Despite clear evidence of fundamental problems in the operations and management of the Federal Emergency Management Agency in its response to the four hurricanes that hit Florida in 2004, when Katrina hit the next year, Congress had still not held oversight hearings. Similarly, Congress missed the fact that various agencies with responsibility for overseeing the banking industry were negligent in identifying looming problems in the financial sector that led to the recession of 2008–2009.

In addition, the majority party largely determines if and when a committee will hold hearings. When the president's party has a majority in a house of Congress, that chamber is generally not aggressive in overseeing the administration because it does not wish to embarrass the president. Democrats were critical of what they regarded as timid Republican oversight of the nation's intelligence establishment and President Bush's planning and implementation of the aftermath of the war in Iraq, including the treatment of prisoners. Nevertheless, the president's partisans resisted holding the White House accountable, fearing that the Democrats would use hearings to discredit Bush. Similarly, critics charge that the failure to discern and make explicit the true costs of policy initiatives—from tax cuts to Medicare prescription drugs to the war in Iraq—made it impossible for a realistic cost–benefit analysis to enter the calculus before Congress approved the policies.[46] Once the Democrats gained majorities in Congress in the 2006 elections, the number of oversight hearings increased substantially.

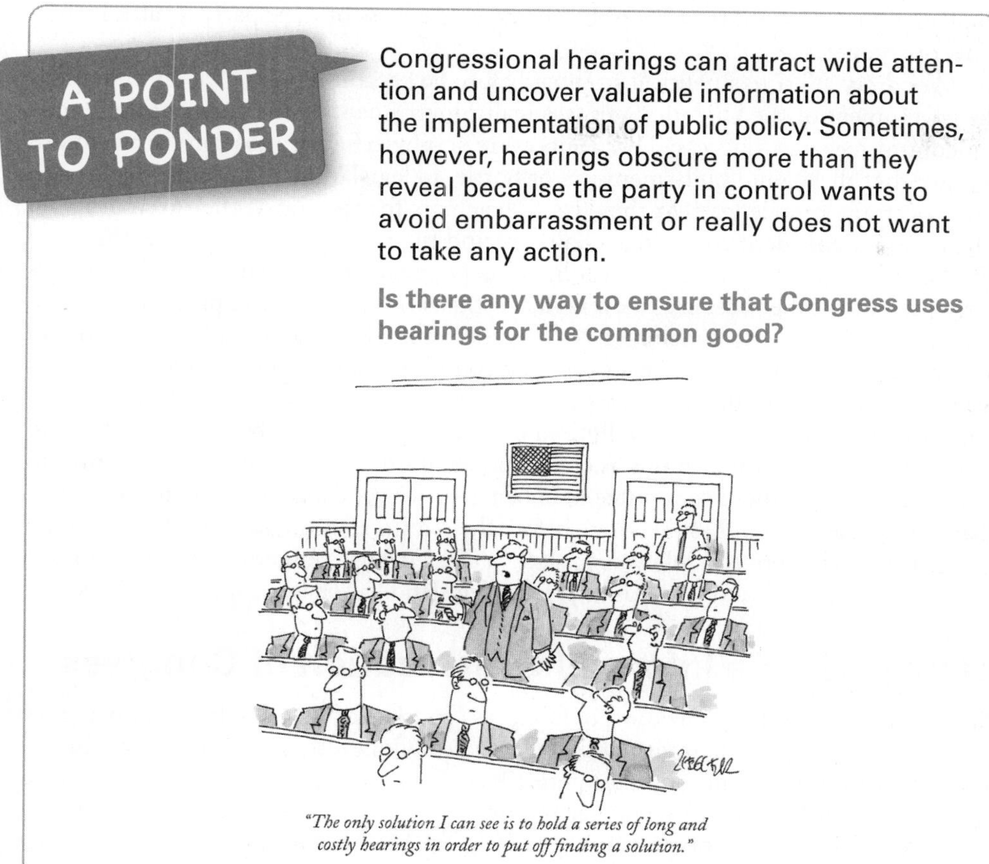

A POINT TO PONDER

Congressional hearings can attract wide attention and uncover valuable information about the implementation of public policy. Sometimes, however, hearings obscure more than they reveal because the party in control wants to avoid embarrassment or really does not want to take any action.

Is there any way to ensure that Congress uses hearings for the common good?

"The only solution I can see is to hold a series of long and costly hearings in order to put off finding a solution."

Getting on a Committee One of the primary objectives of an incoming member of Congress is getting on the right committee. A new member of the House from Iowa would probably prefer to be on the Agriculture Committee while a freshman senator from New York might seek membership on the Banking, Housing, and Urban Affairs Committee. Members seek committees that will help them achieve three goals: reelection, influence in Congress, and the opportunity to make policy in areas they think are important.[47]

Just after their election, new members communicate their committee preferences to their party's congressional leaders and members of their state delegation. Every committee includes members from both parties, but a majority of each committee's members, as well as its chair, come from the majority party in the chamber. Each party in each house has a slightly different way of picking its committee members. Party leaders almost always play a key role.

Those who have supported the leadership are favored in the committee selection process, but generally the parties try to grant members' requests for committee assignments whenever possible. They want their members to please their constituents (being on the right committee should help them represent their constituency more effectively and reinforce their ability to engage in credit claiming) and to develop expertise in an area of policy. The parties also try to apportion the influence that comes with committee membership among the state delegations in order to accord representation to diverse components of the party.[48]

Committee Chairs and the Seniority System If committees are the most important influencers of the congressional agenda, **committee chairs** are the most important influencers of the committee agenda. Committee chairs play dominant roles in scheduling hearings, hiring staff, appointing subcommittees, and managing committee bills when they are brought before the full house.

Until the 1970s, there was a simple way of picking committee chairs: the **seniority system**. If committee members had served on their committee longest and their party

committee chairs
The most important influencers of the congressional agenda. They play dominant roles in scheduling hearings, hiring staff, appointing subcommittees, and managing committee **bills** when they are brought before the full house.

seniority system
A simple rule for picking **committee chairs**, in effect until the 1970s. The member who had served on the committee the longest and whose party controlled the chamber became chair, regardless of party loyalty, mental state, or competence.

controlled the chamber, they got to be chairs—regardless of their party loyalty, mental state, or competence.

Woodrow Wilson, a political scientist before he became a politician, once said that the government of the United States was really government by the chairs of the standing committees of Congress. The chairs were so powerful for most of the twentieth century that they could bully members or bottle up legislation at any time—and with almost certain knowledge that they would be chairs for the rest of their electoral life. The more independent committee chairs are and the more power they have, the more difficult it may be to make coherent policy. Independent and powerful committee chairs can represent another obstacle to overcome in the complex legislative process.

In the 1970s, younger members of Congress revolted, and as a result both parties in both branches permitted members to vote on committee chairs. Today seniority remains the *general rule* for selecting chairs, especially in the Senate, but there are plenty of exceptions. In addition, new rules have limited both committee and subcommittee chairs to three consecutive two-year terms as chair, and committee chairs have lost the power to cast proxy votes for those committee members not in attendance. In general, committee chairs are not as powerful as they were before the reform era. The party leadership in the House has much more control over legislation, often giving committees deadlines for reporting legislation and at times, for its priority legislation, even bypassing committees.

WHY IT MATTERS

The Committee System

The committee system in Congress is highly decentralized. As a result, it is open to the appeals of a wide range of "special" interests, especially those represented by highly paid lobbyists. If Congress were more *centralized* and only those interests cleared by the elected leadership received a hearing, special interests might be constrained. However, there is also a danger that only the interests reflecting the views of the leadership would be heard.

Caucuses: The Informal Organization of Congress

Although the formal organization of Congress consists of its party leadership and its committee structures, the informal organization of Congress is also important. Informal networks of trust and mutual interest have long sprung from numerous sources, including friendship, ideology, and geography.

caucus (congressional) A group of members of Congress sharing some interest or characteristic. Many are composed of members from both parties and from both houses.

Lately, the informal organization of Congress has been dominated by a growing number of caucuses. In this context, a **caucus** is a group of members of Congress who share some interest or characteristic. There are more than 250 caucuses, most of them containing members from both parties and some containing members from both the House and the Senate. The goal of all caucuses is to promote the interests around which they are formed. Caucuses press for committees to hold hearings, push particular legislation, and pull together votes on bills they favor. They are somewhat like interest groups but with a difference: Their members are members of Congress, not petitioners to Congress on the outside looking in. Thus caucuses—interest groups within Congress—are nicely situated to pack more punch.[49]

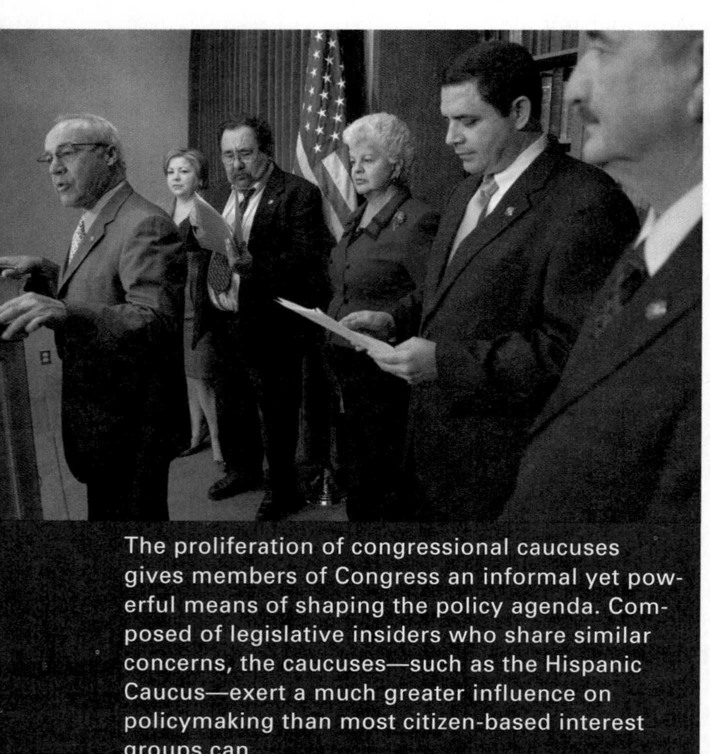

The proliferation of congressional caucuses gives members of Congress an informal yet powerful means of shaping the policy agenda. Composed of legislative insiders who share similar concerns, the caucuses—such as the Hispanic Caucus—exert a much greater influence on policymaking than most citizen-based interest groups can.

This explosion of informal groups in Congress has made the representation of interests in Congress a more direct process. Some caucuses, such as the Black Caucus, the Caucus for Women's Issues, and the Hispanic Caucus, focus on advancing the interests of demographic groups. Others, such as the Sunbelt Caucus, are based on regional groupings. Still others, such as the Republican Study Committee, are ideological groupings. Many caucuses are based on economic interests. For example, the Congressional Bourbon Caucus advocates for the bourbon industry by fighting proposals like a tax increase on liquor, while the Congressional Gaming Caucus deals with issues like reinvigorating the tourism industry and making sure regulations for Internet gambling are fair. Other caucuses focus, for instance, on health issues or on foreign policy matters dealing with specific countries.

Congressional Staff

As we discussed earlier, members of Congress are overwhelmed with responsibilities. It is virtually impossible to master the details of the hundreds of bills on which they must make decisions each year or to prepare their own legislation. They need help to meet their obligations, so they turn to their staff.

Personal Staff Most staff members work in the personal offices of individual members of Congress. The average representative has 17 assistants and the average senator has 40. In total, more than 11,000 individuals serve on the personal staffs of members of Congress. (Another 400 serve the congressional leaders.) In the summer, about 4,000 interns also work in members' offices on Capitol Hill (see "Young People and Politics: Are Opportunities to Intern Biased in Favor of the Wealthy?").

Most of these staffers spend their time on casework, providing services to constituents. They answer mail, communicate the member's views to voters, and help constituents solve problems. Nearly one-half of these House staffers and nearly one-third of the Senate personal staff work in members' offices in their constituencies, not in Washington. This makes it easier for people to make contact with the staff. Other personal staff help members of Congress with legislative functions, including drafting legislation, meeting with lobbyists and administrators, negotiating agreements on behalf of their bosses, writing questions to ask witnesses at committee hearings, summarizing bills, and briefing legislators. Senators, who must cover a wider range of committee assignments than members of the House, are especially dependent on staff. Indeed, members of both houses are now more likely to deal with each other through staff intermediaries than through personal interactions.

Committee Staff The committees of the House and Senate employ another 2,000 or so staff members. These staffers organize hearings, research legislative options, draft committee reports on bills, write legislation, and, as we have seen, keep tabs on the activities of the executive branch. Committee staff members often possess high levels of

Are Opportunities to Intern Biased in Favor of the Wealthy?

Many college students spend their summers working to pay for their studies during the rest of the year. Others, in contrast, serve as interns. Many of the interns have parents who support them financially during the summer. According to some experts, the focus on internships as a tool for professional success has never been greater, and about 80 percent of graduating college seniors have done a paid or unpaid internship. To some, an internship is an essential stepping-stone to career success.

Because Washington internships are in high demand, in most cases they do not pay, or they pay very little. The White House does not pay the interns who work there during the summer; in most cases the Supreme Court does not pay its undergraduate interns; and a vast majority of congressional offices do not pay the 4,000 summer interns who work on Capitol Hill, although a few, mostly on the Senate side, provide a limited stipend. To make matters worse, Washington is an expensive place to live. In some cases, universities or other programs provide some financial help, but most interns are on their own.

As internships become increasingly important to career success, the concern has been raised that they may be creating a class system discriminating against students from less affluent families who must turn down unpaid internships to earn money for college expenses. To the extent that Washington internships serve as a pipeline for people to become policymakers in the nation's capital, critics fear that over time internships, like the rising costs of college tuition, will mean fewer working-class and even middle-class voices in high-level policy debates.

QUESTIONS FOR DISCUSSION

- Is the internship system in Washington likely to bias policymaking in the future?
- Should Congress appropriate funds so internships are more available to students from less wealthy backgrounds?

Source: Jennifer 8. Lee, "Crucial Unpaid Internships Increasingly Separate the Haves from the Have-Nots," *New York Times*, August 10, 2004.

expertise and can become very influential in policymaking. As a result, lobbyists spend a lot of time cultivating these staffers both to obtain information about likely legislative actions and to plant ideas for legislation.

Staff Agencies Finally, Congress has three important staff agencies that aid it in its work. The first is the *Congressional Research Service (CRS),* administered by the Library of Congress and composed of researchers, many with advanced degrees and highly developed expertise. Each year it responds to more than 250,000 congressional requests for information and provides members with nonpartisan studies. CRS also tracks the progress of major bills, prepares summaries of bills, and makes this information available electronically.

The *Government Accountability Office (GAO),* with more than 3,200 employees, helps Congress perform its oversight functions by reviewing the activities of the executive branch to see if it is following the congressional intent of laws and by investigating the efficiency and effectiveness of policy implementation. The GAO also sets government standards for accounting, provides legal opinions, and settles claims against the government.

The *Congressional Budget Office (CBO)* (discussed in more detail in Chapter 14) focuses on analyzing the president's budget and making economic projections about the performance of the economy, the costs of proposed policies, and the economic effects of taxing and spending alternatives.

Committees, caucuses, and individual legislators follow bills from their introduction to their approval. The next section discusses this process, which is often termed "labyrinthine" since getting a bill through Congress is very much like navigating a difficult, intricate maze.

12.4 Outline the path of bills to passage and explain the influences on congressional decision making.

The Congressional Process

Congress's agenda is a crowded one—members introduce about 9,000 bills in each Congress. A **bill** is a proposed law, drafted in precise, legal language. Anyone can draft a bill. The White House and interest groups are common sources of polished bills. However, only members of the House or the Senate can formally submit a bill for consideration. The traditional route for a bill as it works its way through the legislative labyrinth is depicted in Figure 12.2. Most bills are quietly killed off early in the process. Some are introduced mostly as a favor to a group or a constituent; others are private bills, granting citizenship to a constituent or paying a settlement to a person whose car was demolished by a postal service truck. Still other bills may alter the course of the nation.

bill
A proposed law, drafted in legal language. Anyone can draft a bill, but only a member of the House of Representatives or the Senate can formally submit a bill for consideration.

Congress is typically a cumbersome decision-making body. Rules are piled on rules and procedures on procedures.[50] Moreover, legislating has been made more difficult because of the polarized political climate that has prevailed since the 1980s.

Party leaders sought to cope with these problems in various ways, including some already mentioned, and what Barbara Sinclair has termed *unorthodox lawmaking* has become common in the congressional process, especially for the most significant legislation.[51] In both chambers party leaders involve themselves in the legislative process on major legislation earlier and more deeply, using special procedures to aid the passage of legislation. Leaders in the House often refer bills to several committees at the same time, bringing more interests to bear on an issue but complicating the process of passing legislation. Since committee leaders cannot always negotiate compromises *among* committees, party leaders have accepted this responsibility, often negotiating compromises and making adjustments to bills after a committee or committees report legislation. Sometimes for high-priority legislation party leaders simply bypass committees. In the House, special rules from the Rules Committee have become powerful tools for controlling floor consideration of bills and sometimes for shaping the outcomes of votes. Often party leaders from the two chambers negotiate among themselves

FIGURE 12.2 How a Bill Becomes a Law

CONGRESS

Bill introduction

HOUSE	SENATE
 **Bill introduction** Bill is introduced by a member and assigned to a committee, which usually refers it to a subcommittee.	 **Bill introduction** Bill is introduced by a member and assigned to a committee, which usually refers it to a subcommittee.

Committee action

HOUSE	SENATE
Subcommittee Subcommittee performs studies, holds hearings, and makes revisions. If approved, the bill goes to the full committee.	**Subcommittee** Subcommittee performs studies, holds hearings, and makes revisions. If approved, the bill goes to the full committee.
Committee Full committee may amend or rewrite the bill, before deciding whether to send it to the House floor, to recommend its approval, or to kill it. If approved, the bill is reported to the full House and placed on the calendar.	**Committee** Full committee may amend or rewrite the bill, before deciding whether to send it to the Senate floor, to recommend its approval, or to kill it. If approved, the bill is reported to the full Senate and placed on the calendar.
Rules Committee Rules Committee issues a rule governing debate on the House floor and sends the bill to the full House.	**Leadership** Senate leaders of both parties schedule Senate debate on the bill.

Floor action

HOUSE	SENATE
Full House Bill is debated by full House, amendments are offered, and a vote is taken. If the bill passes in a different version from that passed in the Senate, it is sent to a conference committee.	**Full Senate** Bill is debated by full Senate, amendments are offered, and a vote is taken. If the bill passes in a different version from that passed in the House, it is sent to a conference committee.

Conference action

Conference Committee
Conference committee composed of members of both House and Senate meet to iron out differences between the bills. The compromise bill is returned to both the House and Senate for a vote.

HOUSE	SENATE
Full House Full House votes on conference committee version. If it passes, the bill is sent to the president.	**Full Senate** Full Senate votes on conference committee version. If it passes, the bill is sent to the president.

Presidential decision

President
President signs or vetoes the bill. Congress may override a veto by a two-thirds vote in both the House and Senate.

Law

Many bills travel full circle, coming first from the White House as part of the presidential agenda, then returning to the president at the end of the process. In the interim, there are two parallel processes in the Senate and House, starting with committee action. If a committee gives a bill a favorable report, the whole chamber considers it. When the two chambers pass different versions of it, a conference committee drafts a single compromise bill.

instead of creating conference committees. Party leaders also use *omnibus* legislation that addresses numerous and perhaps unrelated subjects, issues, and programs to create winning coalitions, forcing members to support the entire bill to obtain the individual parts.

These new procedures are generally under the control of party leaders in the House, but in the Senate, leaders have less leverage, and *individual* senators have retained substantial opportunities for influence (such as using the filibuster). As a result, it is often more difficult to pass legislation in the Senate.

There are, of course, countless influences on this legislative process. Presidents, parties, constituents, interest groups, the congressional and committee leadership structure—these and other influences offer members cues for their decision making.

Presidents and Congress: Partners and Protagonists

Political scientists sometimes call the president the *chief legislator*, a phrase that might have appalled the Constitution writers, with their insistence on separation of powers. Presidents do, however, help create the congressional agenda. They are also their own best lobbyists.

Presidents have their own legislative agenda, based in part on their party's platform and their electoral coalition. Their task is to persuade Congress that their agenda should also be Congress's agenda, and they have a good chance that Congress will at least give their proposals a hearing.[52]

Presidents have many resources with which to influence Congress. (The next chapter will examine presidential leadership.) They may try to influence members directly—calling up wavering members and telling them that the country's future hinges on their votes, for example—but they do not do this often. If presidents were to pick just one key bill and spend 10 minutes on the telephone with each of the 535 members of Congress, they would spend 89 hours chatting with them. Instead, presidents wisely leave most White House lobbying to staff members and administration officials and work closely with the party's leaders in the House and Senate.

It seems a wonder that presidents, even with all their power and prestige, can push and wheedle anything through the labyrinthine congressional process. The president must usually win at every stage shown in Figure 12.2—in other words, at least 10 times—to achieve policy change. As one scholar put it, presidential leadership of Congress is *at the margins*.[53] In general, successful presidential leadership of Congress has not been the result of the dominant chief executive of political folklore who reshapes the contours of the political landscape to pave the way for change. Rather than creating the conditions for major shifts in public policy, the effective American leader has been the less-heroic *facilitator* who works at the margins of coalition building to recognize and exploit opportunities presented by a favorable configuration of political forces. Of course, presidents can exercise their veto to *stop* legislation they oppose.

As we will show in the next chapter, popular presidents and presidents with a large majority of their party in each house of Congress have a good chance of getting their way. Yet presidents often lose. Ronald Reagan was considered a strong chief executive, and budgeting was one of his principal tools for affecting public policy. Yet commentators typically pronounced the budgets he proposed to Congress DOA, dead on arrival. Members of Congress truly compose an independent branch.

Party, Constituency, and Ideology

Presidents come and go; the parties endure. Presidents do not determine a congressional member's electoral fortunes; constituents do. Where presidents are less influential—on domestic policies especially—party, personal ideology, and constituency are more influential.

Party Influence On some issues, members of the parties stick together like a marching band. They are most cohesive when Congress is electing its official leaders. A vote for Speaker of the House is a straight party-line vote, with every Democrat on one side and every Republican on the other. On other issues, however, the party coalition may come unglued. In the past, votes on civil rights policies, for example, revealed deep divisions within each party.

Differences between the parties are sharpest on questions of economic and social welfare policy (see Chapters 17 and 18).[54] On social welfare issues—for example, the minimum wage, aid to the poor, unemployed, or uninsured, and grants for education—Democrats are more supportive of government action than are Republicans. Democrats are also more supportive of government efforts to regulate the economy in an attempt to alleviate negative consequences of markets or to stimulate economic activity.

Party leaders in Congress help "whip" their members into line. Their power to do so is limited, of course. They cannot drum a recalcitrant member out of the party. Leaders have plenty of influence they can exert, however, including making committee assignments, boosting a member's pet projects, and the subtle but significant influence of providing critical information to a member. Moreover, the congressional parties are a source of funding, as are political action committees (PACs) headed by members of the party leadership.

Polarized Politics Over the past three decades, the distance between the congressional parties has been growing steadily, as you can see in the figure in "A Generation of Change: Polarization in Congress." As the parties pulled apart ideologically, they also became more homogeneous internally. In other words, Republicans in Congress became more consistently conservative, Democrats became more consistently liberal, and the distance between the center of each party increased. As a result of these ideological differences between the parties in Congress, it has been more difficult to reach a compromise—and more difficult for the president to obtain policy support from the opposition party.

Why did this change happen? At the core of the increased ideological distance between the parties have been increasingly divergent electoral coalitions. One important factor is that state legislatures drew the boundaries of House districts so that the partisan divisions in the constituencies of representatives became more one-sided. Most House members no longer had to worry about pleasing the center of the electorate because their own districts were either clearly conservative or clearly liberal.

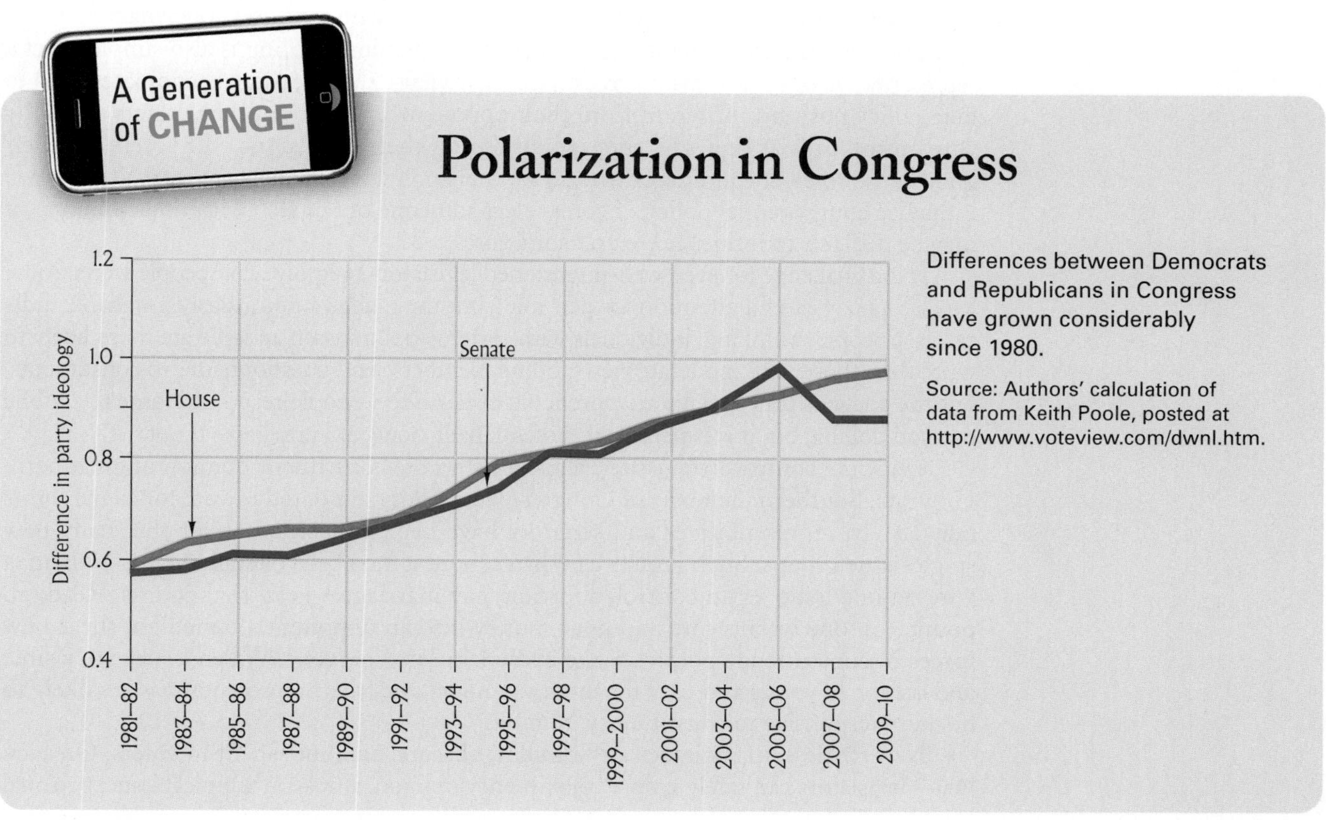

Differences between Democrats and Republicans in Congress have grown considerably since 1980.

Source: Authors' calculation of data from Keith Poole, posted at http://www.voteview.com/dwnl.htm.

In addition, liberal and conservative voters sorted themselves into the Democratic and Republican parties, respectively. There are many fewer liberal Republicans or conservative Democrats than there were a generation ago. Thus, conservatives have been more likely to support the more conservative party and liberals the more liberal party. As supporters of each party have matched their partisan and ideological views, they have made the differences between the parties more distinctive. Moreover, party loyalty among voters in congressional elections also increased, so the relationship between ideology and voting has become notably stronger.

In short, what has happened is the following: Changes in the preferences, behavior, and distribution of congressional voters gave the congressional parties more internally homogeneous, more divergent, and thus more polarized electoral constituencies. These constituencies in turn elected more ideologically polarized representatives in Congress. These new members of Congress have adopted a polarized style that pays little heed to compromise.[55]

Constituency Opinion Versus Member Ideology Members of Congress are representatives; their constituents expect them to represent their interests in Washington. In 1714, Anthony Henry, a member of the British Parliament, received a letter from some of his constituents asking him to vote against an excise tax. He is reputed to have replied in part,

> Gentlemen: I have received your letter about the excise, and I am surprised at your insolence in writing to me at all . . . may God's curse light upon you all, and may it make your homes as open and as free to the excise officers as your wives and daughters have always been to me while I have represented your rascally constituency.[56]

Needless to say, notions of representation have changed since Henry's time.

Sometimes representation requires a balancing act. If some representatives favor more defense spending but suspect that their constituents do not, what are they to do? The English politician and philosopher Edmund Burke advocated the concept of legislators as *trustees*, using their best judgment to make policy in the interests of the people. Others prefer the concept of representatives as *instructed delegates*, mirroring the preferences of their constituents. Actually, members of Congress are *politicos*, adopting both trustee and instructed delegate roles as they strive to be both representatives and policymakers.[57]

The best way constituents can influence congressional voting is also simple: elect a representative or senator who agrees with their views. Congressional candidates tend to take policy positions different from their opponent's. Moreover, the winners generally vote on roll calls as they said they would during their campaigns.[58] If voters use their good sense to elect candidates who share their policy positions, then constituents *can* influence congressional policy. If voters elect someone out of step with their thinking, it may be difficult to influence that person's votes.

It is a challenge for even well-intentioned legislators to know what people want. Some legislators pay careful attention to their mail, but the mail is a notoriously unreliable indicator of people's thinking; individuals with extreme opinions on an issue are more likely to write than those with moderate views. Some members send questionnaires to constituents, but the answers they receive are unreliable because few people respond. Some try public opinion polling, but it is expensive if professionally done and unreliable if not.

On some controversial issues, legislators ignore constituent opinion at great peril. For years, Southern members of Congress would not have dared to vote for a civil rights law. Lately, representatives and senators have been concerned about the many new single-issue groups. Such groups care little about a member's overall record; to them, a vote on one issue—gun control, abortion, gay marriage—is all that counts. Ready to pounce on one wrong vote and pour money into an opponent's campaign, these new forces in constituency politics make every legislator nervous. When issues are visible and salient to voters and easy for them to understand, their representatives are likely to be quite responsive to constituency opinion.[59]

Nevertheless, many issues are complex, obscure, and not salient to voters. On such issues legislators can safely ignore constituency opinion. Thus, on a typical issue, personal ideology is the prime determinant of a congressional member's vote—and it is virtually the only determinant on issues where ideological divisions between the parties are sharp and constituency preferences and knowledge are likely to be weak, such as defense and foreign policy.[60] However, the stronger constituency preferences are on issues and the weaker partisan ideology is, the more likely members are to deviate from their own positions and adopt those of their constituencies.[61] In short, when they have differences of opinion with their constituencies, members of Congress consider constituency preferences but are not controlled by them.[62]

Lobbyists and Interest Groups

The nation's capital is crawling with lawyers, lobbyists, registered foreign agents, public relations consultants, and others—there are about 35,000 registered lobbyists representing 12,000 organizations—all seeking to influence Congress.[63] Lobbyists spent $3.5 billion on lobbying federal officials in 2009—plus millions more in campaign contributions and attempts to try to persuade members' constituents to send messages to Washington.[64]

We saw in the last chapter that lobbyists, some of them former members of Congress, can provide legislators with crucial policy information, political intelligence, and often with assurances of financial aid in the next campaign—making those legislators with whom they agree more effective in the legislative process.[65] (In the debate regarding health care reform in 2009, statements by more than a dozen members of the House were ghostwritten by lobbyists.[66]) Lobbyists work closely with their legislative allies, especially at the committee level.[67] They also often coordinate their efforts at influencing members with party leaders who share their views. Grass-roots lobbying—such as computerized mailings to encourage citizens to pressure their representatives on an issue—is a common activity. These days, groups coordinate their messages across multiple platforms, including television, Web sites, YouTube videos, and social media sites. Interest groups also distribute scorecards of how members of Congress voted on issues important to the groups, threatening members with electoral retaliation if they do not support the groups' stands.

There is some evidence that lobbying pays off,[68] but efforts to change policy usually meet with resistance and most efforts to change the status quo fail. Groups with the most money do not necessarily win.[69] Lobbyists usually make little headway with their opponents: The lobbyist for General Motors arguing against automobile pollution controls will not have much influence with a legislator concerned about air pollution.

Concerned about inappropriate influence from lobbyists, Congress passed a law in 1995 requiring anyone hired to lobby members of Congress, congressional staff members, White House officials, and federal agencies to report what issues they were seeking to influence, how much they were spending on the effort, and the identities of their clients. Congress also placed severe restrictions on the gifts, meals, and expense-paid travel that public officials may accept from lobbyists. In theory, these reporting requirements and restrictions would not only prevent shady deals between lobbyists and members of Congress but also curb the influence of special interests. Nevertheless, slippage occurred. In 2005 and 2006, for example, the country saw some members caught up in bribery scandals. The nation also learned of lobbyist Jack Abramoff's success in charging six Indian tribes more than $80 million for his lobbying services—and of his extraordinary contributions to and expenditures on some representatives and senators. In response, Congress in 2007 passed a new law and the House revised its ethics rules. Together, these measures strengthened public disclosure requirements concerning lobbying activity and funding, placed more restrictions on gifts and travel for members of Congress and their staff, provided for mandatory disclosure of earmarks in expenditure bills, and slowed the revolving door between Congress and the lobbying world.

There are many forces that affect senators and representatives as they decide how to vote on a bill. After his exhaustive study of influences on congressional decision making, John Kingdon concluded that none was important enough to suggest that members of Congress vote as they do because of one influence.[70] The process is as complex for individual legislators as it is for those who want to influence their votes.

A POINT TO PONDER

Interest groups play a central role in the legislative process. They provide valuable information and expertise to lawmakers and help build coalitions. Yet many people see them as "special interests" fighting for narrow interests.

Do organized interests play too great a role in policymaking?

"Mr. Speaker, will the gentleman from Small Firearms yield the floor to the gentleman from Big Tobacco?"

12.5 Assess Congress's role as a representative body and the impact of representation on the scope of government.

Understanding Congress

Congress is a complex institution. Its members want to make sound national policy, but they also want to return to Washington after the next election. How do these sometimes conflicting desires affect American democracy and the scope of American government?

Congress and Democracy

In a large nation, the success of democratic government depends on the quality of representation. Americans could hardly hold a national referendum on every policy issue on the government agenda; instead, they delegate decision-making power to representatives. If Congress is a successful democratic institution, it must be a successful representative institution.

Certainly, some aspects of Congress make it very *un*representative. Its members are an American elite. Its leadership is chosen by its own members, not by any vote of the American people. Voters have little direct influence over the individuals who chair key committees or lead congressional parties. In addition, the Senate is apportioned to represent states, not population, a distribution of power that accords citizens in less populated states a greater say in key decisions. As you can see in "America in Perspective: Malapportionment in the Upper House," malapportionment is high in the U.S. Senate.

Nevertheless, the evidence in this chapter demonstrates that Congress *does* try to listen to the American people. Whom voters elect makes a difference in how congressional votes turn out; which party is in power affects policies. Perhaps Congress could do a better job at representation than it does, but there are many obstacles to improved representation. Legislators find it hard to know what constituents want. Groups may keep important issues off the legislative agenda. Members may spend so much time servicing their constituencies that they have little time left to represent those constituencies in the policymaking process.

Members of Congress are responsive to the people, if the people make clear what they want. For example, in response to popular demands, Congress established a program in 1988 to shield the elderly against the catastrophic costs associated with acute illness. In 1989, in response to complaints from the elderly about higher Medicare premiums, Congress abolished most of what it had created the previous year.

Representativeness Versus Effectiveness The central legislative dilemma for Congress is combining the faithful representation of constituents with making effective public policy. Supporters see Congress as a forum in which many interests compete for a spot on the policy agenda and over the form of a particular policy—just as the Founders intended.

Critics charge that Congress is too representative—so representative that it is incapable of taking decisive action to deal with difficult problems. The agricultural committees busily tend to the interests of farmers, while committees focusing on foreign trade worry about cutting agricultural subsidies. One committee wrestles with domestic unemployment, while another makes tax policy that encourages businesses to open new plants out of the country. One reason why government spends too much, critics say, is that Congress is protecting the interests of too many people. As long as each interest tries to preserve the status quo, Congress cannot enact bold reforms.

On the other hand, defenders of Congress point out that, thanks to its being decentralized, there is no oligarchy in control to prevent the legislature from taking

AMERICA IN PERSPECTIVE

Malapportionment in the Upper House

In a perfectly apportioned system, no citizen's vote weighs more than another's. In a malapportioned system, by contrast, the votes of some citizens weigh more than the votes of others. A number of democracies in developed countries have upper houses with significant powers. The U.S. Senate is the most malapportioned among them.

How content are you with the malapportionment of power in the Senate?

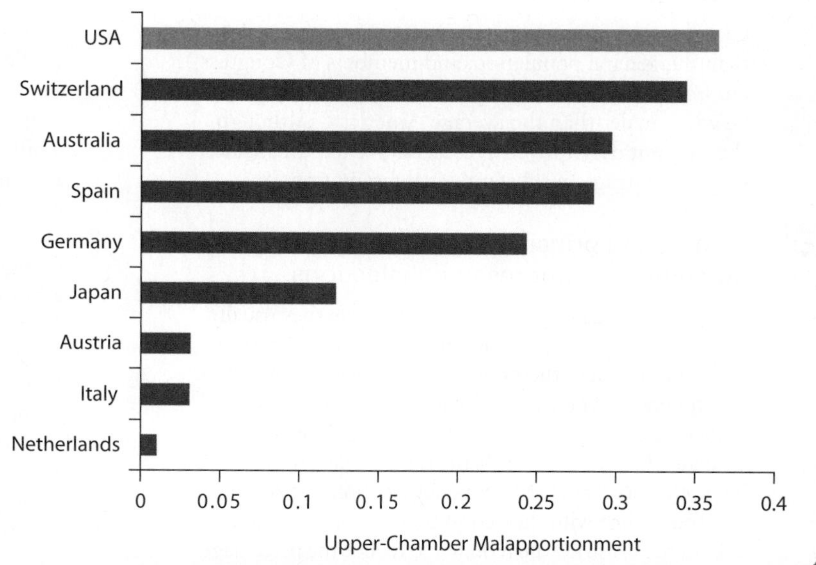

Source: David Samuels and Richard Snyder, "The Value of a Vote: Malapportionment in Comparative Perspective," *British Journal of Political Science* 31 (October 2001), p. 662.

comprehensive action. In fact, Congress has enacted historic legislation such as the huge tax cuts of 1981 and 2001, the comprehensive (and complicated) tax reform of 1986, and various bills structuring the budgetary process designed to balance the budget.[71] In recent years, Congress has also passed health care reform, important trade bills, a prescription drug addition to Medicare, and a major program for elementary and secondary education.

There is no simple solution to Congress's dilemma. It tries to be both a representative and an objective policymaking institution. As long as this is true, it is unlikely that Congress will please all its critics.

Congress and the Scope of Government

Congress is responsive to a multitude of interests, many of which desire government policies. Does this responsiveness predispose the legislature to increase the size of government to please the public? Does providing constituents with pork barrel spending and casework services create too much of an incentive for members of Congress to expand government programs? One can argue that big government helps members of Congress get reelected and gives them good reason to support making it bigger.

Members of Congress vigorously protect the interests of their constituents. At the same time, there are many members who agree with the conservative argument that government is not the answer to problems but rather *is* the problem. These individuals make careers out of fighting against government programs (although these same senators and representatives typically support programs aimed at aiding *their* constituents).

Americans have contradictory preferences regarding public policy. As we have noted in previous chapters, they want to balance the budget and pay low taxes, but majorities also support most government programs. Congress does not impose programs on a reluctant public; instead, it responds to the public's demands for them.

Summary

12.1 Characterize the backgrounds of members of Congress and assess their impact on the ability of members of Congress to represent average Americans.

Congress has proportionately more whites and males than the general population, and members of Congress are wealthier and better educated, and more likely to be white males than the average American. Although they are not descriptively representative of Americans, they may engage in substantive representation.

12.2 Identify the principal factors influencing the outcomes in congressional elections.

Incumbents usually win reelection, because they usually draw weak opponents, are usually better known and better funded than their opponents, typically represent constituencies where a clear majority share their party affiliation, and can claim credit for aiding their constituents. However, incumbents can lose if they are involved in a scandal, if their policy positions are substantially out of line with their constituents, or if the boundaries of their districts are redrawn to reduce the percentage of their constituents identifying with their party.

12.3 Compare and contrast the House and Senate, and describe the roles of congressional leaders, committees, caucuses, and staff.

The House is much larger than the Senate, and is also characterized by greater centralization of power in the party leadership and by more party discipline. Senators are more equal in power and may exercise the option of the filibuster to stop a majority from passing a bill. Congressional leaders are elected by their party members and must remain responsive to them. They cannot always depend on the votes of the members of their party. Committees do most of the work in Congress, considering legislation and overseeing the administration of policy. Although committees are run more democratically than in past decades, chairs have considerable power to set their committees' agendas. Caucuses are part of the informal organization of Congress and are composed of representatives and senators who have a shared interest or characteristic. Personal, committee, and agency staff are crucial components of Congress, providing policy expertise and constituency service.

12.4 Outline the path of bills to passage and explain the influences on congressional decision making.

Congress is typically a cumbersome decision-making body, and the process for considering a bill has many stages. This complexity gives rise to unorthodox lawmaking, in which the congressional leadership bypasses traditional legislative stages. Presidents try to persuade Congress to support their policies, which usually earn space on the congressional agenda. Their ultimate influence on congressional decision making is at the margins, however. Parties have become more homogeneous and more polarized in recent years and provide an important pull on their members on most issues. Constituencies have strong influence on congressional decision making on a few visible issues, while members' own ideologies exert more influence on less visible issues. Interest groups play a key role in informing Congress and sometimes the threat of their opposition influences vote outcomes.

12.5 Assess Congress's role as a representative body and the impact of representation on the scope of government.

Although Congress is an elite institution, it is responsive to the public when the public makes its wishes clear. It is open to influence, an openness that makes it responsive to many interests but also may reduce its ability to make good public policy. Members of Congress often support expanding government to aid their constituents, generally in response to public demands for policy, but many also fight to limit the scope of government.

Chapter Test

12.1 Characterize the backgrounds of members of Congress and assess their impact on the ability of members of Congress to represent average Americans.

1. Which of the following is NOT a reason for the current underrepresentation of women in Congress?
   a. Women are less likely than men to run for office if they feel their chances of winning are poor
   b. Women are less likely than men to become major party nominees
   c. Women are less likely than men to win races they enter
   d. Women are less likely than men to run for office because of childcare responsibilities
   e. All of the above are reasons for the underrepresentation of women in Congress

2. Approximately 25 percent of membership in the House of Representatives is African American.

   True______ False______

3. What is the difference between descriptive and substantive representation? In your opinion, can Congress claim that it does either? Explain why.

12.2 Identify the principal factors influencing the outcomes in congressional elections.

4. All of following are true of incumbents in Congress EXCEPT
   a. Most incumbents decide to run for reelection
   b. Most incumbents' views on policy are well known to their constituents
   c. Most incumbents win reelection with more than 60 percent of the vote
   d. Most incumbents have more campaign contributions to spend than their opponents
   e. Most incumbents have higher levels of name recognition that their opponents

5. Which of the following is most likely to hurt an incumbent legislator's chances for reelection?
   a. The incumbent has gone through a scandalous and public divorce
   b. The incumbent has been in office during an economic downturn
   c. The incumbent has spent more money than his challenger on his reelection campaign
   d. The incumbent has supported the president's policy initiatives
   e. The incumbent has spent considerable time claiming credit for his voting record

6. The vast majority of people are more likely to vote based on party identification than on the candidate's personal characteristics and/or policy platform.

   True______ False______

7. Based on what you know about congressional elections, what do you think are three primary reasons for the incumbency advantage? Generally speaking, do you think the incumbency advantage is good or bad for American democracy? Explain.

12.3 Compare and contrast the House and Senate, and describe the roles of congressional leaders, committees, caucuses, and staff.

8. The filibuster may be considered undemocratic because
   a. It is used in the Senate but not in the House of Representatives
   b. It is used to prevent logrolling in Congress
   c. It is used to undermine the power of the Speaker of the House
   d. It is used by the minority to defeat the majority
   e. It is used by the majority to defeat the minority

9. When the House and the Senate pass different versions of a bill, these versions are to be reconciled by a
   a. Standing committee
   b. Joint committee
   c. Conference committee
   d. Select committee
   e. Reconciliation committee

10. Congressional committee oversight has declined as federal policy responsibilities have increased over time.

    True______ False______

11. Although legislators are often overwhelmed with responsibilities, they have a staff to assist them. What role do personal and committee staffs play in the legislative process? In your opinion, is greater reliance on legislative staff good or bad for representative democracy? Explain your answer.

12. As majority leader of the Senate, Robert Dole once dubbed himself the "Majority Pleader." Based on what you have learned, what supports Senator Dole's assessment, and what contradicts it? How important do you think strong leadership is in the House and in the Senate? Which aspects of leaders' powers would you change, and why?

12.4 Outline the path of bills to passage and explain the influences on congressional decision making.

13. Which of the following best describes the president's influence over congressional decision making?
    a. Presidential influence in Congress regularly directs congressional decision making
    b. Presidential influence in Congress occurs at the margins
    c. Presidential influence in Congress is more pronounced in the Senate than House
    d. Presidential influence in Congress is more likely to occur when interest groups oppose the president's position
    e. Presidential influence in Congress is enhanced by the constitutional separation of powers

14. Only a member of the House or Senate can officially propose a bill.

    True______ False______

15. Constituency opinion is not always the dominant factor that influences a legislator's decision making. Under what circumstances are legislators more likely to respond to constituency opinion and when are they less likely to do so? In your opinion, is it undemocratic when legislators do not respond to constituency opinion in their decision making? Why or why not?

12.5 Assess Congress's role as a representative body and the impact of representation on the scope of government.

16. What are the main arguments in favor of and against the idea that Congress is a representative institution? Which side do you agree more with and why? Are there any ways to make Congress more representative of the American people?

17. Does congressional responsiveness to constituents predispose Congress to increase the scope of government? If so, what can be done to counterbalance this predisposition?

PEARSON mypoliscilab Exercises

Apply what you learned in this chapter on MyPoliSciLab.

Read on **mypoliscilab.com**

eText: Chapter 12

Study and **Review** on **mypoliscilab.com**

Pre-Test
Post-Test
Chapter Exam
Flashcards

Watch on **mypoliscilab.com**

Video: Unknown Wins South Carolina Senate Primary
Video: Kagan Hearing

Explore on **mypoliscilab.com**

Simulation: How a Bill Becomes a Law
Simulation: You Are a Member of Congress
Comparative: Comparing Legislatures
Timeline: The Power of the Speaker of the House
Visual Literacy: Congressional Redistricting
Visual Literacy: Why Is It So Hard to Defeat an Incumbent?

Key Terms

incumbents (336)
casework (339)
pork barrel (339)
bicameral legislature (342)
House Rules Committee (343)
filibuster (343)
Speaker of the House (344)
majority leader (345)
whips (345)
minority leader (346)
standing committees (346)
joint committees (346)
conference committees (346)
select committees (347)
legislative oversight (347)
committee chairs (349)
seniority system (349)
caucus (350)
bill (352)

Internet Resources

www.house.gov
The official House of Representatives Web site contains information on the organization, operations, schedule, and activities of the House and its committees. The site also contains links to the offices of members and committees and enables you to contact your representative directly.

www.senate.gov
The official Senate Web site contains information and links similar to those for the House.

thomas.loc.gov
Information on the activities of Congress, the status and text of legislation, the *Congressional Record*, committee reports, and historical documents.

www.fec.gov
Federal Election Commission data on campaign expenditures.

www.opensecrets.org
The Center for Responsive Politics Web site with data on the role of money in politics.

www.c-span.org
Video coverage of Congress in action.

www.cawp.rutgers.edu
The Center for American Women and Politics Web site, with information on women in politics at all levels of government.

www.congress.org
Nonpartisan news and information on Congress and policy.

www.rollcall.com
Roll Call, the online version of the Capitol Hill newspaper.

thehill.com
News about all aspects of Congress.

For Further Reading

Aberbach, Joel D. ***Keeping a Watchful Eye: The Politics of Congressional Oversight.*** Washington, DC: Brookings Institution, 1990. A thorough study of congressional oversight of the executive branch.

Baumgartner, Frank R., Jeffrey M. Berry, Marie Hohnacki, David C. Kimball, and Beth L. Leech. ***Lobbying and Policy Change: Who Wins, Who Loses, and Why.*** Chicago, IL: University of Chicago Press, 2009. Examines just how influential lobbyists are—and are not.

Binder, Sarah A. ***Stalemate.*** Washington, DC: Brookings Institution, 2003. Discusses the causes and consequences of legislative gridlock.

Dodd, Lawrence C., and Bruce I. Oppenheimer. ***Congress Reconsidered,*** 9th ed. Washington, DC: CQ Press, 2009. Excellent essays covering many aspects of Congress.

Fenno, Richard F., Jr. ***Home Style.*** Boston: Little, Brown, 1978. How members of Congress mend fences and stay in political touch with the folks back home.

Fiorina, Morris P. ***Congress: Keystone of the Washington Establishment,*** 2nd ed. New Haven, CT: Yale University Press, 1989. Argues that members of Congress are self-serving in representing their constituents, ensuring their reelection but harming the national interest.

Jacobson, Gary C. ***The Politics of Congressional Elections,*** 8th ed. New York: Addison-Wesley Longman, 2011. An excellent review of congressional elections.

Koger, Gregory. ***Filibustering.*** Chicago: University of Chicago Press, 2010. Explains the development and uses of the filibuster.

Lee, Frances E. ***Beyond Ideology: Politics, Principles, and Partisanship in the U. S. Senate.*** Chicago: University of Chicago Press, 2009. Argues that many partisan battles are rooted in competition for power rather than disagreement over the proper role of government.

Lee, Frances E., and Bruce I. Oppenheimer. ***Sizing Up the Senate: The Unequal Consequences of Equal Representation.*** Chicago: University of Chicago Press, 1999. How representation in the Senate affects how people are represented, the distribution of government benefits, and the nature of election campaigns.

Mann, Thomas E., and Norman J. Ornstein. ***The Broken Branch.*** New York: Oxford University Press, 2006. How Congress is failing America and how to get it back on track.

Mayhew, David R. ***Congress: The Electoral Connection,*** 2nd ed. New Haven, CT: Yale University Press, 2005. An analysis of Congress based on the premise that the principal motivation of congressional behavior is reelection.

Oleszek, Walter J. ***Congressional Procedures and the Policy Process,*** 8th ed. Washington, DC: CQ Press, 2010. Definitive work on how congressional rules, procedures, and traditions affect legislation.

Sinclair, Barbara. ***Party Wars.*** Norman, OK: University of Oklahoma Press, 2006. The impact of partisan polarization on congressional policy making.

Sinclair, Barbara. ***Unorthodox Lawmaking,*** 3rd ed. Washington, DC: CQ Press, 2007. Explains how Congress tries to cope with decentralization and polarization.

Theriault, Sean M. ***Party Polarization in Congress.*** Cambridge, UK: Cambridge University Press, 2008. Explains the growing partisan polarization in Congress.

Chapter 13

The Presidency

Learning Objectives

13.1 Characterize the expectations for and the backgrounds of presidents and identify paths to the White House and how presidents may be removed.

13.2 Evaluate the president's constitutional powers and the expansion of presidential power.

13.3 Describe the roles of the vice president, cabinet, Executive Office of the President, White House staff, and First Lady.

13.4 Assess the impact of various sources of presidential influence on the president's ability to win congressional support.

13.5 Analyze the president's powers in making national security policy and the relationship between the president and Congress in this arena.

13.6 Identify the factors that affect the president's ability to obtain public support.

13.7 Characterize the president's relations with the press and news coverage of the presidency.

13.8 Assess the role of presidential power in the American democracy and the president's impact on the scope of government.

POLITICS IN ACTION: PRESIDENTIAL POWER

As Barack Obama waited to deliver his State of the Union address in January 2011, he could reflect on his two years as president. They had certainly been eventful. Winning an historic election in 2008, he had hoped to make rapid progress on his agenda for change. Once in office, however, he had to deal first with the greatest financial crisis since the Great Depression. Only then could he turn his attention to health care reform, climate change and energy legislation, immigration, and other crucial matters. Each of these issues presented challenges in forming winning coalitions, especially since Republicans adamantly opposed his proposals.

He was awarded the Nobel Peace Prize. Yet, he also had to make critical and difficult decisions regarding the use of U.S. troops in Iraq and Afghanistan. Stopping the development of nuclear weapons in Iran and North Korea also posed intractable problems. Obtaining global agreement on limiting greenhouses gases was not much easier.

The poor economy, the controversial nature of his proposals for reform, and the strident tone of the opposition all contributed to a decline in both his public approval and his party's chances in the 2010 midterm elections. He had campaigned as an agent of change, and he had proposed many reforms, but he faced the same challenges in accomplishing his goals as his predecessors.

Powerful, strong, leader of the free world, commander in chief—these are common images of the American president. The only place in the world where television networks assign permanent camera crews is the White House. The presidency is power, at least according to popular myth. Problems are brought to the president's desk, the president decides on the right courses of action and issues orders, and an army of aides and bureaucrats carries out these orders.

As Barack Obama and all other presidents soon discover, nothing could be further from the truth. The main reason why presidents have trouble getting things done is that other policymakers with whom they deal have their own agendas, their own interests, and their own sources of power. Presidents operate in an environment filled with checks and balances and competing centers of power. As one presidential aide put it, "Every time you turn around people resist you."[1] Congress is beholden not to the president, but to the individual constituencies of its members. Cabinet members often push on behalf of their departmental interests and constituencies (farmers in the case of the Department of Agriculture, for example). Rarely can presidents rely on unwavering support from their party, the public, or even their own appointees.

As the pivotal leader in American politics, the president is the subject of unending political analysis and speculation. A perennial question focuses on presidential power.

Chapter OUTLINE

World history is replete with examples of leaders who have exceeded the prescribed boundaries of their power. Can the presidency become too powerful and thus pose a threat to democracy? Or is the Madisonian system strong enough to check any such tendencies? On the other hand, is the president *strong enough* to stand up to the diverse interests in the United States? Does the president have enough power to govern on behalf of the majority?

A second fundamental question regarding democratic leaders is the nature of their relationship with the public and its consequences for public policy. The president and vice president are the only officials elected by the entire nation. In their efforts to obtain public support from the broad spectrum of interests in the public, are presidents natural advocates of an expansion of government? Do they promise more than they should in order to please the voters? As they face the frustrations of governing, do presidents seek to centralize authority in the federal government, where they have greater influence, while reducing that of the states? Does the chief executive seek more power through increasing the role of government?

Because not everyone bends easily to even the most persuasive president, the president must be a *leader*. To accomplish policy goals, the president must get other people—important people—to do things they otherwise would not do. Richard Neustadt famously argued that presidents were generally in a weak position to command, so they had to rely on persuasion.[2] George Edwards found that presidents have a difficult time changing people's minds, however, so they have to recognize and exploit opportunities already in their environments.[3] To be effective, the president must have highly developed *political skills* to understand the political forces around him, mobilize influence, manage conflict, negotiate, and fashion compromises. Presidential leadership has varied over the years, depending in large part on the individual who holds our nation's highest office. The following sections explore who presidents are and how they try to lead the nation.

13.1 Characterize the expectations for and the backgrounds of presidents and identify paths to the White House and how presidents may be removed.

The Presidents

The presidency is an institution composed of the roles presidents must play, the powers at their disposal, and the large bureaucracy at their command. It is also a highly personal office. The personality of the individual serving as president makes a difference.

Great Expectations

When a new president takes the oath of office, he faces many daunting tasks. Perhaps the most difficult is living up to the expectations of the American people. Americans expect the chief executive to ensure peace, prosperity, and security.[4] As President Carter remarked, "The President . . . is held to be responsible for the state of the economy . . . and for the inconveniences, or disappointments, or the concerns of the American people."[5] Americans want a good life, and they look to the president to provide it.

Americans are of two minds about the presidency. On the one hand, they want to believe in a powerful president, one who can do good. They look back longingly on the great presidents of the first American century—Washington, Jefferson, Lincoln—and some in the second century as well, especially Franklin D. Roosevelt.

On the other hand, Americans dislike a concentration of power. Although presidential responsibilities have increased substantially since the Great Depression and World War II, there has not been a corresponding increase in presidential authority or administrative resources to meet these new expectations. Americans are basically individualistic and skeptical of authority. According to Samuel Huntington, "The distinctive aspect of the American Creed is its antigovernment character. Opposition to power, and suspicion of government as the most dangerous embodiment of power, are the central themes of American political thought."[6]

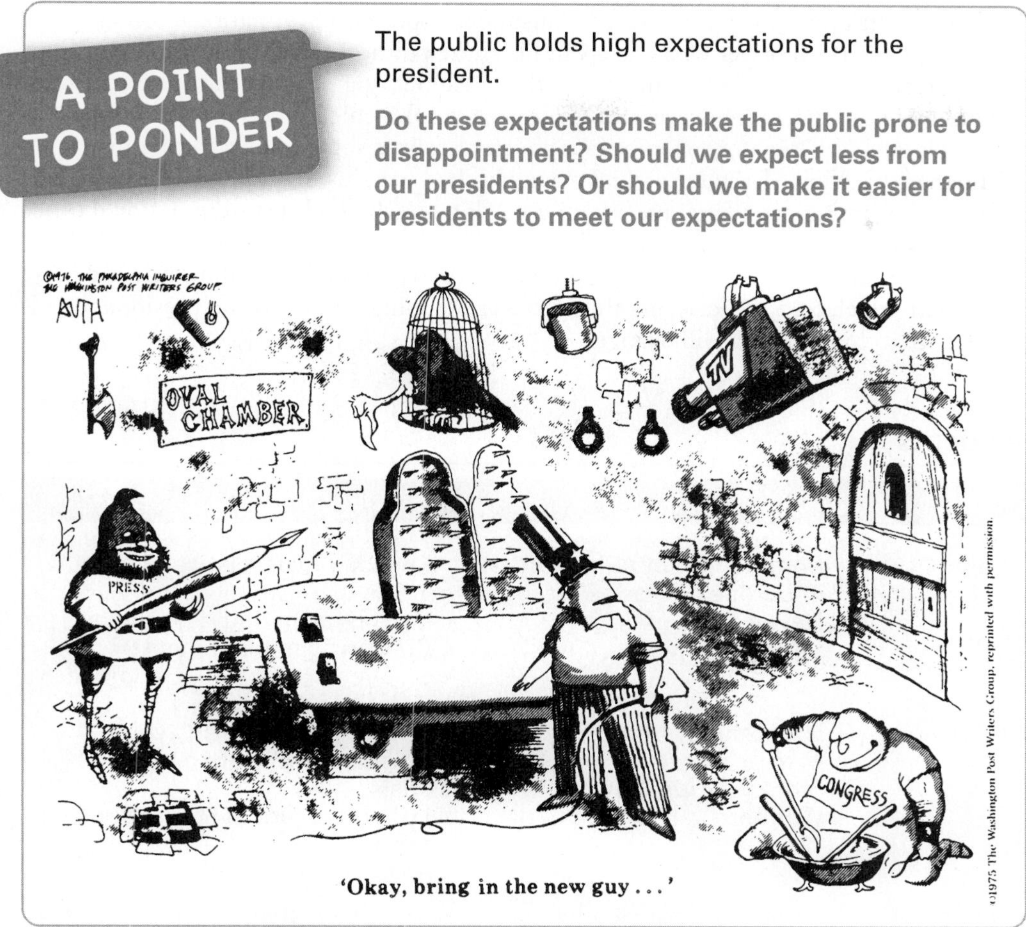

A POINT TO PONDER
The public holds high expectations for the president.
Do these expectations make the public prone to disappointment? Should we expect less from our presidents? Or should we make it easier for presidents to meet our expectations?
AUTH
OVAL CHAMBER
TV
PRESS
CONGRESS

'Okay, bring in the new guy . . .'

Because Americans' expectations of the presidency are so high, who serves as president is especially important. Just who are the people who have occupied the Oval Office?

Who They Are

When Warren G. Harding, one of the least illustrious American presidents, was in office, attorney Clarence Darrow remarked, "When I was a boy, I was told that anybody could become president. Now I'm beginning to believe it." The Constitution simply states that the president must be a natural-born citizen at least 35 years old and must have resided in the United States for at least 14 years. Before Barack Obama was inaugurated as the forty-fourth president in 2009, all American presidents had been white males and, except for John Kennedy, Protestant. This homogeneity conceals considerable variety. Over the years, all manner of men have occupied the Oval Office. Thomas Jefferson was a scientist and scholar who assembled dinosaur bones when presidential business was slack. Woodrow Wilson, the only political scientist ever to become president, combined a Presbyterian moral fervor and righteousness with a professor's intimidating style of leadership and speech making. His successor, Warren G. Harding, became president because Republican leaders thought he looked like one. Poker was his pastime. Out of his element in the job, Harding is almost everyone's choice as the worst American president. His speech making, said opponent William G. McAdoo, sounded "like an army of pompous phrases marching across the landscape in search of an idea." Harding's friends stole the government blind, prompting his brief assessment of the presidency: "God, what a job!"

Since World War II, the White House has been home to a Missouri haberdasher, a war hero, a Boston-Irish politician, a small-town Texas boy who grew up to become the biggest wheeler-dealer in the Senate, a California lawyer described by his enemies as

"Tricky Dick" and by his friends as a misunderstood master of national leadership, a former Rose Bowl player who had spent his entire political career in the House of Representatives, a former governor who had been a Georgia peanut wholesaler, an actor who was also a former governor of California, a CIA chief and ambassador who was the son of a U.S. senator, an ambitious governor from a small state, a former managing director of a Major League baseball team who had won his first election only six years before becoming president, and a young black man who had served in national office for only four years before assuming the role of commander in chief (see Table 13.1).

So far, no woman has served as president. As social prejudices diminish and more women are elected to positions that serve as stepping stones to the presidency, it is likely that this situation will change.

TABLE 13.1 Recent Presidents

PRESIDENT	TERM	PARTY	BACKGROUND	PRESIDENCY
Dwight D. Eisenhower	1953–1961	Republican	• Commander of Allied forces in Europe in World War II • Never voted until he ran for president	• Presided over relatively tranquil 1950s • Conservative domestic policies • Cool crisis management • Enjoyed strong public approval
John F. Kennedy	1961–1963	Democrat	• U.S. senator from Massachusetts • From very wealthy family • War hero	• Known for personal style • Presided over Cuban missile crisis • Ushered in era of liberal domestic policies • Assassinated in 1963
Lyndon B. Johnson	1963–1969	Democrat	• Senate majority leader • Chosen as Kennedy's running mate; succeeded him after the assassination	• Skilled legislative leader with a coarse public image • Launched the Great Society • Won passage of major civil rights laws • Escalated the Vietnam War • War policies proved unpopular; did not seek reelection
Richard M. Nixon	1969–1974	Republican	• U.S. senator from California • Served two terms as Eisenhower's vice president • Lost presidential election of 1960 to John F. Kennedy	• Presided over period of domestic policy innovation • Reopened relations with China • Ended Vietnam War • Resigned as a result of Watergate scandal
Gerald R. Ford	1974–1977	Republican	• House minority leader • First person ever nominated as vice president under Twenty-fifth Amendment	• Pardoned Richard Nixon • Helped heal the nation's wounds after Watergate • Lost election in 1976 to Jimmy Carter
Jimmy Carter	1977–1981	Democrat	• Governor of Georgia • Peanut farmer	• Viewed as honest but politically unskilled • Managed Iranian hostage crisis • Lost bid for reelection in 1980 • Brokered peace between Egypt and Israel
Ronald W. Reagan	1981–1989	Republican	• Governor of California • Well-known actor	• Won a substantial tax cut • Led fight for a large increase in defense spending • Hurt by Iran-Contra scandal • Known as the Great Communicator

George H. W. Bush	1989–1993	Republican	• U.S. representative from Texas • Director of CIA • Ambassador to UN • Served two terms as • Reagan's vice president	• Led international coalition to victory in Gulf War • Presided over end of Cold War • Popular until economy stagnated • Lost reelection bid in 1992
William J. Clinton	1993–2001	Democrat	• Governor of Arkansas • Rhodes Scholar	• Moved Democrats to center • Presided over balanced budget • Benefited from strong economy • Tenure marred by Monica Lewinsky scandal • Impeached but not convicted
George W. Bush	2001–2009	Republican	• Governor of Texas • Son of President George Bush • Elected without plurality of the vote	• Launched war on terrorism • Won large tax cut • Established Department of Homeland Security • Began war with Iraq
Barack Obama	2009–	Democrat	• Senator from Illinois • First African American elected as president	• Dealt with financial crisis • Continued war on terrorism • Won health care reform

How They Got There

Regardless of their ability, background, or character, all presidents must come to the job through one of two basic routes.

Elections: The Typical Road to the White House Most presidents take a familiar journey to 1600 Pennsylvania Avenue: They run for president through the electoral process, which we describe in Chapters 9 and 10. The Constitution guarantees a four-year term once in office (unless the president is convicted in an impeachment trial), but the **Twenty-second Amendment**, ratified in 1951, limits presidents to being elected to only two terms.

Only 13 presidents have actually served two or (in Franklin Roosevelt's case) more full terms in the White House: Washington, Jefferson, Madison, Monroe, Jackson, Grant, Cleveland (whose terms were not consecutive), Wilson, Franklin Roosevelt, Eisenhower, Reagan, Clinton, and George W. Bush. A few—Coolidge, Polk, Pierce, Buchanan, Hayes, and Lyndon Johnson—decided against a second term. Seven others—both the Adamses, Van Buren, Taft, Hoover, Carter, and George H. W. Bush—thought they had earned a second term but found that the voters did not concur.

Succession and Impeachment For more than 10 percent of American history, an individual who was not elected to the office has served as president. About one in five presidents got the job because they were vice president when the incumbent president either died or (in Nixon's case) resigned (see Table 13.2). In the twentieth century, almost one-third (5 of 18) of those who occupied the office were "accidental presidents."

The **Twenty-fifth Amendment**, ratified in 1967, created a means for selecting a new vice president when that office becomes vacant. The president nominates a new vice president, who assumes the office when both houses of Congress approve the nomination by majority vote. President Nixon chose Gerald Ford as vice president when Vice President Spiro Agnew resigned, and Ford then assumed the presidency when Nixon himself resigned. Thus, Ford did not run for either the vice presidency or the presidency before taking office.

Removing a discredited president before the end of a term is not easy. The Constitution prescribes the process of **impeachment**, which is roughly the political equivalent of an indictment in criminal law. The House of Representatives may, by majority vote, impeach the president for "Treason, Bribery, or other high Crimes and

Twenty-second Amendment
Ratified in 1951, this amendment limits presidents to two terms of office.

Twenty-fifth Amendment
Ratified in 1967, this amendment permits the vice president to become acting president if the vice president and the president's cabinet determine that the president is disabled, and it outlines how a recuperated president can reclaim the job.

Standards of Impeachment

It is not easy to impeach a president; the threshold for an impeachable offense is a high one. This standard makes it very difficult to remove a president Congress feels is performing poorly *between* elections. A lower threshold for impeachment would have the potential to turn the United States into a parliamentary system in which the legislature could change the chief executive at any time.

TABLE 13.2 Incomplete Presidential Terms

PRESIDENT	TERM	SUCCEEDED BY
William Henry Harrison	March 4, 1841–April 4, 1841	John Tyler
Zachary Taylor	March 4, 1849–July 9, 1850	Millard Fillmore
Abraham Lincoln	March 4, 1865–April 15, 1865[a]	Andrew Johnson
James A. Garfield	March 4, 1881–September 19, 1881	Chester A. Arthur
William McKinley	March 4, 1901–September 14, 1901[a]	Theodore Roosevelt
Warren G. Harding	March 4, 1921–August 2, 1923	Calvin Coolidge
Franklin D. Roosevelt	January 20, 1945–April 12, 1945[b]	Harry S. Truman
John F. Kennedy	January 20, 1961–November 22, 1963	Lyndon B. Johnson
Richard M. Nixon	January 20, 1973–August 9, 1974[a]	Gerald R. Ford

[a]Second term.
[b]Fourth term.

impeachment
The political equivalent of an indictment in criminal law, prescribed by the Constitution. The House of Representatives may impeach the president by a majority vote for "Treason, Bribery, or other high Crimes and Misdemeanors."

Misdemeanors." Once the House votes for impeachment, the case goes to the Senate, which tries the accused president, with the chief justice of the Supreme Court presiding. By a two-thirds vote, the Senate may convict and remove the president from office.

The House has impeached only two presidents. It impeached Andrew Johnson, Lincoln's successor, in 1868 on charges stemming from his disagreement with Radical Republicans over Civil War reconstruction policies. He narrowly escaped conviction. On July 31, 1974, the House Judiciary Committee voted to recommend that the full House impeach Richard Nixon as a result of the **Watergate** scandal. Nixon escaped a certain vote for impeachment by resigning. In 1998, the House voted two articles of impeachment against President Bill Clinton on party-line votes. The public clearly opposed the idea, however, and the Senate voted to acquit the president on both counts in 1999. In both cases, the question of what constituted an impeachable offense was hotly debated, as you can read in "You Are the Policymaker: What Should Be the Criteria for Impeaching the President?"

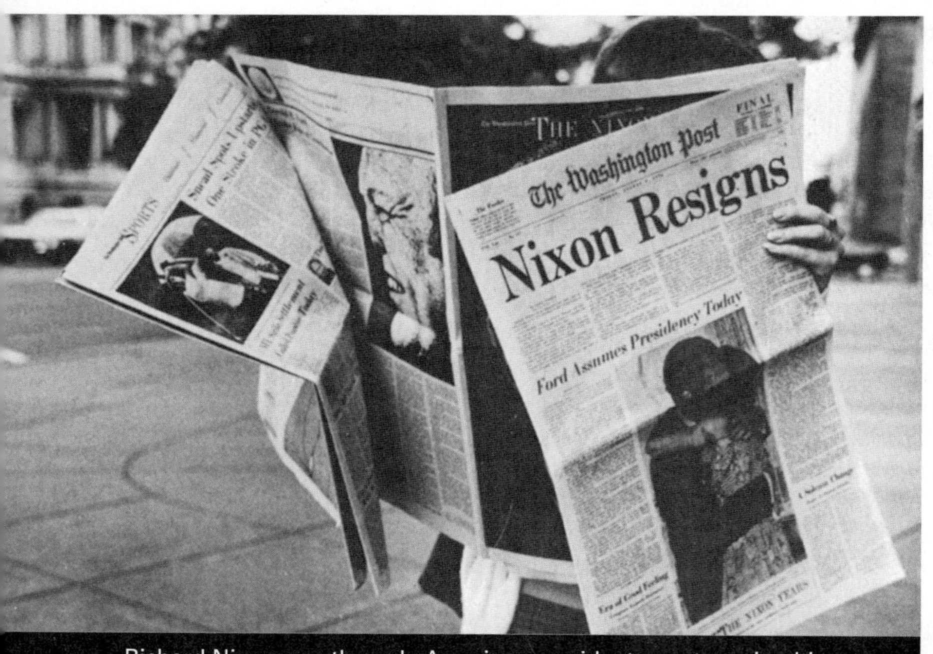

Richard Nixon was the only American president ever to resign his office. Nixon decided to resign rather than face impeachment for his role in the Watergate scandal, a series of illegal wiretaps, break-ins, and cover-ups.

Constitutional amendments cover one other important problem concerning the presidential term: presidential disability and succession. Several times a president has become disabled, incapable of carrying out the job for weeks or even months at a time. After Woodrow Wilson suffered a stroke, his wife, Edith Wilson, became virtual acting president. The Twenty-fifth Amendment clarifies some of the Constitution's vagueness about disability. The amendment permits the vice president to become acting president if the vice president and the president's cabinet determine that the president is disabled or if the president declares his own disability, and it outlines how a recuperated president can reclaim the Oval Office. Other laws specify the order of presidential succession—from the vice president, to the Speaker of the House, to the president pro tempore of the Senate and down through the cabinet members.

YOU ARE THE POLICYMAKER

What Should Be the Criteria for Impeaching the President?

When the Monica Lewinsky story first broke in January 1998, astute political observers immediately perceived that this was more than a lurid sex scandal involving the president. For although the sex angle attracted the most attention, there were also allegations of President Clinton committing perjury when questioned about the affair and obstructing justice by urging Lewinsky to lie under oath. These charges would clearly put any private citizen in danger of being indicted in a criminal court. For a president, who cannot be indicted while in office, it meant possible impeachment by the House of Representatives followed by a Senate trial.

After months of investigation into the allegations, Independent Counsel Kenneth Starr issued a report to Congress accusing President Clinton of 11 counts of possible impeachable offenses, including perjury, obstruction of justice, witness tampering, and abuse of power. The president's detractors used the report as a basis for charging that he had broken the law, failed in his primary constitutional duty to take care that the laws be faithfully executed, betrayed the public's trust, and dishonored the nation's highest office. As a result, they argued the president should be removed from office through the process of impeachment.

The White House fought back. First, the president apologized to the nation, and engaged in a round of expressions of remorse before a variety of audiences. At the same time, the White House accused Starr of an intrusive investigation motivated by a political vendetta against the president. The White House argued that the president made a mistake in his private behavior, apologized for it, and should continue to do the job he was elected to do. Impeachment, the president's defenders said, was grossly disproportionate to the president's offense.

The Constitution provides only the most general guidelines as to the grounds for impeachment. Article II, Section 4, says, "The President, Vice President and all civil Officers of the United States, shall be removed from Office on Impeachment for, and Conviction of, Treason, Bribery, or other high Crimes and Misdemeanors."

There is agreement on at least four points regarding impeachable offenses.

1. Impeachable behavior does not have to be a crime. If, for example, the president refused to work or chose to invade a country solely to increase his public support, his actions could be grounds for impeachment, even though they would not violate the law.
2. The offense should be grave. A poker game in the White House, even though it may violate the law, would not constitute an impeachable offense.
3. A matter of policy disagreement is not grounds for impeachment. When Andrew Johnson was impeached in 1868 and survived conviction by only one vote, the real issue was his disagreement with Congress over the policy of Reconstruction following the Civil War. Johnson's impeachment is widely viewed as an abuse of impeachment power.
4. Impeachment is an inherently political process. The grounds for impeachment are ultimately whatever Congress decides they are because the Constitution assigns these calibrations to members' political judgment.

Beyond these points of agreement, we enter speculative territory. In 1974, the House Judiciary Committee passed three articles of impeachment against President Richard Nixon, but the president resigned before the House took up the charges. The three articles charged that Nixon had (1) obstructed justice, (2) abused his power, and (3) failed to comply with congressional subpoenas. The Democrats on the Judiciary Committee unanimously supported all three articles. In contrast, 10 of the 17 Republicans opposed impeachment, arguing that there needed to be a "smoking gun," demonstrating the president's guilt beyond a doubt. Soon thereafter, the release of another Nixon tape provided enough evidence that even Nixon's defenders on the committee felt was sufficiently convincing, and President Nixon resigned the presidency rather than face a trial in the Senate.

In 1998 and 1999, the tables were turned, as the Republicans supported a lower threshold for an impeachable offense while the Democrats argued for a higher one. In December 1998, the House voted two articles of impeachment against President Clinton on nearly straight party-line votes. The articles charged him with lying to a grand jury and obstructing justice. In the Senate trial that followed, the standards for removing a president from office were hotly debated. Ultimately, neither article received support from even a bare majority of senators, much less the two-thirds threshold necessary to convict him of high crimes and misdemeanors.

What do you think? If you were a member of the House, would *you* have voted to impeach President Clinton?

13.2 Evaluate the president's constitutional powers and the expansion of presidential power.

Watergate
The events and scandal surrounding a break-in at the Democratic National Committee headquarters in 1972 and the subsequent cover-up of White House involvement, leading to the eventual resignation of President Nixon under the threat of **impeachment**.

Presidential Powers

The contemporary presidency hardly resembles the one the Constitution's Framers designed in 1787. The executive office they conceived had more limited authority, fewer responsibilities, and much less organizational structure than today's presidency. The Framers feared both anarchy and monarchy. They wanted an independent executive but disagreed about both the form the office should take and the powers it should exercise. In the end, they created an executive unlike any the world had ever seen[7] (see "America in Perspective: President or Prime Minister?").

Constitutional Powers

The Constitution says remarkably little about presidential power. The discussion of the presidency begins with these general words: "The executive power shall be vested in a president of the United States of America." It goes on to list just a few powers (see Table 13.3). The Framers' invention fit nicely within the Madisonian system of shared power and checks and balances, forcing the president to obtain the support of officials in the other branches of government.

Institutional balance was essential to the convention delegates, who had in mind the abuses of past executives (including both the king and colonial governors) but also the excesses of state legislatures (discussed in Chapter 2). The problem was how to preserve the balance without jeopardizing the independence of the separate branches or impeding the lawful exercise of their authority. The Framers resolved this problem by checking those powers they believed to be most dangerous, the ones that historically had been subject to the greatest abuse (for example, they gave Congress the power to declare war and the Senate the power to approve treaties and presidential appointments), while protecting the general spheres of authority from encroachment (the executive, for instance, was given a qualified veto).

Provisions for reelection and a short term of office also encouraged presidential responsibility. For those executives who flagrantly abused their authority, impeachment was the ultimate recourse.

TABLE 13.3 Constitutional Powers of the President

National Security Powers
Serve as commander in chief of the armed forces
Make treaties with other nations, subject to the agreement of two-thirds of the Senate
Nominate ambassadors, with the agreement of a majority of the Senate
Receive ambassadors of other nations, thereby conferring diplomatic recognition on other governments
Legislative Powers
Present information on the state of the union to Congress
Recommend legislation to Congress
Convene both houses of Congress on extraordinary occasions
Adjourn Congress if the House and Senate cannot agree on adjournment
Veto legislation (Congress may overrule with two-thirds vote of each house)
Administrative Powers
"Take care that the laws be faithfully executed"
Nominate officials as provided for by Congress and with the agreement of a majority of the Senate
Request written opinions of administrative officials
Fill administrative vacancies during congressional recesses
Judicial Powers
Grant reprieves and pardons for federal offenses (except impeachment)
Nominate federal judges, who are confirmed by a majority of the Senate

The Expansion of Power

Today there is more to presidential power than the Constitution alone suggests, and that power is derived from many sources. The role of the president has changed as America has increased in prominence on the world stage; technology has also reshaped the presidency. George Washington's ragtag militias (mostly disbanded by the time the first commander in chief took command) were much different from the mighty nuclear arsenal that today's president commands.

Presidents themselves have taken the initiative to develop new roles for the office. In fact, many presidents have enlarged the power of the presidency by expanding the president's responsibilities and political resources. Thomas Jefferson was the first leader of a mass political party. Andrew Jackson presented himself as the direct representative of the people. Abraham Lincoln mobilized the country for war. Theodore Roosevelt mobilized the public behind his policies. He and Woodrow Wilson set precedents for presidents to serve as world leaders; Wilson and Franklin D. Roosevelt developed the role of the president as manager of the economy.

Perspectives on Presidential Power

During the 1950s and 1960s, it was fashionable for political scientists, historians, and commentators to favor a powerful presidency. Historians rated presidents from strong to weak—and there was no question that "strong" meant good and "weak" meant bad. Political scientists waxed eloquent about the presidency as an institution epitomizing democratic government.[8] By the 1970s, many felt differently. Lyndon Johnson and the unpopular Vietnam War made people reassess the role of presidential power, and Richard Nixon and the Watergate scandal heightened public distrust. The Pentagon Papers, a secret history of the Vietnam War, revealed presidential duplicity. Nixon's "enemies list" and his avowed goal to "screw our enemies" by illegally auditing their taxes,

AMERICA IN PERSPECTIVE

President or Prime Minister?

The Framers selected a presidential system of government for the United States. Most democracies in developed countries, however, have chosen a parliamentary system. In such a system, the members of the legislature, not the voters, select the chief executive, known as the prime minister, from among themselves. More specifically, the majority party (or the largest bloc of votes in the legislature if there is no majority party) votes its party leader to be prime minister. The prime minister may remain in power for a long time—as long as his or her party or coalition has a majority of the seats and supports the leader.

Presidents and prime ministers govern quite differently. Prime ministers never face divided government, for example. Since they represent the majority party or coalition, they can almost always depend on winning votes. In addition, party discipline is better in parliamentary systems than in the United States. Parties know that if the prime minister should lose on an important vote, the government might have to call elections under circumstances unfavorable to the majority. As a result, members of parliament almost always support their leaders.

Prime ministers generally differ in background from presidents as well. They must be party leaders, as we have seen, and they are usually very effective communicators, with skills honed in the rough-and-tumble of parliamentary debate. In addition, they have had substantial experience dealing with national issues, unlike American governors who may move directly into the presidency. Cabinet members, who are usually senior members of parliament, have similar advantages.

So why does the United States maintain a presidential system? The Framers were concerned about the concentration of power and wanted to separate power so that the different branches could check each other. More concerned with the abuse of power than its effective use, they chose a presidential system—the first the world had ever known.

tapping their phones, and using "surreptitious entry" (a euphemism for burglary) asserted that the president was above the law, possessing "inherent powers" that permitted presidents to order acts that otherwise would be illegal.

Early defenders of a strong presidency made sharp turnabouts in their position. In his book *The Imperial Presidency*, historian Arthur Schlesinger argued that the presidency had become too powerful for the nation's own good.[9] (Critics pointed out that Schlesinger did not seem to feel that way when he worked in the Kennedy White House.) Whereas an older generation of scholars had written glowing accounts of the presidency, a newer generation wrote about "The Swelling of the Presidency" and "Making the Presidency Safe for Democracy."[10]

The Nixon era was followed by the presidencies of Gerald Ford and Jimmy Carter, whom many critics saw as weak leaders and failures. Ford himself spoke out in 1980, claiming that Carter's weakness had created an "imperiled" presidency. In the 1980s, Ronald Reagan experienced short periods of great influence and longer periods of frustration as the American political system settled back into its characteristic mode of stalemate and incremental policymaking. The Iran-Contra affair kept concern about a tyrannical presidency alive, while Reagan's inability, in most instances, to sway Congress evoked a desire on the part of some (mostly conservatives) for a stronger presidency. Reagan's immediate successors, George H. W. Bush and Bill Clinton, often found it difficult to get things done.

The presidency of George W. Bush raised anew the issue of presidential power. He asserted an expansive view of the president's constitutional powers, including withholding information from Congress under the doctrine of executive privilege to encourage candid advice from his aides, issuing statements when he signed new laws asserting the right to disregard certain provisions in them, ordering without warrants electronic surveillance of individuals, and holding prisoners without trial for an indefinite period. Once again, critics charged that presidential power threatened the constitutional balance of powers.

13.3 Describe the roles of the vice president, cabinet, Executive Office of the President, White House staff, and First Lady.

Running the Government: The Chief Executive

Although we often refer to the president as the "chief executive," it is easy to forget that one of the president's most important roles is presiding over the administration of government. This role receives less publicity than, for example, appealing to the public for support of policy initiatives, dealing with Congress, or negotiating with foreign powers, but it is of great importance nevertheless.

The Constitution exhorts the president to "take care that the laws be faithfully executed." In the early days of the republic, this clerical-sounding function was fairly easy. Today, the sprawling federal bureaucracy spends more than $3 trillion a year and numbers more than 4 million civilian and military employees. Running such a large organization would be a full-time job for even the most talented of executives, yet it is only one of the president's many jobs.

One of the president's resources for controlling this bureaucracy is the power to appoint top-level administrators. New presidents have about 500 high-level positions available for appointment—cabinet and subcabinet jobs, agency heads, and other non–civil service posts—plus 2,500 lesser jobs. Since passage of the Budgeting and Accounting Act of 1921, presidents have had one other important executive tool: the power to recommend agency budgets to Congress (discussed in detail in Chapter 14).

The vastness of the executive branch, the complexity of public policy, and the desire to accomplish their policy goals have led presidents in recent years to pay even closer attention to appointing officials who will be responsive to the president's policies. Presidents have also taken more interest in the regulations issued by agencies. This trend toward centralizing decision making in the White House pleases those who think the bureaucracy should be more responsive to elected officials. On the other hand, it dismays those who believe that increased presidential involvement in policymaking will undermine the "neutral competence" of professional bureaucrats by encouraging them to follow the president's policy preferences rather than the intent of laws as passed by Congress.

This section focuses on how presidents go about organizing and using the parts of the executive branch most under their control—the vice president, the cabinet, the Executive Office of the President, and the White House staff. (Other aspects the president's role as chief executive are further explored in Chapter 15 on the federal bureaucracy.)

The Vice President

Neither politicians nor political scientists have paid much attention to the vice presidency. Once the choice of a party's "second team" was an afterthought; it has also often been an effort to placate some important symbolic constituency. Jimmy Carter, a moderate southerner, selected as his running mate Walter Mondale, a well-known liberal from Minnesota, and conservative Ronald Reagan chose his chief rival, George Bush, in part to please Republican moderates.[11]

Vice presidents have rarely enjoyed the job. John Nance Garner of Texas, one of Franklin Roosevelt's vice presidents, declared that the job was "not worth a pitcher of warm spit." Some have performed so poorly that they were deemed an embarrassment to the president. After Woodrow Wilson's debilitating stroke, almost everyone agreed that Vice President Thomas Marshall—a man who shirked all responsibility, including cabinet meetings—would be a disaster as acting president. Spiro Agnew, Richard Nixon's first vice president, had to resign and was convicted of evading taxes (on bribes he had accepted).

Before the mid-1970s, vice presidents usually found that their main job was waiting. The Constitution assigns them the minor tasks of presiding over the Senate and voting in case of a tie among the senators. As George H. W. Bush put it when he was vice president, "The buck doesn't stop here." Nonetheless, recent presidents have taken their vice presidents more seriously, involving them in policy discussions and important diplomacy.[12]

The relationship between Jimmy Carter and Walter Mondale marked a watershed in the vice presidency, as Mondale, an experienced senator, became a close advisor to the president, a Washington outsider. In choosing George H. W. Bush, Ronald Reagan also chose a vice president with extensive Washington experience. To become intimates of the president, both vice presidents had to be completely loyal, losing their political independence in the process. Vice President Bush, for example, was accused of knowing more about the Iran-Contra affair than he admitted, but he steadfastly refused to reveal his discussions with President Reagan on the matter.

Although Bush himself chose as vice president Senator Dan Quayle of Indiana, considered by many a political lightweight, Albert Gore, Bill Clinton's vice president, was a Washington insider and played a prominent role in the administration. He met regularly with the president, represented him in discussions with the leaders of numerous countries, and chaired a prominent effort to "reinvent" government.

George W. Bush chose Richard Cheney, who had extensive experience in high-level positions in the national government—including service as White House chief of staff, secretary of defense, and House minority whip—as his vice president and assigned him a central role in his administration. Cheney advised the president on a wide range of issues and chaired task forces dealing with major policy issues. He also was the focus of criticism, especially from those opposed to his support for the aggressive use of military power and an expansive view of presidential power.

Barack Obama chose Senator Joseph Biden of Delaware as his vice president. Biden had substantial experience in government and became a close adviser to the president, especially on foreign policy.

cabinet
A group of presidential advisers not mentioned in the Constitution, although every president has had one. Today the cabinet is composed of 14 secretaries, the attorney general, and others designated by the president.

The Cabinet

Although the Constitution does not mention the group of presidential advisers known as the **cabinet**, every president has had one. The cabinet is too large and too diverse, and its members, heads of the executive departments, are too concerned with representing the interests of their departments for it to serve as a collective board of directors, however. The major decisions remain in the president's hands. Legend has it that Abraham Lincoln asked his cabinet to vote on an issue, and the result was unanimity in opposition to his view. He announced the decision as "seven nays and one aye, the ayes have it."

Members of the president's cabinet are important for both the power they exercise and the status they symbolize. President Barack Obama formed a cabinet that was representative of America's ethnic demographic diversity. Pictured here is President Obama with Attorney General Eric Holder, an African American.

George Washington's cabinet was small, consisting of just three secretaries (state, treasury, and war) and the attorney general. Presidents since Washington have increased the size of the cabinet by requesting Congress to establish new executive departments. Today 14 secretaries and the attorney general head executive departments and constitute the cabinet (see Table 13.4). In addition, presidents may designate other officials (the ambassador to the United Nations is a common choice) as cabinet members.[13]

Even in making his highest-level appointments, the president is subject to the constitutional system of checks and balances. For example, when President George H. W. Bush nominated John Tower, a former senator, as secretary of defense, the Senate handed the president a serious defeat by rejecting Tower after a bitter debate focused on his use of alcohol and relations with women.

The Executive Office

Next to the White House sits an ornate building called the EEOB, or Eisenhower Executive Office Building. It houses a collection of offices and organizations loosely grouped into the Executive Office of the President.[14] Congress has created some of these offices by legislation, and the president has simply organized the rest. The Executive Office started small in 1939, when President Roosevelt established it, but has grown with the rest of government. Three major policymaking bodies are housed in the Executive Office—the National Security Council, the Council of Economic Advisers, and Office of Management and Budget—along with several other units that serve the president (see Figure 13.1).

National Security Council
The committee that links the president's foreign and military policy advisers. Its formal members are the president, vice president, **secretary of state**, and **secretary of defense**, and it is managed by the president's national security assistant.

The **National Security Council** (NSC) is the committee that links the president's key foreign and military policy advisers. Its formal members include the president, vice president, and secretaries of state and defense, but its informal membership is broader. The president's special assistant for national security affairs plays a major role in the NSC, running a staff whose responsibilities include providing the president with information and policy recommendations on national security, aiding the president in national security crisis management, coordinating agency and departmental activities related to national security, and monitoring the implementation of national security policy.

The **Council of Economic Advisers** (CEA) has three members, each appointed by the president, who advise the president on economic policy. They prepare the annual *Economic Report of the President*, which includes data and analysis on the current state and

TABLE 13.4 The Cabinet Departments

DEPARTMENT	YEAR CREATED	FUNCTION
State	1789	Makes foreign policy, including treaty negotiations
Treasury	1789	Serves as the government's banker
Defense	1947	Formed by the consolidation of the former Departments of War and the Navy
Justice	1870	Serves as the government's attorney; headed by the attorney general
Interior	1849	Manages the nation's natural resources, including wildlife and public lands
Agriculture	1862	Administers farm and food stamp programs and aids farmers
Commerce	1903	Aids businesses and conducts the U.S. census
Labor	1913	Formed through separation from the Department of Commerce; runs programs and aids labor in various ways
Health and Human Services	1953	Originally created as the Department of Health, Education, and Welfare, it lost its education function in 1979 and Social Security in 1995
Housing and Urban Development	1966	Responsible for housing and urban programs
Transportation	1966	Responsible for mass transportation and highway programs
Energy	1977	Responsible for energy policy and research, including atomic energy
Education	1979	Responsible for the federal government's education programs
Veterans Affairs	1988	Responsible for programs aiding veterans
Homeland Security	2002	Responsible for protecting against terrorism and responding to natural disasters

future trends of the economy, and help the president make policy on inflation, unemployment, and other economic matters.

The **Office of Management and Budget** (OMB) originated as the Bureau of the Budget (BOB), which was created in 1921. The OMB is composed of a handful of political appointees and more than 600 career officials, many of whom are highly skilled professionals. Its major responsibility is to prepare the president's budget (discussed in Chapter 14). President Nixon revamped the BOB in 1970 in an attempt to make it a managerial as well as a budgetary agency, changing its name in the process to stress its managerial functions.

Because each presidential appointee and department has their own agenda, presidents need a clearinghouse—the OMB. Presidents use the OMB to review legislative proposals from the cabinet and other executive agencies so that they can determine whether they want an agency to propose these initiatives to Congress. The OMB assesses the proposals' budgetary implications and advises presidents on the proposals' consistency with their overall program. The OMB also plays an important role in reviewing regulations proposed by departments and agencies.

Although presidents find that the Executive Office is smaller and more manageable than the cabinet departments, it is still filled with people who often are performing jobs required by law. There is, however, one part of the presidential system that presidents can truly call their own: the White House staff.

Council of Economic Advisers
A three-member body appointed by the president to advise the president on economic policy.

Office of Management and Budget
An office that prepares the president's budget and also advises presidents on proposals from departments and agencies and helps review their proposed regulations.

The White House Staff

Before Franklin D. Roosevelt, the president's personal staff resources were minimal. Only one messenger and one secretary served Thomas Jefferson. One hundred years later the president's staff had grown only to 13. Woodrow Wilson was in the habit of

FIGURE 13.1 Executive Office of the President

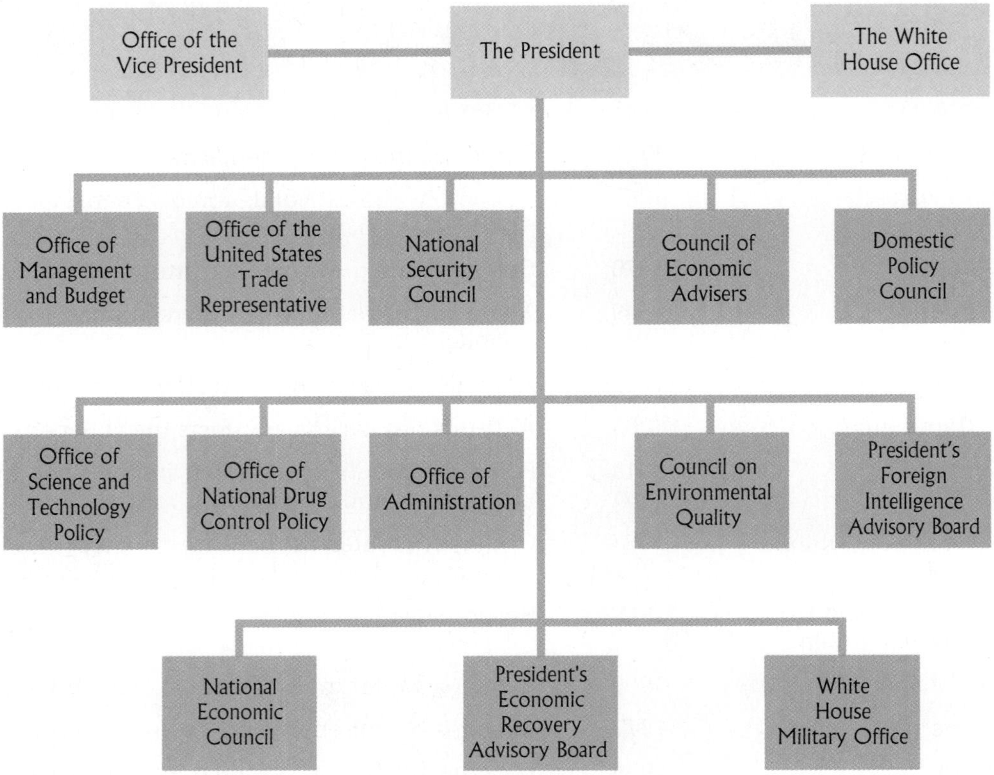

Office of the Vice President
The President
The White House Office

Office of Management and Budget
Office of the United States Trade Representative
National Security Council
Council of Economic Advisers
Domestic Policy Council

Office of Science and Technology Policy
Office of National Drug Control Policy
Office of Administration
Council on Environmental Quality
President's Foreign Intelligence Advisory Board

National Economic Council
President's Economic Recovery Advisory Board
White House Military Office

Source: White House (*www.whitehouse.gov/administration/eop*)

typing his own letters. As recently as the 1920s, the entire budget for the White House staff was no more than $80,000 per year.

Today, the White House staff includes about 600 people—many of whom the president rarely sees—who provide the chief executive with a wide variety of services ranging from making advance travel preparations to answering the avalanche of letters received each year (see Figure 13.2). At the top of the White House staff are the key aides the president sees daily: the chief of staff, congressional liaison aides, a press secretary, a national security assistant, and a few other administrative and political assistants.

The top aides in the White House hierarchy are people who are completely loyal to the president, and the president turns to them for advice on the most serious or mundane matters of governance. Good staff people are self-effacing, working only for the boss and shunning the limelight. The 1939 report of the Brownlow Committee, which served as the basis for the development of the modern White House staff, argued that presidential assistants should have a "passion for anonymity." So important are their roles, though, that the names of top White House aides quickly become well known. Woodrow Wilson's Colonel Edward M. House, Franklin D. Roosevelt's Harry Hopkins, and Richard Nixon's Henry Kissinger, for example, did much to shape domestic and global policy.

Presidents rely heavily on their staffs for information, policy options, and analysis. Different presidents have different relationships with their staffs. They all organize the White House to serve their own political and policy needs and their own decision-making styles. Most presidents end up choosing some form of *hierarchical* organization with a chief of staff at the top, whose job it is to see that everyone else is doing his or her job and that the president's time and interests are protected. A few presidents, such as John F. Kennedy, have employed a *wheel-and-spokes* system of White House management in which many aides have equal status and are balanced against one another in the process of decision making.[15] Whatever the system, White House aides are central

FIGURE 13.2 Principal Offices in the White House

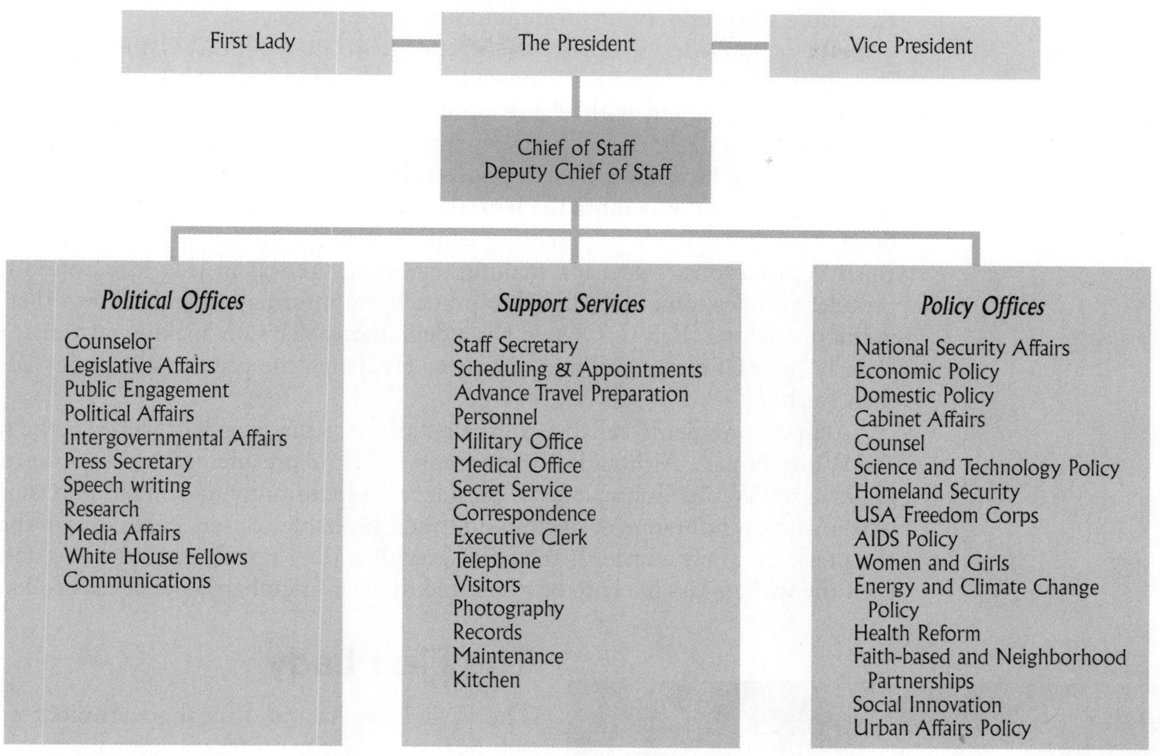

Source: White House (*www.whitehouse.gov/administration/eop*)

A POINT TO PONDER

Presidents rely on their advisors to give them candid opinions. However, even strong and experienced aides at times tell the president what they think he wants to hear rather than what he needs to hear. There is also a danger that the president will not dig beneath the surface to discover what others really think.

How can a president ensure he receives frank advice?

SAY IT AIN'T SO!
YOU'VE GOT TO BE KIDDING!
PERISH THE THOUGHT!
HEAVEN FORBID!
NO! NO! A THOUSAND TIMES NO!

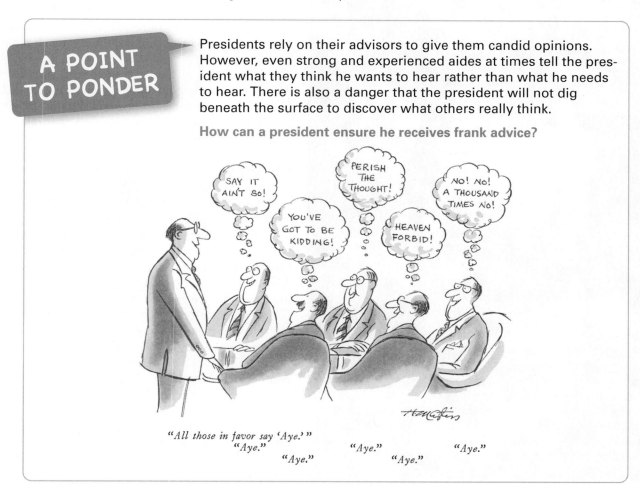

"All those in favor say 'Aye.'"
"Aye." *"Aye."* *"Aye."* *"Aye."* *"Aye."*

in the policymaking process—fashioning options, negotiating agreements, writing presidential statements, controlling paperwork, molding legislative details, and generally giving the president their opinions on most matters.

Recent presidents illustrate significant contrasts in decision-making styles. President Clinton immersed himself in the details of policy. He ran an open White House, dealing directly with a large number of aides and reading countless policy memoranda. His emphasis on deliberation and his fluid staffing system generated criticism that his White House was "indecisive" and "chaotic." George W. Bush took pride in being decisive and was more likely to delegate responsibility than was Clinton. Bush, however, was less likely to persist in asking probing questions. Investigations into the Bush White House's decision making regarding the war in Iraq have found that the president's aides sometimes failed to properly vet information and follow other appropriate procedures. Barack Obama has a deliberative decision-making style that is more orderly than Clinton's and more likely to challenge the premises of policy advocates than Bush's.

Despite presidents' reliance on their staffs, it is the president who sets the tone for the White House. Although it is common to blame presidential advisers for mistakes made in the White House, it is the president's responsibility to demand that staff members analyze a full range of options and their probable consequences before they offer the president their advice. If the chief executive does not demand quality staff work, then the work is less likely to be done, and disaster or embarrassment may follow.

The First Lady

The First Lady has no official government position, yet she is often at the center of national attention. The media chronicles every word she speaks and every hairstyle she adopts. Although some people may think of First Ladies as well-dressed homemakers presiding over White House dinners, there is much more to the job.

Abigail Adams (an early feminist) and Dolley Madison counseled and lobbied their husbands. Edith Galt Wilson was the most powerful First Lady, virtually running the government when her husband, Woodrow, suffered a paralyzing stroke in 1919. Eleanor Roosevelt wrote a nationally syndicated newspaper column and tirelessly traveled and advocated New Deal policies. She became her crippled husband's eyes and ears around the country and urged him to adopt liberal social welfare policies. Lady Bird Johnson chose to focus on one issue, beautification, and most of her successors followed this single-issue pattern. Rosalyn Carter chose mental health, Nancy Reagan selected drug abuse prevention, and Barbara Bush advocated literacy, as did Laura Bush, a former librarian.

In what was perhaps a natural evolution in a society where women have moved into positions formerly held only by males, Hillary Rodham Clinton attained the most responsible and visible leadership position ever held by a First Lady. She was an influential adviser to the president, playing an active role in the selection of nominees for cabinet and judicial posts, for example. Most publicly, she headed the planning for the president's massive health care reform plan in 1993 and became, along with her husband, its primary advocate. Michelle Obama has focused on a range of

Although the First Lady has no official government position, she is often at the center of national attention. In recent years, First Ladies have taken active roles in promoting policies ranging from highway beautification and mental health to literacy and health care. Here First Lady Michelle Obama promotes literacy by reading to schoolchildren. • ***How would things change if a woman were elected president and her spouse were the First Man?***

issues, which have included fighting childhood obesity, supporting military families, helping working women balance career and family, and encouraging national service.

Presidential Leadership of Congress: The Politics of Shared Powers

13.4 Assess the impact of various sources of presidential influence on the president's ability to win congressional support.

Along with their responsibility for running the executive branch, presidents must also deal intensively with the legislative branch. Near the top of any presidential job description would be "working with Congress." The American system of separation of powers is actually one of *shared* powers, so if presidents are to succeed in leaving their stamp on public policy, they must devote much of their time in office to leading the legislature in order to gain support for their initiatives. This effort requires wielding constitutional powers, building party coalitions, exploiting popular support, and exercising legislative skills.

Chief Legislator

Nowhere does the Constitution use the phrase *chief legislator;* it is strictly a phrase invented to emphasize the executive's importance in the legislative process. The Constitution does require that the president give a State of the Union report to Congress and instructs the president to bring other matters to Congress's attention "from time to time." In fact, as noted in Chapter 12, the president plays a major role in shaping the congressional agenda.

The Constitution also gives the president power to **veto** congressional legislation. Once Congress passes a bill, the president may (1) sign it, making it law; (2) veto it, sending it back to Congress with the reasons for rejecting it; or (3) let it become law after 10 working days by not doing anything. Congress can pass a vetoed law, however, if two-thirds of each house votes to override the president. In cases where Congress adjourns within 10 days of submitting a bill, the president can use a **pocket veto**, that is, simply let it die by neither signing nor vetoing it. Table 13.5 shows how frequently recent presidents have used the veto.

veto
The constitutional power of the president to send a bill back to Congress with reasons for rejecting it. A two-thirds vote in each house can override a veto.

pocket veto
A type of veto occurring when Congress adjourns within 10 days of submitting a bill to the president and the president simply lets the bill die by neither signing nor vetoing it.

TABLE 13.5 Presidential Vetoes

PRESIDENT	REGULAR VETOES	VETOES OVERRIDDEN	PERCENTAGE OF VETOES OVERRIDDEN	POCKET VETOES	TOTAL VETOES
Eisenhower	73	2	3	108	181
Kennedy	12	0	0	9	21
Johnson	16	0	0	14	30
Nixon	26	7	27	17	43
Ford	48	12	25	18	66
Carter	13	2	15	18	31
Reagan	39	9	23	39	78
G. H. W. Bush	29	1	3	15	44
Clinton	37	2	5	1	38
G. W. Bush	12	4	33	0	12
Obama*	2	0	0	0	2

*as of January 2011

The President's Veto

Unlike most governors, the president does not have the power to veto parts of a bill. As a result, presidents cannot choose to delete, for example, items in the budget they perceive as wasteful. At the same time, the lack of a line-item veto helps to maintain the delicate balance of separate institutions sharing powers.

The presidential veto is usually effective; Congress has overridden only about 4 percent of all vetoed bills since the nation's founding. Thus, even the threat of a presidential veto can be an effective tool for persuading Congress to give more weight to the president's views. On the other hand, the veto is a blunt instrument. Presidents must accept or reject bills in their entirety; they cannot veto only the parts they do not like (in contrast, most governors have a *line-item veto*, allowing them to veto particular portions of a bill). As a result, the White House often must accept provisions of a bill it opposes in order to obtain provisions that it desires. In recent years, presidents have issued statements when they sign bills, saying they will not comply with certain provisions and, in effect, vetoing parts of bills.

In 1996, Congress passed a law granting the president authority to propose rescinding funds in appropriations bills and also voiding tax provisions that applied to only a few people. Opponents of the law immediately challenged it in the courts as being an unconstitutional grant of power to the president. In 1998 the Supreme Court agreed, voiding the law in *Clinton v. City of New York*.

There are some bills, such as those appropriating funds for national defense, that *must* be passed. Knowing this, the president may veto a version containing provisions he opposes on the theory that Congress does not want to be held responsible for failing to defend the nation. Nevertheless, the presidential veto is an inherently negative resource. It is most useful for preventing legislation. Much of the time, however, presidents are more interested in passing their own legislation. To do so, they must marshal their political resources to obtain positive support for their programs. Presidents' three most useful resources are their party leadership, public support, and their own legislative skills.

Party Leadership

No matter what other resources presidents may have at their disposal, they remain highly dependent on their party to move their legislative programs. Representatives and senators of the president's party usually form the nucleus of coalitions supporting presidential proposals and provide considerably more support than do members of the opposition party. Thus, every president must provide party leadership in Congress, countering the natural tendency toward conflict between the executive and legislative branches that is inherent in the government's system of checks and balances.[16]

The Bonds of Party For most senators and representatives of the president's party, being in the same political party as the president creates a psychological bond. Personal loyalties or emotional commitments to their party and their party leader, a desire to avoid embarrassing "their" administration and thus hurting their chances for reelection, and a basic distrust of the opposition party are inclinations that produce support for the White House. Members of the same party also agree on many matters of public policy, and they are often supported by similar electoral coalitions, reinforcing the pull of party ties. These members also feel they have a collective stake in the president's success.

If presidents could rely on their party members to vote for whatever the White House sent up to Capitol Hill, presidential leadership of Congress would be rather easy. All presidents would have to do is make sure members of their party showed up to vote. If their party had the majority, presidents would always win. If their party was in the minority, presidents would only have to concentrate on converting a few members of the other party.

Slippage in Party Support Things are not so simple, however. Despite the pull of party ties, all presidents experience at least some slippage in the support of their party in Congress. Because presidents cannot always count on their own party members for support, even on key votes, they must be active party leaders and devote their efforts to conversion as much as to mobilization of members of their party.

The primary obstacle to party unity is the lack of consensus on policies among party members, especially in the Democratic Party. Jimmy Carter, a Democrat, remarked, "I learned the hard way that there was no party loyalty or discipline when a complicated or controversial issue was at stake—none."[17]

This diversity of views often reflects the diversity of constituencies represented by party members. The defections of conservative and moderate Democrats from Democratic presidents are a prominent feature of American politics. When constituency opinion and the president's proposals conflict, members of Congress are more likely to vote with their constituents, whom they rely on for reelection. Moreover, if the president is not popular with their constituencies, congressional party members may avoid identifying too closely with the White House.

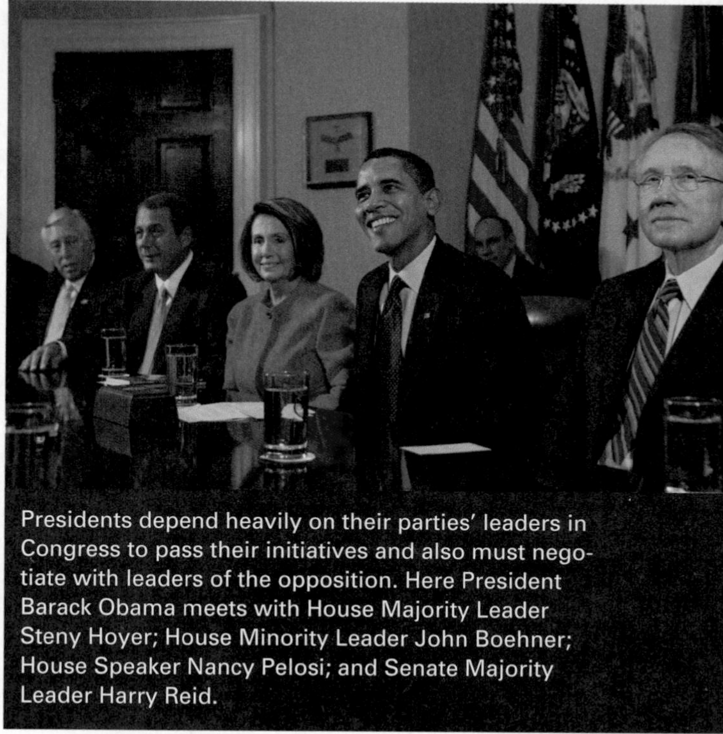
Presidents depend heavily on their parties' leaders in Congress to pass their initiatives and also must negotiate with leaders of the opposition. Here President Barack Obama meets with House Majority Leader Steny Hoyer; House Minority Leader John Boehner; House Speaker Nancy Pelosi; and Senate Majority Leader Harry Reid.

Leading the Party The president has some assets as party leader, including congressional party leaders, services and amenities for party members, and campaign aid. Each asset is of limited utility, however.

The president's relationship with party leaders in Congress is a delicate one. Although the leaders are predisposed to support presidential policies and typically work closely with the White House, they are free to oppose the president or lend only symbolic support; some party leaders may be ineffective themselves. Moreover, party leaders, especially in the Senate, are not in strong positions to reward or discipline members of Congress.

To create goodwill with congressional party members, the White House provides them with many amenities, ranging from photographs with the president to rides on Air Force One. Although this arrangement is to the president's advantage and may earn the benefit of the doubt on some policy initiatives, party members consider it their right to receive benefits from the White House and as a result are unlikely to be especially responsive to the president's largesse. In addition to offering a carrot, the president can, of course, wield a stick in the form of withholding favors, but this is rarely done.

If party members wish to oppose the White House, the president can do little to stop them. The parties are highly decentralized, as we saw in Chapter 8. National party leaders do not control those aspects of politics that are of vital concern to members of Congress—nominations and elections. Members of Congress are largely self-recruited, gain their party's nomination by their own efforts and not the party's, and provide most of the money and organizational support needed for their elections. Presidents can do little to influence the results of these activities.

One way for the president to improve the chances of obtaining support in Congress is to increase the number of fellow party members in the legislature. The phenomenon of **presidential coattails** occurs when voters cast their ballots for congressional candidates of the president's party because those candidates support the president. Most recent studies show a diminishing connection between presidential and congressional voting, however, and few races are determined by presidential coattails.[18] The change in party balance that usually emerges when the electoral dust has settled is strikingly small. In the 15 presidential elections between 1952 and 2008, the party of the winning presidential candidate averaged a net gain of eight seats (out of 435) per election in the House and only one seat in the Senate, where the opposition party actually gained seats in seven of the elections (see Table 13.6).

presidential coattails
These occur when voters cast their ballots for congressional candidates of the president's party because they support the president. Recent studies show that few races are won this way.

What about midterm elections—those held between presidential elections? Can the president depend on increasing the number of fellow party members in Congress then? Actually, the picture is even bleaker than for presidential elections. As you can

TABLE 13.6 Congressional Gains or Losses for the President's Party in Presidential Election Years

Presidents cannot rely on their coattails to carry their party's legislators into office to help pass White House legislative programs. The president's party typically gains few, if any, seats when the president wins election. For instance, the Republicans lost seats in both houses when President George W. Bush was elected in 2000.

YEAR	PRESIDENT	HOUSE	SENATE
1952	Eisenhower (R)	+22	+1
1956	Eisenhower (R)	−2	−1
1960	Kennedy (D)	−22	−2
1964	Johnson (D)	+37	+1
1968	Nixon (R)	+5	+6
1972	Nixon (R)	+12	−2
1976	Carter (D)	+1	0
1980	Reagan (R)	+34	+12
1984	Reagan (R)	+14	−2
1988	G. Bush (R)	−3	−1
1992	Clinton (D)	−10	0
1996	Clinton (D)	+9	−2
2000	G. W. Bush (R)	−2	−4
2004	G. W. Bush (R)	+3	+4
2008	Obama (D)	+21	+8
	Average	+7.9	+1.1

see in Table 13.7, the president's party typically *loses* seats in these elections. For example, in 1986, the Republicans lost eight seats in the Senate, depriving President Reagan of a majority, and in 1994, the Democrats lost eight Senate seats and 52 House seats, losing control of both houses in the process.[19] The president's party is especially likely to lose seats in the House when the president's approval rating is low and when the party gained a lot of seats in the previous election. Thus, the Democrats suffered large losses in the 2010 midterm elections.

Recently, there have been exceptions. In 1998, the Democrats gained five seats in the House, and in 2002, Republicans made small gains in both houses. In 2006, however, George W. Bush's Republicans lost majorities in both houses of Congress.

To add to these party leadership burdens, the president's party often lacks a majority in one or both houses. Since 1953 there have been 30 years in which Republican presidents faced a Democratic House of Representatives and 22 years in which they faced a Democratic Senate. Democrat Bill Clinton faced both a House and a Senate with Republican majorities from 1995 through 2000. Barack Obama had to deal with a Republican majority in the House in 2011–2012.

As a result of election returns and the lack of dependable party support, the president usually has to solicit help from the opposition party. This is often a futile endeavor, however, since the opposition is generally not fertile ground for seeking support. Nevertheless, even a few votes may be enough to give the president the required majority.

TABLE 13.7 Congressional Gains or Losses for the President's Party in Midterm Election Years

For decades the president's party typically lost seats in midterm elections. Thus, presidents could not be certain of helping to elect members of their party once in office. The elections of 1998 and 2002 deviated from this pattern, and the president's party gained a few seats.

YEAR	PRESIDENT	HOUSE	SENATE
1954	Eisenhower (R)	−18	−1
1958	Eisenhower (R)	−47	−13
1962	Kennedy (D)	−4	+3
1966	Johnson (D)	−47	−4
1970	Nixon (R)	−12	+2
1974	Ford (R)	−47	−5
1978	Carter (D)	−15	−3
1982	Reagan (R)	−26	0
1986	Reagan (R)	−5	−8
1990	G. Bush (R)	−9	−1
1994	Clinton (D)	−52	−8
1998	Clinton (D)	+5	0
2002	G. W. Bush (R)	+6	+2
2006	G. W. Bush (R)	−30	−6
2010	Obama (D)	−65*	−6
	Average	−24	−3

*As late as mid-November 2010, votes were still being tallied.

Public Support

One of the president's most important resources for leading Congress is public support. Presidents who enjoy the backing of the public have an easier time influencing Congress. Said one top aide to Ronald Reagan, "Everything here is built on the idea that the president's success depends on grassroots support."[20] Presidents with low approval ratings in the polls find it difficult to influence Congress. As one of President Carter's aides put it when the president was low in the polls, "No president whose popularity is as low as this president's has much clout on the Hill."[21] Members of Congress and others in Washington closely watch two indicators of public support for the president: approval in the polls and mandates in presidential elections.

Public Approval Members of Congress anticipate the public's reactions to their support for or opposition to presidents and their policies. They may choose to be close to or independent of the White House—depending on the president's standing with the public—to increase their chances for reelection. Representatives and senators may also use the president's standing in the polls as an indicator of presidential ability to mobilize public opinion against presidential opponents.

Public approval also makes other leadership resources more efficacious. If the president is high in the public's esteem, the president's party is more likely to be responsive, the public is more easily moved, and legislative skills become more effective. Thus public approval is the political resource that has the most potential to turn a stalemate between the president and Congress into a situation supportive of the president's legislative proposals.

Public approval operates mostly in the background and sets the limits of what Congress will do for or to the president. Widespread support gives the president leeway and weakens resistance to presidential policies. It provides a cover for members of Congress to cast votes to which their constituents might otherwise object. They can defend their votes as support for the president rather than support for a certain policy alone.

Lack of public support strengthens the resolve of the president's opponents and narrows the range in which presidential policies receive the benefit of the doubt. In addition, low ratings in the polls may create incentives to attack the president, further eroding an already weakened position. For example, after the U.S. occupation of Iraq turned sour and the country rejected his proposal to reform Social Security, it became more acceptable in Congress and in the press to raise questions about George W. Bush's capacities as president. Disillusionment is a difficult force for the White House to combat.

The impact of public approval or disapproval on the support the president receives in Congress is important, but it occurs at the margins of the effort to build coalitions behind proposed policies. No matter how low presidential standing dips, the president still receives support from a substantial number of senators and representatives. Similarly, no matter how high approval levels climb, a significant portion of Congress will still oppose certain presidential policies. Members of Congress are unlikely to vote against the clear interests of their constituencies or the firm tenets of their ideology out of deference to a widely supported chief executive, as George W. Bush learned following the terrorist attacks of September 11, 2001. Public approval gives the president leverage, not command.[22]

In addition, presidents cannot depend on having the approval of the public, and it is not a resource over which they have much control, as we will see later. Once again, it is clear that presidents' leadership resources do not allow them to dominate Congress.

Mandates The results of presidential elections are another indicator of public opinion regarding presidents. An electoral mandate—the perception that the voters strongly support the president's character and policies—can be a powerful symbol in American politics. It accords added legitimacy and credibility to the newly elected president's proposals. Moreover, concerns for both representation and political survival encourage members of Congress to support new presidents if they feel the people have spoken.[23]

More important, mandates change the premises of decisions. Following Roosevelt's decisive win in the 1932 election, the essential question became *how* government should act to fight the Depression rather than *whether* it should act. Similarly, following Johnson's overwhelming win in the 1964 election, the dominant question in Congress was not whether to pass new social programs but how many social programs to pass and how much to increase spending. In 1981, the tables were turned; Ronald Reagan's victory placed a stigma on big government and exalted the unregulated marketplace and large defense efforts. Reagan had won a major victory even before the first congressional vote.

Although presidential elections can structure choices for Congress, merely winning an election does not provide presidents with a mandate. Every election produces a winner, but mandates are much less common. Even large electoral victories, such as Richard Nixon's in 1972 and Ronald Reagan's in 1984, carry no guarantee that Congress will interpret the results as mandates from the people to support the president's programs. Perceptions of a mandate are weak if the winning candidate did not stress his policy plans in the campaign or if the voters also elected majorities in Congress from the other party (of course, the winner may *claim* a mandate anyway).[24]

Legislative Skills

Presidential legislative skills come in a variety of forms, including bargaining, making personal appeals, consulting with Congress, setting priorities, exploiting "honeymoon" periods, and structuring congressional votes. Of these skills, bargaining receives perhaps the most attention from commentators on the presidency, and by examining it, one can learn much about the role that a president's legislative skills play in leading Congress.

Bargains occur in numerous forms. Former budget director David Stockman recalled that "the last 10 or 20 percent of the votes needed for a majority of both houses on the 1981 tax cut had to be bought, period." The concessions for members of Congress included special breaks for oil-lease holders, real estate tax shelters, and generous loopholes that virtually eliminated the corporate income tax. "The hogs were really feeding," declared Stockman. "The greed level, the level of opportunities, just got out of control."[25]

Presidents find the role of legislative leader a challenging one. Often they must compromise with opponents in Congress, as President Bill Clinton did in 1996 when he signed the welfare reform bill.

Nevertheless, bargaining, in the form of trading support on two or more policies or providing specific benefits for representatives and senators, occurs less often and plays a less critical role in the creation of presidential coalitions in Congress than one might think. For obvious reasons, the White House does not want to encourage the type of bargaining Stockman describes, and there is a scarcity of resources with which to bargain, especially in an era where balancing the budget is a prominent goal for policymakers (see Chapter 14).

Moreover, the president does not have to bargain with every member of Congress to receive support. On controversial issues on which bargaining may be useful, the president usually starts with a sizable core of party supporters and may add to this group those of the opposition party who provide support on ideological or policy grounds. Others may support the president because of relevant constituency interests or strong public approval. The president needs to bargain only if this coalition does not provide a majority (or two-thirds on treaties and one-third on avoiding veto overrides).

Presidents may improve their chances of success in Congress by making certain strategic moves. It is wise, for example, for a new president to be ready to send legislation to the Hill early during the first year in office in order to exploit the "honeymoon" atmosphere that typically characterizes this period. Obviously, this is a one-shot opportunity.

An important aspect of presidential legislative strategy can be establishing priorities among legislative proposals. The goal of this effort is to set Congress's agenda. If presidents are unable to focus the attention of Congress on their priority programs, these programs may become lost in the complex and overloaded legislative process. Setting priorities is also important because presidents and their staffs can lobby effectively for only a few bills at a time. Moreover, each president's political capital is inevitably limited, and it is sensible to focus on a limited range of personally important issues; otherwise, this precious resource might be wasted.

The president is the nation's key agenda builder; what the administration wants strongly influences the parameters of Washington debate.[26] John Kingdon's careful study of the Washington agenda found that "no other single actor in the political system has quite the capability of the president to set agendas."[27] There are limits to what the president can do, however.

Although the White House can put off dealing with many national issues at the beginning of a new president's term in order to focus on its highest priority legislation, it cannot do so indefinitely. Eventually it must make decisions about a wide range of matters. Soon the legislative agenda is full and more policies are in the pipeline as the administration attempts to satisfy its constituents and responds to unanticipated or simply overlooked problems. Moreover, Congress is quite capable of setting its own agenda, providing competition for the president's proposals.

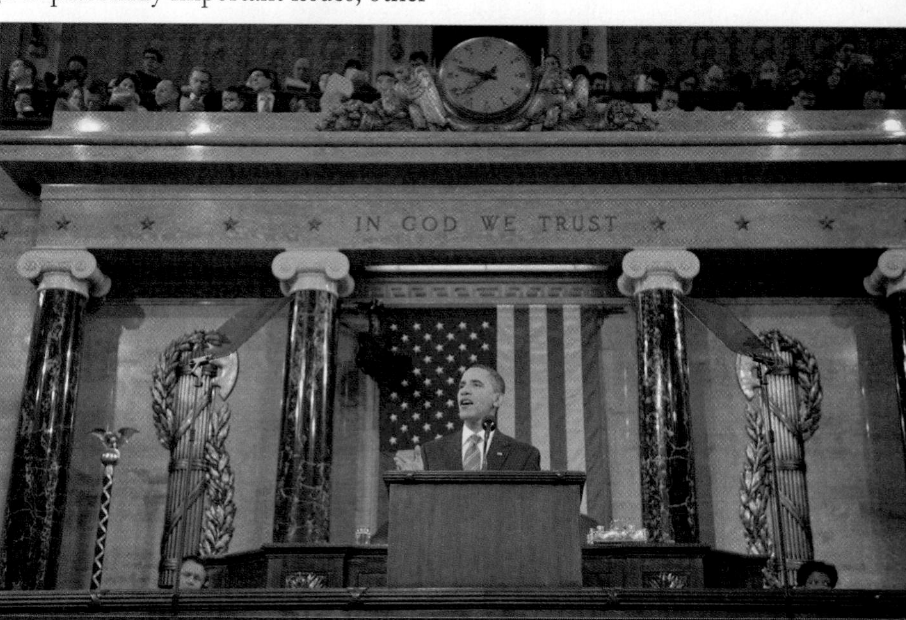

Presidents influence Congress's agenda, but no matter what a president's skills, Congress often follows its own path. Here Barack Obama delivers his State of the Union address.

In general, presidential legislative skills must compete—as presidential public support does—with other, more stable factors that affect voting in Congress: party, ideology, personal views and commitments on specific policies, constituency interests, and so on. By the time a president tries to exercise influence on a vote, most members of Congress have made up their minds on the basis of these other factors.

After accounting for the status of the president's party in Congress and standing with the public, systematic studies have found that presidents known for their legislative skills (such as Lyndon Johnson) are no more successful in winning votes, even close ones, or obtaining congressional support than those considered less adept at dealing with Congress (such as Jimmy Carter).[28] The president's legislative skills are not at the core of presidential leadership of Congress. Even skilled presidents cannot reshape the contours of the political landscape and *create* opportunities for change. They can, however, recognize favorable configurations of political forces—such as existed in 1933, 1965, and 1981—and effectively exploit them to embark on major shifts in public policy.

Perhaps the most important role of presidents—and their heaviest burden—is their responsibility for national security. Dealing with Congress is only one of the many challenges presidents face in the realm of defense and foreign policy.

13.5 Analyze the president's powers in making national security policy and the relationship between the president and Congress in this arena.

The President and National Security Policy

Constitutionally, the president has the leading role in American defense and foreign policy (often termed *national security policy*). Such matters, ranging from foreign trade to war and peace, occupy much of the president's time. There are several dimensions to the president's national security responsibilities, including negotiating with other nations, commanding the armed forces, waging war, managing crises, and obtaining the necessary support in Congress.

Presidents usually conduct diplomatic relations through envoys, but occasionally they engage in personal diplomacy. Here, President Carter celebrates a peace agreement he brokered between Israeli Prime Minister Menachem Begin and Egyptian President Anwar Sadat.

Chief Diplomat

The Constitution allocates certain powers in the realm of national security exclusively to the executive. The president alone extends diplomatic recognition to foreign governments—as Jimmy Carter did on December 14, 1978, when he announced the exchange of ambassadors with the People's Republic of China. The president can also terminate relations with other nations, as Carter did with Iran after Americans were taken hostage in Tehran.

The president also has the sole power to negotiate treaties with other nations, although the Constitution requires the Senate to approve them by a two-thirds vote. Sometimes presidents win and sometimes they lose when presenting a treaty to the Senate. After extensive lobbying, Jimmy Carter persuaded the Senate to approve a treaty returning the Panama Canal to Panama (over objections such as those of one senator who declared, "We stole it fair and square"). Bill Clinton was not so lucky when he sought ratification of the Comprehensive Nuclear Test Ban Treaty. The Senate rejected it in 1999. At other times senators add "reservations" to the treaties they ratify, altering the treaty in the process.[29]

In addition to treaties, presidents also negotiate *executive agreements* with the heads of foreign governments. However, executive agreements do not require Senate ratification (although the president is supposed to report them to Congress and they may require implementing legislation passed by majorities of each house). Most executive agreements are routine and deal with noncontroversial subjects such as food deliveries or customs enforcement, but some, such as the Vietnam peace agreement and the SALT I agreement limiting offensive nuclear weapons, implement important and controversial policies.[30]

Occasionally presidential diplomacy involves more than negotiating on behalf of the United States. Theodore Roosevelt won the Nobel Peace Prize for his role in settling the war between Japan and Russia. One of Jimmy Carter's greatest achievements was forging a peace treaty between Egypt and Israel. For 13 days he mediated negotiations between the leaders of both countries at his presidential retreat, Camp David.

As the leader of the Western world, the president must try to lead America's allies on matters of both economics and defense. This is not an easy task, given the natural independence of sovereign nations, the increasing economic might of other countries, and the many competing influences on policymaking in other nations. Even more than in domestic policymaking, the president must rely principally on persuasion to lead.

In 1950, President Harry Truman fulfilled his role as commander in chief by pinning a distinguished service medal on the shirt of General Douglas MacArthur, who was commanding American troops in Korea. The following year, Truman exercised his powers by dismissing MacArthur for disobeying orders—an unpopular decision given MacArthur's fame as a World War II hero.

Commander in Chief

Because the Constitution's framers wanted civilian control of the military, they made the president the commander in chief of the armed forces. President George Washington actually led troops to crush the Whiskey Rebellion in 1794. Today, presidents do not take the task quite so literally, but their military decisions have changed the course of history.

When the Constitution was written, the United States did not have—nor did anyone expect it to have—a large standing or permanent army. Today the president is commander in chief of about 1.4 million uniformed men and women. In his farewell address, George Washington warned against permanent alliances, but today America has commitments to defend nations across the globe. Even more important, the president commands a vast nuclear arsenal. Never more than a few steps from the president is "the football," a briefcase with the codes needed to unleash nuclear war. The Constitution, of course, states that only Congress has the power to declare war, but it is unreasonable to believe that Congress can convene, debate, and vote on a declaration of war in the case of a nuclear attack.

War Powers

Perhaps no issue of executive–legislative relations generates more controversy than the continuing dispute over war powers. Although charged by the Constitution with declaring war and voting on the military budget, Congress long ago accepted that presidents make short-term military commitments of troops, aircraft, or naval vessels. In recent decades, however, presidents have paid even less attention to constitutional details; for example, Congress never declared war during the conflicts in either Korea or Vietnam.

War Powers Resolution A law passed in 1973, in reaction to American fighting in Vietnam and Cambodia, that requires presidents to consult with Congress whenever possible prior to using military force and to withdraw forces after 60 days unless Congress declares war or grants an extension. However, presidents have viewed the resolution as unconstitutional.

In 1973, Congress passed the **War Powers Resolution** (over President Nixon's veto). A reaction to disillusionment about American fighting in Vietnam and Cambodia, the law was intended to give Congress a greater voice in the introduction of American troops into hostilities. It required presidents to consult with Congress, whenever possible, before using military force, and it mandated the withdrawal of forces after 60 days unless Congress declared war or granted an extension. Congress could at any time pass a concurrent resolution (which could not be vetoed) ending American participation in hostilities.

Congress cannot regard the War Powers Resolution as a success, however. All presidents serving since 1973 have deemed the law an unconstitutional infringement on their powers, and there is reason to believe the Supreme Court would consider the law's use of the **legislative veto** (the ability of Congress to pass a resolution to override a presidential decision) to be a violation of the doctrine of separation of powers. Presidents have largely ignored the law and sent troops into hostilities, sometimes with heavy loss of life, without effectual consultation with Congress. The legislature has found it difficult to challenge the president, especially when American troops were endangered, and the courts have been reluctant to hear a congressional challenge on what would be construed as a political, rather than a legal, issue.[31]

legislative veto
A vote in Congress to override a presidential decision. Although the **War Powers Resolution** asserts this authority, there is reason to believe that, if challenged, the Supreme Court would find the legislative veto in violation of the doctrine of separation of powers.

War Powers

The U.S. has never fully resolved the question of the president's war powers. The ambiguity about presidents' powers frees them from what some see as excessive constraints on their ability to conduct an effective foreign policy. On the other hand, if the president could only send troops into combat after a congressional resolution authorizing the use of force, it is possible that we would be less likely to go to war.

Following numerous precedents, George H. W. Bush took an expansive view of his powers as commander in chief. On his own authority, he ordered the invasion of Panama in 1989 and moved half a million troops to Saudi Arabia to liberate Kuwait after its invasion by Iraq in 1990. Congress averted a constitutional crisis when it passed (on a divided vote) a resolution authorizing the president to use force against Iraq. In a sweeping assertion of presidential authority, Bill Clinton moved toward military intervention in Haiti in 1994 and essentially dared Congress to try to stop him. Congress did nothing but complain to block military action, even though a majority of members of both parties clearly opposed an invasion. In the end, the president avoided an invasion (as opposed to a more peaceful "intervention"), but Congress was unlikely to have cut off funds for such an operation had it occurred. In 1999, the president authorized the United States to take the leading role in a sustained air attack against Serbia, but Congress could not agree on a resolution supporting the use of force.

George W. Bush faced little opposition to responding to the terrorist attacks of September 11, 2001. Congress immediately passed a resolution authorizing the use of force against the perpetrators of the attacks. The next year, Congress passed a resolution authorizing the president to use force against Iraq. However, Congress was less deferential to presidential war powers when the press revealed U.S. mistreatment of prisoners of war and the president's authorization (without a judicial warrant) of the National Security Agency to spy on persons residing within the United States.

Analysts continue to raise questions about the relevance of America's 200-year-old constitutional mechanisms for engaging in war. Some observers worry that the rapid response capabilities afforded the president by modern technology allow him to bypass congressional opposition, thus undermining the separation of powers. Others stress the importance of the commander in chief having the flexibility to meet America's global responsibilities and combat international terrorism without the hindrance of congressional checks and balances. All agree that the change in the nature of warfare brought about by nuclear weapons inevitably delegates to the president the ultimate decision to use such weapons.

Crisis Manager

The president's roles as chief diplomat and commander in chief are related to another presidential responsibility: crisis management. A **crisis** is a sudden, unpredictable, and potentially dangerous event. Most crises occur in the realm of foreign policy. They often involve hot tempers and high risks; quick judgments must be made on the basis of sketchy information. Be it American hostages held in Iran or the discovery of Soviet missiles in Cuba, a crisis challenges the president to make difficult decisions. Crises are rarely the president's doing, but handled incorrectly, they can be the president's undoing. On the other hand, handling a crisis well can remake a president's image, as George W. Bush found following the terrorist attacks of September 11, 2001.

crisis
A sudden, unpredictable, and potentially dangerous event requiring the president to play the role of crisis manager.

Early in American history there were fewer immediate crises. By the time officials were aware of a problem, it often had resolved itself. Communications could take weeks or even months to reach Washington. Similarly, officials' decisions often took weeks or months to reach those who were to implement them. The most famous land battle of the War of 1812, the Battle of New Orleans, was fought *after* the United States had signed a peace treaty with Great Britain. Word of the treaty did not reach the battlefield; thus,

General Andrew Jackson won a victory for the United States that contributed nothing toward ending the war, although it did help put him in the White House as the seventh president.

With modern communications, the president can instantly monitor events almost anywhere. Moreover, because situations develop more rapidly today, there is a premium on rapid action, secrecy, constant management, consistent judgment, and expert advice. Congress usually moves slowly (one might say deliberately), and it is large (making secrecy difficult), decentralized (requiring continual compromising), and composed of generalists. As a result, the president—who can come to quick and consistent decisions, confine information to a small group, carefully oversee developments, and call on experts in the executive branch—has become more prominent in handling crises.

Crisis management may be the most difficult of the president's many roles. By definition, crises are sudden, unpredictable, and dangerous. Here President George W. Bush stands with firefighters and rescue workers at the World Trade Center site three days after the terrorist attacks of September 11, 2001.

Working with Congress

As America moves through its third century under the Constitution, presidents might wish the Framers had been less concerned with checks and balances in the area of national security. In recent years, Congress has challenged presidents on all fronts, including intelligence operations; the treatment of prisoners of war; foreign aid; arms sales; the development, procurement, and deployment of weapons systems; the negotiation and interpretation of treaties; the selection of diplomats; and the continuation of nuclear testing.

Congress has a central constitutional role in making national security policy, although this role is often misunderstood. The allocation of responsibilities for such matters is based on the Founders' apprehensions about the concentration of power and the potential for its abuse. They divided the powers of supply and command, for example, in order to thwart adventurism in national security affairs. Congress can thus refuse to provide the necessary authorizations and appropriations for presidential actions, whereas the chief executive can refuse to act (for example, by not sending troops into battle at the behest of the legislature).

Despite the constitutional role of Congress, the president is the driving force behind national security policy, providing energy and direction. Congress is well organized to deliberate openly on the discrete components of policy, but it is not well designed to take the lead on national security matters. Its role has typically been overseeing the executive rather than initiating policy.[32] Congress frequently originates proposals for domestic policy, but it is less involved in national security policy.[33]

The president has a more prominent role in foreign affairs as the country's sole representative in dealing with other nations and as commander in chief of the armed forces (functions that effectively preclude a wide range of congressional diplomatic and military initiatives). In addition, the nature of national security issues may make the failure to integrate the elements of policy more costly than in domestic policy. Thus, members of Congress typically prefer to encourage, criticize, or support the president rather than to initiate their own national security policy. If leadership occurs, it is usually centered in the White House.

Commentators on the presidency often refer to the "two presidencies"—one for domestic policy and the other for national security policy.[34] By this phrase they mean that the president has more success in leading Congress on matters of national security than on matters of domestic policy. The typical member of Congress, however, supports the president on roll-call votes about national security only slightly more than half the time. There is a significant gap between what the president requests and what members of Congress are willing to give. Certainly the legislature does not accord the president automatic support on national security policy.[35] Nevertheless, presidents do end up obtaining much, often most, of what they request from Congress on national security issues. Some of the support they receive is the result of agreement on policy; other support comes from the president's ability to act first, placing Congress in a reactive position and opening it to the charge that it is undermining U.S. foreign policy if it challenges the president's initiatives.

Presidents need resources to influence others to support their policies. One important presidential asset can be the support of the American people. The following sections will take a closer look at how the White House tries to increase and use public support.

13.6 Identify the factors that affect the president's ability to obtain public support.

Power from the People: The Public Presidency

"Public sentiment is everything. With public sentiment nothing can fail; without it nothing can succeed." These words, spoken by Abraham Lincoln, pose what is perhaps the greatest challenge to any president—to obtain and maintain the public's support. Because presidents are rarely in a position to command others to comply with their wishes, they must rely on persuasion. Public support is perhaps the greatest source of influence a president has, for it is more difficult for other power holders in a democracy to deny the legitimate demands of a president with popular backing.

Going Public

Presidents are not passive followers of public opinion. The White House is a virtual whirlwind of public relations activity.[36] John Kennedy, the first "television president," held considerably more public appearances than did his predecessors. Kennedy's successors, with the notable exception of Richard Nixon, have been even more active in making public appearances. Indeed, they have averaged more than one appearance every weekday of the year. Bill Clinton and George W. Bush invested enormous time and energy in attempting to sell their programs to the public.

Often the White House stages the president's appearances purely to get the public's attention. George W. Bush chose to announce the end of major combat in Iraq on board the aircraft carrier the *Abraham Lincoln*. The White House's Office of Communications choreographed every aspect of the event, including positioning the aircraft carrier so the shoreline could not be seen by the camera when the president landed, arraying members of the crew in coordinated shirt colors over Bush's right shoulder, placing a banner reading "Mission Accomplished" to perfectly capture the president and the celebratory two words in a single camera shot, and timing the speech so the sun cast a golden glow on the president. In such a case, the president could have simply made an announcement, but the need for public support drives the White House to employ public relations techniques similar to those used to publicize commercial products.

Presidents often use commercial public relations techniques to win support for their policy initiatives. President George W. Bush, for example, used the backdrop of an aircraft carrier to announce the end of the war in Iraq and obtain support for his stewardship.

In many democracies, different people occupy the jobs of head of state and head of government. For example, the queen is head of state in England, but she holds little power in government and politics. In America, these roles are fused. As head of state, the president is America's ceremonial leader and symbol of government. Trivial but time-consuming activities—tossing out the first baseball of the season, lighting the White House Christmas tree, meeting an extraordinary Boy or Girl Scout—are part of the ceremonial function of the presidency. Meeting foreign heads of state, receiving ambassadors' credentials, and making global goodwill tours represent the international side of this role. Presidents rarely shirk these duties, even when they are not inherently important. Ceremonial activities give them an important symbolic aura and a great deal of favorable press coverage, contributing to their efforts to build public support.

Presidential Approval

Much of the energy the White House devotes to public relations is aimed at increasing the president's public approval. The White House believes that the higher the president stands in the polls, the easier it is to persuade others to support presidential initiatives. Because of the connection between public support and presidential influence, the press, members of Congress, and others in the Washington political community closely monitor the president's standing in the polls. For years, the Gallup Poll has asked Americans, "Do you approve or disapprove of the way [name of president] is handling his job as president?" You can see the results for presidents beginning with Eisenhower in Figure 13.3.

Presidents frequently do not have widespread public support, often failing to win even majority approval. Figure 13.3 includes the presidents' average approval levels. For Presidents Nixon, Ford, Carter, and George W. Bush, this average approval level was under 50 percent, and for Ronald Reagan it was only 52 percent. Although George H. W. Bush enjoyed much higher average approval levels for three years, in his fourth year his ratings dropped below 40 percent. Bill Clinton struggled to rise above the 50 percent mark in his first term. George W. Bush's approval level skyrocketed after 9/11 but then steadily diminished, falling well below 50 percent. Barack Obama ended his first year with the support of barely half the public.

Presidential approval is the product of many factors.[37] Political party identification provides the basic underpinning of approval or disapproval and mediates the impact of other factors. Partisans are not inclined to approve presidents of the other party. Historically, those who identify with the president's party give the president approval more than 40 percentage points higher than do those who identify with the opposition party. In the more polarized times under George W. Bush and Barack Obama, this difference rose as high as 70 percentage points.

FIGURE 13.3 Presidential Approval

Most presidents seem to be most popular when they first enter office; later on, their popularity often erodes. Bill Clinton was an exception, enjoying higher approval in his second term than in his first. George W. Bush had high approval following 9/11, but public support diminished steadily after that.

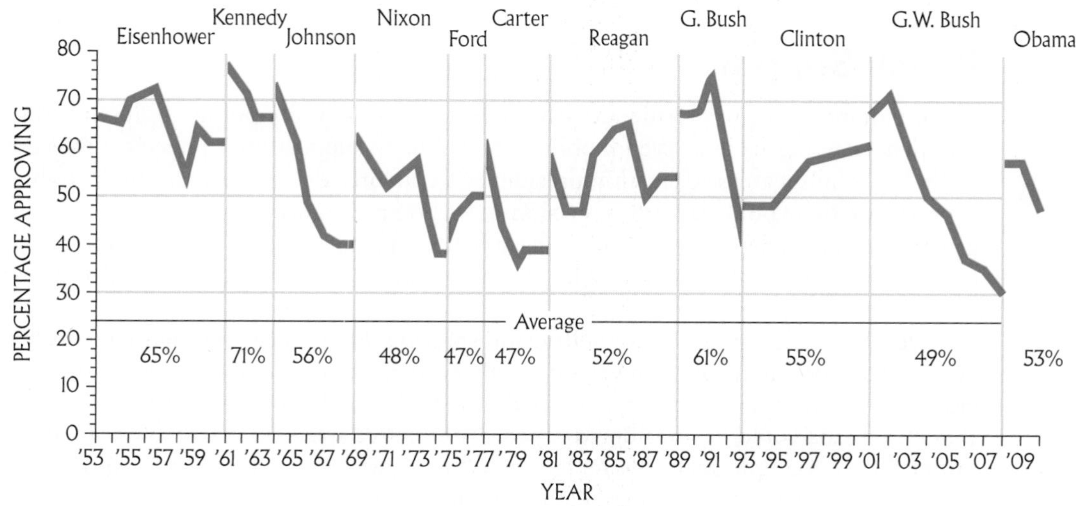

Source: George C. Edwards III, *Presidential Approval* (Baltimore, MD: Johns Hopkins University Press, 1990); updated by the authors.

Presidents usually benefit from a "honeymoon" with the American people after taking office. Some observers believe that "honeymoons" are a fleeting phenomenon, with the public affording new occupants of the White House only a short grace period before they begin their inevitable descent in the polls. You can see in Figure 13.3 that declines do take place, but they are neither inevitable nor swift. Throughout his two terms in office, Ronald Reagan experienced considerable volatility in his relations with the public, but his record certainly shows that support can be revived; Bill Clinton enjoyed more approval in his second term than in his first.

Changes in approval levels appear to reflect the public's evaluation of how the president is handling policy areas such as the economy, war, and foreign affairs. Different policies are salient to the public at different times. For example, if international acts of terrorism on American interests are increasing, then foreign policy is likely to dominate the news and to be on the minds of Americans. If the economy turns sour, then people are going to be concerned about unemployment.

Contrary to conventional wisdom, citizens seem to focus on the president's efforts and stands on issues rather than on personality ("popularity") or simply how presidential policies affect them (the "pocketbook"). Job-related personal characteristics of the president, such as integrity and leadership skills, also play an important role in influencing presidential approval.

Sometimes public approval of the president takes sudden jumps. One popular explanation for these surges of support is "rally events," which John Mueller defined as events that are related to international relations, directly involve the United States and particularly the president, and are specific, dramatic, and sharply focused.[38] A classic example is the 18-percentage-point rise in President George H. W. Bush's approval ratings immediately after the Gulf War began in 1991. George W. Bush's approval shot up 39 percentage points in September 2001. Such occurrences are unusual and isolated events, however; they usually have little enduring impact on a president's public approval. George H. W. Bush, for example, dropped precipitously in the polls and lost his bid for reelection in 1992.

The criteria on which the public evaluates presidents—such as the way they are handling the economy, where they stand on complex issues, and whether they are "strong" leaders—are open to many interpretations. Different people see things differently (see "Young People and Politics: The Generation Gap in Presidential Approval"). The modern White House makes extraordinary efforts to control the context in which presidents appear in public and the way they are portrayed by the press in order to try to influence how the public views them. The fact that presidents are frequently low in the polls anyway is persuasive testimony to the limits of presidential leadership of the public. As one student of the public presidency put it, "The supply of popular support rests on opinion dynamics over which the president may exert little direct control."[39]

Policy Support

Commentators on the presidency often refer to it as a "bully pulpit," implying that presidents can persuade or even mobilize the public to support their policies if they are skilled communicators. Certainly presidents frequently do attempt to obtain public support for their policies with television or radio appearances and speeches to large groups.[40] All presidents since Truman have had media advice from experts on lighting, makeup, stage settings, camera angles, clothing, pacing of delivery, and other facets of making speeches.

Despite this aid and despite politicians' speaking experience, presidential speeches designed to lead public opinion have typically been rather unimpressive. In the modern era, only Franklin D. Roosevelt, John Kennedy, Ronald Reagan, Bill Clinton, and Barack Obama could be considered especially effective speakers. Partly because of his limitations as a public speaker, George H. W. Bush waited until he had been in office for over seven months before making his first nationally televised address.

Moreover, the public is not always receptive to the president's message. For the most part, Americans are not especially interested in politics and government; thus, it is

The Generation Gap in Presidential Approval

Presidential approval is not uniform across different groups in society. Young people approve of President Obama at higher rates than do other age groups, and especially more than those 65 or older. The higher approval could be because the younger generation is more liberal than are their elders, because it includes a higher percentage of minorities, because the president has made a special effort to reach out to young people via the Internet, or because of some other reason.

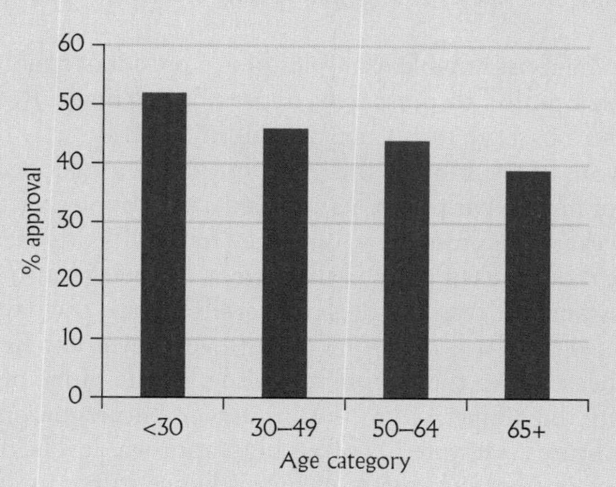

Question: Do you approve or disapprove of the way Barack Obama is handling his job as president?

QUESTIONS FOR DISCUSSION

- Why do you think young people are more supportive of President Obama than are their elders?
- Do you think policymakers pay as much attention to the opinions of young people as to the opinions of those over 65?

Source: Gallup Poll, for week of October 25–31, 2010.

not easy to get their attention. Citizens also have predispositions about public policy (however ill informed) that filter presidential messages. Evan Parker-Stephen suggests that when people encounter political information, they must balance two conflicting roles: as "updaters" who want to perceive the world objectively and as "biased reasoners" who distort information to make it consistent with their political preferences. The more salient their partisan identities, which are especially heightened during the long campaign periods in the United States, the more difficult it is for the president to get his message through to the public.[41]

The public may even get its basic facts wrong, making it difficult to evaluate policies sensibly. Before the war with Iraq in 2003, two-thirds of the public expressed the belief that Iraq played an important role in the 9/11 terrorist attacks. After the war, substantial percentages of the public believed that the United States had found clear evidence that Saddam Hussein was working closely with al Qaeda, that the United States had found weapons of mass destruction in Iraq, and that world opinion favored the United States going to war in Iraq.[42] All of these beliefs were inaccurate.

Ronald Reagan, sometimes called the "Great Communicator," was certainly interested in policy change and went to unprecedented lengths to influence public opinion on behalf of such policies as deregulation, decreases in spending on domestic policy, and increases in the defense budget. Bill Clinton, also an extraordinarily able communicator, traveled widely and spoke out constantly on behalf of his policies, such as those dealing with the economy, health care reform, and free trade. Nevertheless, both presidents were typically unable to obtain the public's support for their initiatives.[43] More recently, George W. Bush made an extraordinary effort to obtain public backing for his stewardship of the war in Iraq and his proposal to reform Social Security and failed.[44] Barack Obama was not able to rally the public behind his efforts to reform health care. In the absence of national crises, most people are unreceptive to political appeals.

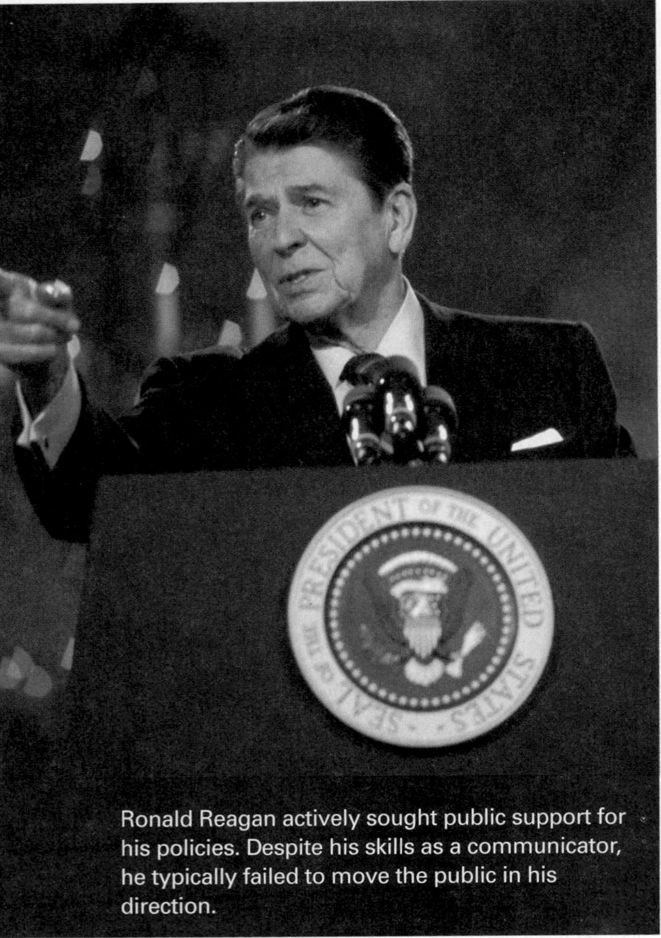
Ronald Reagan actively sought public support for his policies. Despite his skills as a communicator, he typically failed to move the public in his direction.

Mobilizing the Public

Sometimes merely changing public opinion is not sufficient—the president wants the public to communicate its views directly to Congress. Mobilization of the public may be the ultimate weapon in the president's arsenal of resources with which to influence Congress. When the people speak, especially when they speak clearly, Congress listens.

Mobilizing the public involves overcoming formidable barriers and accepting substantial risks. It entails the double burden of obtaining both opinion support and political action from a generally inattentive and apathetic public. If the president tries to mobilize the public and fails, the lack of response speaks clearly to members of Congress.

Among the most notable examples of the president's mobilization of public opinion to pressure Congress was Ronald Reagan's effort to obtain passage of his tax-cut bill in 1981. Shortly before the crucial vote in the House, the president made a televised plea for support of his tax-cut proposals and asked the people to let their representatives in Congress know how they felt. Evidently Reagan's plea worked; thousands of phone calls, letters, and telegrams poured into congressional offices. The president easily carried the day.

Reagan's success was an anomaly, however—even for Reagan. He went repeatedly to the people regarding a wide range of policies, including the budget, aid to the Contras in Nicaragua, and defense expenditures. Despite his often high approval levels, he was never again able to arouse many in his audience to communicate their support of his policies to Congress. Substantial tax cuts hold more appeal to the public than most other issues.

13.7 Characterize the president's relations with the press and news coverage of the presidency.

The President and the Press

Despite all their efforts to lead public opinion, presidents do not directly reach the American people on a day-to-day basis. The mass media provide people with most of what they know about chief executives and their policies. The media also interpret and analyze presidential activities, even the president's direct appeals to the public. The press is thus the principal intermediary between the president and the public, and relations with the press are an important aspect of the president's efforts to lead public opinion.[45]

No matter who is in the White House or who reports on presidential activities, presidents and the press tend to be in conflict. George Washington complained that the "calumnies" against his administration were "outrages of common decency." Thomas Jefferson once declared that "nothing in a newspaper is to be believed." Presidents are policy advocates and thus want to control the amount and timing of information about their administration. The press, in contrast, wants all the information that exists without delay. As long as their goals are different, presidents and the media are likely to be adversaries.

Because of the importance of the press to the president, the White House monitors the media closely. Some presidents have installed special televisions so they can watch the news on all the networks at once. The White House also goes to great lengths to encourage the media to project a positive image of the president's activities and policies. About one-third of the high-level White House staff members are directly involved in media relations and policy of one type or another, and most staff members are involved at some time in trying to influence the media's portrayal of the president.

The person who most often deals directly with the press is the president's *press secretary*, who serves as a conduit of information from the White House to the press. Press secretaries conduct daily press briefings, giving prepared announcements and answering questions. They and their staff also arrange private interviews with White House officials (often done on a background basis, in which the reporter may not attribute remarks to the person being interviewed), photo opportunities, and travel arrangements for reporters when the president leaves Washington.

The press secretary is the primary channel through which the White House communicates with the media. Here, President Barack Obama's press secretary, Robert Gibbs, responds to reporters' questions.

The best-known direct interaction between the president and the press is the formal presidential press conference. Since the presidency of George H. W. Bush, however, prime-time televised press conferences have become rare events. Bill Clinton, who took office with an antagonistic attitude toward the national media, planned to bypass the press conference rather than use it as part of his political strategy. After a rocky start in his press relations, however, he made himself somewhat more accessible to the national press. George W. Bush also relied more on travel around the country to gain television time to spread his message than on formal press conferences.

Most of the news coverage of the White House comes under the heading "body watch." In other words, reporters focus on the most visible layer of the president's personal and official activities and provide the public with step-by-step accounts. They are interested in what presidents are going to do, how their actions will affect others, how they view policies and individuals, and how they present themselves, rather than in the substance of policies or the fundamental processes operating in the executive branch. Former ABC White House correspondent Sam Donaldson tells of covering a meeting of Western leaders on the island of Guadeloupe. It was a slow news day, so Donaldson did a story on the roasting of the pig the leaders would be eating that night, including "an exclusive look at the oven in which the pig would be roasted."[46] Because there are daily deadlines to meet and television reporters must squeeze their stories into sound bites measured in seconds, not minutes, there is little time for reflection, analysis, or comprehensive coverage.

Bias is the most politically charged issue in relations between the president and the press. A large number of studies have concluded that the news media, including the television networks and major newspapers, are not biased *systematically* toward a particular person, party, or ideology, as measured in the amount or favorability of coverage.[47] Cable news channels, especially Fox and MSNBC are another story, and have numerous commentators who approach the news from an ideological perspective.

To conclude that most news outlets contain little explicitly partisan or ideological bias is not to argue that the news does not distort reality in its coverage of the president. As the following excerpt from Jimmy Carter's diary regarding a visit to a U.S. Army base in Panama in 1978 illustrates, "objective" reporting can be misleading:

> I told the Army troops that I was in the Navy for 11 years, and they booed. I told them that we depended on the Army to keep the Canal open, and they cheered. Later, the news reports said that there were boos and cheers during my speech.[48]

We saw in Chapter 7 that the news is fundamentally superficial, oversimplified, and often overblown, all of which means it provides the public with a distorted view of, among other things, presidential activities, statements, policies, and options. We also saw that the press prefers to frame the news in themes, which both simplifies complex issues and events and provides continuity of persons, institutions, and issues. Once these themes are established, the press tends to maintain them in subsequent stories. Of necessity, themes emphasize some information at the expense of other information, often determining what is covered and the context in which it is presented. For example, once a stereotype of President Ford as a "bumbler" was established, his every stumble was magnified as the press emphasized behavior that fit the mold. He was repeatedly forced to defend his intelligence, and many of his acts and statements were reported as efforts to "act" presidential.[49]

News coverage of the presidency often tends to emphasize the negative (even if the presentation is seemingly neutral).[50] In the 1980 election campaign, the press portrayed President Carter as mean and Ronald Reagan as imprecise rather than Carter as precise and Reagan as pleasant. The emphasis, in other words, was on the candidates' negative qualities. George H. W. Bush received extraordinarily negative press coverage during the 1992 election campaign, with the television networks' portrayal of the economy getting worse even as the economy was improving to a robust rate of growth![51] President Clinton received mostly negative coverage during his tenure in office, with a ratio of negative to positive comments on network television of about 2 to 1.[52] When the story broke regarding his affair with Monica Lewinsky, the press engaged in a feeding frenzy, providing an extraordinary amount of information on both the affair and the president's attempts to cover it up.[53] The trend of negative coverage continued in the George W. Bush presidency.[54]

In the past, most editors were reluctant to publish analyses sharply divergent from the president's position without direct confirmation from an authoritative source who would be willing to go on the record in opposition to the White House. This approach restrained media criticism of the president. During the famous investigation of the Watergate scandal, the *Washington Post* verified all information attributed to an unnamed source with at least one other independent source. It also did not print information from other media outlets unless its reporters could independently verify that information.[55] Things have changed, however.

The press relied on analysis, opinion, and speculation as much as on confirmed facts in its coverage of President Clinton's relations with Monica Lewinsky. Even the most prominent news outlets disseminated unsubstantiated reports of charges that those originally carrying the story had not independently verified. If one news outlet carried a charge, the rest, which did not wish to be scooped, soon picked it up. For example, the media widely reported unsubstantiated charges that members of the Secret Service had found the president and Ms. Lewinsky in a compromising position. Such reporting helped sensationalize the story, keeping it alive and undermining the president's efforts to focus the public's attention on matters of public policy.

Similarly, in 2004, the press gave immediate attention to a story on the CBS television program *60 Minutes* that revealed documents regarding President George W. Bush's service in the National Guard. The documents purported to show dissatisfaction with the president's performance—or nonperformance. On closer scrutiny, however, it turned out that the documents were forgeries.

On the other hand, the president has certain advantages in dealing with the press. The White House largely controls the environment in which the president meets the press—even going so far as to have the Marine helicopters revved as Ronald Reagan approached them so that he could not hear reporters' questions and give unrehearsed responses. The press typically portrays the president with an aura of dignity and treats him with deference.[56] According to Sam Donaldson, who was generally considered an aggressive White House reporter, "For every truly tough question I've put to officials, I've asked a dozen that were about as tough as Grandma's apple dumplings."[57]

Thus, when Larry Speakes left after serving as President Reagan's press secretary for six years, he told reporters they had given the Reagan administration "a fair shake."[58] Scott McClellan, a George W. Bush press secretary, concluded that media bias was not a problem and that any bias had minimal impact on the way the public was informed.

The "Bush administration had no difficulty in getting our messages across to the American people," he declared.[59]

Understanding the American Presidency

13.8 Assess the role of presidential power in the American democracy and the president's impact on the scope of government.

Because the presidency is the single most important office in American politics, there has always been concern about whether the president, with all of his power, is a threat to democracy. The importance of the president has raised similar concerns about the scope of government in America.

The Presidency and Democracy

From the time the Constitution was written, there has been a fear that the presidency would degenerate into a monarchy or a dictatorship. Even America's greatest presidents have heightened these fears at times. Despite George Washington's well-deserved reputation for peacefully relinquishing power, he also had certain regal tendencies that fanned the suspicions of the Jeffersonians. Abraham Lincoln, for all his humility, exercised extraordinary powers at the outbreak of the Civil War. Over the past century and a half, political commentators have alternated between extolling and fearing a strong presidency.

Concerns over presidential power are generally closely related to policy views. Those who oppose the president's policies are the most likely to be concerned about *too much* presidential power. As you have seen, however, aside from the possibility of a president's acting outside the law and the Constitution—as became a concern during the administration of George W. Bush with regard to the holding of prisoners and the interception of communications—there is little prospect that the presidency will be a threat to democracy. The Madisonian system of checks and balances remains intact.

This system is especially evident in an era characterized by divided government—government in which the president is of one party and a majority in each house of Congress is of the other party. Some observers are concerned that there is too much checking and balancing and too little capacity to act on pressing national challenges. It is true that more potentially important legislation fails to pass under divided government than when one party controls both the presidency and Congress.[60] However, major policy change *is* possible under a divided government. One author found that major change is just as likely to occur when the parties share control as when one party holds both the presidency and a majority in each house of Congress.[61]

The Presidency and the Scope of Government

Some of the most noteworthy presidents in the twentieth century (including Theodore Roosevelt, Woodrow Wilson, and Franklin Roosevelt) successfully advocated substantial increases in the role of the national government. Supporting an increased role for government is not inherent in the presidency, however; leadership can move in many directions. The presidents following Lyndon Johnson for the most part have championed constraints on government and limits on spending, especially in domestic policy. It is often said that the American people are ideologically conservative and operationally liberal. If so, for most of the past generation, it has been their will to choose presidents who reflected their ideology and a Congress that represented their appetite for public service. It has been the president more often than Congress who has said "no" to government growth.

Summary

13.1 Characterize the expectations for and the backgrounds of presidents and identify paths to the White House and how presidents may be removed.

Americans have high expectations of their presidents, who have come from a relatively wide range of backgrounds. Most presidents are elected by the public, but about one in five succeeded to the presidency when the president died or resigned. No president has been removed for disability, as provided by the Twenty-fifth Amendment, which also provides the mechanism for filling vacancies in the office of vice president, or by conviction of impeachment, although two presidents were impeached.

13.2 Evaluate the president's constitutional powers and the expansion of presidential power.

The Constitution gives the president a few national security, legislative, administrative, and judicial powers, some of which are quite general. Presidential power has increased over time, through the actions of presidents and because of factors including technology and the increased prominence of the United States, and the assertion of presidential power has at time created controversy regarding the constitutional balance of powers.

13.3 Describe the roles of the vice president, cabinet, Executive Office of the President, White House staff, and First Lady.

One of the president's principal responsibilities is to manage the executive branch. The vice president has played a central role in recent administrations. Cabinet members focus on running executive departments but play only a modest role as a unit. The Executive Office includes the Council of Economic Advisers, the National Security Council, which helps organize the president's national security decision making process, and the Office of Management and Budget, which prepares the budget and evaluates regulations and legislative proposals. Presidents rely heavily on the White House staff for information, policy options, and analysis. The First Lady has no official position but may play an important role in advocating on particular issues.

13.4 Assess the impact of various sources of presidential influence on the president's ability to win congressional support.

The veto is a powerful tool for stopping legislation the president opposes. The president's role as party leader is at the core of presidents' efforts to assemble a winning legislative coalition behind their proposals, but party members sometimes oppose the president, and presidents cannot do much to increase the number of fellow party members in the legislature, in presidential or midterm election years. Moreover, the president frequently faces an opposition majority in Congress. Presidents rarely enjoy electoral mandates for their policies, but they can benefit from high levels of public approval. A variety of presidential legislative skills, ranging from bargaining to setting priorities, contribute only marginally to the president's success with Congress.

13.5 Analyze the president's powers in making national security policy and the relationship between the president and Congress in this arena.

The president is the chief diplomat, commander in chief, and crisis manager. Presidents have substantial formal and informal powers regarding going to war, and these powers remain a matter of controversy. Congress has a central constitutional role in making national security policy, but leadership in this area is centered in the White House, and presidents usually receive the support they seek from Congress.

13.6 Identify the factors that affect the president's ability to obtain public support.

Presidents invest heavily in efforts to win the public's support, but they often have low approval levels. Approval levels are affected by party identification, by evaluations of the president's performance on the economy, foreign affairs, and other policy areas, and by evaluations of the president's character and job-related skills. Presidents typically fail to obtain the public's support for their policy initiatives and rarely are able to mobilize the public to act on behalf of these initiatives.

13.7 Characterize the president's relations with the press and news coverage of the presidency.

The press is the principal intermediary between the president and the public. Presidents and the press are frequently in conflict over the amount, nature, and the tone of the coverage of the presidency. Much of the coverage is superficial and without partisan or ideological bias, but there has been an increase in the negativity of coverage and there are an increasing number of ideologically biased sources of news.

13.8 Assess the role of presidential power in the American democracy and the president's impact on the scope of government.

The fear of a presidential power harmful to democracy is always present, but there are many checks on presidential power. Support of increasing the scope of government is not inherent in the presidency, and presidents have frequently been advocates of limiting government growth.

Chapter Test

13.1 Characterize the expectations for and the backgrounds of presidents and identify paths to the White House and how presidents may be removed.

1. Which of the following statements is true concerning presidential selection and tenure?
   a. Approximately half of the presidents in U.S. history have served two or more terms
   b. Impeachment has led to the removal of two presidents
   c. Nearly all presidents have won the office through election
   d. Several vice presidents have assumed the office when the president became incapacitated
   e. None of the above is true

2. The American public tends to expect presidents to be powerful while disliking a concentration of power.

   True______ False______

3. In your opinion, does presidential background matter to the office of the presidency? If so, which aspects are most important? If it does not matter, why doesn't it matter?

13.2 Evaluate the president's constitutional powers and the expansion of presidential power.

4. The ability to nominate ambassadors, who are to be approved by a majority of the Senate, falls into what category of presidential powers?
   a. Administrative powers
   b. Legislative powers
   c. National security powers
   d. Judicial powers
   e. Organizational powers

5. Political scientists and historians have consistently supported a strong presidency model beginning with the latter half of the twentieth century.

   True______ False______

6. What are at least three different factors that have contributed to the expansion of presidential power over time? In what ways have these factors enabled expansion of presidential powers beyond the Founding Fathers' intentions? Do you think that these developments are for the better or worse? Why?

13.3 Describe the roles of the vice president, cabinet, Executive Office of the President, White House staff, and First Lady.

7. Which of the following statements best describes the role of the vice president today?
   a. The vice president's main job is waiting
   b. The vice president's main job is casting tie-breaking votes in the Senate
   c. The vice president's main job is to balance the presidential ticket during the election
   d. The vice president's main job is to play a central role in administration policy and advising
   e. The vice president's main job is to negotiate treaties with other nations

8. The First Lady fulfills an official government position at the side of her husband.

   True______ False______

9. Briefly explain the make-up and functions of the National Security Council, the Council of Economic Advisers, and the Office of Management and Budget.

10. Does the president's cabinet serve as a "collective board of directors"? Explain your answer.

13.4 Assess the impact of various sources of presidential influence on the president's ability to win congressional support.

11. Which of the following statements about changes in Congress in presidential election years from 1952 through 2008 is NOT true?
    a. Over the period, the president's party averaged a very small net gain in the Senate
    b. The president's party made significant gains when the president was reelected
    c. In some elections the party that won the presidency lost seats in both houses
    d. Over the period, the president's party averaged a small net gain in the House
    e. In some elections, the party that won the presidency picked up seats in both houses

12. Merely winning the election provides presidents with a governing mandate.

    True______ False______

13. What are the primary constitutional tools available to presidents as chief legislators? Can you think of any changes that might be made to the Constitution to strengthen the president as chief legislator? How might this change help the president?

14. The president's ability to win congressional support is predicated on a handful of factors. Explain how three of these factors may help the president win congressional support. In what ways are these factors limited in assisting the president in the legislative arena? Which single factor do you think is most important for the president in Congress? Explain your answer.

13.5 Analyze the president's powers in making national security policy and the relationship between the president and Congress in this arena.

15. Executive agreements require
    a. Ratification by the House of Representatives
    b. Ratification by the Senate
    c. Ratification by both houses of Congress
    d. Support of the cabinet
    e. None of the above

16. The War Powers Resolution has succeeded in giving Congress a greater voice in the introduction of American troops into hostilities.

    True______ False______

17. Checks and balances and the separation of powers were central elements in the framing of the U.S. Constitution. Based on your understanding of the Constitution and foreign affairs, do you think the president and Congress act to uphold the separation of powers and checks and balances concerning foreign policy? Do you think that the president has usurped Congress' constitutional influence over foreign affairs and issues of war? If so, is this justified and what are some pros and cons for the U.S. government?

13.6 Identify the factors that affect the president's ability to obtain public support.

18. Which of the following is true regarding presidents' mobilization of the public?
    a. Presidents are rarely successful mobilizing the public
    b. Presidents rarely attempt to mobilize the public
    c. Presidents have often lacked the communication skills to mobilize the public
    d. Presidents need congressional support to be effective mobilizing the public
    e. None of the above

19. Presidential approval ratings mainly reflect the public's views of the president's personality.

    True______ False______

20. What are at least three different factors that influence a president's public approval ratings?

13.7 Characterize the president's relations with the press and news coverage of the presidency.

21. Which of the following statements concerning presidential news coverage is true?
    a. The press has a liberal bias that tends to put Republican presidents at a disadvantage
    b. The press devotes ample time to analysis and comprehensive coverage of the presidency
    c. The press tends to emphasize the superficial in its coverage of the presidency
    d. The press tends to emphasize the positive in its coverage of the presidency
    e. None of the above is true

22. The White House is effective in controlling the environment in which the president meets the press.

    True______ False______

23. Based on your understanding of presidential–press relations, do you think that the framers of the Constitution would be pleased with current news coverage of the presidency? Explain your answer.

13.8 Assess the role of presidential power in the American democracy and the president's impact on the scope of government.

24. Which of the following two statements do you agree with more? Explain your answer.
    (1) Excessive presidential power undermines American democracy.
    (2) A powerful president promotes democratic values.

25. What role has the presidency played in the expansion of the scope of government? In your opinion has the president worked more to expand or limit the role of the federal government? Explain your answer.

PEARSON mypoliscilab™ Exercises

Apply what you learned in this chapter on MyPoliSciLab.

Read on **mypoliscilab.com**

eText: Chapter 13

Study and **Review** on **mypoliscilab.com**

Pre-Test
Post-Test
Chapter Exam
Flashcards

Watch on **mypoliscilab.com**

Video: Bush and the Congress
Video: The Government Bails Out Automakers

Explore on **mypoliscilab.com**

Simulation: Presidential Leadership: Which Hat Do You Wear?
Simulation: You Are a President During a Nuclear Power Plant Meltdown
Comparative: Comparing Chief Executives
Timeline: The Executive Order Over Time
Visual Literacy: Presidential Success in Polls and Congress

Key Terms

Twenty-second Amendment (369)
Twenty-fifth Amendment (369)
impeachment (370)
Watergate (372)
cabinet (376)
National Security Council (376)
Council of Economic Advisers (377)
Office of Management and Budget (377)
veto (381)
pocket veto (381)
presidential coattails (383)
War Powers Resolution (389)
legislative veto (390)
crisis (390)

Internet Resources

www.whitehouse.gov/
Links to presidential speeches, documents, schedules, radio addresses, federal statistics, and White House press releases and briefings.

www.whitehouse.gov/administration/eop
Information about the Executive Office of the President.

www.ibiblio.org/lia/president/
Links to presidents and presidential libraries.

www.ipl.org/div/potus
Background on presidents and their administrations.

www.lib.umich.edu/govdocs/fedprs.html
Wide range of documents regarding the president's activities.

www.presidency.ucsb.edu/
Presidential papers, documents, and data.

www.archives.gov/federal-register/publications/weekly-compilation.html
The *Weekly Compilation of Presidential Documents*, the official publication of presidential statements, messages, remarks, and other materials released by the White House Press Secretary.

www.youtube.com/whitehouse?gl=GB&user=whitehouse
White House YouTube channel.

www.presidentialrhetoric.com/
Presidential rhetoric, including videos of presidential speeches.

For Further Reading

Burke, John P. *The Institutional Presidency,* 2nd ed. Baltimore: Johns Hopkins University Press, 2000. Examines the organization of the White House and presidential advising.

Burke, John P., and Fred I. Greenstein. ***How Presidents Test Reality.*** New York: Russell Sage Foundation, 1989. Excellent work on presidential decision making.

Cohen, Jeffrey E. ***The Presidency in the Era of 24-Hour News.*** Princeton, NJ: Princeton University Press, 2008. Explores how changes in the news media have affected the relationship between the president and the press.

Cooper, Phillip J. ***By Order of the President.*** Lawrence: University Press of Kansas, 2002. The use and abuse of executive direct action.

Edwards, George C., III. ***At the Margins: Presidential Leadership of Congress.*** New Haven, CT: Yale University Press, 1989. Examines the presidents' efforts to lead Congress and explains their limitations.

Edwards, George C., III. ***On Deaf Ears: The Limits of the Bully Pulpit.*** New Haven, CT: Yale University Press, 2003. The effect of presidents' efforts to change public opinion in the White House's pursuit of popular support.

Edwards, George C., III. ***The Strategic President: Persuasion and Opportunity in Presidential Leadership.*** Princeton, NJ: Princeton University Press, 2009. Argues that presidential power is not the power to persuade.

Fisher, Louis. ***Constitutional Conflicts Between Congress and the President,*** 5th ed. rev. Lawrence: University Press of Kansas, 2007. Presents the constitutional dimensions of the separation of powers.

Greenstein, Fred. ***The Presidential Difference,*** 3rd ed. Princeton, NJ: Princeton University Press, 2009. Leadership styles of modern presidents.

Howell, William G. ***Power Without Persuasion.*** Princeton, NJ: Princeton University Press, 2003. Focuses on the use of the president's discretionary power.

Howell, William G., and Jon C. Pevehouse. ***While Dangers Gather.*** Princeton, NJ: Princeton University Press, 2007. Congressional checks on presidential war powers.

Jacobson, Gary C. ***A Divider, Not a Uniter: George W. Bush and the American Public,*** 3rd ed. New York: Longman, 2010. Examines the polarization of public opinion in the Bush presidency.

Kumar, Martha. ***Managing the President's Message: The White House Communications Operation.*** Baltimore, MD: Johns Hopkins University Press, 2007. Explains White House communications and media operations.

Neustadt, Richard E. ***Presidential Power and the Modern Presidents.*** New York: Free Press, 1990. The most influential book on the American presidency; argues that presidential power is the power to persuade.

Rudalevige, Andrew. ***The New Imperial Presidency: Renewing Presidential Power After Watergate.*** Ann Arbor: University of Michigan Press, 2005. The expansion of presidential power in recent decades.

Chapter 14

Congress, the President, and the Budget

The Politics of Taxing and Spending

Learning Objectives

14.1 Describe the sources of funding for the federal government and assess the consequences of tax expenditures and borrowing.

14.2 Analyze federal expenditures and the growth of the budget.

14.3 Outline the budgetary process and explain the role that politics plays.

14.4 Assess the impact of democratic politics on budgetary growth and of the budget on scope of government.

POLITICS IN ACTION: THE POLITICS OF BUDGETING

In February 2010, President Obama proposed his budget for Fiscal Year 2011, calling for spending more than $3.8 *trillion*—and running a deficit of nearly $1.3 trillion. A similar budget the previous year, his first in office, had triggered a backlash by sometimes rowdy "Tea Party" protestors, who take their name from the colonists who famously threw British tea into Boston harbor. Moreover, the size of the budget and fears of the growing national debt had hindered his ability to obtain support for his signature programs, such as health care reform. Yet the president felt that he needed to spend heavily to stimulate the economy, and he also knew that there was little chance of increasing taxes.

Politicians who attempt to make tough decisions about the budget risk incurring voters' wrath. In 1985, Republican senators took the lead with a reform that was designed to balance the budget. In the 1986 congressional elections, Republicans lost control of the Senate. In 1990, President George H. W. Bush bit the bullet and reversed his pledge not to raise taxes. He agreed to a budget deal with the congressional Democrats that succeeded in reducing the deficit and limiting spending. In 1992, he lost his bid for reelection. In 1993, President Clinton followed Bush's precedent and reversed his promise to lower taxes, with a program of higher taxes and spending constraints. In the 1994 elections, Republicans won majorities in both houses of Congress for the first time since 1952. And so it goes.

The budget is almost invariably a key issue in presidential elections. In the election of 2008, John McCain argued that we should make the large temporary tax cuts passed during the presidency of George W. Bush permanent and that we should decrease the size of the federal government. Barack Obama, on the other hand, proposed increasing taxes on the wealthiest Americans and adding to the services government provides.

It is not surprising that the battle of the budget remains at the center of American politics. Two questions are central to public policy: *Who bears the burdens of paying for government?* and *Who receives the benefits?*

Some observers who have considered these two questions are concerned that democracy could distort budgeting. Do politicians seek to "buy" votes by spending public funds on things voters will like and will remember on Election Day? Or is spending, instead, simply the rational response to demands made on government services by the many segments of American society? Do politicians pander to a perceived public desire to "soak the rich" with taxes that redistribute income?

Budgets are central to our theme of the scope of government. Indeed, for many programs, budgeting *is* policy: The amount of money spent on a program determines how many people are served, how well they are served, how much of something (weapons, vaccines, and so on) the government can purchase. The bigger the budget, the bigger the government. But is the growth of the government's budget inevitable? Or are the battles over the allocation of scarce public resources actually a *constraint* on government?

The Constitution allocates various tasks to both the president and Congress, but it generally leaves to each branch the decision of whether to exercise its power to perform a certain task. There is an exception, however. Every year the president and Congress must appropriate funds. If they fail to do so, the government will come to a standstill. The army will be idled, Social Security offices will close, and food stamps will not be distributed to the poor.

Chapter **OUTLINE**

budget
A policy document allocating burdens (taxes) and benefits (expenditures).

deficit
An excess of federal **expenditures** over federal **revenues**.

expenditures
Government spending. Major areas of federal spending are social services and national defense.

revenues
The financial resources of the government. The individual income tax and Social Security tax are two major sources of the federal government's revenue.

Everyone has a basic understanding of budgeting. Public budgets are superficially like personal budgets. There is more to public budgets than bookkeeping, however, because such a **budget** is a policy document allocating burdens (taxes) and benefits (expenditures). Thus, "budgeting is concerned with translating financial resources into human purposes" and a budget "may also be characterized as a series of goals with price tags attached."[1]

Over the past 30 years, with the exception of 1998–2001, the national government has run up large annual budget deficits. A budget **deficit** occurs when **expenditures** exceed **revenues** in a fiscal year, in other words, when the national government spends more money than it receives in taxes. As a result of this succession of annual deficits, the total national debt rose sharply during the 1980s and then again since 2001, increasing from less than $1 trillion in 1980 to about $15 trillion by 2011. About 7 percent of all current budget expenditures go to paying just the *interest* on this debt.[2]

The president and Congress have often been caught in a budgetary squeeze: Americans want them to balance the budget, maintain or increase the level of government spending on most policies, and keep taxes low. As a result, the president and Congress are preoccupied with budgeting, trying to cope with these contradictory demands.

In this chapter, you will learn how the president and Congress produce a budget, making decisions on both taxes and expenditures. In short, you will look at how government manages its money—which is, of course, really *your* money.

14.1 Describe the sources of funding for the federal government and assess the consequences of tax expenditures and borrowing.

Federal Revenue and Borrowing

"Taxes," said Supreme Court Justice Oliver Wendell Holmes, Jr., "are what we pay for civilization." Although he asserted, "I like to pay taxes," most taxpayers throughout history have not shared his sentiment. The art of taxation, said Jean-Baptiste Colbert, Louis XIV's finance minister, is in "so plucking the goose as to procure the largest quantity of feathers with the least possible amount of hissing."[3] In Figure 14.1, you can see where the federal government has been getting its feathers. The three major sources of federal revenue are personal income taxes, corporate income taxes, and social insurance taxes. A small share comes from receipts from such sources as excise taxes (a tax levied on the manufacture, transportation, sale, or consumption of a good—for example, taxes on gasoline).

Personal and Corporate Income Tax

income tax
Shares of individual wages and corporate revenues collected by the government. The **Sixteenth Amendment** explicitly authorized Congress to levy a tax on income.

Sixteenth Amendment
The constitutional amendment adopted in 1913 that explicitly permitted Congress to levy an **income tax**.

Every April 15, millions of bleary-eyed American taxpayers struggle to mail or submit online their income tax forms before midnight. Most individuals are required to pay the government a portion of the money they earn; this portion is an **income tax**. In the early years of the nation, long before the days of a large national defense, Social Security, and the like, fees collected on imported goods financed most of the federal government. Congress briefly adopted an income tax to pay for the Civil War, but the first peacetime income tax was enacted in 1894. Even though the tax was only 2 percent of income earned beyond the then-magnificent sum of $4,000, a lawyer opposing it called the tax the first step of a "communist march." The Supreme Court wasted little time in declaring the tax unconstitutional in *Pollock v. Farmer's Loan and Trust Co.* (1895). In 1913, the **Sixteenth Amendment** was added to the Constitution, explicitly permitting Congress to levy an income tax. Today, the Internal Revenue Service (IRS), established to collect income tax, receives more than 143 million individual tax returns each year.[4]

The income tax is generally *progressive,* meaning that those with more taxable income not only pay more taxes but also pay higher *rates* of tax. Those with lower

FIGURE 14.1 Federal Revenues

Individual income taxes make the largest contribution to federal revenues, but more than a third of federal revenues comes from social insurance taxes. This is a stacked graph in which the *difference* between the lines indicates the revenues raised by each tax.

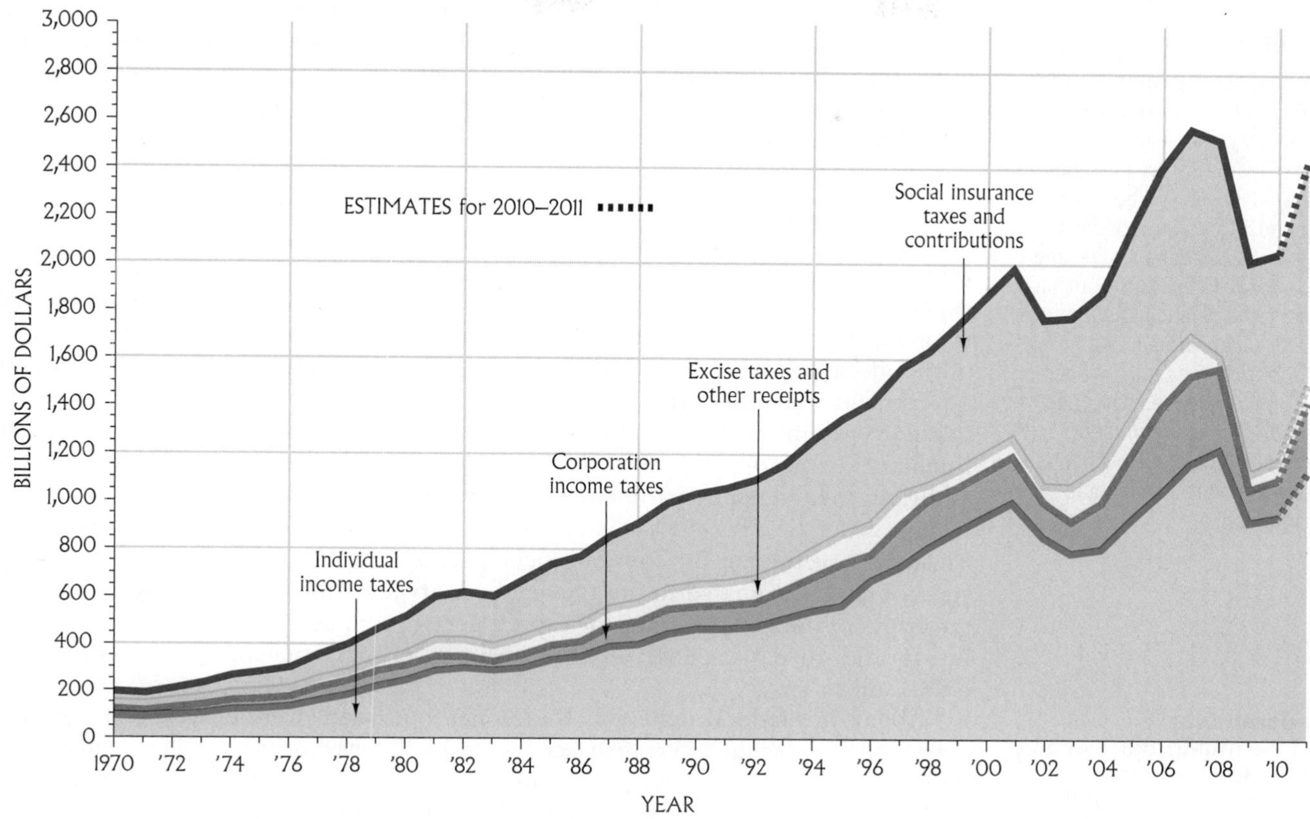

Source: *Budget of the United States Government, Fiscal Year 2011: Historical Tables* (Washington, DC: U.S. Government Printing Office, 2010), Table 2.1.

incomes pay at a 10 percent rate, while those with high incomes pay at a 35 percent rate. About one-third of those filing income tax returns pay no income tax at all. As a result, the 1 percent of taxpayers with the highest taxable incomes pay about 40 percent of all the federal income taxes, more than the bottom 95 percent of tax filers. The top 10 percent pay more than 70 percent of all federal income taxes, while those in the bottom 50 percent of taxable income pay about 3 percent.[5] Some people feel that a progressive tax is the fairest type of taxation because those who have the most pay higher rates. Others, however, have proposed a "flat" tax, with everyone taxed at the same rate; still others have suggested that we abandon the income tax and rely on a national sales tax, much like the sales taxes in most states. It is easy to criticize the income tax but difficult to obtain agreement on a replacement.

Corporations, like individuals, pay income taxes. Although corporate taxes once yielded more revenues than individual income taxes, this has not been true since 1943. In 2010, corporate taxes yielded about 12 cents of every federal revenue dollar, compared with 44 cents from individual income taxes.[6]

The Progressive Income Tax

The income tax is progressive in that those with higher incomes typically pay a higher rate of taxes. Most people would probably find it unfair to pay taxes at the same rate as a millionaire. If a uniform tax rate were set at a level that everyone could afford to pay, it would have to be set very low. In this case there may not be sufficient revenues to fund critical government programs.

Social Insurance Taxes

Both employers and employees pay Social Security and Medicare taxes. Money for these social insurance taxes is deducted from employees' paychecks and matched by their employers. Unlike other taxes, these payments are earmarked for a specific purpose: the Social Security trust funds, which pay benefits to the elderly, the disabled, and the widowed and help support state unemployment programs; and the Medicare trust funds, which pay for medical care for seniors. In 2010, employees and employers each paid a Social Security tax equal to 6.2 percent of the first $106,800 of earnings, and for Medicare they paid another 1.45 percent on all earnings.

As presidents and Congress have cut income taxes and as the large baby boomer generation has hit its peak work years, social insurance taxes have grown faster than any other source of federal revenue. In 1957, these taxes made up a mere 12 percent of federal revenues; today they account for about 36 percent.

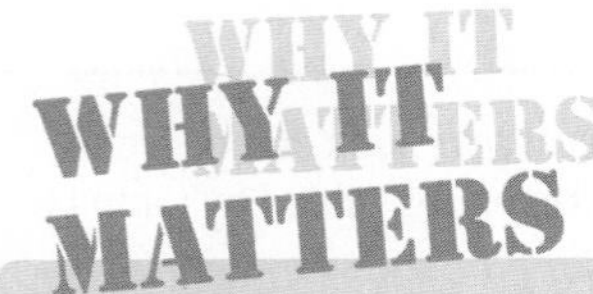

Deficit Spending

The federal government can run a deficit and borrow money to pay its current expenses. States and cities can only borrow (by issuing bonds) for long-term capital expenses such as roads and schools. If the Constitution required a balanced budget, the federal government could not borrow money to provide increased services during an economic downturn, nor could it cut taxes to stimulate the economy in such a situation.

Borrowing

As we have noted, tax revenues normally do not cover the the federal government's expenditures. Like families and firms, the federal government may borrow money to make ends meet. When families and firms need money, they go to their neighborhood bank, savings and loan association, or moneylender. When the federal government wants to borrow money, the Treasury Department sells bonds, guaranteeing to pay interest to bondholders. Citizens, corporations, mutual funds, other financial institutions, and even foreign governments may purchase these bonds. In addition, the federal government has "intragovernmental debt" on its books. This debt is what the Treasury owes various Social Security and other trust funds because the government uses for its general purposes revenue collected from social insurance taxes designated to fund Social Security and other specific programs. Most government borrowing is not for capital needs (such as buildings and machinery) but for day-to-day expenses—farm subsidies, military pensions aid to states and cities, and so on.

federal debt
All the money borrowed by the federal government over the years and still outstanding. Today the federal debt is about $15 trillion.

Today the **federal debt**—all the money borrowed over the years that is still outstanding—is about *$15 trillion* (see Figure 14.2). Seven percent of all federal expenditures go to paying interest on this debt. Borrowing money shifts the burden to future taxpayers, who will have to service the debt, with every dollar the government borrows costing taxpayers many more dollars in interest. Dollars spent servicing the debt cannot be spent on health care, education, or infrastructure. Paying the interest on the debt is not optional.

Many economists and policymakers are concerned about the national debt.[7] Some believe that government borrowing may crowd out private borrowers, both individuals and businesses, from the loan marketplace. Over the past 70 years, a substantial percentage of all the net private savings in the country have gone to the federal government. Most economists believe that under some conditions the government's competing to borrow money may lead to increased interest rates, making it more difficult, for example, for businesses to invest in capital expenditures (such as new plants and equipment) that produce economic growth, and raising the costs to individuals of financing homes or credit card purchases. Large deficits also make the American government dependent on foreign investors, including other governments, to fund its debt—not a favorable position for a superpower. Foreign investors currently hold a majority of the federal government's public debt. If they stop lending us money, perhaps to gain leverage in foreign policy, interest rates would rise and the economy would be depressed.

Sometimes politicians complain that, since families and businesses and even state and local governments balance their budgets, the federal government ought to be able to do the same. Such statements reflect a fundamental misunderstanding of budgeting, however. Most families do *not* balance their budgets. They use credit cards to give themselves instant loans, and they go to the bank to borrow money for major purchases such as automobiles and, most important, homes, with mortgages on homes being debts they carry for years. And state and local governments and private businesses differ from the federal government in having a *capital budget*, a budget for expenditures on

FIGURE 14.2 Total National Debt

The national debt climbed steadily throughout the 1980s, leveled off in the 1990s, and has risen sharply since 2001.

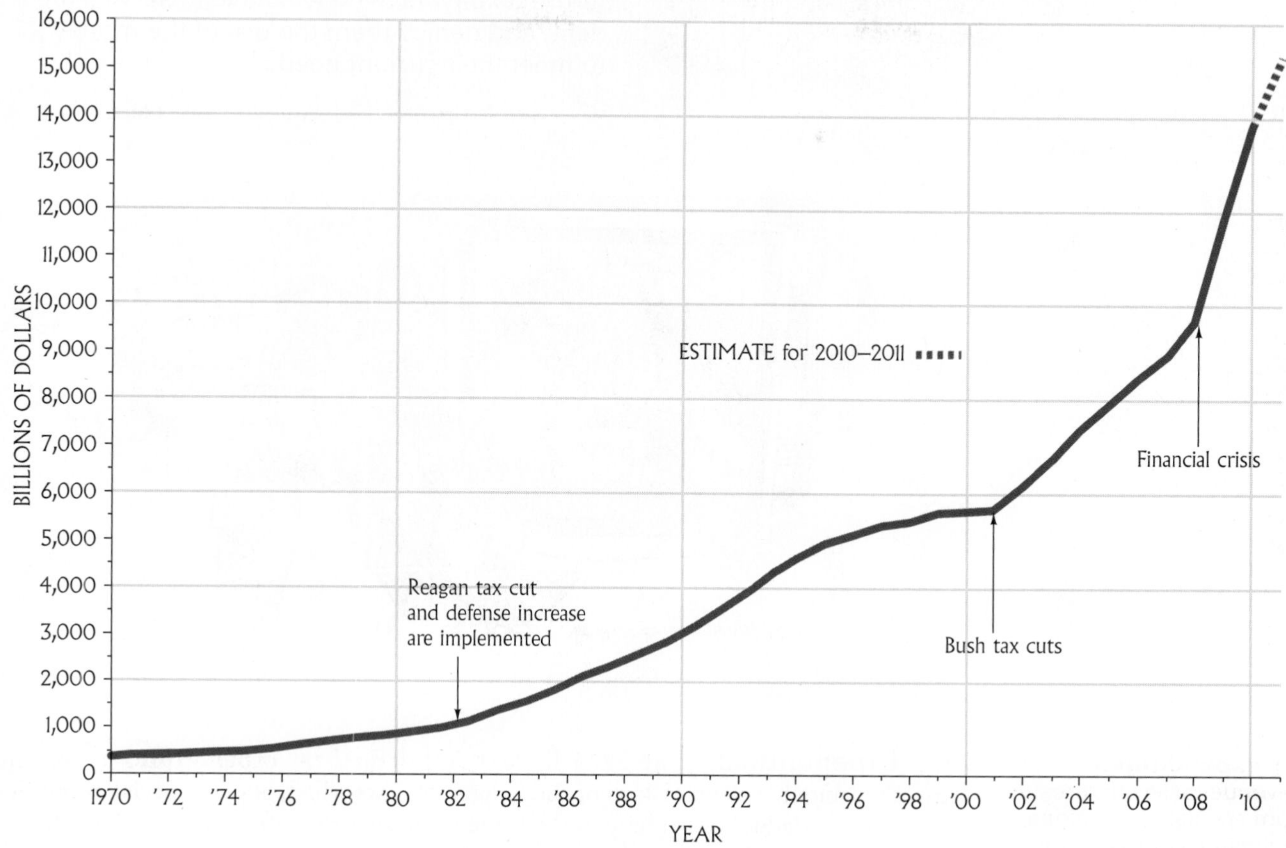

Source: *Budget of the United States Government, Fiscal Year 2011: Historical Tables* (Washington, DC: U.S. Government Printing Office, 2010), Table 7.1.

items that will serve for the long term, such as equipment, roads, and buildings. Thus, for example, when airlines purchase new airplanes or when school districts build new schools, they do not pay for them out of current income. Instead, they borrow money, often through issuing bonds, and these debts do not count against the operating budget. In contrast, when the federal government purchases new jets for the air force or new buildings for medical research, these purchases are counted as current expenditures and run up the deficit.

Despite its borrowing, most of the government's expenditures are still paid by taxes. Few government policies provoke more heated discussion than policy related to taxation.

Taxes and Public Policy

It's not surprising that tax policy provokes heated discussion—no other area of government policy affects as many Americans. In addition to raising revenues to finance its services, the government can use taxes to make citizens' incomes more nearly or less nearly equal, to encourage or discourage growth in the economy, and to promote specific interests. Whereas Chapters 17 and 18 discuss how taxes affect economic and equality issues, here we focus on how tax policies can promote the interests of particular groups or encourage specific activities.

A POINT TO PONDER
The U.S. deficit has grown rapidly in recent years. Borrowing money shifts the burden to future taxpayers, who will have to service the debt, and denies them the use of the money to meet their current needs.
Why do you think the government relies so heavily on deficit spending?
DEBT
DEFICITS
BAILOUTS
I WANT YOU TO PAY ATTENTION— YOU'LL BE PAYING FOR THIS.

tax expenditures
Revenue losses that result from special exemptions, exclusions, or deductions allowed by federal tax law.

Tax Expenditures The 1974 Budget Act defines **tax expenditures** as "revenue losses attributable to provisions of the federal tax laws which allow a special exemption, exclusion, or deduction." These expenditures represent the difference between what the government actually collects in taxes and what it would have collected without special exemptions. Thus, tax expenditures amount to subsidies for different activities. Here are some examples:

- The government permits taxpayers to deduct their contributions to charities from their income, thus encouraging charitable contributions and in effect giving charities a subsidy.
- The government permits homeowners to deduct from their income the billions of dollars they collectively pay each year in mortgage interest, encouraging home ownership and in effect giving homeowners a subsidy.
- The government allows businesses that invest in new plants and equipment to deduct these expenses from their taxes at a more rapid rate than they deduct other expenses, encouraging investment in new plants and equipment. In effect, the owners of these businesses, including stockholders, get a subsidy that is unavailable to owners of other businesses.

Tax expenditures are among the most obscure aspects of a generally obscure budgetary process, partly because they receive no regular review by Congress—a great advantage for those who benefit from a tax expenditure. Although few ordinary citizens seem to realize it, the magnitude of tax expenditures is enormous, as you can see in Table 14.1.

On the whole, tax expenditures benefit middle- and upper-income taxpayers and corporations. Poorer people, who tend not to own homes, can take little advantage of provisions that permit homeowners to deduct mortgage interest payments. Likewise, poorer people in general can take less advantage of the exclusion of taxes on contributions to individual retirement accounts or interest on state and local bonds. Students, however, are an exception to this generalization (see "Young People and Politics: Education and the Federal Tax Code" on page 412).

TABLE 14.1 Tax Expenditures: The Money Government Does Not Collect

Tax expenditures are essentially money that government could collect but does not because they are exempted from taxation. The Office of Management and Budget estimated that the total tax expenditures in 2011 would be about $1.063 trillion—an amount equal to more than 40 percent of the total federal receipts. Individuals receive most of the tax expenditures, and corporations get the rest. Here are some of the largest tax expenditures and their cost to the treasury:

TAX EXPENDITURE	COST
Exclusion of employer contributions to health care and insurance	$171 billion
Deduction of mortgage interest on owner-occupied houses	$105 billion
Exclusion of IRA and 401(k) retirement account contributions and earnings	$81 billion
Deductions for state and local taxes	$70 billion
Deductions for charitable contributions	$54 billion
Capital gains (nonhome)	$45 billion
Exclusion of company contributions to pension funds	$45 billion
Capital gains at death	$45 billion
Exclusion of net imputed rental income	$38 billion
Deferral of income from controlled foreign corporations	$33 billion
Exclusion of capital gains on home sales	$31 billion
Exclusion for interest earned on state and local government bonds	$29 billion
Treatment of qualified dividends	$27 billion
Exclusion of interest on life insurance savings	$23 billion
Exclusion of Social Security and disability benefits	$22 billion
Child credit	$19 billion

Source: *Budget of the United States Government, Fiscal Year 2011: Analytical Perspectives* (Washington, DC: U.S. Government Printing Office, 2010), Tables 16.1 and 16.3.

Government could lower overall tax rates by taxing things it does not currently tax, such as Social Security benefits, pension fund contributions, charitable contributions, and the like. You can easily figure out, though, that these are not popular items to tax, and doing so would evoke strong opposition from powerful interest groups.

To some, tax expenditures such as business-related deductions, tuition tax credits, and capital gains tax rates are "loopholes." To others, they are public policy choices that support a social activity worth subsidizing. Sometimes, deductions can be abused. One billionaire made a charitable donation in her will of as much as $8 billion for the care and welfare of dogs. The estate tax on the $8 billion would have been $3.6 billion, but because she took a charitable deduction, her estate paid no tax. Thus, her deduction constituted a subsidy from the federal government, which means from all taxpayers. The money the treasury lost was approximately half what the government spends on Head Start, a program that benefits 900,000 children.[8]

Regardless of how they are viewed, tax expenditures amount to the same thing: revenues that the government loses because certain items are exempted from normal taxation or are taxed at lower rates. The Office of Management and Budget estimates that were there no tax expenditures, the federal government's total tax receipts would be increased by 40 percent.

Tax Reduction Perennially popular with the public, tax reduction tends to have different consequences for different groups. Early in his administration, President Reagan proposed a massive tax-cut bill, which Congress obligingly passed in July 1981. As a result of this legislation, the federal tax bills of Americans were reduced 25 percent, corporate income taxes were also reduced, new tax incentives were provided for personal savings and corporate investment, and taxes were *indexed* to the cost of living. With the

Education and the Federal Tax Code

If you think that the federal income tax is something that does not affect you much as a student, you are wrong. For example, if you are footing the costs of higher education, education tax credits can help offset these costs. But the rules for obtaining a tax credit are far from simple.

First, there is the American Opportunity Credit, which applies only for the first four years of postsecondary education, whether in a college or a vocational school. The American Opportunity Credit can be worth up to $2,500 per eligible student, per year to a family. It does not apply for education beyond these four years, however, and you must be enrolled at least half time to receive the credit.

The Lifetime Learning Credit applies to undergraduate, graduate, and professional degree courses, including instruction to acquire or improve your job skills. If you qualify, your credit equals 20 percent of the first $10,000 of postsecondary tuition and fees you pay during the year for all eligible students in a family, for a maximum credit of $2,000 per tax return.

The American Opportunity Credit and the Lifetime Learning Credit are education credits you can subtract in full from your federal income tax, not just deduct from your taxable income.

Naturally, there are restrictions on claiming these credits. To qualify for either credit, you must pay postsecondary tuition and fees for yourself, your spouse, or your dependent. The credit may be claimed by the parent or the student but not by both. However, if the student was claimed as a dependent, the student cannot claim the credit. Moreover, you cannot claim both the American Opportunity Credit and the Lifetime Learning Credit for the same student (such as yourself) in the same year. Parents with children or attending school themselves can claim more than one American Opportunity Credit but only one Lifetime Learning Credit.

These credits are not for everyone. The American Opportunity Credit is gradually reduced for those with modified adjusted gross income (MAGI) between $80,000 and $90,000 ($160,000 and $180,000 for married filing jointly) and eliminated completely for those with MAGI exceeding those amounts. The comparable figures for the Lifetime Learning Credit are $50,000 and $60,000 for individuals and $100,000 and $120,000 for married filing jointly. If a taxpayer is married, the credit may be claimed only on a joint return. In addition, the American Opportunity Credit is not allowed for a student convicted of a felony drug offense while in school.

A taxpayer may also take a deduction for up to $4,000 of higher-education expenses, but only when opting not to use the education credits. A different deduction lets taxpayers recoup some of the cost of student loan interests. It and other deductions and credits also begin to diminish as taxpayers earn more.

Welcome to the federal tax code. As you can see, Congress has chosen to give students benefits in the tax code, but it has also been concerned that people do not abuse these benefits. Thus, even students have to face the intricacies of the federal tax code and work out the myriad tax credits and deductions that help defray the costs of a college education. In the end, however, most people agree that it is worth the effort.

QUESTIONS FOR DISCUSSION

- Why doesn't Congress simply appropriate money for students and send them a check instead of relying on the tax code?
- What are the obstacles to simplifying the tax code?

indexing of taxes, beginning in 1985, inflation could no longer push income into higher brackets, and, since people in higher brackets pay a higher *percentage* of their incomes in taxes, tax revenues were less than they would have been without indexing.

Families with high incomes saved many thousands of dollars on taxes, but those at the lower end of the income ladder saw little change in their tax burden because of increases in social insurance and excise taxes (which fall disproportionately on those with lower incomes). Moreover, the massive deficits which began in the 1980s were at least in part a consequence of the 1981 tax cuts, as government continued to spend while reducing its revenues.

In 1993, President Clinton, seeking to deal with these deficits, persuaded Congress to raise the income tax rate on those in the top 2 percent of income and the top corporate income tax rate. However, when budget surpluses materialized (briefly) in the late 1990s, tax reduction once again became a popular rallying cry. In 2001, at the behest of

George W. Bush, Congress enacted a tax cut that gradually lowered tax rates over the next 10 years; in 2003 Congress reduced the tax rates on capital gains and dividends.

Some claim that cutting taxes is a useful way to limit government expansion, or to "starve the beast." In reality, however, government often *grows* more rapidly following substantial tax cuts.[9] For example, the 2001 tax cuts were followed by the reappearance of massive deficits when the president asked Congress to fund two wars and an expensive prescription drug addition to the Social Security program. Moreover, despite the clamor for tax reduction, as you can see in "America in Perspective: How Big Is the Tax Burden?" among democracies with developed economies, America has one of the *smallest* tax burdens.

Federal Expenditures

14.2 Analyze federal expenditures and the growth of the budget.

In 1932, when President Franklin D. Roosevelt took office in the midst of the Great Depression, the federal government was spending just over $3 billion a year. Today, the federal government spends that much in a single morning. Program costs once measured in the millions are now measured in billions. You can see in Figure 14.3 how the federal budget has grown in actual dollars in recent decades and how the various categories of expenditures have grown.

Figure 14.3 makes two interesting points. First, expenditures keep rising (although the rise would not look so steep if we control for the changes in the value of the dollar). Second, the policies and programs on which the government spends

AMERICA IN PERSPECTIVE

How Big Is the Tax Burden?

Americans commonly complain that taxes are too high. Yet the figures in the graph show that the governments in the United States (national, state, and local) tax a smaller percentage of the resources of the country than do those in almost all other democracies with developed economies. Looked at in this perspective, the tax burden in the United States is rather modest public sector. Sweden and Denmark, at the other extreme, take about half the wealth of the country in taxes each year.

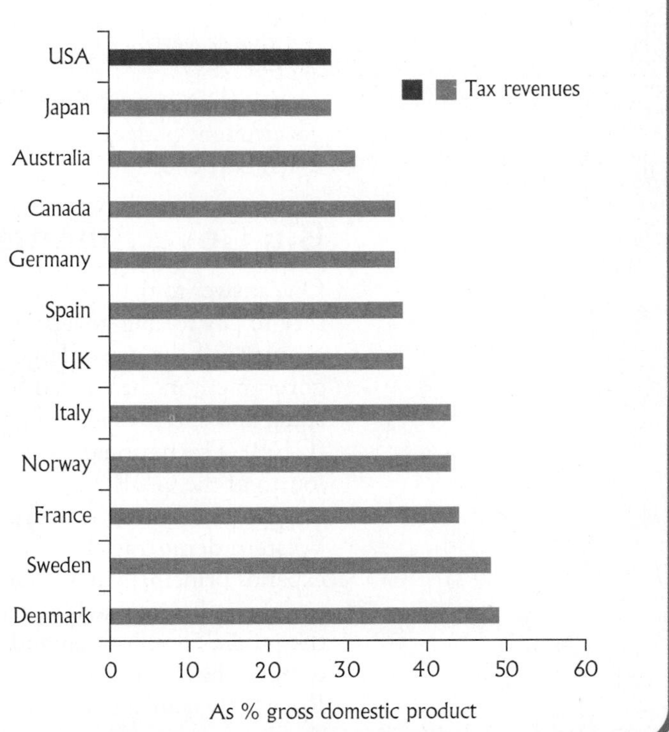

Source: Organization for Economic Cooperation and Development *Factbook 2009.*

FIGURE 14.3 Federal Expenditures

The biggest category of federal expenditures is payments to individuals, composing more than 60 percent of the budget. National defense accounts for about one-fifth of the budget. This is a stacked graph in which the *difference* between the lines indicates the amount spent on each category. The economic crisis of 2008–2009 led to a dramatic increase in the budget.

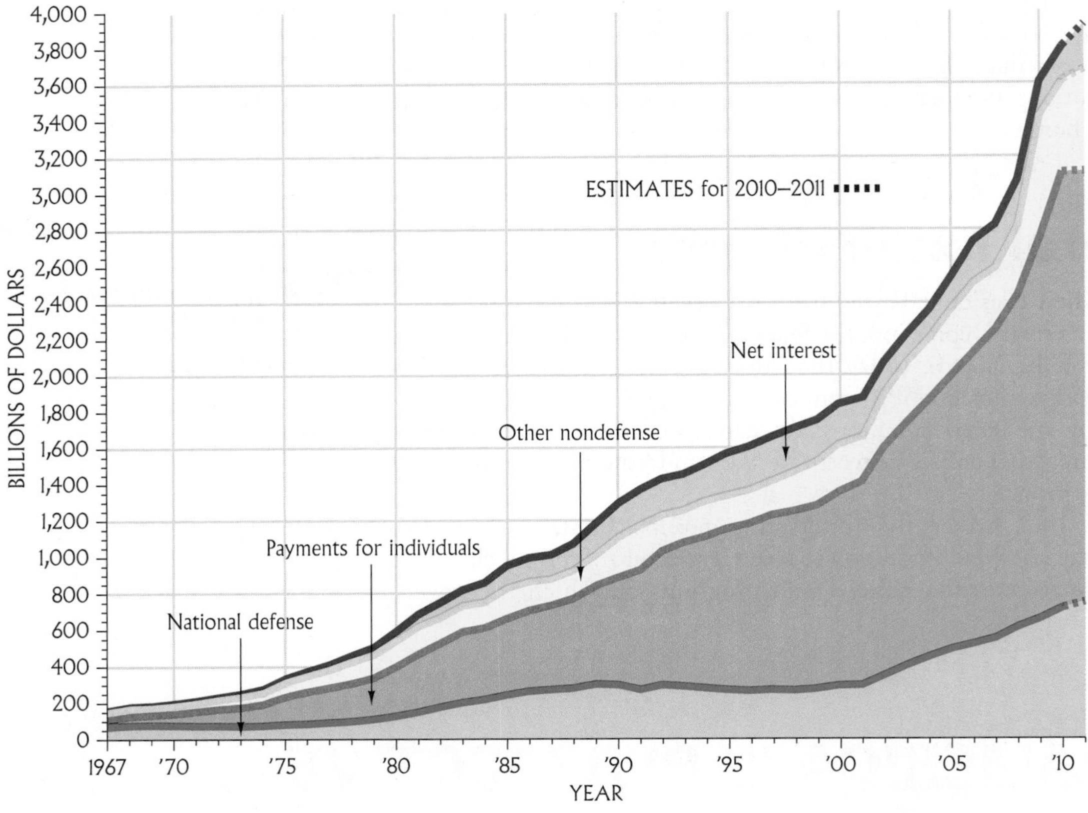

Source: *Budget of the United States Government, Fiscal Year 2011: Historical Tables* (Washington, DC: U.S. Government Printing Office, 2010), Table 6.1.

money change over time. This section explores three important questions: Why are government budgets so big? Where does the money go? Why is it difficult to control federal expenditures?

Big Governments, Big Budgets

One answer to the question of why budgets are so large is simple: Big budgets are necessary to pay for big governments. Among the most important changes of the twentieth century was the rise of large governments.[10] As in other Western nations, the growth of government in the United States has been dramatic. American governments—national, state, and local—spend an amount equal to one-third of the gross domestic product (GDP). The national government's expenditures alone currently represent about one-fourth of the GDP.[11]

No one knows for sure exactly why government has grown so rapidly in all the Western democracies. William Berry and David Lowery found that the public sector expands principally in response to the public's preferences and changes in economic and social conditions, such as economic downturns, urbanization, or pollution, that affect the public's level of demand for government activity.[12] This is why the rise of big government has been strongly resistant to reversal: Citizens like government services. Even Ronald Reagan, a strong leader with an antigovernment orientation, succeeded only in slowing the growth of government, not in actually trimming its size. When he left office, the federal government employed more people and spent more money than when he was inaugurated.

Two developments associated with government growth in America are the rise of the national security state and the rise of the social service state.

The Rise of the National Security State

Before World War II, the United States had customarily disbanded a large part of its military forces at the end of a war. After World War II, however, the Cold War with the Soviet Union resulted in the growth of a permanent military establishment and increased acquisition of expensive military technology. Fueling this military machine greatly increased the cost of government. It was President Eisenhower, a five-star general, who coined the phrase *military-industrial complex* to characterize—and warn against—the close relationship between the military hierarchy and the defense industry that supplies its hardware needs.

In the 1950s and early 1960s, spending for past and present wars amounted to more than half the federal budget. The Department of Defense, in other words, received the majority of federal dollars. A common liberal complaint was that government was shortchanging the poor while lining the pockets of defense contractors. The situation soon changed, however. From the late 1960s through the 1970s, defense expenditures measured in constant dollars (dollars adjusted for inflation) crept downward (see Figure 14.4); meanwhile, as we shall see below, social welfare expenditures were rapidly increasing.

FIGURE 14.4 Trends in National Defense Spending

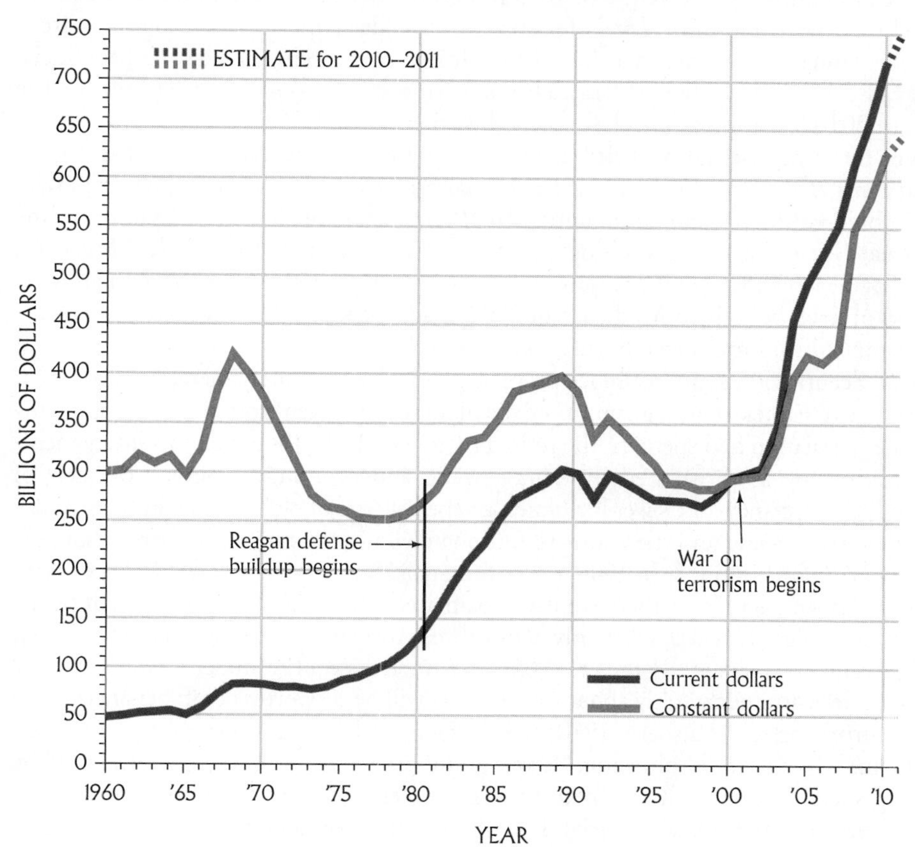

Defense expenditures increased rapidly during the Reagan administration, and declined with the end of the Cold War. They increased again after the September 11, 2001, terrorist attacks and the invasion of Iraq in 2003.

Source: *Budget of the United States Government, Fiscal Year 2011: Historical Tables* (Washington, DC: U.S. Government Printing Office, 2010), Table 6.1.

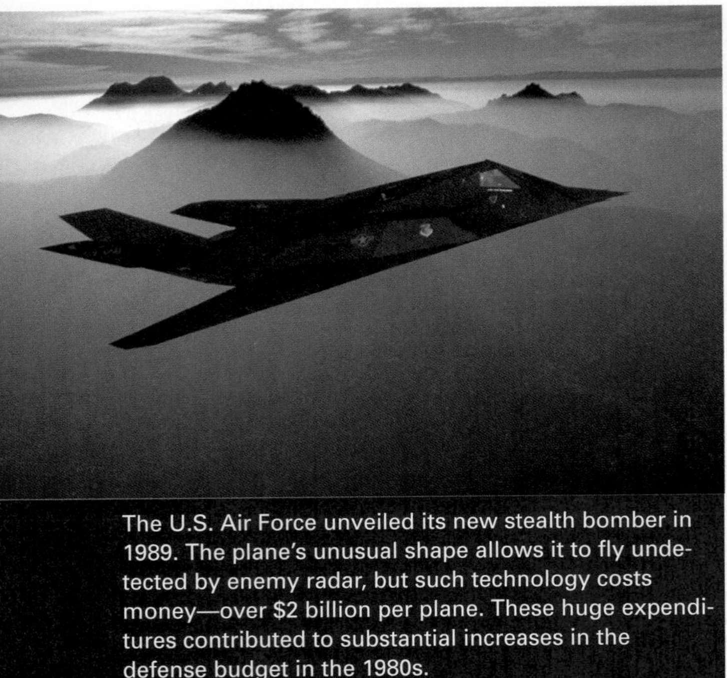

The U.S. Air Force unveiled its new stealth bomber in 1989. The plane's unusual shape allows it to fly undetected by enemy radar, but such technology costs money—over $2 billion per plane. These huge expenditures contributed to substantial increases in the defense budget in the 1980s.

At President Reagan's urging, Congress increased the defense budget substantially, mostly during his first term. Although in the 1990s defense expenditures decreased in response to the end of the Cold War and reduced tensions in Europe (discussed in Chapter 20), they increased again following the terrorist attacks of September 11, 2001, and especially with the war in Iraq. Nevertheless, the budget of the Department of Defense, once the driving force in the expansion of the federal budget, now constitutes only about one-fifth of all federal expenditure.

Payrolls and pensions for the more than 7 million persons who work for the Pentagon, serve in the reserves, or receive military retirement pay, veterans' pensions, or disability compensation constitute a large component of the defense budget. So do the research, development, and *procurement* (purchasing) of military hardware. The costs of procurement are high, and advanced technology makes any weapon, fighter plane, or component more expensive than its predecessors. Moreover, cost overruns are common. The American fleet of stealth bombers cost several times the original estimate—over $2 *billion* each.

The Rise of the Social Service State

The biggest slice of the budget pie, once reserved for defense, now belongs to *income security* expenditures, a bundle of policies extending direct and indirect aid to the elderly, the poor, and the needy. In 1935, during the Great Depression and the administration of President Franklin D. Roosevelt, Congress passed the **Social Security Act**. The act was intended to provide a minimal level of sustenance to older Americans, saving them from poverty. In January 1940, the treasurer of the United States sent the nation's first Social Security check to Ida Fuller of Brattleboro, Vermont—a payment of $22.54 for the month. In 2010, the average check for retired workers was $1,164 a month.

Social Security Act
A 1935 law intended to provide a minimal level of sustenance to older Americans and thus save them from poverty.

Over the years, Social Security has undergone various expansions. In the 1950s, disability insurance became a part of the Social Security program; thus, workers who were disabled could also collect benefits. In 1965, as part of President Lyndon Johnson's Great Society programs, Congress expanded the system to include **Medicare**, which provides both hospital and physician coverage to the elderly. Congress added a prescription drug benefit to Medicare in 2003. Today, about 58 million Americans receive payments from the Social Security system each month.

Medicare
A program added to the Social Security system in 1965 that provides health insurance for the elderly, covering hospitalization, doctor fees, and other health expenses.

Social Security is less an insurance program than a kind of intergenerational contract. Essentially, as Chapter 18 explains in more detail, money is taken from the working members of the population and spent on the retired members. Today, however, this intergenerational relationship is threatened by demographic and economic realities. Because of increased life expectancy and lower birthrates, the percentage of older people in the population has been increasing and there are proportionately fewer working members to support proportionately more retirees. In 1940, the entire Social Security system was financed with a 3 percent tax on payrolls, as there were approximately 50 workers to support each Social Security beneficiary. In 1990, with only about three workers supporting each beneficiary, the tax exceeded 15 percent. By the year 2055, when today's college students will be getting their Social Security checks, only about two workers will be supporting each beneficiary.

Not surprisingly, by the early 1980s the Social Security program faced a problem. In scholar Paul Light's candid phrasing, "It was going broke fast."[13] Congress responded by increasing social insurance taxes—hence the 15 percent rate—so that more would continue to come into the Social Security Trust Fund than would be being spent. The goal was to create a surplus to help finance payments when the baby boomers retired.

In 1999, with a budget surplus having materialized, President Clinton proposed allocating much of the surplus to Social Security and investing some of the Social Security funds in the stock market. Everyone agreed that saving Social Security was a high priority, but not everyone agreed with the president's solutions. As a result, no major changes occurred. George W. Bush faced similar resistance to his proposals for investing part of individuals' social insurance tax payments in the stock market. Nevertheless, the fiscal clock keeps ticking, and it will not be long before Social Security's costs will begin to exceed its income from tax collections. Medicare is in even greater fiscal jeopardy; its costs will exceed its income even sooner, and the trust fund for the hospital insurance part of Medicare will be depleted by the end of the next decade. In short, financing Social Security and Medicare remains a great challenge.

President Harry S. Truman proposed national health care for senior citizens in 1949. Here President Lyndon B. Johnson signs the Medicare bill in Truman's presence in 1965.

Social Security is the largest social policy of the federal government (Social Security and Medicare account for about one-third of the federal budget).[14] However, in the decades since the enactment of the Great Society programs, increasing expenditures in health, education, job training, and many other areas have also contributed significantly to the rise of the social service state and to America's growing budget. No brief list can do justice to the range of government social programs, which provide funds for the elderly, businesses run by minority entrepreneurs, consumer education, drug rehabilitation, environmental education, food subsidies for the poor, guaranteed loans to college students, housing allowances for the poor, inspections of hospitals, and so on. Liberals tend to favor these programs to assist individuals and groups in society, conservatives to see them as a drain. In any event, they cost money—a lot of it (see Figure 14.5).

The rise of the social service state and the rise of the national security state are linked with much of American governmental growth since the end of World War II. Although American social services expanded less than similar services in Western European nations, for most of the postwar period American military expenditures expanded more rapidly. Together, these factors help explain why the budget is the center of attention in American government today. Why is it so difficult to bring this increasing federal budget under control?

Incrementalism

Sometimes political scientists use the term *incrementalism* to describe the spending and appropriations process. **Incrementalism** means simply that the best predictor of this year's budget is last year's budget plus a little bit more (an increment). According to Wildavsky and Caiden, "The largest determining factor of the size and content of this year's budget is last year's. Most of each budget is a product of previous decisions."[15] Incremental budgeting has several features:

incrementalism
A description of the budget process where the best predictor of this year's **budget** is last year's budget, plus a little bit more (an increment). According to Aaron Wildavsky, "Most of the budget is a product of previous decisions."

- Policymakers focus little attention on the budgetary base—the amounts agencies have had over the previous years.
- Usually, agencies can safely assume they will get at least the budget they had the previous year.
- Most of the debate and most of the attention of the budgetary process focus on the proposed increment.
- The budget for any given agency tends to grow by a little bit every year.

This picture of the federal budget is one of constant growth. Expenditures mandated by an existing law or obligation (such as Social Security) are particularly likely to follow a neat pattern of increase. There are exceptions, however. Paul Schulman observed that budgets for the National Aeronautics and Space Administration (NASA)

FIGURE 14.5 Trends in Social Service Spending

Social service spending, principally on health, education, and income security, has increased rapidly since the 1960s and now makes up about two-thirds of the budget.

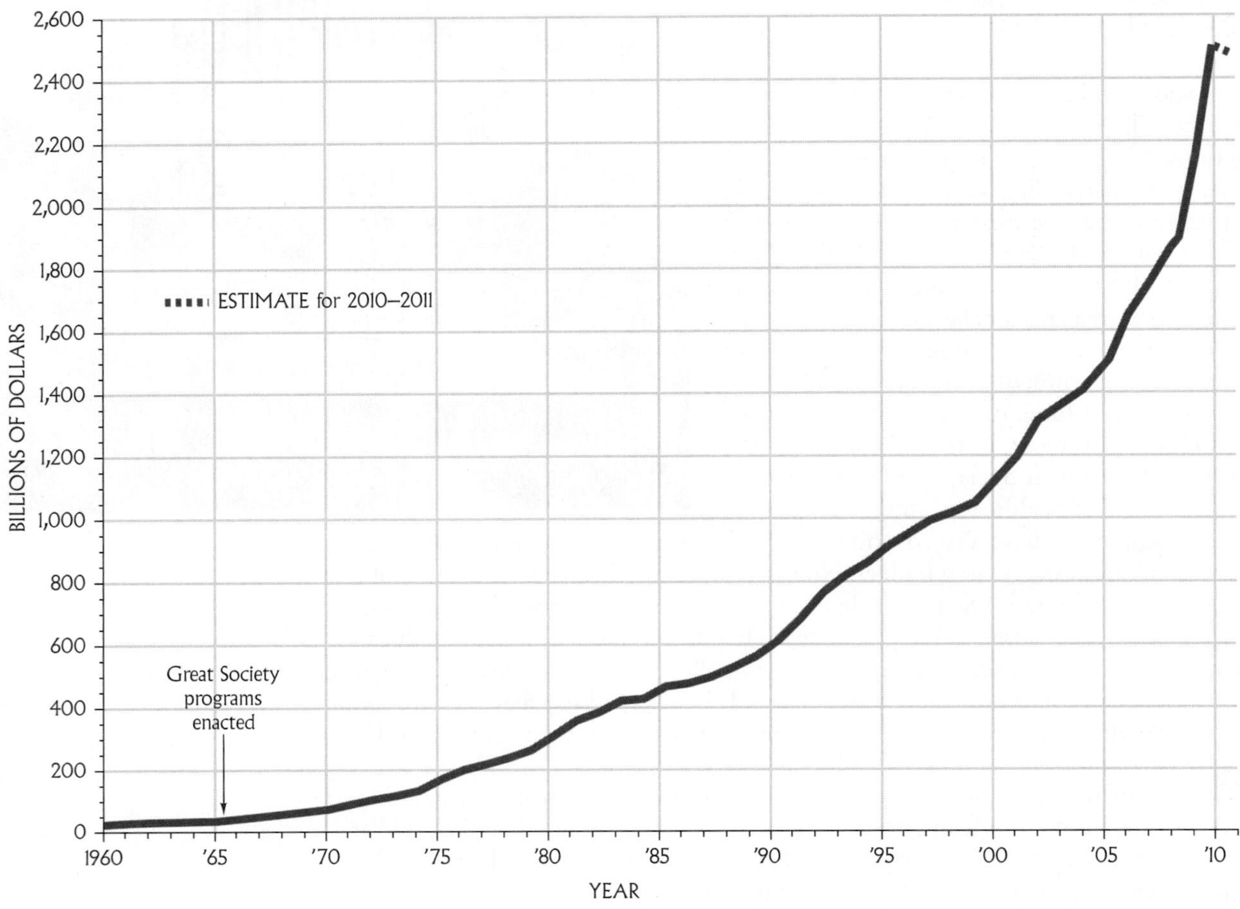

Source: *Budget of the United States Government, Fiscal Year 2011: Historical Tables* (Washington, DC: U.S. Government Printing Office, 2010), Table 3.1.

were hardly incremental; they initially rose as fast as a NASA rocket but later plummeted to a fraction of their former size.[16] Incrementalism may be a general tendency of the budget, but it does not fully describe all budgetary politics.[17]

Because so much of the budgetary process looks incremental, there is a never-ending call for budgetary reform. The idea is always to make it easier to compare programs so that the "most deserving" ones can be supported and the "wasteful" ones cut. Nevertheless, the budgetary process, like all aspects of government, is affected by groups with interests in taxes and expenditures. These interests make it difficult to pare the budget. In addition, the budget is too big to review from scratch each year, even for the most systematic and conscientious members of Congress. The federal budget is a massive document, detailing annual outlays larger than the entire economies of all but the largest countries. Although efforts to check incrementalism have failed, so have attempts to reduce programs whose costs are rising rapidly. Much of the federal budget has become "uncontrollable."

"Uncontrollable" Expenditures

At first glance, it is hard to see how one could call the federal budget uncontrollable. After all, Congress has the constitutional authority to budget—to add or subtract money from an agency. Indeed, all recent presidents have proposed and Congress has adopted some proposals to cut the growth of government spending. How, then, can one speak of an uncontrollable budget?

A POINT TO PONDER

Spending on national defense, interest on the debt, and, especially, Social Security and health care accounts for most of the federal budget, and these expenditures have grown rapidly in recent years.

Is there any way to bring these expenditures under control?

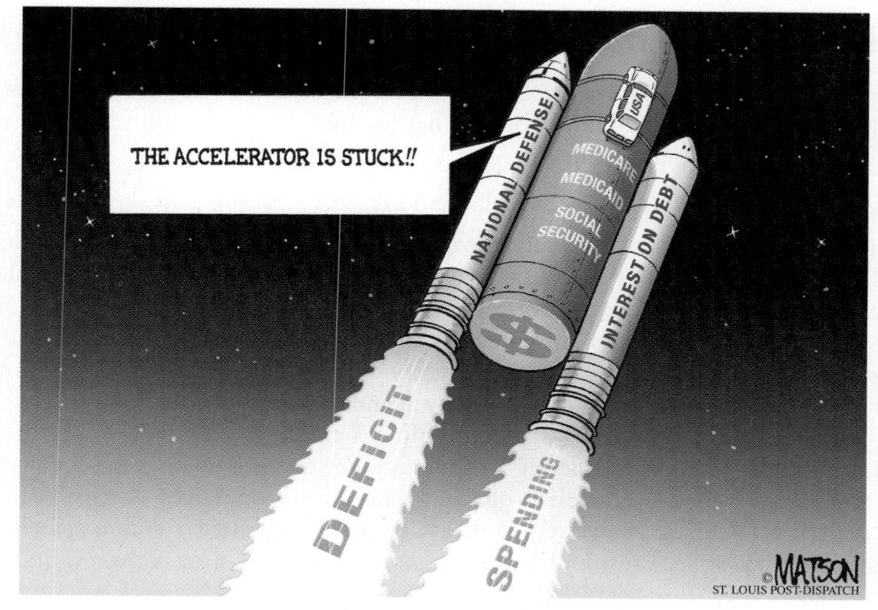

uncontrollable expenditures
Expenditures that are determined by how many eligible beneficiaries there are for a program or by previous obligations of the government and that Congress therefore cannot easily control.

entitlements
Policies for which Congress has obligated itself to pay *X* level of benefits to *Y* number of recipients. Social Security benefits are an example.

The problem is that much of the government's budget does not fit what we might call the "allowance model" of the budget. According to this model, just as Mom and Dad give Mary Jean and Tommy a monthly allowance, of, say, $10 each, with the stern admonition, "Make that last to the end of the month because that's all we're giving you until then," so Congress allocates a lump sum—say, $5.2 billion—to an agency and instruct it to meet its expenses throughout the fiscal year. When most Americans think of the government's budget, they envision the budget as a kind of allowance to the agencies. However, about two-thirds of the government's budget does not work this way at all. **Uncontrollable expenditures** result from policies that make some group automatically eligible for some benefit, such as Social Security or veterans' benefits, or from previous obligations of the government, such as interest on the national debt. The government does not decide each year, for example, whether it will pay the interest on the debt or send checks to Social Security recipients.

Many expenditures are uncontrollable because Congress has in effect obligated itself to pay *X* level of benefits to *Y* number of recipients. Congress writes the eligibility rules; the number of people eligible and their level of guaranteed benefits determine how much Congress must spend. Such policies are called **entitlements**, and they range from agricultural subsidies to veterans' aid. Each year, Congress's bill is a straightforward function of the *X* level of benefits times the *Y* beneficiaries. The biggest uncontrollable expenditure of all is the Social Security system, including Medicare, which in 2011 cost about $1.2 *trillion* dollars for the year. Individuals who are eligible automatically receive Social Security payments. Of course, Congress can, if it desires, cut Social Security benefits or tighten eligibility restrictions. Doing so, however, would provoke a monumental outcry from millions of elderly voters.

WHY IT MATTERS

"Uncontrollable" Spending

Much of the federal budget is "uncontrollable" in the sense that it does not come up for reauthorization on a regular basis. If entitlement programs were subject to the same annual authorizations that most other programs receive, they would probably have less secure funding. We might spend less money on them and more on other services. This flexibility might please some people, especially those not receiving entitlement benefits, but those receiving Social Security and Medicare payments, for example, prefer more reliable funding.

14.3 Outline the budgetary process and explain the role that politics plays.

The Budgetary Process

The distribution of the government's budget is the outcome of a very long, complex process that starts and ends with the president and has Congress squarely in the middle. Because budgets are so important to almost all other policies, the budgetary process is the center of political battles in Washington and involves nearly everyone in government. Nestled inside the tax and expenditures figures are thousands of policy choices, each prompting plenty of politics.

Budgetary Politics

Public budgets are the supreme example of Harold Lasswell's definition of politics as "who gets what, when, and how." Budget battles are fought over contending interests, ideologies, programs, and agencies.

Stakes and Strategies Every political actor has a stake in the budget. Mayors want to keep federal grants-in-aid flowing in, defense contractors like a big defense budget, and scientists push for a large budget for the National Science Foundation. Agencies within the government also work to protect their interests. Individual members of Congress act as policy entrepreneurs for new ideas and support constituent benefits, both of which cost money. Presidents try to use budgets to manage the economy and leave their imprint on Congress's policy agenda.

Think of budgetary politics as resembling a game in which players adopt various strategies.[18] Agencies pushing their budgetary needs to Congress, for instance, try to link the benefits of their program to a senator's or representative's electoral needs. Often, agencies pad their requests a bit, hoping that the almost inevitable cuts will be bearable. President John Adams justified this now common budgetary gambit by saying to his cabinet, "If some superfluity not be given Congress to lop off, they will cut into the very flesh of the public necessities." Interest groups try to identify their favorite programs with the national interest. Mayors tell Congress not how much they like to receive federal aid but how crucial cities are to national survival. Farmers stress not that they like federal aid but that feeding a hungry nation and world is the main task of American agriculture. In the game of budgetary politics, there are plenty of players, all with their own strategies.

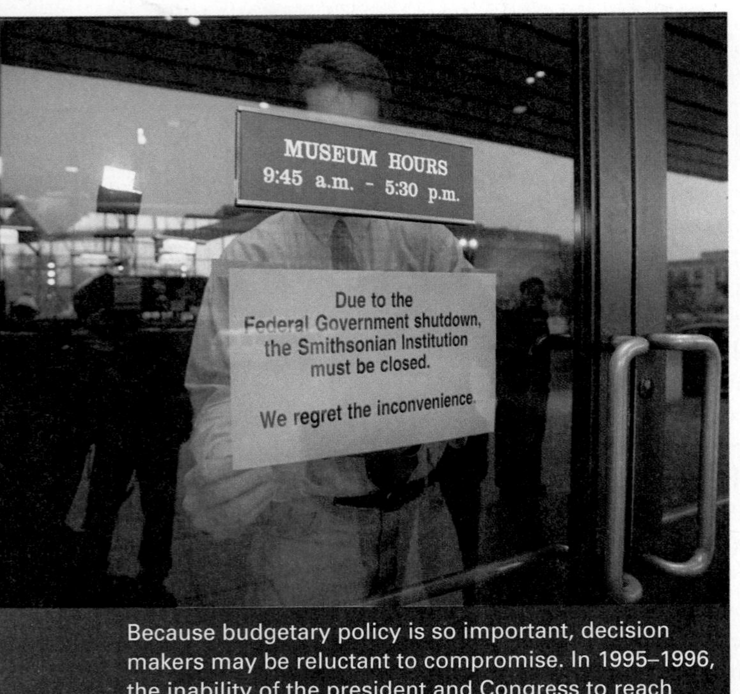

MUSEUM HOURS
9:45 a.m. - 5:30 p.m.
Due to the
Federal Government shutdown,
the Smithsonian Institution
must be closed.
We regret the inconvenience.

Because budgetary policy is so important, decision makers may be reluctant to compromise. In 1995–1996, the inability of the president and Congress to reach agreement led to the shutdown of much of the federal government.

The Players Deciding how to spend trillions of dollars is a process likely to attract plenty of interest—from those formally required to participate in the process as well as those whose stakes are too big to ignore it. Here are the main actors in the budgetary process:

- ***Interest groups.*** No lobbyist worth his or her pay would ignore the budget. Lobbying for a group's needs takes place in the agencies, with presidents (if the lobbyist has access to them), and before congressional committees. A smart agency head will be sure to involve interest groups in defending the agency's budget request.
- ***Agencies.*** Convinced of the importance of their mission, the heads of agencies almost always push for higher budget requests. They send their requests to the Office of Management and Budget and later get a chance to present themselves before congressional committees as well.[19]

- ***The Office of Management and Budget (OMB).*** The OMB is responsible to the president, its boss, but no president has the time to understand and make decisions about the billions of dollars in the budget—parceled out to hundreds of agencies, some of which the chief executive knows little or nothing about. The director and staff of the OMB have considerable independence from the president, which makes them major actors in the budget process.
- ***The president.*** The president makes final decisions on what to propose to Congress. In early February, the president unveils the proposed budget; the president then spends many a day trying to ensure that Congress will stick close to the recommendations.
- ***Tax committees in Congress.*** The government cannot spend money it does not have (or cannot borrow). The **House Ways and Means Committee** and the **Senate Finance Committee** write the tax codes, subject to the approval of Congress as a whole.
- ***Budget Committees and the Congressional Budget Office (CBO).*** The CBO—which is the congressional equivalent of the OMB—and its parent committees, the Senate and House Budget Committees, set the parameters of the congressional budget process through examining revenues and expenditures in the aggregate and proposing resolutions to bind Congress within certain limits.
- ***Subject-matter committees.*** Committees of Congress, ranging from Agriculture to Veterans Affairs, write new laws, which require new expenditures. Committee members may use hearings either to publicize the accomplishments of their pet agencies, thus supporting larger budgets for them, or to question agency heads about waste or overspending.
- ***Appropriations Committees and their subcommittees.*** The Appropriations Committee in each house decides who gets what. These committees take new or old policies coming from the subject-matter committees and decide how much to spend. Appropriations subcommittees hold hearings on specific agency requests.
- ***Congress as a whole.*** The Constitution requires that Congress as a whole approve taxes and appropriations, and senators and representatives have a strong interest in delivering federal dollars to their constituents. A dam here, a military base there, and a job-training program somewhere else—these are items that members look for in the budget.
- ***The Government Accountability Office (GAO).*** Congress's role does not end when it has passed the budget. The GAO works as Congress's eyes and ears, auditing, monitoring, and evaluating what agencies are doing with their budgets.

House Ways and Means Committee
The House of Representatives committee that, along with the **Senate Finance Committee**, writes the tax codes, subject to the approval of Congress as a whole.

Senate Finance Committee
The Senate committee that, along with the **House Ways and Means Committee**, writes the tax codes, subject to the approval of Congress as a whole.

Budgeting involves a cast of thousands. However, their roles are carefully scripted, and their time on stage is limited because budget making is both repetitive (the same things must be done each year) and sequential (actions must occur in the proper order and more or less on time). The budget cycle begins in the executive branch a full 19 months before the fiscal year begins.

The President's Budget

Until 1921, the various agencies of the executive branch sent their budget requests to the secretary of the treasury, who in turn forwarded them to Congress. Presidents played a limited role in proposing the budget; sometimes they played no role at all. Agencies basically peddled their own budget requests to Congress. In 1921 Congress, concerned about retiring the debt the country had accumulated during World War I, passed the Budget and Accounting Act, which required presidents to propose an executive budget to Congress, and created the Bureau of the Budget to help them. In the 1970s, President Nixon reorganized the Bureau of the Budget and gave it a new name,

TABLE 14.2 The President's Budget: An Approximate Schedule

SPRING Budget policy developed	The OMB presents the president with an analysis of the economic situation, and the budgetary outlook and policies are discussed. The OMB then gives guidelines to the agencies, which in turn review current programs and submit to the OMB their projections of budgetary needs for the coming year. The OMB reviews these projections and prepares recommendations to the president on final policy, programs, and budget levels. The president establishes guidelines and targets.
SUMMER Budget decisions conveyed to agencies	The OMB conveys the president's decisions to the agencies and advises and assists them in preparing their budgets.
FALL Estimates reviewed	The agencies submit to the OMB formal budget estimates for the coming fiscal year, along with projections for future years. The OMB holds hearings, reviews its assessment of the economy, and prepares budget recommendations for the president. The president reviews these recommendations and decides on the agencies' budgets and overall budgetary policy. The OMB advises the agencies of these decisions.
WINTER President's budget determined and submitted	The agencies revise their estimates to conform with the president's submitted decisions. The OMB once again reviews the economy and then drafts the president's budget message and prepares the budget document. The president revises and approves the budget message and transmits the budget document to Congress.

the Office of Management and Budget (OMB). The OMB, whose director is a presidential appointee requiring Senate approval, now supervises preparation of the federal budget and advises the president on budgetary matters.

It takes a long time to prepare a presidential budget.[20] By law, the president must submit a budget by the first Monday in February. The process begins almost a year before (see Table 14.2), when the OMB communicates with each agency, sounding out their requests and issuing tentative guidelines. By the summer, the president has decided on overall policies and priorities and has established guidelines and general targets for the budget. These are then communicated to the agencies.

The budget makers now get down to details. During the fall, the agencies submit formal, detailed estimates for their budgets, zealously pushing their needs to the OMB. Budget analysts at the OMB pare, investigate, weigh, and meet on agency requests. Often, the agency heads ask for hefty increases; sometimes they threaten to go directly to the president if their priorities are not met by the OMB. As the Washington winter sets in, the budget document is readied for final presidential approval. There is usually some last-minute juggling—agencies may be asked to change their estimates to conform with the president's decisions, or cabinet members may make a last-ditch effort to bypass the OMB and convince the president to increase their funds. With only days—or hours—left before the submission deadline, the budget document is rushed to the printers. Then the president sends it to Capitol Hill. The next steps are up to Congress.

Congress and the Budget

According to the Constitution, Congress must authorize all federal appropriations. Thus, Congress always holds one extremely powerful trump card in national policymaking: the power of the purse.[21] This year, Congress will decide how to spend nearly $4 trillion.

Reforming the Process For years Congress budgeted in a piecemeal fashion. A subcommittee of the House and Senate Appropriations Committees handled each agency request; then all these appropriations were added to produce a total budget. People never quite knew what the budget's bottom line would be until all the individual bills were totaled up. What Congress spent had little to do with any overall judgment of how much it should spend.

The **Congressional Budget and Impoundment Control Act of 1974** was designed to reform the congressional budgetary process. Its supporters hoped that it would also make Congress less dependent on the president's budget and more able to set and meet its own budgetary goals. The act established the following:

Congressional Budget and Impoundment Control Act of 1974
An act designed to reform the congressional budgetary process, including by forcing Congress to look at the budget as a whole. It was intended to make Congress less dependent on the president's budget and better able to set and meet its own budgetary goals.

- ***A fixed budget calendar.*** In the past, Congress sometimes failed to appropriate money to agencies until after the fiscal year was over, leaving agencies drifting for months with no firm budget. The act mandated a timetable, which has since been amended several times. Each step in the budgetary process has an established completion date (see Table 14.3).
- ***A budget committee in each house.*** The two Budget Committees are supposed to recommend target figures to Congress for the total budget size (with expenditures for major categories and projected revenues) by April 1 of each year. By April 15, Congress is to agree on the total size of the budget, which guides the Appropriations Committees in juggling figures for individual agencies. In doing this, Congress agrees on a budget resolution.
- ***A congressional budget office.*** The **Congressional Budget Office** (CBO) advises Congress on the probable consequences of its budget decisions, forecasts revenues, and is a counterweight to the president's OMB.

Congressional Budget Office
Advises Congress on the probable consequences of its decisions, forecasts revenues, and is a counterweight to the president's Office of Management and Budget.

One purpose of the new budgeting system was to force Congress to consider the budget (both projected expenditures and projected revenues) as a whole rather than in bits and pieces as it had done before. An important part of the process of establishing a budget is to set limits on expenditures on the basis of revenue projections—a step that

TABLE 14.3 The Congressional Budget Process: Targets and Timetables

DATE	ACTION TO BE COMPLETED
First Monday in February	Congress receives the president's budget.
February 15	The CBO submits a budget report to the House and Senate Budget Committees, including an analysis of the president's budget.
February 25	Other committees submit reports on outlays and revenues to Budget Committees in each house.
April 1	Budget Committees report concurrent resolution on the budget, which sets a total for budget outlays, an estimate of expenditures for major budget categories, and the recommended level of revenues. This resolution acts as an agenda for the remainder of the budgetary process.
April 15	Congress completes action on concurrent resolution on the budget.
May 15	Annual appropriations bills may be considered in the House.
June 10	House Appropriations Committee reports last annual appropriations bill.
June 15	Congress completes action on reconciliation legislation, bringing budget totals into conformity with established ceilings.
June 30	House completes action on annual appropriation bills.
October 1	The new fiscal year begins.

budget resolution
A resolution binding Congress to a total expenditure level, supposedly the bottom line of all federal spending for all programs.

is supposed to be done through a **budget resolution**. Thus, in April of each year, as you just saw, both houses are expected to agree on a budget resolution—thereby binding Congress to a total expenditure level that should form the bottom line of all federal spending for all programs. Only then is Congress supposed to begin acting on the individual appropriations.

To use as an analogy a family budget, suppose Family A budgets by adding up all its needs and wants and calling that its budget. Such a strategy almost guarantees overspending the family income. Family B, though, might begin by looking at its revenue in order to determine what its expenditures can total before dealing with its individual expenditure decisions. With its 1974 reforms, Congress was trying to force itself to behave more like Family B than Family A.

The congressional budget resolution often requests that certain changes be made in law, primarily to achieve savings incorporated into the spending totals and thus meet the budget resolution. These changes are legislated in two separate ways.

reconciliation
A congressional process through which program authorizations are revised to achieve required savings. It usually also includes tax or other revenue adjustments.

First is budget **reconciliation**, a process by which program authorizations are revised to achieve required savings; it frequently also includes tax or other revenue adjustments. Usually reconciliation comes near the end of the budgetary process, although occasionally the president and Congress have sought to use it in place of the regular lawmaking process.

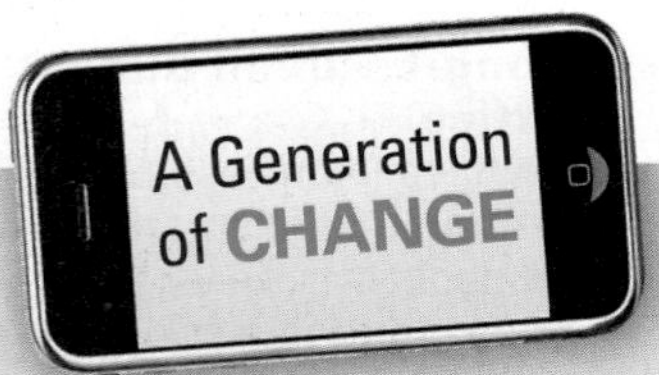

Fluctuating Deficits

Annual federal deficits mushroomed during the Reagan administration (1981–1988), despite the president's oft-repeated commitment to a balanced budget. The deficit disappeared during the Clinton administration, and the nation began running a surplus in fiscal year 1998. By 2002, however, the United States was back in the red. Annual deficits grew even larger beginning in 2009 as the government dealt with the financial crisis that hit the United States in 2008.

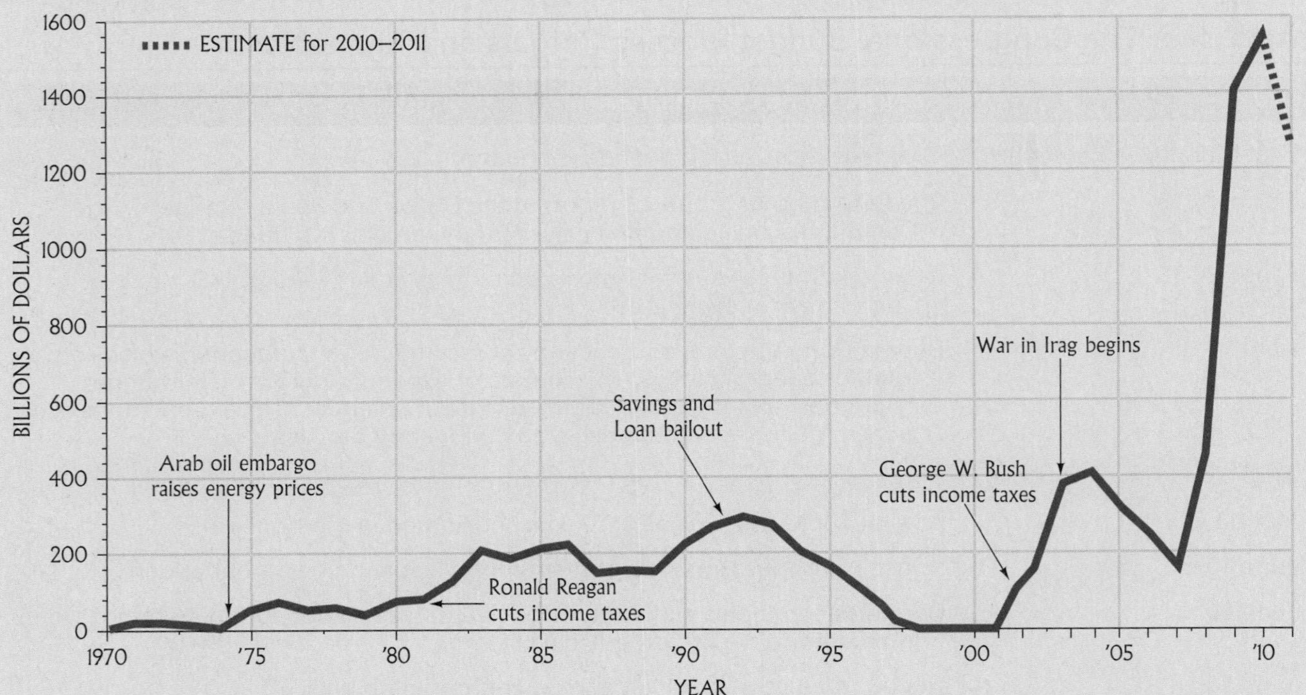

Source: *Budget of the United States Government, Fiscal Year 2011: Historical Tables* (Washington, DC: U.S. Government Printing Office, 2010), Table 1.1.

The second way that laws are changed to meet the budget resolution (or to create or change programs for other reasons) involves more narrowly drawn legislation. An **authorization bill** is an act of Congress that establishes or changes a government program. Authorizations specify program goals and, for discretionary programs, set the maximum amount that they may spend. For entitlement programs, an authorization sets or changes eligibility standards and benefits that must be provided by the program. Authorizations may be for one year, or they may run for a specified or indefinite number of years.

authorization bill
An act of Congress that establishes, continues, or changes a discretionary government program or an entitlement. It specifies program goals and maximum expenditures for discretionary programs.

Congress must pass an additional measure, termed an **appropriations bill**, to fund programs established by authorization bills. For example, if Congress authorizes expenditures on building highways, Congress must pass another bill to appropriate the funds to build them. Appropriations bills usually fund programs for one year and cannot exceed the amount of money authorized for a program; in fact, they may appropriate *less* than was authorized.

appropriations bill
An act of Congress that actually funds programs within limits established by authorization bills. Appropriations usually cover one year.

Evaluating the 1974 Reforms Have these reforms worked? If means that Congress has brought its spending into line with its revenues, then the reforms have been almost a total failure. Congressional budgets were in the red every year between the 1974 amendments and 1998. In fact, the red ink grew from a puddle to an ocean (see "A Generation of Change: Fluctuating Deficits"). Presidents made matters worse, submitting budget proposals that contained large deficits.

In addition, Congress has often failed to meet its own budgetary timetable. There has been too much conflict over the budget for the system to work according to design. Moreover, in many instances Congress has not been able to reach agreement and pass appropriations bills at all and has instead resorted to **continuing resolutions**—laws that allow agencies to spend at the previous year's level. Sometimes, as in 1986 and 1987, and 2007, appropriations bills have been lumped together in one enormous and complex bill (rather than in the 13 separate appropriations bills covering various components of the government that are supposed to pass), precluding adequate review by individual members of Congress and forcing the president either to accept unwanted provisions or to veto the funding for the entire government. These omnibus bills may also become magnets for unrelated and controversial pieces of legislation that could not pass on their own.

continuing resolutions
When Congress cannot reach agreement and pass appropriations bills, these resolutions allow agencies to spend at the level of the previous year.

On the other hand, the 1974 reforms have helped Congress view the entire budget early in the process; now Congress can at least see the forest as well as the trees. The problem is not so much the procedure as disagreement over how scarce resources should be spent. In the meantime, the budget deficit continues to be a source of conflict (see "You Are the Policymaker: Balancing the Budget").

YOU ARE THE POLICYMAKER

Balancing the Budget

You have seen that the national government is running large budget deficits and that the national debt continues to grow. Here is the situation you would face as a budget decision maker: According to the OMB, in fiscal year 2011 the national government will have revenues (including Social Security taxes) of about $2.567 trillion. Mandatory expenditures for domestic policy (entitlements such as Social Security and other prior obligations) total about $2.165 trillion. Nondiscretionary payments on the national debt will cost another $251 billion. National defense will cost an additional $750 billion. That leaves you with a deficit of $599 billion. Moreover, you have yet to spend on discretionary domestic policy programs. The president's proposals for these discretionary programs will take $671 billion. If you spend this amount, you will run a deficit of $1.267 trillion—and you will not even have had a chance to fund any significant new programs. Moreover, you may have to ask Congress for additional funds to pay for the wars in Iraq and Afghanistan.

What do you think? Would you drastically reduce defense expenditures? Or would you leave them alone and close down substantial portions of the rest of the government, such as programs for space and science, transportation and public works, economic subsidies and development, education and social services, health research and services, or law enforcement and other core functions of government—programs that have broad public support? Perhaps you would show great political courage and seek a tax increase to pay for these programs.

14.4 Assess the impact of democratic politics on budgetary growth and of the budget on scope of government.

Understanding Budgeting

Citizens and politicians alike fret about whether government is too big. There is agreement on the centrality of budgeting to modern government and politics, however.

Democracy and Budgeting

Almost all democracies have seen a substantial growth in government in the twentieth century. Economists Allan Meltzer and Scott Richard have argued that government grows in a democracy because of the equality of suffrage. Each voter has one vote, so those with less income have considerable clout. Parties must appeal to a majority of the voters. Hence, claim Meltzer and Richard, less-well-off voters will always use their votes to support public policies that redistribute benefits from the rich to the poor.[22] Many politicians willingly cooperate with the desire of voters to expand their benefits because voters return the favor at election time. Not surprisingly, the most rapidly growing areas of expenditures are Social Security, Medicaid, Medicare, and social welfare programs, which benefit the working and middle classes more than the rich.

Many believe that elites, particularly corporate elites, oppose big government. However, large banks and financial institutions and corporations such as Lockheed, United Airlines, and General Motors have appealed to the government for large bailouts when times got rough. Corporations support a big government that offers them contracts, subsidies, and other benefits. A $189 billion procurement and research-and-development budget at the Department of Defense[23] benefits defense contractors, their workers, and their shareholders.

Low-income and wealthy voters alike have voted for parties and politicians who promised them benefits. Citizens are not helpless victims of big government and its big taxes; they are at least coconspirators. When the air is foul, Americans expect government to help clean it up. When Americans get old, they expect a Social Security check. In a democracy, what people want affects what government does.

Government also grows by responding to groups and their demands. The parade of political action committees is one example of groups asking government for assistance. From agricultural lobbies supporting loans to zoologists pressing for aid from the National Science Foundation, groups seek to expand their favorite part of the budget. They are aided by committees and government agencies that work to fund projects favored by supportive groups (see the discussion on iron triangles in Chapter 15).

You have also seen, however, that some politicians compete for votes by promising not to spend money. After all, Ronald Reagan and George W. Bush did not each win election to the presidency twice by promising to raise taxes and provide more services, nor did the Republicans who took control of Congress in 1995. Among democratic nations, the proportionate size of

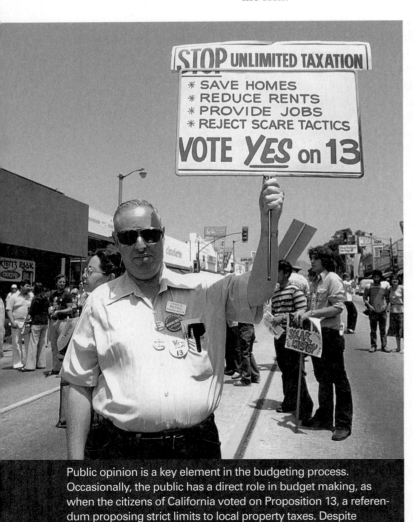

Public opinion is a key element in the budgeting process. Occasionally, the public has a direct role in budget making, as when the citizens of California voted on Proposition 13, a referendum proposing strict limits to local property taxes. Despite protests against the proposed legislation—many citizens argued that tax limits would restrict many government services—the proposition was passed.

The opposition to tax increases constrains the adoption or expansion of many programs. This opposition also makes it difficult to balance the budget.

How can we reconcile our preference for low taxes with our demands for government services?

"I like the concept if we can do it with no new taxes."

government budgets varies widely, and while no country has a more open political system than the United States, Americans have chosen to tax less and spend less on public services than almost all other democracies with developed economies. Interestingly, within the United States, most of the states with lower average incomes vote for candidates promising the least in the way of government benefits. In short, democracy may encourage government spending, but it does not compel it.

Among the most common criticisms of government is that it fails to balance the budget. Public officials are often criticized for lacking the will to deal with the problem, yet it is not lack of resolve that prevents a solution to enormous budget deficits. Instead, it is a lack of consensus on policy. Americans want to spend money on programs but not pay taxes,[24] and, being a democracy, this is exactly what the government does. The inevitable result is red ink.

The Budget and the Scope of Government

Issues regarding the scope of government have pervaded this chapter. The reason is obvious—in many ways, the budget *is* the scope of government. The bigger the budget, the bigger the government. When the country has seen a need, whether to defend itself or to provide for the elderly, it has found a way to pay for it. Even presidents, such as Ronald Reagan and George W. Bush, who led the fight to cut taxes, also wanted to substantially expand at least part of the government. It may seem, then, that there is no limit to budgetary growth.

The budgetary process can also limit government, however. Because of the emphasis on tax cuts, one could accurately characterize policymaking in the American government since 1980 as the "politics of scarcity"—scarcity of funds, that is. Thus, the budget can be a force for reining in the government as well as for expanding its role.[25] For example, President Bill Clinton came into office hoping to make new investments in education, worker training, and the country's physical infrastructure, such as roads and bridges, and to expand health care coverage. He soon found, however, that there was no money to fund new programs. Instead, he had to emphasize cutting the budget deficit. Much of the opposition to Barack Obama's proposal for health care reform was inspired by a fear of increasing the national debt. Thus, America's large budget deficits have been as much a constraint on government as they have been evidence of a burgeoning public sector.

Summary

14.1 Describe the sources of funding for the federal government and assess the consequences of tax expenditures and borrowing.

The personal income tax is the largest source of revenue for the federal government, with social insurance taxes a close second. Other revenue comes from the corporate income tax and excise taxes. Borrowing plays a major role in funding the government, and the national debt has grown rapidly in the past decade, as have government expenditures. Interest on this debt will eat up an increasing portion of future budgets. Tax expenditures represent an enormous drain on revenues but subsidize many popular activities.

14.2 Analyze federal expenditures and the growth of the budget.

Budgets have grown with the rise of the national security state and the social service state. National security and, especially, social services such as Social Security and Medicare, plus interest on the debt, make up most of the budget. Much of the budget represents uncontrollable expenditures, primarily entitlements to payments that the government has committed to make at a certain level and that are difficult to limit. Expenditures for most policies grow incrementally, with each year's budget building on the previous year's, and many interests ask Congress and the president to spend more on their favorite policies.

14.3 Outline the budgetary process and explain the role that politics plays.

The budgetary process is a long and complex one that involves the president, agencies, Congress as a whole, and many important congressional committees. The president submits the budget to Congress, whose reformed budgetary process has nonetheless not brought spending in line with revenues. Because budgets are central for most policies, politics is pervasive in the budgetary process as players battle over contending interests, ideologies, programs, and agencies.

14.4 Assess the impact of democratic politics on budgetary growth and of the budget on scope of government.

Budgets in democracies grow because the public and organized interests demand new and larger public services. However, some politicians compete for votes by promising to limit budgets. Increasing budgets increase the scope of government, but decreases in taxes and increases in debt make it more difficult to add or expand programs.

Chapter Test

14.1 Describe the sources of funding for the federal government and assess the consequences of tax expenditures and borrowing.

1. Approximately what percentage of federal expenditures goes to paying interest on the federal debt?
   a. 1 percent
   b. 7 percent
   c. 15 percent
   d. 25 percent
   e. 40 percent

2. A flat tax is a type of progressive income tax.

   True______ False______

3. Taxes on corporate income generate more revenue than individual income taxes.

   True______ False______

4. How do tax policies promote the interests of particular groups or encourage specific activities? How do tax expenditures amount to government subsidies for different activities? Give specific examples in your answer.

14.2 Analyze federal expenditures and the growth of the budget.

5. Which of the following comprises the largest slice of the budgetary pie?
   a. Defense expenditures
   b. Income security expenditures
   c. Foreign aid expenditures
   d. Domestic policy expenditures other than for income security
   e. Interest expenditures

6. Incrementalism requires budget makers to build the budget anew for each fiscal year.

   True______ False______

7. Federal budgetary expenditures are often deemed uncontrollable. What aspects of the budget contribute to this perception? Are there any ways that you can think of that might lead to greater control of the federal budget?

14.3 Outline the budgetary process and explain the role that politics plays.

8. Which of the following statements accurately characterizes the politics of budgeting?
   a. Agencies within the government work to protect their interest over the budget
   b. Members of Congress act as policy entrepreneurs to support constituent benefits
   c. Presidents try to use budgets to manage the economy
   d. State politicians request grants-in-aid to assist local economies
   e. All of the above, as every political actor has a stake in the budget

9. Congress drafts a budget resolution establishing a total expenditure level before it embarks on making the actual budget.

   True______ False______

10. There are many different players in the national budgetary process. Name three of these players, indicating their role in the process.

11. In 1974, Congress reformed the budgetary process. What are some of the key aspects of the reformed budgetary process and what were some of the reform's goals? How successful have these reforms been? How does politics undermine an effective budgetary process?

14.4 Assess the impact of democratic politics on budgetary growth and of the budget on scope of government.

12. What are some of the primary incentives for politicians to advocate a larger federal budget? Would you conclude that democracy itself promotes budgetary growth or can more limited government coincide with democratic values in the United States today? Defend your answer with specific examples.

13. How may the budget constrain the scope of government? Provide specific examples in your answer.

PEARSON mypoliscilab Exercises

Apply what you learned in this chapter on MyPoliSciLab.

Read on **mypoliscilab.com**

eText: Chapter 14

Study and **Review** on **mypoliscilab.com**

Pre-Test
Post-Test
Chapter Exam
Flashcards

Watch on **mypoliscilab.com**

Video: The Stimulus Breakdown

Explore on **mypoliscilab.com**

Simulation: You Are the President and Need to Get a Tax Cut Passed

Timeline: Growth of the Budget and Federal Spending

Key Terms

budget (406)
deficit (406)
expenditures (406)
revenues (406)
income tax (406
Sixteenth Amendment (406)
federal debt (408)
tax expenditures (410)
Social Security Act (416)
Medicare (416)
incrementalism (417)
uncontrollable expenditures (419)
entitlements (419)
House Ways and Means Committee (421)
Senate Finance Committee (421)
Congressional Budget and Impoundment Control Act of 1974 (423)
Congressional Budget Office (423)
budget resolution (424)
reconciliation (424)
authorization bill (425)
appropriations bill (425)
continuing resolutions (425)

Internet Resources

www.gpoaccess.gov/eop/
The Economic Report of the President and the federal government's budget.

www.irs.ustreas.gov
The Internal Revenue Service home page, containing a wealth of information about taxes.

www.whitehouse.gov/omb
The Office of Management and Budget home page. Clicking on the current year's budget takes you to all the current budget documents.

www.cbo.gov
Congressional Budget Office home page, containing budgetary analyses and data.

www.taxpolicycenter.org
A joint venture of the Urban Institute and the Brookings Institution, containing many studies of budgets and taxes.

www.taxfoundation.org
The Tax Foundation site, with a wealth of tax information.

www.concordcoalition.org
The nonpartisan Concord Coalition provides studies of budgetary issues.

www.cbpp.org
The Center on Budget and Policy Priorities focuses on how fiscal policy and public programs affect low-and moderate-income families and individuals.

For Further Reading

Bennett, Linda L. M., and Stephen Earl Bennett. ***Living with Leviathan.*** Lawrence: University Press of Kansas, 1990. Examines Americans' coming to terms with big government and their expectations of government largesse.

Berry, William D., and David Lowery. ***Understanding United States Government Growth.*** New York: Praeger, 1987. An empirical analysis of the causes of the growth of government in the period since World War II.

Jones, Bryan D., and Walter Williams. ***The Politics of Bad Ideas.*** New York: Pearson Longman, 2007. Shows that there are many bad ideas regarding budgetary policy and explains why they persist.

King, Ronald F. ***Money, Taxes, and Politics.*** New Haven, CT: Yale University Press, 1993. Explains why democratically elected officials approve tax policies that make rich people richer.

Rubin, Irene S. ***The Politics of Public Budgeting: Getting and Spending, Borrowing and Balancing***, 6th ed. Washington, DC: Congressional Quarterly Press, 2009. Shows how politics pervades budgetary decisions at every stage.

Schick, Allen. ***The Federal Budget***, 3rd ed. Washington, DC: Brookings Institution, 2007. A useful, "hands-on" view of federal budgeting.

Wildavsky, Aaron, and Naomi Caiden. ***The New Politics of the Budgetary Process***, 5th ed. New York: Longman, 2004. The standard work on the budgetary process.

Chapter 15

The Federal Bureaucracy

Learning Objectives

15.1 Describe the federal bureaucrats and the ways in which they obtain their jobs.

15.2 Differentiate the four types of agencies into which the federal bureaucracy is organized.

15.3 Identify the factors that influence the effectiveness of bureaucratic implementation of public policy.

15.4 Describe how bureaucracies regulate, and assess deregulation and alternative approaches to regulation.

15.5 Assess means of controlling unelected bureaucrats in American democracy and the impact of the bureaucracy on the scope of government.

Chapter **OUTLINE**

POLITICS IN ACTION: REGULATING FOOD

Americans do not want to worry about the safety of the food they eat. Indeed, food safety is something we take for granted. But who assures this safety? Bureaucrats. It is their job to keep our food safe from contamination. Although we rarely think about food inspections, they represent one of the most important regulatory functions of government. The fact that we rarely think about food safety is testimony to the success of bureaucrats in carrying out their tasks.[1]

Policing the food supply is not a straightforward task, however. It involves a complex web of federal agencies with overlapping jurisdictions. At least 12 agencies and 35 statutes regulate food safety. Eggs in the shell fall under the purview of the Food and Drug Administration (FDA), but once cracked and processed, they come under the jurisdiction of the U.S. Department of Agriculture (USDA). The USDA is responsible for regulating meat and poultry, while the FDA handles most other food products, including seafood and produce. Cheese pizzas are the FDA's responsibility, but if they have pepperoni on top, Agriculture inspectors step in.

Other parts of the government also play a prominent role in enforcing food safety laws. For example, the Environmental Protection Agency oversees pesticides applied to crops, the Centers for Disease Control and Prevention track food-related illnesses, and the Department of Homeland Security coordinates agencies' safety and security activities.

Is this complex system the result of bureaucratic maneuvering? No—Congress created the system layer on top of layer, with little regard to how it should work as a whole. Critics argue that the system is outdated and that it would be better to create a single food safety agency that could target inspections, streamline safety programs, and use resources more efficiently. Such proposals have generated little enthusiasm in Congress, however, where committees are sensitive about losing jurisdiction over agencies. (For example, in the House, the Energy and Commerce Committee has oversight over the FDA while the Agriculture Committee has responsibility for the USDA.) Furthermore, growers and manufacturers fear a single agency would impose onerous new regulations, product recalls, and fines and could be used by empire-building bureaucrats to expand their budget and regulatory authority. So, little change occurs.

Bureaucrats face other challenges in insuring safe food. The FDA is so short of staff that it can inspect the average U.S. food company just once every 10 years. Even worse, it can inspect less than 1 percent of all food imports—despite repeated problems with contaminated products. Indeed, only 20 percent of food imports appear in its computer system for review by the field inspection force.

Bureaucrats are central to our lives. They provide essential public services. They possess crucial information and expertise that make them partners with the president and Congress in decision making about public policy. Who knows more than bureaucrats about Social Security recipients or the military capabilities of China? Bureaucrats are also central to politics. They do much more than simply follow orders. Because of their expertise, bureaucrats inevitably have discretion in carrying out policy decisions, which is why congressional committees and interest groups take so much interest in what they do.

Bureaucratic power extends to every corner of American economic and social life, yet bureaucracies are scarcely hinted at in the Constitution. Congress creates each bureaucratic agency, sets its budget, and writes the policies it administers. Most agencies are responsible to the president, whose constitutional responsibility to "take care that the laws shall be faithfully executed" sheds only a dim light on the problems of managing so large a government. How to manage and control bureaucracies is a central problem of democratic government.

Reining in the power of bureaucracies is also a common theme in debates over the scope of government in America. Some political commentators see the bureaucracy as the prime example of a federal government growing out of control. They view the bureaucracy as acquisitive, constantly seeking to expand its size, budgets, and authority while entangling everything in red tape and spewing forth senseless regulations. Others see the bureaucracy as laboring valiantly against great odds to fulfill the missions elected officials have assigned it. Where does the truth lie? The answer is less obvious than you may think. Clearly, bureaucracies require closer examination.

The German sociologist Max Weber advanced his classic conception of bureaucracy, stressing that the bureaucracy was a "rational" way for a modern society to conduct its business.[2] According to Weber, a **bureaucracy** depends on certain elements: It has a *hierarchical authority structure*, in which power flows from the top down and responsibility flows from the bottom up; it uses *task specialization* so that experts instead of amateurs perform technical jobs; and it develops extensive *rules*, which may seem extreme at times, but which allow similar cases to be handled similarly instead of capriciously.

bureaucracy
According to Max Weber, a hierarchical authority structure that uses task specialization, operates on the merit principle, and behaves with impersonality.

Bureaucracies operate on the *merit principle*, in which entrance and promotion are awarded on the basis of demonstrated abilities rather than on "who you know." Bureaucracies behave with *impersonality* so that they treat all their clients impartially. Weber's classic prototype of the bureaucratic organization depicts the bureaucracy as a well-constructed machine with plenty of (hierarchical) working parts.

15.1 Describe the federal bureaucrats and the ways in which they obtain their jobs.

The Bureaucrats

Bureaucrats are typically much less visible than the president or members of Congress. As a result, Americans usually know little about them. This section examines some myths about bureaucrats and explains who they are and how they got their jobs.

Some Bureaucratic Myths and Realities

Bureaucrat baiting is a popular American pastime. Even presidential candidates have climbed aboard the antibureaucracy bandwagon. Jimmy Carter complained about America's "complicated and confused and overlapping and wasteful" bureaucracies; Gerald Ford spoke of the "dead weight" of bureaucracies; and Ronald Reagan insisted that bureaucrats "overregulated" the American economy, causing a decline in productivity.

Any object of such unpopularity will spawn plenty of myths. The following are some of the most prevalent myths about bureaucracy:

- ***Americans dislike bureaucrats.*** Despite the rhetoric about bureaucracies, Americans are generally satisfied with bureaucrats and the treatment they get from them. Americans may dislike bureaucracies, but they like individual bureaucrats. Surveys have found that two-thirds or more of those who have had encounters with a bureaucrat evaluate these encounters positively. In most instances, people describe bureaucrats as helpful, efficient, fair, courteous, and working to serve their clients' interests.[3]
- ***Bureaucracies are growing bigger each year.*** This myth is half true and half false. The number of government employees has been expanding, but not the number of *federal* employees. Almost all the growth in the number of public employees has

occurred in state and local governments; this number more than doubled in a 40-year period beginning in 1965 while the number of federal employees remained constant. Today, the approximately 20 million state and local public employees far outnumber the approximately 2.8 million civilian (including postal) and 1.4 million military federal government employees. As a percentage of America's total workforce, *federal* government civilian employment has been shrinking, not growing; it now accounts for about 2 percent of all civilian jobs.[4]

Of course, many state and local employees work on programs that are federally funded, and the federal government hires many private contractors to provide goods and services ranging from hot meals to weapons systems.[5] Such people provide services directly to the federal government or to citizens on its behalf.

- ***Most federal bureaucrats work in Washington, D.C.*** Fewer than one in five federal civilian employees work in the Washington, D.C., metropolitan area. "My State: Federal Civilian Employees" shows how they are distributed within the nation. In addition, nearly 90,000 federal civilian employees work in foreign countries and American territories.[6] If you look in your local phone book under "U.S. Government," you will probably find listings for the local offices of the Postal Service, the Social Security Administration, the FBI, the Department of Agriculture's county agents, recruiters for the armed services, air traffic controllers, the Internal Revenue Service (IRS), and many others.
- ***Bureaucracies are ineffective, inefficient, and always mired in red tape.*** No words describing bureaucratic behavior are better known than "red tape."[7] Bureaucracy, however, is simply a way of organizing people to perform work. General Motors,

Federal Civilian Employees

Federal employees are distributed throughout the country. California leads the nation with 153,000 federal civilian nonpostal employees. Texas has 124,000 and New York has 67,000. Reflecting their proximity to Washington, D.C., Virginia has 133,000 federal civilian employees and Maryland has 113,000.

QUESTIONS FOR DISCUSSION

- How does your state rank in terms of federal employment?
- Why do you think some states have more federal employees than others? Are the differences only the result of differences in population?
- Is it important for a state to have a substantial number of federal employees?

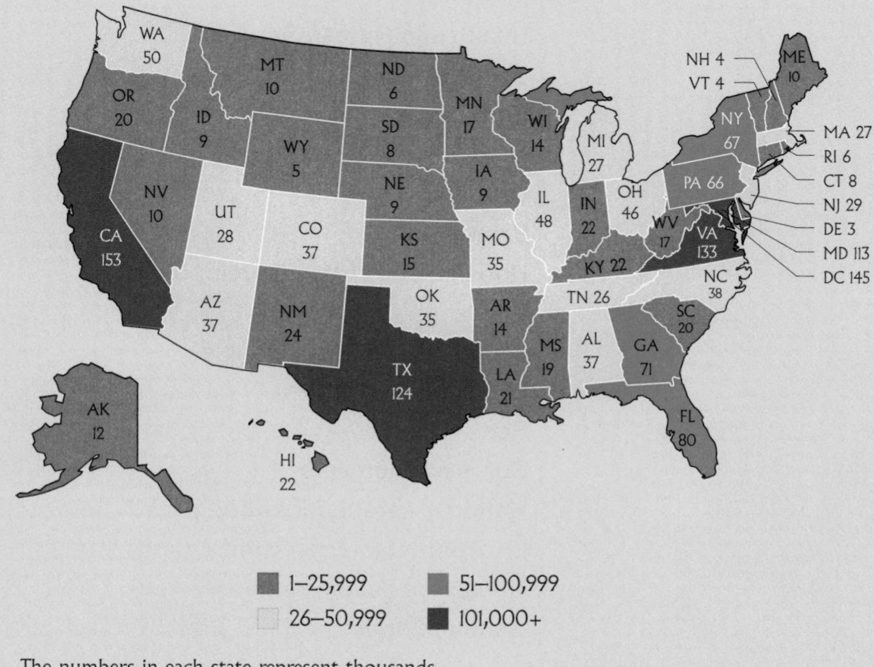

The numbers in each state represent thousands.

Source: U.S. Department of Commerce, *Statistical Abstract of the United States, 2010* (Washington, DC: U.S. Government Printing Office, 2010), Table 486.

a college or university, the U.S. Army, the Department of Health and Human Services, and the Roman Catholic Church are all bureaucracies. Bureaucracies are a little like referees: When they work well, no one gives them much credit, but when they work poorly, everyone calls them unfair, incompetent, or inefficient. Bureaucracies may be inefficient at times, but no one has found a substitute for them, and no one has yet demonstrated that government bureaucracies are more or less inefficient, ineffective, or mired in red tape than private bureaucracies.[8]

Anyone who looks with disdain on American bureaucracies should contemplate life without them. Despite all the complaining about bureaucracies, the vast majority of tasks carried out by governments at all levels are noncontroversial. Bureaucrats deliver mail, test milk, issue Social Security and student loan checks, run national parks, and perform other routine governmental tasks in a perfectly acceptable manner.

Most federal civilian employees work for just a few of the agencies (see Table 15.1). The Department of Defense employs about 25 percent of federal *civilian* workers in addition to the more than 1.4 million men and women in uniform. Altogether, the department makes up more than half the federal bureaucracy. The Postal Service accounts for an additional 28 percent of the federal civilian employees, and the Department of Veterans Affairs, clearly related to national defense, accounts for about 10 percent of

TABLE 15.1 Federal Civilian Employment

EXECUTIVE DEPARTMENTS	NUMBER OF EMPLOYEES[a]
Defense (military functions)	708,000
Veterans Affairs	279,200
Homeland Security	176,100
Justice	119,400
Treasury	113,000
Agriculture	95,300
Interior	70,100
Health and Human Services	65,000
Transportation	57,000
Commerce	141,400**
State	33,600
Labor	18,000
Energy	16,900
Housing and Urban Development	9,700
Education	4,300
Larger Noncabinet Agencies	
U.S. Postal Service	656,800
Social Security Administration	68,300
Corps of Engineers	21,700
National Aeronautics and Space Administration	18,700
Environmental Protection Agency	17,500
Tennessee Valley Authority	12,400
General Services Administration	12,600

[a]Figures are for 2010.

**Figure includes approximately 90,000 temporary employees for the 2010 census.

Source: *Budget of the United States Government, Fiscal Year 2011: Analytical Perspectives* (Washington, DC: U.S. Government Printing Office, 2010), Tables 23-1 and 23-2.

employees. All other functions of government, including homeland security, are handled by the remaining quarter or so of federal employees.

Civil Servants

Given the size of the bureaucracy, it is difficult to imagine a statistically typical bureaucrat. As a whole, however, the permanent bureaucracy is more broadly representative of the American people than are legislators, judges, or presidential appointees in the executive branch[9] (see Figure 15.1).

The diversity of bureaucratic jobs mirrors the diversity of private-sector jobs, including occupations literally ranging from A to Z. Accountants, bakers, census analysts, defense procurement specialists, electricians, foreign service officers, guards in federal prisons, home economists, Indian Affairs agents, judges, kitchen workers, lawyers, missile technologists, narcotics agents, ophthalmologists, postal carriers, quarantine specialists, radiologists, stenographers, truck drivers, underwater demolition experts, virologists, wardens, X-ray technicians, youth counselors, and zoologists all work for the government.

Until little more than a hundred years ago, a person got a job with the government through the patronage system. **Patronage** is a hiring and promotion system based on political factors rather than on merit or competence. Working in a congressional campaign, making large donations, and having the right connections helped people secure jobs with the government. Nineteenth-century presidents staffed the government with their friends and allies, following the view of Andrew Jackson that "to the victors belong the spoils." Scores of office seekers would swarm the White House after Inauguration Day. It is said that during a bout with malaria, Lincoln told an aide to "send in the office seekers" because he finally had something to give them.

A disappointed office seeker named Charles Guiteau helped end this "spoils system" of federal appointments in 1881. Frustrated because President James A. Garfield would not give him a job, Guiteau shot and killed Garfield. Vice President Chester A. Arthur, who then became president, had been known as the Prince of Patronage; he had been collector of the customs for New York, a patronage-rich post. To the surprise of his critics, Arthur encouraged passage of the **Pendleton Civil Service Act** (1883), which created the federal civil service. Today, most federal agencies are covered by some sort of civil service system.

All **civil service** systems are designed to hire and promote members of the bureaucracy on the basis of merit and to create a nonpartisan government service. The **merit principle**—using entrance exams and promotion ratings to reward qualified individuals—is intended to produce an administration of people with talent and

patronage
A system in which jobs and promotions are awarded for political reasons rather than for merit or competence Compare **civil service** and the **merit principle**.

Pendleton Civil Service Act
Passed in 1883, an act that created a federal **civil service** so that hiring and promotion would be based on merit rather than **patronage**.

civil service
A system of hiring and promotion based on the **merit principle** and the desire to create a nonpartisan government service.

merit principle
The idea that hiring should be based on entrance exams and promotion ratings to produce administration by people with talent and skill.

FIGURE 15.1 Characteristics of Federal Nonpostal Civilian Employees

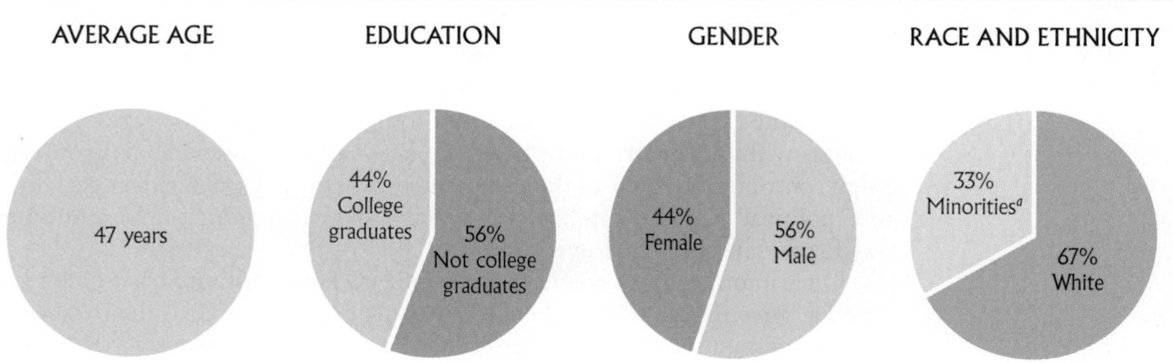

[a]Includes African Americans, Asian Americans, Native Americans, and Hispanics.

Source: United States Office of Personnel Management, *Profile of Federal Civilian Non-Postal Employees,* September 30, 2008

The Merit System

People obtain positions in the federal bureaucracy through a merit system and are protected against losing their jobs because of their political views. If the president could appoint a substantial percentage of bureaucrats, it is likely that they would be more responsive to the president but also likely that they would be less qualified to serve the public interest than today's bureaucrats.

Hatch Act
A federal law prohibiting government employees from active participation in partisan politics while on duty or for employees in sensitive positions at any time.

Office of Personnel Management
The office in charge of hiring for most agencies of the federal government, using elaborate rules in the process.

GS (General Schedule) rating
A schedule for federal employees, ranging from GS 1 to GS 18, by which salaries can be keyed to rating and experience.

Senior Executive Service
An elite cadre of about 9,000 federal government managers at the top of the civil service system.

skill. Creating a nonpartisan civil service means insulating government workers from the risk of being fired when a new party comes to power. At the same time, the **Hatch Act**, originally passed in 1939 and amended most recently in 1993, prohibits civil service employees from actively participating in partisan politics while on duty. While off duty they may engage in political activities, but they cannot run for partisan elective offices or solicit contributions from the public. Employees with sensitive positions, such as those in the national security area, may not engage in political activities even while off duty.

The **Office of Personnel Management** (OPM) is in charge of hiring for most federal agencies. The president appoints its director, who is confirmed by the Senate. The OPM has elaborate rules about hiring, promotion, working conditions, and firing. To get a civil service job, usually candidates must first take a test. If they pass, their names are sent to agencies when jobs requiring their particular skills become available. For each open position, the OPM will send three names to the agency. Except under unusual circumstances, the agency must hire one of these three individuals. Each job is assigned a **GS (General Schedule) rating** ranging from GS 1 to GS 18. Salaries are keyed to rating and experience.

At the very top of the civil service system (GS 16–18) are about 9,000 members of the **Senior Executive Service**, the "cream of the crop" of the federal employees. These executives earn high salaries, and the president may move them from one agency to another as leadership needs change.

After a probationary period, civil servants are protected by the civil service system—overprotected, critics claim. Protecting all workers against political firings—a prerequisite for a nonpartisan civil service—may also protect a few from dismissal for good cause. Firing incompetents is hard work and is unusual. Employees are entitled to appeal, and these appeals can consume weeks, months, or even years. More than one agency has decided to tolerate incompetents, assigning them trivial or no duties, rather than invest its resources in the task of discharging them. In the case of female, minority, or older workers, appeals can also be based on antidiscrimination statutes, making dismissal potentially even more difficult.

Sometimes presidents seek more control over federal employees. President George W. Bush proposed to limit job protection for employees in the Department of Homeland Security. After a protracted battle, Congress agreed, although implementation of this change has been slow and opposed by employee unions.

Political Appointees

As an incoming administration celebrates its victory and prepares to take control of the government, Congress publishes the *Plum Book*, which lists top federal jobs (that is, "plums") available for direct presidential appointment, often with Senate confirmation. There are about 500 of these top policymaking posts (mostly cabinet secretaries, undersecretaries, assistant secretaries, and bureau chiefs) and about 2,500 lesser positions.

All incoming presidents launch a nationwide talent search for qualified personnel. Presidents seek individuals who combine executive talent, political skills, and sympathy for policy positions similar to those of the administration. Often, the president tries to ensure some diversity and balance in terms of gender, ethnicity, region, and different interests within the party. Some positions, especially ambassadorships, go to large campaign contributors. A few of these appointees will be civil servants, temporarily elevated to a "political" status; most, however, will be political appointees, "in-and-outers" who stay for a while and then leave.[10]

Once in office, these administrative policymakers constitute what Hugh Heclo has called a "government of strangers." Their most important trait is their transience. The average assistant secretary or undersecretary lasts less than two years.[11] Few top officials stay long enough to know their own subordinates well, much less people in other agencies. Administrative routines, budget cycles, and legal complexities are often new to

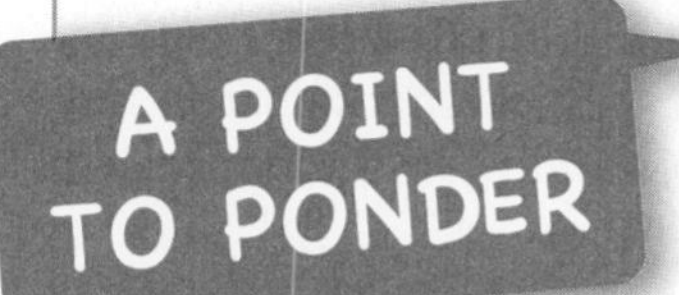

All presidents want to appoint talented men and women to positions in the executive branch. Yet many people receive jobs primarily because of their campaign activities and political loyalty. Major campaign contributors are especially likely to receive choice positions if they wish them.

Do you think this is a good system?

Doonesbury BY GARRY TRUDEAU

them. And although these *Plum Book* appointees may have the outward signs of power, many of them find it challenging to exercise real control over much of what their subordinates do and have difficulty leaving their mark on policy. They soon learn that they are dependent on senior civil servants, who know more, have been there longer, and will outlast them.

Although analytical intelligence, substantive expertise, and managerial skills may be crucial to implementing policies effectively, presidents usually place a premium on personal loyalty and commitment to their programs when evaluating candidates for positions in the bureaucracy. The White House wants bureaucratic responsiveness to its policies, but evidence indicates that bureaucratic resistance to change does not pose a substantial obstacle to presidents' achieving their goals and that career civil servants are more effective than political appointees at managing agencies.[12]

If policy loyalty can be problematic as a criterion for filling key positions, even more potentially problematic are the practices of using these positions to reward political associates and key campaign contributors and of satisfying the desire of high-level appointees to name their own subordinates. Such factors were, for example, behind George W. Bush's nomination of Michael Brown, the former president of the Arabian Horse Association, to head the Federal Emergency Management Agency—an appointment that came back to haunt him in the wake of the agency's performance in dealing with the destruction caused by Hurricane Katrina.

How Bureaucracies Are Organized

15.2 Differentiate the four types of agencies into which the federal bureaucracy is organized.

A complete organizational chart of the American federal government would occupy a large wall. You could pore over this chart, trace the lines of responsibility and authority, and see how government is organized—at least on paper. A very simplified organizational chart appears in Figure 15.2. A much easier way to look at how the federal executive branch is organized is to group agencies into four basic types: cabinet departments, independent regulatory commissions, government corporations, and independent executive agencies.

FIGURE 15.2 Organization of the Executive Branch

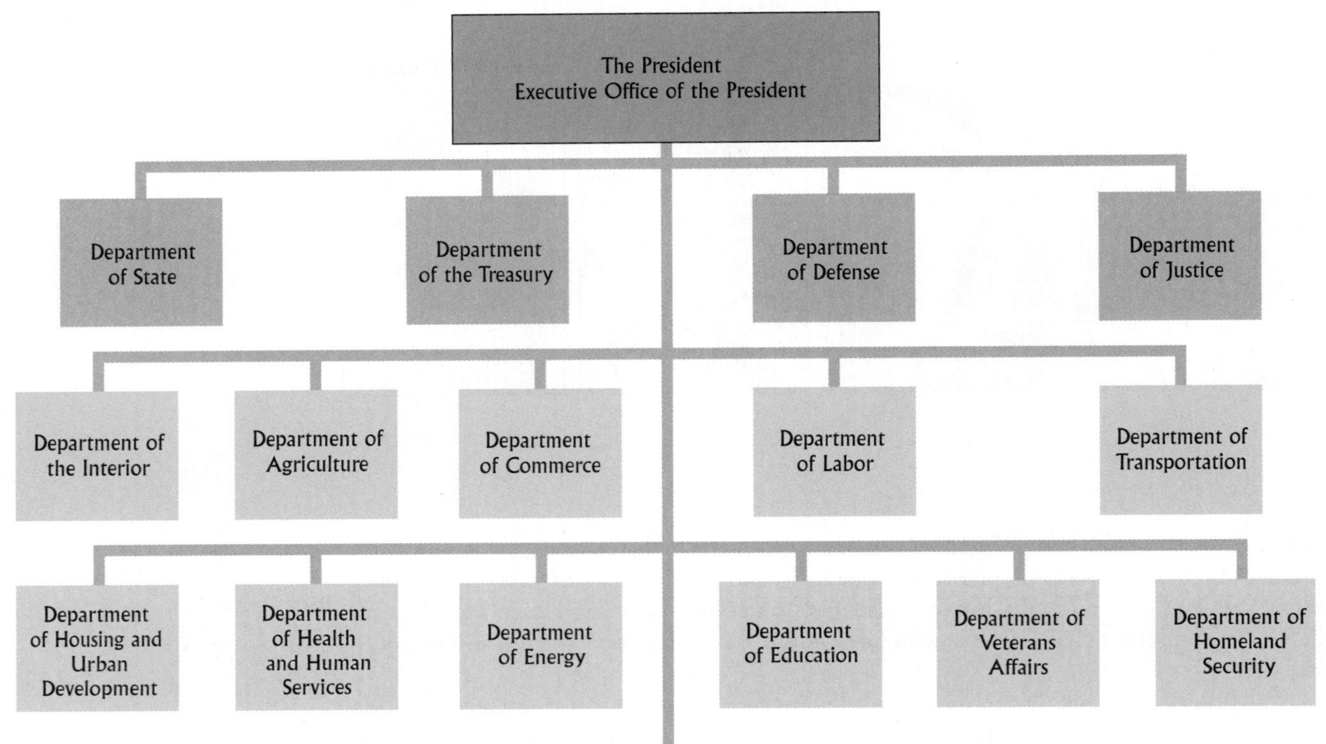

INDEPENDENT ESTABLISHMENTS AND GOVERNMENT CORPORATIONS

African Development Foundation
Broadcasting Board of Governors
Central Intelligence Agency
Commodity Futures Trading Commission
Consumer Product Safety Commission
Corporation for National and Community Service
Defense Nuclear Facilities Safety Board
Environmental Protection Agency
Equal Employment Opportunity Commission
Export-Import Bank of the United States
Farm Credit Administration
Federal Communications Commission
Federal Deposit Insurance Corporation
Federal Election Commission
Federal Housing Finance Board
Federal Labor Relations Authority
Federal Maritime Commission
Federal Mediation and Conciliation Service
Federal Mine Safety and Health Review Commission
Federal Reserve System
Federal Retirement Thrift Investment Board
Federal Trade Commission
General Services Administration
Inter-American Foundation
Merit Systems Protection Board
National Aeronautics and Space Administration
National Archives and Records Administration
National Capital Planning Commission
National Credit Union Administration
National Foundation on the Arts and Humanities
National Labor Relations Board
National Mediation Board
National Railroad Passenger Corporation (Amtrak)
National Science Foundation
National Transportation Safety Board
Nuclear Regulatory Commission
Occupational Safety and Health Review Commission
Office of the Director of National Intelligence
Office of Government Ethics
Office of Personnel Management
Office of Special Counsel
Overseas Private Investment Corporation
Peace Corps
Pension Benefit Guaranty Corporation
Postal Rate Commission
Railroad Retirement Board
Securities and Exchange Commission
Selective Service System
Small Business Administration
Social Security Administration
Tennessee Valley Authority
Trade and Development Agency
U.S. Agency for International Development
U.S. Commission on Civil Rights
U.S. International Trade Commission
U.S. Postal Service

Source: Office of the Federal Register, *United States Government Manual 2009–2010* (Washington, DC: U.S. Government Printing Office, 2010), 21.

Cabinet Departments

Each of the 15 cabinet departments is headed by a secretary (except the Department of Justice, which is headed by the attorney general), who has been chosen by the president and approved by the Senate. Undersecretaries, deputy undersecretaries, and assistant secretaries report to the secretary. Each department manages specific policy areas (see the list in Table 13.4, page 377), and each has its own budget and its own staff.

Each department has a unique mission and is organized somewhat differently. The Department of the Interior, charged with overseeing the nation's natural resources and administering policies that affect Native Americans, is an example of a well-established and traditional department (see Figure 15.3). The real work of a department is done in the bureaus, which divide the work into more specialized areas (a bureau is sometimes called a *service*, *office*, *administration*, or other name).

Sometimes status as a cabinet department can be controversial. For several years, Republicans tried to disband the Education, Energy, and Commerce departments, arguing that they wasted tax dollars and implemented policies that should be terminated.

FIGURE 15.3 Organization of the Department of the Interior

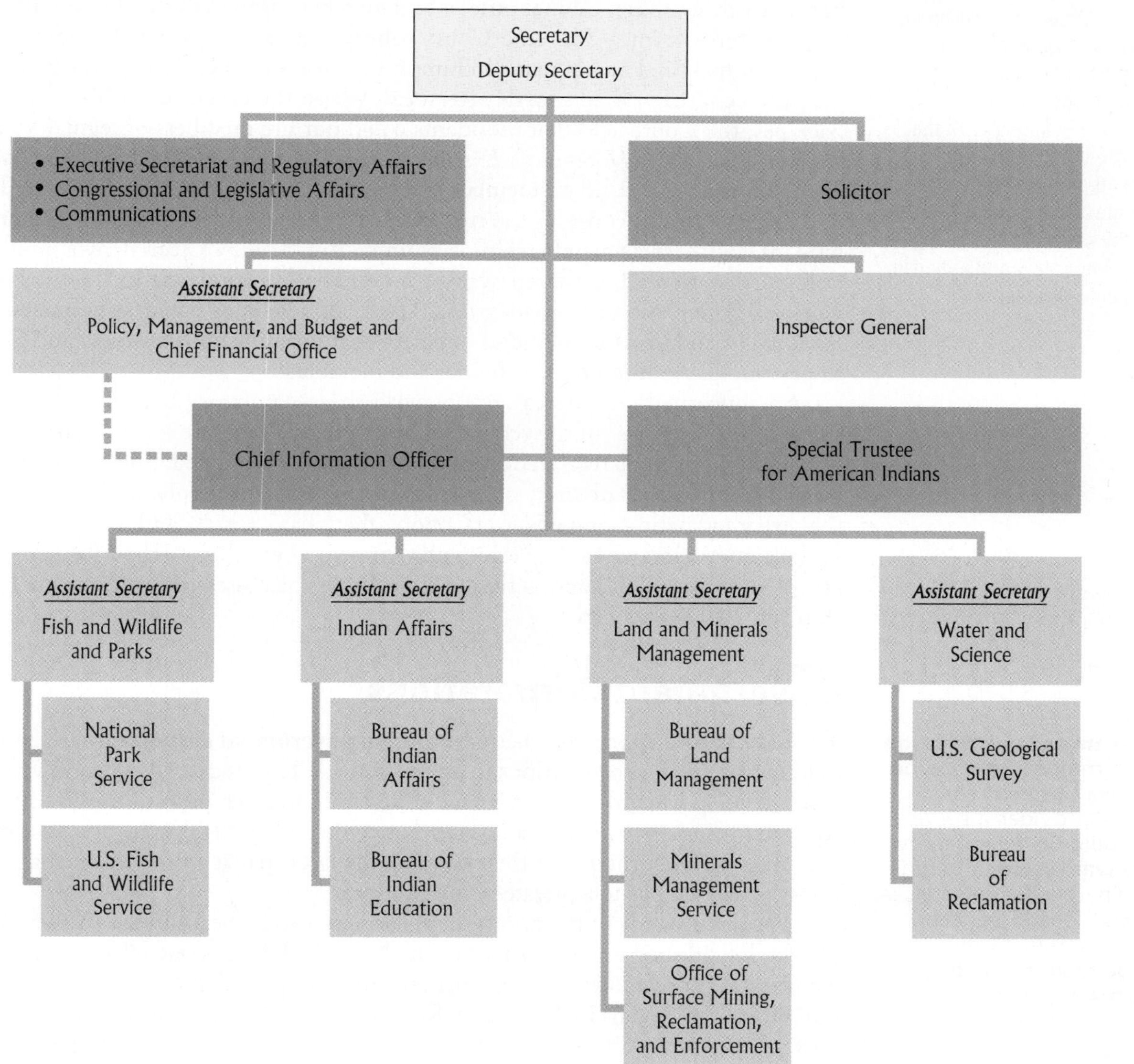

Source: Office of the Federal Register, *United States Government Manual 2009–2010* (Washington, DC: U.S. Government Printing Office, 2010), 240.

Independent Regulatory Commissions

independent regulatory commission
A government agency with responsibility for making and enforcing rules to protect the public interest in some sector of the economy and for judging disputes over these rules.

Each **independent regulatory commission** has responsibility for making and enforcing rules to protect the public interest in a particular sector of the economy, as well as for judging disputes over these rules.[13] The independent regulatory commissions are sometimes called the alphabet soup of American government because most of them are known by their initials. Some examples follow:

- *FRB* (*Federal Reserve Board*), charged with governing banks and, even more important, regulating the supply of money and thus interest rates
- *NLRB* (*National Labor Relations Board*), created to regulate labor–management relations
- *FCC* (*Federal Communications Commission*), charged with licensing radio and TV stations and regulating their programming in the public interest as well as with regulating interstate long-distance telephone rates, cable television, and the Internet
- *FTC (Federal Trade Commission)*, responsible for regulating business practices and controlling monopolistic behavior, and now involved in policing the accuracy of advertising
- *SEC (the Securities and Exchange Commission)*, created to police the stock market

Independent Regulatory Commissions

Independent regulatory commissions, such as the Federal Reserve Board, are designed to be somewhat insulated from the influence of politics. Their independence makes them less responsive to the president and Congress than other agencies. It also provides the potential—but not the certainty—of taking a long-range view and acting in the public interest.

Each of these independent regulatory commissions is governed by a small number of commissioners, usually 5 to 10 members appointed by the president and confirmed by the Senate for fixed terms. The president cannot fire regulatory commission members as easily as he can cabinet officers and members of the White House staff. The difference stems from a Supreme Court ruling in a case in which President Franklin Roosevelt had fired a man named Humphrey from the FTC. Humphrey had taken the matter to court but died shortly afterward. When the executors of his estate sued for back pay, the Court held that presidents could not fire members of regulatory agencies without just cause (*Humphrey's Executor v. United States*, 1935). "Just cause" has never been defined clearly, and no member of a regulatory commission has been fired since.

Interest groups consider the rule making by independent regulatory commissions (and, of course, their membership) very important. The FCC can deny a multimillion-dollar TV station a license renewal—a power that certainly sparks the interest of the National Association of Broadcasters. The FTC regulates business practices, ranging from credit and loans to mergers—a power that prompts both business and consumers to pay careful attention to its activities and membership.

So concerned are interest groups with these regulatory bodies that some critics speak of the "capture" of the regulators by the regulatees.[14] It is common for members of commissions to be recruited from the ranks of the regulated. Sometimes, too, members of commissions or staffs of these agencies move on to jobs in the very industries they were regulating. Some lawyers among them use contacts and information gleaned at the commission when they leave and represent clients before their former employers at the commission. A later section of this chapter discusses the bureaucracy's relationship with interest groups.

Government Corporations

government corporation
A government organization that, like business corporations, provides a service that could be delivered by the private sector and typically charges for its services. The U.S. Postal Service is an example. Compare **independent regulatory commission** and **independent executive agency**.

The federal government also has a handful of **government corporations.** These are not exactly like private corporations in which you can buy stock and collect dividends, but they are like private corporations—and different from other parts of the government—in two ways. First, they provide a service that could be handled by the private sector. Second, they typically charge for their services, though often at rates cheaper than those the consumer would pay to a private-sector producer.

The granddaddy of the government corporations is the Tennessee Valley Authority (TVA). Established in 1933 as part of the New Deal, it has controlled floods, improved navigation, protected the soil against erosion, and provided inexpensive electricity to millions of Americans in Tennessee, Kentucky, Alabama, and neighboring states. The post office, one of the original cabinet departments (first headed by Benjamin Franklin), has become the government's largest corporation: the U.S. Postal Service. Occasionally the government has taken over a "sick industry" and turned it into a government corporation. Amtrak, the railroad passenger service, is one example.

The Independent Executive Agencies

The **independent executive agencies** are essentially all the rest of the government—the agencies that are not cabinet departments, regulatory commissions, or government corporations. Their administrators typically are appointed by the president and serve at his will. Some 45 to 50 such agencies are listed in the current United States Government Manual. Among the biggest (in size of budget) are the following:

- *General Services Administration (GSA)*, the government's landlord, which handles buildings, supplies, and purchasing
- *National Science Foundation (NSF)*, the agency supporting scientific research
- *National Aeronautics and Space Administration (NASA)*, the agency that takes Americans to the moon and points beyond

independent executive agency
The government agencies not accounted for by **cabinet** departments, **independent regulatory commissions,** and **government corporations.** Administrators are typically appointed by the president and serve at the president's pleasure. NASA is an example.

Bureaucracies as Implementors

15.3 Identify the factors that influence the effectiveness of bureaucratic implementation of public policy.

Bureaucracies are essentially *implementors* of policy. They take congressional, presidential, and sometimes even judicial pronouncements and develop procedures and rules for implementing policy goals. They also manage the routines of government, from delivering mail to collecting taxes to training troops.

What Implementation Means

Public policies are rarely self-executing. Congress typically announces the goals of a policy in broad terms, sets up an administrative apparatus, and leaves the bureaucracy the task of working out the details of the program. In other words, the bureaucracy is left to implement the program. **Policy implementation** is the stage of policymaking between the establishment of a policy (such as the passage of a legislative act, the issuing of an executive order, the handing down of a judicial decision, or the promulgation of a regulatory rule) and the results of the policy for individuals.[15] In other words, implementation is a critical aspect of policymaking. At a minimum, implementation includes three elements:

1. Creation of a new agency or assignment of a new responsibility to an old agency
2. Translation of policy goals into operational rules and development of guidelines for the program
3. Coordination of resources and personnel to achieve the intended goals[16]

policy implementation
The stage of policymaking between the establishment of a policy and the consequences of the policy for the people affected. Implementation involves translating the goals and objectives of a policy into an operating, ongoing program.

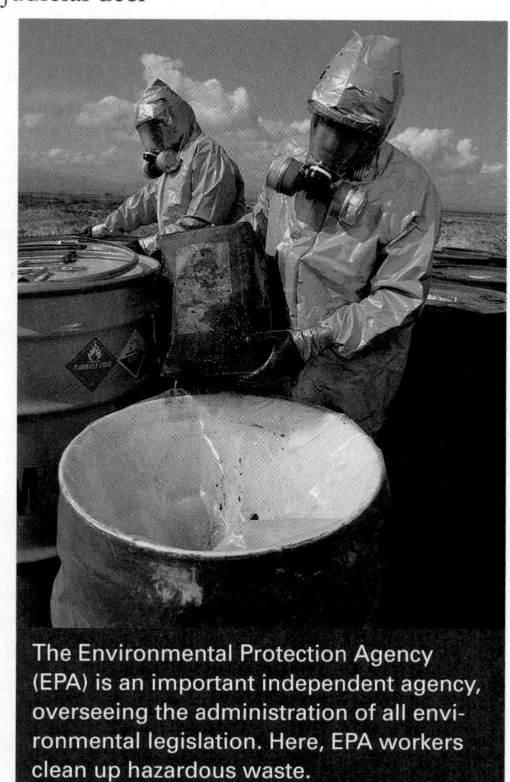

The Environmental Protection Agency (EPA) is an important independent agency, overseeing the administration of all environmental legislation. Here, EPA workers clean up hazardous waste.

Why the Best-Laid Plans Sometimes Flunk the Implementation Test

The Scottish poet Robert Burns once wrote, "The best laid schemes o' mice and men/Gang aft a-gley [often go awry]." So, too, with the best intended public policies. Policies that people expect to work often fail. Congress overwhelmingly passed a bill to guarantee health insurance to millions of Americans when they change or lose their jobs or lose coverage. Yet the law has been ineffective because insurance companies often charge these individuals premiums far higher than standard rates.[17] High expectations followed by dashed hopes are the frequent fate of well-intended public policies. Analysis reveals that implementation can break down for any of several reasons.

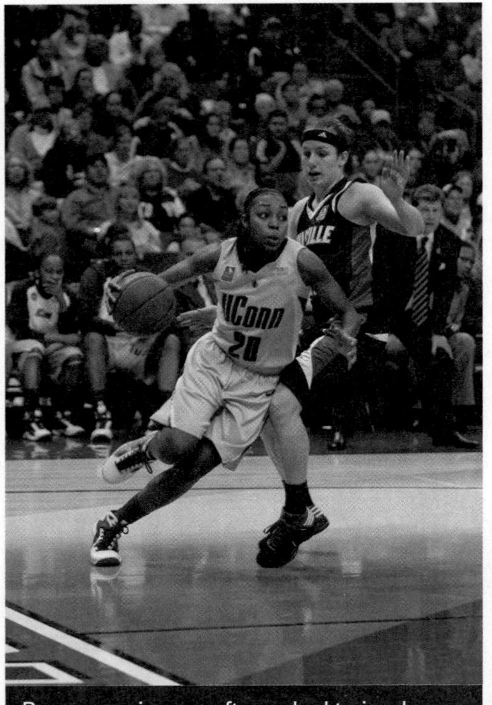

Bureaucracies are often asked to implement unclear laws. When Congress decided to prohibit gender discrimination in college athletics, for example, it left bureaucrats the task of creating guidelines that would end discrimination while addressing the diverse needs of different sports. It took years—and several lawsuits—to establish the law's meaning.

Program Design One reason implementation can break down is faulty program design. "It is impossible," said Eugene Bardach, "to implement well a policy or program that is defective in its basic theoretical conception." Consider, he suggested, the following hypothetical example:

> If Congress were to establish an agency charged with squaring the circle with compass and straight edge—a task mathematicians have long ago shown is impossible—we could envision an agency coming into being, hiring a vast number of consultants, commissioning studies, reporting that progress was being made, while at the same time urging in their appropriations request for the coming year that the Congress augment the agency's budget.

And the circle would remain round.[18]

Lack of Clarity Congress is fond of stating a broad policy goal in legislation and then leaving implementation up to the bureaucracies. Members of Congress can thus escape messy details and place blame for the implementation decisions elsewhere (see "Young People and Politics: Drug Offenses and Financial Aid").

Such was the case with the controversial Title IX of the Education Act of 1972,[19] which said, "No person in the United States shall, on the basis of sex, be excluded from participation in, be denied the benefits of, or be subjected to discrimination under any education program or activity receiving federal financial assistance." Because almost every college and university receives some federal financial assistance, almost all were thereby forbidden to discriminate on the basis of gender. Interest groups supporting women's athletics convinced Congress to include a provision about college athletics. Thus, Section 844 reads,

> The Secretary of [Health, Education, and Welfare (HEW) then, today of Education] shall prepare and publish . . . proposed regulations implementing the provisions of Title IX . . . relating to prohibition of sex discrimination in Federally assisted education programs which shall include with respect to intercollegiate athletic activities reasonable provisions considering the nature of the particular sports.

Just what does this section mean? Proponents of women's athletics thought it meant that discrimination against women's sports was also prohibited. Some, with good reason, looked forward to seeing women's sports funded on an equal footing with men's. A member of the House–Senate Conference Committee, however, proposed language specifically excluding from consideration "revenue-producing athletics," meaning men's football and basketball. The committee rejected this suggestion, but to colleges and universities with big-time athletic programs and to some alumni, the vague Section 844 called for equality in golf and swimming, not men's football and basketball programs, which could continue to have the lion's share of athletic budgets.

Joseph Califano, President Carter's secretary of HEW, was the man in the middle on this tricky problem. His staff developed a "policy interpretation" of the legislation that he announced in December 1978. HEW's interpretation of the 100 or so words of Section 844 of Title IX numbered 30 pages. The interpretation recognized that football was "unique" among college sports. If football was unique, then the interpretation implied (but did not directly say) that male-dominated football programs could continue to outspend women's athletic programs.

Supporters of equal budgets for male and female athletics were outraged. Charlotte West of the Association for Intercollegiate Athletics for Women called HEW's interpretation "a multitude of imprecise and confusing explanations, exceptions, and caveats." Even the football-oriented National Collegiate Athletic Association was wary of the interpretation. One of its lawyers allowed, "They are trying to be fair. The

Drug Offenses and Financial Aid

In 1998, Congress included in a law governing financial aid for college students a provision that prohibited students convicted of drug offenses from receiving grants and loans from the federal government—even if the offense was relatively minor or the conviction happened years ago. A student convicted of a drug offense as an adult could be denied financial aid from one year to life, depending on the number of offenses and severity of conviction. Not surprisingly, the provision became a matter of contention.

The provision itself might seem a bit severe, but there is more. Someone convicted of armed robbery, rape, or even murder, once out of prison, is entitled to government grants and loans with no questions asked. And yet drug offenses were enough to deny tens of thousands of would-be college students financial aid.

Members of Congress accused the Department of Education, under Clinton and Bush, of distorting the law's intent. They argued that the department, which administers financial aid programs, was being too strict in its interpretation. The department responded that Congress had written a vague law—one that simply referred to "a student who has been convicted," and that it was faithfully implementing the letter of the law. In effect, the department argued that it had no discretion in the matter and could not act on its own to make financial aid policy more just.

The George W. Bush administration suggested ending the prohibition on aid for those who violated drug laws before entering college. However, it wanted to continue the aid ban for those who commit such crimes while enrolled in college. Its goal, the administration said, was to discourage students from using drugs. The problem, as others saw it, was that such a rule would still impose stiffer penalties for drug use than for any other crime. It would also have the effect of barring some first-time, minor offenders from getting financial aid while restoring it for more serious drug lawbreakers.

Eight years after passing the original ban on financial aid for drug use, Congress revised the law. The new statute allowed students with past drug convictions to receive student aid, but current students who are convicted of drug offenses will still lose their federal aid—for a year for a first offense, two years for a second offense, and indefinitely for a third offense.

Anticipating implementation problems is difficult. Putting together coalitions within Congress is also difficult. One consequence of these difficulties is that laws are often vague—and often have unintended consequences as well.

QUESTIONS FOR DISCUSSION

- How much discretion should a bureaucratic unit have to correct injustices in laws?
- Why is it so difficult for Congress to anticipate problems implementing laws?

question is how successful they are." A 100-word section in a congressional statute, which prompted a 30-page interpretation by the bureaucracy, in turn prompted scores of court cases. The courts have had to rule on such matters as whether Title IX requires that exactly equivalent dollar amounts be spent on women's and men's athletics. Litigation continues to this day.

The complex case of implementing Title IX for intercollegiate athletics contains an important lesson: Policy problems that Congress cannot resolve are not likely to be easily resolved by bureaucracies.

Bureaucrats receive not only unclear orders but also contradictory ones. James Q. Wilson points out that the Immigration and Naturalization Service (INS) was supposed to keep out illegal immigrants but let in necessary agricultural workers, to carefully screen foreigners seeking to enter the country but facilitate the entry of foreign tourists, and to find and expel undocumented aliens but not break up families, impose hardships, violate civil rights, or deprive employers of low-paid workers. "No organization can accomplish all of these goals well, especially when advocates of each have the power to mount newspaper and congressional investigations of the agency's 'failures.'"[20] Similarly, Congress has ordered the National Park Service to preserve the environmental quality of national parks *and* to keep the parks accessible to tourists. The Forest

Service is supposed to help timber companies exploit the lumber potential in the national forests *and* to preserve the natural environment.

Lack of Resources As noted earlier, we often hear the charge that bureaucracies are bloated. The important issue, however, is not the size of the bureaucracy in the abstract but whether it is the appropriate size for the job the bureaucracy has been assigned to do.[21] As big as a bureaucracy may seem in the aggregate, it frequently lacks the staff—along with the necessary staff training, funding, supplies, and equipment—to carry out the tasks it has been assigned. Recently, for example, the news has been filled with stories of serious problems, many of them ongoing, such as the following:

- U.S. troops in Iraq had insufficient numbers of body armor and armored Humvees and trucks to protect them against roadside bombs.
- After the invasion of Iraq in March 2003, the United States had too few troops to devote to fighting the Taliban in Afghanistan.
- Although 80 percent of the nation's drug supply and a large percentage of its medical devices and food are now imported, the Federal Drug Administration lacks the personnel and computer systems to identify, much less inspect, the plants producing these items.
- Because of a lack of funding, the popular Head Start program serves only about half the children who are eligible to participate.
- Because of a lack of personnel, the Social Security Administration takes well over a year to process claims for Disability Insurance.
- The U.S. Immigration and Customs Enforcement (ICE) lacks the personnel to track most of the millions of aliens who overstay their visas or engage in suspicious activities. The ICE also lacks the resources even to identify, much less deport, more than 10 percent of the 200,000 convicted criminal aliens in the United States.
- In their inspections of facilities handling and storing hazardous wastes, inadequately trained inspectors for the Environmental Protection Agency (EPA) overlooked more than half the serious violations. The computer system the EPA uses to track and control water pollution is obsolete and full of faulty data and does not take into account thousands of significant pollution sources.
- The FBI headquarters lacks computers that would allow the agency to search its own databases for multiple terms such as "aviation" and "schools," which would have helped in identifying the 9/11 terrorists. Only about 50 agents can converse in Arabic, and the agency has a serious shortage of translators for intercepted communications.
- National Guard units have only a third of the equipment they need to respond to domestic disasters and terrorist attacks.
- The Federal Aviation Administration (FAA) lacks the proper personnel and equipment to direct the nation's air traffic safely.
- The Department of Homeland Security could not deploy new machines for detecting smuggled nuclear bombs because the United States had run out of a crucial element, helium 3.
- The IRS lacks the appropriate computer systems to integrate the dozens of databases that contain the information necessary to collect the more than $2 trillion in taxes that finance the federal government.
- There is a shortage of epidemiologists who are trained to recognize and investigate the outbreak of infectious disease.

Why does Congress not simply give the bureaucracies more resources? Some well-organized interests fight against adding resources to certain agencies because they do not wish to be inspected or regulated and prefer an ineffective bureaucracy. Equally important is the battle over scarce budgetary resources. Pressures to allocate personnel to direct services—for example, to the provision of agricultural expertise to farmers—limit the staff available to implement other policies. In addition, the irresistible urge of policymakers to provide services to the public helps to ensure that the bureaucracies will have more programs than they have resources to adequately implement. Finally, in an age when "big government" is under attack, there are strong political incentives to downsize government bureaucracy.

WHY IT MATTERS

Bureaucratic Resources

A case can be made that some bureaucracies are too small. It is likely that a substantial increase in the resources available to those who implement policies would result in improved quality of government services and in the increased ability of agencies to appropriately implement the policies established by Congress and the president.

Agencies may also lack the *authority* necessary to meet their responsibilities. In 2008, we learned that the Securities and Exchange Commission's supervision of Wall Street's largest investment banks was on a "voluntary" basis. Another example is provided by the FDA, which, according to many observers, lacks adequate powers to protect the public from dangerous drugs such as the sleeping pill Halcion and the sedative Versed. The FDA does no testing of its own and must rely entirely on the test results submitted by manufacturers. Yet it lacks the subpoena power to obtain documents when it suspects that drug companies are withholding data about adverse drug reactions or misrepresenting test results. It often lacks access even to company documents used as evidence in private product-liability cases. Similarly, the Department of Agriculture lacks authority to close meat processing plants—even those with serious violations of food safety standards.

As we saw in Chapter 3, many policies are implemented by state and local governments. The federal government may try to influence elementary and secondary education, for example, but it is the state and local governments that provide the actual services. Federal influence over these governments is indirect, at best. Other policies, ranging from safety in the workplace to pollution control, are implemented by thousands of private individuals, groups, and businesses.[22] With such implementers, bureaucrats are more likely to request, educate, and negotiate than to issue orders and institute legal proceedings.

Administrative Routine For most bureaucrats, administration is a routine matter most of the time. They follow **standard operating procedures**, better known as SOPs, to help them make numerous everyday decisions. Standard rules save time. If a Social Security caseworker had to take the time to invent a new rule for every potential client and clear it at higher levels, few clients would be served. Thus, agencies write detailed manuals to cover as many particular situations as officials can anticipate. The regulations elaborating the Internal Revenue Code compose an IRS agent's bible. Similarly, a customs agent has binders filled with rules and regulations about what can and cannot be brought into the United States duty free.

standard operating procedures
Better known as SOPs, these procedures for everyday decision making enable bureaucrats to bring efficiency and uniformity to the running of complex organizations. Uniformity promotes fairness and makes personnel interchangeable. See also **administrative discretion**.

In addition, SOPs bring uniformity to complex organizations. Justice is better served when officials apply rules uniformly, as in the implementation of welfare policies that distribute benefits to the needy or in the levying of fines for underpayment of taxes. Uniformity also makes personnel interchangeable. The army, for example, can transfer soldiers to any spot in the world, and they can find out how to do their job by referring to the appropriate manual.

Routines are essential to bureaucracy. Yet, when not appropriate to a situation, they can become frustrating "red tape" or even potentially dangerous obstacles to action. An October 1983 terrorist attack on their barracks outside Beirut, Lebanon, killed 241 Marines while they slept. A presidential commission appointed to examine the causes of the tragedy concluded that, among other factors, the Marines in the peacekeeping force were "not trained, organized, staffed, or supported to deal effectively with the terrorist threat."[23] In other words, they had not altered their SOPs regarding security, which is basic to any military unit, to meet the unique challenges of a terrorist attack.

The FAA's protocols (routines) for hijackings assumed that the pilot of a hijacked aircraft would notify an air traffic controller that there had been a hijacking, that the FAA could identify the plane, that there would be time for the FAA and NORAD (North American Aerospace Defense Command) to address the issue, and that the hijacking would not be a suicide mission. As the 9/11 Commission put it, these SOPs were "unsuited in every respect" for the 9/11 terrorist hijackings.[24]

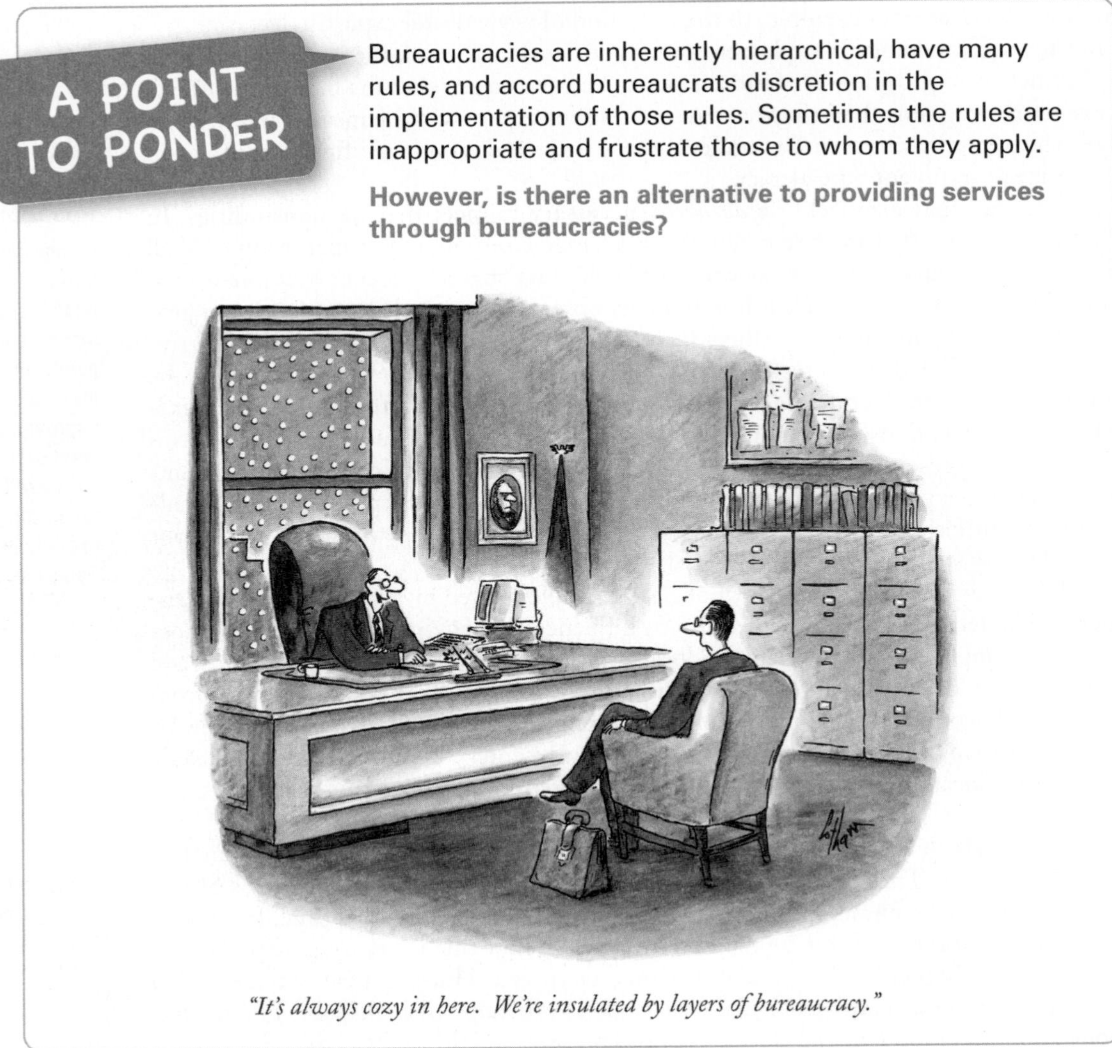

A POINT TO PONDER
Bureaucracies are inherently hierarchical, have many rules, and accord bureaucrats discretion in the implementation of those rules. Sometimes the rules are inappropriate and frustrate those to whom they apply.
However, is there an alternative to providing services through bureaucracies?

"It's always cozy in here. We're insulated by layers of bureaucracy."

Sometimes an agency simply fails to establish routines that are necessary to complete its tasks. For example, in late 1997, the General Accounting Office found that the FAA failed to determine whether the violations its inspectors uncovered at aircraft repair stations were ever corrected. The FAA did not keep the proper paperwork for adequate follow-up activities.

Administrators' Dispositions Paradoxically, bureaucrats operate not only within the confines of routines, but often with considerable discretion to behave independently. **Administrative discretion** is the authority of administrative actors to select among various responses to a given problem.[25] Discretion is greatest when rules do not fit a particular case, and this is often the case—even in agencies with elaborate rules and regulations.

administrative discretion The authority of administrative actors to select among various responses to a given problem. Discretion is greatest when routines, or **standard operating procedures**, do not fit a case.

Some administrators exercise more discretion than others. Michael Lipsky coined the phrase **street-level bureaucrats** to refer to those bureaucrats who are in constant contact with the public (often a hostile one) and have considerable discretion; they include police officers, welfare workers, and lower-court judges.[26] No amount of rules, not even in the thousands of pages as with IRS rules, will eliminate the need for bureaucratic discretion on some policies. It is up to the highway patrol officer who stops you to choose whether to issue you a warning or a ticket.

street-level bureaucrats A phrase coined by Michael Lipsky, referring to those bureaucrats who are in constant contact with the public and have considerable **administrative discretion**.

Ultimately, the way bureaucrats use discretion depends on their dispositions toward the policies and rules they administer. Some of these policies and rules may conflict with their views or their personal or organizational interests. When people are asked to execute orders with which they do not agree, slippage is likely to occur between policy decisions and performance. A great deal of mischief may occur as well.

On one occasion, President Nixon ordered Secretary of Defense Melvin Laird to bomb a Palestine Liberation Organization hideaway, a move Laird opposed. According to the secretary, "We had bad weather for forty-eight hours. The Secretary of Defense can always find a reason not to do something."[27] The president's order was stalled for days and eventually rescinded.

Controlling the exercise of discretion is a difficult task. It is not easy to fire bureaucrats in the civil service, and removing appointed officials may be politically embarrassing to the president, especially if those officials have strong support in Congress and among interest groups. In the private sector, leaders of organizations provide incentives such as pay raises to encourage employees to perform their tasks in a certain way. In the public sector, however, special bonuses are rare, and pay raises tend to be small and across the board. Moreover, there is not necessarily room at the top for qualified bureaucrats. Unlike a typical private business, a government agency cannot expand just because it is performing a service effectively and efficiently.

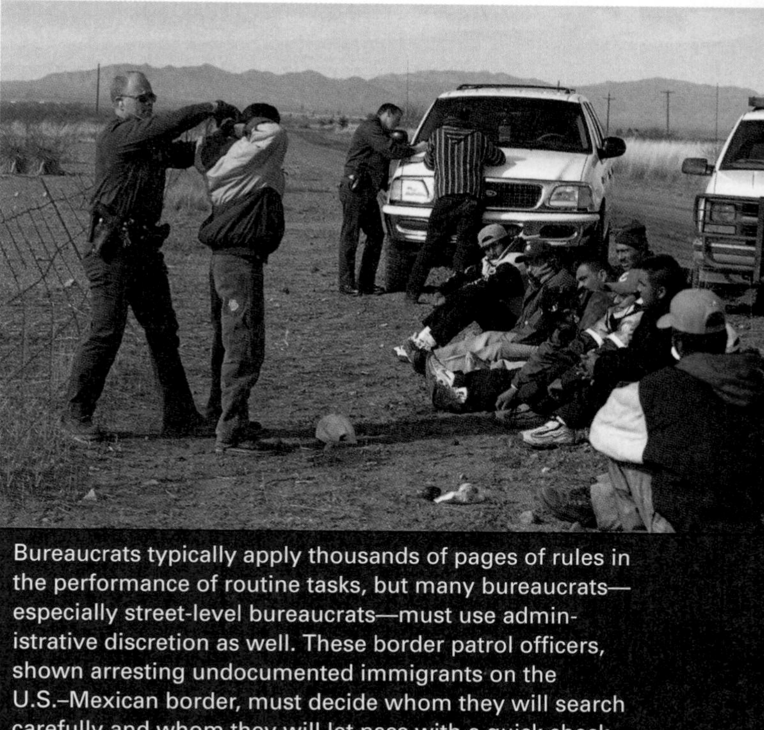

Bureaucrats typically apply thousands of pages of rules in the performance of routine tasks, but many bureaucrats—especially street-level bureaucrats—must use administrative discretion as well. These border patrol officers, shown arresting undocumented immigrants on the U.S.–Mexican border, must decide whom they will search carefully and whom they will let pass with a quick check.

In the absence of positive and negative incentives, the government relies heavily on rules to limit the discretion of implementors. As former Vice President Al Gore put it in a report issued by the National Performance Review,

> Because we don't want politicians' families, friends, and supporters placed in "no-show" jobs, we have more than 100,000 pages of personnel rules and regulations defining in exquisite detail how to hire, promote, or fire federal employees. Because we don't want employees or private companies profiteering from federal contracts, we create procurement processes that require endless signatures and long months to buy almost anything. Because we don't want agencies using tax dollars for any unapproved purpose, we dictate precisely how much they can spend on everything from telephones to travel.[28]

Often these rules end up creating new obstacles to effective and efficient governing, however. As U.S. forces were streaming toward the Persian Gulf in the fall of 1990 to liberate Kuwait from Iraq, the air force placed an emergency order for 6,000 Motorola commercial radio receivers. But Motorola refused to do business with the air force because of a government requirement that the company set up separate accounting and cost-control systems to fill the order. The only way the U.S. Air Force could acquire the much-needed receivers was for Japan to buy them and donate them to the United States!

Fragmentation Sometimes, as we saw in the regulation of food, responsibility for a policy is dispersed among several units within the bureaucracy. The federal government has had as many as 96 agencies involved with the issue of nuclear proliferation. Similarly, in the field of welfare, 10 different departments and agencies administer more than 100 federal human services programs. The Department of Health and Human Services has responsibility for basic welfare grants to the states to aid families, the Department of Housing and Urban Development provides housing assistance for the poor, the Department of Agriculture runs the food stamp program, and the Department of Labor administers training programs and provides assistance in obtaining employment.

The resources and authority necessary for the president to attack a problem comprehensively are often distributed among many bureaucratic units. In 2009, the National Security Agency, the State Department, and the CIA had separate bits of information that Umar Farouk Abdulmutallab was a potential threat to the United

States. Nevertheless, on Christmas Day he was allowed to board a plane to the United States with explosives hidden in his underclothing. The agencies had failed to share and "connect the dots" among the various pieces of information.

More broadly, consider border security, an important element of homeland security. Table 15.2 lists the agencies with responsibilities for border control in 2002, prior to the establishment of the Department of Homeland Security. As you can see, at least 33 departments and agencies had responsibility for protecting America's borders, focusing on threats ranging from illegal immigrants and chemical toxins to missiles and electronic sabotage. It is difficult to coordinate so many different agencies, especially

TABLE 15.2 Departments and Agencies with Responsibility for Border Security in 2002

Department of Agriculture
Animal and Plant Health Inspection Service
Central Intelligence Agency
Department of Commerce
Critical Infrastructure Assurance Office
National Oceanic and Atmospheric Administration
Department of Defense
Defense Intelligence Agency
Inspector General
National Guard
National Reconnaissance Office
National Security Agency
North American Aerospace Defense Command
Department of Energy
Office of Science and Technology Policy
Environmental Protection Agency
Office of International Activities
Department of Justice
Bureau of Alcohol, Tobacco, and Firearms
Drug Enforcement Administration
Federal Bureau of Investigation
Immigration and Naturalization Service
Marshals Service
Office of Special Investigations
Department of State
Bureau of Consular Affairs
Bureau of Intelligence and Research
Bureau of Population, Refugees, and Migration
Bureau for International Narcotics and Law Enforcement Agencies
Passport Office
Postal Service
Department of Treasury
Customs Service
Financial Crimes Enforcement Network
Internal Revenue Service
Office of the Inspector General
Secret Service
Department of Transportation
Coast Guard
Federal Aviation Administration
Federal Motor Carrier Administration
Maritime Administration

when they lack a history of trust and cooperation. Moreover, there are often physical obstacles to cooperation, such as the largely incompatible computer systems of the ICE and the Coast Guard. Once the borders have been breached and an attack has occurred, many other offices get involved in homeland security, including hundreds of state and local agencies.

If fragmentation is a problem, why not reorganize the government? The answer lies in hyperpluralism and the decentralization of power. Congressional committees recognize that they would lose jurisdiction over agencies if these agencies were merged with others. Interest groups do not want to give up the close relationships they have developed with "their" agencies. Agencies themselves do not want to be submerged within a broader bureaucratic unit. Moreover, as with the agencies listed in Table 15.2, most bureaucratic units have multiple responsibilities, making it difficult to subsume them under one organizational umbrella. All these forces fight reorganization, and they usually win.[29] President Clinton's proposal to merge the Drug Enforcement Administration and the Customs Service, two of the agencies in Table 15.2, met with immediate opposition from the agencies and their congressional allies. Pursuing the merger became too costly for the president, who had to focus on higher-priority issues.

Nevertheless, under the right conditions, reorganization is possible. Following the attacks of September 11, 2001, President George W. Bush concluded, in the summer of 2002, that the only way to overcome the fragmentation of agencies involved in providing homeland security was to create a new department, one that combined many of the agencies listed in Table 15.2. Congress created the Department of Homeland Security at the end of 2002, the largest reorganization of the federal government in half a century.

Fragmentation not only disperses responsibility but also allows agencies to work at cross-purposes. For years, one agency supported tobacco farmers while another discouraged smoking. One agency encouraged the redevelopment of inner cities while another helped build highways making it easier for people to live in the suburbs. One agency helped farmers grow crops more efficiently while another paid them to produce less. As long as Congress refuses to make clear decisions about priorities, bureaucrats will implement contradictory policies.

A Case Study of Successful Implementation: The Voting Rights Act of 1965

Even when a policy is controversial, implementation can be effective if goals are clear and there are adequate means to achieve them. In 1965, Congress, responding to generations of discrimination against prospective African American voters in the South, passed the Voting Rights Act. The act outlawed literacy tests and other tests previously used to discriminate against African American registrants. Congress singled out six states in the Deep South in which the number of registered African American voters was minuscule and ordered the Justice Department to send federal registrars to each county in those states to register qualified voters. Those who interfered with the work of federal registrars were to face stiff penalties.

Congress charged the attorney general, as the head of the Justice Department, with implementing the Voting Rights Act. He acted quickly and dispatched hundreds of registrars—some protected by U.S. marshals—to Southern counties. Within seven and a half months of the act's passage, more than 300,000 new African American voters were on the rolls. The proportion of African Americans in the South who were registered to vote increased from 43 percent in 1964 to 66 percent in 1970, partly because of the Voting Rights Act.[30]

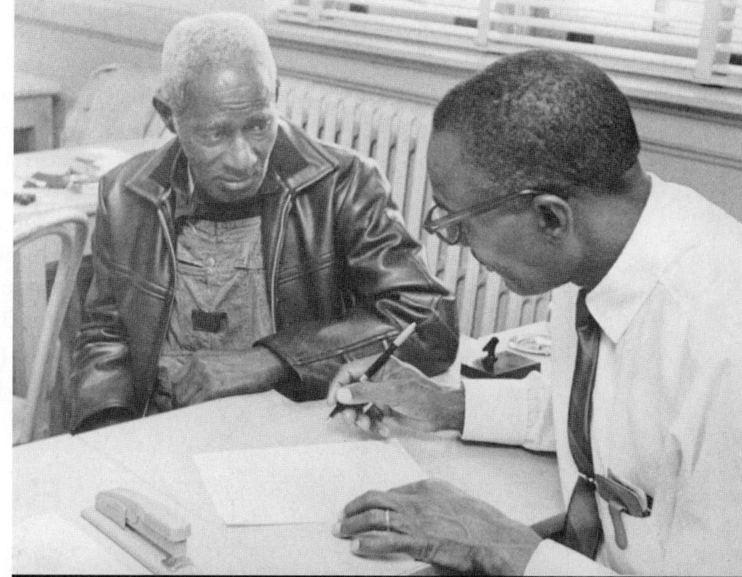

The Voting Rights Act of 1965 was successfully implemented because its goal was clear: to register African Americans to vote in Southern counties where their voting rights had been denied for years. In addition, implementators had the authority to do the job. This federal registrar, along with hundreds of others working for the Department of Justice, helped bring the vote to some 300,000 African Americans in less than a year.

The Voting Rights Act was a successful case of implementation by any standard, but not because it was popular with everyone. Southern representatives and senators were outraged by the bill, and a filibuster had delayed its passage in the Senate. It was successful because its goal was clear (to register large numbers of African American voters), its implementation was straightforward (sending out people to register them), and the authority of the implementors was clear (they had the support of the attorney general and even U.S. marshals) and concentrated in the Justice Department, which was disposed to implementing the law vigorously.

Privatization

A movement to "reinvent government" started in the 1980s. At the heart of this endeavor were efforts to decentralize authority within agencies to provide more room for innovation and to provide performance incentives for government bureaucracies through market competition with private contractors, which could bid to provide government services. Since that time private contractors have become a virtual fourth branch of the national government, which spends nearly half a trillion dollars a year on them. The war in Iraq, increased emphasis on domestic security, and the aftermath of Hurricane Katrina all gave this trend a further impetus.

Everyone seems to agree that the government cannot operate without contractors, which provide the surge capacity to handle crises without expanding the permanent bureaucracy. Moreover, contractors may provide specialized skills that the government lacks. Some government executives favor contractors because they find the federal bureaucracy slow, inflexible or incompetent. Using contractors also allows officials to brag about cutting the federal work force while actually expanding the number of people working for the government.[31]

The theory behind contracting for services is that competition in the private sector will result in better service at lower costs than that provided by public bureaucracies, who have traditionally had a monopoly on providing services. Although there is evidence that some local governments have saved money on services such as garbage collection, there is no evidence that private contractors have provided services more efficiently at the federal level. Moreover, competition is not always present. One study found that fewer than half of the new contracts and payments against existing contracts are now subject to full and open competition.[32] For example, the government has spent billions of dollars in no-bid contracts for companies such as Halliburton to rebuild Iraq.

Contracting also almost always leads to less public scrutiny, as government programs are hidden behind closed corporate doors. Companies, unlike agencies, are not subject to the Freedom of Information Act, which allows the public to gain access to government documents. Members of Congress have sought unsuccessfully for years to get the Army to explain the contracts for Blackwater USA security officers in Iraq, which involve several costly layers of subcontractors. Partly because of the relative lack of openness, efforts to privatize public services have been marked by extensive corruption and sometimes by extensive cost overruns.

15.4 Describe how bureaucracies regulate, and assess deregulation and alternative approaches to regulation.

Bureaucracies as Regulators

regulation
The use of governmental authority to control or change some practice in the private sector.

Government **regulation** is the use of governmental authority to control or change some practice in the private sector. Regulations by government, filling hundreds of volumes, pervade Americans' everyday lives and the lives of businesses, universities, hospitals, and other institutions. (You can see the trend in the volume of regulations in "A Generation of Change: Trends in Regulation.") Regulation may be the most controversial role of the bureaucracies. Congress gives bureaucrats broad mandates to regulate activities as diverse as interest rates, the location of nuclear power plants, and food additives.

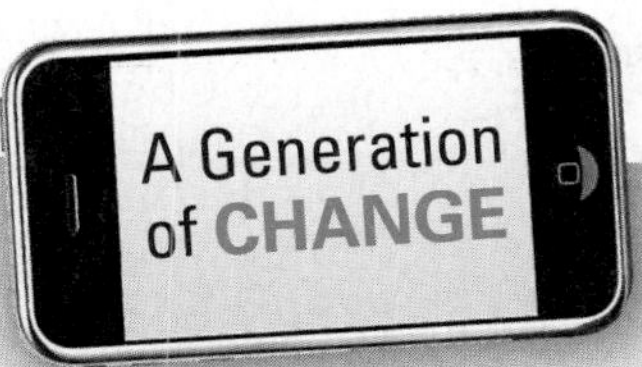

Trends in Regulation

Some people call the *Federal Register* the bureaucracy's bulletin board because it is where new regulations are posted. You can see that the number of pages of regulations fell sharply in 1981 at the beginning of the Reagan administration and then gradually increased. Every White House wants to put its stamp on regulatory policies.

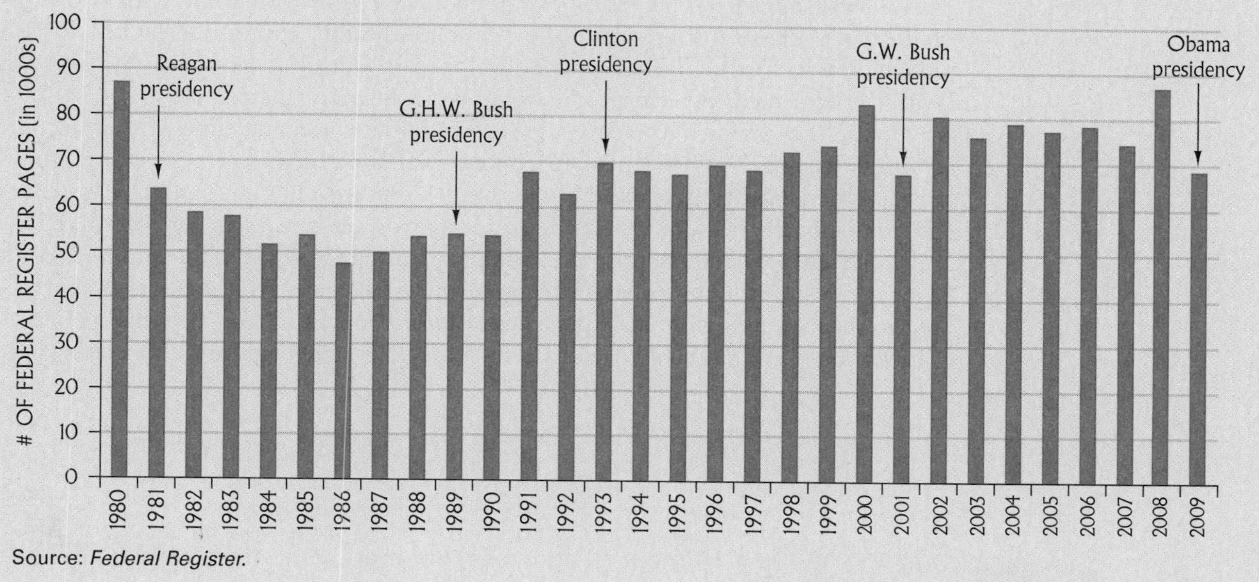

Source: *Federal Register*.

Regulation in the Economy and in Everyday Life

The notion that the American economy is largely a "free enterprise" system, unfettered by government intervention, is about as up to date as a Model T Ford. You can begin to understand the sweeping scope of governmental regulation by examining how the automobile industry is regulated:

- The Securities and Exchange Commission regulates buying and selling stock in an automobile corporation.
- Relations between the workers and managers of the company come under the scrutiny of the National Labor Relations Board.
- The Department of Labor and the Equal Employment Opportunity Commission mandate affirmative action in hiring workers in automobile production plants because automakers are major government contractors.
- The EPA, the National Highway Traffic Safety Administration, and the Department of Transportation require that cars include pollution-control, energy-saving, and safety devices.
- Unfair advertising and deceptive consumer practices in marketing cars come under the watchful eye of the FTC.

From the beginnings of the American republic until 1887, the federal government made almost no regulatory policies. The little regulation that was produced originated with state and local authorities, and opponents disputed even the minimal regulatory powers of state and local governments. In 1877, the Supreme Court upheld the right of government to regulate the business operations of a firm. The case, *Munn v. Illinois*, involved the right of the state of Illinois to regulate the charges and services of a Chicago warehouse. Farmers at this time were seething about alleged overcharging by railroads, grain elevator companies, and other business firms. In 1887—a decade after *Munn*—Congress created the first regulatory agency, the Interstate Commerce Commission (ICC), and charged it with regulating the railroads, their prices, and their services to farmers; the ICC thus set the precedent for regulatory policymaking.

As regulators, bureaucratic agencies typically operate with a large grant of power from Congress, which may detail goals to be achieved but permit the agencies to sketch out the regulatory means. In 1935, for example, Congress created the National Labor Relations Board to control "unfair labor practices," but the NLRB had to play a major role in defining "fair" and "unfair." Most agencies charged with regulation must first develop a set of rules, often called *guidelines*. The appropriate agency may specify how much food coloring it will permit in a hot dog, how many contaminants it will allow an industry to dump into a stream, how much radiation from a nuclear reactor is too much, and so forth. Guidelines are developed in consultation with—and sometimes with the agreement of—the people or industries being regulated.

Next, the agency must apply and enforce its rules and guidelines, either in court or through its own administrative procedures. Sometimes it waits for complaints to come to it, as the Equal Employment Opportunity Commission does; sometimes it sends inspectors into the field, as OSHA does; and sometimes it requires application for a permit or license to demonstrate performance consistent with congressional goals and agency rules, as the FCC does. Often government agencies take violators to court, hoping to secure a judgment and fine against an offender (see "You Are the Policymaker: How Should We Regulate?"). Whatever strategy Congress permits a regulating agency

A POINT TO PONDER

Almost all agencies, not merely the ones called independent regulatory commissions, issue regulations. These regulations pervade everyday life.

It is easy to complain about regulations, but would we really want to give them up?

Source: Frank Cotham, *The New Yorker,* March 17, 1997.

YOU ARE THE POLICYMAKER

How Should We Regulate?

Almost every regulatory policy was created to achieve some desirable social goal. When more than 6,000 people are killed annually in industrial accidents, who would disagree with the goal of a safer workplace? Who would dissent from greater highway safety, when more than 40,000 die each year in automobile accidents? Who would disagree with policies to promote equality in hiring, given the history of discrimination against women and minorities in the workplace? Who would disagree with policies to reduce industrial pollution, when pollution threatens health and lives? However, there may be more than one way to achieve these—and many other—desirable social goals.

On reviewing the regulatory activities of the EPA and OSHA, Charles L. Schultze, who chaired President Carter's Council of Economic Advisors, concluded that neither agency's policies had worked very well. He described their regulations as **command-and-control policy**: The government tells business how to reach certain goals, checks that these commands are followed, and punishes offenders.

Schultze advocated an **incentive system**. He argued that instead of telling construction businesses how their ladders must be constructed, measuring the ladders, and charging a small fine for violators, it would be more efficient and effective to levy a high tax on firms with excessive worker injuries. Instead of trying to develop standards for about 100,000 pollution sources, it would be easier and more effective to levy a high tax on those who cause pollution. The government could even provide incentives in the form of rewards for such socially valuable behavior as developing technology to reduce pollution. Incentives, Schultze argued, use marketlike strategies to regulate industry and are more effective and efficient than command-and-control regulation.

Not everyone is as keen on the use of incentives. Defenders of the command-and-control system of regulation compare the present system to preventive medicine—it is designed to minimize pollution or workplace accidents before they become too severe. Defenders of the system argue, too, that penalties for excessive pollution or excessive workplace accidents would be imposed only after substantial damage had been done. They add that if taxes on pollution or unsafe work environments were merely externalized (that is, passed along to the consumer as higher prices), they would not be much of a deterrent. Moreover, it would take a large bureaucracy to carefully monitor the level of pollution discharged, and it would require a complex calculation to determine the level of tax necessary to encourage businesses not to pollute.

What do you think? The issue of the manner of regulation is a complex one. Is the command-and-control system the best way of achieving regulatory goals, or might an incentive system be more effective?

Source: Charles L. Schultze, *The Public Use of the Private Interest* (Washington, DC: Brookings Institution, 1977); Steven Kelman, *What Price Incentives? Economists and the Environment* (Boston: Auburn House, 1981).

to use, all regulation contains these elements: (1) *a grant of power and set of directions from Congress*, (2) *a set of rules and guidelines* by the regulatory agency itself, and (3) *some means of enforcing compliance* with congressional goals and agency regulations.

Government regulation of the American economy and society has grown in recent decades. The budgets of regulatory agencies, their level of employment, and the number of rules they issue have all been increasing—and have done so even during conservative administrations. As we have seen, few niches in American society are *not* affected by regulation. Not surprisingly, this situation has led to charges that government is overdoing it.

command-and-control policy
The typical system of **regulation** whereby government tells business how to reach certain goals, checks that these commands are followed, and punishes offenders. Compare **incentive system**.

incentive system
An alternative to **command-and-control**, with marketlike strategies such as rewards used to manage public policy.

deregulation
The lifting of government restrictions on business, industry, and professional activities.

Deregulation

With the growth of regulation, **deregulation**—the lifting of government restrictions on business, industry, and professional activities—became a fashionable term.[33] The idea behind deregulation is that the number and complexity of regulatory policies have made regulation too complicated and burdensome. To critics, regulation distorts market forces and has the following problems:

- ***Raising prices.*** If the producer is faced with expensive regulations, the cost will inevitably be passed on to the consumer in the form of higher prices.

- ***Hurting America's competitive position abroad.*** Other nations may have fewer regulations on pollution, worker safety, and other business practices than the United States. Thus, American products may cost more in the international marketplace, undermining sales in other countries.
- ***Failing to work well.*** Tales of failed regulatory policies are numerous. Regulations may be difficult or cumbersome to enforce. Critics charge that regulations sometimes do not achieve the results that Congress intended and maintain that they simply create massive regulatory bureaucracies.

Not everyone, however, believes that deregulation is in the nation's best interest.[34] For example, critics point to severe environmental damage resulting from lax enforcement of environmental protection standards during the Reagan administration. Similarly, many observers attribute much of the blame for the enormously expensive bailout of the savings and loan industry in 1989 to deregulation in the 1980s. Californians found that deregulation led to severe power shortages in 2001. The burst of the real estate bubble in 2007 and 2008 and the resulting financial crisis and bailouts led to demands for increased regulation of financial institutions.

In addition, many regulations have proved beneficial to Americans. To give just a few examples, as a result of government regulations, we breathe cleaner air,[35] we have lower levels of lead in our blood, miners are safer at work,[36] seacoasts have been preserved,[37] and children are more likely to survive infancy.[38]

15.5 Assess means of controlling unelected bureaucrats in American democracy and the impact of the bureaucracy on the scope of government.

Understanding Bureaucracies

As both implementors and regulators, bureaucracies are making public policy, not just administering someone else's decisions. The fact that bureaucrats, who are not elected, compose most of the government raises fundamental issues about who controls governing and about the proper role of bureaucracies.

Bureaucracy and Democracy

Bureaucracies constitute one of America's two unelected policymaking institutions (courts, which we look at in Chapter 16, being the other). In democratic theory, popular control of government depends on elections, but we could not possibly elect the millions of federal civilian and military employees, or even the few thousand top bureaucrats, though they spend more than $3 trillion of the American gross domestic product. Furthermore, the fact that voters do not elect civil servants does not mean that bureaucracies cannot respond to and represent the public's interests. And as we saw earlier, in their backgrounds, bureaucrats are more representative of the American people than are elected officials. Much depends on whether bureaucracies are effectively controlled by the policymakers citizens do elect—the president and Congress.[39]

Presidents Try to Control the Bureaucracy Chapter 13 looked at some of the frustrations presidents endure in trying to control the government they are elected to run. Presidents try hard—not always with success—to impose their policy preferences on agencies (although their frustrations might be less than those of leaders in some other countries, as you can see from "America in Perspective: Influencing Independent Agencies"). Following are some of their tactics:

- ***Appoint the right people to head the agency.*** Normally, presidents control the appointments of agency heads and subheads. Putting their people in charge is one good way for presidents to influence agency policy,[40] yet even this can have its problems. President Reagan's efforts to whittle the powers of the EPA led him to appoint as its head the controversial Anne Gorsuch, who had previously supported policies contrary to the agency's goals. When she attempted to implement her policies, legal squabbles with Congress and political controversy ensued, ultimately leading to her resignation. To patch up the damage Gorsuch had done to his reputation, Reagan named a moderate and seasoned administrator, William Ruckelshaus, to run the agency. Ruckelshaus demanded—and got—more freedom from the White House than Gorsuch had sought. President Clinton had no use for his FBI Director, Louis Freeh, who would barely talk to him, but did not fire Freeh, for fear of being denounced as purging an enemy.

executive orders
Regulations originating with the executive branch. Executive orders are one method presidents can use to control the bureaucracy.

- ***Issue orders***. Presidents can issue **executive orders** to agencies. These orders carry the force of law and are used to implement statutes, treaties, and provisions of the Constitution.[41] Sometimes presidential aides simply pass the word that the president wants something done. These messages usually suffice, although agency heads are reluctant to run afoul of Congress or the press on the basis of a broad presidential hint. The president's rhetoric in speeches outside the bureaucracy may also influence the priorities of bureaucrats.[42]
- ***Alter an agency's budget***. The Office of Management and Budget (OMB) is the president's own final authority on any agency's budget. The OMB's threats to cut here or add there will usually get an agency's attention. Each agency, however, has its constituents within and outside of Congress, and Congress, not the president, does the appropriating.
- ***Reorganize an agency***. Although President Reagan promised, proposed, and pressured to abolish the Department of Energy

Louis Freeh (pictured here), director from 1993 to 2001, had a poisonous relationship with President Bill Clinton, who viewed him as insubordinate and not competent. The president was unable to fire Freeh, however, because of the FBI's investigations of the White House and Freeh's powerful Republican allies.

AMERICA IN PERSPECTIVE

Influencing Independent Agencies

We often think of the president as head of the executive branch, but there are agencies, such as the Federal Reserve Board, that are very powerful and are generally free from the chief executive's direction. This often leaves presidents frustrated, as when they wish the Federal Reserve Board to lower interest rates to stimulate the economy. There are even more autonomous agencies in Latin America, however—agencies removed from the direct control of the president and the legislature.

Why would Latin American governments create agencies they cannot control? The primary reason is to protect a new agency providing a new service from changes in policy made by future decision makers. Those who create an agency fear that its policies will be undone by a new administration or legislature, so they make it autonomous.

These autonomous agencies often have their own sources of revenue and thus can increase their budgets without going through the public and controversial process of government budget debates. They are also freer from legislative oversight and formal presidential controls than are regular agencies, and conflict over their programs is less visible. Until recently, expenditures for autonomous agencies also allowed the government to engage in creative financing because when these agencies contracted debt, it did not count against the central government's debt (which is substantial in some Latin American countries).

Autonomy is decidedly a mixed blessing, however. Creative financing is not necessarily good for a nation, nor is the difficulty policymakers have in consolidating bureaucracies and increasing their efficiency. The lack of traditional means of influence also makes it difficult to alter the priorities of agencies, such as shifting the emphasis from building roads to building apartments.

Sources: Michelle M. Taylor, "When Are Juridically Autonomous Agencies Responsive to Elected Officials? A Simulation Based on the Costa Rican Case," *Journal of Politics* 57 (November 1995): 1070–92; Bruce M. Wilson, Juan Carlos Rodríguez Cordero, and Roger Handberg, "The Best Laid Schemes . . . Gang Aft A-gley: Judicial Reform in Latin America—Evidence from Costa Rica," *Journal of Latin American Studies* 36 (August 2004).

and the Department of Education, he never succeeded—largely because each department was in the hands of an entrenched bureaucracy backed by elements in Congress and strong constituent groups. Reorganizing an agency is hard to do if it is a large and strong agency, and reorganizing a small and weak agency is often not worth the trouble. Nevertheless, as we saw, a massive reorganization occurred in 2002 with the creation of the Department of Homeland Security. It is not clear, however, that this reorganization has improved the implementation of policy.

Congress Tries to Control the Bureaucracy Congress exhibits a paradoxical relationship with the bureaucracies. On the one hand (as we have seen), members of Congress may find a big bureaucracy congenial.[43] Big government provides services to constituents, who may show their appreciation at the polls. Moreover, when Congress lacks the answers to policy problems, it hopes the bureaucracies will find them. Unable itself, for example, to resolve the touchy issue of equality in intercollegiate athletics, Congress passed the ball to the Department of Health, Education, and Welfare. Unable to decide how to make workplaces safer, Congress produced OSHA. As you saw in Chapter 12, Congress is increasingly the problem-identifying branch of government, setting the bureaucratic agenda but letting the agencies decide how to implement the goals it sets.

On the other hand, Congress has found it hard to control the government it helped create. There are several measures Congress can take to oversee the bureaucracy:

- ***Influence the appointment of agency heads.*** Even when the law does not require senatorial approval of a presidential appointment, members of Congress are not shy in offering their opinions about who should and should not be running the agencies. When congressional approval is required, members are doubly influential. Committee hearings on proposed appointments are almost guaranteed to produce lively debates if some members find the nominee's probable orientations objectionable.

- ***Alter an agency's budget.*** With the congressional power of the purse comes a mighty weapon for controlling bureaucratic behavior. At the same time, Congress knows that many agencies perform services that its constituents demand. Too much budget cutting may make an agency more responsive—at the price of losing an interest group's support for a reelection campaign.

- ***Hold hearings.*** Committees and subcommittees can hold periodic hearings as part of their oversight responsibilities, and in these hearings they may parade flagrant agency abuses of congressional intent in front of the press. However, the very committee that created a program usually has responsibility for oversight of it and thus has some stake in showing the agency in a favorable light. Furthermore, as we saw in Chapter 12, members of Congress have other disincentives for vigorous oversight, including a desire not to embarrass the chief executive.

- ***Rewrite the legislation or make it more detailed.*** Every statute is filled with instructions to its administrators. To limit bureaucratic discretion and make its instructions clearer, Congress can write new or more detailed legislation. Still, even voluminous detail can never eliminate discretion.

Through these and other devices, Congress tries to keep bureaucracies under its control. Never entirely successful, Congress faces a constant battle to limit and channel the vast powers that it delegated to the bureaucracy in the first place.

Sometimes these efforts are detrimental to bureaucratic performance. In 2008, about 80 House and Senate committees and subcommittees claimed jurisdiction over a portion of homeland security issues. Officials in the Department of Homeland Security have to spend a large percentage of their time testifying to these committees, and the balkanized jurisdiction has undermined the ability of Congress to perform comprehensive oversight. Moreover, different committees may send different signals to the same agency. One may press for stricter enforcement of regulations, for example, while another seeks for more exemptions.

Iron Triangles and Issue Networks Agencies' strong ties to interest groups on the one hand and to congressional committees and subcommittees on the other further complicate efforts to control the bureaucracy. Chapter 11 illustrated that bureaucracies often enjoy cozy relationships with interest groups and with committees or subcommittees of Congress. When agencies, groups, and committees all depend on one another and are in close, frequent contact, they form what are sometimes called **iron triangles** or subgovernments—triads that have advantages for all sides (see Figure 15.4). Thus, for example, a subcommittee on aging, senior citizens' interest groups, and the Social Security Administration are likely to agree on the need for more Social Security benefits. Richard Rettig has recounted how an alliance slowly jelled around the issue of fighting cancer. It rested on three pillars: cancer researchers, agencies within the National Institutes of Health, and members of congressional health subcommittees.

iron triangles
Also known as subgovernments, a mutually dependent, mutually advantageous relationship between bureaucratic agencies, interest groups, and congressional committees or subcommittees. Iron triangles dominate some areas of domestic policymaking.

When these iron triangles shape policies for senior citizens, the fight against cancer, tobacco, or any other interest, officials in the different triangles make each policy independently of the others, sometimes even in contradiction to other policies. For example, for years the government supported tobacco farmers in various ways while encouraging people not to smoke. Moreover, the iron triangles' decisions tend to bind

FIGURE 15.4 Iron Triangles: One Example

Iron triangles—composed of bureaucratic agencies, interest groups, and congressional committees or subcommittees—have dominated some areas of domestic policymaking by combining internal consensus with a virtual monopoly on information in their area. The tobacco triangle is one example; there are dozens more. Iron triangles are characterized by mutual dependency in which each element provides key services, information, or policy for the others. The arrows indicate some of these mutually helpful relationships. In recent years, a number of well-established iron triangles, including the tobacco triangle, have been broken up.

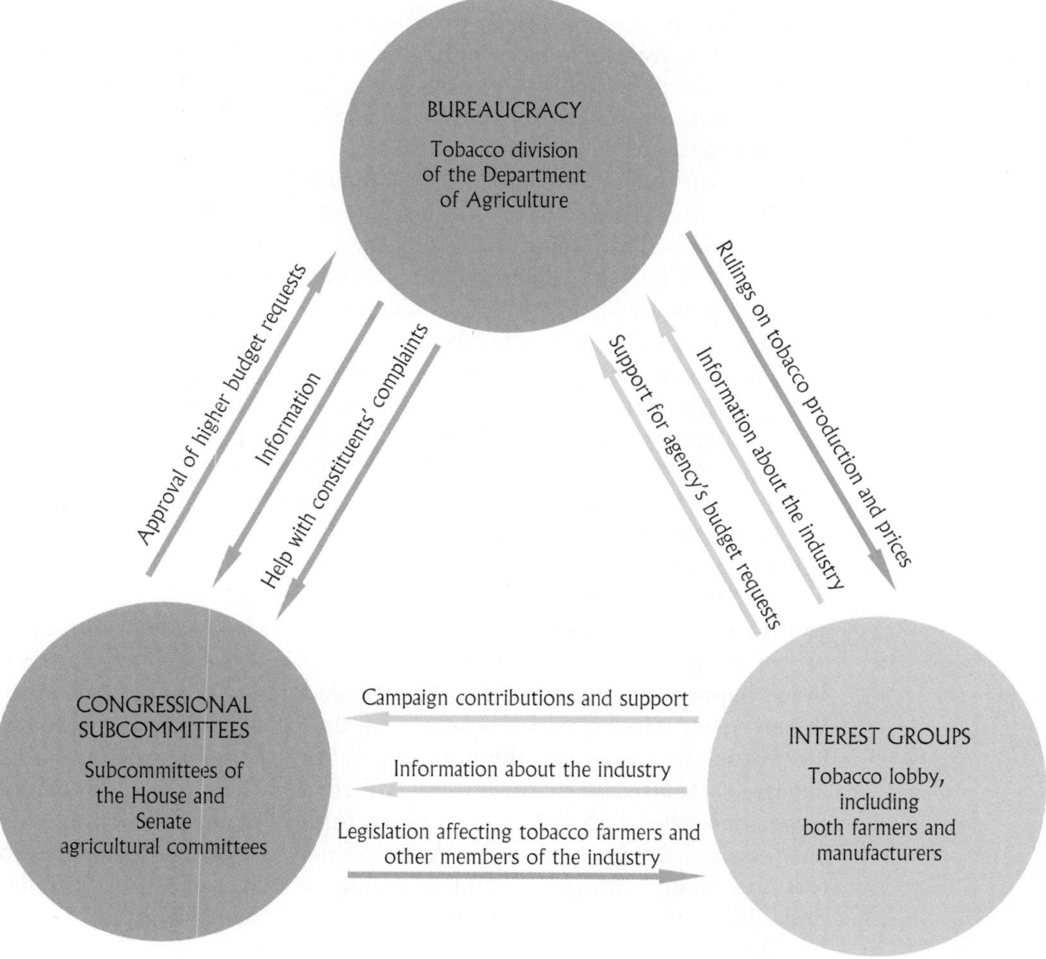

larger institutions, such as Congress and the White House. Congress often defers to the decisions of committees and subcommittees, especially on less visible issues. The White House may be too busy wrestling with global concerns to fret over agricultural issues or cancer. Emboldened by this lack of involvement, subgovernments flourish and add a strong decentralizing and fragmenting element to the policymaking process.

There is often a cozy relationship between the components of three sides of a subgovernment. For example, in 2003, Congress added a massive prescription drug benefit under Medicare. Representative Billy Tauzin shepherded the drug bill through the House as chair of the Energy and Commerce Committee. He then retired from Congress to head the Pharmaceutical Research and Manufacturers of America, a powerful industry lobby group, for an estimated $2 million a year. Thomas Scully, the Medicare administrator and lead negotiator for the administration, resigned his position within weeks after the passage of the bill to join a lobbying firm that represented several health care industry companies significantly affected by the new law. He also announced he would be working part time for an investment firm with interests in several more companies affected by the new law.

The system of subgovernments is now overlaid with an amorphous system of *issue networks*. These networks have led to more widespread participation in bureaucratic policymaking, including by many who have technical policy expertise and are drawn to issues because of intellectual or emotional commitments rather than material interests. Those concerned with environmental protection, for example, have challenged formerly closed subgovernments on numerous fronts (see Chapter 19). This opening of the policymaking process complicates the calculations and decreases the predictability of those involved in the stable and relatively narrow relationships of subgovernments.[44]

Although subgovernments are often able to dominate policymaking for decades, they are not indestructible.[45] For example, the subgovernment pictured in Figure 15.4 long dominated smoking and tobacco policy, focusing on crop subsidies to tobacco farmers. But increasingly, these policies came under fire from health authorities, who were not involved in tobacco policymaking in earlier years. Similarly, Congress no longer considers pesticide policy, once dominated by chemical companies and agricultural interests, separately from environmental and health concerns.

An especially vivid example of the death of an iron triangle is the case of nuclear power.[46] During the 1940s and 1950s, Americans were convinced that the technology that had ended World War II could also serve peaceful purposes. Nuclear scientists spoke enthusiastically about harnessing the atom to achieve all sorts of goals, eventually making electricity so inexpensive that it would be "too cheap to meter." Optimism in progress through science was the rule, and the federal government encouraged the development of nuclear power through a powerful iron triangle.

Congress established a special joint committee, the Joint Committee on Atomic Energy, with complete control over questions of nuclear power. It also created a new executive agency, the Atomic Energy Commission (AEC). The committee, the commission, the private companies that built nuclear power plants, and the electrical utilities that operated them together formed a powerful subgovernment. America built more nuclear power plants than any other country in the world, and American technology was exported overseas to dozens of nations.

Nuclear power today—after the accidents at Three Mile Island and Chernobyl and the various cost overruns associated with the industry—bears almost no resemblance to nuclear power in the early 1960s when the iron triangle was at its peak. What happened? Before the 1960s had ended, the experts had begun to lose control. When critics raised questions concerning the safety of the plants and were able to get local officials to question the policies publicly, the issue grew into a major political debate, associated with the growth of environmentalism. Opposition to nuclear power destroyed two of the most powerful legs of the iron triangle. Congress disbanded the Joint Committee on Atomic Energy; a variety of congressional committees now claim some jurisdiction over nuclear power questions. Similarly, Congress replaced the AEC with two new agencies: the Nuclear Regulatory Commission and the Department of Energy.

The nuclear power industry was devastated: No new nuclear power plants have been started in the United States since 1978, and almost all those under construction at that time have been abandoned at huge financial loss. Nuclear power provides only about 12 percent of our total energy production. In sum, the wave of environmental concern that developed in the late 1960s swept away one of the most powerful iron triangles in recent American history.

This is not the end of the story, however. The extraordinarily high price of gasoline and heating fuel since 2005 and concerns over global warming have encouraged a reconsideration of nuclear power. The Gallup Poll has found, for example, that a majority of the public supports the use of nuclear energy to produce electricity.

If the nuclear power industry should revive, there will be renewed calls for strict regulation—from both the bureaucracy and Congress. Whether an iron triangle reemerges from this change will depend on whether the public is attentive to the issue of nuclear power and whether it allows experts to define safety concerns as technical matters appropriate only for experts to decide.

Bureaucracy and the Scope of Government

To many, the huge American bureaucracy is the prime example of the federal government growing out of control. As this chapter discussed earlier, some observers view the bureaucracy as acquisitive, constantly seeking to expand its size, budgets, and authority. Much of the political rhetoric against big government also adopts this line of argument, along with complaints about red tape, senseless regulations, and the like. It is easy to take potshots at a faceless bureaucracy that usually cannot respond.

One should keep in mind, however, that the federal bureaucracy has not grown over the past 40 years. Moreover, since the population of the country has grown significantly during this period, the federal bureaucracy has actually *shrunk* in size relative to the population it serves.

Originally, the federal bureaucracy had the modest role of promoting the economy, defending the country, managing foreign affairs, providing justice, and delivering the mail. Its role gradually expanded to include providing services to farmers, businesses, and workers. As the discussion of federalism in Chapter 3 showed, with social and economic changes in the United States, a variety of interests placed additional demands on government. We now expect government—and the bureaucracy—to play an active role in dealing with social and economic problems. A good case can be made that the bureaucracy is actually too *small* for many of the tasks currently assigned to it—tasks ranging from the control of illicit drugs to protection of the environment.

In addition, it is important to remember that when the president and Congress have chosen to deregulate certain areas of the economy or cut taxes, the bureaucracy could not and did not prevent them from doing so. The question of what and how much the federal government should do—and thus how big the bureaucracy should be—is answered primarily at the polls and in Congress, the White House, and the courts—not by faceless bureaucrats.

Summary

15.1 Describe the federal bureaucrats and the ways in which they obtain their jobs.

Bureaucrats perform most of the vital services the federal government provides, although their number has not grown, even as the population has increased and the public has made additional demands on government. Bureaucrats shape policy as administrators, as implementors, and as regulators. Most federal bureaucrats get their jobs through the civil service system; as a group, these civil servants are broadly representative of the American people. The top policymaking posts, however, are filled through presidential appointments, often with Senate confirmation.

15.2 Differentiate the four types of agencies into which the federal bureaucracy is organized.

The organization of the federal bureaucracy is most easily understood by categorizing agencies into four types: cabinet departments, independent regulatory commissions, government corporations, and independent executive agencies. The 15 cabinet departments each manage a specific policy area. Independent regulatory commissions make and enforce rules in a particular sector of the economy. Government corporations provide services that could be handled by the private sector and charge for their services. Independent executive agencies account for most of the rest of the federal bureaucracy.

15.3 Identify the factors that influence the effectiveness of bureaucratic implementation of public policy.

As policy implementors, bureaucrats translate legislative policy goals into programs. The effectiveness of policy implementation is influenced by various factors: the policy or program design; the clarity of the legislation or regulations being implemented; the resources available for implementation; the ability of administrators to depart from SOPs when necessary; the disposition of administrators toward the policy they implement; and the extent to which responsibility for policy implementation is concentrated rather than dispersed across agencies.

15.4 Describe how bureaucracies regulate, and assess deregulation and alternative approaches to regulation.

Congress increasingly delegates large amounts of power to bureaucratic agencies to develop rules regulating practices in the private sector. Agencies apply and enforce their rules, in court or through administrative procedures. Regulation affects most areas of American society, and criticism that regulations are overly complicated and burdensome has led to a movement to deregulate. However, many regulations have proved beneficial, and deregulation has itself resulted in policy failures.

15.5 Assess means of controlling unelected bureaucrats in American democracy and the impact of the bureaucracy on the scope of government.

Although bureaucrats are not elected, bureaucracies are not necessarily undemocratic. Bureaucrats are competent and reasonably representative of Americans. Bureaucracies also may be controlled by elected decision makers, although the president and Congress face challenges to their control, including iron triangles. The role of government and hence the size of the bureaucracy depends more on voters than on bureaucrats.

Chapter Test

15.1 Describe the federal bureaucrats and the ways in which they obtain their jobs.

1. The civil service system was designed for which of the following purposes?
   a. To hire and promote bureaucrats on the basis of merit
   b. To produce an administration with talent and skill
   c. To limit bureaucrats' participation in partisan politics
   d. To protect workers from politically motivated firings
   e. All of the above

2. The permanent bureaucracy tends to be less broadly representative of the American people than are legislators, judges, or presidential appointees.

   True______ False______

3. What is the Office of Personnel Management and what is its primary function?

4. How might the current system of political appointments undermine or benefit effective policy implementation? In your opinion, in what ways should this system be reformed to ensure that the most talented and skilled not only work in the bureaucracy but lead it as well?

15.2 Differentiate the four types of agencies into which the federal bureaucracy is organized.

5. Which of the following statements best characterizes the functioning of government corporations?
   a. They help regulate corporations and businesses in the private sector.
   b. They provide and charge for services that could be provided by the private sector.
   c. They help the government hire talented workers from the private sector.
   d. They help manage the government's many buildings, archives, and storage facilities.
   e. They implement congressional policies in the economic domain.

6. The president appoints and the Senate confirms both members of independent regulatory commissions and cabinet secretaries for fixed terms.

   True______ False______

7. Why are independent regulatory commissions prone to "capture"? How might capture undermine effective policy implementation and, ultimately, democracy?

15.3 Identify the factors that influence the effectiveness of bureaucratic implementation of public policy.

8. That the Federal Drug Administration lacks the computer systems to inspect plants that produce food imported into the United States is an example of
   a. A fragmented policy area
   b. An ineffective set of standard operating procedures
   c. A lack of administrative discretion
   d. A lack of bureaucratic resources
   e. A lack of legislative clarity

9. An example of a street-level bureaucrat is a police officer.
   True______ False______

10. What are three main factors that make policy implementation difficult? Which of these do you think is most problematic, and why? Would you favor increasing the president's control over the bureaucracy to reduce the difficulties of policy implementation? Why or why not?

15.4 Describe how bureaucracies regulate, and assess deregulation and alternative approaches to regulation.

11. Which of the following is true about bureaucracies as regulators?
    a. Bureaucratic agencies must adhere to strict guidelines mandated by Congress
    b. Bureaucratic agencies regulate products without consulting the industries being regulated
    c. Bureaucratic agencies have a grant of power and set of directions from Congress
    d. Bureaucratic agencies' regulation of society has declined in recent decades
    e. Bureaucratic agencies' regulatory activity increases only during liberal administrations

12. The EPA's requirement that cars include pollution-control devices is an example of government deregulation.
    True______ False______

13. Compare and contrast the command-and-control and incentive systems of regulation and provide an example of each. In your opinion, which is the more efficient approach, and why?

14. What are the advantages and problems generally connected with regulation? Do you think that in general we need more or less regulation of the economy and society? Explain your answer, drawing on the text and giving examples.

15.5 Assess means of controlling unelected bureaucrats in American democracy and the impact of the bureaucracy on the scope of government.

15. The development of subgovernments to include a system of issue networks has accomplished which of the following?
    a. It ensures that presidents are actively involved in most policy areas
    b. It ensures that subgovernments will be virtually impossible to dismantle
    c. It ensures that policymaking is stable and predictable
    d. It ensures more widespread participation in the policy process
    e. It ensures that the bureaucracy is more independent of elected branches of government

16. Because it is unelected, the federal bureaucracy is often criticized as undemocratic. How do the elected branches of government—Congress and the presidency—exert control over the federal bureaucracy? How might they exert more control over the bureaucracy so that the system will be more democratic?

17. A common perception of the federal bureaucracy is that it epitomizes out-of-control government growth. Based on your reading of the textbook, make an argument that this perception is incorrect, citing specific evidence and examples.

PEARSON mypoliscilab Exercises

Apply what you learned in this chapter on MyPoliSciLab.

Read on **mypoliscilab.com**

eText: Chapter 15

Study and **Review** on **mypoliscilab.com**

Pre-Test
Post-Test
Chapter Exam
Flashcards

Watch on **mypoliscilab.com**

Video: The CDC and the Swine Flu
Video: Internal Problems at the FDA

Explore on **mypoliscilab.com**

Simulation: You Are a Deputy Director of the Census Bureau
Simulation: You Are the Head of FEMA
Simulation: You Are a Federal Administrator
Simulation: You Are the President of MEDICORP
Comparative: Comparing Bureaucracies
Timeline: The Evolution of the Federal Bureaucracy
Visual Literacy: The Changing Face of the Federal Bureaucracy

Key Terms

bureaucracy (434)
patronage (437)
Pendleton Civil Service Act (437)
civil service (437)
merit principle (437)
Hatch Act (438)
Office of Personnel Management (438)
GS (General Schedule) rating (438)
Senior Executive Service (438)
independent regulatory commission (442)
government corporations (442)
independent executive agency (443)
policy implementation (443)
standard operating procedures (447)
administrative discretion (448)
street-level bureaucrats (448)
regulation (452)
deregulation (455)
command-and-control policy (455)
incentive system (455)
executive orders (457)
iron triangles (459)

Internet Resources

www.gpoaccess.gov/gmanual/index.html
U.S. Government Manual, which provides information on the organization of the U.S. government.

www.gpoaccess.gov/fr/index.html
The *Federal Register*, which provides information on U.S. laws and regulations.

www.whitehouse.gov/government/cabinet.html
Information on federal cabinet departments.

www.usa.gov/Agencies/Federal/All_Agencies/index.shtml
Information on all federal departments, independent agencies, and commissions.

www.opm.gov/feddata/
Federal employment statistics.

www.opm.gov
Office of Personnel Management Web site, with information on federal jobs and personnel issues.

www.govexec.com
The Web site for *Government Executive* magazine.

www.gpoaccess.gov/plumbook/2008/index.html
The *Plum Book* of presidential appointments.

For Further Reading

Aberbach, Joel D., and Bert A. Rockman. ***In the Web of Politics.*** Washington, DC: Brookings Institution, 2000. Examines federal executives and the degree to which they are representative of the country and responsive to elected officials.

Arnold, Peri E. ***Making the Managerial Presidency,*** 2nd ed. Princeton, NJ: Princeton University Press, 1996. A careful examination of efforts to reorganize the federal bureaucracy.

Derthick, Martha, and Paul J. Quirk. ***The Politics of Deregulation.*** Washington, DC: Brookings Institution, 1985. Explains why advocates of deregulation prevailed over the special interests that benefited from regulation.

Edwards, George C., III. ***Implementing Public Policy.*** Washington, DC: Congressional Quarterly Press, 1980. A good review of the issues involved in implementation.

Goodsell, Charles T. ***The Case for Bureaucracy,*** 4th ed. Washington, DC: CQ Press, 2004. A strong case on behalf of the effectiveness of bureaucracy.

Gormley, William T., Jr. ***Taming the Bureaucracy.*** Princeton, NJ: Princeton University Press, 1989. Examines remedies for controlling bureaucracies.

Gormley, William T., Jr., and Steven J. Balla. ***Bureaucracy and Democracy: Accountability and Performance,*** 2nd ed. Washington, DC: CQ Press, 2007. Discusses the accountability of unelected bureaucrats in a democracy.

Heclo, Hugh M. ***Government of Strangers: Executive Politics in Washington.*** Washington, DC: Brookings Institution, 1977. A study of the top executives of the federal government, who constitute (says the author) a "government of strangers."

Kerwin, Cornelius M. ***Rulemaking: How Government Agencies Write Law and Make Policy,*** 4th ed. Washington, DC: CQ Press, 2010. Explains how agencies write regulations to implement laws.

Kettl, Donald F. ***System Under Stress: Homeland Security and American Politics,*** 2nd ed. Washington, DC: CQ Press, 2007. Evaluates the consequences of bureaucratic reorganization in response to crises.

Lewis, David E. ***The Politics of Presidential Appointments.*** Princeton, NJ: Princeton University Press, 2008. Analyszes how presidential appointments are made and what difference they make.

Meier, Kenneth J., and Laurence J. O'Toole. ***Bureaucracy in a Democratic State.*** Baltimore, MD: Johns Hopkins University Press, 2006. Argues that bureaucracy can promote democracy.

Osborne, David, and Peter Plastrik. ***Banishing Bureaucracy,*** 2nd ed. David Osborne, 2006. Five strategies for reinventing government.

Savas, E. S. ***Privatization: The Key to Better Government.*** Chatham, NJ: Chatham House, 1987. A conservative economist's argument that many public services performed by bureaucracies would be better handled by the private sector.

Wilson, James Q. ***Bureaucracy.*** New York: Basic Books, 1989. Presents a "bottom-up" approach to understanding how bureaucrats, managers, and executives decide what to do.

Chapter 16

The Federal Courts

Learning Objectives

16.1 Identify the basic elements of the American judicial system and the major participants in it.

16.2 Outline the structure of the federal court system and the major responsibilities of each component.

16.3 Explain the process by which judges and justices are nominated and confirmed.

16.4 Describe the backgrounds of judges and justices and assess the impact of background on their decisions.

16.5 Outline the judicial process at the Supreme Court level and assess the major factors influencing decisions and their implementation.

16.6 Trace the Supreme Court's use of judicial review in major policy battles in various eras of American history.

16.7 Assess the role of unelected courts and the scope of judicial power in American democracy.

POLITICS IN ACTION: APPEALING TO THE SUPREME COURT

Say that you are involved in a lawsuit regarding the application of an affirmative action policy in your college or university. A trial is held in a federal district court. After the trial, a verdict is rendered, and you lose. You are not content to accept this decision, and you appeal to the court of appeals. Once again, you lose. Now your only options are to either accept the decision or appeal to the U.S. Supreme Court. You decide to appeal, and of the thousands of petitions for hearings the Court receives in a year, yours is one of the few dozen it selects.

On the day of the oral argument (there are no trials in the Supreme Court), you walk up the steep steps of the Supreme Court building, the impressive "Marble Palace" with the motto "Equal Justice Under Law" engraved over its imposing columns. The Court's surroundings and procedures suggest the nineteenth century. The justices, clothed in black robes, take their seats at the bench in front of a red velvet curtain. Behind the bench there are still spittoons, one for each justice. (Today, the spittoons are used as wastebaskets.)

Your case, like most of the cases the Court selects for oral arguments, is scheduled for about an hour. Lawyers arguing before the Court often wear formal clothing. They find a goose quill pen on their desk (and may take the pen with them as a memento of their day in court). Each side is allotted 30 minutes to present its case. The justices may—and do—interrupt the lawyers with questions. When the time is up, a discreet red light goes on at your lawyer's lectern, and he immediately stops talking.

That is the end of the hearing, but not the end of the process. You have asked the Court to overrule a policy established by your state legislature. As the Court considers doing so, it recognizes that its decision will become precedent for all such policies across the nation. Months will go by, as the justices deliberate and negotiate an opinion, before the Court announces its decision. If you win, it will take many more months for your university, aided by lower courts, to interpret the decision and implement it.

The scope of the Supreme Court's power is great, extending even to overruling the decisions of elected officials. Despite the trappings of tradition and majesty, however, the Court does not reach its decisions in a political vacuum. Instead, it works in a context of political influences and considerations, a circumstance that raises important questions about the role of the judiciary in the U.S. political system.

The federal courts pose a special challenge to American democracy. Although it is common for state judges to be elected in one fashion or another, federal judges are *appointed* to their positions—for life. The Framers of the Constitution purposefully insulated federal judges from the influence of public opinion. How can we reconcile powerful courts populated by unelected judges with American democracy? Do they pose a threat

Chapter OUTLINE

to majority rule? Or do the federal courts actually function to protect the rights of minorities and thus maintain the type of open system necessary for democracy to flourish?

The power of the federal courts also raises the issue of the appropriate scope of judicial power in our society. Federal courts are frequently in the thick of policymaking on issues ranging from affirmative action and abortion to physician-assisted suicide and the financing of public schools. Numerous critics argue that judges should not be actively involved in determining public policy—that they should leave policy to elected officials, focusing instead on settlement of routine disputes. On the other hand, advocates of a more aggressive role for the courts emphasize that judicial decisions have often met pressing needs—especially needs of the politically or economically powerless—left unmet by the normal processes of policymaking. For example, we have already seen the leading role that the federal courts played in ending legally supported racial segregation in the United States. To determine the appropriate role of the courts in our democracy, we must first understand the nature of our judicial system.

However impressive the Supreme Court may be, it makes only the tiniest fraction of American judicial policy. The Court decides a handful of issues each year—albeit often key issues, with some decisions shaping people's lives and perhaps even determining matters of life and death. In addition to the Supreme Court, there are 12 federal courts of appeal plus a Court of Appeals for the Federal Circuit, 91 federal district courts, and thousands of state and local courts. Most of America's legal business is transacted in these less august courts. In Chapter 21, you will read about state and local courts. This chapter focuses on federal courts and the judges who serve on them—the men and women in black robes who are important policymakers in the American political system.

16.1 Identify the basic elements of the American judicial system and the major participants in it.

The Nature of the Judicial System

The judicial system in the United States is, at least in principle, an adversarial one in which the courts provide an arena for two parties to bring their conflict before an impartial arbiter (a judge). The system is based on the theory that justice will emerge out of the struggle between two contending points of view. The task of the judge is to apply the law to the case, determining which party is legally correct. In reality, most cases never go to trial because they are settled by agreements reached out of court.

There are two basic kinds of cases: criminal law cases and civil law cases. In a *criminal law* case, the government charges an individual with violating specific laws, such as those prohibiting robbery. The offense may be harmful to an individual or to society as a whole, but in either case it warrants punishment, such as imprisonment or a fine. A *civil law* case involves a dispute between two parties (one of whom may be the government itself) over a wide range of matters including contracts, property ownership, divorce, child custody, mergers of multinational companies, and personal and property damage. Civil law consists of both statutes (laws passed by legislatures) and common law (the accumulation of judicial decisions about legal issues).

Just as it is important not to confuse criminal and civil law, it is important not to confuse state and federal courts. The vast majority of all criminal and civil cases involve state law and are tried in state courts. Criminal cases such as burglary and civil cases such as divorce normally begin and end in the state, not the federal, courts.

Participants in the Judicial System

Every case has certain components in common, including litigants, attorneys, and judges; in some cases organized groups also become directly involved. Judges are the policymakers of the American judicial system, and we examine them extensively in later sections of this chapter. Here we will discuss the other regular participants in the judicial process.

Litigants Federal judges are restricted by the Constitution to deciding "cases" or "controversies"—that is, actual disputes rather than hypothetical ones. Judges do not issue advisory opinions on what they think (in the abstract) may be the meaning or constitutionality of a law. The judiciary is essentially passive, dependent on others to take the initiative.

Thus, two parties must bring a case to the court before it may be heard. Every case is a dispute between a *plaintiff* and a *defendant,* in which the former brings some charge against the latter. Sometimes the plaintiff is the government, which may bring a charge against an individual or a corporation. The government may charge Smith with a brutal murder or charge the XYZ Corporation with illegal trade practices. All cases are identified with the name of the plaintiff first and the defendant second, for example, *State v. Smith* or *Anderson v. Baker.* In many (but not all) cases, a *jury,* a group of citizens (usually 12), is responsible for determining the outcome of a lawsuit.

Litigants end up in court for a variety of reasons. Some are reluctant participants—the defendant in a criminal case, for example. Others are eager for their day in court. For some, the courts can be a potent weapon in the search for a preferred policy.

Not everyone can challenge a law, however. Plaintiffs must have what is called **standing to sue**; that is, they must have serious interest in a case, which is typically determined by whether they have sustained or are in immediate danger of sustaining a direct and substantial injury from another party (such as a corporation) or an action of government. Except in cases pertaining to governmental support for religion, merely being a taxpayer and being opposed to a law do not provide the standing necessary to challenge that law in court. Nevertheless, Congress and the Supreme Court have liberalized the rules for standing, making it somewhat easier for citizens to challenge governmental and corporate actions in court.

standing to sue
The requirement that plaintiffs have a serious interest in a case, which depends on whether they have sustained or are likely to sustain a direct and substantial injury from another party or from an action of government.

The courts have broadened the concept of standing to sue to include **class action suits**, which permit a small number of people to sue on behalf of all other people in similar circumstances. These suits may be useful in cases as varied as civil rights, in which a few persons seek an end to discriminatory practices on behalf of all who might be discriminated against, and environmental protection, in which a few persons may sue a polluting industry on behalf of all who are affected by the air or water that the industry pollutes.

class action suits
Lawsuits in which a small number of people sue on behalf of all people in similar circumstances.

Conflicts must not only arise from actual cases between litigants with standing to sue, but they must also be **justiciable disputes**—issues that are capable of being settled by legal methods. For example, one would not go to court to determine whether Congress should fund missile defense, for the matter could not be resolved through legal methods or knowledge.

justiciable disputes
Issues capable of being settled as a matter of law.

Attorneys Lawyers are indispensable actors in the judicial system. Law is one of the nation's largest professions, with about a million attorneys practicing in the United States today.[1] Although lawyers were once available primarily to the rich, today the federally funded Legal Services Corporation employs lawyers to serve the legal needs of the poor and state and local governments provide public defenders for poor people accused of crimes. Moreover, some employers and unions now provide legal insurance, through which individuals who have prepaid can secure legal aid when needed. That access to lawyers has become more equal does not, of course, mean that quality of representation is equal. The wealthy can afford high-powered attorneys who can invest many hours in their cases and arrange for testimony by expert witnesses. The poor are often served by overworked attorneys with few resources to devote to an individual case.

Groups Because they recognize the courts' ability to shape policy, interest groups often seek out litigants whose cases seem particularly strong. Few groups have been more successful in finding good cases and good litigants than the National Association for the Advancement of Colored People (NAACP), which decided to sue the

Linda Brown (left), shown here outside her segregated school, was the plaintiff challenging legal segregation in public education.

school board of Topeka, Kansas, on behalf of a young schoolgirl named Linda Brown in *Brown v. Board of Education* (1954). The NAACP was seeking to end the policy of "separate but equal"—meaning racially segregated—public education, and NAACP legal counsel Thurgood Marshall believed that Topeka represented a stronger case than did other school districts because the city provided segregated facilities that were otherwise genuinely equal. The courts could not resolve the case simply by insisting that expenditures for schools for white and African-American children be equalized.

The American Civil Liberties Union (ACLU) is another interest group that is always seeking cases and litigants to support in its defense of civil liberties. One ACLU attorney, stressing that principle took priority over a particular client, even admitted that some of ACLU's clients are "pretty scurvy little creatures. It's the principle that we're going to be able to use these people for that's important."[2] (For an example, review the case in Chapter 4 of the Nazis who tried to march in Skokie, Illinois.)

At other times groups do not directly argue the case for litigants, but support them instead with ***amicus curiae*** **("friend of the court") briefs**, which attempt to influence the Court's decision, raise additional points of view, and present information not contained in the briefs of the attorneys for the official parties to the case. In controversial cases, many groups may submit such briefs to the Court: 102 briefs were presented in the University of Michigan case on affirmative action in 2003.

amicus curiae **briefs**
Legal briefs submitted by a "friend of the court" for the purpose of influencing a court's decision by raising additional points of view and presenting information not contained in the briefs of the formal parties.

All these participants—plaintiffs, defendants, lawyers, and interest groups—play a role in the judicial drama, as do, in many instances, the public and the press. Much of the drama takes place outside the courtroom. How these participants arrive in the courtroom and which court they go to reflect the structure of the court system.

16.2 Outline the structure of the federal court system and the major responsibilities of each component.

The Structure of the Federal Judicial System

The Constitution is vague about the structure of the federal court system. Specifying only that there would be a Supreme Court, the Constitution left it to Congress's discretion to establish lower federal courts of general jurisdiction. In the Judiciary Act of 1789, Congress created these additional *constitutional courts*, and although the system has been altered over the years, the United States has never been without them. The current organization of the federal court system is displayed in Figure 16.1.

Congress has also established *legislative courts* for specialized purposes. These courts include the Court of Military Appeals, the Court of Claims, the Court of International Trade, and the Tax Court. Legislative courts are staffed by judges who have fixed terms of office and who lack the protections against removal or salary reductions that judges on constitutional courts enjoy. The judges apply a body of law within their area of jurisdiction but cannot exercise the power of judicial review (of finding the actions of the legislative or executive branch unconstitutional).

In this section, we focus on the constitutional courts, that is, on the courts of general jurisdiction—district courts, courts of appeal, and the Supreme Court—which hear a wide range of cases. First, we must clarify another difference among courts. Courts with **original jurisdiction** are those in which a case is heard first, usually in a trial. These are the courts that determine the facts about a case, whether it is a criminal charge or a civil suit. More than 90 percent of court cases begin and end in the court of original jurisdiction. Lawyers can sometimes appeal an adverse decision to a higher

original jurisdiction
The jurisdiction of courts that hear a case first, usually in a trial. These are the courts that determine the facts about a case.

FIGURE 16.1 Organization of the Federal Court System

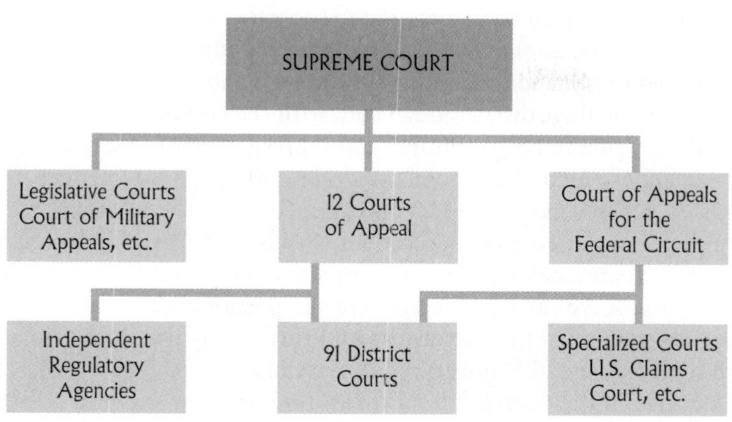

The federal court system is composed of both constitutional courts (the Supreme Court, the courts of appeals, and the district courts) and legislative courts, which have specialized jurisdictions. Losers in cases before independent regulatory commissions may appeal to the courts of appeals.

court for another decision. Courts with **appellate jurisdiction** hear cases brought to them on appeal from a lower court. Appellate courts do not review the factual record, only the legal issues involved. At the state level, the appellate process normally ends with the state's highest court of appeal, which is usually called the state supreme court. Appeals from a state high court can be taken only to the U.S. Supreme Court.

appellate jurisdiction
The jurisdiction of courts that hear cases brought to them on appeal from lower courts. These courts do not review the factual record, only the legal issues involved.

District Courts

The entry point for most litigation in the federal courts is one of the **district courts**, of which there are 91, with at least one in each state, in addition to one in Washington, D.C., and one in Puerto Rico (there are also three somewhat different territorial courts for Guam, the Virgin Islands, and the Northern Mariana Islands). The district courts are courts of original jurisdiction; they hear no appeals. They are the only federal courts that hold trials and impanel juries. The 678 district court judges usually preside over cases alone, but certain rare cases require that three judges constitute the court. Each district court has between 2 and 28 judges, depending on the amount of judicial work within its territory.

district courts
The 91 federal courts of **original jurisdiction**. They are the only federal courts in which trials are held and in which juries may be impaneled.

The jurisdiction of the district courts extends to the following:

- Federal crimes
- Civil suits under federal law
- Civil suits between citizens of different states where the amount in question exceeds $75,000
- Supervision of bankruptcy proceedings
- Review of the actions of some federal administrative agencies
- Admiralty and maritime law cases
- Supervision of the naturalization of aliens

Keep in mind that about 98 percent of all the criminal cases in the United States are heard in state and local court systems, not in the federal courts. Moreover, only a small percentage of the persons convicted of federal crimes in the federal district courts actually have a trial. Most enter guilty pleas as part of a bargain to receive lighter punishment.

State and local courts also handle most civil suits in the United States. And, as with criminal cases, only a small percentage of those civil cases that commence in the federal courts are decided by trial—about 2 percent of the nearly 250,000 civil cases resolved each year;[3] in the vast majority of cases, litigants settle out of court instead.

Diversity of citizenship cases are civil suits in which the parties are U.S. citizens of different states (such as a Californian suing a Texan) or one party is a citizen of a foreign nation and in which the matter in question exceeds $75,000. Congress established this jurisdiction to protect against the possible bias of a state court in favor of a citizen from that state. In these cases, federal judges are to apply the appropriate state laws.

District judges are assisted by an elaborate supporting cast, including clerks, bailiffs, law clerks, stenographers, court reporters, and probation officers. U.S. marshals are assigned to each district to protect the judicial process and to serve the writs that the judges issue. Federal magistrates, appointed to eight-year terms, issue warrants for arrest, determine whether to hold arrested persons for action by a grand jury, and set bail. They also hear motions subject to review by their district judge and, with the consent of both parties in civil cases and of defendants in petty criminal cases, preside over some trials. As the workload for district judges increases (more than 338,000 cases commenced in 2008),[4] magistrates are becoming essential components of the federal judicial system.

Another important player at the district court level is the U.S. attorney. Each of the 91 regular districts has a U.S. attorney who is nominated by the president and confirmed by the Senate and who serves at the discretion of the president (U.S. attorneys do not have lifetime appointments). These attorneys and their staffs prosecute violations of federal law and represent the U.S. government in civil cases.

Most of the cases handled in the district courts are routine, and few result in policy innovations. Usually district court judges do not even publish their decisions. Although most federal litigation ends at this level, a large percentage of the cases that district court judges actually decide (as opposed to those settled out of court or by guilty pleas) are appealed by the losers. A distinguishing feature of the American legal system is the relative ease of appeals. U.S. law gives everyone a right to an appeal to a higher court. The loser in a case only has to request an appeal to be granted one. Of course, the loser must pay a substantial legal bill to exercise this right.

Courts of Appeal

courts of appeal
Appellate courts empowered to review all final decisions of **district courts**, except in rare cases. In addition, they also hear appeals to orders of many federal regulatory agencies.

Congress has empowered the U.S. **courts of appeal** to review all final decisions of district courts, except in rare instances in which the law provides for direct review by the Supreme Court (injunctive orders of special three-judge district courts and certain decisions holding acts of Congress unconstitutional). Courts of appeal also have authority to review and enforce orders of many federal regulatory agencies, such as the Securities and Exchange Commission and the National Labor Relations Board. About 75 percent of the more than 61,000 cases filed in the courts of appeal each year come from the district courts.[5]

FIGURE 16.2 The Federal Judicial Circuits

The 12 judicial circuits differ considerably in size. Not shown in the map are Puerto Rico (part of the First Circuit), the Virgin Islands (in the Third Circuit), and Guam and the Northern Mariana Islands (in the Ninth Circuit).

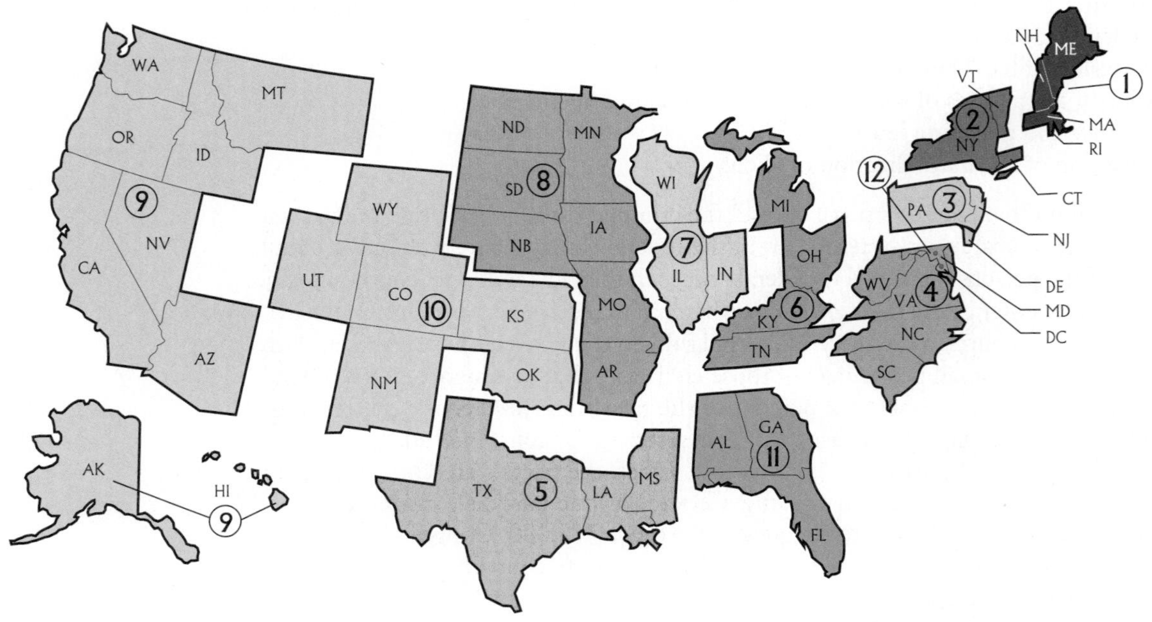

The United States is divided into 12 judicial circuits, including one for the District of Columbia (see Figure 16.2). Each circuit serves at least two states and has between 6 and 28 permanent circuit judgeships (178 in all), depending on the amount of judicial work in the circuit. Each court of appeal normally hears cases in rotating panels consisting of three judges but may sit *en banc* (with all judges present) in particularly important cases. Decisions in either arrangement are made by majority vote of the participating judges.

There is also a special appeals court called the U.S. Court of Appeals for the Federal Circuit. Congress established this court, composed of 12 judges, in 1982 to hear appeals in specialized cases, such as those regarding patents, claims against the United States, and international trade.

The courts of appeal focus on correcting errors of procedure and law that occurred in the original proceedings of legal cases, such as when a district court judge gave improper instructions to a jury or misinterpreted the rights provided under a law. These courts are appellate courts and therefore hold no trials and hear no testimony. Their decisions set precedent for all the courts and agencies within their jurisdictions.

The Supreme Court

Sitting at the pinnacle of the American judicial system is the U.S. **Supreme Court**. The Court does much more for the American political system than decide individual cases. Among its most important functions are resolving conflicts among the states and maintaining national supremacy in the law. The Supreme Court also plays an important role in ensuring uniformity in the interpretation of national laws. For example, in 1984 Congress created a federal sentencing commission to write guidelines aimed at reducing the wide disparities in punishment for similar crimes tried in federal courts. By 1989, more than 150 federal district judges had declared the law unconstitutional, and another 115 had ruled it valid. Only the Supreme Court could resolve this inconsistency in the administration of justice, which it did when it upheld the law.

Supreme Court
The pinnacle of the American judicial system. The Court ensures uniformity in interpreting national laws, resolves conflicts among states, and maintains national supremacy in law. It has both **original jurisdiction** and **appellate jurisdiction**.

There are nine justices on the Supreme Court: eight associates and one chief justice (only members of the Supreme Court are called justices; all others are called judges). The Constitution does not require this number, however, and there have been as few as 6 justices and as many as 10. Congress altered the size of the Supreme Court many times between 1801 and 1869. In 1866, it reduced the size of the Court from 10 to 7 members so that President Andrew Johnson could not nominate new justices to fill two vacancies. When Ulysses S. Grant took office, Congress increased the number of justices to nine because it was confident that he would nominate members to its liking. Since then, the number of justices has remained stable.

All nine justices sit together to hear cases and make decisions. But they must first decide which cases to hear. A familiar battle cry for losers in litigation in lower courts is, "I'll appeal this all the way to the Supreme Court!" In reality, this is unlikely to happen. Unlike other federal courts, the Supreme Court decides which cases it will hear.

You can see in Figure 16.3 that the Court does have an original jurisdiction, yet very few cases arise under it, as Table 16.1 illustrates. Almost all the business of the Court comes from the appellate process, and litigants may appeal cases from both federal and state courts. In the latter instance, however, a "substantial federal question" must be involved; in deference to the states, the Supreme Court hears cases from state courts only if they involve federal law, and then only after the petitioner has exhausted all the potential remedies in the state court system. (Losers in a case in the state court system can appeal only to the Supreme Court, and not to any other federal court.) The Court will not try to settle matters of state law or determine guilt or innocence in state criminal proceedings. To obtain a hearing in the Supreme Court, a defendant convicted in a state court might demonstrate, for example, that the trial was not fair as required by the Bill of Rights, which was extended to cover state court proceedings by the due process clause of the Fourteenth Amendment. As you can see in Table 16.1, the vast majority of cases heard by the Supreme Court come from the lower federal courts.

FIGURE 16.3 How Cases Reach the Supreme Court

There are three routes to the U.S. Supreme Court. The first is through its original jurisdiction, where the Court hears a case in the first instance. Very few cases fall into this category, however. Most cases reach the Court through appeals from decisions in lower federal courts. Some cases also reach the Court as appeals from the highest state court that can hear a state case.

TABLE 16.1 Sources of Full Opinions in the Supreme Court, 2008

TYPE OF CASE	NUMBER OF CASES
Original jurisdiction	1
Civil actions from lower federal courts	42
Federal criminal cases	13
Federal *habeas corpus* cases	7
Civil actions from state courts	7
State criminal cases	8
Total	78

Source: "The Supreme Court, 2008 Term: The Statistics," 123 (November 2009): 393–396.

Most cases that reach the Supreme Court are appeals from lower federal courts. Federal *habeas corpus* is a procedure under which a federal court may review the legality of an individual's incarceration.

The central participants in the judicial system are, of course, the judges. Once on the bench, they inevitably draw on their backgrounds and beliefs in their decision making. Some, for example, will be more supportive of abortion rights or of prayer in the public schools than others. Because presidents and others involved in the appointment process know that judges are not neutral automatons who literally interpret the law, they work diligently to place candidates sympathetic to presidential policies on the bench. Who are the men and women who serve as federal judges and justices, and how did they obtain their positions?

The Politics of Judicial Selection

16.3 Explain the process by which judges and justices are nominated and confirmed.

Nominating federal judges and Supreme Court justices is a president's chance to leave an enduring mark on the American legal system. Guaranteed by the Constitution the right to serve "during good behavior," federal judges and justices enjoy, for all practical purposes, lifetime positions. They may be removed only by conviction of impeachment, which has occurred a mere seven times in over two centuries. Congress has never removed a Supreme Court justice from office, although it tried but did not convict Samuel Chase in 1805. Nor can Congress reduce the salaries of judges, a stipulation that further insulates them from political pressures. The president's discretion is actually less than it appears, however, since the Senate must confirm each nomination by majority vote. Because the judiciary is a coequal branch, the upper house of the legislature sees no reason to be especially deferential to the executive's recommendations.

WHY IT MATTERS

Judicial Election

The public directly elects most state and local judges. All federal judges and justices are nominated by the president and confirmed by the Senate for lifetime tenures. If we elected federal judges, their decisions on highly visible issues might be more responsive to the public—but less responsive to the Constitution.

The Lower Courts

The customary manner for the Senate's consideration of state-level federal judicial nominations to the district courts and courts of appeal is **senatorial courtesy**.[6] Under this unwritten tradition, the Senate does not confirm nominees for district court positions if they are opposed by a senator of the president's party from the state in which the nominee is to serve or nominees for courts of appeal if opposed by a senator of the president's party from the state of the nominee's residence. To invoke the right of senatorial courtesy, the relevant senator usually simply states a general reason for opposition. Other senators then honor their colleague's views and oppose the nomination, regardless of their personal evaluations of the candidate's merits.

senatorial courtesy
An unwritten tradition whereby nominations for state-level federal judicial posts are usually not confirmed if they are opposed by a senator of the president's party from the state in which the nominee will serve. The tradition also applies to courts of appeal when there is opposition from a senator of the president's party who is from the nominee's state.

Because of the strength of this informal practice, presidents usually check carefully with the relevant senator or senators ahead of time to avoid making a nomination that will fail to be confirmed. In many instances, this is tantamount to giving the power of nomination to these senators. Typically, when there is a vacancy for a federal district judgeship, the relevant senator or senators from the state where the judge will serve suggest one or more names to the attorney general and the president. If neither senator is of the president's party, then the party's state congresspersons or other state party leaders may make suggestions. Other interested senators may also try to influence a selection.[7]

The White House, the Department of Justice, and the Federal Bureau of Investigation conduct competency and background checks on persons suggested for judgeships, and the president usually selects a nominee from those who survive the screening process. If one of these survivors was recommended by a senator to whom senatorial courtesy is due, it is difficult for the president to reject the recommendation in favor of someone else who survived the process. Thus, senatorial courtesy turns the Constitution on its head, and in effect the Senate ends up making nominations and the president then approving them.

WHY IT MATTERS

Senatorial Courtesy

Because of the practice of senatorial courtesy, senators in effect end up nominating persons to be district court judges. If the Senate abolished this practice, it would give presidents greater freedom in making nominations and more opportunity to put their stamp on the judiciary.

Others have input in judicial selection as well. The Department of Justice may ask sitting judges, usually federal judges, to evaluate prospective nominees. Sitting judges may also initiate recommendations, advancing or retarding someone's chances of being nominated. In addition, candidates for the nomination are often active on their own behalf. They have to alert the relevant parties that they desire the position and may orchestrate a campaign of support. As one appellate judge observed, "People don't just get judgeships without seeking them."[8]

The president usually has more influence in the selection of judges to the federal courts of appeal than to federal district courts. The decisions of appellate courts are generally more significant than those of lower courts, so the president naturally takes a greater interest in appointing people to these courts. At the same time, individual senators are in a weaker position to determine who the nominee will be because the jurisdiction of an appeals court encompasses several states. Although custom and pragmatic politics require that these judgeships be apportioned among the states in a circuit, the president has some discretion in doing this and therefore has a greater role in recruiting appellate judges than in recruiting district court judges. Even here, however, senators of the president's party from the state in which the candidate resides may be able to veto a nomination.

Traditionally, the Senate confirmed lower federal court nominations swiftly and unanimously. However, the increasing polarization of partisan politics in recent years has affected judicial nominations, especially those for the courts of appeal. Increasingly, lower court confirmations have become lengthy and contentious proceedings. Interest groups opposed to nominations have become more active and encouraged senators aligned with them to delay and block nominations.[9] As a result, there has been a dramatic increase in the time for confirmation,[10] which has in turn has decreased the chances of confirmation. Since 1992, the Senate has confirmed only 60 percent of nominees to the courts of appeal.[11]

Senators of the opposition party filibustered or otherwise derailed the confirmations of a number of high-profile nominations of Presidents Clinton and George W. Bush, in response appointed some judges to the courts of appeals as recess appointments. Such appointments are unusual and good only for the remainder of a congressional term. They are also likely to anger opposition senators. After the Republicans nearly voted to end the possibility of filibustering judicial nominations, 14 senators from both parties forged a deal without White House approval that allowed some—but not all—of Bush's stalled judicial nominees to receive floor votes.

The Supreme Court

The president is vitally interested in the Supreme Court because of the importance of its work and is usually intimately involved in recruiting potential justices. Nominations to the Court may be a president's most important legacy to the nation.

A president cannot have much impact on the Court unless there are vacancies to fill. Although on the average there has been an opening on the Supreme Court every two years, there is a substantial variance around this mean.[12] Franklin D. Roosevelt had to wait five years before he could nominate a justice; in the meantime, he was faced with a Court that found much of his New Deal legislation unconstitutional. Jimmy Carter was never able to nominate a justice. Between 1972 and 1984, there were only two vacancies on the Court. Nevertheless, Richard Nixon was able to nominate four justices in his first three years in office, and Ronald Reagan had the opportunity to add three new members.

When the chief justice's position is vacant, the president may nominate either someone already on the Court or someone from outside to fill the position. Usually presidents choose the latter course to widen their range of options, but if they decide to elevate a sitting associate justice—as President Reagan did with William Rehnquist in 1986—the nominee must go through a new confirmation hearing by the Senate Judiciary Committee.

The president operates under fewer constraints in nominating persons to serve on the Supreme Court than in nominations for the lower courts. Although many of the same actors are present in the case of Supreme Court nominations, their influence is typically quite different. The president usually relies on White House aides and the attorney general and the Department of Justice to identify and screen candidates for the Court. Sitting justices often try to influence the nominations of their future colleagues, but presidents feel little obligation to follow their advice. Senators also play a lesser role in the recruitment of Supreme Court justices than in the selection of lower-court judges, as the jurisdiction of the Court obviously goes beyond individual senators' states or regions. Thus presidents typically consult with senators from the state of residence of a nominee after they have decided whom to select. At this point, senators are unlikely to oppose a nomination because they like having their state receive the honor and are well aware that the president can simply select someone from another state.

Candidates for nomination usually keep a low profile. They can accomplish little through aggressive politicking, and because of the Court's standing, actively pursuing the position might offend those who play important roles in selecting nominees. The American Bar Association's Standing Committee on the federal judiciary has played a varied but typically modest role at the Supreme Court level. Presidents have not generally been willing to allow the committee to prescreen candidates before their nominations are announced. George W. Bush chose not to seek its advice at all.

Through 2010, there have been 153 nominations to the Supreme Court, and 112 people have served on the Court. Four people were nominated and confirmed twice, eight declined appointment or died before beginning service on the Court, and 29 failed to secure Senate confirmation. Presidents have failed 20 percent of the time to appoint the nominees of their choice to the Court—a percentage much higher than for any other federal position.

Although home-state senators do not play prominent roles in the selection process for the Court, the Senate as a whole does. In particular, through its Judiciary Committee, it may probe a nominee's judicial philosophy in great detail.

For most of the twentieth century, confirmations of Supreme Court nominees were routine affairs. Only one nominee failed to win confirmation in the first two-thirds of the century. But, as Table 16.2 shows, the situation changed beginning in the 1960s, tumultuous times that bred ideological conflict. Although John F. Kennedy had no trouble with his two nominations to the Court—Byron White and Arthur Goldberg—his successor, Lyndon Johnson, was less fortunate. In the face of strong opposition, Johnson had to withdraw his nomination of Abe Fortas (already serving on the Court) to serve as chief justice; as a result, the Senate never voted on Homer Thornberry, Johnson's nominee to replace Fortas as an associate justice. Richard Nixon, the next president, had two nominees in a row rejected after bruising battles in the Senate.

Two of President Reagan's nominees proved unsuccessful. In 1987, Reagan nominated Robert H. Bork to fill the vacancy created by the resignation of Justice Lewis Powell. Bork testified before the Senate Judiciary Committee for 23 hours. A wide range of interest groups entered the fray, mostly in opposition to the nominee, whose views they claimed were extremist. In the end, following a bitter floor debate, the Senate rejected the president's nomination by a vote of 42 to 58. Six days after the Senate vote on Bork, the president nominated Judge Douglas H. Ginsburg to the high court. Just nine days later, however, Ginsburg withdrew his nomination after disclosures that he had used marijuana while a law professor at Harvard.

In June 1991, when Associate Justice Thurgood Marshall announced his retirement from the Court, President George H. W. Bush announced his nomination of another African American, federal appeals judge Clarence Thomas, to replace Marshall. Thomas was a conservative, so this decision was consistent with the Bush

TABLE 16.2 Unsuccessful Supreme Court Nominees Since 1900

NOMINEE	YEAR	PRESIDENT
John J. Parker	1930	Hoover
Abe Fortas[a]	1968	Johnson
Homer Thornberry[b]	1968	Johnson
Clement F. Haynesworth, Jr.	1969	Nixon
G. Harrold Carswell	1970	Nixon
Robert H. Bork	1987	Reagan
Douglas H. Ginsburg[a]	1987	Reagan
Harriet Miers[a]	2005	G. W. Bush

[a]Nomination withdrawn. Fortas was serving on the Court as an associate justice and was nominated to be chief justice.

[b]The Senate took no action on Thornberry's nomination.

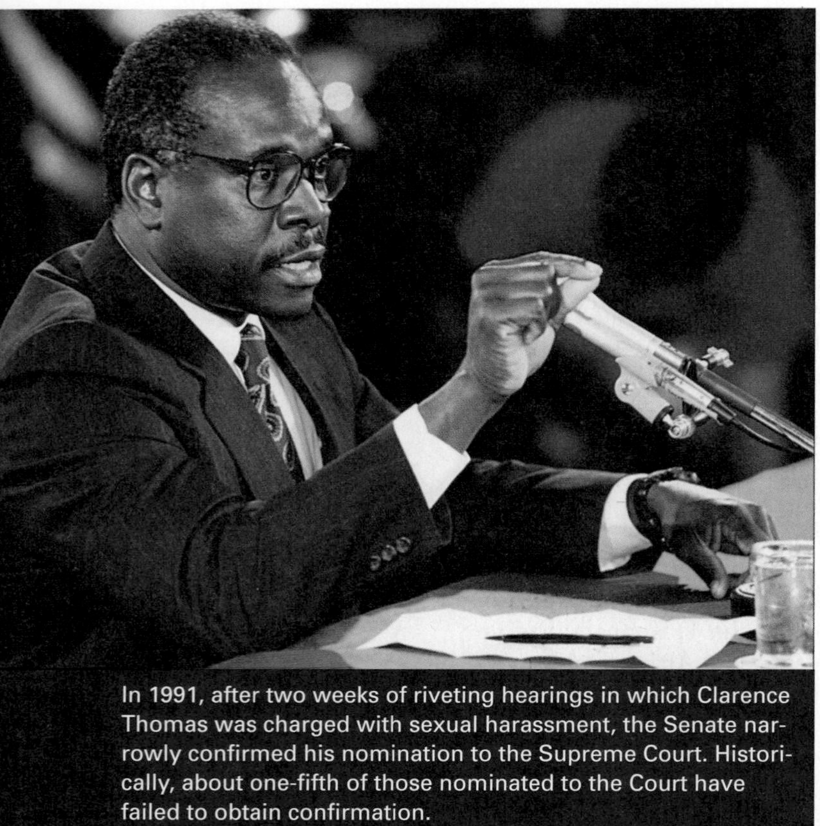

In 1991, after two weeks of riveting hearings in which Clarence Thomas was charged with sexual harassment, the Senate narrowly confirmed his nomination to the Supreme Court. Historically, about one-fifth of those nominated to the Court have failed to obtain confirmation.

administration's emphasis on placing conservative judges on the federal bench. Liberals were placed in a dilemma. On the one hand, they favored a minority group member serving on the nation's highest court, and particularly an African American replacing the Court's only African American. On the other hand, Thomas was unlikely to vote the same way as Thurgood Marshall had voted, and was likely instead to strengthen the conservative trend in the Court's decisions. This ambivalence inhibited spirited opposition to Thomas, who was circumspect about his judicial philosophy in his appearances before the Senate Judiciary Committee. Thomas's confirmation was nearly derailed, however, by charges of sexual harassment leveled against him by University of Oklahoma law professor Anita Hill. Ultimately, following Hill's testimony and Thomas's denial of the charges, he was confirmed in a 52-to-48 vote—the closest margin by which a Supreme Court nomination had been confirmed in more than a century.

President Clinton's two nominees—Ruth Bader Ginsburg and Stephen Breyer—did not cause much controversy and were readily confirmed Similarly, the Senate easily confirmed George W. Bush's nomination of John Roberts as chief justice to succeed William Rehnquist. Indeed, he was not an easy target to oppose. His pleasing and professional personal demeanor and his disciplined and skilled testimony before the Senate Judicial Committee gave potential opponents little basis for opposition.

Ideological conflict returned to the fore, however, when Bush then nominated White House counsel Harriet Miers to replace Justice Sandra Day O'Connor. By settling on a loyalist with no experience as a judge and little substantive record on abortion, affirmative action, religion, and other socially divisive issues, the president shied away from a direct confrontation with liberals and in effect asked his base on the right to trust him on his nomination. However, many conservatives, having hoped and expected that he would make an unambiguously conservative choice to fulfill their goal of clearly altering the Court's balance, were bitterly disappointed and highly critical. They demanded a known conservative. The nomination also smacked of cronyism, with the president selecting a friend rather than someone of obvious merit, and the comparison with Roberts underscored the thinness of Miers's qualifications. In short order, Miers withdrew from consideration, and the president nominated Samuel Alito.

Alito was clearly a traditional conservative and had a less impressive public presence than Roberts. Response to him followed party lines, but he appeared too well qualified and unthreatening in his confirmation hearings to justify a filibuster, and without one, his confirmation was assured. The Senate confirmed Alito by a vote of 58 to 42.

President Obama made his first nomination to the Court in 2009, selecting Sonia Sotomayor. Although conservatives raised questions about some of her previous statements and decisions, she was confirmed by a vote of 68 to 31, largely along party lines. When she took the oath of office, she became the first Hispanic justice. In 2010, the president nominated solicitor general Elena Kagan to the Court. She was confirmed by a vote of 63 to 37, once again largely along party lines.

It is difficult to predict the politics surrounding future nominations to the Supreme Court. One prediction seems safe, however: As long as Americans are polarized around social issues and as long as the Court makes critical decisions about these issues, the potential for conflict over the president's nominations is always present.

Nominations are most likely to run into trouble under certain conditions. Presidents whose parties are in the minority in the Senate or who make a nomination at the end of their terms face a greatly increased probability of substantial opposition.[13] Presidents whose views are more distant from the norm in the Senate or who are appointing a person who might alter the balance on the Court are also likely to face additional opposition. However, opponents of a nomination usually must be able to question a nominee's legal competence or ethics in order to defeat the nomination. Most people do not consider opposition to a nominee's ideology a valid reason to vote against confirmation. For example, liberals disagreed strongly with the views of William Rehnquist, but he was easily confirmed as chief justice. By raising questions about competence or ethics, opponents are able to attract moderate senators to their side and to make ideological protests seem less partisan.

The Backgrounds of Judges and Justices

16.4 Describe the backgrounds of judges and justices and assess the impact of background on their decisions.

The Constitution sets no special requirements for judges or justices, but most observers conclude that the federal judiciary comprises a distinguished group of men and women. Competence and ethical behavior are important to presidents for reasons beyond merely obtaining Senate confirmation of their judicial nominees. Skilled and honorable judges and justices reflect well on the president and are likely to do so for many years, and, of course, they can more effectively represent the president's views. The criteria of competence and ethics, however, still leave a wide field from which to choose; other characteristics also carry considerable weight.

The judges serving on the federal district and circuit courts are not a representative sample of the American people. They are all lawyers (although this is not a constitutional requirement), and they are overwhelmingly white males. Jimmy Carter appointed 40 women, 37 African Americans, and 16 Hispanics to the federal bench, more than all previous presidents combined. Ronald Reagan did not continue this trend, although he was the first to appoint a woman to the Supreme Court. In screening candidates, his administration placed a higher priority on ideology than on diversity. From 1989 to 1992, George H. W. Bush continued to emphasize placing conservatives on the bench. Bill Clinton's nominees were more liberal than were the nominees of Reagan and Bush, and a large percentage of them were women and minorities. George W. Bush's nominees were more diverse than those of his father although less so than were those of Clinton and Carter.[14] Women and minorities are likely to serve on all federal courts more frequently in the future because of their increased numbers in the legal profession as well as because of their increasing political clout.

Federal judges have typically held office as a judge or prosecutor, and often they have been involved in partisan politics. This involvement is generally what brings them to the attention of senators and the Department of Justice when they seek nominees for judgeships. As former U.S. Attorney General and Circuit Court Judge Griffin Bell once remarked, "For me, becoming a federal judge wasn't very difficult. I managed John F. Kennedy's presidential campaign in Georgia. Two of my oldest and closest friends were senators from Georgia. And I was campaign manager and special unpaid counsel for the governor."[15]

Like their colleagues on the lower federal courts, Supreme Court justices are not a representative sample of the population (see Table 16.3 for the current justices). To date, all justices have been lawyers. All but six (Thurgood Marshall, nominated in 1967; Sandra Day O'Connor, nominated in 1981; Clarence Thomas, nominated in 1991; Ruth Bader Ginsburg, nominated in 1993; Sonia Sotomayor, nominated in 2009; and Elena Kagan, nominated in 2010) have been white males. Most have been in their fifties and sixties when they took office, from the upper-middle or upper class, and Protestants.[16]

Geography was once a prominent criterion for selection to the Court, but it is no longer very important. Presidents do like to spread the slots around, however, as when Richard Nixon decided that he wanted to nominate a Southerner. At various times there

TABLE 16.3 Supreme Court Justices, 2010

NAME	YEAR OF BIRTH	PREVIOUS POSITION	NOMINATING PRESIDENT	YEAR OF CONFIRMATION
John G. Roberts, Jr.	1955	U.S. Court of Appeals	G. W. Bush	2005
Antonin Scalia	1936	U.S. Court of Appeals	Reagan	1986
Anthony M. Kennedy	1936	U.S. Court of Appeals	Reagan	1988
Clarence Thomas	1948	U.S. Court of Appeals	G. H. W. Bush	1991
Ruth Bader Ginsburg	1933	U.S. Court of Appeals	Clinton	1993
Stephen G. Breyer	1938	U.S. Court of Appeals	Clinton	1994
Samuel A. Alito, Jr.	1950	U.S. Court of Appeals	G. W. Bush	2006
Sonia Sotomayor	1954	U.S. Court of Appeals	Obama	2009
Elena Kagan	1960	U.S. Solicitor General	Obama	2010

have been what some have termed a "Jewish seat" and a "Catholic seat" on the Court, but these guidelines are not binding on the president. For example, after a half-century of having a Jewish justice, the Court did not have one from 1969 to 1993. And although only 12 Catholics have served on the Court, 6 of the current justices are Catholic.

The backgrounds of federal judges are not representative of Americans. Sonia Sotomayor is the first Hispanic American to serve on the Supreme Court.

Typically, justices have held high administrative or judicial positions before moving to the Supreme Court. Most have had some experience as a judge, often at the appellate level, and many have worked for the Department of Justice. Some have held elective office, and a few have had no government service but have been distinguished attorneys. The fact that many justices, including some of the most distinguished ones, have not had previous judicial experience may seem surprising, but the unique work of the Court renders this background much less important than it might be for other appellate courts.

Partisanship is another important influence on the selection of judges and justices. Only 13 of 112 members of the Supreme Court have been nominated by presidents of a different party. Moreover, many of the 13 exceptions were actually close to the president in ideology, as was the case in Richard Nixon's appointment of Lewis Powell. Herbert Hoover's nomination of Benjamin Cardozo seems to be one of the few cases in which partisanship was completely dominated by merit as a criterion for selection. Usually, close to 90 percent of presidents' judicial nominations are of members of their own parties.

The role of partisanship is really not surprising. Most of a president's acquaintances are made through the party, and there is usually a certain congruity between party and political views. Most judges and justices have at one time been active partisans—an experience that gave them visibility and helped them obtain the positions from which they moved to the courts. Moreover, judgeships are considered very prestigious patronage plums. Indeed, the decisions of Congress to create new judgeships—and thus new positions for party members—are closely related to whether the majority party in Congress is the same as the party of the president. Members of the majority party in the legislature want to avoid providing an opposition party president with new positions to fill with their opponents.

Ideology is as important as partisanship in the selection of judges and justices. Presidents want to appoint to the federal bench people who share their views. In effect, all presidents try to "pack" the courts. They want more than "justice"; they want policies with which they agree. Presidential aides survey candidates' decisions (if they have served on a lower court),[17] speeches, political stands, writings, and other expressions of opinion. They also glean information from people who know the candidates well. Although it is considered improper to question judicial candidates about upcoming court cases, it is appropriate to discuss broader questions of political and judicial philosophy. The Reagan administration was especially concerned about such matters and had each potential nominee fill out a lengthy questionnaire and be interviewed by a special committee in the Department of Justice. Both George H. W. Bush and George W. Bush were also attentive to appointing conservative judges. Bill Clinton was less concerned with appointing liberal judges, at least partly to avoid costly confirmation fights, and instead focused on identifying persons with strong legal credentials, especially women and minorities.

The U. S. Supreme Court, 2011: Front row, left to right: Clarence Thomas, Antonin Scalia, John G. Roberts, Anthony M. Kennedy, and Ruth Bader Ginsburg. Second row, left to right: Sonia Sotomayor, Stephen G. Breyer, Samuel Alito, and. Elena Kagan.

Members of the federal bench also play the game of politics, of course, and may try to time their retirements so that a president with compatible views will choose their successor and perhaps a like-minded Senate will vote on the nomination. For example, it appears that Justice David Souter timed his retirement in 2009 so that Barack Obama rather than George W. Bush would name a new justice. This concern about a successor is one reason why justices remain on the Supreme Court for so long, even when they are clearly infirm.[18]

Presidents are typically pleased with the performance of their nominees to the Supreme Court and through them have slowed or reversed trends in the Court's decisions. Franklin D. Roosevelt's nominees substantially liberalized the Court, whereas Richard Nixon's turned it in a conservative direction, from which it has yet to move.

Nevertheless, it is not always easy to predict the policy inclinations of candidates, and presidents have been disappointed in their nominees about one-fourth of the time. President Eisenhower, for example, was displeased with the liberal decisions of both Earl Warren and William Brennan. Once, when asked whether he had made any mistakes as president, Eisenhower replied, "Yes, two, and they are both sitting on the Supreme Court."[19] Richard Nixon was certainly disappointed when Warren Burger, whom he had nominated as chief justice, wrote the Court's decision calling for immediate desegregation of the nation's schools shortly after his confirmation. This turn of events did little for the president's "Southern strategy." Burger also wrote the Court's opinion in *United States v. Nixon*, which forced the president to release the Watergate tapes. Nixon's resignation soon followed.

Presidents influence policy through the values of their judicial nominees, but this impact is limited by numerous legal and "extralegal" factors beyond the chief executive's control. As Harry Truman put it, "Packing the Supreme Court can't be done . . . I've tried it and it won't work. . . . Whenever you put a man on the Supreme Court, he ceases to be your friend. I'm sure of that."[20]

Although women and people of different ethnicities and religions may desire to have people in their group appointed to the federal bench—at the very least, judgeships have symbolic importance for them[21]—the real question is what, if any, policy differences result. The number of female and minority group judges is too few and their service too recent to serve as a sound basis for broad generalizations about their decisions. There is evidence, however, that female judges on the courts of appeal are more likely than are male judges to support charges of sex discrimination and sexual harassment, and they seem to influence the male judges deciding the cases with them.[22] Similarly, racial and ethnic minority judges on these courts are more likely to find for minority plaintiffs in voting rights cases and also to influence the votes of white judges sitting with them.[23] At the level of the Supreme

Court, conservative Justice Antonin Scalia has said that Justice Thurgood Marshall "could be a persuasive force just by sitting there. He wouldn't have to open his mouth to affect the nature of the conference and how seriously the conference would take matters of race."[24] It is true, of course, that Justice Clarence Thomas, the second African-American justice, is one of the most conservative justices since the New Deal, illustrating that not everyone from a particular background has a particular point of view.

Many members of each party have been appointed, of course, and it appears that Republican judges in general are somewhat more conservative than are Democratic judges. Former prosecutors serving on the Supreme Court have tended to be less sympathetic toward defendants' rights than have other justices. It seems, then, that background does make some difference,[25] yet for reasons that we examine in the following sections, on many issues party affiliation and other characteristics are imperfect predictors of judicial behavior.

The Courts as Policymakers

16.5 Outline the judicial process at the Supreme Court level and assess the major factors influencing decisions and their implementation.

"Judicial decision making," a former Supreme Court law clerk wrote in the *Harvard Law Review*, "involves, at bottom, a choice between competing values by fallible, pragmatic, and at times nonrational men and women in a highly complex process in a very human setting."[26] This is an apt description of policymaking in the Supreme Court and in other courts, too. The next sections look at how courts make policy, paying particular attention to the role of the U.S. Supreme Court. Although it is not the only court involved in policymaking and policy interpretation, its decisions have the widest implications for policy.

Accepting Cases

Deciding what to decide about is the first step in all policymaking. Courts of original jurisdiction cannot very easily refuse to consider a case; appeals courts, including the U.S. Supreme Court, have much more control over their agendas. The approximately 8,000 cases submitted annually to the U.S. Supreme Court must be read, culled, and sifted. Figure 16.4 shows the stages of this process. At least once each week, the nine justices meet in conference. With them in the conference room sit some 25 carts, each wheeled in from the office of one of the nine justices and each filled with petitions, briefs, memoranda, and every item the justices are likely to need during their discussions. These meetings operate under the strictest secrecy; only the justices themselves attend.

At these weekly conferences the justices have two important tasks. The first is to establish an agenda: The justices consider the chief justice's "discuss list" and decide

FIGURE 16.4 Obtaining Space on the Supreme Court's Docket

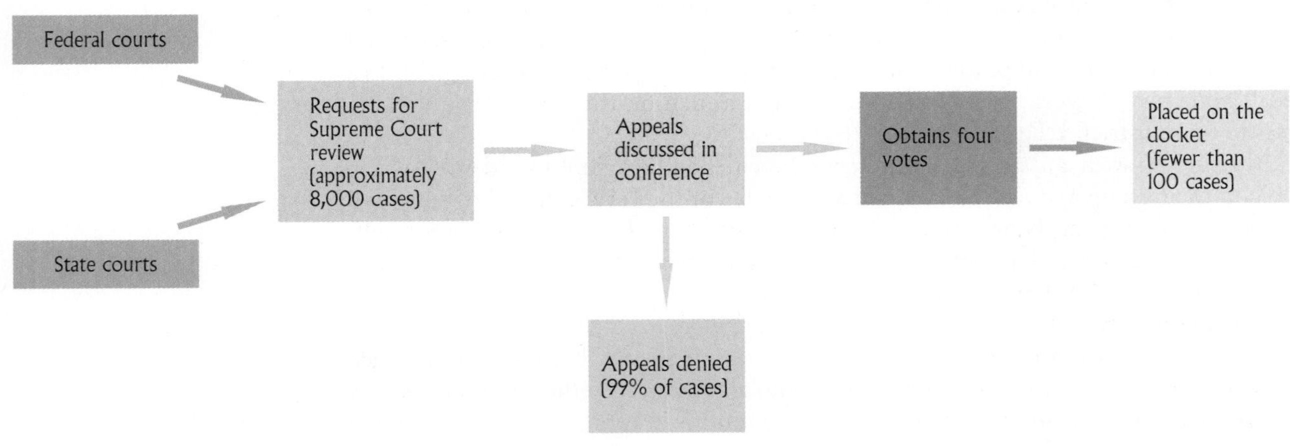

which cases they want to review, or place on the docket. Because few of the justices can take the time to read materials on every case submitted to the Court, most rely heavily on law clerks (each justice has up to four to assist them in considering cases and writing opinions) to screen each case. If four justices agree to grant review of a case (in what is known as the "rule of four"), it can be scheduled for oral argument and the Court typically issues to the relevant lower federal or state court a *writ of certiorari*, a formal document calling up the case. In some instances, the Court will instead decide a case on the basis of the written record already on file with the Court.

Until 1988, some cases—principally those in which federal laws had been found unconstitutional, in which federal courts had concluded that state laws violated the federal Constitution, or in which state laws had been upheld in state courts despite claims that they violated federal law or the Constitution—were technically supposed to be heard by the Court "on appeal." In reality, however, the Court always exercised broad discretion over hearing these and other cases.

The cases most likely to be selected are those that involve major issues—especially civil liberties, conflict between different lower courts on the interpretation of federal law (as when a court of appeals in Texas prohibits the use of affirmative action criteria in college admissions and a court of appeals in Michigan approves their use), or disagreement between a majority of the Supreme Court and lower-court decisions.[27]

Because getting into the Supreme Court is half the battle, it is important to remember this chapter's earlier discussion of standing to sue (litigants must have serious interest in a case, having sustained or being in immediate danger of sustaining a direct and substantial injury from another party or an action of government)—a criterion the Court often uses to decide whether to hear a case. As we discuss later in this chapter, the Court will sometimes avoid hearing cases that are too politically "hot" to handle or that divide the Court too sharply.[28]

Another important influence on the Supreme Court's decisions to accept cases is the solicitor general. As a presidential appointee and the third-ranking official in the Department of Justice, the **solicitor general** is in charge of the appellate court litigation of the federal government. The solicitor general and a staff of about two dozen experienced attorneys have four key functions: (1) to decide whether to appeal cases the government has lost in the lower courts, (2) to review and modify the briefs presented in government appeals, (3) to represent the government before the Supreme Court, and (4) to submit an *amicus curiae* brief on behalf of a litigant in a case in which the government has an interest but is not directly involved.[29] Unlike attorneys for private parties, the solicitors general are careful to seek Court review only of important cases. By avoiding frivolous appeals and displaying a high degree of competence, they typically earn the confidence of the Court, which in turn grants review of a large percentage of the cases they submit.[30]

solicitor general
A presidential appointee and the third-ranking office in the Department of Justice. The solicitor general is in charge of the appellate court litigation of the federal government.

Ultimately, the Supreme Court decides very few cases. In recent years, the Court has made about 80 formal written decisions per year in which their opinions could serve as precedent and thus as the basis of guidance for lower courts. In a few dozen additional cases, the Court reaches a *per curiam decision*—that is, a decision without explanation. Such decisions resolve the immediate case but have no value as precedent because the Court does not offer reasoning that would guide lower courts in future decisions.[31]

Making Decisions

The second task of the justices' weekly conferences is to discuss cases actually accepted and argued before the Court. From the first Monday in October until June, the Court hears oral arguments in two-week cycles: two weeks of courtroom arguments followed by two weeks of reflecting on cases and writing opinions about them. Figure 16.5 shows the stages in this process.

Before the justices enter the courtroom to hear the lawyers for each side present their arguments, they have received elaborately prepared written briefs from each party

FIGURE 16.5 The Supreme Court's Decision-Making Process

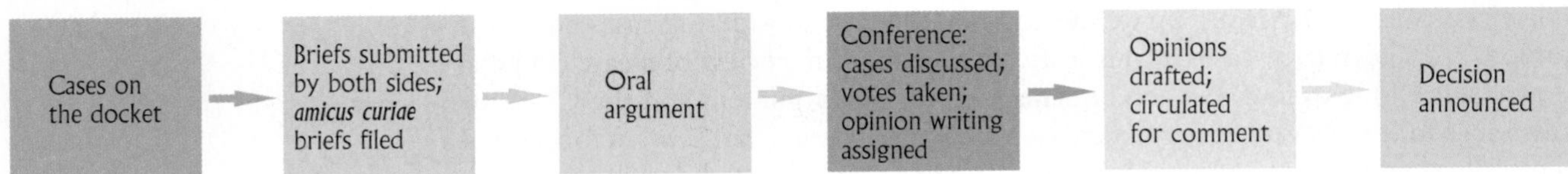

involved. They have also probably received several *amicus curiae* briefs from parties (often groups) who are interested in the outcome of the case but who are not formal litigants. As already noted, *amicus curiae* briefs may be submitted by the government, under the direction of the solicitor general, in cases in which it has an interest. For instance, if a case between two parties involves the question of the constitutionality of a federal law, the federal government naturally wants to have its voice heard. Administrations also use these briefs to urge the Court to change established doctrine. For example, the Reagan administration frequently submitted *amicus curiae* briefs to the Court to try to change the law dealing with defendants' rights.

In most instances, the attorneys for each side have only a half-hour to address the Court. During this time they summarize their briefs, emphasizing their most compelling points.[32] The justices may listen attentively, interrupt with penetrating or helpful questions, request information, talk to one another, read (presumably briefs), or simply gaze at the ceiling. After 25 minutes, a white light comes on at the lectern from which the lawyer is speaking, and five minutes later a red light signals the end of that lawyer's presentation, even if he or she is in midsentence. Oral argument is over.[33]

opinion
A statement of legal reasoning behind a judicial decision. The content of an opinion may be as important as the decision itself.

Back in the conference room, the chief justice, who presides over the Court, raises a particular case and invites discussion, turning first to the senior associate justice. Discussion can range from perfunctory to profound and from courteous to caustic. If the votes are not clear from the individual discussions, the chief justice may ask each justice to vote. Once a tentative vote has been reached on a case, it is necessary to write an **opinion**, a statement of the legal reasoning behind the decision for the case.

Opinion writing is no mere formality. In fact, the content of an opinion may be as important as the decision itself. Broad and bold opinions have far-reaching implications for future cases; narrowly drawn opinions may have little impact beyond the case being decided. Tradition in the Supreme Court requires that the chief justice, if in the majority, write the opinion or assign it to another justice in the majority. The chief justice often writes the opinion in landmark cases, as Earl Warren did in *Brown v. Board of Education* and Warren Burger did in *United States v. Nixon*. If the chief justice is part of the minority, the senior associate justice in the majority assigns the opinion. The person assigned to write an opinion circulates drafts within the Court, justices make suggestions, and they all conduct negotiations among themselves.[34] The content of the opinion can win or lose votes. A justice must redraft an opinion that proves unacceptable to the majority of his or her colleagues on the Court.

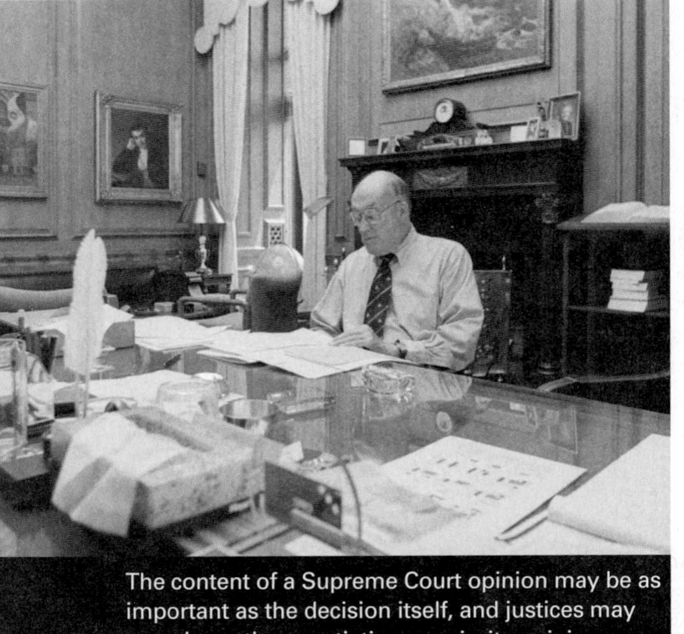
The content of a Supreme Court opinion may be as important as the decision itself, and justices may spend months negotiating a majority opinion. Here, William H. Rehnquist, former chief justice of the Supreme Court, prepares a written opinion.

Justices are free to write their own opinions, to join in other opinions, or to associate themselves with part of one opinion and part of another. Justices opposed to all or part of the majority's decision write *dissenting opinions*. *Concurring opinions* are those written not only to support a majority decision but also to stress a different constitutional or legal basis for the judgment.

When the justices have written their opinions and taken the final vote, they announce their decision. At least six justices must participate in a case, and decisions are made by majority vote. If there is a tie (because of a vacancy on the Court or because a justice chooses not to participate), the decision of the lower court from which the case came is sustained. Five votes in agreement on the reasoning underlying an opinion are necessary for the logic to serve as precedent for judges of lower courts.

The vast majority of cases that reach the courts are settled on the principle of ***stare decisis*** ("let the decision stand"), meaning that an earlier decision should hold for the case being considered. All courts rely heavily on **precedent**—the way similar cases were handled in the past—as a guide to current decisions. Lower courts, of course, are expected to follow the precedents of higher courts in their decision making. If the Supreme Court, for example, rules in favor of the right to abortion under certain conditions, it has established a precedent that lower courts are expected to follow. Lower courts have much less discretion than the Supreme Court.

stare decisis
A Latin phrase meaning "let the decision stand." Most cases reaching appellate courts are settled on this principle.

precedent
How similar cases have been decided in the past.

The Supreme Court is in a position to overrule its own precedents, and it has done so more than 200 times.[35] One of the most famous of such instances occurred with *Brown v. Board of Education* (1954), in which the court overruled *Plessy v. Ferguson* (1896) and found that segregation in the public schools violated the Constitution.

What happens when precedents are unclear? This is especially a problem for the Supreme Court, which is more likely than other courts to handle cases at the forefront of the law, where precedent is typically less firmly established. Moreover, the justices are often asked to apply to concrete situations the vague phrases of the Constitution ("due process of law," "equal protection," "unreasonable searches and seizures") or vague statutes passed by Congress. This ambiguity provides leeway for the justices to disagree (only about one-third of the cases in which full opinions are handed down are decided unanimously) and for their values to influence their judgment. In contrast, when precedents are clear and legal doctrine is well established, legal factors are more likely to play a preeminent role in Supreme Court decision making.[36]

A POINT TO PONDER

Supreme Court justices have substantial discretion in deciding constitutional issues.

Are you content with this judicial freedom? Is there any way to constrain Court decisions?

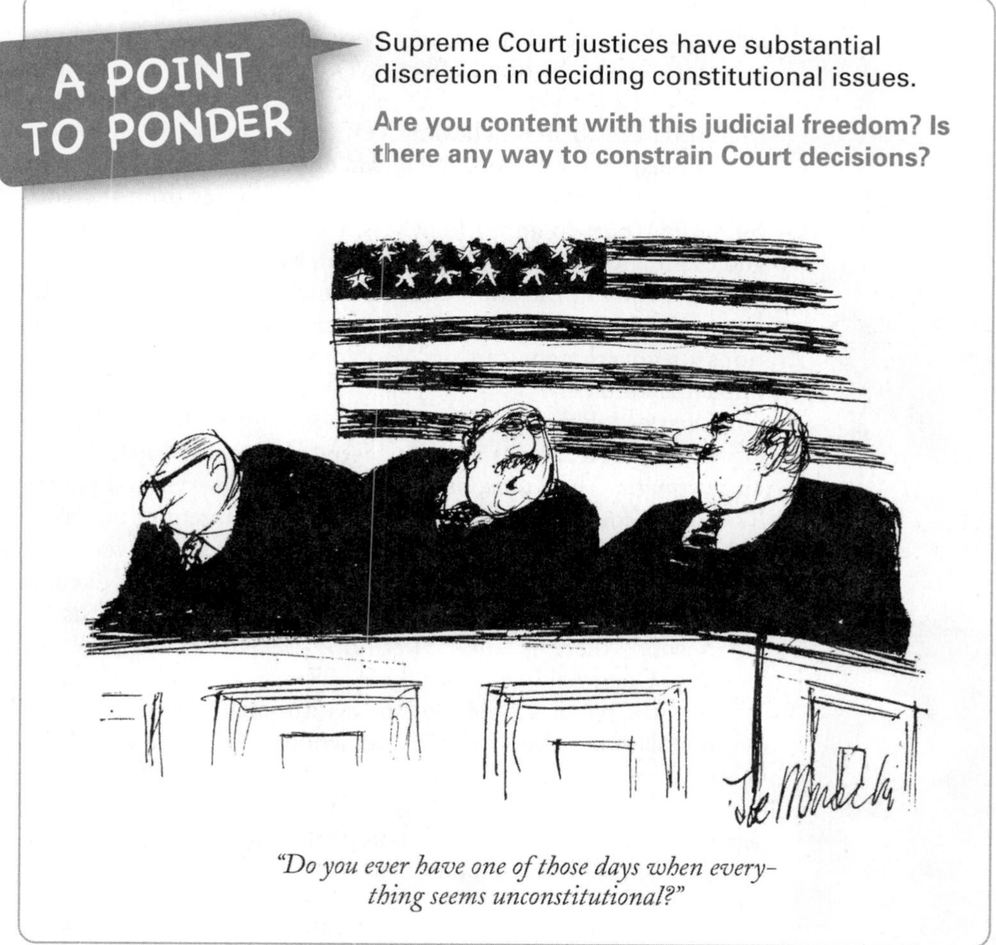

"Do you ever have one of those days when everything seems unconstitutional?"

Perhaps not surprisingly, consistent patterns related to values and ideology—to conservative versus liberal positions—are often evident in the decisions of justices. For example, if there is division on the Court, indicating that precedent is not clear, and you can identify a conservative side to the issue at hand, it is likely that Clarence Thomas will be on that side. Ruth Bader Ginsburg may very well be voting on the other side of the issue. In other words, policy preferences do matter in judicial decision making, especially on the nation's highest court[37] (see "You Are the Policymaker: The Debate over Original Intentions").

The Court conveys its decisions to the press and the public through formal announcements in open court. Media coverage of the Court remains primitive—short and shallow. Doris Graber reports that "much reporting on the courts—even at the Supreme Court level—is imprecise and sometimes even wrong."[38] More important to the legal community, the decisions are bound weekly and made available to every law library and lawyer in the United States. There is, of course, an air of finality to the public announcement of a decision. In fact, however, even Supreme Court decisions are not self-implementing; they are actually "remands" to lower courts, instructing them to act in accordance with the Court's decisions.

judicial implementation
How and whether court decisions are translated into actual policy, thereby affecting the behavior of others. The courts rely on other units of government to enforce their decisions.

original intent
A view that the Constitution should be interpreted according to the original intent of the Framers. Many conservatives support this view.

Implementing Court Decisions

Reacting bitterly to one of Chief Justice Marshall's decisions, President Andrew Jackson is said to have grumbled, "John Marshall has made his decision; now let him enforce it." Court decisions carry legal, even moral, authority, but courts must rely on other units of government to enforce their decisions. **Judicial implementation** refers to how and whether court decisions are translated into actual policy, thereby affecting the behavior of others.

Judicial decision is the end of one process—the litigation process—and the beginning of another process—the process of judicial implementation. Sometimes delay and stalling follow even decisive court decisions. There is, for example, the story of the tortured efforts of a young African American named Virgil Hawkins to get himself admitted to the University of Florida Law School. Hawkins's efforts began in 1949, when he first applied for admission, and ended unsuccessfully in 1958, after a decade of court decisions. Despite a 1956 order from the U.S. Supreme Court to admit Hawkins, legal skirmishing continued and eventually produced a 1958 decision by a U.S. district court in Florida ordering the admission of nonwhites but upholding the denial of admission to Hawkins. Other courts and other institutions of government can be roadblocks in the way of judicial implementation.

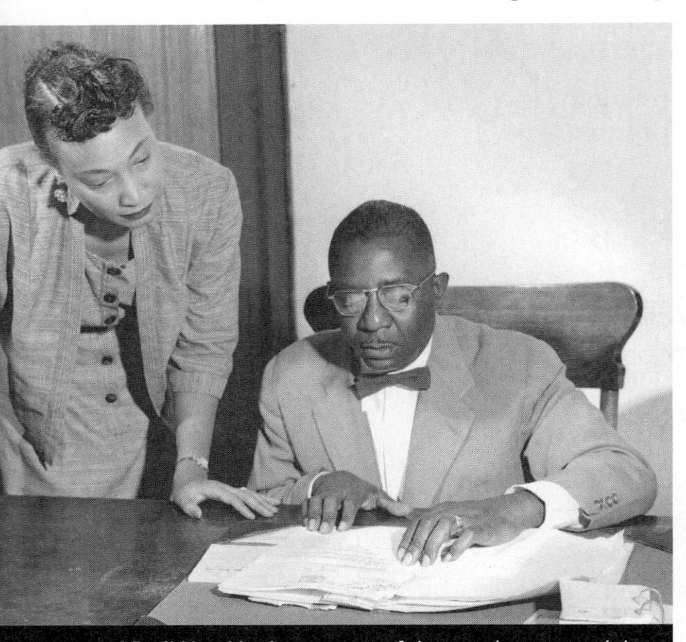

Virgil Hawkins's unsuccessful struggle to attend the all-white University of Florida Law School illustrates how judicial implementation can affect the impact of court decisions. The Supreme Court ordered the school to admit Hawkins in 1956, but the school and state refused to implement the ruling, and continued to appeal the case. Two years later a Florida district court again denied admission to Hawkins, although it did order the school's desegregation.

Charles Johnson and Bradley Canon suggest that implementation of court decisions involves several elements.[39] First, there is an *interpreting population*, heavily composed of lawyers and judges. They must correctly understand and reflect the intent of the original decision in their subsequent actions. Usually lower-court judges do follow the Supreme Court, but sometimes they circumvent higher-court decisions to satisfy their own policy interests.[40]

Second, there is an *implementing population*. Suppose the Supreme Court held (as it did) that prayers organized by school officials in the public schools are unconstitutional. The implementing population (school boards and school administrators whose schools are conducting prayers) must then actually abandon prayers. Police departments, hospitals, corporations, government agencies—all may be part of the implementing population. With so many implementors, many of whom may disagree with a decision, there is plenty of room for "slippage" between what the Supreme Court decides and what actually occurs (as there has been

YOU ARE THE POLICYMAKER

The Debate over Original Intentions

The most contentious issue involving the courts is the role of judicial discretion. According to Christopher Wolfe, "The Constitution itself nowhere specifies a particular set of rules by which it is to be interpreted. Where does one go, then, in order to discover the proper way to interpret the Constitution?"

Some jurists have argued for a jurisprudence of **original intent**, sometimes referred to as *strict constructionism*. This view holds that judges and justices should attempt to determine the intent of the Framers of the Constitution regarding a particular matter and decide cases in line with that intent. Such a view is popular with conservatives.

Advocates of strict constructionism view it as a means of constraining the exercise of judicial discretion, which they see as the foundation of the liberal decisions, especially on matters of civil liberties, civil rights, and defendants' rights (discussed in Chapters 4 and 5).

They also see following original intent as the only basis of interpretation consistent with democracy. Judges, they argue, should not dress up constitutional interpretations with *their* views on "contemporary needs," "today's conditions," or "what is right." It is the job of legislators, not judges, to make such judgments.

Other jurists disagree. They maintain that what appears to be deference to the intentions of the Framers is simply a cover for making conservative decisions. Opponents of original intent assert that the Constitution is subject to multiple meanings by thoughtful people in different ages. Judges will differ in time and place about what they think the Constitution means. Thus, basing decisions on original intent is not likely to have much effect on judicial discretion.

In addition, these jurists contend that the Constitution is not like a paint-by-numbers kit. Trying to reconstruct or guess the Framers' intentions is very difficult. Recent key cases before the Supreme Court have concerned issues such as school busing, abortions, the Internet, and wiretapping that the Framers could not have imagined; there were no public schools or buses, no contraceptives or modern abortion techniques, and certainly no computers or electronic surveillance equipment or telephones in 1787.

The Founders embraced general principles, not specific solutions, when they wrote the Constitution. They frequently lacked discrete, discoverable intent. Moreover, there is often no record of their intentions, nor is it clear whose intentions should count—those of the writers of the Constitution, those of the more than 1,600 members who attended the ratifying conventions, or those of the voters who sent them there. This problem grows more complex when you consider the amendments to the Constitution, which involve thousands of additional "Framers."

Historian Jack N. Rakove points out that there is little historical evidence that the Framers believed that their intentions should guide later interpretations of the Constitution. In fact, there is some evidence for believing that Madison—the key delegate—left the Constitutional Convention bitterly disappointed with the results. What if Madison had one set of intentions but—like anyone working in a committee—got a different set of results?

The lines are drawn. On one side is the argument that any deviation from following the original intentions of the Constitution's Framers is a deviation from principle, leaving unelected judges to impose their views on the American people. If judges do not follow original intentions, then on what do they base their decisions?

On the other side is the counterargument that it is often impossible to discern the views of the Framers and that there is no good reason to be constrained by the views of the eighteenth century, which reflect a more limited conception of constitutional rights. How can the nation cope with its evolving needs unless the principles in the Constitution are adapted to the demands of each era?

What do you think? The choice here is at the very heart of the judicial process. If you were a justice sitting on the Supreme Court and were asked to interpret the meaning of the Constitution, what would *you* do?

Sources: Christopher Wolfe, *The Rise of Modern Judicial Review* (New York: Basic Books, 1986); Raoul Berger, *Government by Judiciary: The Transformation of the Fourteenth Amendment* (Cambridge, MA: Harvard University Press, 1977); Traciel V. Reid, "A Critique of Interpretivism and Its Claimed Influence upon Judicial Decision Making," *American Politics Quarterly* 16 (July 1988): 329–56; Jack N. Rakove, ed., *Interpreting the Constitution* (Boston: Northeastern University Press, 1990); Arthur S. Miller, "In Defense of Judicial Activism," in *Supreme Court Activism and Restraint*, ed. Stephen C. Halpern and Charles M. Lamb (Lexington, MA: D.C. Heath, 1982); Stephen Breyer, *Active Liberty: Interpreting Our Democratic Constitution* (New York: Knopf, 2005); Antonin Scalia, *A Matter of Interpretation: Federal Courts and the Law* (Princeton, NJ: Princeton University Press, 1998).

The Lack of a Judicial Bureaucracy

The federal courts lack a bureaucracy to implement their decisions. In fact, some of the Supreme Court's most controversial decisions, such as those dealing with school integration and school prayers, have been implemented only with great difficulty. If the courts had a bureaucracy to enforce their decisions, justice might be better served, but such a bureaucracy would have to be enormous to monitor, for example, every school or every police station.

with school prayers[41]). Judicial decisions are more likely to be implemented smoothly if implementation is concentrated in the hands of a few highly visible officials, such as the president or state legislators. Even then, the courts may face difficulties. Responding to the *Brown* decision ending legal segregation in the nation's public schools, in 1959 the Board of Supervisors for Prince Edward County, abetted by changes in Virginia laws, refused to appropriate *any* funds for the County School Board at all. This action effectively closed all public schools in the county to avoid integrating them. The schools remained closed for five years until the legal process finally forced them to reopen.

Third, every decision involves a *consumer population*. For example, the consumer population of an abortion decision are those who may want to have an abortion (and those who oppose them); the consumers of the *Miranda* decision (see Chapter 4) are criminal defendants and their attorneys. The consumer population must be aware of its newfound rights and stand up for them.

Congress and presidents can also help or hinder judicial implementation. When the Supreme Court, the year after its 1954 decision in *Brown v. Board of Education*, ordered public schools desegregated "with all deliberate speed," President Eisenhower refused to state clearly that Americans should comply, which may have encouraged local school boards to resist the decision. Congress was not much help either; only a decade later, in the wake of the civil rights movement, did it pass legislation denying federal aid to segregated schools. Different presidents have different commitments to a particular judicial policy. After years of court and presidential decisions supporting busing to end racial segregation, in December 1984 the Reagan administration went before the Supreme Court and argued *against* school busing in a case in Norfolk, Virginia.

16.6 Trace the Supreme Court's use of judicial review in major policy battles in various eras of American history.

The Courts and Public Policy: An Historical Review

Like all policymakers, the courts are choice takers. Ultimately, the choices they take affect us all (see "Young People and Politics: The Supreme Court Is Closer Than You Think"). Confronted with controversial policies, they make controversial decisions that leave some people winners and others losers. The courts have made policy about slavery and segregation, corporate power and capital punishment, and dozens of other controversial matters.

Until the Civil War, the dominant questions before the Court concerned slavery and the strength and legitimacy of the federal government; these latter issues were resolved in favor of the supremacy of the federal government. From the Civil War until 1937, questions of the relationship between the federal government and the economy predominated. During this period, the Court restricted the power of the federal government to regulate the economy. From 1938 to the present, the paramount issues before the Court have concerned personal liberty and social and political equality. In this era, the Court has enlarged the scope of personal freedom and civil rights and has removed many of the constitutional restraints on the regulation of the economy.

Few justices played a more important role in making the Court a significant national agenda setter than John Marshall, chief justice from 1801 to 1835. His successors have continued not only to respond to the political agenda but also to shape discussion and debate about it.

John Marshall and the Growth of Judicial Review

Scarcely was the government housed in its new capital when Federalists and Democratic-Republicans clashed over the courts. In the election of 1800, Democratic-Republican Thomas Jefferson beat Federalist incumbent John Adams. Determined to leave at least the judiciary in trusted hands, Adams tried to fill it with Federalists. He is alleged to have stayed at his desk until 9:00 P.M. on his last night in the White House signing commissions (March 3, 1801).

The Supreme Court Is Closer Than You Think

The Supreme Court of the United States may seem remote and not especially relevant to a college student. Yet a surprising number of its most important decisions have been brought by young adults seeking protection for their civil rights and liberties. For example, we saw in Chapter 5 that in *Rostker v. Goldberg* (1981) several young men filed a suit claiming that the Military Selective Service Act's requirement that only males register for the draft was unconstitutional. Although the Court held that the requirement was constitutional, draft registration was suspended temporarily during the suit.

Students were the center of two cases we discussed in Chapter 4: In *Board of Regents of University of Wisconsin System v. Southworth* (2000), the Court upheld the University of Wisconsin's requirement of a fee to fund speakers on campus, even if the speakers advocated views that offended some students; in *Zurcher v. Stanford Daily* (1978), the Court decided against a campus newspaper which sought to shield its files from a police search. In 1992, the Supreme Court ruled that legislatures and universities may not single out racial, religious, or sexual insults or threats for prosecution as "hate speech" or "bias crimes" (*R.A.V. v. St. Paul*). In cases such as those stemming from Gregory Johnson's burning an American flag at the 1984 Republican National Convention to protest nuclear arms buildup (which the Court protected in *Texas v. Johnson* [1989]) and David O'Brien's burning a draft card (which the Court did not protect in *United States v. O'Brien* [1968]), young adults have also been pioneers in the area of symbolic speech.

Issues of religious freedom have also prominently featured college students. In *Widmar v. Vincent* (1981), the Court decided that public universities that permit student groups to use their facilities must allow student religious groups on campus to use the facilities for religious worship. In 1995, the Court held that the University of Virginia was constitutionally required to subsidize a student religious magazine on the same basis as other student publications (*Rosenberger v. University of Virginia*). However, in 2004 the Court held that the state of Washington was within its rights when it excluded students pursuing a devotional theology degree from its general scholarship program (*Locke v. Davey*).

Thus, the Supreme Court has a long history of dealing with issues of importance to young adults. Often it is young adults themselves who initiate the cases—and who take them all the way to the nation's highest court.

QUESTIONS FOR DISCUSSION

- Why do you think cases involving young people tend to involve civil liberties issues?
- What other issues of particular importance to young people should the Supreme Court decide?

In the midst of this flurry, Adams appointed William Marbury to the minor post of justice of the peace in the District of Columbia. In the rush of last-minute business, however, Secretary of State John Marshall failed to deliver commissions to Marbury and 16 others. He left the commissions to be delivered by the incoming secretary of state, James Madison.

Madison and Jefferson were furious at Adams's actions and refused to deliver the commissions. Marbury and three others in the same situation sued Madison, asking the Supreme Court to order Madison to give them their commissions. They took their case directly to the Supreme Court under the Judiciary Act of 1789, which gave the Court original jurisdiction in such matters.

The new chief justice was none other than Adams's former secretary of state and arch-Federalist John Marshall, himself one of the "midnight appointments" (he took his seat on the Court barely three weeks before Adams's term ended). Marshall and his Federalist colleagues were in a tight spot. Threats of impeachment came from Jeffersonians fearful that the Court would vote for Marbury. Moreover, if the Court ordered Madison to deliver the commissions, he was likely to ignore the order, putting the prestige of the nation's highest court at risk over a minor issue. Marshall had no means of compelling Madison to act. The Court could also deny Marbury's claim. Taking that option, however, would concede the issue to the Jeffersonians and give the appearance of retreat in the face of opposition, thereby reducing the power of the Court.

John Marshall, chief justice from 1801 to 1835, established the Supreme Court's power of judicial review in the 1803 case *Marbury v. Madison.* In their ruling on the case, Marshall and his associates declared that the Court has the power to determine the constitutionality of congressional actions.

Marshall devised a shrewd solution to the case of ***Marbury v. Madison***. In February 1803, he delivered the unanimous opinion of the Court. First, Marshall and his colleagues argued that Madison was wrong to withhold Marbury's commission. The Court also found, however, that the Judiciary Act of 1789, under which Marbury had brought suit, contradicted the plain words of the Constitution about the Court's original jurisdiction. Thus, Marshall dismissed Marbury's claim, saying that the Court, according to the Constitution, had no power to require that the commission be delivered.

Conceding a small battle over Marbury's commission (he did not get it), Marshall won a much larger war, asserting for the courts the power to determine what is and what is not constitutional. As Marshall wrote, "An act of the legislature repugnant to the Constitution is void," and "it is emphatically the province and duty of the judicial department to say what the law is." The chief justice established the power of **judicial review**, the power of the courts to hold acts of Congress and, by implication, the executive in violation of the Constitution.

Marbury v. Madison was part of a skirmish between the Federalists on the Court and the Democratic-Republican–controlled Congress. Partly to rein in the Supreme Court, for example, the Jeffersonian Congress in 1801 abolished the lower federal appeals courts and made the Supreme Court judges return to the unpleasant task of "riding circuit"—serving as lower-court judges around the country. This was an act of studied harassment of the Court by its enemies.

After *Marbury*, angry members of Congress, together with other Jeffersonians, claimed that Marshall was a "usurper of power," setting himself above Congress and the president. This view, however, was unfair. State courts, before and after the Constitution, had declared acts of their legislatures unconstitutional. In the *Federalist Papers*, Alexander Hamilton had expressly assumed the power of the federal courts to review legislation. And in fact the federal courts had already used this power: *Marbury* was not even the first case to strike down an act of Congress, as a lower federal court had done so in 1792, and the Supreme Court itself had approved a law after a constitutional review in 1796. Marshall was neither inventing nor imagining his right to review laws for their constitutionality.

Marbury v. Madison
The 1803 case in which Chief Justice John Marshall and his associates first asserted the right of the Supreme Court to determine the meaning of the U.S. Constitution. The decision established the Court's power of **judicial review** over acts of Congress, in this case the Judiciary Act of 1789.

judicial review
The power of the courts to determine whether acts of Congress and, by implication, the executive are in accord with the U.S. Constitution. Judicial review was established by John Marshall and his associates in ***Marbury v. Madison***.

The case illustrates that the courts must be politically astute in exercising their power over the other branches. By in effect reducing its *own* power—the authority to hear cases such as Marbury's under its original jurisdiction—the Court was able to assert the right of judicial review in a fashion that the other branches could not easily rebuke.

More than any other power of the courts, judicial review has embroiled them in policy controversy. Before the Civil War, the Supreme Court, headed by Chief Justice Roger Taney, held the Missouri Compromise unconstitutional because it restricted slavery in the territories. The decision was one of many steps along the road to the Civil War. After the Civil War, the Court was again active, this time using judicial review to strike down dozens of state and federal laws curbing the growing might of business corporations.

The "Nine Old Men"

Never was the Court as controversial as during the New Deal. At President Roosevelt's urging, Congress passed dozens of laws designed to end the Depression. However, conservatives (most nominated by Republican presidents), who viewed federal intervention in the economy as unconstitutional and tantamount to socialism, dominated the Court.

The Supreme Court began to dismantle New Deal policies one by one. The National Industrial Recovery Act was one of a string of anti-Depression measures. Although this act was never particularly popular, the Court sealed its doom in *Schechter Poultry Corporation v. United States* (1935), declaring it unconstitutional because it regulated purely local business that did not affect interstate commerce.

Incensed, Roosevelt in 1937 proposed what critics called a "court-packing plan." Noting that the average age of the Court was over 70, Roosevelt railed against those "nine old men." The Constitution gave the justices lifetime jobs (see "America in Perspective: The Tenure of Supreme Court Judges"), but Congress can determine the number of justices. Thus, FDR proposed that Congress expand the size of the Court, a move that would have allowed him to appoint additional justices sympathetic to the New Deal. Congress objected and never passed the plan. It became irrelevant, however, when two justices, Chief Justice Charles Evans Hughes and Associate Justice Owen Roberts, began switching their votes in favor of New Deal legislation. (One wit called it the "switch in time that saved nine.") Shortly thereafter, Associate Justice William Van Devanter retired, and Roosevelt got to make the first of his many appointments to the Court.

The Warren Court

Few eras of the Supreme Court have been as active in shaping public policy as that of the Warren Court (1953–1969), presided over by Chief Justice Earl Warren. Scarcely had President Eisenhower appointed Warren when the Court faced the issue of school segregation. In 1954, it held that laws requiring segregation of the public schools were unconstitutional. Later it expanded the rights of criminal defendants, extending the right to counsel and protections against unreasonable search and seizure and self-incrimination (see Chapter 4). It ordered states to reapportion both their legislatures

AMERICA IN PERSPECTIVE

The Tenure of Supreme Court Judges

The U.S. Supreme Court plays a crucial role in American government, and federal judges, including Supreme Court justices, have tenure for life. As a result, the average age of U.S. justices is high, and there are typically many justices who are over 75 years old. Life tenure also means that there are fewer changes of justices than there would be in a system with shorter terms.

Interestingly, *every* other established democracy provides for some limits on the tenure of judges on its highest constitutional court. Here are some examples:

Country	Term for Judges on Highest Constitutional Court
France	9-year, nonrenewable term
Italy	9-year, nonrenewable term
Portugal	9-year, nonrenewable term
Spain	9-year, nonrenewable term
Germany	12-year term, must retire at 68
Japan	10-year term, must retire at 70; voters vote to renew justices every 10 years
India	serve under good behavior up to age 65
Australia	serve under good behavior up to age 70
Canada	serve under good behavior up to age 75

DISCUSSION QUESTIONS:

- If a constitutional convention were reconvened today, would we still opt for life tenure?
- Do you agree with Alexander Hamilton's argument in *Federalist #78* that life tenure was an excellent means of securing "a steady, upright, and impartial administration of the laws"?

Source: Steven G. Calabresi and James Lindgren, "Term Limits for the Supreme Court: Life Tenure Reconsidered," *Harvard Journal of Law and Public Policy* 29 (Summer 2006), pp. 819–822.

and their congressional districts according to the principle of one person, one vote, and it prohibited organized prayer in public schools. So active was the Warren Court that right-wing groups, fearing that it was remaking the country, posted billboards all over the United States urging Congress to "Impeach Earl Warren."[42]

The Burger Court

Warren's retirement in 1969 gave President Richard Nixon his hoped-for opportunity to appoint a "strict constructionist"—that is, one who interprets the Constitution narrowly—as chief justice. He chose Minnesotan Warren E. Burger, then a conservative judge on the District of Columbia Court of Appeals. As Nixon hoped, the Burger Court turned out to be more conservative than the liberal Warren Court. It narrowed defendants' rights, though it did not overturn the fundamental contours of the *Miranda* decision. The conservative Burger Court, however, also wrote the abortion decision in *Roe v. Wade*, required school busing in certain cases to eliminate historic segregation, and upheld affirmative action programs in the *Weber* case (see Chapter 5). One of the most notable decisions of the Burger Court weighed against Burger's appointer, Richard Nixon. At the height of the Watergate scandal (see Chapter 13), the Supreme Court was called on to decide whether Nixon had to turn his White House tapes over to the courts. It unanimously ordered him to do so in *United States v. Nixon* (1974), thus hastening the president's resignation.

The Rehnquist and Roberts Courts

By the early 1990s, the conservative nominees of Republican presidents, led by Chief Justice William Rehnquist, composed a clear Supreme Court majority. In 2005, John Roberts replaced Rehnquist as chief justice, but the basic divisions on the Court have remained relatively stable. Like the Burger Court, the Supreme Court in recent years has been conservative, and like both the Warren and the Burger Courts, it has been neither deferential to Congress nor reluctant to enter the political fray. The Court's decision in *Bush v. Gore* (2000) that decided the 2000 presidential election certainly represents a high point of judicial activism.

However one evaluates the Court's direction, in most cases in recent years the Court has not created a revolution in constitutional law. Instead, as discussed in Chapters 4 and 5, it has limited, rather than reversed, rights established by liberal decisions such as those regarding defendants' rights and abortion. Although its protection of the First Amendment rights of free speech and free press has remained robust, the Court has tended no longer to see itself as the special protector of individual liberties and civil rights for minorities and has raised important obstacles to affirmative action programs. In the area of federalism, however, the Court has blazed new paths in constraining the federal government's power over the states, as we saw in Chapter 3.

16.7 Assess the role of unelected courts and the scope of judicial power in American democracy.

Understanding the Courts

Powerful courts are unusual; few nations have them. The power of American judges raises questions about the compatibility of unelected courts with a democracy and about the appropriate role for the judiciary in policymaking.

The Courts and Democracy

Announcing his retirement in 1981, Justice Potter Stewart made a few remarks to the handful of reporters present. Embedded in his brief statement was this observation: "It seems to me that there's nothing more antithetical to the idea of what a good judge should be than to think it has something to do with representative democracy." He meant that judges should not be subject to the whims of popular majorities. In a nation that insists so strongly that it is democratic, where do the courts fit in?

In some ways, the courts are not a very democratic institution. Federal judges are not elected and are almost impossible to remove. Indeed, their social backgrounds probably make the courts the most elite-dominated policymaking institution. If democracy requires that key policymakers always be elected or be continually responsible to those who are, then the courts diverge sharply from the requirements of democratic government.

The Supreme Court frequently makes controversial decisions regarding important matters of politics and public policy. Critics often argue that unelected judges are making policy decisions that should be made by elected officials. Here, demonstrators express their opinions about the Supreme Court's abortion decisions.

As you saw in Chapter 2, the Constitution's Framers wanted it that way. Chief Justice Rehnquist, a judicial conservative, put the case as follows: "A mere change in public opinion since the adoption of the Constitution, unaccompanied by a constitutional amendment, should not change the meaning of the Constitution. A merely temporary majoritarian groundswell should not abrogate some individual liberty protected by the Constitution."[43]

The courts are not entirely independent of popular preferences, however. Turn-of-the-twentieth-century Chicago humorist Finley Peter Dunne had his Irish saloonkeeper character "Mr. Dooley" quip that "th' Supreme Court follows th' iliction returns." Many years later, political scientists have found that the Court usually reflects popular majorities.[44] Even when the Court seems out of step with other policymakers, it eventually swings around to join the policy consensus,[45] as it did in the New Deal. A study of the period from 1937 to 1980 found that the Court was clearly out of line with public opinion only on the issue of prayers in public schools.[46]

Despite the fact that the Supreme Court sits in a "marble palace," it is not as insulated from the normal forms of politics as one might think. For example, when the Court took up *Webster v. Reproductive Health Services* (1989), the two sides in the abortion debate flooded the Court with mail, targeted it with advertisements and protests, and bombarded it with 78 *amicus curiae* briefs. Members of the Supreme Court are unlikely to cave in to interest group pressures, but they are aware of the public's concern about issues, and this awareness becomes part of their consciousness as they decide cases. Political scientists have found that the Court is more likely to hear cases for which interest groups have filed *amicus curiae* briefs.[47]

Interest groups often use the judicial system to pursue their policy goals, forcing the courts to rule on important social issues. Some Hispanic parents, for example, have successfully sued local school districts to compel them to offer bilingual education.

Courts can also promote pluralism. When groups go to court, they use litigation to achieve their policy objectives.[48] Both civil rights groups and environmentalists, for example, have blazed a path to show how interest groups can effectively use the courts to achieve their policy goals. Thurgood Marshall, the legal wizard of the NAACP's litigation strategy, not only won most of his cases but also won for himself a seat on the Supreme Court. Almost every major policy decision these days ends up in court. Chances are good that some judge can be found who will rule in an interest group's favor. On the other hand, agencies and businesses commonly find themselves ordered by different courts to do opposite things. The habit of always turning to the courts as a last resort can add to policy delay, deadlock, and inconsistency.

The Scope of Judicial Power

The courts, Alexander Hamilton wrote in the *Federalist Papers*, "will be least in capacity to annoy or injure" the people and their liberties.[49] Throughout American history, critics of judicial power have disagreed. They see the courts as too powerful for their own—or the nation's—good. Yesterday's critics focused on John Marshall's "usurpations" of power, on the proslavery decision in *Dred Scott*, or on the efforts of the "nine old men" to kill off Franklin D. Roosevelt's New Deal legislation. Today's critics are never short of arguments to show that courts go too far in making policy.[50]

Courts make policy on both large and small issues. In the past few decades, courts have made policies on major issues involving school busing, abortion, affirmative action, nuclear power, legislative redistricting, bilingual education, prison conditions, counting votes in the 2000 presidential election, and many other key issues.[51]

judicial restraint
A judicial philosophy in which judges play minimal policymaking roles, leaving that duty strictly to the legislatures.

There are strong disagreements about the appropriateness of allowing the courts to have a policymaking role. Many scholars and judges favor a policy of **judicial restraint**, in which judges adhere closely to precedent and play minimal policymaking roles, leaving policy decisions strictly to the legislatures. These observers stress that the federal courts, composed of unelected judges, are the least democratic branch of government

Courts in the U.S. are often involved in key questions of public policy.

Is this a good way to make public policy?
Are powerful unelected judges compatible with democracy?

and question the qualifications of judges for making policy decisions and balancing interests. Advocates of judicial restraint believe that decisions such as those on abortion and prayer in public schools go well beyond the "referee" role they say is appropriate for courts in a democracy.

On the other side are proponents of **judicial activism**, in which judges make bolder policy decisions, even charting new constitutional ground with a particular decision. Advocates of judicial activism emphasize that the courts may alleviate pressing needs—especially needs of those who are politically or economically weak—left unmet by the majoritarian political process.

judicial activism
A judicial philosophy in which judges make bold policy decisions, even charting new constitutional ground. Advocates of this approach emphasize that the courts can correct pressing needs, especially those unmet by the majoritarian political process.

It is important not to confuse judicial activism or restraint with liberalism or conservatism. In Table 16.4, you can see the varying levels of the Supreme Court's use of judicial review to void laws passed by Congress in different eras. In the early years of the New Deal (falling within the 1930–1936 period in the table), judicial activists were conservatives. During the tenure of Earl Warren as chief justice (1953–1969), activists made liberal decisions. The Courts under Chief Justices Warren Burger (1969–1986) and William Rehnquist (1986–2005), and John Roberts (2005–), composed of mostly conservative nominees of Republican presidents, marked the most active use in the nation's history of judicial review to void congressional legislation.[52]

The problem remains of reconciling the American democratic heritage with an active policymaking role for the judiciary. The federal courts have developed a doctrine of **political questions** as a means to avoid deciding some cases, principally those that involve conflicts between the president and Congress. The courts have shown no willingness, for example, to settle disputes regarding the constitutionality of the War Powers Resolution (see Chapter 13).

political questions
A doctrine developed by the federal courts and used as a means to avoid deciding some cases, principally those involving conflicts between the president and Congress.

Similarly, judges typically attempt, whenever possible, to avoid deciding a case on the basis of the Constitution, preferring less contentious "technical" grounds. They also employ issues of jurisdiction, mootness (whether a case presents a real controversy in which a judicial decision can have a practical effect), standing, ripeness (whether the issues of a case are clear enough and evolved enough to serve as the basis of a decision), and other conditions to avoid adjudication of some politically charged cases. The Supreme Court refused to decide, for example, whether it was legal to carry out the war in Vietnam without an explicit declaration of war from Congress.

As you saw in the discussion of *Marbury v. Madison*, from the earliest days of the Republic, federal judges have been politically astute in their efforts to maintain the legitimacy of the judiciary and to conserve their resources. (Remember that judges are typically recruited from political backgrounds.) They have tried not to take on too many politically controversial issues at one time. They have also been much more likely to find state and local laws unconstitutional (about 1,100) than federal laws (fewer than 200, as shown in Table 16.4).

Another factor that increases the acceptability of activist courts is the ability to overturn their decisions. First, the president and the Senate determine who sits on the federal bench. Second, Congress, with or without the president's urging, can begin the process of amending the Constitution to overcome a constitutional decision of the Supreme Court. Although this process does not occur rapidly, it is a safety valve. The Eleventh Amendment in 1795 reversed the decision in *Chisolm v. Georgia*, which permitted an individual to sue a state in federal court; the Fourteenth Amendment in 1868 reversed the decision in *Scott v. Sandford*, which held African Americans not to be citizens of the United States; the Sixteenth Amendment in 1913 reversed the decision in *Pollock v. Farmer's Loan and Trust Co.*, which prohibited a federal income tax; and the Twenty-sixth Amendment in 1971 reversed part of *Oregon v. Mitchell*, which voided a congressional act according 18- to 20-year-olds the right to vote in state elections.

Even more drastic options are available as well. Just before leaving office in 1801, the Federalists created a tier of circuit courts and populated them with Federalist judges; the Jeffersonian Democrats took over the reins of power and promptly

TABLE 16.4 Supreme Court Rulings in Which Federal Statutes Have Been Found Unconstitutional[a]

PERIOD	STATUTES VOIDED
1798–1864	2
1864–1910	33 (34)[b]
1910–1930	24
1930–1936	14
1936–1953	3
1953–1969	25
1969–1986	35
1986–present	41
Total	177

[a]In whole or in part.
[b]An 1883 decision in the *Civil Rights Cases* consolidated five different cases into one opinion declaring one act of Congress void. In 1895, *Pollock v. Farmers Loan and Trust Co.* was heard twice, with the same result both times.

Source: Henry J. Abraham, *The Judicial Process: An Introductory Analysis of the Courts of the United States, England, and France*, 7th ed. (Oxford: Oxford University Press, 1998), p. 309. Used by permission of Oxford University Press, Inc. Updated by the authors.

abolished the entire level of courts. In 1869, the Radical Republicans in Congress altered the appellate jurisdiction of the Supreme Court to prevent it from hearing a case (*Ex parte McCardle*) that concerned the Reconstruction Acts. This kind of alteration is rare, but it occurred recently. The George W. Bush administration selected the naval base at Guantánamo as the site for a detention camp for terrorism suspects in the expectation that its actions would not be subject to review by federal courts. In June 2004, however, the Supreme Court ruled that the naval base fell within the jurisdiction of U.S. law and that the *habeas corpus* statute that allows prisoners to challenge their detentions was applicable. In 2005 and again in 2006, Congress stripped federal courts from hearing habeas corpus petitions from the detainees in an attempt to thwart prisoners from seeking judicial relief. In the end, however, the Supreme Court held Congress's actions to be unconstitutional.

statutory construction
The judicial interpretation of an act of Congress. In some cases where statutory construction is an issue, Congress passes new legislation to clarify existing laws.

Finally, if the issue is one of **statutory construction**, in which a court interprets an act of Congress, then the legislature routinely passes legislation that clarifies existing laws and, in effect, overturns the courts.[53] In 1984, for example, the Supreme Court ruled in *Grove City College v. Bell* that when an institution receives federal aid, only the program or activity that actually gets the aid, not the entire institution, is covered by four federal civil rights laws. In 1988, Congress passed a law specifying that the entire institution is affected. Congress may also pass laws with detailed language to constrain judicial decision making.[54] The description of the judiciary as the "ultimate arbiter of the Constitution" is hyperbolic; all the branches of government help define and shape the Constitution.

Summary

16.1 Identify the basic elements of the American judicial system and the major participants in it.

The vast majority of cases are tried in state, not federal, courts. Courts can only hear "cases" or "controversies" between plaintiffs and defendants. Plaintiffs must have standing to sue, and judges can only decide justiciable disputes. Attorneys also play a central role in the judicial system. Interest groups sometimes promote litigation and often file *amicus curiae* briefs in cases brought by others.

16.2 Outline the structure of the federal court system and the major responsibilities of each component.

The district courts are courts of original jurisdiction and hear most of the federal criminal and civil cases and diversity of citizenship cases, supervise bankruptcy proceedings, and handle naturalization, admiralty and maritime law, and review the actions of some federal administrative agencies. Circuit courts hear appeals from the district courts and from many regulatory agencies. They focus on correcting errors of procedure and law that occurred in the original proceedings of legal cases. The Supreme Court sits at the pinnacle of the system, deciding individual cases, resolving conflicts among the states, maintaining national supremacy in the law, and ensuring uniformity in the interpretation of national laws. Most Supreme Court cases come from the lower federal courts, but some are appeals from state courts and a very few are cases for which the Court has original jurisdiction.

16.3 Explain the process by which judges and justices are nominated and confirmed.

The president nominates and the Senate confirms judges and justices. Senators from the relevant state play an important role in the selection of district court judges, as a result of senatorial courtesy, while the White House has more discretion with appellate judges and, especially, Supreme Court justices. Although the Senate confirms most judicial nominations, it has rejected or refused to act on many in recent years, especially for positions in the higher courts.

16.4 Describe the backgrounds of judges and justices and assess the impact of background on their decisions.

Judges and justices are not a representative sample of the American people. They are all lawyers and are disproportionately white males. They usually share the partisan and ideological views of the president who nominated them, and these views are often reflected in their decisions, especially in the higher courts. Other characteristics such as race and gender are also seen to influence decisions.

16.5 Outline the judicial process at the Supreme Court level and assess the major factors influencing decisions and their implementation.

Accepting cases is a crucial stage in Supreme Court decision making, and the Court is most likely to hear cases on major issues, when it disagrees with lower court decisions, and when the federal government, as represented by the solicitor general, asks for a decision. Decisions, announced once justices have written opinions and taken a final vote, in most cases follow precedent, but the Court can overrule precedents, and decisions where the precedents are less clear often reflect the justices' values and ideologies. The implementation of Court decisions depends on an interpreting population of judges and lawyers, an implementing population ranging from police officers and school boards to state legislatures and the president, and a consumer population of citizens affected by the decision.

16.6 Trace the Supreme Court's use of judicial review in major policy battles in various eras of American history.

Since its astute first overturning a congressional statute in *Marbury v. Madison*, the Court has exercised judicial review to play a key role in many of the major policy battles in American history. Until the Civil War, the dominant questions before the Court concerned slavery and the strength and legitimacy of the federal government, with the latter questions resolved in favor of the supremacy of the federal government. From the Civil War until 1937, questions of the relationship between the federal government and the economy predominated, with the Court restricting the government's power to regulate the economy. From 1938 until the present, the paramount issues before the Court have concerned personal liberty and social and political equality. In this era, the Court has enlarged the scope of personal freedom and civil rights and has removed many of the constitutional restraints on the regulation of the economy. In recent years, the Court has been less aggressive in protecting civil rights for minorities but has constrained the federal government's power over the states.

16.7 Assess the role of unelected courts and the scope of judicial power in American democracy.

Judges and justices are not elected and are difficult to remove, but they are not completely insulated from politics and often have acted to promote openness in the political system. They also have a number of tools for avoiding making controversial decisions, which they often employ, and there are a number of means more democratically selected officials can use to overturn Court decisions.

Chapter Test

16.1 Identify the basic elements of the American judicial system and the major participants in it.

1. Who can challenge a law in an American court?
   a. Any citizen can challenge any law
   b. Any tax-paying citizen can challenge any law
   c. Only a person who has a serious interest in a case can challenge a law
   d. Only a person who is included in a class action suit can challenge a law
   e. Only a lawyer can challenge a law
2. Which of the following is NOT a civil case?
   a. A company's CEO is charged with embezzlement of funds
   b. An employee of a business brings discrimination charges against his superior
   c. A wife sues her husband for child support
   d. A merger of two firms is investigated for its legality
   e. A married couple files for divorce
3. Access to lawyers and quality legal counsel has become more equal over time.

   True______ False______
4. What role do interest groups play in the American judicial system? In your opinion, is this involvement of interest groups more of a positive or a negative? Explain your answer.

16.2 Outline the structure of the federal court system and the major responsibilities of each component.

5. Which of the following was actually specified in the U.S. Constitution?
   a. Constitutional courts
   b. The federal courts system
   c. The Court of Military Appeals
   d. The Tax Court
   e. The U.S. Supreme Court
6. Suppose a person commits murder in a national park. Where would this murder case first be heard?
   a. The U.S. Supreme Court
   b. The U.S. Court of Appeals for the Federal Circuit
   c. A U.S. district court in the district where the crime took place
   d. A legislative court
   e. The U.S. court of appeals in the circuit where the crime took place
7. Only a small percentage of people convicted of federal crimes in the federal district courts actually have a trial.

   True______ False______
8. Why is jurisdiction important to the structure of the federal judicial system? In your answer, be sure to identify each federal court level and explain the type or types of jurisdiction each court has.

16.3 Explain the process by which judges and justices are nominated and confirmed.

9. Which of the following is true about the norm of senatorial courtesy for district court nominees?
   a. The Senate invokes this courtesy only when a majority of senators agrees to invoke it
   b. The Senate invokes this courtesy if a nominee is opposed by a senator of the president's party from the state in which the nominee is to serve
   c. The Senate invokes this courtesy only when a majority of the Senate judiciary committee agrees to invoke it
   d. The Senate invokes this courtesy when the president encourages the Senate to do so
   e. The Senate is less likely to invoke this courtesy for district court nominees than it is to invoke it for appellate court nominees
10. Summarize the different criteria that have been used for selecting judges and justices to the federal courts. What is the primary criterion used to select judges and justices? How has the relative importance of the criteria changed as politics has become more partisan? In your opinion, on what basis should federal judges and justices be selected, and why? What criteria do you think should not be the basis for judicial selection? Explain your answer.

16.4 Describe the backgrounds of judges and justices and assess the impact of background on their decisions.

11. All of the following are true of the backgrounds of federal judges EXCEPT
    a. They typically have been white males
    b. They typically have been from the appointing president's region of the country
    c. They typically share the appointing president's political party affiliation
    d. They typically share the appointing president's ideology
    e. They typically have held administrative or judicial positions
12. The decision of Congress to create new judgeships is related strongly to whether the majority party in Congress is the same as the party of the president.

    True______ False______
13. Why is it difficult to predict the future policy decisions of federal judges and Supreme Court justices? Based on your understanding of the role the courts play in our system of checks and balances, how might this actually be good for American democracy? Do you think that the system should be changed to make judicial behavior more predictable? Explain.

16.5 Outline the judicial process at the Supreme Court level and assess the major factors influencing decisions and their implementation.

14. Under which of the following scenarios is the Court most likely to decide to accept a case?
    a. When at least three justices decide the case has merit
    b. When the justices have additional clerks to help read numerous appeals
    c. When the case is appealed from a state supreme court
    d. When the Solicitor General's Office decides to appeal a case the government has lost in lower court
    e. When the attorneys for the parties in the case make a personal appeal for a hearing

15. At least six justices must participate in a case before the U.S. Supreme Court.

    True______ False______

16. Most cases reaching appellate courts are settled on the principle of *stare decisis*.

    True______ False______

17. Based on what you know about the Supreme Court and American politics, what are three possible reasons why the Court might decide to overturn a previous decision? Do you think the Supreme Court's tendency to overturn precedent helps or hurts its authority? Explain your answer.

18. Explain the three separate populations—implementing population, the interpreting population, and the consumer population—that carry out judicial decisions. Why are each of these populations necessary for judicial implementation and how might each hinder the successful implementation of a decision?

16.6 Trace the Supreme Court's use of judicial review in major policy battles in various eras of American history.

19. A historical review of the Supreme Court reveals that the Court
    a. Has expanded the power of the federal government to regulate the economy
    b. Has expanded the scope of civil liberties afforded to U.S. citizens
    c. Has expanded its use of judicial review primarily after the New Deal
    d. Has expanded its own use by being politically astute in exercising power over other branches
    e. All of the above are true

20. The Rehnquist and Roberts Courts have mostly leaned in a liberal direction in their decisions concerning civil rights and liberties.

    True______ False______

21. Explain the concept of judicial review, including how and when it was first established, and how it has been used at different periods in U.S. history.

22. How have historical eras defined the role of the US Supreme Court in our system of government? Take two historical eras and explain the main issues considered by the Court and how the Court generally decided these cases.

16.7 Assess the role of unelected courts and the scope of judicial power in American democracy.

23. What are the central arguments made by supporters of judicial activism and judicial restraint? Which side do you agree with more, and why? Do you think it is possible for justices to apply original intent in their rulings? Why or why not?

24. In your opinion, what are three pros and three cons of federal judges and justices holding what essentially amounts to lifetime positions? Would you change this system? Why, or why not?

PEARSON mypoliscilab Exercises

Apply what you learned in this chapter on MyPoliSciLab.

Read on **mypoliscilab.com**

eText: Chapter 16

Study and **Review** on **mypoliscilab.com**

Pre-Test
Post-Test
Chapter Exam
Flashcards

Watch on **mypoliscilab.com**

Video: Court Rules on Hazelton's Immigration Laws
Video: Prosecuting Corruption
Video: Prosecuting Cyber Crime
Video: Most Significant Abortion Ruling in 30 Years

Explore on **mypoliscilab.com**

Simulation: You Are a Young Lawyer
Simulation: You Are the President and Need to Appoint a Supreme Court Justice
Simulation: You Are a Clerk to Supreme Court Justice Judith Gray
Comparative: Comparing Judiciaries
Timeline: Chief Justices of the Supreme Court
Visual Literacy: Case Overload

Key Terms

standing to sue (469)
class action suits (469)
justiciable disputes (469)
***amicus curiae* briefs** (470)
original jurisdiction (470)
appellate jurisdiction (471)
district courts (471)
courts of appeal (472)
Supreme Court (473)
senatorial courtesy (475)
solicitor general (483)
opinion (484)
stare decisis (485)
precedent (485)
judicial implementation (486)
original intent (486)
Marbury v. Madison (490)
judicial review (490)
judicial restraint (494)
judicial activism (495)
political questions (495)
statutory construction (496)

Internet Resources

www.supremecourtus.gov
Official site of the U.S. Supreme Court, with information about its operations.

www.fjc.gov
Federal Judicial Center Web site, with information on all federal judges, landmark legislation, and other judicial matters.

www.oyez.org/oyez/frontpage
Web site that allows you to hear oral arguments before the Supreme Court. Also provides information on the Supreme Court and its docket.

www.cnn.com/JUSTICE
Information on recent trials.

www.uscourts.gov
Explains the organization, operation, and administration of federal courts.

www.justice.gov/olp/judicialnominations111.htm
Information on current judicial nominations.

bjs.ojp.usdoj.gov
Bureau of Justice Statistics provides data on all aspects of the U.S. judicial system.

jurist.law.pitt.edu/clerk.htm
Law clerks and clerking at the U.S. Supreme Court.

www.justice.gov/osg
Office of the U.S. solicitor general.

For Further Reading

Abraham, Henry J. ***Justices, Presidents, and Senators: A History of the U.S. Supreme Court Appointments from Washington to Bush II,*** *5th ed.* Lanham, MD: Rowman & Littlefield, 2008. A readable history of the relationships between presidents and the justices they appointed.

Baum, Lawrence. ***The Supreme Court,*** 10th ed. Washington, DC: CQ Press, 2010. An excellent work on the operations and impact of the Court.

Binder, Sarah A., and Forrest Maltzman. ***Advice and Dissent: The Struggle to Shape the Federal Judiciary.*** Washington, DC: Brookings Institution, 2009. The best work on the process of judicial confirmations.

Breyer, Stephen. ***Active Liberty: Interpreting Our Democratic Constitution.*** New York: Knopf, 2005. Presents the "contextual" view of how justices should decide cases.

Carp, Robert A., Ronald Stidham, and Kenneth L. Manning. ***Judicial Process in America,*** 8th ed. Washington, DC: CQ Press, 2010. An overview of federal and state courts.

Ely, John Hart. ***Democracy and Distrust.*** Cambridge, MA: Harvard University Press, 1980. An appraisal of judicial review and an effort to create a balanced justification for the role of the courts in policymaking.

Epstein, Lee, and Jack Knight. ***The Choices Justices Make.*** Washington, DC: CQ Press, 1997. A strategic account of Supreme Court decision making.

Epstein, Lee, and Joseph F. Kobylka. ***The Supreme Court and Legal Change.*** Chapel Hill: University of North Carolina Press, 1992. Examines how interest groups propelled issues regarding abortion and the death penalty to the Supreme Court and how the way they framed their legal arguments affected outcomes on these issues.

Goldman, Sheldon. ***Picking Federal Judges.*** New Haven, CT: Yale University Press, 1997. The definitive work on backgrounds and the politics of recruiting lower-court judges.

Greenhouse, Linda. ***Becoming Justice Blackmun.*** New York: Times Books, 2005. Inside story of the career and daily work of a long-serving justice.

Jacob, Herbert. ***Law and Politics in the United States,*** 2nd ed. Boston: Longman, 1995. An introduction to the American legal system with an emphasis on linkages to the political arena.

Johnson, Charles A., and Bradley C. Canon. ***Judicial Policies: Implementation and Impact,*** 2nd ed. Washington, DC: CQ Press, 1999. One of the best overviews of judicial policy implementation.

O'Brien, David M. ***Storm Center,*** 8th ed. New York: Norton, 2008. An overview of the Supreme Court's role in American politics.

Rowland, C. K., and Robert A. Carp. ***Politics and Judgment in Federal District Courts.*** Lawrence: University Press of Kansas, 1996. An important work on the operations of the federal district courts.

Scalia, Antonin. ***A Matter of Interpretation: Federal Courts and the Law.*** Princeton, NJ: Princeton University Press, 1998. Presents the "original intentions" view of how justices should decide cases.

Segal, Jeffrey A., and Harold J. Spaeth. ***The Supreme Court and the Attitudinal Model.*** Cambridge, MA: Cambridge University Press, 1993. Examines how the attitudes and values of justices affect their decisions.

Sunstein, Cass R., David Schkade, Lisa M. Ellman, and Andrews Sawicki. ***Are Judges Political?*** Washington, DC: Brookings Institution, 2006. An analysis of politics on the federal courts of appeal.

Whittington, Keith E. ***Political Foundations of Judicial Supremacy.*** Princeton, NJ: Princeton University Press, 2007. Argues that presidents and political leaders have encouraged the Supreme Court to be the ultimate interpreters of the Constitution.

Chapter 17

Economic Policymaking

Learning Objectives

17.1 Assess the role that government plays in our mixed economy.

17.2 Identify the two main policy tools that American government can employ to address economic problems.

17.3 Analyze the impact of the global economy on American economic policymaking.

17.4 Describe the economic policy interests of business, labor unions, and consumers.

17.5 Assess the impact of economic policies on the scope of government and democracy in America.

POLITICS IN ACTION: HOW THE GOVERNMENT BAILED OUT WALL STREET WITH TARP

In baseball, the tarp (short for tarpaulin) is pulled out to protect the infield from getting ruined when it rains heavily. In American economic policymaking, the TARP (short for Temporary Asset Relief Program) was conceived to prevent the financial system from ruin in the fall of 2008. Warning of clogged credit markets and an economic shutdown that could rival the depression of the 1930s, Treasury Secretary Henry Paulson told President Bush and congressional leaders that immediate action was necessary to save financial institutions crippled by bad real estate investments. His plan, which came to be known as TARP, involved having the federal government purchase troubled mortgage-related assets from firms such as Bank of America, Wells Fargo, Citigroup, AIG, and many others. Paulson argued that without help from the government, these companies would be unable to continue to loan money to businesses and consumers, and that the American economy would soon not just decline, but crash.

The TARP plan was stunning and unprecedented in two major respects. First, never before had the federal government intervened so deeply in the American financial system. Many observers noted that until these companies could pay back the funds they received through TARP, the federal government would effectively be their major shareholder. Second, Secretary Paulson requested $700 billion; never before had Congress been asked to allocate so much money in one fell swoop.

Despite its unprecedented cost and scope, TARP quickly picked up significant bipartisan support. Barack Obama and John McCain stood on opposite sides of most issues as their race for the presidency neared its end, but both agreed to vote for TARP in the Senate. Similarly, liberals like House Speaker Nancy Pelosi and conservatives like Republican House leader John Boehner signaled their intention to support Paulson's proposal. Most importantly, President Bush went on national television to tell the American people that "the government's top economic experts warn that, without immediate action by Congress, America could slip into a financial panic, and a distressing scenario would unfold." Bush warned about the prospect of plummeting home values, rising foreclosures, business failures, and millions of jobs lost.

Nevertheless, opposition to TARP arose from rank-and-file members of Congress on both sides of the ideological divide. Many conservatives objected to the wholesale intervention of the government in the workings of financial companies. For example, Representative Mike Pence of Indiana urged his colleagues to oppose the package, saying, "If you came here because you believe in limited government and the freedom of the American marketplace, vote in accordance with those convictions." Jeb Hensarling of Texas denounced TARP as a "step down the slippery slope to socialism." On the liberal side, objections centered on concerns about the government offering a lifeline to Wall Street executives and speculators who had taken big risks in pursuit of lottery-style payoffs. Representative William Clay of Missouri argued that his constituents were solidly against bailing out Wall Street. Clay said, "They don't think it's right. They have paid their bills on time. They haven't gotten into risky mortgages. They think Wall Street took the risk.

Chapter **OUTLINE**

That's their attitude—and I agree with them." Senator Bernie Sanders of Vermont said he was opposed because "under this bill, the C.E.O.s and the Wall Street insiders will still, with a little bit of imagination, continue to make out like bandits."

This unusual coalition of liberals and conservatives dealt the bailout bill a serious setback when it was first voted on in the House of Representatives. A total of 95 House Democrats and 133 Republicans voted against their leaders, as the House voted down TARP by a margin of 228 to 205. The reaction of the financial markets was immediate and chilling. After watching the televised House vote, stunned traders on the floor of the New York Stock Exchange immediately began to sell furiously. At the end of the day, the Dow Jones industrial average had fallen 777 points, the largest one-day point drop ever.

Just as Secretary Paulson deemed many of America's financial institutions "too big to fail," so congressional leaders deemed TARP too important to let die. They immediately started to rework the package with new provisions that might entice some members to change their vote, such as increasing the maximum federally insured bank deposit for individual account owners. Moreover, as America's economic situation further deteriorated, more members came to reluctantly accept the necessity of bailing out Wall Street. Republican Sue Myrick of North Carolina said she decided to change her vote after conversations with small businesspeople in her district who could not get credit. Democrat John Lewis of Georgia, an icon of the civil rights movement, switched after hearing how his constituents were seeing their retirement savings slipping away. His conclusion was that "the cost of doing nothing is greater than the cost of doing something." In the end, this sentiment carried the day and the TARP bill became the law of the land.

The extraordinary efforts that went into passing TARP illustrate the great importance that policymakers place on assisting the American economy in today's world. Liberals and conservatives often disagree about how the government can best promote economic growth, as we will see in this chapter, but everyone agrees that the government must play an important role in guiding the economy. Few areas of public policy so directly touch on the fundamental questions of "who gets what, when, and how" as economic policymaking; businesses, labor unions, and consumers all have their competing priorities that policymakers must take into consideration.

If George Washington was the father of the country and James Madison the father of the Constitution, then Alexander Hamilton was the father of the American economy. Bright, arrogant, and with a good head for numbers, Hamilton was the first U.S. secretary of the treasury. We may remember Thomas Jefferson better because he became president, but his economic ideas favoring farmers and small towns quickly became outmoded.

The word "capitalism" wasn't even introduced until the mid-nineteenth century, but Hamilton's economic policies laid the basis for the development of American capitalism. **Capitalism** is an economic system in which individuals and corporations own the principal means of production and compete in a free market to reap profits, with this competition determining the amount of production and prices. It is important to note that the American economic system was never one of pure capitalism. Instead, Hamilton's policies created a **mixed economy**, in which capitalism coexists with and is tempered by government involvement in the economy. Written in an agrarian era, the Constitution nonetheless gave large powers over the economy to the new national government. Hamilton's task and achievement was to put these powers into operation.

capitalism
An economic system in which individuals and corporations, not the government, own the principal means of production and seek profits.

mixed economy
An economic system in which the government is deeply involved in economic decisions (as through its roles as regulator, consumer, subsidizer, taxer, employer, and borrower).

multinational corporations
Businesses with vast holdings in many countries.

Farsighted as he was, even Hamilton would not recognize today's interplay between government and the economy—an interplay grounded in the global economy in which we live, with all its problems and opportunities. This economy is dominated by **multinational corporations**—businesses with vast holdings in many countries, such as Disney, Coca-Cola, and Microsoft. It is characterized by the flow of products between regions and by the movement of jobs to regions where they can be performed more cheaply. Your phone call to a service desk is likely to be answered by one of the quarter-million or so people in India to whom this work has been outsourced.[1] Your neighborhood Wal-Mart is one of the biggest distributors of products made in China. In this challenging global environment, government and the economy have become more closely intertwined. So have politics and the economy: People expect government to keep the economy moving; rightly or wrongly, voters often punish politicians when the economy turns sour.

Government, Politics, and the Economy

17.1 Assess the role that government plays in our mixed economy.

The American economy is made up of countless decisions made by corporations, workers, producers, consumers, regulators, and policymakers. Such decisions are the subject matter of an entire academic discipline, economics, and in one chapter we could not possibly give you more than a hint of how the economy works. But our goal here is more specific: We are interested in understanding how American government and its policies affect the economy and how economics affect policymakers and politicians.

To do this, we'll begin with an institution almost all Americans are familiar with: Wal-Mart. A look at Wal-Mart will illustrate two key points. First, it shows the effects of the government's long arm of regulation on companies (discussed in Chapter 15). Second, Wal-Mart epitomizes the embedding of the U.S. economy in the global economy, a development that has had an enormous impact on the domestic economy and the politics of economic policy.

Economic Policy at Work: Wal-Mart

Headquartered in tiny Bentonville, Arkansas, Wal-Mart is the world's third-largest company, generating $406 billion in revenue in 2009. Wal-Mart's success stems largely from its low prices, achieved in part through tough negotiations with suppliers and relatively low wages for workers. In fact, Wal-Mart's size and impact are such that Wal-Mart has helped keep the inflation rate in the United States low; according to one estimate, Wal-Mart was responsible for 12 percent of all productivity growth in the United States during the 1990s.[2]

Securities and Exchange Commission
The federal agency created during the New Deal that regulates the stock market.

minimum wage
The legal minimum hourly wage to which most workers are entitled.

Government Regulation of Business

Government regulation affects the way in which companies do business in the United States. One government regulatory agency crucially involved in the regulation of big business is the **Securities and Exchange Commission** (SEC), which was created in 1934 and regulates stock transactions and the stock market. Wal-Mart is a publicly traded company, listed on the New York Stock Exchange (its "ticker symbol" is WMT), and thus the trading of its stock is regulated by the SEC. Wal-Mart's officers cannot, for example, enrich themselves by buying and selling Wal-Mart stock on the basis of insider knowledge. Buyers of Wal-Mart stock are entitled to accurate knowledge from the company, and Wal-Mart is required to hire an auditor and publish an annual review.

Wal-Mart's business practices have been amazingly successful, but they have also generated controversy. Here, the group "Jobs with Justice" can be seen expressing their view that Wal-Mart fails to provide adequate healthcare coverage for its employees.

Government also regulates business in the area of labor practices. About 1.4 million people work for Wal-Mart—about 1 out of every 100 workers in the United States. Most American workers, including Wal-Mart's employees, are entitled to a **minimum wage,** $7.25 per hour

labor union
An organization of workers intended to engage in collective bargaining.

collective bargaining
Negotiations between representatives of labor unions and management to determine pay and acceptable working conditions.

in 2010. A 1935 law protects the right of workers to form and join **labor unions** to engage in **collective bargaining** about wages and working conditions with their employers under rules controlled by the National Labor Relations Board, an agency that the law established. However, Wal-Mart has discouraged its employees from joining labor unions, and, indeed, the rise of companies like Wal-Mart, along with the decline of the manufacturing sector, has contributed to a decline in labor union membership and power in the United States. Nonetheless, workers at Wal-Mart, as at other companies, are protected by government regulations governing worker safety and hiring and other employment policies. Worker safety, for example, is governed by the rules of the Occupational Safety and Health Administration. American companies cannot employ undocumented workers, and in 2003, federal immigration officers raided 67 Wal-Marts, arresting 250 illegal aliens working on cleaning crews. Because of yet other regulations, Wal-Mart cannot discriminate on the basis of a person's sex, race, or age in hiring, firing, and promoting employees.

Wal-Mart and the World Economy No institution better epitomizes globalization and America's embedding in the world economy than Wal-Mart. Despite a "Made in America" Wal-Mart advertising campaign in the mid-1980s, most of the merchandise in Wal-Mart comes from other countries. In 2002, for example, Wal-Mart is estimated to have imported $12 billion in goods from China, one-tenth of China's total exports to the United States that year. The repercussions for American consumers and workers are considerable. According to economist C. Fred Bergsten, the elimination of trade barriers among nations, by reducing the cost of products, has in effect added about $2,000 to the annual income of the average U.S. family.[3] Wal-Mart has played a major role in enabling families to achieve that benefit. By the same token, however, according to *Business Week,* Wal-Mart's "hard line on costs has forced many factories to move overseas."[4] A company that sells about a quarter of the toothpaste sold in the United States (and a similar share of almost every other consumer product) has real clout. And, as you can see in "America in Perspective: Manufacturing Workers' Compensation in Developing Countries as Compared to the U.S.," labor costs are substantially less in developing countries like China and Mexico.

In short, Wal-Mart in many ways symbolizes the new U.S. economy.[5] It is a major player in the globalization of the economy, and is enmeshed in challenges and opportunities of this globalization. At the same time, as this illustration showed, Wal-Mart, like other businesses, is subject to many federal government rules and regulations. As we will see throughout this chapter, when it comes to the economy, policies and politics matter.

"It's the Economy, Stupid": Voters, Politicians, and Economic Policy

Perhaps the most famous motto of any recent presidential campaign was the 1992 Clinton campaign's saying of "It's the economy, stupid." In running against the incumbent president, George H. W. Bush, Bill Clinton constantly hammered home his message that Bush wasn't using the power of the federal government to try to alleviate the economic pain of the middle-class. Like most politicians, Clinton knew that voters pay attention to what President Truman called "the most sensitive part of their anatomies," their pocketbooks. As discussed earlier in the book, economic conditions affect both voting behavior (see Chapter 10) and presidential approval (see Chapter 13). Voters, the parties, and politicians are riveted on economic issues, especially at election time. Countless studies by political scientists have reaffirmed the wisdom of Truman's observations about voters and their pocketbooks. Summarizing a generation of research, two political scientists put it plainly: "There is little doubt that economic conditions profoundly affect voters' electoral decisions."[6] Economic conditions are the best single predictor of voters' evaluation of how the president is doing his job.[7] Voters may (as we will see) exaggerate the importance of politicians in shaping the economy, but the more sophisticated the voter, the more likely he or she is to engage in "pocketbook voting."[8]

Manufacturing Workers' Compensation in Developing Countries as Compared to the U.S.

In the graph below, you can see how much manufacturers pay workers in developing countries as compared to the United States. For example, the index value of 4 for the Philippines means that it would cost a manufacturer 25 times more in terms of labor costs to produce the same product in the United States. This graph makes it is easy to see why companies have decided to move the production of goods like shoes and children's toys to places like China. The costs of shipping these goods into America are far outweighed by the savings on labor.

QUESTIONS FOR DISCUSSION

- Think about when you buy something made in one of these developing countries and it seems ridiculously cheap. Do you feel that you are taking advantage of the people earning low wages to make this product or, rather, that you are helping them by giving business to their developing economy?
- Some people say that American companies have a responsibility to ensure that the goods that they import are not made with child labor or in unsafe conditions. How much effort, if any, do you think our government should be taking to make sure that countries we trade with do not permit such practices?

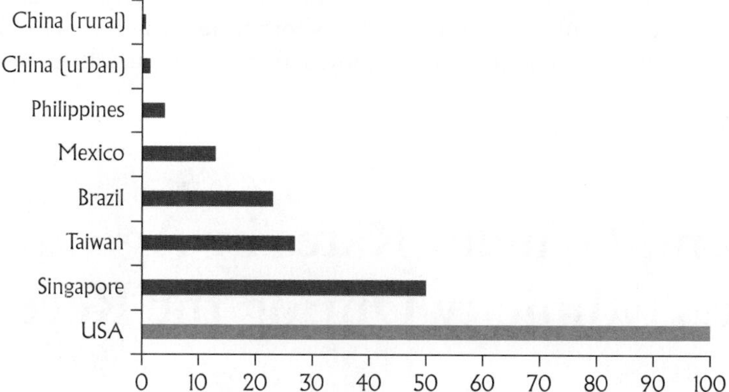

Source: U.S. Bureau of Labor Statistics, "International Comparisons of Hourly Compensation Costs in Manufacturing, 2007" (published March 26, 2009); Erin Lett and Judith Banister, "China's Manufacturing Employment and Compensation Costs: 2002–06," *Monthly Labor Review*, April 2009: 30–38.

With all the bad economic news in 2008, the presidential election of that year was no exception to the centrality of economic issues. As Lewis-Beck and Nadeau write, "Gloom over the American economy found no precedent in contemporary times. This gloomy view translated itself sharply into a vote against McCain, for many felt the incumbent Republican administration was responsible."[9] David Plouffe, Obama's 2008 campaign manager, resurrected the old slogan from the 1992 Clinton campaign, and even titled one chapter of his book about the campaign, "It's the Economy, Stupid."[10]

The connection between economic conditions and voting is real but complex. Mary may lose her job, but she does not quickly jump to the conclusion that the president deserves to be thrown out. Rather, voters tend to engage is what political scientists call "sociotropic" voting, assessing the overall rate of employment and unemployment more than their individual circumstances.[11] Furthermore, as political scientists Suzanna De Boef and Paul M. Kellstedt have shown, the "pictures in their heads" that American voters have of the economy are shaped not only by real economic conditions but also by politics and by news coverage of the economy.[12]

Like voters, the parties are economic animals. The two parties have different economic centers of gravity. Democrats are more likely to stress the importance of keeping unemployment low, whereas Republicans are worried about inflation. This difference in priorities reflects their constituencies, since Democrats appeal particularly to working-class voters concerned about employment and Republicans appeal particularly to voters with more money to save and invest who may worry that inflation will erode their savings. Let us look at the twin economic—and political—concerns of unemployment and inflation.

Two Major Worries: Unemployment and Inflation

unemployment rate
As measured by the Bureau of Labor Statistics, the proportion of the labor force actively seeking work but unable to find jobs.

The **unemployment rate** is the percentage of Americans seeking work who are unable to find it. Measuring how many and what types of workers are unemployed is one of the major jobs of the Bureau of Labor Statistics (BLS) in the Department of Labor. To carry out this task, the BLS conducts a huge statistical survey of 60,000 households every month. It then announces the nation's unemployment rate. The number of U.S. jobs has to increase by about 125,000 every month just to keep up with new entrants into the labor force (college graduates, for example) and thus avoid an increase in the unemployment rate.

Of course, the unemployment rate varies from time to time and group to group. For example, it rose to 10 percent in late 2009 with the economic recession, and it tends to be higher for young adults than for other groups (see "Young People and Politics: Unemployment Rates by Age and Race/Ethnicity During the Recession"). Most people are out of work for only a short time (which is why the connection between the poverty rate and the unemployment rate is weak). Even so, the official unemployment

Unemployment Rates by Age and Race/Ethnicity During the Recession

The unemployment rate is one of the nation's most important economic indicators and a political issue as well. Although Americans sometimes think of unemployment as mainly a problem for middle-aged people, in actuality unemployment rates are much higher for young Americans age 16 to 24. This is especially true during times of recession, as young entrants to the job market find that there are few new jobs available at a time when many companies are laying people off. Young blacks and Hispanics face a double whammy in their search for a job, as you can see by their very high unemployment rates during the recessionary year of 2009 shown to the right.

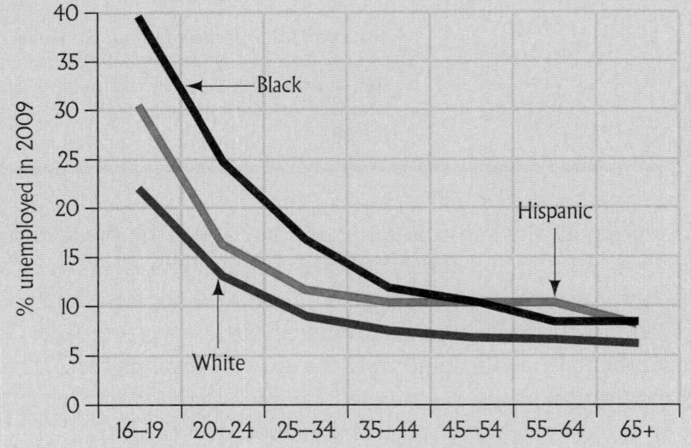

Source: Bureau of Labor Statistics.

QUESTION FOR DISCUSSION

- Some policymakers have suggested that the minimum wage should be reduced just for young people during recessions in order to give businesses a special incentive to hire them. Others oppose this step as likely to force many young people to accept extremely low wages. What do you think—would you favor a lower minimum wage for young Americans when jobs are scarce?

rate underestimates unemployment because it leaves out "discouraged workers," who have given up their job search or have only been able to obtain a part-time job. The BLS also now releases what is known as the **underemployment rate**, which includes both the unemployed and discouraged workers. In July 2010, the national unemployment rate was 9.5 percent while the underemployment rate was 16.5 percent. When the unemployment rate increases, public opinion often pushes policymakers to "do more" to "expand employment."[13]

underemployment rate
As measured by the Bureau of Labor Statistics, a statistic that includes, along with the unemployed, discouraged workers and people who are working part-time because they cannot find full-time work.

Inflation, the other major economic worry of policymakers, is a rise in prices for goods and services. For decades, the BLS has also kept tabs on inflation, using the **consumer price index** (CPI), which measures the change in the cost of buying a fixed basket of goods and services. Each month, BLS data gatherers fan out over the country looking at the prices of some 80,000 items from eggs to doctor visits. The goal of the CPI is to create a measure that reflects changes over time in the amount that consumers need to spend to achieve a certain standard of living.

inflation
A rise in price of goods and services.

consumer price index
The key measure of inflation—the change in the cost of buying a fixed basket of goods and services.

Inflation has risen sharply during three periods since 1970, with each of these sharp rises tied to soaring prices for energy. The first inflationary shock occurred in 1973 and 1974, when Arab oil-producing nations cut off the flow of oil to the United States to protest American support for Israel during its war with Egypt and Syria. The second occurred when the Iranian revolution of 1979 again disrupted the flow of oil from the Persian Gulf. Long lines and higher prices at the gas pumps were accompanied by an annual rate of inflation of 11 percent in 1979 and 14 percent during the election year of 1980. Finally, in 1991 when Iraq's invasion of Kuwait led to the Gulf War, there was a moderate surge in inflation as oil prices increased in anticipation of possible shortages (which actually never occurred). Since then, the annual inflation rate in the United States has consistently been below 4 percent. However, in the summer of 2008, the specter of high inflation suddenly loomed as the inflation rate briefly exceeded 5 percent for a couple months due to the surge of world-wide oil prices to over $100 a barrel. At that point in the campaign, John McCain was planning to make this a major issue. Had this proven to be the prime economic concern of the electorate in November rather than Wall Street's collapse and rising unemployment, McCain would probably have had a better chance to win in 2008.

Policies for Controlling the Economy

17.2 Identify the two main policy tools that American government can employ to address economic problems.

Voters take economic performance into account at the polling booth because they expect politicians to use the power of the federal government to try to control the economy. The time when government could assert that the private marketplace could handle economic problems has long passed, if it ever really existed. When the stock market crash of 1929 sent unemployment soaring, President Herbert Hoover clung to **laissez-faire**—the principle that government should not meddle with the economy. In the next presidential election, Hoover was handed a crushing defeat by Franklin D. Roosevelt, whose New Deal programs experimented with dozens of new federal policies to put the economy back on track. Since the New Deal, policymakers have been actively involved in trying to control the economy. The American political economy offers two important tools to steer the economy: monetary policy and fiscal policy.

laissez-faire
The principle that government should not meddle in the economy.

Monetary Policy and the "Fed"

In February 2006, the new chairman took over at the Federal Reserve Board, thereby becoming the world's most important economist and one of the most powerful figures in American government. Ben Bernanke's only regret was that his new job, unlike his

In 2006, Ben Bernanke, who had been chair of the economics department at Princeton, became the chair of the Federal Reserve Board, the most important economic policymaking position in the United States. He was subsequently reappointed by President Obama for another four-year term as Fed Chairman.

previous job as chair of the economics department at Princeton, required him to wear a suit and tie to work every day. The chair of the Fed has more power over the U.S. economy than does any other person, including the president. A few choice words from him (thus far there has not been a female head of the Fed) can send financial markets either soaring or reeling. For example, long-time Fed Chair Alan Greenspan once rhetorically asked in a speech whether the stock market might be displaying "irrational exuberance" and "unduly escalating asset values." An instant reaction was felt round the world, as the major stock markets immediately fell between 2 and 4 percent. All these markets interpreted Greenspan's remark to mean that he thought stocks were overvalued and that the Fed might raise American interest rates to cool down escalating stock prices and prevent an inflationary spiral.

Such is the power that the chair of the Fed can exercise at any time. Unlike the president, the Fed doesn't have to get congressional support for actions that are likely to impact the economy. And unlike Congress, the Fed deliberates in secret, making every public statement by its leader a potentially valuable clue as to how it might act. But what is the Fed, and what does it do?

monetary policy
Government manipulation of the supply of money in private hands—one of two important tools by which the government can attempt to steer the economy.

monetarism
An economic theory holding that the supply of money is the key to a nation's economic health, with too much cash and credit in circulation producing inflation.

Federal Reserve System
The main instrument for making monetary policy in the United States. It was created by Congress in 1913 to regulate the lending practices of banks and thus the money supply.

The most important tool government has to manage the economy is its control over the money supply. The government's main economic policy is **monetary policy**, that is, manipulation of the supply of money and credit in private hands. An economic theory called **monetarism** holds that the supply of money is the key to the nation's economic health. Monetarists believe that having too much cash and credit in circulation generates inflation. Essentially, they advise that the rate of growth in the money supply should not exceed the rate of growth of the gross domestic product (GDP). Politicians worry constantly about the money supply because it affects the rate of interest that their constituents have to pay for home, car, business, and other loans. If there is too little money in circulation, credit tightens, economic growth is slowed, and employment levels fall.

The main agency for making monetary policy is the **Federal Reserve System**, commonly known as the Fed. Created by Congress in 1913 to regulate the lending practices of banks and thus the money supply, the Fed is intended to be formally beyond the control of the president and Congress. Its seven-member Board of Governors—appointed by the president and confirmed by the Senate—is expected to do its job without regard to partisan politics. Accordingly, members of the Fed's Board of Governors are given 14-year terms designed to insulate them from political pressures.

The Fed has several tools for affecting the supply of money and credit. Its policymaking body, the Federal Open Market Committee (FOMC), meets eight times a year and, taking into consideration a vast amount of economic data, sets a target for the "federal funds rate," the interest rate banks can charge each other for overnight loans. The Fed also buys and sells government bonds, and by doing this, determines whether banks have more or less money to lend out. The more money banks have to lend, the cheaper borrowing is; if banks have less to lend, borrowing becomes more expensive, and interest rates rise.

In this way, the complicated financial dealings of the Fed affect the amount of money available and interest rates, which in turn impact inflation and the availability of jobs. Because the Fed can profoundly influence the state of the economy, it is no wonder that its every move attracts intense attention from the financial markets as well as politicians—and that presidents try to persuade the Fed to pursue policies in line with presidential plans for the country.

In general, the Fed has been found to be fairly responsive to the White House, though not usually to the extent of trying to influence election outcomes.[14] Nevertheless, even the chief executive can be left frustrated by the politically insulated decisions of the Fed. Some have called for more openness in its decision-making process, whereas others have proposed more direct political control of the Fed through shorter terms for its Board of Governors.

WHY IT MATTERS

Interest Rates

Interest rates are the amount you pay to borrow money for a house or a car, for example. Banks or finance companies charge you these rates, but how high they are is strongly influenced by decisions of the Fed. Even a great credit rating cannot get you a low interest rate if the Federal Reserve Board is keeping the money supply tight.

Fiscal Policy: Keynesian Versus Supply-Side Economics

The second tool for steering the nation's economy is **fiscal policy**, or use of the federal budget—taxing, spending, and borrowing—to influence the economy. In contrast to monetary policy, fiscal policy is shaped mostly by Congress and the president. Moreover, the use of fiscal policy is influenced by political ideology and views of the appropriate scope of government.

fiscal policy
Use of the federal budget—taxes, spending, and borrowing—to influence the economy; along with monetary policy, a main tool by which the government can attempt to steer the economy. Fiscal policy is almost entirely determined by Congress and the president.

One position on fiscal policy is that of **Keynesian economic theory**, named after English economist John Maynard Keynes. Keynes's landmark book, *The General Theory of Employment, Interest, and Money*, was published during the Depression of the 1930s, and Keynesianism soon became the dominant economic philosophy in America. His theory emphasized that government spending could help an economy weather the bad times that were part of the normal ups and downs of the business cycle. Keynes argued that government could spend its way out of the Depression by stimulating the economy through an infusion of money from government programs. If businesses were not able to expand, the government would need to pick up the slack, he claimed—even if it meant running up a substantial budget deficit. If there were no jobs available for people, the government should create some—building roads, dams, houses, or whatever seemed most appropriate. The key would be to get money back in the consumers' pockets, because if few people have money to buy goods, demand for goods will be weak, production will be slowed, and the economic situation will worsen. Thus, the main goal of fiscal policy in the view of Keynesian economic theory is to increase demand. More recently, when President Obama took office in January 2009 in the midst of a severe recession, the first major bill that he signed was a $787 billion stimulus package that contained funding for numerous projects that the Democrats believed would combat the downturn and get millions of Americans back to work.

Whereas the Keynesian approach has been associated primarily with Democrats, the second approach to fiscal policy has been associated primarily with Republicans. The premise of **supply-side economics** is that the key task for fiscal policy is to stimulate the supply of goods, not their demand. First adopted during the presidency of Ronald Reagan,[15] supply-side economics maintains that big government soaks up too much of the GDP. By spending too freely and also taxing too heavily and regulating too tightly, government actually curtails economic growth. Supply-siders argue that lowering tax rates stimulates the supply of goods, as people are motivated to work longer, increase their savings and investments, and produce

Following the advice of Keynesian economics, the federal government has recently spent money in various ways to stimulate consumer demand. One of the most innovative programs was known as "cash for clunkers," in which the federal government spent $4 billion to give people rebates for turning in their old gas guzzlers when they purchased a new more energy-efficient car.

A POINT TO PONDER

Do you think the Keynesian and supply-side approaches—portrayed here in their most extreme version—are really fantasies, or do you think one is fairly reasonable?

If you think neither one is reasonable, can you envision a third way that falls somewhere in the middle?

Keynesian economic theory
Named after English economist John Maynard Keynes, the theory emphasizing that government spending and deficits can help the economy deal with its ups and downs. Proponents of this theory advocate using the power of government to stimulate the economy when it is lagging.

supply-side economics
An economic theory, first applied during the Reagan administration, holding that the key task for fiscal policy is to stimulate the supply of goods, as by cutting tax rates.

WHY IT MATTERS

Keynesian Versus Supply-Side Economics

Supply-side economic theory, as advocated by Presidents Ronald Reagan and George W. Bush, represents a great departure from Keynesian economic theory, which has guided Democratic economic policymaking ever since the New Deal. Whereas Keynesian theory recommends government spending to combat economic downturns by increasing demand, supply-side economics advocates tax cuts in order to stimulate the supply of goods. The scope of government expands when Keynesian policies are enacted, but contracts when supply-side economics is put into effect.

more. Economist Arthur Laffer proposed (legend says he did so on the back of a cocktail napkin) a curve suggesting that the more government taxed, the less people worked and thus the smaller the government's tax revenues. In its most extreme form, this theory held that by taking a smaller percentage of people's income, the government would actually get more total revenue as production increased. Thus, tax cuts, such as the $152 billion tax rebate that President George W. Bush passed in early 2008 to deal with the beginning of the recession, are a key tool of the supply-side approach.

Clearly, the Keynesian and supply-side approaches to fiscal policy make diametrically different assumptions about how the tools of fiscal policy should be used and, more generally, about the appropriate scope of government. Despite disagreements about approach, there is now clear agreement on one fundamental point: It is the government's responsibility to use fiscal policy to try to control the economy. But like controlling the weather, this is much easier said than done.

Why It Is Hard to Control the Economy

Many politicians and voters—and even some political scientists—seem to believe that the economy can be easily controlled. Thus, some political scientists have argued that politicians manipulate the economy for short-run advantage to win elections, in a sort of "political business cycle."[16] Presidents, their argument goes, take special care to get the economy moving nicely just before elections, putting more money in voters' hands through either tax cuts or transfer payments such as Social Security and veterans' benefits. A neat trick if you can do it—controlling economic conditions precisely in order to facilitate reelection. However, as economist Robert Samuelson points out, "If presidents could create jobs, the unemployment rate would rarely exceed 3.5 percent."[17]

Part of the problem is that trying to control economic indicators like unemployment and inflation with precision is like attempting to stop on an economic dime. Government makes economic policy very slowly. Most policies must be decided on a considerable time before they can be implemented, let alone have their full impact on the economy. The president's budget, for example, is prepared many months in advance of its enactment into law, and once enacted, it is usually quite a while before new policies will have their full impact on the economy. Furthermore, as we saw in Chapter 14, the budgetary process is dominated by "uncontrollable expenditures," which are mandated by law, and many benefits such as Social Security go up automatically as the cost of living increases.

The American free enterprise system imposes the biggest restraint on controlling the economy. The billions of economic choices made by consumers and businesses are more important in their impact than are government policies. Because the private sector is much larger than the public sector, it dominates the economy. Big as the federal government is, it still spends only about a quarter of our GDP. Consumers and businesses make the vast majority of our economic decisions. Fiscal and monetary policy can influence these decisions—but not control them.

Politics, Policy, and the International Economy

17.3 Analyze the impact of the global economy on American economic policymaking.

Policymakers' difficulties in controlling the U.S. economy are compounded in this era of increasing globalization. Today's economy is worldwide.[18] The U.S. economy depends heavily on international trade, as do other countries' economies; roughly a quarter of the world GDP is based on exports. Foreign-owned assets in the United States totaled $23,357 billion at the end of 2008; at the same time, Americans owned $19,888 billion in assets in other countries.[19] "American" cars have U.S. brands on them but may be made almost entirely abroad; "foreign" cars have a Japanese, German, or Korean brand but may be made mostly in the United States. In short, what U.S. policymakers' decisions about the economy can never again be made in a vacuum. (We will return to these issues in Chapter 20.)

Most developing countries want to follow an economic policy of **protectionism**, letting their fragile economies grow while keeping out products from other countries. Ours was no exception in its formative years. Alexander Hamilton, our first secretary of the treasury, was our first protectionist. In the very first Congress, he supported a set of tariffs (essentially taxes) on products imported into the United States. For most of the nineteenth century, the tariff was the major source of federal revenues. In recent times, however, economists have been virtually united against tariffs and protectionism. And, although tariffs are often tempting to politicians whose constituents' jobs may be jeopardized by cheap imports, one country's tariff is likely to provoke retaliation from another country.

protectionism
Economic policy of shielding an economy from imports.

After World War II, the world's governments moved slowly but steadily toward free trade and the reductions of tariffs, in what has been called a "growing willingness

The Growing Trade Deficit

The graph below compares the total of imports into the United States and exports from the United States to other countries as a percentage of the gross domestic product (GDP). As international trade has taken off, both imports and exports have accounted for a larger portion of the GDP over time. But imports have risen faster, thereby resulting in a growing trade deficit. Notably, imports and exports both fell off in 2009 as a result of the recession.

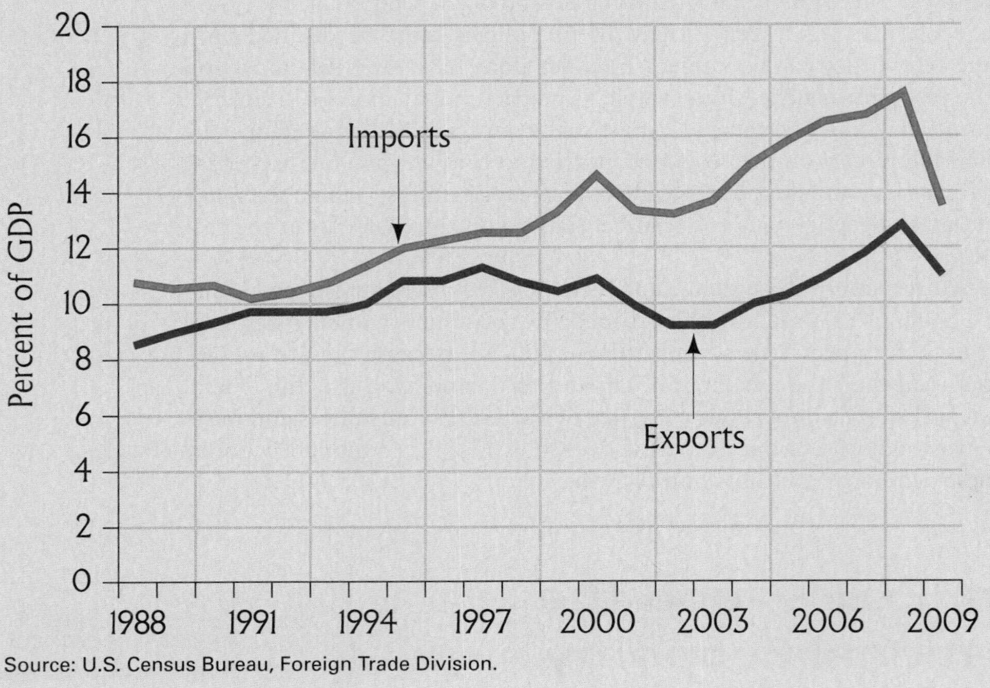

Source: U.S. Census Bureau, Foreign Trade Division.

of national governments to open up their national economy to global market forces."[20] In the United States, this process was, politically speaking, harder for Democrats, whose labor union supporters were concerned about job losses to other countries than for Republicans, whose business supporters wanted new markets. President Clinton had to overcome the resistance of unions and many of his fellow Democrats to pass the World Trade Agreement Treaty, creating a **World Trade Organization** (WTO), an organization promoting free trade and punishing protectionist restrictions. Unions feared that free trade would essentially promote "a race to the bottom," where massive international corporations would "constantly ransack the globe searching for low costs and high returns."[21]

World Trade Organization
International organization that promotes free trade.

"Not so fast," said most economists. Jobs lost to foreign trade are only half the story, as jobs are also gained from international trade. Thus, for example, Catherine Mann, an economist with the Institute for International Economics, predicts that increased trade will lead to a new surge of technology employment in the United States.[22] As *New York Times* columnist Thomas Friedman points out, although customer service jobs may have been outsourced to India, employees at Indian call centers are running Microsoft Windows, sitting in air conditioning generated by Carrier units, and drinking Cokes.[23] American exports to India have increased from $2.5 billion in 1990 to $16.5 billion in 2009.[24] International trade almost usually creates long-term gain. But it may also well create short-term pain. Markets that are gained for American businesses in developing countries may come at the cost of jobs at home. Such tradeoffs present policymakers with difficult value judgments to make.

For American policymakers, the difficulty of these value judgments is increased by the fact that the United States has long imported more than it has exported. Moreover, as you can see in "A Generation of Change: The Growing Trade Deficit," the gap between imports and exports has increased substantially in recent years. The problem that many policymakers see with this development is that billions of U.S. dollars are being sent overseas each year to pay for our trade deficit. Essentially, foreigners are loaning the United States money by accepting our currency in return for their goods. Many analysts are concerned about U.S. reliance on other countries to fund its national debt.

Arenas of Economic Policymaking

17.4 Describe the economic policy interests of business, labor unions, and consumers.

When the government spends one-fourth of America's gross domestic product and regulates much of the other three-fourths, its economic policies will surely provoke much debate. Liberals tend to favor active government involvement in the economy and higher taxes in order to smooth out the unavoidable inequality of a free enterprise system. Conservatives maintain that the most productive economy is one in which the government exercises a hands-off policy of minimal regulation and taxation. Business, consumers, and labor are three of the major actors in, and objects of, government economic policy. Our Wal-Mart illustration introduced some issues relevant to the business and labor arenas. Here, we look at public policy in the business and labor arenas more systematically, as well as at public policy in the consumer arena.

Business and Public Policy

The corporation has long stood at the center of the American economy. At the turn of the twentieth century, powerful corporate titans took control of entire industries. After they eliminated competitors, they could charge customers essentially whatever they wanted. John D. Rockefeller's control of oil refining and processing was the most famous example. This was the era of the trusts, as monopolies were then called. Government regulation of business is at least as old as the first antitrust act, the Sherman Act of 1890. The purpose of **antitrust policy** is to ensure competition and prevent monopoly (control of a market by one company). Today, antitrust legislation permits the Justice Department to sue in federal court to break up companies that control too much of the market.

antitrust policy
Policy designed to ensure competition and prevent monopoly.

In general, Democratic administrations tend to pursue more antitrust actions than do Republican administrations. The transition from Bush to Obama certainly illustrates this pattern. During the administration of George W. Bush, the Justice Department's antitrust division took a largely hands-off approach to corporate mergers. In 2007, Jonathan Baker and Carl Shapiro asked 20 of the country's top antitrust lawyers whether mergers between firms in the same industry were more likely to be approved than they were a decade earlier. On a scale of 1 to 5, with 5 being "significantly more likely," the average score was 4.8.[25] These experts agreed that the Department of Justice under President Bush was highly supportive of the argument that "market concentration is *not* a good basis for predicting competitive effects"[26]—in other words, that a situation in which few companies control a market does not necessarily hurt consumers. In contrast, the Obama administration has made the opposite assertion and thus pledged to step up antitrust enforcement. Assistant Attorney General Christine Varney announced this policy change in May 2009, stating that "we need to bring the focus of the economic discourse back to the basic and practical principle: when markets are competitive, the consumer wins."[27]

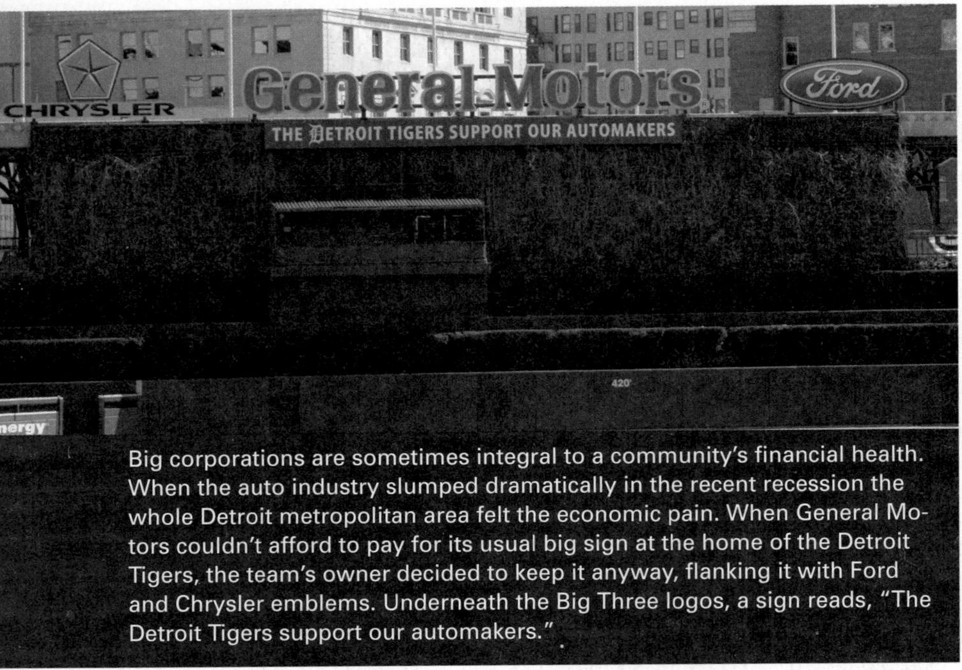

Big corporations are sometimes integral to a community's financial health. When the auto industry slumped dramatically in the recent recession the whole Detroit metropolitan area felt the economic pain. When General Motors couldn't afford to pay for its usual big sign at the home of the Detroit Tigers, the team's owner decided to keep it anyway, flanking it with Ford and Chrysler emblems. Underneath the Big Three logos, a sign reads, "The Detroit Tigers support our automakers."

In the 1990s, the corporations and their chief executive officers (CEOs) were the modern symbols of American success, as profits soared and CEO salaries averaged over 10 million dollars.[28] However, in the first decade of the twenty-first century, they seemed, instead, symbols of American excess. A go-go time for the stock market turned into a plummeting earnings loss for millions of American investors and retirees, with major downturns in 2001 and then again in 2008. Although there were many culprits, corporate corruption played a significant part in the stock market's troubles. Early in the decade, a string of corporate leaders from Enron, Tyco, HealthSouth, and other companies were charged with fraud, and many went to prison. In 2002, the Brookings Institution estimated that the first-year fallout of corporate accounting scandals would cost the American economy around $35 billion—about what the country was spending on homeland security.[29] In 2010, corporate fraud was again in the news, as Goldman Sachs—the nation's largest investment institution—agreed to pay a $550 million fine after the SEC charged that it had defrauded investors by failing to disclose a conflict of interest on mortgage investments it sold as the housing market went sour. Not surprisingly, these reports of corporate scandals led to calls for tightening up disclosure requirements for corporations, by Democrats and Republicans alike.

In 2008, when the government was compelled to bail out the financial services industry, as discussed at the outset of this chapter, large compensation packages for CEOs and other top executives became the focus of public fury—particularly when they were going to executives of companies receiving taxpayer funds. Moreover, President Obama argued that executive pay packages had encouraged excessive risk and led to the practices largely responsible for this downturn. His administration has looked for ways to curb executive pay, or at the very least ensure that such compensation packages are properly disclosed to and approved by corporate shareholders. In contrast, supporters of current CEO pay levels argue that executive compensation should be determined by the free market, and that high levels of compensation are commensurate with the billions in shareholder wealth that successful CEOs create.

It is important to keep in mind that government doesn't just regulate business—businesses also get some substantial benefits from government. One of the oldest protections that government gives to business is found in the Constitution: protection for inventions and creative works in the form of patents and copyrights. The Department of Commerce collects data on products and markets through the Census Bureau, helps businesses export their wares, and protects inventions through the Patent Office. The Small Business Administration is the government's counselor, adviser, and loan maker to small businesses. Various agencies fund research that is valuable to businesses in a wide range of areas, including natural resources, transportation, electronics, and health. In fact, the federal government is the principal source of research and development funding in the United States.

President Calvin Coolidge's saying "The business of America is business" rings particularly true when Republican administrations are in office, but some would argue that it applies almost all the time. As discussed in Chapter 11, business lobbyists in Washington are well organized and well funded. In fact, domestic and foreign corporations and their trade associations "account for the preponderance of politically active groups within the United States."[30] Keep in mind, though, that while the business lobby is unified on some issues (low taxes on business low, less regulation), much business lobbying pits one interest against another—cable TV versus broadcast networks, for example.

Consumer Policy: The Rise of the Consumer Lobby

Consumer policymaking is a relatively recent phenomenon, as for many years the governing principle was simply "let the buyer beware." The first major consumer protection policy in the United States was the Food and Drug Act of 1906, which prohibited the interstate transportation of dangerous or impure foods and drugs. Today, the **Food and Drug Administration** (FDA) has broad regulatory powers over the manufacturing, contents, marketing, and labeling of food and drugs. It is the FDA's responsibility to ascertain the safety and effectiveness of new drugs before approving them for marketing in the United States.

Food and Drug Administration
The federal agency formed in 1913, with broad regulatory powers over the manufacturing, contents, marketing, and labeling of foods and drugs sold in the United States.

Consumerism was a sleeping political giant until the 1960s, when consumer activists such as Ralph Nader uncovered and publicized clear cases of unsafe products and false advertising and argued that it was the government's responsibility to protect consumers. As these activists garnered broad public support, the 1960s and 1970s saw a flood of consumer protection legislation. Created in 1972, the Consumer Product Safety Commission (CPSC) has broad powers to ban hazardous products from the market. Today the CPSC regulates the safety of items ranging from toys to lawn mowers. The Federal Trade Commission (FTC), traditionally responsible for regulating trade practices, become a defender of consumer interests in truth in advertising and has issued regulations on such matters as product labeling, exaggerated product claims, and the use of celebrities in advertising.

In response to practices that contributed to the downturn of 2008, the landmark financial reform bill that President Obama signed into law in 2010 created the Consumer Financial Protection Bureau. The bureau's mandate is to make sure that consumers can make informed decisions about financial products and services and to protect them from unfair lending practices. Financial transactions falling under its jurisdiction include mortgages, credit cards, student loans, auto loans, and payday loans. The bureau works to ban deceptive practices, to ensure the safety and fairness of new consumer financial products that come on to the market, and to promote equal access to financial services for all consumers.

Labor and Government

Throughout most of the nineteenth century and well into the twentieth, the federal government allied with business elites to squelch labor unions. The courts interpreted the antitrust laws as applying to unions as well as businesses. Until the Clayton Antitrust Act of 1914 exempted unions from antitrust laws, the mighty arm of the federal government was busier busting unions than trusts.

The major turnabout in government policy toward labor took place during the New Deal. In 1935, Congress passed the **National Labor Relations Act**, often called the Wagner Act after its sponsor, Senator Robert Wagner of New York. As we saw in the discussion of Wal-Mart, the Wagner Act guaranteed workers the right of collective bargaining—the right to have labor union representatives negotiate with management to determine working conditions. It also established rules to protect unions and organizers, to be adjudicated by the National Labor Relations Board, which the act established. For example, under the Wagner Act, an employer cannot fire or discriminate against a worker who advocates unionizing.

National Labor Relations Act
A 1935 law, also known as the Wagner Act, that guarantees workers the right of collective bargaining, sets down rules to protect unions and organizers, and created the National Labor Relations Board to regulate labor–management relations.

After World War II, a series of strikes and a new Republican majority in Congress tilted federal policy somewhat back in the direction of management. The Taft-Hartley Act of 1947 continued to guarantee unions the right of collective bargaining, but it prohibited various unfair practices by unions as well. The act also gave the president power

YOU ARE THE POLICYMAKER

Should the Minimum Wage Be Raised?

In May 2007, Congress enacted the first increase in the federal minimum wage in 10 years. This law increased the minimum wage from $5.15 to $7.25 an hour in three stages between 2007 and 2009. The debate on the bill had centered on what really was best for people in low-wage jobs. Liberals argued that the increase was long overdue given the rise in the cost of living, since Congress had last adjusted the minimum wage a decade earlier. Furthermore, they stressed that over a third of minimum-wage workers were the sole breadwinners in their families and would be living in poverty even with this increase (which brought their yearly income up to $15,000). In contrast, conservatives argued that this was likely to be a job-killing bill that would cost many of these workers what little they had. They cited data from the National Restaurant Association that the previous minimum wage increase had cost the restaurant industry 146,000 jobs and led restaurant owners to put off hiring another 106,000 during the following year. Some conservatives, such as President Bush, ended up supporting the increase after $5 billion in tax breaks were added for small businesses to help them offset the costs of paying minimum wage workers more.

Barely had the ink dried on the new law before the issue of the minimum wage became an issue once again: During the 2008 presidential campaign. Barack Obama proposed that the minimum wage be increased to $9.50 by 2011 and that further increases be pegged to changes in the cost of living. Republican nominee John McCain, however, firmly opposed this proposal. He argued that low-wage workers would be better served by corporate tax cuts and expanded job training programs.

What do you think? Would you favor further increases in the minimum wage? Do you think that the minimum wage should be adjusted yearly for inflation, just like Social Security benefits?

to halt major strikes by seeking a court injunction for an 80-day "cooling off" period. Most important, section 14B of the law permitted states to adopt what union opponents call right-to-work laws. Such laws forbid labor contracts from requiring workers to join unions to hold their jobs.

Unions have had some notable successes over the years, promoting labor-friendly policies that have become crucial components of the economy. First, partly as the result of successful union lobbying, the government provides unemployment compensation—paid for by workers and employers—to cushion the blows of unemployment (see Chapter 18 for more information on this policy). Second, since the New Deal, the government has guaranteed a minimum wage, setting a floor on the hourly wages earned by employees. In 2007, President George W. Bush signed into law a substantial increase in the minimum wage, and in the 2008 campaign, Barack Obama and John McCain debated the wisdom of a further increase (see "You Are the Policymaker: Should the Minimum Wage Be Raised?").

17.5 Assess the impact of economic policies on the scope of government and democracy in America.

Understanding Economic Policymaking

The minimum wage and unemployment compensation are just two of many economic policies that contradict Karl Marx's assumptions of how a free enterprise system inevitably exploits ordinary workers. Looking at mid-nineteenth-century business practices, Marx saw an economic system in which working conditions were long, hard, and miserable. Most workers barely managed to earn a meager livelihood while the rich got richer off their labor. In a completely free economic system, there was no way to compel the owners of the factories to treat the workers better. Exploitation would continue, and even get worse, Marx felt. His radical solution was for the state to assume all power over the economy in a revolution of the proletariat (i.e., the masses). In the communist system envisioned by Marx, all the means of production would be owned by the state and each citizen would be an equal shareholder. In practice, however, the state-run economy of the Soviet Union did not provide the necessary incentives to get people to work productively and American-style free enterprise prevailed in the Cold War.

The solutions to many of the problems of the free enterprise economy were achieved in America through the democratic process. A large part of this effort involved expanding the scope of government, which conservatives would like to see at least partially rolled back in today's economy.

As American workers have gained more political power, they have demanded government action to improve working conditions and regulate business practices. No longer can children be found working in factories, as did this 11-year-old girl in a Tennessee textile mill around 1910.

Democracy and Economic Policymaking

As the voting power of the ordinary worker grew, so did the potential for government regulation of the worst ravages of the free enterprise system. Political pressure grew for action to restrict unfair business practices and protect individual rights. Over time, the state assumed responsibility for setting the age at which one could work, determining the normal work week, establishing standards for safety on the job, protecting pension funds, and many other aspects of economic life. Just as the right of free speech is not interpreted so as to allow someone to shout "Fire!" in a crowded movie theater, so the right to free enterprise is no longer interpreted as a giving businesses the right to employ 10-year-olds, or to have employees work in unsafe conditions. It is now generally agreed that such practices should be forbidden by the government. Through their choices at the ballot box, Americans essentially decided to give up certain economic freedoms for the good of society as a whole. As former Bush Treasury Secretary Henry Paulson writes in his memoir about the financial crisis of 2008, "The history of capitalism in America has been one of striking the right balance between profit-driven market forces and the array of regulations and laws necessary to harness these forces for the common good."[31]

It would be a vast exaggeration, however, to say that democracy regularly facilitates an economic policy that looks after the general rather than specific interests. As you have seen throughout this text, the decentralized American political system often works against efficiency in government. In particular, groups that may be adversely affected by an economic policy have many avenues through which they can work to block it. Therefore, one of the consequences of democracy for economic policymaking is that it is difficult to make decisions that hurt particular groups or that involve accepting short-term pain in return for long-term gain. Of course, this is the way most Americans presumably want it to be.

Economic Policymaking and the Scope of Government

Liberals and conservatives fundamentally disagree about the scope of government involvement in the economy. In general, liberals look to the writings of economists such as John Maynard Keynes and Robert Solow, whose work offers justification for an expanded role of government in stimulating the economy. Conservatives, on the other hand, rely on Friedrich Hayek's influential theories on the free market and on Milton Friedman's arguments against government intervention. Whereas liberals focus on the imperfections of the market and what government can do about them, conservatives focus on the imperfections of government. For example, while liberals often propose government spending to create new jobs, conservatives argue that businesses can create new jobs and prepare people for them if government will just get out of the way.

It should be noted that the disagreement about the scope of government in economic policymaking is one concerning the means rather than the ends. This could even be seen in the responses of President Clinton and Republican congressional leaders to the longest baseball strike ever, in the mid-1990s. When Clinton failed to broker an agreement between the players and the owners, he called upon Congress to pass legislation authorizing him to compel both sides to accept binding arbitration. Republican leaders Dole and Gingrich responded that, in their view, it would be unwise for the government to interfere in any labor dispute not related to national security—the free market would have to be relied upon to work out the problem. But they also stated emphatically that they—like President Clinton—wanted to see the baseball strike resolved as soon as possible.

Summary

17.1 Assess the role that government plays in our mixed economy.

The federal government regulates stock transactions and corporate accounting practices. It also regulates labor practices, protecting workers' collective bargaining rights and setting the minimum wage. Voters expect politicians to keep the economy humming along, and will often vote them out of office if they fail to do. Two particular concerns of voters and politicians alike are unemployment and inflation. Democrats tend to focus more on keeping unemployment low, whereas Republicans tend to place more emphasis on keeping inflation in check.

17.2 Identify the two main policy tools that American government can employ to address economic problems.

Two major instruments are available to government for managing the economy: monetary policy and fiscal policy. Republicans have become the party of supply-side economics, believing that tax cuts will lead to economic growth and jobs. Democrats disagree, sticking to Keynesian economic theory, which recommends government spending in order to stimulate demand for goods during economic downturns.

17.3 Analyze the impact of the global economy on American economic policymaking.

The American economy has become quite dependent on trade with other countries. Both imports and exports now constitute over 10 percent of the nation's gross domestic product (GDP), with imports regularly exceeding exports. American jobs are often lost when we import goods that are made more cheaply in countries with low labor costs. On the other hand, by sending American dollars overseas we are opening foreign markets for American companies to sell their products to, thereby creating new jobs.

17.4 Describe the economic policy interests of business, labor unions, and consumers.

Businesses generally want lower taxes and less regulation by the government. Yet, they sometimes profit from government antitrust actions, which ensure that individual companies do not control too much of the market. In 2008, the government stepped in to prevent many firms in the financial services industry from going bankrupt. Labor unions are interested in seeing to it that their ability to organize workers is facilitated. More specifically, they seek government support for a high minimum wage and ample unemployment insurance benefits. Consumer groups seek government protection from business practices that can harm the buying public, such as the defective products or deceptive lending practices.

17.5 Assess the impact of economic policies on the scope of government and democracy in America.

Liberal economic policies focus on the problems of a free enterprise system and tend to involve expanding the scope of government; conservative economic policies focus on the problems that can arise from excessive government intervention in the economy and hence tend to involve reducing the scope of government. Through the democratic process, Americans seek to enact regulations that will protect businesses, labor, and consumers alike without impinging upon fundamental economic freedoms.

Chapter Test

17.1 Assess the role that government plays in our mixed economy.

1. In their economic policies, Democrats have tended to focus on ______ whereas Republicans have tended to focus on ______.
   a. Inflation; employment
   b. Employment; inflation
   c. Trade; business practices
   d. Business practices; trade
   e. Investment; subsidies

2. Voters typically reward and punish politicians at election time based on how voters feel about the performance of the economy.

   True______ False______

3. Thinking of the Wal-Mart example in the chapter, analyze how it shows that the United States has a mixed economy. What are some examples of how government economic policies have influenced Wal-Mart?

17.2 Identify the two main policy tools that American government can employ to address economic problems.

4. The most important tool the government has for directing the economy is
   a. Its control over trade policy
   b. Its control over government subsidies
   c. Its control over labor laws
   d. Its control over the money supply
   e. Its control over investment practices

5. Keynesian economic theory has as a central idea that
   a. The government should not interfere with business practices
   b. The government should decentralize economic policymaking
   c. The government should take an activist role in managing the economy
   d. The government should manage interest rates in economic policymaking
   e. The government should erect trade barriers to protect the economy

6. Compare and contrast Keynesian and supply-side approaches to economic policy.

17.3 Analyze the impact of the global economy on American economic policymaking.

7. In recent years the gap between U.S. imports and exports has generally widened.

   True______ False______

8. Identify two positive and two negative aspects of economic globalization. How has the global economy affected American economic policymaking?

17.4 Describe the economic policy interests of business, labor unions, and consumers.

9. Antitrust legislation is intended to restrict
   a. The influence of business lobbyists
   b. Unethical management practices of businesses
   c. The nationalization of businesses
   d. The establishment of monopolies by businesses
   e. Excessively risky investment practices by businesses

10. Antitrust legislation is designed to limit not only businesses but also labor unions.

    True______ False______

11. Compare and contrast the roles that business, labor unions, and the consumer lobby play in American economic policymaking. What are some of the ways in which business, labor, and consumers are each affected by economic policies?

17.5 Assess the impact of economic policies on the scope of government and democracy in America.

12. In your opinion, does economic policymaking in the United States promote democratic values? Develop specific examples to support your answer.

13. Discuss the differences between the liberal and conservative views concerning the government's role in the economy, using some specific examples from today's economy. Which view do you agree with more and why?

PEARSON mypoliscilab Exercises

Apply what you learned in this chapter on MyPoliSciLab.

Read on **mypoliscilab.com**

eText: Chapter 17

Watch on **mypoliscilab.com**

Video: Recession Hits Indiana

Video: Economic Policy Debate at the G20

Video: Fed Approves Mortgage Crackdown

Study and Review on mypoliscilab.com

Pre-Test
Post-Test
Chapter Exam
Flashcards

Explore on mypoliscilab.com

Simulation: Making Economic Policy
Comparative: Comparing Economic Policy
Visual Literacy: Evaluating Federal Spending and Economic Policy
Visual Literacy: Where the Money Goes

Key Terms

capitalism (504)
mixed economy (504)
multinational corporations (504)
Securities and Exchange Commission (505)
minimum wage (505)
labor union (506)
collective bargaining (506)
unemployment rate (508)
underemployment rate (509)
inflation (509)
consumer price index (509)
laissez-faire (509)
monetary policy (510)
monetarism (510)
Federal Reserve System (510)
fiscal policy (511)
Keynesian economic theory (512)
supply-side economics (512)
protectionism (513)
World Trade Organization (514)
antitrust policy (515)
Food and Drug Administration (517)
National Labor Relations Act (517)

Internet Resources

www.whitehouse.gov/cea
Reports of the President's Council of Economic Advisers, such as the annual Economic Report of the President.

www.federalreserve.gov
Information about the activities of the Federal Reserve Board.

www.cbpp.org
The Council on Budget and Policy Priorities presents information and research on economics and the budget from a liberal perspective.

www.cato.org
The Cato Institute is a conservative organization with plenty of papers and data on the economy.

For Further Reading

Barber, Benjamin. ***Jihad vs. McWorld.*** New York: Ballentine Books, 1996. A very readable account of globalization and its consequences.

Friedman, Thomas, L. ***The World Is Flat.*** New York: Farrar, Straus, and Giroux, 2005. The *New York Times* global affairs columnist takes a look at the plusses and minuses of globalization.

Gilder, George. ***Wealth and Poverty.*** New York: Basic Books, 1981. A supply-sider's bible.

Gosling, James J. ***Economics, Politics, and American Public Policy.*** New York: M.E. Sharpe, 2007. A brief introduction to the politics of economic policy.

Greider, William. ***Secrets of the Temple: How the Federal Reserve Runs the Country.*** New York: Simon and Schuster, 1987. A book that demystifies the Fed.

Krugman, Paul. ***The Return of Depression Economics and the Crisis of 2008.*** New York: Norton, 2009. The Nobel Prize–winning economist and *New York Times* columnist analyzes the economic downturn, which began in 2008, from a liberal perspective.

Mishel, Lawrence et al., ***The State of Working America, 2010–2011.*** Ithaca, NY: ILR Press, 2011. Prepared biennially by the Economic Policy Institute, this book includes a wide variety of data on family incomes, wages, taxes, unemployment, and other aspects of the American economy.

Paulson, Henry M., Jr. ***On the Brink: Inside the Race to Stop the Collapse of the Global Financial System.*** New York: Business Plus, 2010. The former treasury secretary tells the inside story of how the federal government took emergency action to prevent an economic catastrophe in the fall of 2008.

Posner, Richard A. ***A Failure of Capitalism: The Crisis of '08 and the Descent into Depression.*** Cambridge, MA: Harvard University Press, 2009. A prominent judge and an expert on law and economics, Posner analyzes the economic downturn, which began in 2008, from a conservative perspective.

Sloan, John. ***The Reagan Effect.*** Lawrence: University Press of Kansas, 1999. The enduring effect of Ronald Reagan's supply-side economics on the economy and political system.

Vavarek, Lynn. ***The Message Matters: The Economy and Presidential Campaigns.*** Princeton, NJ: Princeton University Press, 2009. An excellent analysis of how presidential candidates have dueled over the economy in recent campaigns.

Yergin, Daniel, and Joseph Stanislaw. ***The Commanding Heights: The Battle for the World Economy.*** New York: Touchstone, 2002. A good exposition of the new global economy.

Chapter 18

Social Welfare Policymaking

Learning Objectives

18.1 Compare and contrast entitlement and means-tested social welfare programs.

18.2 Assess the extent of economic inequality in America and the role of government in lessening it.

18.3 Trace the changes over time in major federal welfare programs.

18.4 Outline how America's Social Security program works and the challenge of keeping it financially solvent in the coming years.

18.5 Distinguish American social welfare policy from that of other established democracies.

18.6 Assess the impact of social welfare policies on democracy and the scope of government in America.

POLITICS IN ACTION: THE DEBATE OVER EXTENDING UNEMPLOYMENT INSURANCE

Jim Bunning was a Hall of Fame pitcher in his days in professional baseball. His celebrity helped get him elected to the Senate from Kentucky. But in March 2010, in the eyes of many observers he became a candidate for the political "Hall of Shame" when he single-handedly held up the extension of unemployment benefits to hundreds of thousands of Americans. Bunning wanted the $10 billion price of extending these benefits offset by reductions in spending elsewhere in the budget, so as to not drive up the deficit. By repeatedly objecting to a unanimous consent motion in the Senate, he was able to prevent the Senate from taking up the measure on an emergency basis.

This action drew national attention to Senator Bunning, as well as to the plight of many unemployed Americans who faced the loss of further compensation from the government. ABC News staked out Bunning's Washington office, repeatedly trying in vain to get him to comment on camera about the controversy. At one point, Jonathan Karl of ABC News tried to force his way into a senators-only elevator to confront Bunning. As the senator dodged his pleas for a comment, Karl yelled, "We wanted to ask the senator why he is blocking a vote that would extend unemployment benefits to more than 340,000 Americans, including Brenda Wood, a teacher in Austin, Texas, who has been out of work for two years." Jon Stewart paid him a great deal of attention on *The Daily Show*, calling him derogatory names that can't be repeated here. Back in Kentucky, Bunning's regional offices received bomb threats. His staff spokesperson reported that the phones had been ringing off the hook all day, with many irate calls. White House Press Secretary Robert Gibbs denounced Bunning's actions in his daily press briefing, saying that he was hurting the unemployed, who needed these benefits as they continued to look for work.

On the other side of the political fence, Senator Bunning did have his defenders. The *Wall Street Journal* editorialized that this was Mr. Bunning's "finest hour," praising his principled stand on behalf of fiscal responsibility. In addition, some prominent conservatives used this debate to question the wisdom and effectiveness of extending unemployment benefits. Senator Jon Kyl of Arizona, the second-ranking Republican in the Senate, argued that unemployment insurance "doesn't create new jobs. In fact, if anything, continuing to pay people unemployment compensation is a disincentive for them to seek new work." Former Republican House leader Tom Delay told CNN that "there's an argument to be made that these extension of unemployment benefits keeps people from going and finding jobs." And Representative Steven King of Iowa remarked, "We shouldn't turn the safety net into a hammock."

Ultimately, Senator Bunning realized that his point had been made and relented on his objection, and the Senate passed the extension of unemployment benefits by a vote of 78 to 19. The overwhelming support for unemployment benefits and the outrage that Senator Bunning's action engendered make it clear just how much Americans have come to count on social welfare programs to help them through difficult times. Many social welfare

Chapter OUTLINE

Food Stamps help put healthy food on your table

SOCIAL SECURITY FIX IT.

policies are also referred to as "social insurance," because social welfare policies are intended to insure people against, or at least minimize some consequences of, certain of life's crises—serious illness, disability, problems of aging, or job loss. People can rightly count on social welfare policies, say liberals; however, say conservatives, perhaps they count on them too much for their own good. Most people agree that social welfare policies should provide a helping hand, not a handout. But, as we will see in this chapter, determining the line between these two is a matter of great political controversy.

The United States is a diverse nation whose citizens and groups achieve quite different levels of material success. The fact that such differences exist in American democracy, however, raises important political questions: What are the economic differences among Americans, and why do they exist? Are they acceptable? What role should the government play in helping those who are less fortunate? What are the most effective government policies?

social welfare policies Policies that provide benefits, cash or in-kind, to individuals, based on either entitlement or means testing.

The answers that Americans provide to these questions determine the nation's approach to **social welfare policies**. Social welfare policies attempt to provide assistance and support to specific groups in society through cash and other benefits. Who gets these benefits and what level of support is provided are issues that must be resolved by the political system. How America resolves these issues depends on how its leaders, political parties, interest groups, and citizens view the nature and distribution of poverty, the role of government, and the effectiveness of various social welfare programs.

18.1 Compare and contrast entitlement and means-tested social welfare programs.

Types of Social Welfare Policies

Our lives are affected by a wide range of government policies, but it is social welfare policies that most directly affect us as individuals. Such policies include hundreds of programs through which government provides support and assistance to specific groups of people—for example, Social Security checks for retired workers, food stamp benefits for poor families, and Medicare and Medicaid coverage of medical expenses for the retired and the poor, respectively. Not surprisingly, social welfare policies are expensive. Expenditures on social programs dwarf what government spends on anything else, including national defense.

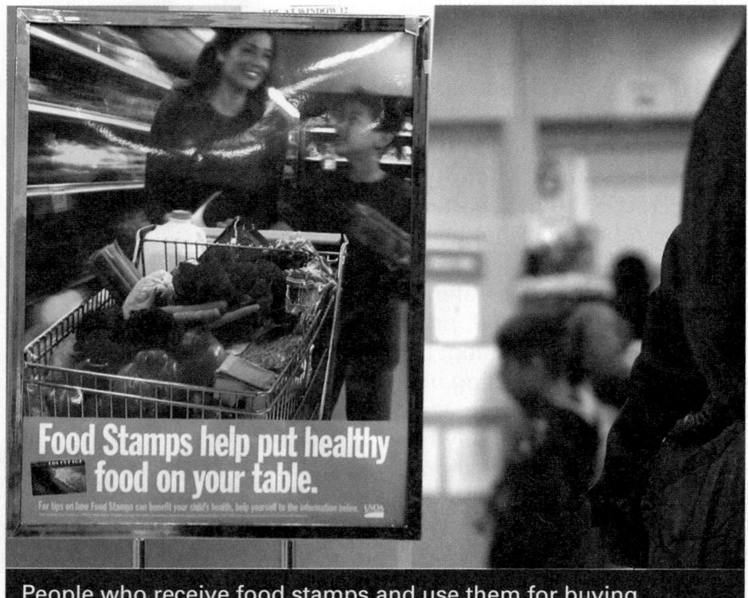
Food Stamps help put healthy food on your table.

People who receive food stamps and use them for buying groceries must pass a means test in order to receive this government benefit. As America plunged into recession, the number of Americans receiving food stamps rose from 31 million in November 2008 to 40 million in April 2010.

No area of public policy causes more confusion or stimulates more argument than does social welfare. One common misperception is to equate social welfare with government aid to the poor. In fact, these programs distribute far more money to the nonpoor than to people below the poverty line. Political scientist Martin Gilens notes that about five-sixths of all money for social programs goes to programs that everyone is eligible for, such as Social Security and Medicare; only 17 percent of social spending goes to programs that target the poor.[1] Few Americans have qualms about assisting older Americans through government programs. Government assistance to the poor is a different matter, however. As political scientists Stanley Feldman and Marco Steenbergen put it, Americans may be humanitarians, but they are not egalitarians.[2] To clarify the picture, it is useful to distinguish between two types of programs that social welfare policies consist of.

Entitlement programs provide benefits to individuals regardless of need. They are sometimes called "social insurance" programs because typically people (and their employers) pay into them and later get money from them. Thus, you don't have to be poor to get an entitlement, nor does being rich disqualify you. The two main entitlement programs, Social Security and Medicare, are the largest and most expensive social welfare programs in America. These programs have had a positive effect on the health and income of older Americans, who receive more and better medical treatment as a result of Medicare and in many cases are kept out of poverty by Social Security payments. Entitlement programs are rarely controversial and are often overwhelmingly popular (perhaps because everyone is *entitled* to them).

entitlement programs
Government programs providing benefits to qualified individuals regardless of need.

WHY IT MATTERS

Perceptions of Poverty

Some people see the poor as lazy; others believe that most of the people who are poor are victims of circumstance. These perceptions of the poor affect the kinds of social welfare policies they favor. Conservatives tend to believe that means-tested welfare programs only discourage people from working. Liberals are more likely to see these programs as helping people weather difficult circumstances.

In contrast, **means-tested programs**, such as Food Stamps and Medicaid, provide benefits only to people with specific needs. To be eligible for means-tested programs, people have to prove that they qualify for them. Means-tested programs generate much political controversy, with the positions taken depending largely on how people see the poor and the causes of poverty. Poverty may be seen as largely as consequence of the individual's decisions and behaviors, that is, largely beyond the individual's control. When the poor are seen as victims of forces beyond their control (loss of a breadwinner, disabilities, poor economic opportunities), government programs are relatively uncontroversial, for liberals and conservatives alike. However, when the poor are seen as responsible for their poverty, by conservatives in particular, government programs tend to be seen as encouraging dependency. As Weil and Finegold summarize the situation, American welfare policy is frequently caught between two competing values: "the desire to help those who could not help themselves, and the concern that charity would create dependency."[3]

Let's look, therefore, at income and poverty and at what public policy has to do with each.

Income, Poverty, and Public Policy

18.2 Assess the extent of economic inequality in America and the role of government in lessening it.

The United States has one of the world's highest per capita incomes, and when cost of living and tax rates are taken into account, only a few small countries (for example, Norway, Brunei, and Luxembourg) rank ahead of the United States in terms of purchasing power. According to the Census Bureau, in 2009, the median American household income was \$49,777—that is, half of American households made more than \$49,777, and half made less. Thus, Americans are an affluent people. Yet, no industrialized country has wider extremes of income than the United States—and the extremes in the United States have been widening. Timothy Smeeding, one of the leading researchers on poverty in America, points out that "over the last four decades, the United States has seen large increases in income inequality" and that "many developed countries have experienced at least modest increases in the inequality of . . . income, but none so sustained as in the United States."[4] Income is important to politics, just as it is important to people. McCarty, Poole, and Rosenthal argue that American politics is becoming more polarized and that the main "conflict is basically over income redistribution."[5] Liberals and conservatives are divided about many things, but "who gets what" in terms of income is a major battleground.

means-tested programs
Government programs providing benefits only to individuals who qualify based on specific needs.

Who's Getting What?

The novelist F. Scott Fitzgerald once wrote to his friend Ernest Hemingway, "The rich are different from you and me." "Yes," replied Hemingway, "they have more money." Like Hemingway, social scientists focus on the monetary difference. They use the concept of **income distribution** to describe how the national income is divided up. If we divide the population into groups based on income, say, into fifths, income distribution tells us what share goes to each group, from the bottom one-fifth to the top one-fifth.

income distribution
The way the national income is divided into "shares" ranging from the poor to the rich.

In the United States, the distribution of income across groups is quite uneven. The repercussions of different income distribution patterns can be considerable. Thomas B. Edsall remarks that "the distribution of income and wealth in a democratic country goes to the heart of its political ethic, defining the basic contours of a nation's sense of justice and equality."[6]

Income distribution in the United States has changed considerably in recent decades, as you can see in Table 18.1. During the 1960s and 1970s, the distribution of income was rather constant. Since the 1980s, however, the old adage has proved true: The rich have gotten richer, and the poor have gotten poorer. This change in the distribution of income can contribute to a situation known as **relative deprivation**, in which people believe they are not doing well compared to some reference group. For many observers, a sense of relative deprivation is becoming common in America as the super-rich have grown richer while average working Americans have seen their income stagnate.

relative deprivation
A perception by an individual that he or she is not doing well economically in comparison to others.

So far we have focused on **income**, the amount of money collected between two points in time. Income is different from **wealth**, the value of one's assets, including stocks, bonds, bank accounts, cars, houses, and so forth. Studies of wealth show even more inequality than those of income: one-third of America's wealth is held by the wealthiest 1 percent of the population, another one-third is held by the next 9 percent, and the remaining one-third is held by the other 90 percent.

income
The amount of money collected between any two points in time.

wealth
The value of assets owned.

Who's Poor in America?

Counting the poor may seem easy, but it is not. First one needs to define poverty. Compared with most people in Haiti, poor Americans seem almost prosperous. Russia is a poor country by American standards, but it is not afflicted with the poverty of rural Mexico. Mexico City may look poor to an American visitor, but many people come there from the Mexican countryside seeking prosperity—relatively speaking.

To define this inherently relative concept, the U.S. Census Bureau is charged with determining the **poverty line**, the income threshold below which an individual is considered impoverished. This official statistic was designed by Mollie Orshansky, a statistician with the Social Security Administration who realized that in order for politicians to do something about poverty, they first needed to have a way of measuring it. From earlier work for the Department of Agriculture, Orshansky had learned that a family barely managing to make ends meet spent roughly one-third of its money on food. To set the poverty level, she took the cost of the Department of Agriculture's subsistence diet and multiplied it by three. The federal government adopted this formula as its official measure of the poverty threshold in the mid-1960s, and has continued to update the formula every year by factoring in inflation.

poverty line
The income threshold below which people are considered poor, based on what a family must spend for an "austere" standard of living, traditionally set at three times the cost of a subsistence diet.

TABLE 18.1 Who Gets What? Income Shares of American Households, 1960–2008

The table demonstrates how much of the nation's income is received by people within each quintile (or fifth) of the population. Thus, in 2008, for example, people whose income placed them in the lowest 20 percent of households received just 3.4 percent of the nation's income while those in the highest 20 percent got half of the nation's income. In recent decades, the share of the highest fifth has grown while those of the lowest fifths have gotten smaller. What do you think accounts for this growing divide between rich and poor?

INCOME QUINTILE	1960	1970	1980	1990	1998	2008
Lowest fifth	4.9	5.5	5.1	4.6	4.2	3.4
Second fifth	11.8	12.0	11.6	10.8	9.9	8.6
Third fifth	17.6	17.4	17.5	16.6	15.7	14.7
Fourth fifth	23.6	23.5	24.3	23.8	23.0	23.3
Highest fifth	42.0	41.6	41.6	44.3	47.3	50.0

Source: U.S. Census Bureau. The 2008 data can be found in the Census Bureau's report entitled "Income, Poverty, and Health Insurance Coverage in the United States: 2008," p. 10. This report is posted online at http://www.census.gov/prod/2009pubs/p60-236.pdf.

Orshansky never intended to create a permanent formula. She believed that if spending habits changed, then the measurement of poverty ought to be adjusted accordingly. Many scholars believe that today, because the cost of food has declined relative to the cost of other goods, an income equal to three times a subsistence food budget leaves a family in need of many necessities. For years, experts on the subject of poverty have called for a return to Mollie Orshansky's basic concept: what it really takes to maintain an austere standard of living. Moreover, in the decades since Orshansky's basic work was done, the Census Bureau has expanded its data collection routines to assemble much more detailed information about spending patterns and income, thereby making possible a more complex and refined measurement of poverty. In March 2010, the Obama administration announced that it had settled on an alternative measure, which takes into account a wide range of expenses, such as housing, utilities, child care, and medical treatment, as well as variations in the cost of living in different parts of the country. At least in its first year (2011), this new measure will not be used to determine eligibility for any federal programs.[7]

Few events in recent American history highlighted the gap between the well-off and the poor more than Hurricane Katrina, which hit New Orleans and its suburbs hard in 2005. Rebuilding in the prosperous suburban areas proceeded quickly, as evidenced by the number of people waiting to tour a model home in the upper picture. But in the poor areas, such as the Lower Ninth Ward, scenes such as that in the lower picture remained all too common for years after the hurricane.

Officially, 43.6 million Americans, or about 14.3 percent of the population, were poor in 2009, according to the traditional measure employed by the Census Bureau. However, the official poverty counts tend to *underestimate* poverty in America, not only for the reasons discussed above but, more generally, because it is a snapshot in time rather than a moving picture. That is, a count of the poor at any one point in time can conceal millions who quickly drop into and out of poverty. Divorce, the loss of a breadwinner, job setbacks, and a new mouth to feed can precipitate a fall below the poverty line. Economic insecurity—the chance of suddenly falling into a much lower income bracket—is higher in the United States than in most industrialized countries. Over half of all Americans between the ages of 25 and 75 will spend at least one year in poverty during their lives, according to Jacob Hacker's analysis.[8] Journalist Barbara Ehrenreich chronicled the life of the "near poor" in America[9] by taking on a string of low-wage jobs—working at lower-end retail stores and doing janitorial work, for example—and piecing together a meager living. As she documented, contrary to popular impression, most poor and near-poor are gainfully employed in low-wage jobs that often fail to take them above the poverty line.[10]

Who's officially poor? Although the poor are a varied group, poverty is more associated with certain demographic characteristics, as you can see in Figure 18.1. Poverty rates are higher for African Americans, Hispanics, unmarried women, children, and inner-city residents. African Americans and Hispanics have a more than 20 percent chance of living in poverty, as opposed to a less than 10 percent chance for white, non-Hispanics. Although poverty had long been a problem especially for the elderly, the creation of Social Security in 1935 and its expansion over time significantly reduced poverty among the elderly. Today, poverty is particularly a problem for unmarried women and their children. Scholar Harrell Rodgers tellingly titled his study of contemporary poverty *Poor Women, Poor Children,*[11] and experts often refer to the

FIGURE 18.1 Poverty Rates for Persons with Selected Characteristics, 2009

Below, you can see the poverty rates for various groups as determined by surveys conducted by the Census Bureau in 2009. Whether the Census Bureau classifies a person as living in poverty depends on how his or her family's income falls with regard to the poverty threshold, which varies according to the number of adults and children in the family. In 2009, the poverty threshold for a single adult was $11,161, for two adults it was $14,366, and for a single parent with two children it was $17,268.

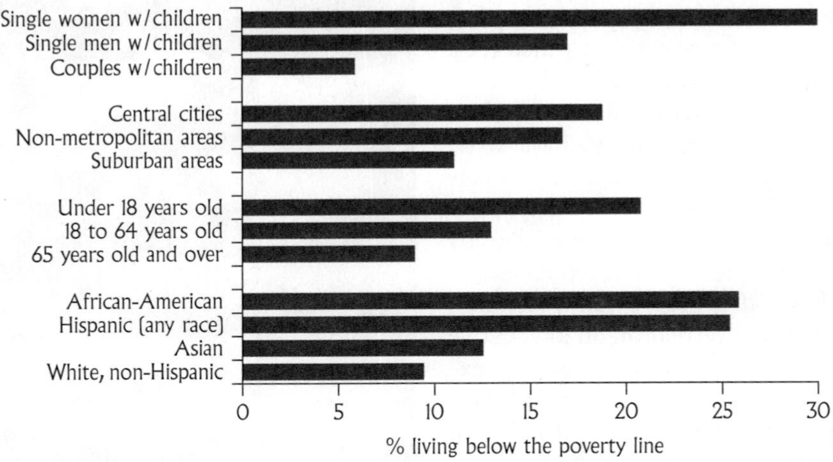

Source: U.S. Census Bureau, "Income, Poverty, and Health Insurance Coverage in the United States: 2009," p. 15.

feminization of poverty
The increasing concentration of poverty among women, especially unmarried women and their children.

feminization of poverty. The poverty rate for female-headed families is almost 30 percent, as opposed to less than 6 percent for families with two parents. Having children out of wedlock, Rodgers says, is the "superhighway to poverty."[12]

How Public Policy Affects Income

To eradicate poverty, some people believe, the government should ensure that everyone has a minimal level of income. But, of course, income is determined by many factors that are clearly not subject to governmental control— how hard people work, what opportunities are available in the area where they reside, what kind of education parents could afford to provide. However, because government (national, state, and local) spends one of out every three dollars in the American economy, it is bound to have a major impact on citizens' income and wealth. There are two principal ways in which government affects a person's income. One is through its taxing powers; the other is through its expenditure policies.

progressive tax
A tax by which the government takes a greater share of the income of the rich than of the poor—for example, when a rich family pays 50 percent of its income in taxes, and a poor family pays 5 percent.

proportional tax
A tax by which the government takes the same share of income from everyone, rich and poor alike.

regressive tax
A tax in which the burden falls relatively more heavily on low-income groups than on wealthy taxpayers. The opposite of a progressive tax, in which tax rates increase as income increases.

Taxation "Nothing," said Benjamin Franklin, "is certain in life but death and taxes." Taxes can be termed progressive, proportional, or regressive, depending on their effects on citizens' incomes. A **progressive tax** takes a bigger bite from the incomes of the rich than from those of the poor, for example, charging millionaires 50 percent of their income and the poor 5 percent of theirs. A **proportional tax** takes the same percentage from everyone, rich and poor alike. And, finally, a **regressive tax** takes a higher percentage from those at lower income levels than from the well-to-do.

A tax is rarely advocated or defended because it is regressive, but some taxes do take a bigger bite from the poor than the rich. Chief among these are sales taxes, from which many states derive more than half their revenues. A sales tax looks proportional—6 percent of every purchase, for example, is taxed. However, since poor families spend a higher percentage of their income on purchases—of food, clothing, school supplies, and other necessities—they wind up paying a higher percentage of their incomes in sales taxes than do the rich.

Federal income taxes are progressive; you only have to look at the rates on your tax forms to see this. The rich send a bigger proportion of their incomes to Washington

A POINT TO PONDER

Liberals often claim that the relatively high level of economic inequality in America is due to our relatively low tax rates, in particular for those in the upper brackets. They would like to see the government invest more in treating the symptoms of poverty, even if it means higher tax rates. Conservatives counter that tax cuts create economic incentives that help everyone, and reject the message of cartoons such as this one.

What do you think? Do you agree with the premise of this cartoon?

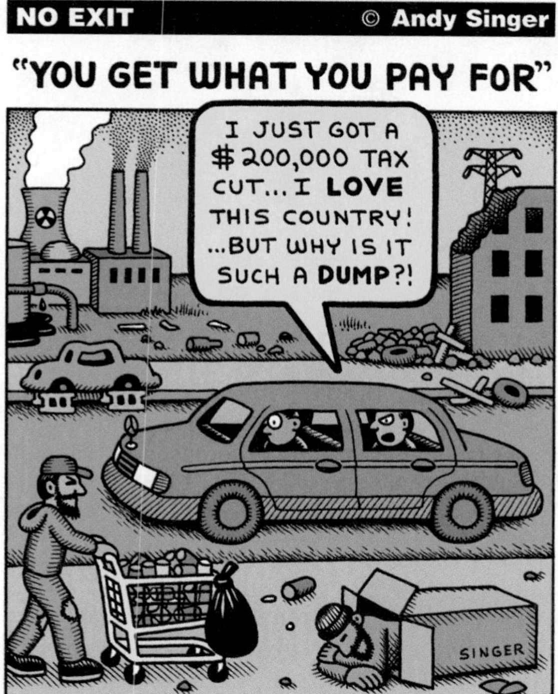

than the poor. In 2006, Americans who earned over a million dollars paid an average of 23 percent of their adjusted gross income in federal income taxes. By comparison, individuals in the $40,000 to $50,000 income range paid an average of 8 percent.[13] If your income is low enough, you can even get money back from the government rather than paying income tax. The **Earned Income Tax Credit** (EITC) is a special tax benefit for working people who earn low incomes. In 2010, workers who were raising one child in their home and had family incomes of less than $16,420 could get an EITC of up to $3,043. Estimates indicate that the EITC puts as much as $20 billion a year into the hands of poor and near-poor families.[14]

Earned Income Tax Credit
The Earned Income Tax Credit, or the EITC, is a refundable federal income tax credit for low- to moderate-income working individuals and families, even if they did not earn enough money to be required to file a tax return.

Government Expenditures The second way in which government can affect personal income is through its expenditures. Each year millions of government checks are mailed to Social Security beneficiaries, retired government employees, veterans, and others. Unemployed workers receive payments through state-run unemployment insurance programs. The government also provides "in-kind" benefits, which provide assistance in ways other than simply writing a check. Food stamps and low-interest college loans are both examples of in-kind benefits. These and other benefits—cash and in-kind—are called

How Unemployment Insurance Benefits Vary

The map classifies the 50 states according to the maximum weekly benefit that they offered unemployed workers as of June 2009. In many states, the maximum benefit can only be obtained if the unemployed worker has dependents, such as children, at home. You can find the specific details for your state at the web link in the source information below.

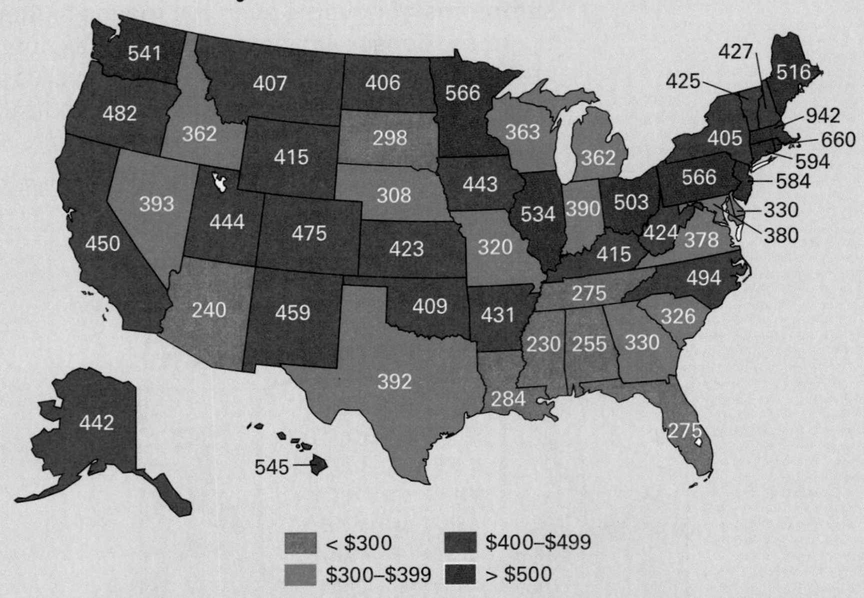

Source: "The Boundaries of Unemployment," *Wall Street Journal,* June 23, 2009. This information can be found online at http://online.wsj.com/article/SB124571390708339073.html#articleTabs_interactive%26articleTabs%3Dinteractive.

QUESTIONS FOR DISCUSSION

- One of the reasons that unemployment insurance benefits are set by states is that the cost of living varies greatly amongst the states. Taking into account the cost of living in your state, do you think that the unemployment insurance benefits that are available are adequate to keep someone afloat financially between jobs?
- Clearly, lower benefits tend to be found in Republican-leaning states whereas higher benefits tend to be found in Democratic-leaning states. Why do you think this is the case?

transfer payments Benefits given by the government directly to individuals—either cash transfers, such as Social Security payments, or in-kind transfers, such as food stamps and low-interest college loans.

transfer payments; they transfer money from federal and state treasuries to individuals. In the case of state-run programs, such as unemployment insurance, benefits vary widely amongst the states. You can see how your state ranks in terms of weekly checks to workers who have lost their jobs in "My State: How Unemployment Benefits Vary."

It is clear that many recipients are better off after these transfers than before, particularly the elderly, whose poverty rate declined from 35 percent in 1959 to 10 percent in 2008 primarily because of Social Security payments and Medicare. Many of the poor have been raised above the poverty line by these cash and in-kind transfers. In April 2010, a record 40.4 million Americans were receiving food stamps. The average monthly benefit of about $130 per person helped many families weather the worst of the recession. A recent study by sociologists Mark Rank and Mark Hirschl startled some policymakers in finding that half of Americans receive food stamps, at least briefly, by the time they turn 20. Among black children, the figure was 90 percent.[15]

Table 18.2 summarizes the major government social welfare programs that affect our incomes, both programs providing cash benefits and those providing in-kind benefits. We have already mentioned Social Security and Medicare as entitlement programs; notice that unemployment insurance is the other major entitlement program. The other programs are means tested and are available only to the near-poor or the poor. In addition to Medicaid and food stamps, they include Temporary Assistance for Needy Families and Supplementary Security Income, providing cash to needy families and the needy with disabilities, and the Children's Health Insurance Program, subsidizing health care for children in poor families.

TABLE 18.2 The Major Social Welfare Programs

PROGRAM	DESCRIPTION	BENEFICIARIES	FUNDING
Entitlement Programs—"Social Insurance"			
Social Security	Monthly payments	Retired or disabled people and surviving members of their families	Payroll tax on employees and employers
Medicare (Part A)	Partial payment of cost of hospital care	Retired and disabled people	Payroll taxes on employees and employers
Medicare (Part B)	Voluntary program of medical insurance (pays physicians)	Persons 65 or over and disabled Social Security beneficiaries	Beneficiaries pay premiums
Unemployment Insurance (UI)	Weekly payments; benefits vary by state	Workers who have been laid off and cannot find work	Taxes on employers; states determine benefits
The Means-Tested Programs			
Medicaid	Medical and hospital aid	The very poor	Federal grants to state health programs
Food stamps	Coupons that can be used to buy food	People whose income falls below a certain level	General federal revenues
Temporary Assistance for Needy Families (TANF)	Payment	Families with children, either one-parent families or, in some states, two-parent families where the breadwinner is unemployed	Paid partly by states and partly by the federal government
Supplementary Security Income (SSI)	Cash payments	Elderly, blind, or disabled people whose income is below a certain amount	General federal revenue
Children's Health Insurance Program (CHIPs)	Subsidies for insurance	Poor families with children	Federal and state revenues

Helping the Poor? Social Policy and the Needy

18.3 Trace the changes over time in major federal welfare programs.

Historically, societies considered family welfare a private concern. Children were to be nurtured by their parents and, in turn, care for them in their old age. Governments took little responsibility for feeding and clothing the poor or anyone else. The life of the poor was grim almost beyond our imagining. In England, governments passed Poor Laws providing "relief" for the poor but intended, historians argue, to make the life of the poor so miserable that people would do almost anything to avoid the specter, disgrace, and agony of poverty.[16] It was scarcely better in the United States as late as the Great Depression, in the 1930s.

"Welfare" as We Knew It

The administration of Franklin D. Roosevelt implemented a host of policies to deal with the Depression, thus establishing a safety net for less fortunate Americans. The most important piece of this New Deal legislation was the **Social Security Act of 1935**. In addition to creating the Social Security entitlement program for the aged, this bill also created a program to assist some of the nation's poor. Known eventually as "Aid to Families with Dependent Children," this program brought various state

Social Security Act of 1935
Created both the Social Security program and a national assistance program for poor families, usually called Aid to Families with Dependent Children.

programs together under a single federal umbrella to help poor families that had no breadwinner and had children to care for. The federal government established some uniform standards for the states and subsidized their efforts to help families. However, states were free to give generous or skimpy benefits, and payments ranged widely. For the first quarter-century of the program, enrollments remained small. Spurred in part by the civil rights movement, in 1964 President Lyndon Johnson declared a national "War on Poverty," and added food stamps and other programs to the arsenal of poverty-fighting policies. These programs—collectively called "welfare"—came to bitterly divide Republicans from Democrats and conservatives from liberals.

If Lyndon Johnson had declared war on poverty, President Ronald Reagan declared war on antipoverty programs. In 1981, he persuaded Congress to cut welfare benefits and lower the number of Americans on the welfare rolls, arguing that welfare had proved to be a failure. Conservative economist Charles Murray offered an influential and provocative argument that the social welfare programs that began with Johnson's War on Poverty not only failed to curb the advance of poverty but actually made the situation worse.[17] The problem, Murray maintained, was that these public policies discouraged the poor from solving their problems. He contended that welfare programs made it profitable to be poor and thus discouraged people from pursuing means by which they could rise out of poverty. For example, Murray claimed, since poor couples could obtain more benefits if they weren't married, most would not marry and the result would be further disintegration of the family. Many scholars disagreed,[18] but their arguments and interpretations of the data were overwhelmed by the public's extremely negative perception of welfare. "Deadbeat dads" who ran out on their families, leaving them on welfare, and "welfare queens" who collected money they didn't deserve became common images of a broken system.[19]

WHY IT MATTERS

The 1996 Reform of Welfare

Because, since the reform, the states have been faced with fixed amounts to spend on welfare and individuals limited in terms of how long they could receive benefits, the percentage of poor people who receive welfare assistance has declined markedly. Many liberals are concerned that a hole has been opened in the safety net; conservatives tend to be pleased that incentives for the poor to find gainful employment have been increased.

No one was clearer or blunter about American antipathy toward welfare than political scientist Martin Gilens.[20] He found that despite the clear evidence to the contrary, Americans tended to see welfare recipients as overwhelmingly African American. Whites' welfare attitudes were strongly influenced by whether they held negative stereotypes of African Americans, for example, perceiving them as "lazy."[21] Negative views of African American welfare mothers generated opposition to welfare in a way that views of white welfare mothers did not. Moreover, when Gilens counted magazine and newspaper stories about poor people over a period of several decades, he found that although only a third of all welfare recipients were African American, about three-quarters of these stories concerned African Americans.[22] Attitudes toward welfare, in short, became "race coded" and it was commonly concluded that many "undeserving poor" were on welfare.

The stage for a major welfare reform was set when Bill Clinton pledged to reform America's system of welfare in his successful bid for the presidency in 1992.

Since 1996, welfare reform policies have tried to reduce the welfare rolls and get recipients to work. The young single woman pictured here said that she had gained new hope from the Climb Wyoming job training program that she was enrolled in while temporarily receiving welfare payments. You can find out about this program for single mothers at http://www.climbwyoming.org/.

Ending Welfare as We Knew It: The Welfare Reform of 1996

Bill Clinton was determined to be a "centrist" president, fearing the "tax and spend" label Republicans applied to liberal Democrats. Clinton promised to "end welfare as we know it" by providing welfare recipients with two years of support—training, child care, and health care—in exchange for an agreement to find work. Republicans in Congress were even more enthusiastic about welfare reform than the new president. In August 1996, the president and congressional Republicans completed a welfare reform bill that received almost unanimous support from the Republicans but was opposed by about half of the congressional Democrats. Under the lofty name of the **Personal Responsibility and Work Opportunity Reconciliation Act** (PRWORA), this bill provided that (1) each state would receive a *fixed* amount of money to run its own welfare programs, (2) people on welfare would have to find work within two years or lose all their benefits, and (3) there would be a lifetime maximum of five years for welfare. With the reform, the name of welfare was also changed, from Aid to Families with Dependent Children to **Temporary Assistance for Needy Families** (TANF).

Personal Responsibility and Work Opportunity Reconciliation Act
The welfare reform law of 1996, which implemented the Temporary Assistance for Needy Families program.

Temporary Assistance for Needy Families
Replacing Aid to Families with Dependent Children as the program for public assistance to needy families, TANF requires people on welfare to find work within two years and sets a lifetime maximum of five years.

Today, the benefits from this means-tested program for the poorest of the poor are small and declining. Recipient families collect an average of about $363 monthly in TANF benefits. The number of families receiving aid has also declined: As you can see in "A Generation of Change: The Decline of America's Welfare Rolls," the welfare reform bill has had its intended effect of dramatically reducing the percentage of the population receiving welfare benefits.

Today, welfare spending remains unpopular compared to most other governmental expenditures. The 2008 General Social Survey asked a random sample of the public whether spending should be increased or decreased in 22 categories. Education ranked as the American public's top priority for more spending; welfare ranked nineteenth with only aid to big cities, space exploration, and foreign aid ranking lower.[23]

One reason that welfare remains unpopular may be that TANF, along with food stamps and health benefits, is seen as contributing to a flood of immigrants. In some states, controversial policies have been considered which would deny benefits to people who cannot prove that they are legal residents, as you can read about in "You Are the Policymaker: Should Government Benefits Be Denied to Illegal Immigrants?"

How Welfare Reform Drastically Reduced the Welfare Rolls

For the decade prior to the welfare reform bill of 1996, an average of 4.8 percent of the population had been receiving welfare benefits through the Aid to Families with Dependent Children (AFDC) program. Under the new Temporary Aid to Needy Families (TANF) program, the average declined to just 1.7 percent between 2000 and 2009. Notably, even as the worst recession since World War II hit the United States in 2009, the welfare rolls grew by only a slight percentage. The fact that states have only a fixed amount of money to dole out under the TANF greatly restricted their ability to expand the distribution of welfare benefits during the recession. Many advocates for the poor argued that this result demonstrated that welfare's original purpose of being a safety net in bad times had been undermined. Conservatives responded that it was a good thing that fewer people were dependent on the government so that more had great incentive to work hard at obtaining gainful employment during the recession.

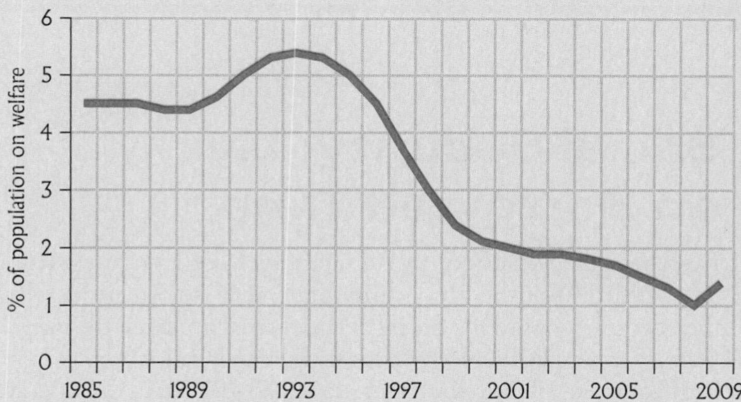

Source: "Indicators of Welfare Dependence," U.S. Department of Health and Human Services, *Annual Report to Congress*, 2008. Updated by the authors based on caseload data reported by the U.S. Department of Health and Human Services' Administration for Children and Families.

What do you think: Has the decline in the welfare rolls, even during a major recession, been a positive or a negative development?

YOU ARE THE POLICYMAKER

Should Government Benefits Be Denied to Illegal Immigrants?

In states such as Texas and California, which have experienced an influx of illegal immigrants particularly from Mexico and Central America, there is concern that providing public services to illegal immigrants is seriously draining state resources. The issue gained prominence as early as 1994, when Californians voted on Proposition 187. labeled by its proponents as the "Save Our State Initiative." This measure sought to cut illegal immigrants off from public services and benefits, such as education, and welfare benefits. Not only would Proposition 187 save the state treasury, its proponents argued, but it would discourage illegal immigrants, who came largely to take advantage of the free goods offered.

Opponents replied that although illegal immigration is surely a problem, the idea of cutting off public services could easily do more harm than good. They pointed out the public-health risks of denying illegal immigrants basic health care, such as immunizations that help control communicable diseases. If denied an education, some children of illegal immigrants, with nothing to do all day, they argued, would turn to crime. They also had a fairness argument: By paying sales taxes and rent, part of which goes to landlords' property taxes, illegal immigrants contribute to the tax base that pays for public services and thus should be entitled to make use of them.

The proponents of Proposition 187 won at the ballot box. However, they lost in their attempts to get the measure enforced. When Hispanic groups challenged the law, the courts ruled that the proposition violated the rights of illegal immigrants, as well as national laws concerning eligibility for federally funded benefits. Overall, the proposition was held to be an unconstitutional state scheme to regulate immigration.

California's experience with Proposition 187 has not stopped other states from trying to follow a similar course. In 2007, Oklahoma Governor Brad Henry signed into law the "Taxpayer and Citizen Protection Act," which many advocates of cracking down on illegal immigration highly praised. Like California's Proposition 187, this act was designed to deny illegal immigrants the right to receive services and benefits such as welfare benefits, scholarships, and medical care other than emergency care. The act also made it a crime to transport or house illegal immigrants in Oklahoma. As with California's law, the Oklahoma law was successfully challenged in court by Hispanic groups on the grounds that responsibility for enforcing immigration laws belongs to the federal government, not the states.

Until the federal government comes up with a comprehensive immigration reform package, it is likely that states will continue to experiment with ways in which to deal with undocumented immigrants. For example, in 2010 Arizona passed a controversial law requiring immigrants to carry their alien registration documents at all times and requiring police to question people if they have a reason to suspect they are in the U.S. illegally.

What do you think? Should illegal immigrants be denied government benefits, such as welfare and in-state tuition? Or should illegal immigrants who have paid their fair share of taxes receive some or all of the benefits that American citizens do? What are the advantages and disadvantages of each approach?

18.4 Outline how America's Social Security program works and the challenge of keeping it financially solvent in the coming years.

Social Security: Living on Borrowed Time

Every year, the Social Security Administration sends out over 100 million letters titled "Your Social Security Statement" to Americans detailing their contributions to the **Social Security trust fund** and the likely benefits they can expect to receive from it when they retire. About 75 million baby boomers will be retiring between 2010 and 2030. Chances are that they will live longer and healthier lives than previous generations—and run up bigger costs for Social Security. Many experts, as well as politicians, believe that Social Security is badly in need of reform. They argue that it is moving inexorably toward a day, not very far off, when the income being paid into the program will not be enough for paying out benefits, at least not at the level that people have come to expect from their yearly Social Security statement. But what exactly is Social Security? Let's look at its history—and at its future.

The Growth of Social Security

Social Security, officially called Old Age, Survivors and Disability Insurance (OASDI), has proved to be a highly successful and popular program. Year after year, more than 90 percent of people polled support Social Security. Although its benefits are relatively modest—the average monthly check for a retired worker in 2010 was about $1,100—Social Security has lifted many elderly out of poverty. Social Security taxes and benefits have both grown over the years because the program worked.

Social Security, now the most expensive public policy in the United States, began modestly enough, as part of Franklin Roosevelt's New Deal. President Roosevelt famously said that he wanted the fiscal basis to be so solid that "no damn politician can ever scrap my social security program." The fiscal soundness derived from the fact that, before money could go out to the beneficiaries, it would have to come into the federal treasury in payroll taxes. Indeed, over the years, Americans have tended to look on their Social Security benefits as getting back what they paid in. But from the start, taxes and benefits were not necessarily equivalent. The first Social Security recipient, a woman named Ida May Fuller from Brattleboro, Vermont, contributed a mere $22.54 and received benefits totaling $22,888.92, because she lived to an old age.[24] Today, however, a worker in his or her twenties may be facing the prospect of paying in more than he or she can expect to get back. To understand the problem, we have to look at how Social Security works.

Government taxes employees and their employers a percentage of the employee's income up to a maximum contribution. Both employee and employer contributions are paid into the **Social Security Trust Fund**. Current payroll taxes are 12.4 percent. If you work, you are contributing 6.2 percent of your wages (up to $102,000), and your employer matches it. (If you are making $102,000, you and Bill Gates are paying the same dollar amount into Social Security.) Your contributions, as well as those of all other workers, go into the Social Security Trust Fund.

Social Security Trust Fund
The "account" into which Social Security employee and employer contributions are "deposited" and used to pay out eligible recipients.

As long as more money is being paid in than is going out, the Trust Fund stays in the black. Although the sums are huge, the math is not all that complicated. Today's average monthly Social Security payment to recipients is equal to about 31 percent of the average monthly wage. Currently, there are about three workers per recipient. Thus, a recipient's benefits require a Social Security payroll tax of 10.3 percent per worker (31/3 = 10.3). Since current payroll taxes are 12.4 percent, for the moment more money is going into the Trust Fund than is being paid out. By law, the Trust Fund must invest this money in U.S. Treasury bonds, an investment that has typically been earning about 6 percent a year, although since the onset of the recession in 2008 this yield has been substantially less.

Essential to this arithmetic is the ratio of workers to beneficiaries. Suppose, for instance, that instead of three workers per beneficiaries, there are only two. The cost to each worker rises to 15.5 percent of earnings (31/2 = 15.5). Assuming the same payroll tax, Social Security eventually turns from black to red ink, once the excess funds accumulated in the Trust Fund have been used. As you can see in Figure 18.2, the ratio

FIGURE 18.2 Number of Covered Workers per Social Security Beneficiary, 1960–2080

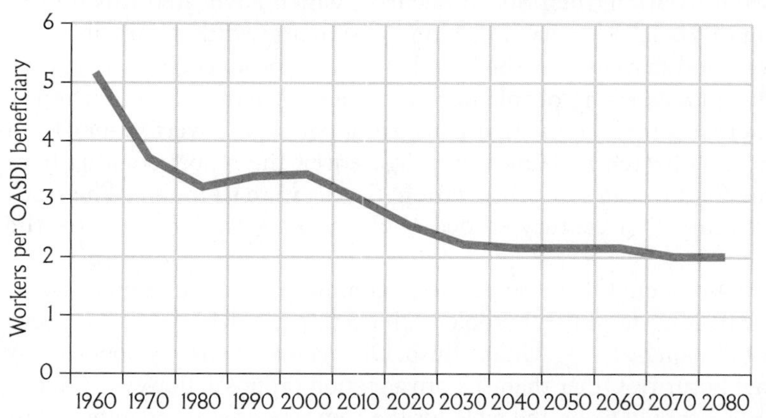

To the left, you can see how the average number of workers per Social Security (OASDI) beneficiary has fallen between 1960 and 2010, and is projected to continue to fall through 2080. Keep in mind that projections for the future are subject to demographers' best estimates of life expectancies, birth rates, and immigration rates. Should any of these factors change, then these estimates will change also.

Source: 2009 "Social Security Trustees Report," Table IV.B2. This table can be found online at http://www.ssa.gov/OACT/TR/2009/IV_LRest.html#345423.

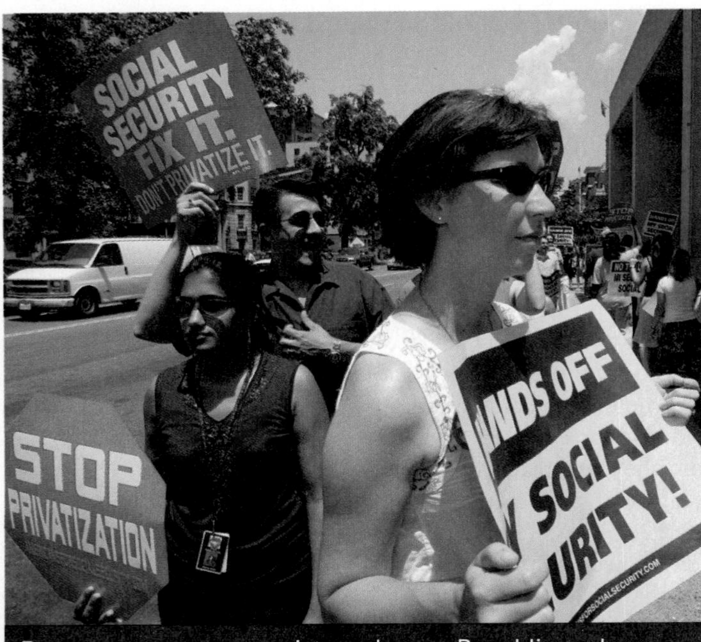

For years, some economists and many Republicans have advocated the partial "privatization" of Social Security. George W. Bush pushed the idea throughout two terms, never successfully. These protesters in Washington, D.C., want to leave Social Security untouched.

of workers to Social Security beneficiaries has been heading downwards for quite some time, and is projected to fall yet more in the future. Thus, the Social Security program may be living on borrowed time.

Various demographic factors explain the changing ratio. When Social Security was established, average life expectancy for Americans was lower than the 65 years at which workers could begin to collect benefits. With medical advances, average life expectancy has soared to 78 years. The bottom line is that, while the number of Social Security contributors (the workers) is growing slowly, the number of Social Security recipients (the retired) is growing rapidly.

In short, as the number of retirees grows (and their average benefit is increased to adjust for inflation, in what are called cost-of-living adjustments), Social Security payouts will exceed income, and within a number of years, the Trust Fund will be depleted. At that point, Congress would have to also use regular appropriations to pay out benefits to retirees—monies that thus would not be available for other purposes. There is no politically pleasant solution to this Social Security dilemma. Some experts say benefits must be cut; others say the rate of Social Security taxes must be increased; and yet others believe that both measures will be necessary. Hard choices lie ahead. And many young Americans suspect that Social Security is not going to be around for them anyway. (See "Young People and Politics: Social Security and UFOs.")

Reforming Social Security

Politicians tread gingerly on the terrain of Social Security, fearing a backlash from older Americans,[25] a concern accentuated by the fact that older Americans are an age group with a high voting rate.[26] Nonetheless, the looming problems of Social Security are so serious that recent presidents have tried their hands at reform.

President George W. Bush proposed diverting about a third of individuals' Social Security contribution to private retirement funds. The idea was that individuals could reduce their contribution and put that part of the money into a private account, a stock, a bond, or another investment and then collect their gains—or perhaps face their losses—when they were eligible to collect Social Security. President Bush appointed a Commission to Strengthen Social Security, which advocated this idea of limited privatization of Social Security. The Commission argued that contributions put into the stock or bond market over the long haul would produce greater returns, making it possible for today's young people to receive more benefits when they retire. Critics countered that the problem was that permitting people to divert money from the system would merely hasten its bankruptcy. Moreover, the report couldn't have come at a worse time for advocates of privatization: Stocks were slumping. The stock slump of the early twenty-first century eroded public and political support for the whole idea.

In February 2010, President Obama appointed a commission to draft a proposal for dealing with the nation's long-term fiscal problems, including the deficit that the Social Security Trust Fund will soon be facing. Unlike Bush, Obama has adamantly opposed any privatization of Social Security. Other than the privatization proposal, however, Obama has insisted that all ideas should be on the table for the commission's consideration. The

Social Security and UFOs

The story that more young adults believe in UFOs than in the future of Social Security was repeated so often that it became an urban legend. President Clinton told an audience at the University of Illinois that "there are polls that say that young people in their twenties think it's more likely that they will see UFOs than that they will ever collect Social Security." Countless other politicians, on various TV news shows, also told the story. How did such an odd, erroneous story arise?

A group called Third Millennium that favors Social Security reform commissioned two surveys in 1994, one of Americans 65 and older and one of young adults. Pollster Frank Luntz, who conducted the surveys, asked the young adults if they thought Social Security would exist by the time they retired: only 28 percent said yes. At the end of the questionnaire, he asked: "And one final question, and I ask you to take this seriously—Do you think UFOs exist?" Some 46 percent said yes. That was the basis for the claim that young people believe more in UFOs than in Social Security (or, in President Clinton's embellishment, that "they will see UFOs").

There was a little more to the survey than that. Interestingly, young people were more likely than were seniors themselves (48 to 35 percent) to think that older people were getting "less than their fair share of government benefits." But the quirky finding about UFOs became a part of national lore. Anyone with a complaint about Social Security could trot out the isolated numbers and make something out of them.

In 1998, precisely because this story was still being told, the Employee Benefit Research Institute, in surveying people ages 18 to 34, asked "Which do you have greater confidence in, receiving Social Security benefits after retirement or that alien life from outer space exists?" It found that 63 percent have greater confidence in getting their Social Security and 33 percent thought alien life was more likely.

Whether or not young people are more likely to be believe in extra-terrestial life or getting Social Security benefits today, the evidence is clear that there is much skepticism about the latter, as you can see from the July 2010 Gallup poll results shown in the figure below.

QUESTIONS FOR DISCUSSION

- What do you think the chances are that your generation will receive Social Security benefits when you reach retirement age?
- Experts recommend some combination of higher taxes and lower benefits in order to put the Social Security program on firm footing for the future. Do you think such changes would be fair to young Americans?

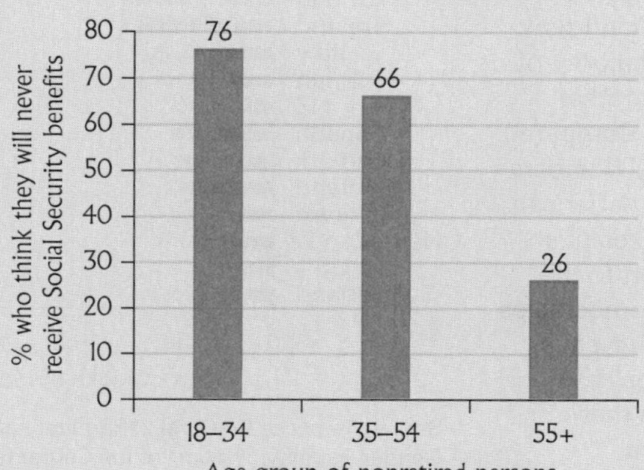

Source: Frank Newport, "Six in 10 Workers Hold No Hope of Receiving Social Security." Gallup public opinion report, July 20, 2010.

Republican co-chair of the commission, former Wyoming Senator Alan Simpson, took the president's challenge to examine politically painful options to heart. In accepting his charge to lead this commission, he colorfully said, "You have two choices with Social Security. You either raise the payroll tax, or decrease the benefits—or start affluence testing [i.e., denying benefits to affluent retirees]. The rest of it is B.S. And if the people are really ingesting B.S. all day long, their grandchildren will be picking grit with the chickens."[27] Which option, or combination thereof, that the commission recommends may well determine the future of America's most popular social welfare policy.

18.5 Distinguish American social welfare policy from that of other established democracies.

Social Welfare Policy Elsewhere

Most industrial nations tend to be far more generous with social welfare programs than is the United States. This greater generosity is evident in programs related to health, child care, unemployment compensation, and the elderly. Europeans often think of their countries as "welfare states," with all the generous benefits—and, by U.S. standards, staggering taxes—that this implies.[28] One example can be seen in "America in Perspective: Parental Leave Policies."

Americans tend to see poverty and social welfare needs as individual concerns, whereas European nations tend to support greater governmental responsibility for these problems. For example, 71 percent of Americans believe that the poor could escape

AMERICA IN PERSPECTIVE

Parental Leave Policies

Since 1993, U.S. federal law has required employers with 50 or more employees to provide workers (both women and men) with up to 12 weeks of *unpaid* leave for the birth or adoption of a child or the illness of a close family member. When President Clinton signed this law he hailed this as a landmark piece of legislation, whereas the majority of Republicans denounced it as yet another example of intrusive government. Compared to all other advanced industrialized democracies, though, the provisions of the American Family and Medical Leave Act are relatively meager. As you can see in the chart to the right all of the other established democracies provide for at least 10 weeks of *paid* leave for a two-parent family to care for a new child and most allow *unpaid* leave that greatly exceeds what American law provides for.

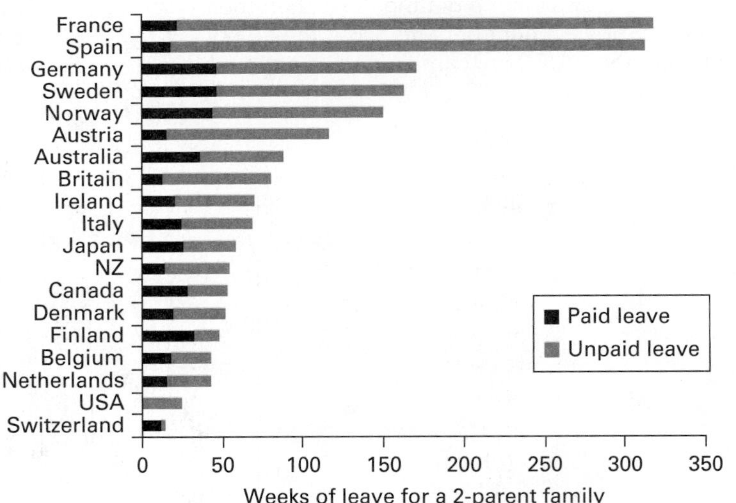

Source: Rebecca Ray et al., "Parental Leave Policies: Assessing Generosity and Gender Equality," Report of the Center for Economic and Policy Research, June 2009, p. 6. Updated by the authors for Australia, which implemented its first *paid* family leave in 2011.

During the 2008 presidential campaign, Barack Obama proposed that *unpaid* family leave in America be extended to companies with at least 25 employees, and that the federal government provide grants to states to help them implement programs to provide *paid* family leave. Would you favor or oppose these proposals? If you favor them, would you go even further and bring American family leave policy into line with the norm in other advanced industrialized democracies?

poverty if they worked hard enough, compared to just 40 percent of Europeans.[29] Also, Europeans often have a more positive attitude toward government, whereas Americans are more likely to distrust government action in areas such as social welfare policy.

Most Americans would be amazed at the range of social benefits in the average European country. French parents, for example, are guaranteed the right to put their toddlers in *crèches* (day care centers), regardless of whether the parents are rich or poor, at work or at home. French unemployment benefits are generous by American standards, although French unemployment rates are considerably higher than ours. In many European countries, free or low-cost government health care policies even include treatments at health spas.

Europeans pay a high price for generous benefits. Tax rates in Western European nations far exceed those in the United States (see Chapter 14); in some cases top tax rates exceed 50 percent of income. Moreover, the problems that the United States faces in funding Social Security occur to an even greater extent in many European countries, not only because of the level of benefits but also because their populations are shrinking due to very low birthrates, which compounds the issue of fewer taxpayers supporting an aging population.

Understanding Social Welfare Policy

18.6 Assess the impact of social welfare policies on democracy and the scope of government in America.

Social welfare policies are bound to be controversial in a capitalist, democratic political system. Very few issues divide liberals and conservatives more sharply. Americans struggle to balance individual merit and the rewards of initiative with the reality of systemic inequalities and the need to provide support to many. Citizens disagree on how much government can or should do to even out the competition and protect those who are less able or too old to compete. In short, Americans seek to retain a commitment to both competition and compassion. Sorting out the proper balance of these values is at the heart of policy disagreements about social welfare programs.

Democracy and Social Welfare

In a democracy, competing demands are resolved by government decision makers. But these policymakers do not act in a vacuum. They are aligned with and pay close attention to various groups in society. These groups include members of their legislative constituencies, members of their electoral coalitions, and members of their political party. Many of these groups provide the financial assistance that the decision makers need to seek and retain political office.

In the social welfare policy arena, the competing groups are often quite unequal in terms of political resources. For example, the elderly are relatively well organized and often have the resources needed to wield significant influence in support of programs they desire. As a result, they are usually successful in protecting and expanding their programs. For the poor, however, influencing political decisions is more difficult. They vote less frequently and lack strong, focused organizations and money. Larry Bartels finds that elected officials are often unresponsive to the policy preferences of low-income citizens.[30]

Although government benefits are difficult to obtain, especially for the poor, the nature of democratic politics also makes it difficult to withdraw benefits once they are established. Policymaking in the United States is very incremental in nature. Once put into place, policies develop a life of their own. They engage supporters in the public, in Congress, in the bureaucracy, and among key interest groups. Tremendous pressures come from these supporters to expand, or at least keep, existing programs. These pressures persist even when the size and costs of programs seem to have grown beyond anything originally envisioned, as has often been the case with social welfare programs.

Social Welfare Policy and the Scope of Government

Nothing more clearly accounts for the growth of government in America than social welfare spending, although Americans tend to overestimate spending on the poor while underestimating entitlement spending. Ever since the New Deal and the creation of Social Security, the growth of government has been driven by the growth of social welfare policies. Conservatives complain about the "welfare state." Even if ours is small relative to those of other nations, the American social welfare system grows generation by generation. American attitudes toward the growth of social welfare often depend on their assessment of what Schneider and Ingram call "target groups."[31] The elderly and the "deserving poor"—groups viewed favorably—are one thing; the "undeserving poor" are quite another. The debate about the scope of social welfare policies is influenced by a debate about how deserving various groups are, as well as by the political resources of potential beneficiaries.

Summary

18.1 Compare and contrast entitlement and means-tested social welfare programs.

Means-tested social welfare programs provide benefits only to people who qualify for them based on specific needs. In contrast, entitlement programs provide benefits to individuals without regard to need. Because entitlement programs can provide benefits to everyone, they are generally more popular with the public than means-tested programs.

18.2 Assess the extent of economic inequality in America and the role of government in lessening it.

Despite America's affluence, the extent of inequality—the disparity between incomes—is quite substantial and has been increasing in recent decades. America's means-tested social welfare programs help to reduce inequality by helping the poorest individuals. Progressive taxes, such as the federal income tax, also alleviate inequality by taking a bigger bite out of the rich than the middle class.

18.3 Trace the changes over time in major federal welfare programs.

The Aid to Families with Dependent Children (AFDC) program was begun during FDR's New Deal, greatly expanded during the period of LBJ's Great Society, and then reduced in scope by the Reagan administration. When he ran for president in 1992, Bill Clinton promised to "end welfare as we know it." With the help of a Republican majority in Congress in 1996, this was accomplished as the AFDC program was replaced by Temporary Assistance to Needy Families (TANF). The major innovation of the new law was that recipients of aid can only be on the welfare rolls for two consecutive years and five years during their lifetime.

18.4 Outline how America's Social Security program works and the challenge of keeping it financially solvent in the coming years.

The Social Security program collects a payroll tax from workers and their employers each month and pays out monthly benefits to retirees. It has proved to be a highly successful and popular program. However, demographic trends have put the program in danger, as soon there will not be enough workers per beneficiary to keep the program solvent. The government will soon face the painful choice between raising taxes or cutting benefits to senior citizens.

18.5 Distinguish American social welfare policy from that of other established democracies.

Most established democracies have more expensive and generous social welfare programs than does the United States. In particular, European governments provide citizens with benefits, such as paid parental leave upon the birth of a child, that are unheard of in the United States. Taxes in Europe have to be higher than taxes in the United States in order to pay for these benefits.

18.6 Assess the impact of social welfare policies on democracy and the scope of government in America.

As in most policy arenas, groups with ample political resources tend to get more of what they want in the battle over social welfare policies. Thus, the elderly have been very successful in preserving their Social Security and Medicare benefits, whereas the poor have faced difficulties in getting increased funding for TANF. Overall, the growth in social welfare spending, particularly for Social Security and Medicare, accounts for much of the increase in the scope of government in recent decades.

Chapter Test

18.1 Compare and contrast entitlement and means-tested social welfare programs.

1. Which of the following is characterized as an entitlement program?
   a. Medicaid
   b. Medicare
   c. Supplemental Security Income
   d. Children's Health Insurance Program
   e. Food stamps

2. Compare and contrast entitlement and means-tested social welfare programs. How does each type balance "the desire to help those who could not help themselves, and the concern that charity would create dependency"? Explain your answer.

18.2 Assess the extent of economic inequality in America and the role of government in lessening it.

3. Among which of the following groups is poverty most common?
   a. Unmarried women with children
   b. Inner-city residents
   c. African Americans
   d. Hispanics
   e. Older Americans

4. Changes in income distribution in the United States over the past few decades have led to an increased sense of relative deprivation among U.S. citizens.

   True______ False______

5. Compare and contrast the ways in which the government can affect personal income and income distribution through taxation. Provide an example of each, and explain which you think is the fairest form of taxation.

6. How accurate is the poverty line as a measure of poverty? What are some problems with the measure and how has the Obama administration attempted to resolve these problems?

18.3 Trace the changes over time in major federal welfare programs.

7. Which of the following is NOT true about welfare reform legislation passed in 1996 and its consequences?
   a. Benefits for the poor have declined
   b. The number of families receiving aid has declined
   c. The role of state governments in welfare has declined
   d. The number of years for which families are eligible for benefits has declined
   e. The amount of money spent on welfare benefits has declined.

8. The government spends more money on transfer payments for the poor than on transfer payments for other citizens.

   True______ False______

9. Discuss the history of major federal welfare programs for the poor. Based on evidence provided in the textbook, how successful have these welfare programs been? In your opinion, what is the likely future of welfare programs in the United States?

18.4 Outline how America's Social Security program works and the challenge of keeping it financially solvent in the coming years.

10. Social Security is currently the most expensive social welfare policy in the United States.

    True______ False______

11. What are the primary reasons why the Social Security Trust Fund faces insolvency in the near future? In your opinion, what should be done to reform Social Security so that funds will be available for future generations? Explain what obstacles you think your proposal faces and why you think it might work.

18.5 Distinguish American social welfare policy from that of other established democracies.

12. Most European nations tend to be much more generous with social welfare programs than the United States is.

    True______ False______

13. How do social welfare programs in Europe compare with those in the United States? Provide a specific example.

18.6 Assess the impact of social welfare policies on democracy and the scope of government in America.

14. How does political participation affect the distribution of social welfare benefits in the United States? Do you think that this is a problem for America's democracy?

15. How do social welfare policies contribute to the scope of government in the United States? How might efforts to reform social welfare programs be complicated by the groups who benefit from them?

PEARSON mypoliscilab™ Exercises

Apply what you learned in this chapter on MyPoliSciLab.

Read on **mypoliscilab.com**

eText: Chapter 18

Study and **Review** on **mypoliscilab.com**

Pre-Test
Post-Test
Chapter Exam
Flashcards

Watch on **mypoliscilab.com**

Video: Raising the Minimum Wage

Explore on **mypoliscilab.com**

Comparative: Comparing Social Welfare Systems
Timeline: The Evolution of Social Welfare Policy

Key Terms

social welfare policies (526)
entitlement programs (527)
means-tested programs (527)
income distribution (527)
relative deprivation (528)
income (528)
wealth (528)
poverty line (528)
feminization of poverty (530)
progressive tax (530)
proportional tax (530)
regressive tax (530)
Earned Income Tax Credit (531)
transfer payments (532)
Social Security Act of 1935 (533)
Personal Responsibility and Work Opportunity Reconciliation Act (535)
Temporary Assistance for Needy Families (535)
Social Security Trust Fund (537)

Internet Resources

www.aspe.hhs.gov/hsp/indicators-rtc/index.shtml
The Department of Health and Human Services issues an annual report to Congress on indicators of welfare dependence, which it posts at this site.

www.aecf.org
The Annie E. Casey Foundation produces a wealth of information about America's children, including its *Kids Count* data book.

www.fairus.org
FAIR—the Federation for American Immigration Reform—has data on immigration in the United States.

www.ssa.gov
The official site of the Social Security Administration, where you can read about the history of the program and learn how to calculate your own benefits.

For Further Reading

Alesina, Alberto, and Edward L. Glaeser. ***Fighting Poverty in the US and Europe: A World of Difference.*** New York: Oxford University Press, 2005. A systematic analysis of different approaches to the problems of domestic inequality and poverty.

Bartels, Larry M. ***Unequal Democracy: The Political Economy of the New Gilded Age.*** Princeton, NJ: Princeton University Press, 2008. A very influential analysis of the political causes and consequences of America's growing income gap.

Campbell, Andrea Louise. ***How Policies Make Citizens: Senior Political Activism and the American Welfare State.*** Princeton, NJ: Princeton University Press, 2003. How Social Security created a new class of elderly political activists.

Correspondents of the *New York Times*. *Class Matters*. New York: Times Books, 2005. A team of *New York Times* reporters explores the ways in which social class influences destiny in a society that likes to think of itself as a land of unbounded opportunity.

Diamond, Peter A., and Peter R. Orszag. ***Saving Social Security: A Balanced Approach.*** Washington, DC: Brookings Institution, 2005. The authors, one of whom was Obama's first budget director, argue that Social Security needs lots of minor surgeries but not major surgery.

Ehrenreich, Barbara. ***Nickel and Dimed: On (Not) Getting By in America.*** New York: Henry Holt, 2008. A well-educated journalist experiences the difficulties of getting by in America while working a string of low-wage jobs.

Gilens, Martin. ***Why Americans Hate Welfare: Race, Media, and the Politics of Antipoverty Policy.*** Chicago: University of Chicago Press, 1999. Gilens argues that public opposition to welfare is fed by a combination of racial and media stereotyping about the true nature of America's poor.

Hacker, Jacob S. ***The Great Risk Shift.*** New York: Oxford University Press, 2006. Why Americans have to rely more and more on their own resources for health, retirement security, and everything else.

Haskins, Ron. ***Work over Welfare: The Inside Story of the 1996 Welfare Reform Law.*** Washington, DC: Brookings Institution, 2007. The most authoritative account of the passage of the landmark reform of welfare.

Iceland, John. ***Poverty in America: A Handbook***, 2nd ed. Berkeley, CA: University of California Press, 2006. A comprehensive review of poverty in America, examining how poverty is measured and understood, as well as how public policies have dealt with it over time.

Page, Benjamin I., and Lawrence R. Jacobs. ***Class War?*** Chicago: University of Chicago Press, 2009. An examination of what Americans think about economic equality, and what they think the government should do about it.

Rodgers, Harrell, Jr. ***American Poverty in a New Era of Reform***, 2nd ed. New York: M. E. Sharpe, 2006. Discusses what has happened to poverty since the welfare reforms.

Chapter 19

Policymaking for Health Care, the Environment, and Energy

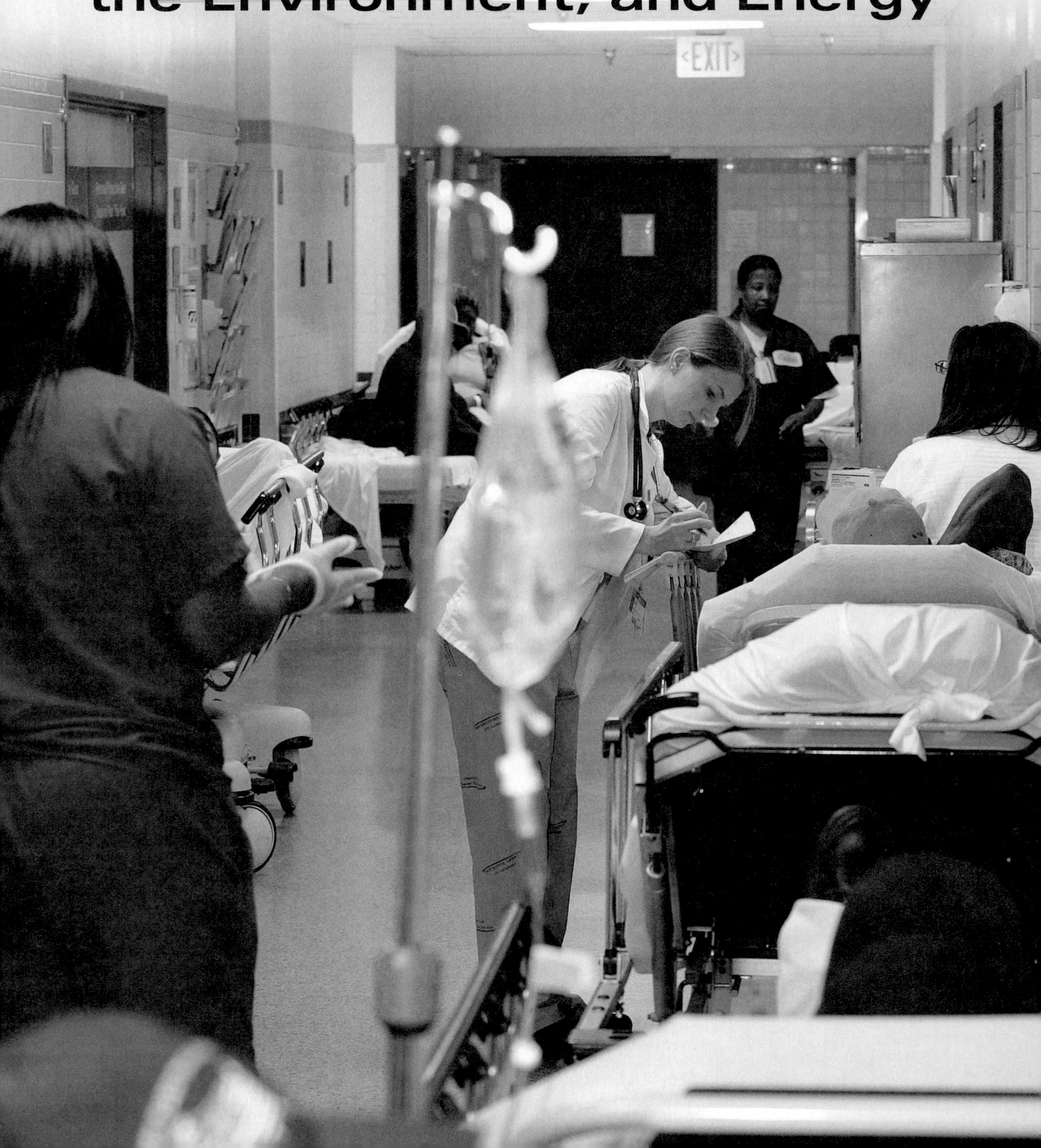

Learning Objectives

19.1 Outline the problems of health care in America and the role of government in health care.

19.2 Analyze the conflicts between economic growth and environmental protection, and identify the major national environmental protection policies.

19.3 Evaluate the advantages and disadvantages of each of the principal sources of energy in the United States.

19.4 Assess the role of democratic politics in making health care, environmental, and energy policy and the effect of these policies on the scope of government.

POLITICS IN ACTION: THE PRESIDENT TRIES TO REFORM HEALTH CARE

On September 9, 2009, President Barack Obama addressed a joint session of Congress on health care. He pointed out that it had been nearly a century since Theodore Roosevelt had called for health care reform. A bill for comprehensive reform was introduced in 1943 by John Dingell, Sr., and his son, who replaced him in the House, had been introducing the same bill for half a century. The health care system, the president said, was at the breaking point. Too many people lacked access to health care, and the costs for everyone were out of control. "We are . . . the only advanced democracy on Earth," the president proclaimed, "that allows such hardship for millions of its people." The president proposed a solution to the problems he identified, but many in the Congress and the public were not convinced. After a protracted battle, and despite significant public opposition, the president prevailed. The political cost of this victory remains to be seen.

Passage of major legislation in the areas of the environment and energy has also proved difficult. President Obama proposed a plan to deal with greenhouse emissions and global warming, but it failed to pass. And nothing like a comprehensive national energy policy has ever passed, either.

Health, the environment, and energy all are central to human well-being and thus highly salient to both the pubic and policymakers. They are also highly technical areas requiring complex policies that are difficult for most people to understand and evaluate. In addition, these policy areas cut across the rest of American society. For example, the environment and energy production affect health and also economic development. Equally important, these areas seem to call for government action to solve problems that appear intractable.

Yet government action is difficult on such complex matters that involve so many segments of American life so fundamentally. These policy areas thus raise profound questions. Is American democracy capable of resolving such complex matters? And just what should the government's role be in dealing with them?

Chapter OUTLINE

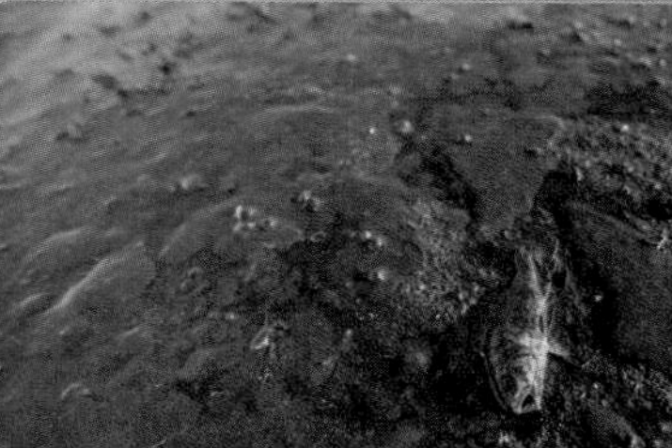

19.1 Outline the problems of health care in America and the role of government in health care.

Health Care Policy

There are few things more important to people than their health. Americans tend to believe they enjoy the best health care in the world. But is this true? What are the measures of health care? Do Americans enjoy the best health? And just how much are Americans paying for their health care? To what extent does everyone have access to state-of-the-art medical technology? And what role does government play in the financing, delivery, and regulation of health care? How does it make policy regarding health care?

Although Americans are generally healthy, which is unsurprising given the country's wealth, they lag behind a number of other countries in some key health care categories, such as life expectancy and the infant mortality rate (see "America in Perspective: The Costs and Benefits of Health Care"). The average life expectancy of 78 years is slightly lower than that in Canada and most other developed nations. A nation's *infant mortality rate*—the proportion of babies who do not survive the first five years of life—is considered a key indicator of the nation's health. The chances of a baby born in the United States dying in the first five years of life are more than 50 percent higher than those of a baby born in Japan. Yet the United States spends more per person on health care than any other country. If there is a gap between U.S. expenditures on health care and results in terms of health, this gap may be partly explained by the U.S. health care system.

The Cost of Health Care

American health care costs are both staggering and soaring. Americans now spend more than $2.5 *trillion* a year on health care. Health expenditures are one of the largest components of America's economy, accounting in 2009 for more than *one-sixth* (17 percent) of the gross domestic product (GDP),[1] a higher proportion than in any other country. Other democracies with developed economies, including Canada, Japan, the United Kingdom, France, and Germany, spend much less of their wealth on health care while providing universal health care coverage for their citizens.

AMERICA IN PERSPECTIVE

The Costs and Benefits of Health Care

American health care presents a paradox: As a nation, we spend a far larger share of our national income on health than any other industrialized country, in terms of both per capita spending and percentage of gross domestic product (GDP) spent on health care, yet we are far from having the healthiest population, as indicated by both life expectancy and the infant mortality rate.

Country	Per Capita Spending in U.S. Dollars (2006)	Percent of GDP Spent on Health	Life Expectancy in Years (Men/Women)	Infant Mortality Rate (Deaths of Children Under 5 per 1,000 Live Births)
United States	6,714	15.3	75/80	7
Canada	3,912	10.0	78/82	5
France	4,056	11.1	77/84	4
Germany	3,669	10.4	77/82	4
Japan	2,690	7.9	79/86	3
United Kingdom	3,361	8.4	77/81	5

Source: World Health Organization, 2009.

The costs of health care are a major obstacle to balancing the federal budget and to investing in the economy. Indeed, nearly one-fourth of all federal expenditures go for health care.[2] As President Clinton said shortly before taking office, "If I could wave a magic wand tomorrow and do one thing for this economy, I would bring health costs in line with inflation . . . because . . . that would free more money for people to invest in the plants and the production and the jobs of the future."[3]

Why are health care expenditures in the United States so high? Americans do not have more doctor visits or hospital stays than people in other countries. For example, Germans, the British, and others spend more nights in the hospital than Americans. And doctor visits per person have actually been declining in the United States.[4]

Other factors are behind the high cost of health care in America. American health providers have overbuilt medical care facilities (a substantial percentage of all hospital beds are vacant on any given day), and doctors and hospitals have few incentives to be more efficient. New technologies, drugs, and procedures often add to the cost of health care, including by addressing previously untreatable conditions and by providing better but more expensive care. Thus, much of the money that Americans pay for health care is spent on procedures and treatments, such as kidney dialysis and organ transplants, that may not be widely available in other countries and that may cost a lot, sometimes hundreds of thousands of dollars.

Part of the reason health care in the United States may rely excessively on expensive high-tech solutions is that medical bills are paid by a mixture of government funds, private insurance, and individuals' out-of-pocket payments; no one has primary responsibility for paying—or controlling—health care costs. In countries with national health care systems (or national health insurance), government policymakers have focused more on containing costs, especially administrative costs, as well as on ensuring equality of care. In the United States, cost containment and, as we will discuss, equality of care have taken a back seat to technological advances. To give one example, competition among urban hospitals to provide the most advanced care has led to duplication of expensive equipment and thus higher health costs.

Because insurance companies and government programs pay for most health care expenses, most patients have no reason to ask for cheaper care—they do not face the full financial consequences of their care. The providers of health care, such as physicians, are also insulated from competing with each other to offer less expensive care. In fact, with the rise in medical malpractice suits, doctors may be ordering extra tests, however expensive they may be, to ensure that they cannot be sued—an approach that is sometimes called "defensive medicine." Such practices drive up the costs of medical care for everyone. As doctors are hit with higher and higher costs for insurance against malpractice suits, they increase their fees to pay their premiums. Because insurance companies pay the bills, patients do not protest. However, increased costs associated with medical care are making insurance rates skyrocket.

Business groups are increasingly calling for relief from the high costs of health care. For example, they complain that their foreign competitors avoid the high costs of private insurance premiums because in many other countries governments, rather than employers, cover health insurance costs. And as many people who must seek medical care are uninsured and underinsured, employers complain that the rising insurance rates they must pay represent inflated premiums inteded to cover the costs of care for the uninsured and underinsured. To combat rising rates, some employers attempt to reduce their burden by cutting out benefits, particularly benefits covered by government programs. At the same time, employers defend the $171 billion tax break, or subsidy, that they receive for providing health insurance to their employees. Yet employer-provided insurance often has high administrative costs, discourages labor mobility as employees fear losing their insurance, and continues to insulate people from the consequences of their health care costs.

Not only are health care costs high but they have also been rising rapidly, as Figure 19.1 shows. At this rate of increase, we will likely be spending 19 percent of our GDP for health care by 2019.[5] The cost of premiums for employer-based insurance has increased by over 100 percent since 2000.[6] Because government is so deeply

FIGURE 19.1 The Rising Costs of Health Care

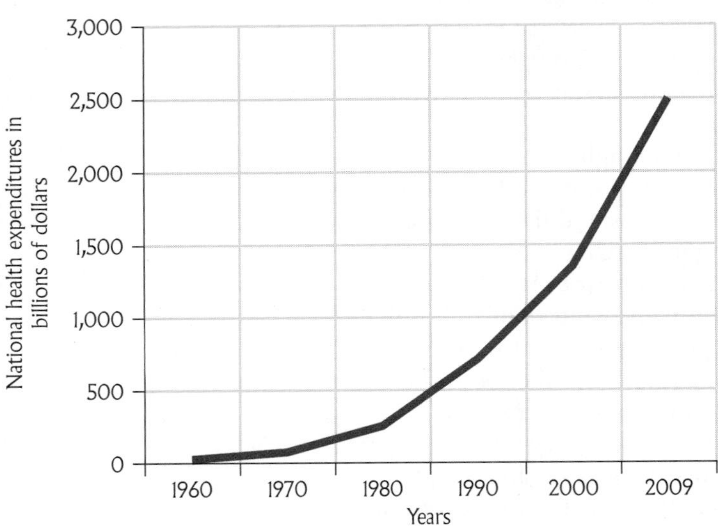

The United States spends an enormous amount on health care, and these expenditures have risen rapidly over the past 50 years. Getting health care expenditures under control is one of the greatest challenges of both government and the health care industry.

Source: Centers for Medicare and Medicaid Services, 2010.

involved in health care, government's burden will soar as well. The two major government health care programs—Medicare and Medicaid—could amount to 22 percent of the GDP by 2050.

The inefficiencies of the U.S. health care system are part of the explanation for the gap between the high costs that Americans pay for health care and the health benefits they derive, a gap made clear by comparisons with other countries. Another part of the explanation can be found in Americans' unequal access to health care.

Access to Health Care

Inequalities in health care and hence in health are a serious problem in America. Although the world's highest-quality care is available to some citizens, many poor and working-class Americans are relegated to an inferior health care system, because access to health insurance is not universal in the United States as it is in many countries.

Americans gain access to health care in a variety of ways. The most common means of access is through private health insurance plans, generally obtained through employers, sometimes obtained individually. Individual policies are often significantly more expensive than policies obtained through employers, as employers are able to bargain for group rates with insurers. Two-thirds of Americans have private health insurance of some kind.

The traditional form of private insurance plans is the fee-for-service health insurance policy, in which a policyholder pays an annual premium and then is entitled to have the insurance company pay a certain amount of each medical service obtained during the year. This traditional system posed problems for cost containment in that it gave doctors incentives to provide additional, and perhaps unnecessary, services; in effect, the more treatments doctors provided, the more money they made. Moreover, doctors insisted that patients be able to choose their own doctors without restrictions, which made it impossible to contract with groups of doctors to provide services more economically.

health maintenance organization
Organization contracted by individuals or insurance companies to provide health care for a yearly fee. Such network health plans limit the choice of doctors and treatments. More than half of Americans are enrolled in health maintenance organizations or similar programs.

In recent years, private market forces changed the country's health care system dramatically, through the growth of managed care. Today, private insurance often takes the form of contracting with a **health maintenance organization** (HMO), a network of health care providers that directly provides all or most of a person's health care for a yearly fee. More than half of Americans are enrolled in HMOs or other forms of network health plans.

Managed care grew on the strength of its claims to provide better service at a lower cost. By focusing on prevention rather than treatment and by designating a single doctor as a patient's primary care provider, rather than having patients treated by different specialists with no central coordination or oversight, managed care was intended to improve health care and contain costs. Insurers negotiate with physician groups and hospitals on fees and costs, and try to monitor care to control unnecessary use. At least three-fourths of all doctors have joined networks, signing contracts covering at least some of their patients to cut their fees and accept oversight of their medical decisions. Of course, HMOs have done nothing to ease the plight of those without health insurance.

Other Americans have access to health care through government programs. Nearly everyone 65 and older participates in Medicare, a government-subsidized program. About 43 million of those with low incomes are covered by Medicaid, another government program.[7] (We discuss both these programs in the next section.) Many children are covered by the Children's Health Insurance Program.

More than 46 million people—15 percent of the public—are without health insurance coverage for the entire year. With Medicare covering those over 65, the uninsured are disproportionately young. Included among the ininsured are more than 7 million children under the age of 18, and 29 percent of young adults, aged 18 to 24. In addition, millions of others are without health insurance for shorter periods. The uninsured who are not covered by government programs must pay all their health care expenses out of their own pocket. Because hospitals set a standard rate for each procedure and then bargain for group rates with insurance companies, the uninsured pay the full cost. This makes insurance the ticket to medical care in America.

Getting and keeping health insurance are often linked to having a job, especially a high-paying job. The reason is a historical quirk: During World War II, the federal government imposed a wage freeze, and to attract workers, many employers paid health benefits. Thus was forged the link between one's job and one's health insurance. Today, 58 percent of Americans get their health insurance from the workplace.[8] Often, the lack of health insurance is associated with short periods of unemployment—or with working part time, as part-time employees may not be eligible for employer insurance plans.

Although insurance is linked to employment, the majority of the nation's uninsured are full-time workers (and their families), most of whom work for companies with 100 or fewer employees and earn low wages. Small companies have to pay more for health insurance than larger companies do, mostly because health risks and marketing and administrative costs cannot be spread as broadly. Thus, many small companies find providing health insurance too costly. In addition, some companies have cut back on benefits to dependents of workers. As a result, even if parents have coverage through their employers, their children may be uninsured.

Millions of Americans have inadequate insurance and receive less and poorer quality health care than do those with more comprehensive insurance. These individuals, much like those without insurance, often postpone treatment until illnesses worsen and require more expensive emergency treatment. Insurance can also be inadequate because of the share of the cost that people have to pay themselves, costs that can leave policyholders with significant debt should a medical crisis occur. In part because of such problems, many workers who are offered health insurance by their employers or unions do not take it.

As the foregoing discussion suggests, access to health insurance in the United States is closely tied to income. Twenty-five percent of those with household incomes of less than $25,000 per year lack health insurance, despite the existence of government-subsidized programs such as Medicaid and Medicare. Among these low-income households are many single-mother households; the ininsured include, as mentioned above, approximately 7 million children, although the percentage of children who are uninsured varies considerably from state to state (see "My State: Children Without Health Insurance"). The higher a family's income, the more likely it is that its members are insured.[9] Access to health insurance is also tied to race and ethnicity. Thus, 31 percent of Hispanics and 19 percent of African Americans lack health insurance for the entire year, compared to 15 percent of non-Hispanic whites.

Children Without Health Insurance

Children without health insurance are more likely to go without medical treatment. Eleven million poor children are covered by a joint state–federal program called CHIP (Children's Health Insurance Program). Still, over 7 million children do not have health insurance. The percentage of children who are uninsured varies significantly from state to state.

QUESTIONS FOR DISCUSSION

- How does your state rank in terms of uninsured children?
- Why do you think some states have better insurance coverage of children than others?

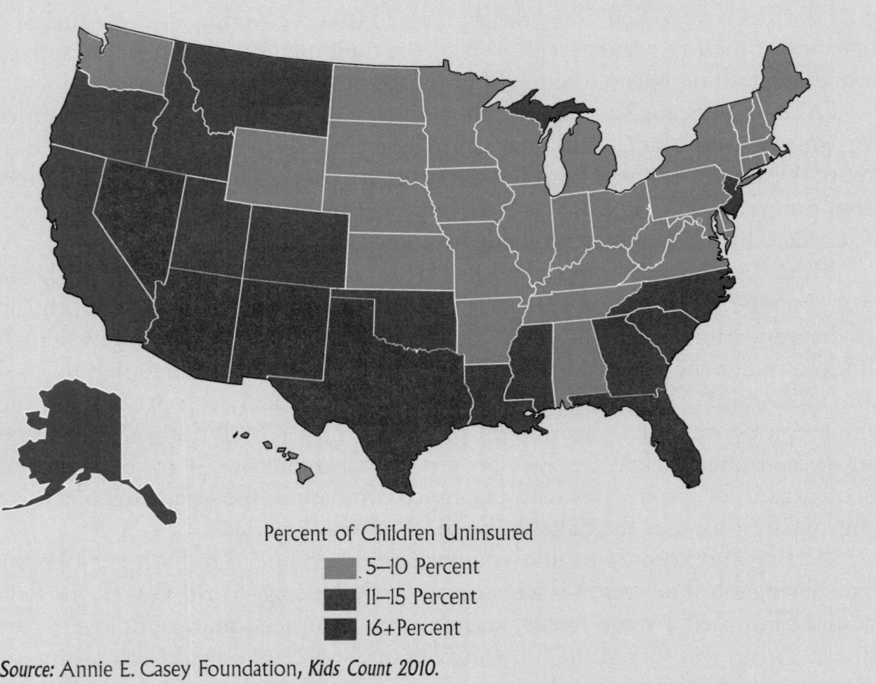

Source: Annie E. Casey Foundation, *Kids Count 2010.*

For Americans who lack health insurance, the problem is not lack of access to the most up-to-date research and equipment but, rather, the more fundamental problem of lack of access to a family doctor or someone to administer prenatal and neonatal care. Americans without insurance tend not to see health care professionals regularly and are less likely to receive preventive care; children have less access to well-child care, immunizations, basic dental services, and prescription medication.[10] Studies have found that many Americans do without health care, postpone it, or resort to emergency rooms for minor illnesses[11] (see "Young People and Politics: Health Insurance, Emergency Rooms, and Young Americans"). To an even greater extent than with the underinsured, when the uninsured receive care, the care is typically poorer quality, and medical problems can quickly lead to medical debt.[12] Some Americans who lack their insurance and are confronted with serious illness have resorted to "medical migration," outsourcing their medical care to cheaper foreign hospitals, for example, in India.[13]

The uninsured are more likely to be hospitalized for conditions that could have been prevented, and more likely to die in the hospital than those with insurance.[14] Lack of health insurance has been estimated to cause tens of thousands of preventable deaths each year.[15] Long-term studies show that people without health insurance face a 25 percent higher risk of dying than those with insurance.[16]

The racial and ethnic disparaties in access to health care are reflected in differences between groups in measures of health. Average life expectancy is five years longer for whites than for African Americans. In fact, average life expectancy for African-American males is lower than average life expectancy in many Eastern European and less developed countries. Not all of this difference can be explained by variances in lifestyles and nutrition. Similarly, African-American infant mortality is over twice as high as that for whites.[17] For both life expectancy and infant mortality, lack of insurance appears to play a significant role in explaining the differences.

Factors affecting health in early childhood and throughout life begin prenatally, but, as a result of lack of access to health care, many pregnant women, especially in the

Health Insurance, Emergency Rooms, and Young Americans

Health insurance usually costs considerable sums, and young people often lack discretionary income. For this reason, and because they are less likely to be in jobs with benefits than are older adults and less likely to worry about health issues, young Americans between 18 and 35 are disproportionately uninsured. Twenty-seven percent of those in this age group lack health insurance.

Although young people are less likely to become seriously ill than older adults (chances of getting heart disease or cancer increase with age), they are more likely to be injured, particularly in traffic accidents—and these often require expensive emergency care. Teens are also twice as likely as adults to be hurt on the job. Except for the very old (those over 75), young adults are the biggest users of emergency rooms.

In response to charges that emergency rooms were denying service to patients unable to pay, Congress in 1986 passed the Emergency Medical Treatment and Labor Act (EMTALA). EMTALA makes it illegal for emergency rooms to turn away people. The emergency room is therefore the only place in the American health care system that is required by law to treat you. Still, as a patient in the emergency room, one of the first questions you are likely to be asked is, "What insurance do you have?" Because young adults have a harder time answering that question than is any other age group, a trip to the emergency room can leave them with big medical debts at a time when they are trying to establish a good credit history.

Emergency rooms provide critical care, but they are the most expensive single component of the health care system. In addition, when people cannot pay their bills, often because they lack health insurance, the costs of providing emergency care are shifted to others using the hospital. In effect, many young adults shift the burden of paying for their health care to older adults.

QUESTIONS FOR DISCUSSION

- Should young Americans—or all Americans—be required to purchase health insurance, just as they are required to purchase collision insurance on their cars?
- Should emergency rooms be required by law to treat everyone who comes in?

Sources: U.S. Census Bureau, Current Population Survey, 2009, *Annual Social and Economic Supplement;* Centers for Disease Control and Prevention, *Emergency Department Visit Data*, 2010.

nation's inner cities, do not obtain the care needed to ensure that their babies will be born healthy. Lacking an obstetrician or family doctor (poor neighborhoods, urban and rural, have too few doctors), these women may not get prenatal care for most of their preganancy. This is yet another example of the point made above: Often, availability of family doctors and routine hospital services is more important in determining the quality of a nation's health care than is availability of high-tech medical equipment.

Disparities in access together with the great cost of many potentially lifesaving procedures of modern medicine raise important and complicated questions of public policy. Dollars spent on expensive procedures to save a few lives cannot be spent on other pressing health care needs. Thus, for example, when the government allows Medicare payments for certain procedures, less money may be available for rural hospitals or for health clinics in poor areas of the nation's cities.

Although many Americans vehemently oppose "rationing" of medical care, such rationing in effect goes on all the time in our system.[18] Much rationing is informal; physicians and families quietly agree not to provide further care to a loved one. Some of it is formal. Virtually every insurance plan sets limits to the services for which it will pay and for total payments. Medical boards have elaborate rules for allocating donated organs. Oregon has taken the lead on the issue of rationing health care, trying to set priorities for medical treatments under its Medicaid program. By not providing some costly treatments that might save or prolong people's lives, the Oregon program is able to use its resources to provide medical care for a larger pool of people. Evidence shows that Oregon's effort works well and that patient satisfaction is higher than before the plan was implemented.[19]

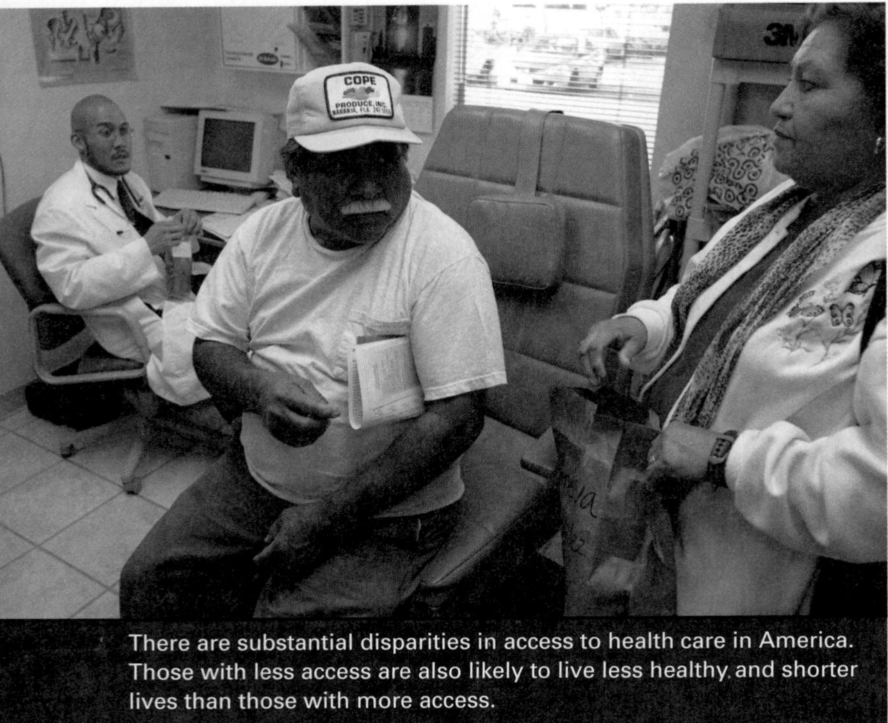
There are substantial disparities in access to health care in America. Those with less access are also likely to live less healthy and shorter lives than those with more access.

The Role of Government in Health Care

Americans often think insurance companies pay most health care costs, but in fact the government pays more of the costs than does the private insurance industry. As already mentioned, many Americans' access to health care is through Medicare and Medicaid. National, state, and local governments pay for 42 percent of the total cost of health services and supplies. Moreover, as discussed in Chapter 14, the government subsidizes employer-provided health insurance with tax breaks worth about $171 billion per year. Many hospitals are connected to public universities, and much medical research is financed through the National Institutes of Health and other federal agencies. More than 20,000 physicians work for the federal government, most providing health care for the armed forces and veterans, and nearly all the rest receive payments from it. The government thus plays an important health care role in America, although less so than in other countries.

Medicare
A program added to the Social Security system in 1965 that provides hospitalization insurance for the elderly and permits older Americans to purchase inexpensive coverage for doctor fees and other medical expenses.

Passed by Congress in 1965, **Medicare**, health care insurance for the elderly, is part of the Social Security system and covers 43 million people, or about 14 percent of the population. As with Social Security, paycheck deductions include payments into Medicare and, when a person becomes eligible, he or she receives the benefits. Part A of Medicare provides hospitalization insurance and short-term nursing care; Part B, which is voluntary, permits older Americans to purchase inexpensive coverage for doctor fees and other nonhospital medical expenses. Part D, which went into effect in 2006, covers much of the cost of prescription drugs.

In another parallel with Social Security, Medicare costs are outrunning tax contributions to the Medicare Trust Fund. Medicare is the most rapidly increasing component of the federal budget. It currently costs about $500 billion, accounting for about 13 percent of the budget,[20] and without reform, this percentage will soar. To save money, Medicare has frequently cut back on the fees it pays doctors and hospitals. As a result, some doctors and hospitals do not accept Medicare patients, because Medicare payments for services do not cover their costs.

Despite such cuts, Medicare expenditures keep growing, in part because of Medicare's vocal constituency. The elderly are one of the most powerful voting and lobbying forces in American politics. AARP, formerly known as the American Association of Retired Persons, has grown from about 150,000 members in 1959 to nearly 40 million today, making it the largest voluntary association in the world. This single group now can claim to represent one American in eight, and its numbers may swell as the baby-boom generation reaches retirement. Not only does AARP relentlessly advocate increasing Medicare benefits but elderly Americans dependent on Social Security and Medicare actively participate in American elections.[21] In addition, powerful organizations representing hospitals and doctors lobby for Medicare to pay for the latest techniques and procedures. Health care policy that favors the elderly is one of the results of this interest group activity. When Congress, in 1989, passed a Social Security surtax designed to pay for new catastrophic illness coverage, the elderly objected, and the next year Congress repealed the tax.

For workers in low-paying service jobs that do not include health insurance, and for those who are unemployed and cannot afford private health insurance, there is no organization capable of exerting such influence in government. Because many of these people do not vote, the bias in representation is even greater. Nevertheless, the nation has spent substantial sums to provide health care for the poor.

Medicaid, the program designed to provide health care for the poor, also passed in 1965 and, like Medicare, serves about 43 million people, or about 14 percent of the public. Its current cost to the federal government is about $300 billion (like other public assistance programs, Medicaid is funded by both the states and the national government).[22] Unlike Medicare, which goes to elderly Americans regardless of their income, Medicaid is a means-tested program. In fact, Medicaid is for the poorest of the poor (only about half of the people below the poverty line qualify for Medicaid). As with Medicare, rising medical costs have led both to soaring expenditures and to cuts in fees that mean fewer providers will accept patients.

Medicaid
A public assistance program designed to provide health care for poor Americans and funded by both the states and the national government.

Originally created in 1997, the *Children's Health Insurance Program* (CHIP) is a state and federal partnership that targets uninsured children and pregnant women in families with incomes too high to qualify for most state Medicaid programs but, often, too low to afford private coverage. It serves about 11 million children. Within federal guidelines, each state determines the design of its CHIP program, including eligibility parameters, benefit packages, payment levels for coverage, and administrative procedures.

Reform Efforts

More than 60 years ago, Harry S. Truman called for **national health insurance**, a compulsory insurance program to finance all Americans' medical care. The idea was strongly opposed by the American Medical Association, the largest physicians' interest group, which disparaged it as "socialized medicine" because the program would be government run. Truman's proposal went nowhere. While every other industrial nation in the world adopted some form of national health insurance, the United States remained the exception.

national health insurance
A compulsory insurance program for all Americans that would have the government finance citizens' medical care. First proposed by President Harry S. Truman.

Bill Clinton Nearly a half-century later, President Clinton made health care reform the centerpiece of his first administration. His five-pound, 1,342-page Health Security Act proposal in 1993 was an effort to deal with the two great problems of health care policy: costs and access. The difficulties the president faced with this proposal reveal much about the challenge of reforming health care in America.[23]

Clinton's main concern was guaranteeing health care coverage for all Americans. His plan would particularly have benefited people without any health insurance, but it would also have extended coverage for millions of others with inadequate health insurance.

Paying for the plan would have necessitated either broad-based taxes, which were politically unpalatable, or a requirement that employers provide health insurance for their employees or pay a premium into a public fund (which would also cover Medicaid and Medicare recipients). The president chose the employer insurance option, but the small business community was adamantly opposed to bearing the cost of providing health insurance. The president also proposed raising taxes on cigarettes, which angered the tobacco industry, and imposing a small tax on other large companies.

Because the White House reform plan for health care was bureaucratic and complicated, it was easy for opponents to label it a government takeover of the health care system. An aggressive advertising campaign mounted by the health insurance industry characterized the president's plan as being expensive and experimental, as providing lower-quality and rationed care, and as killing jobs. The health insurance industry's famous "Harry and Louise" ads—in which Harry and Louise, sitting at their kitchen table, mull over the Clinton plan and conclude, "There's got to be a better way"—were one of the most effective policy-oriented campaigns in history.

In addition, the middle class felt its health care threatened. Gallup polls found that the public saw Clinton's health care reform proposal as a Democratic social welfare program that would help the poor, hurt the middle class, and create bigger government. In the end, there was more concern about too much government with the plan than there was about too little health insurance without it.[24] After a long and tortuous battle, the plan died in Congress.

National Health Insurance

The United States, unlike all other developed nations, does not have national health insurance. Would Americans have more access to health care if we adopted such a system? Would they receive better or worse quality of care under a policy of national health insurance?

Barack Obama Early in his administration, Barack Obama made comprehensive health care reform a top priority in domestic policy. Like Clinton, he focused on both increasing access to health care and containing its costs. For those who already had health insurance, the president proposed to end discrimination by health insurance companies against people with preexisting conditions and to prevent insurance companies from dropping coverage when people became sick and needed it most. He also wanted to cap out-of-pocket expenses for the insured and eliminate extra charges for preventive care like mammograms, flu shots, and diabetes tests. And he sought to close a gap in Medicare's coverage for prescription drugs. Most Americans supported such measures.

The most resistance came when the president proposed to substantially increase the number of people with health insurance. First, he wanted to create a new insurance marketplace—the Exchange—that would allow people without insurance, as well as small businesses, to compare plans and buy insurance at competitive prices. Next, he proposed providing new tax credits to help people buy insurance and to help small businesses cover their employees. Offering a public health insurance option to provide the uninsured who could not find affordable coverage with a real choice and to provide price competition with private health insurance plans proved to be highly controversial. So did the requirements that large employers cover their employees and for individuals who could afford it to buy insurance so that everyone would contribute to the pool of resources for health care.

Opponents charged that a public option for health insurance would constitute a government takeover of health care, pushing out private health insurance companies. In addition, critics claimed, a public option would be very costly. Businesses complained about the costs of covering employees in the midst of a recession and in the face of international competition. Others criticized the requirement that everyone have health insurance as limiting individuals' freedom of choice. Although Obama claimed that his reform proposal would not add to the budget deficit and that it was possible to cut costs by identifying and removing waste, fraud, and abuse in the health care system and reforming medical malpractice law, not everyone agreed.

Despite voting for a presidential candidate espousing change, the public had not changed its basic skepticism of government or its resistance to paying for it. Obama faced a strategic problem in attempting to reform the health care system without igniting fears that people could lose what they like about their own health care. Although there was widespread agreement that substantial change in the health care system was necessary, most people were reasonably satisfied with the quality of their own medical care and were anxious about government involvement. Most people were worried that if the government guaranteed health coverage, they would see declines in the quality of their own care, limits on their ability to choose doctors and get needed treatment, and increases in their out-of-pocket health costs and tax bills.[25]

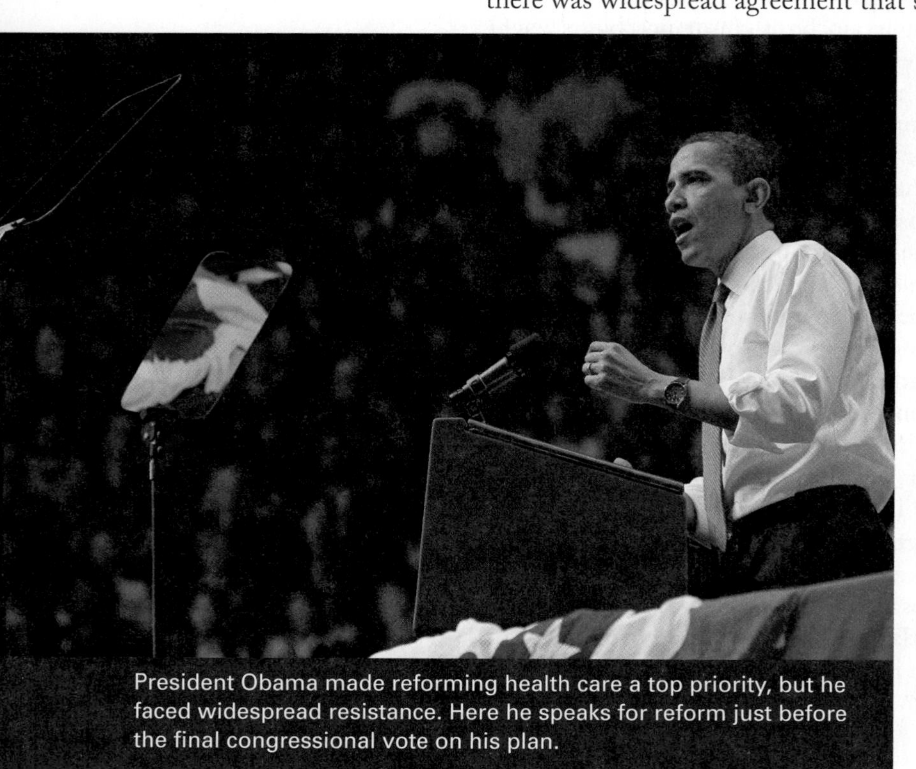
President Obama made reforming health care a top priority, but he faced widespread resistance. Here he speaks for reform just before the final congressional vote on his plan.

Perhaps equally important as an obstacle to reforming health care in 2009–2010 was the general political climate. We have seen in Chapter 14 on the budget that the president had to propose enormous expenditures to combat the economic crisis he inherited, running up record deficits in the process. These policies made the country risk averse. Moreover, comprehensive reform of such a large sector of the economy is inherently complex policy, making it difficult to explain and easy for opponents to caricature.

Despite all his and his administration's efforts, the president never obtained majority—or even plurality—support among the public for health care reform. Nevertheless, the White

House and the Democratic majorities in Congress pushed through an historic comprehensive health care reform bill (without the public option) in 2010.

Environmental Policy

19.2 Analyze the conflicts between economic growth and environmental protection, and identify the major national environmental protection policies.

The natural environment might seem to be above politics. After all, public opinion analyst Louis Harris reported that "the American people's desire to battle pollution is one of the most overwhelming and clearest we have ever recorded in our 25 years of surveying public opinion."[26] Concern for the environment is further reflected in the rapid growth of environmental groups.

As in other areas, however, there is significant politically charged debate over the environment. Attempts to control air quality or limit water pollution often encounter political opposition because of their impact on business, economic growth, and jobs; hence, policymaking choices are involved. And although Americans may be generally in favor of "doing something" about the environment, specific proposals, for example, to limit suburban growth, encourage carpooling, increase taxes on gasoline, or limit access to national parks, have met with strong resistance.

Economic Growth and the Environment

Nobody is against cleaning up and preserving the environment. Political questions arise because environmental concerns often conflict with equally legitimate concerns about economic growth and jobs. Pollution is generated in the course of making cars, producing electricity, and providing food and the consumer products that Americans take for granted. On federally owned land, including national parks and forests, there has long been a policy of multiple use whereby mining, lumbering, and grazing leases are awarded to private companies or ranchers at very low cost. Often the industries supported by these arrangements are important sources of jobs in otherewise depressed areas, and they may also help lessen the country's dependence on foreign sources of oil and minerals. For most of American history, pollution was seen simply as an inevitable byproduct of economic growth.

Although the conservation movement began in the nineteenth century, it was in the 1960s and 1970s that environmental interest groups exploded in both size and number. Today, for example, the National Wildlife Federation has nearly 4.5 million members; Greenpeace USA, the World Wildlife Fund, and the Conservation Foundation have more than a million members each; and the Sierra Club, the Clean Water Action Project, the Nature Conservancy, and the National Audubon Society have more than a half-million members each. And there are numerous other environmental groups, ranging from the Wilderness Society to the Center for Health, Environment & Justice.

As old groups evolved into active political organizations and as new groups formed and grew, the environment became a more important policymaking concern. If at first many politicians viewed these new lobbyists with skepticism, over time the environmental movement became more influential. Now politicians of both parties seek the support of environmental groups when they run for office. Issues once considered only from the standpoint of jobs and economic growth are now also considered from an environmental standpoint.

The fact that environmental considerations now come into play is apparent, for example, in debates about local and state economic development. As you saw in Chapter 3, in the federal system, states compete for economic advantage. States and cities push to attract large investments, such as automobile plants, as new business can be a boon to their economies. Business elites can argue that stringent pollution-control laws will prevent new businesses from coming and drive businesses away by driving up their costs. But states with lax pollution enforcement may find their citizens unhappy and residents of other states, including those who might relocate with new businesses, reluctant to move there. Moreover, costs to a state of enforcing pollution legislation may be offset by savings

Coastal states often desire the jobs provided by offshore drilling. Yet they may also find their coast lines covered with oily sludge, and their tourism and fishing industries adversely affected.

in health care costs achieved by reducing health risks to residents. Thus, state competition does not always work against pollution standards. In fact, sometimes states compete with each other to enforce tighter pollution and land use controls. Many states today—including California, which has the most stringent antipollution laws in the country—are betting that legislation designed to achieve environmental goals will not have a negative economic impact on the state.

Conflicts between economic growth and environmental goals are apparent in Alaska and the Northwest, with political battles pitting lumbering interests against national and local environmental groups. Lumbering provides jobs, but it decimates old-growth trees in Alaska's Tongass National Forest and on public lands in Oregon and Washington. Environmentalists complain that some of the few remaining large tracts of virgin forest are being felled by logging companies operating under generous lease agreements with the U.S. government. Similarly, oil exploration on public lands and off shore in coastal waters brings the goals of environmental protection and economic growth into conflict. The spill of the *Exxon Valdez* off the coast of Alaska in 1989 demonstrated the environmental risks of oil exploration. Yet Alaskans are keen on the jobs oil fields provide and the revenues from oil that keeps their taxes low.

The very success of the environmental movement in passing laws designed to protect public health and to preserve or restore the environment has spawned a backlash. Opponents of strict environmental protection laws demand evidence that policies are accomplishing their goals. Arguing that the effects of environmental regulations on employment, economic growth, and international competitiveness must be part of the policymaking equation, they insist that Congress and the bureaucracy subject regulations to cost–benefit analysis to determine that they do not cost more than the benefits they create. Others, especially ranchers, miners, farmers, and the timber industry, demand inexpensive access to public land and the right to use their own property as they wish or else be compensated by government for being prohibited from doing so.

In arguing for a more cautious approach to environmental protection, opponents also point to mistakes that have been made. For example, in the early 1980s, government scientists argued that exposure to asbestos could cause thousands of cancer deaths. Because asbestos was used as insulation in schools and public buildings, parents and others reacted with alarm. In 1985, Congress approved a sweeping law that led cities and states to spend between $15 billion and $20 billion to remove asbestos from public buildings. But in 1990, Environmental Protection Agency officials admitted that ripping out the asbestos had been an expensive mistake; the removal often sent tiny asbestos fibers into the air. Now the agency's advice is that, unless asbestos is damaged or crumbling, it be left untouched.

Environmental Protection Agency
The largest federal independent regulatory agency, created in 1970 to administer much of U.S. environmental protection policy.

National Environmental Policy Act
Passed in 1969, the centerpiece of federal environmental policy, which requires agencies to file **environmental impact statements.**

environmental impact statement
A detailing of a proposed policy's environmental effects, which agencies are required to file with the EPA every time they propose to undertake a policy that might be disruptive to the environment.

Environmental Policies in America

Until the early 1960s, what environmental policies existed focused largely on conservation and the national parks. It was President Richard Nixon who pressed for most of the nation's first environmental legislation. Created in 1970, the **Environmental Protection Agency** (EPA) is now the nation's largest federal regulatory agency. The EPA has a wide-ranging mission; it is charged with administering policies dealing with land use, air and water quality, and wilderness and wildlife preservation.

Environmental Impacts The centerpiece of federal environmental policy is the **National Environmental Policy Act** (NEPA), passed in 1969.[27] This law requires government agencies to file an **environmental impact statement** (EIS) with the EPA every time they propose to undertake a policy that is potentially disruptive to the natural environment. The EIS details possible environmental effects of the proposed policy. Big dams and small post offices, major port construction and minor road widening—proposals for all these projects must include an EIS.

Strictly speaking, an environmental impact statement is merely a procedural requirement. In practice, the filing of impact statements alerts environmentalists to proposed projects. Environmentalists can then take agencies to court for violating the act's procedural requirements if the agencies file incomplete or inaccurate impact statements. Because environmental impacts are usually so complicated and difficult to predict, it is relatively easy to argue that the statements are either incomplete or inaccurate in some way. Agencies have often abandoned proposed projects to avoid prolonged court battles with environmental groups.

The law does not give the environmental groups the right to stop any environmentally unsound activities, but it does give them the opportunity to delay construction so much that agencies simply give up. Chances are that many of the biggest public works projects of the past century—including the Hoover Dam, Kennedy Airport, Cape Canaveral's space facility, and most Tennessee Valley Authority projects—would not have survived the environmental scrutiny to which they would have been subject had they been undertaken after the NEPA was enacted. In any case, the NEPA has been an effective tool in preventing environmental despoliation.

Clean Air Another landmark piece of legislation affecting the environment is the **Clean Air Act of 1970**, which charges the EPA with protecting and improving the quality of the nation's air, to minimize people's exposure to airborne contaminants. Among its provisions is that the Department of Transportation (DOT) undertake to reduce automobile emissions. For years after the act's passage, fierce battles raged between the automakers and the DOT about how stringent the requirements had to be. Automakers claimed it was impossible to meet DOT standards; the DOT claimed that automakers were dragging their feet in the hope that Congress would delay or weaken the requirements. Although Congress did weaken the requirements, the smaller size of American cars, the use of unleaded gasoline, and the lower gas consumption of new cars are all due in large part to DOT regulations.

Clean Air Act of 1970
The law aimed at combating air pollution, by charging the EPA with protecting and improving the quality of the nation's air.

Water Pollution Control Act of 1972
A law intended to clean up the nation's rivers and lakes, by enabling regulation of point sources of pollution.

Over time, Congress has reauthorized the Clean Air Act and significantly increased the controls on cars, oil refineries, chemical plants, and coal-fired utility plants. In particular, the reauthorization in 1990 was the strongest step forward in the fight to clean the air since the bill's original passage. As a result of federal policies, air pollution from toxic organic compounds and sulfur dioxide has decreased substantially since 1970.

Clean Water Congress acted to control pollution of the nation's lakes and rivers with the **Water Pollution Control Act of 1972**. This law was enacted in reaction to the tremendous pollution of Northeastern rivers and the Great Lakes. Since its passage, water quality has improved dramatically. In 1972, only one-third of U.S. lakes and rivers were safe for fishing and drinking. Today, the fraction has doubled to two-thirds. And with less polluted waters, the number of waterfowl has increased substantially.

Nevertheless, federal laws regulate only "point sources"—places where pollutants can be dumped in the water, such as a paper mill along a river. What is hard to regulate is the most important cause of water pollution, "runoff" from streets, roads, fertilized lawns, and service stations.

Polluted air harms not only the humans that breathe it but also trees, such as those pictured here that were damaged by acid rain. Nevertheless, some people fear lost jobs if refineries, coal-burning power plants, and other sources of air pollution have to clean the air they discharge.

Wilderness Preservation One component of the environment that has received special attention is wilderness—those areas that are largely untouched by human activities. Wilderness preservation is important to biodiversity and for recreational purposes and symbolic reasons as well. The founding of the National Park System in 1916 put the United States in the forefront of wilderness preservation. Among the most consistently successful environmental campaigns have been those aimed at preserving wild lands,[28] and there are now 378 national parks and 155 national forests. Still, only about 4 percent of the land in the United States is designated as wilderness, and half of that is in Alaska. The strains of overuse may make it necessary to restrict the public's access to national parks so they may be preserved for future generations. And wilderness areas come under increasing pressure from those, such as logging and mining interests, who stress the economic benefits lost by keeping them intact.

Endangered Species Act of 1973
A law requiring the federal government to protect all species listed as endangered.

Endangered Species Preserving wilderness areas indirectly helps protect wildlife. National policy protects wildlife in other, more direct ways as well. The **Endangered Species Act of 1973**, for example, created an endangered species protection program in the U.S. Fish and Wildlife Service. More important, the law required the government to actively protect each of the hundreds of species listed as endangered, regardless of the economic consequences for the areas that were the habitats of the species. During the Reagan administration, the act was amended to allow exceptions in cases of overriding national or regional interest. A cabinet-level committee, quickly labeled "The God Squad," was established to decide such cases. As EPA chief William Reilly explained, "The God Squad is a group of people, of which I am a minor divinity, which has the power to blow away a species."[29]

Because endangered species are increasingly threatened by expanding human populations and growing demands for development, implementation of the act has often been controversial. Bringing back the wolves in Yellowstone has a certain appeal to many Americans but not to neighboring ranchers. As of 2009, the endangered species list included 1,215 animal and 752 plant species.[30] (For a look at policy issues related to saving a particular species, see "You Are the Policymaker: How Much Should We Do to Save a Species? The Florida Manatee.")

Toxic Wastes Long before the environmental movement began, polluters created problems that are still unresolved. For example, during the 1940s and 1950s, Hooker Chemical Company dumped toxic wastes near the shores of the Love Canal in New York. In 1953, the company generously donated a 16-acre plot next to the canal to build a school. Thereafter, tons of chemicals, some in rotting barrels, were discovered, and children and adults were later found to have developed liver, kidney, and other health problems. The level of contamination was high, and Hooker Chemical Company had gone out of business. With Love Canal, and the identification of a huge number of other toxic waste dumps, popular outcry led to action from Washington.[31]

Superfund
A fund created by Congress in 1980 to clean up hazardous waste sites. Money for the fund comes from taxing chemical products.

In 1980, Congress established a **Superfund**, a fund to clean up toxic waste sites, created by taxing chemical products. The law that established the fund specified that polluters were responsible for paying for cleanups; the fund was to be used when polluters could not be identified. A controversial retroactive liability provision held companies liable even for legal dumping prior to 1980. The law also contained strict provisions for liability, under which the government could hold a single party liable for cleaning up an entire site that had received waste from many sources.

The Comprehensive Environmental Response, Compensation, and Liability Act (the formal name of the Superfund law) has virtually eliminated haphazard dumping of toxic wastes, including through prohibitions and requirements it established, but it has been less successful in cleaning up existing waste. In endless rounds of litigation that ensued, companies facing multimillion-dollar cleanup bills tried to recover some of their costs by suing smaller companies that had contributed to the hazardous waste, and companies fought with their insurers over whether policies written in the early 1980s covered Superfund-related costs.[32]

YOU ARE THE POLICYMAKER

How Much Should We Do to Save a Species? The Florida Manatee

The manatee is a plump, squinty-eyed, walrus-like freshwater mammal, 9 to 10 feet in length and weighing in at about 1,000 pounds. Manatees are friendly and intelligent animals that spend most of the day sleeping in the water, surfacing for air regularly at intervals no greater than 20 minutes and grazing in shallow waters at depths of 3 to 7 feet. They may live up to 60 years. Because manatees cannot survive very long in water below 68 degrees Fahrenheit, Florida is the manatee's natural winter range. They congregate around warm water springs and man-made sources of warm water such as power plant discharges.

One of the major killers of manatees is the propellers on the thousands of boats in Florida's lakes and rivers. Biologists even use scar patterns from the propellers to identify individual manatees. Another significant threat is loss of reliable warm water habitats that allow manatees to survive the cold in winter. Natural springs are threatened by increased demands for water supply, and aging power plants may need to be replaced. Sea grass and other aquatic foods that manatees depend on are affected by water pollution.

The manatee is one of the charter members of the endangered species list. They are also protected under the Federal Marine Mammal Protection Act. Thus, two federal laws make it illegal to harm, harass, injure, or kill manatees. In addition, Florida passed laws, including the Florida Manatee Sanctuary Act, to protect its unique marine mammal.

If a species is on the endangered species list, both the federal and state governments must enact policies to protect its habitat. Nearly one-quarter of Florida's canals, rivers, and lakes were designated as manatee protection areas. Any construction project had to come to a halt if a manatee appeared within 100 feet and could resume only if the animal left—as the regulation put it—"of its own volition." Boating was curtailed. Fishing was limited. Canal locks were refitted at a substantial cost.

In this case, then, as often occurs, the Endangered Species Act collided with other interests—economic growth, property rights, and recreational activities. The Coastal Conservation Association of Florida, a pro-fishing group, produced data to show that the manatee population was increasing, and that regulations should be reduced and the habitat restrictions eased. (Environmentalists challenged the data.) Developers wanted more flexibility to develop property. One state legislator compared environmentalists to watermelons ("green on the outside and red on the inside"). The direct costs of protecting the manatee so far have been about a half-billion dollars. Some people think the money could be better spent.

What do you think? Do we want to save every species? (There may be 100 million of them.) When have we done enough to save a species? How much should we sacrifice to save a species?

Sources: U.S. Fish and Wildlife Service, *Federal and State Endangered and Threatened Species Expenditures, Fiscal Year 2007;* Craig Pittman, "Fury over a Gentle Giant," *Smithsonian Magazine*, February 2004, 55–59.

The EPA, which administers the Superfund law, has located and analyzed tens of thousands of hazardous waste sites. Cleaning up sites can take many years and cost millions of dollars each. About 1,100 sites have been cleaned, and work is going on at more than 400 additional sites. Nevertheless, there are additional sites requiring cleaning in 49 states and the District of Columbia. Originally, a tax on oil and chemical companies funded the Superfund, but these taxes expired in 1995. The fund now depends on general revenues, which have been in short supply, slowing the rate of cleanup.

Policies in addition to the Superfund law also require monitoring and regulation of the use and disposal of hazardous wastes. Regulations mandated by the Resource Conservation and Recovery Act of 1977, for example, require "cradle-to-grave" tracking of many toxic chemicals, specify how these chemicals are to be handled while in use or in transit, and prescribe certain disposal techniques.

Nuclear Waste Another serious environmental challenge is the disposal of nuclear waste, such as that from nuclear reactors and the production of nuclear weapons. Nuclear waste must be isolated to protect not only us but also people in the distant future, as these

WHY IT MATTERS

"Nimby"

Most Americans say "NIMBY"—not in my backyard—when government proposes locating unwanted waste dumps, toxic disposal sites, and other unhealthy land uses near their homes. Should government give every neighborhood a veto over having to house wastes? If every community, even sparsely populated areas, had a veto, where would society dispose of its hazardous materials?

materials can take millennia to decay to the point where they are safe. Tens of thousands of tons of highly radioactive nuclear waste are sitting in temporary sites around the country, most of them near nuclear power plants. Congress has studied, debated, and fretted for years over where to store the nation's nuclear waste. In the 1980s, Congress envisioned that spent nuclear fuel would be consolidated and permanently buried. It designated Yucca Mountain in Nevada as the provisional site in 1987. Questions about the safety and cost of the site and the vehement opposition from Nevada's congressional delegation have delayed the implementation of the plan. Although President Bush signed off on the plan in 2002, President Obama reversed the decision in 2009.

Although it is not surprising that no state is eager to have a storage area for nuclear wastes within its boundaries, the problem is that nuclear waste keeps accumulating. Widening opposition to potentially hazardous industrial facilities, such as toxic or nuclear waste dumps, has further complicated environmental policymaking in recent years. Local groups have often successfully organized resistance to planned development, rallying behind the cry, "Not In My Back Yard!"[33] The so-called NIMBY phenomenon highlights another difficult dilemma in environmental policy: How can government equitably distribute the costs associated with society's seemingly endless demand for new technologies, some of which turn out to be environmentally threatening? If, for example, we are to use nuclear power to keep our lights on, the waste it produces must go in someone's backyard. But whose?

Global Warming

global warming
The increase in the earth's temperatures that, according to most scientists, is occurring as a result of the carbon dioxide that is produced when fossil fuels are burned collecting in the atmosphere and trapping energy from the sun.

One of the most intractable and potentially most serious environmental issues is **global warming**. When fossil fuels (coal, oil, and natural gas—the remnants of ancient plants and animals) are burned, they produce carbon dioxide. It, along with smaller quantities of methane and other gases, collects in the atmosphere, wrapping the earth in an added layer of insulation and heating the climate. The "greenhouse effect" occurs when energy from the sun is trapped under the atmosphere and warms the earth as a result, much as in a greenhouse. The deforestation of trees capable of absorbing pollutants, mainly carbon dioxide, reinforces this effect.[34]

Most scientists agree that the earth is warming at a rapid rate and will be between 2 and 6 degrees warmer by the year 2100. This may not seem like a major change, but the world is now only 5 to 9 degrees warmer than during the depths of the last ice age, 20,000 years ago. Scientists predict that if the warming trend is not reversed, seas will rise (gobbling up shorelines and displacing millions of people), severe droughts, rainstorms, heat waves, and floods will become more common, and broad shifts in climatic and agricultural zones will occur, bringing famine, disease, and pestilence to some areas.

There is no technology to control carbon emissions, so the principal way to reduce greenhouse gases is to burn less fuel or find alternative sources of energy. In 1992, industrialized countries met in Rio de Janeiro and voluntarily agreed to cut greenhouse gas emissions to 1990 levels by the year 2000. None of the countries came close to meeting these goals. In 1997, 150 nations met in Kyoto, Japan, and agreed in principle to require 38 industrial nations to reduce their emissions of greenhouse gases below 1990 levels by about 2010. Few came close to meeting their goal. President Clinton never submitted the treaty to the Senate, and President George W. Bush renounced it. Meetings in Bali in 2007 and Copenhagen, Denmark, in 2009, could not produce a binding treaty.

Opponents of cutting greenhouse gases fear it will cost a staggering sum. Industries that have to adjust their emissions may become less competitive and jobs may be lost as a result. Moreover, the costs of taking action are immediate, but carbon dioxide lingers in the atmosphere for over 100 years, so the benefits of reductions would not be felt for decades.

Disputes have arisen between industrialized and developing nations over distributing the burden of cutting greenhouse gas emissions. The former group argue that developing nations produce more emissions per dollar of gross domestic product than do developed countries. The latter counter that the rich countries got rich by burning coal and oil and still produce most of the emissions today. (The United States alone, with only 4 percent of the world's population, produces more than 20 percent of the gases that cause global warming.) Thus, the developing nations argue, developed nations should bear most of the burden of reducing global warming. The developing nations also point out that in many cases they are the ones who would be hurt worst by climate changes and that they are hard-pressed enough as it is.

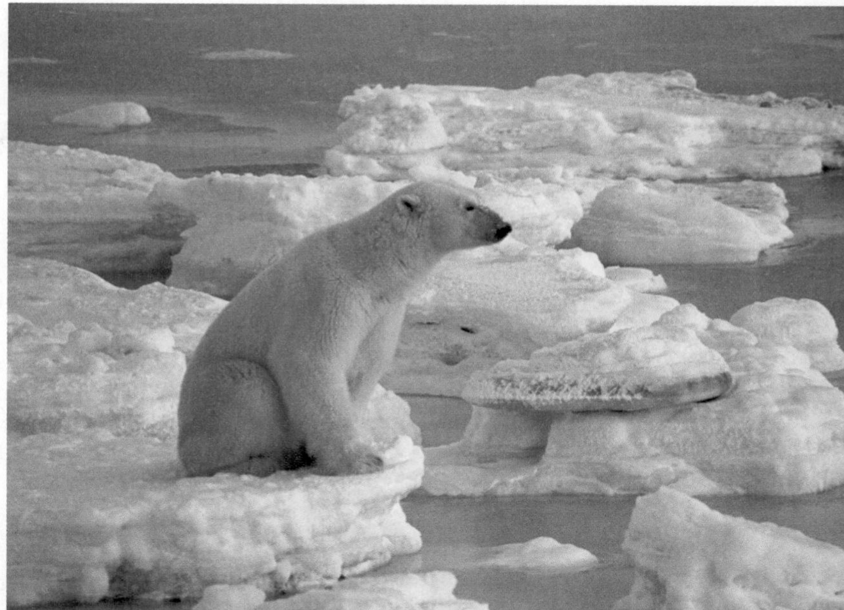

Global warming has many consequences, including the melting of polar ice. As a result, polar bears lose their access to seals, a primary source of food.

In addition, not everyone is convinced that the earth's warming is the result of greenhouse gases. Some politicians in the United States believe that scientific support for the global warming hypothesis is weak. Senator James Inhofe of Oklahoma has called global warming "the greatest hoax ever perpetrated on the American people." Scientific uncertainty in a technological age undermines efforts to deal with problems caused by technology.

President Obama has proposed to stem carbon dioxide emissions through a market-based cap-and-trade system in which the government sets a mandatory cap on emissions and then issues companies or other groups credits for a certain amount of emissions. Companies that need to increase their emission allowance must buy credits from those who pollute less. In effect, the buyer is paying a charge for polluting, while the seller is being rewarded for having reduced emissions by more than was needed. Thus, in theory, those who can reduce emissions most cheaply will do so, achieving the pollution reduction at the lowest cost to society. The goal is to encourage the development of the most innovative and efficient means of limiting emissions without inhibiting economic growth. An early example of an emission trading system was the sulphur dioxide trading system under the framework of the Acid Rain Program of the 1990 Clean Air Act, which has reduced these emissions by 50 percent since 1980. Several states, led by California, have set up emissions trading systems.

Some critics of cap and trade worry that it leaves too much to chance and that it is too difficult to hold polluters accountable. Others argue that the costs of emissions controls will be passed on to consumers in the form of higher energy costs, amounting to a tax on all energy use. Such a tax increase, they claim, could lead to either a loss of jobs and an erosion of the American family's budget.

As a result of the conflicting views regarding global warming and the burden of reducing it, little progress has been made in the United States. The issues and problems become further apparent when we look at energy policy.

WHY IT MATTERS

Global Warming

Many scientists believe that global warming will have dire consequences for the entire world. Because of its advanced economic system, the United States produces a larger quantity of greenhouse gases per person than does any other nation. At the same time, no one can force the United States to reduce its emissions. What are our responsibilities to other peoples? How much cost, if any, should the American people bear to benefit the rest of the world, as well as the United States?

Energy Policy

19.3 Evaluate the advantages and disadvantages of each of the principal sources of energy in the United States.

Modern American society depends on the availability of abundant energy. Yet energy use is tied to emission of pollutants and greenhouse gases, and America's energy resources are limited. The challenge of sustaining Americans' standard of living and accustomed patterns of life in the face of both these sets of issues presents policymakers with thorny problems to resolve.

Once Americans used wood, animals, water, and people power for energy. Today 83 percent of the nation's energy comes from coal, oil, and natural gas (see Figure 19.2). Americans search continually for new and more efficient sources of energy, both to increase supplies and to reduce pollution. Much of this research on new energy sources and efficiencies comes from the federal government.

Coal

Coal is America's most abundant fuel. An estimated 90 percent of the country's energy resources are in coal deposits—enough to last hundreds of years. Coal accounts for 22 percent of the energy Americans use, and it produces 48 percent of its electricity. Although coal may be the nation's most plentiful fuel, unfortunately it is also the dirtiest. It contributes to global warming and smog, and it is responsible for the "black lung" health hazard to coal miners and for the soot-blackened cities of the Northeast. In addition, the burning of coal to produce electricity is largely responsible for acid rain.

Petroleum and Natural Gas

In many ways the lifeblood of America's economy, petroleum, or oil, currently supplies 37 percent of our total energy needs and almost all the fuel we use in our cars and trucks.[35] Natural gas produces 21 percent of our electricity. Natural gas and petroleum are somewhat cleaner than coal, but they both contribute to global warming. In addition, transporting oil can result in spills that cause serious environmental damage, and refining oil pollutes the air. Moreover, although the United States once produced most of its own oil, today 57 percent of the oil we use is imported,[36] and our dependence on other nations for oil is increasing (see "A Generation of Change: Importing Petroleum"). In payment for imported oil, the United States sends enormous amounts of cash to other nations, increasing its balance of trade deficit, and, as some of these nations are not too friendly to the United States, helping to fund potential adversaries. Finally, in today's world many countries compete for oil, and, in particular, surging economic growth in China and India is increasing demand and hence prices.

Dependence on foreign oil and natural gas also places the United States at the mercy of actions of other nations. Much of the world's natural gas and oil reserves are in Russia and in Middle Eastern countries—countries on which the United States cannot necessarily rely for dependable supplies of fuel. When the United States supported Israel in the Yom Kippur War in 1973, Arab nations proclaimed an embargo on oil shipments to the United States. High prices, which hurt the economy, and long lines at the gas pump resulted. When Iraq invaded oil-rich Kuwait in 1990, the United States went to war to drive the Iraqis out and deny them the possibility of controlling another 10 percent of the world's oil supply.

FIGURE 19.2 Sources of America's Energy

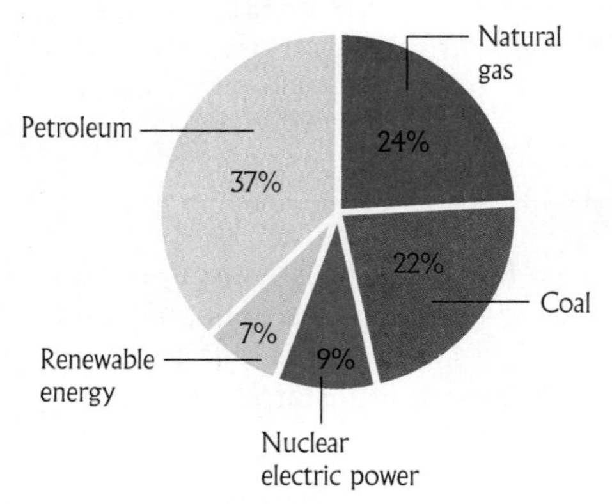

Despite the technological advances of society, America still relies on traditional sources for its energy: coal, oil, and natural gas. Coal generates nearly half of our electricity; oil fuels our cars, trucks, and planes. Only 7 percent of our energy comes from renewable sources, mainly hydroelectric and geothermal power.

Source: Energy Information Administration, 2010.

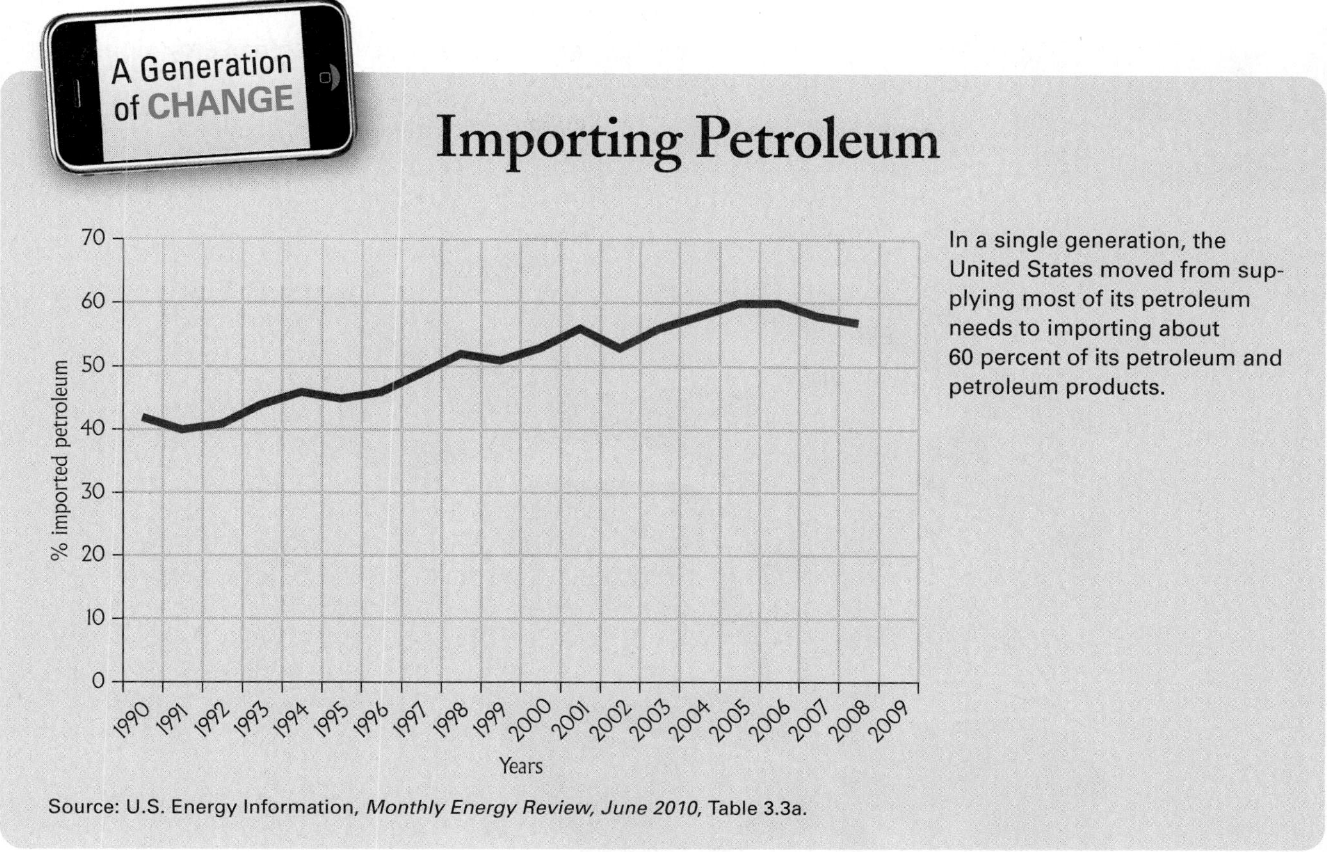

Source: U.S. Energy Information, *Monthly Energy Review, June 2010*, Table 3.3a.

In the event that the United States is confronted with a serious disruption in oil supplies today, the Strategic Petroleum Reserve, which was established following the embargo, can provide an emergency supply of crude oil. The reserve, maintained by the Department of Energy, consists of oil that is stockpiled in underground salt caverns along the Gulf of Mexico coastline. In addition, the Department of Energy maintains an emergency supply of heating oil for consumers in the Northeast, who depend on this fuel for much of their heating needs. Two million barrels of this heating oil are stored in commercial terminals and can be released quickly should severe weather or other emergencies create life-threatening shortages.

One way to minimize the effects of an oil supply disruption is to ensure that our domestic production of oil is maintained. Remaining U.S. oil fields are becoming increasingly costly to produce because much of the easy-to-find oil has already been recovered. Yet, for every barrel of oil that flows from U.S. fields, nearly two barrels remain in the ground. Higher oil prices encourage the development of technology to find and produce much of this "left-behind" oil.

Oil exploration on public lands and offshore in coastal waters also has potential to increase America's oil supplies. However, this drilling also raises issues of environmental protection. Energy companies and environmentalists have battled over Alaska's reserves for years, stalling drilling there. In 2010, President Obama announced opening large areas of the American coastline to offshore drilling.

Two months later, an offshore oil rig exploded in the Gulf of Mexico, setting off the largest oil spill in history. It is clear that regulators in the Department of Interior had failed to do their jobs and that BP, the operator of the well, had not followed industry standards. The Obama administration quickly reorganized the bureaucracy dealing with offshore drilling, but this could not prevent environmental damage from the spilled oil. The president put further deep water drilling on hold pending a thorough investigation.

A POINT TO PONDER

Effectively conserving energy (and limiting greenhouse gas emissions) requires sacrifices by every citizen.

Do you think Americans will be willing to make such sacrifices?

Nuclear Energy

The most controversial energy source is nuclear power. During the 1940s and 1950s, Americans were convinced that the technology that had ended World War II could be made to serve peaceful purposes. Nuclear scientists spoke enthusiastically about harnessing the atom to produce electricity that would be "too cheap to meter." These claims, however, were met with increasing skepticism in the light both of huge cost overruns in the construction of nuclear power plants and of the accidents at Three Mile Island and Chernobyl, in 1979 and 1986, respectively. Perhaps the most significant blow of all to the nuclear power industry was the wave of environmental concern that developed in the late 1960s.[37] Environmentalists opposed nuclear power because of radiation leaks in the mining, transportation, and use of atomic fuel; because of the enormous problem of nuclear waste disposal; and because of the inherent difficulty of regulating such complex technology. No new nuclear power plants have been started in the United States since 1978, and almost all those under construction at that time have been abandoned at huge financial loss.[38]

Nevertheless, defenders of nuclear energy continued to argue that burning coal and oil to generate electricity blackens miners' lungs, causes acid rain that defoliates forests and kills lakes, adds to global warming, and creates other problems. And in recent years, the high price of gasoline and heating fuel and concerns over global warming have encouraged a reconsideration of nuclear power. Leaders of both political parties and the American public support increasing the percentage of electricity produced by nuclear energy from the current 21 percent.

Renewable sources of energy such as solar power offer hope for cleaner air in the future. However, the contribution of renewable sources of energy to America's energy supply is likely to remain small for the foreseeable future.

Renewable Sources of Energy

Renewable energy sources include water, wind, the sun, geothermal sources, hydrogen, and biomass. Using water to drive turbines, hydroelectric power facilities in the United States generate about 6 percent of our electricity. Wind power, harnessed with modern windmills, generates about 1 percent of our electricity and is one of the nation's fastest-growing sources of energy. Biomass power is obtained from plants and plant-derived materials and can be used to produce electricity (biopower) and liquid fuels (biofuels). It now ranks second to hydropower as a renewable source of energy in the United States, accounting for about 3 percent of energy produced. However, although they may ultimately play a significant role, the contribution of renewable sources of energy to America's energy supply is likely to remain small for the foreseeable future.

Understanding Health Care, Environmental, and Energy Policy

19.4 Assess the role of democratic politics in making health care, environmental, and energy policy and the effect of these policies on the scope of government.

Health care, environmental, and energy issues have at least three things in common. First, they involve human health and welfare and thus are highly salient to both the pubic and policymakers. Second, they are highly technical areas in which ordinary people are ill equipped to make policy. Finally, dealing with them requires expanding the scope of government.

Democracy, Health Care, and Environmental Policy

High-tech issues, more than any others, strain the limits of public participation in a democracy. Whether it be the ethical issues raised by machines and devices that can keep patients alive indefinitely or the threats to public safety inherent in an accident at a nuclear power plant, governments are constantly called on to make decisions that involve tremendously complex technologies. Does unavoidable ignorance about complex technological issues involved in health care and environmental and energy policy mean that citizens cannot participate effectively in the public policy debates on these areas of policy?

Most Americans do not want to leave these issues to "experts" to decide, and they do not. When the president proposes complex health care reform, the public takes a stand. When there are tradeoffs to be made between economic growth and clean air, average citizens express their opinions. Sometimes these opinions are ill-informed, but democracy, as we have seen, is often a messy business. In addition, the public often relies on group representation to help them out with technical issues. Interest groups—associations of professionals and citizens—play an active role in making the complicated decisions that will affect Americans for generations and thus help translate public opinion into policy.

The Scope of Government and Health Care, Environmental, and Energy Policy

In the area of health care, the scope of the federal government has grown. Medicare for the elderly, Medicaid for the poor, and tax subsidies for employer-provided health insurance are large, expensive public policies. Adding prescription drug coverage for the elderly was a huge increase in the cost of governmentally supported medicine. The health care reform bill passed in 2010 added yet additional government responsibilities to ensure that all American have access to health care and to regulate private health insurance companies. Nonetheless, health care policy is the most important single policy difference between the United States and other industrialized democracies. We have a mixed, mostly private system; many other industrialized democracies have an almost entirely public one.

Similarly, in the past three decades, concerns for environmental protection have placed additional demands on the federal government. Volumes of regulations and billions of dollars spent on environmental protection have enlarged the scope of government's environmental policy. Responding to the issue of global warming will require yet additional regulations. Developing and protecting sources of energy also requires government subsidies, and sometimes even war. Moreover, pollution, a byproduct of energy use, raises issues of government protection of the nation's health and environment. It would be convenient to ignore these policy demands, but the public expects the government to act.

Summary

19.1 Outline the problems of health care in America and the role of government in health care.

America's health costs are both extremely high and increasing at a rapid rate. The health care system provides few incentives for controlling costs, and Americans who can afford it demand the most advanced care. There are severe inequalities in health care and hence in health in America. Insurance has been mainly obtainable as a benefit from employers, and many poor and working-class Americans, uninsured or underinsured, have been relegated to an inferior health care system. The government provides health care for the elderly and the poor through Medicare and Medicaid, and since the reforms of 2010, intended to increase access and help control costs, it provides subsidies for health insurance to small businesses and individuals.

19.2 Analyze the conflicts between economic growth and environmental protection, and identify the major national environmental protection policies.

Environmental concerns often conflict with equally legitimate concerns about economic growth and jobs. Interest groups advocating environmental protection now play a critical role in environmental policymaking. The Environmental Protection Agency is charged with administering policies dealing with land use, air and water quality, and wilderness and wildlife preservation. The National Environmental Policy Act requires the federal government to file an environmental impact statement with the EPA every time it proposes to undertake a policy that is potentially disruptive to the environment. The Clean Air Act charges the EPA with protecting and improving the quality of the nation's air, while the Water Pollution Control Act aims to clean the nation's water. Yet other policies, such as the Endangered Species Act, seek to preserve wilderness areas and wildlife. The disposal of toxic wastes, including nuclear waste, continues to challenge policymakers, although the Superfund has helped to clean up toxic waste sites. Global warming is another intractable issue, as there is disagreement over the role of carbon emissions in warming the earth and there is no agreed-upon approach to controlling them.

19.3 Evaluate the advantages and disadvantages of each of the principal sources of energy in the United States.

Coal is America's most abundant fuel and produces nearly half our electricity, but it is the dirtiest source of energy. Petroleum supplies most of our motor fuel, and natural gas produces over a fifth of our electricity. Although they are somewhat cleaner than coal, they both contribute to global warming and drilling, transporting, and refining of oil and gas are also sources of pollution. Moreover, the United States is dependent on other nations to supply much of its oil and gas. Nuclear power is clean and provides more than a fifth of our electricity. However, many question its safety and the storage of nuclear waste has proven to be an intractable problem. Renewable energy sources, including water, wind, solar, geothermal, hydrogen, and biomass, will probably play an important role at some point, but for the foreseeable future, their contribution to America's energy supply is likely to remain small.

19.4 Assess the role of democratic politics in making health care, environmental, and energy policy and the effect of these policies on the scope of government.

High-tech issues strain the limits of public participation in a democracy, but most Americans do not leave these issues to "experts" to decide. The public often relies on group representation to help them out with technical issues.

The scope of the federal government has grown as it has provided health care for the elderly, the poor, and, more recently, those who simply cannot afford health insurance. Health is the most rapidly growing public policy and poses a long-term challenge for budgeters. Similarly, concerns for environmental protection have placed additional demands on the federal government, increasing its regulatory reach. The public also expects the government to ensure a sufficient supply of energy and to deal with its polluting byproducts.

Chapter Test

19.1 Outline the problems of health care in America and the role of government in health care.

1. Which of the following is a reason health care in the United States is so costly compared to health care in other countries?
   a. Americans visit the doctor more frequently than do citizens of other nations
   b. Americans spend more time in the hospital than do citizens of other nations
   c. Americans have access to fewer health facilities than do citizens of other nations
   d. Americans have fewer incentives to seek out low-cost health care than do citizens of other nations
   e. Americans have coverage for a greater proportion of their population than do citizens of other nations

2. Access to health care in the United States is most commonly tied to employment.

   True______ False______

3. Compare and contrast Medicare and Medicaid. How is each of these programs funded, and how are the two programs threatened by increased health care costs?

4. Briefly discuss presidents' efforts to reform health care in the United States, beginning with Harry Truman's effort of over 60 years ago. What problems have these reform efforts attempted to solve? In your opinion, can government reform of health care solve these problems? Why or why not?

19.2 Analyze the conflicts between economic growth and environmental protection, and identify the major national environmental protection policies.

5. How have environmental impact statements been an important tool in preventing environmental despoliation?
   a. By restricting businesses from undertaking any project that would negatively affect the environment
   b. By alerting environmentalists to projects that might negatively affect the environment
   c. By ensuring that projects follow EPA guidelines for avoiding environmental damage
   d. By giving Congress a means to more effectively oversee environmental policy
   e. All of the above

6. The federal government's attempts to combat air pollution include market-based solutions, such as trading emissions credits.

   True______ False______

7. Why do economic growth and environmental protection come into conflict? How does the textbook illustrate that economic growth and environmental protection can both be pursued? What are some examples of policies that might promote both economic growth and environmental protection?

8. In your estimation, what is the biggest environmental problem facing the United States in the twenty-first century? What are some steps the federal government has taken thus far to address this problem, and what remains to be done? Based on what you have learned from the textbook, what type of solution seems most promising?

19.3 Evaluate the advantages and disadvantages of each of the principal sources of energy in the United States.

9. Like natural gas and petroleum, nuclear power contributes to global warming.

   True______ False______

10. Pick two sources of energy and assess their advantages and disadvantages in terms of both the economics of their use and the environment. In your opinion, which source of energy available to the United States holds the most promise to continue strong economic growth while protecting the environment? Explain your answer.

19.4 Assess the role of democratic politics in making health care, environmental, and energy policy and the effect of these policies on the scope of government.

11. Does the complex nature of health care, environmental, and energy policies necessarily undermine public participation in these policy debates? Why or why not?

12. How have health care, environmental, and energy policies each contributed to the growth in the scope of government in recent years? Do you think these policies inevitably lead to a larger government? Explain your answer.

PEARSON mypoliscilab™ Exercises

Apply what you learned in this chapter on MyPoliSciLab.

Read on **mypoliscilab.com**

eText: Chapter 19

Study and **Review** on **mypoliscilab.com**

Pre-Test
Post-Test
Chapter Exam
Flashcards

Watch on **mypoliscilab.com**

Video: Health Care Plan
Video: Three Mile Island
Video: Making Environmental Policy

Explore on **mypoliscilab.com**

Simulation: You Are an Environmental Activist
Comparative: Comparing Health Systems

Key Terms

health maintenance organization (550)
Medicare (554)
Medicaid (555)
national health insurance (555)
Environmental Protection Agency (558)
National Environmental Policy Act (558)
environmental impact statements (558)
Clean Air Act of 1970 (559)
Water Pollution Control Act of 1972 (559)
Endangered Species Act of 1973 (560)
Superfund (560)
global warming (562)

Internet Resources

www.kff.org
Kaiser Family Foundation Web site, with excellent studies of health care-related issues.

www.cms.hhs.gov
Centers for Medicare and Medicaid Services Web site, with information on the two largest government health programs.

www.who.int/whosis/en/index.html
World Health Organization Web site, with information on health care around the world.

www.epa.gov
Official site for the Environmental Protection Agency, which provides information on policies and current environmental issues.

www.sierraclub.org
Web site for the Sierra Club, one of the most active environmental protection organizations.

www.epa.gov/superfund/
Environmental Protection Agency information about toxic waste sites and their cleanup.

www.algore.com
A Web site by Al Gore, a leading advocate for combating climate change.

www.epa.gov/climatechange/
Environmental Protection Agency information on climate change.

www.eia.doe.gov
The best source of information on energy sources, consumption, and policy.

www.fws.gov
U.S. Fish and Wildlife Service, the protector of endangered species.

www.energy.gov
U.S. Department of Energy Web site, featuring information on a wide range of energy-related topics.

For Further Reading

Casamayou, Maureen Hogan. ***The Politics of Breast Cancer.*** Washington, DC: Georgetown University Press, 2001. How women's groups and others organized to elevate breast cancer research on the policy agenda.

Kraft, Michael E. ***Environmental Policy and Politics,*** 5th ed. New York: Longman, 2011. Overview of environmental policy and policymaking.

Morone, James A., Theodor J. Litman, and Leonard S. Robins. ***Health Politics and Policy,*** 4th ed. Boston: Cengage, 2008. The politics and policy of health care.

Patel, Kant, and Mark Rushefsky. ***Health Care in America: Separate and Unequal.*** Armonk, NY: M.E. Sharpe, 2008. Examines the causes of the inequalities of the American health care system and discusses various policy alternatives.

Rabe, Barry G. ***Statehouse and Greenhouse: The Emerging Politics of American Climate Change.*** Washington, DC: Brookings Institution, 2004. Many states have taken the policy lead in reducing greenhouse gases even as the federal government has been mired in gridlock about the issue.

Rosenbaum, Walter A. ***Environmental Politics and Policy,*** 8th ed. Washington, DC: CQ Press, 2010. The actors, institutions, processes, and polices involved in environmental policymaking.

Shaffer, Brenda. ***Energy Politics.*** Philadelphia: University of Pennsylvania Press, 2009. An excellent introduction to the international politics of energy.

Skocpol, Theda. ***Boomerang: Health Care Reform and the Turn Against Government.*** New York: Norton, 1996. Why Clinton's health care reforms boomeranged.

Smith, Zachary A. ***The Environmental Policy Paradox,*** 5th ed. New York: Longman, 2009. An introduction to environmental policymaking.

Vanderheiden, Steve. ***Atmospheric Justice: A Political Theory of Climate Change.*** New York: Oxford University Press, 2008. An incisive examination of the public policy challenges of global warming via the conceptual frameworks of justice, equality, and responsibility.

Vig, Norman J., and Michael E. Kraft, ed. ***Environmental Policy,*** 7th ed. Washington, DC: CQ Press, 2009. Useful articles on a range of environmental policy issues.

Chapter 20

National Security Policymaking

Learning Objectives

20.1 Identify the major instruments and actors in making national security policy.

20.2 Outline the evolution of and major issues in American foreign policy through the end of the Cold War.

20.3 Explain the major obstacles to success in the war on terrorism.

20.4 Identify the major elements of U.S. defense policy.

20.5 Analyze the evolving challenges for U.S. national security policy.

20.6 Assess the role of democratic politics in making national security policy and the role of national security policy in expanding government.

Chapter OUTLINE

POLITICS IN ACTION: A NEW THREAT

On September 11, 2001, America trembled. Terrorist attacks on the World Trade Center in New York and the Pentagon in Washington killed thousands and exposed the nation's vulnerability to unconventional attacks.

Less than 12 years after the fall of the Berlin Wall and the diminishment of Communism as a threat, the United States could no longer take comfort in its status as the world's only superpower. Suddenly the world seemed a more threatening place, with dangers lurking around every corner.

Pursuing its new foreign policy emphasis on ending terrorism, the United States launched wars against Afghanistan and Iraq. The United States won the battles quite easily, but the aftermath of the wars led to more deaths than the fighting itself and forced America to invest tens of billions of dollars in reconstruction and military occupation. Particularly because Iraq had in fact had little or no connection to al Qaeda, the terrorist organization behind the September 11 attacks, debate rages as to whether U.S. actions dealt terrorists a severe blow or had the effect of radicalizing opponents and recruiting new terrorists to their cause. At the same time, "rogue" states like Iran and North Korea have continued their development of nuclear weapons, threatening to make the world even less stable.

Answering the question of the appropriate role of the national government in the area of national security policy has become more important and perhaps more difficult than ever. America's status in the world makes leadership unavoidable. What should be the role of the world's only remaining superpower? What should we do with our huge defense establishment? Should we go it alone, or should we work closely with our allies on issues ranging from fighting terrorism and stopping nuclear proliferation to protecting the environment and encouraging trade? At the same time, a number of critical areas of the world, most notably the Middle East, have a frightening potential for conflict. Should the United States get involved in trying to end conflicts resulting from ethnic and religious differences and regional issues? Does the United States have a choice about involvement when the conflict could affect its ability to fight terrorism or prevent the use of nuclear weapons?

And just how should we decide about national security policy? Should the American people and their representatives participate as fully in the policymaking process as they do for domestic policy? Or should they delegate discretion in this area to officials who seem at home with the complex and even exotic issues of defense and foreign policy? Can the public and its representatives in Congress or in interest groups even exert much influence on the elites who often deal in secrecy with national security policy?

National security is as important as ever. New and complex challenges have emerged to replace the conflict with communism. Some of these challenges, such as the fight against terrorism, are traceable to a malevolent enemy—but many others are not.

20.1 Identify the major instruments and actors in making national security policy.

American Foreign Policy: Instruments, Actors, and Policymakers

foreign policy
Policy that involves choice taking about relations with the rest of the world. The president is the chief initiator of U.S. foreign policy.

Foreign policy, like domestic policy, involves making choices—but the choices involved are about relations with the rest of the world. Because the president is the main force behind foreign policy, every morning the White House receives a highly confidential intelligence briefing that might cover monetary transactions in Tokyo, last night's events in some trouble spot on the globe, or Fidel Castro's health. The briefing is part of the massive informational arsenal the president uses to manage American foreign policy.

Instruments of Foreign Policy

The instruments of foreign policy are different from those of domestic policy. Foreign policies depend ultimately on three types of tools: military, economic, and diplomatic.

Military Among the oldest instruments of foreign policy are war and the threat of war. German General Karl von Clausewitz once called war a "continuation of politics by other means." The United States has been involved in only a few full-scale wars. It has often employed force to influence actions in other countries, however. Historically, most such use of force has been close to home, in Central America and the Caribbean.

In recent years, the United States has used force to influence actions in a range of trouble spots around the world—not only to topple Saddam Hussein's regime in Iraq and the Taliban regime in Afghanistan but also, for example, to oppose ethnic cleansing in the Kosovo province of the former Yugoslavia, to prevent the toppling of the democratic government of the Philippines, to assist a UN peacekeeping mission in Somalia, and to rescue stranded foreigners and protect our embassy in Liberia. The United States also employed military force to aid the democratic transfer of power in Haiti and for humanitarian relief operations in Iraq, Somalia, Bangladesh, Russia, and Bosnia and elsewhere in the former Yugoslavia.

Economic Today, economic instruments are becoming weapons almost as potent as those of war. The control of oil can be as important as the control of guns. Trade regulations, tariff policies, and monetary policies are other economic instruments of foreign policy. A number of studies have called attention to the importance of a country's economic vitality to its long-term national security.[1]

Diplomacy Diplomacy is the quietest instrument of influence. It is the process by which nations carry on relationships with each other. Although diplomacy often evokes images of ambassadors at chic cocktail parties, the diplomatic game is played for high stakes. Sometimes national leaders meet in summit talks. More often, less prominent negotiators work out treaties covering all kinds of national contracts, from economic relations to aid for stranded tourists.

Actors on the World Stage

If all the world's a stage, then there are more actors on it—governmental and otherwise—than ever before. More than 125 nations have emerged since 1945. Once foreign relations were almost exclusively transactions among nations, in which leaders used military, economic, or diplomatic methods to achieve foreign policy goals. Although nations remain the main actors, the cast has become more varied.

International Organizations Most of the challenges in international relations, ranging from peacekeeping and controlling weapons of mass destruction to protecting the environment and maintaining stable trade and financial networks, require the cooperation of many nations. It is not surprising that international organizations play an increasingly important role on the world stage.

The best-known international organization is the **United Nations** (UN). The UN was created in 1945 and has its headquarters in New York. Its members agree to renounce war and to respect certain human and economic freedoms (although they sometimes fail to keep these promises). In addition to its peacekeeping function, the UN runs programs in areas including economic development and health, education, and welfare.

The most prominent international organization is the United Nations. Here, the General Assembly meets to discuss climate change.

The UN *General Assembly* is composed of 192 member nations, each with one vote. Although not legally binding, General Assembly resolutions can achieve a measure of collective legitimization when a broad international consensus is formed on some matter concerning relations among states. It is the *Security Council,* however, that is the seat of real power in the UN. Five of its 15 members (the United States, Great Britain, China, France, and Russia) are permanent members; the others are chosen from session to session by the General Assembly. Each permanent member has a veto over Security Council decisions, including any decisions that would commit the UN to a military peacekeeping operation. The *Secretariat* is the executive arm of the UN and directs the administration of UN programs. Composed of about 9,000 international civil servants, it is headed by the secretary-general.

United Nations
Created in 1945 and currently including 192 member nations, with a central peacekeeping mission and programs in areas including economic development and health, education, and welfare. The seat of real power in the UN is the Security Council.

Since 1948, there have been 63 UN peacekeeping operations, including 50 created by the Security Council since 1988. In 2010, there were 16 such operations underway—in Sudan, Haiti, Timor-Leste, the Democratic Republic of the Congo, Western Sahara, Afghanistan, India and Pakistan, Syria, Ivory Coast, Liberia, Chad and the Central African Republic, Lebanon, Cyprus, Kosovo, Darfur, and the Middle East generally.

The United States often plays a critical role in implementing UN policies, although U.S. attitudes toward the UN have varied. President Clinton envisioned an expanded role for UN peacekeeping operations at the beginning of his term but later concluded that the UN is often not capable of making and keeping peace, particularly when hostilities among parties still exist. He also backtracked on his willingness to place American troops under foreign commanders—always a controversial policy. George W. Bush sought but did not receive UN sanction for the war with Iraq. He, too, expressed skepticism of the organization's ability to enforce its own resolutions. Nevertheless, many countries feel the legitimacy of the UN is crucial for their participation in peacekeeping or other operations requiring the use of force.

The UN is only one of many international organizations. The International Monetary Fund, for example, helps regulate the chaotic world of international finance; the World Bank finances development projects in new nations; the World Trade Organization attempts to regulate international trade; and the Universal Postal Union helps get the mail from one country to another.

Regional Organizations The post–World War II era has seen a proliferation of *regional organizations*—organizations of several nations bound by a treaty, often for military reasons. The **North Atlantic Treaty Organization** (NATO) was created in 1949. Its members—the United States, Canada, most Western European nations, and Turkey—agreed to combine military forces and to treat a war against one as a war against all. During the Cold War, more than a million NATO troops (including about 325,000 Americans) were spread from West Germany to Portugal as a deterrent to foreign aggression. To counter the NATO alliance, the Soviet Union and its Eastern

North Atlantic Treaty Organization
A regional organization that was created in 1949 by nations including the United States, Canada, and most Western European nations for mutual defense and has subsequently been expanded.

European allies formed the Warsaw Pact. With the thawing of the Cold War, however, the Warsaw Pact was dissolved and the role of NATO changed dramatically. In 1999, Poland, Hungary, and the Czech Republic, former members of the Warsaw Pact, became members of NATO. Since then, eight additional Eastern European countries—Slovakia, Slovenia, Bulgaria, Romania, Latvia, Estonia, Lithuania, and Croatia—have joined the alliance.

Regional organizations can have economic as well as military and political functions. The **European Union** (EU) is a transnational government composed of most European nations. The EU coordinates monetary, trade, immigration, and labor policies so that its members have become one economic unit, just as the 50 states of the United States are an economic unit. Most EU nations have adopted a common currency, the euro. Other economic federations exist in Latin America, Africa, and Asia, although none is as unified as the EU.

European Union
A transnational government composed of most European nations that coordinates monetary, trade, immigration, and labor policies, making its members one economic unit.

Multinational Corporations Chapter 17 discussed the potent *multinational corporations* (MNCs). Today, a large portion of the world's industrial output comes from these corporations, and they account for more than one-tenth of the global economy and one-third of world exports. Sometimes more powerful (and often much wealthier) than the governments under which they operate, MNCs have voiced strong opinions about governments, taxes, and business regulations. They have even linked forces with agencies such as the Central Intelligence Agency (CIA) to overturn governments they disliked. In the 1970s, for example, several U.S.-based multinationals worked with the CIA to "destabilize" the democratically elected Marxist government in Chile, which Chile's military then overthrew in 1973. Although rarely so heavy-handed, MNCs are forces to be reckoned with in nearly all nations.

Nongovernmental Organizations Groups that are not connected with governments, known as *nongovernmental organizations* (NGOs), are also actors on the global stage. Churches and labor unions have long had international interests and activities. Today, environmental and wildlife groups, such as Greenpeace, have also proliferated internationally, as have groups interested in protecting human rights, such as Amnesty International.

Terrorists Not all groups, however, are committed to saving whales, oceans, or even people. Some are committed to the overthrow of particular governments and operate as terrorists around the world. Airplane hijackings, and assassinations, bombings, and similar terrorist attacks have made the world a more unsettled place. Conflicts within a nation or region may spill over into world politics. Terrorism in the Middle East, for example, affects the price of oil in Tokyo, New York, and Berlin. Civil war in southeastern Europe may strain relations between the West and Russia.

Individuals Finally, *individuals* are international actors. Tourism sends Americans everywhere and brings to America legions of tourists from around the world. Tourism creates its own costs and benefits and thus can affect international relations and the international economic system. It may enhance friendship and understanding among nations. However, more tourists traveling out of the country than arriving in the country can create problems with a country's balance of payments (discussed later in this chapter). In addition to tourists, growing numbers of students are going to and coming from other nations; they are carriers of ideas and ideologies. So are immigrants and refugees, who also place new demands on public services.

Just as there are more actors on the global stage than in the past, there are also more American decision makers involved in foreign policy problems.

The Policymakers

There are many policymakers involved with national security policy, but any discussion of foreign policymaking must begin with the president.

The President The president, as you know from Chapter 13, is the main force behind foreign policy. As chief diplomat, the president negotiates treaties; as commander in chief of the armed forces, the president deploys American troops abroad. The president also appoints U.S. ambassadors and the heads of executive departments (with the consent of the Senate), and has the sole power to accord official recognition to other countries and receive (or refuse to receive) their representatives.

Presidents make some foreign policy through the formal mechanisms of treaties or executive agreements. Both are written accords in which the parties agree to specific actions and both have legal standing, but only treaties require Senate ratification. Thus, presidents usually find it more convenient to use executive agreements. Since the end of World War II, presidents have negotiated thousands of executive agreements but only about 800 treaties. Most executive agreements deal with routine and noncontroversial matters, but they have also been used for matters of significance, as in the case of the agreement ending the Vietnam War and arms control agreements.

The president combines constitutional prerogatives with greater access to information than other policymakers and can act with speed and secrecy if necessary. The White House also has the advantages of the president's role as a leader of Congress and the public and of the president's ability to commit the nation to a course of action. Presidents do not act alone in foreign policy, however. They are aided (and sometimes thwarted) by a huge national security bureaucracy. In addition, they must contend with the views and desires of Congress, which also wields considerable clout in the foreign policy arena—sometimes in opposition to a president.

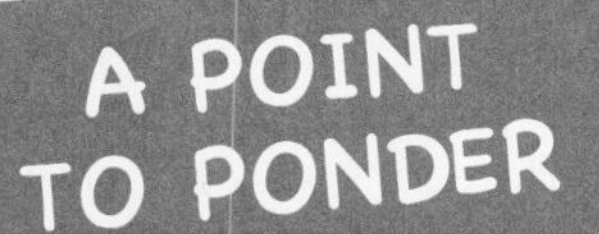

The president is at the center of national security policymaking, and juggling a wide range of international problems, often not of his making, is inevitably at the top of the White House's agenda.

Is it possible for one person, no matter how capable, to devote the necessary attention to such an array of issues?

Source: Robert Ariail, *The State* (Columbia SC) May 28, 2009.

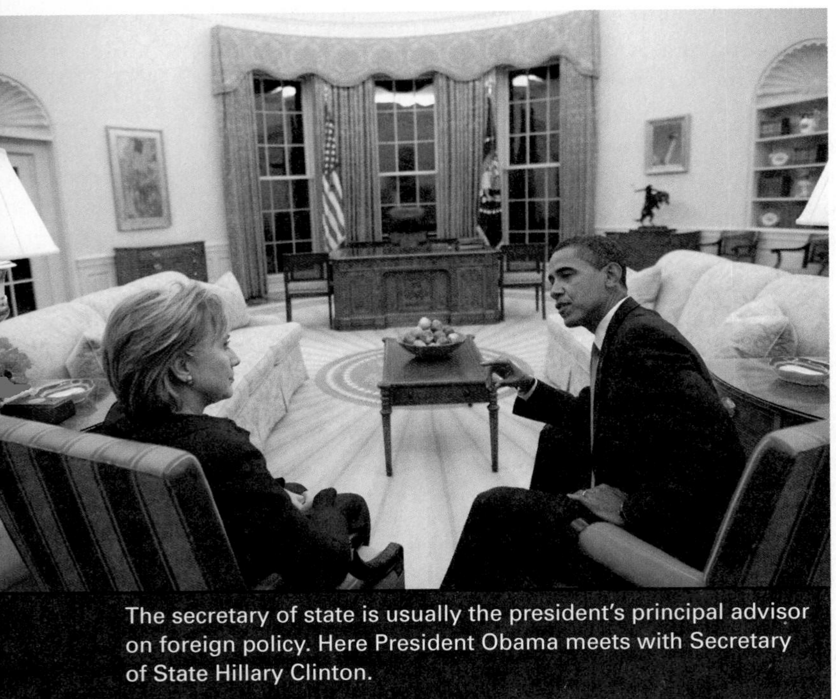
The secretary of state is usually the president's principal advisor on foreign policy. Here President Obama meets with Secretary of State Hillary Clinton.

The Diplomats The State Department is the foreign policy arm of the U.S. government. Its head is the **secretary of state** (Thomas Jefferson was the first). Traditionally, the secretary of state has been the key adviser to the president on foreign policy matters. In countries from Albania to Zimbabwe, the State Department staffs over 300 U.S. embassies, consulates, and other posts, representing the interests of Americans. Once a dignified and genteel profession, diplomacy is becoming an increasingly dangerous job. The 1979 seizure of the American embassy in Tehran, Iran, and the 1998 bombing of the American embassy in Nairobi, Kenya, are extreme examples of the hostilities diplomats can face.

The approximately 34,000 State Department employees are organized into functional areas (such as economic and business affairs and human rights and humanitarian affairs) and area specialties (a section on Middle Eastern affairs, one on European affairs, and so on), each nation being handled by a "country desk." The political appointees who occupy the top positions in the department and the highly select members of the Foreign Service who compose most of the department are heavily involved in formulating and executing American foreign policy.

secretary of state
The head of the Department of State and traditionally the key adviser to the president on **foreign policy**.

Many recent presidents have found the State Department too bureaucratic and intransigent. Even its colloquial name of "Foggy Bottom," taken from the part of Washington where it is located, conjures up less than an image of proactive cooperation. Some presidents have bypassed institutional arrangements for foreign policy decision making and have instead established more personal systems for receiving policy advice. Presidents Nixon and Carter, for example, relied more heavily on their assistants for national security affairs than on their secretaries of state. Thus, in their administrations, foreign policy was centered in the White House and was often disconnected from what was occurring in the State Department. Critics, however, charged that this situation led to split-level government and chronic discontinuity in foreign policy.[2] In most recent presidencies, the secretary of state has played a lead role in foreign policy making.

The National Security Establishment Foreign policy and military policy are closely linked. Thus, a key foreign policy actor is the Department of Defense, often called "the Pentagon" after the five-sided building in which it is located. Created by Congress after World War II, the department collected together the U.S. Army, Navy, and Air Force. The services have never been thoroughly integrated, however, and critics contend that they continue to plan and operate too independently of one another, although reforms made under the Goldwater-Nichols Defense Reorganization Act of 1986 increased interservice cooperation and centralization of the military hierarchy. The **secretary of defense** manages a budget larger than the entire budget of most nations and is the president's main civilian adviser on national defense matters.

secretary of defense
The head of the Department of Defense and the president's key adviser on military policy and, as such, a key **foreign policy** actor.

Joint Chiefs of Staff
A group that consists of the commanding officers of each of the armed services, a chairperson, and a vice chairperson, and advises the president on military policy.

The **Joint Chiefs of Staff** is made up of the commanding officers of each of the services, along with a chairperson and vice chairperson. American military leaders are sometimes portrayed as aggressive hawks in policymaking. However, Richard Betts carefully examined the Joint Chiefs' advice to the president in many crises and found them to be no more likely than civilian advisers to push an aggressive military policy.[3]

High-ranking officials are supposed to coordinate American foreign and military policies. Congress formed the *National Security Council* (NSC) in 1947 for this purpose. The NSC is composed of the president, the vice president, the secretary of defense, and the secretary of state. The president's assistant for national security—a position that first gained public prominence with the flamboyant, globe-trotting Henry Kissinger during President Nixon's first term—manages the NSC staff.

Despite the coordinating role assigned to the NSC, conflict within the foreign policy establishment remains common. The NSC staff has sometimes competed with, rather than integrated policy advice from, cabinet departments—particularly State and Defense. It has also become involved in covert operations. In 1986, officials discovered that NSC staff were secretly selling battlefield missiles to Iran in return for help in gaining the release of hostages held by Iranian-backed terrorists in Lebanon and then were secretly funneling some of the money from the sale to anticommunist rebels (called *Contras*) fighting the Nicaraguan government, despite a congressional ban on such aid. The scandal that erupted, termed the Iran-Contra affair, resulted in the resignation of the president's assistant for national security affairs, Vice Admiral John Poindexter, and the sacking of a number of lower-level NSC officials.

All policymakers require information to make good decisions. Information on the capabilities and intentions of other nations is often difficult to obtain. As a result, governments resort to intelligence agencies to obtain and interpret such information. Congress created the **Central Intelligence Agency** (CIA) after World War II to coordinate American information- and data-gathering intelligence activities abroad and to collect, analyze, and evaluate its own intelligence.

Central Intelligence Agency
An agency created after World War II to coordinate American intelligence activities abroad and to collect, analyze, and evaluate intelligence.

The CIA plays a vital role in providing information and analysis necessary for effective development and implementation of national security policy. Most of its activities are uncontroversial because the bulk of the material it collects and analyzes comes from readily available sources, such as government reports and newspapers. Also generally accepted is its use of espionage to collect information—when the espionage is directed against foreign adversaries. However, in the 1970s, Congress discovered that at times the agency had also engaged in wiretaps, interception of mail, and the infiltration of interest groups in the United States. These actions violated the CIA's charter, and revelations of spying on Americans who disagreed with the foreign policy of the administration badly damaged the agency's morale and external political support.

The CIA also has a long history of involvement in other nations' internal affairs. After the end of World War II, for example, the CIA provided aid to anticommunist parties in Italy and West Germany. It was no less busy in developing countries, where, for example, it nurtured coups in Iran in 1953 and in Guatemala in 1954. The CIA has also trained and supported armies—most notably, in Vietnam. In the 1980s, a major controversy surrounded the CIA's activities, when congressional inquiries into the Iran-Contra affair, discussed above, suggested that the agency, under Director William Casey, had been quietly involved in covert operations to assist the Contra rebels.[4]

Since the end of the Cold War, there has been substantial debate on the role of the CIA. The end of the Cold War reduced pressure for covert activities and brought a climate more conducive to focusing on conventional intelligence gathering. Currently, Congress requires the CIA to inform relevant congressional committees promptly of existing and anticipated covert operations. However, the failure to predict the terrorist attacks on September 11, 2001, changed the tenor of the debate, with many leaders calling for an increase in covert capabilities. Perhaps more disconcerting was the CIA's conclusion that Iraq possessed weapons of mass destruction. Destroying these weapons became the principal justification for the war, and their absence was a major embarrassment for the agency and the Bush administration.

There are numerous other components of America's intelligence community, which has a combined budget of about $50 billion per year. For example, the National Reconnaissance Office uses imagery satellites to monitor missile sites and other military activities around the world. The *National Security Agency* (NSA) is on the cutting edge of electronic eavesdropping capabilities and produces foreign signals intelligence. It also works to protect against foreign adversaries' gaining access to sensitive or classified national security information. In 2005, debate erupted over the NSA's monitoring of communications between the United States and overseas. Although the interception of communications focused on identifying contacts between those in the United States and terrorists abroad, there was inevitably some slippage. Critics

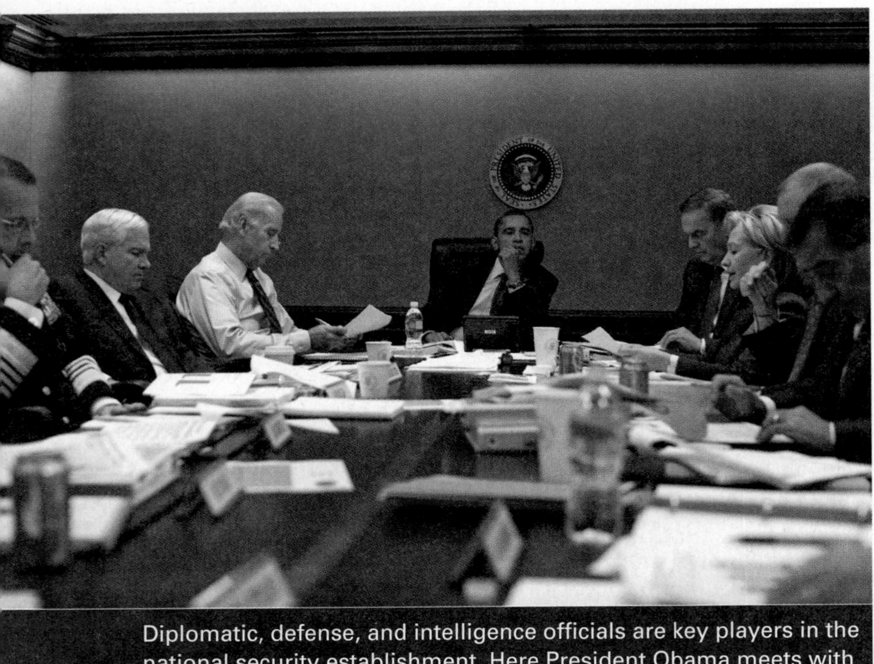
Diplomatic, defense, and intelligence officials are key players in the national security establishment. Here President Obama meets with top national security officials in the White House Situation Room.

charged President Bush with violating Americans' privacy and the legal mandate that the NSA obtain a warrant before listening to private messages. The White House claimed that the president possessed the power to authorize the interceptions without a warrant, that the NSA was careful to protect civil liberties, and that the program was necessary to protect Americans against terrorism. As we saw in Chapter 4, in 2008, Congress allowed officials the use of broad warrants to eavesdrop on large groups of foreign targets at once rather than requiring individual warrants for wiretapping purely foreign communications.

To better coordinate the nearly 100,000 people working in 16 agencies involved in intelligence and oversee the more than $50 billion intelligence budget, Congress in 2004 created a director of national intelligence. The person filling this position is to be the president's chief adviser on intelligence matters. It is not easy to manage such a large number of diverse agencies, spread across numerous departments, and there have been growing pains and slips in the process of improving coordination, as when the intelligence community failed to prevent a terrorist with explosives hidden in his clothing from boarding a plane to Detroit on Christmas day in 2009.

Congress The U.S. Congress shares with the president constitutional authority over foreign and defense policy (see Chapters 12 and 13). Congress has sole authority, for example, to declare war, raise and organize the armed forces, and appropriate funds for national security activities. The Senate determines whether treaties will be ratified and ambassadorial and cabinet nominations confirmed. The "power of the purse" (see Chapter 14) and responsibilities for oversight of the executive branch give Congress considerable clout, and each year senators and representatives carefully examine defense budget authorizations.[5]

Congress's important constitutional role in foreign and defense policy is sometimes misunderstood. It is a common mistake among some journalists, executive officials, and even members of Congress to believe that the Constitution vests foreign policy decisions solely in the president. Sometimes this erroneous view leads to perverse results, such as the Iran-Contra affair, discussed above, in which officials at high levels in the executive branch "sought to protect the president's 'exclusive' prerogative by lying to Congress, to allies, to the public, and to one another." Louis Fisher suggests that such actions undermined the "mutual trust and close coordination by the two branches that are essential attributes in building a foreign policy that ensures continuity and stability."[6]

20.2 Outline the evolution of and major issues in American foreign policy through the end of the Cold War.

American Foreign Policy Through the Cold War

Until the mid-twentieth century, American foreign policy for the most part emphasized keeping a distance from the affairs of other countries, with the exception of its neighbors to the south, in whose affairs it intervened frequently. Following World War II, the United States, which had emerged as the dominant power, became locked in an ideological conflict with the Soviet Union.

Isolationism

Throughout most of its history, the United States followed a foreign policy course called **isolationism**. This policy, articulated by George Washington in his farewell address, directed the country to stay out of other nations' conflicts, particularly European wars. The famous *Monroe Doctrine,* enunciated by President James Monroe, reaffirmed America's intention to stay out of Europe's affairs but warned European nations to stay out of Latin America. The United States—believing that its own political backyard included the Caribbean and Central and South America—did not hesitate to send marines, gunboats, or both to intervene in Central American and Caribbean affairs (for interventions since 1900, see Figure 20.1). When European nations were at war, however, Americans relished their distance from the conflicts. So it was until World War I (1914–1918).

isolationism
The **foreign policy** course the United States followed throughout most of its history whereby it tried to stay out of other nations' conflicts, particularly European wars.

In the wake of World War I, President Woodrow Wilson urged the United States to join the League of Nations, a forerunner to the UN. The U.S. Senate refused to ratify the League of Nations treaty, indicating that the country was not ready to abandon the long-standing American habit of isolationism, and that the Senate was not ready to relinquish any of its war-making authority to an international body. It was World War II, which forced the United States into a global conflict, that dealt a deathblow to American isolationism. Most nations signed a charter for the UN at a conference in San Francisco in 1945. The United States was an original signatory and soon donated land to house the UN permanently in New York City.

FIGURE 20.1 U.S. Military Interventions in Central America and the Caribbean Since 1900

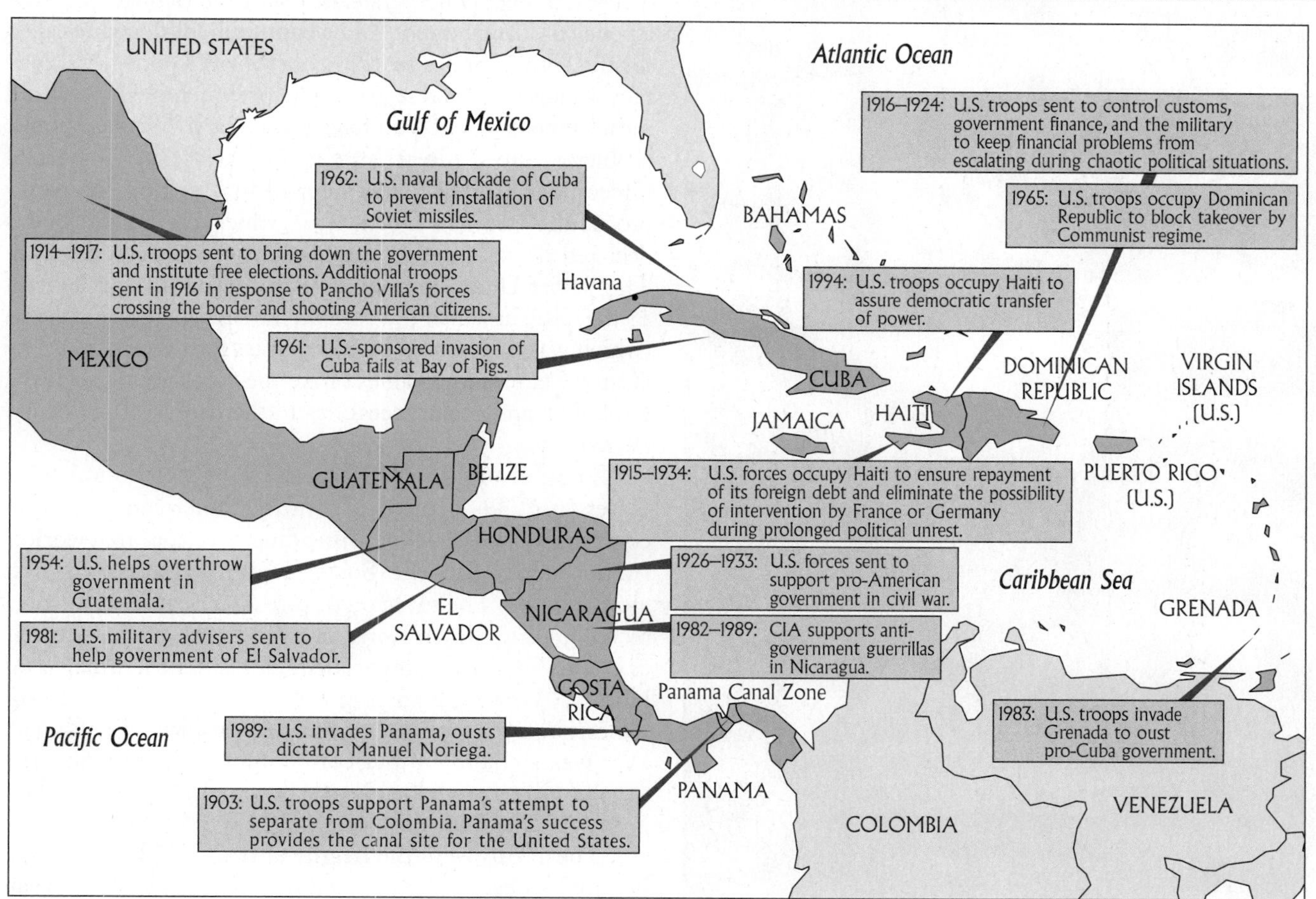

The Cold War

At the end of World War II, the Allies had vanquished Germany and Japan, and much of Europe was strewn with rubble. The United States was unquestionably the dominant world power both economically and militarily. It not only had helped to bring the war to an end but also had inaugurated a new era in warfare by dropping the first atomic bombs on Japan in August 1945. Because only the United States possessed nuclear weapons, Americans looked forward to an era of peace secured by their nuclear umbrella.

containment doctrine
A **foreign policy** strategy advocated by George Kennan that called for the United States to isolate the Soviet Union, "contain" its advances, and resist its encroachments by peaceful means if possible but by force if necessary.

Cold War
The hostility between the United States and the Soviet Union, which often brought them to the brink of war and which spanned the period from the end of World War II until the collapse of the Soviet Union and Eastern European communist regimes in 1989 and the years following.

After World War II, the United States forged strong alliances with the nations of Western Europe. To help them rebuild their economies, the United States poured billions of dollars into war-ravaged European nations through a program known as the Marshall Plan—named after its architect, Secretary of State George C. Marshall. A military alliance was also forged; the creation of NATO in 1949 affirmed the mutual military interests of the United States and Western Europe, and NATO remains a cornerstone of American foreign and defense policy.

Containment Although many Americans expected cooperative relations with the Soviet Union, their wartime ally, they soon abandoned these hopes. There is still much dispute about how the Cold War between the United States and the Soviet Union started.[7] Even before World War II ended, some American policymakers feared that the Soviets were intent on spreading communism not only to their neighbors but around the globe. All of Eastern Europe fell under Soviet domination as World War II ended. In 1946, Winston Churchill warned that the Russians had sealed off Eastern Europe with an "iron curtain."

President John F. Kennedy looks over the Berlin Wall in 1963. The Soviet Union built the wall to separate communist East Berlin from the western sectors of the city. It stood as the most palpable symbol of the Cold War for almost 30 years until it was torn down in 1989.

Communist support of a revolt in Greece in 1946 compounded fears of Soviet aggression. Writing in *Foreign Affairs* in 1947, foreign policy strategist George F. Kennan proposed a policy of "containment."[8] His **containment doctrine** called for the United States to isolate the Soviet Union—to "contain" its advances and resist its encroachments—by peaceful means if possible but with force if necessary. When economic problems forced Great Britain to decrease its support of Greece, the United States stepped in based on the newly proclaimed Truman Doctrine, in which the United States declared it would help other nations oppose communism. The Soviet Union responded with the Berlin Blockade of 1948–1949, in which it closed off land access to West Berlin (which was surrounded by communist East Germany). The United States and its allies broke the blockade by airlifting food, fuel, and other necessities to the people of the beleaguered city.

The fall of China to Mao Zedong's communist-led forces in 1949 seemed to confirm American fears that communism was a cancer spreading over the "free world." In the same year, the Soviet Union exploded its first atomic bomb. The invasion of pro-American South Korea by communist North Korea in 1950 further fueled American fears of Soviet imperialism. President Truman said bluntly, "We've got to stop the Russians now," and sent American troops to Korea under UN auspices. The Korean War was a chance to put containment into practice. Involving China as well as North Korea, the war dragged on until July 27, 1953.

The 1950s were the height of the **Cold War**; though hostilities never quite erupted into armed battle between them, the United States and the Soviet Union were often on the brink of war. John Foster Dulles, secretary of state under Eisenhower, proclaimed a policy often referred to as "brinkmanship," in which the United States was to be prepared to use nuclear weapons in order to *deter* the Soviet Union and communist China from taking aggressive actions.

By the 1950s, the Soviet Union and the United States were engaged in an **arms race**. One side's weaponry goaded the other side to procure yet more weaponry, as one missile led to another. By the mid-1960s, the result of the arms race was a point of *mutual assured destruction* (MAD), in which each side had the ability to annihilate the other even after absorbing a surprise attack. These nuclear capabilities also served to deter the use of nuclear weapons. Later sections of this chapter will examine efforts to control the arms race.

arms race
A tense relationship beginning in the 1950s between the Soviet Union and the United States whereby one side's weaponry became the other side's goad to procure more weaponry, and so on.

The Vietnam War The Korean War and the 1949 victory of communist forces in China fixed the U.S. government's attention on Asian communism. In 1950, President Truman decided to aid France's effort to retain its colonial possessions in Southeast Asia, but the Vietnamese communists finally defeated the French in a battle at Dien Bien Phu in 1954. The morning after the battle, peace talks among the participants and other major powers began in Geneva, Switzerland. Although a party to the resultant agreements, which stipulated that the country be temporarily divided into north and south regions and national elections be held throughout Vietnam in 1956, the United States never accepted them. Instead, it began supporting one noncommunist leader after another in South Vietnam, each seemingly more committed than the last to defeating communist forces in the North.[9]

Unable to contain the forces of the communist guerillas and the North Vietnamese army with American military advisers, President Lyndon Johnson sent in American troops—more than 500,000 at the peak of the undeclared war. He dropped more bombs on communist North Vietnam than the United States had dropped on Germany in all of World War II. These American troops and massive firepower failed to contain the North Vietnamese, however. At home, widespread protests against the war contributed to Johnson's decisions not to run for reelection in 1968 and to begin peace negotiations.

The new Nixon administration prosecuted the war vigorously, in Cambodia as well as in Vietnam, but also negotiated with the Vietnamese communists. A peace treaty was signed in 1973, but few expected it to hold. South Vietnam's capital, Saigon, finally fell to the North Vietnamese army in 1975. South and North Vietnam were reunited into a single nation, and Saigon was renamed Ho Chi Minh City in honor of the late leader of communist North Vietnam.

Looking back on the Vietnam War, most Americans question its worth. It divided the nation and made citizens painfully aware of the government's ability to lie to them—and (perhaps worse) to itself. It reminded Americans that even a "great power" cannot prevail in a protracted military conflict against a determined enemy unless there is a clear objective and unless the national will is sufficiently committed to expend vast resources on the task.

The Era of Détente Even while the United States was waging the Vietnam War, Richard Nixon—a veteran fighter of the Cold War—supported a new policy that came to be called *détente*. The term was popularized by Nixon's national security adviser and later secretary of state, Henry Kissinger.

Détente represented a slow transformation from conflict thinking to cooperative thinking in foreign policy strategy. It sought a relaxation of tensions between the superpowers, coupled with firm guarantees of mutual security. The policy assumed that the United States and the Soviet Union had no permanent, immutable sources of conflict; that both had an interest in peace and world stability; and that a nuclear war was—and should be—unthinkable. Thus, foreign policy battles between the United States and the Soviet Union were to be waged with diplomatic, economic, and propaganda weapons; the threat of force was downplayed.

détente
A policy, beginning in the early 1970s, that sought a relaxation of tensions between the United States and the Soviet Union, coupled with firm guarantees of mutual security.

One major initiative emerging from détente was the *Strategic Arms Limitation Talks* (SALT). These talks represented a mutual effort by the United States and the Soviet Union to limit the growth of their nuclear capabilities, with each power maintaining sufficient nuclear weapons to deter a surprise attack by the other. Nixon signed the first SALT accord in 1972, and negotiations for a second agreement, SALT II, soon followed. After six years of laborious negotiations, President Carter finally signed the agreement and sent it to the Senate in 1979. The Soviet invasion of Afghanistan that year caused Carter to withdraw the treaty from Senate consideration, however, even though both he and Ronald Reagan insisted that they would remain committed to the agreement's limitations on nuclear weaponry.

The United States applied the philosophy of détente to the People's Republic of China as well as to the Soviet Union. After the fall of the pro-American government in 1949, the United States had refused to extend diplomatic recognition to the world's most populous nation, recognizing instead the government in exile on the nearby island of Taiwan. As a senator in the early 1950s, Richard Nixon had been an implacable foe of "Red China," even suggesting that the Democratic administration had traitorously "lost" China. Nevertheless, two decades later this same Richard Nixon became the first president to visit the People's Republic and sent an American mission there. President Jimmy Carter extended formal diplomatic recognition to China in 1979. Over time, cultural and economic ties between the United States and China increased greatly.

Not everyone favored détente, however. Even Carter called for a substantial increase in defense spending after the Soviet Union invaded Afghanistan in 1979. Few people saw more threats from the Soviet Union than did Ronald Reagan, who called it the "Evil Empire." He viewed the Soviet invasion of Afghanistan as typical Russian aggression that, if unchecked, could only grow more common. He hailed anticommunist governments everywhere and pledged to increase American defense spending.

The Reagan Rearmament From the mid-1950s to 1981 (with the exception of the Vietnam War), the defense budget had generally been declining as a percentage of both the total federal budget and the GDP. In 1955, during the Eisenhower administration, defense accounted for 61 percent of the federal budget and about 10 percent of the GDP. By the time President Reagan took office in 1981, the two numbers had dropped to 23 and 5.2 percent, respectively. These figures reflected a substantial cut indeed, although the decrease came about more because levels of social spending had increased than because military spending had declined.

According to Reagan, America faced a "window of vulnerability" because the Soviet Union was galloping ahead of the United States in military spending and, as a result, the United States had to build its defenses before it could negotiate arms control agreements. Reagan proposed the largest peacetime defense spending increase in American history: a five-year defense buildup costing $1.5 trillion. Defense officials were ordered to find places to spend more money.[10] These heady days for the Pentagon lasted only through the first term of Reagan's presidency, however. In his second term, concern over huge budget deficits brought defense spending to a standstill. Once inflation is taken into account, Congress appropriated no increase in defense spending at all from 1985 to 1988.

In 1983 President Reagan added another element to his defense policy—a new plan for defense against missiles. He called it the Strategic Defense Initiative (SDI); critics quickly renamed it "Star Wars." Reagan's plans for SDI proposed creating a global umbrella in space wherein computers would scan the skies and use various high-tech devices to destroy invading missiles. The administration proposed a research program that would have cost tens of billions of dollars over the next decade.

In the face of an onslaught of criticism regarding the feasibility of SDI, its proponents reduced their expectations about the size and capabilities of any defensive shield that could be erected over the next generation. Talk of a smaller system—capable of protecting against an accidental launch of a few missiles or against a threat by some Third World country with nuclear weapons—replaced the dream of an impenetrable umbrella over the United States capable of defeating a massive Soviet nuclear strike.

Beginning in 1989, communism in the Soviet Union and in Eastern Europe suddenly began to crumble. The end of the Cold War between East and West reduced the threat of nuclear war between the superpowers, but it also left a host of difficult new national security issues in its wake. Here, workers dismantle the head from a huge granite statue of Lenin in Berlin in 1991.

The Final Thaw in the Cold War On May 12, 1989, in a commencement address at Texas A&M University, President George H. W. Bush announced a new era in American foreign policy. He termed this an era "beyond containment" and declared the goal of the United States would shift from containing Soviet expansion to seeking the integration of the Soviet Union into the community of nations.

The Cold War ended as few had anticipated—spontaneously. Suddenly, the elusive objective of 40 years of post–World War II U.S. foreign policy—freedom and self-determination for Eastern Europeans and Soviet peoples and the reduction of the military threat from the East—was achieved. Forces of change sparked by Soviet leader Mikhail Gorbachev led to a staggering wave of upheaval that shattered communist regimes and the postwar barriers between Eastern and Western Europe. The Berlin Wall, the most prominent symbol of oppression in Eastern Europe, came tumbling down on November 9, 1989, and East and West Germany formed a unified, democratic republic. The Soviet Union split into 15 separate nations, and non-communist governments formed in most of them. Poland, Czechoslovakia (soon splitting into the Czech Republic and Slovakia), and Hungary established democratic governments, and reformers overthrew the old-line communist leaders in Bulgaria and Romania.

In 1989, reform seemed on the verge of occurring in China as well. That spring in Tiananmen Square, the central meeting place in Beijing, thousands of students held protests on behalf of democratization. Unable to tolerate challenges to their rule any longer, the aging Chinese leaders forcibly—and brutally—evacuated the square, crushing some protestors under armored tanks. It is still not clear how many students were killed and how many others arrested, but the reform movement in China received a serious setback. This suppression of efforts to develop democracy sent a chill through what had been a warming relationship between the United States and the People's Republic of China.

Reform continued elsewhere, however. On June 17, 1992, Boris Yeltsin addressed a joint session of the U.S. Congress. When the burly, silver-haired president of the new Russian republic entered the House chamber, members of Congress greeted him with chants of "Bo-ris, Bo-ris" and hailed him with numerous standing ovations.

Yeltsin proclaimed to thunderous applause,

> The idol of communism, which spread *everywhere* social strife, animosity and unparalleled brutality, which instilled fear in humanity, has collapsed . . . I am here to assure you that we will not let it rise again in our land.

The Cold War that had been waged for two generations had ended, and the West, led by the United States, had won.

20.3 Explain the major obstacles to success in the war on terrorism.

American Foreign Policy and the War on Terrorism

The end of the Cold War raised hopes that a long era of relative tranquility would follow. Although in many parts of the world, conflicts continued and new conflicts arose, Americans experienced a sense of diminished danger. This sense was shattered by the events of September 11, 2001, however, and terrorism moved to the fore as a foreign policy concern.

The Spread of Terrorism

Perhaps the most troublesome issue in the national security area is the spread of terrorism—the use of violence to demoralize and frighten a country's population or government. Terrorism takes many forms, including the bombing of buildings (such as the attacks on the World Trade Center and the Pentagon on September 11, 2001; on the American embassy in Kenya in 1998; and on the World Trade Center in 1993) and ships (such as the USS *Cole* in Yemen in 2000), the assassinations of political leaders (as when Iraq attempted to kill former president George Bush in 1993), and the kidnappings of diplomats and civilians (as when Iranians took Americans hostage in 1979).

It is difficult to defend against terrorism, especially in an open society. Terrorists have the advantage of stealth and surprise and, often, of a willingness to die for their cause. Improved security measures and better intelligence gathering can help. So, perhaps, can punishing governments and organizations that engage in terrorist activities. In 1986, the United States launched an air attack on Libya in response to Libyan-supported acts of terrorism; in 1993, the United States struck at Iraq's intelligence center in response to a foiled plot to assassinate former president George Bush; and in 1998, the United States launched an attack in Afghanistan on Osama bin Laden, the leader of the terrorist organization al Qaeda.

Afghanistan and Iraq

Following the September 11, 2001, attacks, the United States declared war on terrorism. President George W. Bush made the war the highest priority of his administration, and the United States launched an attack on bin Laden and al Qaeda and on the

Terrorism takes many forms, including the bombing of buildings and ships. Shown here are terrorist attacks on the World Trade Center in New York in 2001, the American embassy in Kenya in 1998, and the USS *Cole* in Yemen in 2000.

Taliban regime that had been harboring them. The Taliban fell in short order, although many suspected members of al Qaeda escaped. In the meantime, the president declared that Iran, Iraq, and North Korea formed an "axis of evil" and began laying plans to remove Iraqi president Saddam Hussein from power. In 2003, a U.S.-led coalition toppled Hussein.

In the 2000 presidential campaign, George W. Bush had spoken of "humility" in foreign affairs and cautioned against overextending America's military. He had also warned against "nation building," which involves installing institutions of a national government in a country and often requires massive investment and military occupation. However, in the wake of the September, 11, 2001, attacks, the threat of terrorism caused the president to rethink these views, and the administration began talking about meeting America's "unparalleled responsibilities." With the invasion of Iraq, one of those responsibilities became to rebuild and democratize Iraq.

There is broad consensus that the planning for postwar Iraq was poor. The administration presumed that Americans would be welcomed as liberators, that Iraqi oil would pay for most (if not all) of the necessary reconstruction of the country, and that the Iraqis possessed the necessary skills and infrastructure to do the job. These premises proved to be faulty, and the United States faced first chaos and then a protracted insurrection, especially in the "Sunni triangle" around Baghdad. Five years after the end of the official fighting, 140,000 American troops were still stationed in Iraq, straining our defense resources. As both U.S. expenditures on reconstruction and American casualties mounted, the public's support for the effort declined substantially, and President Bush experienced a corresponding drop in his approval ratings.

Although President Bush often declared that postwar Iraq was the front line in the global war on terror, his critics responded that the war proved a boon for extremists. Muslims consider Iraq, the seat of Islamic power for five centuries, sacred ground. The presence of foreign, non-Muslim occupiers made the country a magnet for militants who opposed their presence and welcomed an opportunity to kill Americans and other Westerners.

Moreover, since the war in Afghanistan, al Qaeda has transformed itself into an umbrella organization that provides an inspirational focal point for loosely affiliated terrorist groups in dozens of countries worldwide. Some view this transformed threat as potentially more dangerous than the one posed by the original al Qaeda. A "decapitation" strategy, focusing on the elimination of a small group of senior figures in the original al Qaeda network, may no longer be an adequate or appropriate strategy for dealing with a threat that has, in effect, metastasized.

Because of the increasingly decentralized nature of the terrorist threat, the military component of the global counterterrorism campaign is more likely to resemble a war of attrition on multiple fronts than a limited number of surgical strikes against a single adversary. One consequence is that the war on terrorism is likely to persist for many years. There were approximately 11,800 terrorist attacks worldwide during 2008, resulting in over 54,000 deaths, injuries, and kidnappings. Most of the deaths occurred in Iraq, Pakistan, and Afghanistan. Approximately 40 percent of these attacks occurred in Iraq and the Near East, and 35 percent occurred in South Asia, especially in Afghanistan and Pakistan.[11] Most of the deaths occurred in Iraq, Pakistan, and Afghanistan.

Nor is it likely that the use of military force alone will suffice. Some observers argue that relying primarily on the use of force to combat terrorism is responding to a tactic (terrorism) rather than to the forces that generate it. Traditionally, winning a war involved defeating an enemy nation on the battlefield and forcing it to accept political terms. In contrast, winning the war on terror, involving as it does terrorist groups and not enemy states, will require political changes that erode and ultimately undermine support for the ideology and strategy of those determined to destroy the United States and its allies. The war will be won not when Washington and its allies kill or capture all terrorists or potential terrorists but when the ideology the terrorists espouse is discredited; when their tactics are seen to have failed; and when potential terrorists find more promising paths to the dignity, respect, and opportunities they crave.

In 2007, President Bush ordered a troop "surge" in Iraq. It was designed to quell violence and give Iraqis the opportunity to establish a democratic government, train forces to assume police and defense responsibilities, and engage in national reconciliation among the major religious and ethnic groups. The first goal was met, as violence was reduced. Progress on the other goals has been much slower, however. Nevertheless, President Obama has been substantially reducing U.S. troop levels.

Obama has turned America's attention to Afghanistan, which continues to be threatened by Taliban insurgents and religious extremists, some of whom are linked to al Qaeda and to sponsors outside the country. Ensuring legitimate and effective governance in Afghanistan, delivering relief assistance, and countering the surge in narcotics cultivation remain major challenges for the international community. In 2009, President Obama announced an increase of 30,000 U.S. troops in Afghanistan. Although his goal was to begin removing them after a short period, success has been elusive.

To compound the problem, a terrorist haven emerged in Pakistan's remote tribal belt. As Pakistan is understandably sensitive to another country's military operating within its borders, the U.S. military has been hampered in conducting the sort of missions that would disrupt terrorist activity there. In addition, it appears that there is substantial sympathy for the Taliban among many Pakistani military and intelligence officials, which constrains Pakistan's own efforts to fight the terrorists.

Whatever the current issues in the debate over the war on terrorism, there is no doubt that the need to fight terrorists has forced Americans to rethink some of the basic tenets of U.S. national security policy.

20.4 Identify the major elements of U.S. defense policy.

Defense Policy

The politics of national defense involves high stakes—the nation's security, for example. Domestic political concerns, budgetary limitations, and ideology all influence decisions on the structure of defense policy and negotiations with allies and adversaries. All public policies include budgets, people, and equipment. In the realm of national defense, these elements are especially critical because of the size of the budget and the bureaucracy as well as the destructive potential of modern weapons. The goals of American defense policy are to win the war on terrorism, defend American territory against new threats, and, if necessary, conduct a number of smaller military actions around the world. A large military infrastructure is necessary to meet these goals.

Defense Spending

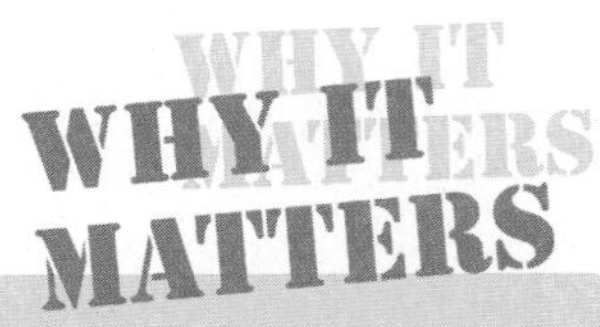

The Defense Budget

In the twenty-first century, the United States spends about one-fifth of its national budget on defense to support a large defense establishment. This expenditure contributes to large annual budget deficits, although some argue that we should spend even more to protect the country against terrorism.

Defense spending now makes up about one-fifth of the federal budget. Although this is a much smaller percentage than in earlier years (see Figure 20.2), vast sums of money and fundamental questions of public policy are still involved (see Figure 14.4). Some scholars have argued that America faces a trade-off between defense spending and social spending. A nation, they claim, must choose between guns and butter, and more guns means less butter. Evidence supporting the existence of such a trade-off is mixed, however. In general, defense and domestic policy expenditures appear to be independent of each other.[12] Ronald Reagan's efforts to increase military budgets while cutting back on domestic policy expenditures seem to have stemmed more from his own ideology than from any inevitable choice between the two.

Defense spending is a thorny political issue, entangled with ideological disputes. Conservatives advocate increases in defense spending and insist that America maintain its readiness at a high level. They point out that many nations and terrorist organizations retain potent military capability and that wars on a significant scale are still possible. Liberals have supported increased defense spending for the war on terrorism but more generally are skeptical of defense spending. They maintain that the Pentagon wastes money and that the United States buys too many guns and too little butter. The

FIGURE 20.2 Trends in Defense Spending

John F. Kennedy took office in 1961 at the height of the Cold War. National defense was the dominant public policy for the U.S. government; it accounted for half of all the money that the government spent ("outlays") that year. Things have changed dramatically since then, however. Although defense spending continued to increase until the 1990s, spending on other policies increased even more. As a result, defense spending is now only about one-fifth of the budget. Still, at more than $600 billion per year (counting the cost of occupation of Iraq), it remains a significant sum, one over which battles continue to be fought in Congress.

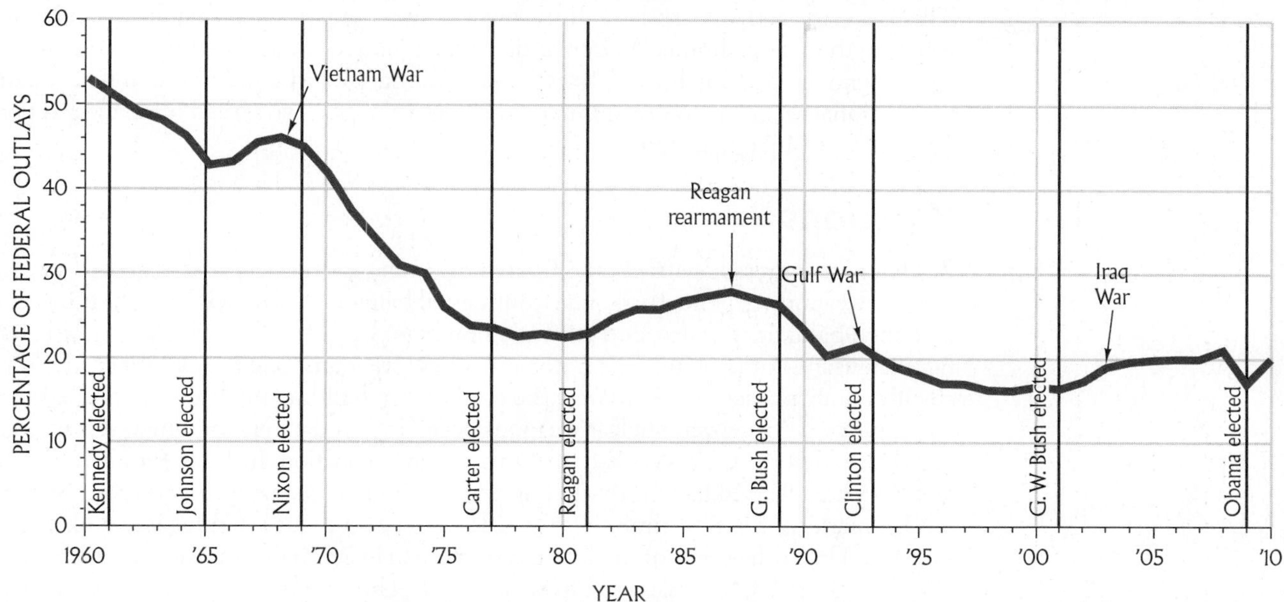

Source: *Budget of the United States Government, Fiscal Year 2011: Historical Tables* (Washington, DC: U.S. Government Printing Office, 2010), Table 3.1.

most crucial aspect of national defense, they argue, is a strong economy, which is based on investments in "human capital" such as health and education.

In the 1990s, the lessening of East–West tensions gave momentum to significant reductions in defense spending, which some called the *peace dividend.* Changing spending patterns was not easy, however. For example, military hardware developed during the early 1980s has proven to be increasingly expensive to purchase and maintain. And when the assembly lines at weapons plants close down, submarine designers, welders, and many others lose their jobs. These programs become political footballs as candidates compete over promises to keep weapons systems in production. Ideology plays a crucial role in the basic decisions members of Congress make regarding defense spending, but once these decisions are made, liberal as well as conservative representatives and senators fight hard to help constituencies win and keep defense contracts.[13]

The trend of reductions in defense spending reversed abruptly in 2001 following the September 11 terrorist attacks. Whatever the proper level of spending, there is no question that the United States spends more on defense than the next 15 or 20 biggest spenders combined. The United States has overwhelming nuclear superiority, the world's dominant air force, the only navy with worldwide operations (which also has impressive airpower), and a unique capability to project power around the globe. No other country in modern history has come close to this level of military predominance, and the gap between the United States and other nations is increasing. Moreover, the military advantages are even greater when one considers the quality as well as the quantity of U.S. defense capabilities. America has exploited the military applications of advanced communications and information technology and has developed the ability to coordinate and process information about the battlefield and to destroy targets from afar with extraordinary precision.

Personnel

Crucial to the structure of America's defense is a large standing military force. The United States has about 1.4 million men and women on active duty and about 845,000 in the National Guard and reserves (see Figure 20.3). There are about 300,000 active-duty troops deployed abroad; many of these troops are serving in Iraq and Afghanistan, although there is also a substantial U.S. presence in Europe, Japan, and South Korea.[14] This is a very costly enterprise and the ongoing wars in particular frequently evoke calls to bring the troops home. As demands have increased on active-duty personnel, the military now relies much more heavily on National Guard and reserve units to maintain national security; National Guard and reserve units have served for extended periods in Iraq and Afghanistan.

Weapons

To deter an aggressor's attack, the United States has relied on possession of a triad of nuclear weapons: ground-based intercontinental ballistic missiles (ICBMs), submarine-launched ballistic missiles, and strategic bombers. Both the United States and Russia have thousands of large nuclear warheads. These weapons, like troops, are costly: Each stealth bomber costs over $2 *billion*; the total cost of building nuclear weapons has been $5.5 *trillion*.[15] Moreover, nuclear weapons pose obvious dangers to human survival.

The end of the Cold War led to a focus on arms reduction. In 1988, President Reagan and Soviet leader Mikhail Gorbachev agreed to eliminate *intermediate-range nuclear forces* (INF), marking the first time the two sides agreed to reduce current levels of nuclear weapons. Under the terms of the INF treaty, more than 2,500 nuclear weapons with ranges between 300 and 3,400 miles were to be destroyed. Three years later, presidents Gorbachev and George H. W. Bush signed the *Strategic Arms Reduction Treaty* (START). The treaty had the distinction of being the first accord mandating the elimination of strategic nuclear weaponry. In 1993, President Bush and President Boris Yeltsin of Russia signed an agreement (START II) to cut the U.S. and Russian nuclear arsenals (with the latter including those of Ukraine, Belarus, and Kazakhstan) to a total of no more than 6,500 weapons by the year 2003—less than one-third of the 20,000 long-range nuclear weapons the two possessed at the time. The agreement banned large, accurate ICBMs with multiple warheads

FIGURE 20.3 Size of the Armed Forces*

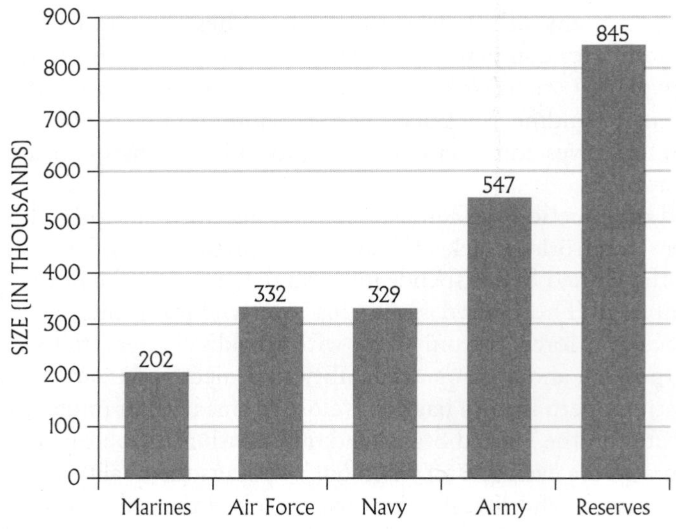

*2010 estimates

Sources: Office of Management and Budget, *Budget of the United States Government, Fiscal Year 2011: Appendix* (Washington, DC: U.S. Government Printing Office, 2010), 239.

altogether. In 2002, President George W. Bush and President Vladimir Putin signed a treaty to limit strategic nuclear weapons to no more than 2,200 for each country by 2012. In 2010, President Obama and Russian President Dmitry Medvedev went even further, agreeing to limit strategic weapons to 1,550 warheads for each nation.

President Reagan and Soviet President Mikhail Gorbachev signed a treaty eliminating intermediate-range nuclear missiles from Europe. The INF treaty marked the first time an American president had agreed to reduce current levels of nuclear weapons.

Even while negotiating reductions on nuclear arsenals, President George W, Bush stepped up efforts begun by Ronald Reagan to build a national missile defense. To pursue this system, in December 2001, the president withdrew the United States from the Anti-Ballistic Missile Treaty, part of the SALT accord that the United States and the Soviet Union had signed in 1972.

Nuclear weapons are the most destructive in America's arsenal, but they are by no means the only weapons. Jet fighters, aircraft carriers, and even tanks are extraordinarily complex as well as extraordinarily costly. The perception that space-age technology helped win the Gulf War in "100 hours" and topple the Taliban regime in Afghanistan and Saddam Hussein in Iraq with few American casualties, along with the fact that producing expensive weapons provides jobs for American workers, mean that high-tech weapons systems will continue to play an important role in America's defense posture.

Reforming Defense Policy

The rethinking of national security policy that has been prompted by the changing nature of threats to America's security has led to a reforming of the nation's military. Reevaluating weapons systems is part of this effort. So is changing the force structure to make the armed forces lighter, faster, and more flexible. Yet other changes include more effectively coupling intelligence with an increasingly agile military and a greater use of Special Forces, elite, highly trained tactical teams that conduct specialized operations such as reconnaissance, unconventional warfare, and counterterrorism actions. New approaches to military conflict inevitably follow from such transformations.

Although the United States has unsurpassed military strength, many international matters clamor for attention. Even the mightiest nation can be mired in intractable issues.

The New National Security Agenda

20.5 Analyze the evolving challenges for U.S. national security policy.

The national security agenda is changing rapidly. To begin with, the role of military power is changing, and more countries now possess nuclear weapons. Moreover, international economic issues are increasingly important. Dealing with China and India on trade and finance has become as crucial as negotiating arms reductions with Russia. Economic competition with other countries has increased, as has the economic vulnerability of the United States. Oil supply lines, for example, depend on a precarious Middle Eastern peace and on the safe passage of huge tankers through a sliver of water called the Strait of Hormuz. In an interdependent world, our dependence on trade places us at the mercy of interest rates in Germany, restrictive markets in Japan, currency values in China, and so on. In addition, we sometimes appear to be losing the war on drugs to an international network of wealthy drug lords. And determining policy regarding the global environment has taken on new prominence. Inevitably, the national security agenda is having ever-greater repercussions for domestic policymaking.

The Changing Role of Military Power

Harvard political scientist Stanley Hoffman likened the plight of the United States to that of Jonathan Swift's fictional character, Gulliver, the traveler seized and bound by the tiny Lilliputians.[16] For Americans, as for Gulliver, merely being big and powerful is no guarantee of dominance. Time after time and place after place, so it seems, the American Gulliver is frustrated by the Lilliputians.

Although the United States is the world's mightiest military power, there are limits to what military strength can achieve. In the long and controversial Vietnam War, for example, 500,000 American troops were not enough. Our military might did not protect us from the deadly terrorist attacks on September 11, 2001. Military strength, in short, is only one part of the equation. Moreover, force is often not an appropriate way of achieving other goals—such as economic and ecological welfare—that are becoming more important in world affairs.[17] Economic conflicts do not yield to high-tech weapons. America cannot persuade nations to sell it cheap oil, or prop up the textile industry's position in world trade, by resorting to military might. The United States is long on firepower at the very time when firepower is decreasing in its utility as an instrument of foreign policy.

The Only Superpower

The United States is the world's only superpower. This puts us in a strong position to defend ourselves against other nations. It also means, however, that the United States comes under more pressure to intervene in the world's hot spots. Furthermore, being a superpower does not protect us against attacks by nonstate actors, such as terrorists.

Although the United States is militarily supreme, it is becoming increasingly dependent on other countries to defeat terrorism, protect the environment, control weapons of mass destruction, regulate trade, and deal with other problems that cross national boundaries. Even the effective use of U.S. military power requires military bases, ports, airfields, fuel supplies, and overflight rights that only its allies can provide.[18]

According to Joseph Nye, it is "soft power"—the ability of a country to persuade others to do what it wants without force or coercion—that is often crucial to national security. Countries need to be able to exert this soft power as well as hard power; that is, security hinges as much on winning hearts and minds as it does on winning wars.[19] Indeed, American culture, ideals, and values have been important to helping Washington attract partners and supporters, to shaping long-term attitudes and preferences in a way that is favorable to the United States.

Despite these changes, military power remains an important element in U.S. foreign policy. One reason is that the end of the Cold War emboldened local dictators and reignited age-old ethnic rivalries that had been held in check by the Soviet Union, resulting in a greatly increased number of regional crises posing a threat to peace. The status of the United States as the only superpower meant that people were more likely to look to it for help when trouble erupted, as in the case of the former Yugoslavia. Thus, a difficult foreign policy problem is deciding when to involve U.S. troops.

Humanitarian Interventions On various occasions in recent decades, the United States and its allies have used military force to accomplish humanitarian ends. Notable examples include the efforts to distribute food and then oust a ruthless and unprincipled warlord in Somalia in 1992 and 1993; restore the elected leader of Haiti in 1994; stop the ethnic warfare in Bosnia by bombing the Serbs in 1995; protect ethnic Albanians in Kosovo by bombing Serbs in 1999; and provide food, housing, and medical care in the aftermath of a severe earthquake in Haiti in 2010.

Such interventions are often controversial, because they may involve violating a nation's sovereignty with the use of force. And the United States is usually hesitant to intervene, as American lives may be lost and there may be no clear ending point for the mission. Nevertheless, demands for humanitarian intervention continue to arise. For example, in recent years, the crisis in Darfur in western Sudan—where, since February

2003, more than 250,000 people have been killed and nearly 3 million displaced—prompted new calls for international humanitarian intervention.

Economic Sanctions An ancient tool of diplomacy, sanctions are nonmilitary penalties imposed on a foreign government in an attempt to modify its behavior. A wide range of penalties are possible—for example, a cutoff of aid, a ban on military sales, restrictions on imports, or a total trade embargo. The implied power behind sanctions that the United States imposes is U.S. economic muscle and access to U.S. markets.

Economic sanctions are often a first resort in times of crises, as a less risky and extreme measure than sending in troops. In many cases, they are the outgrowth of pressure from well-organized domestic political groups concerned about another country's policies related to ethnic or religious groups, the environment, human rights, or economic or other issues. These groups and government officials, in seeking sanctions, may want to curb unfair trade practices, end human rights abuses and drug trafficking, promote environmental initiatives, or stop terrorism.

Some economic sanctions have accomplished their intended goals; for example, sanctions levied against South Africa in the mid-1980s contributed to the demise of apartheid. Most experts, however, view these tools as having limited effect. The economic sanctions on Iran have not prevented it from seeking to build nuclear weapons.

To succeed, sanctions generally must have broad international support, which is rare. Unilateral sanctions are doomed to failure. The barriers of sanctions leak, and the real losers may be, say, U.S. companies that are forced to cede lucrative markets to competitors around the globe. For example, when President Carter imposed a grain embargo on the Soviet Union in 1980 in retaliation for the Soviet invasion of Afghanistan, only U.S. farmers were hurt; the Soviet Union simply bought grain elsewhere.

In addition, critics argue that sanctions are counterproductive because they can provoke a nationalist backlash. The decades-old sanctions against Cuba did not oust Marxist dictator Fidel Castro, and the perennial threats of sanctions against China typically result in a hardening of China's attitude regarding human rights and other matters.

Nuclear Proliferation

The spread of technology has enabled more countries to build nuclear weapons and the missiles to deliver them. Policymakers in the United States and other countries have sought to halt the spread of nuclear weapons, notably through the framework of the Nuclear Non-Proliferation Treaty, signed in 1968. The primary means of accomplishing this goal has been to encourage nations to agree that they would not acquire—or, at least, would not test—nuclear weapons. As you can see in Figure 20.4, only eight countries have declared that they have nuclear weapons capacities: the United States, Russia, Britain, France, China, India, Pakistan, and North Korea. Israel is widely suspected of having nuclear weapons. South Africa and three countries that used to be part of the Soviet Union—Belarus, Kazakhstan, and Ukraine—have given up nuclear weapons. Algeria, Argentina, Brazil, Libya, South Korea, Sweden, and Taiwan have ended their nuclear weapons programs.

Currently, policymakers are most concerned about North Korea and about Iran, which is actively developing nuclear weapons capabilities. These nations pose serious threats to their neighbors and perhaps to the United States as well. Over the last two decades, the United States has promised a range of aid and other benefits to North Korea in return for ending its nuclear weapons program. These incentives have not worked, as North Korea tested a nuclear weapon in 2006 and now possesses a few nuclear weapons. Iran does not yet possess nuclear weapons, although it has taken a defiant stance and refused to cooperate fully with international weapons inspectors. In response, the U.S. has aggressively pushed for economic sanctions against Iran to encourage it to end its pursuit of nuclear weapons. These U.S. efforts have received wide support but have been opposed by Russia and China. Iran is likely to occupy a prominent position on the foreign policy agenda for some time (see "You Are the Policymaker: Defanging a Nuclear Threat").

FIGURE 20.4 The Spread of Nuclear Weapons

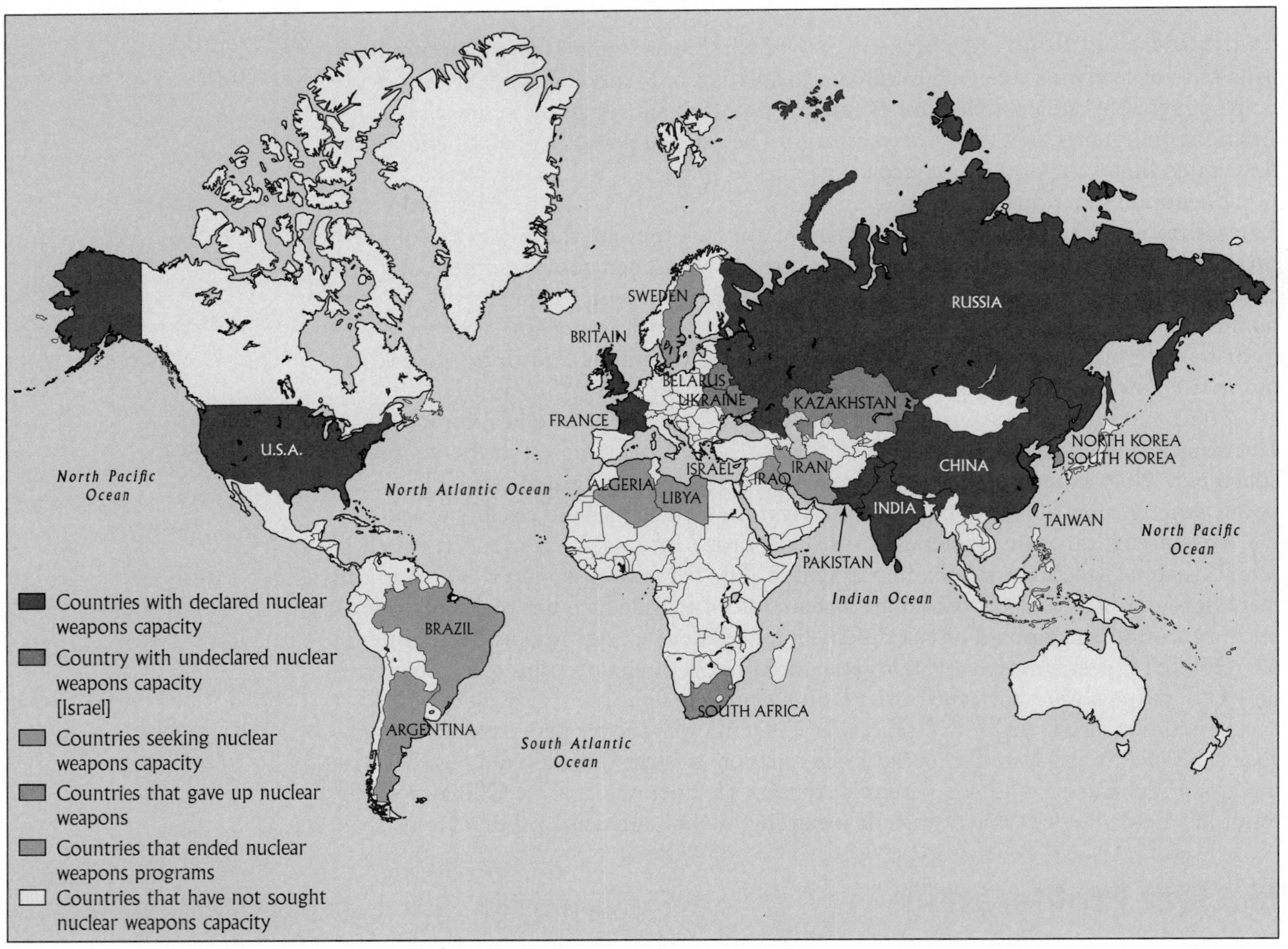

Source: *CQ Weekly*, May 23, 1998, 1,366. Updated by authors.

Other nations have serious security concerns when faced with hostile neighbors possessing nuclear weapons, concerns that can contribute to nuclear proliferation. When India resumed testing of nuclear weapons in 1998, neighboring Pakistan quickly tested its first nuclear weapons. The two nations' possession of nuclear weapons is a matter of special concern because of their history of conflict over Kashmir. In addition, political instability in Pakistan raises concern over the government's control of its nuclear weapons.

The International Economy

interdependency Mutual reliance, as in the economic realm, in which actions in nations reverberate and affect the economic well-being of people in other nations.

At one time, nations' international economic policymaking centered largely on erecting high barriers to fend off foreign products. Such economic isolationism would no longer be feasible in today's international economy, characterized above all by **interdependency**, a mutual reliance in which actions in a country reverberate and affect the economic well-being of people in other countries. The health of the American economy depends increasingly on the prosperity of its trading partners and on the smooth flow of trade and finance across borders (see "Young People and Politics: Embracing Globalization").

The *International Monetary Fund* (IMF) is a cooperative international organization of 185 countries intended to stabilize the exchange of currencies and the world economy. From 1997 to 1998, the decline of currencies in a number of Asian countries,

YOU ARE THE POLICYMAKER

Defanging a Nuclear Threat

One of the highest priorities of U.S. foreign policy is stopping the spread of nuclear weapons, especially to countries hostile to America. Some experts estimate that Iran will need only a few more years to build its first nuclear bomb.

Nuclear weapons in Iranian hands is not a comforting thought. The State Department has designated Iran as the world's leading sponsor of terrorism. The mullahs running the country support organizations such as Hamas, Hezbollah, and the Islamic Jihad; may be providing weapons and training to terrorists inside Iraq; and have sheltered senior members of al Qaeda. The current president, Mahmoud Ahmadinejad, has declared that Israel should be "wiped off the map." Iran has missiles that can now reach Israel and U.S. forces in Iraq and Afghanistan and is developing missiles that can reach Western Europe and North America.

How should we deal with this threat? The first response was diplomacy. The United States and its Western European allies sought to convince Iran to stop its nuclear research, and the International Atomic Energy Agency sealed some nuclear research facilities. In 2006, however, Iran removed the seals and declared that it had every right to develop atomic energy.

We could embargo Iran's main export, oil, but that would drive up energy prices everywhere and is unlikely to receive the international support necessary for economic sanctions to succeed. Curtailing foreign travel will have little impact on a people who currently do not travel much outside their borders.

Another option is ordering the CIA and other agencies to encourage an overthrow of the government. The chances of succeeding in such a venture are small, however.

There are also military options. In theory, the United States could invade, but the U.S. military is overstretched with its responsibilities in Iraq and Afghanistan. That leaves only one serious option—air strikes by Israel or the United States, possibly accompanied by commando raids. It is doubtful that bombs could eradicate Iran's nuclear program (much of which is underground), but it is possible they could set it back for years, possibly long enough for the regime to implode.

Of course, Iran is not likely to react passively to such a strike; the mullahs would almost certainly order terrorist retaliation against the United States and Israel and increase their efforts to sabotage our activities in next-door Afghanistan and Iraq. Iran could also become a rallying point for the Islamic world, which already is deeply suspicious and often disdainful of American policy. One result could be a further radicalization of millions of Muslims and an increase in the pool of potential recruits to terrorism.

What do you think? President Obama faces a dilemma regarding Iran. If you were president, what would *you* do?

including South Korea, Thailand, Indonesia, and the Philippines, threatened to force these nations to default on their debts—and, in the process, throw the international economy into turmoil. To stabilize these currencies, the IMF, to which the United States is by far the largest contributor, arranged for loans and credits of more than $100 billion. The IMF's intervention seems to have been successful, but the necessity of making the loans dramatically illustrates the world's economic interdependence.

Economic Interdependence

The world economy is increasingly interdependent. This increased interdependence means, for example, that investments and markets in other countries provide economic opportunities for Americans but also that Americans are more dependent on the strength of other countries' economies and that U.S. products and workers face increased competition.

International Trade Since the end of World War II, trade among nations has grown rapidly. American exports and imports have increased twenty-fold since 1970 alone. Among the largest U.S. exporters are grain farmers, producers of computer hardware and software, aircraft manufacturers, moviemakers, heavy construction companies, and purveyors of accounting and consulting services. Foreign tourist spending bolsters the U.S. travel, hotel, and recreation industries. American colleges and universities derive a significant portion of their revenue from educating foreign students. The globalization of finances has been even more dramatic than the growth of trade. Worldwide computer and communications networks link financial markets in all parts of the globe instantaneously, making it easier to move capital across national boundaries but also increasing the probability that, say, a steep decline on Wall Street will send the Japanese stock market plummeting.

Coping with foreign economic issues is becoming just as difficult—and, increasingly, just as important—as coping with domestic ones. In a simpler time, the main

Embracing Globalization

The protests that regularly occur during economic summit meetings of the leaders of the world's most economically developed countries might lead you to conclude that young adults are in the forefront of opposition to globalization, the process by which national economies, societies, and cultures have become integrated through a globe-spanning network of communication and trade. Actually, the facts are quite different, according to the Pew *Global Attitudes Project* surveys.

In every country, globalization has produced some political tensions. However, strong majorities in all regions believe that increased global interconnectedness is a good thing, and in most regions young people are more likely than their elders to see advantages in increased global trade and communication, and they are more likely to support "globalization."

The hesitation among some older citizens to embrace the movement toward globalization may be due in part to national pride. Although people in all countries and of all ages are proud of their cultures, in North America and Western Europe in particular, that pride is markedly stronger among the older generations, with younger people tending to be less wedded to their cultural identities. In the United States, 68 percent of those aged 65 and older agree with the statement "our people are not perfect, but our culture is superior," while only 49 percent of those aged 18 to 29 agree. The generation gap in Western Europe is similar.

Despite the general attraction of globalization, solid majorities everywhere think their way of life needs to be protected against foreign influence. Again, that desire cuts across all age groups everywhere, but in the United States and Western Europe, there is a generation gap, with older people much more worried than are the young about protecting their country's way of life. In the United States, 71 percent of people aged 65 and older agree that they want to shield their way of life from foreign influence, while just 55 percent of those ages 18 to 29 agree. This generation gap is even greater in France, Germany, and Britain, where older people are twice as likely as young people to be worried about erosion of their way of life.

Skepticism about foreign influence is evident in widespread, intense antipathy toward immigration. Majorities in nearly every country surveyed support tougher restrictions on people entering their countries. Again, however, age makes a difference. Immigrants are particularly unpopular across Europe, especially among the older generation, where half of those surveyed said they agreed completely with the statement that additional immigration controls were needed. In the United States, for example, 50 percent of those aged 65 and older indicate strong support for additional controls compared to only 40 percent of young people.

There are many reasons why young adults may be more supportive of globalization than are their elders. Better educated, more widely traveled, and more accustomed to the Internet, young adults seem to be less parochial, have less fear of change, and have more appreciation for the benefits of other cultures. Partially as a result of these attitudes, we should expect the trend toward globalization to accelerate over the coming decades.

QUESTION FOR DISCUSSION

- Do you think young people fear foreign competition?
- Do you agree that education and experience are the best explanations for the greater support of globalization among young people?

tariff
A special tax added to imported goods to raise their price, thereby protecting businesses and workers from foreign competition.

instrument of international economic policy was the **tariff**, a special tax added to the cost of imported goods. Tariffs are intended to raise the price of imported goods and thereby protect the country's businesses and workers from foreign competition. Tariff making, though, is a game everyone can play. High U.S. tariffs encourage other nations to respond with high tariffs on American products. The high tariffs that the government enacted early in the Great Depression (and that some say aggravated this economic crisis) were the last of their kind. Since that time, the world economy has moved from high tariffs and protectionism to lower tariffs and freer trade. In recent decades, various agreements have lowered barriers to trade, including the 1993 *North American Free Trade Agreement (NAFTA)* with Canada and Mexico, the 1994 *General*

Agreement on Tariffs and Trade (GATT), and the 2005 Central American–Dominican Republic Free Trade Agreement.

However, nontariff barriers such as quotas, subsidies, and quality specifications for imported products are common means of limiting imports. In recent decades, for example, the United States has placed quotas on the amount of steel that could be imported and has negotiated voluntary limits on the importation of Japanese automobiles. Such policies do save American jobs involved in producing steel and automobiles, but they also raise the price of steel and automobiles that Americans buy, and, since increased steel prices raise the costs of making products that use steel, they also wind up costing American jobs. Both the United States and European countries provide significant subsidies for a range of agricultural products, subsidies that have sometimes proved to be obstacles to negotiating tariff reductions.

More foreign-owned companies are building factories in the United States—just as American companies have plants around the globe. Thus, many Hondas and Toyotas are made in the United States. Foreign-owned firms in the United States employ about 5 percent of the workforce and account for a significant percentage of research-and-development spending and investment in plants and equipment. These firms also pay more on average than do their counterparts in the rest of the U.S. economy.[20] You can see employment by foreign companies in your state in "My State: U.S. Employment of Foreign Multinational Companies." As a result of the foreign investments in the U.S., it is increasingly difficult to define "imports."

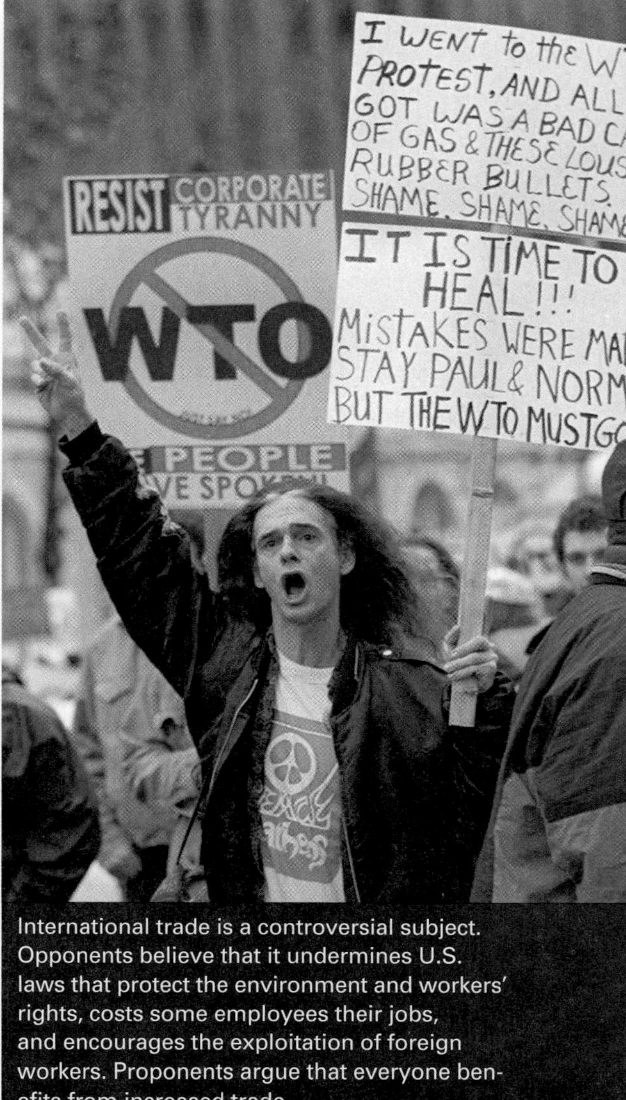

International trade is a controversial subject. Opponents believe that it undermines U.S. laws that protect the environment and workers' rights, costs some employees their jobs, and encourages the exploitation of foreign workers. Proponents argue that everyone benefits from increased trade.

Balance of Trade When Americans purchase foreign products, they send dollars out of the country. Thus, for example, when a tanker of oil from Saudi Arabia arrives in Houston, dollars travel to Saudi Arabia. If other nations do not buy as much from us as as we buy from them, then the United States is paying out more than it is taking in. A country's **balance of trade** is the ratio of what a country pays for imports to what it earns from exports. When a country imports more than it exports, it has a balance-of-trade *deficit*. Year after year, the American balance of trade has been preceded by a minus sign; in 2009, for example, the deficit for the balance of trade was $379 billion.[21]

balance of trade
The ratio of what is paid for imports to what is earned from exports. When more is paid than earned, there is a balance-of-trade deficit.

A balance of trade deficit can lead to a decline in the value of a nation's currency. If the dollar's buying power declines against other currencies, Americans pay more for goods that they buy from other nations. This decline in the value of the dollar, however, also makes American products cheaper abroad, thereby increasing our exports. Since the late 1980s, the United States has experienced an export boom, reaching nearly $1.6 trillion in 2009.[22] Exports account for about 10 percent of the GDP. About 5 percent of all civilian employment in the United States is related to manufacturing exports. A substantial amount of white-collar employment—in the area of financial services, for example—is also directly tied to exports.

Energy

In 1973, the **Organization of Petroleum Exporting Countries** (OPEC) responded to American support of Israel in its war against Egypt that year by embargoing oil shipments to the United States and Western European nations. The fuel shortages and long lines at gas stations that resulted from the 1973 oil embargo convincingly illustrated the growing interdependency of world politics.

Organization of Petroleum Exporting Countries
An economic organization consisting primarily of Middle Eastern nations that seeks to control the amount of oil its members produce and sell to other nations and hence the price of oil.

More than half the world's recoverable reserves of oil lie in the Middle East; Saudi Arabia alone controls much of this resource. Within the United States, states such as

U.S. Employment of Foreign Multinational Companies*

Foreign investment in the United States is substantial. With investment, comes jobs for Americans. Foreign companies now employ a significant number of people in every state.

*2007

Source: U.S. Department of Commerce. Bureau of Economic Analysis, 2008.

Texas, Oklahoma, Louisiana, and Alaska produce considerable amounts of oil but far from enough to meet the country's needs. America imports more than half of its annual consumption of oil from other countries, particularly from countries in the Middle East. The United States is less dependent on foreign sources of oil than are many European countries, like France or Italy, which have virtually no oil of their own, or Japan, which imports all its oil. On the other hand, America's dependence on foreign oil is growing every year. This dependence makes the United States vulnerable, especially because the Middle East remains unstable. The decision to respond to Iraq's invasion of Kuwait in 1990 was based in large part on the fact that Kuwait produces about 10 percent of the world's oil, and its neighbor, Saudi Arabia, also vulnerable to attack by Iraq, possesses about a quarter of the world's proven oil reserves.

Foreign Aid

Presidents of both parties have pressed for aid to nations in the developing world. Aside from simple humanitarian concern, these requests have been motivated by, for example, a desire to stabilize nations that were friendly to the United States or that possessed supplies of vital raw materials. Sometimes aid has been given in the form of grants, but often it has taken the form of credits and loan guarantees to purchase American goods, loans at favorable interest rates, and forgiveness of previous loans. At other times, the United States has awarded preferential trade agreements for the sale of foreign goods in the United States.

A substantial percentage of foreign aid is in the form of military assistance and is targeted to a few countries the United States considers to be of vital strategic significance: Israel, Egypt, Turkey, and Greece have received the bulk of such assistance in recent years. Foreign aid programs have also assisted with goals, including agricultural modernization and irrigation as well as family planning in countries where high population growth rates are a problem. Food for Peace programs have subsidized the sale of American agricultural products to poor countries (and simultaneously given an economic boost to American farmers). Peace Corps volunteers have fanned out over the globe to provide medical care and other services in less developed nations.

Nevertheless, foreign aid has never been very popular with Americans. It is not surprising that Congress typically cuts the president's foreign aid requests; such requests lack an electoral constituency to support them, and many people believe that aid provided to developing nations serves only to further enrich their elites without helping the poor. Currently, Congress appropriates less than 1 percent of the federal budget for economic and humanitarian foreign aid. Although the United States donates more total aid (both for economic development and military assistance) than any other country, it devotes a smaller share of its GDP to foreign economic development than any other developed nation (see "America in Perspective: Ranking Largesse"). It is important to note, however, that the United States provides a great deal more aid through grants from private voluntary organizations, foundations, religious organizations, corporations, universities, and individuals.[23]

Understanding National Security Policymaking

20.6 Assess the role of democratic politics in making national security policy and the role of national security policy in expanding government.

Although national security policy deals with issues and nations that are often far from America's shores, it is crucially important to all Americans. And the themes that have guided your understanding of American politics throughout *Government in America*—democracy and the scope of government—can also shed light on the topic of international relations.

National Security Policymaking and Democracy

To some commentators, the conduct of America's international relations is undemocratic in the sense of having little to do with public opinion. Because domestic issues are closer to their daily lives and easier to understand, Americans are usually more interested in domestic policy than in foreign policy. This preference would seem to give public officials more discretion in making national security policy. In addition, some say, those with the discretion are elites in the State Department and unelected military officers in the Pentagon.

There is little evidence, however, that policies at odds with the wishes of the American people can be sustained; civilian control of the military is unquestionable. When the American people hold strong opinions regarding international relations—as when they first supported and later opposed the war in Vietnam—policymakers are usually responsive. Citizens in democracies do not choose to fight citizens in other democracies, and studies have found that well-established democracies rarely go to war against one another.[24]

In addition, the system of separation of powers plays a crucial role in foreign as well as domestic policy. The president takes the lead on national security matters, but you saw in Chapter 12 that Congress has a central role in matters of international relations. Whether treaties are ratified, defense budgets are appropriated, weapons systems are authorized, or foreign aid is awarded is ultimately at the discretion of Congress, the government's most representative policymaking body. Specific issues such as the proper funding for the Strategic Defense Initiative rarely determine congressional elections, but public demands for and objections to policies are likely to be heard in Washington.

When it comes to the increasingly important arena of American international economic policy, pluralism is pervasive. Agencies and members of Congress, as well as

AMERICA IN PERSPECTIVE

Ranking Largesse

The United States is the largest donor of foreign aid, but it ranks lower than almost all other industrialized nations in the percentage of its gross national income (GNI) it spends on economic development aid for needy nations. American private giving, which is not reflected in these figures, is substantial, however, and is typically much greater than private giving from other nations.

DISCUSSION QUESTIONS

- Which is the more informative measure of a nation's giving, total aid or percent of GNI?
- Should the United States be giving more aid to underdeveloped nations?

Source: Organization for Economic Cooperation and Development, *OECD in Figures, 2009 Edition* (Paris: Organization for Economic Cooperation and Development, 2010).

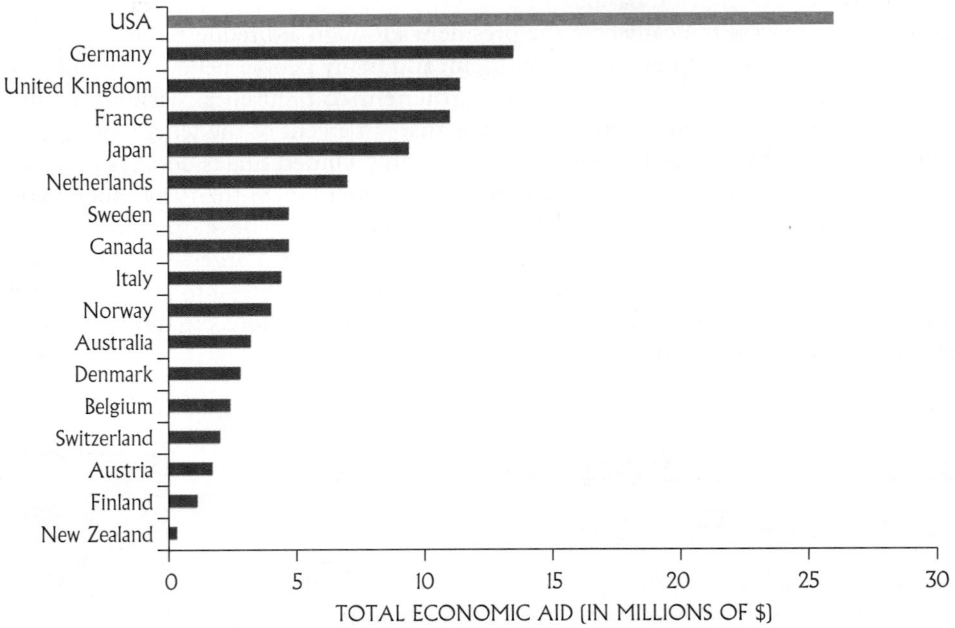

USA
Germany
United Kingdom
France
Japan
Netherlands
Sweden
Canada
Italy
Norway
Australia
Denmark
Belgium
Switzerland
Austria
Finland
New Zealand
0 5 10 15 20 25 30
TOTAL ECONOMIC AID (IN MILLIONS OF $)

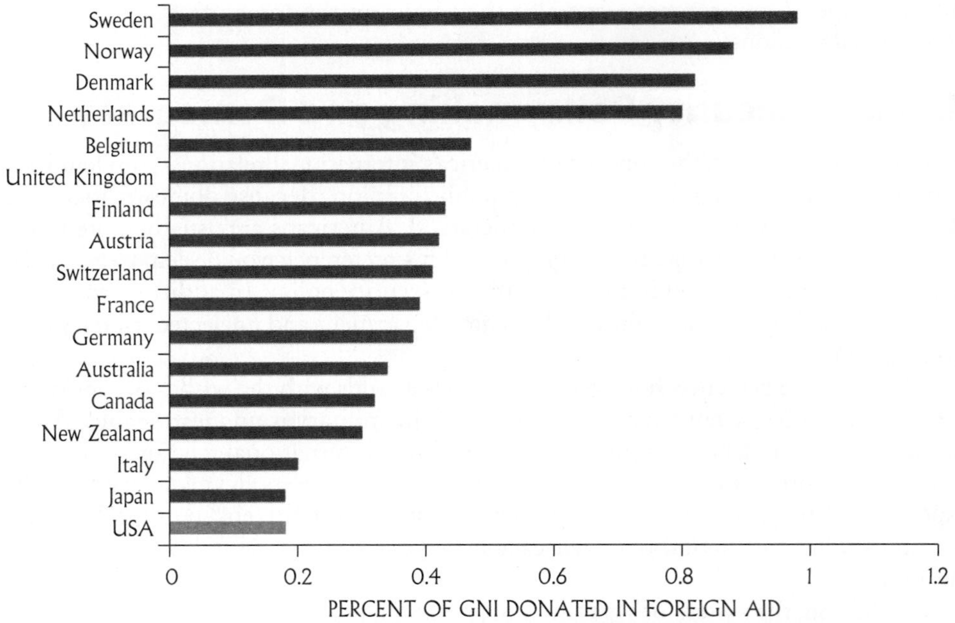

Sweden
Norway
Denmark
Netherlands
Belgium
United Kingdom
Finland
Austria
Switzerland
France
Germany
Australia
Canada
New Zealand
Italy
Japan
USA
0 0.2 0.4 0.6 0.8 1 1.2
PERCENT OF GNI DONATED IN FOREIGN AID

their constituents, all pursue their own policy goals. For example, the Treasury Department and the Federal Reserve Board worry about the negative balance of trade, and the Department of Defense spends billions in other countries to maintain American troops abroad. The Department of Agriculture and Department of Commerce and their constituents—farmers and businesspeople—want to peddle American products abroad and generally favor freer trade. The Department of Labor and the unions worry that the nation may export not only products but also jobs to other countries where labor costs are low. Jewish citizens closely monitor U.S. policy toward Israel, while Cuban Americans aggressively seek to influence U.S. policy toward Cuba. Even foreign governments hire lobbying firms and join in the political fray. As a result, a wide range of interests are represented in the making of foreign policy.

National Security Policymaking and the Scope of Government

America's status and involvements as a superpower have many implications for how active the national government is in the realm of foreign policy and national defense. The war on terrorism, treaty obligations to defend allies around the world, the nation's economic interests in an interdependent global economy, and pressing new questions on the global agenda such as global warming all demand government action.

By any standard, the scope of government in these areas is large. The national defense consumes about a fifth of the federal government's budget and requires more than 2 million civilian and military employees for the Department of Defense. The United States has a wide range of political, economic, and other interests to defend around the world. As long as these interests remain, the scope of American government in foreign and defense policy will be substantial.

Summary

20.1 Identify the major instruments and actors in making national security policy.

The use and potential use of military force, economic policies, and diplomacy are the main instruments of national security policy. Nations, international and regional organizations, multinational corporations, nongovernmental organizations, terrorists, and individuals influence American national security policy. The president is the main force in national security policymaking, and he is assisted by the Departments of State and Defense and by the CIA and the rest of the intelligence establishment. Congress also plays an important role in national security policy.

20.2 Outline the evolution of and major issues in American foreign policy through the end of the Cold War.

Until the mid-twentieth century, American foreign policy emphasized keeping a distance from the affairs of other countries, with the notable exception of countries in Latin America. Following World War II, the United States became locked in an ideological conflict with the Soviet Union and focused its foreign policy on containing communism and Soviet expansion. This competition came to include a nuclear arms race and U.S. involvement in wars in Korea and Vietnam against communist forces, but never war between the United States and the Soviet Union. There were efforts to relax tensions, but the Cold War did not end until the breakup of the Soviet Union and the liberalization of governments in Eastern Europe. Nevertheless, the United States maintained an enormous defense capability.

20.3 Explain the major obstacles to success in the war on terrorism.

The U.S. defense capability has been put to new use with the war on terrorism, the struggle that is at the top of America's national security priorities. It is difficult to defend against terrorism in an open society. Terrorists have the advantage of stealth and surprise and, often, of a willingness to die for their cause. They are also generally decentralized, so we cannot defeat them simply by attacking another nation. Moreover, winning the war on terrorism requires political as well as military successes. The United States' wars with Iraq and Afghanistan were motivated by the fight against terrorists. However, ensuring legitimate, effective governance remains difficult, and a terrorist haven has emerged in remote regions of Pakistan.

20.4 Identify the major elements of U.S. defense policy.

The United States spends about one-fifth of its budget on national defense, and has 1.4 million men and women in the active duty armed services and another 845,000 on the National Guard and reserves. Modern weapons systems are sophisticated, expensive, and dangerous, and the United States has entered a number of important agreements to reduce nuclear weapons. Recent reforms in defense policy, intended to reshape it for changed threats, have placed more emphasis on lighter, faster, and more flexible forces, the more effective use of intelligence, the use of Special Forces, and counterterrorism.

20.5 Analyze the evolving challenges for U.S. national security policy.

Although the United States has great military power, many of the issues facing the world today are not military issues. Nuclear proliferation and terrorism present new challenges to national security, challenges not easily met by advanced weaponry alone. Global interdependency in economics, energy, the environment, and other areas has also become important, revealing new vulnerabilities and thus additional challenges for national security policy. The effective use of foreign aid is also a perennial policy concern.

20.6 Assess the role of democratic politics in making national security policy and the role of national security policy in expanding government.

Although there are different opinions over how much discretion to accord policymakers in national security policy, policies at odds with the public's wishes cannot be sustained, and Congress can be a crucial check on the executive. As long as the United States is fighting a war on terrorism, has treaty obligations to defend allies around the world, participates actively in an interdependent global economy, and must deal with pressing questions such as energy supplies, global warming, and nuclear proliferation, the scope of American government in foreign and defense policy will be substantial.

Chapter Test

20.1 Identify the major instruments and actors in making national security policy.

1. Which of the following is NOT true concerning the United Nations?
   a. The United States often plays an important role in implementing UN policies
   b. The Security Council is the key decision-making body in the UN
   c. General Assembly resolutions are legally binding on its members
   d. Peacekeeping is an important function of the UN
   e. The General Assembly includes almost 200 nations

2. Which of the following organizations was created to help the president coordinate American foreign and military policies?
   a. The Department of Defense
   b. The National Security Council
   c. The State Department
   d. The North Atlantic Treaty Organization
   e. The Senate Committee on Foreign Relations

3. Economic instruments have become almost as important as military power in a nation's foreign policy.

   True______ False______

4. What role does Congress play in American foreign policy and what role does the president play? Do these roles ensure a balance of power between the legislative and the executive in the area of foreign policy? Why or why not?

20.2 Outline the evolution of and major issues in American foreign policy through the end of the Cold War.

5. Concerning the policy of détente, which of the following is NOT true?
   a. It represented a turn toward more cooperative thinking in U.S. foreign policy
   b. It sought to relax tensions between the United States and the Soviet Union
   c. It assumed that a nuclear war should be unthinkable
   d. It sought firm guarantees of mutual security
   e. It represented an era of increased defense spending in the United States

6. The policy of containment called for the United States to stop the spread of terrorism.

   True______ False______

7. What goals were pursued during the era of détente and during the Reagan rearmament? Briefly describe the situation and major issues in these two time periods. What foreign policy actors and tools were especially involved in these eras and what role did they play?

20.3 Explain the major obstacles to success in the war on terrorism.

8. The end of the Cold War resulted in the emergence of global terrorism.

   True______ False______

9. Compare and contrast the challenges of the Cold War with the challenges of combating global terrorism. What makes terrorism so difficult to defend against? Support your answer with examples from the text.

20.4 Identify the major elements of U.S. defense policy.

10. Evidence shows that there is a clear trade-off between defense and domestic policy expenditures.

    True______ False______

11. What position do conservatives and liberals each take on defense spending and what arguments do they make in support of their position? Whom do you agree with more and why?

12. How have defense policy experts suggested that the U.S. military be reformed? Explain the various factors that have led to these suggestions.

20.5 Analyze the evolving challenges for U.S. national security policy.

13. To succeed, economic sanctions typically have to
    a. Have broad international support
    b. Follow targeted military strikes
    c. Have support within the targeted nation
    d. Involve the nations of North America
    e. None of the above

14. Currently, efforts to stop the proliferation of nuclear weapons are focused mainly on Iran and North Korea.

    True______ False______

15. U.S. foreign aid has typically received widespread support from the American people.

    True______ False______

16. Why is America's dependence on foreign oil increasingly relevant to American foreign policy? What are some examples of how energy has affected U.S. foreign policy, both militarily and economically?

17. How has role of U.S. military power as a tool of influence over global affairs changed over time? What are the pros and cons of two other tools besides military power that the United States can use to influence global affairs? Why is a combination of tools likely to be needed?

20.6 Assess the role of democratic politics in making national security policy and the role of national security policy in expanding government.

18. Assess the extent to which U.S. national security policymaking is undemocratic. If a foreign policy decision is seen to be undemocratic, what is the likelihood that such a policy can be maintained by policymakers? Explain your answer.

19. How does national security policy contribute to an expanded scope of government? Can you think of any ways to reduce spending on national defense? In your opinion, would it be wise to do so? Why or why not?

PEARSON mypoliscilab Exercises

Apply what you learned in this chapter on MyPoliSciLab.

Read on **mypoliscilab.com**

eText: Chapter 20

Study and **Review** on **mypoliscilab.com**

Pre-Test
Post-Test
Chapter Exam
Flashcards

Watch on **mypoliscilab.com**

Video: Three Vivid Years – But Progress?
Video: NYC's Subway Surveillance System
Video: Sanctions on Iran

Explore on **mypoliscilab.com**

Simulation: You Are President John F. Kennedy
Simulation: You Are the President of the United States
Comparative: Comparing Foreign and Security Policy
Timeline: The Evolution of Foreign Policy
Visual Literacy: Evaluating Defense Spending

Key Terms

foreign policy (574)
United Nations (575)
North Atlantic Treaty Organization (575)
European Union (576)
secretary of state (578)
secretary of defense (578)
Joint Chiefs of Staff (578)
Central Intelligence Agency (579)
isolationism (581)
containment doctrine (582)
Cold War (582)
arms race (583)
détente (583)
interdependency (594)
tariff (596)
balance of trade (597)
Organization of Petroleum Exporting Countries (597)

Internet Resources

www.state.gov
Information about the Department of State and current foreign policy issues.

www.defenselink.mil
Information about the Department of Defense and current issues in national security policy.

https://www.cia.gov/library/publications/the-world-factbook/index.html
The *CIA World Factbook.*

www.oecd.org/home
The Organization for Economic Cooperation and Development provides a wealth of economic information on the world's nations.

www.nato.int
Contains background and activities of NATO.

www.un.org/en
Background on the United Nations and its varied programs.

www.cfr.org
The Council on Foreign Relations is the most influential private organization in the area of foreign policy. Its Web site includes a wide range of information on foreign policy.

www.whitehouse.gov/nsc
Information about the members and functions of the National Security Council.

www.foreignaffairs.com
Foreign Affairs, the leading magazine on foreign relations.

www.nctc.gov
The National Counterterrorism Center, with information on terrorism and on responses to terrorism.

For Further Reading

Brzezinski, Zbigniew. ***The Choice: Global Domination or Global Leadership.*** New York: Basic Books, 2004. An important critique of the Bush administration's national security strategy.

Easterly, William. ***The White Man's Burden.*** New York: Penguin, 2006. Why the West's efforts to aid the rest of the world have not been more effective.

Gordon, Philip H. ***Winning the Right War.*** New York: Times Books, 2007. A new way of thinking about the war on terror and a new strategy for winning it.

Howell, William G., and Jon C. Pevehouse. ***While Dangers Gather: Congressional Checks on Presidential War Powers.*** Princeton, NJ: Princeton University Press, 2007. Shows how Congress can influence decisions on war.

Huntington, Samuel P. ***The Clash of Civilizations and the Remaking of World Order.*** New York: Simon and Schuster, 1996. Argues that civilizational identities built on religious empires of the past will be the source of international turmoil in the next century.

Kagan, Donald. ***On the Origins of War and the Preservation of Peace.*** New York: Doubleday, 1995. Provides insights gleaned from studying the origins of great wars.

Mandelbaum, Michael. ***The Case for Goliath: How America Acts as the World's Government in the Twenty-First Century.*** New York: Public Affairs, 2006. Explains the ways in which the United States provides the world critical services, ranging from physical security to commercial regulation and financial stability.

Mead, Walter Russell. ***Power, Terror, Peace, and War.*** New York: Alfred A. Knopf, 2004. Analyzes America's grand strategy in national security.

Nye, Joseph S., Jr. ***The Paradox of American Power: Why the World's Only Superpower Can't Go It Alone.*** New York: Oxford University Press, 2002. Although the United States is militarily and economically supreme, it is increasingly dependent on other nations to accomplish its goals.

Nye, Joseph S., Jr. ***Soft Power: The Means to Success in World Politics.*** Cambridge, MA: Harvard University Press, 2004. Argues that national security hinges as much on winning hearts and minds as it does on winning wars.

Woodward, Bob. ***State of Denial.*** New York: Simon and Schuster, 2006. The inside story of decision making regarding the war with Iraq and its aftermath.

Yergin, Daniel. ***Shattered Peace: The Origins of the Cold War and the National Security State.*** Boston: Houghton Mifflin, 1977. An excellent political history of the early years of the Cold War and containment.

Zelizer, Julian. ***Arsenal of Democracy: The Politics of National Security—From World War II to the War on Terrorism.*** New York: Basic Books, 2009. Makes the case that domestic politics shapes foreign policies.

Chapter 21

The New Face of State and Local Government

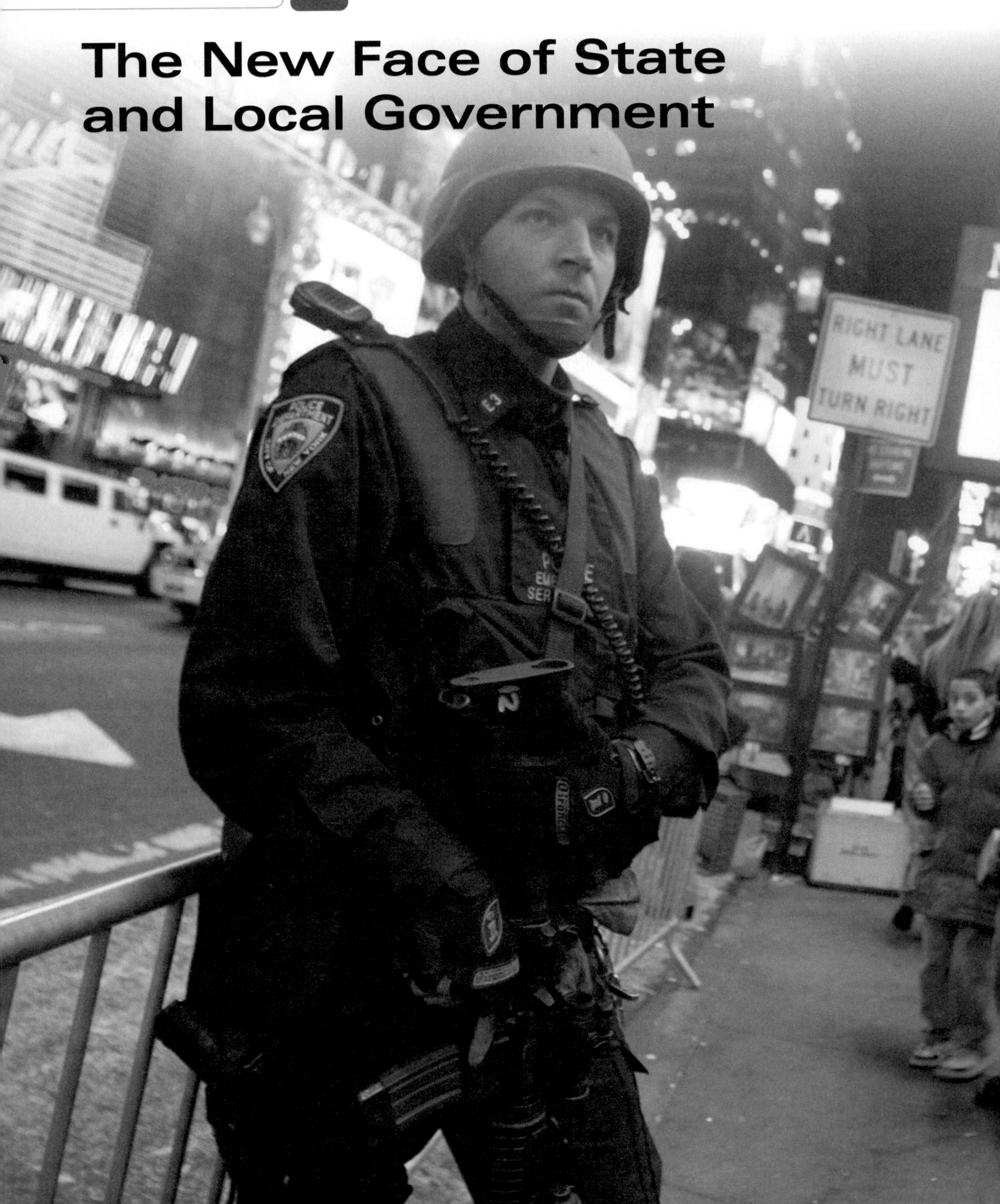

Learning Objectives

21.1 Describe how state constitutions differ and a common process for amending state constitutions.

21.2 Summarize recent patterns in partisan competition in state elections and party control in state government.

21.3 Outline the roles of responsibilities of governors and distinguish their formal and informal powers.

21.4 Describe the functions of state legislatures and contrast state legislators today with those of the past.

21.5 Outline the basic elements of most state court systems, and describe the various methods for selecting state judges.

21.6 Differentiate types of direct democracy, and evaluate direct democracy.

21.7 Explain Dillon's rule, and differentiate five types of local government.

21.8 Contrast state revenue and expenditures with local revenue and expenditures and outline ways state and local governments have tried to increase revenue.

21.9 Assess the democratic elements and the problems of state and local government.

POLITICS IN ACTION: SUBNATIONAL GOVERNMENTS AND HOMELAND SECURITY

Following the attacks of September 11, 2001, the national government passed laws that created new categories of crime for terrorist acts and increased the power of national law enforcement agencies. At the same time, state governments adopted laws regarding terrorist acts, consolidated agencies charged with law enforcement and emergency response, and took new steps to slow the flood of undocumented immigrants.

Traditionally, state and local governments have been responsible for most criminal justice policy and for maintaining the civil order in situations contained within state borders. However, the national government response to September 11 reflects growing national involvement in criminal justice policy. The states have been reluctant to forfeit their policymaking role or their role in prosecuting criminals. This competition has led some to suggest that states should maintain their traditional dominant role in criminal justice policy but defer to the national government in criminal justice issues involving national security, including terrorism, or confusion will abound.[1] Such an example occurred in 2002 as Maryland and Virginia argued with the national government over who would be the first to prosecute the accused terrorist in the Washington, D.C.-area sniper case, with Virginia arguing it should go first and make use of its new antiterrorism law.

The debate over government jurisdiction in criminal justice policy is important for several reasons. First, maintaining the civil order is the primary purpose for any government. Second, the ultimate power of the government comes from its ability to take away the rights and liberties of individuals. Our fear of this power led us to place limits on the government and to keep this power close at hand—with state and local governments.

Does increasing national involvement in criminal justice policy, from drug crimes to carjacking to terrorism, threaten our liberties more than traditional state and local government involvement in this area? If local and state officials are closer to citizens, do we lose some accountability over officials if the states defer to the national government? On the other hand, are state governments threatening the security of our homeland by adopting their own policies? Clearly there are no simple answers, but the questions reflect the tensions within our federalist system between levels of government and the difficulty of establishing distinct policy jurisdictions.

Chapter OUTLINE

subnational governments
State and local governments, which, with reform, modernization, and changing intergovernmental relations, have assumed new responsibilities and importance since the 1960s.

State and local governments, or **subnational governments**, touch our lives every day. They pick up our garbage, educate us, keep us safe from criminals, protect our water supply, and perform a myriad of other vital services. Odds are that you are attending a state or city university right now. You will drive home on locally maintained streets. Subnational governments regulate a wide range of business activities, from generating electric power to cutting hair. The state government is also the single largest employer in every state; moreover, local governments, taken together, employ even more people than do the states. So, as a consumer of government services, as a regulated businessperson, and/or as an employee, we live lives that are intimately touched by subnational governments.

WHY IT MATTERS

State Boundaries and Public Policy

State boundaries typically result from historical accidents rather than efforts to define regions that have similar interests and needs. For example, the people of the Florida Panhandle probably have more in common with those of southern Alabama and Georgia than those of South Florida. But what if the states were reconstructed so as to make them more homogeneous and therefore more different from one another? How do you think this would affect state policy? For example, would state policies also be more dissimilar? Would citizens be happier with the policies in their state?

Nonetheless, not that long ago, some political observers predicted that state governments would soon cease to exist.[2] The states seemed to them archaic accidents of history rather than meaningful political entities. For example, how could one possibly equate Wyoming, with just over a half million people and 5 people per square mile, to California, with over 36 million people and 234 people per square mile? What do Hawaii and Alaska have in common with Rhode Island and Louisiana as political entities? Some critics in the 1950s and 1960s thought, "Not much." State governments were ridiculed as being "horse-and-buggy" institutions in an era of space travel.[3] Their institutions were seen as weak, outdated, resource poor, and simply not up to the task of running a modern government. Moreover, social liberals saw the states as obstacles to addressing the grievances of racial and ethnic minorities and urban dwellers—witness Governor George Wallace's stand against the racial integration of Alabama schools (Chapter 3). The national government was seen as the driver of progressive policymaking, and the states were encouraged to step aside or get replaced.

But as Mark Twain said about his mistaken obituary, these reports of the death of the states were greatly exaggerated. Through a process of reform, modernization, and changing intergovernmental relations since the 1960s, subnational governments have become more vital to our democratic system than ever. They have assumed new and costly responsibilities in areas such as social welfare, education, health, issues related to immigration, economic development, and criminal justice. (To read about state action on immigration, see "My State: How Have States Responded to Illegal Immigration?") States and localities have also gained importance as national policymakers have confronted budgetary limits and policymakers have recognized the virtues of grass-roots democracy—of giving decision-making power to governments closer to the people.

In this chapter, we discuss subnational government with an eye toward two important characteristics: *revitalization* and *diversity*. Since the early 1960s, the states have become revitalized in their institutions, their personnel, and their role in the federal system.[6] State legislatures, governors' offices, courts, and even bureaucracies have undergone dramatic changes that have allowed them to move forward as strong and active players in the U.S. policymaking process. The people involved in governing the states and localities are more representative of their constituents than was previously the case, and they tend to be better educated and more professionalized and have greater policy expertise. With the weight of the philosophical argument about where policymaking power should lie in the federal system swinging mostly toward the states for the past four decades (Chapter 3), the national government has provided states and localities with increasing control over many policy areas.

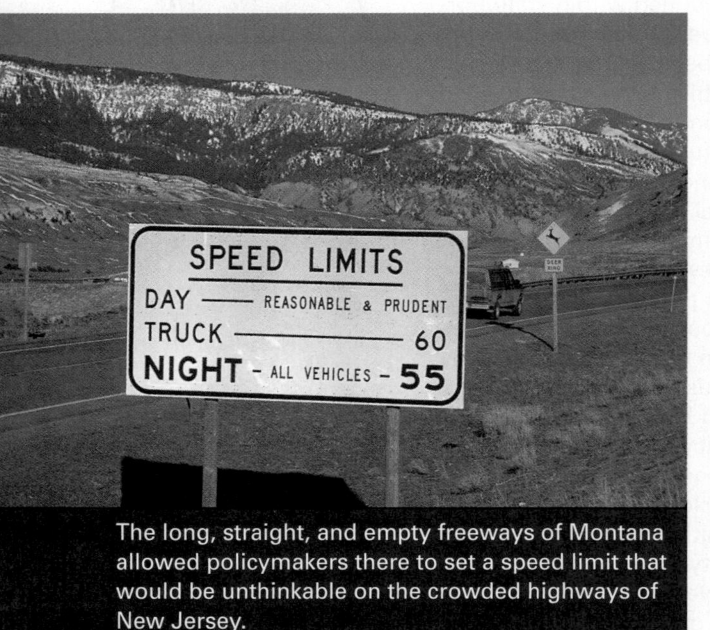

The long, straight, and empty freeways of Montana allowed policymakers there to set a speed limit that would be unthinkable on the crowded highways of New Jersey.

The second characteristic important to understanding subnational government in the United States is diversity. As anyone who has ever traveled outside his or her hometown knows, government, policy, and political behavior differ from place to place. For example, in California, citizens can propose and pass laws through the ballot box; in Delaware, they can't. On the freeways of New Jersey, you may legally drive no faster than 65 miles per hour, whereas until recently in Montana, the only limit was your own judgment and the power of your car's engine. In South Dakota, almost twice

How Have States Responded to Illegal Immigration?

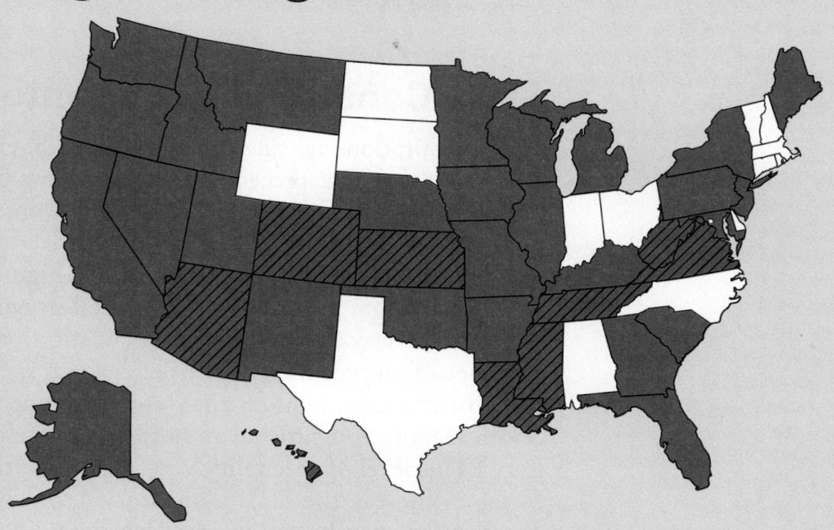

Source: National Conference of State Legislatures, "State Laws related to Immigration and Immigrants," August 9, 2010. http://www.ncsl.org/default.aspx?tabid=19897.

Estimates suggest that more than 12 million people illegally reside in the United States. Despite an increase in illegal immigration, the national government has not adopted any significant policies to address the issue since the late 1980s. In 2006 and 2007, as Congress again failed to act on this issue, states began to adopt new policies to address local problems stemming from illegal immigration. Some of these policies try to address problems faced by children whose parents are illegal immigrants; for example, in 2008, six states adopted policies to provide health insurance to the children of illegal immigrants. Others aim to discourage illegal immigration; for example, by 2009, Missouri, Mississippi, Utah, and South Carolina joined a growing list of states that imposed new requirements on employers to check the identities of job applicants. During the 2009 state legislative sessions, the 50 states considered over 1,500 bills and resolutions related to immigration, nearly three times the number considered in 2006. At least 353 of these bills and resolutions were adopted.[4] The map shows states that enacted immigration laws related to hiring unauthorized workers, including employment eligibility verification requirements and penalties, as well as measures that limit or eliminate unemployment benefits and worker's compensation, from 2006 to August 2010; a total of 110 such laws were enacted in 36 states. Shaded states adopted some employment related law while shaded states with lines adopted laws that provide specific and direct penalties above and beyond federal law, such as fines or loss of license, to private companies found to be employing illegal or undocumented workers.[5]

QUESTIONS FOR DISCUSSION

- Making use of the Immigration Policy page at the National Conference of State Legislatures Web page (www.ncsl.org), investigate what employment related immigration legislation your state considered in recent legislative sessions. What legislation has it adopted since 2006? If none, what actions have neighboring states taken on this issue? Do you observe any regional patterns in the policies adopted?
- What problems does immigration pose in your state?
- How does your state benefit from immigration?

the proportion of eligible voters cast votes as in Louisiana during any given election. To understand this diversity among the states is to understand the politics and history of the United States better. Why do these differences exist and what effects do they have?

State Constitutions

> **21.1** Describe how state constitutions differ and a common process for amending state constitutions.

Each state is governed by a separate and unique constitution that spells out the basic rules of that state's political game. Thus, although every state elects a governor as its chief executive officer and every state except Nebraska has a legislature with two chambers, the states endow their governors with different powers and organize and elect their legislatures differently. Each state's constitution was written under unique historical conditions and with a unique set of philosophical principles in mind. Each is different in its length and provisions. Some are modern documents with recent revisions; others were written 200 years ago and are largely unchanged. The differences among these documents also reflect the diversity—social, economic, geographic, historic, and political—of the states.[7]

State Constitutions in Context

State constitutions are subordinate to the U.S. Constitution and the laws of the United States, but they take precedence over state law. State constitutions share many features with the U.S. Constitution. Like the U.S. Constitution, they provide for separation of powers—for executive, judicial, and legislative branches, and for means of taxation and finance—and they include a bill of rights. Figure 21.1 shows how the Texas state constitution arranges the state's governmental structure.

The key way in which the state constitutions differ from the U.S. Constitution is that they often provide far more detail about specific policies. The Oklahoma constitution, for example, requires that "stock feeding" be taught in public schools, and the South Dakota constitution authorizes a twine and cordage plant at its state penitentiary.[8] This level of specificity leads to constitutions that are long and sometimes confusing. Whereas the U.S. Constitution is a brief document of 8,700 words, state constitutions can be as long as Alabama's 220,000-word tome. (In Southern states, where most constitutions were rewritten after the Civil War, state constitutions tend to be longer and more particularistic.) A few states, however, try to stick to the point as closely as the national constitution does—Vermont's constitution, adopted in 1793, is a model of brevity with only 6,880 words.

Why do some states try to embed specific policy into what is supposed to be a document detailing fundamental principles and government organization? It has long been argued that powerful interest groups have encouraged lengthy constitutions in order to protect their interests. That is, it is far more difficult to amend a state constitution than to change a law, so activists try to include policy statements in the constitution in order to guard against their future repeal. Even so, because the amendment process is often difficult, some argue that longer constitutions help limit government interference with Americans' valued individualism.[9]

Amending State Constitutions

Periodically, a state considers changes to the basic rules of its political game. Most avoid the politically difficult process of writing an entirely new constitution. Massachusetts, for example, is still governed by a constitution written in 1780. Mississippi, Nebraska, New York, and Utah are among 29 states that have nineteenth-century constitutions. Although a few states have attempted to write entirely new constitutions since World War II (the most recent successful attempt being Georgia in 1983), most states have adapted their governing documents to modern times by the "cut-and-paste" method of constitutional amendment. Indeed, California has amended its constitution 493 times since 1879.

The most common way that state constitutions are amended is through a two-step process (usually referred to as a referendum) by which the legislature "proposes" an amendment (usually by passing a resolution to this effect by a vote of two-thirds of the legislature and in 12 states doing so in two consecutive sessions) and a majority vote in the next general election "ratifies" it. Although this process is difficult, it is used every election year, typically for taxation and public debt issues. In many states, constitutions may also be amended through citizen-proposed initiatives, either direct (from voters and directly to the ballot) or indirect (from voters to the legislature first), approved by a

FIGURE 21.1 Government Under the Texas State Constitution

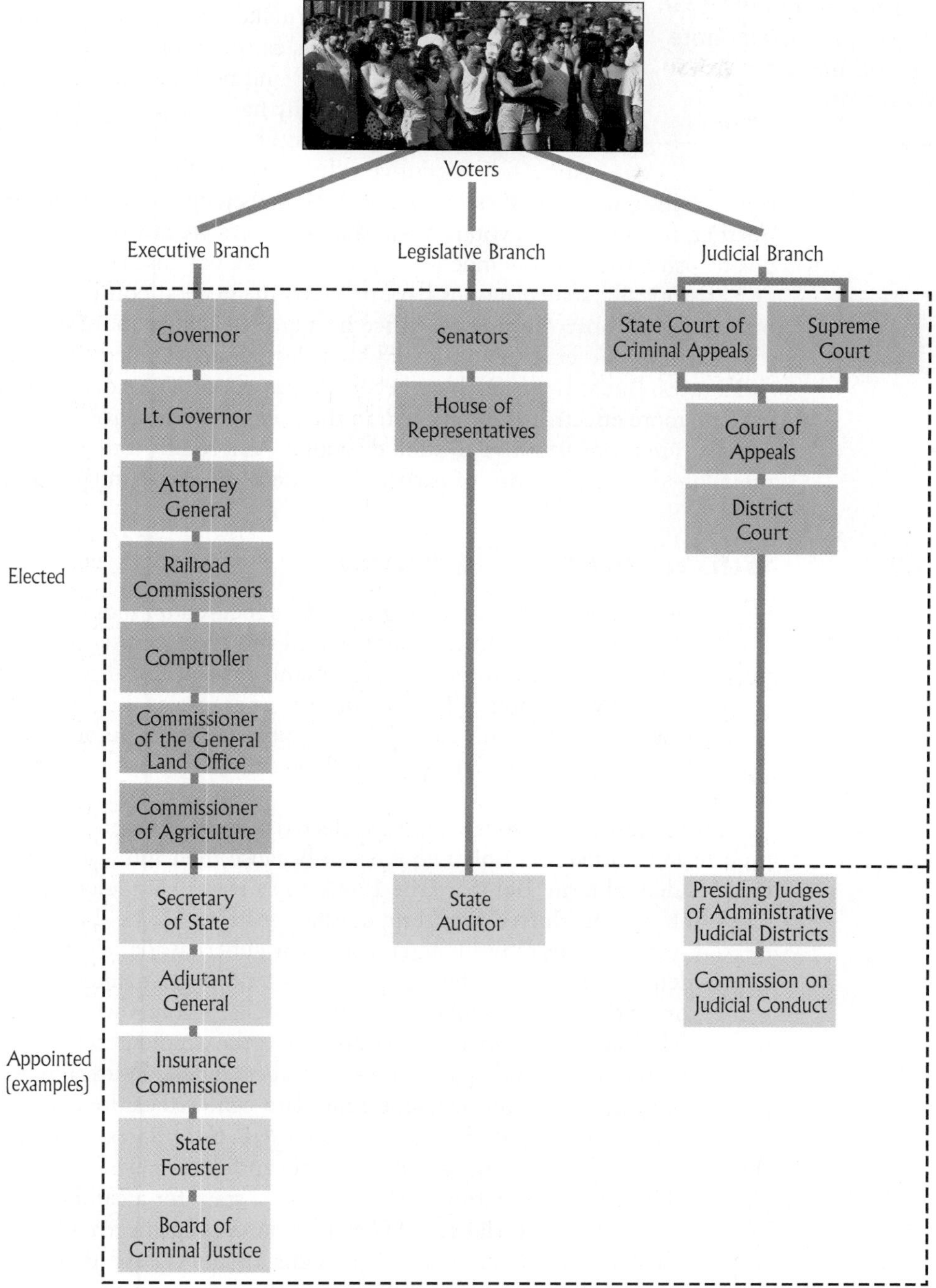

Source: Council of State Governments, 2008.

majority vote in the next general election. Across all states between 1898 and 1998, 827 initiatives and referenda for constitutional amendments were proposed and voters approved 343 (42 percent) of the measures.[10] Although rarely used, a constitutional convention is another tool for amending state constitutions; for example, in 2004 and 2005 Massachusetts legislators invoked a constitutional convention, in which they attempted, but failed, to amend the constitution and overturn a court ruling that allowed same-sex marriage.

21.2 Summarize recent patterns in partisan competition in state elections and party control in state government.

State Elections

Most top-level state policymakers are elected to office. Thus, whereas at the national level voters can elect only one member of the executive branch (the president) and no member of the judicial branch, at the state level voters usually have far more power to determine who governs them. For example, in California, voters select eight statewide executive officers (including the governor, treasurer, and even the insurance commissioner) as well as many judges down to the trial court level.[11] Further, in some states, voters are authorized to make law directly through the ballot box by using the direct democracy mechanisms we will discuss shortly.

Historically, state elections have reflected the general political mood of the country or state, with those running for office having little ability to influence their own electoral fortunes. Voters cared little and knew less about state legislative or even gubernatorial races. But as the states have become more important and as their institutions have become more effective and respected in the past generation, average voters and political activists are more attentive to state elections. As a result, state officials look more like their constituents, in terms of partisanship, ideology, and demographics.

Gubernatorial Elections

Gubernatorial races have increasingly become focused on individual candidates rather than party affiliations. Political scientists call this the "presidentialization" of gubernatorial elections since they have come to resemble the personality-focused modern campaigns for the White House. This has occurred because of the increasing importance to gubernatorial campaigns of television and, subsequently, of money, and because of the decoupling of gubernatorial races from presidential races and state political party organizations.[12]

Historically, most governors were elected during presidential years, either because their term of office was only two years or because their four-year term coincided with the presidential term. But since the 1960s, most states have adopted a four-year gubernatorial term and shifted that term so that elections are held during nonpresidential election years. Today, only 11 states hold their gubernatorial elections at the same time as presidential elections.[13] The change means that in most states the gubernatorial race is the "top of the ticket," which makes it more likely voters will pay attention and that races will be decided on what voters think about the candidates, rather than on the popularity or unpopularity of a party's presidential candidate. Political scientists refer to the pattern of running on your own as a "candidate-centered campaign."[14]

In order to run on their own, gubernatorial candidates have taken to television advertising in a big way, just as presidential candidates have, and largely for the same reasons. There are simply too many people in a state for a candidate to meet them all face-to-face. Gubernatorial candidates hire nationally known advertising agencies to develop slick ad campaigns. These campaigns are not cheap; use of television is one of the main reasons why the costs of gubernatorial campaigns have skyrocketed. For elections between 1977 and 1980, the total cost of gubernatorial primary and general elections was $524 million (adjusted to 2006 dollars); for elections between 2003 and 2006, that cost increased by 107 percent, to $1,084 million. Although the largest states have some of the most expensive elections overall, if we adjust for the cost per general election vote, we find that 2002-2006 election costs were the highest in New Hampshire at $47.16 per vote, and much less in a larger state like Virginia at $24.03 per vote. However, collectively the elections in California and Texas are the most expensive, with the average costs of the last five races in California at $114 million and in Texas at $59 million, and the California gubernatorial recall election in 2003 alone costing nearly $204 million.[15]

Most of this money has to be raised by the candidates themselves. At one time, state political party organizations had a strong hand both in funding these campaigns and in selecting the party nominees. Those days are long gone in most states. With the

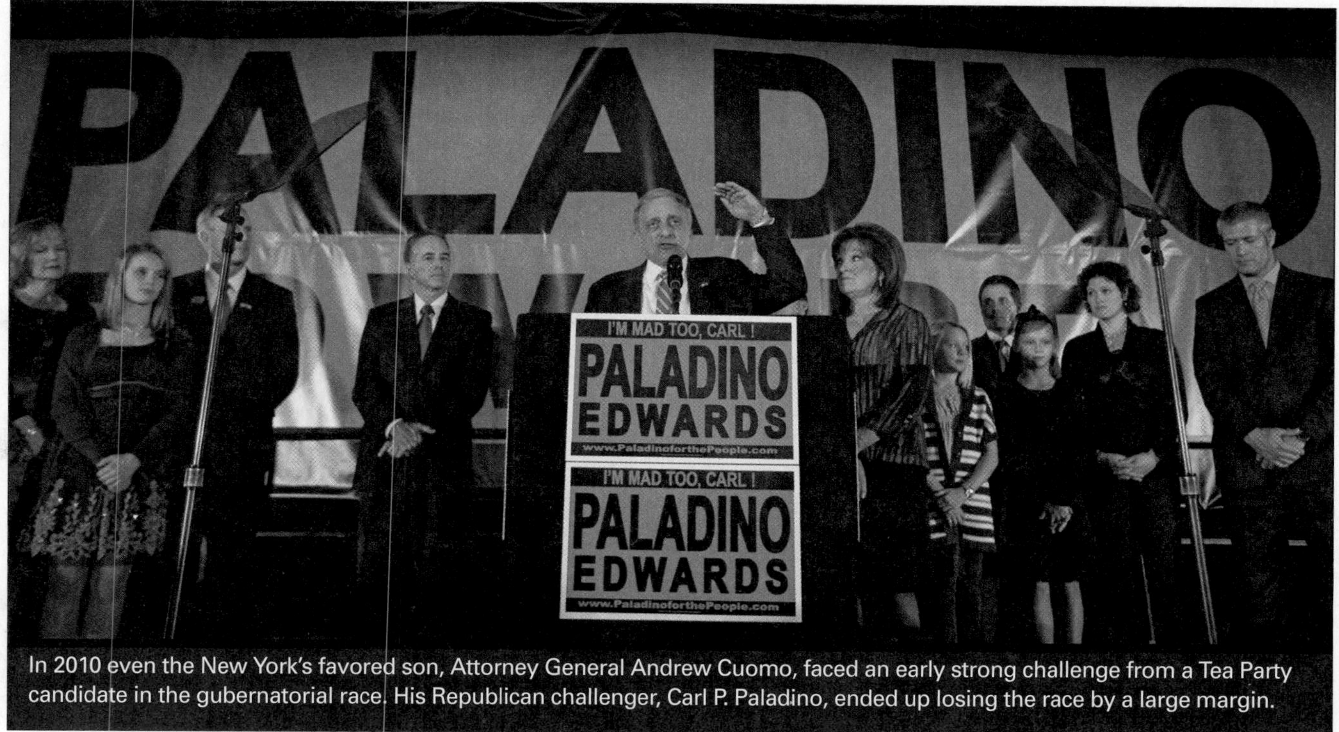

In 2010 even the New York's favored son, Attorney General Andrew Cuomo, faced an early strong challenge from a Tea Party candidate in the gubernatorial race. His Republican challenger, Carl P. Paladino, ended up losing the race by a large margin.

advent of the direct primary for nominating party candidates, a person who wants to become governor must organize and fund a major campaign in the primary. And by the time a candidate wins the primary, he or she has built a solid campaign organization and has little need for the party's help in the general election.

One result of the personalization of gubernatorial elections has been that parties have a harder time predicting their success. Because voters now become familiar with gubernatorial candidates during campaigns, they more frequently vote based on their attitude toward the candidates rather than on party loyalty. This can lead to ticket splitting and divided government, as votes for less well-known state legislative candidates do tend to be based on party affiliation.[16] We see the results of this when states whose voters are predominantly of one party elect governors of the other party. For example, in 2009, New Jersey voters elected Republican Christopher Christie to the governorship, even though registered Democratic voters outnumber registered Republicans in the state, and Democrats maintained majorities in the 2008–2010 state legislative session. At the extreme, this has led to four Independent governors being elected since 1992, including true independents Angus King of Maine (Independent) and Jesse Ventura of Minnesota (Reform Party).

State Legislative Elections

Of all state- and national-level officials, state legislators have the smallest constituencies, ranging from fewer than 3,000 people in a New Hampshire House of Representatives district to almost 800,000 people in a California Senate district, but with an average size of about 50,000 for state house districts and 140,000 for state senate districts.[17] By comparison, governors (600,000 to 57 million constituents) and members of the U.S. House of Representatives (average 646,952 constituents) need to respond to considerably more constituents.

Reapportionment and Campaign Finance As the twentieth century progressed, it was clear that state legislatures were becoming horribly malapportioned, giving greater representation to rural areas than their population warranted. Districts were often constructed on the basis of the boundaries of some local government, such as a county, regardless of how many people lived there. In the nineteenth century, most

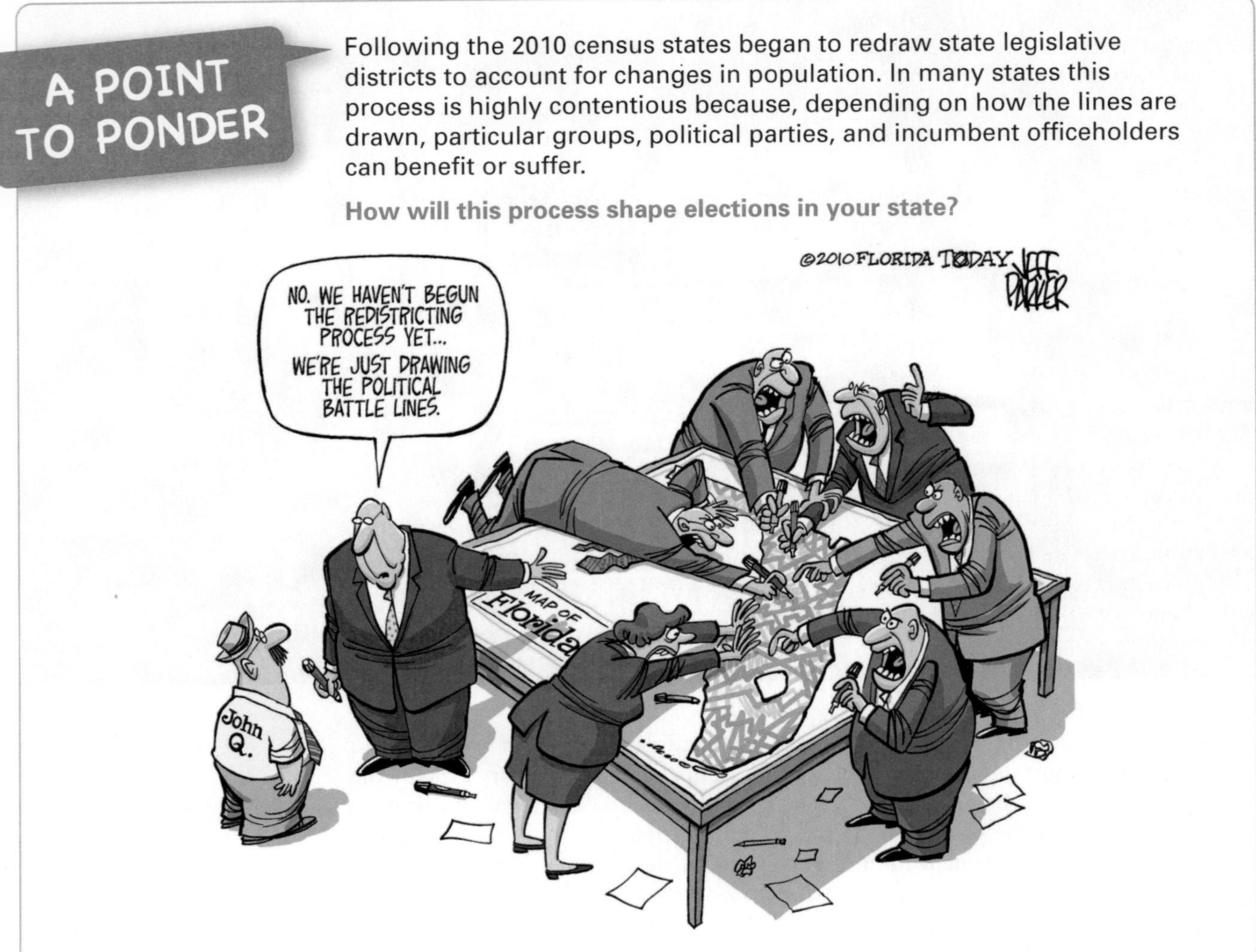

Following the 2010 census states began to redraw state legislative districts to account for changes in population. In many states this process is highly contentious because, depending on how the lines are drawn, particular groups, political parties, and incumbent officeholders can benefit or suffer.

How will this process shape elections in your state?

state legislators represented rural areas and that was where people lived. By the 1960s, the population had become overwhelmingly urban; however, since the legislative district boundaries had rarely changed, state legislatures continued to be dominated by rural politicians. With counties as the basis of districts, in many states rural counties with a few thousand residents and urban counties with hundreds of thousands of residents all had the same representation in the state legislature.

In 1962, after decades of avoiding the issue, the U.S. Supreme Court ruled that the districts of the lower chamber of state legislatures must be based on the number of people living in them. This landmark decision in *Baker v. Carr* established the principle of "one person, one vote" in drawing up state house districts. Two years later, the Court ruled in *Reynolds v. Sims* that state senates must also be apportioned in this fashion.

These cases dramatically changed the face of state legislatures. Gone was the rural dominance of these chambers. New representatives arrived from the central cities and suburbs. Urban and metropolitan area problems became the focus of state legislatures.

Periodic redrawing of legislative districts is required as population shifts. This is now done following every decennial census, further changing the composition of state legislatures. The late-twentieth-century migration of citizens to the suburbs resulted in new voting power for suburban metropolitan interests and a decline in the power of central cities.

Ironically, although state legislators have the smallest districts, they are the elected officials that voters know the least well. This is largely due to the historic lack of media coverage given to state legislatures and lack of campaign resources of candidates for the office. The result is that races for state legislature tended to be decided on the basis of forces beyond candidates' control—party identification of district voters and the parties' candidates in the race for governor and president.[18]

But with the recent shifting of more policy responsibilities to the states and increases in state legislative salaries (discussed shortly) making the office both more important and more attractive, campaigns for the state legislature have started to become more candidate-centered, although not nearly to the extent that gubernatorial campaigns have. This "congressionalization" of state legislative races—the emergence of more-candidate-centered campaigns, in which, as with congressional races, parties nonetheless do play an important role—is encouraged by increased resources (mainly staff and time) available to incumbent legislators seeking to retain their seats, and by the increasing willingness of political action committees (PACs) at the state level to contribute to expensive campaigns.[19] Campaign costs skyrocketed for state legislative campaigns beginning in the 1980s and continue to be high today, with candidates in large states such as California and Illinois finding it necessary to raise at least $200,000; highly competitive races might cost over $2 million. Although it is still possible to run a less closely contested campaign in a less populous state for only several thousand dollars, this is no longer the norm.[20]

The need to raise and spend more money on these campaigns favors incumbent legislators. Incumbents can use the resources and prestige of office both to enhance their visibility with their constituents and to attract campaign contributions from PACs and others interested in garnering favor in the legislature. State legislative leaders also help incumbents through their own PACs and party funds in order to enhance their personal influence as leaders and the prospects of their party retaining or regaining control of their chamber.[21]

Partisan Competition, Legislative Turnover, and Term Limits Recent decades have seen trends in state legislatures toward increasing party competition, closer partisan splits, and changing party control. Much of the increase in party competition has occurred as a result of Republican gains in the South (for example, both the lower and upper chambers of the South Carolina and Florida state legislatures now have a majority of Republicans), although Northern states have also been experiencing increasingly competitive elections. Nevertheless, Democrats have recently regained a slight advantage in partisan control of state legislative seats nationally; following the 2008–2009 elections, Democrats held 55 percent of all seats in state legislatures, stemming what had been a downward trend since the 1980s.[22]

Although some state legislative chambers have very lopsided partisan splits (for example, in the Idaho state senate Republicans hold 80 percent of the seats, and in the Massachusetts state senate Democrats hold 87 percent), others are closely divided. In 15 legislative chambers (of 99), four or fewer seats separate the parties. The Alaska senate is an extreme case, with exactly 10 Republicans and 10 Democrats. And, following the 2008–2009 elections, 10 chambers changed majority party control or are now equally split between the parties.[23] However, consistent with the trend mentioned above, even as party competition has increased in some states, such as Maine, it has declined in others, such as Illinois. And the percentage of contested legislative seats varies widely across the states, with some states seeing a large increase in contested seats (Missouri) from the 1970s to the 2000s but others actually seeing significant declines (Pennsylvania).[24]

Divided government exists when a single party does not control both chambers of the state legislature and the governor's office. With divided government, it is usually much more difficult for coherent policy action to take place because the parties that control the different components of state government have conflicting policy and electoral goals. Increased party competition and switching of party control have inevitably led to more divided control of state government than in the past, when party affiliation of voters within states was more stable and electorates more homogeneous.[25] After the 2008–2009 elections, 23 states had divided government (see Table 21.1); in contrast, in 1946 only 7 states did. The increase in divided government, along with the increases in

TABLE 21.1 The Balance of Power, 2010

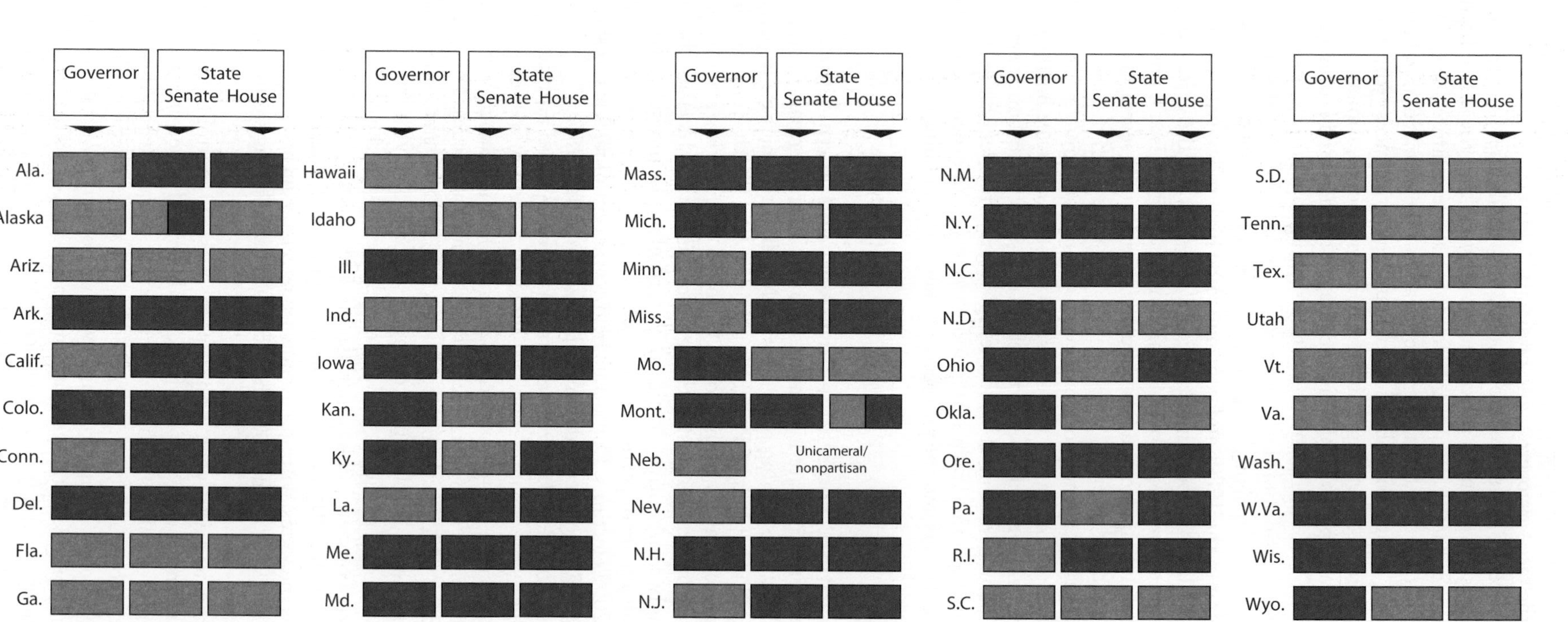

Source: National Conference of State Legislatures. 2010. "2008–09 (Post-election) Partisan Composition of State Legislatures," February 10, 2010, http://ecom.ncsl.org/programs/legismgt/statevote/partycomptable2009print.htm.

party competition and switching of party control, has tended to increase legislative partisan voting behavior and polarize legislative deliberations, thereby making compromise harder to come by. Further, this sort of swinging from party to party can lead to a lack of policy continuity in a state. On the other hand, high levels of party competition tend to make elected officials more attentive and responsive to voters.[26]

Aside from partisan change, there is the question of turnover in state legislatures. Turnover levels—the rate that state legislators are replaced from election to election—give us an understanding both of how much experience and expertise state legislators have relative to other political actors in the states and of how closely they are connected to their constituencies.

Recent history suggests that in any 10-year period, about 75 percent of state senate and 77 percent of state house legislative seats are turned over.[27] Thus, significant change in the people holding state legislative office is the norm. The current average annual turnover rate in any election year is about 26 percent in lower chambers and 23 percent in upper chambers.[28] Pennsylvania and Missouri had the lowest average percent turnover, in their senates—less than 10 percent. Oregon and Colorado had the highest average turnover rates, also in their senates—48 and 35 percent, respectively.[29]

In recent years, voters in many states have attempted to increase turnover rates by legally restricting the number of terms a member may serve. Increasingly, voters appear to support the argument that professional, career-oriented legislators become so entrenched and difficult to unseat that they lose touch with their constituents and instead pander to special interests. Since 1990, 21 states have adopted term limits for state legislators, almost exclusively through direct democracy mechanisms (discussed shortly). However, six states have seen their term limits overturned, either in court or by the state legislature, leaving only 15 term-limit laws intact.[30] The number of terms permitted varies from state to state. California, for example, limits its assembly (lower house) members to six years (three terms) and its senators to eight years (two terms).[31] The effect of term limits also varies. In the 2002 elections, term-limited states had turnover rates in lower chambers that were 13 percent higher than those of non–term-limited states and turnover rates in upper chambers that were 9 percent higher. In some states the effects of term limits is quite dramatic. For example, 40 percent of Michigan House members were term-limited out of office in 2008.[32]

The Changing Face of State Elected Officials

In 1996, Washington state voters chose Gary Locke as its governor, and he became the first Asian American to be elected governor of one of the 48 contiguous states. And in 2007 Piyush "Bobby" Jindal was elected governor of Louisiana, becoming the first American governor of Indian-American descent as well as the first nonwhite governor of that state. Although governors have traditionally been white men (generally married, often lawyers), state voters are increasingly electing a wider variety of people as governors and other state officials.

In 1998, women were elected to all five statewide executive offices in Arizona—governor, secretary of state, treasurer, superintendent of public instruction, and attorney general. The so-called Fab Five were sworn into office by another powerful Arizona female—U.S. Supreme Court Justice Sandra Day O'Connor.

Women have made strong inroads into the governors' offices (see Figure 21.2). Before 1974, only a few women had ever been governors, and those were elected because they were married to a former governor who could not run again. But in 1974, Ella Grasso was elected to the governor's office of Connecticut in her own right, and in 1976 Dixie Lee Ray followed her in Washington. Since 1925, a total of 33 women have served as governors

FIGURE 21.2 Female Representation in State Government

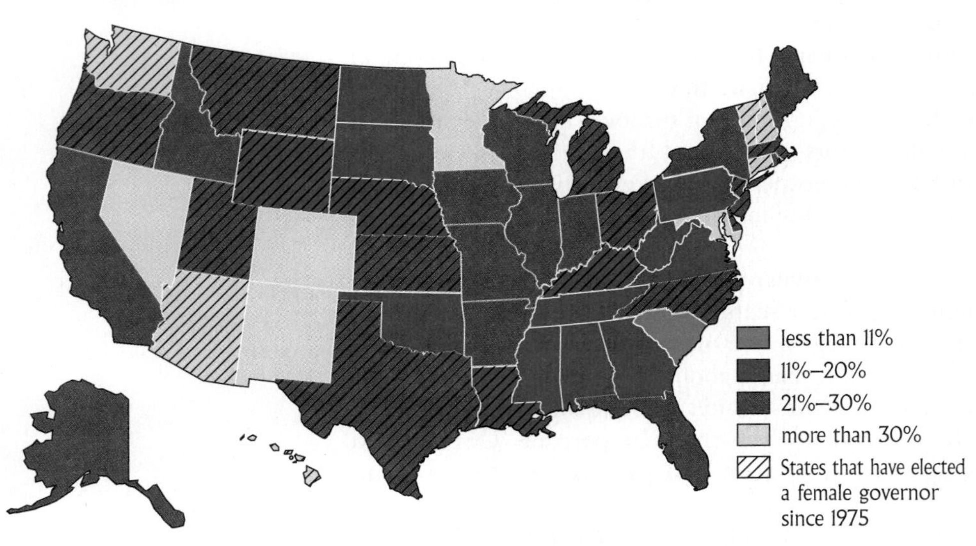

Percentage of females in the state legislature in 2009.

Source: Center for American Women and Politics, "Facts on Women Officeholders," August 7, 2010, http://www.cawp.rutgers.edu/fast_facts/index.php.

(29 since 1975) in states as varied as Delaware, Oregon, Kansas, and Kentucky, representing both the Democratic and Republican parties. In 2006, 36 states held gubernatorial elections; women ran in nine of these elections, winning in six of the nine. In 2010, there were six female state governors and 13 female lieutenant governors.

State legislatures, too, have been looking more and more like the diverse population of the United States.[33] In 2010, 24.3 percent of all state legislators were women, a tremendous increase over the 1969 figure of about 4 percent.[34] Women are also taking more leadership roles in state legislatures, serving in such positions as senate or house majority leader. In 2010, for example, there were 58 women in legislative leadership positions. However, as you can see in Figure 21.2, state legislatures do vary widely in the percentage of female legislators; during the 2010 legislative session, this figure ranged from almost 38 percent in New Hampshire to just 10 percent in South Carolina. The number and percentage of state legislators who are African American have also been increasing over this same period, so that in 2009, for example, 628, or 9 percent, of state legislators were African Americans. Latinos and Asians have also been increasing in their state legislative representation, primarily in Florida and the Western states; in 2009, 3 percent of state legislators were Latino, and in 2008, 1 percent of state legislators were Asian American.[35]

Although at historic highs, the percentages of women and ethnic minorities in state elected positions are still less than representative, showing the slowness with which progress is made. Yet the inroads that women and minorities are making in state and local offices may well also lead to them being elected more frequently to national positions. For example, a sharp jump in the number of women in the U.S. Senate in the 1990s was encouraged by increases in women being elected to state legislative positions in the 1970s and 1980s.

21.3 Outline the roles of responsibilities of governors and distinguish their formal and informal powers.

Governors and the Executive Branch

During his first several months as governor of California in 2003 and 2004, Arnold Schwarzenegger traveled to Israel, Japan, and China to promote investment in California industries, such as biotechnology, and to promote trade between those countries and his state.

Schwarzenegger also appeared in television commercials aired oversees that promoted California. Such actions are becoming increasingly common for governors who are interested in creating more economic growth, even though they have no legal capacity to sign formal trade agreements with foreign nations.

Governors' involvement in promoting economic growth highlights the modern role of the governor. Not only is the governor the chief executive officer of a state, with the responsibility to execute the laws passed by the legislature, but he or she is also the best-known state public official, to whom the public looks for leadership, assurance, conflict resolution, and policy initiatives. If administering public policy is the governor's main constitutional responsibility, then promoting his or her vision of what public policy ought to be is the modern governor's primary responsibility to the public.

The Job of Governor

Like presidents, governors are expected to wear many hats—sometimes fulfilling constitutionally assigned duties, sometimes performing political tasks. But the powers of governors are not always commensurate with citizens' expectations. State constitutions often hamstring a governor, dividing executive power among many different administrative actors and agencies. To some extent, a generation of modernization and reform has resulted in enhanced powers for governors by reducing the number of independently elected officials and independent boards and commissions in the state executive branch, as well as by enhancing governors' other formal powers.[36] These reforms have established clearer lines of authority and enhanced the governor's appointment, reorganization, and budgetary powers. Most states have also increased the number of years a governor can serve and increased their salaries. Nevertheless, the limited formal powers of governors make it very difficult for them to fulfill their responsibilities to the state without resorting to more "informal powers," such as the use of the media and a public relations staff.

How powerful are the nation's governors? Political scientist Thad Beyle has devoted considerable attention to this subject. He has rated the institutional powers of the governor of each of the states, based on an analysis of gubernatorial powers outlined in state constitutions and statutes and on the strength of the governor's party in the state legislature. Figure 21.3 displays these ratings, which may change from year to year but reflect in a general way the governor's ability to stay in office, make major appointments, prepare

FIGURE 21.3 Institutional Powers of the Governors

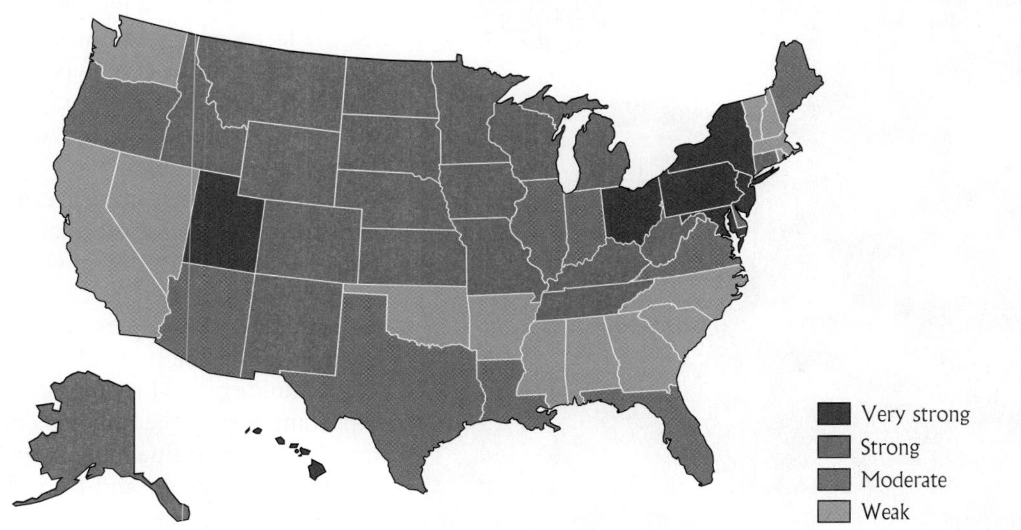

Source: Adapted from Thad Beyle and Margaret Ferguson, "Governors and the Executive Branch," in *Politics in the American States*, 9th ed., ed. Virginia Gray and Russell L. Hanson (Washington, DC: Congressional Quarterly Press, 2008), 192–228.

the state budget, veto legislation, and direct political parties. Governors of seven states—Hawaii, Maryland, New Jersey, New York, Ohio, Pennsylvania, and Utah—have very strong powers. Of the other governors, 18 have strong powers, 10 have moderate powers, and 15—in states as diverse as Massachusetts, California, and Nevada—have only weak powers.[37]

Two of a governor's most important formal powers for controlling state government are the veto and the executive budget. The governor's veto is similar to that of the president—a governor can refuse to sign a bill passed by the state legislature, blocking it from becoming law. But in most states, the governor's veto power is far more potent than the president's. First, gubernatorial vetoes have been very difficult for state legislatures to override historically, and this remains true today.[38] Although state legislatures have become more aggressive in overriding vetoes in recent years, still less than 10 percent of gubernatorial vetoes are overridden.

line-item veto
The power possessed by 42 state governors to veto only certain parts of a bill while allowing the rest of it to pass into law.

Further, 42 state governors have the **line-item veto**, which allows them to veto only certain parts of a bill while allowing the rest of the bill to pass into law. This keeps the legislature from being able to force the governor to sign a popular bill with a provision that the governor thinks is unwise. The line-item veto is especially useful on appropriations bills, allowing the governor to trim pork barrel spending as he or she sees fit. In Wisconsin, the governor is even allowed to veto individual words and letters from a bill, sometimes changing its basic meaning. In 1987, newly elected Governor Tommy Thompson, a Republican, used this power over 350 times on the budget passed by Wisconsin's Democratic legislature.[39] With the power of the line-item veto, a governor with a sizable minority in the legislature to support him or her can force or cajole the legislature into passing much of his or her agenda.

In almost all states, the governor also has the power to initiate the state budget process. This process, which usually begins with an annual "State of the State" address, allows the governor to set the agenda for what is by far the most important bill(s) of the state legislative session. The budget details how state tax dollars are going to be spent—it is where state public policy "puts up or shuts up." Although the legislature may amend and must pass the governor's proposal as it does any other bill, the limited staff and session time of most state legislatures, especially compared to that available to the governor, makes the massive budget sent by the governor difficult to change substantially. Further, since the governor has the ability to veto—and sometimes line-item veto—the budget passed by the legislature, he or she also has the last word in the process. This enables a governor to gain help for his or her policy goals from both state legislators and bureaucrats interested in furthering their own policy goals through state spending.

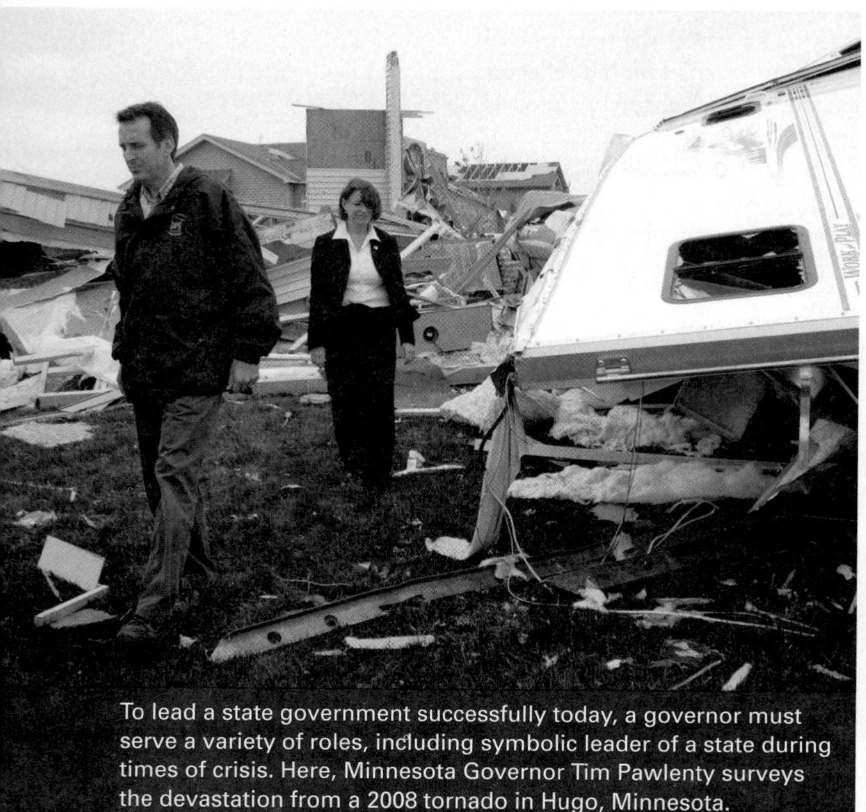
To lead a state government successfully today, a governor must serve a variety of roles, including symbolic leader of a state during times of crisis. Here, Minnesota Governor Tim Pawlenty surveys the devastation from a 2008 tornado in Hugo, Minnesota.

To enhance their influence, governors supplement their formal institutional powers with more "personal powers."[40] A governor's real power depends on the way he or she uses character, leadership style, and persuasive abilities in conjunction with the formal prerogatives of the office. Building public support is an increasingly important part of the policymaking process. It is important for influencing legislative decision making in all states—and for influencing citizen behavior in states with direct democracy mechanisms. For example, in 2004, California Governor Schwarzenegger expended most of his informal powers in a failed attempt to generate public support for ballot propositions concerning government finances rather than trying to influence legislators.

Not surprisingly, public relations and media experts have become a key part of many governors' staffs. Although press coverage of state politics is intermittent at best, focusing on only the most salient controversies and such predictable events as the governor's State of the State Address, a savvy governor can create media events and opportunities that enhance his or her popularity and political clout. Whether it is Texas Governor Rick Perry meeting with the president of Mexico or Florida Governor Charlie Crist attending a rally with President Obama on federal stimulus funds for the states, the media image of a caring, active, busy governor can be parlayed into political clout with the legislature and executive agencies. Of course, governors must also use their media experts to try to control media frenzies, including situations of their own creation. South Carolina Governor Mark Sanford faced rabid media attention following a reporter's discovery that he took a secret trip to Argentina in 2009 to continue an extramarital affair. With media savvy, Governor Sanford survived an impeachment resolution in the legislature; his marriage was not as resilient.

lieutenant governor
In many states, the second-highest executive official government, elected with the governor as a ticket in some states and separately in others. She or he may have legislative and executive branch responsibilities.

After languishing for most of the twentieth century as a political backwater office where political hacks, business leaders, and others went to cap off their careers before retiring to the country club, governorships today tend to be filled by politically savvy and active leaders with strong policy agendas.[41,42] Modern governors are likely to highly educated, experienced, and capable of managing the diverse problems of a state. In addition to being better educated than their predecessors, recent governors have often had previous experience as a statewide elected official or held a national position.

In short, today's governors increasingly have the tools and skills to control state government and guide the state in the policy directions they think are best. The esteem in which the modern governorship is held is illustrated by the fact that in the last quarter of the twentieth century, the U.S. president was a former governor in all but five years. In each presidential race in this period, at least one of the major party nominees was a sitting or former governor.

As the state's legal counsel, the attorney general watches out for the state's legal interests. In 2008, Texas Attorney General Greg Abbott (R) led 30 other state attorney generals in filing a legal brief before the Supreme Court urging the Court to invalidate the District of Columbia's ban on handguns. The Court struck down the ban.

Other Executive Officers

Unlike the U.S. president, most governors must work with an array of independently elected executive branch officials in conducting the affairs of state government. At various times, these officials may assist or oppose the governor. Voters in 43 states choose a **lieutenant governor**, a second-highest executive. The governor and lieutenant governor are elected as a team in 24 states but independently in the other states. In the latter case, it is possible for the two top state executives to be political rivals or even members of different political parties. This can result in some real battles between them. For example, in 1990 when Governor (and Democrat) Michael Dukakis of Massachusetts left the state on an international trade mission, (Republican) Lieutenant Governor Evelyn Murphy initiated major cuts in public employment in an attempt to jump-start her floundering campaign for governor. Perhaps in anticipation of such antics, when Republican Steve Windom became lieutenant governor of Alabama, the Democrat-dominated state legislature and Democratic governor promptly stripped the office of almost all its powers.[43] Most lieutenant governors have few formal duties aside from presiding over the state senate and being in the succession path for governor.

Other major executive positions, elected in some states and appointed in others, include the following:

- Attorney general—the state's legal counsel and prosecutor (elected in 43 states)
- Treasurer—the manager of the state's bank accounts (elected in 38 states)
- Secretary of state—in charge of elections and record-keeping (elected in 36 states)
- Auditor—financial comptroller for the state (elected in 25 states)

Other officials, elected in fewer states, include education secretary and commissioners for land, labor, mines, agriculture, and utilities, among others.[44]

So many independent executives, commissions, and boards work within state governments that many politicians and scholars have called for major state government reorganization to allow governors more control and to increase efficiency generally. Every state has undertaken some kind of reorganization of the executive branch in the past 40 years. However, research shows that the expected benefits of reorganized state governments are not always achieved. Such reorganization only sometimes increases accountability and seldom results in cost saving and efficiency—benefits often promised by its proponents.[45] Moreover, although state residents may value smaller governments, in many states they clearly prefer having electoral control over all of the leaders of state executive branches, even if this structure is less efficient.

21.4 Describe the functions of state legislatures and contrast state legislators today with those of the past.

State Legislatures

State legislatures are often easy targets for criticism. Their work is not well understood, and the institution does not typically receive the public attention that the governor's office or national institutions do. Further, until fairly recent decades, state legislatures and legislators had a history of poor performance, which still haunts them. They were "malapportioned, unrepresentative, dominated by their governors and/or special interests, and unable and unwilling to deal with the pressing issues of the day."[46]

But between 1965 and 1985, many state legislatures underwent a metamorphosis into more full-time, professional bodies, in some cases becoming like state-level congresses. According to political scientist Alan Rosenthal, "They increased the time they spent on their tasks; they established or increased their professional staffs; and they streamlined their procedures, enlarged their facilities, invigorated their processes, attended to their ethics, disclosed their finances, and reduced their conflicts of interest."[47] As a result, state legislatures are far more active, informed, representative, and democratic today than they were 45 years ago.

State legislatures serve the same basic function in state government as Congress does in the national government, and they do it with the same basic mechanisms. State legislatures make almost all the basic laws of the state by approving identical bills in both their chambers (except in the case of Nebraska's unicameral legislature). They appropriate the money that is needed for the state government to function. They oversee the activities of the executive branch through confirming gubernatorial appointments, controlling the budgets of the agencies, and investigating complaints and concerns of citizens and the press. State legislators themselves attend closely to the needs of their constituents, whether through voting on bills in line with their constituents' interests or chasing down problems a citizen has with a bureaucratic agency.

Members of the state legislature are at the front line of interaction between citizens and government. Because most state legislatures meet for only a limited number of months each year and because state capitals are typically not too distant from their districts, state legislators usually live among the people they represent. They are closely involved with their constituents not only at election time but throughout the year. They coach basketball and run restaurants, they teach school and preach at local churches, and they are local attorneys and bankers. In short, the state legislature in almost all states comes closest to the sort of citizen-directed government envisioned by Thomas Jefferson over 200 years ago.

The reforms discussed above, collectively called *legislative professionalism*, were designed to improve the efficiency and effectiveness of state legislatures.[48] That is, they were designed "to enhance the capacity of the legislature to perform its role in the policymaking process with an expertise, seriousness, and effort comparable to that of other actors in the process."[49] Changes have been primarily in three areas.

First, legislative sessions were lengthened to give legislators more time to deal with the increasingly complex problems of the states. Before 1965, most state legislatures met for only several weeks each year, and many would meet only every other year. In 2010, 44 state legislatures had annual sessions, usually meeting for between three and five months, with a few (such as in Michigan, Massachusetts, and Wisconsin) effectively meeting year-round.

The second legislative professionalism reform was to increase legislators' salaries so they could devote more of their time to considering the state's business and less to their "regular" job. The idea was also that if service in the state legislature paid a living wage, legislators would have fewer conflicts of interest and a wider variety of people would be willing to serve. For instance, the only people who could afford to serve in the West Virginia state legislature in 1960 for a salary of $1,500 for a 90-day legislative session were those who had an outside source of income or were independently wealthy. In 2010, the roughly $80,000 a Michigan state representative earned could allow him or her to focus full-time on legislative duties throughout the year.

The third professionalism reform was the increase in the staff available to help legislators in their duties. Since 1979, permanent state legislative staff has increased over 60 percent.[50] Along with the increases in session length and salary, this increase in staff has dramatically increased state legislatures' ability to have an impact on the state policymaking process.

Not all the effects of this drive toward legislative professionalism are seen as positive. Some argue that professionalism leads to an overemphasis on reelection, inflated campaign costs, and lack of leadership in the lawmaking process.[51] Legislative professionalism threatens the existence of the "citizen legislature," in which people leave their job for a couple of months each year to serve the state and inject some "common sense" into government. The recent spate of state term limits laws indicates the esteem in which many Americans hold this sort of nonprofessional state legislature. There is also some evidence that increased professionalism does not enhance some of the aspects of the process that proponents argued it would, such as increasing membership diversity in state legislatures.[52]

Moreover, not all states have professionalized their legislatures to the same level. As already noted, not all state legislatures are in any sense full-time, professional bodies. For example, members of the New Hampshire House of Representatives earn $200 for a two-year term (with no per diem), which consists of only one 30-day period of service in each year. On the other hand, across the border in Massachusetts, state legislators earn over $61,000 and meet virtually the entire year. Figure 21.4 shows which states have professionalized legislatures, which still have citizen legislatures, and which have legislatures that are hybrids, having some characteristics of both. Professional legislatures tend to developed mainly in states with large and heterogeneous populations that both need and can afford them, although there is a regional effect that may have to do with political preferences for a professional government.[53]

Although it is difficult to assess the effects of legislative professionalism, there is some evidence that more professionalism leads to more liberal policies, more spending on social welfare programs, and perhaps more divided government in the states.[54]

We may now be seeing the beginning of a "deprofessionalizing" trend in some states, a hearkening back to the Jeffersonian ideal of the citizen legislature. Term limits laws are the most obvious manifestation of this trend, but recent laws in California limiting legislative staffing and in Colorado limiting the powers of the legislative leadership may also signal that the legislative professionalism movement is cyclical.[55]

FIGURE 21.4 Legislative Professionalism

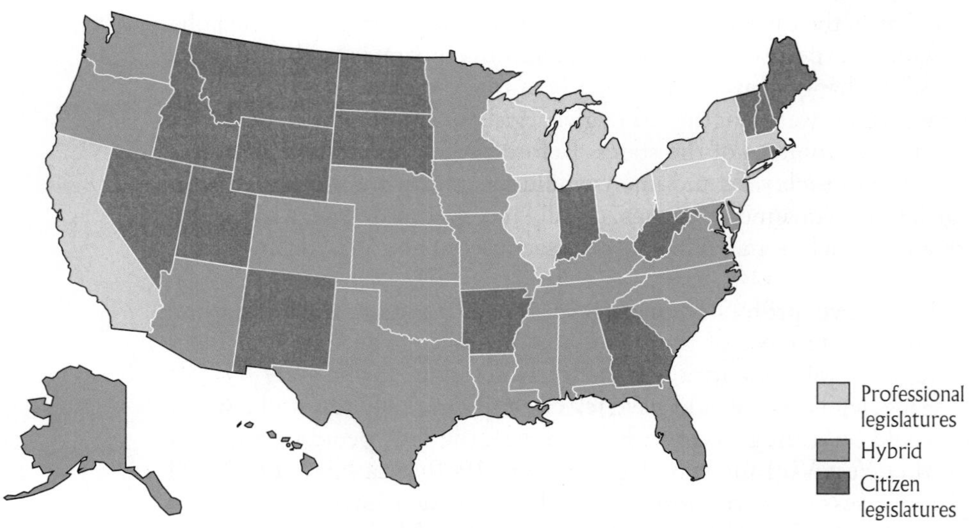

Source: Adapted from Keith E. Hamm and Gary F. Moncrief, "Legislative Politics in the States," in *Politics in the American States*, 9th ed., ed. Virginia Gray and Russell L. Hanson (Washington, DC: Congressional Quarterly Press, 2008), 154–91.

21.5 Outline the basic elements of most state court systems, and describe the various methods for selecting state judges.

State Court Systems

The organization of the states' courts reflects two major influences: (1) the model established by the national courts and (2) the judicial preferences of each state's citizens as manifested in state constitutions and statutes. State courts are far more involved in administering justice than is the national judiciary. Indeed, 98 percent of all litigation in the United States is settled in state courts. Recent data show that state courts have 52 times as many criminal cases as national courts and 27 times as many civil cases, with only 24 times as many judges.[56] In addition, state court workloads have been increasing in both criminal and civil cases, forcing states to experiment with alternatives to trial courts like mediation, arbitration, and plea bargaining. The volume of cases heard by state courts is significant, but courts are also policymaking bodies. Particularly when the highest court in the state rules on a case, judges are doing more than just interpreting the law; they are often making policy in the same fashion as the U.S. Supreme Court.[57]

Since World War II, many state court systems have undergone reforms designed to modernize and rationalize their procedures and structure, much like the reforms in the states' governors' offices and legislatures. These include reforms both of organizational structure and judicial selection.

State Court Organization

State court systems often developed as a hodgepodge of individual courts set up at odd times and for odd reasons at the subnational level. Many states have low-level courts, such as justices of the peace or magistrate courts, whose presiding officials may not even be lawyers. Many states developed a variety of specialized courts to deal with specific judicial matters involving traffic, family, or taxes. These systems, which included courts that were completely independent of any higher authority, often led to confusion, duplication of effort, and unfair treatment of cases and people.

In the past generation, efforts have been made to consolidate and coordinate many state courts systems so that they parallel the federal system, discussed in Chapter 16. First, specialized courts have been consolidated and subsumed into trial courts with more general jurisdiction. These courts are usually established for county-sized areas and are the setting for most trials. They are known by a variety of labels—district courts, circuit courts, superior courts, and (in the case of New York) supreme courts.

Judges assigned to these trial courts often work in only one county and specialize in criminal, juvenile, or civil litigation. A single judge presides over each case, and citizens may be called on to serve as jurors and members of grand jury panels.

Many states have also moved toward coordinating their court systems through their court of last resort, usually called the state supreme court. Under a coordinated system, the state supreme court not only serves as the court of final appeal for all cases in the state court system but also has the responsibility for administering and regulating the justice system in the state. This usually involves appointing a chief court administrator to handle the day-to-day budgeting, operations, and organization of all the courts in the state, and establishing boards to oversee and deal with complaints against lawyers and judges in the states.

A major innovation adopted by most states in the past 30 years is an *intermediate court of appeal*. Like national appeals courts, these courts are organized on a regional basis and with judges working together in panels of three or more, with a majority deciding each case. No witnesses are called before appellate courts, and juries are not used. Instead, judges read briefs and hear lawyers' arguments on whether the law was appropriately applied at the trial court level and whether due process of law was followed. The job of judges at this level is not to determine the facts of a case but to interpret the laws and the state or national constitution as they apply to the case.

The organizational purpose of an intermediate court of appeal is to reduce the pressure on the state supreme court of the many "routine" appeals of trial court decisions (see Figure 21.5). These are appeals that have few implications for state policy or procedure, primarily impacting only the case at hand. The state supreme court is thus freed up to consider only those cases with statewide policy importance. Twelve states, all with small populations, do not have intermediate courts of appeal,[58] so the appellate work in these states falls solely to the supreme court, reducing its ability to concentrate on making policy through judicial interpretation.

FIGURE 21.5 Prototypical Modern State Court System

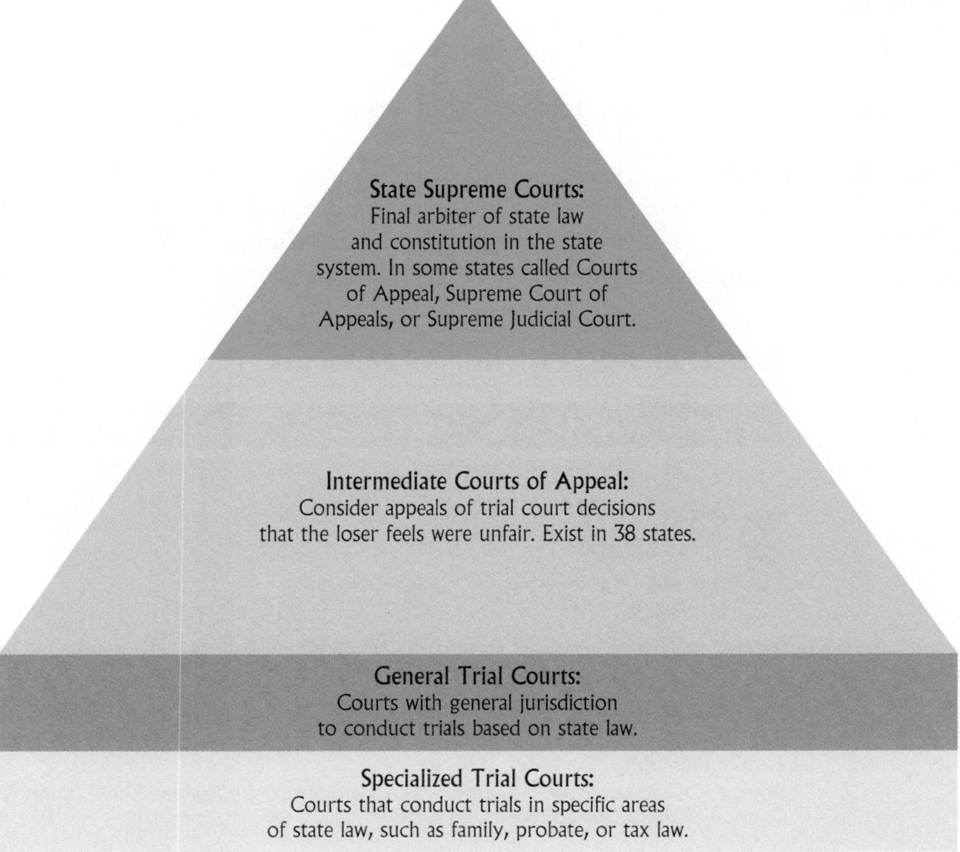

State Supreme Courts:
Final arbiter of state law
and constitution in the state
system. In some states called Courts
of Appeal, Supreme Court of
Appeals, or Supreme Judicial Court.
Intermediate Courts of Appeal:
Consider appeals of trial court decisions
that the loser feels were unfair. Exist in 38 states.
General Trial Courts:
Courts with general jurisdiction
to conduct trials based on state law.
Specialized Trial Courts:
Courts that conduct trials in specific areas
of state law, such as family, probate, or tax law.

Selecting Judges

In contrast to national judges, all of whom are appointed by the president for life, judges rise to the bench in the states in a variety of ways (see Table 21.2). These judicial selection mechanisms are each relics of values that were manifested in a series of reform movements over the past 200 years.

At the founding of the country, almost all state judges were appointed, as in the federal system, either by the governor or the state legislature, and 15 states still use this method of judicial selection for some or all their judges. With the Jacksonian democratic impulse of the early to mid nineteenth century, states began to select their judges by partisan ballot, just as other state officials were selected. Currently, 11 states select some or all of their judges this way. In the Progressive Era (1890–1920), reformers argued that to be administered fairly, justice should be nonpartisan because a judge elected on a party platform might be more biased in his or her decisions. Persuaded by this argument, many states changed their judicial selection mechanism to that of nonpartisan election, where candidates ran against one another but without a party label. Nineteen states still use nonpartisan elections to select some or all their judges. Election as a method of choosing judges remains both common and controversial.[59]

In the most recent wave of judicial selection reforms, since World War II, 16 states have adopted a hybrid system of appointment and election known as the **Merit Plan**. In this system, the governor appoints the state's judges from a list of persons recommended by the state bar or a committee of jurists and other officials. Each appointed judge then serves a short "trial run" term, usually one year, in which citizens may assess the judge's performance. After this, an election is held in which voters are asked whether the judge should be retained in office—they simply vote yes or no, not for one candidate or another. If voters approve retention by a majority vote (Illinois requires 60 percent), then the judge continues in office for a lengthy term (usually 6 to 12 years), after which another retention election is held if the judge wishes to continue serving. Few judges lose in this type of retention election, which raises the question of whether the Merit Plan's democratic component truly enhances responsiveness to citizens. Indeed, recent research suggests merit judges are no more or less responsive to changes in public preferences.[60]

Merit Plan
Method for selecting state judges in which governors appoint persons based on the recommendations of a committee; usually, after serving a short term, the judge faces a retention election.

direct democracy
Government controlled directly by citizens. Procedures in some states such as the initiative, the referendum, and the recall give voters a direct impact on policymaking and the political process by means of the voting booth and can therefore be considered forms of direct democracy.

21.6 Differentiate types of direct democracy, and evaluate direct democracy.

Direct Democracy

A method of policymaking that in the United States is unique to subnational governments is **direct democracy**. Three procedures—the initiative, the referendum, and the recall—provide citizens with ways they can directly impact policymaking and the political

TABLE 21.2 State Judicial Selection Mechanisms

APPOINTMENT	ELECTION	MERIT PLAN
By Governor: DE, ME, MD, MA, NH, NM NJ, NY, RI, VT	Partisan: AL, AR, IL, IN, MS, NY, NC, PA, TN, TX, WV	AK, AZ, CA, CO, FL, IN, IA, KS, MD, MO, NE, OK, SD, TN, UT, WY
By Legislature: CT, HI, RI, SC, VA	Nonpartisan: AZ, CA, FL, GA, ID, KS, KY, LA, MI, MN, MT, NV, NM, ND, OH, OK, OR, SD, WA	

Note: States may appear more than once, since some states select different types of judges through different mechanisms. Minor local judges, such as justices of the peace, are not considered in this table.

Source: Council of State Governments, *The Book of the States, 2009 Edition* (Washington, DC: Council of State Governments, 2010), 297.

process through the voting booth. One or more of these procedures is available in all states except Alabama. The referendum is the most commonly used, especially for ratifying constitutional amendments. Less widely available are the more proactive procedures—the initiative (used in 24 states) and the recall (used in 17 states) (see Table 21.3). The initiative and recall were developed in the Progressive Era largely in the Western and Midwestern states as a way to bring more power to the people by cutting out the middle persons in the policymaking system—political parties, politicians, and interest groups.

The **initiative** is the purest form of direct democracy. Although its details vary from state to state, the basic procedure is as follows. First, a citizen decides that he or she wants to see a law passed. The specific language of that proposal is then registered with a state official (typically the secretary of state), and permission to circulate a petition is given. The advocates of the proposal then try to get a specified number of eligible voters (typically 5 to 10 percent of those voting in the previous election) to sign a petition saying they would like to see the proposal on the ballot. When the appropriate number of signatures has been verified, the proposal is placed on the next general election ballot for an approve/disapprove vote. If a majority of voters approve it, the proposal becomes law. Between 1904 and 2006, at least 2,155 initiatives were placed on state ballots, and 41 percent of these passed. Both the average number and the passage rate of initiatives have increased since 1990.[61]

initiative
A process permitted in some states whereby voters may place proposed changes to state law on the ballot if sufficient signatures are obtained on petitions calling for such a vote.

The initiative allows for the adoption of policy that might otherwise be ignored or opposed by policymakers in the state legislature and governor's offices. The best example of this is the state legislative term-limits movement of the 1990s. Since this policy would directly and negatively affect some state legislators, it is easy to see why such a policy would be difficult to pass through the state legislature. Of the 21 states that have passed such limits, only Louisiana does not have the initiative. Perhaps just as telling, of the 24 states that have the initiative in some form, only four (Alaska, Illinois, Mississippi, and North Dakota) have not passed term limits. Other sorts of ideas that, for good or ill, became state law through this process but might not otherwise have done so, include everything from property tax limitations in many states in the 1970s and 1980s to legalization of marijuana for medical purposes in California and seven other states more recently. Some research even suggests that legislatures in states with the initiative may pass laws more in line with citizen preferences because the threat of the initiative is present,[62] but other research disputes this finding.[63]

Direct Democracy

Direct democracy has a special appeal to Americans, who believe in government by the people. But what if all laws passed by a state legislature had to be approved by the voters? We might adopt many policies that infringe on the rights of numerical minorities. We would also have to vote more often and spend more time voting. Extensive voting demands might decrease citizen participation and lead to ill-informed policy choices. At the same time, citizens would likely view government actions as more legitimate.

Perhaps not surprisingly, there is considerable debate over the wisdom of making state law through citizen-initiated proposals. Constitutional amendments and legislation passed through initiative are often poorly drafted and may contain ambiguous or contradictory provisions. As a result, initiatives often create new problems, leading to lawsuits and court interpretation and, often, action by the legislature.

TABLE 21.3 Direct Democracy Mechanisms

INITIATIVE[a]	LEGISLATIVE REFERENDUM[b]	RECALL
AK, AZ, AR, CA, CO, FL, ID,	AZ, AR, CA, DE, ID, IL, KY,	AK, AZ, CA, GA, ID, KS,
IL, ME, MA, MI, MS, MO, MT,	ME, MD, MA, MI, MO, MT,	LA, MI, MN, MT, NV, NM,
NE, NV, ND, OH, OK, OR, SD,	NE, NV, NM, ND, OH, OK, OR,	ND, OR, SD, WA, WI
UT, WA, WY	SD, UT, WA	

[a]These states have at least one of the several forms of initiative.

[b]All states except Alabama allow or require a referendum for state constitutional amendments. The states listed in this column also allow referenda on the passage of legislative issues that are not constitutional amendments.

Source: Council of State Governments, *The Book of the States, 2009 Edition* (online only) (Washington, DC: Council of State Governments, 2010), February 26, 2010, http://www.csg.org/knowledgecenter/docs/6-9OnlineOnly.pdf.

During the 2004 primary and general elections, 13 states passed constitutional amendments banning same-sex marriage via the referendum process. Here, State Representative Nan Orrock (D-Atlanta) addresses an October 27, 2004, rally against the Georgia referendum (Amendment 1), which passed a week later by 76 to 24 percent.

It is also unclear to what extent the initiative process empowers citizens as opposed to merely giving new tools to well-financed interest groups. In larger states, special interests can pay professional firms to gather the required number of signatures. Monied interests also have the advantage in mounting expensive television advertising campaigns. These ads can present voters with a biased or incomplete set of facts on an issue they know little about. For example, in the 1998 California initiative campaign to legalize Indian tribal casinos, the gambling industry spent more than $71 million on *both sides* of the issue, with advertisements that were often confusing to citizens.[64] All too often, complex public policy questions are reduced to simplistic sloganeering. As Ann O' M. Bowman and Richard C. Kearney argue:

> Seldom are issues so simple that a yes-or-no ballot question can adequately reflect appropriate options and alternatives. A legislative setting, in contrast, fosters the negotiation and compromise that produce workable solutions. Legislatures are deliberative bodies, not instant problem solvers.[65]

referendum
A state-level method of direct legislation that gives voters a chance to approve or disapprove legislation or a constitutional amendment proposed by the state legislature.

A hybrid of legislative and direct democratic policymaking is the **referendum**. Whereas the initiative is proposed by a citizen or group, the referendum begins life as a legislative resolution. Typically, the state legislature deliberates on and passes the proposal in both chambers in identical form, as required for any bill to become law, but then, instead of a bill going to the governor for his or her approval, the proposal is presented to the voters in a general election. If a majority of voters approve it, it becomes law; otherwise, it does not. In all states except Alabama, this procedure is required for amendments to the state constitution, and in many subnational governments referenda are required for bond issues (government debt), tax changes, and other fiscal matters.

recall
A procedure that allows voters to call a special election for a specific official in an attempt to throw him or her out of office before the end of term. Recalls are permitted in only 17 states, seldom used because of their cost and disruptiveness, and rarely successful.

The **recall** is different than the initiative or referendum because it is about elected officials rather than public policy. In essence, the recall allows voters to call a special election for a specific official in an attempt to throw him or her out of office before the end of his or her term. The process involves gathering signatures on a petition of voters in the jurisdiction of the official being recalled, much like an initiative. Once enough signatures are gathered, a special election is held, usually within three months of official confirmation of the valid number of signatures, in which the official being recalled runs against any forthcoming challenger(s), if he or she desires to do so.

Needless to say, this is a drastic action and it is infrequently undertaken successfully. It is disruptive of the routine political process and very costly for the jurisdiction having to hold the special election. Because of this, only 17 states allow for the recall, and these states make it difficult to undertake, with the required number of signatures being much higher than that for an initiative. Historically, those who have been recalled have been accused of a serious breach of propriety, morals, or ethics and have tended to be judges or other local officials serving long terms. For example, in 1982 a district judge in Madison, Wisconsin, made the highly publicized and inflammatory statement that he thought a very young victim in a sexual assault case appeared promiscuous; the judge was recalled and removed from office.[66] However, in recent years, some state and local officials have been recalled for more policy-oriented reasons, such as for supporting tax increases in Michigan, a stadium sales tax in Wisconsin, and gun control in California. Most dramatically, in 2003 California Governor Gray Davis was recalled after voters came to believe that he had failed to solve the state's energy and fiscal crisis, and action-movie star Arnold Schwarzenegger was chosen to replace him. This was the first successful recall of a governor since North Dakota voters recalled Governor Lynn Frazier in 1921.

Local Governments

21.7 Explain Dillon's rule, and differentiate five types of local government.

In Chapter 3, you read about the concept of federalism and how the nation's Founders tried to strike a balance between the powers of the central government and those of the states. This state–federal *intergovernmental relationship* has evolved in the past 200 years through statutes passed by Congress, constitutional amendments and their interpretation by the U.S. Supreme Court, civil war, and tradition. The relationship between the states and the national government is both contentious and one of the defining characteristics of government in the United States.

The intergovernmental relationship between the states and their local governments is no less important in defining how our government works. But this relationship is far less ambiguous and involves no balance and little interpretation.

The basic relationship is that local governments are totally subservient to the state government. According to **Dillon's Rule** (after Iowa Judge John Dillon, who expressed this idea in an 1868 court decision), local governments have only those powers that are explicitly given to them by the states. Dillon argued definitively that local governments were "creatures of the state" and that the state legislature gave local governments the "breath of life without which they cannot exist."[67] This means that local governments have very little discretion over which policies they pursue or how they pursue them. In fact, the states have been known to take away policymaking and administrative power from local governments completely, as when the state of Missouri took over a school district that state officials felt was being run improperly. An extreme case of state usurpation of local power took place in 1997 when the Massachusetts state legislature actually *abolished* Middlesex County because of mismanagement and corruption.[68]

Dillon's Rule
The idea (named for Iowa Judge John Dillon, who expressed it in an 1868 decision) that local governments have only those powers that are explicitly given them by the states. This means that local governments have very little discretion over what policies they pursue or how they pursue them.

The basis of this shocking imbalance of power is the U.S. Constitution. Although the Constitution discusses at length the role of the states and the relationship between the states and the central government, local governments are never explicitly mentioned. The establishment and supervision of local government has been interpreted to be one of the "reserve powers" for the states, under the Tenth Amendment of the Bill of Rights. The idea is that states have certain responsibilities and policy goals that they must fulfill, but that sometimes the best way to do this is through local units of government that they establish. For example, the states have the responsibility to educate children, but each state except Hawaii has opted to establish regional school districts to do this for the state.

Although local governments have no constitutional sovereignty, local government officials are certainly not powerless in their efforts to control their own destiny. But, rather than formal power, local governments have power that arises from informal political clout. First, many people feel more strongly connected to their local governments than to the state. After all, it is the local government officials they see most frequently—the police officer responding to an emergency call, the teacher in the school educating their child, or the city council member helping to get the potholes filled in the street. State officials understand the sympathy (and political clout) that these officials have among citizens, so they do not try to rile them without good reason. Further, local government officials of all stripes form interest groups to lobby state officials. In all states, organizations of local officials, such as the Wisconsin League of Municipalities or the Texas Association of Counties, are among the most powerful interest groups in the state capitol.[69]

Many cities have also managed to get state legislatures to grant them a degree of autonomy through a **local charter**. Such a charter is an organizational statement and grant of authority from the state to a local government, much like a state or national constitution. States sometimes allow cities to write their own charters and, within limits, to change them without permission from the state legislature. Today, this practice of **home rule** is widely used to organize and modernize city government.

local charter
An organizational statement and grant of authority from the state to a local government, much like a state or national constitution. States sometimes allow municipalities to write their own charters and, within limits, to change them without permission of the state legislature.

home rule
The practice by which municipalities are permitted by the states to write their own charters and, within limits, change them without permission of the state legislature. Today this practice is widely used to organize and modernize municipal government.

Number and Types of Local Governments

The U.S. Bureau of the Census counts not only people but also governments. Its latest count revealed an astonishing 89,476 American local governments (see Table 21.4). In addition to being a citizen of the United States and of a state, the average citizen also resides within the jurisdiction of perhaps 10 to 20 local governments. (Some of these local governments offer particularly good opportunities for young people to participate in politics, as discussed in "Young People and Politics: Public Service Through Elective Office.") The state of Illinois holds the current record for the largest number of local governments: 6,994 at the latest count. The six-county Chicago metropolitan area alone has more than 1,200 governments.

The sheer number of governments in the United States is, however, as much a burden as a boon to democracy. Citizens are governed by a complex maze of local governments—some with broad powers, others performing very specialized services. This plethora of local governments creates voter overload and ignorance, thereby defeating the democratic purpose of citizen control.

Local governments can be classified into five types based on their legal purpose and the scope of their responsibilities: counties, townships, municipalities, school districts, and special districts.

Counties The largest geographic unit of government at the local level is the *county* government (called "parishes" in Louisiana and "boroughs" in Alaska). Texas has the most counties with 254, while Delaware and Hawaii have only 3 each. Los Angeles County, the most populous county, serves over 9.5 million residents, whereas Loving County, Texas, serves only 67 residents.

The 3,033 county governments are administrative arms of state government. Typically, counties are responsible for keeping records of births, deaths, and marriages; establishing a system of justice and law enforcement; maintaining roads and bridges; collecting taxes; conducting voter registration and elections; and providing for public welfare and education. Rural residents more often rely on county governments for services because they have fewer local governments to turn to than city dwellers.

County governments usually consist of an elected *county commission*, the legislative body that makes policy, and a collection of "row officers," including sheriffs, prosecutors, county clerks, and assessors, who run county services. Some urban counties, such as Milwaukee County, St. Louis County, and Wayne (Detroit) County, now elect a county executive (like a mayor or governor). In some counties, such as Dade (Miami) County and Sacramento County, the county commission appoints a county administrator to take responsibility for the administration of county policies.

Townships *Township* governments are found in only 20 states, including Maine, Michigan, New Hampshire, New York, Vermont, and Wisconsin. Most of the 16,519 township governments have limited powers and primarily just assist with county

TABLE 21.4 Local Governments in the United States

TYPE OF GOVERNMENT	1962	2007	% CHANGE, 1962–2007
All local governments	91,186	89,476	–1.1%
General-purpose governments			
County	3,043	3,033	–0.03%
Municipal	18,000	19,492	+7.7%
Township	17,142	16,519	–3.6%
Single-purpose governments			
School district	34,678	13,051	–66.4%
Special district	18,323	37,381	+49.0%

Source: U.S. Bureau of the Census, "Local Governments and Public School Systems by Type and State: 2007," August 11, 2010, http://www.census.gov/govs/www/cog2007.html

Public Service Through Elective Office

Many young Americans are concerned about particular issues and government policy, and some are inspired to mobilize other young adults to register to vote, attend city council meetings, and sign petitions. However, even though issues such as public spending on education, economic development, and the drinking age have a direct impact on youth, few young people are motivated enough about these issues to run for public office. And because of age restrictions, most national and statewide offices are closed to young adults. However, in most states there are no age requirements for state and local legislative positions, and some young adults successfully run for these offices.

In Kansas, 20-year-old Tanner Fortney ran for the Spring Hill city council in February 2001 after becoming interested in public policy through his high school debate team and, later, through an internship with Congressman Dennis Moore (D-Kans.) and through his political science classes at the University of Kansas. Fortney survived the primary election for the city council but lost the general election by 75 votes. After the election, Fortney did not wallow in defeat. Instead, he gained an appointment to the Spring Hill planning commission and immersed himself in the details of zoning and infrastructure.

Fortney's vigor impressed the town's mayor, and when a city council member resigned in October 2001, Mayor Mark Squire appointed Fortney to the council. The appointment made Fortney the council's youngest member ever. Fortney focused his attention on development and economic growth issues, trying to make sure the town balanced residential and commercial development. Fortney's hard work, zeal, and fresh perspective helped to revitalize city government in the sleepy suburb of 3,000 near Kansas City.

Fortney was reelected in 2003 and became president of the council in 2005. Although he was not reelected for another term in 2007, Fortney's example clearly demonstrates that young people can become involved and make a difference.

QUESTIONS FOR DISCUSSION

- What are the minimum age limits for running for local and state offices in your state? Do you think they are too low or too high?
- Would you ever consider running for local or state office? Why or why not? Would a specific issue or desire for a policy change encourage you to run? Explain.
- If you did run for office at a young age, what steps would you take to encourage more young people to become involved in politics?

services in rural areas; however, some, such as those in New England, function much like city governments. Voters typically elect a township board, a supervisor, and perhaps a very small number of other executives. Township officers oversee public highways and local law enforcement, keep records of vital statistics and tax collections, and administer elections. However, most lack the power to pass local ordinances since they serve as administrative extensions of state and county governments.

Municipalities Cities are more formally referred to as municipal governments or *municipalities*, and they supply most local programs and services for 19,492 communities in the United States. In most states, municipalities, more so than other local governments, provide police and fire protection, street maintenance, solid waste collection, water and sewer works, park and recreation services, and public planning. Some larger cities also run public hospitals and health programs, administer public welfare services, operate public transit and utilities, manage housing and urban development programs, and even run universities. Because of this significant involvement in service delivery, municipal politics often revolves around citizen satisfaction with the delivery of services.

Originally, many municipalities in the United States were run with a special form of direct democracy—the **town meeting**. Under this system, all voting-age adults in a community gathered once a year to make public policy such as passing new local laws, approving a town budget, and electing a small number of local residents to serve as town officials. But as cities became too large for the town meeting style of governance, three modern forms of municipal government developed.

town meeting
A special form of direct democracy under which all voting-age adults in a community gather once a year to make public policy. Now used only in a few villages in New England.

Mayor–Council Government In a typical mayor–council government (Figure 21.6), local residents elect a mayor and a city council. In "strong mayor" cities, such as New York City, the city council makes public policy, and the mayor and city bureaucrats who report to the mayor are responsible for policy implementation. Strong mayors may also veto actions of the city council. In "weak mayor" cities, most power is vested in the city council, which directs the activities of the city bureaucracy. The mayor serves as the presiding officer for city council meetings and as the ceremonial head of city government. Most mayor–council cities have this weak mayor form of governance because most of the numerous small cities of 10,000 or fewer residents use this system. San Diego is one major city that uses the weak mayor form of government.

Council–Manager Government. In this form of municipal government, voters elect a city council and sometimes a mayor, who often acts as both presiding officer and voting member of the council (see Figure 21.7). The council is responsible for setting policy for the city. The implementation and administration of the council's actions are placed in the hands of an appointed **city manager**, who is expected to carry out policy with the aid of city bureaucracy. More than one-third of cities use this form of government, including such major cities as Dallas, Kansas City, and Phoenix.

city manager
An official appointed by the city council who is responsible for implementing and administering the council's actions. More than one-third of U.S. cities use the council–manager form of government.

Commission Government. In commission government, voters elect a panel of city commissioners, each of whom serves as both legislator and executive. These officials make public policy just as city council members do in the other two forms of government. However, each member is also elected as a commissioner of a functional area of city government (for example, public safety), and bureaucrats report to a single commissioner. Among the few cities that still use a commission government are Vicksburg, Mississippi, and St. Petersburg, Florida.[70]

Most city council members and many mayors are elected in nonpartisan elections. Traditionally, city council members represented a district or ward of the city—a practice that permitted ward-based machine party bosses to control elections and to try to create public policies that were good for individual wards rather than for the city as a whole. Reformers advocated at-large city elections, with all members of the city council chosen by voters throughout the city. These at-large representatives could not create

FIGURE 21.6 Mayor–Council Government

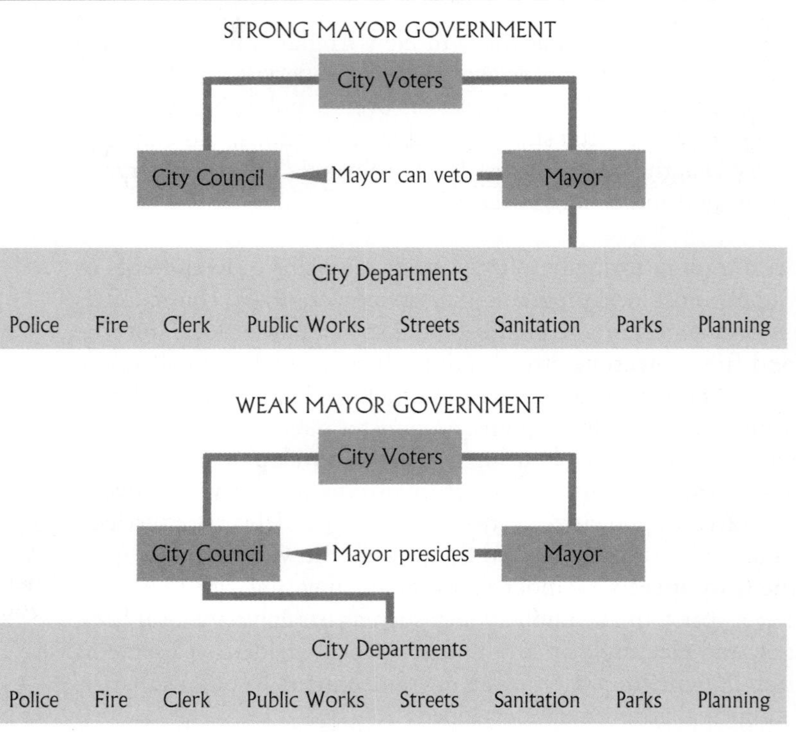

FIGURE 21.7 Council–Manager Government

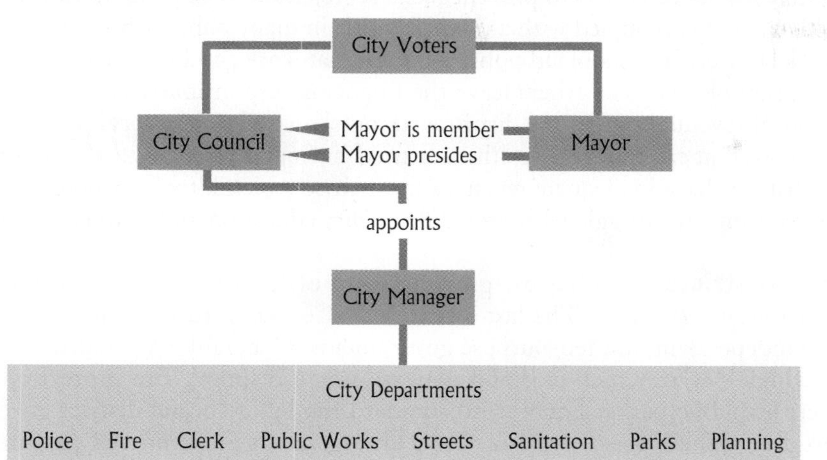

public policies to benefit only their own neighborhoods because they would have to answer to all the city's voters. A majority of cities use at-large elections today.

A consequence of at-large elections is that they make it more difficult for minority group members to be elected to the city council. This is because African American and other ethnic minorities in U.S. cities have tended to live in more or less homogeneous neighborhoods. Therefore, although they may be a minority of the entire city's population (and so fail to generate a majority in at-large elections), they may be a majority in smaller sections of the city, and so could elect candidates to pursue their interests in district-based electoral systems. Cities that employ district elections may have a greater degree of representational equity for African Americans and Hispanics on city councils than cities that use at-large elections.[71]

School Districts The nation's 13,051 *school districts* are responsible for educating children. Although some cities, counties, townships, and one state (Hawaii) operate dependent public school systems (a total of 1,510), school districts are run as independent local governments. Consolidation of small, often rural, districts into larger ones is the major reason for the 66 percent drop in the number of school districts that you saw in Table 21.4.

In an independent school district, voters within a geographically defined area are responsible for their own public education system, including electing a board of education, selecting administrators and teachers, building and operating schools, designing and running education programs, and raising the revenues to meet a locally adopted school budget. Because the states are ultimately responsible for public education, state governments adopt general standards for education, mandate certain school programs, and provide a system of state financial assistance to public schools. But within the guidelines of state policy and the parameters of state funding, locally elected school boards and their appointed administrators deliver education services to the nation's children.

School districts have become the focus for many emotionally charged issues at the local level. Prayer in public schools, sex education, equity in school funding, English as a second-language classes, charter schools, gay and lesbian student groups, and lingering racial discrimination are just a few of the more explosive issues surrounding schools in the 2000s. For example, although the Supreme Court declared that states have a responsibility to eliminate discrimination in education, in such important decisions as *Brown v. Board of Education* (1954) and *Swann v. Charlotte-Mecklenberg County Schools* (1971) (see Chapter 5), inequities in the public school systems persist, with racial minorities still encountering poorly funded public education in many instances. In fact, political scientists have discovered an extensive pattern of second-generation discrimination—a shortage of minority teachers "which leads to negative outcome for minority students."[72] Furthermore, in 2007 the Supreme Court ruled that public schools cannot use race as a criterion when assigning children to schools. The ruling overturned policies that attempted to create racial diversity across and within schools (*Parents Involved in Community Schools v. Seattle School Dist. No. 1*). How this ruling may influence efforts to prevent racial segregation in the long term is not clear.

This inequity is coupled with a financial crisis in many public school systems. States have widely divergent school aid policies—some states are good providers to their neediest local schools, whereas others leave the financing responsibility largely to local districts. Local revenue sources are disproportionately based on the local property tax—a policy choice that can result in wealthier districts having an abundance of resources while poorer districts have inadequate revenues for their schoolchildren.[73] Schools around the country continue to struggle with providing quality education with limited resources.

Special Districts The fastest-growing form of local government in the United States is the *special district*. The last official U.S. Census Bureau count showed 37,381 of these independent, limited-purpose governments. Generally, special districts provide only a single service, such as flood control, waste disposal, fire protection, public libraries, or public parks. There is no standard model of special district government organization—the types of organizational arrangements are almost as plentiful as the number of districts. Some districts have elected policymaking boards; a governor or mayor appoints others. Special districts are highly flexible units of local government because their boundary lines can be drawn across the usual municipal, county, and township borders. By providing services on a larger scale—whether fire protection, drinking water, or even sports stadiums—they help localities realize certain economies and efficiencies and can address problems that cross multiple political jurisdictions.

However, important questions about democracy are inherent in the growth of special districts. Special districts are, to a great extent, invisible governments; the local press rarely covers their operations, and there is little direct public participation in their decision making. Most citizens do not even know who serves on these district boards or when the boards meet. As a result, the public has great difficulty holding special districts accountable even though these districts often, for example, have the power to increase taxes in order to provide services.

Fragmentation, Cooperation, and Competition

Local Services

The multitude of local governments with independent authority can make the delivery of public services in a metropolitan area inefficient, contentious, and just plain confusing. If all government services in a metropolitan area were taken over by a single government entity, such as the county, then these services might be provided more effectively and at a lower cost. And inequities in services between wealthy neighborhoods and poor neighborhoods might be resolved. However, such consolidation would allow fewer access points to government, perhaps making it less democratic.

Each governing body in a fragmented metropolis tends to look at problems from its own narrow perspective. As a result, local bodies fail to cooperate with one another and plan effectively for the region's future needs. For example, the development of an effective mass transit system is often hindered when not all communities are willing to share in financing a new metropolitan bus network or light rail system, or when a narrowly focused special district devoted to maintaining the region's road network proves unwilling to divert its funds to help finance new rail construction.

Traditionally, regional cooperation on specific policy areas has been undertaken through the use of special districts. For example, local water and sewer needs transcend municipality borders, and so, in most metropolitan areas, special sewer and water districts have been set up to coordinate the delivery of this service.

But there are limits to the number of special districts that can be established efficiently and the level of coordination these districts can achieve. What can be done to coordinate a variety of public services in a metropolitan area? A few areas have developed *super-locals*, institutional arrangements that act almost as general-purpose governments for an entire region. Seattle, Miami, and Minneapolis–St. Paul each have a metropolitan council that serves such a function. For example, the Minneapolis–St. Paul Metropolitan Council operates the region's bus service, provides sewer and water services, operates a regional housing and development authority, and funds and plans regional parks and trails, all activities that cut across traditional local governments' physical and policy area boundaries.

But examples of institutionalized regional coordination are the exception rather than the rule. For the most part, the prospects for promoting regional cooperation to correct the inequalities and coordination problems that result from metropolitan fragmentation have been dim. Generally speaking, the United States lacks the strong tradition of regional planning evident in Europe (see "America in Perspective: Urban

AMERICA IN PERSPECTIVE

Urban Planning in the European Union and the United States

The nations of the European Union play a much stronger role in guiding urban development than does the United States. Europe's strong planning has helped to preserve cities, control the pace of development, protect agricultural land and the environment, and minimize urban sprawl to a degree that is hardly imaginable in the United States. Typically, these urban planning actions are initiated by regional agencies that get their authority from the central government.

In Great Britain, planners prevented the overgrowth of London by encircling the city with a "green belt"—a designated area in which the countryside would be preserved and no new development permitted. The growth of the region's population was absorbed in planned "new towns" that were built some distance from the central city. The result was a mixture of city and countryside in a metropolitan area and the avoidance of American-style urban sprawl.

Faced with the prospect of excessive growth in Paris, France's national agency for development steered new industries into the suburbs and more distant cities. Still the lure of Paris proved irresistible. In response, central government and regional planners built two new towns of high-rise office buildings, convention centers, and hotels in different spots just outside the city's borders. These towns became the main office centers of the metropolitan Paris area. High-rise residential new towns were built in a ring around Paris to absorb the area's rapidly growing population. These new commercial and residential centers were connected to the old city by a new commuter rail system.

The Netherlands has also relied on strong government planning and controls over land use to prevent the country's limited supply of land from being eaten up by rapid urbanization. Dutch planners saved valuable agricultural land and recreational space in a "green heart" in the midst of the metropolitan Amsterdam–The Hague–Rotterdam Randstad ("Ring City") area, one of the most densely populated areas in the world. Riding a train through the area today, you can easily see exactly where the city ends and the land designated for agricultural purposes begins. The planning boundaries are extremely clear and well guarded.

European planners now confront new problems. With the globalization of their economies, cities in Europe find that they are increasingly competing with one another for new business. As a result, spatial planning considerations are sometimes sacrificed in order to give a corporation a site it desires. Citizens' demands for individual homes of their own have also led to pressures for continued suburban development, sometimes compromising the integrity of regional land-use plans. Rush-hour traffic jams have become increasingly common in major European metropolises.

Despite these new problems, European nations have been able to ward off the ills of uncontrolled growth. In the United States, by contrast, the private sector and the free market—not government—play the dominant role in deciding where growth will occur. Compared to Europe, regional planning in the United States is essentially toothless.

Sources: Peter Hall, *Urban and Regional Planning*, 4th ed. (Independence, KY: Routledge, 2002); H. V. Savitch, *Post-Industrial Cities: Politics and Planning in New York, Paris, and London* (Princeton, NJ: Princeton University Press, 1988); Hans Thor Andersen and Ronald Van Kempen, *Governing European Cities: Social Fragmentation, Social Exclusion and Urban Governance* (London: Ashgate, 2000).

Planning in the European Union and the United States"). In large part, this reflects the strong localism inherent in American democracy. In the United States, there is a tradition of people being able to "vote with their feet," that is, of people moving to the place where the government's policies best reflect their values and provide the desired type and level of services.[74] This exacerbates the problem of regional coordination by making local governments in different parts of the same metropolitan area more likely to disagree over solutions to regional problems, such as transportation or sewer services—disagreement that results in a situation where all regional residents suffer, regardless of the jurisdiction in which they reside.

A good (if disturbing) example of this is seen in the conflict over the racial integration of the Milwaukee public schools. When its schools were ordered to desegregate in the 1970s and 1980s, many white families moved out of the school district into neighboring suburban districts. In a classic case of "white flight," white student enrollment in the Milwaukee public schools dropped rapidly. In response, the federal court that issued the original desegregation order then expanded its order to include other school districts

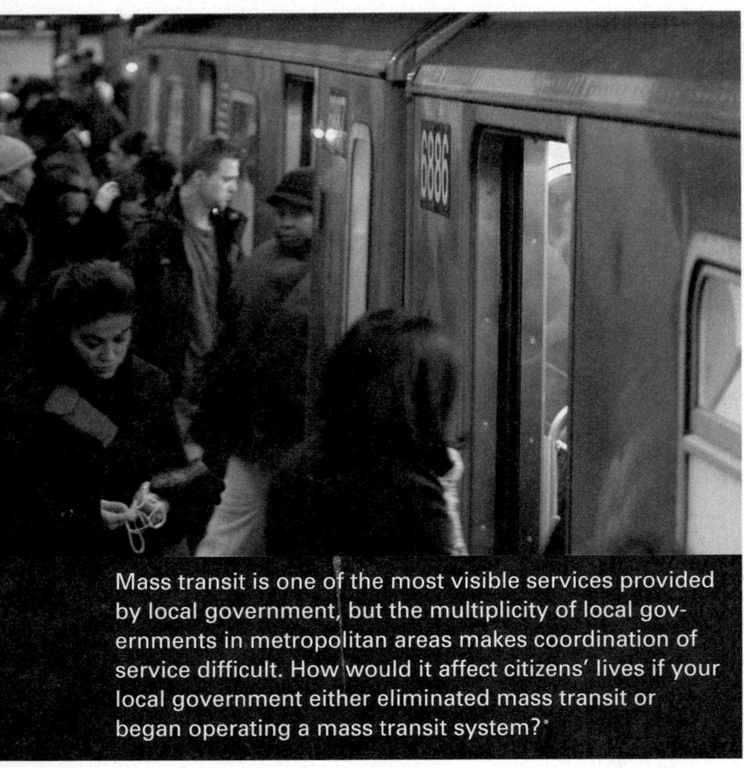

Mass transit is one of the most visible services provided by local government, but the multiplicity of local governments in metropolitan areas makes coordination of service difficult. How would it affect citizens' lives if your local government either eliminated mass transit or began operating a mass transit system?

within Milwaukee County, thus attempting to force a regional coordination for educational policy by judicial fiat and with the backing of the national government. But again, many white families voted with their feet and left the county entirely, making the attempt at coordination a failure.

Conflicts between the preferences and needs of suburbanites and those of city dwellers typically involve taxes, roads, and central city services. Many people move to the suburbs because property taxes are lower and land is cheaper. The denser population of an urban area creates a need for higher levels of most local government services and therefore a higher tax burden. Regional coordination often looks to suburbanites to subsidize the taxes of the urban dwellers they left behind. Because suburbanites live more spread out and often far away from their jobs, they need plenty of good roads and highways on which to commute. Meanwhile, urban dwellers prefer that more transportation money be spent on mass transit, which is economical for dense populations. Urban dwellers also complain that suburbanites drive into the central city each workday, using city services like roads, police, water, and so forth, and then take themselves and their tax dollars back to the suburbs at night. These examples offer the barest outline of the differences in preferences and viewpoints of people in different areas of a metropolis. It is easy to understand why coordination and cooperation are hard to come by.

Local governments are also engaged in serious competition for economic development. That is, they try to expand their tax base through commercial and residential development. Although some analysts conclude that cities are actually quite limited in their ability to control economic change within their borders, local officials often believe that development policies are a community's lifeblood.[75] A business owner can simply threaten to leave a community or locate facilities in another town if he or she is unhappy with local policies. Thus, business owners and corporate officials have great leverage to extract concessions from local officials because no local government wants to face the loss of jobs or tax base. As a result, cities compete with one another for desirable business facilities by offering tax reductions, promises of subsidized infrastructure development, and other services demanded by business.

However, local governments can cooperate with one another when they find it in their mutual interest to do so. Central cities and suburbs are often willing, for instance, to share the costs of a new sewage disposal facility. They may also cooperate in ventures to attract a major new employer to the area, or to keep one, as in the case of the massive efforts by local governments in the Chicago metropolitan area to construct a new baseball stadium to keep the White Sox from leaving town in the late 1980s. Sometimes two or more governments may cooperate informally to share equipment and services. In many areas of the country, a **council of governments** (frequently referred to as a COG) brings officials from various localities together to discuss mutual problems and plan joint, cooperative action. These COGs are often formally very weak, underfunded, poorly staffed, and lacking in any real legislative or taxing power.

council of governments Councils in many areas of the country where officials from various localities meet to discuss mutual problems and plan joint, cooperative action.

21.8 Contrast state revenue and expenditures with local revenue and expenditures and outline ways state and local governments have tried to increase revenue.

State and Local Finance Policy

When a state or local government approves its budget for the next year, the basic policy objectives of the government have also been approved. These objectives are contained in the taxing and spending plans that make up the budget. Lofty speeches can be made and bills passed into law, but without some significant and specific budgetary commitment, a policy will usually have little impact on citizens' lives. Taxpayers increasingly demand more accountability and efficiency from their subnational governments, forcing officials to squeeze services and programs out of limited revenue dollars. Figure 21.8 shows how state governments get their money and how they spend it. Although precise proportions of the categories of sources of revenue and of expenditures vary from year to year, the 2007 data in the figure reflect the basic pattern.

State government revenues are derived from a variety of sources. States receive the largest share of revenue, 40.1 percent in the figure, from taxes. States' major sources of tax revenue are sales taxes, income taxes, and motor vehicle and fuel taxes. The second-largest source of state revenue is intergovernmental revenue (23.6 percent)—almost all as grants from the national government. Nearly as large a source of revenue is state insurance programs (20.7 percent), which are contributions to state programs such as employee pension funds, pollution liability funds, among many others. Charges and fees for services such as state hospitals, college courses, and state parks have become an increasingly important source of revenue for states in the past 20 years (14.4 percent, along with miscellaneous revenue, including gaming proceeds, as discussed in "A Generation of Change: The Fruits of Devolution" and "You Are the Policymaker: Should Your State Take a Chance on Gambling?").

Over the past 40 years, changes in their constitutions, including allowing for sales taxes and income taxes, have given states wider access to revenue. Today, 45 states levy a general sales tax; Alaska, Delaware, Montana, New Hampshire, and Oregon are the only holdouts. Only seven states—Alaska, Florida, Nevada, South Dakota, Texas, Washington, and Wyoming—do not have a personal income tax, although New Hampshire and Tennessee have only a limited form of income tax. The modernization of state revenue structures gives the states new money to finance the public programs demanded by citizens.

How do states spend their money? Most of the states' money—about 50 percent—goes to operate state programs (in public safety, education, health and social services, and so on), construct state buildings, and provide direct assistance to individuals. Another 28 percent is allocated as aid to local governments. Since so much of the money that states spend is given to local governments (and since so much of the local governments' revenue comes from the states), the states have even more leverage over the locals than is given to them by Dillon's Rule.

Local government finances can be confusing because of the fragmentation of local governments and the varied ways in which states support and constrain their local governments and in which states and local governments have sorted out the assignment of

FIGURE 21.8 State Government Revenues and Expenditures

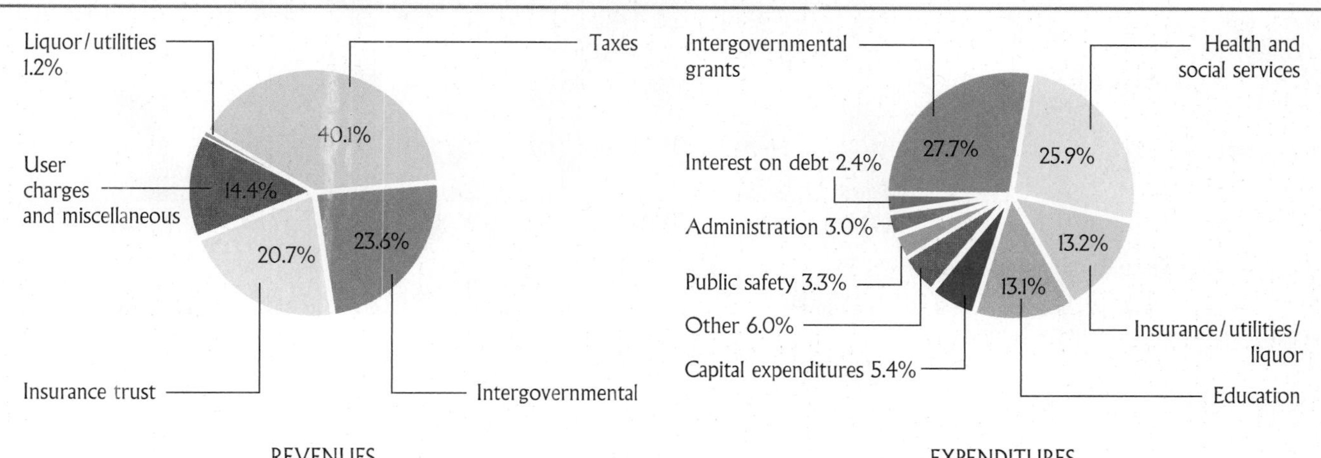

Source: U.S. Bureau of the Census, "State and Local Government Finances, 2006, February 17, 2010, http://www.census.gov/compendia/statab/cats/state_local_govt_finances_employment/state_government_finances.html.

The Fruits of Devolution

Although a "devolution revolution" of power and responsibility back to the states began under President Nixon in the 1970s, it was President Reagan's policies in the 1980s that solidified this trend. Nevertheless, few observers in the 1980s foresaw just how important state and local politics and policymaking were becoming.

State experiments with education, health care, and social welfare policy, conducted throughout the 1990s, provided the foundation for national policy change in the late 1990s and the 2000s. Meanwhile, governors, with new broader authority and policy agendas, were increasingly in the national spotlight as potential presidential candidates and possible appointees to executive branch positions. Consider that from 1992 through 2004, voters preferred presidential candidates who had been governors to opponents with Washington insider credentials.

Likewise, apart from the war on terrorism and related national security issues, the most prominent national issues have arisen from ongoing debates in the states. From illegal immigration to abortion, religion in schools, health care reform, carbon emissions, and same-sex marriage, it has been the actions of state legislatures, state courts, and direct democracy proposals placed on state ballots that have shaped national debate. Meanwhile, state governments have continued to play a primary role in implementing national regulations, including environmental protection, at the same time that some have pursued more stringent regulations than those outlined by the national government.

As their policymaking role and responsibility have expanded, states have also found an increasing need for new sources of revenue. In seeking solutions states have (inadvertently) provided the basis for a gambling revolution in America. Since the 1980s, state governments around the country have increasingly expanded legal gambling in the form of lotteries, tribal casinos, and privately managed casinos. Indeed, there are few areas left in the country where citizens cannot at least buy lottery tickets, and revenues (fees, taxes, and direct profit revenue) from gambling have given many states new pots of money for spending on basic services, including education. The figure shows that in Indiana, gambling revenues for the state increased from $165.3 million in 1994 to $775 million in 2003. The majority of this revenue goes to the state's Build Indiana Fund, which was created to keep local property taxes down by paying for capital projects in communities across the state.

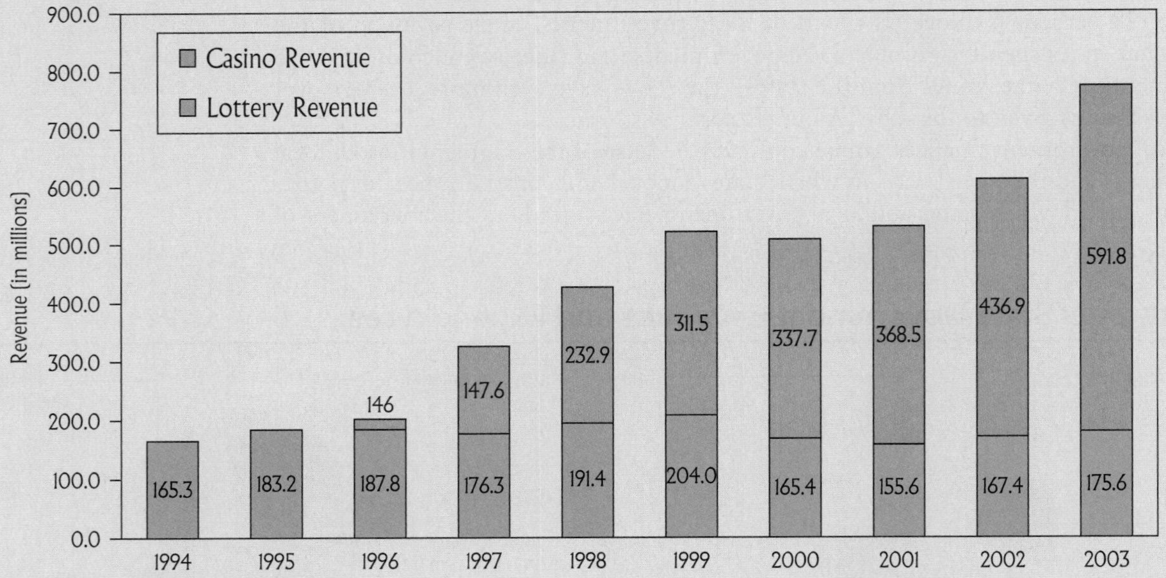

Indiana State Gaming Revenue

Source: Comparative Lottery Analysis: The Impact of Casinos on Lottery Revenues and Total Gaming Revenues, 2004, www.umassd.edu/cfpa/docs/casinolottery.pdf.

YOU ARE THE POLICYMAKER

Should Your State Take a Chance on Gambling?

No one likes taxes, but government services have to be paid for somehow. Since the 1980s, many states have tried to earn money for state programs "painlessly" through legalized gambling. Thirty years ago, only Nevada allowed most forms of gambling; in some states children couldn't even enter a sweepstakes on the back of a cereal box. Today, many states not only allow a variety of types of gambling but even sponsor and earn money from such activities. Various states run lotteries and allow casino and riverboat gambling, horse and dog racing, slot machines, video lottery, bingo, and other forms of what proponents call "gaming."

Suppose you are a state legislator faced with the question of legalizing gambling in your state in order to earn extra revenue without raising taxes. To what extent are you willing to accept the negative aspects of gambling in order to gain its monetary rewards?

States earn money from gambling in three main ways. First, states may run a gambling operation outright. State lotteries are the best example. States skim off as much as 50 percent of the receipts from lottery tickets, offering most of the rest as prize money. Second, states may earn money from gambling by taxing bets and winnings heavily, as is commonly done with casino and racetrack gambling. Third, states can levy a variety of fees, including licensing fees.

This sort of revenue is a very attractive alternative to direct taxation as a way to help states fund public services. First, it is seen as a voluntary source of revenue rather than mandatory taxation. Some characterize it as a tax on stupidity. Second, some argue, certain forms of gambling encourage economic development in local areas and are thereby a positive good quite apart from contributing revenue. The prosperity that some Native American tribes have gained through opening casinos (allowed by the national government since 1988) is evidence in favor of this position. Third, there are those who view gambling as a harmless recreational activity that the state has no business banning anyway—why not make a little money on it?

Even though all states except Utah and Hawaii have legalized some form of gambling in the past 25 years, not all states collect much revenue from gambling, and not all people are convinced that it is good public policy. One argument against legalized gambling is that it is a regressive form of taxation because the people who gamble the highest proportions of their incomes are those who are relatively poor. There has been increasing concern about compulsive gambling, a psychological disorder akin to alcoholism that drives people to gamble incessantly. Like alcoholism, compulsive gambling can lead to financial ruin and the destruction of families. There are also those who argue that gambling is simply immoral and that legalizing and especially encouraging it (as in state lottery TV commercials) leads people to pursue false hope and a destructive lifestyle. Finally, there is some debate as to just how much money a state can actually earn from gambling. For example, beyond the economic benefits of employment and spin-off businesses, commercial casinos in the states contributed about $5.7 billion in direct gaming-related taxes in 2008; state-run lotteries are estimated to have produced almost $16 billion in state revenues in 2005 and almost $18 billion in 2008. However, as economic conditions declined in 2007 to 2009, people spent less on gaming and states saw less revenue from gaming-related activities. Some observers argue that the market for gaming is reaching a saturation point. Legalized gaming can certainly be a significant source of funds, but in many states the potential proportional contribution to the budget is fairly small, at less than 10 percent.

What do you think? As a state legislator, you must weigh the benefits of "painless" gambling revenue against the arguments of those who oppose it. Should your state legalize gambling? If so, in what form? Should it run a lottery? Should it allow casinos and tax them? What difference does it make if neighboring states do or do not have legalized gambling? What would *you* do?

policy responsibilities among local governments. Figure 21.9 offers a snapshot of local government finances—combining county, city, township, school, and special district budgets—across the United States. Local governments receive their revenues from three main sources: intergovernmental aid, taxes, and user charges. Intergovernmental aid (primarily from the states) and taxes each represent about one-third of local government revenue, again showing the great dependence of local governments on their states. Local taxes are mainly property taxes, but sales and income taxes also contribute to the revenue of some local governments. Charges on the use of certain services, such as libraries and recreation facilities, provide another 20 percent of local government revenue. About 8 percent of their revenue comes from municipally owned utilities and liquor sales.

FIGURE 21.9 Local Government Revenues and Expenditures

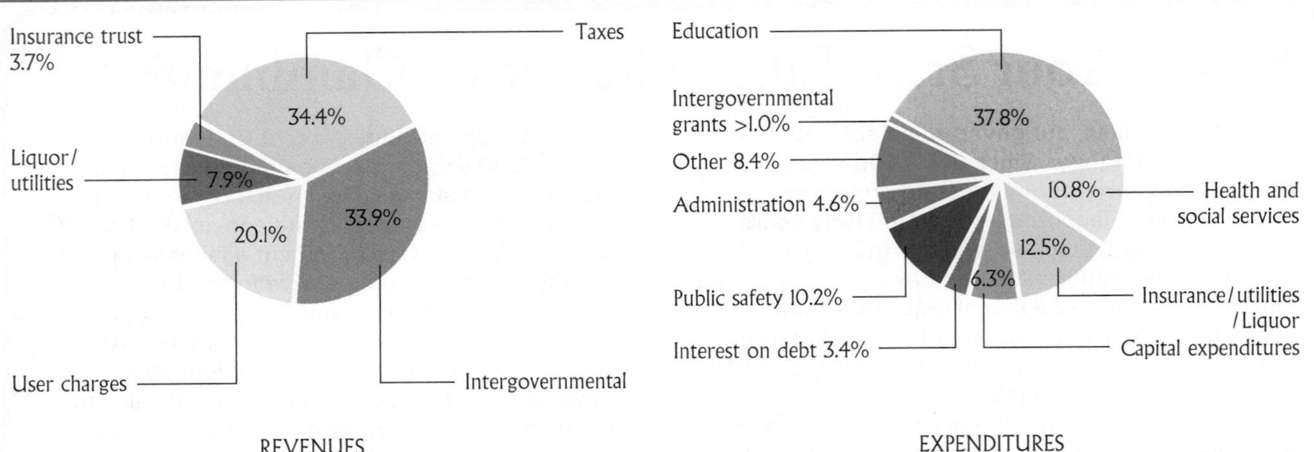

Source: U.S. Bureau of the Census, "State and Local Government Finances, 2006," February 17, 2010, http://www.census.gov/compendia/statab/cats/state_local_govt_finances_employment/state_government_finances.html.

Local governments allocate their monies to a range of services, but the main areas are public education (38 percent), health and social services (11 percent), and public safety (10 percent). These are services that citizens need on a regular basis and expect local governments to provide.

The difference between state and local expenditures reflects the distribution of public services between these levels of government that has developed over the course of the history of the United States. Local government is expected to provide two of the most important and broadly used services of all government in the United States—education and public safety (police and fire protection). State governments, on the other hand, are mainly in charge of making sure that the poorest of the state's citizens have their basic physical needs met. Further, the state is charged with gathering the state's resources and distributing them where they are most needed via intergovernmental grants. While local governments are busy providing direct citizen service, the state governments can take a broader view to enhance equity in public service.

21.9 Assess the democratic elements and the problems of state and local government.

Understanding State and Local Governments

A full understanding of the complexity of subnational government cannot be gleaned from a single textbook chapter, but you should remember a few important points about these 89,476 governments.

Democracy at the Subnational Level

The very existence of so many governments to handle complex as well as ordinary—but needed—services, testifies to the health of our democracy. States have been willing to decentralize their governing arrangements to permit the creation of local governments to address citizens' policy demands. Today, local voters choose their own representatives to serve on county commissions, city councils, school boards, and some special district boards. As small legislatures elected from among the community's residents, these governing bodies are usually the policymaking institutions closest and most open to all citizens. In many ways, local governments encourage individual participation in government and promote the value of individualism at the local level.

The states also operate in an open policymaking environment. Many of the most important of state officials are elected to office, far more than in the national government.

Direct primaries permit voters to select nominees for state offices. The recall even allows voters to oust an official from office before his or her term is over in about one-third of the states. The initiative and the referendum permit voters in many states to make policy or amend their state constitutions directly. In most states, voters have a far more direct role in selecting judges than is the case in the national court system. And by the 1990s, subnational elections were producing a group of officials who demographically were far more representative of the U.S. population.

Even so, subnational politics may not be as democratic as this initial assessment would seem to indicate. Politics at the state level is poorly covered by the media and, as a result, is relatively invisible to the public. Voters can hardly hold elected officials accountable if they know little about what is going on in the state capital. Even at the local level, there is little press coverage of anything other than the results of city council meetings or a mayor's actions—and that doesn't even happen regularly in smaller communities or in suburbs (and increasingly cities) that lack their own daily newspaper.

When, as is often the case, only 30 to 35 percent of voters participate in statewide elections and fewer than 20 percent turnout for local elections, there are real concerns about the health of our grass-roots governments. In one effort to boost citizen participation, states have begun experimenting with vote-by-mail elections. Instead of having to show up on a specific day to cast a ballot, in 1996 citizens in Oregon were able to mail in their ballots, and two years later Oregon voters passed an initiative making vote-by-mail the only way to vote for every election. Further, in a small number of cities throughout the United States, including Birmingham, Dayton, Milwaukee, and St. Paul, vigorous programs of neighborhood democracy have been developed where citizen participation in public affairs goes far beyond voting. In these cities, neighborhood boards are given control over meaningful policy decisions and program resources (such as rent assistance, childcare, and a variety of youth programs), and their actions are not merely advisory. These cities also reward municipal officials who listen to the views of these neighborhood bodies. The experience in these and other cities shows that citizens will devote the considerable time necessary to participate in public affairs if they are convinced that participation is meaningful and that city officials are not just manipulating them.[76]

Competition between subnational governments for economic development also raises significant questions about democracy. As a result of this competition, state and local governments have subsidized business growth and economic development, often at the expense of redistribution services and human resource needs. Business interests have substantial leverage in state and city affairs as a result of their ability to threaten to leave or locate facilities in another jurisdiction. The increasing importance of money in subnational elections has only added to the influence that special interests exert in state and local affairs.

The workings of democracy are often difficult to see in the judicial branch of government. Because most citizens do not attend trials and only lawyers and judges are directly involved in the appeals process, the proceedings of the judiciary are seldom visible to the public until a significant case or decision is announced. This judicial process is not subject to quite the same scrutiny as the legislative and executive functions of state governments. Even though most state and local judges and justices must face the voters to gain or retain their positions, the lack of information that voters have about the judicial process makes the level of true democracy in this process suspect. Citizens will have to take more interest in the crucial role of courts in our democracy in order for courts to assume the same political importance in states as the other branches of government.

The Scope of Subnational Government

Growth in subnational government employment has proceeded at a pace exceeding that of the national government for most of the past 100 years, as you learned in Chapter 15. Most of this growth has been driven by citizen demand for more government services. Although most American voters want their elected representatives to control the size of government, voters also want government to provide them with more and better programs to solve problems, especially in areas where the national government has left gaps or failed to act.

Have the reform and professionalization of subnational government in recent decades made any difference for taxpayers? In most cases, they have not resulted in smaller government. By its very nature, legislative professionalism costs tax dollars and leads to a legislature that is more permanent and continuous. Although school district consolidation has reduced the number of school districts by 66 percent over the past 45 years, during this same period other types of special district governments, responding to a growing demand, have increased by nearly 50 percent.

Most state governments have experimented with *sunset legislation*, which involves periodically reviewing agencies to control the growth of government and eliminate unneeded programs. States have also empowered their legislatures to review executive branch regulations and rules to ensure that citizens or businesses are not overregulated by government. These practices help limit the scope of governments.

But as citizen demand in recent decades led to growth and development in the areas of technology, communications, and public health and safety, subnational governments have had to grow, not diminish. More police, more health care providers, more computer technicians, and more social welfare caseworkers have been needed to meet the expanding range of problems that confront people daily. Although some local governments are barely able to fulfill their basic responsibilities for public safety and maintenance of the local infrastructure, other cities and counties have become much more competent at managing local affairs. Indeed, recent research suggests that local governments often lead their states and the nation in devising innovative ways to deliver public services.[77, 78]

In sum, with the greater responsibilities thrust on them by the national government and the demands of their citizens, subnational governments have responded by enhancing their capacity to provide services to their citizens. In the past 40 years, the enhanced capacity of democratically elected officials in the states, especially state legislators and governors, and the greater use of direct democracy mechanisms have led to stronger and more effective subnational governments that are also more extensive and expensive.

Summary

21.1 Describe how state constitutions differ and a common process for amending state constitutions.

State constitutions vary a great deal in terms of length and level of detail, as well as in their provisions. For example, most Southern states have relatively long and detailed constitutions written following the Civil War. State constitutions can be amended through several processes, but most often a referendum vote by citizens is required.

21.2 Summarize recent patterns in partisan competition in state elections and party control in state government.

Competition between the main political parties has been on the rise across the country for the last 20 years, with a greater number of contested seats and relatively close outcomes in general elections. However, there are still many local and state offices that are dominated by one party. Party control of state government has been trending towards the Democratic party in the 2000s, but state governments have also faced an extended period of divided government, where at least one legislative chamber is controlled by one party and the other party controls the other chamber or the governorship.

21.3 Outline the roles of responsibilities of governors and distinguish their formal and informal powers.

Governors are expected to wear many hats, but many have limited powers. Governors serve as the head of state, are chief law enforcers, and are expected to set policy priorities for state government. In most states this means that the governors play a significant role in the budget process, can appoint individuals within the executive branch, can veto legislation, and can reorganize the executive branch. Governors' formal powers, such as budgetary and appointment powers, are often less important for getting things done than their informal powers, such as public support and the strength of their party in the state legislature.

21.4 Describe the functions of state legislatures and contrast state legislators today with those of the past.

State legislatures are the primary mechanism for creating almost all the basic laws of the state. They appropriate the money that is needed for the state government to function. Legislatures are also responsible for overseeing the activities of the executive branch, including confirming gubernatorial appointments. Since the 1960s, legislatures are not dominated by rural interests and have become considerably more diverse, with greater numbers of women and racial and ethnic minorities.

21.5 Outline the basic elements of most state court systems, and describe the various methods for selecting state judges.

Most state court systems are organized as a hierarchy, with specialized trial courts at the bottom, general trial courts next, intermediate courts of appeal, and a supreme court at the top. States use various selection methods for judges, including appointment by the governor or the legislature, partisan and nonpartisan elections, and, in many states, a combination of political appointment followed by a retention election after a period of service.

21.6 Differentiate types of direct democracy, and evaluate direct democracy.

Direct democracy refers to direct citizen control of the government and includes initiatives and referenda as well as recall. Initiatives and referenda allow citizens to make law (statutory or constitutional) at the ballot box. Because direct democracy relies on majority rule, some observers express concern that minority interests are not protected in this process.

21.7 Explain Dillon's rule, and differentiate five types of local government.

According to Dillon's rule, local governments are "creatures of the state" and have only the powers explicitly granted them by the state. These powers are usually established by a charter granted to a local government by a state. Local governments all exist to help govern an area smaller than a state. Some, such as counties and municipalities, exist to provide a broad array of services to citizens. Others, such as school and special districts, are tasked with a specific purpose, such as providing education or drinking water. Many local governments have a board or commission that functions as a legislature and an executive whose powers relative to the legislature vary greatly. Many local legislatures appoint a manager to handle day-to-day executive decisions.

21.8 Contrast state revenue and expenditures with local revenue and expenditures and outline ways state and local governments have tried to increase revenue.

Local governments rely more heavily than states on intergovernmental transfers for revenue; state governments rely more on a variety of taxes, including income taxes. Most local government expenditures go to education and health and social services; most state expenditures are in fact intergovernmental grants to local governments. State and local governments have tried to improve their revenue streams by adding targeted sales taxes and user fees and by legalizing various forms of gaming.

21.9 Assess the democratic elements and the problems of state and local government.

State and local governments offer the potential for idealized democratic governance with the reality of locally elected representatives solving local problems. Having so many local governments gives citizens greater access to policymaking and allows for policy experimentation on solving problems. However, the great number of local govern-ments also makes for a confusing system that tends to receive little attention from the media or voters, threatening the very notion of responsiveness in a democracy. And, as state and local governments have steadily grown and increased their responsibilities, the high degree of fragmentation and sometimes competition between governments has created a variety of governance problems.

Chapter Test

21.1 Describe how state constitutions differ and a common process for amending state constitutions.

1. Which of the following is NOT true of state constitutions?
   a. They provide for a separation of power
   b. They create executive, legislative, and judicial branches
   c. They include a bill of rights
   d. They tend to be much longer than the U.S. Constitution
   e. They take precedence over federal law

2. Most state constitutions are amended directly through the initiative process.

   True______ False______

3. What are some of the primary differences between state constitutions and the U.S. Constitution? Why do you think these differences exist?

21.2 Summarize recent patterns in partisan competition in state elections and party control in state government.

4. The condition of divided government occurs when
   a. There is a high level of turnover in state legislatures
   b. There is a high level of competition for positions in the state legislature
   c. There is a high level of disagreement between two parties in a state legislature
   d. There is a high level of demographic diversity of elected officials
   e. None of the above

5. By far, the best predictor of the outcome of gubernatorial races is the partisan makeup of the state.

   True______ False______

6. Compare and contrast state legislative and gubernatorial elections. How have both types of elections become more candidate-centered? What are some consequences of these changes? In your opinion, is the current trend toward candidate-centered elections harmful or beneficial to representative democracy?

7. Compare and contrast the pros and cons of instituting term limits for state legislatures. What impact would term limits have on party control in state government? Based on your answer, do you think term limits would be harmful or beneficial to state government? Explain.

21.3 Outline the roles of responsibilities of governors and distinguish their formal and informal powers.

8. Which of the following is NOT typically a formal power granted to state governors?
   a. Governors have the power to appoint
   b. Governors have the power to veto
   c. Governors have the power to initiate the state budget process
   d. Governors have the power to sign trade agreements between their state and foreign nations
   e. Governors have all formal powers listed above

9. Controlling the media has become increasingly important to state governors.

   True______ False______

10. Compare and contrast governors' formal and informal powers. Which of the various powers that governors have do you perceive as the most effective for governors and why?

21.4 Describe the functions of state legislatures and contrast state legislators today with those of the past.

11. Which of the following is a characteristic of a citizen legislator?
    a. Citizen legislators closely interact with their constituents throughout the year
    b. Citizen legislators rely on an extensive legislative staff
    c. Citizen legislators are paid a generous annual salary
    d. Citizen legislators work in the legislature nearly year-round
    e. All of the above are characteristics of citizen legislators

12. What are some of the primary changes associated with legislative professionalism over time? Do you think these changes have produced a more effective state legislature? Why or why not?

21.5 Outline the basic elements of most state court systems, and describe the various methods for selecting state judges.

13. Which of the following methods is used to select state judges?
    a. Judges are appointed by governors or legislatures
    b. Judges are elected by voters in nonpartisan elections
    c. Judges are elected by voters in partisan elections
    d. Judges are appointed by governors, then elected by voters after a year in office
    e. All of the above

14. Intermediate courts of appeals are designed to dispose of routine appeals of trial court decisions.

    True______ False______

21.6 Differentiate types of direct democracy, and evaluate direct democracy.

15. A referendum begins in the state legislature.

    True______ False______

16. What are some of the benefits of three forms of direct democracy (e.g., referendums, initiatives, and recall) in the United States? What are some of the costs? In your opinion, does direct democracy actually empower citizens? Why or why not?

21.7 Explain Dillon's rule, and differentiate five types of local government.

17. The interrelationships between state and local governments are stipulated in the U.S. Constitution.

    True______ False______

18. All but which of the following are basic types of local governments?
    a. Counties
    b. Townships
    c. Mayor–council governments
    d. Municipalities
    e. School districts

19. What does Dillon's Rule stipulate? How is it important to state and local governmental relations? How is it allowed under the U.S. Constitution?

20. What are some potential consequences of the fragmented local governing structures that most metropolitan areas have? Can you think of any solutions that will lead to more effective government and policy at the local level? Explain your answer.

21.8 Contrast state revenue and expenditures with local revenue and expenditures and outline ways state and local governments have tried to increase revenue.

21. Which is the largest share of revenue for states?
    a. Intergovernmental revenue
    b. State insurance programs
    c. Traffic and parking tickets

d. Taxes
e. Federal grants

22. Local governments spend the largest percentage of their budget on health services.

    True______ False______

23. How have local governments sought to increase revenue? Why do local governments need to raise additional monies?

21.9 Assess the democratic elements and the problems of state and local government.

24. Do you think that subnational politics promotes or hinders participatory democracy? If it promotes democracy, in what ways does it do so? If it hinders democracy, how might subnational politics be altered to improve participation?

25. What is the primary reason behind recent patterns of growth in state and local government? In your opinion, is the growth in state and local government good or bad for American citizens? Explain your answer.

PEARSON mypoliscilab™ Exercises

Apply what you learned in this chapter on MyPoliSciLab.

Read on **mypoliscilab.com**

eText: Chapter 21

Study and **Review** on **mypoliscilab.com**

Pre-Test
Post-Test
Chapter Exam
Flashcards

Watch on **mypoliscilab.com**

Video: Wisconsin Governor Seeks to Remove 'Sexting' DA
Video: Battling City Corruption

Explore on **mypoliscilab.com**

Simulation: You Are Attempting to Revise the Texas Constitution
Simulation: You Are a Governor
Simulation: You Are a State Legislator
Simulation: You Are the Mayor and Need to Get a Town Budget Passed
Simulation: You Are the Director of Economic Development for Los Angeles
Comparative: Comparing Executive Branches
Comparative: Comparing Judicial Systems
Comparative: Comparing State and Local Governments
Timeline: Initiatives and Referendums
Visual Literacy: Explaining Differences in State Laws

Key Terms

subnational governments (608)
line-item veto (620)
lieutenant governor (621)
Merit Plan (626)
direct democracy (626)
initiative (627)
referendum (628)
recall (628)
Dillon's Rule (629)
local charter (629)
home rule (629)
town meeting (631)
city manager (632)
council of governments (636)

Internet Resources

http://www.csg.org
Web site of the Council of State Governments, with information on states and state public policies.

www.ncsl.org
Web site of the National Conference of State Legislatures, with information on state legislatures, elections, and members.

www.ncsconline.org
Web site of the National Center for State Courts.

www.nga.org
Web site of the National Governors Association, with links to Web sites for each state.

www.usmayors.org
Web site of the United States Conference of Mayors.

www.census.gov
Web site of the U.S. Census Bureau, with links to sites with data on states and local areas.

www.stateline.org
Web site of the Pew Center on the States, with lots of general and state-specific policy information.

For Further Reading

Brooks, Clayton McClure, ed. ***A Legacy of Leadership: Governors and American History.*** Philadelphia: University of Pennsylvania Press, 2008. A timely collection of essays on how governors and their offices have changed in the last 100 years.

The Council of State Governments. ***The Book of the States*** (annual). Lexington, KY: Council of State Governments. An overview of annual developments in state government.

Gray, Virginia, and Russell L. Hanson, eds. ***Politics in the American States: A Comparative Analysis.*** 9th ed. Washington, DC: Congressional Quarterly Press, 2008. A superb collection of essays that review the empirical literature on state politics.

Hedge, David M. ***Governance and the Changing American States: Transforming American Politics.*** Washington, DC: Congressional Quarterly Press, 1998. An in-depth and balanced assessment of the literature on the resurgence of state government institutions.

Hovey, Hal A., and Kendra A. Hovey. ***CQ's State Fact Finder: Rankings Across America*** (semi-annual). Washington, DC: Congressional Quarterly Press. A data book with hundreds of state-by-state comparisons on economic, demographic, political, and policy variables.

International City/County Management Association. ***The Municipal Year Book*** (annual). Washington, DC: ICMA. Excellent current affairs updates on local governments and informative directories on civic affairs and public officials.

Kantor, Paul P., and Dennis R. Judd. ***Urban Politics in a Global Age.*** New York: Longman, 2009. An important review and analysis of urban government today.

Rosenthal, Alan. ***Engines of Democracy: Politics and Policymaking in State Legislatures.*** Washington, DC: Congressional Quarterly Press, 2008. A detailed examination and evaluation of the state legislatures by a leading analyst of those bodies.

Squire, Peverill. ***State Legislatures Today: Politics Under the Domes.*** New York: Prentice Hall, 2009. Explores the evolution of state legislatures, elections, the changing nature of the job, and the process of policymaking.

Weber, Ronald E., and Paul Brace, eds. ***American State and Local Politics: Directions for the 21st Century.*** Chatham, NJ: Chatham House, 1999. A collection of essays by top scholars focusing on recent reforms and their implications.

Appendix

THE DECLARATION OF INDEPENDENCE*

In Congress, July 4, 1776

The Unanimous Declaration of the Thirteen United States of America

When in the Course of human events it becomes necessary for one people to dissolve the political bands which have connected them with another, and to assume among the powers of the earth, the separate and equal station to which the Laws of Nature and of Nature's God entitle them, a decent respect to the opinions of mankind requires that they should declare the causes which impel them to the separation.

We hold these truths to be self-evident, that all men are created equal, that they are endowed by their Creator with certain unalienable Rights, that among these are Life, Liberty and the pursuit of Happiness.—That to secure these rights, Governments are instituted among Men, deriving their just powers from the consent of the governed,—That whenever any Form of Government becomes destructive of these ends, it is the Right of the People to alter or to abolish it, and to institute new Government, laying its foundation on such principles and organizing its powers in such form, as to them shall seem most likely to effect their Safety and Happiness. Prudence, indeed, will dictate that Governments long established should not be changed for light and transient causes; and accordingly all experience hath shewn that mankind are more disposed to suffer, while evils are sufferable, than to right themselves by abolishing the forms to which they are accustomed. But when a long train of abuses and usurpations, pursuing invariably the same Object evinces a design to reduce them under absolute Despotism, it is their right, it is their duty, to throw off such Government, and to provide new Guards for their future security.

Such has been the patient sufferance of these Colonies; and such is now the necessity which constrains them to alter their former Systems of Government. The history of the present King of Great Britain is a history of repeated injuries and usurpations, all having in direct object the establishment of an absolute Tyranny over these States. To prove this, let Facts be submitted to a candid world.

He has refused his Assent to Laws, the most wholesome and necessary for the public good.

He has forbidden his Governors to pass Laws of immediate and pressing importance, unless suspended in their operation till his Assent should be obtained; and when so suspended, he has utterly neglected to attend to them.

He has refused to pass other Laws for the accommodation of large districts of people, unless those people would relinquish the right of Representation in the Legislature, a right inestimable to them and formidable to tyrants only.

He has called together legislative bodies at places unusual, uncomfortable, and distant from the depository of their Public Records, for the sole purpose of fatiguing them into compliance with his measures.

He has dissolved Representative Houses repeatedly, for opposing with manly firmness his invasions on the rights of the people.

He has refused for a long time, after such dissolutions, to cause others to be elected; whereby the Legislative Powers, incapable of Annihilation, have returned to the People at large for their exercise; the State remaining in the mean time exposed to all the dangers of invasion from without, and convulsions within.

He has endeavored to prevent the population of these States; for that purpose obstructing the Laws for Naturalization of Foreigners; refusing to pass others to encourage their migration hither, and raising the conditions of new Appropriations of Lands.

He has obstructed the Administration of Justice, by refusing his Assent to Laws for establishing Judiciary powers.

He has made Judges dependent on his Will alone, for the tenure of their offices, and the amount and payment of their salaries.

He has erected a multitude of New Offices, and sent hither swarms of Officers to harass our people, and eat out their substance.

He has kept among us, in times of peace, Standing Armies without the Consent of our legislatures.

He has affected to render the Military independent of and superior to the Civil power.

*This text retains the spelling, capitalization, and punctuation of the original.

He has combined with others to subject us to a jurisdiction foreign to our constitution, and unacknowledged by our laws; giving his Assent to their Acts of pretended Legislation:

For quartering large bodies of armed troops among us:

For protecting them, by a mock Trial, from punishment for any Murders which they should commit on the Inhabitants of these States:

For cutting off our Trade with all parts of the world:

For imposing Taxes on us without our Consent:

For depriving us in many cases, of the benefits of Trial by Jury:

For transporting us beyond Seas to be tried for pretended offences:

For abolishing the free System of English Laws in a neighboring Province, establishing therein an Arbitrary government, and enlarging its Boundaries so as to render it at once an example and fit instrument for introducing the same absolute rule into these Colonies:

For taking away our Charters, abolishing our most valuable Laws, and altering fundamentally the Forms of our Governments:

For suspending our own Legislatures, and declaring themselves invested with power to legislate for us in all cases whatsoever.

He has abdicated Government here, by declaring us out of his Protection and waging War against us.

He has plundered our seas, ravaged our Coasts, burnt our towns, and destroyed the lives of our people.

He is at this time transporting large Armies of foreign Mercenaries to compleat the works of death, desolation and tyranny, already begun with circumstances of Cruelty & perfidy scarcely paralleled in the most barbarous ages, and totally unworthy the Head of a civilized nation.

He has constrained our fellow Citizens taken Captive on the high Seas to bear Arms against their Country, to become the executioners of their friends and Brethren, or to fall themselves by their Hands.

He has excited domestic insurrections amongst us, and has endeavored to bring on the inhabitants of our frontiers, the merciless Indian Savages, whose known rule of warfare, is an undistinguished destruction of all ages, sexes and conditions.

In every stage of these Oppressions We have Petitioned for Redress in the most humble terms: Our repeated Petitions have been answered only by repeated injury. A Prince, whose character is thus marked by every act which may define a Tyrant, is unfit to be the ruler of a free people.

Nor have We been wanting in attention to our British brethren. We have warned them from time to time of attempts by their legislature to extend an unwarrantable jurisdiction over us. We have reminded them of the circumstances of our emigration and settlement here. We have appealed to their native justice and magnanimity, and we have conjured them by the ties of our common kindred to disavow these usurpations, which would inevitably interrupt our connections and correspondence. They too have been deaf to the voice of justice and consanguinity. We must, therefore, acquiesce in the necessity, which denounces our Separation, and hold them, as we hold the rest of mankind, Enemies in War, in Peace Friends.

We, therefore, the Representatives of the United States of America, in General Congress, Assembled, appealing to the Supreme Judge of the world for the rectitude of our intentions, do, in the Name, and by Authority of the good People of these Colonies, solemnly publish and declare, That these United Colonies are, and of Right ought to be Free and Independent States; that they are Absolved from all Allegiance to the British Crown, and that all political connection between them and the State of Great Britain, is and ought to be totally dissolved; and that as Free and Independent States, they have full Power to levy War, conclude Peace, contract Alliances, establish Commerce, and to do all other Acts and Things which Independent States may of right do. And for the support of this Declaration, with a firm reliance on the protection of divine Providence, we mutually pledge to each other our Lives, our Fortunes and our sacred Honor.

John Hancock

NEW HAMPSHIRE
Josiah Bartlett,
Wm. Whipple,
Matthew Thornton.

MASSACHUSETTS BAY
Saml. Adams,
John Adams,
Robt. Treat Paine,
Elbridge Gerry.

RHODE ISLAND
Step. Hopkins,
William Ellery.

CONNECTICUT
Roger Sherman,
Samuel Huntington,
Wm. Williams,
Oliver Wolcott.

NEW YORK
Wm. Floyd,
Phil. Livingston,
Frans. Lewis,
Lewis Morris.

NEW JERSEY
Richd. Stockton,
Jno. Witherspoon,
Fras. Hopkinson,
John Hart,
Abra. Clark.

PENNSYLVANIA
Robt. Morris,
Benjamin Rush,
Benjamin Franklin,
John Morton,
Geo. Clymer,
Jas. Smith,
Geo. Taylor,
James Wilson,
Geo. Ross.

DELAWARE
Caesar Rodney,
Geo. Read,
Tho. M'kean.

MARYLAND
Samuel Chase,
Wm. Paca,
Thos. Stone,
Charles Caroll of
Carrollton.

VIRGINIA
George Wythe,
Richard Henry Lee,
Th. Jefferson,
Benjamin Harrison,
Thos. Nelson, jr.,
Francis Lightfoot Lee,
Carter Braxton.

NORTH CAROLINA
Wm. Hooper,
Joseph Hewes,
John Penn.

SOUTH CAROLINA
Edward Rutledge,
Thos. Heyward, Junr.,
Thomas Lynch, jnr.,
Arthur Middleton.

GEORGIA
Button Gwinnett,
Lyman Hall,
Geo. Walton.

THE FEDERALIST NO. 10

James Madison

November 22, 1787

To the People of the State of New York.

Among the numerous advantages promised by a well constructed Union, none deserves to be more accurately developed than its tendency to break and control the violence of faction. The friend of popular governments, never finds himself so much alarmed for their character and fate, as when he contemplates their propensity to this dangerous vice. He will not fail therefore to set a due value on any plan which, without violating the principles to which he is attached, provides a proper cure for it. The instability, injustice and confusion introduced into the public councils, have in truth been the mortal diseases under which popular governments have every where perished; as they continue to be the favorite and fruitful topics from which the adversaries to liberty derive their most specious declamations. The valuable improvements made by the American Constitutions on the popular models, both ancient and modern, cannot certainly be too much admired; but it would be an unwarrantable partiality, to contend that they have as effectually obviated the danger on this side as was wished and expected. Complaints are every where heard from our most considerate and virtuous citizens, equally the friends of public and private faith, and of public and personal liberty; that our governments are too unstable; that the public good is disregarded in the conflicts of rival parties; and that measures are too often decided, not according to the rules of justice, and the rights of the minor party; but by the superior force of an interested and over-bearing majority. However anxiously we may wish that these complaints had no foundation, the evidence of known facts will not permit us to deny that they are in some degree true. It will be found indeed, on a candid review of our situation, that some of the distresses under which we labor, have been erroneously charged on the operation of our governments; but it will be found, at the same time, that other causes will not alone account for many of our heaviest misfortunes; and particularly, for that prevailing and increasing distrust of public engagements, and alarm for private rights, which are echoed from one end of the continent to the other. These must be chiefly, if not wholly, effects of the unsteadiness and injustice, with which a factious spirit has tainted our public administrations.

By a faction I understand a number of citizens, whether amounting to a majority or minority of the whole, who are united and actuated by some common impulse of passion, or of interest, adverse to the rights of other citizens, or to the permanent and aggregate interests of the community.

There are two methods of curing the mischiefs of faction: the one, by removing its causes; the other, by controlling its effects.

There are again two methods of removing the causes of faction: the one by destroying the liberty which is essential to its existence; the other, by giving to every citizen the same opinions, the same passions, and the same interests.

It could never be more truly said than of the first remedy, that it is worse than the disease. Liberty is to faction, what air is to fire, an aliment without which it instantly expires. But it could not be a less folly to abolish liberty, which is essential to political life, because it nourishes faction, than it would be to wish the annihilation of air, which is essential to animal life, because it imparts to fire its destructive agency.

The second expedient is as impracticable, as the first would be unwise. As long as the reason of man continues fallible, and he is at liberty to exercise it, different opinions will be formed. As long as the connection subsists between his reason and his self-love, his opinions and his passions will have a reciprocal influence on each other; and the former will be objects to which the latter will attach themselves. The diversity in the faculties of men from which the rights of property originate, is not less an insuperable obstacle to a uniformity of interests. The protection of these faculties is the first object of Government. From the protection of different and unequal faculties of acquiring property, the possession of different degrees and kinds of property immediately results: and from the influence of these on the sentiments and views of the respective proprietors, ensues a division of the society into different interests and parties.

The latent causes of faction are thus sown in the nature of man; and we see them every where brought into different degrees of activity, according to the different circumstances of civil society. A zeal for different opinions concerning religion, concerning Government and many other points, as well of speculation as of practice; an attachment to different leaders ambitiously contending for pre-eminence and power; or to persons of other descriptions whose fortunes have been interesting to the human passions, have in turn divided mankind into parties, inflamed them with mutual animosity, and rendered them much more disposed to vex and oppress each other, than to co-operate for their common good. So strong is this propensity of mankind to fall into mutual animosities, that where no substantial occasion presents itself, the most frivolous and fanciful distinctions have been sufficient to kindle their unfriendly passions, and excite their most violent conflicts. But the most common and durable source of factions, has been the various and unequal distribution of property. Those who hold, and those who are without property, have ever formed distinct interests in society. Those who are creditors, and those who are debtors, fall under a like discrimination. A landed interest, a manufacturing interest, a mercantile interest, a monied interest, with many lesser interests, grow up of necessity in civilized nations, and divide them into different classes, actuated by different sentiments and views. The regulation of these various and interfering interests forms the principal task of modern Legislation, and involves the spirit of party and faction in the necessary and ordinary operations of Government.

No man is allowed to be a judge in his own cause; because his interest would certainly bias his judgment, and, not improbably, corrupt his integrity. With equal, nay with greater reason, a body of men, are unfit to be both judges and parties, at the same time; yet, what are many of the most important acts of legislation, but so many judicial determinations, not indeed concerning the rights of single persons, but concerning the rights of large bodies of citizens, and what are the different classes of legislators, but advocates and parties to the causes which they determine? Is a law proposed concerning private debts? It is a question to which the creditors are parties on one side, and the debtors on the other. Justice ought to hold the balance between them. Yet the parties are and must be themselves the judges; and the most numerous party, or, in other words, the most powerful faction must be expected to prevail. Shall domestic manufactures be encouraged, and in what degree, by restrictions on foreign manufactures? are questions which would be differently decided by the landed and the manufacturing classes; and probably by neither, with a sole regard to justice and the public good. The apportionment of taxes on the various descriptions of property, is an act which seems to require the most exact impartiality; yet, there is perhaps no legislative act in which greater opportunity and temptation are given to a predominant party, to trample on the rules of justice. Every shilling with which they over-burden the inferior number, is a shilling saved to their own pockets.

It is in vain to say, that enlightened statesmen will be able to adjust these clashing interests, and render them all subservient to the public good. Enlightened statesmen will not always be at the helm: Nor, in many cases, can such an adjustment be made at all, without taking into view indirect and remote considerations, which will rarely prevail over the immediate interest which one party may find in disregarding the rights of another, or the good of the whole.

The inference to which we are brought, is, that the causes of faction cannot be removed; and that relief is only to be sought in the means of controlling its effects.

If a faction consists of less than a majority, relief is supplied by the republican principle, which enables the majority to defeat its sinister views by regular vote: It may clog the administration, it may convulse the society; but it will be unable to execute and mask its violence under the forms of the Constitution. When a majority is included in a faction, the form of popular government on the other hand enables it to sacrifice to its ruling passion or interest, both the public good and the rights of other citizens. To secure the public good, and private rights, against the danger of such a faction, and at the same time to preserve the spirit and the form of popular government, is then the great object to which our enquiries are directed: Let me add that it is the great desideratum, by which alone this form of government can be rescued from the opprobrium under which it has so long labored, and be recommended to the esteem and adoption of mankind.

By what means is this object attainable? Evidently by one of two only. Either the existence of the same passion or interest in a majority at the same time, must be prevented; or the majority, having such co-existent passion or interest, must be rendered, by their number and local situation, unable to concert and carry into effect schemes of oppression. If the impulse and the opportunity be suffered to coincide, we well know that neither moral nor religious motives can be relied on as an adequate control. They are not found to be such on the injustice and violence of individuals, and lose their efficacy in proportion to the number combined together; that is, in proportion as their efficacy becomes needful.

From this view of the subject, it may be concluded, that a pure Democracy, by which I mean, a Society, consisting of a small number of citizens, who assemble and administer the Government in person, can admit of no cure for the mischiefs of faction. A common passion or interest will, in almost every case, be felt by a majority of the whole; a communication and concert results from the form of Government itself; and there is nothing to check the inducements to sacrifice the weaker party, or an obnoxious individual. Hence it is, that such Democracies have ever been spectacles of turbulence and contention; have ever been found incompatible with personal security, or the rights of property; and have in general been as short in their lives, as they have been violent in their deaths. Theoretic politicians, who have patronized this species of Government, have erroneously supposed, that by reducing mankind to a perfect equality in their political rights, they would, at the same time, be perfectly equalized and assimilated in their possessions, their opinions, and their passions.

A republic, by which I mean a government in which the scheme of representation takes place, opens a different prospect, and promises the cure for which we are seeking. Let us examine the points in which it varies from pure democracy, and we shall comprehend both the nature of the cure and the efficacy which it must derive from the union.

The two great points of difference, between a democracy and a republic, are, first, the delegation of the government, in the latter, to a small number of citizens, elected by the rest; secondly, the greater number of citizens, and greater sphere of country, over which the latter may be extended.

The effect of the first difference is, on the one hand, to refine and enlarge the public views, by passing them through the medium of a chosen body of citizens, whose wisdom may best discern the true interest of their country, and whose patriotism and love of justice, will be least likely to sacrifice it to temporary or partial considerations. Under such a regulation, it may well happen, that the public voice, pronounced by the representatives of the people, will be more consonant to the public good, than if pronounced by the people themselves, convened for the purpose. On the other hand the effect may be inverted. Men of factious tempers, of local prejudices, or of sinister designs, may by intrigue, by corruption, or by other means, first obtain the suffrages, and then betray the interest of the people. The question resulting is, whether small or extensive republics are most favorable to the election of proper guardians of the public weal, and it is clearly decided in favor of the latter by two obvious considerations.

In the first place, it is to be remarked that, however small the republic may be, the representatives must be raised to a certain number, in order to guard against the cabals of a few; and that however large it may be, they must be limited to a certain number, in order to guard against the confusion of a multitude. Hence, the number of representatives in the two cases not being in proportion to that of the constituents, and being proportionally greatest in the small republic, it follows, that if the proportion of fit characters be not less in the large than in the small republic, the former will present a greater option, and consequently a greater probability of a fit choice.

In the next place, as each Representative will be chosen by a greater number of citizens in the large than in the small Republic, it will be more difficult for unworthy candidates to practise with success the vicious arts, by which elections are too often carried; and the suffrages of the people being more free, will be more likely to center on men who possess the most attractive merit, and the most diffusive and established characters.

It must be confessed, that in this, as in most other cases, there is a mean, on both sides of which inconveniences will be found to lie. By enlarging too much the number of electors, you render the representative too little acquainted with all their local circumstances and lesser interests; as by reducing it too much, you render him unduly attached to these, and too little fit to comprehend and pursue great and national objects. The Federal Constitution forms a happy combination in this respect; the great and aggregate interests being referred to the national, the local and particular, to the state legislatures.

The other point of difference is, the greater number of citizens and extent of territory which may be brought within the compass of Republican, than of Democratic Government; and it is this circumstance principally which renders factious combinations less to be dreaded in the former, than in the latter. The smaller the society, the fewer probably will be the distinct parties and interests composing it; the fewer the distinct parties and interests, the more frequently will a majority be found of the same party; and the smaller the number of individuals composing a majority, and the smaller the compass within which they are placed, the more easily will they concert and execute their plans of oppression. Extend the sphere, and you take in a greater variety of parties and interests; you make it less probable that a majority of the whole will have a common motive to invade the rights of other citizens; or if such a common motive exists, it will be more difficult for all who feel it to discover their own strength, and to act in unison with each other. Besides other impediments, it may be remarked, that where there is a consciousness of unjust or dishonorable purposes, communication is always checked by distrust, in proportion to the number whose concurrence is necessary.

Hence it clearly appears, that the same advantage, which a Republic has over a Democracy, in controlling the effects of faction, is enjoyed by a large over a small Republic—is enjoyed by the Union over the States composing it. Does this advantage consist in the substitution of Representatives, whose enlightened views and virtuous sentiments render them superior to local prejudices, and to schemes of injustice? It will not be denied, that the Representation of the Union will be most likely to possess these requisite endowments. Does it consist in the greater security afforded by a greater variety of parties, against the event of any one party being able to outnumber and oppress the rest? In an equal degree does the increased variety of parties, comprised within the Union, increase this security? Does it, in fine, consist in the greater obstacles opposed to the concert and accomplishment of the secret wishes of an unjust and interested majority? Here, again, the extent of the Union gives it the most palpable advantage.

The influence of factious leaders may kindle a flame within their particular States, but will be unable to spread a general conflagration through the other States: a religious sect may degenerate into a political faction in a part of the Confederacy but the variety of sects dispersed over the entire face of it, must secure the national Councils against any danger from that source: a rage for paper money, for an abolition of debts, for an equal division of property, or for any other improper or wicked project, will be less apt to pervade the whole body of the Union, than a particular member of it; in the same proportion as such a malady is more likely to taint a particular county or district, than an entire State.

In the extent and proper structure of the Union, therefore, we behold a Republican remedy for the diseases most incident to Republican Government. And according to the degree of pleasure and pride, we feel in being Republicans, ought to be our zeal in cherishing the spirit, and supporting the character of Federalists.

PUBLIUS

THE FEDERALIST NO. 51

James Madison

February 6, 1788

To the People of the State of New York.

To what expedient then shall we finally resort for maintaining in practice the necessary partition of power among the several departments, as laid down in the constitution? The only answer that can be given is, that as all these exterior provisions are found to be inadequate, the defect must be supplied, by so contriving the interior structure of the government, as that its several constituent parts may, by their mutual relations, be the means of keeping each other in their proper places. Without presuming to undertake a full development of this important idea, I will hazard a few general observations, which may perhaps place it in a clearer light, and enable us to form a more correct judgment of the principles and structure of the government planned by the convention.

In order to lay a due foundation for that separate and distinct exercise of the different powers of government, which to a certain extent, is admitted on all hands to be essential to the preservation of liberty, it is evident that each department should have a will of its own; and consequently should be so constituted, that the members of each should have as little agency as possible in the appointment of the members of the others. Were this principle rigorously adhered to, it would require that all the appointments for the supreme executive, legislative, and judiciary magistracies, should be drawn from the same fountain of authority, the people, through channels, having no communication whatever with one another. Perhaps such a plan of constructing the several departments would be less difficult in practice than it may in contemplation appear. Some difficulties however, and some additional expense, would attend the execution of it. Some deviations therefore from the principle must be admitted. In the constitution of the judiciary department in particular, it might be inexpedient to insist rigorously on the principle; first, because peculiar qualifications being essential in the members, the primary consideration ought to be to select that mode of choice, which best secures these qualifications; secondly, because the permanent tenure by which the appointments are held in that department, must soon destroy all sense of dependence on the authority conferring them.

It is equally evident that the members of each department should be as little dependent as possible on those of the others, for the emoluments annexed to their offices. Were the executive magistrate, or the judges, not independent of the legislature in this particular, their independence in every other would be merely nominal.

But the great security against a gradual concentration of the several powers in the same department, consists in giving to those who administer each department, the necessary constitutional means, and personal motives, to resist encroachments of the others. The provision for defense must in this, as in all other cases, be made commensurate to the danger of attack. Ambition must be made to counteract ambition. The interest of the man must be connected with the constitutional right of the place. It may be a reflection on human nature, that such devices should be necessary to control the abuses of government. But what is government itself but the greatest of all reflections on human nature? If men were angels, no government would be necessary. If angels were to govern men, neither external nor internal controls on government would be necessary. In framing a government which is to be administered by men over men, the great difficulty lies in this: You must first enable the government to control the governed; and in the next place, oblige it to control itself. A dependence on the people is no doubt the primary control on the government; but experience has taught mankind the necessity of auxiliary precautions.

This policy of supplying by opposite and rival interests, the defect of better motives, might be traced through the whole system of human affairs, private as well as public. We see it particularly displayed in all the subordinate distributions of power; where the constant aim is to divide and arrange the several offices in such a manner as that each may be a check on the other; that the private interest of every individual, may be a sentinel over the public rights. These inventions of prudence cannot be less requisite in the distribution of the supreme powers of the state.

But it is not possible to give to each department an equal power of self defense. In republican government the legislative authority, necessarily, predominates. The remedy for this inconveniency is, to divide the legislature into different branches; and to render them by different modes of election, and different principles of action, as little connected with each other, as the nature of their common functions, and their common dependence on the society, will admit. It may even be necessary to guard against dangerous encroachments by still further precautions. As the weight of the legislative authority requires that it should be thus divided, the weakness of the executive may require, on the other hand, that it should be fortified. An absolute negative, on the legislature, appears at first view to be the natural defense with which the executive magistrate should be armed. But perhaps it would be neither altogether safe, nor alone sufficient. On ordinary occasions, it might not be exerted with the requisite firmness; and on extraordinary occasions, it might be perfidiously abused. May not this defect of an absolute negative be supplied, by some qualified connection between this weaker department, and the weaker branch of the stronger department, by which the latter may be led to support the constitutional rights of the former, without being too much detached from the rights of its own department?

If the principles on which these observations are founded be just, as I persuade myself they are, and they be applied as a criterion, to the several state constitutions, and to the federal constitution, it will be found, that if the latter does not perfectly correspond with them, the former are infinitely less able to bear such a test.

There are moreover two considerations particularly applicable to the federal system of America, which place that system in a very interesting point of view.

First. In a single republic, all the power surrendered by the people, is submitted to the administration of a single government; and usurpations are guarded against by a division of the government into distinct and separate departments. In the compound republic of America, the power surrendered by the people, is first divided between two distinct governments, and then the portion allotted to each, subdivided among distinct and separate departments. Hence a double security arises to the rights of the people. The different governments will control each other; at the same time that each will be controlled by itself.

Second. It is of great importance in a republic, not only to guard the society against the oppression of its rulers; but to guard one part of the society against the injustice of the other part. Different interests necessarily exist in different classes of citizens. If a majority be united by a common interest, the rights of the minority will be insecure. There are but two methods of providing against this evil: The one by creating a will in the community independent of the majority, that is, of the society itself, the other by comprehending in the society so many separate descriptions of citizens, as will render an unjust combination of a majority of the whole, very improbable, if not impracticable. The first method prevails in all governments possessing an hereditary or self appointed authority. This at best is but a precarious security; because a power independent of the society may as well espouse the unjust views of the major, as the rightful interests, of the minor party, and may possibly be turned against both parties. The second method will be exemplified in the federal republic of the United States. While all authority in it will be derived from and dependent on the society, the society itself will be broken into so many parts, interests and classes of citizens, that the rights of individuals or of the minority, will be in little danger from interested combinations of the majority. In a free government, the security for civil rights must be the same as for religious rights. It consists in the one case in the multiplicity of interests, and in the other, in the multiplicity of sects. The degree of security in both cases will depend on the number of interests and sects; and this may be presumed to depend on the extent of country and number of people comprehended under the same government. This view of the subject must particularly recommend a proper federal system to all the sincere and considerate friends of republican government: Since it shows that in exact proportion as the territory of the union may be formed into more circumscribed confederacies or states, oppressive combinations of a majority will be facilitated, the best security under the republican form, for the rights of every class of citizens, will be diminished; and consequently, the stability and independence of some member of the government, the only other security, must be proportionally increased. Justice is the end of government. It is the end of civil society. It ever has been, and ever will be pursued, until it be obtained, or until liberty be lost in the pursuit. In a society under the forms of which the stronger faction can readily unite and oppress the weaker, anarchy may as truly be said to reign, as in a state of nature where the weaker individual is not secured against the violence of the stronger: And as in the latter state even the stronger individuals are prompted by the uncertainty of their condition, to submit to a government which may protect the weak as well as themselves: So in the former state, will the more powerful factions or parties be gradually induced by a like motive, to wish for a government which will protect all parties, the weaker as well as the more powerful. It can be little doubted, that if the state of Rhode Island was separated from the confederacy, and left to itself, the insecurity of rights under the popular form of government within such narrow limits, would be displayed by such reiterated oppressions of factious majorities, that some power altogether independent of the people would soon be called for by the voice of the very factions whose misrule had proved the necessity of it. In the extended republic of the United States, and among the great variety of interests, parties and sects which it embraces, a coalition of a majority of the whole society could seldom take place on any other principles than those of justice and the general good; and there being thus less danger to a minor from the will of the major party, there must be less pretext also, to provide for the security of the former, by introducing into the government a will not dependent on the latter; or in other words, a will independent of the society itself. It is no less certain than it is important, notwithstanding the contrary opinions which have been entertained, that the larger the society, provided it lie within a practicable sphere, the more duly capable it will be of self government. And happily for the *republican cause*, the practicable sphere may be carried to a very great extent, by a judicious modification and mixture of the *federal principle.*

PUBLIUS

THE CONSTITUTION OF THE UNITED STATES OF AMERICA*

(Preamble)

We the People of the United States, in Order to form a more perfect Union, establish Justice, insure domestic Tranquility, provide for the common defence, promote the general Welfare, and secure the Blessings of Liberty to ourselves and our Posterity, do ordain and establish this Constitution for the United States of America.

ARTICLE I.

(The Legislature)

Section 1. All legislative Powers herein granted shall be vested in a Congress of the United States, which shall consist of a Senate and House of Representatives.

*This text retains the spelling, capitalization, and punctuation of the original. Brackets indicate passages that have been altered by amendments.

Section 2. The House of Representatives shall be composed of Members chosen every second Year by the People of the several States, and the Electors in each State shall have the Qualifications requisite for Electors of the most numerous Branch of the State Legislature.

No person shall be a Representative who shall not have attained to the Age of twenty five Years, and been seven Years a Citizen of the United States, and who shall not, when elected, be an Inhabitant of that State in which he shall be chosen.

Representatives and direct [Taxes][1] shall be apportioned among the several States which may be included within this Union, according to their respective Numbers [which shall be determined by adding to the whole Number of free Persons, including those bound to Service for a Term of Years, and excluding Indians not taxed, three fifths of all other Persons].[2] The actual Enumeration shall be made within three Years after the first Meeting of the Congress of the United States, and within every subsequent Term of ten Years, in such Manner as they shall by Law direct. The Number of Representatives shall not exceed one for every thirty Thousand, but each State shall have at Least one Representative; and until such enumeration shall be made, the State of New Hampshire shall be entitled to chuse three, Massachusetts eight, Rhode-Island and Providence Plantations one, Connecticut five, New-York six, New Jersey four, Pennsylvania eight, Delaware one, Maryland six, Virginia ten, North Carolina five, South Carolina five, and Georgia three.

When vacancies happen in the Representation from any State, the Executive Authority thereof shall issue Writs of Election to fill such Vacancies.

The House of Representatives shall chuse their speaker and other Officers; and shall have the sole Power of Impeachment.

Section 3. The Senate of the United States shall be composed of two Senators from each State [chosen by the Legislature thereof],[3] for six Years; and each Senator shall have one Vote.

Immediately after they shall be assembled in Consequence of the first Election, they shall be divided as equally as may be into three Classes. The Seats of the Senators of the first Class shall be vacated at the Expiration of the second year, of the second Class at the Expiration of the fourth Year, and of the third Class at the Expiration of the sixth Year, so that one third may be chosen every second Year [and if Vacancies happen by Resignation, or otherwise, during the Recess of the Legislature of any State, the Executive thereof may make temporary Appointments until the next Meeting of the Legislature, which shall then fill such Vacancies].[4]

No Person shall be a Senator who shall not have attained to the Age of thirty Years, and been nine Years a Citizen of the United States, and who shall not, when elected, be an Inhabitant of that State for which he shall be chosen.

The Vice President of the United States shall be President of the Senate, but shall have no Vote, unless they be equally divided.

The Senate shall chuse their other Officers, and also a President pro tempore, in the Absence of the Vice President, or when he shall exercise the Office of President of the United States.

The Senate shall have the sole Power to try all Impeachments. When sitting for that Purpose, they shall be on Oath or Affirmation. When the President of the United States is tried, the Chief Justice shall preside: And no Person shall be convicted without the Concurrence of two thirds of the Members present.

Judgment in Cases of Impeachment shall not extend further than to removal from Office, and disqualification to hold and enjoy any Office of honor, Trust or Profit under the United States; but the Party convicted shall nevertheless be liable and subject to Indictment, Trial, Judgment and Punishment, according to Law.

Section 4. The Times, Places and Manner of holding Elections for Senators and Representatives, shall be prescribed in each State by the Legislature thereof; but the Congress may at any time by Law make or alter such Regulations, except as to the Places of chusing Senators.

[The Congress shall assemble at least once in every Year, and such Meeting shall be on the first Monday in December, unless they shall by Law appoint a different Day.][5]

Section 5. Each House shall be the Judge of the Elections, Returns and Qualifications of its own Members, and a Majority of each shall constitute a Quorum to do Business; but a smaller Number may adjourn from day to day, and may be authorized to compel the Attendance of absent Members, in such Manner, and under such Penalties as each House may provide.

Each House may determine the Rules of its Proceedings, punish its Members for disorderly Behaviour, and, with the Concurrence of two thirds, expel a Member.

Each House shall keep a Journal of its Proceedings, and from time to time publish the same, excepting such Parts as may in their judgment require Secrecy; and the Yeas and Nays of the Members of either House on any question shall, at the Desire of one fifth of those present, be entered on the Journal.

Neither House, during the Session of Congress, shall, without the Consent of the other, adjourn for more than three days, nor to any other Place than that in which the two Houses shall be sitting.

Section 6. The Senators and Representatives shall receive a Compensation for their Services, to be ascertained by Law, and paid out of the Treasury of the United States. They shall in all Cases, except Treason, Felony and Breach of the Peace, be privileged from Arrest during their Attendance at the Session of their respective Houses, and in going to and returning from the same; and for any Speech or Debate in either House, they shall not be questioned in any other Place.

No Senator or Representative shall, during the Time for which he was elected, be appointed to any civil Office under the Authority of the United States, which shall have been created, or the Emoluments whereof shall have been encreased during such time; and no Person holding any Office under the United States, shall be a Member of either House during his Continuance in Office.

Section 7. All Bills for raising Revenue shall originate in the House of Representatives; but the Senate may propose or concur with Amendments as on other Bills.

Every Bill which shall have passed the House of Representatives and the Senate, shall, before it becomes a Law, be presented to the President of the United States; If he approves he shall sign it, but if not he shall return it, with his Objections to that House in which it shall have originated, who shall enter the Objections at

[1]See Amendment XVI.
[2]See Amendment XIV.
[3]See Amendment XVII.
[4]See Amendment XVII.
[5]See Amendment XX.

large on their Journal, and proceed to reconsider it. If after such Reconsideration two thirds of that House shall agree to pass the Bill, it shall be sent, together with the Objections, to the other House, by which it shall likewise be reconsidered, and if approved by two thirds of that House, it shall become a Law. But in all such Cases the Votes of both Houses shall be determined by yeas and Nays, and the Names of the Persons voting for and against the Bill shall be entered on the Journal of each House respectively. If any Bill shall not be returned by the President within ten Days (Sundays excepted) after it shall have been presented to him, the Same shall be a Law, in like Manner as if he had signed it, unless the Congress by their Adjournment prevent its Return, in which Case it shall not be a Law.

Every Order, Resolution, or Vote to which the Concurrence of the Senate and House of Representatives may be necessary (except on a question of Adjournment) shall be presented to the President of the United States; and before the Same shall take Effect, shall be approved by him, or being disapproved by him, shall be repassed by two thirds of the Senate and House of Representatives, according to the Rules and Limitations prescribed in the Case of a Bill.

Section 8. The Congress shall have Power To lay and collect Taxes, Duties, Imposts and Excises, to pay the Debts and provide for the common Defence and general Welfare of the United States; but all Duties, Imposts and Excises shall be uniform throughout the United States;

To borrow Money on the credit of the United States;

To regulate Commerce with foreign Nations, and among the several States, and with the Indian Tribes;

To establish a uniform Rule of Naturalization, and uniform Laws on the subject of Bankruptcies throughout the United States;

To coin Money, regulate the Value thereof, and of foreign Coin, and fix the Standard of Weights and Measures;

To provide for the Punishment of counterfeiting the Securities and current Coin of the United States;

To establish Post Offices and post Roads;

To promote the Progress of Science and useful Arts, by securing for limited Times to Authors and Inventors the exclusive Right to their respective Writings and Discoveries;

To constitute Tribunals inferior to the supreme Court;

To define and punish Piracies and Felonies committed on the high Seas, and Offences against the Law of Nations;

To declare War, grant Letters of Marque and Reprisal, and make Rules concerning Captures on Land and Water;

To raise and support Armies, but no Appropriation of Money to that Use shall be for a longer Term than two Years;

To provide and maintain a Navy;

To make Rules for the Government and Regulation of the land and naval Forces;

To provide for calling forth the Militia to execute the Laws of the Union, suppress Insurrections and repel Invasions;

To provide for organizing, arming, and disciplining, the Militia, and for governing such Part of them as may be employed in the Service of the United States, reserving to the States respectively, the Appointment of the Officers, and the Authority of training the Militia according to the discipline prescribed by Congress;

To exercise exclusive Legislation in all Cases whatsoever, over such District (not exceeding ten Miles square) as may, by Cession of particular States, and the Acceptance of Congress, become the Seat of the Government of the United States, and to exercise like Authority over all Places purchased by the Consent of the Legislature of the State in which the Same shall be, for the Erection of Forts, Magazines, Arsenals, dock-Yards, and other needful Buildings;—And

To make all Laws which shall be necessary and proper for carrying into Execution the foregoing Powers, and all other Powers vested by this Constitution in the Government of the United States, or in any Department or Officer thereof.

Section 9. The Migration or Importation of such Persons as any of the States now existing shall think proper to admit, shall not be prohibited by the Congress prior to the Year one thousand eight hundred and eight, but a Tax or duty may be imposed on such Importation, not exceeding ten dollars for each Person.

The Privilege of the Writ of Habeas Corpus shall not be suspended, unless when in Cases of Rebellion or Invasion the public Safety may require it.

No Bill of Attainder or ex post facto Law shall be passed.

[No Capitation, or other direct, Tax shall be laid, unless in Proportion to the Census or Enumeration herein before directed to be taken.][6]

No Tax or Duty shall be laid on Articles exported from any State.

No Preference shall be given by any Regulation of Commerce or Revenue to the Ports of one State over those of another; nor shall Vessels bound to, or from, one State, be obliged to enter, clear, or pay Duties in another.

No Money shall be drawn from the Treasury, but in Consequence of Appropriations made by Law; and a regular Statement and Account of the Receipts and Expenditures of all public Money shall be published from time to time.

No Title of Nobility shall be granted by the United States: And no Person holding any Office of Profit or Trust under them, shall, without the Consent of the Congress, accept of any present, Emolument, Office, or Title, of any kind whatever, from any King, Prince, or foreign State.

Section 10. No State shall enter into any Treaty, Alliance, or Confederation; grant Letters of Marque and Reprisal; coin Money; emit Bills of Credit; make any Thing but gold and silver Coin a Tender in Payment of Debts; pass any Bill of Attainder, ex post facto Law, or Law impairing the Obligation of Contracts, or grant any Title of Nobility.

No State shall, without the Consent of the Congress, lay any Imposts or Duties on Imports or Exports, except what may be absolutely necessary for executing its inspection Laws: and the net Produce of all Duties and Imposts, laid by any State on Imports or Exports, shall be for the Use of the Treasury of the United States; and all such Laws shall be subject to the Revision and Controul of the Congress.

No State shall, without the Consent of Congress, lay any Duty of Tonnage, keep Troops, or Ships of War in time of Peace, enter into any Agreement or Compact with another State, or with a foreign Power, or engage in War, unless actually invaded, or in such imminent Danger as will not admit of delay.

ARTICLE II.

(The Executive)

Section 1. The executive Power shall be vested in a President of the United States of America. He shall hold his Office during the

[6]See Amendment XVI.

Term of four Years, and, together with the Vice President, chosen for the same Term, be elected, as follows.

Each State shall appoint, in such Manner as the Legislature thereof may direct, a Number of Electors, equal to the whole Number of Senators and Representatives to which the State may be entitled in the Congress; but no Senator or Representative, or Person holding an Office of Trust or Profit under the United States, shall be appointed an Elector.

[The Electors shall meet in their respective States, and vote by Ballot for two Persons, of whom one at least shall not be an Inhabitant of the same State with themselves. And they shall make a List of all the Persons voted for, and of the Number of Votes for each; which List they shall sign and certify, and transmit sealed to the Seat of the Government of the United States, directed to the President of the Senate. The President of the Senate shall, in the Presence of the Senate and House of Representatives, open all the Certificates, and the Votes shall then be counted. The Person having the greatest Number of Votes shall be the President, if such Number be a Majority of the whole Number of Electors appointed; and if there be more than one who have such Majority, and have an equal Number of Votes, then the House of Representatives shall immediately chuse by Ballot one of them for President; and if no Person have a Majority, then from the five highest on the List the said House shall in like Manner chuse the President. But in chusing the President, the Votes shall be taken by States, the Representation from each State having one Vote; A quorum for this Purpose shall consist of a Member or Members from two thirds of the States, and a Majority of all the States shall be necessary to a Choice. In every Case, after the Choice of the President, the Person having the greatest Number of Votes of the Electors shall be the Vice President. But if there should remain two or more who have equal Votes, the Senate shall chuse from them by Ballot the Vice President.][7]

The Congress may determine the Time of chusing the Electors, and the Day on which they shall give their Votes; which Day shall be the same throughout the United States.

No Person except a natural born Citizen, or a Citizen of the United States, at the time of the Adoption of this Constitution, shall be eligible to the Office of President; neither shall any Person be eligible to that Office who shall not have attained to the Age of thirty five Years, and been fourteen Years a Resident within the United States.

[In Case of the Removal of the President from Office, or of his Death, Resignation, or Inability to discharge the Powers and Duties of the said Office, the Same shall devolve on the Vice President, and the Congress may by Law provide for the Case of Removal, Death, Resignation or Inability, both of the President and Vice President, declaring what Officer shall then act as President, and such Officer shall act accordingly, until the Disability be removed, or a President shall be elected.][8]

The President shall, at stated Times, receive for his Services, a Compensation, which shall neither be encreased nor diminished during the Period for which he shall have been elected, and he shall not receive within that Period any other Emolument from the United States, or any of them.

Before he enter on the Execution of his Office, he shall take the following Oath or Affirmation:—"I do solemnly swear (or affirm) that I will faithfully execute the Office of President of the United States, and will to the best of my Ability, preserve, protect and defend the Constitution of the United States."

[7]See Amendment XII.
[8]See Amendment XXV.

Section 2. The President shall be Commander in Chief of the Army and Navy of the United States, and of the Militia of the several States, when called into the actual Service of the United States; he may require the Opinion, in writing, of the principal Officer in each of the executive Departments, upon any Subject relating to the Duties of their respective Offices, and he shall have Power to grant Reprieves and Pardons for Offences against the United States, except in Cases of Impeachment.

He shall have Power, by and with the Advice and Consent of the Senate, to make Treaties, provided two thirds of the Senators present concur; and he shall nominate, and by and with the Advice and Consent of the Senate, shall appoint Ambassadors, other public Ministers and Consuls, Judges of the supreme Court, and all other Officers of the United States, whose Appointments are not herein otherwise provided for, and which shall be established by Law: but the Congress may by Law vest the Appointment of such inferior Officers, as they think proper, in the President alone, in the Courts of Law, or in the Heads of Departments.

The President shall have Power to fill up all Vacancies that may happen during the Recess of the Senate, by granting Commissions which shall expire at the end of their next Session.

Section 3. He shall from time to time give to the Congress Information of the State of the Union, and recommend to their Consideration such Measures as he shall judge necessary and expedient; he may, on extraordinary Occasions, convene both Houses, or either of them, and in Case of Disagreement between them, with Respect to the Time of Adjournment, he may adjourn them to such Time as he shall think proper; he shall receive Ambassadors and other public Ministers; he shall take Care that the Laws be faithfully executed, and shall Commission all the Officers of the United States.

Section 4. The President, Vice President and all civil Officers of the United States, shall be removed from Office on Impeachment for, and Conviction of, Treason, Bribery, or other high Crimes and Misdemeanors.

ARTICLE III.

(The Judiciary)

Section 1. The judicial Power of the United States, shall be vested in one supreme Court, and in such inferior Courts as the Congress may from time to time ordain and establish. The Judges, both of the supreme and inferior Courts, shall hold their Offices during good Behaviour, and shall, at stated Times, receive for their Services, a Compensation, which shall not be diminished during their Continuance in Office.

Section 2. The judicial Power shall extend to all Cases, in Law and Equity, arising under this Constitution, the Laws of the United States, and Treaties made, or which shall be made, under their Authority;—to all Cases affecting Ambassadors, other public Ministers and Consuls;—to all Cases of admiralty and maritime Jurisdiction;—to Controversies to which the United States shall be a Party;—to Controversies between two or more States; [—between a State and Citizens of another State;—][9] between Citizens of

[9]See Amendment XI.

different States,—between Citizens of the same State claiming Lands under Grants of different States, [and between a State, or the Citizens thereof, and foreign States, Citizens or Subjects.][10]

In all Cases affecting Ambassadors, other public Ministers and Consuls, and those in which a State shall be Party, the supreme Court shall have original Jurisdiction. In all the other Cases before mentioned, the supreme Court shall have appellate Jurisdiction, both as to Law and Fact, with such Exceptions, and under such Regulations as the Congress shall make.

The Trial of all Crimes, except in Cases of Impeachment, shall be by Jury; and such Trial shall be held in the State where the said Crimes shall have been committed; but when not committed within any State, the Trial shall be at such Place or Places as the Congress may by Law have directed.

Section 3. Treason against the United States, shall consist only in levying War against them, or in adhering to their Enemies, giving them Aid and Comfort. No Person shall be convicted of Treason unless on the Testimony of two Witnesses to the same overt Act, or on Confession in open Court.

The Congress shall have Power to declare the Punishment of Treason, but no Attainder of Treason shall work Corruption of Blood, or Forfeiture except during the Life of the Person attainted.

ARTICLE IV.

(Interstate Relations)

Section 1. Full Faith and Credit shall be given in each State to the public Acts, Records, and judicial Proceedings of every other State. And the Congress may by general Laws prescribe the Manner in which such Acts, Records and Proceedings shall be proved, and the Effect thereof.

Section 2. The Citizens of each State shall be entitled to all Privileges and Immunities of Citizens in the several States.

A Person charged in any State with Treason, Felony, or other Crime, who shall flee from Justice, and be found in another State, shall on Demand of the executive Authority of the State from which he fled, be delivered up, to be removed to the State having Jurisdiction of the Crime.

[No Person held to Service or Labour in one State under the Laws thereof, escaping into another, shall, in Consequence of any Law or Regulation therein, be discharged from such Service or Labour, but shall be delivered up on Claim of the Party to whom such Service or Labour may be due.][11]

Section 3. New States may be admitted by the Congress into this Union; but no new State shall be formed or erected within the Jurisdiction of any other State; nor any State be formed by the Junction of two or more States, or Parts of States, without the Consent of the Legislatures of the States concerned as well as of the Congress.

The Congress shall have Power to dispose of and make all needful Rules and Regulations respecting the Territory or other Property belonging to the United States; and nothing in this Constitution shall be so construed as to Prejudice any Claims of the United States, or of any particular State.

Section 4. The United States shall guarantee to every State in this Union a Republican Form of Government, and shall protect each of them against Invasion, and on Application of the Legislature, or of the Executive (when the Legislature cannot be convened) against domestic Violence.

ARTICLE V.

(Amending the Constitution)

The Congress, whenever two thirds of both Houses shall deem it necessary, shall propose Amendments to this Constitution, or, on the Application of the Legislatures of two thirds of the several States, shall call a Convention for proposing Amendments, which, in either Case, shall be valid to all Intents and Purposes, as Part of this Constitution, when ratified by the Legislatures of three fourths of the several States, or by Conventions in three fourths thereof, as the one or the other Mode of Ratification may be proposed by the Congress; Provided that no Amendment which may be made prior to the Year One thousand eight hundred and eight shall in any Manner affect the first and fourth Clauses in the Ninth Section of the first Article; and that no State, without its Consent, shall be deprived of its equal Suffrage in the Senate.

ARTICLE VI.

(Debts, Supremacy, Oaths)

All Debts contracted and Engagements entered into, before the Adoption of this Constitution, shall be as valid against the United States under this Constitution, as under the Confederation.

This Constitution, and the laws of the United States which shall be made in Pursuance thereof; and all Treaties made, or which shall be made, under the Authority of the United States, shall be the supreme Law of the Land; and the Judges in every State shall be bound thereby, any Thing in the Constitution or Laws of any State to the Contrary notwithstanding.

The Senators and Representatives before mentioned, and the Members of the several State Legislatures, and all executive and judicial Officers, both of the United States and of the several States, shall be bound by Oath or Affirmation, to support this Constitution; but no religious Test shall ever be required as a Qualification to any Office or public Trust under the United States.

ARTICLE VII.

(Ratifying the Constitution)

The Ratification of the Conventions of nine States, shall be sufficient for the Establishment of this Constitution between the States so ratifying the Same.

Done in Convention by the Unanimous Consent of the States present the Seventeenth Day of September in the Year of our Lord one thousand seven hundred and Eighty seven and of the Independence of the United States of America the Twelfth. IN WITNESS whereof we have hereunto subscribed our Names.

Go. WASHINGTON
Presid't. and deputy from Virginia

[10]See Amendment XI.
[11]See Amendment XIII.

ATTTEST
William Jackson
Secretary

DELAWARE
Geo. Read
Gunning Bedford jun
John Dickinson
Richard Basset
Jaco. Broom

MASSACHUSETTS
Nathaniel Gorbam
Rufus King

CONNECTICUT
Wm. Saml. Johnson
Roger Sherman

NEW YORK
Alexander Hamilton

NEW JERSEY
Wh. Livingston
David Brearley
Wm. Paterson
Jona. Dayton

PENNSYLVANIA
B. Franklin
Thomas Mifflin
Robt. Morris
Geo. Clymer
Thos. FitzSimons
Jared Ingersoll
James Wilson
Gouv. Morris

NEW HAMPSHIRE
John Langdon
Nicholas Gilman

MARYLAND
James McHenry
Dan of St. Thos. Jenifer
Danl. Carroll

VIRGINIA
John Blair
James Madison Jr.

NORTH CAROLINA
Wm. Blount
Richd. Dobbs Spaight
Hu. Williamson

SOUTH CAROLINA
J. Rutledge
Charles Cotesworth Pinckney
Charles Pinckney
Pierce Butler

GEORGIA
William Few
Abr. Baldwin

Articles in addition to, and amendment of the Constitution of the United States of America, proposed by Congress and ratified by the Legislatures of the several states, pursuant to the Fifth Article of the original Constitution.

(The first ten amendments were passed by Congress on September 25, 1789, and were ratified on December 15, 1791.)

Amendment I—Religion, Speech, Assembly, Petition

Congress shall make no law respecting an establishment of religion, or prohibiting the free exercise thereof; or abridging the freedom of speech, or of the press; or the right of the people peaceably to assemble, and to petition the Government for a redress of grievances.

Amendment II—Right to Bear Arms

A well regulated Militia, being necessary to the security of a free State, the right of the people to keep and bear Arms, shall not be infringed.

Amendment III—Quartering of Soldiers

No Soldier shall, in time of peace be quartered in any house, without the consent of the Owner, nor in time of war, but in a manner to be prescribed by law.

Amendment IV—Searches and Seizures

The right of the people to be secure in their persons, houses, papers, and effects, against unreasonable searches and seizures, shall not be violated, and no warrants shall issue, but upon probable cause, supported by Oath or affirmation, and particularly describing the place to be searched, and the persons or things to be seized.

Amendment V—Grand Juries, Double Jeopardy, Self-incrimination, Due Process, Eminent Domain

No person shall be held to answer for a capital, or otherwise infamous crime, unless on a presentment or indictment of a Grand Jury, except in cases arising in the land or naval forces, or in the Militia, when in actual service in time of War or public danger; nor shall any person be subject for the same offence to be twice put in jeopardy of life or limb; nor shall be compelled in any criminal case to be a witness against himself, nor be deprived of life, liberty, or property, without due process of law; nor shall private property be taken for public use, without just compensation.

Amendment VI—Criminal Court Procedures

In all criminal prosecutions, the accused shall enjoy the right to a speedy and public trial, by an impartial jury of the State and district wherein the crime shall have been committed, which district shall have been previously ascertained by law, and to be informed of the nature and cause of the accusation; to be confronted with the witnesses against him; to have compulsory process for obtaining witnesses in his favor, and to have the assistance of counsel for his defence.

Amendment VII—Trial by Jury in Common-law Cases

In Suits at common law, where the value in controversy shall exceed twenty dollars, the right of trial by jury shall be preserved, and no fact tried by a jury, shall be otherwise re-examined in any Court of the United States, than according to the rules of the common law.

Amendment VIII—Bails, Fines, and Punishment

Excessive bail shall not be required, nor excessive fines imposed, nor cruel and unusual punishments inflicted.

Amendment IX—Rights Retained by the People

The enumeration in the Constitution, of certain rights, shall not be construed to deny or disparage others retained by the people.

Amendment X—Rights Reserved to the States

The powers not delegated to the United States by the Constitution, nor prohibited by it to the States, are reserved to the States respectively, or to the people.

Amendment XI—Suits Against the States (Ratified February 7, 1795)

The Judicial power of the United States shall not be construed to extend to any suit in law or equity, commenced or prosecuted against one of the United States by Citizens of another State, or by Citizens or Subjects of any Foreign State.

Amendment XII—Election of the President and Vice-President (Ratified June 15, 1804)

The Electors shall meet in their respective states, and vote by ballot for President and Vice-President, one of whom, at least, shall not be an inhabitant of the same state with themselves; they shall name in their ballots the person voted for as President, and in distinct ballots the person voted for as Vice-President, and they shall make distinct lists of all persons voted for as President, and of all persons voted for as Vice-President, and of the number of votes for each, which lists they shall sign and certify, and transmit sealed to the seat of the government of the United States, directed to the President of the Senate;—The President of the Senate shall, in the presence of the Senate and House of Representatives, open all the certificates and the votes shall then be counted;—The person having the greatest number of votes for President, shall be the President, if such number be a majority of the whole number of Electors appointed; and if no person have such majority, then from the persons having the highest numbers not exceeding three on the list of those voted for as President, the House of Representatives shall choose immediately, by ballot, the President. But in choosing the President, the votes shall be taken by states, the representation from each state having one vote; a quorum for this purpose shall consist of a member or members from two-thirds of the states, and a majority of all the states shall be necessary to a Choice. [And if the House of Representatives shall not choose a President whenever the right of choice shall devolve upon them, before the fourth day of March next following, then the Vice-President shall act as President, as in the case of the death or other constitutional disability of the President.][12]—The person having the greatest number of votes as Vice-President, shall be the Vice-President, if such number be a majority of the whole number of Electors appointed, and if no person have a majority, then from the two highest numbers on the list, the Senate shall choose the Vice- President; a quorum for the purpose shall consist of two-thirds of the whole number of Senators, and a majority of the whole number shall be necessary to a choice. But no person constitutionally ineligible to the office of President shall be eligible to that of Vice-President of the United States.

Amendment XIII—Slavery (Ratified on December 6, 1865)

Section 1. Neither slavery nor involuntary servitude, except as a punishment for crime whereof the party shall have been duly convicted, shall exist within the United States, or any place subject to their jurisdiction.

Section 2. Congress shall have power to enforce this article by appropriate legislation.

Amendment XIV—Citizenship, Due Process, and Equal Protection of the Laws (Ratified on July 9, 1868)

Section 1. All persons born or naturalized in the United States, and subject to the jurisdiction thereof, are citizens of the United States and of the State wherein they reside. No State shall make or enforce any law which shall abridge the privileges or immunities of citizens of the United States; nor shall any State deprive any person of life, liberty, or property, without due process of law; nor deny to any person within its jurisdiction the equal protection of the laws.

Section 2. Representatives shall be apportioned among the several States according to their respective numbers, counting the whole number of persons in each State, excluding Indians not taxed. But when the right to vote at any election for the choice of electors for President and Vice President of the United States, Representatives in Congress, the Executive and Judicial officers of a State, or the members of the Legislature thereof, is denied to any of the male inhabitants of such State, being twenty-one years of age, and citizens of the United States, or in any way abridged, except for participation in rebellion, or other crime, the basis of representation therein shall be reduced in the proportion which the number of such male citizens shall bear to the whole number of male citizens twenty-one years of age in such State.

Section 3. No person shall be a Senator or Representative in Congress, or elector of President and Vice President, or hold any office, civil or military, under the United States, or under any State, who, having previously taken an oath, as a member of Congress, or as an officer of the United States, or as a member of any State legislature, or as an executive or judicial officer of any State, to support the Constitution of the United States, shall have engaged in insurrection or rebellion against the same, or given aid or comfort to the enemies thereof. But Congress may by a vote of two-thirds of each House, remove such disability.

Section 4. The validity of the public debt of the United States, authorized by law, including debts incurred for payment of pensions and bounties for services in suppressing insurrection or rebellion, shall not be questioned. But neither the United States nor any State shall assume or pay any debt or obligation incurred in aid of insurrection or rebellion against the United States, or any claim for the loss or emancipation of any slave, but all such debts, obligations and claims shall be held illegal and void.

Section 5. The Congress shall have power to enforce, by appropriate legislation, the provisions of this article.

Amendment XV—The Right To Vote (Ratified on February 3, 1870)

Section 1. The right of citizens of the United States to vote shall not be denied or abridged by the United States or by any State on account of race, color, or previous condition of servitude.

Section 2. The Congress shall have power to enforce this article by appropriate legislation.

Amendment XVI—Income Taxes (Ratified on February 3, 1913)

The Congress shall have power to lay and collect taxes on incomes, from whatever source derived, without apportionment among the several States, and without regard to any census or enumeration.

Amendment XVII—Election of Senators (Ratified on April 8, 1913)

The Senate of the United States shall be composed of two Senators from each State, elected by the people thereof, for six years; and each Senator shall have one vote. The electors in each State shall have the qualifications requisite for electors of the most numerous branch of the State legislatures.

When vacancies happen in the representation of any State in the Senate, the executive authority of such State shall issue writs of election to fill such vacancies: *Provided*, That the legislature of any State may empower the executive thereof to make temporary

[12]Amendment XX.

appointments until the people fill the vacancies by election as the legislature may direct.

This amendment shall not be so construed as to affect the election or term of any Senator chosen before it becomes valid as part of the Constitution.

Amendment XVIII—Prohibition (Ratified on January 16, 1919)

Section 1. After one year from the ratification of this article the manufacture, sale, or transportation of intoxicating liquors within, the importation thereof into, or the exportation thereof from the United States and all territory subject to the jurisdiction thereof for beverage purposes is hereby prohibited.

Section 2. The Congress and the several States shall have concurrent power to enforce this article by appropriate legislation.

Section 3. This article shall be inoperative unless it shall have been ratified as an amendment to the Constitution by the legislatures of the several States, as provided in the Constitution, within seven years from the date of the submission hereof to the States by the Congress.[13]

Amendment XIX—Women's Right To Vote (Ratified on August 18, 1920)

The right of citizens of the United States to vote shall not be denied or abridged by the United States or by any State on account of sex.

Congress shall have power to enforce this article by appropriate legislation.

Amendment XX—Terms of Office, Convening of Congress, and Succession (Ratified February 6, 1933)

Section 1. The terms of the President and Vice President shall end at noon on the 20th day of January, and the terms of Senators and Representatives at noon on the 3d day of January, of the years in which such terms would have ended if this article had not been ratified; and the terms of their successors shall then begin.

Section 2. The Congress shall assemble at least once in every year, and such meeting shall begin at noon on the 3d day of January, unless they shall by law appoint a different day.

Section 3. If, at the time fixed for the beginning of the term of the President, the President elect shall have died, the Vice President elect shall become President. If a President shall not have been chosen before the time fixed for the beginning of his term, or if the President elect shall have failed to qualify, then the Vice President elect shall act as President until a President shall have qualified; and the Congress may by law provide for the case wherein neither a President elect nor a Vice President elect shall have qualified, declaring who shall then act as President, or the manner in which one who is to act shall be selected, and such person shall act accordingly until a President or Vice President shall have qualified.

Section 4. The Congress may by law provide for the case of the death of any of the persons from whom the House of Representatives may choose a President whenever the rights of choice shall have devolved upon them, and for the case of the death of any of the persons from whom the Senate may choose a Vice President whenever the right of choice shall have devolved upon them.

Section 5. Sections 1 and 2 shall take effect on the 15th day of October following the ratification of this article.

Section 6. This article shall be inoperative unless it shall have been ratified as an amendment to the Constitution by the legislatures of three-fourths of the several States within seven years from the date of its submission.

Amendment XXI—Repeal of Prohibition (Ratified on December 5, 1933)

Section 1. The eighteenth article of amendment to the Constitution of the United States is hereby repealed.

Section 2. The transportation or importation into any State, Territory, or possession of the United States for delivery or use therein of intoxicating liquors, in violation of the laws thereof, is hereby prohibited.

Section 3. This article shall be inoperative unless it shall have been ratified as an amendment to the Constitution by conventions in the several States, as provided in the Constitution, within seven years from the date of the submission hereof to the States by the Congress.

Amendment XXII—Number of Presidential Terms (Ratified on February 27, 1951)

No person shall be elected to the office of the President more than twice, and no person who has held the office of President, or acted as President, for more than two years of a term to which some other person was elected President shall be elected to the office of the President more than once. But this Article shall not apply to any person holding the office of President when this Article was proposed by the Congress, and shall not prevent any person who may be holding the office of President, or acting as President, during the term within which this Article becomes operative from holding the office of President or acting as President during the remainder of such term.

Amendment XXIII—Presidential Electors for the District of Columbia (Ratified on March 29, 1961)

Section 1. The District constituting the seat of Government of the United States shall appoint in such manner as the Congress may direct:

A number of electors of President and Vice President equal to the whole number of Senators and Representatives in Congress to which the District would be entitled if it were a State, but in no event more than the least populous State; they shall be in addition to those appointed by the States, but they shall be considered, for the purposes of the election of President and Vice President, to be electors appointed by a State; and they shall meet in the District and perform such duties as provided by the twelfth article of amendment.

[13]Amendment XXI.

Section 2. The Congress shall have power to enforce this article by appropriate legislation.

Amendment XXIV—Poll Tax (Ratified on January 23, 1964)

Section 1. The right of citizens of the United States to vote in any primary or other election for President or Vice President, for electors for President or Vice President, or for Senator or Representative in Congress, shall not be denied or abridged by the United States or any State by reason of failure to pay any poll tax or other tax.

Section 2. The Congress shall have power to enforce this article by appropriate legislation.

Amendment XXV—Presidential Disability and Vice Presidential Vacancies (Ratified on February 10, 1967)

Section 1. In case of the removal of the President from office or of his death or resignation, the Vice President shall become President.

Section 2. Whenever there is a vacancy in the office of the Vice President, the President shall nominate a Vice President who shall take office upon confirmation by a majority vote of both Houses of Congress.

Section 3. Whenever the President transmits to the President pro tempore of the Senate and the Speaker of the House of Representatives his written declaration that he is unable to discharge the powers and duties of his office, and until he transmits to them a written declaration to the contrary, such powers and duties shall be discharged by the Vice President as Acting President.

Section 4. Whenever the Vice President and a majority of either the principal officers of the executive departments or of such other body as Congress may by law provide, transmit to the President pro tempore of the Senate and the Speaker of the House of Representatives their written declaration that the President is unable to discharge the powers and duties of his office, the Vice President shall immediately assume the powers and duties of the office as Acting President.

Thereafter, when the President transmits to the President pro tempore of the Senate and the Speaker of the House of Representatives his written declaration that no inability exists, he shall resume the powers and duties of his office unless the Vice President and a majority of either the principal officers of the executive department or of such other body as Congress may by law provide, transmit within four days to the President pro tempore of the Senate and the Speaker of the House of Representatives their written declaration that the President is unable to discharge the powers and duties of his office. Thereupon Congress shall decide the issue, assembling within forty-eight hours for that purpose if not in session. If the Congress, within twenty-one days after receipt of the latter written declaration, or, if Congress is not in session, within twenty-one days after Congress is required to assemble, determines by two-thirds vote of both Houses that the President is unable to discharge the powers and duties of his office, the Vice President shall continue to discharge the same as Acting President; otherwise, the President shall resume the powers and duties of his office.

Amendment XXVI—Eighteen-year-old Vote (Ratified on July 1, 1971)

Section 1. The right of citizens of the United States, who are eighteen years of age or older, to vote shall not be denied or abridged by the United States or by any State on account of age.

Section 2. The Congress shall have power to enforce this article by appropriate legislation.

Amendment XXVII—Congressional Salaries (Ratified on May 18, 1992)

Section 1. No law varying the compensation for the services of the Senators and Representatives, shall take effect, until an election of Representatives shall have intervened.

Presidents of the United States

YEAR	PRESIDENTIAL CANDIDATES	POLITICAL PARTY	ELECTORAL VOTE	PERCENTAGE OF POPULAR VOTE
1789	**George Washington**	—	69	—
	John Adams		34	
	Others		35	
1792	**George Washington**	—	132	—
	John Adams		77	
	Others		55	
1796	**John Adams**	Federalist	71	—
	Thomas Jefferson	Democratic-Republican	68	
	Thomas Pinckney	Federalist	59	
	Aaron Burr	Democratic-Republican	30	
	Others		48	
1800	**Thomas Jefferson**	Democratic-Republican	73	—
	Aaron Burr	Democratic-Republican	73	
	John Adams	Federalist	65	
	C. C. Pinckney	Federalist	64	
	John Jay	Federalist	1	
1804	**Thomas Jefferson**	Democratic-Republican	162	—
	C. C. Pinckney	Federalist	14	
1808	**James Madison**	Democratic-Republican	122	—
	C. C. Pinckney	Federalist	47	
	George Clinton	Independent-Republican	6	
1812	**James Madison**	Democratic-Republican	128	—
	De Witt Clinton	Federalist	89	
1816	**James Monroe**	Democratic-Republican	183	—
	Rufus King	Federalist	34	
1820	**James Monroe**	Democratic-Republican	231	—
	John Q. Adams	Independent-Republican	1	
1824	**John Q. Adams**	Democratic-Republican	84	30.9
	Andrew Jackson	Democratic-Republican	99	
	Henry Clay	Democratic-Republican	37	
	W. H. Crawford	Democratic-Republican	41	
1828	**Andrew Jackson**	Democratic	178	56.0
	John Q. Adams	National Republican	83	
1832	**Andrew Jackson**	Democratic	219	54.2
	Henry Clay	National Republican	49	
	William Wirt	Anti-Masonic	7	
	John Floyd	Independent Democrat	11	
1836	**Martin Van Buren**	Democratic	170	50.8
	William H. Harrison	Whig	73	
	Hugh L. White	Whig	26	
	Daniel Webster	Whig	14	
1840	**William H. Harrison***	Whig	234	52.9
	Martin Van Buren	Democratic	60	
	(John Tyler, 1841)			
1844	**James K. Polk**	Democratic	170	49.5
	Henry Clay	Whig	105	
1848	**Zachary Taylor***	Whig	163	47.3
	Lewis Cass	Democratic	127	
	(Millard Fillmore, 1850)			
1852	Franklin Pierce	Democratic	254	50.8
	Winfield Scott	Whig	42	
1856	**James Buchanan**	Democratic	174	45.3
	John C. Fremont	Republican	114	
	Millard Fillmore	American	8	
1860	**Abraham Lincoln**	Republican	180	39.8
	J. C. Breckinridge	Democratic	72	
	Stephen A. Douglas	Democratic	12	
	John Bell	Constitutional Union	39	

Note: Presidents are shown in boldface.

*Died in office, succeeding vice president shown in parentheses.

(*continues*)

Presidents of the United States (continued)

YEAR	PRESIDENTIAL CANDIDATES	POLITICAL PARTY	ELECTORAL VOTE	PERCENTAGE OF POPULAR VOTE
1864	**Abraham Lincoln***	Republican	212	55.1
	George B. McClellan	Democratic	21	
	(Andrew Johnson, 1865)			
1868	**Ulysses S. Grant**	Republican	214	52.7
	Horatio Seymour	Democratic	80	
1872	**Ulysses S. Grant**	Republican	286	55.6
	Horace Greeley	Democratic	**	
1876	**Rutherford B. Hayes**	Republican	185	48.0
	Samuel J. Tilden	Democratic	184	
1880	**James A. Garfield***	Republican	214	48.3
	Winfield S. Hancock	Democratic	155	
	(Chester A. Arthur, 1881)			
1884	**Grover Cleveland**	Democratic	219	48.5
	James G. Blaine	Republican	182	
1888	**Benjamin Harrison**	Republican	233	47.8
	Grover Cleveland	Democratic	168	
1892	**Grover Cleveland**	Democratic	277	46.0
	Benjamin Harrison	Republican	145	
	James B. Weaver	People's	22	
1896	**William McKinley**	Republican	271	51.1
	William J. Bryan	Democratic	176	
1900	**William McKinley***	Republican	292	51.7
	William J. Bryan	Democratic	155	
	(Theodore Roosevelt, 1901)			
1904	**Theodore Roosevelt**	Republican	336	56.4
	Alton B. Parker	Democratic	140	
1908	**William H. Taft**	Republican	321	51.6
	William J. Bryan	Democratic	162	
1912	**Woodrow Wilson**	Democratic	435	41.8
	Theodore Roosevelt	Progressive	88	
	William H. Taft	Republican	8	
1916	**Woodrow Wilson**	Democratic	277	49.2
	Charles E. Hughes	Republican	254	
1920	**Warren G. Harding***	Republican	404	60.3
	James M. Cox	Democratic	127	
	(Calvin Coolidge, 1923)			
1924	**Calvin Coolidge**	Republican	382	54.0
	John W. Davis	Democratic	136	
	Robert M. LaFollette	Progressive	13	
1928	**Herbert C. Hoover**	Republican	444	58.2
	Alfred E. Smith	Democratic	87	
1932	**Franklin D. Roosevelt**	Democratic	472	57.4
	Herbert C. Hoover	Republican	59	
1936	**Franklin D. Roosevelt**	Democratic	523	60.8
	Alfred M. Landon	Republican	8	
1940	**Franklin D. Roosevelt**	Democratic	449	54.7
	Wendell L. Willkie	Republican	82	
1944	**Franklin D. Roosevelt***	Democratic	432	53.4
	Thomas E. Dewey	Republican	99	
	(Harry S Truman, 1945)			
1948	**Harry S Truman**	Democratic	303	49.5
	Thomas E. Dewey	Republican	189	
	J. Strom Thurmond	States' Rights	39	
1952	**Dwight D. Eisenhower**	Republican	442	55.1
	Adlai E. Stevenson	Democratic	89	
1956	**Dwight D. Eisenhower**	Republican	457	57.4
	Adlai E. Stevenson	Democratic	73	
1960	**John F. Kennedy***	Democratic	303	49.7
	Richard M. Nixon	Republican	219	
	(Lyndon B. Johnson, 1963)			

**Horace Greeley died between the popular vote and the meeting of the presidential electors.

YEAR	PRESIDENTIAL CANDIDATES	POLITICAL PARTY	ELECTORAL VOTE	PERCENTAGE OF POPULAR VOTE
1964	**Lyndon B. Johnson**	Democratic	**486**	**61.1**
	Barry M. Goldwater	Republican	**52**	
1968	**Richard M. Nixon**	Republican	**301**	**43.4**
	Hubert H. Humphrey	Democratic	**191**	
	George C. Wallace	American Independent	**46**	
1972	**Richard M. Nixon†**	Republican	**520**	**60.7**
	George S. McGovern	Democratic	**17**	
	(Gerald R. Ford, 1974)‡			
1976	**Jimmy Carter**	Democratic	**297**	**50.1**
	Gerald R. Ford	Republican	**240**	
1980	**Ronald Reagan**	Republican	**489**	**50.7**
	Jimmy Carter	Democratic	**49**	
	John B. Anderson	Independent	—	
1984	**Ronald Reagan**	Republican	**525**	**58.8**
	Walter Mondale	Democratic	**13**	
1988	**George Bush**	Republican	**426**	**53.4**
	Michael Dukakis	Democratic	**112**	
1992	**Bill Clinton**	Democratic	**370**	**43.0**
	George Bush	Republican	**168**	
	H. Ross Perot	Independent	—	
1996	**Bill Clinton**	Democratic	**379**	**49.2**
	Robert Dole	Republican	**159**	
	H. Ross Perot	Reform	—	
2000	**George W. Bush**	Republican	**271**	**47.9**
	Al Gore	Democratic	**266**	
	Ralph Nader	Green	—	
	Patrick J. Buchanan	Reform	—	
2004	**George W. Bush**	Republican	**286**	**50.7**
	John Kerry	Democratic	**251**	
	Ralph Nader	Independent	—	
2008	**Barack Obama**	Democratic	**365**	**52.9**
	John McCain	Republican	**173**	

†Resigned

‡Appointed vice president

Party Control of the Presidency, Senate, and House of Representatives in the Twentieth and Twenty-first Centuries

CONGRESS	YEARS	PRESIDENT	SENATE D	SENATE R	SENATE OTHER*	HOUSE D	HOUSE R	HOUSE OTHER*
57th	1901–03	McKinley T. Roosevelt	29		3	153	198	5
58th	1903–05	T. Roosevelt	32	58	—	178	207	—
59th	1905–07	T. Roosevelt	32	58	—	136	250	—
60th	1907–09	T. Roosevelt	29	61	—	164	222	—
61st	1909–11	Taft	32	59	—	172	219	—
62d	1911–13	Taft	42	49	—	228‡	162	1
63d	1913–15	Wilson	51	44	1	290	127	18
64th	1915–17	Wilson	56	39	1	230	193	8
65th	1917–19	Wilson	53	42	1	200	216	9
66th	1919–21	Wilson	48	48‡	1	191	237‡	7
67th	1921–23	Harding	37	59	—	132	300	1
68th	1923–25	Coolidge	43	51	2	207	225	3
69th	1925–27	Coolidge	40	54	1	183	247	5
70th	1927–29	Coolidge	47	48	1	195	237	3
71st	1929–31	Hoover	39	56	1	163	267	1
72d	1931–33	Hoover	47	48	1	216‡	218	1
73d	1933–35	F. Roosevelt	59	36	1	313	117	5
74th	1935–37	F. Roosevelt	69	25	2	322	103	10
75th	1937–39	F. Roosevelt	75	17	4	333	89	13
76th	1939–41	F. Roosevelt	69	23	4	262	169	4
77th	1941–43	F. Roosevelt	66	28	2	267	162	6
78th	1943–45	F. Roosevelt	57	38	1	222	209	4
79th	1945–47	Truman	57	38	1	243	190	2
80th	1947–49	Truman	45	51‡	—	188	246‡	1
81st	1949–51	Truman	54	42	—	263	171	1
82d	1951–53	Truman	48	47	1	234	199	2
83d	1953–55	Eisenhower	47	48	1	213	221	1
84th	1955–57	Eisenhower	48‡	47	1	232‡	203	—
85th	1957–59	Eisenhower	49‡	47	—	234‡	201	—
86th†	1959–61	Eisenhower	64‡	34	—	283‡	154	—
87th	1961–63	Kennedy	64	36	—	263	174	—
88th	1963–65	Kennedy Johnson Johnson	67	33	—	258	176	—
89th	1965–67	Johnson	68	32	—	295	140	—
90th	1967–69	Johnson	64	36	—	248	187	—
91st	1969–71	Nixon	58‡	42	—	243‡	192	—
92d	1971–73	Nixon	55‡	45	—	255‡	180	—
93d	1973–75	Nixon Ford	57‡	43	—	243‡	192	—
94th	1975–77	Ford	61‡	38	—	291‡	144	—
95th	1977–79	Carter	62	38	—	292	143	—
96th	1979–81	Carter	59	41	—	277	158	—
97th	1981–83	Reagan	47	53	—	243‡	192	—
98th	1983–85	Reagan	46	54	—	269‡	166	—
99th	1985–87	Reagan	47	53	—	253‡	182	—
100th	1987–89	Reagan	55‡	45	—	258‡	177	—
101st	1989–91	Bush	55‡	45	—	260‡	175	—
102d	1991–93	Bush	56‡	44	—	267‡	167	1
103d	1993–95	Clinton	57	43	—	258	176	1
104th	1995–97	Clinton	46	54‡	—	202	232‡	1
105th	1997–99	Clinton	45	55‡	—	206	228‡	1
106th	1999–01	Clinton	45	55‡	—	211	223‡	1
107th	2001–03	G. W. Bush	50	49	1	212	221	2
108th	2003–05	G. W. Bush	48	51	1	205	229	1
109th	2005–07	G. W. Bush	44	55	1	202	232	11
110th	2007–09	G. W. Bush	50‡	49	1	233‡	202	—
111th	2009–11	Obama	58	40	2	257	178	—
112th	2011–13	Obama	51	47	2	191**	244‡	—

*Excludes vacancies at beginning of each session. Party balance immediately following election.

†The 437 members of the House in the 86th and 87th Congresses are attributable to the at-large representative given to both Alaska (January 3, 1959) and Hawaii (August 21, 1959) prior to redistricting in 1962.

‡Chamber controlled by party other than that of the president.

**As late as mid-November 2010, votes were still being tallied.

D= Democrat R= Republican

Supreme Court Justices Serving in the Twentieth and Twenty-first Centuries

NAME	NOMINATED BY	SERVICE
John M. Harlan	Hayes	**1877–1911**
Horace Gray	Arthur	**1882–1902**
Melville W. Fuller*	Cleveland	**1888–1910**
David J. Brewer	Harrison	**1890–1910**
Henry B. Brown	Harrison	**1890–1906**
George Shiras, Jr.	Harrison	**1892–1903**
Edward D. White	Cleveland	**1894–1910**
Rufus W. Peckham	Cleveland	**1895–1909**
Joseph McKenna	McKinley	**1898–1925**
Oliver W. Holmes	T. Roosevelt	**1902–1932**
William R. Day	T. Roosevelt	**1903–1922**
William H. Moody	T. Roosevelt	**1906–1910**
Horace H. Lurton	Taft	**1910–1914**
Edward D. White	Taft	**1910–1921**
Charles E. Hughes	Taft	**1910–1916**
Willis Van Devanter	Taft	**1911–1937**
Joseph R. Lamar	Taft	**1911–1916**
Mahlon Pitney	Taft	**1912–1922**
James C. McReynolds	Wilson	**1914–1941**
Louis D. Brandeis	Wilson	**1916–1939**
John H. Clarke	Wilson	**1916–1922**
William H. Taft	Harding	**1921–1930**
George Sutherland	Harding	**1922–1938**
Pierce Butler	Harding	**1922–1939**
Edward T. Sanford	Harding	**1923–1930**
Harlan F. Stone	Coolidge	**1925–1941**
Charles E. Hughes	Hoover	**1930–1941**
Owen J. Roberts	Hoover	**1930–1945**
Benjamin N. Cardozo	Hoover	**1932–1938**
Hugo L. Black	F. Roosevelt	**1937–1971**
Stanley F. Reed	F. Roosevelt	**1938–1957**
Felix Frankfurter	F. Roosevelt	**1939–1962**
William O. Douglas	F. Roosevelt	**1939–1975**
Frank Murphy	F. Roosevelt	**1940–1949**
Harlan F. Stone	F. Roosevelt	**1941–1946**
James F. Byrnes	F. Roosevelt	**1941–1942**
Robert H. Jackson	F. Roosevelt	**1941–1954**
Wiley B. Rutledge	F. Roosevelt	**1943–1949**
Harold H. Burton	Truman	**1945–1958**
Fred M. Vinson	Truman	**1946–1953**
Tom C. Clark	Truman	**1949–1967**
Sherman Minton	Truman	**1949–1956**
Earl Warren	Eisenhower	**1953–1969**
John M. Harlan	Eisenhower	**1955–1971**
William J. Brennan, Jr.	Eisenhower	**1956–1990**
Charles E. Whittaker	Eisenhower	**1957–1962**
Potter Stewart	Eisenhower	**1958–1981**
Byron R. White	Kennedy	**1962–1993**
Arthur J. Goldberg	Kennedy	**1962–1965**
Abe Fortas	Johnson	**1965–1969**
Thurgood Marshall	Johnson	**1967–1991**
Warren E. Burger	Nixon	**1969–1986**
Harry A. Blackmun	Nixon	**1970–1994**
Lewis F. Powell, Jr.	Nixon	**1971–1987**
William H. Rehnquist	Nixon	**1971–1986**
John Paul Stevens	Ford	**1975–2010**
Sandra Day O'Connor	Reagan	**1981–2006**
William H. Rehnquist	Reagan	**1986–2005**
Antonin Scalia	Reagan	**1986–**
Anthony M. Kennedy	Reagan	**1988–**
David H. Souter	Bush	**1990–2010**
Clarence Thomas	Bush	**1991–**
Ruth Bader Ginsburg	Clinton	**1993–**
Stephen G. Breyer	Clinton	**1994–**
John G. Roberts, Jr.	G. W. Bush	**2005–**
Samuel A. Alito, Jr.	G. W. Bush	**2006–**
Sonia Sotomayor	Obama	**2009–**
Elena Kagan	Obama	**2010–**

*Boldface type indicates service as chief justice.

Glossary

501(c) groups. Groups that are exempted from reporting their contributions and can receive unlimited contributions. Section 501c of the tax code specifies that such groups cannot spend more than half their funds on political activities.

527 groups. Independent political groups that are not subject to contribution restrictions because they do not directly seek the election of particular candidates. Section 527 of the tax code specifies that contributions to such groups must be reported to the IRS.

A

actual group. The people in the **potential group** who actually join. See also **interest group.**

Adarand Constructors v. Pena. A 1995 Supreme Court decision holding that federal programs that classify people by race, even for an ostensibly benign purpose such as expanding opportunities for minorities, should be presumed to be unconstitutional.

administrative discretion. The authority of administrative actors to select among various responses to a given problem. Discretion is greatest when routines, or **standard operating procedures**, do not fit a case.

affirmative action. A policy designed to give special attention to or compensatory treatment for members of some previously disadvantaged group.

agenda. See **policy agenda.**

Americans with Disabilities Act of 1990. A law passed in 1990 that requires employers and public facilities to make "reasonable accommodations" for people with disabilities and prohibits discrimination against these individuals in employment.

***amicus curiae* briefs.** Legal briefs submitted by a "friend of the court" for the purpose of influencing a court's decision by raising additional points of view and presenting information not contained in the briefs of the formal parties.

Anti-Federalists. Opponents of the **U.S. Constitution** at the time when the states were contemplating its adoption. See also **Federalists.**

antitrust policy. Policy designed to ensure competition and prevent monopoly.

appellate jurisdiction. The jurisdiction of courts that hear cases brought to them on appeal from lower courts. These courts do not review the factual record, only the legal issues involved. Compare **original jurisdiction.**

appropriations bill. An act of Congress that actually funds programs within limits established by **authorization bills**. Appropriations usually cover one year.

arms race. A tense relationship beginning in the 1950s between the Soviet Union and the United States whereby one side's weaponry became the other side's goad to procure more weaponry, and so on.

Articles of Confederation. The first constitution of the United States, adopted by Congress in 1777 and enacted in 1781. The Articles established a national legislature, the Continental Congress, but most authority rested with the state legislatures.

authorization bill. An act of Congress that establishes, continues, or changes a discretionary government program or an entitlement. It specifies program goals and maximum expenditures for discretionary programs. Compare **appropriations bill.**

B

balance of trade. The ratio of what is paid for imports to what is earned from exports. When more is paid than earned, there is a balance-of-trade deficit.

Barron v. Baltimore. The 1833 Supreme Court decision holding that the **Bill of Rights** restrained only the national government, not the states and cities. See also *Gitlow v. New York.*

beats. Specific locations from which news frequently emanates, such as Congress or the White House. Most top reporters work a particular beat, thereby becoming specialists in what goes on at that location.

bicameral legislature. A legislature divided into two houses. The U.S. Congress and all state legislatures except Nebraska's are bicameral.

bill. A proposed law, drafted in legal language. Anyone can draft a bill, but only a member of the House of Representatives or the Senate can formally submit a bill for consideration.

Bill of Rights. The first 10 amendments to the **U.S. Constitution**, drafted in response to some of the **Anti-Federalist** concerns. These amendments define such basic liberties as freedom of religion, speech, and press and guarantee defendants' rights.

block grants. Federal grants given more or less automatically to states or communities to support broad programs in areas such as community development and social services. Compare **categorical grants.**

Blue Dog Democrats. Fiscally conservative Democrats who are mostly from the South and/or rural parts of the United States.

Brown v. Board of Education. The 1954 Supreme Court decision holding that school segregation was inherently unconstitutional because it violated the **Fourteenth Amendment**'s guarantee of **equal protection**. This case marked the end of legal segregation in the United States. See also ***Plessy v. Ferguson.***

budget. A policy document allocating burdens (taxes) and benefits (expenditures).

budget resolution. A resolution binding Congress to a total expenditure level, supposedly the bottom line of all federal spending for all programs.

bureaucracy. According to Max Weber, a hierarchical authority structure that uses task specialization, operates on the merit principle, and behaves with impersonality.

C

cabinet. A group of presidential advisers not mentioned in the Constitution, although every president has had one. Today the cabinet is composed of 14 secretaries, the attorney general, and others designated by the president.

campaign strategy. The master game plan candidates lay out to guide their electoral campaign.

capitalism. An economic system in which individuals and corporations, not the government, own the principal means of production and seek profits. Compare **mixed economy.**

casework. Activities of members of Congress that help constituents as individuals, particularly by cutting through bureaucratic red tape to get people what they think they have a right to get.

categorical grants. Federal grants that can be used only for specific purposes, or "categories," of state and local spending. They come with strings attached, such as nondiscrimination provisions. Compare **block grants.**

caucus (congressional). A group of members of Congress sharing some interest or characteristic. Many are composed of members from both parties and from both houses.

caucus (state party). A system for selecting convention delegates used in about a dozen mostly rural states in which voters must show up at a set time and attend an open meeting to express their presidential preference.

census. An "actual enumeration" of the population, which the Constitution requires that the government conduct every 10 years. The census is a valuable tool for understanding demographic changes. See also **demography.**

Central Intelligence Agency (CIA). An agency created after World War II to coordinate American intelligence activities abroad and to collect, analyze, and evaluate intelligence.

chains. Groups of newspapers published by media conglomerates and today accounting for over four-fifths of the nation's daily newspaper circulation.

checks and balances. Features of the Constitution that limit government's power by requiring that power be balanced among the different governmental institutions. These institutions continually constrain one another's activities. See also **separation of powers.**

city manager. An official appointed by the city council who is responsible for implementing and administering the council's actions. More than one-third of U.S. cities use the council–manager form of government.

civic duty. The belief that in order to support democratic government, a citizen should vote.

civil disobedience. A form of **political participation** based on a conscious decision to break a law believed to be unjust and to suffer the consequences. See also **protest.**

civil liberties. The legal constitutional protections against government. Although our civil liberties are formally set down in the **Bill of Rights**, the courts, police, and legislatures define their meaning.

civil rights. Policies designed to protect people against arbitrary or discriminatory treatment by government officials or individuals.

Civil Rights Act of 1964. The law making racial discrimination in hotels, motels, and restaurants illegal and forbidding many forms of job discrimination.

civil service. A system of hiring and promotion based on the **merit principle** and the desire to create a nonpartisan government service. Compare **patronage.**

class action suits. Lawsuits in which a small number of people sue on behalf of all people in similar circumstances.

Clean Air Act of 1970. The law aimed at combating air pollution, by charging the **Environmental Protection Agency** with protecting and improving the quality of the nation's air.

closed primaries. Elections to select party nominees in which only people who have registered in advance with the party can vote for that party's candidates, thus encouraging greater party loyalty. Compare **open primaries.**

coalition. A group of individuals with a common interest on which every political party depends.

coalition government. When two or more parties join together to form a majority in a national legislature. This form of government is quite common in the multiparty systems of Europe.

Cold War. The hostility between the United States and the Soviet Union, which often brought them to the brink of war and which spanned the period from the end of World War II until the collapse of the Soviet Union and Eastern European communist regimes in 1989 and the years following.

collective bargaining. Negotiations between representatives of **labor unions** and management to determine pay and acceptable working conditions.

collective good. Something of value that cannot be withheld from a potential group member.

command-and-control policy. The typical system of **regulation** whereby government tells business how to reach certain goals, checks that these commands are followed, and punishes offenders. Compare **incentive system**.

commercial speech. Communication in the form of advertising. It can be restricted more than many other types of speech but has been receiving increased protection from the Supreme Court.

committee chairs. The most important influencers of the congressional agenda. They play dominant roles in scheduling hearings, hiring staff, appointing subcommittees, and managing committee **bills** when they are brought before the full house.

committees (congressional). See **conference committees, joint committees, select committees,** and **standing committees.**

conference committees. Congressional committees formed when the Senate and the House pass a particular **bill** in different forms. Party leadership appoints members from each house to iron out the differences and bring back a single bill. See also **joint committees, select committees,** and **standing committees.**

Congressional Budget and Impoundment Control Act of 1974. An act designed to reform the congressional budgetary process, including by forcing Congress to look at the budget as a whole. It was intended to make Congress less dependent on the president's budget and better able to set and meet its own budgetary goals.

Congressional Budget Office. Advises Congress on the probable consequences of its decisions, forecasts revenues, and is a counterweight to the president's **Office of Management and Budget**.

Connecticut Compromise. The compromise reached at the Constitutional Convention that established two houses of Congress: the House of Representatives, in which **representation** is based on a state's share of the U.S. population; and the Senate, in which each state has two representatives. Compare **New Jersey Plan** and **Virginia Plan**.

consent of the governed. The idea that government derives its authority by sanction of the people.

constitution. A nation's basic law. It creates political institutions, assigns or divides powers in government, and often provides certain guarantees to citizens. Constitutions can be either written or unwritten. See also **U.S. Constitution**.

consumer price index (CPI). The key measure of **inflation**—the change in the cost of buying a fixed basket of goods and services.

containment doctrine. A **foreign policy** strategy advocated by George Kennan that called for the United States to isolate the Soviet Union, "contain" its advances, and resist its encroachments by peaceful means if possible but by force if necessary.

continuing resolutions. When Congress cannot reach agreement and pass appropriations bills, these resolutions allow agencies to spend at the level of the previous year.

convention. See **national party convention**.

cooperative federalism. A system of government in which powers and policy assignments are shared between states and the national government. Compare **dual federalism**.

Council of Economic Advisers (CEA). A three-member body appointed by the president to advise the president on economic policy.

council of governments (COG). Councils in many areas of the country where officials from various localities meet to discuss mutual problems and plan joint, cooperative action.

courts of appeal. Appellate courts empowered to review all final decisions of **district courts**, except in rare cases. In addition, they also hear appeals to orders of many federal regulatory agencies.

Craig v. Boren. In this 1976 ruling, the Supreme Court established the "intermediate scrutiny" standard for determining gender discrimination.

crisis. A sudden, unpredictable, and potentially dangerous event requiring the president to play the role of crisis manager.

critical election. An electoral "earthquake" where new issues emerge, new coalitions replace old ones, and the majority party is often displaced by the minority party. Critical election periods are sometimes marked by a national crisis and may require more than one election to bring about a new **party era**. See also **party realignment.**

cruel and unusual punishment. Court sentences prohibited by the **Eighth Amendment**. Although the Supreme Court has ruled that mandatory death sentences for certain offenses are unconstitutional, it has not held that the death penalty itself constitutes cruel and unusual punishment. See also ***Gregg v. Georgia*** and ***McClesky v. Kemp***.

D

Declaration of Independence. The document approved by representatives of the American colonies in 1776 that stated their grievances against the British monarch and declared their independence.

deficit. An excess of federal **expenditures** over federal **revenues**. See also **budget.**

democracy. A system of selecting policymakers and of organizing government so that policy represents and responds to the public's preferences.

demography. The science of population changes.

deregulation. The lifting of government restrictions on business, industry, and professional activities.

détente. A policy, beginning in the early 1970s, that sought a relaxation of tensions between the United States and the Soviet Union, coupled with firm guarantees of mutual security.

devolution. Transferring responsibility for policies from the federal government to state and local governments.

Dillon's Rule. The idea (named for Iowa Judge John Dillon, who expressed it in an 1868 decision) that local governments have only those powers that are explicitly given them by the states. This means that local governments have very little discretion over what policies they pursue or how they pursue them.

direct democracy. Government controlled directly by citizens. Procedures in some states such as the initiative, the referendum, and the recall give voters a direct impact on policymaking and the political process by means of the voting booth and can therefore be considered forms of direct democracy.

direct mail. A method of raising money for a political cause or candidate, in which information and requests for money are sent to people whose names appear on lists of those who have supported similar views or candidates in the past.

district courts. The 91 federal courts of **original jurisdiction**. They are the only federal courts in which trials are held and in which juries may be impaneled. Compare **courts of appeal**.

dual federalism. A system of government in which both the states and the national government remain supreme within their own spheres, each responsible for some policies. Compare **cooperative federalism.**

due process clause. Part of the **Fourteenth Amendment** guaranteeing that persons cannot be deprived of life, liberty, or property by the United States or state governments without due process of law. See also ***Gitlow v. New York***.

E

Earned Income Tax Credit (EITC). A refundable federal income tax credit for low- to moderate-income working individuals and families, even if they did not earn enough money to be required to file a tax return.

Eighth Amendment. The constitutional amendment that forbids **cruel and unusual punishment**, although it does not define this phrase. Through the **Fourteenth Amendment**, this provision applies to the states.

elastic clause. The final paragraph of Article I, Section 8, of the Constitution, which authorizes Congress to pass all laws "necessary and proper" to carry out the enumerated powers. See also **implied powers.**

electioneering. Direct group involvement in the electoral process, for example, by helping to fund campaigns, getting members to work for candidates, and forming **political action committees**.

Electoral College. A unique American institution, created by the Constitution, providing for the selection of the president by electors. Although the Electoral College vote usually reflects a popular majority, less populated states are overrepresented and the winner-take-all rule concentrates campaigns on close states.

electronic media. Television, radio, and the Internet, as compared with **print media**.

elitism. A theory of government and politics contending that an upper-class elite will hold most of the power and thus in effect run the government. Compare **hyperpluralism** and **pluralism.**

Endangered Species Act of 1973. A law requiring the federal government to protect all species listed as endangered.

Engel v. Vitale. The 1962 Supreme Court decision holding that state officials violated the **First Amendment** when they wrote a prayer to be recited by New York's schoolchildren.

entitlement programs. Government programs providing benefits to qualified individuals regardless of need.

entitlements. Policies for which Congress has obligated itself to pay *X* level of benefits to *Y* number of recipients. Social Security benefits are an example.

enumerated powers. Powers of the federal government that are specifically addressed in the Constitution; for Congress, including the powers listed in Article I, Section 8, for example, to coin money and regulate its value and impose taxes. Compare **implied powers**.

environmental impact statement (EIS). A detailing of a proposed policy's environmental effects, which agencies are required to file with the **Environmental Protection Agency** every time they propose to undertake a policy that might be disruptive to the environment.

Environmental Protection Agency (EPA). The largest federal independent regulatory agency, created in 1970 to administer much of U.S. environmental protection policy.

equal protection of the laws. Part of the **Fourteenth Amendment** emphasizing that the laws must provide equivalent "protection" to all people.

Equal Rights Amendment (ERA). A constitutional amendment originally introduced by Congress in 1923 and passed by Congress in 1972, stating that "equality of rights under the law shall not be denied or abridged by the United States or by any state on account of sex." The amendment fell short of the three-fourths of the state legislatures required for passage.

establishment clause. Part of the **First Amendment** stating that "Congress shall make no law respecting an establishment of religion."

European Union (EU). A transnational government composed of most European nations that coordinates monetary, trade, immigration, and labor policies, making its members one economic unit.

exclusionary rule. The rule that evidence cannot be introduced into a trial if it was not constitutionally obtained. The rule prohibits use of evidence obtained through **unreasonable search and seizure**.

executive agency. See **independent executive agency.**

executive orders. Regulations originating with the executive branch. Executive orders are one method presidents can use to control the bureaucracy.

exit poll. Public opinion surveys used by major media pollsters to predict electoral winners with speed and precision.

expenditures. Government spending. Major areas of federal spending are social services and national defense.

extradition. A legal process whereby a state surrenders a person charged with a crime to the state in which the crime is alleged to have been committed.

F

factions. Parties or interest groups that James Madison saw as arising from the unequal distribution of property or wealth and attacked as having the potential to cause instability in government.

federal debt. All the money borrowed by the federal government over the years and still outstanding. Today the federal debt is about $15 trillion.

Federal Election Campaign Act. A law passed in 1974 for reforming campaign finances. The act created the **Federal Election Commission**, provided public financing for presidential primaries and general elections, limited presidential campaign spending, required disclosure, and attempted to limit contributions.

Federal Election Commission (FEC). A six-member bipartisan agency created by the **Federal Election Campaign Act** of 1974. The Federal Election Commission administers and enforces campaign finance laws.

Federal Reserve System. The main instrument for making **monetary policy** in the United States. It was created by Congress in 1913 to regulate the lending practices of banks and thus the money supply.

federalism. A way of organizing a nation so that two or more levels of government have formal authority over the same land and people. It is a system of shared power between units of government. Compare **unitary government.**

Federalist Papers. A collection of 85 articles written by Alexander Hamilton, John Jay, and James Madison under the name "Publius" to defend the Constitution in detail.

Federalists. Supporters of the **U.S. Constitution** at the time the states were contemplating its adoption. See also **Anti-Federalists.**

feminization of poverty. The increasing concentration of poverty among women, especially unmarried women and their children.

Fifteenth Amendment. The constitutional amendment adopted in 1870 to extend **suffrage** to African Americans.

Fifth Amendment. A constitutional amendment designed to protect the rights of persons accused of crimes, including protection against double jeopardy, **self-incrimination**, and punishment without due process of law.

filibuster. A strategy unique to the Senate whereby opponents of a piece of legislation use their right to unlimited debate to prevent the Senate from ever voting on a **bill**. Sixty members present and voting can halt a filibuster.

First Amendment. The constitutional amendment that establishes the four great liberties: freedom of the press, of speech, of religion, and of assembly.

fiscal federalism. The pattern of spending, taxing, and providing grants in the federal system; it is the cornerstone of the national government's relations with state and local governments.

fiscal policy. Use of the federal budget—taxes, spending, and borrowing—to influence the economy; along with **monetary policy**, a main tool by which the government can attempt to steer the economy. Fiscal policy is almost entirely determined by Congress and the president. See also **Keynesian economic theory.**

Food and Drug Administration (FDA). The federal agency formed in 1913, with broad regulatory powers over the manufacturing, contents, marketing, and labeling of foods and drugs sold in the United States.

foreign policy. Policy that involves choice taking about relations with the rest of the world. The president is the chief initiator of U.S. foreign policy.

formula grants. Federal **categorical grants** distributed according to a formula specified in legislation or in administrative regulations.

Fourteenth Amendment. The constitutional amendment adopted after the Civil War that declares "No State shall make or enforce any law which shall abridge the privileges or immunities of citizens of the United States; nor shall any state deprive any person of life, liberty, or property, without due process of law; nor deny to any person within its jurisdiction the **equal protection of the laws**." See also **due process clause**.

free exercise clause. A **First Amendment** provision that prohibits government from interfering with the practice of religion.

free-rider problem. For a group, the problem of people not joining because they can benefit from the group's activities without joining. See also **interest group.**

frontloading. The recent tendency of states to hold primaries early in the calendar in order to capitalize on media attention.

full faith and credit. A clause in Article IV of the Constitution requiring each state to recognize the public acts, records, and judicial proceedings of all other states.

G

gender gap. The regular pattern in which women are more likely to support Democratic candidates, in part because they tend to be less conservative than men and more likely to support spending on social services and to oppose higher levels of military spending.

Gibbons v. Ogden. A landmark case decided in 1824 in which the Supreme Court interpreted very broadly the clause in Article I, Section 8, of the Constitution giving Congress the power to regulate interstate commerce, as encompassing virtually every form of commercial activity.

Gideon v. Wainwright. The 1963 Supreme Court decision holding that anyone accused of a felony where imprisonment may be imposed, however poor he or she might be, has a right to a lawyer. See also **Sixth Amendment**.

Gitlow v. New York. The 1925 Supreme Court decision holding that freedoms of press and speech are "fundamental personal rights and liberties protected by the due process clause of the **Fourteenth Amendment** from impairment by the states" as well as by the federal government. Compare ***Barron v. Baltimore***.

global warming. The increase in the earth's temperatures that, according to most scientists, is occurring as a result of the carbon dioxide that is produced when fossil fuels are burned collecting in the atmosphere and trapping energy from the sun.

government. The institutions and processes through which **public policies** are made for a society.

government corporation. A government organization that, like business corporations, provides a service that could be delivered by the private sector and typically charges for its services. The U.S. Postal Service is an example. Compare **independent regulatory commission** and **independent executive agency**.

Gregg v. Georgia. The 1976 Supreme Court decision that upheld the constitutionality of the death penalty, stating, "It is an extreme sanction, suitable to the most extreme of crimes." The Court did not, therefore, believe that the death sentence constitutes **cruel and unusual punishment**.

gross domestic product (GDP). The sum total of the value of all the goods and services produced in a year in a nation.

GS (General Schedule) rating. A schedule for federal employees, ranging from GS 1 to GS 18, by which salaries can be keyed to rating and experience. See **civil service.**

H

Hatch Act. A federal law prohibiting government employees from active participation in partisan politics while on duty or for employees in sensitive positions at any time.

health maintenance organization (HMO). Organization contracted by individuals or insurance companies to provide health care for a yearly fee. Such network health plans limit the choice of doctors and treatments. More than half of Americans are enrolled in health maintenance organizations or similar programs.

Hernandez v. Texas. A 1954 Supreme Court decision that extended protection against discrimination to Hispanics.

high-tech politics. A politics in which the behavior of citizens and policymakers and the political agenda itself are increasingly shaped by technology.

home rule. The practice by which municipalities are permitted by the states to write their own charters and, within limits, change them without permission of the state legislature. Today this practice is widely used to organize and modernize municipal government.

House Rules Committee. The committee in the House of Representatives that reviews most **bills** coming from a House committee before they go to the full House.

House Ways and Means Committee. The House of Representatives committee that, along with the **Senate Finance Committee**, writes the tax codes, subject to the approval of Congress as a whole.

hyperpluralism. A theory of government and politics contending that groups are so strong that government, seeking to please them all, is thereby weakened. See also **elitism** and **pluralism**.

I

ideology. See **political ideology.**

impeachment. The political equivalent of an indictment in criminal law, prescribed by the Constitution. The House of Representatives may impeach the president by a majority vote for "Treason, Bribery, or other high Crimes and Misdemeanors."

implied powers. Powers of the federal government that go beyond those enumerated in the Constitution, in accordance with the statement in the Constitution that Congress has the power to "make all laws necessary and proper for carrying into execution" the powers enumerated in Article I. See also ***McCulloch v. Maryland*, elastic clause,** and **enamerated powers.**

incentive system. An alternative to **command-and-control**, with market-like strategies such as rewards used to manage public policy.

income. The amount of money collected between any two points in time. Compare **wealth.**

income distribution. The way the national income is divided into "shares" ranging from the poor to the rich.

income tax. Shares of individual wages and corporate revenues collected by the government. The **Sixteenth Amendment** explicitly authorized Congress to levy a tax on income.

incorporation doctrine. The legal concept under which the **Supreme Court** has nationalized the **Bill of Rights** by making most of its provisions applicable to the states through the **Fourteenth Amendment**.

incrementalism. A description of the budget process where the best predictor of this year's **budget** is last year's budget, plus a little bit more (an increment). According to Aaron Wildavsky, "Most of the budget is a product of previous decisions."

incumbents. Those already holding office. In congressional elections, incumbents usually win.

independent executive agency. The government agencies not accounted for by **cabinet** departments, **independent regulatory commissions**, and **government corporations**. administrators are typically appointed by the president and serve at the president's pleasure. NASA is an example.

independent regulatory commission. A government agency with responsibility for making and enforcing rules to protect the public interest in some sector of the economy and for judging disputes over these rules. Compare **government corporation** and **independent executive agency**.

inflation. A rise in price of goods and services.

initiative. A process permitted in some states whereby voters may place proposed changes to state law on the ballot if sufficient signatures are obtained on petitions calling for such a vote.

initiative petition. A process permitted in some states whereby voters may put proposed changes in the state law to a vote if sufficient signatures are obtained on petitions.

interdependency. Mutual reliance, as in the economic realm, in which actions in nations reverberate and affect the economic well-being of people in other nations.

interest group. An organization of people with shared policy goals entering the policy process at several points to try to achieve those goals. Interest groups pursue their goals in many arenas.

intergovernmental relations. The workings of the federal system—the entire set of interactions among national, state, and local governments, including regulations, transfers of funds, and the sharing of information.

investigative journalism. The use of in-depth reporting to unearth scandals, scams, and schemes, at times putting reporters in adversarial relationships with political leaders.

iron triangles. Also known as *subgovernments*, a mutually dependent, mutually advantageous relationship between interest groups interested in a particular policy, government agencies that administer that policy, and the congressional committees and subcommittees that handle it. Iron triangles dominate some areas of domestic policymaking.

isolationism. The **foreign policy** course the United States followed throughout most of its history whereby it tried to stay out of other nations' conflicts, particularly European wars.

J

Joint Chiefs of Staff. A group that consists of the commanding officers of each of the armed services, a chairperson, and a vice chairperson, and advises the president on military policy.

joint committees. Congressional committees on a few subject-matter areas with membership drawn from both houses. See also **conference committees, standing committees,** and **select committees.**

judicial activism. A judicial philosophy in which judges make bold policy decisions, even charting new constitutional ground. Advocates of this approach emphasize that the courts can correct pressing needs, especially those unmet by the majoritarian political process. Compare **judicial restraint.**

judicial implementation. How and whether court decisions are translated into actual policy, thereby affecting the behavior of others. The courts rely on other units of government to enforce their decisions. See also **judicial review.**

judicial restraint. A judicial philosophy in which judges play minimal policymaking roles, leaving that duty strictly to the legislatures. Compare **judicial activism.**

judicial review. The power of the courts to determine whether acts of Congress and, by implication, the executive are in accord with the **U.S. Constitution**. Judicial review was established by ***Marbury v. Madison***.

justiciable disputes. Issues capable of being settled as a matter of law.

K

Keynesian economic theory. Named after English economist John Maynard Keynes, the theory emphasizing that government spending and deficits can help the economy deal with its ups and downs. Proponents of this theory advocate using the power of government to stimulate the economy when it is lagging. See also **fiscal policy.**

Korematsu v. United States. A 1944 Supreme Court decision that upheld as constitutional the internment of more than 100,000 Americans of Japanese descent in encampments during World War II.

L

labor union. An organization of workers intended to engage in **collective bargaining**.

laissez-faire. The principle that government should not meddle in the economy. See also **capitalism**.

legislative oversight. Congress's monitoring of the bureaucracy and its administration of policy, performed mainly through hearings.

legislative veto. A vote in Congress to override a presidential decision. Although the **War Powers Resolution** asserts this authority, there is reason to believe that, if challenged, the Supreme Court would find the legislative veto in violation of the doctrine of separation of powers.

legitimacy. A characterization of elections by political scientists meaning that they are almost universally accepted as a fair and free method of selecting political leaders. When legitimacy is high, as in the United States, even the losers accept the results peacefully.

Lemon v. Kurtzman. The 1971 Supreme Court decision that established that aid to church-related schools must (1) have a secular legislative purpose; (2) have a primary effect that neither advances nor inhibits religion; and (3) not foster excessive government entanglement with religion.

libel. The publication of false or malicious statements that damage someone's reputation.

lieutenant governor. In many states, the second-highest executive official government, elected with the governor as a ticket in some states and separately in others. She or he may have legislative and executive branch responsibilities.

limited government. The idea that certain restrictions should be placed on government to protect the **natural rights** of citizens.

line-item veto. The power possessed by 42 state governors to veto only certain parts of a bill while allowing the rest of it to pass into law.

linkage institutions. The political channels through which people's concerns become political issues on the **policy agenda**. In the United States, linkage institutions include elections, **political parties, interest groups,** and the **media**.

lobbying. According to Lester Milbrath, a "communication, by someone other than a citizen acting on his or her own behalf, directed to a governmental decision maker with the hope of influencing his or her decision."

local charter. An organizational statement and grant of authority from the state to a local government, much like a state or national constitution. States sometimes allow municipalities to write their own charters and, within limits, to change them without permission of the state legislature. See also **home rule.**

M

majority leader. The principal partisan ally of the **Speaker of the House,** or the party's manager in the Senate. The majority leader is responsible for scheduling **bills**, influencing committee assignments, and rounding up votes in behalf of the party's legislative positions.

majority rule. A fundamental principle of traditional democratic theory. In a democracy, choosing among alternatives requires that the majority's desire be respected. See also **minority rights**.

mandate theory of elections. The idea that the winning candidate has a mandate from the people to carry out his or her platforms and politics. Politicians like the theory better than political scientists do.

Mapp v. Ohio. The 1961 Supreme Court decision ruling that the **Fourth Amendment's** protection against **unreasonable searches and seizures** must be extended to the states.

Marbury v. Madison. The 1803 case in which Chief Justice John Marshall and his associates first asserted the right of the Supreme Court to determine the meaning of the U.S. Constitution. The decision established the Court's power of **judicial review** over acts of Congress, in this case the Judiciary Act of 1789.

mass media. Television, radio, newspapers, magazines, the Internet, and other means of popular communication.

matching funds. Contributions of up to $250 are matched from the Presidential Election Campaign Fund to candidates for the presidential nomination who qualify and agree to meet various conditions, such as limiting their overall spending.

McCleskey v. Kemp. The 1987 Supreme Court decision that upheld the constitutionality of the death penalty against charges that it violated the **Fourteenth Amendment** because minority defendants were more likely to receive the death penalty than were white defendants.

McCulloch v. Maryland. An 1819 Supreme Court decision that established the supremacy of the national government over state governments. The Court, led by Chief Justice John Marshall, held that Congress had certain **implied powers** in addition to the **enumerated powers** found in the Constitution.

McGovern–Fraser Commission. A commission formed at the 1968 Democratic convention in response to demands for reform by minority groups and others who sought better representation.

means-tested programs. Government programs providing benefits only to individuals who qualify based on specific needs.

media events. Events that are purposely staged for the media and that are significant just because the media are there.

Medicaid. A public assistance program designed to provide health care for poor Americans and funded by both the states and the national government.

Medicare. A program added to the Social Security system in 1965 that provides hospitalization insurance for the elderly and permits older Americans to purchase inexpensive coverage for doctor fees and other medical expenses.

melting pot. A term often used to characterize the United States, with its history of immigration and mixing of cultures, ideas, and peoples.

Merit Plan. Method for selecting state judges in which governors appoint persons based on the recommendations of a committee; usually, after serving a short term, the judge faces a retention election.

merit principle. The idea that hiring should be based on entrance exams and promotion ratings to produce administration by people with talent and skill. See also **civil service** and compare **patronage.**

Miami Herald Publishing Company v. Tornillo. A 1974 case in which the Supreme Court held that a state could not force a newspaper to print replies from candidates it had criticized, illustrating the limited power of government to restrict the **print media**. See ***Red Lion Broadcasting Company v. FCC.***

Miller v. California. A 1973 Supreme Court decision that avoided defining obscenity by holding that community standards be used to determine whether material is obscene in terms of appealing to a "prurient interest" and being "patently offensive" and lacking in value.

minimum wage. The legal minimum hourly wage to which most workers are entitled.

minority leader. The principal leader of the minority party in the House of Representatives or in the Senate.

minority majority. The situation, likely beginning in the mid-twenty-first century, in which the non-Hispanic whites will represent a minority of the U.S. population and minority groups together will represent a majority.

minority rights. A principle of traditional democratic theory that guarantees rights to those who do not belong to majorities. See also **majority rule**.

Miranda v. Arizona. The 1966 Supreme Court decision that sets guidelines for police questioning of accused persons to protect them against **self-incrimination** and to protect their right to counsel.

mixed economy. An economic system in which the government is deeply involved in economic decisions (as through its roles as regulator, consumer, subsidizer, taxer, employer, and borrower). Compare **capitalism.**

monetarism. An economic theory holding that the supply of money is the key to a nation's economic health, with too much cash and credit in circulation producing inflation. See also **monetary policy.**

monetary policy. Government manipulation of the supply of money in private hands—along with **fiscal policy,** an important tool by which the government can attempt to steer the economy. See also the **Federal Reserve System.**

Motor Voter Act. A 1993 act that requires states to permit people to register to vote when they apply for their driver's license.

multinational corporations. Businesses with vast holdings in many countries.

N

NAACP v. Alabama. The Supreme Court protected the right to assemble peaceably in this 1958 case when it decided the NAACP did not have to reveal its membership list and thus subject its members to harassment.

narrowcasting. Media programming on cable TV (e.g., on MTV, ESPN, or C-SPAN) or the Internet that is focused on a particular interest and aimed at a particular audience, in contrast to broadcasting.

national chairperson. The national chairperson is responsible for the day-to-day activities of the party and is usually handpicked by the presidential nominee. See also **national committee.**

national committee. One of the institutions that keeps the party operating between conventions. The national committee is composed of representatives from the states and territories. See also **national chairperson.**

national convention. The meeting of party delegates every four years to choose a presidential ticket and write the party's platform.

National Environmental Policy Act (NEPA). Passed in 1969, the centerpiece of federal environmental policy, which requires agencies to file **environmental impact statements.**

national health insurance. A compulsory insurance program for all Americans that would have the government finance citizens' medical care. First proposed by President Harry S. Truman.

National Labor Relations Act. A 1935 law, also known as the Wagner Act, that guarantees workers the right of **collective bargaining**, sets down rules to protect unions and organizers, and created the National Labor Relations Board to regulate labor–management relations.

national party convention. The supreme power within each of the parties. The convention meets every four years to nominate the party's presidential and vice-presidential candidates and to write the party's platform.

national primary. A proposed nationwide primary that would replace the current system of **caucuses** and **presidential primaries**.

National Security Council. The committee that links the president's foreign and military policy advisers. Its formal members are the president, vice president, **secretary of state**, and **secretary of defense**, and it is managed by the president's national security assistant.

natural rights. Rights inherent in human beings, not dependent on governments, which include life, liberty, and property. The concept of natural rights was central to English philosopher John Locke's theories about government and was widely accepted among America's Founders.

Near v. Minnesota. The 1931 Supreme Court decision holding that the protects newspapers from prior restraint.

New Deal coalition. A coalition forged by the Democrats, who dominated American politics from the 1930s to the 1960s. Its basic elements were the urban working class, ethnic groups, Catholics and Jews, the poor, Southerners, African Americans, and intellectuals.

New Jersey Plan. The proposal at the Constitutional Convention that called for equal **representation** of each state in Congress regardless of the state's population. Compare **Virginia Plan** and **Connecticut Compromise.**

New York Times v. Sullivan. Decided in 1964, this case established the guidelines for determining whether public officials and other public figures could win damage suits for **libel**. To do so, individuals must prove that the defamatory statements were made with "actual malice" and reckless disregard for the truth.

Nineteenth Amendment. The constitutional amendment adopted in 1920 that guarantees women the right to vote. See also **suffrage**.

nomination. The official endorsement of a candidate for office by a **political party**. Generally, success in the nomination game requires momentum, money, and media attention.

North Atlantic Treaty Organization (NATO). A regional organization that was created in 1949 by nations including the United States, Canada, and most Western European nations for mutual defense and has subsequently been expanded.

O

Office of Management and Budget (OMB). An office that prepares the president's budget and also advises presidents on proposals from departments and agencies and helps review their proposed regulations. See also **Congressional Budget Office.**

Office of Personnel Management (OPM). The office in charge of hiring for most agencies of the federal government, using elaborate rules in the process.

open primaries. Elections to select party nominees in which voters can decide on Election Day whether they want to participate in the Democratic or Republican contests. Compare **closed primaries.**

opinion. A statement of legal reasoning behind a judicial decision. The content of an opinion may be as important as the decision itself.

Organization of Petroleum Exporting Countries (OPEC). An economic organization consisting primarily of Middle Eastern nations that seeks to control the amount of oil its members produce and sell to other nations and hence the price of oil.

original intent. A view that the Constitution should be interpreted according to the original intent of the Framers. Many conservatives support this view.

original jurisdiction. The jurisdiction of courts that hear a case first, usually in a trial. These are the courts that determine the facts about a case. Compare **appelate jurisdiction.**

P

PACs. See **political action committees (PACs).**

party competition. The battle of the parties for control of public offices. Ups and downs of the two major parties are one of the most important elements in American politics.

party dealignment. The gradual disengagement of people from the parties, as seen in part by shrinking **party identification.**

party eras. Historical periods in which a majority of voters cling to the party in power, which tends to win a majority of the elections. See also **critical election** and **party realignment.**

party identification. A citizen's self-proclaimed preference for one party or the other.

party image. The voter's perception of what the Republicans or Democrats stand for, such as conservatism or liberalism.

party machines. A type of political party organization that relies heavily on material inducements, such as patronage, to win votes and to govern.

party platform. A political party's statement of its goals and policies for the next four years. The platform is drafted prior to the party convention by a committee whose members are chosen in rough proportion to each candidate's strength. It is the best formal statement of a party's beliefs.

party realignment. The displacement of the majority party by the minority party, usually during a **critical election** period. See also **party eras.**

patronage. One of the key inducements used by party machines. A patronage job, promotion, or contract is one that is given for political reasons rather than for merit or competence alone.

Pendleton Civil Service Act. Passed in 1883, an act that created a federal **civil service** so that hiring and promotion would be based on merit rather than **patronage**.

Personal Responsibility and Work Opportunity Reconciliation Act (PRWORA). The welfare reform law of 1996, which implemented the Temporary Assistance for Needy Families program.

Planned Parenthood v. Casey. A 1992 case in which the Supreme Court loosened its standard for evaluating restrictions on abortion from one of "strict scrutiny" of any restraints on a "fundamental right" to one of "undue burden" that permits considerably more regulation.

plea bargaining. A bargain struck between the defendant's lawyer and the prosecutor to the effect that the defendant will plead guilty to a lesser crime (or fewer crimes) in exchange for the state's promise not to prosecute the defendant for a more serious (or additional) crime.

Plessy v. Ferguson. An 1896 Supreme Court decision that provided a constitutional justification for segregation by ruling that a Louisiana law requiring "equal but separate accommodations for the White and colored races" was constitutional.

pluralism. A theory of government and politics emphasizing that many groups, each pressing for its preferred policies, compete and counterbalance one another in the political marketplace. Compare **elitism** and **hyperpluralism.**

pocket veto. A type of veto occurring when Congress adjourns within 10 days of submitting a **bill** to the president and the president simply lets the bill die by neither signing nor vetoing it. See also **veto.**

policy. See **public policy.**

policy agenda. The issues that attract the serious attention of public officials and other people involved in politics at a point in time.

policy entrepreneurs. People who invest their political "capital" in an issue. According to John Kingdon, a policy entrepreneur "could be in or out of government, in elected or appointed positions, in interest groups or research organizations."

policy gridlock. A condition that occurs when interests conflict and no coalition is strong enough to form a majority and establish policy, so nothing gets done.

policy impacts. The effects a policy has on people and problems. Impacts are analyzed to see how well a policy has met its goal and at what cost.

policy implementation. The stage of policymaking between the establishment of a policy and the consequences of the policy for the people affected. Implementation involves translating the goals and objectives of a policy into an operating, ongoing program.

policy voting. Electoral choices that are made on the basis of the voters' policy preferences and where the candidates stand on policy issues.

policymaking institutions. The branches of government charged with taking action on political issues. The U.S. Constitution established three policymaking institutions—Congress, the presidency, and the courts. Today, the power of the bureaucracy is so great that most political scientists consider it a fourth policymaking institution.

policymaking system. The process by which policy comes into being and evolves. People's interests, problems, and concerns create political issues for government policymakers. These issues shape policy, which in turn impacts people, generating more interests, problems, and concerns.

political action committees (PACs). Political funding vehicles created by the 1974 campaign finance reforms. A corporation, union, or some other interest group can create a PAC and register it with the **Federal Election Commission**, which will monitor the PAC's expenditures.

political culture. An overall set of values widely shared within a society.

political efficacy. The belief that one's **political participation** really matters—that one's vote can actually make a difference.

political ideology. A coherent set of beliefs about politics, public policy, and public purpose, which helps give meaning to political events.

political issue. An issue that arises when people disagree about a problem and how to fix it.

political participation. All the activities used by citizens to influence the selection of political leaders or the policies they pursue. The most common means of political participation in a democracy is voting; other means include **protest** and **civil disobedience**.

political party. According to Anthony Downs, a "team of men [and women] seeking to control the governing apparatus by gaining office in a duly constituted election."

political questions. A doctrine developed by the federal courts and used as a means to avoid deciding some cases, principally those involving conflicts between the president and Congress.

political socialization. The process through which individuals in a society acquire political attitudes, views, and knowledge, based on inputs from family, schools, the media, and others.

politics. The process by which we select our governmental leaders and what policies these leaders pursue. Politics produces authoritative decisions about public issues.

poll taxes. Small taxes levied on the right to vote that often fell due at a time of year when poor African American sharecroppers had the least cash on hand. This method was used by most Southern states to exclude African Americans from voting. Poll taxes were declared void by the **Twenty-fourth Amendment** in 1964. See also **white primary.**

pork barrel. Federal projects, grants, and contracts available to state and local governments, businesses, colleges, and other institutions in a congressional district.

potential group. All the people who might be **interest group** members because they share some common interest. Compare **actual group.**

poverty line. The income threshold below which people are considered poor, based on what a family must spend for an "austere" standard of living, traditionally set at three times the cost of a subsistence diet.

precedent. How similar cases have been decided in the past.

presidential coattails. These occur when voters cast their ballots for congressional candidates of the president's party because they support the president. Recent studies show that few races are won this way.

Presidential Election Campaign Fund. Money from the $3 federal income tax check-off goes into this fund, which is then distributed to qualified candidates to subsidize their presidential campaigns.

presidential primaries. Elections in which a state's voters go to the polls to express their preference for a party's nominee for president. Most delegates to the **national party conventions** are chosen this way.

press conferences. Meetings of public officials with reporters.

print media. Newspapers and magazines, as compared with **electronic media**.

prior restraint. A government preventing material from being published. This is a common method of limiting the press in some nations, but it is usually unconstitutional in the United States, according to the **First Amendment** and as confirmed in the 1931 Supreme Court case of ***Near v. Minnesota***.

privileges and immunities. The provision of the Constitution according citizens of each state the privileges of citizens of other states.

probable cause. The situation occurring when the police have reason to believe that a person should be arrested. In making the arrest, police are allowed legally to search for and seize incriminating evidence. Compare **unreasonable searches and seizures.**

progressive tax. A tax by which the government takes a greater share of the income of the rich than of the poor—for example, when a rich family pays 50 percent of its income in taxes, and a poor family pays 5 percent. Compare **regressive tax** and **proportional tax.**

project grants. Federal **categorical grant** given for specific purposes and awarded on the basis of the merits of applications.

proportional representation. An electoral system used throughout most of Europe that awards legislative seats to political parties in proportion to the number of votes won in an election. Compare with **winner-take-all system.**

proportional tax. A tax by which the government takes the same share of income from everyone, rich and poor alike. Compare **progressive tax** and **regressive tax.**

protectionism. Economic policy of shielding an economy from imports.

protest. A form of **political participation** designed to achieve policy change through dramatic and unconventional tactics. See also **civil disobedience.**

public goods. Goods, such as clean air and clean water, that everyone must share.

public interest lobbies. According to Jeffrey Berry, organizations that seek "a collective good, the achievement of which will not selectively and materially benefit the membership or activists of the organization."

public opinion. The distribution of the population's beliefs about politics and policy issues.

public policy. A choice that government makes in response to a political issue. A policy is a course of action taken with regard to some problem.

R

random-digit dialing. A technique used by pollsters to place telephone calls randomly to both listed and unlisted numbers when conducting a survey. See also **random sampling.**

random sampling. The key technique employed by survey researchers, which operates on the principle that everyone should have an equal probability of being selected for the **sample.**

rational-choice theory. A popular theory in political science to explain the actions of voters as well as politicians. It assumes that individuals act in their own best interest, carefully weighing the costs and benefits of possible alternatives.

reapportionment. The process of reallocating seats in the House of Representatives every 10 years on the basis of the results of the census.

recall. A procedure that allows voters to call a special election for a specific official in an attempt to throw him or her out of office before the end of term. Recalls are permitted in only 17 states, seldom used because of their cost and disruptiveness, and rarely successful.

reconciliation. A congressional process through which program authorizations are revised to achieve required savings. It usually also includes tax or other revenue adjustments.

Red Lion Broadcasting Company v. Federal Communications Commission. A 1969 case in which the Supreme Court upheld restrictions on radio and television broadcasting. These restrictions on the broadcast media are much tighter than those on the **print media** because there are only a limited number of broadcasting frequencies available. See also ***Miami Herald Publishing Company v. Tornillo.***

Reed v. Reed. The landmark case in 1971 in which the Supreme Court for the first time upheld a claim of gender discrimination.

referendum. A state-level method of direct legislation that gives voters a chance to approve or disapprove proposed legislation or a proposed constitutional amendment.

Regents of the University of California v. Bakke. A 1978 Supreme Court decision holding that a state university could weigh race or ethnic background as one element in admissions but could not set aside places for members of particular racial groups.

regional primaries. A proposed series of primaries held in each geographic region that would replace the current system of **caucuses** and **presidential primaries.**

regressive tax. A tax in which the burden falls relatively more heavily on low-income groups than on wealthy taxpayers. The opposite of a **progressive tax,** in which tax rates increase as income increases.

regulation. The use of governmental authority to control or change some practice in the private sector.

relative deprivation. A perception by an individual that he or she is not doing well economically in comparison to others.

representation. A basic principle of traditional democratic theory that describes the relationship between the few leaders and the many followers.

republic. A form of government in which the people select representatives to govern them and make laws.

responsible party model. A view about how parties should work, held by some political scientists. According to the model, parties should offer clear choices to the voters, who can then use those choices as cues to their own preferences of candidates. Once in office, parties would carry out their campaign promises.

retrospective voting. A theory of voting according to which voters essentially make their decisions based on their answers to the question "What have you done for me lately?"

revenues. The financial resources of the government. The individual income tax and Social Security tax are two major sources of the federal government's revenue.

right to privacy. The right to a private personal life free from the intrusion of government.

right-to-work laws. A state law forbidding requirements that workers must join a union to hold their jobs. State right-to-work laws were specifically permitted by the Taft-Hartley Act of 1947.

Roe v. Wade. The 1973 Supreme Court decision holding that a state ban on all abortions was unconstitutional. The decision forbade state control over abortions during the first trimester of pregnancy, permitted states to limit abortions to protect the mother's health in the second trimester, and permitted states to ban abortion during the third trimester.

Roth v. United States. A 1957 Supreme Court decision ruling that "obscenity is not within the area of constitutionally protected speech or press."

S

sample. A relatively small proportion of people who are chosen in a survey so as to be representative of the whole.

sampling error. The level of confidence in the findings of a public opinion poll. The more people interviewed, the more confident one can be of the results.

Schenck v. United States. A 1919 decision upholding the conviction of a socialist who had urged young men to resist the draft during World War I. Justice Holmes declared that government can limit speech if the speech provokes a "clear and present danger" of substantive evils.

School District of Abington Township, Pennsylvania v. Schempp. A 1963 Supreme Court decision holding that a Pennsylvania law requiring Bible reading in schools violated the **establishment clause** of the **First Amendment.**

Scott v. Sandford. The 1857 Supreme Court decision ruling that a slave who had escaped to a free state enjoyed no rights as a citizen and that Congress had no authority to ban slavery in the territories.

search warrant. A written authorization from a court specifying the area to be searched and what the police are searching for.

secretary of defense. The head of the Department of Defense and the president's key adviser on military policy and, as such, a key **foreign policy** actor.

secretary of state. The head of the Department of State and traditionally the key adviser to the president on **foreign policy**.

Securities and Exchange Commission (SEC). The federal agency created during the New Deal that regulates the stock market.

select committees. Congressional committees appointed for a specific purpose, such as the Watergate investigation. See also **joint committees, standing committees,** and **conference committees.**

selective benefits. Goods that a group can restrict to those who actually join.

selective perception. The phenomenon that people's beliefs often guide what they pay the most attention to and how they interpret events.

self-incrimination. The situation occurring when an individual accused of a crime is compelled to be a witness against himself or herself in court. The **Fifth Amendment** forbids self-incrimination. See also ***Miranda v. Arizona.***

Senate Finance Committee. The Senate committee that, along with the **House Ways and Means Committee**, writes the tax codes, subject to the approval of Congress as a whole.

senatorial courtesy. An unwritten tradition whereby nominations for state-level federal judicial posts are usually not confirmed if they are opposed by a senator of the president's party from the state in which the nominee will serve. The tradition also applies to courts of appeal when there is opposition from a senator of the president's party who is from the nominee's state.

Senior Executive Service (SES). An elite cadre of about 9,000 federal government managers at the top of the civil service system.

seniority system. A simple rule for picking **committee chairs,** in effect until the 1970s. The member who had served on the committee the longest and whose party controlled the chamber became chair, regardless of party loyalty, mental state, or competence.

separation of powers. A feature of the Constitution that requires each of the three branches of government—executive, legislative, and judicial—to be relatively independent of the others so that one cannot control the others. Power is shared among these three institutions. See also **checks and balances.**

Shays' Rebellion. A series of attacks on courthouses by a small band of farmers led by Revolutionary War Captain Daniel Shays to block foreclosure proceedings.

single-issue groups. Groups that have a narrow interest, tend to dislike compromise, and often draw membership from people new to politics.

Sixteenth Amendment. The constitutional amendment adopted in 1913 that explicitly permitted Congress to levy an **income tax**.

Sixth Amendment. A constitutional amendment designed to protect individuals accused of crimes. It includes the right to counsel, the right to confront witnesses, and the right to a speedy and public trial.

Social Security Act (1935). Created both the Social Security program and a national assistance program for poor families.

Social Security Trust Fund. The "account" into which Social Security employee and employer contributions are "deposited" and used to pay out eligible recipients.

social welfare policies. Policies that provide benefits, cash or in-kind, to individuals, based on either entitlement or means testing.

soft money. Political contributions earmarked for party-building expenses at the grass-roots level or for generic party advertising. Unlike money that goes to the campaign of a particular candidate, such party donations are not subject to contribution limits. For a time, such contributions were unlimited, until they were banned by the McCain-Feingold Act.

solicitor general. A presidential appointee and the third-ranking office in the Department of Justice. The solicitor general is in charge of the appellate court litigation of the federal government.

sound bites. Short video clips of approximately 10 seconds. Typically, they are all that is shown from a politician's speech on the nightly television news.

Speaker of the House. An office mandated by the Constitution. The Speaker is chosen in practice by the majority party, has both formal and informal powers, and is second in line to succeed to the presidency should that office become vacant.

standard operating procedures. Better known as *SOPs*, these procedures for everyday decision making enable bureaucrats to bring efficiency and uniformity to the running of complex organizations. Uniformity promotes fairness and makes personnel interchangeable. See also **administrative discretion**.

standing committees. Separate subject-matter committees in each house of Congress that handle **bills** in different policy areas. See also **joint committees, select committees,** and **conference committees.**

standing to sue. The requirement that plaintiffs have a serious interest in a case, which depends on whether they have sustained or are likely to sustain a direct and substantial injury from another party or from an action of government.

***stare decisis*.** A Latin phrase meaning "let the decision stand." Most cases reaching appellate courts are settled on this principle.

statutory construction. The judicial interpretation of an act of Congress. In some cases where statutory construction is an issue, Congress passes new legislation to clarify existing laws.

street-level bureaucrats. A phrase coined by Michael Lipsky, referring to those bureaucrats who are in constant contact with the public and have considerable **administrative discretion**.

subnational governments. State and local governments, which, with reform, modernization, and changing intergovernmental relations, have assumed new responsibilities and importance since the 1960s.

suffrage. The legal right to vote, extended to African Americans by the **Fifteenth Amendment**, to women by the **Nineteenth Amendment**, and to people over the age of 18 by the Twenty-sixth Amendment.

superdelegates. National party leaders who automatically get a delegate slot at the **national party convention**.

Superfund. A fund created by Congress in 1980 to clean up hazardous waste sites. Money for the fund comes from taxing chemical products.

supply-side economics. An economic theory, first applied during the Reagan administration, holding that the key task for fiscal policy is to stimulate the supply of goods, as by cutting tax rates.

supremacy clause. The clause in Article VI of the Constitution that makes the Constitution, national laws, and treaties supreme over state laws as long as the national government is acting within its constitutional limits.

Supreme Court. The pinnacle of the American judicial system. The Court ensures uniformity in interpreting national laws, resolves conflicts among states, and maintains national supremacy in law. It has both **original jurisdiction** and **appellate jurisdiction**.

symbolic speech. Nonverbal communication, such as burning a flag or wearing an armband. The Supreme Court has accorded some symbolic speech protection under the **First Amendment**. See ***Texas v. Johnson.***

T

talking head. A shot of a person's face talking directly to the camera. Because such shots are visually unstimulating, the major networks rarely show politicians talking for very long.

tariff. A special tax added to imported goods to raise the price, thereby protecting businesses and workers from foreign competition.

tax expenditures. Revenue losses that result from special exemptions, exclusions, or deductions allowed by federal tax law.

Temporary Assistance for Needy Families (TANF). Replacing Aid to Families with Dependent Children as the program for public assistance to needy families, TANF requires people on welfare to find work within two years and sets a lifetime maximum of five years.

Tenth Amendment. The constitutional amendment stating, "The powers not delegated to the United States by the Constitution, nor prohibited by it to the states, are reserved to the states respectively, or to the people."

Texas v. Johnson. A 1989 case in which the Supreme Court struck down a law banning the burning of the American flag on the grounds that such action was **symbolic speech** protected by the **First Amendment**.

third parties. Electoral contenders other than the two major parties. American third parties are not unusual, but they rarely win elections.

Thirteenth Amendment. The constitutional amendment ratified after the Civil War that forbade slavery and involuntary servitude.

ticket splitting. Voting with one party for one office and with another party for other offices. It has become the norm in American voting behavior.

town meeting. A special form of direct democracy under which all voting-age adults in a community gather once a year to make public policy. Now used only in a few villages in New England.

transfer payments. Benefits given by the government directly to individuals—either cash transfers, such as Social Security payments, or in-kind transfers, such as food stamps and low-interest college loans.

trial balloons. Intentional news leaks for the purpose of assessing the political reaction.

Twenty-fifth Amendment. Passed in 1967, this amendment permits the vice president to become acting president if the vice president and the president's cabinet determine that the president is disabled, and it outlines how a recuperated president can reclaim the job.

Twenty-fourth Amendment. The constitutional amendment passed in 1964 that declared **poll taxes** void in federal elections.

Twenty-second Amendment. Passed in 1951, this amendment limits presidents to two terms of office.

U

uncontrollable expenditures. Expenditures that are determined by how many eligible beneficiaries there are for a program or by previous obligations of the government and that Congress therefore cannot easily control.

underemployment rate. As measured by the Bureau of Labor Statistics, a statistic that includes, along with the unemployed, discouraged workers and people who are working part-time because they cannot find full-time work.

unemployment rate. As measured by the Bureau of Labor Statistics, the proportion of the labor force actively seeking work but unable to find jobs.

union shop. A provision found in some collective bargaining agreements requiring all employees of a business to join the union within a short period, usually 30 days, and to remain members as a condition of employment.

unitary governments. A way of organizing a nation so that all power resides in the central government. Most national governments today are unitary governments. Compare **federalism.**

United Nations (UN). Created in 1945 and currently including 192 member nations, with a central peacekeeping mission and programs in areas including economic development and health, education, and welfare. The seat of real power in the UN is the Security Council.

unreasonable searches and seizures. Obtaining evidence in a haphazard or random manner, a practice prohibited by the Fourth Amendment. **Probable cause** and/or a **search warrant** are required for a legal and proper search for and seizure of incriminating evidence.

U.S. Constitution. The document written in 1787 and ratified in 1788 that sets forth the institutional structure of U.S. government and the tasks these institutions perform. It replaced the Articles of Confederation.

V

veto. The constitutional power of the president to send a bill back to Congress with reasons for rejecting it. A two-thirds vote in each house can override a veto. See also **legislative veto** and **pocket veto.**

Virginia Plan. The proposal at the Constitutional Convention that called for **representation** of each state in Congress in proportion to that state's share of the U.S. population. Compare **New Jersey Plan** and **Connecticut Compromise.**

voter registration. A system adopted by the states that requires voters to register prior to voting. Some states require citizens to register as much as 30 days in advance, whereas others permit Election Day registration.

Voting Rights Act of 1965. A law designed to help end formal and informal barriers to African American **suffrage**. Under the law, hundreds of thousands of African Americans were registered, and the number of African American elected officials increased dramatically.

W

War Powers Resolution. A law passed in 1973, in reaction to American fighting in Vietnam and Cambodia, that requires presidents to consult with Congress whenever possible prior to using military force and to withdraw forces after 60 days unless Congress declares war or grants an extension. However, presidents have viewed the resolution as unconstitutional. See also **legislative veto.**

Water Pollution Control Act of 1972. A law intended to clean up the nation's rivers and lakes, by enabling regulation of point sources of pollution.

Watergate. The events and scandal surrounding a break-in at the Democratic National Committee headquarters in 1972 and the subsequent cover-up of White House involvement, leading to the eventual resignation of President Nixon under the threat of **impeachment**.

wealth. The value of assets owned. Compare **income.**

whips. Party leaders who work with the **majority leader** or **minority leader** to count votes beforehand and lean on waverers whose votes are crucial to a **bill** favored by the party.

white primary. Primary elections from which African Americans were excluded, an exclusion that, in the heavily Democratic South, deprived African Americans of a voice in the real contests. The Supreme Court declared white primaries unconstitutional in 1944. See also **poll taxes.**

winner-take-all system. An electoral system in which legislative seats are awarded only to the candidates who come in first in their constituencies. Compare **proportional representation.**

World Trade Organization (WTO). International organization that promotes free trade.

writ of habeas corpus. A court order requiring jailers to explain to a judge why they are holding a prisoner in custody.

Z

Zelman v. Simmons-Harris. The 2002 Supreme Court decision that upheld a state program providing families with vouchers that could be used to pay for tuition at religious schools.

Zurcher v. Stanford Daily. A 1978 Supreme Court decision holding that a proper **search warrant** could be applied to a newspaper as well as to anyone else without necessarily violating the **First Amendment** rights to freedom of the press.

Notes

CHAPTER 1

1. John McCormick, "Lost Obama Interview Provides Portrait of Aspiring Politician," Bloomberg News, August 4, 2009. See http://www.bloomberg.com/apps/news?pid=washingtonstory&sid=aMI4WIB.JTDA.

2. David Von Drehle, "The Year of the Youth Vote," *Time*, January 31, 2008. See http://www.time.com/time/politics/article/0,8599,1708570-2,00.html.

3. Because the level of difficulty of the questions differed somewhat, one should only examine the differences within a year and not necessarily infer that political knowledge as a whole has decreased.

4. For example, younger people have consistently scored much lower than have senior citizens in the Pew Research Center's regular "News IQ" surveys. The reports from these surveys can be found at http://pewresearch.org/politicalquiz/.

5. Stephen Earl Bennett and Eric W. Rademacher, "The Age of Indifference Revisited: Patterns of Political Interest, Media Exposure, and Knowledge Among Generation X," in Stephen C. Craig and Stephen Earl Bennett, eds., *After the Boom: The Politics of Generation X* (Lanham, MD: Rowman & Littlefield, 1997), 39.

6. Michael X. Delli Carpini and Scott Keeter, *What Americans Know About Politics and Why It Matters* (New Haven, CT: Yale University Press, 1996), chap. 6.

7. Data for Presidents Richard Nixon through George W. Bush can be found in Samuel Kernell, *Going Public: New Strategies of Presidential Leadership*, 4th ed. (Washington, DC: CQ Press, 2007), 140. For Obama's Nielsen ratings in 2009, see Martin P. Wattenberg, "The Presidential Media Environment in the Age of Obama," in Thomas R. Dye et al., *Obama Year One* (New York: Longman, 2010), p. 58.

8. Anthony Corrado, "Elections in Cyberspace: Prospects and Problems," in Anthony Corrado and Charles M. Firestone, eds., *Elections in Cyberspace: Toward a New Era in American Politics* (Washington, DC: Aspen Institute, 1996), 29.

9. Jeremy D. Mayer, "Campaign Press Coverage—At the Speed of Light." In Richard J. Semiatin, ed., *Campaigns on the Cutting Edge* (Washington, DC: CQ Press, 2008), 152.

10. Ganesh Sitaraman and Previn Warren, *Invisible Citizens: Youth Politics After September 11* (New York: i Universe, Inc., 2003), ix.

11. Harold D. Lasswell, *Politics: Who Gets What, When, and How* (New York: McGraw-Hill, 1938).

12. Randy Shilts, *And the Band Played On: Politics, People, and the AIDS Epidemic* (New York: Penguin Books, 1987).

13. Robert A. Dahl, *Dilemmas of Pluralist Democracy* (New Haven, CT: Yale University Press, 1982), 6.

14. Robert A. Dahl, *A Preface to Democratic Theory* (Chicago: University of Chicago Press, 1956), 137.

15. Robert Putnam, *Bowling Alone: The Collapse and Revival of American Community* (New York: Simon & Schuster, 2000).

16. Jacob S. Hacker and Paul Pierson, *Off Center: The Republican Revolution and the Erosion of American Democracy* (New Haven, CT: Yale University Press, 2005), 16.

17. American Political Science Association Task Force on Inequality and American Democracy, "American Democracy in an Age of Rising Inequality" (Washington, DC: American Political Science Association, 2004), 2. The entire report can be found at http://www.apsanet.org/imgtest/taskforcereport.pdf.

18. Ronald Inglehart and Christian Welzel, *Modernization, Cultural Change, and Democracy: The Human Development Sequence* (New York: Cambridge University Press, 2005), 2.

19. G. K. Chesterton, *What I Saw in America* (New York: Dodd, Mead & Co., 1922), 7.

20. Seymour Martin Lipset, *American Exceptionalism: A Double-Edged Sword* (New York: Norton, 1996), 31.

21. Ibid., 19

22. Louis Hartz, *The Liberal Tradition in America* (New York: Harcourt, Brace, 1955).

23. Frederick Jackson Turner, *The Significance of the Frontier in American History* (New York: Readex Microprint, 1966), 221.

24. John W. Kingdon, *America the Unusual* (New York: St. Martin's/Worth, 1999), 2.

25. Seymour Martin Lipset, *The First New Nation* (New York: Norton, 1979), 68.

26. James Q. Wilson, "How Divided Are We?" *Commentary*, February 2006, 15.

27. Ibid., 21.

28. Morris P. Fiorina, *Culture War? The Myth of a Polarized America*, 2nd ed. (New York: Longman, 2006), 165.

29. Wayne Baker, *America's Crisis of Values: Reality and Perception* (Princeton, NJ: Princeton University Press, 2005).

30. Dick Armey, *The Freedom Revolution* (Washington, DC: Regnery, 1995), 316.

CHAPTER 2

1. Gordon S. Wood, *The Radicalism of the American Revolution* (New York: Vintage, 1993), 4.

2. Garry Wills, *Inventing America: Jefferson's Declaration of Independence* (New York: Doubleday, 1978), 13, 77.

3. Clinton Rossiter, *1787: The Grand Convention* (New York: Macmillan, 1966), 60.

4. On the Lockean influence on the Declaration of Independence, see Carl L. Becker, *The Declaration of Independence: A Study in the History of Political Ideas* (New York: Random House, 1942).

5. Seymour Martin Lipset, *The First New Nation* (New York: Basic Books, 1963).

6. Gordon S. Wood, *The Creation of the American Republic, 1776–1787* (Chapel Hill: University of North Carolina Press, 1969), 3.

7. On the Articles of Confederation, see Merrill Jensen, *The Articles of Confederation* (Madison: University of Wisconsin Press, 1940).

8. Wood, *The Radicalism of the American Revolution*, 6–7.

9. Calvin C. Jillson and Cecil L. Eubanks, "The Political Structure of Constitution-Making: The Federal Convention of 1787," *American Journal of Political Science* 28 (August 1984): 435–58. See also Calvin C. Jillson, *Constitution Making: Conflict and Consensus in the Federal Convention of 1787* (New York: Agathon, 1988).

10. This representation may have practical consequences. See Frances E. Lee, "Representation and Public Policy: The Consequences of Senate Apportionment for the Geographic Distribution of Federal Funds," *Journal of Politics* 60 (February 1998): 34–62; and Daniel Wirls, "The Consequences of Equal Representation: The Bicameral Politics of NAFTA in the 103rd Congress," *Congress and the President* 25 (Autumn 1998): 129–45.

11. Cecelia M. Kenyon, ed., *The Antifederalists* (Indianapolis: Bobbs- Merrill, 1966), xxxv.

12. Rossiter, *1787.*

13. See Charles A. Beard, *An Economic Interpretation of the Constitution of the United States* (New York: Macmillan, 1913); Robert E. Brown, *Charles Beard and the Constitution* (Princeton, NJ: Princeton University Press, 1956); Forrest B. McDonald, *We the People: The Economic Origins of the Constitution* (Chicago: University of Chicago Press, 1958); and Forrest B. McDonald, *Novus Ordo Seclorum: The Intellectual Origins of the Constitution* (Lawrence: University Press of Kansas, 1986).

14. A brilliant exposition of the Madisonian system is found in Robert A. Dahl, *A Preface to Democratic Theory* (Chicago: University of Chicago Press, 1956).

15. "Federalist #10," in Fairfield, *The Federalist Papers*.

16. "Federalist #51," in Fairfield, *The Federalist Papers*.

17. Quoted in Beard, *An Economic Interpretation of the Constitution of the United States*, 299.

18. See Kenyon, *The Antifederalists.*

19. Jackson Turner Main, *The Antifederalists* (Chapel Hill: University of North Carolina Press, 1961). For more on the Anti-Federalists, see Herbert J. Storing, *What the Anti-Federalists Were For* (Chicago: University of Chicago Press, 1981).

20. The early attempts at ratification of the ERA are recounted in Janet Boles, *The Politics of the Equal Rights Amendment* (New York: Longman, 1978).

21. Jane J. Mansbridge, *Why We Lost the ERA* (Chicago: University of Chicago Press, 1986).

22. See "Federalist #78," in Fairfield, *The Federalist Papers.*

23. See, for example, James MacGregor Burns, *The Deadlock of Democracy* (Englewood Cliffs, NJ: Prentice Hall, 1963), 6.

CHAPTER 3

1. For a study of how different states enforce federal child support enforcement, see Lael R. Keiser and Joe Soss, "With Good Cause: Bureaucratic Discretion and the Politics of Child Support Enforcement," *American Journal of Political Science* 42 (October 1998): 1,133–56.

2. On the states and cities as innovators, see Charles R. Shipan and Craig Volden, "The Mechanisms of Policy Diffusion," *American Journal of Political Science* 52 (October 2008): 840–57; Richard P. Nathan and Fred C. Doolittle, *Reagan and the States* (Princeton, NJ: Princeton University Press, 1987); Virginia Gray, "Innovation in the States: A Diffusion Study," *American Political Science Review* 67 (December 1973): 1,174–85; and Jack L. Walker, "The Diffusion of Innovations in the American States," *American Political Science Review* 63 (September 1969): 880–99.

3. *Alden v. Maine*, (1999). See also *College Savings Bank v. Florida Prepaid Postsecondary Education Expense Board* (1999); and *Florida Prepaid Postsecondary Education Expense Board v. College Savings Bank* (1999).

4. *Federal Maritime Commission v. South Carolina Ports Authority* (2002).

5. The Fourteenth Amendment was passed *after* the Eleventh Amendment, so the Fourteenth is not limited by the Eleventh.

6. *Monroe v. Pape* (1961); *Monell v. New York City Department of Social Welfare* (1978); *Owen v. Independence* (1980); *Maine v. Thiboutot*, (1980); *Oklahoma City v. Tuttle*, (1985); *Dennis v. Higgins* (1991).

7. The transformation from dual to cooperative federalism is described in Walker, *The Rebirth of Federalism*, chap. 4.

8. The classic discussion of cooperative federalism is found in Morton Grodzins, *The American System: A New View of Governments in the United States*, ed. Daniel J. Elazar (Chicago: Rand McNally, 1966).

9. See Pew Research Center poll, September 25–October 31, 1997, and Craig Volden, "Intergovernmental Political Competition in American Federalism," *American Journal of Political Science* 49 (April 2005): 327–42.

10. Office of Management and Budget, *Budget of the United States Government, Fiscal Year 2011: Historical*

Tables (Washington, DC: U.S. Government Printing Office, 2010), Tables 12.1, 12.2, and 15.2.

11. On intergovernmental lobbying, see Donald H. Haider, *When Governments Go to Washington* (New York: Free Press, 1974) and Anne Marie Commisa, *Governments as Interest Groups: Intergovernmental Lobbying and the Federal System* (Westport, CT: Praeger, 1995).

12. For an exception to the general pattern, see Lisa L. Miller, "The Representational Biases of Federalism: Scope and Bias in the Political Process, Revisited," Perspectives on Politics 5 (June 2007): 305–21.

13. Michael A. Bailey, "Welfare and the Multifaceted Decision to Move," *American Political Science Review* 99 (February 2005): 125–35; Michael A. Bailey and Mark Carl Rom, "A Wider Race? Interstate Competition Across Health and Welfare Programs," *Journal of Politics* 66 (May 2004): 326–47; Craig Volden, "The Politics of Competitive Federalism: A Race to the Bottom in Welfare Benefits," *American Journal of Political Science* 46 (April 2002): 352–63; Paul E. Peterson and Mark Rom, "American Federalism, Welfare Policy, and Residential Choices," *American Political Science Review* 83 (September 1989): 711–28. But see William D. Berry, Richard C. Fording, and Russell L. Hanson, "Reassessing the 'Race to the Bottom' in State Welfare Policy," *Journal of Politics* 65 (May 2003): 327–49. Some states limit welfare payments to new residents. On environmental policy, see David M. Konisky, "Regulatory Competition and Environmental Enforcement: Is There a Race to the Bottom? *American Journal of Political Science* 51 (October 2007): 853–72.

14. Office of Management and Budget, *Budget of the United States Government, Fiscal Year 2011: Historical Tables* (Washington, DC: US Government Printing Office, 2010), Table 15.3.

CHAPTER 4

1. James W. Prothro and Charles M. Grigg, "Fundamental Principles of Democracy: Bases of Agreement and Disagreement," *Journal of Politics* 22 (1960): 276–94; John L. Sullivan et al., "The Sources of Political Tolerance: A Multivariate Analysis," *American Political Science Review* 75 (1981): 100–15.

2. Darren W. Davis and Brian D. Silver, "Civil Liberties vs. Security: Public Opinion in the Context of the Terrorist Attacks on America," *American Journal of Political Science* 48 (January 2004): 28–46.

3. *Widmar v. Vincent* (1981).

4. *Westside Community Schools v. Mergens* (1990).

5. *Good News Club v. Milford Central School* (2001).

6. *Lamb's Chapel v. Center Moriches Union Free School* (1993).

7. *Rosenberger v. University of Virginia* (1995).

8. *Locke v. Davey* (2004).

9. *Illinois ex rel McCollum v. Board of Education* (1948).

10. *Zorach v. Clauson* (1952).

11. *Stone v. Graham* (1980).

12. *Lee v. Weisman* (1992).

13. *Santa Fe School District v. Doe* (2000).

14. *Wallace v. Jaffree* (1985).

15. See Kenneth D. Wald and Allison Calhoun-Brown, *Religion and Politics in the United States*, 6th ed. (Lanham, MD: Rowman & Littlefield, 2010).

16. See, for example, Gallup poll of August 8–11, 2005.

17. *Edwards v. Aguillard* (1987).

18. *Epperson v. Arkansas* (1968).

19. *McCreary County v. American Civil Liberties Union of Kentucky* (2005).

20. *Van Orden v. Perry* (2005).

21. *Lynch v. Donelly* (1984).

22. *County of Allegheny v. American Civil Liberties Union* (1989).

23. *Bob Jones University v. United States* (1983).

24. *Wisconsin v. Yoder* (1972).

25. Denying people unemployment compensation is an exception to this rule.

26. *City of Boerne v. Flores* (1997).

27. *Gonzales v. O Centro Espirita Beneficente Uniao do Vegetal* (2006).

28. *Cutter v. Wilkinson* (2005)

29. Charles R. Lawrence III, "If He Hollers Let Him Go: Regulating Racist Speech on Campus," in *Words That Wound: Critical Race Theory, Assaultive Speech, and the First Amendment*, ed. Mari J. Matsuda, Charles R. Lawrence III, Richard Delgado, and Kimberle Crenshaw, (Boulder, CO: Westview, 1993), 67–68.

30. Ira Glasser, "Introduction," in *Speaking of Race, Speaking of Sex: Hate Speech, Civil Rights, and Civil Liberties*, ed. Henry Louis Gates Jr. (New York: New York University Press, 1994), 8.

31. *R.A.V. v. St. Paul* (1992). However, states may impose longer prison terms on people convicted of "hate crimes" (crimes motivated by racial, religious, or other prejudice) without violating their rights to free speech.

32. See Fred W. Friendly, *Minnesota Rag* (New York: Random House, 1981).

33. *Hazelwood School District v. Kuhlmeier* (1988).

34. *Morse v. Frederick* (2007).

35. The Supreme Court upheld the government's suit in *United States v. Snepp* (1980).

36. *McIntyre v. Ohio Elections Commission* (1995).

37. *Hudgens v. National Labor Relations Board* (1976).

38. *Pruneyard Shopping Center v. Robins* (1980).

39. *City of Ladue v. Gilleo* (1994).

40. *Jenkins v. Georgia* (1974).

41. *Schad v. Mount Ephraim* (1981).

42. *Barnes v. Glen Theater, Inc.* (1991); *Erie v. Pap's A.M.* (2000).

43. *Osborne v. Ohio* (1990).

44. *Reno v. ACLU* (1997).

45. *Ashcroft v. Free Speech Coalition* (2002).

46. The story of this case is told in Anthony Lewis, *Make No Law: The Sullivan Case and the First Amendment* (New York: Random House, 1991).

47. Renata Adler, *Reckless Disregard* (New York: Knopf, 1986).

48. *Tinker v. Des Moines Independent School District* (1969).

49. After Congress passed the Flag Protection Act of 1989 outlawing desecration of the American flag, the Supreme Court also found the act an impermissible infringement on free speech in *United States v. Eichman* (1990).

50. *United States v. O'Brien* (1968).

51. *Virginia v. Black* (2003).

52. *Nebraska Press Association v. Stuart* (1972).

53. *Richmond Newspapers v. Virginia* (1980).

54. *Greater New Orleans Broadcasting, Inc. v. United States* (1999).

55. *Central Hudson Gas & Electric Corporation v. Public Service Commission of N.Y.* (1980).

56. *FCC v. Pacifica Foundation* (1978).

57. *Frisby v. Schultz* (1988).

58. *Rumsfeld v. Forum for Academic and Institutional Rights, Inc.* (2006).

59. *Brigham City v. Stuart* (2006).

60. *Michigan v. Sitz* (1990).

61. *Illinois v. Caballes* (2005).

62. *Brendlin v. California* (2007). The police recognized the passenger as a parole violator.

63. *Safford Unified School District #1 v. Redding* (2009).

64. *Knowles v. Iowa* (1998).

65. *Arizona v. Grant* (2009).

66. *City of Indianapolis v. Edmond* (2000).

67. *Florida v. J.L.* (2000).

68. *Kyllo v. U.S.* (2001).

69. *Nix v. Williams* (1984).

70. *United States v. Leon* (1984).

71. *Arizona v. Evans* (1995).

72. *Hudson v. Michigan* (2006).

73. *United States v. Payner* (1980).

74. On the *Miranda* case, see Liva Baker, *Miranda: The Crime, the Law, the Politics* (New York: Atheneum, 1983).

75. *Arizona v. Fulminante* (1991).

76. *Maryland v. Shatzer* (2010).

77. *Berghuis v. Thompkins* (2010)

78. The story of Gideon is eloquently told by Anthony Lewis, *Gideon's Trumpet* (New York: Random House, 1964).

79. *United States v. Gonzalez-Lopez* (2006).

80. David Brereton and Jonathan D. Casper, "Does It Pay to Plead Guilty? Differential Sentencing and the Function of the Criminal Courts," *Law and Society Review* 16 (1981–1982): 45–70.

81. *Batson v. Kentucky* (1986); *Miller-El v. Dretke* (2005).

82. *Apprendi v. New Jersey* (2000); *Blakely v. Washington* (2004); *United States v. Booker* (2005); *Cunningham v. California* (2007).

83. *Crawford v. Washington* (2004).

84. *Melendez-Diaz v. Massachusetts* (2009).

85. Graham v. Florida (2010).

86. Joe Soss, Laura Langbein, and Alan R. Metelko, "Why Do White Americans Support the Death Penalty?" *Journal of Politics* 65 (May 2003): 397–421.

87. *Baze v. Rees* (2008).

88. Guttmacher Institute, 2009.

89. *Madsen v. Women's Health Center* (1994). In 1997, the Court also upheld a 15-foot buffer zone.

90. *Hill v. Colorado* (2000).

91. *National Organization for Women v. Scheidler* (1994).

92. Although, as Chapter 16 on the judiciary will show, there is indirect accountability.

CHAPTER 5

1. For opposing interpretations of the Fourteenth Amendment, see Judith A. Baer, *Equality Under the Constitution: Reclaiming the Fourteenth Amendment* (Ithaca, NY: Cornell University Press, 1983), and Raoul Berger, *Government by Judiciary: The Transformation of the Fourteenth Amendment* (Cambridge, MA: Harvard University Press, 1977).

2. Desmond King, *Separate but Unequal: Black Americans and the US Federal Government* (Oxford: Oxford University Press, 1995).

3. D. Garth Taylor, Paul B. Sheatsley, and Andrew M. Greeley, "Attitudes Toward Racial Integration," *Scientific American* 238 (June 1978): 42–49; Richard G. Niemi, John Mueller, and John W. Smith, *Trends in Public Opinion* (Westport, CT: Greenwood Press, 1989), 180.

4. There are a few exceptions. Religious institutions such as schools may use religious standards in employment. Gender, age, and disabilities may be considered in the few cases where such occupational qualifications are absolutely essential to the normal operations of a business or enterprise, as in the case of a men's restroom attendant.

5. On the implementation of the Voting Rights Act, see Richard Scher and James Button, "Voting Rights Act: Implementation and Impact," in *Implementation of Civil Rights Policy*, ed. Charles Bullock III and Charles Lamb, (Monterey, CA: Brooks/Cole, 1984); Abigail M. Thernstrom, *Whose Votes Count?* (Cambridge, MA: Harvard University Press, 1987); and Chandler Davidson and Bernard Groffman, eds., *Quiet Revolution in the South: The Impact of the Voting Rights Act, 1965–1990* (Princeton, NJ: Princeton University Press, 1994).

6. U.S. Department of Commerce, *Statistical Abstract of the United States, 2010* (Washington, DC: U.S. Government Printing Office, 2010), Table 404. See David Lublin, *The Paradox of Representation: Racial Gerrymandering and Minority Interests in Congress* (Princeton, NJ: Princeton University Press, 1997), on how racial redistricting helped increase the number of minority representatives in Congress.

7. *League of United Latin American Citizens v. Perry* (2006).

8. See Dee Brown, *Bury My Heart at Wounded Knee: An Indian History of the American West* (New York: Holt, Rinehart and Winston, 1970).

9. U.S. Department of Commerce, *Statistical Abstract of the United States, 2010*, Table 405.

10. *White v. Register* (1973).

11. See Eleanor Flexner, *Century of Struggle* (New York: Atheneum, 1971).

12. See J. Stanley Lemons, *The Woman Citizen: Social Feminism in the 1920s* (Urbana: University of Illinois Press, 1973).

13. *Kirchberg v. Feenstra* (1981).

14. *Arizona Governing Committee for Tax Deferred Annuity and Deferred Compensation Plans v. Norris* (1983).
15. *Michael M. v. Superior Court* (1981).
16. *Kahn v. Shevin* (1974).
17. U.S. Department of Labor, Bureau of Labor Statistics, *Women in the Labor Force: A Databook (2009 Edition)*, Tables 1–7.
18. *Cleveland Board of Education v. LaFleur* (1974).
19. *United Automobile Workers v. Johnson Controls* (1991).
20. *Roberts v. United States Jaycees* (1984); *Board of Directors of Rotary International v. Rotary Club of Duarte* (1987); *New York State Club Association v. New York* (1988).
21. *United States v. Virginia et al.* (1996).
22. U.S. Department of Labor, Bureau of Labor Statistics, *Women in the Labor Force: A Databook (2009 Edition)*, Table 16.
23. U.S. Department of Commerce, *Statistical Abstract of the United States, 2010*, Table 498.
24. www.eeoc.gov/laws/types/sexual_harassment.cfm.
25. *Meritor Savings Bank v. Vinson* (1986).
26. See also *Burlington Industries, Inc. v. Ellerth* (1998).
27. *Faragher v. City of Boca Raton* (1998); *Pennsylvania State Police v. Suders* (2004).
28. *Burlington Northern Santa Fe Railway Co. v. White* (2006).
29. *Davis v. Monroe County Board of Education* (1999).
30. U.S. Census Bureau, Current Population Survey, *Annual Social and Economic Supplement, 2009*.
31. *Massachusetts Board of Retirement v. Murgia* (1976).
32. *Smith v. City of Jackson* (2005).
33. *Bregdon v. Abbott* (1998).
34. *Boy Scouts of America v. Dale* (2000).
35. Gallup poll, May 3-6, 2010; Pew Research Center for the People & the Press polls, August 11–17 and August 20–27, 2009.
36. Kenneth D. Wald, James W. Button, and Barbara A. Rienzo, "The Politics of Gay Rights in American Communities: Explaining Antidiscrimination Ordinances and Policies," *American Journal of Political Science* 40 (November 1996): 1152–78, examines why some communities adopt antidiscrimination ordinances and policies that include sexual orientation and others do not.
37. On the affirmative action issues raised by *Bakke* and other cases, see Allan P. Sindler, *Bakke, De Funis and Minority Admissions* (New York: Longman, 1978).
38. *Richmond v. J.A. Croson Co.* (1989).
39. *Fullilove v. Klutznick* (1980).
40. *Metro Broadcasting, Inc. v. Federal Communications Commission* (1990).
41. *Local Number 93 v. Cleveland* (1986); *United States v. Paradise* (1987).
42. *Local 28 of the Sheet Metal Workers v. EEOC* (1986).
43. *Firefighters v. Stotts* (1984).
44. *Wygant v. Jackson Board of Education* (1986).
45. Harry Holzer and David Newmark, "Assessing Affirmative Action," *Journal of Economic Literature* 38 (September 2000): 483–568.
46. See Barbara S. Gamble, "Putting Civil Rights to a Popular Vote," *American Journal of Political Science* 41 (January 1997): 245–69.

CHAPTER 6

1. Nate Silver, "Most Don't Know What 'Public Option' Is," August 27, 2009. See http://www.fivethirtyeight.com/2009/08/poll-most-dont-know-what-public-option.html.
2. See http://2010.census.gov/2010census/why/index.php.
3. John F. Kennedy, *A Nation of Immigrants* (New York: Harper and Row, 1964).
4. See *Statistical Abstract of the United States, 2007* (Washington, DC: U.S. Government Printing Office, 2007), 255.
5. Harold W. Stanley and Richard G. Niemi, *Vital Statistics on American Politics, 2009–2010* (Washington, DC: Congressional Quarterly Press, 2008), 53–54.
6. See Michael Hoefer et al., "Estimates of the Unauthorized Immigrant Population Residing in the United States: January 2009" (Washington, DC: Department of Homeland Security). This report is available online at http://www.dhs.gov/xlibrary/assets/statistics/publications/ois_ill_pe_2009.pdf.
7. On the details of the 1965 Immigration Act and its unintended consequences, see Steven M. Gillon, *That's Not What We Meant to Do: Reform and Its Unintended Consequences in Twentieth-Century America* (New York: Norton, 2000), chap. 4.
8. Ronald T. Takaki, *Strangers from a Different Shore* (Boston: Little, Brown, 1989), chap. 11.
9. See http://www.census.gov/population/www/socdemo/education/cps2008.html.
10. Ellis Cose, *A Nation of Strangers: Prejudice, Politics, and the Populating of America* (New York: William Morrow and Company, 1992), 219.
11. Robert D. Putnam, "E Pluribus Unum: Diversity and Community in the 21st Century: the 2006 Johan Skytte Prize Lecture," *Scandinavian Political Studies*, Vol. 30, Issue 2 (2007): 150.
12. Richard Dawson et al., *Political Socialization*, 2nd ed. (Boston: Little, Brown, 1977), 33.
13. See M. Kent Jennings and Richard G. Niemi, *The Political Character of Adolescence: The Influence of Families and Schools* (Princeton, NJ: Princeton University Press, 1981), chap. 2.
14. See M. Kent Jennings and Richard G. Niemi, *Generations and Politics: A Panel Study of Young Adults and Their Parents* (Princeton, NJ: Princeton University Press, 1981).
15. John R. Alford, Carolyn L. Funk, and John R. Hibbing, "Are Political Orientations Genetically Transmitted?" *American Political Science Review* (May 2005): 153–67.
16. See Martin P. Wattenberg, *Is Voting for Young People?* (New York: Longman, 2008), chaps. 1–3.
17. The figure on the average age of the TV news audience can be found in "The State of the Media: 2009." See http://www.stateofthemedia.org/2009/narrative_networktv_audience.php?cat=2&media=6. The figure for a typical prime-time show is cited in Robert D. Putnam, *Bowling Alone: The Collapse and Revival of American Community* (New York: Simon and Schuster, 2000), 221.
18. Quoted in Sabine Reichel, *What Did You Do in the War Daddy? Growing Up German* (New York: Hill & Wang, 1989), 113.
19. David Easton and Jack Dennis, *Children in the Political System* (New York: McGraw-Hill, 1969), 106–7.
20. Jean M. Converse, *Survey Research in the United States: Roots and Emergence, 1890–1960* (Berkeley: University of California Press, 1987), 116. Converse's work is the definitive study on the origins of public opinion sampling.
21. Herbert Asher, *Polling and the Public: What Every Citizen Should Know* (Washington, DC: Congressional Quarterly Press, 1988), 59.
22. Mark S. Mellman, "Pollsters Cellphonobia Setting In," *The Hill*, May 23, 2007. See http://thehill.com/opinion/columnists/mark-mellman/8579-pollsters-cellphonobia.
23. Knowledge Networks, "Knowledge Networks Methodology, 1. See http://www.knowledgenetworks.com/ganp/docs/Knowledge%20Networks%20Methodology.pdf.
24. Quoted in Norman M. Bradburn and Seymour Sudman, *Polls and Surveys: Understanding What They Tell Us* (San Francisco: Jossey-Bass, 1988), 39–40.
25. Lawrence R. Jacobs and Robert Y. Shapiro, *Politicians Don't Pander* (Chicago: University of Chicago Press, 2000), xiii.
26. Michael D. Shear, "Poll Results Drive Rhetoric of Obama's Health-Care Message." *Washington Post*, July 30, 2009.
27. W. Lance Bennett, *Public Opinion and American Politics* (New York: Harcourt Brace Jovanovich, 1980), 44.
28. E. D. Hirsch Jr., *Cultural Literacy* (Boston: Houghton Mifflin, 1986).
29. Michael X. Delli Carpini and Scott Keeter, *What Americans Know About Politics and Why It Matters* (New Haven, CT: Yale University Press, 1996), chap. 3. For an updated look at this topic, see "Public Knowledge of Current Affairs Little Changed by News and Information Revolutions: What Americans Know: 1989–2007" (report of the Pew Research Center for People & the Press, April 15, 2007). This report can be found online at http://people-press.org/reports/display.php3?ReportID=319.
30. W. Russell Neuman, *The Paradox of Mass Politics: Knowledge and Opinion in the American Electorate* (Cambridge, MA: Harvard University Press, 1986).
31. For a classic example of how voters rationally use group cues, see Arthur Lupia, "Shortcuts Versus Encyclopedias: Information and Voting Behavior in California Insurance Reform Elections," *American Political Science Review*, Vol. 88, No. 1 (March 1994): 63–76.
32. Mark J. Hetherington, *Why Trust Matters* (Princeton, NJ: Princeton University Press, 2005), 4.
33. See, for example, Elaine C. Kamarck, "The Evolving American State: The Trust Challenge," *The Forum*, Vol. 7, Issue 4 (2010): Article 9.
34. See Ronald Inglehart, *Modernization and Postmodernization* (Princeton, NJ: Princeton University Press, 1997), 254–55. Inglehart also shows that the decline of class voting is a general trend throughout Western democracies.
35. See Seymour Martin Lipset and Earl Raab, *Jews and the New American Political Scene* (Cambridge, MA: Harvard University Press, 1995), chap. 6.
36. Angus Campbell et al., *The American Voter* (New York: Wiley, 1960), chap. 10.
37. Norman H. Nie, Sidney Verba, and John R. Petrocik, *The Changing American Voter* (Cambridge, MA: Harvard University Press, 1976), chap. 7.
38. See, for example, John L. Sullivan, James E. Pierson, and George E. Marcus, "Ideological Constraint in the Mass Public: A Methodological Critique and Some New Findings," *American Journal of Political Science* 22 (May 1978): 233–49, and Eric R. A. N. Smith, *The Unchanging American Voter* (Berkeley: University of California Press, 1989).
39. Michael S. Lewis-Beck et al., *The American Voter Revisited* (Ann Arbor, MI: University of Michigan Press, 2008), 279.
40. Morris P. Fiorina, *Culture War? The Myth of a Polarized America*, 2nd ed. (New York: Longman, 2006), 127.
41. Ibid., 8.
42. This definition is a close paraphrase of that in Sidney Verba and Norman H. Nie, *Participation in America* (New York: Harper & Row, 1972), 2.
43. See Verba and Nie, *Participation in America*, and Sidney Verba, Kay Lehman Schlozman, and Henry E. Brady, *Voice and Equality: Civic Voluntarism in American Politics* (Cambridge, MA: Harvard University Press, 1995).
44. See Russell J. Dalton, *The Good Citizen* (Washington, DC: Congressional Quarterly Press, 2008), 60.
45. This letter can be found in Juan Williams, *Eyes on the Prize: America's Civil Rights Years, 1954–1965* (New York: Viking, 1987), 187–89.
46. Verba and Nie, *Participation in America*, 125.
47. Because registration procedures in Louisiana are regulated by the provisions of the Voting Rights Act, registration forms ask people to state their race and the registrars must keep track of this information. Thus, Louisiana can accurately report how many people of each race are registered and voted, which they regularly do. The 2004 data can be found at http://sos.louisiana.gov/stats/Post_Election_Statistics/Statewide/2004_1102_sta.txt.
48. See Verba and Nie, *Participation in America*, chap. 10.
49. Campbell et al., *The American Voter*, 541.
50. Morris P. Fiorina, *Retrospective Voting in American National Elections* (New Haven: Yale University Press, 1981), 5.

CHAPTER 7

1. See Darrell M. West, *Air Wars: Television Advertising in Election Campaigns, 1952–2000*, 3rd ed. (Washington, DC: Congressional Quarterly Press, 2001), 67.
2. Stephen Ansolabehere and Shanto Iyengar, *Going Negative* (New York: Free Press, 1995). But for a different perspective, see John G. Geer, *In Defense of Negativity: Attack Ads in Presidential Campaigns* (Chicago: University of Chicago Press, 2006).

3. December 1, 1969, memo from Nixon to H. R. Haldeman in Bruce Oudes, ed., *From: The President—Richard Nixon's Secret Files* (New York: Harper & Row, 1988), 76–77.

4. Mark Hertsgaard, *On Bended Knee: The Press and the Reagan Presidency* (New York: Farrar, Straus & Giroux, 1988), 34.

5. Bob Woodward, *The Agenda: Inside the Clinton White House* (New York: Simon and Schuster, 1994), 313.

6. Quoted in David Brinkley, *Washington Goes to War* (New York: Knopf, 1988), 171.

7. Sam Donaldson, *Hold On, Mr. President!* (New York: Random House, 1987), 54.

8. Marvin Kalb, *One Scandalous Story: Clinton, Lewinsky, and Thirteen Days That Tarnished American Journalism* (New York: Free Press, 2001), 6.

9. Ibid., 20.

10. Ibid., 138.

11. See the classic report by Michael J. Robinson, "Public Affairs Television and the Growth of Political Malaise: The Case of 'The Selling of the Pentagon,'" *American Political Science Review* 70 (June 1976): 409–32. See also Joseph Cappella and Kathleen Hall Jamieson, *Spiral of Cynicism: The Press and the Public Good* (New York: Oxford University Press, 1997).

12. Quoted in Kathleen Hall Jamieson and Paul Waldman, *Electing the President 2000: The Insider's View* (Philadelphia: University of Pennsylvania Press, 2001), 221.

13. See, for example, Michael X. Delli Carpini and Scott Keeter, *What Americans Know About Politics and Why It Matters* (New Haven, CT: Yale University Press, 1996), and Ruy A. Teixeira, *The Disappearing American Voter* (Washington, DC: Brookings Institution, 1992).

14. Robert D. Putnam, *Bowling Alone: The Collapse and Revival of American Community* (New York: Simon & Schuster, 2000), 218.

15. Leonard Downie Jr. and Robert G. Kaiser, *The News About the News: American Journalism in Peril* (New York: Knopf, 2002), 65.

16. Ibid.

17. Howard Kurtz, "The Press Loves a Hero, but . . . Presidential Commission Won't Save Newspapers," *Washington Post*, August 17, 2009.

18. Russell Baker, *The Good Times* (New York: William Morrow, 1989), 326.

19. For some evidence that indicates Nixon was correct, see James N. Druckman, "The Power of Television Images: The First Kennedy–Nixon Debate Revisited," *Journal of Politics* (May 2003): 559–71.

20. See Walter Cronkite, *A Reporter's Life* (New York: Knopf, 1996), 257–58.

21. Frank Rich, "The Weight of an Anchor," *New York Times*, May 19, 2002.

22. Michael K. Bohn, *Nerve Center: Inside the White House Situation Room* (Dulles, VA: Brassey's, Inc., 2003), 59.

23. Project for Excellence in Journalism, *The State of the News Media, 2004*, www.stateofthenewsmedia.org/index.asp.

24. NBC News, "A Day in the Life of Obama's White House," June 3, 2009. See http://www.msnbc.msn.com/id/31050780/.

25. Thomas Rosenstiel, "The End of Network News," *Washington Post* (September 12, 2004).

26. Matthew Hindman, *The Myth of Digital Democracy* (Princeton, NJ: Princeton University Press, 2009), 61–63.

27. Bruce Bimber and Richard Davis, *Campaigning Online: The Internet in U.S. Elections* (New York: Oxford University Press, 2003), 145.

28. See "Brian Williams Weighs in on the News Media," http://journalism.nyu.edu/pubzone/wewantmedia/node/487.

29. Hindman, 103.

30. Doris A. Graber, *Mass Media and American Politics*, 8th ed. (Washington, DC: Congressional Quarterly Press, 2010), 32.

31. Cited in Downey and Kaiser, *The News About the News*, 239.

32. Edward J. Epstein, *News from Nowhere: Television and the News* (New York: Random House, 1973).

33. Downie and Kaiser, *The News About the News*, 137.

34. Steven Ansolabehere, Roy Behr, and Shanto Iyengar, *The Media Game: American Politics in the Television Age* (New York: Macmillan, 1993), 53.

35. For example, see Leon V. Sigal, *Reporters and Officials: The Organization and Politics of News Reporting* (Lexington, MA: D.C. Heath, 1973), 122.

36. This letter can be found in Hedrick Smith, ed., *The Media and the Gulf War: The Press and Democracy in Wartime* (Washington, DC: Seven Locks Press, 1992), 378–80. Smith's book contains an excellent set of readings on media coverage of the war.

37. Stephen J. Farnsworth and S. Robert Lichter, *The Mediated Presidency: Television News and Presidential Governance* (Lanham, MD: Rowman & Littlefield, 2006), 95–96.

38. A *Los Angeles Times* national poll conducted April 2–3, 2003, asked the following question: "Reporters have been assigned to U.S. military units in the region of Iraq and given unprecedented access to military action and personnel. Which of the following statements comes closer to your view: (1) Greater media coverage of the military action and U.S. personnel in Iraq is good for the country because it gives the American people an uncensored view of events as they unfold; or (2) Greater media coverage of the military action and U.S. personnel in Iraq is bad for the country because it provides too much information about military actions as they unfold"? The results were that 55 percent picked the first alternative, 37 percent picked the second, and 8 percent said they didn't know.

39. Jody Powell, "White House Flackery," in *Debating American Government*, 2nd ed., ed. Peter Woll (Glenview, IL: Scott, Foresman, 1988), 180.

40. Dan Rather, quoted in Hoyt Purvis, ed., *The Presidency and the Press* (Austin, TX: Lyndon B. Johnson School of Public Affairs, 1976), 56.

41. Kathleen Hall Jamieson and Joseph N. Capella, "The Role of the Press in the Health Care Reform Debate of 1993–1994," in *The Politics of News, the News of Politics*, ed. Doris Graber, Denis McQuail, and Pippa Norris (Washington, DC: Congressional Quarterly Press, 1998), 118–19.

42. This point is well argued in Kathleen Hall Jamieson, *Eloquence in an Electronic Age* (New York: Oxford University Press, 1988).

43. Daniel Hallin, "Sound Bite News: Television Coverage of Elections," *Journal of Communications* (Spring 1992); 1992–2004 data from studies by the Center for Media and Public Affairs.

44. Quoted in Austin Ranney, *Channels of Power* (New York: Basic Books, 1983), 116.

45. Walter Cronkite, *A Reporter's Life*, 376–77.

46. "Campaign 2000 Final: How TV News Covered the General Election Campaign," *Media Monitor* 14 (November/December 2000): 3–4.

47. Ibid.

48. Michael Waldman, *POTUS Speaks: Finding the Words That Defined the Clinton Presidency* (New York: Simon and Schuster, 2000), 267.

49. David. H. Weaver, et al., *The American Journalist in the 21st Century* (Mahwah, NJ: Lawrence Erlbaum, 2007), 17.

50. Bernard Goldberg, *Bias: A CBS Insider Exposes How the Media Distort the News* (Washington, DC: Regnery, 2002), 5.

51. Ibid., 119.

52. Ibid., 17.

53. Michael J. Robinson and Margaret Petrella, "Who Won the George Bush-Dan Rather Debate?" *Public Opinion* 10 (March/April 1988): 43.

54. Robinson, "Public Affairs Television, and the Growth of Political Malaise," 428.

55. W. Lance Bennett, *News: The Politics of Illusion*, 2nd ed. (New York: Longman, 1988), 46.

56. See Paul F. Lazarsfeld et al., *The People's Choice* (New York: Columbia University Press, 1944).

57. Shanto Iyengar and Donald R. Kinder, *News That Matters* (Chicago: University of Chicago Press, 1987).

58. Ibid., 118–19.

59. Joanne M. Miller and Jon A. Krosnick, "News Media Impact on the Ingredients of Presidential Evaluations: Politically Knowledgeable Citizens Are Guided by a Trusted Source," *American Journal of Political Science* (April 2000): 301–15.

60. Frederick T. Steeper, "Public Response to Gerald Ford's Statements on Eastern Europe in the Second Debate," in *The Presidential Debates: Media, Electoral, and Public Perspectives*, ed. George F. Bishop, Robert G. Meadow, and Marilyn Jackson-Beeck (New York: Praeger, 1978), 81–101.

61. Jamieson and Waldman, *Electing the President 2000*, 5–6.

62. John W. Kingdon, *Agendas, Alternatives, and Public Policies* (Boston: Little, Brown, 1984), 3.

63. Ibid.

64. See the interview with Richard Valeriani in Juan Williams, *Eyes on the Prize* (New York: Viking, 1987), 270–71.

65. For an interesting study of how hiring a public relations firm can help a nation's TV image, see Jarol B. Manheim and Robert B. Albitton, "Changing National Images: International Public Relations and Media Agenda Setting," *American Political Science Review* 78 (September 1984): 641–57.

66. Bernard Cohen, *The Press and Foreign Policy* (Princeton, NJ: Princeton University Press, 1963), 13.

67. "Public Evaluations of the News Media, 1985–2009" (Pew Research Center for People & the Press, September 12, 2009). This report can be found online at http://people-press.org/reports/pdf/543.pdf.

68. Doris A. Graber, *Mass Media and American Politics*, 8th ed. (Washington, DC: Congressional Quarterly Press, 2010), 240.

69. Ronald W. Berkman and Laura W. Kitch, *Politics in the Media Age* (New York: McGraw-Hill, 1986), 311.

70. Ibid., 313.

71. Matthew Robert Kerbel, *Edited for Television: CNN, ABC, and the 1992 Presidential Campaign* (Boulder, CO: Westview, 1994), 196.

CHAPTER 8

1. E. E. Schattschneider, *Party Government* (New York: Farrar and Rinehart, 1942), 1.

2. Anthony Downs, *An Economic Theory of Democracy* (New York: Harper & Row, 1957).

3. Marjorie Randon Hershey, *Party Politics in America*, 12th ed. (New York: Longman, 2007), 8.

4. Kay Lawson, ed., *Political Parties and Linkage: A Comparative Perspective* (New Haven, CT: Yale University Press, 1980), 3.

5. The major exception to this rule is nominations for the one-house state legislature in Nebraska, which is officially nonpartisan.

6. Downs, *An Economic Theory of Democracy*.

7. Morris P. Fiorina, *Congress: Keystone of the Washington Establishment*, 2nd ed. (New Haven, CT: Yale University Press, 1989), 101.

8. See Adam Cohen and Elizabeth Taylor, *American Pharaoh* (Boston: Little, Brown, 2000), 155–63.

9. Kay Lawson, "California: The Uncertainties of Reform," *Party Renewal in America, ed.* Gerald Pomper (New Brunswick, NJ: Praeger, 1980), chap. 8.

10. John F. Bibby et al., "Parties in State Politics," in *Politics in the American States*, 4th ed., ed. Virginia Gray, Herbert Jacob, and Kenneth Vines (Boston: Little, Brown, 1983), 76–79.

11. Hershey, *Party Politics in America*, 60.

12. John F. Bibby, "State Party Organizations: Coping and Adapting to Candidate-Centered Politics and Nationalization," in *The Parties Respond*, 3rd ed., ed. L. Sandy Maisel (Boulder, CO: Westview, 1998), 34.

13. Comments of Roy Romer and Jim Nicholson at the Bulen Symposium on American Politics, December 1, 1998, as noted by Martin Wattenberg.

14. The term is from V. O. Key. The standard source on critical elections is Walter Dean Burnham, *Critical Elections and the Mainsprings of American Politics* (New York: Norton, 1970).

15. On the origins of the American party system, see William N. Chambers, *Political Parties in a New Nation* (New York: Oxford University Press, 1963).

16. See Richard Hofstader, *The Idea of a Party System: The Rise of Legitimate Opposition in the United States, 1780–1840* (Berkeley: University of California Press, 1969).

17. James W. Ceaser, *Presidential Selection: Theory and Development* (Princeton, NJ: Princeton University Press, 1979), 130.

18. Quoted in James L. Sundquist, *Dynamics of the Party System*, rev. ed. (Washington, DC: Brookings Institution, 1983), 88. Sundquist's book is an excellent account of realignments in American party history.

19. Ibid., 1955.

20. On Boston, see Gerald H. Gamm, *The Making of New Deal Democrats: Voting Behavior and Realignment in Boston, 1920–1940* (Chicago: University of Chicago Press, 1989).

21. See Earl Black and Merle Black, *The Rise of Southern Republicans* (Cambridge, MA: Harvard University Press, 2002).

22. See Morris P. Fiorina, *Divided Government* (New York: Macmillan, 1992).

23. Steven J. Rosenstone, Roy L. Behr, and Edward H. Lazarus, *Third Parties in America* (Princeton, NJ: Princeton University Press, 1984).

24. For discussion of political ambiguity as a strategy, see Kenneth A. Shepsle, "The Strategy of Ambiguity: Uncertainty and Electoral Competition," *American Political Science Review* 66 (June 1972): 555–68, and Benjamin I. Page, *Choices and Echoes in Presidential Elections* (Chicago: University of Chicago Press, 1978), chap. 6.

25. The classic statement on responsible parties can be found in "Toward a More Responsible Two-Party System: A Report of the Committee on Political Parties," American Political Science Association, *American Political Science Review* 44 (1950): supplement, number 3, part 2.

26. See Marian Currinder, *Money in the House: Campaign Funds and Congressional Party Politics*. Boulder, CO: Westview Press, 2009.

27. David R. Mayhew, *Divided We Govern: Party Control, Lawmaking, and Investigations, 1946–1990* (New Haven, CT: Yale University Press, 1991), 199.

28. See Evron M. Kirkpatrick, "Toward a More Responsible Party System: Political Science, Policy Science, or Pseudo-Science?"*American Political Science Review* 65 (1971): 965–90.

CHAPTER 9

1. Karl Rove, "The Endless Campaign," *Wall Street Journal*, December 20, 2007, A17.

2. Anthony King, *Running Scared* (New York: Free Press, 1997).

3. R. W. Apple Jr., "Foley Assesses Presidential Elections and Tells Why He Wouldn't Run," *New York Times*, November 4, 1998, A12.

4. Paul Taylor, "Is This Any Way to Pick a President?" *Washington Post National Weekly Edition*, April 13, 1987, 6.

5. The McGovern Fraser Commission report can be found online today at http://abacus.bates.edu/muskie-archives/ajcr/1971/McGovern%20Commission.shtml.

6. See Byron Shafer, *Quiet Revolution: The Struggle for the Democratic Party and the Shaping of Post-Reform Politics* (New York: Russell Sage Foundation, 1983).

7. William G. Mayer, "Superdelegates: Reforming the Reforms Revisited," in *Reforming the Presidential Nominating Process*, ed. Steven S. Smith and Melanie J. Springer (Washington, DC: Brookings, 2009), 87 and 97.

8. Ibid., p. 103.

9. Thomas E. Mann, "Is This Any Way to Pick a President?" in *Reforming the Presidential Nomination Process*, ed. Steven S. Smith and Melanie J. Springer (Washington, DC: Brookings, 2009), 165.

10. David Plouffe, *The Audacity to Win: The Inside Story and Lessons of Barack Obama's Historic Victory* (New York: Viking, 2009), 176.

11. See Hugh Winebrenner, *The Iowa Precinct Caucuses: The Making of a Media Event* (Ames: Iowa State University Press, 1987).

12. David Yepsen, "Brows Wrinkle, Yet Expect to See a Record Turnout," *Des Moines Register*, January 2, 2008.

13. This tradition extends back to 1916. The early primary date was chosen then to coincide with the already existing town meetings. Town meetings were held in February prior to the thawing of the snow, which in the days of unpaved roads made traveling extremely difficult in the spring. In 1916 no one could have dreamed that by holding the state's primary so early they were creating a mass media extravaganza for New Hampshire.

14. Harold W. Stanley and Richard G. Niemi, *Vital Statistics on American Politics*, 6th ed. (Washington, DC: Congressional Quarterly Press, 1998), 173. The same research also showed that New Hampshire received just 3 percent of the TV coverage during the general election—a figure far more in line with its small population size.

15. Robert Farmer, quoted in Clifford W. Brown Jr., Lynda W. Powell, and Clyde Wilcox, *Serious Money: Fundraising and Contributing in Presidential Nomination Campaigns* (New York: Cambridge University Press, 1995), 1.

16. Frank Bruni, *Ambling into History: The Unlikely Odyssey of George W. Bush* (New York: HarperCollins, 2002), 5.

17. Larry M. Bartels, *Presidential Primaries and the Dynamics of Public Choice* (Princeton, NJ: Princeton University Press, 1988), 269.

18. "CQ Vote Studies—Participation: A Numbers Game," *CQ Weekly*, January 14, 2008, 156.

19. See www.stateofthemedia.org/2005/chartland.asp?id=470&ct=line&dir=&sort=&col1_box=1&col2_box=1.

20. R. W. Apple, "No Decisions, No Drama," *New York Times*, August 1, 2000, A14.

21. Barack Obama, *The Audacity of Hope* (New York: Three Rivers Press, 2006), 358.

22. Thomas E. Patterson, *The Mass Media Election* (New York: Praeger, 1980), 3.

23. Obama, *The Audacity of Hope*, 121.

24. "The Internet and the 2008 Election," Report of the Pew Internet & American Life Project, June 15, 2008, http://www.pewinternet.org/pdfs/PIP_2008_election.pdf.

25. Robert G. Boatright, "Fundraising—Present and Future," in *Campaigns on the Cutting Edge*, ed. Richard J. Semiatin (Washington, DC: Congressional Quarterly Press, 2008).

26. Jonathan S. Krasno and Daniel E. Seltz, "Buying Time: Television Advertising in the 1998 Congressional Elections," www.brennancenter.org/programs/cmag_temp/download.html.

27. David R. Runkel, ed., *Campaign for President: The Managers Look at '88* (Dover, MA: Auburn, 1989), 136.

28. For more information on the legal differences between 501c and 527 independent advocacy groups, see the summary information posted by the Center for Responsive Politics at: http://www.opensecrets.org/527s/types.php.

29. Frank J. Sorauf, *Inside Campaign Finance: Myths and Realities* (New Haven, CT: Yale University Press, 1992), 229.

30. Ibid., 162–63.

31. Archibald Cox and Fred Wertheimer, "The Choice Is Clear: It's People vs. the PACs," in *Debating American Government*, 2nd ed., ed. Peter Woll (Glenview, IL: Scott, Foresman, 1988), 125.

32. This is discussed in Jeffrey M. Berry, *The Interest Group Society*, 3rd ed. (New York: Longman, 1997), 172.

33. Frank J. Sorauf, *Money in American Elections* (Glenview, IL: Scott Foresman, 1988), 312.

34. See http://www.opensecrets.org/news/2008/10/us-election-will-cost-53-billi.html.

35. Bradley A. Smith, *Unfree Speech: The Folly of Campaign Finance Reform* (Princeton, NJ: Princeton University Press, 2001), 173.

36. Gary C. Jacobson, "The Effects of Campaign Spending in House Elections: New Evidence for Old Arguments," *American Journal of Political Science* 34 (May 1990): 334–62.

37. Herbert E. Alexander, *Financing Politics: Money, Elections, and Political Reform*, 4th ed. (Washington, DC: Congressional Quarterly Press, 1992), 96.

38. See Dennis J. McGrath and Dane Smith, *Professor Wellstone Goes to Washington: The Inside Story of a Grassroots U.S. Senate Campaign* (Minneapolis: University of Minnesota Press, 1995).

39. Dan Nimmo, *The Political Persuaders* (Englewood Cliffs, NJ: Prentice Hall, 1970), 5.

40. D. Sunshine Hillygus and Todd G. Shields, *The Persuadable Voter: Wedge Issues in Presidential Campaigns* (Princeton, NJ: Princeton University Press, 2008).

41. Sidney Blumenthal, *The Permanent Campaign* (New York: Simon and Schuster, 1982).

42. See Martin P. Wattenberg, *The Rise of Candidate-Centered Politics: Presidential Elections of the 1980s* (Cambridge, MA: Harvard University Press, 1991).

43. James W. Ceaser, *Presidential Selection: Theory and Development* (Princeton, NJ: Princeton University Press, 1979), 83.

CHAPTER 10

1. Quoted in Stanley G. Kelley Jr., *Interpreting Elections* (Princeton, NJ: Princeton University Press, 1983), 3–4.

2. See Thomas E. Cronin, *Direct Democracy* (Cambridge, MA: Harvard University Press, 1989), chap. 7.

3. Daniel A. Smith, *Tax Crusaders and the Politics of Direct Democracy* (New York: Routledge, 1998).

4. Morton Grodzins, "Political Parties and the Crisis of Succession in the United States: The Case of 1800," in *Political Parties and Political Development*, ed. Joseph LaPalombara and Myron Weiner (Princeton, NJ: Princeton University Press, 1966), 319.

5. In 1804, the Twelfth Amendment to the Constitution changed the procedure to the one we know today, in which each elector votes separately for president and vice president.

6. A summary of these survey results can be found at http://www.census.gov/hhes/www/socdemo/voting/index.html.

7. See Martin P. Wattenberg, "Should Election Day Be a Holiday?" *Atlantic Monthly*, October 1998, 42–46.

8. Anthony Downs, *An Economic Theory of Democracy* (New York: Harper & Row, 1957), chap. 14.

9. See http://www.sos.state.ia.us/pdfs/2006Statewidestats.pdf.

10. See George C. Edwards III, *At the Margins* (New Haven, CT: Yale University Press, 1989), chap. 8.

11. Richard G. Niemi and Herbert F. Weisberg, eds., *Controversies in Voting Behavior*, 2nd ed. (Washington, DC: Congressional Quarterly Press, 1984), 164–65.

12. See Martin P. Wattenberg, *The Decline of American Political Parties, 1952–1996* (Cambridge, MA: Harvard University Press, 1998).

13. Shawn W. Rosenberg with Patrick McCafferty, "Image and Voter Preference," *Public Opinion Quarterly* 51 (Spring 1987): 44.

14. Arthur H. Miller, Martin P. Wattenberg, and Oksana Malanchuk, "Schematic Assessments of Presidential Candidates," *American Political Science Review* 80 (1986): 521–40. For more recent data, see Martin P. Wattenberg, "Personal Popularity in U.S. Presidential Elections,"*Presidential Studies Quarterly* 34 (2004): 119–31.

15. Paul R. Abramson, John H. Aldrich, and David W. Rohde, *Change and Continuity in the 2008 Elections* (Washington, DC: Congressional Quarterly Press, 2010), p. 146.

16. Joan Shorenstein Center, "The Theodore H. White Lecture on Press and Politics with Maureen Dowd," 23. This lecture can be found online at http://www.hks.harvard.edu/presspol/prizes_lectures/th_white_lecture/transcripts/th_white_2007_dowd.pdf.

17. Ibid., chap. 6.

18. See Gary C. Jacobson, *A Divider, Not a Uniter: George W. Bush and the American People* (New York: Longman, 2007).

19. See http://www.gallup.com/poll/125345/Obama-Approval-Polarized-First-Year-President.aspx.

20. American Bar Association, *Electing the President* (Chicago: American Bar Association, 1967), 3.

21. The Twenty-third Amendment (1961) permits the District of Columbia to have three electors even though it has no representatives in Congress.

22. David Plouffe, *The Audacity to Win* (New York: Viking, 2009), p. 247.

23. Benjamin Page, *Choices and Echoes in American Presidential Elections* (Chicago: University of Chicago Press, 1978), 153.

24. See Morris P. Fiorina, *Retrospective Voting in American National Elections* (New Haven, CT: Yale University Press, 1981).

25. V. O. Key, *The Responsible Electorate* (New York: Random House, 1966), 76.

26. Benjamin Ginsberg, *Consequences of Consent* (Reading, MA: Addison-Wesley, 1982), 194.

27. Ibid., 198.

CHAPTER 11

1. See: http://content.nejm.org/cgi/content/full/NEJMp0902392.

2. See: http://www.menshealth.com/men/health/doctors-hospitals/sweet-on-a-soda-tax/article/cf2237c26ab93210VgnVCM10000030281eac.

3. These figures can be found using the search feature on lobbying spending at the Center for Responsive Politics Web site. See http://www.opensecrets.org/lobby/index.php.

4. Kay L. Schlozman and John T. Tierney, *Organized Interests and American Democracy* (New York: Harper & Row, 1986), 1.

5. The 1959 figure is taken from Frank R. Baumgartner and Beth L. Leech, *Basic Interests: The Importance of Groups in Politics and in Political Science* (Princeton, NJ: Princeton University Press, 1998), 109; the 2009 figure is taken from the advertising posted for the most recent edition of *Encyclopedia of Associations: National Organizations of the U.S.*

6. The classic work is David B. Truman, *The Governmental Process*, 2nd ed. (New York: Knopf, 1971).

7. Thomas R. Dye, *Who's Running America?* 5th ed. (Englewood Cliffs, NJ: Prentice Hall, 1990), 170.

8. Robert Engler, *The Brotherhood of Oil* (Chicago: University of Chicago Press, 1977).

9. Theodore J. Lowi, *The End of Liberalism*, 2nd ed. (New York: Norton, 1979).

10. See Lee Fritschler, *Smoking and Politics: Policy Making and the Federal Bureaucracy* (Englewood Cliffs, NJ: Prentice Hall, 1983).

11. E. E. Schattschneider, *The Semisovereign People* (New York: Holt, Rinehart and Winston, 1960), 35.

12. Truman, *The Governmental Process*, 511.

13. Mancur Olson, *The Logic of Collective Action* (Cambridge, MA: Harvard University Press, 1965), especially 9–36.

14. Jeffrey H. Birnbaum and Alan S. Murray, *Showdown at Gucci Gulch: Lawmakers, Lobbyists, and the Unlikely Triumph of Tax Reform* (New York: Vintage, 1987).

15. Ibid., 235.

16. Frank R. Baumgartner et al., *Lobbying and Policy Change: Who Wins, Who Loses, and Why* (Chicago: University of Chicago Press, 2009), 208–09.

17. Ibid., p. 210.

18. Lester W. Milbrath, *The Washington Lobbyists* (Chicago: Rand McNally, 1963), 8.

19. See Public Citizen, "Cashing In," November 19, 2009. This report can be found at http://www.citizen.org/documents/Ca$hing_in.pdf.

20. See https://www.columbiabooks.com/ProductDetail/the-18-0-1/Washington_Representatives_2009.

21. Norman Ornstein and Shirley Elder, *Interest Groups, Lobbying, and Policymaking* (Washington, DC: Congressional Quarterly Press, 1978), 59–60.

22. Peter H. Stone, "Friends, After All," *National Journal*, October 22, 1994, 2440.

23. Rogan Kersh, "The Well-Informed Lobbyist: Information and Interest Group Lobbying" in Allan J. Cigler and Burdett A. Loomis, eds., *Interest Group Politics*, 7th ed. (Washington, DC: Congressional Quarterly Press, 2007), 390.

24. Richard L. Hall and Alan V. Deardorff, "Lobbying as Legislative Subsidy," *American Political Science Review* 100 (February 2006): 69.

25. For a summary of recent studies on the influence of lobbying, see Baumgartner and Leech, *Basic Interests*, 130.

26. See Kelly Patterson and Matthew M. Singer, "Targeting Success: The Enduring Power of the NRA" in Allan J. Cigler and Burdett A. Loomis, eds., *Interest Group Politics*, 7th edition (Washington, DC: Congressional Quarterly Press, 2007): 37–64.

27. See http://www.opensecrets.org/pacs/lookup2.php?strID=C00368142&cycle=2008.

28. Frederic J. Frommer, "Baseball PAC Gives Thousands to Parties," Associated Press, May 13, 2003.

29. See http://www.fec.gov/press/press2009/20090415PAC/20090424PAC.shtml.

30. R. Kenneth Godwin and Barry J. Seldon, "What Corporations Really Want from Government: The Public Provision of Private Goods," in Cigler and Loomis, *Interest Group Politics*, 6th ed., 219.

31. The Sovern story is told in "Taking an Ax to PACs," *Time*, August 20, 1984, 27.

32. Karen Orren, "Standing to Sue: Interest Group Conflict in Federal Courts," *American Political Science Review* 70 (September 1976): 724.

33. Gregory A. Caldeira and John R. Wright, "*Amici Curiae* Before the Supreme Court: Who Participates, When, and How Much," *Journal of Politics* 52 (August 1990): 782–804.

34. Ronald J. Hrebenar and Ruth K. Scott, *Interest Group Politics in America*, 2nd ed. (Englewood Cliffs, NJ: Prentice Hall, 1990), 201.

35. Ken Kollman, *Outside Lobbying: Public Opinion and Interest Group Strategies* (Princeton, NJ: Princeton University Press, 1998), 33.

36. Quoted in Jeffrey M. Berry, *The Interest Group Society*, 2nd ed. (Glenview, IL: Scott Foresman, 1989), 103.

37. Paul Edward Johnson, "Organized Labor in an Era of Blue-Collar Decline," in *Interest Group Politics*, 3rd ed., ed. Allan J. Cigler and Burdett A. Loomis (Washington, DC: Congressional Quarterly Press, 1991), 33–62.

38. Christopher J. Bosso, "The Color of Money: Environmental Groups and the Pathologies of Fund Raising," in *Interest Group Politics*, 4th ed., ed. Allan J. Cigler and Burdett A. Loomis (Washington, DC: Congressional Quarterly Press, 1995), 102.

39. For an interesting analysis of how changes in the regulatory environment, congressional oversight, and public opinion altered the debate on nuclear power, see Frank R. Baumgartner and Bryan D. Jones, *Agendas and Instability in American Politics* (Chicago: University of Chicago Press, 1993).

40. Dona C. Hamilton and Charles V. Hamilton, *The Dual Agenda: Race and Social Welfare Policies of Civil Rights Organizations* (New York: Columbia University Press, 1997), 2.

41. Jeffrey M. Berry, *Lobbying for the People* (Princeton, NJ: Princeton University Press, 1977), 7.

42. Robert H. Salisbury, "The Paradox of Interest Groups in Washington—More Groups, Less Clout," in *The New American Political System*, 2nd ed., ed. Anthony King (Washington, DC: American Enterprise Institute, 1990), 204.

43. Mark J. Rozell, Clyde Wilcox, and David Madland, *Interest Groups in American Campaigns: The New Face of Electioneering*, 2nd ed. (Washington, DC: Congressional Quarterly Press, 2006), 87.

44. Alexis de Tocqueville, *Democracy in America*, vol. 2 (New York: Vintage, 1945), 114.

45. Hrebenar and Scott, *Interest Group Politics in America*, 234.

46. Steven V. Roberts, "Angered President Blames Others for the Huge Deficit," *New York Times*, December 14, 1988, A16.

47. William M. Lunch, *The Nationalization of American Politics* (Berkeley: University of California Press, 1987), 206.

48. Salisbury, "The Paradox of Interest Groups in Washington," 229.

CHAPTER 12

1. See Craig Schultz, ed., *Setting Course: A Congressional Management Guide* (Washington, DC: Congressional Management Foundation, 1994); and David E. Price, *The Congressional Experience: A View from the Hill* (Boulder, CO: Westview Press, 1999).

2. David T. Canon, *Race, Redistricting, and Representation: The Unintended Consequences of Black Majority Districts* (Chicago: University of Chicago Press, 1999).

3. Susan A. Banducci, Todd Donovan, and Jeffrey A. Karp, "Minority Representation, Empowerment, and Participation," *Journal of Politics* 66 (May 2004): 534–56.

4. On the impact of gender on representation, see Brian Frederick, "Are Female House Members Still More Liberal in a Polarized Era?" *Congress & the Presidency* 36 (Fall 2009): 181–202; Leslie A. Schwindt-Bayer and Renato Corbetta, "Gender Turnover and Roll-Call Voting in the U.S. House of Representatives," *Legislative Studies Quarterly* 29 (May 2004): 215–29; Arturo Vega and Juanita M. Firestone, "The Effects of Gender on Congressional Behavior and the Substantive Representation of Women," *Legislative Studies Quarterly* 20 (May 1995): 213–22; and Sue Thomas, "The Impact of Women on State Legislative Policies," *Journal of Politics* 53 (November 1991): 958–76.

5. Christopher Witko and Sally Friedman, "Business Backgrounds and Congressional Behavior," *Congress and the Presidency* 35 (Spring 2008): 71–86.

6. On various views of representation, see Hanna Pitkin, *The Concept of Representation* (Berkeley: University of California Press, 1967).

7. Sally Friedman, "House Committee Assignments of Women and Minority Newcomers, 1965–1994," *Legislative Studies Quarterly* 21 (February 1996): 73–81; Alan Gerber, "African Americans' Congressional Careers and the Democratic House Delegation," *Journal of Politics* 58 (August 1996): 831–45.

8. John L. Sullivan and Eric Uslaner, "Congressional Behavior and Electoral Marginality," *American Journal of Political Science* 22 (August 1978): 536–53.

9. Thomas Mann, *Unsafe at Any Margin* (Washington, DC: American Enterprise Institute, 1978).

10. Glenn R. Parker, *Homeward Bound* (Pittsburgh: University of Pittsburgh Press, 1986); John R. Johannes, *To Serve the People* (Lincoln: University of Nebraska Press, 1984).

11. The *New York Times*/CBS News Poll cited in "Voters Disgusted with Politicians as Election Nears," *New York Times*, November 13, 1994, A10.

12. Patricia Hurley and Kim Q. Hill, "The Prospects for Issue Voting in Contemporary Congressional Elections," *American Politics Quarterly* 8 (October 1980): 446.

13. Mann, *Unsafe at Any Margin*, 37.

14. That presidential elections and congressional elections are not closely related is an argument made in Ray C. Fair, "Presidential and Congressional Vote-Share Equations," *American Journal of Political Science* 53 (January 2009): 55–72; and Lyn Ragsdale, "The Fiction of Congressional Elections as Presidential Events," *American Politics Quarterly* 8 (October 1980): 375–98. For evidence that voters' views of the president affect their voting for senators, see Lonna Rae Atkeson and Randall W. Partin, "Economic and Referendum Voting: A Comparison of Gubernatorial and Senatorial Elections," *American Political Science Review* 89 (March 1995): 99–107. See, however, Fair, "Presidential and Congressional Vote-Share Equations."

15. James E. Campbell, *The Presidential Pulse of Congressional Elections* (Lexington: University Press of Kentucky, 1993), 119; Gary C. Jacobson, "Does the Economy Matter in Midterm Elections?" *American Journal of Political Science* 34 (May 1990): 400–404; Robert S. Erikson, "Economic Conditions and the Congressional Vote: A Review of the Macrolevel Evidence," *American Journal of Political Science* 34 (May 1990): 373–99; Benjamin Radcliff, "Solving a Puzzle: Aggregate Analysis and Economic Voting Revisited," *Journal of Politics* 50 (May 1988): 440–58; John R. Owens and Edward C. Olson, "Economic Fluctuations and Congressional Elections," *American Journal of Political Science* 24 (August 1980): 469–93.

16. David R. Mayhew, *Congress: The Electoral Connection* (New Haven, CT: Yale University Press, 1974).

17. Richard F. Fenno Jr., *Home Style* (Boston: Little, Brown, 1978), 32.

18. Ibid., 106–7.

19. The "service spells success" argument is made in Morris P. Fiorina, *Congress: Keystone of the Washington Establishment*, 2nd ed. (New Haven, CT: Yale University

Press, 1989), and, with a slightly different emphasis, in Glenn R. Parker, "The Advantages of Incumbency in Congressional Elections," *American Politics Quarterly* 8 (October 1980): 449–61.

20. Gary C. Jacobson, *The Politics of Congressional Elections*, 7th ed. (New York: Longman, 2009), 122–33; Stephen Ansolabehere, James M. Snyder Jr., and Charles Stewart III, "Old Voters, New Voters, and the Personal Vote: Using Redistricting to Measure the Incumbency Advantage," *American Journal of Political Science* 44 (January 2000): 17–34.

21. See, for example, Glenn R. Parker and Suzanne L. Parker, "The Correlates and Effects of Attention to District by U.S. House Members," *Legislative Studies Quarterly* 10 (May 1985): 223–42; and John C. McAdams and John R. Johannes, "Congressmen, Perquisites, and Elections," *Journal of Politics* 50 (May 1988): 412–39; and Paul Feldman and James Jondrow, "Congressional Elections and Local Federal Spending," *American Journal of Political Science* 28 (February 1984): 147–63.

22. On strategies of challengers, see Gary C. Jacobson and Samuel Kernell, *Strategy and Choice in Congressional Elections*, 2nd ed. (New Haven, CT: Yale University Press, 1983), and Gary C. Jacobson, "Strategic Politicians and the Dynamics of U.S. House Elections, 1946–1986," *American Political Science Review* 83 (September 1989): 773–94. See also Steven D. Levitt and Catherine D. Wolfram, "Decomposing the Sources of Incumbency Advantage in the U.S. House," *Legislative Studies Quarterly* 22 (February 1997): 45–60.

23. See Gary C. Jacobson, *Money in Congressional Elections* (New Haven, CT: Yale University Press, 1980).

24. On the importance of challenger quality and financing, see Alan I. Abramowitz, Brad Alexander, and Matthew Gunning, "Incumbency, Redistricting, and the Decline of Competition in U.S. House Elections," *Journal of Politics* 68 (February 2006): 75–88; Alan I. Abramowitz, "Explaining Senate Election Outcomes," *American Political Science Review* 82 (June 1988): 385–403; and Donald Philip Green and Jonathan S. Krasno, "Salvation for the Spendthrift Incumbent," *American Journal of Political Science* 32 (November 1988): 884–907.

25. Center for Responsive Politics (www.opensecrets.org); Federal Election Commission (www.fec.gov).

26. Jacobson, *The Politics of Congressional Elections*, 45–51, 133–35. See also Alan Gerber, "Estimating the Effect of Campaign Spending on Senate Election Outcomes Using Instrumental Variables," *American Political Science Review* 92 (June 1998): 401–12; Robert S. Erikson and Thomas R. Palfrey, "Campaign Spending and Incumbency: An Alternative Simultaneous Equation Approach," *Journal of Politics* 60 (May 1998): 355–73; Christopher Kenny and Michael McBurnett, "An Individual-Level Multiequation Model of Expenditure Effects in Contested House Elections," *American Political Science Review* 88 (September 1994): 699–707; and Gary C. Jacobson, "The Effects of Campaign Spending in House Elections: New Evidence for Old Arguments," *American Journal of Political Science* 34 (May 1990): 334–62.

27. Center for Responsive Politics (www.opensecrets.org); Federal Election Commission (www.fec.gov).

28. Bill Bishop, *The Big Sort: Why the Clustering of Like-Minded America Is Tearing Us Apart* (Boston: Houghton Mifflin, 2008).

29. Gary C. Jacobson and Michael A. Dimock, "Checking Out: The Effects of Bank Overdrafts on the 1992 House Elections," *American Journal of Political Science* 38 (August 1994): 601–24. See also Marshal A. Dimock and Gary C. Jacobson, "Checks and Choices: The House Bank Scandal's Impact on Voters in 1992," *Journal of Politics* 57 (November 1995): 1143–59, and Carl McCurley and Jeffrey J. Mondak, "Inspected by #1184063113: The Influence of Incumbents' Competence and Integrity in U.S. House Elections," *American Journal of Political Science* 39 (November 1995): 864–85.

30. Susan Welch and John R. Hibbing, "The Effects of Charges of Corruption on Voting Behavior in Congressional Elections, 1982–1990,"*Journal of Politics* 59 (February 1997): 226–39; and John G. Peters and Susan Welch, "The Effects of Corruption on Voting Behavior in Congressional Elections," *American Political Science Review* 74 (September 1980): 697–708.

31. For a discussion of the politics and process of reapportionment, see Thomas E. Mann, *Redistricting* (Washington, DC: Brookings Institution Press, 2008).

32. On term limits, see Gerald Benjamin and Michael J. Malbin, eds., *Limiting Our Legislative Terms* (Washington, DC: CQ Press, 1992).

33. Said former House Speaker Jim Wright in *You and Your Congressman* (New York: Putnam, 1976), 190. See also Donald R. Matthews and James Stimson, *Yeas and Nays: Normal Decision-Making in the House of Representatives* (New York: Wiley, 1975), and John L. Sullivan et al., "The Dimensions of Cue-Taking in the House of Representatives: Variations by Issue Area," *Journal of Politics* 55 (November 1993): 975–97.

34. Nelson W. Polsby et al., "Institutionalization of the House of Representatives," *American Political Science Review* 62 (1968): 144–68.

35. John R. Hibbing, "Contours of the Modern Congressional Career," *American Political Science Review* 85 (June 1991): 405–28.

36. See Bernard Grofman, Robert Griffin, and Amihai Glazer, "Is the Senate More Liberal Than the House? Another Look," *Legislative Studies Quarterly* 16 (May 1991): 281–96.

37. See Sarah A. Binder and Steven S. Smith, *Politics or Principle? Filibustering in the United States Senate* (Washington, DC: Brookings Institution, 1997).

38. Robert L. Peabody, *Leadership in Congress* (Boston: Little, Brown, 1976), 4.

39. On the increasing importance of party leadership in the House, see David W. Rohde, *Parties and Leaders in the Postreform House* (Chicago: University of Chicago Press, 1991); Barbara Sinclair, "The Emergence of Strong Leadership in the 1980s House of Representatives," *Journal of Politics* 54 (August 1992): 657–84; and Gary W. Cox and Matthew D. McCubbins, *Legislative Leviathan* (Berkley: University of California Press, 1993).

40. For more on congressional oversight, see Diana Evans, "Congressional Oversight and the Diversity of Members' Goals," *Political Science Quarterly* 109 (Fall 1994): 669–87; and Christopher H. Foreman Jr., *Signals from the Hill* (New Haven, CT: Yale University Press, 1988).

41. Joel D. Aberbach, *Keeping a Watchful Eye: The Politics of Congressional Oversight* (Washington, DC: Brookings Institution, 1990).

42. Aberbach, *Keeping a Watchful Eye;* Joel D. Aberbach, "What's Happened to the Watchful Eye?," *Congress and the Presidency* 29 (spring 2002): 3–23.

43. Thomas E. Mann and Norman J. Ornstein, *The Broken Branch* (New York: Oxford University Press, 2006).

44. Richard F. Fenno Jr., *Congressmen in Committees* (Boston: Little, Brown, 1973), 1.

45. Useful studies of committee assignments include Kenneth Shepsle, *The Giant Jigsaw Puzzle* (Chicago: University of Chicago Press, 1978), and Cox and McCubbins, *Legislative Leviathan*, chaps. 1, 7, and 8.

46. See Jennifer Nicoll Victor and Nils Ringe, "The Social Utility of Informal Institutions," *American Politics Research* 37 (September 2009): 742–66; Susan Webb Hammond, *Congressional Caucuses in National Policy Making* (Baltimore: Johns Hopkins University Press, 1998).

47. For a thorough discussion of rule changes and the impact of procedures, see Steven S. Smith, *Call to Order: Floor Politics in the House and Senate* (Washington, DC: Brookings Institution, 1989).

48. Barbara Sinclair, *Unorthodox Lawmaking*, 3rd ed. (Washington, DC: CQ Press, 2007). See also Barbara Sinclair, "Orchestrators of Unorthodox Lawmaking: Pelosi and McConnell in the 110th Congress," *The Forum* 6 (No. 3, 2008).

49. George C. Edwards III and Andrew Barrett, "Presidential Agenda Setting in Congress," in *Polarized Politics: Congress and the President in a Partisan Era*, ed. Jon R. Bond and Richard Fleisher (Washington, DC: CQ Press, 2000).

50. George C. Edwards III, *At the Margins: Presidential Leadership of Congress* (New Haven, CT: Yale University Press, 1989).

51. James M. Snyder Jr. and Tim Groseclose, "Estimating Party Influence in Congressional Roll-Call Voting," *American Journal of Political Science* 44 (April 2000): 187–205; Aage Clausen, *How Congressmen Decide: A Policy Focus* (New York: St. Martin's Press, 1973).

52. Sean M. Theriault, *Party Polarization in Congress* (Cambridge, UK: Cambridge University Press, 2008).

53. Quoted in Peter G. Richards, *Honourable Members* (London: Faber and Faber, 1959), 157.

54. See Roger H. Davidson, *The Role of the Congressman* (New York: Pegasus, 1969), and Thomas E. Cavanaugh, "Role Orientations of House Members: The Process of Representation" (paper delivered at the annual meeting of the American Political Science Association, Washington, DC, August 1979).

55. Tracy Sulkin, "Campaign Appeals and Legislative Action," *Journal of Politics* 71 (July 2009): 1093–1108; John L. Sullivan and Robert E. O'Connor, "Electoral Choice and Popular Control of Public Policy: The Case of the 1966 House Elections," *American Political Science Review* 66 (December 1972): 1256–68.

56. Stephen Ansolabehere and Philip Edward Jones, "Constituents' Responses to Congressional Roll-Call Voting," *American Journal of Political Science* 54 (July 2010): 583–97; Patricia A. Hurley and Kim Quaile Hill, "Beyond the Demand-Input Model: A Theory of Representational Linkages," *Journal of Politics* 65 (May 2003): 304–26; Christopher Wlezien, "Patterns of Representation: Dynamics of Public Preferences and Policy," *Journal of Politics* 66 (February 2004): 1–24.

57. Larry M. Bartels, however, found that members of Congress were responsive to constituency opinion in supporting the Reagan defense buildup. See "Constituency Opinion and Congressional Policy Making: The Reagan Defense Buildup," *American Political Science Review* 85 (June 1991): 457–74.

58. Kim Quaile Hill and Patricia A. Hurley, "Dyadic Representation Reappraised," *American Journal of Political Science* 43 (January 1999): 109–37.

59. On the importance of ideology, see Bernstein, *Elections, Representation, and Congressional Voting Behavior.*

60. *Washington Representatives 2010* (Washington, DC: Columbia Books, 2010); *PoliticalMoneyLine.*

61. Center for Responsive Politics (www.opensecrets.org), 2010; *PoliticalMoneyLine.*

62. Richard L. Hall and Alan V. Deardorff, "Lobbying as Legislative Subsidy," *American Political Science Review* 100 (February 2006): 69–84; and Richard L. Hall and Kristina C. Miler, "What Happens After the Alarm? Interest Group Subsidies to Legislative Overseers," *Journal of Politics* 70 (October 2008): 990–1005.

63. Robert Pear, "In House, Many Spoke with One Voice: Lobbyists'," *New York Times*, November 15, 2009.

64. See Frank R. Baumgartner, Jeffrey M. Berry, Marie Hojnacki, David C. Kimball, and Beth L. Leech, *Lobbying and Policy Change: Who Wins, Who Loses, and Why* (Chicago, IL: University of Chicago Press, 2009).

65. Brian Kelleher Richter, Krislert Samphantharak, Jeffrey F. Timmons, "Lobbying and Taxes," *American Journal of Political Science* 53 (October 2009): 893–909.

66. Baumgartner, Berry, Hojnacki, Kimball, and Leech, *Lobbying and Policy Change,* chaps. 10–12.

67. John W. Kingdon, *Congressmen's Voting Decisions*, 3rd ed. (Ann Arbor: University of Michigan Press, 1989), 242.

68. See M. Darrell West, *Congress and Economic Policymaking* (Pittsburgh: University of Pittsburgh Press, 1987).

CHAPTER 13

1. Quoted in Thomas E. Cronin, *The State of the Presidency*, 2nd ed. (Boston: Little, Brown, 1980), 223.

2. Richard E. Neustadt, *Presidential Power and the Modern Presidents* (New York: Free Press, 1990).

3. George C. Edwards III, *The Strategic President: Persuasion and Opportunity in Presidential Leadership* (Princeton, NJ: Princeton University Press, 2009).

4. On the public's expectations of the president, see George C. Edwards III, *The Public Presidency* (New York: St. Martin's Press, 1983), chap. 5.

5. Office of the White House Press Secretary, *Remarks of the President at a Meeting with Non-Washington Editors and Broadcasters*, September 21, 1979, 12.

6. Samuel P. Huntington, *American Politics: The Promises of Disharmony* (Cambridge, MA: Belknap, 1981), 33.

7. On the creation of the presidency, see Donald L. Robinson, *To the Best of My Ability* (New York: Norton, 1987), and Thomas E. Cronin, ed., *Inventing the American Presidency* (Lawrence: University Press of Kansas, 1989).

8. A good example is Clinton Rossiter, *The American Presidency*, rev. ed. (New York: Harcourt, 1960).

9. Arthur Schlesinger, *The Imperial Presidency* (Boston: Houghton Mifflin, 1973).

10. The titles of chapters 5 and 11 in Thomas E. Cronin, *The State of the Presidency*, 2nd ed. (Boston: Little, Brown, 1980).

11. On the factors important in the presidential nominee's choice of a running mate, see Lee Sigelman and Paul J. Wahlbeck, "The 'Veepstakes': Strategic Choice in Presidential Running Mate Selection," *American Political Science Review* 91 (December 1997): 855–64.

12. See Paul C. Light, *Vice Presidential Power* (Baltimore: Johns Hopkins University Press, 1984).

13. For a study of the backgrounds of cabinet members, see Jeffrey E. Cohen, *The Politics of the U.S. Cabinet* (Pittsburgh: University of Pittsburgh Press, 1988).

14. For background on the Executive Office, see John Hart, *The Presidential Branch*, 2nd ed. (Chatham, NJ: Chatham House, 1995).

15. Two useful books on the history and functions of the White House staff are Hart, *The Presidential Branch*, and Bradley H. Patterson Jr., *The White House Staff* (Washington, DC: Brookings Institution, 2000).

16. For a discussion of presidential party leadership in Congress, see George C. Edwards III, *At the Margins: Presidential Leadership of Congress* (New Haven, CT: Yale University Press, 1989), chaps. 3–5.

17. Jimmy Carter, *Keeping Faith* (New York: Bantam, 1982), 80.

18. For a review of these studies and an analysis showing the limited impact of presidential coattails on congressional election outcomes, see Edwards, *The Public Presidency*, 83–93.

19. For evidence of the impact of the president's campaigning in midterm elections, see Jeffrey E. Cohen, Michael A. Krassa, and John A. Hamman, "The Impact of Presidential Campaigning on Midterm U.S. Senate Elections," *American Political Science Review* 85 (March 1991): 165–78. On the president's effect on congressional elections more broadly, see James E. Campbell, *The Presidential Pulse of Congressional Elections* (Lexington: University Press of Kentucky, 1993).

20. Quoted in Sidney Blumenthal, "Marketing the President," *New York Times Magazine*, September 13, 1981, 110.

21. Quoted in "Slings and Arrows," *Newsweek*, July 31, 1978, 20.

22. Edwards, *At the Margins*, chaps. 6–7.

23. Lawrence J. Grossback, David A. M. Peterson, and James A. Stimson, *Mandate Politics* (New York: Cambridge University Press, 2006).

24. For an analysis of the factors that affect perceptions of mandates, see Edwards, *At the Margins*, chap. 8.

25. David Stockman, *The Triumph of Politics* (New York: Harper & Row, 1986), 251–65; William Greider, "The Education of David Stockman," *Atlantic*, December 1981, 51.

26. George C. Edwards III and Andrew Barrett, "Presidential Agenda Setting in Congress," in *Polarized Politics*, ed. Jon R. Bond and Richard Fleisher (Washington, DC: Congressional Quarterly Press, 2000).

27. John Kingdon, *Agendas, Alternatives, and Public Policies* (Boston: Little, Brown, 1984), 25. On presidential agenda setting, see Paul C. Light, *The President's Agenda* (Baltimore: Johns Hopkins University Press, 1991), and George C. Edwards III and B. Dan Wood, "Who Influences Whom? The President, Congress, and the Media," *American Political Science Review* 93 (June 1999): 327–44.

28. Edwards, *The Strategic President*, chap. 4; Edwards, *At the Margins*, chaps. 9–10; Jon R. Bond and Richard Fleisher, *The President in the Legislative Arena* (Chicago: University of Chicago Press, 1990), chap. 8.

29. See David Auerswald and Forrest Maltzman, "Policymaking Through Advice and Consent: Treaty Considerations by the United States Senate," *Journal of Politics* 65 (November 2003): 1097–110.

30. On treaties and executive agreements, see Glen S. Krutz and Jeffrey S. Peake, *Treaty Politics and the Rise of Executive Agreements* (Ann Arbor: University of Michigan Press, 2009).

31. For an analysis of war powers and other issues related to separation of powers, see Louis Fisher, *Constitutional Conflicts Between Congress and the President*, 5th ed. rev. (Lawrence: University Press of Kansas, 2007), and Louis Fisher, *Presidential War Power*, 2nd ed. rev. (Lawrence: University Press of Kansas, 2004).

32. See William G. Howell and Jon C. Pevehouse, *While Dangers Gather: Congressional Checks on Presidential War Powers* (Princeton, NJ: Princeton University Press, 2007).

33. See Barbara Hinckley, *Less than Meets the Eye* (Chicago: University of Chicago Press, 1994).

34. The phrase was originated by Aaron Wildavsky in "The Two Presidencies," *Trans-Action* 4 (December 1966): 7–14. He later determined that the two presidencies applied mostly to the 1950s. See Duane M. Oldfield and Aaron Wildavsky, "Reconsidering the Two Presidencies," in *The Two Presidencies: A Quarter Century Assessment*, ed. Steven A. Shull (Chicago: Nelson-Hall, 1991), 181–90.

35. Edwards, *At the Margins*, chap. 4.

36. Samuel Kernell, *Going Public*, 4th ed. (Washington, DC: Congressional Quarterly Press, 2004.

37. Edwards, *The Public Presidency*, chap. 6; George C. Edwards III, *Presidential Approval* (Baltimore: Johns Hopkins University Press, 1990).

38. Mueller also included the inaugural period of a president's term as a rally event. See John E. Mueller, *War, Presidents and Public Opinion* (New York: Wiley, 1973), 208–13.

39. Kernell, *Going Public*, 169.

40. On presidents' efforts to build policy support, see Jeffrey K. Tulis, *The Rhetorical Presidency* (Princeton, NJ: Princeton University Press, 1987).

41. Evan Parker-Stephen, "Campaigns, Motivation, and the Dynamics of Political Learning." *Working Paper*, 2008.

42. Steven Kull, Clay Ramsay, and Evan Lewis, "Misperceptions, the Media, and the Iraq War," *Political Science Quarterly* 118 (Winter 2003–2004): 569–598.

43. Useful comparisons over Reagan's and Clinton's tenures can be found in George C. Edwards III, *On Deaf Ears: The Limits of the Bully Pulpit* (New Haven, CT: Yale University Press, 2003), chaps. 2–3.

44. George C. Edwards III, *Governing by Campaigning: The Politics of the Bush Presidency*, 2nd ed. (New York: Longman, 2007).

45. The best source for the White House's relations with the press is Martha Kumar, *Managing the President's Message: The White House Communications Operation* (Baltimore, MD: Johns Hopkins University Press, 2007).

46. Sam Donaldson, *Hold On, Mr. President!* (New York: Random House, 1987), 196–97.

47. Two of the leading studies are found in Michael J. Robinson and Margaret A. Sheehan, *Over the Wire and on TV* (New York: Russell Sage Foundation, 1983), and Daniel C. Hallin, *"The 'Uncensored War': the Media and Vietnam* (New York: Oxford University Press, 1986).

48. Carter, *Keeping Faith*, 179–80.

49. See Mark J. Rozell, *The Press and the Ford Presidency* (Ann Arbor: University of Michigan Press, 1992).

50. Thomas E. Patterson, *Doing Well and Doing Good* (Cambridge, MA: Shorenstein Center, 2000), pp. 10, 12; "Clinton's the One," *Media Monitor* 6 (November 1992): 3–5; S. Robert Lichter and Richard E. Noyes, *Good Intentions Make Bad News,* 2nd ed. (Lanham, MD: Rowman and Littlefield,1996), chaps. 6–7, esp. pp. 288–99; "Campaign 2000 Final: How TV News Covered the General Election Campaign," *Media Monitor* 14 (November/December 2000); Thomas E. Patterson, *Out of Order* (New York: Knopf, 1993), pp. 3–27, chap. 3.

51. Ibid., 113.

52. *Media Monitor*, May/June 1995, 2–5; Thomas E. Patterson, "Legitimate Beef: The Presidency and a Carnivorous Press," *Media Studies Journal*, spring 1994, 21–26; "Sex, Lies, and TV News," *Media Monitor* 12 (September/October 1998); "TV News Coverage of the 1998 Midterm Elections," *Media Monitor* 12 (November/December 1998). See also Andras Szanto, "In Our Opinion . . . : Editorial Page Views of Clinton's First Year,"*Media Studies Journal*, spring 1994, 97–105; Lichter and Noyes, *Good Intentions Make Bad News*, p. 214.

53. See, for example, *Media Monitor*, June/July 1998.

54. Stephen J. Farnsworth and S. Robert Lichter, *The Mediated Presidency: Television News and Presidential Governance* (Lanham, MD: Rowman and Littlefield, 2006), pp. 40–45, chap. 4; Stephen J. Farnsworth and S. Robert Lichter, *The Nightly News Nightmare: Television's Coverage of U.S. Presidential Elections, 1988–2004*, 2nd ed. (Lanham, MD: Rowman & Littlefield, 2007), chap. 4. See also Jeffrey E. Cohen, *The Presidency in the Era of 24-Hour News* (Princeton, NJ: Princeton University Press), chaps. 5–6.

55. Katherine Graham, *Personal History* (New York: Vintage, 1998).

56. Michael Baruch Grossman and Martha Joynt Kumar, *Portraying the President: The White House and the News Media* (Baltimore: Johns Hopkins University Press, 1981), chaps. 10–11.

57. Donaldson, *Hold On, Mr. President!*, 237–38.

58. Quoted in Eleanor Randolph, "Speakes Aims Final Salvo at White House Practices," *Washington Post*, January 31, 1987, A3.

59. Scott McClellan, *What Happened: Inside the Bush White House and Washington's Culture of Deception* (New York: Public Affairs, 2008), pp. 156–58.

60. George C. Edwards III, Andrew Barrett, and Jeffrey S. Peake, "The Legislative Impact of Divided Government," *American Journal of Political Science* 41 (April 1997): 545–63.

61. David R. Mayhew, *Divided We Govern* (New Haven, CT: Yale University Press, 1991).

CHAPTER 14

1. Aaron Wildavsky and Naomi Caiden, *The New Politics of the Budgetary Process*, 5th ed. (New York: Longman, 2004), 2.

2. *Budget of the United States Government, Fiscal Year 2011: Historical Tables* (Washington, DC: U.S. Government Printing Office, 2010), Tables 3.1 and 7.1.

3. Quoted in Gerald Carson, *The Golden Egg: The Personal Income Tax, Where It Came From, How It Grew* (Boston: Houghton Mifflin, 1977), 12.

4. Tax Foundation, 2010.

5. Tax Foundation, 2010.

6. *Budget of the United States Government, Fiscal Year 2011: Historical Tables* (Washington, DC: U.S. Government Printing Office, 2010), Table 2.2.

7. An exception is Robert Eisner, who argues that if the government counted its debt as families and business firms do—that is, by balancing assets against liabilities—the government would be in pretty good shape. See *How Real Is the Federal Deficit?* (New York: Free Press, 1986).

8. Ray D. Madoff, "Dog Eat Your Taxes?," *New York Times*, July 9, 2008.

9. An excellent discussion of such issues is Bryan D. Jones and Walter Williams, *The Politics of Bad Ideas* (New York: Pearson Longman, 2007).

10. For some perspectives on the rise of government expenditures, see David Cameron, "The Expansion of the Public Economy: A Comparative Analysis," *American Political Science Review* 72 (December 1978): 1243–61; and William D. Berry and David Lowery, *Understanding United States Government Growth* (New York: Praeger, 1987).

11. *Budget of the United States Government, Fiscal Year 2011: Historical Tables* (Washington, DC: U.S. Government Printing Office, 2010), Table 1.3.

12. Berry and Lowery, *Understanding United States Government Growth.*

13. Paul Light, *Artful Work: The Politics of Social Security Reform* (New York: HarperCollins, 1992), 82.

14. *Budget of the United States Government, Fiscal Year 2011: Historical Tables* (Washington, DC: U.S. Government Printing Office, 2010), Tables 1.1 and 8.5.

15. Aaron Wildavsky and Naomi Caiden, *The New Politics of the Budgetary Process*, 3rd ed. (New York: Longman, 1997), 45.

16. Paul R. Schulman, "Nonincremental Policymaking: Notes Toward an Alternative Paradigm," *American Political Science Review* 69 (December 1975): 1354–70.

17. See Bryan D. Jones, Frank R. Baumgartner, et al., "A General Empirical Law of Public Budgets: A Comparative Analysis," *American Journal of Political Science* 53 (October 2009): 855–73; Bryan D. Jones and Frank R. Baumgartner, *The Politics of Attention* (Chicago: University of Chicago Press, 2005).

18. A good description of budgetary strategies is in Wildavsky and Caiden, *The New Politics of the Budgetary Process*, chap. 3.

19. For a discussion of the ways in which bureaucracies manipulate benefits to gain advantage with members of Congress, see Douglas Arnold, *Congress and the Bureaucracy* (New Haven, CT: Yale University Press, 1979), and the articles in Barry S. Rundquist, ed., *Political Benefits* (Lexington, MA: D.C. Heath, 1980).

20. A good review of the formation of the budget is Allen Schick, *The Federal Budget: Politics, Policy, Process*, 3rd ed. (Washington, DC: Brookings Institution, 2007).

21. An important work on congressional budget making is Wildavsky and Caiden, *The New Politics of the Budgetary Process*.

22. Allan Meltzer and Scott F. Richard, "Why the Government Grows (and Grows) in a Democracy," *The Public Interest* 52 (summer 1978): 117.

23. *Budget of the United States Government, Fiscal Year 2011* (Washington, DC: U.S. Government Printing Office, 2010), p. 58.

24. See, for example, CBS News/New York Times poll, February 5–10, 2009.

25. See James D. Savage, *Balanced Budgets and American Politics* (Ithaca, NY: Cornell University Press, 1988), for a study of the influence the principle of budget balancing has had on politics and public policy from the earliest days of U.S. history.

CHAPTER 15

1. This example is based on Allan Freedman, "Battles over Jurisdiction Likely to Block Merger of Agencies," *Congressional Quarterly Weekly Report*, May 30, 1998, 1440; Marian Burros, "F.D.A. Inspections Lax, Congress Is Told," *New York Times*, July 18, 2007; Stephen J. Hedges, "How Imports Swamp FDA Thin Line of Defense Against Tainted Food," *Chicago Tribune*, September 2, 2007; Gardiner Harris, "Advisers Say F.D.A.'s Flaws Put Lives at Risk," *New York Times*, December 1, 2007.

2. H. H. Gerth and C. Wright Mills, *From Max Weber: Essays in Sociology* (New York: Oxford University Press, 1958), chap. 8.

3. See Charles T. Goodsell, *The Case for Bureaucracy*, 4th ed. (Washington, DC: CQ Press, 2004), chap. 2. See also Daniel Katz et al., *Bureaucratic Encounters* (Ann Arbor: Institute for Social Research, University of Michigan, 1975).

4. U.S. Department of Commerce, *Statistical Abstract of the United States, 2010* (Washington, DC: U.S. Government Printing Office, 2010), Table 484.

5. See Paul C. Light, *The True Size of Government* (Washington, DC: Brookings Institution, 1999), 1, 44.

6. Office of Personnel Administration, "Federal Civilian Personnel Summary," 2008.

7. See Herbert Kaufman, *Red Tape* (Washington, DC: Brookings Institution, 1977).

8. See Goodsell, *The Case for Bureaucracy*, 48–54.

9. Ibid., chap. 5.

10. Hugh M. Heclo, *A Government of Strangers: Executive Politics in Washington* (Washington, DC: Brookings Institution, 1977).

11. On the transient nature of presidential appointees, see G. Calvin Mackenzie, ed., *The In-and-Outers* (Baltimore: Johns Hopkins University Press, 1987).

12. David E. Lewis, *The Politics of Presidential Appointments* (Princeton, NJ: Princeton University Press, 2008); George C. Edwards III, "Why Not the Best? The Loyalty–Competence Trade-Off in Presidential Appointments," in G. Calvin Mackenzie, ed., *Innocent Until Nominated* (Brookings Institution, 2000).

13. On the independent regulatory agencies, see the classic work by Marver Bernstein, *Regulating Business by Independent Commission* (Princeton, NJ: Princeton University Press, 1955). See also, on regulation, James Q. Wilson, ed., *The Politics of Regulation* (New York: Basic Books, 1980), and A. Lee Fritschler and Bernard H. Ross, *Business Regulation and Government Decision-Making* (Cambridge, MA: Winthrop, 1980).

14. Bernstein, *Regulating Business by Independent Commission*, 90. For a partial test of the capture theory that finds the theory not altogether accurate, see John P. Plumlee and Kenneth J. Meier, "Capture and Rigidity in Regulatory Administration," in *The Policy Cycle*, ed. Judith May and Aaron Wildavsky (Beverly Hills, CA: Russell Sage Foundation, 1978). Another critique of the capture theory is Paul J. Quirk, *Industry Influence in Federal Regulatory Agencies* (Princeton, NJ: Princeton University Press, 1981).

15. George C. Edwards III, *Implementing Public Policy* (Washington, DC: Congressional Quarterly Press, 1980), 1.

16. Lineberry, *American Public Policy*, 70–71.

17. For another dramatic example, see Martha Derthick, *New Towns In-Town* (Washington, DC: Urban Institute Press, 1972).

18. Eugene Bardach, *The Implementation Game* (Cambridge, MA: MIT Press, 1977), 250–51.

19. The implementation of the athletics policy is well documented in two articles by Cheryl M. Fields in the *Chronicle of Higher Education*, December 11 and 18, 1978, on which this account relies.

20. James Q. Wilson, *Bureaucracy* (New York: Basic Books, 1989), 158.

21. A good discussion of how policymakers ignored the administrative capacity of one important agency when assigning it new responsibilities can be found in Martha Derthick, *Agency Under Stress* (Washington, DC: Brookings Institution, 1990).

22. Kenneth J. Meier and Laurence J. O'Toole, *Bureaucracy in a Democratic State* (Baltimore, MD: Johns Hopkins University Press, 2006).

23. Report of the DOD Commission on Beirut International Airport Terrorist Act, October 23, 1983, December 20, 1983, 133.

24. *The 9/11 Commission Report* (New York: Norton, 2004), 17–18.

25. On administrative discretion, see Gary S. Bryner, *Bureaucratic Discretion* (New York: Pergamon Press, 1987).

26. Michael Lipsky, *Street-Level Bureaucracy* (New York: Russell Sage Foundation, 1980).

27. Quoted in Seymour Hersh, *The Price of Power: Kissinger in the Nixon White House* (New York: Summit, 1983), 235–36.

28. Albert Gore, *From Red Tape to Results: Creating a Government That Works Better and Costs Less* (New York: Times Books, 1993), 11.

29. For a careful analysis of efforts to reorganize the federal bureaucracy, see Peri E. Arnold, *Making the Managerial Presidency*, 2nd ed. (Princeton, NJ: Princeton University Press, 1996).

30. On the implementation and impact of the Voting Rights Act, see Charles S. Bullock III and Harrell R. Rodgers, Jr., *Law and Social Change: Civil Rights Laws and Their Consequences* (New York: McGraw-Hill, 1972), chap. 2; Richard Scher and James Button, "Voting Rights Act: Implementation and Impact," in*Implementation of Civil Rights Policy*, ed. C. S. Bullock and C. M. Lamb (Monterey, CA: Brooks/Cole, 1984), chap. 2; and Abigail M. Thernstrom, *Whose Votes Count?* (Cambridge, MA: Harvard University Press, 1987).

31. Light, *The True Size of Government.*

32. Scott Shane and Ron Nixon, "In Washington, Contractors Take on Biggest Role Ever," *New York Times*, February 4, 2007.

33. See Martha Derthick and Paul J. Quirk, *The Politics of Deregulation* (Washington, DC: Brookings Institution, 1985).

34. See, for example, Susan J. Tolchin and Martin J. Tolchin, *Dismantling America: The Rush to Deregulate* (New York: Oxford University Press, 1983).

35. Evan J. Ringquist, "Does Regulation Matter? Evaluating the Effects of State Air Pollution Control Programs," *Journal of Politics* 55 (November 1993): 1022–45.

36. Michael Lewis-Beck and John Alford, "Can Government Regulate Safety? The Coal Mine Example," *American Political Science Review* 74 (September 1980): 745–56.

37. Paul Sabatier and Dan Mazmanian, *Can Regulation Work? Implementation of the 1972 California Coastal Initiative* (New York: Plenum, 1983).

38. Gary Copeland and Kenneth J. Meier, "Gaining Ground: The Impact of Medicaid and WIC on Infant Mortality," *American Politics Quarterly* 15 (April 1987): 254–73.

39. See B. Dan Wood and Richard W. Waterman, *Bureaucratic Dynamics: The Role of Bureaucracy in a Democracy* (Boulder, CO: Westview, 1994).

40. A good work on this point is Richard P. Nathan, *The Administrative Presidency* (New York: Wiley, 1983).

41. See Adam Warber, *Executive Orders and the Modern Presidency* (Boulder, CO: Lynne Rienner Publishers (2006); William G. Howell, *Power Without Persuasion* (Princeton, NJ: Princeton University Press, 2003); and Kenneth R. Mayer, *With the Stroke of a Pen, Executive Orders and Presidential Power* (Princeton, NJ: Princeton University Press, 2001).

42. Matthew Eshbaugh-Soha, *The President's Speeches: Beyond Going Public* (Boulder, CO: Lynne Rienner, 2006); and Andrew B. Whitford and Jeff Yates, "Policy Signals and Executive Governance: Presidential Rhetoric in the War on Drugs," *Journal of Politics* 65 (November 2003): 995–1012.

43. Morris Fiorina, *Congress: Keystone of the Washington Establishment*, 2nd ed. (New Haven, CT: Yale University Press, 1989).

44. Hugh M. Heclo, "Issue Networks and the Executive Establishment," in *The New American Political System*, ed. Anthony King (Washington, DC: American Enterprise Institute, 1978), 87–124. See also William P. Browne and Won K. Paik, "Beyond the Domain: Recasting Network Politics in the Postreform Congress," *American Journal of Political Science* 37 (November 1993): 1054–78, and John P. Heinz, Edward O. Laumann, Robert L. Nelson, and Robert L. Salisbury, *The Hollow Core: Private Interests in National Policy Making* (Cambridge, MA: Harvard University Press, 1993).

45. Frank R. Baumgartner and Bryan D. Jones, *Agendas and Instability in American Politics* (Chicago: University of Chicago Press, 1993).

46. Ibid.

CHAPTER 16

1. U.S. Department of Commerce, *Statistical Abstract of the United States, 2008* (Washington, DC: U.S. Government Printing Office, 2008), Table 598.

2. Quoted in Lawrence C. Baum, *The Supreme Court*, 4th ed. (Washington, DC: CQ Press, 1992), 72.

3. Administrative Office of the United States Courts.

4. Administrative Office of the United States Courts.

5. Administrative Office of the United States Courts.

6. See Sarah A. Binder and Forrest Maltzman, *Advice and Dissent: The Struggle to Shape the Federal Judiciary* (Washington, DC: Brookings Institution, 2009) on the history and procedures regarding judicial nominations.

7. Sarah Binder and Forrest Maltzman, "The Limits of Senatorial Courtesy," *Legislative Studies Quarterly* 29 (February 2004): 5–22. Michael A. Sollenberger, "The Blue Slip: A Theory of Unified and Divided Government, 1979-2009,"*Congress & the Presidency* 37 (May-August 2010): 125-156; Brandon Rottinghaus and Chris Nicholson, "Counting Congress In: Patterns of Success in Judicial Nomination Requests by Members of Congress to Presidents Eisenhower and Ford," *American Politics Research* 38 (July 2010): 691-717.

8. Quoted in J. Woodford Howard Jr., *Courts of Appeals in the Federal Judicial System: A Study of the Second, Fifth, and District of Columbia Circuits* (Princeton, NJ: Princeton University Press, 1981), p. 101.

9. Nancy Scherer, Brandon L. Bartels, and Amy Steigerwalt, "Sounding the Fire Alarm: The Role of Interest Groups in the Lower Federal Court Confirmation Process," *Journal of Politics* 70 (October 2008): 1026–39.

10. Binder and Maltzman, *Advice and Dissent*, 4–6, chaps. 2, 4; Jon R. Bond, Richard Fleisher, and Glen S. Krutz, "Malign Neglect: Evidence That Delay Has Become the Primary Method of Defeating Presidential Appointment," *Congress & the Presidency* (Fall 2009): 226–43; and Lauren Cohen Bell, "Senatorial Discourtesy: The Senate's Use of Delay to Shape the Federal Judiciary," *Political Research Quarterly* 55 (September 2002): 589–607.

11. Binder and Maltzman, *Advice and Dissent*, 2–4, chap. 4.

12. See Gary King, "Presidential Appointments to the Supreme Court: Adding Systematic Explanation to Probabilistic Description,"*American Politics Quarterly* 15 (July 1987): 373–86.

13. Charles R. Shipan and Megan L. Shannon, "Delaying Justice(s): A Duration Analysis of Supreme Court Confirmations," *American Journal of Political Science* 47 (October 2003): 654–68.

14. Sheldon Goldman, Sara Schiavoni, and Elliot Slotnick, "W. Bush's Judicial Legacy," *Judicature* 92 (May–June 2009): 258–88.

15. Quoted in Nina Totenberg, "Will Judges Be Chosen Rationally?," *Judicature* 60 (August/September 1976): 93.

16. See John Schmidhauser, *Judges and Justices: The Federal Appellate Judiciary* (Boston: Little, Brown, 1978).

17. One study found, however, that judicial experience does not help presidents predict justices' decisions on racial equality cases. See John Gates and Jeffrey Cohen, "Presidents, Supreme Court Justices, and Racial Equality Cases: 1954–1984," *Political Behavior* 10 (November 1, 1988): 22–35.

18. On the importance of ideology and partisanship considerations in judicial retirement and resignation decisions, see Kjersten R. Nelson and Eve M. Ringsmuth, "Departures from the Court: The Political Landscape and Institutional Constraints," *American Politics Research* 37 (May 2009): 486–507; and Deborah J. Barrow and Gary Zuk, "An Institutional Analysis of Turnover in the Lower Federal Courts, 1900–1987," *Journal of Politics* 52 (May 1990): 457–76.

19. Quoted in Henry J. Abraham, *Justices and Presidents: A Political History of Appointments to the Supreme Court*, 3rd ed. (New York: Oxford University Press, 1992), 266.

20. Ibid., 70.

21. See, for example, the important role that African American support played in the confirmation of Clarence Thomas even though he was likely to vote against the wishes of leading civil rights organizations. L. Marvin Overby, Beth M. Henschen, Julie Walsh, and Michael H. Strauss, "Courting Constituents: An Analysis of the Senate Confirmation Vote on Justice Clarence Thomas,"*American Political Science Review* 86 (December 1992): 997–1003.

22. Jennifer L. Peresie, "Female Judges Matter: Gender and Collegial: Decisionmaking in the Federal Appellate Courts," *Yale Law Journal* 114 (May 2005): 1759–90.

23. Adam B. Cox and Thomas J. Miles, "Judging the Voting Rights Act," *Columbia Law Review* 108 (January 2008): 1–54.

24. Quoted in Adam Liptak, "The Waves Minority Judges Always Make," ***New York Times***, May 1, 2009.

25. On the impact of the background of members of the judiciary, see Robert A. Carp and C. K. Rowland, *Policymaking and Politics in the Federal District Courts* (Knoxville: University of Tennessee Press, 1983); Thomas G. Walker and Deborah J. Barrow, "The Diversification of the Federal Bench: Policy and Process Ramifications," *Journal of Politics* 47 (May 1985): 596–617; and C. Neal Tate, "Personal Attribute Models of the Voting Behavior of United States Supreme Court Justices: Liberalism in Civil Liberties and Economics Decisions, 1946–1978," *American Political Science Review* 75 (June 1981): 355–67.

26. Quoted in Nina Totenberg, "Behind the Marble, Beneath the Robes," *New York Times Magazine*, March 16, 1975, 37.

27. Ryan C. Black and Ryan J. Owens, "Agenda Setting in the Supreme Court: The Collision of Policy and Jurisprudence," *Journal of Politics* 71 (July 2009): 1062–75; H. W. Perry Jr., *Deciding to Decide: Agenda Setting in the United States Supreme Court* (Cambridge, MA: Harvard University Press, 1991); Doris Marie Provine, *Case Selection in the United States Supreme Court* (Chicago: University of Chicago Press, 1980); Stuart H. Teger and Douglas Kosinski, "The Cue Theory of Supreme Court Certiorari Jurisdiction: A Reconsideration," *Journal of Politics* 42 (August 1980): 834–46.

28. Sidney Ulmer, "The Supreme Court's Certiorari Decisions: Conflict as a Predictive Variable," *American Political Science Review* (December 1984): 901–11.

29. On the solicitor general's *amicus* briefs, see Rebecca E. Deen, Joseph Ignagni, and James Meernik, "Executive Influence on the U.S. Supreme Court: Solicitor General *Amicus* Cases, 1953–1997," *American Review of Politics* 22 (spring 2001): 3–26, and Timothy R. Johnson, "The Supreme Court, the Solicitor General, and the Separation of Powers," *American Politics Research* 31 (July 2001): 426–51.

30. See Rebecca Mae Salokar, *The Solicitor General* (Philadelphia: Temple University Press, 1992).

31. Each year, data on Supreme Court decisions can be found in the November issue of the *Harvard Law Review*.

32. On the influence of oral arguments on the Supreme Court, see Timothy R. Johnson, Paul J. Wahlbeck, and James F. Spriggs II, "The Influence of Oral Arguments on the U.S. Supreme Court," *American Political Science Review* 100 (February 2006): 99–113.

33. A useful look at attorneys practicing before the Supreme Court is Kevin McGuire, *The Supreme Court Bar: Legal Elites in the Washington Community* (Charlottesville: University Press of Virginia, 1993).

34. See, for example, Forrest Maltzman and Paul J. Wahlbeck, "Strategic Policy Considerations and Voting Fluidity on the Burger Court," *American Political Science Review* 90 (September 1996): 581–92; Paul J. Wahlbeck, James F. Spriggs II, and Forrest Maltzman, "Marshalling the Court: Bargaining and Accommodation on the United States Supreme Court," *American Journal of Political Science* 42 (January 1998): 294–315; and James F. Spriggs II, Forrest Maltzman, and Paul J. Wahlbeck, "Bargaining on the U.S. Supreme Court: Justices' Responses to Majority Opinion Drafts," *Journal of Politics* 61 (May 1999): 485–506.

35. A. P. Blaustein and A. H. Field, "Overruling Opinions in the Supreme Court," *Michigan Law Review* 57, no. 2 (1957): 151; David H. O'Brien, *Constitutional Law and Politics*, 3rd ed. (New York: Norton, 1997), 38.

36. See, for example, Brandon L. Bartels, "The Constraining Capacity of Legal Doctrine on the U.S. Supreme Court," *American Political Science Review* 103 (August 2009): 474-495; Michael A. Bailey and Forrest Maltzman, "Does Legal Doctrine Matter? Unpacking Law and Policy Preferences on the U.S. Supreme Court," *American Political Science Review* 102 (August 2008): 369-384.

37. See, for example, Jeffrey A. Segal and Harold J. Spaeth, *The Supreme Court and the Attitudinal Model* (Cambridge: Cambridge University Press, 1993); Jeffrey A. Segal and Albert O. Cover, "Ideological Values and the Votes of U.S. Supreme Court Justices," *American Political Science Review* 83 (June 1989): 557–66; Tracey E. George and Lee Epstein, "On the Nature of Supreme Court Decision Making," *American Political Science Review* 86 (June 1992): 323–37; and Jeffrey A. Segal and Harold J. Spaeth, "The Influence of *Stare Decisis* on the Votes of United States Supreme Court Justices," *American Journal of Political Science* 40 (November 1996): 971–1003.

38. Doris Graber, *Mass Media and American Politics*, 6th ed. (Washington, DC: CQ Press, 2002), 312–13.

39. Charles A. Johnson and Bradley C. Canon, *Judicial Policies: Implementation and Impact*, 2nd ed. (Washington, DC: CQ Press, 1999), chap. 1. See also James F. Spriggs II, "The Supreme Court and Federal Administrative Agencies: A Resource-Based Theory and Analysis of Judicial Impact," *American Journal of Political Science* 40 (November 1996): 1122–51.

40. See Richard L. Pacelle Jr. and Lawrence Baum, "Supreme Court Authority in the Judiciary," *American Politics Quarterly* 20 (April 1992): 169–91, and Donald R. Songer, Jeffrey A. Segal, and Charles M. Cameron, "The Hierarchy of Justice: Testing a Principal-Agent Model of Supreme Court-Circuit Court Interactions," *American Journal of Political Science* 38 (August 1994): 673–96.

41. Kevin T. McGuire, "Public Schools, Religious Establishments, and the U.S. Supreme Court: An Examination of Policy Compliance," *American Politics Research* 37 (January 2009): 50–74.

42. For an excellent overview of the Warren period by former Watergate special prosecutor and Harvard law professor Archibald Cox, see *The Warren Court* (Cambridge, MA: Harvard University Press, 1968).

43. William Rehnquist, "The Notion of a Living Constitution," in *Views from the Bench*, ed. Mark W. Cannon and David M. O'Brien (Chatham, NJ: Chatham House, 1985), 129. One study found, however, that judicial experience is not related to the congruence of presidential preferences and the justices' decisions on racial equality cases. See John Gates and Jeffrey Cohen, "Presidents, Supreme Court Justices, and Racial Equality Cases: 1954–1984," *Political Behavior* 10 (November 1, 1988): 22–35.

44. Richard Funston, "The Supreme Court and Critical Elections," *American Political Science Review* 69 (1975): 810; John B. Gates, *The Supreme Court and Partisan Realignment* (Boulder, CO: Westview, 1992); Thomas R. Marshall, "Public Opinion, Representation, and the Modern Supreme Court," *American Politics Quarterly* 16 (July 1988): 296–316; William Mishler and Reginald S. Sheehan, "The Supreme Court as a Countermajoritarian Institution? The Impact of Public Opinion on Supreme Court Decisions," *American Political Science Review* 87 (March 1993): 87–101; William Mishler and Reginald S. Sheehan, "Public Opinion, the Attitudinal Model, and Supreme Court Decision Making: A Micro-Analytic Perspective," *Journal of Politics* 58 (February 1996): 169–200; Roy B. Flemming and B. Dan Wood, "The Public and the Supreme Court: Individual Justice Responsiveness to American Policy Moods," *American Journal of Political Science* 41 (April 1997): 468–98; Kevin T. McGuire and James A. Stimson, "The Least Dangerous Branch: New Evidence on Supreme Court Responsiveness to Public Preferences," *Journal of Politics* 66 (November 2004): 1018–35.

45. Mario Bergara, Barak Richman, and Pablo T. Spiller, "Modeling Supreme Court Strategic Decision Making: The Congressional Constraint," *Legislative Studies Quarterly* 28 (May 2003) 247–80.

46. David G. Barnum, "The Supreme Court and Public Opinion: Judicial Decision Making in the Post-New Deal Period," *Journal of Politics* 47 (May 1985): 652–62.

47. Gregory A. Caldeira and John R. Wright, "Organized Interests and Agenda Setting in the U.S. Supreme Court," *American Political Science Review* 82 (December 1988): 1109–28.

48. On group use of the litigation process, see Karen Orren, "Standing to Sue: Interest Group Conflict in the Federal Courts,"*American Political Science Review* 70 (September 1976): 723–42; Karen O'Connor and Lee Epstein, "The Rise of Conservative Interest Group Litigation," *Journal of Politics* 45 (May 1983): 479–89; and Lee Epstein and C. K. Rowland, "Debunking the Myth of Interest Group Invincibility in the Courts,"*American Political Science Review* 85 (March 1991): 205–17.

49. "Federalist #78," in Hamilton, Madison, and Jay, *The Federalist Papers*.

50. However, see Gerald N. Rosenberg, *The Hollow Hope: Can Courts Bring About Social Change?* (Chicago: University of Chicago Press, 1991). Rosenberg questions whether courts have brought about much social change.

51. Examples of judicial activism are reported in a critical assessment of judicial intervention by Donald Horowitz, *The Courts and Social Policy* (Washington, DC: Brookings Institution, 1977).

52. Paul Gerwitz and Chad Golder, "So Who Are the Activists?," *New York Times*, July 6, 2005.

53. William N. Eskridge, "Overriding Supreme Court Statutory Interpretation Decisions," *Yale Law Journal* 101 (1991): 331–455; Joseph Ignagni and James Meernik, "Explaining Congressional Attempts to Reverse Supreme Court Decisions,"*Political Research Quarterly* 10 (June 1994): 353–72. See also R. Chep Melnick, *Between the Lines: Interpreting Welfare Rights* (Washington, DC: Brookings Institution, 1994).

54. Kirk A Randazzo, Richard W. Waterman, and Jeffrey A. Fine, "Checking the Federal Courts: The Impact of Congressional Statutes on Judicial Behavior,"*Journal of Politics* 68 (November 2006): 1006–1017.

CHAPTER 17

1. Thomas L. Friedman, *The World Is Flat: A Brief History of the 21st Century* (New York: Ferrar, Straus and Giroux, 2005), 24.

2. "The Wal-Mart You Don't Know," *Fast Company* 77 (December 2003): 68 ff.

3. C. Fred Bergsten, "Foreign Economic Policy for the Next President." *Foreign Affairs* (March/April, 2004), 89.

4. "The Long Arm of Bentonville Arkansas," *Business Week*, October 6, 2003, 103.

5. "The Wal-Martization of America," *New York Times*, November 15, 2003, A12.

6. Brad T. Gomez and J. Matthew Wilson, "Political Sophistication and Economic Voting in the American Electorate: A Theory of Heterogeneous Attribution," *American Journal of Political Science* 45 (October 2001): 899.

7. Robert S. Erikson, Matthew MacKuen, and James L. Stimson, *The Macro Polity* (New York: Cambridge University Press, 2002), 59.

8. Gomez and Wilson, "Political Sophistication and Economic Voting in the American Electorate."

9. Michael S. Lewis-Beck and Richard Nadeau, "Obama and the Economy in 2008." *PS: Political Science & Politics* (July 2009): 483.

10. See David Plouffe, *The Audacity to Win: The Inside Story and Lessons of Barack Obama's Historic Victory* (New York: Viking, 2009), chap. 15.

11. For a summary of economic conditions and voting choice, see Michael S. Lewis-Beck and Mary Stegmaier, "Economic Determinants of Electoral Outcomes," *Annual Review of Political Science* (Palo Alto, CA: Annual Reviews, 2000): 183–219.

12. Suzzana DeBoef and Paul M. Kellstedt, "The Political (and Economic) Origins of Consumer Confidence," *American Journal of Political Science* 48 (October 2004): 633–49.

13. Benjamin I. Page and Robert Y. Shapiro, *The Rational Public: Fifty Years of Trends in America's Policy Preferences* (Chicago: University of Chicago Press, 1992), 122.

14. See William Greider, *Secrets of the Temple: How the Federal Reserve Runs the Country* (New York: Simon and Schuster, 1987); Nathaniel Beck, "Elections and the Fed: Is There a Political Monetary Cycle?," *American Journal of Political Science* 20 (February 1987): 194–216; and Manabu Saeki, "Explaining Federal Reserve Monetary Policy," *Review of Policy Research* 19 (Summer 2002): 129–50.

15. The classic supply-side theory can be found in George Gilder, *Wealth and Poverty* (New York: Basic Books, 1981).

16. The most ardent proponent of this view is Edward Tufte. See his *Political Control of the Economy* (Princeton, NJ: Princeton University Press, 1978).

17. Robert Samuelson, "A Phony Jobs Debate," *Washington Post*, February 25, 2004, A25.

18. The standard and very readable book on globalization is Daniel Yergin and Joseph Stanislaw, *The Commanding Heights* (New York: Touchstone, 2002). See also Benjamin Barber, *Jihad vs. McWorld: How Globalism and Tribalism Are Reshaping the World* (New York: Ballantine, 1996).

19. Bureau of Economic Analysis, "U.S. Net International Investment Position at Yearend 2008," June 26, 2009. This press release can be found on the Web at http://www.bea.gov/newsreleases/international/intinv/intinvnewsrelease.htm.

20. Beth A. Simmons and Zachary Elkins, "The Globalization of Liberalization," *American Political Science Review* 98 (February 2004): 171.

21. Doug Henwood, *After the New Economy* (New York: New Press, 2003), 159.

22. Catherine Mann, "Globalization of IT Services and White Collar Jobs: The Next Wave of Productivity Growth" (Washington, DC: Institute for International Economics, 2004).

23. Friedman, *The World Is Flat.*

24. See the foreign trade statistics with India posted by the U.S. Census bureau at http://www.census.gov/foreign-trade/balance/c5330.html

25. Jonathan B. Baker and Carl Shapiro, "Reinvigorating Horizontal Merger Enforcement." Paper prepared for the Kirkpatrick Conference on the Conservative Economic Influence on U.S. Antitrust Policy, Georgetown University Law School, April 2007, p. 18. This paper can be found online at http://papers.ssrn.com/sol3/papers.cfm?abstract_id=991588.

26. Ibid, p. 25.

27. Christine A. Varney, "Vigorous Antitrust Enforcement in This Challenging Era." Remarks prepared for the United States Chamber of Commerce, May 12, 2009, p. 17. This speech can be found online at http://www.justice.gov/atr/public/speeches/245777.pdf.

28. For some impressive statistics on CEO salaries, see Lawrence Mishel et al., *The State of Working America, 2008/09* (Ithaca, NY: Economic Policy Institute, 2009), 219–23.

29. Carol Graham, Robert Litan, and Sandip Sukhtankar, "The Bigger They Are, the Harder They Fall: An Estimate of the Costs of the Crisis in Corporate Governance" (Washington, DC: Brookings Institution Working Papers, August 30, 2002).

30. Wendy L. Hansen and Neil J. Mitchell, "Disaggregating and Explaining Corporate Political Activity: Domestic and Foreign Corporations in National Politics," *American Political Science Review* 94 (December 2000): 891.

31. Henry M. Paulson, Jr., *On the Brink: Inside the Race to Stop the Collapse of the Global Financial System* (New York: Business Plus, 2010), 438.

CHAPTER 18

1. Martin Gilens, *Why Americans Hate Welfare* (Chicago: University of Chicago Press, 1999).

2. Stanley Feldman and Marco R. Steenbergen, "The Humanitarian Foundation of Public Support for Social Welfare," *American Journal of Political Science* 45 (July 2001): 658–77.

3. Alan Weil and Kenneth Finegold, "Introduction," *Welfare Reform: The Next Act,* ed. Alan Weil and Kenneth Finegold (Washington, DC: Urban Institute Press, 2002), p. xiii.

4. Timothy M. Smeeding, "Public Policy, Income Inequality, and Poverty: The United States in Comparative Perspective," *Social Science Quarterly* 86 (2005): 955. See also Lane Kenworthy and Jonas Pontusson, "Rising Inequality and the Politics of Redistribution in Affluent Countries," *Perspectives on Politics* 3 (September 2005): 449–72.

5. Nolan McCarty, Keith T. Poole, and Howard Rosenthal, *Income Distribution and the Realignment of American Politics* (Washington, DC: American Enterprise Institute, 1977), p. 1. See also their *Polarized America: The Dance of Ideology and Unequal Riches* (Cambridge, MA: MIT Press, 2006).

6. Thomas B. Edsall, *The New Politics of Inequality* (New York: Norton, 1984), p. 18.

7. For more information on this new measure of poverty, see http://www.census.gov/hhes/www/povmeas/SPM_TWGObservations.pdf.

8. Jacob S. Hacker, *The Great Risk Shift* (New York: Oxford University Press, 2008), pp. 24, 32.

9. Barbara Ehrenreich, *Nickel and Dimed: On (Not) Getting By in America* (New York: Owl Books, 2002).

10. See David K. Shipler, *The Working Poor: Invisible in America* (New York: Knopf, 2004).

11. Harrell Rodgers, *Poor Women, Poor Children*, 3rd ed. (New York: M. E. Sharpe, 1996).

12. Harrell Rodgers, *American Poverty in a New Era of Reform* (New York: M. E. Sharpe, 2000), p. 207.

13. See the Statistical Abstract of the United States, 2010, table 476. This can be found online at http://www.census.gov/compendia/statab/2010/tables/10s0476.pdf.

14. Alan Berube and Benjamin Forman, "Rewarding Work: The Impact of the Earned Income Tax Credit." *Brookings Institution Report*, June 2001.

15. Mark R. Rank and Thomas A. Hirschl, "Estimating the Risk of Food Stamp Use and Impoverishment During Childhood," *Archives of American Pediatrics and Adolescent Medicine* (November 2009): 994–99.

16. See, for example, Francis Fox Piven and Richard Cloward, *Regulating the Poor* (New York: Pantheon, 1971). For an empirical analysis of theories of the rise of welfare that finds some support for the Piven and Cloward thesis, see Richard Fording, "The Political Response to Black Insurgency: A Critical Test of Competing Theories of the State," *American Political Science Review* 95 (March 2001): 115–30.

17. Charles Murray, *Losing Ground: American Social Policy, 1950–1980* (New York: Basic Books, 1984). Marvin Olasky, the guru of "compassionate conservatism," makes a similar argument in his *Tragedy of Human Compassion* (Chicago: Regnery, 1992). Doing good for people, especially through government, Olasky argues, is bad for them. For a contrary argument, see Benjamin Page and James R. Simmons, *What Government Can Do: Dealing with Poverty and Inequality* (Chicago: University of Chicago Press, 2000).

18. See, for example, David T. Ellwood and Lawrence H. Summers, "Is Welfare Really the Problem?" *Public Interest* 83 (Spring 1986): 57–78.

19. See Ange-Marie Hancock, *The Politics of Disgust: The Public Identity of the Welfare Queen* (New York: New York University Press, 2004).

20. Martin Gilens, *Why Americans Hate Welfare: Race, Media, and the Politics of Antipoverty Policy* (Chicago: University of Chicago Press, 1999).

21. Gilens, *Why Americans Hate Welfare*, chap. 5.

22. Aristide Zolberg, *A Nation By Design* (Cambridge MA: Harvard University Press, 2006), p. 1.

23. Tom Smith, "Trends in National Spending Priorities, 1973-2008." (Chicago: National Opinion Research Center), p. 31. This report can be found online at http://news.uchicago.edu/images/pdf/090210.SPEND08.pdf.

24. For a good history of the Social Security system, see Sylvester J. Schieber and John B. Shoven, *The Real Deal: The History and Future of Social Security* (New Haven, CT: Yale University Press, 1999).

25. Andrea Louise Campbell explains how Social Security has energized one of America's most important interest groups in her *How Policies Make Citizens* (Princeton, NJ: Princeton University Press, 2002).

26. Martin Wattenberg, *Is Voting for Young People?* (New York: Pearson Longman, 2006), p. 4.

27. See http://tpmdc.talkingpointsmemo.com/2010/02/debt-commission-chairs-on-social-security-changes-everything-is-on-the-table-video.php.

28. Political scientist Benjamin Radcliff developed some empirical data to show that the extent of government welfare provisions is in fact positively related to people's sense of well-being from country to country. See his "Politics, Markets and Life Satisfaction: The Political Economy of Human Happiness," *American Political Science Review* 95 (December 2001): 939–52.

29. See Alberto Alesina and Edward L. Glaeser, *Fighting Poverty in the US and Europe: A World of Difference* (New York: Oxford, 2005), p. 4.

30. See Larry M. Bartels, *Unequal Democracy: The Political Economy of the New Gilded Age* (Princeton, NJ: Princeton University Press, 2008), chap. 9.

31. Anne Schneider and Helen Ingram, "The Social Construction of Target Populations," *American Political Science Review* 87 (1993): 334–47.

CHAPTER 19

1. Centers for Medicare and Medicaid Services, 2010.

2. *Budget of the United States Government, Fiscal Year 2011: Historical Tables* (Washington, DC: U.S. Government Printing Office, 2010), Table 3.1.

3. Quoted in Richard L. Berke, "Clinton Warns That Economy May Still Be Bad," *New York Times*, December 8, 1992, A13.

4. Council of Economic Advisers, *Annual Report 2006*, 88.

5. *NHE Fact Sheet*, Centers for Medicare and Medicaid Services, 2010.

6. Kaiser Family Foundation, Employer Health Benefits Survey 2009.

7. U.S. Census Bureau, Current Population Survey, 2009 Annual Social and Economic Supplement; U.S. Census Bureau, Current Population Survey, *Income, Poverty, and Health Insurance Coverage in the United Sates: 2008*, 2009.

8. U.S. Census Bureau, Current Population Survey, 2009, *Annual Social and Economic Supplement.*

9. *Income, Poverty, and Health Insurance Coverage in the United States: 2008*, 2009.

10. Institute of Medicine, America's Uninsured Crisis: Consequences for Health and Health Care. National Academies Press, February 2009.

11. Sara R. Collins, Jennifer L. Kriss, Michelle M. Doty, and Sheila D. Rustgi, *"Losing Ground: How the Loss of Adequate Health Insurance Is Burdening Working Families,"* Commonwealth Fund, August 2008.

12. Kaiser Family Foundation, The Uninsured: A Primer, Key Facts about Americans Without Health Insurance, Kaiser Family Foundation, 2008.

13. John Lancaster, "Surgeries, Side Trips for 'Medical Tourists,'" *Washington Post*, October 21, 2004, A1.

14. Kaiser Family Foundation, The Uninsured: A Primer, Key Facts About Americans Without Health Insurance. Kaiser Family Foundation, 2008.

15. Institute of Medicine, *Care Without Coverage: Too Little, Too Late (Washington, DC:* National Academy Press, 2002). [[should this be "(City, State: National Academy [or Academies"?] Press), 2002"?]

16. "Care Without Coverage," Institute of Medicine, May 2002, 6.

17. U.S. Department of Commerce, *Statistical Abstract of the United States, 2010* (Washington, DC: U.S. Government Printing Office, 2010), Tables 102 and 112.

18. Robert Blank, *Rationing Medicine* (New York: Columbia University Press, 1988).

19. Howard M. Leichter, "The Poor and Managed Care in the Oregon Experience," *Journal of Health Politics, Policy and Law* 24 (October 1999): 1172–84.

20. *Budget of the United States Government, Fiscal Year 2011: Historical Tables* (Washington, DC: U.S. Government Printing Office, 2010), Table 3.1.

21. Andrea Louise Campbell, "Self-Interest, Social Security, and the Distinctive Political Participation Patterns of Senior Citizens,"*American Political Science Review* 96 (September 2002): 565–74.

22. *Budget of the United States Government, Fiscal Year 2011: Historical Tables* (Washington, DC: U.S. Government Printing Office, 2010), Table 16.1; *Income, Poverty, and Health Insurance Coverage in the United Sates: 2008*, 2009.

23. The story of the Clinton health care plan is told in Theda Skocpol, *Boomerang: Health Care Reform and the Turn Against Government* (New York: Norton, 1996).

24. Polls of August 8-9, 1994, and August 15–16, 1994.

25. See George C. Edwards III, "Strategic Assessments in the Early Obama Administration (paper delivered at the 2009 Annual Meeting of the American Political Science Association, September 2009); George C. Edwards III, "Obama's Leadership of the Public" (paper delivered at the 2009 Annual Meeting of the Midwest Political Science Association, April 2009).

26. Louis Harris, *Washington Post*, January 15, 1982.

27. For a legislative and administrative discussion and evaluation of the NEPA, see Richard A. Loroff, *A National Policy for the Environment: NEPA and Its Aftermath* (Bloomington: Indiana University Press, 1976).

28. Samuel Hays, *Beauty, Health, Permanence* (New York: Cambridge University Press, 1987), 99.

29. Charles P. Alexander, "On the Defensive," *Time*, June 15, 1992, 35.

30. U.S. Fish and Wildlife Service, 2010.

31. On toxic waste and its politics, see Robert Nakamura and Thomas Church, *Taming Regulation* (Washington, DC: Brookings Institution, 2003).

32. On implementing the Superfund law, see Thomas W. Church and Robert T. Nakamura, *Cleaning Up the Mess: Implementation Strategies in Superfund* (Washington, DC: Brookings Institution, 1993).

33. Denis J. Brion, *Essential Industry and the NIMBY Phenomenon* (New York: Quorum Books, 1991); Charles Piller, *The Fail-Safe Society* (New York: Basic Books, 1991); Daniel Mazmanian and David Morell, "The 'NIMBY' Syndrome: Facility Siting and the Failure of Democratic Discourse," in Norman J. Vig and Michael E. Kraft, eds., *Environmental Policy in the 1990s* (Washington, DC: Congressional Quarterly Press, 1990), chap. 6.

34. A good source of information on climate change is the Environmental Protection Agency's Climate Change site at www.epa.gov/climatechange/index.html.

35. A classic study of oil is Daniel Yergin, *The Prize: The Epic Quest for Oil, Money and Power* (New York: Simon and Shuster, 1991).

36. U.S. Energy Information Administration, 2010.

37. Frank R. Baumgartner and Bryan D. Jones, *Agendas and Instability in American Politics* (Chicago: University of Chicago Press, 1993).

38. See John L. Campbell, *Collapse of an Industry: Nuclear Power and the Contradictions of U.S. Policy* (Ithaca, NY: Cornell University Press, 1988).

CHAPTER 20

1. See, for example, Paul Kennedy, *The Rise and Fall of the Great Powers* (New York: Random House, 1987).

2. Raymond Vernon, *In the Hurricane's Eye: The Troubled Prospects of Multinational Enterprises* (Cambridge, MA: Harvard University Press, 1998); United Nations, *World Investment Report, 2005* (New York: United Nations, 2005).

3. I. M. Destler, "National Security Management: What Presidents Have Wrought," *Political Science Quarterly* 95 (Winter 1980–1981): 573–88.

4. Richard Betts, *Soldiers, Statesmen, and Cold War Crises* (Cambridge, MA: Harvard University Press, 1977), 216, Table A.

5. See Bob Woodward, *Veil: The Secret Wars of the CIA, 1981–1987* (New York: Simon and Schuster, 1987).

6. A good study of the role of Congress in setting U.S. foreign policy is James M. Lindsay, *Congress and the Politics of U.S. Foreign Policy* (Baltimore: Johns Hopkins University Press, 1994). Congress's role in the defense budget process is discussed in Ralph G. Carter, "Budgeting for Defense," in *The President, Congress, and the Making of Foreign Policy*, ed. Paul E. Peterson (Norman: University of Oklahoma Press, 1994).

7. Louis Fisher, "Executive-Legislative Revelations in Foreign Policy" (paper presented at the United States–Mexico Comparative Constitutional Law Conference, Mexico City, June 17, 1998), 1.

8. An excellent treatment of the origins of the Cold War is Daniel Yergin, *Shattered Peace: The Origins of the Cold War and the National Security State* (Boston: Houghton Mifflin, 1977).

9. The article was titled "Sources of Soviet Conduct" and appeared in *Foreign Affairs* (July 1947) under the pseudonym *X*.

10. Stanley Karnow, *Vietnam: A History* (New York: Penguin Books, 1983), 43. Karnow's book is one of the best of many excellent books on Vietnam. See also Frances Fitzgerald, *Fire in the Lake* (Boston: Little, Brown, 1972), and David Halberstam, *The Best and the Brightest* (New York: Random House, 1972).

11. Nicholas Lemann, "The Peacetime War," *Atlantic Monthly*, October 1984, 72.

12. National Counterterrorism Center, 2010.

13. See, for example, Bruce Russett, "Defense Expenditures and National Well-Being," *American Political Science Review* 76 (December 1982): 767–77; William K. Domke, Richard C. Eichenberg, and Catherine M. Kelleher, "The Illusion of Choice: Defense and Welfare in Advanced Industrial Democracies, 1948–78," *American Political Science Review* 77 (March 1983): 19–35; and Alex Mintz, "Guns Versus Butter: A Disaggregated Analysis," *American Political Science Review* 83 (December 1989): 1285–96.

14. On the importance of ideology, see studies discussed in Robert A. Bernstein, *Elections, Representation, and Congressional Voting Behavior* (Englewood Cliffs, NJ: Prentice Hall, 1989), 70–76.

15. U.S. Department of Commerce, *Statistical Abstract of the United States, 2010* (Washington, DC: U.S. Government Printing Office, 2010), Table 497.

16. Stephen I. Schwartz, ed., *Atomic Audit: The Costs and Consequences of U.S. Nuclear Weapons Since 1940* (Washington, DC: Brookings Institution, 1998).

17. Stanley Hoffman, *Gulliver's Troubles, or the Setting of American Foreign Policy* (New York: McGraw-Hill, 1968).

18. Robert O. Keohane and Joseph S. Nye Jr., *Power and Independence*, 3rd ed. (New York: Longman, 2000).

19. Joseph S. Nye Jr., *The Paradox of American Power: Why the World's Only Superpower Can't Go It Alone* (New York: Oxford University Press, 2002).

20. Joseph S. Nye Jr., *Soft Power: The Means to Success in World Politics* (Cambridge, MA: Harvard University Press, 2004).

21. Robert M. Kimmit, "Public Footprints in Private Markets," *Foreign Affairs* 87 (January/February 2008): 126.

22. U.S. Census Bureau, Foreign Trade Division, 2010.

23. Ibid.

24. Carol C. Adelman, "The Privatization of Foreign Aid," *Foreign Affairs* 82 (November/ December 2003): 9–14.

25. See Bruce M. Russett, *Controlling the Sword* (Cambridge, MA: Harvard University Press, 1990), chap. 5; Thomas Hartley and Bruce M. Russett, "Public Opinion and the Common Defense: Who Governs Military Spending in the United States?" *American Political Science Review* 86 (December 1992): 905–15; Bruce M. Russett, *Grasping the Democratic Peace* (Princeton, NJ: Princeton University Press, 1993); Spencer R. Weart, *Never at War* (New Haven, CT: Yale University Press, 1998); Michael D. Ward and Kristian S. Gleditsch, "Democratizing Peace," *American Political Science Review* 92 (March 1998): 51–62; and Paul R. Hensel, Gary Foertz, and Paul F. Diehl, "The Democratic Peace and Rivalries," *Journal of Politics* 62 (November 2000): 1173–88.

CHAPTER 21

1. Laura K. Donohue and Juliette N. Kayyem, "Federalism and the Battle over Counterterrorist Law: State Sovereignty, Criminal Law Enforcement, and National Security," *Studies in Conflict and Terrorism* 25 (2002): 1–18.

2. Luther H. Gulick, "Reorganization of the State," *Civil Engineering* (August 1933): 420–21.

3. James N. Miller, "Hamstrung Legislatures," *National Civic Review* (May 1965): 178–87.

4. National Conference of State Legislatures, "2009 State Laws Related to Immigrants and Immigration," April 9, 2010. http://www.ncsl.org/default.aspx?tabid=19232.

5. Other states have laws that make companies ineligible for state or local govenerment contracts if they knowingly employ undocumented or illegal immigrants.

6. Ann O' M. Bowman and Richard C. Kearney, *The Resurgence of the States* (Englewood Cliffs, NJ: Prentice Hall, 1986). For other important statements of the improved capacity of state governments to undertake innovative action, see David Osborne, *Laboratories of Democracy* (Boston: Harvard Business School Press, 1988); David B. Walker, *The Rebirth of Federalism* (Chatham, NJ: Chatham House, 1995); and David M. Hedge, *Governance and the Changing American States* (Boulder, CO: Westview, 1998).

7. See Daniel J. Elazar, "The Principles and Traditions Underlying American State Constitutions," *Publius: The Journal of Federalism* 12 (Winter 1982): 11–25.

8. Mavis Mann Reeves, *The Question of State Government Capability* (Washington, DC: Advisory Commission on Intergovernmental Relations, 1985), 38.

9. Christopher W. Hammons, "Was James Madison Wrong? Rethinking the American Preference for Short,

Framework-Oriented Constitutions,"*American Political Science Review* 93 (December 1999): 837–50.

10. Initiative and Referendum Institute, *I & R Usage, 2000* (Washington, DC: Initiative and Referendum Institute, 2000).

11. Council of State Governments, *The Book of the States, 2003 Edition* (Washington, DC: Council of State Governments, 2004), 235.

12. Thomas M. Carsey, *Campaign Dynamics: The Race for Governor* (Ann Arbor: University of Michigan Press, 1999).

13. Council of State Governments, *The Book of the States, 2003 Edition*, 176.

14. Thomas M. Carsey and Gerald C. Wright, "State and National Factors in Gubernatorial and Senatorial Elections," *American Journal of Political Science* 42 (July 1998): 994–1002.

15. Data are from Thad Beyle and Margaret Ferguson, "Governors and the Executive Branch," in *Politics in the American States*, 9th ed., ed. Virginia Gray and Russell L. Hanson (Washington, DC: Congressional Quarterly Press, 2008), 198–99.

16. Carsey, *Campaign Dynamics*.

17. Note that not all lower chambers of state legislatures are called the "house of representatives," although most are; we refer to them as such in this chapter to avoid confusion. Council of State Governments, *The Book of the States, 2003 Edition*, 108.

18. Alan Rosenthal, *The Decline of Representative Democracy: Process, Participation, and Power in State Legislatures* (Washington, DC: Congressional Quarterly Press, 1998).

19. Sarah McCally Morehouse and Malcolm E. Jewell, *State Politics, Parties, and Policy*, 2nd ed. (Lanham, MD: Rowman & Littlefield, 2003), 197–201.

20. Rosenthal, *The Decline of Representative Democracy*, 179–80; Keith E. Hamm and Gary F. Moncrief, "Legislative Politics in the States," in *Politics in the American States*, 9th ed., ed. Virginia Gray and Russell L. Hanson (Washington, DC: Congressional Quarterly Press, 2008), 154–91; Institute on Money in State Politics, *State Elections Overview 2004* (Helena, MT: The Institute on Money in State Politics, 2005).

21. Morehouse and Jewell, *State Politics, Parties, and Policy*, 199–200.

22. National Conference of State Legislatures, "2008 Partisan Composition of State Legislatures," March 5, 2008, http://www.ncsl.org/statevote/partycomptable2008.htm.

23. National Conference of State Legislatures, 2010, "2008–09 (Post-election) Partisan Composition of State Legislatures," February 10, 2010, http://ecom.ncsl.org/programs/legismgt/statevote/partycomptable2009print.htm.

24. Keith E. Hamm and Gary F. Moncrief, "Legislative Politics in the States," 154–91.

25. Morris P. Fiorina, "Divided Government in the States," in *The Politics of Divided Government*, ed. Gary Cox and Samuel Kernell (Boulder, CO: Westview, 1991).

26. Thomas M. Holbrook and Raymond J. La Raja, "Parties and Elections," in *Politics in the American States*, 9th ed., ed. Virginia Gray and Russell L. Hanson (Washington, DC: Congressional Quarterly Press, 2008), 61–97.

27. Hamm and Moncrief, "Legislative Politics in the States," 154–91.

28. Hamm and Moncrief, "Legislative Politics in the States," 154–91.

29. Gary Moncrief, Richard G. Niemi, and Lynda W. Powell, "Time, Turnover and Term Limits: Trends in Membership Turnover in U.S. State Legislatures" (paper presented at the Annual State Politics and Policy Conference, Tucson, Arizona, March 2003).

30. National Conference of State Legislatures, "Legislative Term Limits: An Overview," June 9, 2004, www.ncsl.org/programs/legman/ABOUT/Termlimit.htm.

31. Alan Rosenthal, "The Legislature: Unraveling of Institutional Fabric," in *The State of the States*, 3rd ed., ed. Carl E. Van Horn (Washington, DC: Congressional Quarterly Press, 1996), 128.

32. Moncrief et al., "Time, Turnover and Term Limits," 17; National Conference of State Legislatures, "Members Termed Out: 1996–2008," April 9, 2010, http://www.ncsl.org/Default.aspx?TabId=14842.

33. Charles E. Menifield, ed., *Representation of Minority Groups in the U.S.: Implications for the Twenty-First Century* (Lanham, MD: Austin & Winfield, 2001).

34. Center for American Women and Politics, "Women in Elective Office," February 17, 2010, http://www.cawp.rutgers.edu/fast_facts/levels_of_office/documents/stleg.pdf.

35. National Conference of State Legislatures, "Legislator Demographics," August 11, 2010, http://www.ncsl.org/default.aspx?tabid=14850.

36. Nelson C. Dometrius, "Governors: Their Heritage and Future," in *American State and Local Politics: Directions for the 21st Century*, ed. Ronald E. Weber and Paul Brace (Chatham, NJ: Chatham House, 1999).

37. Thad Beyle and Margaret Ferguson, "Governors and the Executive Branch," in *Politics in the American States*, 9th ed., ed. Virginia Gray and Russell L. Hanson (Washington, DC: Congressional Quarterly Press, 2008), 192–228.

38. Beyle and Ferguson, "Governors and the Executive Branch," 192–228.

39. Dennis Farney, "When Wisconsin Governor Wields Partial Veto, the Legislature Might as Well Go Play Scrabble," *Wall Street Journal*, July 1, 1993.

40. Beyle and Ferguson, "Governors and the Executive Branch," 192–228.

41. Carsey, *Campaign Dynamics*, 1999.

42. Ann O' M. Bowman and Richard C. Kearney, *State and Local Government*, 4th ed. (Boston: Houghton-Mifflin, 1999), 203–4.

43. Associated Press, "Alabama Lt. Governor Finds Nothing to Do," *New York Times*, February 17, 1999.

44. Council of State Governments, *The Book of the States, 2003 Edition* (Washington, DC: Council of State Governments, 2004), 199–208.

45. Kenneth J. Meier, "Executive Reorganization of Government: Impact on Employment and Expenditures," *American Journal of Political Science* 24 (1980): 396–412.

46. Hedge, *Governance and the Changing American States*, 111.

47. Alan Rosenthal, "The Legislative Institution: Transformed and at Risk," in *The State of the States*, ed. Carl Van Horn (Washington, DC: Congressional Quarterly Press, 1989), 69.

48. Joel A. Thompson and Gary E. Moncrief, "The Evolution of the State Legislature: Institutional Change and Legislative Careers," in *Changing Patterns in State Legislative Careers*, ed. Gary E. Moncrief and Joel A. Thompson (Ann Arbor: University of Michigan Press, 1992).

49. Christopher Z. Mooney, "Measuring U.S. State Legislative Professionalism: An Evaluation of Five Indices," *State and Local Government Review* 26 (Spring 1994): 70–71.

50. National Conference of State Legislatures, "Size of State Legislative Staff: 1979, 1988, 1996, and 2003—Permanent Staff (November 2003)," July 7, 2004, www.ncsl.org/programs/ legman/about/staffcount2003.htm.

51. Alan Rosenthal, *The Decline of Representative Democracy*.

52. Peverill Squire, "Legislative Professionalization and Membership Diversity in State Legislatures, *Legislative Studies Quarterly* 17 (February 1992): 69–79.

53. Christopher Z. Mooney, "Citizens, Structures, and Sister States: Influences on State Legislative Professionalism," *Legislative Studies Quarterly* 20 (February 1995): 47–68.

54. Phillip W. Roeder, "State Legislative Reform: Determinants and Policy Consequences," *American Politics Quarterly* 7 (January 1979): 51–70; Morris P. Fiorina, "Further Evidence of the Partisan Consequences of Legislative Professionalism,"*American Journal of Political Science* 43 (July 1999): 974–77.

55. James King, "Changes in Professionalism in U.S. State Legislatures," *Legislative Studies Quarterly* 25 (2000): 327–43.

56. Robert C. LaFountain, Richard Y. Schauffler, Shauna M. Strickland, William E. Raftery, and Chantal G. Bromage, eds. *Examining the Work of State Courts: A National Perspective from the Court Statistics Project.* (Washington, DC: A joint project of the Conference of State Court Administrators, the Bureau of Justice Statistics, and the National Center for State Courts, 2006).

57. Paul Brace, Melinda Gann Hall, and Laura Langer, "Placing State Supreme Courts in State Politics," *State Politics and Policy Quarterly* 1 (Spring 2001): 81–108.

58. Delaware, Maine, Mississippi, Montana, Nevada, New Hampshire, North Dakota, Rhode Island, South Dakota, Vermont, West Virginia, and Wyoming.

59. Melinda Gann Hall, "State Supreme Courts in American Democracy: Probing the Myths of Judicial Reform," *American Political Science Review* 95 (June 2001): 315–30.

60. Ibid.

61. Initiative and Referendum Institute, *Initiative Use* (Washington, DC: Initiative and Referendum Institute, 2006), www.iandrinstitute.org/Usage.htm.

62. Elisabeth R. Gerber, "Legislative Response to the Threat of Popular Initiatives," *American Journal of Political Science* 40 (February 1996): 99–128.

63. Edward L. Lascher Jr., Michael G. Hagen, and Steven A. Rochlin, "Gun Behind the Door? Ballot Initiatives, State Policies, and Public Opinion," *Journal of Politics* 58 (August 1996): 760–75.

64. Brett Pulley, "The 1998 Campaign: Special Interests; Gambling Proponents Bet $85 Million on Election," *New York Times*, October 31, 1998.

65. Bowman and Kearney, *State and Local Government*, 125.

66. Thomas E. Cronin, *Direct Democracy* (Cambridge, MA: Harvard University Press, 1989), 143.

67. Thomas E. Cronin, *Direct Democracy* (Cambridge, MA: Harvard University Press, 1989), 143.

68. *City of Clinton v. Cedar Rapids and Missouri RR Co.*, 24 Iowa 475 (1868), as quoted in Richard P. Nathan, "The Role of the States in American Federalism," in *The State of the States*, 2nd ed., ed. Carl E. Van Horn (Washington, DC: Congressional Quarterly Press, 1993).

69. Don AuCoin and William F. Doherty, "House Votes to Pull Plug on Middlesex," *Boston Globe*, June 13, 1997, B12.

70. Anthony Nownes, Clive Thomas, and Ronald Hrebenar, "Interest Groups in the States," in Gray and Hanson, *Politics in the American States*, 98–126.

71. *The Municipal Year Book, 1996* (Washington, DC: International City/County Management Association, 1996).

72. David Brockington, Todd Donovan, Shaun Bowler, and Richard Brischetto, "Minority Representation Under Cumulative and Limited Voting," *Journal of Politics* 60 (November 1998): 1108–25.

73. Kenneth J. Meier, Robert D. Wrinkle, and J. L. Polinard, "Representative Bureaucracy and Distributional Equity: Addressing the Hard Question," *Journal of Politics* 61 (November 1999): 1025–39.

74. Kenneth K. Wong, "The Politics of Education," in Gray and Hanson, *Politics in the American States*, 365–71.

75. Thomas R. Dye, *American Federalism* (Lexington, MA: D. C. Heath, 1990).

76. Paul E. Peterson, *City Limits* (Chicago: University of Chicago Press, 1981).

77. Jeffrey Berry, Kent Portney, and Ken Thomson, *The Rebirth of Urban Democracy* (Washington, DC: Brookings Institution, 1993).

78. David Osborne and Ted Gaebler, *Reinventing Government: How the Entrepreneurial Spirit Is Transforming the Public Sector* (Reading, MA: Addison-Wesley, 1992).

Key Terms in Spanish/Palabras importantes en español

A

actual group—grupo actual

administrative discretion—discreción administrativa

affirmative action—acción afirmativa

Americans with Disabilities Act of 1990—disposición legal de 1990 para ciudadanos americanos minusválidos

***amicus curiae* briefs**—instrucciones, informes, de la competencia de amigos del senado.

Anti-Federalists—anti-federalistas

antitrust policy—política antimonopolio

appellate jurisdiction—jurisdicción apelatoria

appropriations bill—proyecto de ley de apropiación

arms race—carrera armamentista

Articles of Confederation—Artículos de la Confederación

authorization bill—estatuto de autorización

B

balance of trade—balance de intercambio comercial

beats—v. derrotar; recorrido de vigilancia policiaca

bicameral legislature—legislatura bi-camaral

bill—proyecto de ley; moción; cuenta

Bill of Rights—proyecto de ley de derechos

block grants—otorgamientos en conjunto

budget—presupuesto

budget resolution—resolución de presupuesto

bureaucracy—burocracia

C

cabinet—gabinete

campaign strategy—estrategia de campaña

capitalism—capitalismo

casework—trabajo de asistencia social

categorical grants—concesiones categorizadas

caucus—reunión del comité central o asamblea local de un partido

census—censo

Central Intelligence Agency (CIA)—Agencia Central de Inteligencia

chains (newspaper chains)—cadena (cadenas periodísticas)

checks and balances—cheques y balances

city manager—aministrador de la ciudad

civic duty—deber cívico

civil disobedience—desobediencia civil

civil liberties—libertades civiles

civil rights—derechos civiles

Civil Rights Act of 1964—ley de Derechos Humanos de 1964

civil rights movement—movimiento de derechos civiles

civil service—administración pública

class action lawsuits—demanda colectiva

Clean Air Act of 1970—ley contra la contaminación del aire de 1970

closed primaries—primarias cerradas

coalition—coalición

coalition government—coalición de gobierno

cold war—guerra fría

collective bargaining—negociación colectiva

collective good—bienestar colectivo

command-and-control policy—política de ordenamiento y control

commercial speech—discurso comercial

committee chairs—presidentes de comité

conference committees—comités de conferencias

Congressional Budget and Impoundment Control Act of 1974—Ley del Presupuesto e Incautación del Congreso de 1974

Congressional Budget Office (CBO)—Oficina de Presupuesto del Congreso

Connecticut Compromise—Compromiso de Connecticut

consent of the governed—consentimiento del gobernado

constitution—constitución

consumer price index (CPI)—índice de precios del consumidor

containment doctrine—doctrina o política de contención

continuing resolutions—resoluciones continuas

cooperative federalism—federalismo cooperativo

Council of Economic Advisers (CEA)—Consejo de Asesores Económicos

council of governments (COG)—consejo de gobiernos

courts of appeal—corte de apelación

crisis—crisis

critical election—elección crítica

cruel and unusual punishment—castigo cruel e inusual

D

Declaration of Independence—Declaración de Indepen-dencia

deficit—déficit

democracy—democracia

demography—demografía

deregulation—desregular, liberalizar

détente—relajación

Dillon's Rule—Regla de Dillon

direct democracy—democracia directa

direct mail—correo directo

district courts—juzgado de distrito

dual federalism—federalismo dual

E

Eighth Amendment—Octava Enmienda (constitucional)

elastic clause—cláusula flexible

electioneering—campaña electoral

Electoral College—colegio electoral

elitism—teoría de la élite

Endangered Species Act of 1973—Ley de Especies en Peligro de Extinción de 1973

entitlements—derechos

enumerated powers—poderes enumerados

environmental impact statement (EIS)—declaración de impacto sobre el ambiente

Environmental Protection Agency (EPA)—Agencia de Protección al Ambiente

equal protection of the laws—igualdad de protección de la ley

Equal Rights Amendment (ERA)—enmienda de Igualdad de Derechos
establishment clause—cláusula de instauración
European Union (EU)—Unión Europea
exclusionary rule—regla de exclusión
executive orders—órdenes ejecutivas
exit poll—conteo de salida de votación
expenditures—gastos
extradition—extradición

F

factions—facciones
federal debt—deuda federal
Federal Election Campaign Act—Ley de la Campaña Federal de Elección
Federal Election Commission (FEC)—Comisión Federal Electoral
Federal Reserve System—Sistema Federal de Reserva
federalism—federalismo
Federalist Papers—Documentos Federalistas
Federalists—federalistas
Fifteenth Amendment—Quinceava Enmienda
Fifth Amendment—Enmienda Quinta
filibuster—intervención parlamentaria con objeto de impedir una votación
First Amendment—Enmienda Primera
fiscal federalism—federalismo fiscal
fiscal policy—política fiscal
Food and Drug Administration (FDA)—Departamento Administrativo de Alimentos y Estupefacientes
foreign policy—política extranjera
formula grants—fórmula de concesión
Fourteenth Amendment—Catorceava Enmienda
free exercise clause—cláusula de ejercicio libre
free-rider problem—problema de polizón
frontloading—carga frontal
full faith and credit—fe y crédito completo

G

gender gap—disparidad de género
government—gobierno
government corporation—corporacion gubernamental
gross domestic product (GDP)—producto doméstico bruto
GS (General Schedule) rating—prorrateo programático general

H

Hatch Act—Ley Hatch
health maintenance organization (HMO)—Organización para el Manteniento de la Salud
high-tech politics—política sobre alta tecnología
home rule—regla de casa (local)
House Rules Committee—Comité de Reglas de la Cámara
House Ways and Means Committee—Comité de Formas y Medios de la Cámara
hyperpluralism—hiperpluralismo; pluralismo en exceso

I

impeachment—juicio de impugnación
implied powers—poderes implícitos
incentive system—sistema de incentivos
income—ingresos de enlace
incorporation doctrine—doctrina de incorporación
incrementalism—incrementalismo
incumbents—titular en función
independent executive agency—agencia ejecutiva independiente
independent regulatory commission—agencia regulatoria independiente
inflation—inflación
initiative—iniciativa
initiative petition—iniciativa de petición
interdependency—interdependencia
interest group—grupos de interés
intergovernmental relations—relaciones intergubernamentales
investigative journalism—periodismo de investigación
iron triangles—triángulos de acero
isolationism—aislacionismo

J

Joint Chiefs of Staff—Junta de Comandantes de las Fuerzas Armadas (Estado Mayor)
joint committees—comisiones
judicial activisim—activismo judicial
judicial implementation—implementación judicial
judicial restraint—restricción judicial
judicial review—revisión judicial
justiciable disputes—conflictos enjuiciables

K

Keynesian economic theory—teoría económica keynesiana

L

laissez-faire—liberalismo económico
legislative oversight—descuido legislativo
legislative veto—Veto legislativo
legitimacy—legitimidad
libel—difamación, calumnia
lieutenant governor—lugarteniente del gobernador
limited government—gobierno limitado
line-item veto—artículo de veto
linkage institutions—instituciones de enlace
lobbying—cabildeo
local charter—estatutos locales; fuero local

M

majority leader—líder de la mayoría
majority rule—gobierno de la mayoría
mandate theory of elections—mandato teórico de elecciones
mass media—medios de difusión (comunicación) masiva
McGovern-Fraser Commission—Comisión *McGovern-Fraser*
media event—evento de los medios de difusión (comunicación)
Medicaid—programa de asistencia médica estatal *Medicaid* para personas de bajos ingresos
Medicare—programa de asistencia médica estatal *Medicare* para personas mayores de 65 años
melting pot—crisol
Merit Plan—plan meritorio (por méritos)
merit principle—principio de mérito
minority leader—líder de la minoría parlamentaria
minority majority—majoria de la minoría
minority rights—derechos de las minorías
mixed economy—economía mixta
monetarism—monetarismo
monetary policy—política monetaria
Motor Voter Act—Ley para promoción del voto
multinational corporations—corporaciones multinacionales

N

narrowcasting—transmisión cerrada; monitoreo cerrado

national chairperson—director/a de comité nacional

national committee—comité nacional

national convention—convención nacional

National Environmental Policy Act (NEPA)—Ley de la Política Ambiental Nacional

national health insurance—seguro de salud nacional

National Labor Relations Act—Ley Nacional de Relaciones Laborales

national party convention—convención nacional del partido

national primary—primaria nacional

National Security Council (NSC)—Consejo Nacional de Seguridad

natural rights—derechos naturales

New Deal coalition—coalición para el Nuevo Tratado

New Jersey Plan—Plan de New Jersey

Nineteenth Amendment—Enmienda Diecinueve

nomination—nominación

North Atlantic Treaty Organization (NATO)—Tratado de las Organizaciones del Atlantico Norte

O

Office of Management and Budget (OMB)—Oficina de Gestión y Presupuesto

Office of Personnel Management (OPM)—Oficina de Gestión de Personal

open primaries—primarias abiertas

opinion—opinión

Organization of Petroleum Exporting Countries (OPEC)—Organización de Países Exportadores de Petróleo

original intent—intento original

original jurisdiction—jurisdicción original

P

party competition—competencia de partido

party dealignment—desalineamiento del partido

party eras—épocas del partido

party identification—identificación partidista

party image—imágen del partido

party machines—maquinaria partidista

party platform—plataforma del partido

party realignment—realinación del partido

patronage—patrocinio

Pendleton Civil Service Act—Ley del Servicio Público de Pendleton

plea bargaining—negociación fiscal-defensa

pluralism—teoría pluralista

pocket veto—veto indirecto del presidente al no firmar dentro de los diez días establecidos

policy agenda—agenda política

policy entrepreneurs—política empresarial

policy gridlock—parálisis política

policy implementation—implementación política

policy voting—política de votación

policymaking institutions—instituciones de normatividad política

policymaking system—sistema de normatividad política

political action committees (PACs)—comités de acción política

political culture—cultura política

political efficacy—eficacia política

political ideology—ideología política

political issue—asunto político

political participation—participación política

political party—partido político

political questions—cuestiones políticas

political socialization—socialización política

politics—política

poll taxes—votación para impuestos

pork barrel—asignación de impuestos estatales para el beneficio de una cierta zona o grupo

potential group—grupo potencial

poverty line—límite económico mínimo para sobrevivencia

precedent—precedente

presidential coattails—acción a la sombra presidencial

presidential primaries—elecciones primarias presidenciales

press conferences—conferencias de prensa

print media—medios de comunicación impresos

prior restraint—restricción anterior

privileges and immunities—privilegios e inmunidades

probable cause—causa probable

progressive tax—impuesto progresivo

project grant—proyecto de concecsión

proportional representation—representación proporcional

proportional tax—impuesto proporcional

protest—n. protesta; v. protestar

public goods—bienes públicos

public interest lobbies—cabildeo por intereses públicos

public opinion—opinión pública

public policy—política pública

R

random-digit dialing—llamadas con números aleatorios

random sampling—muestreo aleatorio

rational-choice theory—teoría de selección racional

reapportionment—nueva distribución en la representación del congreso

recall—retirar

reconciliation—reconciliación

referendum—referendum

regional primaries—elecciones primarias regionales

regressive tax—impuesto regresivo

regulation—norma, regla

relative deprivation—privación relativa

representation—representación

republic—república

responsible party model—modelo de partido responsable

retrospective voting—votación retrospectiva

revenues—ingresos

right to privacy—derecho a la privacidad

right-to-work laws—leyes del derecho al trabajo

S

sample—muestra

sampling error—error de muestreo

search warrant—orden de cateo

secretary of defense—secretario de la defensa

secretary of state—secretario de estado

select committees—comités seleccionados

selective benefits—beneficios selectivos

selective perception—percepción selectiva

self-incrimination—auto incriminación

Senate Finance Committee—Comité Senatorial de Finanzas
senatorial courtesy—cortesía senatorial
Senior Executive Service (SES)—el de más alto rango en el servicio del ejecutivo
seniority system—sistema de antigüedad
separation of powers—separación de poderes
Shays' Rebellion—Rebelion de Shays
single-issue groups—grupos para una sola causa
Sixteenth Amendment—Enmienda Dieciséis
Sixth Amendment—Enmienda Sexta
Social Security Act—Ley de Seguridad Social
social welfare policies—políticas para el bien social
soft money—moneda débil, sin garantía
solicitor general—subsecretario de justicia
sound bites—segmentos de sonido
Speaker of the House—presidente de la cámara
standard operating procedures (SOPs)—procedimientos normales de operación
standing committees—comités permanentes
standing to sue—en posición de entablar demanda
stare decisis—variación de "decisión firme" o "decisión tomada"; la decisión se fundamenta en algo ya decidio.
statutory construction—construcción establecida por ley
Strategic Defense Initiative (SDI)—Iniciativa de Defensa Estratégica
street-level bureaucrats—burócratas de bajo nivel
subnational government—gobierno subnacional
suffrage—sufragio
superdelegates—superdelegados
Superfund—superfondo; fondo de proporciones mayores
supply-side economics—economía de la oferta
supremacy clause—cláusula de supremacía
Supreme Court—Suprema Corte
symbolic speech—discurso simbólico

T

talking head—busto parlante; presentador, entrevistador
tariff—tarifa
tax expenditures—gastos de impuesto
Tenth Amendment—Enmienda Décima
third parties—terceras personas
Thirteenth Amendment—Enmienda Treceava
ticket splitting—votación de candidatos de diferentes partidos para diferentes cargos
town meeting—consejo municipal de vecinos
transfer payments—transferencia de pagos
trial balloons—globo de prueba; proponer algo para conocer la reacción de alguien
Twenty-fifth Amendment—Enmienda veiticincoava
Twenty-fourth Amendment—Enmienda veiticuatrava
Twenty-second Amendment—Enmienda veintidoava

U

U.S. Constitution—Constitución de los Estados Unidos
uncontrollable expenditures—gastos incontrolables
unemployment rate—nivel de desempleo; porcentage de desempleo
union shop—empresa que emplea sólo trabajadores sindicalizados
unitary governments—estados/gobiernos unitarios
United Nations (UN)—Naciones Unidas
unreasonable searches and seizures—cateos y detenciones/embargos irrazonables
urban underclass—urbanita de clase baja

V

veto—veto
Virginia Plan—Plan Virginia
voter registration—registro de votantes
Voting Rights Act of 1965—Ley de Derechos del Elector de 1965

W

War Powers Resolution—Resolución de Poderes de Guerra
Water Pollution Control Act of 1972—Ley para el Control de la Contaminación de Aguas de 1972
wealth—riqueza
whips—miembro de un cuerpo legislativo encargado de hacer observar las consignas del partido
white primary—primaria blanca/ sin novedad
winner-take-all system—sistema en el que el ganador toma todos los votos
writ of habeas corpus—un recurso de hábeas corpus

Answer Key

CHAPTER 1

1. E 2. True 4. True 6. D 8. E
9. False

CHAPTER 2

1. C 4. E 5. False 7. C 8. True
10. C 11. E 12. A 13. A 14. False
16. A 17. False 19. D 20. True 22. True

CHAPTER 3

1. A 2. False 4. B 5. True 6. True
7. C 8. True 10. E

CHAPTER 4

1. C 2. A 4. C 5. B 7. C 8. E
9. True 12. False 14. E 16. C
17. False 20. C

CHAPTER 5

1. True 2. E 4. True 5. B 7. False 9. D
10. False 12. A 13. True 15. D

CHAPTER 6

1. D 2. A 4. False 5. False 7. A
8. False 9. False 11. True 12. True
15. D 16. False

CHAPTER 7

1. D 2. True 4. D 5. False 6. False
9. A 10. True 13. A 15. True 17. E

CHAPTER 8

1. C 2. True 5. False 7. B 8. False
11. True 13. B 16. D 17. False 20. D
21. False

CHAPTER 9

1. D 2. False 3. True 6. E 7. False
9. A 10. True 13. C

CHAPTER 10

1. D 2. True 4. E 5. False 7. B
8. True 9. False 11. D 12. True 14. False

CHAPTER 11

1. True 3. E 4. False 7. C 8. True
11. C 12. False 15. E 16. False

CHAPTER 12

1. C 2. False 4. B 5. A 6. True
8. D 9. C 10. False 13. B 14. True

CHAPTER 13

1. C 2. True 4. C 5. False 7. D
8. False 11. B 12. False 15. E
16. False 18. A 19. False 21. C
22. True

CHAPTER 14

1. B 2. False 3. False 5. B 6. False
8. E 9. True

CHAPTER 15

1. E 2. False 5. B 6. False 8. D
9. True 11. C 12. False 15. D

CHAPTER 16

1. C 2. A 3. True 5. E 6. C
7. True 9. B 11. B 12. True 14. D
15. True 16. True 19. E 20. False

CHAPTER 17

1. B 2. True 4. E 5. True 7. False 9. False
12. True 13. False

CHAPTER 18

1. B 3. A 4. True 7. C 8. False
10. True 12. True

CHAPTER 19

1. D 2. True 5. B 6. True 9. False

CHAPTER 20

1. C 2. B 3. True 5. E 6. False
8. False 10. False 13. A 14. True
15. False

CHAPTER 21

1. E 2. False 4. E 5. False 8. D
9. True 11. A 13. E 14. True 15. True
17. False 18. C 21. D 22. False

Acknowledgments

TEXT ACKNOWLEDGMENTS

Chapter 1: U.S. Census Bureau Current Population Surveys. Data can be found at http://www.census.gov/hhes/www/socdemo/voting/publications/historical/index.html. **Chapter 3:** Office of Management and Budget, Budget of the United States Government, Fiscal Year 2011: Historical Tables (Washington, DC: U.S. Government Printing Office, 2010), Table 12.1. Office of Management and Budget, Budget of the United States Government, Fiscal Year 2011: Historical Tables (Washington, DC: U.S. Government Printing Office, 2010), Table 12.2. Office of Management and Budget, Budget of the United States Government, Fiscal Year 2011: Historical Tables (Washington, DC: U.S. Government Printing Office, 2010), Table 15.3. **Chapter 4:** Gallup Poll, July 17-19, 2009. Used with permission. **Chapter 5:** U.S. Census Bureau, News Release, May 14, 2009. U.S. Department of Labor, Bureau of Labor Statistics, Women in the Labor Force: A Databook (2008 edition), Table 16. **Chapter 6:** Excerpt from "Most Don't Know What 'Public Option' Is," August 27, 2009, http://www.fivethirtyeight.com/2009/08/poll-most-dont-know-what-public-option.html. Used with permission. US Census Bureau, http://www.census.gov/population/www/projections/files/nation/summary/np2008-t4.xls. **Chapter 7:** AMERICAN JOURNALIST IN THE 21ST CENTURY: U.S. NEWS PEOPLE AT THE DAWN OF A NEW MILLENNIUM by David H. Weaver et al.. Copyright 2007 by TAYLOR & FRANCIS GROUP LLC-BOOKS. Reproduced with permission of TAYLOR & FRANCIS GROUP LLC-BOOKS in the format Textbook via Copyright Clearance Center. AMERICAN JOURNALIST IN THE 21ST CENTURY: U.S. NEWS PEOPLE AT THE DAWN OF A NEW MILLENNIUM by David H. Weaver et al. Copyright 2007 by TAYLOR & FRANCIS GROUP LLC-BOOKS. Reproduced with permission of TAYLOR & FRANCIS GROUP LLC-BOOKS in the format Other book via Copyright Clearance Center. "How Network News Broadcasts Are Going the Way of the Dinosaurs." State of the News Media, 2007 and 2009, http://www.stateofthemedia.org/2009/index.htm. Ratings are for November of each year. Used with permission. **Chapter 8:** Courtesy of Pew Research Center. **Chapter 9:** The Pew Research Center's Project for Excellence in Journalism; "Winning the Media Campaign: How the Press Reported the 2008 Presidential General Election," Oct 22, 2008, http://www.journalism.org/sites/journalism.org/files/WINNING%20THE%20MEDIA%20CAMPAIGN%20FINAL.pdf. Federal Election Commission. Copyright Center for Responsive Politics, www.opensecrets.org. **Chapter 11:** Quote from Americans Against Food Taxes ad used with permission. "The Power 25" from FORTUNE, © May 28, 2001 Time Inc. All rights reserved. Used by permission and protected by the Copyright Laws of the United States. The printing, copying, redistribution, or retransmission of the Material without express written permission is prohibited. "The Power 25" from FORTUNE, © May 28, 2001 Time Inc. All rights reserved. Used by permission and protected by the Copyright Laws of the United States. The printing, copying, redistribution, or retransmission of the Material without express written permission is prohibited. Statistical Abstract of the United States, 2010, table 650, http://www.census.gov/compendia/statab/2010/tables/10s0650.pdf. Federal Election Commission. **Chapter 12:** David Samuels and Richard Snyder, "The Value of a Vote: Malapportionment in Comparative Perspective," British Journal of Political Science, v. 31, n. 4, October 2001, p. 662. Copyright © 2001 Cambridge University Press. Reprinted with the permission of Cambridge University Press. David Samuels and Richard Snyder, "The Value of a Vote: Malapportionment in Comparative Perspective," British Journal of Political Science, v. 31, n. 4, October 2001, p. 662. Copyright © 2001 Cambridge University Press. Reprinted with the permission of Cambridge University Press. "Incumbency Factor in Congressional Elections" adapted from Harold W. Stanley and Richard G. Neimi, Vital Statistics on American Politics, 2007-2008, CQ Press, 2008. Used with permission. "Incumbency Factor in Congressional Elections" adapted from VITAL STATISTICS ON CONGRESS by Norman J. Ornstein, Thomas E. Mann, and Michael J. Malbin. Copyright 1998 by AMERICAN ENTERPRISE INST FOR PUBLIC POLICY RES. Reproduced with permission of AMERICAN ENTERPRISE INST FOR PUBLIC POLICY RES in the format Other book via Copyright Clearance Center. **Chapter 13:** White House (www.whitehouse.gov/administration/eop). White House (www.whitehouse.gov/administration/eop). **Chapter 14:** Budget of the United States Government, Fiscal Year 2011: Historical Tables (Washington, DC: U.S. Government Printing Office, 2010), Table 2.1. Budget of the United States Government, Fiscal Year 2011: Historical Tables (Washington, DC: U.S. Government Printing Office, 2010), Table 7.1. Budget of the United States Government, Fiscal Year 2011: Historical Tables (Washington, DC: U.S. Government Printing Office, 2010), Tables 16.1 and 16.3. Budget of the United States Government, Fiscal Year 2011: Historical Tables (Washington, DC: U.S. Government Printing Office, 2010), Table 6.1. Budget of the United States Government, Fiscal Year 2011: Historical Tables (Washington, DC: U.S. Government Printing Office, 2010), Table 3.1. Budget of the United States Government, Fiscal Year 2011: Historical Tables (Washington, DC: U.S. Government Printing Office, 2010), Table 1.1. **Chapter 15:** U.S. Department of Commerce, Statistical Abstract of the United States, 2010 (Washington, DC: U.S. Government Printing Office, 2010), Table 486. Budget of the United States Government, Fiscal Year 2011: Analytical Perspectives (Washington, DC: U.S. Government Printing Office, 2010), Tables 23-1 and 23-2. United States Office of Personnel Management, Profile of Federal Civilian Non-Postal Employees, September 30, 2008. Federal Register. Office of the Federal Register, United States Government Manual 2009-2010 (Washington, DC: U.S. Government Printing Office, 2010), 21. Office of the Federal Register, United States Government Manual 2009–2010 (Washington, DC: U.S. Government Printing Office, 2010), 240. **Chapter 16:** JUDICIAL PROCESS 7E by Abraham (1998) Table 9 p. 309. By permission of Oxford University Press, Inc. Updated by the authors. **Chapter 17:** Bureau of Labor Statistics. U.S. Census Bureau, Foreign Trade Division. **Chapter 18:** U.S. Census Bureau. The 2008 data can be found in the Census Bureau's report entitled "Income, Poverty, and Health Insurance Coverage in the United States: 2008," p. 10. This report is posted online at: http://www.census.gov/prod/2009pubs/p60-236.pdf. U.S. Census Bureau, "Income, Poverty, and Health Insurance Coverage in the United States: 2008," p. 14. "Indicators of Welfare Dependence." U.S. Department of Health and Human Services. Annual Report to Congress, 2008; updated by authors based on caseload data reported by the U.S. Department of Health and Human Services' Administration for Children and Families. Rebecca Ray et al., "Parental Leave Policies: Assessing Generosity and Gender Equality," Report of the Center for Economic and Policy Research, p. 6. © June 2009. Used with permission. Updated by the authors for Australia, which implemented their first paid family leave in 2011. **Chapter 19:** World Health Organization, 2009. Centers for Medicare and Medicaid Services, 2010. Annie E. Casey Foundation, Kids Count, 2010. Used with permission. Energy Information Administration, 2010. **Chapter 20:** Office of Management and Budget, Budget of the United States Government, Fiscal Year 2011: Historical Tables (Washington, DC: U.S. Government Printing Office, 2010), Table 3.1. Office of Management and Budget, Budget of the United States Government, Fiscal Year 2011: Appendix (Washington, DC: U.S. Government Printing Office, 2010), 239. CQ Weekly, May 23, 1998. Updated by the authors. Copyright 1998 by CONGRESSIONAL QUARTERLY INC. Reproduced with permission of CONGRESSIONAL QUARTERLY INC in the format Textbook via Copyright Clearance Center. CQ Weekly, May 23, 1998. Updated by the authors. Copyright 1998 by CONGRESSIONAL QUARTERLY INC. Reproduced with permission of CONGRESSIONAL QUARTERLY INC in the format Other book via Copyright Clearance Center. U.S. Department of Commerce, Bureau of Economic Analysis, 2010. **Chapter 21:** U.S. Bureau of the Census, "Local Governments and Public School Systems by Type and State: 2007," March 7, 2008, http://www.census.gov/govs/www/cog2007.html. U.S. Bureau of the Census, "State and Local Government Finances, 2006," February 17, 2010, http://www.census.gov/compendia/statab/cats/state_local_govt_finances_employment/state_government_finances.html. Comparative Lottery Anaylsis: The Impact of Casinos on Lottery Revenues and Total Gaming Revenues, 2004, www.umassd.edu/cfpa/docs/casinolottery.pdf. Used with permission of the Center for Policy Analysis. U.S. Bureau of the Census, "State and Local Government Finances, 2006.

PHOTO ACKNOWLEDGMENTS

Chapter 1 page 2: Chuck Kennedy/Getty; 3T: AP Photo; 3TC: Getty Images; 3TB: Jewel Samad/Getty Images; 3B: Joseph Sohm/Corbis; 5: Colorblend Images/Getty Images; 7: AFP/Getty Images; 8: AP Photo; 9: AP Photo; 10: AFP Getty Images; 12 AFP Getty Images; 14: Chris Wildt/www.cartoonstock.com; 16: Alex Wong/Getty Images; 18: Joseph Sohm/Corbis; 20: Robert Trippett/Sipa; 21: David Horsey; 23: Jewel Sammad/Getty Imags **Chapter 2** page 28: Jeff Fusco//Getty Images; 29T: US Capitol Historical Society; 29TC: New York Public Library Picture Collection; 29TB: Hulton Picture Archive/Getty Images; 29B: Luke Frazza/Getty Images; 31: Joe Griffiths/Hulton Archive/Getty Images; 32: US Capitol Historical Society; 34L: Brown Brothers; 34R National Archives and Records Administration; 37: Scribner's Popular History of the United States, 1987; 38: Yale University Library, Sterling Memorial Library; 39: New York Public Library, Astor Lenox and Tilden Foundation; 41T: DOONSBURY c GR Trudeau. Reprinted with permission of the Universal Press Syndicate. All Rights Reserved; 42B: New York Public Library Picture Collection; 47 National Geographic Photographer George Mobley/US Capitol Historical Society; 52 Hulton Archive/Getty Images; 55: By permission of Mike Lukovich and Creators Syndicate; 58: Luke Frazza/Getty Images **Chapter 3** page 64: AP Photo; 65T: Joe Raedle/ Getty Images; 65TC: Hulton Archive/Getty Images; 65TB: AP Photo; 65B: Michael Newman/PhotoEdit; 68: Joe Raedle/Getty Images; 73: Hulton Archive/Getty Images; 74: AP Photo; 75 AP Photo; 79: Michael Newman/PhotoEdit; 81: Herb Block Foundation; 82: Ron Sachs/Pool/Getty Images; 87 Tom Cheney/The New Yorker Cartoon Bank. www.cartonbank.com **Chapter 4** page 92: Stefan Zakin/Corbis; 93T: Annie Griffiths Bell/Corbis; 93TC: AP Photo; 93TB: Michael Newman/PhotoEdit; 93B Mobile Press Register/Corbis; 94: AP Photo; 99: Annie Griffiths Bell/Corbis; 101: AP Photo; 104: AP Photo; 105 AP Photo; 107: By permission of John L. Hart FLP and Creators Syndicate Inc. ; 108: Pool/Pool/Getty Images; 110: Getty Images; 111: Jean Yves Rabeuf/The Image Works; 112: Robert Mankoff/ The New Yorker Cartoon Bank. www.cartoonbank.com; 117: Michael Newman/PhotoEdit117B: By permission of John L. Hart FLP and Creators syndicate; 120: AP Photo; 124: Mobile Press Register/Corbis **Chapter 5** page 132: Francis Miller/Time and Life Pictures/Getty Images; 133T: AP Photo; 133TC: Corbis; 133TB: Steve Rubin/The Image Works; 133B AP Photo; 135: AP Photo; 137: Bettmann/Corbis; 142 AP Photo; 145: Reuters/Corbis; 146 Corbis; 149: AP Photo; 150 Mark Wilson/Getty Images; 152: Tribune Media Services, Inc. All Rights Reserved. Reprinted with permission; 154: Steve Rubin/The Image Works; 155: Tribune Media Services, Inc. All Rights Reserved; 156 AP Photo; 158 Tom Cheney/The New Yorker Cartoon Bank. www.cartoonbank.com; **Chapter 6** page 166: AP Photo; 167TR: Bob Daemmrich/The Image Works; 167TC: Sven Hagolan; 167TB: Getty; 167B: AP Photo; 168: Jack Smith/Getty Images; 170: Bob Daemmrich/the Image Works; 172 Virginie Mortet/Getty Images; 177:Sven Hagolan; 180: www.cartoonstock.com; 188: Getty Images; 189 AP Photo; 189T AP Photo; 189B John Filo /Getty **Chapter 7** page 196R: Diana Walker/Getty Images; 196L: Chip Somodevilla/Getty Images; 197T: AP Photo; 197TC: Alex Wong/Getty Images; 197TB: AP Photo; 197B: Reuters/Corbis; 198 AP Photo; 201 Alex Wong/Getty; 205 AP Photo; 209: Used with permission of Matt Wuerker and The Cartoonist Group. All Rights reserved; 210: Robyn Beck/Getty Images; 213: AP Photo; 215: Reuters/Corbis; 220 A. Bacall/www.cartoonstock.com **Chapter 8** page 224: AP Photo 225T: Matt Brewer Hamilton; 224TC: Bettmann/Corbis; 224TB: TOLES c 2000 Washington Post. Reprinted with permission of Universal Press Syndicate; 224B: Neo Images/PhotoEdit; 228: Matt Brewer Hamilton; 232 Jean Claude Lejeune; 230 Bettmaann/Corbis; 234 TOLES c 2000 Washington Post. Reprinted with permission of Universal Press Syndicate; 239 The Granger Collection; 243: Neo Images/PhotoEdit; 247: Robert Mankoff/The New Yorker Cartoon/www.cartoonbank.com **Chapter 9** page 252: Bruce Ely/The Oregonian; 203T: AP Photo; 203TC: Sean Tevis; 203TB: Ken Cordier/Reuters/ HO/Landov; 203B: AP Photo; 255: AP Photo; 257: Jim Ruyman/Landov; 258:AP Photo; 257: John Cole; 263: Howell/Getty Images; 264: Sean Tevis; 270: Reuters/HO/Landov; 272: AP Photo; 275: Used with permission of Matt Wurker and the Cartoonist Group. All Rights Reserved. **Chapter 10** page 280: Robert King/Zuma Press; 281T: AP Photo; 281TC: Library of Congress; 281TB: Joshua Loft/New York Times; 281B: AP Photo; 282 AP Photo; 284: Library of Congress; 287: Joshua Loft/The New York Times; 288 Dennis Renault/Renault; 290: Tim Sloan/Getty Images; 296: The New Yorker Collection 2002 Mike Twohy from Cartoonbank. www.cartoonbank.com; 297: AP Photo; 299: Getty Images. **Chapter 11** page 304: Getty; 305T: AP Photo, 305TC: Jeffrey Markowitz/Corbis; 305TB: Getty Images; 305B: AP Photo; 309: Jim Bourgman. Reprinted with special permission of King Feature Syndicate; 317: AP Photo; 318: Tribune Media Services. All Rights reserved. Reprinted with permission; 320: Jeffrey Markowitz/Corbis; 322:Getty Images; 324: Getty Images; 325: AP Photo; 326 Carlo Aligen/Getty **Chapter 12** page 332: Jewel Sanad/Getty; 333T: Gunther/Sipa Press; 333TB Lifetime TV; 333B Getty Images; 335 Gunther/Sipa Press; 336: Lifetime TV; 344: David Horsey; 345L: AP Photo; 345C: Brendan Hoffman/Getty; 345R: Alex Wong/Getty Images; 349: Jack Ziegler/The New Yorker collection/www.cartoonbank.com; 350: Getty Images; 358: J.B. Handlesman/The New Yorker Cartoon/www.cartoonbank.com **Chapter 13** page 364: Timn Sloan/Pool/Corbis; 365TC: Alex Webb/Magnum Photos; 365TC: Getty Images; TB: AP Photo; 365B: Corbis; 367 Auth c 2002 the Philadelphia Inquirer. Reprinted with permission of Universal Press Syndicate; 368-369 a: Courtesy of the Eisenhower Library; b: AP Photos; c: AP Photos; d: AP Photos; e: AP Photos; f: AP Photos; g: AP Photos; h: AP Photos; i: AP Photos; k: Getty Images; 370 Alex Webb/Magnum Photos; 376 Jim Young Reuters/Corbis; 379: Henry Martin/the New Yorker Collection/ www.cartoonbank.com; 380: Paul J. Richards/Getty; 383: AP Photos; 387T: Stephen Jaffe; 387B Pool/Reuters/Corbis; 388 Corbis; 389: Bettmann/Corbis; 391: AP Photo; 392: AP Photo; 396 Mark Feinstein/ The Image Works; 397 AP Photos **Chapter 14** page 404: AP Photo; 405T: Phillip Wallack/Corbis; 405TC: AP Photos; 405TB: Robert Matson; 405B: Ted Korondy/Corbis; 410 Mike Keefe/The Denver Post; 416: AP Photos; 417: AP Photos; 419: Robert Matson; 420: AP Photos; 426: Ted Korondy/Corbis; 427 Dana Fradon /The New Yorker Cartoon/ www.cartonobank.com **Chapter 15** page 434: AP Photos; 443T: Jim West/The Image Works; 433TC: Chuck Nacke/Woodfin Camp; 433TB: Brian Pohorylo/Corbis; 433B: Jack Kurtz/The Image Works; 440: "Lot #1; 444: Jim west/the Image Works; 443: Chuck Nacke/Woodfin Camp; 444: Brian Pohoryllo/Corbis; 454: Joe Heller; 449: Jack Kurtz/The Image Works; 451: Bettmann/Corbis; 448: Frank Cotham/The New Yorker Collection/www.cartoonbank.com **Chapter 16** page 466: Joe Sohm/The Image Works; 467T: Carol Iwasaki/Getty Images; 466TC: Reuters/New Media/Corbis; 467TB: AP Photo; 467B: David Hume Kennerly/Getty Images; 470: Iwasaki/Getty Images; 478: Reuters/New Media/Corbis; 480: White House handout/Corbis; 481: AP Photos; 484: David Hume Kennerly/Getty Images;485: Joseph Mirachi/The New Yorker Collection/ www.cartoonbank.com; 486: Bettmann/Corbis; 490: Supreme Court Historical; 493T:Alex Wong/Getty Images; 493B: Paul Conklin/ PhotoEdit; 494 By permission of Chuck Assay Creators Syndicate **Chapter 17** page 502: Chip Somodevilla/Getty Images; 503T: Scott Olsen/Getty Images; 503TC: Getty Images; 503TB: AP Photos; 503 B: Lewis Hines/George Eastman House/Getty Images; 505: Scott Olsen/Getty Images; 510: Getty Images; 511: Jonathan Ernst/Corbis; 512: Paul Singer; 516: Paul Sancya/AP Photos; 519: Lewis Hines/George Eastman House/Getty Images;. **Chapter 18** page 524: AP Photos; 525T: Getty Images; 525TC:Mario Thoma/Getty Images; 525TB:Carmel Zucka/Getty Images; 525B: Alex Wong/Getty Images; 526: Getty Images; 529T: Mario Thoma/Getty Images; 529B: Varley Charlie/Sipa; 531: Andy Singer; 534: Carmel Zucka/The New York Times/Redux; 538: Alex Wong/Getty Images **Chapter 19** page 546: AP Photos; 547T: AP Photos; 547TC: Corbis Images; 547TB: Getty Images; 547B: AP Photos; 554: Corbis Images; 556: AP Photos; 558 Corbis Images; 559: Getty Images; 563 Getty Images; 566: Chris Britt and Creators Syndicate; 567: AP Photos **Chapter 20** page 572: Robert Clark/Aurora Photos; 573T: Stan Honda/Getty Images; 573 TC: Bettmann/Corbis: 573 TB: Matthew McDermott/Corbis; 573B: Bettmann/Corbis; 575: Stan Honda/Getty Images; 577 Robert Arial; 578: Corbis Images; 580: Corbis Images; 582T: AP Photos; 582B: Bettmann/Corbis; 585: AP Photos; 586L: Matthew McDermott/Corbis; 586C: AP Photos; 586R: AFP Getty Images; 591: Bettmann/Corbis; 597 Getty Images; **Chapter 21** page 608: AP Photos; 609T: Steven Starr/Stock Boston; 609TC: AP Photos; 609TB: Tim Pawlenty/Landov; 610 Steven Starr/Stock Boston; 613: AP Photo; 616: Jeff Parker; 620: AP Photos; 622: Tim Pawlenty/ Landov; 623: Corbis Images; 630: D. Youngblood/Southern Voice; 638: Bryan Smith/Zuma Press

Index

E

M

S

T

U

V

W

Y

Z